INSTRUCTOR'S RESOURCE MANUAL
FOR
MATERNAL & CHILD· NURSING CARE

SECOND EDITION

LONDON ■ LADEWIG ■ BALL ■ BINDLER

MICHAEL D. ALDRIDGE, MSN, RN, CCRN, CNS
CLINICAL NURSING INSTRUCTOR
THE UNIVERSITY OF TEXAS AT AUSTIN
AUSTIN, TEXAS

MARY DOWELL, PhD
PROFESSOR
UNIVERSITY OF MARY HARDIN BAYLOR
BELTON, TEXAS

BERNADETTE DRAGICH, PhD, APRN, BC
PROFESSOR
BLUEFIELD STATE COLLEGE
BLUEFIELD, WEST VIRGINIA

YVETTE ROLLE, MSN
INSTRUCTOR
HOUSTON COMMUNITY COLLEGE
HOUSTON, TEXAS

PEARSON

Prentice
Hall

Upper Saddle River, New Jersey 07458

Notice: Care has been taken to confirm the accuracy of the information presented in this book. The authors, editors, and the publisher, however, cannot accept any responsibility for errors or omissions or for consequences from application of the information in this book and make no warranty, express or implied, with respect to its contents.

The authors and the publisher have exerted every effort to ensure that drug selections and dosages set forth in this text are in accord with current recommendations and practice at time of publication. However, in view of ongoing research, changes to government regulation, and the constant flow of information relating to drug therapy and drug reactions, the reader is urged to check precautions. This is particularly important when the recommended agent is a new and/or infrequently employed drug.

The authors and publisher disclaim all responsibility for any liability, loss, injury, or damage incurred as a consequence, directly or indirectly, of the use and application of any of the contents of this volume.

All photography/illustrations not credited on page, under or adjacent to the piece, were photographed/rendered on assignment and are the property of Pearson Education/Prentice Hall Health.

Cover and unit opening photographs copyright Nick Zungoli, The Exposures Gallery.

Publisher: Julie Levin Alexander
Assistant to Publisher: Regina Bruno
Editor-in-Chief: Maura Connor
Executive Editor: Pamela Lappies
Associate Editor: Danielle Doller
Editorial Assistant: Joanna Satkowitz
Director of Production and Manufacturing: Bruce Johnson
Managing Production Editor: Patrick Walsh
Production Liaison: Nicholas Radhuber
Production Editor: Lindsey Hancock, Carlisle Publishing Services
Manufacturing Manager: Ilene Sanford
Manufacturing Buyer: Pat Brown
Marketing Manager: Francisco Del Castillo
Marketing Coordinator: Michael Sirinides
Composition: Carlisle Publishing Services
Cover Printer: Phoenix Color
Printer/Binder: Command Web

Pearson Prentice Hall™ is a trademark of Pearson Education, Inc.
Pearson® is a registered trademark of Pearson plc
Prentice Hall™ is a registered trademark of Pearson Education, Inc.

Pearson Education Ltd.
Pearson Education Singapore, Pte. Ltd.
Pearson Education Canada, Ltd.
Pearson Education—Japan
Pearson Education Australia PTY, Limited

Pearson Education North Asia Ltd.
Pearson Education de Mexico, S.A. de C.V.
Pearson Education Malaysia, Pte. Ltd.
Pearson Education, Upper Saddle River, New Jersey

10 9 8 7 6 5 4 3 2 1
ISBN 0-13-198726-7

CONTENTS

PREFACE

As teachers involved in nursing education, you are participants in a rapidly changing environment. Limited clinical sites, nontraditional students with limited time for lengthy assignments, and changing student learning styles are just a few of the factors that demand a rethinking of how you go about the "business" of education. This *Instructor's Resource Manual,* written to accompany *Maternal & Child Nursing Care, Second Edition* by London, Ladewig, Ball, and Bindler, is designed to assist you provide an optimal learning experience for your students and their many learning needs.

Each chapter of the *Instructor's Resource Manual* is thoroughly integrated with the corresponding chapter in the main textbook. Chapters are organized by objectives, and the teaching unit flows from these objectives. You will find the following features to support the objectives:

- **Concepts for Lecture** in the manual may be used in their entirety for class presentation, or they may be merged with the classroom activities for a mixture of teaching styles that will meet the needs of students with various learning styles.

- **Lecture Outlines** can be found on your *Instructor's Resource CD-ROM* as text PowerPoint files to use in the classroom with some integrated art.

- **Image PowerPoints** are figures, tables, and boxes that are from the textbook. These are available in PowerPoint on the *Instructor's Resource CD-ROM*.

- **Suggestions for Classroom and Clinical Activities** attempt to go beyond the traditional activities that have been the mainstay of maternal-newborn & pediatric nursing education for many years. These are designed to help you design appropriate exercises and applications in the classroom, in the skills laboratory, and in the clinical setting and make use of the many media assets and exercises available on the Student CD-ROM and Companion Website.

- **Media Library** is a showcase of all the media and visual assets available for that chapter. These identify for you—the instructor—all the specific media resources and activities available for that chapter on the *Student CD-ROM* and *Companion Website* as well as all the images from the textbook that are included in the Image Bank PowerPoint presentation on the *Instructor's Resource CD-ROM*. Chapter by chapter, the **Media Library** helps you decide what resources from the Student CD-ROM, Companion Website, and Instructor's Resource CD-ROM to assign to enhance your course and your students' ability to apply concepts from the book into practice.

For additional assistance incorporating these resources into your course, please see the sections at the beginning of this manual that provide an overall guide to the media resources and activities available from the Student CD-ROM, Companion Website, Instructor's Resource CD-ROM, and OneKey Online Courses—e.g., Blackboard, WebCt, and CourseCompass.

Finally, the following additional resources are also available to accompany this textbook. For more information or sample copies, please contact your Prentice Hall Sales Representative:

- **Clinical Skills Manual for *Maternal & Child Nursing Care, Second Edition* ISBN: 0131736280**—This colorful skills atlas serves as a portable, quick reference to step-by-step maternal-newborn and pediatric nursing procedures. The second edition of this valuable manual guides you through 150 skills using full-color photographs and rationales, including 30 maternal-newborn skills and over 100 pediatric skills. It also includes chapters on physical assessment, special pain management techniques, cardiorespiratory care, administration of medications—including intravenous access—and other information useful to nurses in the clinical setting. Throughout the companion textbook, *Maternal & Child Nursing Care, Second Edition,* special cross-reference icons refer readers to the complete skill presentation in this manual.

- **Student CD-ROM**—This CD-ROM is packaged with the textbook. It provides an interactive study program that allows students to practice answering bonus NCLEX-RN® questions with rationales for right and wrong answers and new alternate item formats. It contains an audio glossary, a wealth of animations and video tutorials with exercises, and skills. Also included are unique Nursing in Action activities where students answer critical thinking questions based on brief video clips of real nurses and clients as well as a new Critical Thinking in Action end-of-chapter feature that carries over from the textbook. It includes a visual portrayal of the scenario, and short-answer and critical thinking questions to reinforce applications discussed in the text chapter. All activities can be saved to the user's computer or printed with questions and student answers included.

- **Companion Website www.prenhall.com/ london**—This online Study Guide is designed to help students apply the concepts presented in the book. Each chapter-specific module features Objectives, NCLEX-RN® Review with comprehensive rationales and alternate item formats, Case Studies, Care Plan Activities, Critical Thinking Activities, WebLinks, MediaLink Applications, Audio Glossary, useful tools—such as recommended dietary allowances, lab values, growth charts and assessment tools—and more. Faculty adopting this textbook have access to the online *Syllabus Manager* feature of the Companion Website, www.prenhall.com/london. Syllabus Manager offers a whole host of features that facilitate the students' use of the Companion Website, and allows faculty to post syllabi and course information online for their students. For more information or a demonstration of Syllabus Manager, please contact a Prentice Hall Sales Representative.

- **Instructor's Resource CD-ROM ISBN: 0131987275**— This cross-platform CD-ROM provides several tools to aid faculty in teaching. It includes image and integrated illustrations and lectures in Power-Point presentations for use in the classroom. It also contains an electronic test bank and animations and videos from the Student CD-ROM. Also included is a bonus PowerPoint presentation called First Day of Class that is designed to help students and faculty get

the most out of the textbook and its available features. This supplement is available to faculty at no additional cost upon adoption of the textbook.

- **Online Course Management Systems**—Also available are online companions for schools using course management systems. The online course management solutions feature interactive assessment modules, electronic test bank, PowerPoint Images, animations and video clips, and more. For more information about adopting an online course management system to accompany **Maternal & Child Nursing Care, Second Edition,** please contact your http://www.prenhall.com/mischtm/rep_locator_fr.html or go to the appropriate website:

http://cms.prenhall.com/webct/index.html
http://cms.prenhall.com/blackboard/index.html
http://cms.prenhall.com/coursecompass

It is our hope that the information provided in this manual will decrease the time it takes you to prepare for class and will optimize the learning experience for your students.

GUIDELINES FOR INCORPORATING
PRENTICE HALL'S NURSING MEDIA RESOURCES
INTO YOUR COURSE

Media resources for *Maternal & Child Nursing Care* by London, Ladewig, Ball, and Bindler are available for both the instructor and the student. These resources enhance your teaching, as well as help your students visualize and comprehend difficult concepts. Furthermore, the media resources and activities enable your students to apply concepts from the textbook to real nursing scenarios, hone critical thinking skills, and reinforce basic knowledge gained from textbook reading assignments.

The table here identifies where these media resources are available among the free supplements accompanying this textbook. Resources located on the textbook's Companion Website are available to both the instructor and student at www.prenhall. com/london.

Resource	Companion Website	Instructor's Resource cd-rom	Student cd-rom	WebCt Blackboard CourseCompass
Objectives	√	Electronic Instructor's Manual	√	√
Audio Glossary	√		√	√
Practice NCLEX-RN® Review Questions	√		√	√
Animations and/or Video Clips		√	√	√
Chapter Outline	√			√
Toolbox	√		√	√
Case Studies	√			√
Care Plan Activities	√			√
Critical Thinking	√		√	√
Procedures			√	
New York Times Link	√			√
MediaLinks	√			√
MediaLink Applications	√			√
Syllabus Manager™	√ (See guide for using this resource within this Instructor's Resource Manual.)			
Customizable & Printable Instructor's Resource Manual		√		√
PowerPoint Images from the textbook		√		√
PowerPoint Text Slides		√		√
NCLEX-RN®-style Test Items		√		√
Additional Resources		√		√

SUGGESTIONS FOR INCORPORATING THESE MEDIA RESOURCES AND ACTIVITIES INTO YOUR COURSE

1. Students who have difficulty identifying the main idea when reading the full chapter may use the chapter summary on the website to highlight major concepts.

2. Students who are visual learners can use the animations and/or video clips to reinforce their understanding of difficult concepts. Instructors may use the animations and/or video clips to enhance lecture presentations.

3. Students may use practice NCLEX-RN®-style review questions to prepare for course tests and to improve test-taking skills. Students may use these independently on the Companion Website and submit their answers to receive an instant score. Instructors may assign these quizzes and exercises as homework, and ask students to route their answers to the instructor using the Email Results function on the Companion Website. Or, these practice questions may be used as a discussion for the end of the classroom lecture or discussion in small groups.

4. Students may be assigned case studies to analyze as a group and present results to the class in a post-conference activity. They may respond to case study questions to prepare for clinical learning experiences as an independent study activity. Or, instructors may assign these activities as homework and ask students to route their essay-style answers to the instructor using the Email Results function on the Companion Website.

5. Instructors may assign students individually or in groups to build a care plan online for specific clients—emailing the final care plan to the instructor using the Email Results function on the Companion Website.

6. Questions from the class discussion section may be posted on Blackboard, WebCT, or CourseCompass, as well as on the Companion Website. Instructors can assign designated dates for responding to the questions provided. Students may be allowed to have group discussion online or individual exchange with the instructor online.

7. Students may use the MediaLinks as additional resources in support of written assignments or for enhancement of course requirements.

8. Instructors may assign the MediaLink Applications as homework for students to research specific topics on the Web and respond to the critical thinking questions provided on the Companion Website. Students can email their essay-style responses to the instructor using the Email Results function on the Companion Website.

9. Instructors may use PowerPoint images and PowerPoint text slides to enhance classroom presentations and discussions.

HOW TO USE
PRENTICE HALL'S SYLLABUS MANAGER™ AND COMPANION WEBSITE

Syllabus Manager™ provides an easy, step-by-step process to create and revise syllabi, with direct links to the Companion Website and other online content. It can be used by a nontechnical person to build and maintain one or more syllabi on the web. Students may "turn on" an instructor's syllabus from within any Companion Website. Your complete syllabus is hosted on Prentice Hall servers, allowing convenient updates from any computer by only you and your students. Changes you make to your syllabus are immediately available to your students at their next login.

All features and content on the Companion Website were developed in accordance with the chapter and textbook objectives. Thus, all the exercises meet the goals of the objectives, making the Companion Website a pedagogically sound study and teaching tool. The features on the Companion Website for **Maternal & Child Nursing Care, Second Edition** include the following modules for each chapter:

- Objectives
- Audio Glossary
- NCLEX-RN® Review
- Critical Thinking
- Case Study
- Care Plan
- MediaLinks
- MediaLink Applications
- Tools
- *The New York Times* Link

To access Syllabus Manager™, go to the home page for this textbook at *www.prenhall.com/london.* On the top navigation bar, click on **Syllabus.** New users can click on **Instructor Help** for assistance on the syllabus creation process.

To create your own secure course syllabus online, click on **New Account.** After entering your Personal Information, School Information, and Log in Information, click **Continue.** From here, you begin the easy four-step process to creating your syllabus.

STEP 1 COURSE DETAILS

This step allows you to create the basic information for your syllabus: Course Name (including start date and end date), Course Description (including policies and objectives), Class Time and Location, Course Prerequisites, and Grading Policy. Some of the fields have drop-down capability. You can even cut and paste your current syllabus into these fields or link the school's URL to your current syllabus. *Scroll to the bottom of the screen and click on Next, or on the drop-down menu select STEP 2: Assignment Schedule.*

STEP 2 ASSIGNMENT SCHEDULE

On this screen you are choosing dates for the assignments, and making notations about the assignments. It contains the course calendar in a pane on the left side of the page. Notice the days when your class meets are highlighted in blue. When you create assignments, their due dates appear in orange on the calendar. To create an assignment, click on the day of the assignment in the calendar. Next, you will give the assignment a name. Under notes/instructions, you may choose to mention clinical days, guest speakers, activities, or simply describe a set of assignments due that day. Then, you can add a component to the assignment, either from the textbook's Companion Website or a custom assignment from your current syllabus online by adding a link.

To add an activity from the textbook's Companion Website, begin by clicking on **Add CW Resource.** A window opens and displays your Companion Website title and parts. Click through the Companion Website to locate the element you want to include as an assignment resource and then click **Select** to add the component. When the student views your syllabus, they will click on the date of the assignment, and immediately be linked to the exercises you selected on the textbook Companion Website. You may add any combination of components. When you finish creating the assignment click the **Save** button. You may copy this assignment or add additional assignments for other days before clicking on **Next** to continue creating your syllabus. *Click on Next, or on the drop-down menu select STEP 3: Password for Students.*

STEP 3 PASSWORD FOR STUDENTS

You may want to protect this syllabus by entering a password. This password should be given out to only those who should have access to this syllabus. If you choose not to enter any password, your syllabus will be viewable by anyone. On this screen you can designate a secure password so only your students can access this syllabus. You can change the password as often as you like. *Click on Next, or on the drop-down menu select STEP 4: Finish.*

STEP 4 FINISH

Here you designate whether your syllabus is finished and able to be viewed by students, or still under construction and available only to you. *Click on* **Log Off** *to log out of Syllabus Manager™ and return to your Companion Website.*

Your students will now be able to access your course syllabus by searching your name, your email address, or your school name under Student Login. To view or update any of your existing syllabi, begin by logging in under Instructor Login. For additional demonstrations of Syllabus Manager™, or for help in creating your syllabus, please contact your Prentice Hall Sales Representative.

TEACHING CARE TO STUDENTS WHO SPEAK ENGLISH AS A NONNATIVE LANGUAGE

We are fortunate in the 21st century to have so many multinational and multilingual nursing students in the United States. As our classrooms become more diverse, there are additional challenges to communication, but we in the nursing education community are ready. Our goal is to educate competent and caring nurses to serve the health needs of our diverse communities.

We know that English as a nonnative language (ENNL) students experience higher attrition rates than their native English-speaking counterparts. This is a complex problem. However, there are teaching strategies that have helped many students be successful.

The first step toward developing success strategies is understanding language proficiency. Language proficiency has four interdependent components. Each component is pertinent to nursing education. *Reading* is the first aspect of language. Any nursing student will tell you that there are volumes to read in nursing education. Even native speakers of English find the reading load heavy. People tend to read more slowly in their nonnative language. They also tend to recall less. Nonnative speakers often spend inordinate amounts of time on reading assignments. These students also tend to take longer to process exam questions.

Listening is the second component of language. Learning from lectures can be challenging. Some students are more proficient at reading English than at listening to it. It is not uncommon for ENNL students to understand medical terminology, but to become confused by social references, slang, or idiomatic expressions used in class. The spoken language of the teacher may be different in accent or even vocabulary from that experienced by immigrant students in their language education. ENNL students may not even hear certain sounds that are not present in their native languages. Amoxicillin and Ampicillin may sound the same. Asian languages do not have gender-specific personal pronouns (he, she, him, her, etc.). Asian students may become confused when the teacher is describing a case study involving people of different genders.

Speaking is the third component of language proficiency. People who speak with an accent are often self-conscious about it. They may hesitate to voice their questions or to engage in discussion. Vicious cycles of self-defeating behavior can occur in which a student hesitates to speak, resulting in decreased speaking skills, which results in more hesitation to speak. Students may develop sufficient anxiety about speaking that their academic outcomes are affected. Students tend to form study groups with others who have common first languages. Opportunities to practice English are therefore reduced, and communication errors are perpetuated. When the teacher divides students into small groups for projects,

ENNL students often do not participate as much as others. If these students are anxious about speaking, they may withdraw from classroom participation. ENNL students may feel rejected by other students in a small-group situation when their input is not sought or understood.

The fourth aspect of language is *writing*. Spelling and syntax errors are common when writing a nonnative language. Teachers often respond to student writing assignments with feedback that is too vague to provide a basis for correction or improvement by ENNL students. When it comes to writing lecture notes, these students are at risk of missing important details because they may not pick up the teacher's cues about what is important. They might miss information when they spend extra time translating a word or concept to understand it, or they might just take more time to write what is being said.

Another major issue faced by ENNL nursing students is the culture of the learning environment. International students were often educated in settings where students took a passive role in the classroom. They may have learned that faculty are to be respected, not questioned. Memorization of facts may have been emphasized. It may be a shock to them when the nursing faculty expect assertive students who ask questions and think critically. These expectations cannot be achieved unless students understand them.

Finally, the European-American culture, which forms the context for nursing practice, creates challenges. Because they are immersed in Euro-American culture and the culture of nursing, faculty may not see the potential sources of misunderstanding. For example, if a teacher writes a test question about what foods are allowed on a soft diet, a student who understands therapeutic diets may miss the question if he or she does not recognize the names of the food choices. Nursing issues with especially high culture connection are: food, behavior, law, ethics, parenting, games, or choosing the right thing to say. These topics are well represented in psychiatric nursing, which makes it a difficult subject for ENNL students.

MINIMIZING CULTURE BIAS ON NURSING EXAMS

Our goal is not really to eliminate culture from nursing or from nursing education. Nursing exists in a culture-dependent context. Our goal is to practice transcultural nursing and to teach nursing without undue culture bias.

Sometimes our nursing exam questions will relate to culture-based expectations for nursing action. The way to make these questions fair is to teach transcultural nursing and to clarify the cultural expectations of a nursing student in the Euro-American-dominated healthcare system. Students must learn the cultural aspects of the profession before they can practice appropriately within it. Like other cultures, the professional culture of nursing has its own language (medical terminology and nursing diagnosis, of course). We have our own accepted way of dress, our own implements, skills, taboos, celebrations, and behavior. The values accepted by our culture are delineated in the ANA Code of Ethics, and are passed down to our young during nursing education.

It is usually clear to nursing educators that students are not initially aware of all the aspects of the professional culture, and that these must be taught. The social context of nursing seems more obvious to educators, and is often overlooked in nursing education. Some aspects of the social context of nursing were previously mentioned (food, games, social activities, relationships, behavior, what to say in certain situations). Students must also learn these social behaviors and attitudes if they are to function fully in nursing. If they do not already know about American hospital foods, what to say when someone dies, how to communicate with an authority figure, or what game to play with a 5-year-old child, they must learn these things in nursing school.

Try for yourself the following test. It was written without teaching you the cultural expectations first.

CULTURE-BIASED TEST

1. Following radiation therapy, an African American client has been told to avoid using her usual hair care product due to its petroleum content. Which product should the nurse recommend that she use instead?
   A. Royal Crown hair treatment
   B. Dax Wave and Curl
   C. Long Aid Curl Activator Gel
   D. Wave Pomade

2. A Jewish client is hospitalized for Pregnancy Induced Hypertension during Yom Kippur. How should the nurse help this client meet her religious needs based on the tradition of this holy day?
   A. Order meals without meat-milk combinations
   B. Ask a family member to bring a serving of *Marror* for the client
   C. Encourage her to fast from sunrise to sunset
   D. Remind her that she is exempt from fasting

3. Based on the Puerto Rican concept of *compadrazco*, who is considered part of the immediate family and responsible for care of children?
   A. Parents, grandparents, aunts, uncles, cousins, and godparents
   B. Mother and father, older siblings
   C. Mother, father, any blood relative
   D. Parents and chosen friends (*compadres*) who are given the honor of childcare responsibility

4. A 60-year-old Vietnamese immigrant client on a general diet is awake at 11 P.M. on a summer night. What is the best choice of food for the nurse to offer to this client?
   A. Warm milk
   B. Hot tea
   C. Ice cream
   D. Iced tea

5. Which of the following positions is contraindicated for a client recovering from a total hip replacement?
   A. Side-lying using an abductor pillow
   B. Standing
   C. Walking to the restroom using a walker
   D. Sitting in a low recliner

When you took this test, did it seem unfair? It was intended to test nursing behaviors that were based on culture-specific situations. Your immigrant and ENNL students are likely to face questions like these on every exam.

Item #1 is about hair care products for black hair. Option C is the only one that does not contain petroleum products. Students could know this, if they were given the information before the exam. Otherwise the item is culture-biased.

Item #2 is about the Jewish holiday Yom Kippur. To celebrate this holiday, it is customary to fast from sunrise to sunset, but people who are sick, such as the client in the question, are exempted from fasting. This is only unfair if students did not have access to the information.

Item #3 expects you to know about *compadrazco,* in which parents, grandparents, aunts, uncles, cousins, and godparents are all considered immediate family. This can be an important point if you are responsible for visiting policies in a pediatrics unit.

Item #4 tests knowledge about the preferred drink for an immigrant Vietnamese client. Many people in Asia feel comforted by hot drinks and find cold drinks to be unsettling.

Item #5 does not seem so biased. If you understand total hip precautions, it is a pretty simple question, unless you have never heard of a "low recliner." An ENNL student who missed this question said, "I saw the chairs in clinical called 'geri chairs' and I know that the client cannot bend more than 90 degrees, but 'low recliner' was confusing to me. I imagined someone lying down (reclining) and I think this would not dislocate the prosthesis."

The best way to avoid culture bias on exams is to know what you are testing. It is acceptable to test about hip precautions, but not really fair to test about the names of furniture. The same is true of foods. Test about therapeutic diets, but not about the recipes (an African immigrant student advised us to say "egg-based food" instead of custard).

Behavior in social and professional situations is especially culture-bound. Behavior-based questions are common on nursing exams. Make behavior expectations explicit. Especially when a student is expected to act in a way that would be inappropriate in his or her social culture, these are very difficult questions. For example, we expect nurses to act assertively with physicians and clients. It is inappropriate for many Asian students to question their elders. When a client is their elder, these students will choose the option that preserves respect for the client over one that provides teaching. We must make our expectations very clear.

Finally, talk with your ENNL and immigrant students after your exams. They can provide a wealth of information about what confused them or what was ambiguous. Discuss your findings with your colleagues and improve your exams. Ultimately your exams will be clearer and more valid.

SUCCESS STRATEGIES

The following strategies were developed originally to help ENNL students. An interesting revelation is that they also help native English speakers who have learning styles that are not conducive to learning by lecture, or who read slowly, or have learning disabilities or other academic challenges.

STRATEGIES FOR PROMOTING ENNL STUDENT SUCCESS

1. You cannot decrease the reading assignment because some students read slowly, but you can help students prioritize the most important areas.
2. Allow adequate time for testing. The NCLEX is not a 1-minute-per-question test anymore. Usually 1.5 hours is adequate for a 50-item multiple-choice exam.
3. Allow students to tape lectures if they want to. You might have lectures audio-taped and put in the library for student access.
4. Speak clearly. Mumbling and rapid anxious speech are difficult to understand. If you have a problem with clarity, provide handouts containing the critical points. You may want to provide the handouts anyway, as your intent is to teach and test nursing knowledge, not note-taking skills.
5. Avoid slang and idiomatic expressions. When you do use slang, explain it. This is especially important on exams. When in doubt about whether a word is confusing, think about what the dictionary definition would be. If there are two meanings, use another word.
6. Allow the use of translation dictionaries on exams. You can say that students must tell you what they are looking up, so they cannot find medical terminology that is part of the test.
7. Be aware of cultural issues when you are writing exams. Of course you will test on culture-specific issues, but be sure you are testing what you want to test (the student's knowledge of diets, not of recipes).
8. Feel free to use medical terminology; after all, this is nursing school. However, when you use an important new term, write it on the board so students can spell it correctly in their notes.
9. In clinical, make the implied explicit. It seems obvious that safety is the priority, but if a student thinks the priority is respecting her elders, there could be a disaster when a client with a new hip replacement demands to get out of bed.
10. Hire a student who takes clear and accurate lecture notes to post his or her notes for use by ENNL and other students. The students will still attend class and take their own notes, but will have this resource to fill in the details that they miss.
11. SOA (spell out abbreviations).
12. Many international students learned to speak English in the British style. If something would be confusing to a British person, they will find it confusing.
13. Provide opportunities for students to discuss what they are learning with other students and faculty. A faculty member might hold a weekly discussion group where students bring questions. It can be interesting to find a student having no trouble tracing the path of a red cell from the heart to the portal vein, but having difficulty understanding what cream of wheat is ("I thought it was a stalk of grain in a bowl with cream poured on it").
14. Make it clear that questions are encouraged. When a student is not asking, and you think he or she may not understand, ask the student after class if he or she has questions. Make it easier for students to approach you by being approachable. Learn their names, and learn to pronounce them correctly. Hearing you try to pronounce their name might be humorous for them, and it will validate how difficult it is to speak other languages.
15. Take another look at basing grades on class participation. You may be putting inordinate demands on the ENNL students. Of course nurses must learn to work with others, but the nurse who talks most is not necessarily the best.
16. Be a role model for communication skills. You might even say in class when you talk about communication that if you respect a person who is trying to communicate with you, you will persist until you understand the message. Say, "Please repeat that," or "I think you said to put a chicken on my head, is that correct?" or "You want me to do what with the textbook?" It may be considered socially rude to ask people to repeat themselves repeatedly. Make it clear that this is not a social situation. In the professional role, we are responsible for effective communication. We cannot get away with smiling and nodding our heads.
17. In clinical, if a student has an accent that is difficult for the staff to understand, discuss clarification techniques (#16 above) with the student and staff member. Make it explicit that it is acceptable for the student to ask questions and for the staff to ask for clarification.
18. If your college has a writing center where students can receive feedback on grammar and style before submitting papers, have students use it. If you are not so fortunate, view papers as a rough draft instead of a final product. Give specific feedback about what to correct and allow students to resubmit.
19. Make any services available to ENNL students available to all students (such as group discussions and notes). These services may meet the learning needs of many students while preventing the attitude that "they are different and they get something I don't."
20. Faculty attitudes are the most important determinant of a successful program to promote the success of ENNL nursing students. Talk with other faculty about the controversial issues. Create an organized program with a consistent approach among the faculty. The rewards will be well worth the work.

CHAPTER 1
MATERNAL, NEWBORN, AND CHILD HEALTH NURSING

RESOURCE LIBRARY

CD-ROM
NCLEX-RN® Review
Case Study: Cord Blood Banking

COMPANION WEBSITE
Audio Glossary
NCLEX-RN® Review

IMAGE LIBRARY

Figure 1.1 A certified nurse-midwife confers with her client.
Figure 1.2 Children need to be involved actively in decisions regarding their care when appropriate.

Figure 1.3 Uninsured children by race, Hispanic origin, and age: 2003.
Figure 1.4 Infant mortality rates by race: United States, 1940–2002.

LEARNING OBJECTIVE 1
Identify the nursing roles available to the maternal-newborn nurse.

CONCEPTS FOR LECTURE

1. Registered nurses provide nursing care to both inpatient and outpatient women with childbearing or reproductive issues as well as newborns and children.
2. Nurse practitioners provide ambulatory care services to expectant families. They also function in some acute care and high-risk units.
3. Certified nurse-midwives manage the care of women who are at low risk for complications during pregnancy and childbirth.
4. Clinical nurse specialists (CNSs) have a master's degree and specialized knowledge and competence in a specific clinical area.

POWERPOINT LECTURE SLIDES

1 Registered Nurse Provides Care in a Wide Variety of Settings
- Inpatient and outpatient maternal-newborn facilities—nurses play major role in minimizing psychologic and physical distress associated with reproductive issues
- Collaborative care—functions as part of multidisciplinary health team
- Case management—coordinates cost-effective health care based on need
- Client education—client education is a major component of maternal-child nursing

2 Nurse Practitioners Are Part of the Healthcare Team
- Focus on physical and psychosocial assessments
  ○ Conduct some diagnostic tests and procedures
  ○ Obtain historical information
  ○ Perform comprehensive physical examinations
- Make clinical judgments based on assessment data
- Treatment—provide appropriate treatment regimes for diagnosed conditions
- Collaborative practice—seek physician consultation when necessary

3 Certified Nurse-Midwives Are Members of the Caring Team
- Manages independently
  ○ Client with low-risk pregnancy
  ○ Normal newborn

- Collaborative practice
  - Refers high-risk cases to physician
  - Consults with physician when in doubt
- Treatment—provides treatment for childbirth-related problems

3a Certified Nurse-Midwife Confers with Her Client
- (Figure 1.1)

4 Clinical Nurse Specialists Function in Maternal-Newborn Settings
- Clinical nurse specialists (CNSs) have a master's degree and specialized knowledge; competent in specific clinical area
- Often work with maternal-newborn clients on various units
  - Mother-baby units
  - Pediatric units
  - Intensive care units
- Assist unit staff to provide evidenced-based care

SUGGESTIONS FOR CLASSROOM ACTIVITIES

Assign students to work in groups. Allow each group to select one nursing specialty. Instruct members of the individual groups to review the educational preparation and responsibilities for each specialty. Allow each group to present the information to the class.

SUGGESTIONS FOR CLINICAL ACTIVITIES

Place students in clinical areas with nurses of varying specialities. Instruct students to identify the roles and responsibilities of each practitioner and allow them to discuss their findings during post-clinical conference.

LEARNING OBJECTIVE 2

Summarize the use of community-based nursing care in meeting the needs of childbearing and childrearing families.

CONCEPTS FOR LECTURE

1. Primary care includes a focus on health promotion, illness prevention, and individual responsibility for one's own health.
2. Community-based care is important in meeting the needs of the childbearing and childrearing family.
3. The vast majority of care takes place outside of the hospitals.

POWERPOINT LECTURE SLIDES

1 Primary Care Is the Focus of Much Attention
- Services best provided in community-based settings; cost effective
- Focus
  - Health promotion
  - Illness prevention
  - Responsibility for one's own health
- Third-party payers and managed care organizations—beginning to recognize importance of primary care in containing costs
- One challenge that managed care organizations face: How to relate to essential community providers of care

2 Community-based Care Is Important for the Childbearing Family
- Essential element of health care for uninsured or underinsured individuals—geared to needs of specific population
- Part of trend initiated by consumers—request seamless system of family-centered, comprehensive, coordinated health care, health education, and social services

- System requires coordination
  - Clients move from primary care services to acute care facilities and then back into community
  - Nurses can assume this care-management role and perform an important service

3 Places Where Community-based Care Takes Place
- Clinics
- Offices
- Community-based organizations
- Private homes—enables infants, children, and women to remain at home with conditions that formerly would have required hospitalization

SUGGESTIONS FOR CLASSROOM ACTIVITIES

Instruct one group of students to list institutions where community-based services are performed. Instruct another group to list all the services that are available. Allow the students to match the cards according to institutions and services provided.

SUGGESTIONS FOR CLINICAL ACTIVITIES

Schedule students to obtain clinical experience in clinics, doctor's offices, and community organizations involved in providing maternal-child health care. Students may also be assigned to work with perinatal home health nurses.

LEARNING OBJECTIVE 3

Summarize the current status of factors related to health insurance and access to health care.

CONCEPTS FOR LECTURE

1. All pregnant women and children in United States do not have access to health care.
2. Children living in poverty unable to receive basic preventive care.
3. Medicaid is most prevalent form of insurance among the poor.

POWERPOINT LECTURE SLIDES

1 Limited Access to Health Care
- 2003: 15.6% of population (45 million people) without health insurance
- 2002: 83.4% of pregnant women in United States began prenatal care in first trimester
- African American, Hispanic, and Native American women disproportionately less likely to receive early and adequate prenatal care

1a Uninsured Children by Race, Hispanic Origin, and Age: 2003
- (Figure 1.3)

2 Children Living in Poverty
- Children more likely to be uninsured than general population—most of these children had difficulty obtaining the most basic preventive health care, including immunizations
- Congress passed legislation to create the Child Health Insurance Plan in 1997
  - Enable more children to obtain access to essential healthcare services
  - As of the end of September 2002, 5.3 million children were enrolled

3 Availability of Insurance
- In 2003, 8.4 million children, 11.4% of all those younger than 18 years of age, had no health insurance

- For people living in poverty
  - Medicaid is most prevalent form of insurance
  - Covers 12.4% of people (35.6 million) including pregnant women who fall into specified income categories

SUGGESTIONS FOR CLASSROOM ACTIVITIES

Allow students to discuss universal health care and the implications. Ask individuals in the classroom to say whether or not universal health care will increase access to health care for all. Allow them to provide evidence to support their conclusions.

SUGGESTIONS FOR CLINICAL ACTIVITIES

Have students research the requirement for medicaid reimbursement and private insurance in a clinical facility. Allow them to compare and contrast the process.

LEARNING OBJECTIVE 4

Define the following statistical terms relevant to health care: birth rate, infant mortality rate, neonatal mortality rate, and maternal mortality rate.

CONCEPTS FOR LECTURE

1. The birth rate in the United States increased for older women and decreased for teens.
2. Infant mortality rate is increasing in the United States.
3. Neonatal mortality rate increase is most prevalent during the first week of life.
4. Overall maternal mortality rate is decreasing in the United States.

POWERPOINT LECTURE SLIDES

1 Birth Rate
- Number of live births per 1000 people
  - United States in 2002 birth rate of 13.9 reflected steady pattern of decrease seen for past several years
  - Birth rate for teens decreased for 11th straight year to 43 births per 1000 females aged 15 to 19 years
- Increasing birth rates for women aged 35 to 39 (42.4 per 1000)
- Women aged 40 to 44 (8.2 per 1000)

1a Infant Mortality Rates by Race: United States, 1940–2002
- (Figure 1.4)

2 Infant Mortality Rate
- Number of deaths of infants under 1 year of age per 1000 live births—2002 increased from 6.8 in the U.S. to 7.0
- Two key predictors of infant health
- Percentage of infants born preterm (before 37 completed weeks' gestation)
- Percentage of low birth weight (less than 2500 grams) infants

3 Neonatal Mortality Rate
- Neonatal mortality is number of deaths of infants less than 28 days of age per 1000 live births; rate increase concentrated in neonatal period, especially during first week of life
- Predisposing factors
  - Low birth weight
  - Prematurity

POWERPOINT LECTURE SLIDES *continued*

 Maternal Mortality Rate
- Number of deaths from causes related to or aggravated by pregnancy or postpartum period per 100,000 live births
- 2002, 357 women died from maternal causes
- Decrease of 42 deaths from 2001 total (rate of 8.9)
- African American women's rate of death (24.9) in United States was more than 4 times rate for white women (6.0)
- Predisposing factors influencing decrease in maternal deaths
  ◦ Use of hospitals
  ◦ Specialized healthcare personnel

SUGGESTIONS FOR CLASSROOM ACTIVITIES

Lead a discussion among students about the various factors that influence birth rates, neonatal mortality rates, infant mortality rates, and maternal mortality rates. For further review, advise students to visit the Companion Website for cultural and statistical web links.

SUGGESTIONS FOR CLINICAL ACTIVITIES

Allow students to conduct research to identify the birth rate, neonatal mortality rate, infant mortality rate, and maternal mortality rate in their city or state according to race or ethnic origin. Discuss findings during post-clinical conference.

LEARNING OBJECTIVE 5

Identify the goals for patient safety developed by the Joint Commission on the Accreditation of Healthcare Organizations (JCAHO).

CONCEPTS FOR LECTURE

1. In 2005, National Patient Safety Goals were established by The Joint Commission on the Accreditation of Healthcare Organizations' International Center for Patient Safety.

POWERPOINT LECTURE SLIDES

1 Joint Commission on the Accreditation of Healthcare Organizations
- Audits the operation of hospitals and healthcare facilities
- Joint Commission on the Accreditation of Healthcare Organizations' 2005 National Safety Goals
  ◦ Improve accuracy of patient identification
  ◦ Improve effectiveness of communication among caregivers
  ◦ Improve safety of using medications
  ◦ Improve safety of using infusion pumps
  ◦ Reduce risk of healthcare-associated infections
  ◦ Accurately and completely reconcile medications across continuum of care
  ◦ Reduce the risk of patient harm resulting from falls.

SUGGESTIONS FOR CLASSROOM ACTIVITIES

Instruct students to identify and discuss the seven patient-safety national goals. Allow students to discuss how they, as students, may implement the outlined goals.

SUGGESTIONS FOR CLINICAL ACTIVITIES

Ask students to make a list of all client care activities on their assigned units and make a list of all activities that promoted the achievements of the outlined patient-safety goals and all the activities that did not contribute to client safety. Allow students to discuss their observations during post-clinical conference.

LEARNING OBJECTIVE 6

Delineate significant legal and ethical issues that influence the practice of maternal-child nursing.

CONCEPTS FOR LECTURE

1. The fetus is increasingly viewed as a client separate from the mother. Human stem cells can be found in embryonic tissue and in the primordial germ cells of a fetus.
2. Abortion can legally be performed until the fetus reaches the age of viability. The decision to have an abortion is made by a woman in consultation with her physician.
3. Assisted reproductive technology (ART) is the term used to describe highly technologic approaches used to produce pregnancy.
4. Federal "Baby Doe" regulations were developed to protect the rights of infants with severe defects.

POWERPOINT LECTURE SLIDES

 The Unborn Child
- President George W. Bush announced that "unborn children" would qualify for government healthcare benefits.
  - 2002: U.S. federal policy defined childhood as starting at conception
  - Designed to promote prenatal care
- Stem cell research
  - Cultured stem cells can be made to differentiate into other types of cells
  - These cells may be used to treat medical problems

 Abortion
- Legally performed until fetus reaches age of viability; before viability, rights of mother are paramount
- After viability, abortion permissible
  - When life or health of mother is threatened
  - Rights of fetus take precedence

 Assisted Reproductive Technology
- Used to describe highly technologic approaches used to produce pregnancy
  - In vitro fertilization
  - Embryo transfer (IVF-ET)
- Ovulation-inducing medications—produce multiple embryos that are then implanted
- Multiple pregnancy increases the risk of miscarriage, preterm birth, and neonatal morbidity and mortality

 Regulations to Protect the Rights of Infants with Severe Defects
- Parents usually ultimate decision makers about child's care
- Federal regulations require formalized ethical decision-making process
- Conditions considered by members of ethics committee
- Treatment to improve quality of life or save infant's life is often elected

---

SUGGESTIONS FOR CLASSROOM ACTIVITIES

Assign students to review the "Case Study: Cord Blood Banking" activity on the accompanying CD-ROM. Facilitate a classroom discussion about the case study.

SUGGESTIONS FOR CLINICAL ACTIVITIES

Assign students to an ethics committee meeting addressing quality of life issues in the perinatal environment. Students may also research past cases where federal regulations were considered and engage in active discussion during clinical conferences.

LEARNING OBJECTIVE 7

Discuss the role of evidence-based practice in improving the quality of nursing care for childbearing families.

CONCEPTS FOR LECTURE

1. Evidence-based practice refers to clinical practice based on research findings and other available data.
2. Evidence-based practice increases nurses' accountability and results in better client outcomes.

POWERPOINT LECTURE SLIDES

1 Evidence-based Practice
- Nursing interventions supported by current, valid research—emerging as a force in health care
- It provides a useful approach to problem solving/decision making; self-directed, patient-centered, life-long learning
- Builds on actions necessary to transform research findings into clinical practice

2 Evidence-based Practice Results in Better Client Outcomes
- Outcomes improved as a result of quality improvement initiatives
- Nurses need to recognize which practices have conflicting findings as to their effect on client outcomes
- Market pressures also a force in use of evidence-based practice
- Nurses and other healthcare providers forced to evaluate routines to provide better client outcomes

SUGGESTIONS FOR CLASSROOM ACTIVITIES

Lead a discussion on the advantages of evidenced-based practice. Allow students to vocalize their views on that subject. For additional information, web links, and activities, instruct students to visit the Companion Website.

SUGGESTIONS FOR CLINICAL ACTIVITIES

Ask students to inquire about the utilization of evidenced-based practice in healthcare institutions during their clinical rotation. Allow them to discuss their findings with the other students in their clinical groups.

CHAPTER 2
CULTURE AND THE FAMILY

RESOURCE LIBRARY

 CD-ROM

NCLEX-RN® Review
Audio Glossary

COMPANION WEBSITE

NCLEX-RN® Review
MediaLink Applications:
  Critical Thinking: Examine Your Cultural Influences
  Cultural Assessment Tools
Audio Glossary

IMAGE LIBRARY

Figure 2.1 Single-parent families account for nearly one-third of all U.S. families.
Figure 2.2 Preschoolers from various cultural backgrounds play together.
Figure 2.3 Many cultures value the input of grandparents and other elders in the family or group.

Figure 2.4 Today very few communities are limited to one culture.
Figure 2.5 Infant massage.
Figure 2.6 During pregnancy, therapeutic touch is often helpful in easing pain and reducing anxiety.

LEARNING OBJECTIVE 1

Distinguish among several different types of families.

CONCEPTS FOR LECTURE

1. A *family* is defined as individuals who are joined together by marriage, blood, adoption, or residence in the same household. More broadly, bonds of emotional closeness, sharing, and support generally characterize families.
2. There are numerous types of families that are both traditional and nontraditional.

POWERPOINT LECTURE SLIDES

1 What Is a Family?
  • Individuals joined together by:
    ○ Marriage
    ○ Blood
    ○ Adoption
    ○ Residence in the same household

1a Characteristics of Families
  • Emotional closeness
  • Sharing
  • Support

2 Nuclear Family
  • Husband provider
  • Wife who stays home
  • Children
  • Was once the norm in the United States
  • No longer very common

2a Dual-Career/Dual-Earner Family
  • Both parents work
  • Two-thirds of U.S. families are this type

2b Childless Family
  • Growing trend
  • 10% of couples have infertility problems
  • 5% of married couples are voluntarily childless

Extended Families
- Couple shares household and childrearing responsibilities with:
  - Parents
  - Siblings
  - Other relatives
- More common in non-U.S. cultures and in working-class families

 Extended Kin Network Family
- Type of extended family
- Two nuclear families live in close proximity to each other
- Share support, chores, goods, services
- Common in Latino community

 Single-Parent Family
- Head of household is widowed, divorced, abandoned, or separated
- Rare in past, but more common now

Stepfamily
- Biologic parent with children and a new spouse who may or may not have children
- More common due to high rates of divorce and remarriage

 Binuclear Family
- Post-divorce family
- Biologic children are members of two nuclear households (mother and father)
- Children alternate between the two homes

 Nonmarital Heterosexual Cohabitating Family
- Heterosexual couple
- May or may not have children
- Live together outside of marriage

Gay and Lesbian Families
- Same-sex orientation
- Live together
- With or without children

SUGGESTIONS FOR CLASSROOM ACTIVITIES

Pass around blank index cards and ask students to write the type of family they grew up in. Have them turn the cards in. Briefly tally the results of the group and share with the class.

SUGGESTIONS FOR CLINICAL ACTIVITIES

Remind students to explore the type of families their clients come from. This can make a tremendous difference in the nursing care provided, and families may not offer the information if they are not asked.

LEARNING OBJECTIVE 2

Identify the stages of a family life cycle.

CONCEPTS FOR LECTURE

1. Duvall described an eight-stage family life cycle that describes the developmental process that each family encounters. It is based on the nuclear family, and the oldest child serves as the marker except in the last two stages when no children are present. Families with more than one child may overlap stages. *Refer to Table 2.1 for details.*
2. Other family models reflecting the contemporary family have been developed, but are outside the scope of this text.

POWERPOINT LECTURE SLIDES

1 Stages of a Family Life Cycle (Duvall)
- Based on nuclear family
- Oldest child is the marker; last two stages, no children present
- Families with more than one child may overlap stages

1a Eight Stages
- Married couples (no children)
- Childbearing families
- Families with preschool children
- Families with school-age children
- Families with teenagers
- Families launching young adults
- Middle-aged parents
- Aging family members

2 Other Family Models
- Other models have been developed
- Reflect non-nuclear family composition

SUGGESTIONS FOR CLASSROOM ACTIVITIES

Divide the class into eight groups and assign each group one of the eight stages described in the lecture. Have each group identify the tasks and challenges faced by families during that stage. Have each group share their ideas with the class.

SUGGESTIONS FOR CLINICAL ACTIVITIES

Remind students to consider which stage the family they are caring for is in, as well as the tasks and challenges faced during this stage.

LEARNING OBJECTIVE 3

Identify prevalent cultural norms related to childbearing and childrearing.

CONCEPTS FOR LECTURE

1. The culture that a family exists in has a great influence on childbearing practices, including the number of children a family has, the status conferred with the child's gender, and beliefs about contraception.
2. Cultures have different expectations of children, and these impact how families raise their children. *Refer to Table 2.3 for specific details.*

POWERPOINT LECTURE SLIDES

1 Culture and Childbearing Practices
- Children generally valued by all cultures
- Number of children desired
- Gender of child and status
- Beliefs about contraception

1a Beliefs During Pregnancy
- Importance of prenatal care
- Avoidance of doorways, steps
- Bad air (close windows)
- Do not sit or lie down for long periods of time (baby becomes too big)

2 Culture and Childrearing Practices
- African American
- Amish
- Appalachian

- Arab American
- Chinese American
- Mexican American
- Navajo Indian

SUGGESTIONS FOR CLASSROOM ACTIVITIES

Ask students to share cultural practices related to child-bearing or childrearing that they have experienced in their own families.

SUGGESTIONS FOR CLINICAL ACTIVITIES

Discuss possible cultural beliefs that may conflict with nursing. For example, if a family wanted to light candles in their hospital room, how could the nurse address the situation? Why does the family believe that the ritual is important? Is there a way to compromise?

LEARNING OBJECTIVE 4
Summarize the importance of cultural competency in providing nursing care.

CONCEPTS FOR LECTURE

1. Cultural competency is the skills and knowledge necessary to appreciate, respect, and effectively work with individuals from different cultures. It requires self-awareness, an understanding of cultural differences, and the ability to adapt clinical practices into the family's belief system.
2. Biological differences include genetic and physical differences among cultural groups. These differences affect both nursing assessment and patterns of disease.
3. Communication is the method by which members of cultural groups share information. Although language is the most obvious form of communication, factors such as nonverbal communication, touch, and space are also important forms of communication.
4. Time orientation varies greatly among cultures. Cultural groups may place emphasis on events from the past, present, or future. The use of clocks may be limited in certain cultures.
5. Nutrition, and the role of food, plays a large part in many cultures. Nutritional assessments should take culture into account.

POWERPOINT LECTURE SLIDES

1. Cultural Competence
   - Definition
   - Requires:
     - Self-awareness
     - Understanding of cultural differences
     - Ability to adapt clinical practices

2. Biological Differences
   - Genetic differences
   - Physical differences (Example: Mongolian spots)
   - Disease patterns (Example: Hispanics have higher rates of diabetes and lactose intolerance)

3. Communication Patterns
   - Definition
   - Language
     - Interpreters
     - Health literacy/written instructions
     - Use of names
     - Appropriateness of expressing feelings

3a. Other Aspects of Communication
   - Nonverbal communication
   - Touch
   - Space

4. Time Orientation
   - Past, present, or future
   - Use of clocks
   - Implications for health care

5. Nutrition, Food, and Culture
   - Food and culture closely linked
     - Rituals
     - Special occasions/holidays
   - Fasting
   - Value large children—large equals healthy
   - Food in the hospital setting

Suggestions for Classroom Activities

Before class, assign students to complete the exercise, "Critical Thinking: Examine Your Cultural Influences," available on the Companion Website. Use this exercise as a basis for the discussion regarding cultural competence.

Suggestions for Clinical Activities

Have students shadow a dietitian for part of a clinical day. Incorporate cultural preferences for food into the nutritional assessment.

LEARNING OBJECTIVE 5

Discuss the use of a cultural assessment tool as a means of providing culturally sensitive care.

Concepts for Lecture

1. Cultural assessment tools assist the nurse in gathering culturally appropriate information in a succinct, systematic way.

PowerPoint Lecture Slides

1 Cultural Assessment Tools
- Helps the nurse collect information about health practices
- Based on client's:
  - Beliefs
  - Values
  - Customs

1a Examples of Assessment Questions:
- Who in the family must be consulted before decisions are made?
- Does the family see primarily in the present or do they have a futuristic time orientation?
- What type of healthcare provider is preferred?
- Does the family have beliefs or traditions that may impact the plan of care?

Suggestions for Classroom Activities

During class, have students read "Evidence-Based Nursing 2.1: Investigating Culture and Healthcare Barriers." Use the critical thinking questions at the end of the case to discuss how cultural assessment tools could be used to identify barriers to health care.

Suggestions for Clinical Activities

Have students use the cultural assessment tools, which can be located on the Companion Website, to assess a family they are caring for.

LEARNING OBJECTIVE 6

Identify key considerations in providing spiritually sensitive care.

Concepts for Lecture

1. *Religion* and *spirituality* mean different things to different people. The religious beliefs of families can influence their attitudes toward health care, childbearing, and childrearing.
2. There are several strategies that nurses can use to provide spiritually sensitive care. Self-awareness and respect are among the most important.

PowerPoint Lecture Slides

1 Religion and Spirituality
- Religion
  - Faith-based
  - Organized system with a common set of beliefs
  - Usually centered on worship of a supreme being
- Spirituality
  - Individual's concern with the spirit or soul
  - May include a transcendent power

1a Religious Beliefs and Health Care
- Christian Scientists: avoid medical interventions
- Jehovah's Witnesses: may refuse blood transfusions
- Roman Catholics: refuse contraception

1b References to a Higher Power
- Atheists: Believe there is no higher power
- Agnostics: Have doubts about existence of transcendent being
- May be offended by references to God or a higher power

2 Strategies for Providing Spiritually Sensitive Care
- Self-awareness
- Respect for others' beliefs
- Allow access to religious leaders during hospitalization
- Ask rather than assume

SUGGESTIONS FOR CLASSROOM ACTIVITIES	**SUGGESTIONS FOR CLINICAL ACTIVITIES**
Have students identify religious beliefs of families that may conflict with the plan of care. Discuss strategies for accommodating these beliefs.	Members of Jehovah's Witness have hospital liaisons who work to educate healthcare providers about their belief system, as well as to use strategies that decrease the need for blood transfusion. If one of these liaisons exists in your community, invite them to attend clinical conference and discuss these topics with students. Although many students may not agree with the belief, they will have a better understanding of it.

LEARNING OBJECTIVE 7

Distinguish between *complementary* and *alternative therapies*.

CONCEPTS FOR LECTURE

1. *Complementary therapies* are adjuncts to conventional medical treatments. They have been through scientific testing and have demonstrated some degree of reliability. Examples include acupuncture, acupressure, and massage therapy.
2. *Alternative therapies* are substances or procedures that are often used in place of conventional medical therapy. They may not have undergone rigorous scientific testing in the United States, but may have undergone testing in other countries.
3. Some examples of complementary and alternative therapies include homeopathy, naturopathy, traditional Chinese medicine, mind-based therapies, chiropractic, massage therapy, herbal therapy, and therapeutic touch.

POWERPOINT LECTURE SLIDES

1 Complementary Therapies
- Adjunct to conventional medical treatment
- Scientific testing demonstrates reliability
- Examples:
  - Acupuncture
  - Acupressure
  - Massage therapy
- May have acceptance in hospital setting
- May be covered by insurance plans

2 Alternative Therapies
- Used in place of conventional medical treatment
- Lack of rigorous scientific testing in the United States—may have been thoroughly tested in other countries
- Examples:
  - Magnet therapy
  - Herbal therapy
  - Aromatherapy
  - Many others
- May not be accepted in the hospital setting
- Not usually covered by insurance plans

3 Examples of Complementary and Alternative Therapies
- Homeopathy
- Naturopathy

- Traditional Chinese medicine
- Mind-based therapies
- Chiropractic
- Massage therapy
- Herbal therapy
- Therapeutic touch

SUGGESTIONS FOR CLASSROOM ACTIVITIES

Before class, divide students into groups and assign each group a complementary or alternative therapy discussed in the text. Have each group prepare a brief summary of the therapy, along with specific considerations regarding childbearing and childrearing families. Have each group present their findings to the class.

SUGGESTIONS FOR CLINICAL ACTIVITIES

Some hospitals are becoming more accepting of complementary and alternative therapies. Determine what the policy is in your local clinical setting.

LEARNING OBJECTIVE 8

Identify the benefits and risks of complementary and alternative therapies.

CONCEPTS FOR LECTURE

1. Complementary and alternative therapies have many potential benefits for women and children, including an emphasis on health promotion and wellness, low risk of side effects, and affordability.
2. Complementary and alternative therapies carry some risk to women and children, including lack of standardization, lack of research, and a poor understanding of potential side effects of some substances. Herbal therapy has particular risks for childbearing women.

POWERPOINT LECTURE SLIDES

1 Benefits of Complementary and Alternative Therapies
- Many emphasize promotion of wellness
- High value on holistic healing
- Many are non-invasive
- Many have few side effects
- May be more affordable than conventional treatments

2 Risks of Complementary and Alternative Therapies
- Lack of standardization and regulation
- Lack of research to substantiate effectiveness—particularly in children
- Inadequate training of some healers
- Financial risks of unproven methods ("snake oil")

2a Herbal Therapy and Pregnancy: Guidelines
- Avoid herbs during first trimester
- Avoid highly concentrated extracts; side effects tend to be higher
- Avoid herbs that
  - Induce abortion or menstruation
  - Stimulate the nervous system
  - Stimulate the gastrointestinal tract

SUGGESTIONS FOR CLASSROOM ACTIVITIES

Identify specific herbs that should be avoided during pregnancy. Locate reliable resources on the world wide web that students can use, and share these websites with the class.

SUGGESTIONS FOR CLINICAL ACTIVITIES

As an alternative clinical experience, assign students to observe with a practitioner of alternative or complementary therapies. If students have never seen a chiropractic adjustment or an acupuncture session, it can be very revealing. They may be surprised to learn that many practitioners also treat women and children.

LEARNING OBJECTIVE 9

Discuss complementary therapies appropriate for the nurse to use with childbearing and childrearing families.

CONCEPTS FOR LECTURE

1. Nurses who choose to use complementary and alternative therapies should only use methods that are within their scope of nursing practice. Therapies should generally be non-invasive and somewhat mainstream. Such therapies should be documented within the context of nursing practice.

POWERPOINT LECTURE SLIDES

1 Using Complementary and Alternative Therapies
- Must be within scope of nursing practice
- Cannot infringe upon licensure of others (Example: Massage therapy)
- Should be non-invasive
- Should be somewhat mainstream

1a Examples
- Acupuncture wristbands for nausea during pregnancy
- Progressive relaxation
- Therapeutic touch
- Visualization and guided imagery
- Meditation, prayer
- Others

1b Documentation
- Document within context of nursing practice
- Example: Music therapy for the child having acute pain

SUGGESTIONS FOR CLASSROOM ACTIVITIES

Invite a nurse who practices complementary and alternative therapies to speak to the class about his or her experiences.

SUGGESTIONS FOR CLINICAL ACTIVITIES

Determine if the hospital or clinical setting has a policy regarding nurses practicing complementary or alternative therapies.

CHAPTER 3
REPRODUCTIVE ANATOMY AND PHYSIOLOGY

RESOURCE LIBRARY

CD-ROM

NCLEX-RN® Review
Audio Glossary
Activity: Female Reproductive System
Activity: Ovulation
Activity: Male Reproductive System
Animations:
  3-D Female Pelvis
  3-D Male Pelvis

COMPANION WEBSITE

Additional NCLEX Review-RN®
MediaLink Applications:
  Case Study: Sex Education for Teens
  Care Plan Activity: Irregular Menses in a Client with Anxiety

IMAGE LIBRARY

Figure 3.1 Sexual differentiation.
Figure 3.2 Physiologic changes leading to onset of puberty.
Figure 3.3 Female external genitals, longitudinal view.
Figure 3.4 Female internal reproductive organs.
Figure 3.5 Structures of the uterus.
Figure 3.6 Pelvic blood supply.
Figure 3.7 Uterine muscle layers.
Figure 3.8 Uterine ligaments.
Figure 3.9 Fallopian tubes and ovaries.
Figure 3.10 Pelvic bones with supporting ligaments.
Figure 3.11 Muscles of the pelvic floor.
Figure 3.12 Female pelvis.
Figure 3.13 Pelvic planes: Coronal section and diameters of the bony pelvis.

Figure 3.14 Anatomy of the breast: Sagittal view of left breast.
Figure 3.15 Female reproductive cycle: Interrelationships of hormones with the four phases of the uterine cycle and the two phases of the ovarian cycle in an ideal 28-day cycle.
Figure 3.16 Various stages of development of the ovarian follicles.
Figure 3.17 Blood supply to the endometrium (cross-sectional view of the uterus).
Figure 3.18 Male reproductive system, sagittal view.
Figure 3.19 Schematic representation of a mature spermatozoon.

LEARNING OBJECTIVE 1

Identify the structures and functions of the female and male reproductive systems.

CONCEPTS FOR LECTURE

1. The female reproductive system consists of several organs that work together to facilitate ovulation, fertilization, implantation and fetal development, and birth.
2. The male reproductive organs produce the germ cell and are responsible for transporting it to the site of reproduction.
3. Both male and female reproductive systems produce hormones and secretions to stimulate and support reproduction.

POWERPOINT LECTURE SLIDES

1. Female Reproductive System
   • Internal genitalia
     ◦ Ovaries and fallopian tubes
     ◦ Cervix and uterus
     ◦ Vagina

1a. Female Internal Reproductive Organs
   • (Figure 3.4)

1b Female Reproductive System
- External genitalia/vulva
  ○ Mons pubis
  ○ Labia majora
  ○ Labia minora
  ○ Clitoris
  ○ Urethral meatus and opening of the paraurethral glands
  ○ Vaginal vestibule
- Breasts: Accessories of the reproductive system

1c Female External Genitals, Longitudinal View
- (Figure 3.3)

2 Male Reproductive System
- Testes
- Epididymis, vas deferens, and ejaculatory duct
- Accessory glands
- Penis

2a Male Reproductive System, Sagittal View
- (Figure 3.18)

2b Schematic Representation of a Mature Spermatozoon
- (Figure 3.19)

3 Hormones
- Female hormones
  ○ Estrogen
  ○ Progesterone
  ○ Prostaglandin
- Male hormones
  ○ Testosterone is the most important sex hormone

SUGGESTIONS FOR CLASSROOM ACTIVITIES

Assign students to complete the activities: "Female Reproductive System" and "Male Reproductive System" on the accompanying Student CD-ROM and discuss in class.

SUGGESTIONS FOR CLINICAL ACTIVITIES

Have students view the animations on the Student CD-ROM on the female and male pelvis.

LEARNING OBJECTIVE 2

Summarize the actions of the hormones that affect reproductive functioning.

CONCEPTS FOR LECTURE

1. Estrogen stimulates and supports reproduction in a variety of ways and has several functions in the female reproductive system.
2. Progesterone causes increased proliferation and secretion of glandular tissue in the reproductive system. It is also responsible for decreasing myometrial contractility.
3. Prostaglandins also play a role in reproduction.

POWERPOINT LECTURE SLIDES

1 Estrogen
- Controls development of female secondary sex characteristics
- Assists in the maturation of the ovarian follicles
- Causes endometrial mucosa to proliferate following menstruation
- Causes uterus to increase in size and weight

1a Female Reproductive Cycle
- (Figure 3.15)

1b Estrogen
- Increases myometrial contractility in both the uterus and fallopian tubes
- Increases uterine sensitivity to oxytocin
- Inhibits FSH production
- Stimulates LH production

2 Progesterone
- Decreases uterine motility and contractility
- Facilitates vaginal epithelium proliferation
- Secretion of thick viscous cervical mucus
- Increases breast glandular tissue in preparation for breast feeding

3 Prostaglandin
- Prostaglandin: Increases during follicular maturation
- Causes extrusion of the ovum

SUGGESTIONS FOR CLASSROOM ACTIVITIES

Allow students to use the Companion Website to access the Reproductive Anatomy and Physiology web links for further discussion and review.

SUGGESTIONS FOR CLINICAL ACTIVITIES

Instruct students to go to the Companion Website and complete the "Case Study: Sex Education for Teens Activity." Have them visit the Reproductive Anatomy and Physiology web links on the Companion Website for further review before the next clinical day. Allow students to discuss the case study during pre- or post-clinical conference.

LEARNING OBJECTIVE 3

Identify the two phases of the ovarian cycle and the changes that occur in each phase.

CONCEPTS FOR LECTURE

1. The ovarian cycle has two phases: the follicular phase (days 1 to 14) and the luteal phase (days 15 to 28 in a 28-day cycle). *Figure 3.16 depicts the changes.* Maturation of the ovarian follicle occurs in the follicular phase.

2. The corpus luteum develops during the luteal phase and secretes progesterone during the time the endometrium is favorable for implantation.

POWERPOINT LECTURE SLIDES

 1 Various Stages of Development of the Ovarian Follicles
- (Figure 3.16)

1a Follicular Phase
- Hypothalamus secretes gonadotropin-releasing hormone (GnRH)
- GnRH stimulates the anterior pituitary gland to secrete the gonadotropic hormones, follicle-stimulating hormone (FSH), and luteinizing hormone (LH)
- FSH is primarily responsible for the maturation of the ovarian follicle
- As the follicle matures, it secretes increasing amounts of estrogen
- Final maturation facilitated by LH
- The follicular phase ends with ovulation

 2 Luteal Phase
- Release of ovum
- LH: Corpus luteum develops from ruptured follicle

POWERPOINT LECTURE SLIDES *continued*

- Secretion of progesterone increases
- Fertilized ovum able to implant into endometrium
- Secretion of human chorionic gonadotropin (hCG)
- Absence of fertilization
- Corpus luteum degenerates
- Decrease in estrogen and progesterone
- Increase in LH and FSH

SUGGESTIONS FOR CLASSROOM ACTIVITIES

Assign students to participate in the Ovulation Activity on the Student CD-ROM and discuss their findings.

SUGGESTIONS FOR CLINICAL ACTIVITIES

Divide students into groups and assign each group to present to the rest of the class at least one aspect of ovulation. For example, one group may present the action of the FSH, another the LH hormone, and other groups may discuss the functions of individual hormones and the phases of the ovulation cycle.

LEARNING OBJECTIVE 4

Describe the phases of the menstrual cycle, their dominant hormones, and the changes that occur in each phase.

CONCEPTS FOR LECTURE

1. The menstrual phase is marked by hormonal changes and changes in the myometrium. *Refer to Figure 3.15*.
2. During the proliferative phase several changes take place in the endometrial glands, cervical mucus, and estrogen levels.
3. The secretory phase begins after ovulation and is influenced primarily by progesterone.
4. If fertilization does not occur, the ischemic phase begins. The corpus luteum begins to degenerate, and as a result both estrogen and progesterone levels fall.

POWERPOINT LECTURE SLIDES

1. Menstrual Phase
   - Shedding of the endometrial lining
   - Low estrogen levels

2. Proliferative Phase
   - Enlargement of the endometrial glands
   - Changes in cervical mucus
   - Increasing estrogen levels

3. Secretory Phase
   - Follows ovulation
   - Influenced primarily by progesterone
   - Increase in vascularity of the uterus
   - Increase in myometrial glandular secretions

4. Ischemic Phase
   - If fertilization does not occur, the ischemic phase begins
   - The corpus luteum begins to degenerate
   - Both estrogen and progesterone levels fall
   - Escape of blood into the stromal cells of the endometrium

SUGGESTIONS FOR CLASSROOM ACTIVITIES

Engage students in critical thinking exercises on the Student CD-ROM.

SUGGESTIONS FOR CLINICAL ACTIVITIES

Assign students to complete the "Care Plan Activity: Irregular Menses in a Client with Anxiety" located on the Companion Website.

LEARNING OBJECTIVE 5

Discuss the significance of specific female reproductive structures during childbirth.

CONCEPTS FOR LECTURE

1. The pelvic cavity is divided into the false pelvis and the true pelvis.
2. There are four basic pelvic types. Each type has a characteristic shape, and each shape has implications for labor and birth.

POWERPOINT LECTURE SLIDES

1 Female Pelvis
- (Figure 3.12A)

1a Division of the Pelvis
- False pelvis
  - Part above the pelvic brim
  - Serves to support the weight of the enlarged pregnant uterus
  - Directs the presenting fetal part into the true pelvis
- Inlet: Upper border of pelvis
  - Pelvic cavity: Curved canal with a longer posterior than anterior wall
  - Outlet: Pelvic outlet is at the lower border of the true pelvis

2 Basic Pelvic Types
- Gynecoid
- Android
- Anthropoid
- Platypelloid

SUGGESTIONS FOR CLASSROOM ACTIVITIES

Allow students to review the female pelvis animation on the Student CD-ROM.

SUGGESTIONS FOR CLINICAL ACTIVITIES

Assign students to draw and label a diagram of the female pelvis. Allow students to identify the shape of a client's pelvis and discuss the impact on labor.

LEARNING OBJECTIVE 6

Identify the functions of specific male reproductive structures for reproduction.

CONCEPTS FOR LECTURE

1. Male reproductive structures located in the pelvis and outside of the pelvis also play their part in reproduction.
2. Each structure works together to facilitate reproduction.

POWERPOINT LECTURE SLIDES

1 Male Reproductive Structures
- Penis
- Scrotum
- Testes; seminal fluid

1a Male Reproductive Structures
- Epididymis
- Vas deferens
- Urethra

2 Functions of Male Reproductive Structures
- Penis: Deposits sperm in the vagina for fertilization of the ovum
- Scrotum: Protects testes and sperm by maintaining a temperature lower than the body
- Testes
  - Serve as a site for spermatogenesis
  - Produce testosterone
- Seminal fluid: Transports viable and mobile sperm to female reproductive tract

Functions of Male Reproductive Structures
- Epididymis: Reservoir for maturing spermatozoa
- Vas deferens: Rapidly squeeze sperm from their storage sites into urethra
- Urethra: Passageway for both urine and semen

SUGGESTIONS FOR CLASSROOM ACTIVITIES	**SUGGESTIONS FOR CLINICAL ACTIVITIES**
Instruct students to view animation of the male pelvis on the Student CD-ROM.	Assign students to label a drawing of the male pelvis. Lead a discussion in the function of the male pelvis. Allow students to identify and discuss the functions of organs contained in the male pelvis.

CHAPTER 4
HEALTH PROMOTION FOR WOMEN

RESOURCE LIBRARY

💿 CD-ROM

NCLEX-RN® Review
Audio Glossary
Skill 2-2: Assisting with a Pelvic Examination
Animation: Oral Contraceptive

🌐 COMPANION WEBSITE

NCLEX-RN® Review
Case Study
Thinking Critically

📖 IMAGE LIBRARY

Figure 4.1 Sample basal body temperature chart.
Figure 4.2 A, Unrolled condom with reservoir tip.
B, Correct use of a condom.
Figure 4.3 A, The female condom. B, Remove
condom and applicator from wrapper by pulling up
on the ring. C, Insert condom slowly by gently
pushing the applicator toward the small of the back.
D, When properly inserted, the outer ring should
rest on the folds of skin around the vaginal opening,
and the inner ring (closed end) should fit loosely
against the cervix.
Figure 4.4 Inserting the diaphragm. A, Apply jelly
to the rim and center of the diaphragm. B, Insert
the diaphragm. C, Push the rim of the diaphragm
under the symphysis pubis. D, Check placement
of the diaphragm. Cervix should be felt through the
diaphragm.

Figure 4.5 A cervical cap.
Figure 4.6 The contraceptive sponge is moistened
well with water and inserted into the vagina
with the concave portion positioned over the
cervix.
Figure 4.7 The Mirena Intrauterine System, which
releases levonorgestrel gradually, may be left in place
for up to 5 years.
Figure 4.8 The NuvaRing vaginal contraceptive ring.
Courtesy of Organon, Inc.
Figure 4.9 Positions for inspection of the breasts.
Figure 4.10 Procedure for breast self-examination.
Figure 4.11 Screening for domestic violence should
be done privately.

Nursing Practice

LEARNING OBJECTIVE 1

Summarize information that women may need to implement effective self-care measures for dealing with
menstruation.

CONCEPTS FOR LECTURE

1. Nurses who work with young girls and adolescents
   can implement effective self-care measures for dealing
   with menstruation.
2. Nurses who work with teenagers need to provide basic information about menstruation.

POWERPOINT LECTURE SLIDES

 Menstruation Self-Care Practices
- Choice of sanitary protection
  - Pads: Deodorants added to sanitary napkins
    may prove harmful
  - Change brand if irritation occurs
  - Tampons: Use of super-absorbent tampons has
    been linked to the development of toxic shock
    syndrome
  - Women should avoid their use
  - Use regular-absorbency tampons for heavy
    menstrual flow
  - Use the first 2 or 3 days of the period
- Use of vaginal sprays
  - Not necessary
  - Can cause infections and other problems

1a Menstruation Self-Care Practices
- Douching practices
  - Unnecessary
  - Vagina cleanses itself
  - Douching washes away the natural mucus
  - Makes the vagina more susceptible to infection
- Cleansing methods
  - Use plain soap and water
  - Most effective method of controlling odor
  - Bathing is important
  - Warm tub bath

1b Menstruation Self-Care Practices
- Proper nutrition
  - Vitamins B and E help relieve discomforts
  - Vitamin B6 may help relieve bloating and irritability
- Exercise
  - Regular exercise
  - Helps prevent cramps and other menstrual complaints
- Management of discomforts
  - Balanced diet
  - Vitamins
  - Use of heat and massage
  - Medical management

2 Menstruation: Basic Information
- Menarche: Onset of menses and the menstrual cycle
- Cycle length: Length may vary from 21 to 35 days
- Amount of menstrual flow: Average flow is approximately 25 to 60 mL per period
- Length of menses: Usually lasts from 2 to 8 days

SUGGESTIONS FOR CLINICAL ACTIVITIES

Assign students to prepare a health teaching plan about menstruation to be used to teach adolescent clients in the clinical area.

LEARNING OBJECTIVE 2

Contrast dysmenorrhea and premenstrual syndrome.

CONCEPTS FOR LECTURE

1. Dysmenorrhea, or painful menstruation, occurs at, or a day before, the onset of menstruation and disappears by the end of menses.

POWERPOINT LECTURE SLIDES

1 Dysmenorrhea
- Signs and symptoms—painful cramps
- Treatment
  - Oral contraceptives
  - Prostaglandin inhibitors

2. Premenstrual syndrome (PMS) refers to a symptom complex associated with the luteal phase of the menstrual cycle (2 weeks prior to the onset of menses).

- ○ Self-care measures
- ○ Biofeedback

 Dysmenorrhea
- • Self-care measures
  - ○ Good nutrition
  - ○ Regular exercise
  - ○ Heat application
  - ○ Massage
  - ○ Rest

 Premenstrual Syndrome
- • Signs and symptoms
  - ○ Psychologic: Mood and sleep disorders
  - ○ Neurologic: Migraine, vertigo, and syncope
  - ○ Respiratory: Rhinitis, hoarseness, and occasionally asthma
  - ○ Gastrointestinal: Nausea, vomiting, and other disorders
  - ○ Urinary: Retention, oliguria
  - ○ Dermatologic: Acne
  - ○ Mammary: Swelling and tenderness

2a Premenstrual Syndrome
- • Treatment: Self-care
  - ○ Nutrition
  - ○ Aerobic exercise
- • Medical treatment
  - ○ Progesterone agonists
  - ○ Prostaglandin inhibitors
  - ○ Diuretics
  - ○ Serotonin agents
  - ○ Oral contraceptives
- • Nursing management
  - ○ Education and emotional support
  - ○ Administration of treatments and drugs

SUGGESTIONS FOR CLASSROOM ACTIVITIES

Encourage students to explore additional interactive resources on the Companion Website through the Women's Health web links in preparation for class lecture.

SUGGESTIONS FOR CLINICAL ACTIVITIES

Allow for clinical review of the Critical Thinking in Action case study in the textbook and have students watch the corresponding video and answer the questions located on the Student CD-ROM.

LEARNING OBJECTIVE 3

Compare the advantages, disadvantages, and effectiveness of the various methods of contraception available today.

CONCEPTS FOR LECTURE

1. There are various contraceptive methods with varying degrees of effectiveness. They can be described in terms of advantages, disadvantages, and effectiveness.

POWERPOINT LECTURE SLIDES

1 Methods of Contraception
- • Fertility awareness methods
  - ○ Advantages: Natural and noninvasive
  - ○ Disadvantages: Requires extensive initial counseling
  - ○ Effectiveness: Couples must practice abstinence

- Barrier contraceptives
  - Advantages: Easy to use with no side effects
  - Condoms prevent spread of most venereal diseases
  - Disadvantages: Some types must be fitted by a physician
  - Must be placed prior to intercourse
  - Must be used with spermacides
  - Effectiveness: Excellent when used correctly

1a Cervical Cap
- (Figure 4.5)

1b Inserting Diaphragm
- (Figure 4.4)

1c Two Views: Unrolled Condom and Use of Condom
- (Figure 4.2)

1d Methods of Contraception
- Spermacides
  - Advantages: Inexpensive and easy to obtain
  - Disadvantages: Must be applied prior to intercourse
  - Considered "messy" by many people
  - Effectiveness: Minimally effective when used alone
- Intrauterine devices
  - Advantages: Effective for up to 5 years without removal
  - Disadvantages: May cause cramping and bleeding for first 3 to 6 months
  - Woman must check for proper placement after each menses
  - Does not protect from STDs
  - Predispose woman to PID

1e Mirena Intrauterine System
- (Figure 4.7)

1f Methods of Contraception
- Hormonal contraceptives
  - Advantages: Menstrual symptoms lessened
  - Predictable menstruation
  - Disadvantages: May increase chance of blood clots
  - Contraindicated: Smokers
  - Clients with cardiovascular disorders
  - Previous history of thrombembolic disease
  - Does not protect from STDs
  - Effectiveness: Very effective when used correctly

1g Methods of Contraception
- Sterilization
  - Advantages: Permanent form of birth control
  - No cost once procedure is completed
  - Disadvantages: Nonreversible
  - Requires general anesthesia for the woman
  - Requires local anesthesia for the man
  - Vasectomy does not produce immediate sterility
  - Semen sample must be clear before stopping other method
  - Does not protect against STDs

SUGGESTIONS FOR CLASSROOM ACTIVITIES

View the animation on oral contraceptives on the Student CD-ROM in class. Allow students to engage in discussion about contraceptive forms and use.

SUGGESTIONS FOR CLINICAL ACTIVITIES

Assign students to a health clinic to shadow healthcare providers engaged in contraceptive counseling.

LEARNING OBJECTIVE 4

Delineate basic gynecologic screening procedures indicated for well women.

CONCEPTS FOR LECTURE

1. Monthly breast self-examination (BSE) is the best method for detecting breast masses.
2. A mammogram is a soft tissue x-ray of the breast that can detect lesions in the breast before they can be felt.
3. Pap smear detects cellular abnormalities at the cervix.
4. Pelvic examination allows for the detection of abnormalities of the reproductive organs and lower abdominal area. *Refer to "Skill 2-2: Assisting with a Pelvic Exam" in the Skills Manual.*

POWERPOINT LECTURE SLIDES

1 Breast Examination
- Monthly breast self-examination (BSE)
  - Best method for detecting breast masses early
  - Recommend women develop the habit of routine BSE
- Effectiveness of BSE
  - Determined by correct procedure
  - BSE should be performed on a regular monthly basis
  - About 1 week after each menstrual period
- Clinical breast examination by a trained healthcare provider
  - Suspicious or worrisome findings
  - Diagnostic procedures
  - Referral

1a Positions for Inspection of the Breasts
- (Figure 4.9)

1b Procedure for Breast Self-examination
- (Figure 4.10)

2 Mammography
- Effective screening tool for breast cancer
- American Cancer Society recommendation: All women age 40 and over have an annual mammogram

- The National Cancer Institute and ACOG
  - Recommend mammograms every 1 to 2 years for women ages 40 to 49
  - Annually for all women age 50 and older

 Pap Smear
- A form of cervical cytology testing
  - Examination of cells from the cervix and endocervical canal
  - Detects cellular abnormalities
  - Early detection of cervical cancer
  - Decreases incidence of cervical cancer deaths
  - Yearly Pap smear recommended

3a Nursing Practice
- ("Nursing Practice")

4 Pelvic Examination
- Detection of abnormalities
  - Vagina
  - Uterus
  - Ovaries
  - Lower abdomen
- Perceptions
  - Uncomfortable
  - Embarrassing
- Recommended strategies: Allow client to visualize the procedure in a mirror

---

SUGGESTIONS FOR CLASSROOM ACTIVITIES

Facilitate in-class discussion of "Skill 2-2: Assisting with a Pelvic Examination" on the Student CD-ROM and Clinical Skills Manual.

SUGGESTIONS FOR CLINICAL ACTIVITIES

Assign students to women's health clinics. Allow them to observe healthcare providers performing and assisting with pelvic examinations.

LEARNING OBJECTIVE 5

Discuss the physical and psychologic aspects of menopause.

CONCEPTS FOR LECTURE

1. During menopause the female experiences a variety of physical changes
2. Psychological changes also affect the post-menopausal female.

POWERPOINT LECTURE SLIDES

 Physical Aspects
- Ovulation ceases 1 to 2 years prior to menopause
- Gradual atrophy of reproductive organs
  - Other atrophic changes
  - Urethra
  - Trigonal area of the bladder
- FSH levels rise
- Less estrogen is produced

1a Physical Aspects
- Vasomotor disturbances
  - "Hot flashes"
  - Sweating and sleep disturbances
- Thinning of pubic hair
  - Turns gray or white
  - May ultimately disappear

- Decreased pelvic support
- Decrease in breast firmness: Pendulous and decrease in size

 Physical Aspects
- Possible development of osteoporosis
  - ○ Decrease in the bony skeletal mass
  - ○ Associated with lowered estrogen and androgen levels
  - ○ Lack of physical exercise
  - ○ Chronic low intake of calcium
- Increased risk of coronary heart disease— estrogen deprivation
- Loss of protein from the skin and supportive tissues—wrinkling
- Weight gain
  - ○ Frequent gain weight
  - ○ Excessive caloric intake
  - ○ Lower caloric need with the same level of intake

 Psychological Aspects
- Possible helpless feelings due to physical changes
- Fatigue from lack of sleep due to hot flashes
- Possible increase in enjoyment of sexual intercourse due to lack of worry about pregnancy
- Psychologic adaptation influenced by
  - ○ Her own expectations and knowledge
  - ○ Physical well-being
  - ○ Family views
  - ○ Marital stability
  - ○ Sociocultural expectations

SUGGESTIONS FOR CLASSROOM ACTIVITIES

Assign students to review "Evidence-Based Nursing: Prevention of Osteoporosis" in preparation for in-class completion of the critical thinking exercise EBN 4.1.

SUGGESTIONS FOR CLINICAL ACTIVITIES

Suggest that students review "Complementary Care: Phytoestrogens." Encourage them to access the Women's Health web links for additional information. Allow students to observe post-menopausal counseling at a women's health clinic or doctor's office.

LEARNING OBJECTIVE 6

Explain the cycle of violence and its application to battered women, including pregnant women.

CONCEPTS FOR LECTURE

1. Battering takes place in a cyclic fashion through three phases.
2. Early identification of battered females and treatment is indicated for all females facing physical violence and psychological abuse.

POWERPOINT LECTURE SLIDES

 Cycle of Violence
- Tension-building phase: Batterer demonstrates power and control
- Acute battering incident:
  - ○ Triggered by an external event or internal state of batterer
  - ○ Episode of acute violence

- Tranquil phase: Kind and loving behavior on part of batterer as a way to make up for violence

 Cycle of Violence
- Application to battered women
  - Woman may have been raised to be:
  - Submissive
  - Passive dependent
  - Developed a sense of hopelessness
  - Incidents may increase during pregnancy
- Physically abusive partners nearly always experience psychologic abuse
- Universal screening recommended for all female clients at every health encounter

 Treatment
- Medical treatment for injuries
- Temporary shelter for her and her children
- Counseling
- Legal assistance
- Financial assistance
- Job training
- Employment counseling
- Enrollment in ongoing support group with counseling

SUGGESTIONS FOR CLASSROOM ACTIVITIES

Have students view the video on spousal abuse on the Student CD-ROM. Utilize role play in the classroom to assist students in identifying the behavior of the abuser and the victim.

SUGGESTIONS FOR CLINICAL ACTIVITIES

Schedule students to visit a homeless shelter for abused and battered women. Allow them to observe the activities that the clients engage in and the counseling that they receive.

LEARNING OBJECTIVE 7

Delineate the nurse's role in working with women who have experienced intimate partner violence or rape.

CONCEPTS FOR LECTURE

1. The nurse caring for a victim of violence or rape functions in a variety of roles.

POWERPOINT LECTURE SLIDES

 The Nurses's Role
- Coordinate the care of survivors of sexual assault
- Create a safe, secure milieu
- Obtain a careful, detailed history
- Gather necessary forensic evidence—complete physical examination

 The Nurses's Role
- Complete a forensic chart and kit
- Explain all procedures
- Reassure the survivor
- Act as the survivor's advocate—provide support without usurping decision making

POWERPOINT LECTURE SLIDES *continued*

 The Nurses's Role
- Offers prophylactic treatment for STIs
- Offers postcoital contraceptive therapy
- Provides sexual assault counseling
- Cares for family members—reduces their anxiety

SUGGESTIONS FOR CLASSROOM ACTIVITIES

Identify a specially trained sexual assault nurse examiner (SANE) in your community. Invite her to talk about her role in the community in relation to the care of victims of violence or rape in your classroom.

SUGGESTIONS FOR CLINICAL ACTIVITIES

Identify case studies of female victims of violence or rape. Allow students to participate in open discussion. Let them explore strategies to decrease domestic violence and rape.

CHAPTER 5
COMMON GYNECOLOGIC PROBLEMS

RESOURCE LIBRARY

CD-ROM
NCLEX-RN® Review
Audio Glossary

IMAGE LIBRARY

Figure 5.1 Depiction of the clue cells characteristically seen in bacterial vaginosis.
Figure 5.2 The hyphae and spores of *Candida albicans,* the fungus responsible for vulvovaginal candidiasis.
Figure 5.3 Microscopic appearance of *Trichomonas vaginalis.*

COMPANION WEBSITE
NCLEX-RN® Review
The Bethesda System for Classifying Pap Smears

Figure 5.4 Condylomata acuminata on the vulva.
Figure 5.5 The nurse provides information for the woman during preoperative teaching.

Table 5.1 The Bethesda System for Classifying Pap Smears
Nursing Practice
Teaching Highlights: Preventing Cytitis

LEARNING OBJECTIVE 1
Contrast the common benign breast disorders.

CONCEPTS FOR LECTURE

1. Fibrocystic breast changes, the most common of the benign breast disorders, are most prevalent in women 30 to 50 years of age.
2. Fibroadenoma is a common benign tumor seen in women in their teens and early twenties. It is potentially malignant.
3. Intraductal papillomas are tumors in the terminal portion of a duct associated with menopause.
4. Duct ectasis (comedomastitis) is an inflammatory condition of the ducts behind the nipple commonly occurring during or near the onset of menopause.

POWERPOINT LECTURE SLIDES

1 Fibrocystic Breast Changes
- May be caused by an imbalance in progesterone and estrogen—breast tissue thickens
- Symptoms: Cyclic increased breast tenderness and swelling before beginning of menses
- Findings on physical examination
  - Mild signs of irregularity and nodularity
  - Possible expressible nipple discharge
- Treatment: Sodium and caffeine restriction may help

2 Fibroadenoma
- Typical characteristics
  - Freely movable solid benign tumor
  - Well defined, rounded with a rubbery texture
  - Asymptomatic and nontender
- Treatment
  - Watchful observation
  - Possible surgical excision

3 Intraductal Papilloma
- Tumor within the ductal system of the breast
  - Prevalent during menopause
  - Have the potential to become malignant

- Typical characteristics
  - Most frequent cause of nipple discharge in nonpregnant, nonlactating females
  - Small ball-like solitary nodules
- Treatment
  - Excision
  - Follow-up care

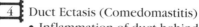 Duct Ectasis (Comedomastitis)
- Inflammation of duct behind nipple
  - Occurs during or near menopause
  - Not associated with malignancy
- Typical characteristics
  - Thick, sticky nipple discharge
  - Burning pain, pruritus, and inflammation
  - Nipple retraction may also occur
- Treatment: Drug therapy for symptom relief or surgical removal
- Nursing management for benign breast disorders
  - Formulation of nursing diagnosis and therapeutic communication
  - Emotional support and education
  - Specific interventions and evaluation

SUGGESTIONS FOR CLASSROOM ACTIVITIES

In class have students engage in role play and vocalize specific signs and symptoms of each benign breast disorder. Students may be assigned to play the role of the clients with the various conditions or the healthcare provider recommending treatment options.

SUGGESTIONS FOR CLINICAL ACTIVITIES

- Arrange for students to spend several hours in a breast health clinic. Encourage students to observe the different screening procedures as well as the emotional reactions of the clients.
- Contact a school nurse who works with high school students. Arrange for nursing students to present a class on breast self-examination techniques to either female junior or senior high school students. The class would include a discussion on the importance of breast self-exam and a demonstration/practice session using a breast self-exam model.

LEARNING OBJECTIVE 2

Discuss the signs and symptoms, medical therapy, and implications for fertility of endometriosis.

CONCEPTS FOR LECTURE

1. Endometriosis is a condition characterized by the presence of endometrial tissue outside of the uterine cavity. It may occur at any age after puberty, but is most common in women between ages 20 and 45. The most common symptom is pelvic pain.
2. Treatment may be medical, surgical, or a combination of the two.

POWERPOINT LECTURE SLIDES

Signs and Symptoms
- Pelvic pain—related to menstrual cycle
- Dyspareunia—painful intercourse
- Abnormal uterine bleeding
- Bimanual examination
  - Fixed, tender, retroverted uterus
  - Palpable nodules in cul-de-sac
  - Diagnosis confirmed by laparoscopy

3. The condition is often diagnosed when the woman seeks evaluation for infertility.

 Treatment Options
- Surgical removal of visible endometrial tissue
  - Excision, endocoagulation, electrocautery, or laser vaporization
  - Surgery is effective in relieving pain
- Surgical removal of uterus and ovaries
- Hormonal therapy
- Women with minimal symptoms—observation, analgesics, nonsteroidal and anti-inflamatory drugs

[3] Implications for Fertility
- Infertility
  - Clients with endometriosis may have difficulty becoming pregnant
  - The client then seeks intervention for infertility
  - Endometriosis diagnosed during infertility evaluation
- Hormonal therapy or oral contraceptives
  - Suppresses the menstrual cycle
  - Pregnancy must be delayed until oral contraceptive or hormonal therapy is completed

[3a] Nursing Management
- Assessment—signs and symptoms, knowledge of condition, and treatment options
- Nursing diagnosis
  - Formulate diagnosis based on assessment data
  - Most common nursing diagnosis: Pain
- Planning and implementation—give explanations and provide treatment
- Evaluation
  - Outcomes include pain relief
  - The ability to choose appropriate treatment options

SUGGESTIONS FOR CLASSROOM ACTIVITIES

Contact a women's healthcare provider to obtain the name of a woman with endometriosis who would speak to the class on her personal experiences.

SUGGESTIONS FOR CLINICAL ACTIVITIES

Arrange for students to attend a self-help group for women who experience endometriosis.

LEARNING OBJECTIVE 3

Identify the risk factors, treatment options, and nursing interventions for a woman with toxic shock syndrome.

CONCEPTS FOR LECTURE

1. Toxic shock syndrome (TSS) is primarily a disease of women at or near menses or during the postpartum period. The causative organism is *Staphylococcus aureus*. Several factors place the woman at risk for this condition.
2. Early diagnosis and treatment are important in preventing death.

POWERPOINT LECTURE SLIDES

[1] Risk Factors
- Use of superabsorbent tampons
- Use of cervical cap or diaphragm during menses
- Colonization of *Staphylococcus aureus*

 Early Diagnosis
- Identification of signs and symptoms
- Most common signs of TSS include:
  - Fever (often greater than 38.9°C [102°F])
  - Rash on the trunk initially

CONCEPTS FOR LECTURE *continued*

3. Education of women is key to preventing toxic shock syndrome (TSS).

POWERPOINT LECTURE SLIDES *continued*

- ○ Desquamation of the skin, especially the palms and soles; occurs 1 to 2 weeks after the onset of symptoms
- ○ Hypotension and dizziness
- ○ Systemic symptoms—vomiting, diarrhea, severe myalgia, and inflamed mucous membranes
- ○ Disorders of the central nervous system— alterations in consciousness, disorientation, and coma

 Treatment Options
- • Hydration—intravenous fluids
- • Broad-spectrum antibiotics including antistaphylococcal agents
- • Nursing interventions—treatment and prevention through education

 Education
- • Instruct women about correct use of:
  - ○ Superabsorbent tampons
  - ○ Cervical caps and diaphragms
  - ○ Instruct women not to use tampons for first 6 to 8 weeks after childbirth

SUGGESTIONS FOR CLASSROOM ACTIVITIES

- • Recommend that students review Critical Thinking in Action feature in the book and view the video and answer questions on the Student CD-ROM. Assign the case study on the Companion Website on TSS for homework.
- • Divide the students into two groups. Have one group go online to find statistics regarding the incidence and mortality rate associated with toxic shock syndrome in the United States. Have another group go online to obtain information from two tampon manufacturers regarding the self-care measures that women can utilize to prevent TSS. In class, each group will present their findings.

LEARNING OBJECTIVE 4

Compare vulvovaginal candidiasis and bacterial vaginosis.

CONCEPTS FOR LECTURE

1. Signs and symptoms of vaginitis are the most common reasons women seek gynecologic care.
2. It may be caused by an infection or by an alteration of normal flora, as in the case of bacterial vaginosis and *Candida albicans. Refer also to "Drug Guide: Metronidazole," Ladewig, 6e, page 118*

POWERPOINT LECTURE SLIDES

1 Symptoms of Vaginitis or Vulvovaginitis
- • Increased vaginal discharge
- • Vulvar irritation
- • Pruritis and foul odor
- • Pain

2 Bacterial Vaginosis
- • Caused by alteration in normal vaginal bacterial flora
- • Signs and symptoms
  - ○ Thin, watery white or gray vaginal discharge
  - ○ Vaginal discharge has a "fishy" smell
  - ○ "Clue" cells are seen on wet-mount preparation
- • Treatment
  - ○ Metronidazole (Flagyl)

   ○ Alternate use of clindamycin (Cleocin) vaginal cream
   ○ Oral clindamycin

 Depiction of Clue Cells Characteristically Seen in Bacterial Vaginosis
   • (Figure 5.1)

 Vulvovaginal Candidiasis
   • Most common form of vaginitis related to use of:
      ○ Oral contraceptives
      ○ Immunosuppressants
      ○ Antibiotics
   • Signs and Symptoms
      ○ Thick, curdy vaginal discharge
      ○ Severe itching
      ○ Dysuria and dyspareunia

 Hyphae and Spores of *Candida Albicans*
   • (Figure 5.2)

Vulvovaginal Candidiasis
   • Diagnosis
      ○ Signs and symptoms
      ○ Microscopic examination of vaginal discharge
      ○ Hyphae and spores seen on wet-mount preparation
   • Treatment
      ○ Antifungal drugs
      ○ Intravaginal butoconazole, miconozole
      ○ Nystatin suppositories, cream, or tablets
   • Recurrent episodes of infection
      ○ Monitor blood glucose levels for glycosuria
      ○ Diabetic or prediabetic condition may exist

SUGGESTIONS FOR CLASSROOM ACTIVITIES

For homework have students complete the NCLEX-RN® review questions on the Student CD-ROM and Companion Website specific to lecture topics.

SUGGESTIONS FOR CLINICAL ACTIVITIES

Assign students to clinical areas where females commonly seek health care for vaginal infections. Allow students to teach clients how to prevent vaginal infections.

LEARNING OBJECTIVE 5

Describe the common sexually transmitted infections.

CONCEPTS FOR LECTURE

1. Sexually transmitted infections (STIs) are the most common reasons for outpatient, community-based treatment of women. Trichomoniasis is an infection caused by a microscopic motile protozoan.
2. Chlamydial infection is the most common bacterial STI in the United States. Gonorrhea is an infection also of bacterial origin.

POWERPOINT LECTURE SLIDES

 Trichomoniasis
   • Organism: *Trichomonas vaginalis,* a microscopic motile protozoan
   • Common symptoms: Yellow-green, frothy, odorous discharge and vaginal itching

3. Herpes genitalia is caused by a virus. Condylomata acuminata (venereal warts) is relatively common. This infection is also caused by a virus. Another sexually transmitted infection of viral origin is acquired immun-odeficiency syndrome (AIDS).

4. Syphilis is a chronic STI caused by a spirochete.

- Diagnosis and treatment
  - *Trichomonas vaginalis* seen under the microscope on a wet-mount preparation of vaginal discharge confirms the diagnosis
  - Most males asymptomatic. Both partners are treated with metronidazole (Flagyl) administered in a single 2-g dose; a 7-day regimen is also available

 Microscopic Appearance of *Trichomonas Vaginalis*
- (Figure 5.3)

 Chlamydia and Gonorrhea Infection
- Chlamydia: Causative organism—*Chlamydia trachomatis*
  - Often asymptomatic
  - May cause ophthalmia neonatorum in the newborn
  - Erythromycin ophthalmic ointment prophylaxis at birth
  - Both partners are treated with doxycycline or azithromycin
- Diagnosis symptoms and treatment
  - Thin or purulent discharge
  - Dysuria
  - Lower abdominal pain
  - Diagnosis: Antigen detection, deoxyribonucleic acid (DNA) probe assays, and polymerase chain reaction (PCR)
  - Treatment: Single dose of azithromycin orally or doxycycline orally twice daily for 7 days
  - Sexual partners are also treated; couples should abstain from intercourse for 7 days
  - Pregnant women are treated with erythromycin ethylsuccinate or amoxicillin

 Gonorrhea
- Gonorrhea
  - Organism: *Neisseria gonorrhoeae*
  - Signs and symptoms: Purulent, green-yellow discharge, dysuria, and urinary frequency
  - Both partners are treated with antibiotics: Cefixime and doxycycline
- Diagnosis and treatment
  - Positive cervical culture and signs and symptoms
  - Both partners are treated with antibiotics: Cefixime and doxycycline
  - Gonorrhea and chlamydia may cause pelvic inflammatory disease

 Herpes Genitalia
- Herpes genitalia causative organism: Herpes Simplex Virus (HSV)
  - Development of single or multiple blister-like vesicles on the genitals
  - Results in inflammation and pain

- ○ Flulike symptoms may develop
- ○ Diagnosis: Appearance of lesions, pap smear or culture of lesions
- ○ Treatment: Acyclovir and other antiherpes viral drugs
- ○ Cannot be cured
- ○ Recurrences may be triggered by physical and/or emotional stress—may cause fatal fetal infection if herpes lesion is present in genital tract during childbirth

 Condylomata Acuminata
- • Condylomata acuminata causative organism: Human Papilloma Virus (HPV)
  - ○ Cauliflower-like lesions on penis or in genital area
  - ○ Linked with cervical cancer
  - ○ Biopsy and treatment
  - ○ Provider-administered therapies: Cryotherapy, intralesional interferon; surgical removal, curettage, or laser surgery
  - ○ Imiquimod, podophylin, and podofilox are not used during pregnancy
  - ○ Thought to be teratogenic
  - ○ Large doses have been associated with fetal death

 Condylomata Acuminata on Vulva
- • (Figure 5.4)

 Acquired Immunodeficiency Syndrome
- • Acquired immunodeficiency syndrome
  - ○ Fatal disorder caused by the human immunodeficiency virus (HIV): Has profound implications for the fetus if infected woman is pregnant

 Syphilis
- • Chronic STI caused by the Spirochete *Treponema pallidum*
  - ○ Primary: Chancre at site of entry and flulike symptoms; Secondary: 6 weeks to 6 months chancre disappears and wartlike skin eruptions appear with other systemic reactions
  - ○ Transplacental transmission may occur
  - ○ Serologic testing for every pregnant woman is mandated in some states

 Syphilis
- • Diagnosis
  - ○ Dark-field examination for spirochetes
  - ○ Blood tests: Venereal disease research laboratory (VDRL)
  - ○ Rapid plasma reagin (RPR)
  - ○ Treponemal antibody-absorption (FTA-ABS) test
  - ○ Nonpregnant and pregnant women with syphilis of less than a year
  - ○ CDC (2002) recommends 2.4 million units of benzathine penicillin G administered intramuscularly in a single dose

○ For syphilis more than one year duration, 2.4 million units of benzathine penicillin G given intramuscularly once a week for 3 weeks

○ Nonpregnant women allergic to penicillin: treat with Doxycycline or tetracycline

○ Pregnant woman allergic to penicillin: Desensitized to penicillin and then treatment recommended by CDC

○ Maternal serologic testing may remain positive for 8 months

○ Newborn may have a positive test for 3 months

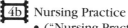 4b Nursing Practice
- ("Nursing Practice")

SUGGESTIONS FOR CLASSROOM ACTIVITIES

- Invite a nurse from the county/state STI clinic to come to class to speak about strategies for working with clients with an STI.
- Assign the care plan activity on gynecologic infection on the Companion Website for homework.

SUGGESTIONS FOR CLINICAL ACTIVITIES

If possible, assign at least one or two students to clients with STI. Allow them to discuss the nursing management of the individual clients during post-clinical conference.

LEARNING OBJECTIVE 6

Summarize the health teaching a nurse needs to provide to a woman with a sexually transmitted infection.

CONCEPTS FOR LECTURE

1. The nurse must actively engage in teaching the client diagnosed with a sexually transmitted infection about all aspects of the infection. *See "Teaching Highlights: Preventing STIs and Their Consequences."*

POWERPOINT LECTURE SLIDES

1 Health Teaching
- Provide information about the infection
- Methods of transmission
- Implications for pregnancy
- Implications for future fertility
- Portray an attitude of acceptance

1a Health Teaching
- Importance of thorough treatment
- Importance of ensuring the partner is treated
- Need to abstain from sexual activity during treatment
- Availability of treatment and cure for some STIs
- Ability to control symptoms but not cure some STIs
- Importance of prevention
- Use of condoms to decrease the incidence of infection
- Provide information about support groups

SUGGESTIONS FOR CLASSROOM ACTIVITIES

Encourage students to review "Teaching Highlights: Preventing STIs and Their Consequences" before the lecture. Allow open class discussion following the lecture.

SUGGESTIONS FOR CLINICAL ACTIVITIES

Assign students into groups. Instruct each group to select a sexually transmitted disease and to formulate a teaching plan and present it to a group of clients.

LEARNING OBJECTIVE 7

Relate the implications of pelvic inflammatory disease (PID) for future fertility to its pathology, signs and symptoms, and treatment.

CONCEPTS FOR LECTURE

1. The greatest problem of pelvic inflamatory disease is post-infection tubal damage often caused by chlamydia and gonorrhea.
2. The woman who is acutely ill will have obvious signs and symptoms. A low grade infection may be more difficult to detect.
3. Several combinations of therapy are utilized to treat this condition.
4. Women of reproductive age are most at risk for pelvic inflammatory disease.

POWERPOINT LECTURE SLIDES

1 Pathology
- Often caused by chlamydia or gonorrhea—usually produces tubal infection (salpingitis)
- Infection may cause:
  - Scarring of fallopian tubes
  - Prevention of union between sperm and ova
  - Prevention of the mobility of the fertilized ova through the fallopian tubes
  - Problems with fertility

2 Signs and Symptoms
- Chills and fever
- Bilateral sharp cramping pain of the lower abdomen
- Purulent vaginal discharge
- Irregular vaginal bleeding
- Nausea and vomiting
- Malaise
- Sometimes asymptomatic with normal lab values

3 Diagnosis and Treatment
- Diagnosis
  - Physical examinations
  - Positive cervical cultures for gonorrhea or chlamydia
  - CBC with differential
  - Laparoscopy
  - Signs and symtoms
- Treatment
  - Intravenous fluids
  - Analgesics
  - Intravenous antibiotics
  - Treatment of sexual partner
  - Removal of IUD 24 to 48 hours after beginning antibiotics

4 Risk Factors and Nursing Management
- Sexually active females ages 15 to 39
- Multiple sexual partners
- Early onset of sexual activity
- Recent gynecologic procedure
- IUD insertion
- Nursing management
  - Identify females at risk
  - Education to aim at prevention
  - Discuss signs and symptoms
  - Administer treatments
  - Reinforce the importance of completing antibiotic therapy
  - Discuss the possible effects on fertility

LEARNING OBJECTIVE 8

Identify the implications of an abnormal finding during a pelvic examination.

CONCEPTS FOR LECTURE

1. A Papanicolaou (Pap) smear is a test done to screen for the presence of cellular anomalies of the cervix and cervical cancer.
2. Ovarian masses may be palpated during the pelvic examinations.
3. Fibroid tumors/leiomyomas are the most common benign uterine mass in women.
4. Endometrial cancer, most commonly a disease of postmenopausal women, has a high rate of cure if detected early.

POWERPOINT LECTURE SLIDES

1 Abnormal Pap Smear Results
- Detects variety of abnormalities
- Greatest impact on detection of cervical cancer
- Bethesda system most widely used Pap smear reporting system: Early detection allows changes to be treated before precancerous or cancerous cells develop
- Notification: Source of anxiety for woman
- Deliver results in a caring way
- Need for accurate and complete information about meaning of results—need to provide information about next steps to be taken
- Give client time to ask questions and express concerns
- Therapeutic or diagnostic procedures
  - Repetition of Pap Smear, colposcopy, endocervical biopsy
  - Cryotherapy, laser conization, or large loop excision of transformation zone

1a Bethesda System for Classifying Pap Smears
- (Table 5.1)

2 Ovarian Masses
- May be palpated during a pelvic exam
- Between 70% and 80% of ovarian masses are benign
- More than 50% are functional cysts
- Occur most commonly in women 20 to 40 years of age
- May be asymptomatic or symptomatic
- Symptoms: Cramping, dyspareunia, irregular bleeding
- Treatment: Oral contraceptives, surgery considered for large masses
- Most ovarian cysts resolve on their own
- Ovarian cancer is the most fatal of all cancers in women
- Difficult to diagnose
- Often spreads throughout the pelvis before it is detected

POWERPOINT LECTURE SLIDES *continued*

 Uterine Masses
- Fibroid tumors/leiomyomas
- Most common benign disease entities in women
- Most common reason for gynecologic surgery
- Between 20% and 50% of women develop leiomyomas by age 40
- Common in women of African heritage
- Frequently asymptomatic
- Symptoms include: Lower abdominal pain, fullness or pressure, menorrhagia, dysmenorrhea
- Diagnosis: Ultrasonography revealing masses or nodules
- Masses or nodules involving the uterus palpated on pelvic examination
- Treatment: None, drug therapy, or surgery

Endometrial Cancer
- Most common disease of postmenopausal women
- High rate of cure if detected early
- Hallmark sign is vaginal bleeding in postmenopausal women not treated with hormone replacement therapy
- Diagnosis: Endometrial biopsy, transvaginal ultrasound
- Posthysterectomy pathology examination of the uterus
- Treatment: Total abdominal hysterectomy (TAH) and bilateral salpingo-oophorectomy (BSO)
- Radiation therapy may also be indicated
- Nursing management
  - Inform client of etiology, symptoms, and treatment options
  - Schedule follow-up appointments
  - Provide emotional support and counseling

SUGGESTIONS FOR CLASSROOM ACTIVITIES

- Have students refer to the Bethesda System for Classifying Pap Smears that is available on the Companion Website.
- Invite students to share experiences of their first pelvic exam in class. Allow students to discuss methods that could be used to decrease a client's anxiety regarding their first pelvic exam.

SUGGESTIONS FOR CLINICAL ACTIVITIES

Provide pelvic models and speculums for student practice.

LEARNING OBJECTIVE 9

Contrast cystitis and pyelonephritis.

CONCEPTS FOR LECTURE

1. Cystitis is an infection of lower urinary tract or the bladder.
2. Pyelonephritis is an infection of the upper urinary tract or the kidneys.

POWERPOINT LECTURE SLIDES

 Cystitis ("Teaching Highlights: Preventing Cytitis")
- Most common organisms: *Escherichia coli, Klebsiella,* and *Proteus*

- Symptoms
  - Dysuria, urgency, frequency
  - Low-grade fever
- Diagnosis
  - Symptoms
  - Urine culture
- Treatment: PO antibiotics

 Pyelonephritis
- Less common and more severe than cystitis
  - May be preceded by lower urinary tract infection
  - Sudden onset: Chills, high temperature, flank pain, dysuria, urgency, and frequency
  - May cause nausea, vomiting, and general malaise
- Treatment
  - Hospitalization
  - Intravenous antibiotics or oral antibiotics

Suggestions for Classroom Activities

- In-class review of "Teaching Highlights: Preventing Cystitis."
- Divide students into pairs and let them practice teaching each other ways to avoid cystitis.

Suggestions for Clinical Activities

Allow students to utilize "Teaching Highlights: Preventing Cystitis" in the clinical area as a health teaching tool for clients at the clinical site.

CHAPTER 6
SPECIAL REPRODUCTIVE ISSUES FOR FAMILIES

RESOURCE LIBRARY

CD-ROM

Audio Glossary
NCLEX-RN® Review
Activity: Ovulation
Skill 2–5: Assisting During Amniocentesis

COMPANION WEBSITE

Thinking Critically
NCLEX-RN® Review
MediaLink Applications:
    Case Study: Infertility
    Care Plan: Infertile Couple

IMAGE LIBRARY

Figure 6.1 Flow chart for management of the infertile couple.
Figure 6.2 A, A monophasic, anovulatory basal body temperature (BBT) chart. B, A biphasic BBT chart illustrating probable time of ovulation, the different types of testing, and the time in the cycle that each would be performed.
Figure 6.3 A, Spinnbarkeit (elasticity). B, Ferning pattern. C, Lack of ferning.
Figure 6.4 Sperm passage through cervical mucus.
Figure 6.5 Assisted reproductive techniques.
Figure 6.6 Normal female karyotype.
Figure 6.7 Normal male karyotype.
Figure 6.8 Karyotype of a male who has trisomy 21, Down syndrome.
Figure 6.9 A boy with Down syndrome.
Figure 6.10 Infant with Turner syndrome at 1 month of age.

Figure 6.11 Autosomal dominant pedigree.
Figure 6.12 Autosomal recessive pedigree.
Figure 6.13 X-linked recessive pedigree.
Figure 6.14 A, Genetic amniocentesis for prenatal diagnosis is done at 14 to 16 weeks' gestation. B, Chorionic villus sampling is done at 8 to 10 weeks, and the cells are karyotyped within 48 to 72 hours.
Figure 6.15 Dermatoglyphic patterns of the hands in A, a normal individual, and B, a child with Down syndrome.
Figure 6.16 Screening pedigree.

Table 6.1 Possible Causes of Infertility.
Table 6.2 Fertility Awareness.
Table 6.3 Initial Infertility Physical Workup and Laboratory Evaluation.
Table 6.4 Normal Semen Analysis.

LEARNING OBJECTIVE 1

Identify the essential components of fertility.

CONCEPTS FOR LECTURE

1. Essential components present in the female are vital for fertility.
2. There are elements in the male that facilitate fertility.

POWERPOINT LECTURE SLIDES

1 Female
- Cervical mucus must be favorable
- Fallopian tubes must be patent
- Functional hypothalamic-pituitary axis
- Ovaries must produce and release ova in a regular, cyclic fashion

- Endometrium must be prepared for implantation of the blastocyst
- Adequate reproductive hormones must be present

1a Possible Causes of Infertility
- (Table 6.1)

1b Fertility Awareness
- (Table 6.2)

2 Male
- Functional reproductive organs
  - Testes must produce adequate numbers of sperm
  - Unobstructed genital tract
  - Genital tract secretions must be normal
  - Ejaculated sperm must reach cervix

Suggestions for Classroom Activities

Facilitate an in-class review of "Complementary Care: Common Treatments for Infertility" and Tables 6.1 and 6.2.

Suggestions for Clinical Activities

Have students complete the Ovulation exercise on the Student CD-ROM and discuss their findings. View the animations on cell division and conception in clinical.

Learning Objective 2

Describe the elements of the preliminary investigation of infertility.

Concepts for Lecture

1. There are several elements to consider when performing a preliminary investigation of the infertile couple. *Refer to Table 6.3.*
2. A fertility problem is a deeply personal, emotion-laden area in a couple's life.

PowerPoint Lecture Slides

1 Preliminary Investigation
- Information about most fertile times for intercourse
- Explanation of basic infertility workup
- Basic assessments
  - Ovarian function
  - Cervical mucus adequacy
  - Semen analysis
  - Tubal patency
  - General condition of pelvic organs

1a Preliminary Investigation
- Complete physical examination of both partners
- Laboratory examination
  - CBC
  - UA
  - Hormonal assays

1b Initial Infertility Physical Workup and Laboratory Evaluation
- (Table 6.3)

2 Psychosocial Support
- Provide comfort to couples; offer a sympathetic ear
- Nonjudgmental approach
- Provide appropriate information and instructions

- Establish rapport—elicit relevant information from couples

[2a] Flow Chart for Management of the Infertile Couple
- (Figure 6.1)

SUGGESTIONS FOR CLASSROOM ACTIVITIES

- Recommend students prepare for an in-class discussion about "Case Study: Infertility" by reviewing the activity on the companion website.
- Invite a nurse practitioner who works with infertile couples to speak on the elements of the intial infertility assessment.

SUGGESTIONS FOR CLINICAL ACTIVITIES

Assign students the care plan activity at the Companion Website, "Infertile Couple," in preparation for clinical discussion.

LEARNING OBJECTIVE 3

Summarize the indications for the tests and associated treatments, including assisted reproductive technologies, that are done in an infertility workup.

CONCEPTS FOR LECTURE

1. There are several indications for tests and treatments for infertility.

POWERPOINT LECTURE SLIDES

[1] Indications for Tests and Treatments
- If lack of ovarian function is suspected
  - Basal body temperature recording
  - Hormonal assessments
  - Endometrial biopsy
  - Transvaginal ultrasound
- If cervical problems are suspected
  - Ferning capacity of cervical mucus

[1a] Indications for Tests and Treatments
- If tubal or uterine problems are suspected
  - Hysterosalpingography
  - Hysteroscopy
  - Laparoscopy
- If male's fertility is suspected
  - Semen analysis
  - Screening for antisperm antibodies

[1b] Normal Semen Analysis
- (Table 6.4)

[1c] Indications for Tests and Treatments
- Pharmacologic intervention is prescribed
  - Abnormal ovarian or endometrial function
- Therapeutic insemination
  - Indicated for low or abnormal sperm counts
  - Structural defects in the male reproductive tract

[1d] Tasks of the Infertile Couple

[1e] Indications for Tests and Treatments
- Indications for in vitro fertilization (IVF)
  - Infertility from tubal factors
  - Mucus abnormalities
  - Male infertility

  ○ Female immunologic infertility
  ○ Cervical factors
- Pharmacological agents
  ○ Danazol (Danocrine)
  ○ Oral contraceptives
  ○ Ovulation-induction agents

SUGGESTIONS FOR CLASSROOM ACTIVITIES

- Utilize the infertility questionnaire as a tool for students to use during a role play depicting an infertile couple at their first interview.
- Divide students into groups of three or four. Assign each group a different pharmacological agent used to manage infertility. Have each group present information related to the purpose, mechanism of action, side effects, and nursing considerations. Allow time for students to present their findings.

SUGGESTIONS FOR CLINICAL ACTIVITIES

Recommend that students review "Developing Cultural Competence: Infertility Treatments." Arrange for students to shadow a healthcare provider at a fertility clinic serving multicultural clients.

LEARNING OBJECTIVE 4

Explore the couple's psychological reactions related to infertility issues.

CONCEPTS FOR LECTURE

1. Infertility therapy taxes a couple's financial, physical, and psychological resources.

POWERPOINT LECTURE SLIDES

1 Psychological Reactions
- Development of lack of spontaneity of sexual intercourse
  ○ Constant attention to temperature charts
  ○ Instructions about their sex life from an outsider
- Feelings of loss of control
- Feelings of reduced competency
- Loss of status and ambiguity as a couple— infertility often becomes central focus for role identity

1a Psychological Reactions
- Sense of social stigma
  ○ Feelings of guilt or shame
- Stress on marital and sexual relationship
  ○ Heighten feelings of frustration or anger between partners
- Strained relationship with healthcare providers
- Tasks of the infertile couple

SUGGESTIONS FOR CLASSROOM ACTIVITIES

- Suggest that students complete the Case Study: Infertility exercise on the Companion Website in preparation for class.
- Invite a couple who has had infertility problems to speak to your class on the physical, emotional, and financial costs of infertility.

SUGGESTIONS FOR CLINICAL ACTIVITIES

Students may access the Reproductive web links on the Companion Website for additional information in preparation for post-clinical conference.

LEARNING OBJECTIVE 5

Describe the nurse's role as counselor, educator, and advocate for couples during infertility evaluation and treatment.

CONCEPTS FOR LECTURE

1. As nurses care for infertile couples, they function in a variety of roles.

POWERPOINT LECTURE SLIDES

1 Nurse's Roles
- Counselor
  - ○ Supports the couple as they make decisions
  - ○ Helps the couple to recognize feelings
  - ○ Facilitates the free expressions of feelings
  - ○ Facilitates partner communication
- Educator
  - ○ Provides accurate information
  - ○ Gives extensive and repeated explanations
  - ○ Ensures couples have written instructions
  - ○ Helps them to understand the process

1a Nurse's Roles
- Advocate
  - ○ Helps the couple identify alternatives
  - ○ Helps the couple to understand motives
  - ○ Provides resources
  - ○ Gives infertile couples a sense of control

SUGGESTIONS FOR CLASSROOM ACTIVITIES

Invite a registered nurse or nurse practitioner who specializes in caring for infertile couples to speak to your class about the roles of nurses caring for infertile couples.

SUGGESTIONS FOR CLINICAL ACTIVITIES

Arrange for students to rotate to a fertility clinic. Assign them to observe the various roles that nurses play in the management of infertility. Allow them to discuss their observations during post-clinical conference.

LEARNING OBJECTIVE 6

Discuss the indications for preconceptual chromosomal analysis and prenatal testing.

CONCEPTS FOR LECTURE

1. Preconceptual chromosomal analysis and prenatal testing is important to identify congenital abnormalities and chromosomal defects.

POWERPOINT LECTURE SLIDES

1 Indications for Testing
- Advanced maternal age—age 35 or older
- Family history
  - ○ Chromosomal disorder
  - ○ Birth defects
  - ○ Mental retardation
- Parent with balanced translocation (chromosomal abnormality)—risk that approximately 10% to 15% children will be affected
- If the father is the carrier, 2% to 5% risk

1a Indications for Testing
- Previous child with chromosomal disorder—1% to 2% risk of future child having chromosomal abnormality
- Mother carrying an X-linked disease—risk of affected male fetus is 50%
- Ethnic group with history of chromosomal disorders

POWERPOINT LECTURE SLIDES *continued*

- Parents carrying an inborn error of metabolism—may be diagnosed in utero

 Indications for Testing
- Couples with a history of two or more first trimester spontaneous abortions
- Both parents carrying an autosomal recessive disease—sickle cell disease
- Women with an abnormal serum alpha-fetoprotein test

 Couples Who May Benefit from Prenatal Diagnosis

SUGGESTIONS FOR CLASSROOM ACTIVITIES

- Assign students to gather additional information about genetic testing like the Human Genome Project from web links at the Companion Website. Allow class discussion of information gathered.
- Invite a couple/person who have a child with a genetic defect to share their experience with the class. Prior to class, have students learn about the genetic defect that the couple/person will be discussing.

SUGGESTIONS FOR CLINICAL ACTIVITIES

Arrange for students to rotate to a clinic that screens for birth defects and provides counseling and treatment options for clients. Allow them to observe the process from admission through testing and counseling.

LEARNING OBJECTIVE 7

Identify the characteristics of autosomal dominant, autosomal recessive, and X-linked (sex-linked) recessive disorders.

CONCEPTS FOR LECTURE

1. A person is said to have an autosomal dominantly inherited disorder if the disease trait is heterozygous; that is, the abnormal gene overshadows the normal gene of the pair to produce the trait.
2. In an autosomal recessive inherited disorder, the person must have two abnormal genes to be affected.
3. X-linked, or sex-linked, disorders are those for which the abnormal gene is carried on the X chromosome. *Refer to Figure 6.13.*

POWERPOINT LECTURE SLIDES

Autosomal Dominant Disorders
- Affected person
  - Generally has an affected parent
  - One child may have more severe form of disorder
  - 50% chance of having an affected child with each pregnancy
- Males and females are equally affected
- Father can pass abnormal gene on to son

 Autosomal Dominant Disorders
- Common disorders
  - Huntington disease
  - Polycystic kidney disease
  - Neurofibromatosis (von Recklinghausen disease)
  - Achondroplastic dwarfism

 Autosomal Dominant Pedigree
- (Figure 6.11)

 Autosomal Recessive Disorder
- Both parents must be carriers
  - Must have two abnormal genes to be affected
  - Each offspring has 25% chance of having disease
  - 50% chance of being carrier

- Common disorders
  - Cystic fibrosis
  - Sickle cell anemia
  - Tay-Sachs disease
  - Most metabolic disorders

`2a` Autosomal Recessive Pedigree
- (Figure 6.12)

`3` X-Linked Recessive Disorders
- No male-to-male transmission
  - X-linked dominant
  - Effects limited to males
  - 50% chance carrier mother passes abnormal gene to son
  - 50% chance daughter of a carrier mother will be a carrier
  - 100% chance that daughters of affected fathers will be a carrier
- Common disorders
  - Hemophilia
  - Duchenne muscular dystrophy
  - Color blindness

`3a` X-Linked Recessive Pedigree
- (Figure 6.13)

SUGGESTIONS FOR CLASSROOM ACTIVITIES

Invite a healthcare provider who specializes in genetic disorders to talk to students about the prevalence and management of genetic disorders.

SUGGESTIONS FOR CLINICAL ACTIVITIES

Arrange for clinical rotation at a genetic clinic. In preparation for clinical conference, advise students to complete the NCLEX-RN® review questions and to review the web links for this chapter on the Companion Website or Student CD-ROM.

LEARNING OBJECTIVE 8

Compare prenatal and postnatal diagnostic procedures used to determine the presence of genetic disorders.

CONCEPTS FOR LECTURE

1. The ability to diagnose certain genetic diseases has enormous implications for the practice of preventive health care. Several methods are available for prenatal diagnosis. Refer to "Skill 2-5: Assisting During Amniocentesis" in the Clinical Skills Manual.
2. When a child is born with anomalies, has a stormy newborn period, or does not progress as expected, a genetic evaluation may be warranted during the postnatal period.

POWERPOINT LECTURE SLIDES

`1` Prenatal Diagnostic Tests
- Genetic ultrasound
  - To assess the fetus for genetic or congenital problems
- Genetic amniocentesis
  - Helps in the identification of genetic disorders
- Percutaneous umbilical blood sampling
  - To obtain fetal blood
  - Facilitates rapid chromosome diagnosis and genetic studies

`1a` Genetic Amniocentesis
- (Figure 6.14)

`1b` Prenatal Diagnostic Tests
- Chorionic villus sampling
  - Diagnostic information available at 8 to 10 weeks' gestation
  - Products of conception tested directly

- Alpha-fetoprotein
  - Done at 15 to 22 weeks' gestation
  - High levels associated with open neural tube defects
  - Low levels associated with Down syndrome

2️⃣ Postnatal Diagnostic Tests
- Complete and detailed history
  - Determines whether the problem is prenatal
  - Assists in identifying if the problem is postnatal
  - Helps to determine familial origin
- Physical examination

2a Postnatal Diagnostic Tests
- Dermatoglyphics analysis
- Laboratory analysis
  - Chromosome analysis
  - Enzyme assay
  - Antibody titers for infectious teratogens
  - DNA studies

2b Dermatoglyphic Patterns of the Hands
- (Figure 6.15A and Figure 6.15B)

2c Screening Pedigree
- (Figure 6.16)

SUGGESTIONS FOR CLASSROOM ACTIVITIES

When preparing for lecture, advise students to review "Skill 2-5: Assisting During Aminocentesis," on the Student CD-ROM and Clinical Skills Manual.

SUGGESTIONS FOR CLINICAL ACTIVITIES

Assign students to prenatal testing centers. Facilitate their involvement in caring for clients having genetic tests. Arrange to have students discuss their observations and experiences during post-clinical conference.

LEARNING OBJECTIVE 9

Explore the emotional impact on a couple undergoing genetic testing or coping with the birth of a baby with a genetic disorder and explain the nurse's role in supporting the family undergoing genetic counseling.

CONCEPTS FOR LECTURE

1. Parents experience grief, fear, and anger when they discover that their baby has been born with a defect or a genetic disease.
2. The nurse's role involves clarifying issues for the family.

POWERPOINT LECTURE SLIDES

1️⃣ Emotional Impact
- Concern for infant's survival
- Anger
- Grief
- Guilt
- Strife within the family
- Possibility of lifelong difficulties
- Fear of results of testing
- Blame for infant's disorder

2️⃣ The Nurse's Role
- Supports the family decisions
- Helps families to acquire adequate information
- Clarifies issues for the family
- Helps them understand information
- Acts as a liaison between family and genetic counselor

POWERPOINT LECTURE SLIDES *continued*

2a The Nurse's Role
- Provides information about support groups
- Provides continuity of care to the family
- Provides follow-up care
- Uses appropriate referral systems

SUGGESTIONS FOR CLASSROOM ACTIVITIES	**SUGGESTIONS FOR CLINICAL ACTIVITIES**
Invite a registered nurse or nurse practitioner who is experienced in caring for clients who require genetic testing to talk to your students about the emotional impact to clients and the roles nurses play when caring for those clients.	Arrange for students to shadow a healthcare provider at a genetic clinic. Allow them to follow clients through the initial assessment and follow-up.

© 2007 Pearson Education, Inc. Chapter 6/Objective 9 **51**

CHAPTER 7
CONCEPTION AND FETAL DEVELOPMENT

RESOURCE LIBRARY

💿 CD-ROM

Animations:
  Conception
  Cell Division
  Oogenesis
  Spermatogenesis
  Oogenesis and Spermatogenesis Compared
  Matching Oogenesis and Spermatogenesis
  Placenta Formation
  Embryonic Heart Formation and Circulation
  Fetal Circulation

🌐 COMPANION WEBSITE

Audio Glossary
Thinking Critically
Additional NCLEX-RN® Review
MediaLink Applications:
  Case Study: Teaching about Pregnancy
  Care Plan Activity: Client Fearful of Multiple
    Gestation

📖 IMAGE LIBRARY

Figure 7.1 Gametogenesis involves meiosis within the ovary and testis.
Figure 7.2 Sperm penetration of an ovum.
Figure 7.3 During ovulation the ovum leaves the ovary and enters the fallopian tube.
Figure 7.4 Formation of primary germ layers.
Figure 7.5 Endoderm differentiates to form the epithelial lining of the digestive and respiratory tracts and associated glands.
Figure 7.6 Early development of primary embryonic membranes.
Figure 7.7 A, Formation of faternal twins (note separate placentas.) B, Formation of identical twins.
Figure 7.8 Maternal side of placenta (Dirty Duncan).
Figure 7.9 Fetal side of placenta (Shiny Shultz).

Figure 7.10 Vascular arrangement of the placenta.
Figure 7.11 Fetal circulation.
Figure 7.12 The actual size of a human conceptus from fertilization to the early fetal stage.
Figure 7.13 The embryo at 5 weeks.
Figure 7.14 The embryo at 7 weeks.
Figure 7.15 The fetus at 9 weeks.
Figure 7.16 The fetus at 14 weeks.
Figure 7.17 The fetus at 20 weeks weighs 435 to 465 g and measures about 19 cm.

Table 7.1 Comparison of Meiosis and Mitosis.
Table 7.2 Derivation of Body Structures from Primary Cell Layers.
Table 7.4 Fetal Development: What Parents Want to Know.

LEARNING OBJECTIVE 1

Compare the difference between meiotic cellular division and mitotic cellular division.

CONCEPTS FOR LECTURE

1. Each human begins life as a single cell called a fertilized ovum or zygote. Cells multiply through the process of cellular division. One type of cellular reproduction is called mitosis.
2. Meiosis is another process of cellular reproduction that is necessary for reproduction of the species.

POWERPOINT LECTURE SLIDES

 Mitosis
  • Process of cellular division
    ○ Results in daughter cells that are exact copies of the original cell
    ○ Identical to parent cell and to each other
    ○ Contain a full set of chromosomes or genetic material
    ○ Refered to as diploid cells
    ○ Somatic cells continue to reproduce and replace each other

1a Mitosis
- The cell undergoes several changes ending in cell division
  - At the last phase of cell division, a furrow develops in the cell cytoplasm
  - The parent cell divides into two daughter cells
  - Each daughter cell has its own nucleus
  - They are identical to the parent cell
  - They have the same diploid number of chromosomes (46) and same genetic makeup as the cell from which they came

2 Meiosis
- Type of cell division that produces reproductive cells called gametes (sperm and ova)—each cell contains half genetic material of parent cell (haploid)
- Meiosis consists of two successive cell divisions
  - First division: Chromosomes replicate
  - Second division: Chromatids of each chromosome separate and move to opposite poles of each of the daughter cells
  - Cellular division results in formation of four cells
  - Each cell contains haploid number of chromosomes
  - Daughter cells contain only half the DNA of normal somatic cell

2a Comparison of Meiosis and Mitosis
- (Table 7.1)

SUGGESTIONS FOR CLASSROOM ACTIVITIES

Have students access the Student CD-ROM to view the cell division animation and discuss in class.

SUGGESTIONS FOR CLINICAL ACTIVITIES

Allow students to draw labeled diagrams and discuss both types of cellular division. Refer to Table 7.1 when discussing.

LEARNING OBJECTIVE 2

Compare the processes by which ova and sperm are produced.

CONCEPTS FOR LECTURE

1. Oogenesis is a process that ends with the development of the ovum.
2. Spermatogenes is the production of the male gamete or sperm. This process begins during puberty.

POWERPOINT LECTURE SLIDES

1 Oogenesis
- Process that produces the female gamete, called an ovum (egg), that begins to develop early in the fetal life of the female
  - Ovaries begin to develop early in the fetal life of the female
  - All ova that female will produce in her lifetime are present at birth—ovary gives rise to oogonial cells, which develop into oocytes
  - During puberty: Mature primary oocyte continues through first meiotic division in ovary
  - Haploid cells released at ovulation

1a Oogenesis
- The first meiotic division
  - Two cells of unequal size produced with same number of chromosomes

- One cell is secondary oocyte, other is minute polar body
- Secondary oocyte and polar body each contain 22 double-structured autosomal chromosomes and one double-structured sex chromosome (X)
- During puberty: Mature primary oocyte continues through first meiotic division in ovary

2 Spermatogenesis
- Production of the male gamete, or sperm, during puberty
- The spermatogonium (primordial germ cell)
  - Begins with complete set of genetic material—diploid number of chromosomes
  - Cell replicates before it enters first meiotic division
  - Cell is now primary spermatocyte
  - During second meiotic division, divide to form four spermatids, each with haploid number of chromosomes
- During the first meiotic division
  - Spermatogonium forms two cells called secondary spermatocytes
  - Each contains 22 double-structured autosomal chromosomes and either double-structured X sex chromosome or double-structured Y sex chromosome

---

SUGGESTIONS FOR CLASSROOM ACTIVITIES

Instruct students to review the following animations: oogenesis, spermatogenesis, oogenesis and spermatogenesis compared, matching oogenesis and spermatogenesis and discuss in class.

SUGGESTIONS FOR CLINICAL ACTIVITIES

Students may engage in a health teaching assignment related to the lecture topic in the clinical area.

LEARNING OBJECTIVE 3

Describe the components of the process of fertilization.

CONCEPTS FOR LECTURE

1. Preparation is the first component of fertilization.
2. Moment of fertilization is the second component of fertilization.

POWERPOINT LECTURE SLIDES

1 Preparation for Fertilization
- Preparation is the first component of fertilization
  - Ovum released into fallopian tube—viable for 24 hours
  - Sperm deposited into vagina—viable for 48 to 72 hours (highly fertile for 24 hours)
  - Sperm must undergo capacitation and acrosomal reaction

2 Moment of Fertilization
- Sperm penetration causes chemical reaction that blocks more sperm penetration

- Sperm enters ovum, chemical signal prompts secondary oocyte to complete second meiotic division
- True moment of fertilization occurs as nuclei unite
- Chromosomes pair up to produce diploid zygote
- Each nucleus contains haploid number of chromosomes (23)
- Union restores diploid number (46)
- Zygote contains new combination of genetic material
- Sex of zygote determined at moment of fertilization
- Two chromosomes of twenty-third pair (sex chromosomes)—either XX or XY— determine sex of individual
- Females have two X chromosomes, males have an X and a Y chromosome

 Sperm Penetration of Ovum
- (Figure 7.2A and Figure 7.2B)

 Fertilization
- (Figure 7.3)

Suggestions for Classroom Activities

Allow students to view conception animation on the Student CD-ROM. To reinforce lecture information, assign from the Companion Website that students explore the Conception and Fetal Development MediaLinks at home and attempt the critical thinking exercises.

Suggestions for Clinical Activities

Have students review "Case Study: Teaching About Pregnancy" on the Companion Website and discuss the case study in pre- or post-clinical conference.

Learning Objective 4

Describe in order of increasing complexity the structures that form during the cellular multiplication and differentiation stages of intrauterine development.

Concepts for Lecture

1. Cellular multiplication begins as the zygote moves through the fallopian tube toward the cavity of the uterus.
2. About the tenth to fourteenth day after conception, the homogeneous mass of blastocyst cells differentiates into the primary germ layers. *Refer to Table 7.3.*

PowerPoint Lecture Slides

 Cell Multiplication
- Rapid mitotic division—cleavage
- Blastomeres grow to morula (solid ball of 12 to 16 cells)
- Morula divides into solid mass (blastocyst); surrounded by outer layer of cells (trophoblast)
- Implantation; occurs in 7 to 10 days

 Cell Differentiation
- 10 to 14 days (ectoderm, mesoderm, and endoderm) from which all tissues, organs, and organ systems develop
  - Blastocyst differentiates into three primary germ layers (ectoderm, mesoderm, and endoderm)
  - All tissues, organs, and organ systems develop from these primary germ cell layers
- Embryonic membranes form at implantation
  - The chorion and the amnion

2a Derivation of Body Structures from Primary Cell Layers
- (Table 7.2)

2b Cell Differentiation
- Amniotic Fluid: Created when amnion and chorion grow and connect and form amniotic sac to produce fluid
- Yolk sac
  ○ Develops as part of the blastocyst
  ○ Produces primitive red blood cells
  ○ Soon incorporated into the umbilical cord

2c Formation of Primary Germ Layers
- (Figure 7.4)

2d Cell Differentiation
- Ectoderm
- Mesoderm
- Endoderm—differentiation of endoderm results in formation of epithelium lining respiratory and digestive tracts

2e Endoderm Differentiation
- (Figure 7.5)

SUGGESTIONS FOR CLASSROOM ACTIVITIES

Suggest that students explore the Conception and Fetal Development web links on the Companion Website. Allow students to review the cell division animation on the Student CD-ROM

LEARNING OBJECTIVE 5

Describe the development, structure, and functions of the placenta and umbilical cord during intrauterine life.

CONCEPTS FOR LECTURE

1. The umbilical cord connects the fetus to the placenta and facilitates fetal circulation.
2. The placenta allows metabolic and nutrient exchange between the embryonic and maternal circulations.

POWERPOINT LECTURE SLIDES

1 Umbilical Cord
- Develops from amnion
  ○ Body stalk attaches embryo to yolk sac, fuses with embryonic portion of placenta
  ○ Provides pathway from chorionic villi to embryo
- Contains two arteries and one vein; surrounded by Wharton's jelly to protect vessels
  ○ Wharton's jelly: Specialized connective tissue
  ○ Protects blood vessels
- Function of umbilical cord: Provides circulatory pathway to embryo

2 Placenta
- Placental development
  ○ Begins at third week of embryonic development
  ○ Develops at site where embryo attaches to uterine wall
- Function: Metabolic and nutrient exchange between embryonic and maternal circulations
- Placenta has two parts
  ○ Maternal
  ○ Fetal

2a Placenta
- Maternal portion
  - Consists of decidua basalis and its circulation
  - Surface appears red and flesh-like
- Fetal portion
  - Consists of the chorionic villi and their circulation
  - The fetal surface of the placenta is covered by the amnion
  - Appears shiny and gray

2b Maternal Side of Placenta
- (Figure. 7.8)

2c Fetal Side of Placenta
- (Figure 7.9)

SUGGESTIONS FOR CLASSROOM ACTIVITIES	SUGGESTIONS FOR CLINICAL ACTIVITIES
Facilitate in-class review of the placenta formation and fetal circulation animations on the Companion Website.	Assign students to identify the stage of development of the placenta and its current function when caring for prenatal clients.

LEARNING OBJECTIVE 6

Identify the differing processes by which fraternal (dizygotic) and identical (monozygotic) twins are formed.

CONCEPTS FOR LECTURE

1. Identical twins are unique in that they come from a single fertilized ovum.
2. Fraternal twins come from two separate fertilized ova. Dizygotic twinning increases with maternal age up to about age 35 and then decreases abruptly.

POWERPOINT LECTURE SLIDES

1 Formation of Twins
- (Figure 7.7)

1a Identical Twins
- Develop from single fertilized ovum
- Of same sex and have same genotype
- Identical twins usually have common placenta; monozygosity is not affected by environment, race, physical characteristics, or fertility
- Both fetus are same sex with same characteristics
- Single placenta

1b Identical Twins
- Number of amnions and chorions present—depends on timing of division
- Division within 3 days of fertilization; two embryos, two amnions, and two chorions will develop
- Division about 5 days after fertilization
  - Two embryos develop with separate amniotic sacs
  - Sacs will eventually be covered by a common chorion
  - Monochorionic-diamniotic placenta

- If amnion already developed, division approximately 7 to 13 days after fertilization
  - Two embryos with common amniotic sac and common chorion
  - Monochorionic-monoamniotic placenta
  - Occurs about 1% of the time

 Fraternal Twins
- Also referred to as dizygotic
  - Arise from two separate ova fertilized by two separate spermatozoa
  - Two placentas, two chorions, and two amnions
  - Sometimes placentas fuse and appear to be one
- Fraternal twins
  - No more similar to each other than singly born siblings
  - May be of same or different sex

SUGGESTIONS FOR CLASSROOM ACTIVITIES

Use clay to demonstrate the different process between dizygotic and monozygotic twinning.

SUGGESTIONS FOR CLINICAL ACTIVITIES

Assign "Care Plan Activity: Client Fearful of Multiple Gestation" found on the Companion Website.

LEARNING OBJECTIVE 7

Summarize the significant changes in growth and development of the fetus in utero at 4, 6, 12, 16, 20, 24, 28, 36, and 40 weeks' gestation.

CONCEPTS FOR LECTURE

1. Significant changes take place in fetal development during weeks 4 through 16.
2. Progressive changes continue from 20 through 40 weeks.

POWERPOINT LECTURE SLIDES

1 Human Conceptus from Fertilization to the Early Fetal Stage.
- (Figure 7.12)

1a Fetus Growth and Development
- 4 weeks: 4–6 mm, brain formed from anterior neural tube, limb buds seen, heart beats, GI system begins
- 6 weeks: 12 mm, primitive skeletal shape, chambers in heart, respiratory system begins, ear formation begins
- 12 weeks: 8 cm, ossification of skeleton begins, liver produces red cells, palate complete in mouth, skin pink, thyroid hormone present, insulin present in pancreas
- 16 weeks: 13.5 cm, teeth begin to form, meconium begins to collect in intestines, kidneys assume shape, hair present on scalp

2 20-Week Embryo
- (Figure 7.17)

2a Fetus Growth and Development
- 20 weeks: 19 cm, myelination of spinal cord begins, suck and swallow begins, lanugo covers body, vernix begins to protect the body
- 24 weeks: 23 cm, respiration and surfactant production begins, brain appears mature

- 28 weeks: 27 cm, nervous system begins regulation of some functions, adipose tissue accumulates; nails, eyebrows, and eyelids are present; eyes are open
- 36 weeks: 35 cm, earlobes soft with little cartilage, few sole creases

 Fetus Growth and Development
- 40 weeks : 40 cm, adequate surfactant, vernix in skin folds and lanugo on shoulders, earlobes firm, sex apparent
  - Weight about 3,000 to 3,600 g (6 lb., 10 oz. to 7 lb., 15 oz.)
  - Varies in different ethnic groups
  - Skin has a smooth, polished look
  - Hair on head is coarse and about 1 inch long
  - Body and extremities are plump

 Fetal Development: What Parents Want to Know
- (Table 7.4)

SUGGESTIONS FOR CLASSROOM ACTIVITIES

Have students review the embryonic heart formation and circulation animation on the Student CD-ROM and discuss in class.

SUGGESTIONS FOR CLINICAL ACTIVITIES

- Instruct students to prepare a health teaching assignment about fetal development for clients during clinical rotation.
- During clinical, if experiencing prenatal clients, identify and document stage and system growth for the time period.

CHAPTER 8
PREPARATION FOR PARENTHOOD

RESOURCE LIBRARY

 CD-ROM

Audio Glossary
NCLEX-RN® Review

COMPANION WEBSITE

Care Plan: Preconception Counseling
Case Study: Preparing for Pregnancy
Further Information about Parteras
NCLEX-RN® Review

IMAGE LIBRARY

Figure 8.1 Birth preference sheet.
Figure 8.2 In a group setting with a nurse-instructor, expectant parents share information about pregnancy and childbirth.
Figure 8.3 It is especially important that siblings be well prepared when they are going to be present for the birth.

Figure 8.4 Effleurage is light stroking of the abdomen with the fingertips.

LEARNING OBJECTIVE 1

Provide a rationale for preconception counseling.

CONCEPTS FOR LECTURE

1. Preconception counseling is necessary to assist couples in taking steps to ensure that they are in the best possible physical and mental health when pregnancy occurs.

POWERPOINT LECTURE SLIDES

1 Reasons for Preconception Counseling
- To recognize environmentalal hazards—limit exposure to environmental hazards
- To identify lifestyle hazards—take steps to change lifestyle habits
- Identify any health problems—treat healthcare problems
- Identify problems with fertility
  ○ Treatment
  ○ Exploration of fertility options

1a Reasons for Preconception Counseling
- To provide information
  ○ Contraception
  ○ Fertility
- Comprehensive history—identification of health problems
- Comprehensive physical examination—identification of health problems
- Nutrition
  ○ Ensure adequate nutrients
  ○ Average weight for woman's body build and height

1b Reasons for Preconception Counseling
- Exercise: Improves the woman's circulation and general health

- Contraception: Stop using the hormonal birth control before attempting to conceive
- Conception: Identifying the woman's most fertile period
- Exploration of options
  - Healthcare provider
  - Suitable birth setting
  - Labor support and sibling preparation

Suggestions for Classroom Activities

Facilitate in-class review and discussion of "Care Plan: Preconception Counseling" activity found on the Companion Website and "Complementary Care: Ayurveda and Preconception Lifestyle" in the text.

Suggestions for Clinical Activities

Arrange for students to attend a preconception class. Assign the "Case Study: Preparing for Pregnancy" activity on the Companion Website in advance of discussion.

Learning Objective 2

Delineate the many issues related to pregnancy, labor, and birth that require decision making by the parents.

Concepts for Lecture

1. Couples are faced with making decisions about a multitude of issues related to pregnancy and the birthing process. *Refer to Table 8.1*.

PowerPoint Lecture Slides

1 Issues Related to Pregnancy
- Choice of a healthcare provider
  - Explaining the various options
  - Outline what can be expected
  - Advise to conduct research before selection
- Birth experience plan
  - Consider choices in the community
- Choice of birth setting
  - Tour facilities
  - Talk with nurses
  - Talk to recent parents

 1a Issues Related to the Birthing Process
- Choice of support person during labor
  - Spousal support
  - Friend
  - Family member
  - Volunteer
  - Doula support
- Choice of who should be present during the birth
  - Family members
  - Siblings

Suggestions for Classroom Activities

- Provide examples of birthing plans for students to view.
- Invite a certified nurse-midwife who works at a birthing center to talk to the class about her or his role. Ask the midwife to discuss the advantages and differences between delivering a newborn at a birthing center or at an acute care setting.

Suggestions for Clinical Activities

Have students complete the MediaLink Application activity on the Companion Website and discuss their findings and formulate a teaching plan for a pregnant client at the clinical site.

LEARNING OBJECTIVE 3

Describe the types of antepartal education programs available to expectant couples and their families.

CONCEPTS FOR LECTURE

1. Prenatal education programs provide important opportunities to share information about pregnancy and childbirth and to enhance the parents' decision-making skills.
2. Prenatal classes are often divided into early and late classes.

POWERPOINT LECTURE SLIDES

 Prenatal Education Programs
- Class content—directed by the overall goals of the program
- A nurse may direct expectant parents to education programs
- Programs must meet client's special needs and learning goals
- Purpose
  - Provide information about childbirth
  - Assists clients in the decision-making process

 Early Prenatal Classes
- Focus on the description of each stage of pregnancy
  - Early gestational changes
  - Self-care during pregnancy
  - Fetal development and environmental dangers
- Sexuality in pregnancy
- Birth settings and care providers
- Nutrition, rest, exercise, and discomforts

 Late Prenatal Classes
- Focus on preparation for the birth—birth choices
- Postpartum and newborn period
  - Postpartum self-care
  - Infant care and feeding
  - Newborn safety issues—importance of car seats
- Parenting skills and neonatal bonding
  - Infant stimulation concepts
  - Neonatal bonding
  - Parenting skills
- Sibling preparation

 Prenatal Classes
- Preparation for a cesarean section
- Breastfeeding
- Grandparent role preparation
- Adolescent parenting classes

 Group Setting
- (Figure 8.2)

SUGGESTIONS FOR CLASSROOM ACTIVITIES

- Select students from the class to present and facilitate class discussion of the content outlined in Figure 8.1.
- Invite a lactation consultant to class to share her experiences providing breastfeeding teaching sessions to expectant couples. Ask the speaker to include information regarding the cost of classes, class content, and class length/duration.

SUGGESTIONS FOR CLINICAL ACTIVITIES

Arrange for students to attend a childbirth education class: sibling preparation, adolescent, childbirth preparation.

LEARNING OBJECTIVE 4

Compare methods of childbirth preparation.

CONCEPTS FOR LECTURE

1. There are many different methods to prepare clients for childbirth. They all emphasize measures that help to decrease anxiety and pain. *Refer to Table 8.3.*

POWERPOINT LECTURE SLIDES

1 Methods of Childbirth Preparation
- Lamaze
  - Uses breathing patterns
  - Controlled muscular relaxation techniques
  - Disassociation relaxation
  - Use of gentle touch and verbal cues
  - Relaxation may also be promoted by cutaneous stimulation
  - Abdominal effleurage

1a Effleurage
- (Figure 8.4)

1b Methods of Childbirth Preparation
- Bradley
  - Partner-coached childbirth
  - Educational component
- Kitzinger: Sensory-memory techniques

SUGGESTIONS FOR CLASSROOM ACTIVITIES

- Allow in-class review of Table 8.3. Ask students to identify the differences and the similarities of each method.
- Have students bring pillows and blankets to class. Divide students into groups of two—one student will be the coach, the other student the pregnant woman. Acting as the childbirth educator, have students practice progressive relaxation exercises, touch relaxation, effleurage, and two breathing techniques.

SUGGESTIONS FOR CLINICAL ACTIVITIES

Assign students to labor and delivery. Select one group of students to care for clients who had no childbirth preparation classes. Assign another group to clients who had childbirth preparation classes. During post-clinical conference allow students to describe, compare, and contrast clients' coping behavior during the birthing process.

LEARNING OBJECTIVE 5

Identify ways in which the nurse conveys respect for client individuality in preparing for childbirth.

CONCEPTS FOR LECTURE

1. Nurses must convey respect for clients during childbirth preparation classes.

POWERPOINT LECTURE SLIDES

1 Strategies for Conveying Respect
- Stress value of individuality when providing information to expectant parents—goal is to encourage women to incorporate their own natural responses into coping with the pain of labor and birth
- Emphasize the uniqueness of each birth experience—encourage self-care activities like vocalization or "sounding"
- Provide the client with tools and knowledge for decision making—make informed choices

1a Strategies for Conveying Respect
- Encourage expectant mothers and couples to make birth a personal experience
  - Items from home may help create a more personal birthing space

- Many expectant parents enjoy listening to music or watching home videos
- Personalization of birth experience may give expectant parents feelings of increased serenity and empowerment

Suggestions for Classroom Activities

- Suggest that students review "Developing Cultural Competence Birth Choices" from the text in preparation for in-class discussion. Allow students to explain how cultural competence can assist in conveying respect to clients when teaching childbirth preparation classes.
- Invite a massage therapist, reflexologist, acupuncturist, and hypnotist to speak to the class on how their techniques provide comfort and pain reduction to the laboring woman. Ask the speakers to demonstrate their technique(s) in class.

Suggestions for Clinical Activities

Assign a group of students to a prenatal clinic. Instruct students to prepare a childbirth preparation teaching plan for presentation at the clinic.

CHAPTER 9
PHYSICAL AND PSYCHOLOGIC CHANGES OF PREGNANCY

RESOURCE LIBRARY

💿 CD-ROM

Audio Glossary
NCLEX-RN® Review

🌐 COMPANION WEBSITE

Care Plan: Preparing Siblings for New Baby
Case Study: Prenatal Education
Thinking Critically
NCLEX-RN® Review

📖 IMAGE LIBRARY

Figure 9.1 Vena caval syndrome.
Figure 9.2 Linea nigra.
Figure 9.3 Postural changes during pregnancy.
Figure 9.4 Hegar's sign, a softening of the isthmus of the uterus, can be determined by the examiner during a vaginal examination.

Figure 9.5 Approximate height of the fundus at various weeks of pregnancy.

Table 9.1 Differential Diagnosis of Pregnancy-Subjective Changes
Table 9.2 Differential Diagnosis of Pregnancy-Objective Changes

---

LEARNING OBJECTIVE 1
Identify the anatomic and physiologic changes that occur during pregnancy.

CONCEPTS FOR LECTURE

1. Several anatomic and physiological changes take place during pregnancy.

POWERPOINT LECTURE SLIDES

[1] Anatomic and Physiologic Changes
- Uterus: Increased amounts of estrogen and growing fetus
  - Enlargement in size
  - Increase in weight, strength, elasticity, and vascularity
- Cervix: Increased estrogen levels
  - Hyperplasia
  - Formation of mucous plug
  - Mucous plug prevents organisms entering uterus

[1a] Anatomic and Physiologic Changes
- Vagina: Increased estrogen levels
  - Increased thickness of mucosa
  - Increased vaginal secretions to prevent bacterial infections
  - Connective tissue relaxes
- Breasts: Increased estrogen and progesterone levels
  - Increase in size and number of mammary glands

POWERPOINT LECTURE SLIDES *continued*

- ○ Nipples more erectile and areolas darken
- ○ Colostrum produced during third trimester

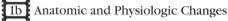 Anatomic and Physiologic Changes
- • Respiratory system: Increasing levels of progesterone causes:
  - ○ Increased volume of air
  - ○ Decreased airway resistance
  - ○ Increased anteroposterior diameter
  - ○ Thoracic breathing occurs as uterus enlarges

 Anatomic and Physiologic Changes
- • Cardiovascular system: Increased levels of estrogen and progesterone
  - ○ Cardiac output and blood volume increases
  - ○ Increased size of uterus interferes with blood return from lower extremities
  - ○ Increased level of red cells to increase oxygen delivery to cells
  - ○ Clotting factors increase

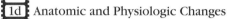 Anatomic and Physiologic Changes
- • GI system: Action of increasing levels of progesterone
  - ○ Delayed gastric emptying
  - ○ Decreased peristalsis
- • GU system: Increased blood volume
  - ○ Glomerular filtration rate increases
  - ○ Renal tubular reabsorption increases

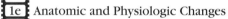 Anatomic and Physiologic Changes
- • Skin and Hair: Increased skin pigmentation caused by increased estrogen and progesterone
- • Musculoskeletal: Relaxation of joints caused by increased estrogen and progesterone
- • Metabolism: Increased during pregnancy
  - ○ Demands of the growing fetus and its support system
- • Weight Gain: Recommended 25 to 35 lb
  - ○ Overweight, recommended gain is 15 to 25lb.
  - ○ Underweight: Gain weight needed to reach ideal weight plus 25 to 35 lb

1f Anatomic and Physiologic Changes
- • Endocrine System
  - ○ Thyroid
  - ○ Pituitary
  - ○ Adrenals
  - ○ Pancreas

SUGGESTIONS FOR CLASSROOM ACTIVITIES

Provide a drawing of the female anatomy showing all organ systems. Instruct students to highlight each organ system that is affected during pregnancy, label each organ, and list the changes that occur in each organ system.

SUGGESTIONS FOR CLINICAL ACTIVITIES

Have students attend prenatal appointments with several women. In post-conference identify different system alterations in the three trimesters.

LEARNING OBJECTIVE 2

Relate these anatomic and physiologic changes to the signs and symptoms that develop in the woman.

CONCEPTS FOR LECTURE

1. Anatomical and physiological changes are responsible for the development of the signs and symptoms of pregnancy.

POWERPOINT LECTURE SLIDES

 Signs and Symptoms
- Uterus: Enlargement of abdomen
  - Increased strength and elasticity: Allows uterus to contract
  - Fetus expelled during labor
- Cervix: Mucous plug expelled as labor begins
  - Increased vascularity may cause bleeding after vaginal exams
- Vagina: Acid pH increases chance of vaginal yeast infections
- Breasts: Increase in size causes soreness
  - Colostrum may be present during the third trimester

 Signs and Symptoms
- Respiratory system
  - Increased size of uterus may cause shortness of breath
  - Increased vascularity may cause nasal stuffiness and nosebleeds
- Cardiovascular system: Decreased blood return from lower extremities
  - Varicose veins
  - Hemorrhoids
- Pressure on vena cava by the enlarged uterus
  - Dizziness
  - Decreased blood pressure

 Signs and Symptoms
- Skin and Hair: Increased skin pigmentation
  - Causes linea nigra and chloasma
- GI system: Increased levels of estrogen cause:
  - Nausea and vomiting
  - Constipation
  - Slow peristalsis and motility
- GU system: Increased urination caused by:
  - Increasing size of uterus
  - Pressure on bladder
  - Increased blood volume and glomerular filtration
- Musculoskeletal: Action of estrogen and progesterone
  - Relaxation of joints: Lordosis of lumbosacral spine

1c Approximate Height of the Fundus at Various Weeks of Pregnancy
- (Figure 9.5)

1d Linea Nigra
- (Figure 9.2)

1e Vena Caval Syndrome
- (Figure 9.1)

1f Postural Changes During Pregnancy
- (Figure 9.3)

SUGGESTIONS FOR CLASSROOM ACTIVITIES

Divide students into two groups. One group will identify the anatomical and physiological change specific to one body system, and the other group will respond by stating the corresponding signs and symptoms. In preparation for this exercise, recommend that students access the Physical and Psychological Changes of Pregnancy web links on the Companion Website.

SUGGESTIONS FOR CLINICAL ACTIVITIES

Select prenatal clinics for clinical rotation. Allow students to participate in the admission process of a client's first prenatal visit. Ask them to identify some of the visible changes associated with pregnancy. Also allow them to identify some of the client's complaints that are also associated with the physiological effects of pregnancy.

LEARNING OBJECTIVE 3

Compare subjective (presumptive), objective (probable), and diagnostic (positive) changes of pregnancy.

CONCEPTS FOR LECTURE

1. Many of the changes women experience during pregnancy are used to diagnose the pregnancy itself. They are called the subjective, or presumptive, changes; the objective, or probable, changes; and the diagnostic, or positive, changes of pregnancy. *Refer to "Nursing Practice 9.1 and 9.2."*

POWERPOINT LECTURE SLIDES

1 Changes of Pregnancy
- Subjective (presumptive) changes
  - Amenorrhea
  - Nausea and vomiting
  - Fatigue
  - Urinary frequency
  - Breast changes
  - Quickening

1a Differential Diagnosis of Pregnancy—Subjective Changes
- (Table 9.1)

1b Changes of Pregnancy
- Objective (probable) changes
  - Goodell's and Chadwick's sign
  - Hegar's and McDonald's sign
  - Enlargement of the abdomen
  - Braxton Hicks contractions
  - Uterine soufflé
  - Skin pigmentation changes
  - Pregnancy tests

1c Hegar's Sign
- (Figure 9.4)

1d Differential Diagnosis of Pregnancy—Objective Changes
- (Table 9.2)

1e Changes of Pregnancy
- Diagnostic (positive) changes
  - Fetal heartbeat
  - Fetal movement
  - Visualization of the fetus

SUGGESTIONS FOR CLASSROOM ACTIVITIES

Ask for a volunteer who has been pregnant from your group of students to share her experience with the rest of the class. Allow her to highlight the subjective and presumptive signs and symptoms that she experienced. Allow students to use Tables 9.1 and 9.2 to develop a list of differential diagnoses relative to the information that the selected student provides.

SUGGESTIONS FOR CLINICAL ACTIVITIES

Schedule students to rotate to an antepartum unit or prenatal clinic. Select a client and demonstrate the positive signs of pregnancy. Allow students to listen to the fetal heart rate, palpate fetal movements, and visualize the fetus via ultrasound.

LEARNING OBJECTIVE 4

Contrast the various types of pregnancy tests.

CONCEPTS FOR LECTURE

1. A variety of assay techniques are available to detect hCG during early pregnancy. They include a series of urine and serum tests.

POWERPOINT LECTURE SLIDES

 Pregnancy Tests
- Urine tests
  - Hemagglutination-inhibition test (Pregnosticon R test)
  - Latex agglutination test (Gravindex and Pregnosticon Slide tests)
  - The first two are done on first early morning urine specimen
  - Positive within 10 to 14 days after the first missed period
  - Detect hCG during early pregnancy

[1a] Pregnancy Tests
- Serum tests
  - β-subunit radioimmunoassay: Positive a few days after presumed implantation
  - Immunoradiometric assay (IRMA) (Neocept, Pregnosis); requires only about 30 minutes to perform
  - Enzyme-linked immunosorbent assay (ELISA) (Model Sensichrome, Quest Confidot): Detects hCG levels as early as 7 to 9 days after ovulation and conception, 5 days before the first missed period
  - Fluoroimmunoassay (FIA) (Opus hCG, Stratus hCG); takes about 2 to 3 hours to perform; used primarily to identify and follow hCG concentrations

 Pregnancy Tests
- Over-the-counter pregnancy tests
  - Enzyme immunoassay tests
  - Performed on urine
  - Sensitive
  - Detect even low levels of hCG
  - Can detect a pregnancy as early as first day of missed period
  - Negative result, test may be repeated in 1 week if period has not occurred

SUGGESTIONS FOR CLASSROOM ACTIVITIES	SUGGESTIONS FOR CLINICAL ACTIVITIES
Invite a laboratory technologist skilled in performing pregnancy tests to describe the most common pregnancy tests used to diagnose pregnancy in your community.	Allow students to observe how urine and serum tests are done at a lab in a prenatal clinic to diagnose pregnancy.

LEARNING OBJECTIVE 5

Discuss the emotional and psychological changes that commonly occur in a woman, her partner, and her family during pregnancy.

CONCEPTS FOR LECTURE

1. During pregnancy, the expectant mother faces significant changes and must deal with major psychosocial adjustments.
2. During pregnancy, the expectant father also has to go through a period of psychosocial adjustments.
3. Pregnancy can be considered a maturational crisis since it is a common event in the normal growth and development of the family.

POWERPOINT LECTURE SLIDES

1. Mother's Emotional and Psychological Changes
   - First trimester: Disbelief and ambivalence
   - Second trimester: Quickening; helps mother to view fetus as separate from herself
   - Third trimester: Anxiety about labor and birth; nesting (bursts of energy) occurs
   - Rubin's four tasks: Ensuring safe passage through pregnancy, labor, and birth
     - Seeking acceptance of this child by others
     - Seeking commitment and acceptance of herself as mother to infant
     - Learning to give of oneself on behalf of one's child

2. Father/Partner's Emotional and Psychologic Changes
   - First trimester
     - May feel left out
     - Disbelief
     - May be confused by his partner's mood changes
     - Might resent the attention she receives
   - Second trimester: Begins to decide which behaviors of own father he wants to imitate or discard
   - Third trimester: Anxiety about labor and birth

3. Family's Emotional and Psychologic Changes
   - Siblings
     - May view baby as threat to security of their relationships with parents
     - Reaction depends on age of siblings
     - Preparation for birth is essential
   - Grandparents
     - Usually supportive
     - Excited about the birth
     - May be unsure about how deeply to become involved

SUGGESTIONS FOR CLASSROOM ACTIVITIES

For classroom activity, allow students to go to the Companion Website to review "Care Plan: Preparing Siblings for New Baby." Encourage class participation and discussion. Assign the "Case Study: Prenatal Education" activity for homework.

SUGGESTIONS FOR CLINICAL ACTIVITIES

Assign students to a prenatal clinic. Allow them to conduct surveys on newly diagnosed pregnant couples. The surveys should focus on how the mother and father feel about the pregnancy. If grandparents and siblings are present, recommend that the survey include them. At the end of the clinical day at post-clinical conference, allow students to discuss their findings in terms of the emotional and psychological changes in the family during pregnancy.

LEARNING OBJECTIVE 6

Summarize cultural factors that may influence a family's response to pregnancy.

CONCEPTS FOR LECTURE

1. Cultural assessment is an important aspect of prenatal care.
2. Cultural assessment will help to identify cultural factors that will impact the family's plan for the pregnancy.

POWERPOINT LECTURE SLIDES

 1 Cultural Assessment
- Determines
  - Main beliefs
  - Wishes
  - Traditions of the family
  - Values
  - Behaviors about pregnancy and childbearing
- Helps to explore woman's (or family's) expectations of healthcare system
- Allows nurse to provide care that is appropriate and responsive to family needs

2 Cultural Factors
- Factors that will impact the family's plans for the pregnancy
  - Religious preferences
  - Language
  - Communication style
  - Common etiquette practices
  - Ethnic background
  - Amount of affiliation with the ethnic group
  - Patterns of decision making

SUGGESTIONS FOR CLASSROOM ACTIVITIES

Conduct a class review of "Complementary Care: Herbs During Pregnancy." Allow students to discuss the implications of the use of herbs during pregnancy.

SUGGESTIONS FOR CLINICAL ACTIVITIES

Assign students to care for clients from multicultural backgrounds. Ask students to find out about birth practices specific to each client's culture.

CHAPTER 10
ANTEPARTAL NURSING ASSESSMENT

RESOURCE LIBRARY

 CD-ROM

Audio Glossary
NCLEX-RN® Review

 COMPANION WEBSITE

Thinking Critically
NCLEX-RN® Review
Case Study: Initial Prenatal Assessment
Care Plan Activity: Initial Assessment of Primigravida

 **IMAGE LIBRARY**

Figure 10.1 The TPAL approach provides detailed information about the woman's pregnancy history.
Figure 10.2 The EDB wheel can be used to calculate the due date.
Figure 10.3 A cross-sectional view of fetal position when McDonald's method is used to assess fundal height.
Figure 10.4 Listening to the fetal heartbeat with a Doppler device.

Figure 10.5 Manual measurement of inlet and outlet.
Figure 10.6 Use of a closed fist to measure the outlet.

Table 10.2 Danger Signs in Pregnancy

Complementary Care: Yoga During Pregnancy

LEARNING OBJECTIVE 1

Summarize the essential components of a prenatal history.

CONCEPTS FOR LECTURE

1. The history is essentially a screening tool to identify factors that may place the mother or fetus at risk during the pregnancy. *Refer to Table 10.1.*

POWERPOINT LECTURE SLIDES

 1 Prenatal History
- Details of current pregnancy
  - First day of last normal menstrual period (LMP)
  - Presence of complications
  - Attitude toward pregnancy
  - Results of pregnancy tests, if completed
  - Presence of discomforts since LMP
  - Number of pregnancies and number of living children
  - Number of abortions, spontaneous or induced

1a Prenatal History
- History of previous pregnancies
  - Length of pregnancy
  - Length of labor and birth
  - Type of birth
  - Type of anesthesia used (if any)
  - Woman's perception of the experience
  - Complications associated with childbirth
  - Neonatal complications

1b Prenatal History
- Gynecologic history
  - Date of last Pap smear—any history of abnormal Pap smear
  - Previous infections: Vaginal, cervical, tubal, or sexually transmitted
  - Previous surgery

- ○ Age at menarche and sexual history
- ○ Regularity, frequency, and duration of menstrual flow
- ○ History of dysmenorrhea and contraceptive history

1c Prenatal History
- • Current medical history
  - ○ General health: Weight, nutrition, and regular exercise program
  - ○ Blood type and Rh factor, if known
  - ○ General health: Nutrition and regular exercise program
  - ○ Medications and use of herbal medication during pregnancy
  - ○ Previous or present use of alcohol, tobacco, or caffeine
  - ○ Illicit drug use and drug allergies and other allergies

1d Prenatal History
- • Current medical history
  - ○ Potential teratogenic insults to this pregnancy
  - ○ Presence of disease conditions such as diabetes
  - ○ Immunizations (especially rubella)
  - ○ Presence of any abnormal symptoms

1e Prenatal History
- • Past medical history
  - ○ Childhood diseases
  - ○ Past treatment for any disease condition
  - ○ Surgical procedures
  - ○ Presence of bleeding disorders or tendencies (Has she received blood transfusions?)

1f Prenatal History
- • Family medical history
  - ○ Presence of chronic or acute systemic diseases
  - ○ Complications associated with childbirth: Preeclampsia
  - ○ Occurrence of multiple births
  - ○ History of congenital diseases or deformities
  - ○ Occurrence of cesarean births and cause, if known

1g Prenatal History
- • Religious preference and religious beliefs related to health care and birth:
  - ○ Prohibition against receiving blood products
  - ○ Dietary considerations or circumcision rites
- • Practices that are important to maintain her spiritual well-being
- • Practices in her culture or that of her partner that will influence care

POWERPOINT LECTURE SLIDES *continued*

1h Prenatal History
- Occupational history: Physical demands of present job
- Partner's history: Genetic conditions and blood type
- Woman's demographic information
  - Age, educational level
  - Ethnic background
  - Socioeconomic status

SUGGESTIONS FOR CLASSROOM ACTIVITIES

At the end of the lecture select two students. One student will play the role of a pregnant client. The other will obtain a complete comprehensive prenatal history based on the information obtained in the lecture and textbook from the "pregnant client." The other students will observe and critique the process. Assign the "Case Study: Initial Prenatal Assessment" activity on the Companion Website for homework.

SUGGESTIONS FOR CLINICAL ACTIVITIES

Arrange to have students work with a healthcare provider at a prenatal clinic. Allow them to observe and participate in the history-taking process during an initial visit. Encourage students to also participate and observe subsequent prenatal visits. At the end of the clinical allow them to compare and contrast the essential elements of both types of visits.

LEARNING OBJECTIVE 2
Define common obstetric terminology found in the history of maternity clients.

CONCEPTS FOR LECTURE

1. The following terms are used in recording the history of maternity clients.

POWERPOINT LECTURE SLIDES

 Common Obstetric Terminology
- Gravida: Any pregnancy, regardless of duration, includes the current pregnancy
- Parity: Birth after 20 weeks' gestation; infant may be born alive or dead
- TPAL
  - **T**: Number of term infants born
  - **P**: Number of preterm infants
  - **A**: Number of pregnancies ending in either spontaneous or therapeutic abortion
  - **L**: Number of currently living children

 TPAL
- (Figure 10.1)

 Common Obstetric Terminology
- Gestation: Number of weeks since the first day of the last menstrual period
- Abortion: Birth occurring before the end of 20 weeks' gestation
- Term: Normal duration of pregnancy (38 to 42 weeks' gestation)

- Antepartum: Time between conception and the onset of labor
- Intrapartum: Period from the onset of true labor until the birth of the infant and placenta

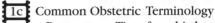 Common Obstetric Terminology
- Postpartum: Time from birth until the woman's body returns to prepregnant condition
- Preterm or premature labor: Labor that occurs after 20 weeks' gestation but before completion of 37 weeks' gestation
- Nulligravida: Woman who has never been pregnant
- Primigravida: Woman pregnant for the first time

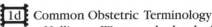 Common Obstetric Terminology
- Nullipara: Woman who has had no births at more than 20 weeks' gestation
- Primipara: Woman who has had one birth at more than 20 weeks' gestation
- Multipara: Woman who has had two or more births at more than 20 weeks' gestation
- Stillbirth: Infant born dead after 20 weeks' gestation
- Multigravida: Woman in second or any subsequent pregnancy

SUGGESTIONS FOR CLASSROOM ACTIVITIES

Present the class with a list of pregnancy histories using the obstetrical terms. Have them describe in narrative what the history terms mean.

SUGGESTIONS FOR CLINICAL ACTIVITIES

On the clinical unit have students review pregnancy histories of the women who have given birth. Discuss the findings in post-conference.

LEARNING OBJECTIVE 3

Identify factors related to the father's health that are generally recorded on the prenatal record.

CONCEPTS FOR LECTURE

1. Information about the father is also documented on the prenatal record. This information will assist in the identification of risk factors.

POWERPOINT LECTURE SLIDES

Father's Information
- Existing medical conditions
- History of chronic illness—father or immediate family member
- Blood type and Rh factor
- Age
- Occupation
- Current use of recreational drugs

Father's Information
- Present use of tobacco and alcohol
- Genetic disorders
- Educational level
- Methods by which he learns best
- Attitude toward the pregnancy

SUGGESTIONS FOR CLASSROOM ACTIVITIES

Present several case studies to the class, each involving a pregnant couple. In each situation have a significant factor related to the father—a genetic disease in his family history, a history of cocaine use, an Rh positive blood type, a history of domestic violence, or others. Ask students to evaluate the potential impact of this factor on the pregnancy and future of the couple and child.

SUGGESTIONS FOR CLINICAL ACTIVITIES

Allow students to continue to shadow a prenatal healthcare provider during initial prenatal visits and subsequent visits. Assign students to generate a list of risk factors for each client seen based on the prenatal history of both parents.

LEARNING OBJECTIVE 4

Describe areas that should be evaluated as part of the initial assessment of psychosocial and cultural factors related to a woman's pregnancy.

CONCEPTS FOR LECTURE

1. The prenatal assessment holistically focuses on the woman by considering cultural and psychosocial factors that influence her health.

POWERPOINT LECTURE SLIDES

[1] Cultural and Psychosocial Factors
- Language preference
- Religious preference
- Socioeconomic status
- Psychological status
- Educational needs
- Support system

[1a] Cultural and Psychosocial Factors
- Determine food preferences
- Determine significant people to client—assess degree of involvement of those people
- Assess family functioning
  - Level of involvement
  - Stability of living conditions
- Be aware of the practices of various cultural groups

[1b] Complementary Care (Yoga)
- ("Complementary Care: Yoga During Pregnancy")

SUGGESTIONS FOR CLASSROOM ACTIVITIES

Invite a healthcare provider from a different culture to discuss prenatal care in the context of the health provider's culture. Recommend that students review "Complementary Care: Yoga." Assign the "Care Plan: Initial Assessment of Primigravida" on the Companion Website for homework.

SUGGESTIONS FOR CLINICAL ACTIVITIES

Rotate students to a prenatal clinic that serves a diverse group of clients. Recommend that students interact with clients and obtain information about the individual client's diet, religion, language, and customs surrounding pregnancy and childbirth. Allow students to discuss their findings.

LEARNING OBJECTIVE 5

Describe the normal physiologic changes one would expect to find when performing a physical assessment of a pregnant woman.

CONCEPTS FOR LECTURE

1. During a physical assessment, several normal physiological changes can be identified. *Refer to "Assessment Guides 10.1 and 10.2."*

POWERPOINT LECTURE SLIDES

[1] Normal Physiological Changes
- Pulse may increase by 10 beats per minute
- Respiration may be increased and thoracic breathing predominant
- Temperature and blood pressure within normal limits

- Weight varies: Should be proportional to the gestational age of the fetus
- Nose: Nasal stuffiness
- Chest and lungs: Transverse diameter greater than anterior-posterior diameter

1a Normal Physiological Changes
- Skin:
  - Linea nigra
  - Striae gravidarum
  - Melasma
  - Spider nevi
- Mouth: Gingival hypertrophy
- Neck: Slight hyperplasia of thyroid in the third trimester—small, nontender nodes

1b Normal Physiological Changes
- Breasts
  - Increasing size
  - Pigmentation of nipples and areola
  - Tubercles of Montgomery enlarge
  - Colostrum appears in third trimester

1c Normal Physiological Changes
- Abdomen
  - Progressive enlargement
  - Fetal heart rate heard at approximately 12 weeks' gestation
- Extremities: Possible edema late in pregnancy
- Spine: Lumbar spinal curve may be accentuated
- Pelvic area: Vagina without significant discharge

1d Normal Physiological Changes
- Cervix closed
- Uterus shows progressive growth
- Laboratory tests
  - Physiologic anemia may occur (decrease in hemoglobin and hematocrit)
  - Small degree of glycosuria may occur

SUGGESTIONS FOR CLASSROOM ACTIVITIES

Provide drawings of the pregnant female anatomy. Divide students into groups. Assign a body system to individual groups. Group members will highlight the body system they have been assigned and make a list of all the normal physiological changes that may be assessed during a prenatal visit.

SUGGESTIONS FOR CLINICAL ACTIVITIES

Allow students to accompany healthcare providers performing physical assessments on pregnant females. With the help of the healthcare provider, they should try to identify some of the normal assessment findings.

LEARNING OBJECTIVE 6

Compare the methods most commonly used to determine the estimated date of birth.

CONCEPTS FOR LECTURE

1. Historically the due date has been called the estimated date of confinement (EDC), and different methods may be used to estimate the date of birth (EDB).

POWERPOINT LECTURE SLIDES

1 Commonly Used Methods
- Nägele's rule
  - Begin with the first day of the LMP
  - Subtract 3 months, and add 7 days

- Physical Examination—fundal height:
  Measurement of uterine size
- Ultrasound: Method used to measure fetal parts
  - Crown-to-rump measurements
  - Biparietal diameter (BPD) measurements

1a EDB Wheel
- (Figure 10.2)

1b Fetal Position When McDonald's Method Used
- (Figure 10.3)

SUGGESTIONS FOR CLASSROOM ACTIVITIES

Provide expected date of birth (EDB) wheels in the classroom for student manipulation. Demonstrate the use of the wheel to calculate the expected date of delivery from the last menstrual period. List a number of LMPs and ask students to calculate the expected due dates using Nägele's rule. Assign students to review the MediaLink Application activity on the Companion Website for homework.

SUGGESTIONS FOR CLINICAL ACTIVITIES

At a prenatal clinic or antepartum unit, allow students to practice using the wheel and Nägele's rule to calculate the EDB using the last menstrual period. Ask them to identify any differences in the expected date of delivery obtained from using the wheel and Nägele's rule.

LEARNING OBJECTIVE 7

Develop an outline of the essential measurements that can be determined by clinical pelvimetry.

CONCEPTS FOR LECTURE

1. The pelvis can be measured to determine whether its size is adequate for a vaginal birth.

POWERPOINT LECTURE SLIDES

1 Pelvic Measurements
- Pelvic inlet
  - Diagonal conjugate
  - Measure at least 11.5 cm
- Obstetric conjugate—10 cm or more

1a Manual Measurement of Inlet and Outlet
- (Figure 10.5)

1b Pelvic Measurements
- Pelvic outlet
  - Anteroposterior diameter should be 9.5 to 11.3 cm
  - Transverse diameter should be 8 to 10 cm

1c Closed Fist to Measure Outlet
- (Figure 10.6)

SUGGESTIONS FOR CLASSROOM ACTIVITIES

Bring a pelvic model to the class. Demonstrate the measurements of the pelvic inlet and outlet. Let the students practice performing those measurements.

SUGGESTIONS FOR CLINICAL ACTIVITIES

Assign students to shadow a prenatal healthcare provider during measurements of the pelvis of the pregnant female. If permissible, allow them to also participate in that activity. At the end of clinical conference, students may discuss their findings and observations.

LEARNING OBJECTIVE 8

Delineate the possible causes of the danger signs of pregnancy.

CONCEPTS FOR LECTURE

1. Infections may complicate the pregnancy. Healthcare providers must be able to identify signs of infection. *Refer to "Evidence-Based Practice: Guidelines for Prevention of Perinatal Group B Streptococcal Disease."*

2. It is important to identify early signs of anemia, pulmonary, and cardiovascular problems for early treatment and prevention of complications.

3. Other signs may indicate problems with other body systems.

POWERPOINT LECTURE SLIDES

1 Signs of Infection or Cancer
- Elevation in vital signs
- Urine with elevated white blood cells
- High white blood cell count in the blood
- Lesions in the genital area
- Excessive malodorous vaginal discharge
- Positive tests for sexually transmitted infections

1a Signs of Infection or Cancer
- Tender, hard fixed nodes in the neck
- Abnormal lung sounds
- Breast lumps
- Nipple discharge
- Redness and tenderness of breast tissue

2 Signs of Anemia or Cardiopulmonary Problems
- Pale mucous membranes
- Skin pallor
- Signs of nutrition deficiency
- Low hemoglobin and hematocrit levels
- Elevations in blood pressure
- Edema
- More than expected weight gain

2a Signs of Cardiopulmonary Problems
- Abnormal lung sounds
- Increased respiratory rate
- Abnormal heart rhythm
- Extra heart sounds

3 Other Danger Signs
- Less than expected weight gain
- Petechiae or bruises
- Inflamed gingival tissue
- Enlarged thyroid
- Abdominal tenderness or mass
- Lack of peripheral pulses

3a Other Danger Signs
- Failure to detect fetal heart rate
- Abnormal spinal curves
- Hyperactive reflexes
- Below normal pelvic measurements
- Hemorrhoids

3b Danger Signs in Pregnancy
- (Table 10.2)

SUGGESTIONS FOR CLASSROOM ACTIVITIES

Divide students into two groups. Let one group of students use note cards to list about four danger signs. Members of the other group will list the possible causes of four danger signs on note cards. Allow students to match note cards, signs with possible causes. Recommend they utilize Table 10.2 for this exercise. Assign students to complete the critical thinking exercise at the end of "Evidence-Based Nursing Practice: Guidelines for Prevention of Perinatal Group B Streptococcal Disease."

SUGGESTIONS FOR CLINICAL ACTIVITIES

Rotate students to a high-risk prenatal clinic or antepartum unit. Allow them to work with prenatal healthcare providers and collect subjective and objective data to formulate care plans to address danger signs identified in the clients they are caring for.

LEARNING OBJECTIVE 9

Relate the components of the subsequent prenatal history and assessment to the progress of pregnancy.

CONCEPTS FOR LECTURE

1. Recommendations are in place to guide the frequency of antepartal visits in an uncomplicated pregnancy.
2. Subsequent prenatal assessment provides a systematic approach to the regular physical examinations the pregnant woman should undergo for optimal antepartal care and also provides a model for evaluating both the pregnant woman and the expectant father, if he is involved in the pregnancy.

POWERPOINT LECTURE SLIDES

1. Subsequent Prenatal Assessment
   - Prenatal visits
     - Every 4 weeks for the first 28 weeks' gestation
     - Every 2 weeks from 28 weeks' until 36 weeks' gestation
     - After week 36, every week until childbirth

2. Subsequent Prenatal Assessment
   - Assessments during prenatal visits
     - Vital signs and weight
     - Edema
     - Uterine size and fetal heartbeat
     - Urinalysis
     - Blood tests for AFP, glucose
     - Vaginal swab for group B strep
     - Expected psychological stage of pregnancy

SUGGESTIONS FOR CLASSROOM ACTIVITIES

Have students develop a timeline for prenatal visits and the assessments and teaching appropriate at each visit.

SUGGESTIONS FOR CLINICAL ACTIVITIES

Have students attend a prenatal clinic and teach pregnant women about the assessments and care they receive at that visit, and about screening tests that will be performed at their next visit.

CHAPTER 11
THE EXPECTANT FAMILY: NEEDS AND CARE

RESOURCE LIBRARY

CD-ROM

Audio Glossary
NCLEX-RN® Review

📖 IMAGE LIBRARY

Figure 11.1 The Empathy Belly® is a pregnancy simulator that allows men and women to experience some of the symptoms of pregnancy.

Figure 11.2 Acupressure wristbands are sometimes used to help relieve nausea during early pregnancy.

Figure 11.3 Swelling and discomfort from varicosities can be decreased by lying down with the legs and one hip elevated (to avoid compression of the vena cava).

Figure 11.4 When picking up objects from floor level or lifting objects, the pregnant woman must use proper body mechanics.

Figure 11.5 The expectant father can help relieve the woman's painful leg cramps by flexing her foot and straightening her leg.

Figure 11.6 Fetal movement assessment method: The Cardiff Count-to-Ten scoring card (adaptation).

🌐 COMPANION WEBSITE

NCLEX-RN® Review
Case Study: First Trimester Client
Thinking Critically

Figure 11.7 This breast shield is designed to increase the protractility of inverted nipples.

Figure 11.8 Position for relaxation and rest as pregnancy progresses.

Figure 11.9 A, Starting position when the pelvic tilt is done on hands and knees. B, A prenatal yoga instructor offers pointers for proper positioning for the first part of the tilt: head up, neck long and separated from the shoulders, buttocks up, and pelvis thrust back, allowing the back to drop and release on an inhaled breath. C, The instructor helps the woman assume the correct position for the next part of the tilt. D, Proper posture.

Figure 11.10 Kegel exercises.

Figure 11.11 For many older couples, the decision to have a child may be very rewarding.

Teaching Highlights: Assessing Fetal Activity.

LEARNING OBJECTIVE 1

Describe actions that the nurse can take to help maintain the well-being of the expectant father and siblings during a family's pregnancy.

CONCEPTS FOR LECTURE

1. Anticipatory guidance of the expectant father, if he is involved in the pregnancy, is a necessary part of any plan of care.
2. Children may feel less neglected and more secure if they know that their parents are willing to help with their anger and aggressiveness.

POWERPOINT LECTURE SLIDES

1 Care of the Expectant Father
- Asses father's intended degree of participation
- If culturally appropriate, recommend childbirth classes
- Provide information about expected changes (physical and emotional) during pregnancy
- Allow father to express feelings:
  ○ About pregnancy
  ○ Related topics: Feeding, ability to parent, and sexual activity

1a The Empathy Belly
- (Figure 11.1)

1b Relieving Painful Leg Cramps
- (Figure 11.5)

2 Care of the Siblings
- Discuss negative feelings of siblings that may occur at birth of a new child:
  - Helps children master their feelings
  - Children may feel less neglected and more secure
  - Helps them to work on their feelings of anger and resentment

SUGGESTIONS FOR CLASSROOM ACTIVITIES	SUGGESTIONS FOR CLINICAL ACTIVITIES
Invite a certified nurse-midwife to talk to your class about strategies that the midwife has utilized in practice to care for couples and siblings during a pregnancy.	Assign students to attend a childbirth class. Observe the interactions between the couples and outline the information presented during the childbirth class. Compare the information provided with the information presented in lecture format and outlined in the book. Allow students to identify similarities and new information.

LEARNING OBJECTIVE 2

Explain the causes of the common discomforts of pregnancy.

CONCEPTS FOR LECTURE

1. The common discomforts of pregnancy result from physiologic and anatomic changes and are fairly specific to each of the three trimesters.

POWERPOINT LECTURE SLIDES

 1 Causes of Discomforts of Pregnancy: First Trimester
- Nausea and vomiting: Multifactorial
  - Elevated human chorionic gonadotropin (hCG) level
  - Changes in carbohydrate metabolism
  - Emotional factors
- Urinary frequency: Enlarging uterus puts pressure on bladder
- Fatigue: May be caused by urinary frequency at night

1a Causes of Discomforts of Pregnancy: First Trimester
- Increased estrogen and progesterone levels causes:
  - Nasal stuffiness and epistaxis
  - Breast tenderness
  - Increased vaginal discharge
  - Cervical hyperplasia
  - Increased production of mucus by endocervical gland

 1b Causes of Discomforts of Pregnancy: Second and Third Trimesters
- Heartburn: Increasing levels of progesterone—decreased gastric motility
- Ankle edema: Slow venous return
  - Increased capillary permeability
  - Increased levels of sodium
- Varicose veins: Venous congestion and weight gain
- Hemorrhoids: Constipation and slow venous return of blood

1c Causes of Discomforts of Pregnancy: Second and Third Trimesters
- Backache: Increased lumbosacral vertebrae curve due to enlarging uterus
- Leg cramp: Imbalance of calcium and phosphorus
- Fatigue and poor lower extremity circulation

1d Causes of Discomforts of Pregnancy: Second and Third Trimesters
- Trimester flatulence: Decreased gastric motility and air swallowing
- Faintness: Sudden change of position, which precipitates postural hypotension
- Dyspnea: Decreased vital capacity due to increasing size of uterus
- Carpal tunnel syndrome: Compression of median nerve precipitated by edema

SUGGESTIONS FOR CLASSROOM ACTIVITIES

Assign students to complete the "Case Study: First Trimester Client" activity on the Companion Website and discuss their answers in class.

SUGGESTIONS FOR CLINICAL ACTIVITIES

Arrange for clinical rotation at a prenatal clinic or antepartum unit. Ask students to make a list of their client's discomforts associated with the pregnancy and develop an individual plan of care.

LEARNING OBJECTIVE 3

Identify appropriate relief measures for the common discomforts of pregnancy.

CONCEPTS FOR LECTURE

1. Appropriate relief measures are available to deal with the common discomforts associated with pregnancy. *Refer to "Complementary Care: Ginger and Acupressure for Morning Sickness" and Table 11.2.*

POWERPOINT LECTURE SLIDES

1 Appropriate Relief Measures
- Nausea and vomiting
  - Avoid odors, eat dry crackers in the morning
  - Avoid greasy foods and drink fluids between meals
- Heartburn
  - Eat small, frequent meals
  - Avoid overeating and lying down after a meal
- Flatulence: Chew food completely and avoid gas-forming foods
- Dyspnea
  - Use good posture to sit and stand
  - Sleep in a semi-Fowler's position

1a Accupressure Wrist Bands
- (Figure 11.2)

1b Appropriate Relief Measures
- Constipation
  - Increase fluid and fiber in diet
  - Develop regular bowel habits
- Faintness
  - Change positions slowly
  - Avoid standing for long periods

- Backache
  - Use good body mechanics
  - Practice pelvic tilt exercises
- Leg cramps: Apply heat to affected muscles and dorsiflex feet

`1c` Proper Body Mechanics
- (Figure 11.4)

`1d` Appropriate Relief Measures
- Ankle edema
  - Elevate legs while sitting or standing
  - Dorsiflex feet frequently
- Varicose veins
  - Elevate legs as much as possible
  - Wear support hose
- Hemorrhoids
  - Avoid constipation
  - Use ice packs or sitz baths as necessary

`1e` Relief of Swelling and Discomfort
- (Figure 11.3)

`1f` Position for Relaxation
- (Figure 11.8)

`1g` Appropriate Relief Measures
- Urinary frequency
  - Increase fluid intake during day
  - Decrease fluid intake in the evening
- Fatigue: Plan rest periods and ask for help from family or support persons
- Breast tenderness: Wear well-supporting bra
- Increased vaginal discharge: Bathe daily and wear cotton underwear
- Nasal stuffiness and epistaxis: Use cool mist vaporizer
- Carpal tunnel syndrome: Avoid repetitive hand movement and elevate arm as needed

SUGGESTIONS FOR CLASSROOM ACTIVITIES

Divide students into two groups. Assign group A to write problems related to pregnancy on individual note cards. Then, assign group B to write treatment options on individual note cards. Place all the note cards at a central location. Allow students to match note cards, problem to treatment options. Assign students to review and complete the Critical Thinking in Action activity for homework.

SUGGESTIONS FOR CLINICAL ACTIVITIES

Schedule students' clinical at a prenatal clinic to work with a nurse practitioner or certified nurse-midwife. Instruct students to document all clients' complaints associated with pregnancy and the treatments recommended by the advanced-practice nurse. Allow for discussion of findings during post-clinical conference.

LEARNING OBJECTIVE 4

Discuss the basic information that a nurse should provide to the expectant family to enable them to carry out appropriate self-care.

CONCEPTS FOR LECTURE

1. Many caregivers encourage pregnant women to monitor their unborn child's well-being by regularly assessing fetal activity beginning at 28 weeks' gestation.

2. Whether the pregnant woman plans to bottle- or breastfeed her infant, support of the breasts is important to promote comfort, retain breast shape, and prevent back strain.

3. Information about several other factors has to be considered to maintain a healthy pregnancy and facilitate maternal well-being. *Refer to Table 11.2.*

POWERPOINT LECTURE SLIDES

1 Fetal Activity Monitoring
- Cardiff Counting Method
  - Focus on counting fetal movements and keeping a record
  - Client should feel at least 10 fetal movements in 3 hours
  - Vigorous activity generally provides reassurance of fetal well-being
  - Decrease or cessation of movement may signal a problem

1a Assessing Fetal Activity
- ("Teaching Highlights: Assessing Fetal Activity")

1b Fetal Movement Assessment
- (Figure 11.6)

2 Breast Care
- Recommend: Wear bra with good support and fit
  - If breastfeeding, avoid soap on breasts
  - Nipple preparation: Go braless to toughen nipples
  - Roll nipples or oral stimulation by partner to prepare for breastfeeding
  - Should be avoided in women who have had previous preterm labor

3 Information About Other Factors
- Clothing: Non-constricting
- Shoes: Low heeled
- Bathing: Be aware of cultural norms and avoid falls
- Employment
  - No complications, work until labor
  - Assess for fetotoxic hazards
- Travel: Complicated pregnancy, avoid travel
- Dental Care: Maintain regular dental checkups
- Immunizations: Avoid live virus vaccines

3a Information About Other Factors
- Activity and Rest
  - Regular exercise in uncomplicated pregnancy
  - Rest periods
- Exercises to prepare for childbirth: Pelvic tilt
- Perineal exercises: Kegel
- Inner thigh exercises
- Sexual activity: Consider alternative positions for intercourse
- Avoid: Medications not prescribed, alcohol, tobacco, and illicit drugs
- Risks and benefits of homeopathic remedies and herbs

3b Pelvic Tilt
- (Figure 11.9A, D)

3c Kegel Exercise
- (Figure 11.10)

SUGGESTIONS FOR CLASSROOM ACTIVITIES	SUGGESTIONS FOR CLINICAL ACTIVITIES
Ask students to complete the Companion Website activity, "Thinking Critically: Counseling About Strenuous Physical Activity." Facilitate a class discussion about the content.	Schedule students to work with advanced practice nurses providing prenatal care. Let the students focus on the self-care instructions that these nurses provide for their clients.

LEARNING OBJECTIVE 5

Delineate some of the concerns that an expectant couple might have about sexual activity.

CONCEPTS FOR LECTURE

1. Couples usually have many questions and concerns about sexual activity during pregnancy. They should be provided with accurate information about sexual activity during pregnancy. *Refer to "Teaching Highlights: Sexual Activity During Pregnancy."*

POWERPOINT LECTURE SLIDES

1 Concerns and Information About Sexual Activity
- Concerns
  - Possible injury to the baby or the woman during intercourse
  - Changes in the desire each partner feels for the other
  - Communication of desire and need
- Information
  - Partners need to communicate feelings and needs
  - Healthy pregnancy: No reason to limit sexual activity

1a Accurate Information About Sex During Pregnancy
- Information
  - Complicated pregnancy
  - Limit sexual activity
- Contraindicated for sexual activity
  - Multiple pregnancy
  - Threatened abortion

1b Accurate Information About Sex During Pregnancy
- Contraindicated for sexual activity
  - Incompetent cervix
  - Sexually transmitted infection
  - Miscarriage following orgasm
  - Rupture of membranes
  - Preterm labor

SUGGESTIONS FOR CLASSROOM ACTIVITIES	SUGGESTIONS FOR CLINICAL ACTIVITIES
Facilitate a review and discussion among students of "Teaching Highlights: Sexual Activity During Pregnancy."	As students continue their clinical rotation at a prenatal clinic with an advanced-practice nurse, recommend that they pay attention and record strategies utilized by the advanced-practice nurses when they engage in providing information about sexual activity during pregnancy to clients.

LEARNING OBJECTIVE 6

Summarize the medical risks and special concerns of the older expectant woman and her partner.

CONCEPTS FOR LECTURE

1. There are medical risks associated with pregnancy after age 35.
2. There are also special concerns associated with pregnancy after age 35.

POWERPOINT LECTURE SLIDES

 Medical Risks
- Fetal death risk is increased for all women older than 35
- Mother is more likely to have chronic medical conditions
- Chronic medical conditions could pose a risk to the fetus
- Increased risk for cesarian section
- Increased risk for Down syndrome
- Increased risk for autosomal dominant inherited disorders

 Special Concerns
- Parents' ability to meet needs of child
- Not doing same things as peers
- Social isolation may occur
- Concern that "biological clock" continues to tick
- Fear of own mortality

 Older Couples
- (Figure 11.11)

SUGGESTIONS FOR CLASSROOM ACTIVITIES

Invite an older couple to share their experiences about their pregnancy with your students, including their physical and emotional responses, their concerns related to their age, the labor and delivery process, and their adjustment to parenthood.

SUGGESTIONS FOR CLINICAL ACTIVITIES

Assign students to a prenatal clinic or doctor's office. Allow them to shadow a prenatal provider caring for mothers over age 35. Allow students to interview clients and inquire about the client's experiences during the pregnancy.

CHAPTER 12
MATERNAL NUTRITION

RESOURCE LIBRARY

 CD-ROM

NCLEX-RN® Review
Audio Glossary

 COMPANION WEBSITE

NCLEX-RN® Review
Case Study: Maternal Weight Gain
Thinking Critically
Care Plan Activity: Maternal Nutrition

IMAGE LIBRARY

Figure 12.1 "MyPyramid: Steps to a Healthier You" identifies the basic food groups and provides guidance about healthful eating.
Figure 12.2 The vegetarian food pyramid.
Figure 12.3 Food preferences and habits are affected by cultural factors.
Figure 12.4 Sample nutritional questionnaire used in nursing management of a pregnant woman.

Table 12.2 Vegetarian Food Groups
Nursing Practice
Evidence-Based Nursing: Folate Supplementation in Pregnancy
Developing Cultural Competence: Kosher Diets

LEARNING OBJECTIVE 1

Delineate recommended levels of weight gain during pregnancy.

CONCEPTS FOR LECTURE

1. Maternal weight gain is an important factor in fetal growth and infant birth weight

POWERPOINT LECTURE SLIDES

1 Weight Gain Recommendations
- Optimal weight gain
  - Depends on the woman's weight for height
  - Prepregnant nutritional state
  - Underweight: 28 to 40 lb
  - Normal weight: 25 to 35 lb
  - Overweight: 15 to 25 lb
  - Obese: Approximately 15 lb

1a Weight Gain Recommendations
- Pattern of weight gain is important
  - First trimester: 3.5 to 5 lb
  - Second and third trimester: About 1 lb weekly
- Twins: Second and third trimesters: 1.5 lbs per week
- Dieting during pregnancy can result in maternal ketosis

1b Weight Gain
- ("Nursing Practice")

SUGGESTIONS FOR CLASSROOM ACTIVITIES

Use "Nursing Practice" as a focus for a class discussion about the distribution of weight during pregnancy. Assign the "Case Study: Maternal Weight Gain" exercise on the Companion Website for homework.

SUGGESTIONS FOR CLINICAL ACTIVITIES

During clinical rotation at the prenatal clinic, assign students to participate in weighing pregnant females. Ask them to note the weight gained for each client weighed. Compare that weight to the recommended weight gain and note any deviations. Allow students to discuss their findings at the end of clinical conference.

LEARNING OBJECTIVE 2

Identify the role of specific nutrients in the diet of the pregnant woman.

CONCEPTS FOR LECTURE

1. The RDA for almost all nutrients increases during pregnancy, although the amount of increase varies with each nutrient. These increases reflect the additional requirements of both the mother and the developing fetus.

POWERPOINT LECTURE SLIDES

1 Role of Nutrients
- Carbohydrates
  - Main source of energy as well as fiber
  - Promotes maternal, fetal, and placenta weight gain
- Protein: Supplies needed amino acids for growth of uterus and breast tissue
- Magnesium: Promotes cellular metabolism
- Iron: Prevents maternal anemia
- Maintains fetal and infant stores of iron

1a Role of Nutrients
- Fat: Promotes fetal fat deposits
- Calcium and phosphorus: Promote mineralization of fetal bones and teeth
- Iodine: Promotes fetal thyroid gland function
- Sodium: Regulates fluid balance and metabolism in the mother
- Zinc: Promotes growth of fetus and sufficient lactation
- Vitamins: Maintain good maternal health
- Folic acid: May prevent neural tube defects in the fetus

1b Folate Supplementation in Pregnancy
- ("Evidence-Based Nursing: Folate Supplementation in Pregnancy")

SUGGESTIONS FOR CLASSROOM ACTIVITIES

Allow students to review "Evidence-Based Nursing: Folate Supplementation in Pregnancy." Assign them to complete the critical thinking activity that follows it.

SUGGESTIONS FOR CLINICAL ACTIVITIES

Assign students to work with a nutritionist or dietician who educates pregnant females about nutrition during pregnancy.

LEARNING OBJECTIVE 3

Compare nutritional needs during pregnancy, the postpartum period, and lactation with nonpregnant requirements.

CONCEPTS FOR LECTURE

1. During pregnancy and lactation, nutritional requirements increase significantly from nonpregnant requirements. *Refer to Table 12.1.*

POWERPOINT LECTURE SLIDES

1 Nutritional Requirements
- Calories in second and third trimester
  - Increase by 300 kcal/day

    ◦ During lactation: Increase by another 200 kcal/day
- Protein increases by 14 mg to 60 mg/day

1a Nutritional Requirements
- Calcium increases to 1000 to 1300 mg/day
- Magnesium increases to 350 mg/day
- Iron increases to 27 mg/day
- Iodine increases to 220 mcg/day

1b Nutritional Requirements
- Zinc increases to 11 mg/day during pregnancy and 12 mg/day during lactation
- Vitamin A increases to 770 mcg/day
- Vitamin D increases to 5 mcg/day
- Vitamin C increases from 75 to 85 mg/day
- Thiamine increases from 1.1 to 1.4 mg/day
- Riboflavin increases from 1.1 to 1.4 mg/day

1c Nutritional Requirements
- Niacin increases from 14 to 18 mg/day
- Pantothenic acid increases to 5 mg/day
- Vitamin B12 increases from 2.4 to 2.6 mcg/day
- Fluid needs increase to 8 to 10 glasses of noncaffeinated beverages/day
- For nonnursing mothers, during postpartum period nutritional requirements return to prepregnancy levels

1d MyPyramid
- (Figure 12.1)

SUGGESTIONS FOR CLASSROOM ACTIVITIES

- Allow students to make a list of foods that are rich in all the nutrients outlined in the lecture. Assign the "Care Plan: Maternal Nutrition" activity on the Companion Website for homework.
- Provide a sample meal plan for a nonpregnant client. Have students divide into two groups. Each group will adapt the meal plan to meet the additional calorie requirements for the pregnant mother and the breast-feeding mother. Ensure that the additional needs for carbohydrates, proteins, and minerals are reflected in the meal plan.

SUGGESTIONS FOR CLINICAL ACTIVITIES

Ask students to use Figure 12.4 as a guide to obtaining a diet history from a pregnant female in the prenatal unit or the antepartum unit. After obtaining the information, allow students to analyze the information based on the recommended pyramid guide.

LEARNING OBJECTIVE 4

Plan adequate prenatal vegetarian diets based on the nutritional requirements of pregnancy.

CONCEPTS FOR LECTURE

1. The expectant woman who is vegetarian must eat the proper combination of foods to obtain adequate nutrients.

POWERPOINT LECTURE SLIDES

1 Vegetarian Diets During Pregnancy
- There are different types of vegetarian diets
  - ◦ Lacto-ovo vegetarians: Dairy and egg products
  - ◦ Lacto-vegetarians: Dairy products but no eggs
  - ◦ Vegans: No foods from animal sources

- Most vegans need additional supplementation—vitamins B12, D, and calcium

[1a] Vegetarian Diets During Pregnancy
- Vegetarians' daily food requirements are:
  - 6 to 11 servings of whole grains, cereal, pasta, and rice
  - 2 to 4 servings of fruit
  - 3 to 5 servings of vegetables
  - 2 to 3 servings of legumes, nuts, seeds, and meat alternatives
  - 2 to 3 servings of milk products (unless vegan)

[1b] Vegetarian Food Pyramid
- (Figure 12.2)

[1c] Vegetarian Food Groups
- (Table 12.2)

SUGGESTIONS FOR CLASSROOM ACTIVITIES

Invite a nutritionist to talk to your students about vegetarian diets and the implications for pregnancy. Be sure to discuss the need for vitamin supplementation of a pregnant client who is a vegetarian.

SUGGESTIONS FOR CLINICAL ACTIVITIES

Assign students to shadow a dietician in a prenatal environment educating pregnant vegetarian clients about the recommended food choices to sustain a healthy mother and fetus.

LEARNING OBJECTIVE 5

Describe ways in which various physical, psychosocial, and cultural factors can affect nutritional intake and status.

CONCEPTS FOR LECTURE

1. Cultural, ethnic, and religious backgrounds determine people's experiences with food and influence food preferences and habits.

POWERPOINT LECTURE SLIDES

[1] Factors Affecting Nutritional Intake
- Nausea, vomiting, and heartburn
- Lactose intolerance may cause diarrhea or bloating after dietary intake
- Cultural, ethnic, and religious influences may prohibit use of foods needed for adequate nutrition

[1a] Factors Affecting Nutritional Intake
- Socioeconomic level may limit availability of nutritious foods
- Lack of knowledge about proper nutrition may limit woman's ability to prepare nutritional foods
- Clients with eating disorders may have nutritional and electrolyte imbalances
- Pica may result in iron deficiency anemia

[1b] Food Preferences and Habits Are Affected by Cultural Factors
- (Figure 12.3)

[1c] Developing Cultural Competence
- ("Developing Cultural Competence: Kosher Diets")

SUGGESTIONS FOR CLASSROOM ACTIVITIES

Invite a nutritionist to your class to discuss diets reflective of clients from diverse cultural backgrounds within your community and the implications for pregnancy.

SUGGESTIONS FOR CLINICAL ACTIVITIES

Assign students to clients from different cultures. Allow them to obtain diet, histories from their individual clients. Allow them to review the most common food groups in the client's diet, and based on the food pyramid guide determine whether their diets are meeting the nutrition requirements for pregnancy.

LEARNING OBJECTIVE 6

Compare recommendations for weight gain and nutrient intakes in the pregnant adolescent with those for the mature pregnant adult.

CONCEPTS FOR LECTURE

1. Many factors that affect the weight gain of the adolescent during pregnancy need to be assessed in order to facilitate early intervention.
2. Nutritional care of the pregnant adolescent is of particular concern to healthcare professionals.

POWERPOINT LECTURE SLIDES

 Factors to Assess
- Factors to assess in pregnant adolescents
  ○ Low prepregnant weight and anemia
  ○ Low weight gain during pregnancy and eating disorders
  ○ Young age at menarche
  ○ Unhealthy lifestyle: Smoking, alcohol, and illicit drug use
  ○ Excessive prepregnant weight
  ○ Chronic disease

 Weight Gain and Nutrient Intake
- Weight gain: Recommended weight gain of the adult pregnancy plus the expected gain of the adolescent
- Nutrient needs—adolescent needs more iron, calcium, and folic acid than adult pregnant woman
- Caloric needs
  ○ Vary widely
  ○ Figures as high as 50 kcal/kg have been suggested
  ○ Satisfactory weight gain usually confirms an adequate caloric intake

SUGGESTIONS FOR CLASSROOM ACTIVITIES

Assign students to write a paper describing some of the factors that interfere with the ability of the pregnant teenager to gain weight during pregnancy.

SUGGESTIONS FOR CLINICAL ACTIVITIES

Arrange for students to participate in weighing pregnant adolescent clients at a prenatal clinic. Allow students to compare their individual client's weight with the recommended weight gain according to gestational age for each client. Allow them to discuss their findings during a post-clinical conference.

LEARNING OBJECTIVE 7

Discuss basic factors a nurse should consider when offering nutritional counseling to a pregnant adolescent.

CONCEPTS FOR LECTURE

1. Counseling about nutrition and healthy eating practices is an important element of care for pregnant teenagers that nurses can effectively provide in a community setting.

POWERPOINT LECTURE SLIDES

 Nutritional Counseling
- Basic factors to consider
  - Number of years since adolescent reached menarche
  - Whether growth has been completed
  - Most adolescents have irregular eating patterns
  - Adolescent may not be the one who regularly prepares meals
  - Individual who prepares meals should be included in nutritional counseling
  - Teens are present, not future, oriented, which impacts nutritional counseling

[1a] Nutritional Counseling
- May be helpful to involve the expectant father
  - Clinics and schools often offer classes
  - Provides focused activities designed to address this topic
- Pregnant teenager will soon become a parent—her understanding of nutrition may influence her well-being but also that of her child
- Counseling may be individualized
- May involve other teens
- May provide a combination of both approaches

SUGGESTIONS FOR CLASSROOM ACTIVITIES

Ask students to write a paper describing why counseling about nutrition is essential for pregnant teenagers. Assign students to review and complete the Critical Thinking in Action activity before class and discuss their findings.

SUGGESTIONS FOR CLINICAL ACTIVITIES

During clinical rotation at a prenatal clinic, assign students to work with a prenatal advanced-practice provider as she or he provides nutritional counseling for teenage pregnant females.

LEARNING OBJECTIVE 8

Compare nutritional counseling issues for breastfeeding and formula-feeding mothers.

CONCEPTS FOR LECTURE

1. After birth, the formula-feeding mother's dietary requirements return to prepregnancy levels.
2. Breastfeeding mothers need an increase in nutrient intake. *Refer to Table 12.1.*

POWERPOINT LECTURE SLIDES

 Formula-Feeding Mothers
- Eat a well-balanced diet
- Dietary requirements are the same as before pregnancy
- Weight loss of 1 to 2 pounds/week is acceptable
- Advise her to reduce her daily caloric intake by about 300 kcal

- Excessive weight gain: Refer to dietician
- The dietician can design healthy weight-reduction diets

 Breastfeeding Mothers
- Calorie requirements increase by 200 kcal/day over needs during pregnancy
- Need 2500 to 2700 kcal/day
- Need 65 g/day of protein
- Need 1000 mg/day of calcium
- Should avoid foods that irritate the infant

SUGGESTIONS FOR CLASSROOM ACTIVITIES	**SUGGESTIONS FOR CLINICAL ACTIVITIES**
• Instruct students to use Table 12.1 to develop a meal plan for a lactating female. • Display various commercial formulas and have students read the ingredients for each formula.	Assign students to work with a dietician. Allow students to observe a dietician developing meal plans for lactating females in a hospital setting.

CHAPTER 13
ADOLESCENT PREGNANCY

RESOURCE LIBRARY

 CD-ROM

NCLEX-RN® Review
Audio Glossary

 COMPANION WEBSITE

NCLEX-RN® Review
MediaLink Applications:
    Case Study: Adolescent Pregnancy
    Care Plan: Adolescent Pregnancy
Thinking Critically

📖 IMAGE LIBRARY

Figure 13.1 The nurse gives this young mother an opportunity to listen to her baby's heartbeat.
Figure 13.2 Young adolescents may benefit from prenatal classes designed for them.

Evidence-Based Nursing: Screening for Sexually Transmitted Infections During Pregnancy.

Developing Cultural Competence: Impact of Education on Marriage and Childbearing.

LEARNING OBJECTIVE 1

Define the scope of the problem of adolescent pregnancy.

CONCEPTS FOR LECTURE

1. Adolescents progress through three stages of psycho-social development. *Refer to Table 13.1 and Table 13.2.*
2. More than half the teens that become pregnant give birth and keep their babies. Very few adolescents give up their babies for adoption.

POWERPOINT LECTURE SLIDES

1 Caption Stages of Development
- Early adolescence (age 14 and under)— conformity to peer group
- Middle adolescence (ages 15 to 17 years)
  ○ Seeks independence
  ○ Turns increasingly to peer groups
- In late adolescence (ages 18 to 19 years)— understands and accepts consequences for behavior

2 Scope of the Problem
- United States: Each year about 900,000 teenage girls become pregnant
- Adolescent pregnancy rate
  ○ 43 per 1,000 females
  ○ Rate declining
  ○ Still has the highest rate among industrialized nations

2a Scope of the Problem
- One-third of teen pregnancies are terminated
- About 14% end in miscarriage

- Higher adolescent birth rates
  - African-American teens
  - The rate for black teens ages 15 to 17 has declined by 50%
  - Hispanic teens
  - Pregnancy rates in all groups are declining

SUGGESTIONS FOR CLASSROOM ACTIVITIES

Facilitate student access to the Adolescent Pregnancy web links to obtain additional information about the prevalence of adolescent pregnancy in the United States and the strategies that are being utilized to decrease the incidence of teenage pregnancies.

SUGGESTIONS FOR CLINICAL ACTIVITIES

- Arrange to have students rotate to an adolescent prenatal clinic. Allow them to work with and observe prenatal healthcare providers.
- Have each clinical group research the number of teen deliveries and pregnancy terminations at the agency where they have their student clinical experience.

LEARNING OBJECTIVE 2

Summarize factors contributing to adolescent pregnancy.

CONCEPTS FOR LECTURE

1. Many factors contribute to teenage pregnancies.

POWERPOINT LECTURE SLIDES

`1` Contributing Factors
- First sexual experience at an early age
- Lack of information about contraception
- Inability to access contraceptives easily
- In some communities, less stigma

 `1a` Contributing Factors
- Lack of adult supervision
- Repeat pregnancy risk is higher if the teen lives with sexual partner
- High-risk behaviors: Premarital sexual activity; multiple partners
- Psychosocial factors

 `1b` Contributing Factors
- Poverty
- Early school failure
- Early childhood sexual abuse
- Religious factors
- Inconsistent contraceptive use

SUGGESTIONS FOR CLASSROOM ACTIVITIES

Assign students to write a paper about the factors that contribute to teen pregnancy in their community or state. Ask them to include information about the prevalence based on ethnic background and race. Allow students to present the information in the classroom.

SUGGESTIONS FOR CLINICAL ACTIVITIES

Schedule students to prenatal childbirth classes for pregnant teens. Instruct students to make a list of the strategies utilized by the presenter to engage the pregnant teens.

LEARNING OBJECTIVE 3

Discuss the physical, psychologic, and sociologic risks a pregnant adolescent faces.

CONCEPTS FOR LECTURE

1. Unfortunately, adolescents typically begin prenatal care later in pregnancy than any other age group, which places them at risk for physical problems.
2. Teens also face psychosocial risks during pregnancy.

POWERPOINT LECTURE SLIDES

1 Physical Risks
- Preterm labor
- Low birth weight infant
- Cephalopelvic disproportion
- Iron deficiency anemia
- Preeclampsia
- Sexually transmitted infections (STIs)

1a STD Screening
- ("Evidence-Based Nursing: Screening for Sexually Transmitted Infections During Pregnancy.")

2 Psychosocial Risks
- Interruption of the developmental tasks of adolescence
- More likely to drop out of school
- Need for public assistance
- Low-paying employment
- Single parenthood
- Increased domestic violence

2a Psychosocial Risks
- Lack of stable relationships
- Lack of economic and social stability
- Failure to establish a stable family
- Majority of adolescent marriages end in divorce
- Lack of maturity in dealing with an intimate relationship

SUGGESTIONS FOR CLASSROOM ACTIVITIES

Plan an organized classroom review and discussion about the contents of "Evidence-Based Nursing: Screening for Sexually Transmitted Infections During Pregnancy." Allow students to complete the critical thinking activity.

SUGGESTIONS FOR CLINICAL ACTIVITIES

Allow students to utilize data on prenatal records to generate a list of physical and psychosocial risks for individual clients at a prenatal pregnant teen clinic.

LEARNING OBJECTIVE 4

Delineate characteristics of the fathers of children of adolescent mothers.

CONCEPTS FOR LECTURE

1. There are characteristic features associated with fathers of children of adolescent mothers.

POWERPOINT LECTURE SLIDES

1 Characteristics of Fathers
- 50% of the fathers are not teens
- They are usually 20 years of age or older
- Generally from similar backgrounds
- Often a victim of early school failure
- Usually unemployed
- Not more likely to support the mother

1a Characteristics of Fathers
- Adult paternity common in some other cultures
- Adolescent fathers tend to be less educated than older fathers

- Often marry at a younger age than older fathers
- Often have more children
- Male partners may be very involved in the pregnancy
- May be present for the birth

SUGGESTIONS FOR CLASSROOM ACTIVITIES

Open a class discussion about fathers of babies by adolescent mothers and their involvement in the pregnancy. Ask students to state whether or not they support an active role for the father. Allow students to state reasons for their answers.

SUGGESTIONS FOR CLINICAL ACTIVITIES

Suggest that students identify partners of adolescent pregnant females in the teen clinic and observe their involvement in childbirth classes or prenatal visits.

LEARNING OBJECTIVE 5

Discuss the range of reactions of the adolescent's family and social network to her pregnancy.

CONCEPTS FOR LECTURE

1. The family and social network experience a range of reactions towards an adolescent pregnancy.

POWERPOINT LECTURE SLIDES

1 Reactions to Pregnancy
- Anger
- Shock
- Sorrow
- Teens may use abortion—unless prohibited by culture or religion

1a Developing Cultural Competence
- ("Developing Cultural Competence: Impact of Education on Marriage and Childbearing.")

1b Reactions to Pregnancy
- May receive more support from family and friends—where teen pregnancy is socially acceptable
- Adolescent fathers may view pregnancy as a sign of adult status
- Sign of increased sexual power
- The mother of the pregnant adolescent usually provides the most support

SUGGESTIONS FOR CLASSROOM ACTIVITIES

At the end of the lecture allow students to review and complete the "Thinking Critically" activity and discuss their answers.

SUGGESTIONS FOR CLINICAL ACTIVITIES

At the teen clinic, allow students with the guidance of the instructor or preceptor to review prenatal records of adolescent clients and conduct interviews. Instruct students to review data collected and formulate an individual, psychosocial nursing diagnosis.

LEARNING OBJECTIVE 6

Formulate a plan of care to meet the needs of a pregnant adolescent.

CONCEPTS FOR LECTURE

1. It is necessary to set goals for prenatal classes when preparing to meet the health needs of the pregnant adolescent.

POWERPOINT LECTURE SLIDES

1 Goals for Prenatal Classes
- Provide anticipatory guidance about pregnancy
- Prepare participants for labor and birth

2. The pregnant adolescent has the same care needs as any pregnant woman.
3. The adolescent's mother is often present during the teen's labor and birth. The father of the baby may also be involved.
4. During the postpartum period, most teens do not foresee that they will become sexually active in the near future.

- Help participants identify the problems
- Help them to identify conflicts associated with teenage pregnancy
- Assist them to recognize and deal with parenting conflicts

1a Goals for Prenatal Classes
- Promoting increased self-esteem
- Providing information about available community resources
- Helping participants develop adaptive coping skills
- Providing information about available community resources
- Helping participants develop adaptive coping skills

1b Listening to Baby's Heartbeat
- (Figure 13.1)

1c Adolescent Prenatal Classes
- (Figure 13.2)

2 Nursing Care
- Provide information about the following:
  ○ Regular prenatal visits
  ○ Signs of complications
  ○ Sexually transmitted diseases
  ○ Substance abuse

2a Nursing Care
- Obtain consent for care
- Develop a trusting relationship
- Promote self-esteem and problem-solving skills
- Promote the physical health of the adolescent
- Promoting family adaptation
- Facilitate prenatal education

3 Care During Labor
- Admission
  ○ Ask teen who will be her primary support person
  ○ Find out who she wants involved in labor and birth
- During labor
  ○ Be readily available to answer questions
  ○ Offer support
  ○ Help adolescent's support people to understand their roles
  ○ Encourage partner at his own level of comfort

4 Postpartum Care
- Predischarge teaching
  ○ Resumption of ovulation
  ○ Importance of contraception
  ○ Provide information about contraception to her sexual partner
  ○ Give information about peer group postpartum classes
  ○ Such classes address a variety of topics: Postpartum adaptation
  ○ Infant and child development and parenting skills

SUGGESTIONS FOR CLASSROOM ACTIVITIES

Let students review and discuss "Case Study: Adolescent Pregnancy," activity in the classroom. This case study can be accessed on the Companion Website.

SUGGESTIONS FOR CLINICAL ACTIVITIES

Students may complete "Care Plan: Adolescent Pregnancy," activity on the Companion Website. At the teen clinic, allow students with the guidance of the instructor or preceptor to review prenatal records and conduct interviews and physical assessments. Instruct students to analyze the information and formulate physical and psychosocial nursing diagnoses based on collected assessment data.

LEARNING OBJECTIVE 7

Describe successful community approaches for the prevention of adolescent pregnancy.

CONCEPTS FOR LECTURE

1. Effective adolescent pregnancy prevention programs are long-term and intensive.

POWERPOINT LECTURE SLIDES

 Community Approaches
- 1996: National Campaign to Prevent Teen Pregnancy
- Aim: Reduce teenage pregnancy one-third by 2005
- Decision of the organization
  ○ Best approach is community-wide involvement
  ○ Programs directed at the multiple causes of the problem

 Community Approaches
- Some groups believe that abstinence is the only answer
- Other groups advocate sex education; easy availability of contraception
- Many parents advocate an "abstinence-plus" approach
- Research suggests effective programs focus more on societal problems

 Community Approaches
- Effective programs
  ○ Are long-term and intensive
  ○ Involve adolescents in program planning
  ○ Include good role models from the same cultural and racial backgrounds
  ○ Include a focus on the adolescent male

SUGGESTIONS FOR CLASSROOM ACTIVITIES

Assign students to prepare a presentation outlining all the adolescent pregnancy prevention programs that are available in their local community. Suggest they work in small groups. Allow students to present the information in the classroom.

SUGGESTIONS FOR CLINICAL ACTIVITIES

Assign students to spend four or more hours at a community organization that works to prevent adolescent pregnancies. Instruct students to write a paper detailing the strategies utilized by the organization to prevent teenage pregnancy.

Chapter 14
Pregnancy at Risk: Pregestational Problems

Resource Library

 CD-ROM

NCLEX-RN® Review
Audio Glossary

 COMPANION WEBSITE

NCLEX-RN® Review
MediaLink Applications:
    Case Study: Client with Gestational Diabetes
    Care Plan: Woman with Diabetes Mellitus
    Care Plan Activity: Antepartal Client at Risk
Thinking Critically

📖 IMAGE LIBRARY

Figure 14.1 Percentages of past month illicit drug use among women ages 15 to 44, by pregnancy status, age, and race/ethnicity: 2002.

Figure 14.2 During labor the nurse closely monitors the blood glucose levels of the woman with diabetes mellitus.

Figure 14.3 The nurse teaches the pregnant woman with gestational diabetes mellitus how to do home glucose monitoring.

Figure 14.4 When a woman with heart disease begins labor, the nursing students and instructor monitor her closely for signs of congestive heart failure.

Table 14.3 White's Classification of Diabetes in Pregnancy.

Complementary Care: Garlic Supplements Interfere with HIV Medication.

Learning Objective 1

Summarize the effects of alcohol and illicit drugs on the childbearing woman and her fetus/newborn.

Concepts for Lecture

1. Illicit drug use during pregnancy, particularly in the first trimester, may have a negative effect on the health of the woman and the growth and development of the fetus. *See Table 14.1*
2. The effects of alcohol on the fetus may result in a group of signs known as fetal alcohol syndrome (FAS).

PowerPoint Lecture Slides

1 Effects of Drug Use: Cocaine and Crack
- Adverse maternal effects
  - Seizures and hallucinations
  - Pulmonary edema and cerebral hemorrhage
  - Respiratory failure and heart problems
  - Increased incidence of spontaneous abortion
  - Abruptio placentae, preterm birth, and stillbirth

1a Effects of Drug Use: Cocaine and Crack
- Fetal neonatal effects
  - Increased risk of intrauterine growth restriction (IUGR)
  - Small head circumference
  - Cerebral infarctions
  - Altered brain development
  - Shorter body length
  - Malformations of the genitourinary tract
  - Lower Apgar scores

- May have neurobehavioral disturbances
- Marked irritability
- An exaggerated startle reflex
- Labile emotions

 Effects of Drug Use: Cocaine and Crack
- Newborns exposed to cocaine in utero
  - Increased risk of sudden infant death syndrome (SIDS)
  - Cocaine crosses into breast milk
  - May cause symptoms in the breastfeeding infant
  - Extreme irritability and vomiting
  - Diarrhea, dilated pupils, and apnea
  - Cocaine use after childbirth: Prohibits breastfeeding

 Effects of Drug Use: Marijuana
- Associated with impaired coordination, memory, and critical thinking ability
- No strong evidence that marijuana is teratogenic
- Risks are dose related
- Increased risk of intrauterine growth restriction
- Sudden infant death syndrome (SIDS) in infants born to heavy users
- Impact of heavy marijuana use on pregnancy is difficult to evaluate
- Variety of social factors may influence the results

 Effects of Drug Use: Ecstasy
- MDMA (methylenedioxymethamphetamine)
- It produces euphoria and feelings of empathy for others
- Deaths have occurred among users
- Little is yet known about the effects of MDMA on pregnancy
- Ecstasy use may be critical issue during fetal brain development

 Effects of Drug Use: Heroin
- CNS depressant narcotic
- Alters perception and produces euphoria
- An addictive drug, generally IV-administered
- Associated with malnutrition
- Fetus of heroin-addicted woman—increased risk for IUGR and meconium aspiration

 Effects of Drug Use: Heroin
- Hypoxia
- Restlessness and shrill, high-pitched cry
- Irritability and fist sucking
- Vomiting and seizures
- Signs of withdrawal usually appear within 72 hours
- May last for several days

 Effects of Drug Use: Methadone
- Most commonly used for women dependent on opioids

- Blocks withdrawal symptoms
- Reduces or eliminates the craving for narcotics
- Crosses the placenta
- Associated with pregnancy complications and abnormal fetal presentation
- Prenatal exposure: Reduced head circumference and lower birth weight
- Newborn may experience withdrawal symptoms

 Effects of Alcohol Use
- Central nervous system (CNS) depressant
- Potent teratogen
- Maternal effects
  - Malnutrition
  - Bone marrow suppression
  - Increased incidence of infections
  - Liver disease
  - Withdrawal seizures

2a Effects of Alcohol Use
- Physical abnormalities
- Mental abnormalities
- Newborn may suffer from withdrawal syndrome
- Excessive alcohol consumption
  - May intoxicate the infant
  - May inhibit the maternal letdown

2b Percentages of Illicit Drug Use Among Women
- (Figure 14.1)

SUGGESTIONS FOR CLASSROOM ACTIVITIES

Allow for in-class review of data displayed in Figure 14.1. Facilitate a discussion about the contents of Table 14.1.

SUGGESTIONS FOR CLINICAL ACTIVITIES

Arrange for students to work with a prenatal provider who cares for pregnant clients with substance abuse problems in a prenatal or antepartum environment.

LEARNING OBJECTIVE 2

Relate the pathology and clinical treatment of diabetes mellitus in pregnancy to the implications for nursing care.

CONCEPTS FOR LECTURE

1. Diabetes mellitus (DM), an endocrine disorder of carbohydrate metabolism, results from inadequate production or use of insulin. States of altered carbohydrate metabolism have been classified in several ways.
2. Pregnancy can affect diabetes significantly because the physiologic changes of pregnancy can drastically alter insulin requirements.
3. The pregnancy of a woman who has diabetes carries a higher risk of complications, especially perinatal mortality and congenital anomalies.
4. Clinical therapy begins with glucose screening and aims to control blood glucose levels

POWERPOINT LECTURE SLIDES

 Pathophysiology
- DM: Endocrine disorder
  - Inadequate production or use of insulin
  - Glucose metabolism is impaired
  - Cells break down stores of fats and protein for energy
  - Result: Negative nitrogen balance and ketosis
- Cardinal signs and symptoms of DM: Polyuria
  - Polydipsia
  - Polyphagia
  - Weight loss

1a Classification
- Type 1 diabetes: Absolute insulin deficiency

- Type 2 diabetes
  - Insulin secretory defect
  - Insulin resistance
- Other specific types
- White's classification: Describes the extent of DM
- Gestational diabetes mellitus
  - Glucose intolerance
  - First diagnosed during pregnancy

1b Etiologic Classification of Diabetes Mellitus

1c White's Classification of Diabetes in Pregnancy

2 Influence of Pregnancy on Diabetes
- DM may be difficult to control
- Insulin requirements vary during pregnancy
- Risk of ketoacidosis
- Progression of vascular disorders
- Hypertension may occur
- Nephropathy may result from renal impairment
- Retinopathy may develop

3 Influence of Diabetes on Pregnancy Outcome
- Maternal risks
  - Hydramnios
  - Preeclampsia-eclampsia
  - Ketoacidosis
  - Infections
- Fetal-neonatal risks—congenital anomalies

3a Influence of Diabetes on Pregnancy Outcome
- Fetal-neonatal risks
  - Macrosomia
  - Intrauterine growth restriction (IUGR)
  - Respiratory Distress Syndrome
  - Polycythemia
  - Hyperbilirubinemia

4 Clinical Therapy
- Goal: Scrupulous maternal plasma glucose control
  - Screening: 1-hour GTT (24 to 28 weeks)
  - Diagnosis: 3-hour oral GTT
  - Blood glucose monitoring
  - Assessment of long-term glucose control: HbA_{1c}
  - Diet and insulin
  - Fetal assessments

4a Monitoring Blood Glucose Levels
- (Figure 14.2)

4b Teaching Home Glucose Monitoring
- (Figure 14.3)

Suggestions for Classroom Activities

Facilitate review and discussion of "Case Study: Client with Gestational Diabetes" activity in the classroom. This case study can be found on the Companion Website.

Suggestions for Clinical Activities

Schedule clinical rotation at a high-risk antepartum unit. Assign students to work with registered nurses caring for clients with diabetes during pregnancy. Instruct students to develop an individual care plan for each client they were assigned to care for. Students may utilize "Care Plan: Woman with Diabetes Mellitus" on the Companion Website as a template for developing the care plans.

LEARNING OBJECTIVE 3

Discriminate among the types of anemia associated with pregnancy regarding signs, treatment, and implications for pregnancy.

CONCEPTS FOR LECTURE

1. Anemia indicates inadequate levels of hemoglobin in the blood. There are characteristic signs and symptoms associated with a diagnosis of anemia.
2. There are different types of anemia associated with pregnancy complications. Early recognition and treatment of anemia reduces pregnancy complications. *Refer to Table 14.4.*

POWERPOINT LECTURE SLIDES

1. Anemia
   - Definition: Hemoglobin (Hb) less than 10 g/dL
   - Signs: Fatigue
     - Paleness
     - Lack of energy
   - Implications for the infant: Low birth weight
     - Prematurity
     - Stillbirth

2. Types of Anemia
   - Iron deficiency—most common
   - Folic acid deficiency
   - Sickle cell anemia
   - Thalassemia

Suggestions for Classroom Activities

- Ask students to use Table 14.4 to outline the maternal and fetal risks associated with each type of anemia.
- Divide students into two groups. Have one group develop a menu that includes foods high in iron and the other group develop a menu that includes foods high in folic acid.

Suggestions for Clinical Activities

Allow students to review the hemoglobin levels of a group of clients at a prenatal clinic. Ask them to identify the clients with anemia based on hemoglobin levels. Students should be encouraged to get additional information from the prenatal chart and prenatal healthcare provider to determine the type of anemia each client was diagnosed with.

LEARNING OBJECTIVE 4

Discuss acquired immunodeficiency syndrome (AIDS), including care of the pregnant woman who has tested positive for the human immunodeficiency virus (HIV), fetal/neonatal implications, and ramifications for the childbearing family.

CONCEPTS FOR LECTURE

1. Human immunodeficiency virus (HIV) infection is one of today's major health concerns. It leads to a progressive disease that ultimately results in acquired immunodeficiency syndrome.

POWERPOINT LECTURE SLIDES

1. Human Immunodeficiency Virus (HIV) Infection
   - 18% of cases in the United States are women
   - HIV-1 virus affects specific T cells
   - Suppresses body's immune responses
   - Affected person susceptible to opportunistic infections

2. Many women who are HIV positive choose to avoid pregnancy because of the risk of infecting the fetus.

3. There are established guidelines for the management of pregnant women with HIV infection. *Refer to "Evidence-Based Nursing: Use of Antiretroviral Drugs in Pregnant Women Who Are HIV-1 Infected" and "Nursing Care Plan: The Woman with HIV Infection."*

- The individual develops detectable antibodies
- Diagnosis
  - Enzyme-linked immunosorbent assay (ELISA)
  - Confirmed with the Western blot test

 Human Immunodeficiency Virus (HIV) Infection
- Modes of transmission
  - Exposure to contaminated blood and body fluids
  - Sexual intercourse
  - IV drug abuse: Use of contaminated needles
  - Blood transfusion
  - Placental transmission
  - Breast milk

 Maternal-Fetal Neonatal Risks
- Maternal development of AIDS and opportunistic infections
- Fetal neonatal risk
  - HIV/AIDS disease in the newborn
  - Antiretroviral therapy has decreased infection rates
  - Following birth: Positive antibody titer
  - Reflects the passive transfer of maternal antibodies
  - Does not indicate HIV infection

 Clinical Therapy
- Clinical evaluation of the HIV disease stage
- Assess CD4$^+$ count
- Evaluate the risk of disease progression
- Document history of antiretroviral therapy
- Discuss risks and benefits of therapy during pregnancy
- Provide counseling about risk factors
- Three-part ZDV prophylaxis regimen

 Clinical Therapy
- Three-part ZDV prophylaxis regimen
  - Oral ZDV daily
  - Intravenous ZDV during labor and until birth
  - Oral ZDV for the infant
  - Start 8 to 12 hours after birth
  - Continue for 6 weeks

 Nursing Management
- Education
  - Nutrition and ZDV prophylaxis
  - Teaching for self-care
- Monitor for signs and symptoms of complications
- Review laboratory findings
  - May indicate complications
  - May indicate disease progression
- Adhere to universal precautions
- Provide family support and referral to social services

 Complementary Care
- ("Complementary Care: Garlic Supplements Interfere with HIV Medication.")

Start the lecture with a discussion on evidence-based practice. Instruct students to review "Evidence-Based Nursing" and complete the critical thinking activity at the end.

Assign students to a prenatal HIV clinic. Request that students review the prenatal records of their individual clients before participating in the care of the client. Instruct them to utilize the subjective and objective data collected to outline a nursing care plan for each client.

LEARNING OBJECTIVE 5

Describe the effects of various heart disorders on pregnancy, including their implications for nursing care.

CONCEPTS FOR LECTURE

1. The woman with heart disease has decreased cardiac reserve, making it more difficult for her heart to handle the higher workload of pregnancy.
2. The pathology found in a pregnant woman with heart disease varies with the type of disorder.
3. The primary goal of clinical therapy is early diagnosis and ongoing management of the woman with cardiac disease.

POWERPOINT LECTURE SLIDES

1 Heart Disease
- Complicates about 1% of pregnancies
- Pregnancy increased
  - Cardiac output
  - Heart rate
  - Blood volume
- Heart disease
  - Decreased cardiac reserve
  - Diminished capacity to handle pregnancy workload

2 Heart Disorders
- Congenital heart defects
  - Atrial septal and ventricular septal defects
  - Patent ductus arteriosus
  - Coarctation of the aorta, and tetralogy of Fallot
- Rheumatic heart disease—mitral stenosis
- Mitral valve prolapse
- Peripartum cardiomyopathy

3 Clinical Therapy
- Diagnosis
  - Echocardiogram and chest x-ray
  - Auscultation of heart sounds
  - Sometimes cardiac catheterization
- Classification of functional capacity
  - Class 1 through 4
- Drug therapy

3a Nursing Management
- Assess the stress of pregnancy on the heart's functioning
- Limitation of activity
- Monitor for signs of impending cardiac failure
- Health teaching
- Evaluate maternal vital signs
- Maintain an atmosphere of calm
- Fetal assessment
- Family support

3b Monitoring the Woman with Heart Disease
- (Figure 14.4)

SUGGESTIONS FOR CLASSROOM ACTIVITIES

Invite a cardiologist to talk to the students about heart disease and the implications for pregnancy.

SUGGESTIONS FOR CLINICAL ACTIVITIES

Arrange for students to spend some clinical time in a high-risk perinatal care unit. If possible, assist in the selection of pregnant or laboring females who have been diagnosed with cardiac disease. Each student should be paired with an experienced perinatal registered nurse. The students should focus on observing the overall clinical and nursing management of their individual clients.

LEARNING OBJECTIVE 6

Delineate the effects of selected pregestational medical conditions on pregnancy.

CONCEPTS FOR LECTURE

1. A woman with a preexisting medical condition needs to be aware of the possible impact of pregnancy on her condition, as well as the impact of her condition on the successful outcome of her pregnancy. *Refer to Table 14.5.*

POWERPOINT LECTURE SLIDES

1 Impact on Mother and Pregnancy
- All women with chronic medical conditions need increased vigilance during pregnancy
- Most chronic medical conditions
  - Will have some effect on the mother

1a Impact on Newborn
- Chronic maternal medical conditions
  - May increase risks to the newborn
  - Premature birth
  - Low birth weight
  - Growth retardation

SUGGESTIONS FOR CLASSROOM ACTIVITIES

Begin the class by talking about the most common medical conditions that may complicate a pregnancy. Utilize Table 14.5 to focus on the common conditions listed in the book.

SUGGESTIONS FOR CLINICAL ACTIVITIES

Students should continue their clinical experience at the high-risk perinatal unit. Assign students to shadow registered nurses caring for pregnant clients with medical conditions. Select one student to present subjective and objective data collected on the client. Allow the other students to use the data presented to identify a list of nursing diagnosis for that client.

CHAPTER 15
PREGNANCY AT RISK: GESTATIONAL ONSET

RESOURCE LIBRARY

⊙ CD-ROM

NCLEX-RN® Review
Skill 2-3: Assessing Deep Tendon Reflexes and Clonus
Skill 2-4: Administration of Rh Immune Globulin
  (RhIgG) (RhoGAM, HypoRho-D)
Animation: Early Premature Labor
Audio Glossary

🌐 COMPANION WEBSITE

NCLEX-RN® Review
Media Link Application:
  Case Study: Client with Preclampsia
  Care Plan Activity: Client at Risk for Preterm Labor
Case Study

📖 IMAGE LIBRARY

Figure 15.1 Types of spontaneous abortion.
Figure 15.2 Hydatidiform mole.
Figure 15.3 A cerclage or purse-string suture is inserted in the cervix to prevent preterm cervical dilatation and pregnancy loss.
Figure 15.4 To elicit clonus, with the knee flexed and the leg supported, sharply dorsiflex the foot, hold it momentarily, and then release it.
Figure 15.5 Rh alloimmunization sequence.

Table 15.1 Risk Factors for Spontaneous Preterm Labor
Table 15.2 Self-Care Measure to Prevent Preterm Labor
Table 15.3 Deep Tendon Reflex Rating Scale
Table 15.4 Rh Alloimmunization
Pathophysiology Illustrated: Ectopic Pregnancy
Pathophysiology Illustrated: Preclampsion

LEARNING OBJECTIVE 1

Contrast the etiology, medical therapy, and nursing interventions for the various bleeding problems associated with pregnancy.

CONCEPTS FOR LECTURE

1. During the first and second trimesters, abortion is the major cause of bleeding.
2. Other complications that may cause bleeding in the first half of pregnancy are ectopic pregnancy and gestational trophoblastic disease.
3. In the second half of pregnancy, particularly in the third trimester, the two major causes of bleeding are placenta previa and abruptio placentae.
4. The nurse has certain general responsibilities in providing nursing care for clients experiencing bleeding during pregnancy.

POWERPOINT LECTURE SLIDES

1 Causes of Bleeding During the First and Second Trimester
- Abortion: Expulsion of the fetus before 20 weeks' gestation
  - Expulsion of fetus less than 500 g
  - Spontaneous: Occur naturally
  - Induced: Caused by medical or surgical means
- Medical therapy: Bed rest and abstinence from sex
  - Persistent bleeding: Hospitalization
  - IV therapy or blood transfusions
  - Dilatation and curettage (D&C) or suction evacuation

1a Types of Spontaneous Abortion
- (Figure 15.1)

2 Causes of Bleeding During First Half of Pregnancy
- Ectopic pregnancy
  - Implantation of fertilized ovum in site other than uterus

- ○ Mortality rates declined almost 90%
- ○ Initially symptoms of pregnancy
- ○ Positive hCG present in blood and urine
- ○ Chorionic villi grow into tube wall or implantation site
- ○ Rupture and bleeding into the abdominal cavity occurs

 Causes of Bleeding During First Half of Pregnancy
- Ectopic pregnancy
  - ○ Result is sharp unilateral pain and syncope
  - ○ Referred shoulder pain
  - ○ Lower abdominal pain
  - ○ Vaginal bleeding
- Medical therapy: Intramuscular methotrexate if future pregnancy desired
- Surgical therapy: Salpingostomy or salpingectomy

 Ectopic Pregnancy
- ("Pathophysiology Illustrated: Ectopic Pregnancy")

 Causes of Bleeding During First Half of Pregnancy
- Gestational trophoblastic disease
  - ○ Pathologic proliferation of trophoblastic cells
  - ○ Includes hydatidiform mole
  - ○ Invasive mole (chorioadenoma destruens)
  - ○ Choriocarcinoma, a form of cancer
  - ○ Initially, clinical picture similar to pregnancy
  - ○ Classic signs: Uterine enlargement greater than gestational age, vaginal bleeding

 Causes of Bleeding During First Half of Pregnancy
- Classic signs
  - ○ Present in about 50% of cases
  - ○ May pass hydropic vesicles
  - ○ Hyperemesis gravidarum
  - ○ Higher serum hCG levels
- Therapy: Suction evacuation of the mole
  - ○ Uterine curettage for removal of placental fragments
  - ○ Hysterectomy for excessive bleeding

 Hydatidiform Mole
- (Figure 15.2)

 Causes of Bleeding During Second Half of Pregnancy
- Bleeding during second half of pregnancy
  - ○ Placenta previa
  - ○ Abruptio placentae
- Nursing Interventions: Initial assessment of bleeding
  - ○ Monitor blood pressure and pulse frequently
  - ○ Observe for signs of shock
  - ○ Assess amount of bleeding over a time period
  - ○ Prepare for intravenous (IV) therapy

 Nursing Responsibilities
- Assess fetal heart tones

- Prepare equipment for examination
- Have oxygen available
- Collect and organize all data
- Notify other members of healthcare team
- Obtain an order to type and cross match for blood
- Assess coping mechanisms of woman in crisis
- Assess the family's response to situation

SUGGESTIONS FOR CLASSROOM ACTIVITIES

Discuss the pathophysiology of ectopic pregnancy. Utilize "Pathophysiology Illustrated: Ectopic Pregnancy" to do so.

SUGGESTIONS FOR CLINICAL ACTIVITIES

Schedule students' clinical time at a high-risk prenatal clinic or an antepartum unit. Arrange for them to care for clients diagnosed with bleeding during pregnancy along with a primary nurse. They should participate in assessment data collection. Ask them to make a list of the nursing interventions carried out or observed during their clinical rotation.

LEARNING OBJECTIVE 2

Identify the medical therapy and nursing interventions indicated in caring for a woman with an incompetent cervix.

CONCEPTS FOR LECTURE

1. Incompetent cervix refers to the premature dilatation of the cervix, usually in the fourth or fifth month of pregnancy.
2. Incompetent cervix is managed with the help of surgical procedures.
3. The nurse plays an active role in caring for clients with incompetent cervix.

POWERPOINT LECTURE SLIDES

1 Incompetent Cervix
- Associated with repeated second trimester abortions
- Possible causes
  - Cervical trauma
  - Infection
  - Congenital cervical or uterine anomalies
  - Increased uterine volume (as with a multiple gestation)
- Diagnosis: Positive history of repeated second trimester abortions

2 Treatment: Surgical Procedures
- Shirodkar procedure (cerclage)
- Modification of it by McDonald
- Reinforces the weakened cervix
- Purse-string suture is placed in cervix
- Done in first trimester or early in second trimester
- Cesarean birth may be planned
- Suture may be cut at term and vaginal birth permitted

2a A Cerclage
- (Figure 15.3)

3 Nursing Interventions
- Monitor women for premature labor
- Monitor for premature rupture of membranes

- Teach client
  - Signs of premature labor
  - Signs of premature rupture of membranes
- Tell client to contact healthcare provider if membranes rupture or labor begins

SUGGESTIONS FOR CLASSROOM ACTIVITIES

Invite an obstetrician to talk to your class about the management of a woman with incompetent cervix. Be sure to discuss collecting a prenatal history on this client.

SUGGESTIONS FOR CLINICAL ACTIVITIES

Continue clinical rotation at a high-risk clinic or antepartum unit. Assign students to observe and participate in the care of a client diagnosed with incompetent cervix. Allow students to create a health-teaching plan for a client who is going to have a cerclage or had the procedure done.

LEARNING OBJECTIVE 3

Discuss the medical therapy and nursing care of a woman with hyperemesis gravidarum.

CONCEPTS FOR LECTURE

1. Hyperemesis gravidarum, a relatively rare condition, is excessive vomiting during pregnancy.
2. Treatment of hyperemesis gravidarum is aimed at controlling vomiting and maintaining fluid and electrolyte status.
3. The nurse's role in caring for a client diagnosed with hyperemesis gravidarum is multifaceted.

POWERPOINT LECTURE SLIDES

1. Hyperemesis Gravidarum
   - Exact cause of hyperemesis is unclear
   - Increased levels of hCG may play a role
   - Severe cases: Causes dehydration
     - Fluid-electrolyte imbalance
     - Alkalosis
     - Metabolic acidosis
     - Decreased urinary output

2. Aim of Treatment
   - Control vomiting: Antiemetics
   - Correct fluid and electrolyte imbalance—potassium chloride
   - Correct dehydration: Intravenous (IV) fluids
   - Improve nutritional statatus
     - Vitamin supplements
     - Total parenteral nutrition

3. Nursing Care
   - Supportive
   - Directed at maintaining a relaxed environment
   - Maintaining oral hygiene
   - Monitoring weight
   - Monitoring for signs of complications
   - Once oral feedings resume, food needs to be attractively served

SUGGESTIONS FOR CLASSROOM ACTIVITIES

Instruct students to make a list of nursing diagnoses that applies to a client diagnosed with hyperemesis gravidarum. Tell the students to write a minimum of two nursing interventions for each listed nursing diagnoses.

SUGGESTIONS FOR CLINICAL ACTIVITIES

Arrange for clinical rotation at an antepartum unit. Assign students to observe and participate in the care of clients diagnosed with hyperemesis gravidarum. Allow students to formulate care plans for each assigned client.

Delineate the nursing care needs of a woman experiencing premature rupture of the membranes (PROM) or preterm labor.

CONCEPTS FOR LECTURE

1. Premature rupture of membranes (PROM) nursing care focuses on prevention of infection.
2. Nursing care during preterm labor focuses on administration of tocolytics and monitoring for progression of labor. *Refer to "Drug Guide: Betamethasone" in the book.*

POWERPOINT LECTURE SLIDES

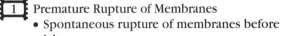 **Premature Rupture of Membranes**
- Spontaneous rupture of membranes before labor
- Preterm PROM (PPROM): Rupture of membranes before term
- Maternal risk of infection increases
- Risk of abruptio placentae
- Fetal-newborn: Risk of respiratory distress syndrome
- Fetal sepsis, malpresentation and prolapse of umbilical cord
- Increased perinatal morbidity and mortality

1a Premature Rupture of Membranes
- Prevention of infection
  ○ Use sterile speculum to detect amniotic fluid
  ○ Limit digital vaginal examinations
- If maternal signs of infection evident, antibiotic therapy started immediately
- Upon admission to nursery: Infant assessed for sepsis, placed on antibiotic

1b Premature Rupture of Membranes
- Absence of infection and gestation age less than 37
  ○ Hospitalization and bed rest
  ○ Complete blood cell count (CBC)
  ○ C-reactive protein and urinalysis
  ○ Continuous or intermittent fetal monitoring
  ○ Regular nonstress tests (NSTs) or biophysical profiles
  ○ Maternal vital signs assessed every 4 hours
  ○ Regular laboratory evaluations

1c Premature Rupture of Membranes
- Absence of infection /gestation age less than 37 weeks
  ○ Fetal lung maturity studies
  ○ Maternal corticosteroid administration
- If sent home: Discharge instructions
  ○ Bed rest with bathroom privileges
  ○ Monitor temperature and pulse every 4 hours
  ○ Keep fetal movement chart and have weekly NST
  ○ Call healthcare provider for signs of complications

2 Preterm Labor
- Labor that occurs between 20 and 37 weeks gestation

- Documented uterine contractions
  (4 in 20 minutes or 8 in 1 hour)
- Documented cervical change
- Cervical dilatation of greater than 1 cm
- Cervical effacement of 80% or more

 Preterm Labor
- Management
  - Assessment of cervicovaginal fibronectin
  - Assessment of cervical length via ultrasound
  - Obtaining history of previous preterm birth
  - Assess for the presence of infections
  - Educating clients about preterm labor
  - Assessing for early signs and symptoms
  - Maternal laboratory studies

 Preterm Labor
- Management
  - IV infusion: Promotes maternal hydration
  - Tocolysis: Medications used to stop labor
- Tocolytics
  - β-adrenergic agonists and magnesium sulfate
  - Prostaglandin synthetase inhibitors
  - Calcium channel blockers

 Preterm Labor
- Nursing management
  - Identify woman at risk
  - Assess the progress of labor
  - Administration of medications
- Assess impact of labor on mother and fetus
  - Teach how to recognize onset of labor
  - Provide information about community
    resources

2d Risk Factors for Spontaneous Preterm Labor
- (Table 15.1)

2e Self-Care Measures to Prevent Preterm Labor
- (Table 15.2)

SUGGESTIONS FOR CLASSROOM ACTIVITIES

Towards the end of the lecture ask students to review and discuss "Evidence-Based Nursing: Preterm Birth Prevention." Have students identify community resources that are currently in use to decrease the incidence of preterm labor. Assign "Care Plan: Client at Risk for Preterm Labor" activity on the Companion Website for homework.

SUGGESTIONS FOR CLINICAL ACTIVITIES

Arrange for clinical rotation at an antepartum unit. Assign students clients with a diagnosis of preterm labor. Instruct students to review the medical records to identify risk factors associated with clients' diagnoses. Tell the students to use "Teaching Highlights: Preterm Labor" as a template for client teaching. Students may also view the premature labor animation on the Student CD-ROM for reference.

LEARNING OBJECTIVE 5

Describe the development and course of hypertensive disorders associated with pregnancy.

CONCEPTS FOR LECTURE

1. A number of hypertensive disorders can occur during pregnancy.
2. Hypertensive disorders that occur during pregnancy place the pregnant female, the fetus, or the newborn at risk for complications.
3. Clinical manifestations depend on whether the condition is mild, severe, or complicated with the occurrence of eclampsia.
4. Clinical and nursing management is dependent on the severity of the disease. *See "Nursing Care Plan for a Woman with Preeclampsia" and "Drug Guide: Magnesium Sulfate."*

POWERPOINT LECTURE SLIDES

1 Classification and Pathophysiology
- Classification
  - Gestational (or transient) hypertension
  - Preeclampsia-eclampsia
  - Chronic hypertension
  - Chronic hypertension with superimposed preeclampsia or eclampsia

1a Classification and Pathophysiology
- Pathophysiology
  - Decreased levels of vasodilators
  - Loss of normal vasodilation capability
  - Increased levels of vasoconstrictors (partially produced by placenta)
  - Concurrent vasospasm
  - BP begins to rise after 20 weeks' gestation

1b Pathophysiology Illustrated: Preeclampsia
- ("Pathophysiology Illustrated: Preeclampsia")

2 Maternal Risks
- Hyperreflexia and headache
- Seizures, renal failure, and abruptio placentae
- Disseminated intravascular coagulation (DIC)
- Ruptured liver and pulmonary embolism
- HELLP syndrome (**H**emolysis, **E**levated **L**iver enzymes, and **L**ow **P**latelet count)

2a Fetal-Neonatal Risks
- Small for gestational age (SGA)
- Premature
- Hypermagnesemia (magnesium sulfate administration to mother)
- Increased morbidity and mortality

3 Clinical Manifestations and Diagnosis
- Mild preeclampsia
  - BP 140/90 mm Hg or higher
  - 1+ proteinuria may occur
  - Liver enzymes may be elevated minimally
  - Edema may be present

- Severe preeclampsia
  - BP 160/110 mm Hg or higher
  - measurements, 6 hours apart

3a Clinical Manifestations and Diagnosis
- Severe preeclampsia
  - Proteinuria ≥5 g in a 24-hour urine collection
  - Dipstick urine protein 3+ to 4+ on 2 random samples

- ○ Samples must be obtained at least 4 hours apart
- ○ Visual or cerebral disturbances
- Eclampsia
  - ○ Grand mal convulsion
  - ○ May occur antepartum, intrapartum, or postpartum

 Management
- Home care of mild preeclampsia
  - ○ Client monitors her blood pressure
  - ○ Measures weight and tests urine protein daily
  - ○ Remote NSTs performed daily or biweekly
  - ○ Advised to report signs of worsening preeclampsia
- Hospital care of mild preeclampsia
  - ○ Bed rest and moderate to high protein diet
  - ○ Fetal evaluation

 Management
- Severe preeclampsia
  - ○ Bed rest
  - ○ Diet: High-protein, moderate-sodium
  - ○ Anticonvulsants: Magnesium sulfate
  - ○ Fluid and electrolyte replacement
  - ○ Corticosteroids and antihypertensive drugs

 Management
- Eclampsia
  - ○ Anticonvulsants: Bolus of magnesium sulfate
  - ○ Sedation and other anticonvulsants: Dilantin
  - ○ Diuretics to treat pulmonary edema
  - ○ Furosemide (Lasix)
  - ○ Digitalis: For circulatory failure
  - ○ Strict monitoring of intake and output

 Management
- Nursing care: Assessment
  - ○ Formulation of nursing diagnoses
  - ○ Set goals and outcome criteria
  - ○ Implement specific nursing interventions
  - ○ Interventions are aimed at meeting goals
  - ○ Evaluation of nursing interventions

 Management
- Nursing care
  - ○ Monitor vital signs and auscultate lungs
  - ○ Evaluate fetal heart rate patterns
  - ○ Monitor urinary output and urine protein hourly
  - ○ Check specific gravity of the urine hourly
  - ○ Weigh the woman daily at the same time
  - ○ Assess deep tendon reflexes and clonus

 Deep Tendon Reflex Rating Scale
- (Table 15.3)

 To Elicit Clonus
- (Figure 15.4)

LEARNING OBJECTIVE 6

Explain the cause and prevention of hemolytic disease of the newborn secondary to Rh incompatibility.

CONCEPTS FOR LECTURE

1. Rh alloimmunization (sensitization), also called isoimmunization, most often occurs when an Rh-negative woman carries an Rh-positive fetus, either to term or to termination by miscarriage or induced abortion.

POWERPOINT LECTURE SLIDES

 Rh Alloimmunization: Causes
- Rh-negative woman carries an Rh-positive fetus
- Fetal red blood cells cross into maternal circulation
- Response: Production of Rh antibodies
- Transfer of RBCs usually occurs at birth
- The first child is not affected
- Subsequent pregnancy
  - Rh antibodies enter the fetal circulation
  - Result: Hemolysis of fetal red blood cells and fetal anemia

1a Rh Alloimmunization Sequence
- (Figure 15.5)

1b Rh Alloimmunization: Fetal and Neonatal Risks
- Anemia
- Hemolytic syndrome
- Erythroblastosis fetalis
  - Marked fetal edema, called hydrops fetalis
  - Congestive heart failure
  - Marked jaundice

1c Rh Alloimmunization: Prevention
- Screen for Rh incompatibility and sensitization
  - Take a history
  - Identify Rh-negative woman
  - Antibody screen (indirect Coombs' test)
  - Identifies if woman is sensitized
  - Give injection of 300 mcg Rh immune globulin

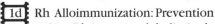 Rh Alloimmunization: Prevention
- Give Rh immune globulin in the following cases
  - Pregnant Rh-women who have no antibody titer
  - At 28 weeks' gestational age
  - Mother whose baby's father is Rh positive or unknown

POWERPOINT LECTURE SLIDES *continued*

- ○ After each abortion and within 72 hours postpartum
- ○ Amniocentesis and placenta previa
- ○ Invasive procedures that may cause bleeding

 Rh Alloimmunization
- • (Table 15.4)

SUGGESTIONS FOR CLASSROOM ACTIVITIES	SUGGESTIONS FOR CLINICAL ACTIVITIES
Utilize Figure 15.5 to illustrate Rh alloimmunization. Allow for in-class review of Table 15.5.	Students should be allowed to participate in the screening, identification, education, and nursing management of pregnant women who have Rh-negative blood. They may do so at a prenatal clinic or an antepartum, intrapartum, or postpartum unit under the supervision of a preceptor or clinical instructor.

LEARNING OBJECTIVE 7

Compare Rh incompatibility to ABO incompatibility with regard to occurrence, treatment, and implications for the fetus or newborn.

CONCEPTS FOR LECTURE

1. In most cases, ABO incompatibility is limited to type O mothers with a type A, B, or AB fetus. Unlike Rh incompatibility, no treatment exists to prevent the occurrence.

POWERPOINT LECTURE SLIDES

 ABO Incompatibility
- • Cause: Mother has type O blood and infant has A, B, or AB
  - ○ Anti-A and anti-B antibodies occur naturally
  - ○ During pregnancy maternal antibodies cross placenta
  - ○ Cause hemolysis of the fetal red blood cells
  - ○ Unlike Rh incompatibility, first infant is often involved, no evidence of repeated sensitization, no antepartal treatment

 ABO Incompatibility
- • Creates hyperbilirubinemia in the infant
- • Hyperbilirubinemia is treated with phototherapy
- • Assess for potential for ABO incompatibility— type O mother and type A or B father
- • Following birth
  - ○ Newborn assessed carefully
  - ○ Assess for development of hyperbilirubinemia
- • Unlike Rh incompatibility, it cannot be prevented

SUGGESTIONS FOR CLASSROOM ACTIVITIES	SUGGESTIONS FOR CLINICAL ACTIVITIES
Allow for in-class review of "Skill 2.4: Administration of Rh Immune Globulin (RhIgG, RhoGAM, HypRho-D)." This skill can be found on the Student CD-ROM and in the *Clinical Skills Manual*.	Before clinical, assign students to review information about RhoGAM by writing up a drug card outlining the name of the drug, the classification, recommended dosage, route of administration, desired effect, adverse reactions and nursing implications. Allow students to give RhoGAM shots under the supervision of an assigned preceptor or clinical instructor.

LEARNING OBJECTIVE 8

Summarize the effects of surgical procedures on pregnancy and explain ways in which pregnancy may complicate diagnosis.

CONCEPTS FOR LECTURE

1. Elective surgery poses some risks and should be delayed until the postpartum, but essential surgery can generally be done during pregnancy.
2. Special considerations must be kept in mind whenever the surgical client is pregnant.

POWERPOINT LECTURE SLIDES

1 Effects of Surgical Procedures
- First trimester surgery: Increase incidence of abortion
- Increased incidence of fetal mortality
- Low-birth-weight (less than 2500 g) infants
- Increased incidence of preterm labor
- Increased incidence of intrauterine growth restriction
- Inability to perform some diagnostic procedures (x-ray)—may hinder diagnosis of disease during pregnancy

2 Special Considerations
- Surgery during early second trimester decreases risk of complication
- During surgery, wedge placed under mother's hip prevents uterine compression of major blood vessels
- Insertion of nasogastric tube to decrease vomiting
- An indwelling catheter
  - Prevents bladder distension
  - Facilitates monitoring of output

2a Special Considerations
- Fetal heart rate must be monitored electronically during and after surgery
- Postoperatively
  - Encourage to turn, breathe deeply, and cough
  - Encourage use of ventilation therapy
  - Early ambulation to prevent complications
- Discharge teaching is very important

SUGGESTIONS FOR CLASSROOM ACTIVITIES

Ask students to make a list of all the physiological changes according to body systems associated with pregnancy and for each change show how surgery may impact the physiological status of the pregnant female. Allow guided classroom discussion.

SUGGESTIONS FOR CLINICAL ACTIVITIES

Arrange for students to observe and participate in caring for pregnant clients during the preoperative, intraoperative, and postoperative phases of surgery under the guidance of a clinical instructor. Instruct students to write about the observations that they made and to identify actual or potential problems associated with their client's surgery.

LEARNING OBJECTIVE 9

Discuss the impact of trauma due to an accident on the pregnant woman or her fetus.

CONCEPTS FOR LECTURE

1. Trauma complicates 6% to 7% of pregnancies and is the leading nonobstetric cause of maternal death. When major blunt trauma to the mother occurs in the second or third trimester the risk of fetal loss is 40% to 50%.

POWERPOINT LECTURE SLIDES

1 Impact of Trauma During Pregnancy
- Types of trauma
  - Blunt trauma
  - Penetrating injuries
  - Gunshot wounds

2. Treatment of major injuries during pregnancy focuses initially on life-saving measures for the woman and the fetus.

- Causes: Motor vehicle accident—most common
  - Falls
  - Direct assaults
- Impact
  - Maternal shock
  - Premature labor or spontaneous abortion

 Impact of Trauma During Pregnancy
- Maternal mortality: From head trauma or hemorrhage
  - Uterine rupture is rare
  - Placental abruption (abruptio placentae)
- Traumatic separation of the placenta
  - High rate of fetal mortality
  - Premature birth
- Early rupture of membranes

 Treatment
- Major injuries
  - Life-saving measures for woman
  - Establishing an airway
  - Control external bleeding
  - Administer IV fluid to alleviate shock
  - Kept on her left side to prevent further hypotension
  - Oxygen is administered at 100%
  - Exploratory surgery may be necessary

 Treatment
- Fetus near term and uterus damaged: Cesarean section
- Fetus immature
  - Uterus can be repaired
  - Pregnancy continue to term
- Evaluation of fetal heart rate and movement
- Minor injuries
  - Fetal monitoring for minimum of 4 hours
  - Signs of obstetric complications such as uterine bleeding
  - Monitoring for 24 hours is recommended

SUGGESTIONS FOR CLASSROOM ACTIVITIES

In preparation for this lecture, assign students to obtain information about the prevalence and causes of trauma during pregnancy in their local community. Allow students to discuss their findings in the classroom.

SUGGESTIONS FOR CLINICAL ACTIVITIES

Arrange to have students gain clinical experience in an obstetric triage unit. Assign students to shadow a prenatal healthcare provider who evaluates pregnant clients involved in motor vehicle accidents or sustained trauma by other means. Instruct students to write a paper describing the evaluation process for each client observed.

LEARNING OBJECTIVE 10

Explain the needs and care of the pregnant woman who experiences abuse.

CONCEPTS FOR LECTURE

1. Domestic violence, most often the intentional injury of a woman by her partner, often begins or increases during pregnancy.

POWERPOINT LECTURE SLIDES

 Physical Abuse During Pregnancy
- Incidence: 4% to 8%
- May result in loss of pregnancy

2. The goals of treatment are to identify the woman at risk, to increase her decision-making abilities to decrease the risk for further abuse, and to provide a safe environment for the woman and her unborn child.

- Preterm labor, low-birth-weight infants, and fetal death
- Abused women have higher rates of complications
  - Anemia, infection, and low weight gain
  - First- and second-trimester bleeding
- Be alert for nonspecific signs

 Physical Abuse During Pregnancy
- Management: Early detection
- Ask about abuse at several prenatal visits
- Client may only disclose abuse after knowing her caregivers
- Assess old scars on parts of the body
- Be alert for signs of bruising: Target areas of violence during pregnancy
  - Client's breasts
  - Abdomen or genitalia

 Treatment
- Create an accepting, nonjudgmental environment
- Allow client to express her concerns
- Client needs to be aware of community resources
  - Emergency shelters
  - Police, legal, and social services
  - Counseling
- Client has to make decision to seek assistance

SUGGESTIONS FOR CLASSROOM ACTIVITIES

Invite a social worker to talk to the students about the incidence of spousal abuse in the local community and the strategies currently utilized in the local community to address this problem.

SUGGESTIONS FOR CLINICAL ACTIVITIES

As part of the students' clinical assignment, allow them to gather information in their local community about the community resources available to pregnant females facing physical abuse. Students should also be allowed to spend some time at a shelter for pregnant abused clients. Students should focus on the services available to help pregnant, physically abused females at the shelter they have been assigned to.

LEARNING OBJECTIVE 11

Describe the effects of infections on the pregnant woman and her unborn child.

CONCEPTS FOR LECTURE

1. Infections acquired during pregnancy may have an impact on the fetus. *Refer to Table 15.5.*

POWERPOINT LECTURE SLIDES

 Prenatal Infections
- Toxoplasmosis: Protozoan *Toxoplasma gondii*
- Transmission
  - Eating raw or undercooked meat
  - Contact with the feces of infected cats
- Fetal-neonatal risks
  - Fetal infection
  - Severe fetal disease or death
- Severe neonatal disorders
- Treatment
  - Sulfadiazine and pyrimethamine
  - Given after the first trimester

Prenatal Infections
- Rubella: Virus
- Transmission: Across placenta to fetus
  - Fetal neonatal infection
  - Infant should be isolated
  - Rubella syndrome
- Treatment: Prevention
  - Vaccination of all children
  - Vaccination of women of reproductive age

 Prenatal Infections
- Cytomegalovirus: Virus
- Transmission
  - Across placenta to fetus
  - Cervical route during birth
- Fetal infection
- Fetal death
- Neonatal disorders
- Treatment: Currently none exist

 Prenatal Infections
- Herpes simplex virus: HSV-1 or HSV-2
- Transmission: Ascending infection during birth
  - After membranes rupture
  - Transplacental: Rare
- Neonatal infection
- Treatment: Antiviral therapy (acyclovir)
- Active herpes lesion: Cesarean section
- No evidence of genital infection exists, vaginal birth is preferred

 Prenatal Infections
- Group B streptococcal infection (GBS)—bacterial infection
- Transmission: Vertical from mother during birth
  - From colonized nursing personnel
  - From colonized infants
- Neonatal infection treated with antibiotics
- Prevention
  - Early identification
  - Antibiotic prophylaxis

 Prenatal Infections
- Other Infections
  - Urinary tract infections
  - Vaginal infections
  - Sexually transmitted infections
- Maternal infections may cause spontaneous abortions.
- Some evidence links infection and prematurity
- Risk of maternal and fetal morbidity and mortality
- Early diagnosis and treatment is necessary

SUGGESTIONS FOR CLASSROOM ACTIVITIES

During the lecture, facilitate review of the contents in Table 15.5. At the end of the lecture, instruct students to complete "Thinking Critically."

SUGGESTIONS FOR CLINICAL ACTIVITIES

Assign students to an antepartum unit or prenatal clinic. Allow them to review prenatal or medical records of the clients they have been assigned to care for. They should pay particular attention to subjective and objective information including laboratory results. Instruct them to utilize the assessment data to identify clients with prenatal infections or clients at risk for prenatal infections. Allow them to make a list of possible nursing diagnoses for each of their clients.

CHAPTER 16
ASSESSMENT OF FETAL WELL-BEING

RESOURCE LIBRARY

CD-ROM
NCLEX-RN® Review
Skill 2–5: Assisting During Amniocentesis
Skill 2–8: Biophysical Profile (BPP)
Audio Glossary

IMAGE LIBRARY

Figure 16.1 Ultrasound scanning permits visualization of the fetus in utero.
Figure 16.2 Ultrasound of fetal face.
Figure 16.5 Example of a reactive nonstress test (NST).
Figure 16.6 Example of a nonreactive NST.
Figure 16.7 NST management scheme.
Figure 16.8 Example of a positive contraction stress test (CST).
Figure 16.9 Amniocentesis

COMPANION WEBSITE
NCLEX-RN® Review
MediaLink Applications:
   Case Study: Client Undergoing Contraction Stress Test
   Care Plan Activity: Assessment of Fetal Well-Being

Table 16.2 Sample Nursing Approaches to Pretest Teaching
Table 16.4 Criteria for Biophysical Profile Scoring
Table 16.5 Contraction Stress Test
Table 16.6 Lecithin/Sphingomyelin (L/S) Ratio and Phosphatidylglycerol (PG)

Nursing Practice

LEARNING OBJECTIVE 1

Identify pertinent information to be discussed with the woman regarding her own assessment of fetal activity and methods of recording fetal activity.

CONCEPTS FOR LECTURE

1. Clinicians now generally agree that vigorous fetal activity provides reassurance of fetal well-being.
2. The expectant mother's perception of fetal movements and her commitment to completing a fetal movement record may vary.

POWERPOINT LECTURE SLIDES

1 Fetal Activity
  • Vigorous fetal activity—provides reassurance of fetal well-being
  • Marked decrease or cessation in activity
    ○ May indicate possible fetal compromise
    ○ May require immediate follow-up
  • Assessment of fetal activity (from week 28 to week 38)—noninvasive method of monitoring the fetus

2 Fetal Activity Record: Pertinent Information
  • The purpose of the assessment
  • How to complete the form
  • Whom to call with questions
  • What to report
  • Provide the opportunity for follow-up during each visit

SUGGESTIONS FOR CLASSROOM ACTIVITIES

Instruct students to prepare a teaching plan for instructing pregnant clients how to monitor and record fetal activity. Assign "Care Plan: Assessment of Fetal Well-Being" activity on the Companion Website for homework.

SUGGESTIONS FOR CLINICAL ACTIVITIES

Allow students to engage in teaching pregnant clients about the monitoring and recording of fetal activity in a prenatal environment. Review Skill 2-8: Assessment of Fetal Well-Being: Biophysical Profile (BPP) in the Clinical Skills Manual.

LEARNING OBJECTIVE 2

Identify indications and interpret findings for ultrasound examination during pregnancy.

CONCEPTS FOR LECTURE

1. Valuable information about the fetus may be obtained from ultrasound testing.

POWERPOINT LECTURE SLIDES

1 Ultrasound
- Confirmation of pregnancy and fetal presentation
- Evaluation of fetal heartbeat and fetal respiration
- Identification of more than one embryo or fetus
- For examination of anatomical fetal structures
- To estimate gestational age, fetal weight, and growth
- Location of the placenta and amniotic fluid volume
- Accompanying invasive procedures

1a Ultrasound
- Means of assessing the fetus over a period of time
- It is noninvasive and painless
- Allows midwife or physician to study the gestation serially
- It is nonradiating to both the woman and her fetus
- It has no known harmful effects
- The nurse provides an opportunity for the woman to ask questions
- The nurse acts as an advocate

1b Ultrasound Scanning Permits Visualization of the Fetus in Utero
- (Figure 16.1)

1c Ultrasound of Fetal Face
- (Figure 16.2)

SUGGESTIONS FOR CLASSROOM ACTIVITIES

Discuss evidence-based nursing. Allow students to review "Evidence-Based Nursing: Ultrasound for Fetal Assessment in Early Pregnancy." Ask them to complete the critical thinking exercise at the end.

SUGGESTIONS FOR CLINICAL ACTIVITIES

Assign students to an antenatal testing clinic that also performs prenatal ultrasounds. The aim of this experience is for students to observe the responsibilities of the nurse before, during, and after the ultrasound of a pregnant client.

LEARNING OBJECTIVE 3

Compare and contrast the procedure and information obtained from Doppler velocity, nonstress test, contraction stress test, and biophysical profile tests.

CONCEPTS FOR LECTURE

1. Doppler blood flow studies are used to assess placental function and sufficiency.
2. A nonstress test is based on the knowledge that the FHR normally increases in response to fetal activity and to sound stimulation.
3. Biophysical profile is a combination of an ultrasound and a nonstress test used to assess fetal well-being.
4. A contraction stress test evaluates respiratory function of the placenta.

POWERPOINT LECTURE SLIDES

1 Doppler Blood Flow Studies
- Noninvasive: Can be initiated at 16 to 18 weeks
- Can be scheduled at regular intervals for women at risk
- Measures blood flow changes in maternal and fetal circulation
- Allows for assessment of placental function
- Normal S/D ratio is below 2.6 by 26 weeks
- S/D ratio is below 3 at term
- Increase in placental bed resistance = an elevated S/D ratio

1a Umbilical Artery Velocity Waveforms

1b Examples of Abnormal Umbilical Artery Velocity Waveforms

2 Nonstress Test
- Used to assess fetal status using an electronic fetal monitor
- Based on the knowledge
  ○ Well-oxygenated fetus has adequate oxygenation
  ○ Intact central nervous system
  ○ Increase in fetal heart rate (FHR) with fetal movement
- Reactive NST: Two accelerations of FHR over 20 minutes
- Nonreactive: Less than 2 accelerations over 40 minutes
- Unsatisfactory: Cannot be interpreted

2a Reactive Nonstress Test (NST)
- (Figure 16.5)

2b Example of a Nonreactive NST
- (Figure 16.6)

2c NST Management Scheme
- (Figure 16.7)

3 Biophysical Profile
- Comprehensive assessment of five biophysical variables
  ○ Fetal breathing movement
  ○ Fetal movements of body or limbs

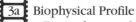

- ○ Fetal tone (extension and flexion of extremities)
- ○ Amniotic fluid volume (visualized as pockets of fluid around the fetus)
- ○ Reactive FHR with activity (reactive NST)

3a Biophysical Profile
- For each normal finding, score of 2 is assigned
- Maximum score of 10 is possible
- For each abnormal finding, a score of 0 is assigned
- Combination of an ultrasound and a nonstress test
- Helps to identify healthy or compromised fetus
- Indicated when risk of placental insufficiency
- When risk of fetal compromise

3b Criteria for Biophysical Profile Scoring
- (Table 16.4)

4 Contraction Stress Test
- Enables identification of fetal risk for asphyxia
- Fetal monitor is used
- Fetal heart rate response to contractions is noted
- Healthy fetus usually tolerates contractions
- If placental reserve is insufficient
  - ○ Fetal hypoxia
  - ○ Depression of the myocardium
  - ○ Decrease in FHR

4a Positive Contraction Stress Test (CST)
- (Figure 16.8)

4b Contraction Stress Test
- (Table 16.5)

SUGGESTIONS FOR CLASSROOM ACTIVITIES

Ask students to compare and discuss nursing care for the following procedures: Doppler velocimetry, nonstress test, contraction stress test, and biophysical profile tests. End the lecture with an in-class review of Tables 16.3, 16.4, and 16.5. Assign "Case Study: Client Undergoing Contraction Stress Test" activity on the Companion Website for homework.

SUGGESTIONS FOR CLINICAL ACTIVITIES

Allow students to observe a contraction stress test from the preparation phase to the end of the procedure. Have them turn in a written paper describing the experience using the following headings: Indication, Definition, Client Preparation, Description of Contraction Stress Test Procedure, Post-Procedure Care, Reportable Signs and Symptoms, and Significance of Contraction Stress Test.

LEARNING OBJECTIVE 4

Discuss the use of amniocentesis as a diagnostic tool.

CONCEPTS FOR LECTURE

1. A number of studies can be performed on amniotic fluid to determine fetal health. *See "Nursing Practice."*

POWERPOINT LECTURE SLIDES

 Amniocentesis
- Procedure used to obtain amniotic fluid
- Allows for testing of amniotic fluid
- These tests can provide information about genetic disorders
- May be used in screening for the following
  ○ Down syndrome (trisomy 21)
  ○ Trisomy 18 and neural tube defects (NTDs)
  ○ Can provide information about fetal lung maturity
- Helps to evaluate fetal health

1a Amniocentesis
- Nursing care: Assist the physician during amniocentesis
  ○ Support the woman undergoing the procedure
  ○ Obtain informed consent
  ○ Clarify the physician's instructions or explanations
  ○ Obtain baseline vital signs
  ○ Obtain baseline fetal heart rate
  ○ After procedure, review reportable side effects
  ○ Assess vital signs and fetal heart rate

1b Amniocentesis
- (Figure 16.9)

SUGGESTIONS FOR CLASSROOM ACTIVITIES

Facilitate in-class review of "Skill 2–5: Assisting During Amniocentesis." This activity can be found on the Student CD-ROM and in the Clinical Skills Manual.

SUGGESTIONS FOR CLINICAL ACTIVITIES

During clinical rotation at the prenatal testing clinic, allow students to observe an amniocentesis. Assign students to write a paper about the procedure utilizing the following headings, Indication, Definition, Client Preparation, Description of Amniocentesis Procedure, Post-Amniocentesis Care, Reportable Signs and Symptoms, and Significance of Amniocentesis. The paper should be based on the student's observations in the clinical area.

LEARNING OBJECTIVE 5

Describe the tests that can be done on amniotic fluid.

CONCEPTS FOR LECTURE

1. Concentrations of certain substances in amniotic fluid provide information about the health status of the fetus. *Refer to "Nursing Practice."*

POWERPOINT LECTURE SLIDES

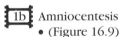 Amniotic Fluid Analysis
- The triple test and quadruple screen
  ○ Measure substances in the amniotic fluid
  ○ Information helps identify fetal anomalies

- Fetal lung maturity is determined by
  ○ The lecithin/sphingomyelin ratio
  ○ Presence of phosphatidylglycerol
  ○ Level of lamellar body counts

1a L/S Ratio and PG
- (Table 16.6)

1b Amniotic Fluid Analysis
- Triple test assesses for
  ○ Appropriate levels of alpha-fetoprotein (AFP)
  ○ Human chorionic gonadotropin (hCG)
  ○ Unconjugated estriol (UE3)
- Triple test is most widely used test to screen for Down syndrome (trisomy 21)

1c Amniotic Fluid Analysis
- Triple test is most widely used test to screen for trisomy 18, and neural tube defects (NTDs)
- Quadruple screen
  ○ Measurement of Diameric Inhibin-A
  ○ More sensitive accurate detector of trisomy 21
  ○ Will replace the triple screen in the near future

SUGGESTIONS FOR CLASSROOM ACTIVITIES

Review Table 16.6 and "Nursing Practice" in the classroom. Discuss various complications that may occur following an amniocentesis.

SUGGESTIONS FOR CLINICAL ACTIVITIES

Allow students to review their assigned clients' laboratory results from an amniocentesis test. Instruct students to utilize a diagnostic textbook and a perinatal healthcare provider (NP, CNM, MD) to assist them in the interpretation of the test results.

LEARNING OBJECTIVE 6

Identify the advantages and disadvantages of chorionic villus sampling (CVS).

CONCEPTS FOR LECTURE

1. Chorionic villus sampling (CVS) involves obtaining a small sample of chorionic villi from the developing placenta. CVS is performed in some medical centers for first-trimester diagnosis of genetic, metabolic, and deoxyribonucleic acid (DNA) studies. *Review "Nursing Practice" and Table 16.1.*

POWERPOINT LECTURE SLIDES

1 Chorionic Villus Sampling
- Can be performed transabdominally or transcervically
- Performed between 10 and 12 weeks
- Performed for first trimester diagnostic studies
- Advantages
  ○ Allows for early detection of fetal disorders
  ○ Short waiting time for results

1a Chorionic Villus Sampling
- Disadvantages
  ○ Increased risk of injury to fetus
  ○ Inability to detect neural tube defects
  ○ Potential for repeated invasive procedures
  ○ Risk of failure to obtain placental tissue
  ○ Risk of contamination of specimen

    ○ Risk of leakage of amniotic fluid
    ○ Risk of intrauterine infection
    ○ Risk of Rh alloimmunization

 Sample Nursing Approaches to Pretest Teaching
• (Table 16.2)

SUGGESTIONS FOR CLASSROOM ACTIVITIES	SUGGESTIONS FOR CLINICAL ACTIVITIES
Discuss the contents of Table 16.1 and Table 16.2 in the classroom. Invite students to participate in the discussion. Include information outlined in "Nursing Practice."	Instruct students to prepare a generic health-teaching plan for clients undergoing prenatal testing. Allow students to participate in teaching clients before prenatal testing under the guidance of a perinatal healthcare provider.

CHAPTER 17
PROCESSES AND STAGES OF LABOR AND BIRTH

RESOURCE LIBRARY

CD-ROM

Animations:
  Rupturing Membranes
  Vaginal Birth
  Placenta Delivery
Videos:
  Fetal Lie
  First Stage of Labor and Transition
  Second Stage of Labor
  Third Stage of Labor
Audio Glossary

📖**IMAGE LIBRARY**

COMPANION WEBSITE

NCLEX-RN® Review
Case Study
Thinking Critically
MediaLink Applications:
  Case Study: Client in First Stage of Labor
  Care Plan Activity: Client in Uncomplicated Labor
  Care Plan Activity: Labor Progress

Figure 17.1 Comparison of Caldwell-Moloy pelvic types.
Figure 17.2 Superior view of the fetal skull.
Figure 17.3 Lateral view of the fetal skull, identifying the landmarks that have significance during birth.
Figure 17.4 A, Typical anteroposterior diameters of the fetal skull. B, Transverse diameters of the fetal skull.
Figure 17.5 Fetal attitude.
Figure 17.6 Cephalic presentation.
Figure 17.7 Process of engagement in cephalic presentation.
Figure 17.8 Measuring the station of the fetal head while it is descending.
Figure 17.9 Categories of presentation.
Figure 17.10 Characteristics of uterine contractions.
Figure 17.11 Effacement of the cervix in the primigravida.

Figure 17.13 Mechanisms of labor.
Figure 17.14 Placental separation and expulsion.
Figure 17.15 Distribution of labor pain during the later phase of the first stage and early phase of the second stage.
Figure 17.16 Distribution of labor pain during the later phase of the second stage and actual birth.

Table 17.1 Critical Factors in Labor
Table 17.2 Implications of Pelvic Type for Labor and Birth
Table 17.3 Factors Associated with a Positive Birth Experience
Table 17.4 Comparison of True and False Labor
Table 17.5 Characteristics of Labor

LEARNING OBJECTIVE 1

Examine the five critical factors that influence labor.

CONCEPTS FOR LECTURE

1. Birth passage: The ability of the pelvis and cervix to accommodate the passage of the fetus.
2. Fetus: The ability of the fetus to complete the birth process.
3. Relationship between the passage and the fetus: The position of the fetus in relation to the pelvis.
4. Physiologic forces of labor: Characteristics of contractions and the effectiveness of expulsion methods.
5. Psychosocial considerations: Understanding and preparing for the childbirth experience. Amount of support from other. Present emotional Status. Beliefs and values.

POWERPOINT LECTURE SLIDES

 The Birth Passage
  • Ability of pelvis and cervix to accommodate passage of fetus
  • True pelvis
    ○ Forms bony canal through which fetus must pass
    ○ Divided into three sections: inlet, pelvic cavity, outlet
  • Four classical types of pelvis
    ○ Gynecoid
    ○ Android

○ Anthropoid
○ Platypelloid

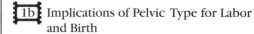 Comparison of Cladwell-Moloy Pelvic Types
• (Figure 17.1)

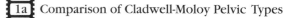 Implications of Pelvic Type for Labor and Birth
• (Table 17.2)

▣2 The Fetus
• Ability of fetus to complete birth process
• Fetal skull has three major parts
  ○ Face
  ○ Base of skull
  ○ Vault of cranium
• Molding: Cranial bones overlap under pressure of the powers of labor and demands of unyielding pelvis

▣2a Superior View of Skull
• (Figure 17.2)

▣3 Relationship Between the Passage and the Fetus
• Position of fetus in relation to pelvis
• Fetal attitude refers to relation of fetal parts to one another
• Fetal lie refers to relationship of cephalocaudal axis of fetus to cephalocaudal axis of woman
• Fetal presentation determined by fetal lie and by body part of fetus that enters pelvic passage first—this portion of fetus called presenting part
• Relationship of maternal pelvis and presenting part—engaement of presenting part occurs when largest diameter of presenting part reaches or passes through pelvic inlet
• Station refers to relationship of presenting part to imaginary line drawn between ischial spines of maternal pelvis

 Fetal Attitude
• (Figure 17.5)

▣3b Process of Engagement in Cephalic Presentation
• (Figure 17.7)

▣3c Measuring the Station of Fetal Head
• (Figure 17.8)

▣4 Physiologic Forces of Labor
• Characteristics of contractions and effectiveness of expulsion methods
• Primary and secondary forces work together to achieve birth of fetus, fetal membranes, placenta
  ○ Primary force is uterine muscular contractions
  ○ Secondary force is use of abdominal muscles to push during second stage of labor

▣4a Characteristics of Uterine Contractions
• (Figure 17.10)

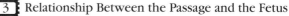

5 Psychosocial Considerations
- Understanding and preparing for childbirth experience
- Amount of support from others
- Present emotional status
- Beliefs and values

SUGGESTIONS FOR CLASSROOM ACTIVITIES

Bring a fetal model and plastic pelvis to class. Demonstrate attitude, lie, and presentation. Review the video "Fetal Lie" on the Student CD-ROM.

SUGGESTIONS FOR CLINICAL ACTIVITIES

Ask students to identify the diameter of the fetal head, fontanels, and sutures of their assigned baby in the nursery

LEARNING OBJECTIVE 2

Describe the physiology of labor.

CONCEPTS FOR LECTURE

1. Progesterone causes relaxation of smooth muscle tissue. Estrogen causes stimulation of uterine muscle contractions. Connective tissue loosens and permits the softening, thinning, and opening of the cervix.
2. Muscles of the upper uterine segment shorten and cause the cervix to thin and flatten. Fetal body is straightened as the uterus elongates with each contraction.
3. Pressure of the fetal head causes cervical dilation. Rectum and vagina are drawn upward and forward with each cotnraction. During the second stage, the anus everts.

POWERPOINT LECTURE SLIDES

1 Progesterone and Estrogen
- Progesterone causes relaxation of smooth muscle tissue
- Estrogen causes stimulation of uterine muscle contractions
- Connective tissue loosens and permits softening, thinning, opening of cervix

2 Thinning of Cervix
- Muscles of upper uterine segment shorten and cause cervix to thin and flatten
- Fetal body straightened as uterus elongates with each contraction

3 Contraction
- Pressure of fetal head causes cervical dilation
- Rectum and vagina are drawn upward and forward with each contraction
- During second stage, anus everts

SUGGESTIONS FOR CLASSROOM ACTIVITIES

Discuss and demonstrate the cardinal movements of labor with a fetal model and plastic pelvis. View the video "First Stage of Labor and Transition" from the Student CD-ROM in class.

SUGGESTIONS FOR CLINICAL ACTIVITIES

Have students develop a care map on the physiology of labor and how it impacts each body system.

LEARNING OBJECTIVE 3

Discuss the premonitory signs of labor.

CONCEPTS FOR LECTURE

1. Lightening—Braxton Hicks contractions.
2. Cervical changes—bloody show.
3. Rupture of membranes—sudden burst of energy.
4. Other signs may occur prior to the onset of labor.

POWERPOINT LECTURE SLIDES

1. Premonitory Signs of Labor
   - Lightening: Fetus descends into pelvic inlet
   - Braxton Hicks contractions
     - Irregular, intermittent contractions that occur during pregnancy
     - Cause more discomfort closer to onset of labor

2. Premonitory Signs of Labor
   - Cervical changes: Cervix begins to soften and weaken (ripening)
   - Bloody show
     - Loss of cervical mucous plug
     - Causes blood-tinged discharge

3. Premonitory Signs of Labor
   - Rupture of membranes: If rupture prior to onset of labor, good chance labor will begin within 24 hours
   - Sudden burst of energy
     - Known as nesting
     - Usually occurs 24 to 48 hours before start of labor

4. Other Premonitory Signs of labor
   - Loss of 1 to 3 pounds
   - Diarrhea, indigestion, nausea, vomiting may occur prior to onset of labor

SUGGESTIONS FOR CLASSROOM ACTIVITIES

- Discuss the human needs an expectant mother has when experiencing the premonitory signs of labor. Review the animation "Rupturing Membrances" on the Student CD-ROM.
- Have students suck on Lifesavers candies and note how the candy thins and the center hole enlarges. Compare to cervical changes prior to and during labor.

SUGGESTIONS FOR CLINICAL ACTIVITIES

Ask students to design a teaching plan regarding the signs and symptoms of labor. Have them teach an expectant mother and her partner at an antepartum clinic.

LEARNING OBJECTIVE 4

Differnitate between false and true labor.

CONCEPTS FOR LECTURE

1. True labor is characterized by: Contractions that occur at regular intervals and increase in duration and intensity; discomfort that begins in the back and radiates to the front of the abdomen; walking intensifies contractions; resting or relaxing in warm water does not decrease the intensity of contractions; contractions that produce cervical dilatation.

POWERPOINT LECTURE SLIDES

1. True Labor
   - Characterized by
     - Contractions at regular intervals—increase in duration and intensity
     - Discomfort begins in back and radiates to front of abdomen
     - Walking intensifies contractions

CONCEPTS FOR LECTURE *continued*

2. False labor is characterized by: Irregular contractions that do not increase in duration or intensity; contractions that are lessened by walking, rest, or warm water; discomfort that is felt primarily in the abdomen; contractions that produce no effect on cervix.

POWERPOINT LECTURE SLIDES *continued*

- ○ Resting or relaxing in warm water does not decrease intensity
- ○ Contractions produce cervical dilatation

 False Labor
- • Characterized by
  - ○ Irregular contractions that do not increase in duration or intensity
  - ○ Contractions are lessened by walking, rest, or warm water
  - ○ Discomfort felt primarily in abdomen
  - ○ Contractions produce no effect on cervix

 Comparsion of True and False Labor
- • (Table 17.4)

SUGGESTIONS FOR CLASSROOM ACTIVITIES

Discuss the psychological needs of an expectant mother who has experienced false labor. Have students prepare a one-page teaching pamphlet to use with prenatal clients when teaching them to differentiate between false and true labor.

SUGGESTIONS FOR CLINICAL ACTIVITIES

Have students attend a childbirth class. Ask them to document what the expectant mothers learn about true and false labor.

LEARNING OBJECTIVE 5

Describe the physiologic and psychologic changes occrring in each of the stages of labor.

CONCEPTS FOR LECTURE

1. Latent phase physiologic changes: Regular, mild contractions begin and increase in intensity and frequency; cervical effacement and dilation begins. Latent phase psychologic changes: Relief that labor has begun; high excitement with some anxiety.
2. Active phase physiologic changes: Contractions increase in intensity, frequency, and duration; cervical dilation increases from 4 to 7 cm; fetus begins to descend into the pelvis. Active phase psychologic changes: fear of loss of control; anxiety increases; possible decrease in coping skills.
3. Transition phase physiologic changes: Contractions continue to increase in intensity, duration, and frequency; cervix dilates from 8 to 10 cm; fetus descends rapidly into the birth passage; woman may experience rectal pressure; woman may experience nausea and/or vomiting. Transition phase psychologic changes: increased feelings of anxiety; irritability; eager to complete birth experience; need to have support person or nurse at bedside.

POWERPOINT LECTURE SLIDES

 Latent Phase
- • Latent phase physiologic changes
  - ○ Regular, mild contractions begin and increase in intensity and frequency
  - ○ Cervical effacement and dilation begins
- • Latent phase psychologic changes
  - ○ Relief that labor has begun
  - ○ High excitement with some anxiety

 Active Phase
- • Active phase physiologic changes
  - ○ Contractions increase in intensity, frequency, and duration
  - ○ Cervical dilation increases from 4 to 7 cm
  - ○ Fetus begins to descend into the pelvis
- • Active phase psychologic changes:
  - ○ Fear of loss of control
  - ○ Anxiety increases

 Transition Phase
- • Transition phase physiologic changes
  - ○ Contractions continue to increase in intensity, duration, and frequency
  - ○ Cervix dilates from 8 to 10 cm
  - ○ Fetus descends rapidly into the birth passage
  - ○ Woman may experience rectal pressure
  - ○ Woman may experience nausea and/or vomiting

4. Second stage physiologic changes: Begins with complete cervical dilation and ends with the birth of the infant; woman pushes due to pressure of fetal head on sacral and obturator nerves; woman uses intra-abdominal pressure; perineum begins to bulge, flatten, and move anteriorly as fetus descends. Second stage psychologic changes: May feel a sense of purpose; may feel out of control, frightened, and irritable.

5. Third stage physiologic changes: Placental separation—uterus contracts and the placenta begins to separate; placental delivery—woman bears down and delivers the placenta. Physician may put slight traction on the cord to assist the delivery of the placenta. Third stage psychologic changes: Woman may feel relief at the completion of the birth; woman is usually focused on welfare of the infant and may not recognize that placental expulsion is occurring.

6. Fourth stage physiologic changes: Woman experiences increased pulse and decreased blood pressure due to redistribution of blood from uterus and blood loss; uterus remains contracted and is located between umbilicus and symphysis pubis; woman may experience a shaking chill; urine may be retained due to decreased bladder tone and possible trauma to the bladder. Fourth stage psychologic changes: May experience euphoria and energized at birth of child; may be thirsty and hungry.

- Transition phase psychologic changes
  - Increased feelings of anxiety
  - Irritability
  - Eager to complete birth experience
  - Need to have support person or nurse at bedside

 Characteristics of Labor
- (Table 17.5)

 Second Stage Physiologic Changes
- Second stage physiologic changes
  - Begins with complete cervical dilation and ends with birth of infant
  - Woman pushes due to pressure of fetal head on sacral and obturator nerves
  - Woman uses intra-abdominal pressure
  - Perineum begins to bulge, flatten, and move anteriorly as fetus descends
- Second stage psychologic changes
  - May feel a sense of purpose
  - May feel out of control, frightened, and irritable

 Third Stage
- Third stage physiologic changes
  - Placental separation: Uterus contracts and placenta begins to separate
  - Placental delivery: Woman bears down and delivers placenta—physician may put slight traction on cord to assist delivery of placenta
- Third stage psychologic changes
  - Woman may feel relief at completion of birth
  - Woman usually focused on welfare of infant and may not recognize that placental expulsion is occurring

 Fourth Stage of Labor
- Fourth stage physiologic changes
  - Woman experiences increased pulse and decreased blood pressure due to redistribution of blood from uterus and blood loss
  - Uterus remains contracted and located between umbilicus and symphysis pubis
  - Woman may experience a shaking chill
  - Urine may be retained due to decreased bladder tone and possible trauma to the bladder
- Fourth stage psychologic changes
  - May experience euphoria and be energized at birth of child
  - May be thirsty and hungry

SUGGESTIONS FOR CLASSROOM ACTIVITIES

In class, show the Vaginal Birth Animation from the Student CD-ROM. Discuss the complementary therapies that may be of value to a mother during birth. Have students view the videos "Second Stage of Labor" and "Third Stage of Labor" as well as the animation "Placental Delivery" on the Student CD-ROM for review.

SUGGESTIONS FOR CLINICAL ACTIVITIES

Assign students to write a reflective journal after they have observed a vaginal delivery. Have them elaborate on the role of the nurse. Assign "Case Study: Client in First Stage of Labor" and "Care Plans: Client in Uncomplicated Labor Progress" activities on the Companion Website for homework.

LEARNING OBJECTIVE 6

Summarize maternal systemic responses to labor.

CONCEPTS FOR LECTURE

1. Cardiovascular changes: Increase in cardiac output; blood pressure—rises with each contraction and may rise further with pushing; respiratory system—increase in oxygen demand and consumption. Mild respiratory acidosis usually occurs by time of birth.
2. Renal system: Increase in renin, plasma renin activity, and angiotensinogen. Edema may occur at base of bladder due to pressure of fetal head.
3. Gastrointestinal system: Gastric motility decreased. Gastric emptying is prolonged. Gastric volume remains increased—immune system and other blood values: WBC count increases. Blood glucose decreases.
4. Pain: In the first stage, it arises from dilation of cervix, stretching of lower uterine segment, pressure, and hypoxia of uterine muscle cells during contractions. In the second stage, it arises from hypoxia of contracting uterine muscle cells, distention of the vagina and perineum, and pressure. In the third stage, it arises from contractions and dilation of cervix as placenta is expelled.

POWERPOINT LECTURE SLIDES

1. Cardiovascular and Respiratory Changes
   - Cardiovascular changes: Cardiac output
   - Blood pressure
     ○ Rises with each contraction
     ○ May rise further with pushing
   - Respiratory system
     ○ Increase in oxygen demand and consumption
     ○ Mild respiratory acidosis usually occurs by the time of birth

2. Renal Changes
   - Renal system
     ○ Increase in renin, plasma renin activity, angiotensinogen
     ○ Edema may occur at base of bladder due to pressure of fetal head

3. GI and Immune System
   - Gastrointestinal system
     ○ Gastric motility decreased
     ○ Gastric emptying is prolonged
     ○ Gastric volume remains increased
   - Immune system and other blood values
     ○ WBC count increases
     ○ Blood glucose decreases

4. Pain
   - First stage: Arises from dilation of cervix, stretching of lower uterine segment, pressure, and hypoxia of uterine muscle cells during contractions
   - Second stage: Arises from hypoxia of contracting uterine muscle cells, distention of vagina and perineum, and pressure
   - Third stage: Arises from contractions and dilation of cervix as placenta is expelled

4a. Placental Separation and Expulsion
   - (Figure 17.14)

SUGGESTIONS FOR CLASSROOM ACTIVITIES

Discuss priority nursing assessments and interventions during the fourth stage of labor. Include nutritional needs of the mother at this time.

SUGGESTIONS FOR CLINICAL ACTIVITIES

Assign students to care for mothers during the fourth stage of labor. Ask them to develop one physical and one psychosocial nursing diagnosis with interventions.

LEARNING OBJECTIVE 7

Explore fetal responses to labor.

CONCEPTS FOR LECTURE

1. Labor may cause no adverse effects in the healthy fetus. Fetal heart rate may decrease as the head pushes against the cervix. Blood flow decreases to the fetus at the peak of each contraction leading to a decrease in pH. Further decrease of pH occurs during pushing due to the woman holding her breath.

POWERPOINT LECTURE SLIDES

1. Fetal Responses
   - Labor may cause no adverse effects in healthy fetus
   - Fetal heart rate may decrease as head pushes against cervix
   - Blood flow decreases to fetus at peak of each contraction leading to decrease in pH
   - Further decrease of pH occurs during pushing due to woman holding her breath

SUGGESTIONS FOR CLASSROOM ACTIVITIES

- Discuss the following physiologic changes in the fetus and which adverse effects can occur in each category: heart rate changes, acid-base changes in labor, hemodynamic changes, and fetal sensation.
- Place plastic figurine and rope into a balloon. Partially fill the balloon with water and seal. Have students observe the results of "contractions" on the figurine when balloon is intact, and again when fluid is released through a pinhole. Relate this rupture of membranes and effects of increased pressure on the fetal head and cord.

SUGGESTIONS FOR CLINICAL ACTIVITIES

Assign students to care for clients in a variety of labor situations, noting and comparing the influence of latent phase versus transitional or second stage contractions on fetal heart tracings. In post-clinical conferences, ask students to discuss what sensations the fetus experiences during labor.

Chapter 18
Intrapartal Nursing Assessment

RESOURCE LIBRARY

CD-ROM

Skill 3-1: Performing an Intrapartal Vaginal Examination
Skill 3-3: Performing Leopold's Maneuvers
Skill 3-4: Auscultation of Fetal Heart Rate
Skill 3-5: External Electronic Fetal Monitoring
Skill 3-6: Electronic Fetal Monitoring
Audio Glossary
NCLEX-RN® Review

COMPANION WEBSITE

Thinking Critically
NCLEX-RN® Review
MediaLink Applications:
   Case Study: Maternal Assessment during Labor
   Care Plan Activity: Client with Decelerations

IMAGE LIBRARY

Figure 18.1 Woman in labor with external monitor applied.

Figure 18.2 To gauge cervical dilatation, the nurse places the index and middle fingers against the cervix and determines the size of the opening.

Figure 18.3 Palpating the presenting part (portion of the fetus that enters the pelvis first).

Figure 18.4 Top: The fetal head progressing through the pelvis. Bottom: The changes the nurse will detect on palpation of the occiput through the cervix while doing a vaginal examination.

Figure 18.5 Leopold's maneuvers for determining fetal position and presentation.

Figure 18.6 Location of FHR in relation to the more commonly seen fetal positions.

Figure 18.7 Electronic fetal monitoring by external technique.

Figure 18.8 Technique for internal, direct fetal monitoring.

Figure 18.9 Normal FHR pattern obtained by internal monitoring.

Figure 18.10 Variability.

Figure 18.11 Types and characteristics of early, late, and variable decelerations.

Table 18.2 Contraction and Labor Progress Characteristics

Teaching Highlights

LEARNING OBJECTIVE 1

Discuss high-risk screening and intrapartal assessment of maternal physical and psychosociocultural factors.

CONCEPTS FOR LECTURE

1. High-risk screening is an integral aspect of assessing a woman in labor. There are multiple factors that contribute to high-risk intrapartal situations. *See Table 18.1.*

2. A physical assessment is part of the admission process and assists in screening for high-risk factors.

3. Sociocultural variables such as poverty, nutrition, or the amount of prenatal care may precipitate a high-risk condition.

4. Psychosocial assessment and communication are integral elements of this assessment.

POWERPOINT LECTURE SLIDES

 High-Risk Screening
- Obtain maternal history and note presence of any high-risk factors
  - Name and age of mother
  - Last menstrual period (LMP) and estimated date of birth (EDB)
  - Attending physician or certified nurse-midwife (CNM)

- Personal Data
  - Blood type
  - Rh factor
  - Results of serological testing
  - Prepregnant and present weight
  - Allergies to medications, foods, and other substances
  - Note prescribed and over-the-counter (OTC) medications taken during pregnancy, and history of substance abuse, use of alcohol and tobacco

 Physical Assessment
- Integral part of admission procedure and essential for ongoing care
  - Assessment of body systems
  - Actual labor process and fetal status
- Laboratory Findings
  - Evaluate hemoglobin for decreased oxygen-carrying capacity
  - Evaluate complete blood count (CBC) for signs of infection, blood dyscrasia, or coagulation problems
  - Evalaute results of serologic testing
  - Assess Rh factor in Rh-negative woman
  - Assess urine for glucose, ketones, protein—evaluate for possible urinary tract infections and instruct woman in collection techniques

 Cultural Assessment
- Address and honor values and beliefs of laboring woman
- Nurses more effective when aware of
  - Cultural beliefs of specific group
  - The impact individual differences may have on laboring mother
- Challenging for nurses to achieve balance between cultural awareness and risk of stereotyping

 Psychosocial Assessment
- Laboring client has previous ideas, knowledge, and fears about childbearing—using assessment techniques, nurse can meet laboring client's needs for information and support
- Support system
  - Father or support person—what are their caretaking activities, such as soothing conversation and touching?
  - Does relationship involve interactions? Is support person in close proximity?

POWERPOINT LECTURE SLIDES *continued*

- Need to consider possibility that woman has experienced domestic violence—use ACOG(1998) guidelines when interviewing and interview alone
  - Has anyone close to you ever threatened to harm you?
  - Have you ever been hit, kicked, slapped, or choked. If yes, by whom ? What is the total number of times?
  - Has anyone, including your partner, ever forced you to have sex?
  - Are you afraid of your partner or anyone else?
- Anxiety
  - Observe for rapid breathing, nervous tremors, frowning, grimacing, clenching of teeth, thrashing, crying, and increased pulse and respiration
  - Provide support, information, and encourage client
  - Teach relaxation and breathing techniques
  - May need to provide a paper bag if client's lips are tingling (hyperventilating)

SUGGESTIONS FOR CLASSROOM ACTIVITIES

Discuss various risk factors and the implications of these risk factors for the mother and fetus. Incorporate the "Thinking Critically" scenario in lecture. Have students review Skill 3-1: Performing an Intrapartal Vaginal Examination on the Student CD-ROM and in the Clinical Skills Manual.

SUGGESTIONS FOR CLINICAL ACTIVITIES

Have students assist with the admission of a laboring client. Have students rotate through a healthcare provider's office.

LEARNING OBJECTIVE 2

Summarize methods used to evaluate labor.

CONCEPTS FOR LECTURE

1. Asessment of contractions for frequency, strength, and intensity of contractions. *See "Skills 3-4 & 3-5: Electronic Fetal Monitoring."*
2. Cervical dilatation and effacement are evaluated directly by vaginal examination. *See "Skill 3-1: Performing an Intrapartal Vaginal Examination."*
3. Vaginal examination assists in the evaluation of descent and status of membranes. *See "Skill 3-3: Auscultation Fetal Heart Rate."*

POWERPOINT LECTURE SLIDES

1 Assessment of Contractions
- Uterine contractions assessed by palpation or continous electronic monitoring
  - Assess at least three successive contractions
  - Good time to assess laboring mother's perception of pain (note and chart woman's response to contraction and her affects)

Assessment of Contractions by Palpation
- Palpation
  - Assess contractions for frequency, duration, and intensity by placing one hand on uterine fundus
  - Keep hand relatively still as excessive movement may stimulate contractions or cause discomfort
- Determine frequency—noting time from beginning of one contraction to beginning of next contraction
- Determine contraction duration
  - Note time when tensing of fundus is first felt and again as relaxation occurs
  - Intensity of contraction can be evaluated by estimating indentability of fundus

 Contraction and Labor Progress Characteristics
- (Table 18.2)

 Electronic Fetal Monitoring
- Provides continous data and is routine for high-risk clients
  - Also used for women experiencing an induction of labor
  - May be done externally or with an internal monitor
- External Monitoring
  - Device placed against maternal abdomen (tocodynamometer) positioned against fundus, held in place with belt
  - Device has flexible disk, responds to pressure
  - When fundus contracts, pressure applied; "toco" and contraction displayed as pattern on monitor
  - External monitoring does not accurately record intensity of uterine contraction
  - May be difficult to obtain fetal heart rate (hydramnios with very active fetus)
  - Belt will require frequent readjustment

 External Fetal Monitoring
- (Figure 18.1)

 Internal Direct Fetal Monitoring
- (Figure 18.8)

 Accurate Measurement of Uterine Contraction Intensity
- Used when imperative to have accurate intrauterine pressure readings; important to palpate intensity and resting tone of uterine fundus
  - Procedure

      ○ Membranes need to be ruptured

      ○ Physician or CNM inserts intrauterine pressure catheter into uterine cavity and connects by cable to electronic fetal monitor

      ○ Small micropressure device located in catheter measures pressure within uterus in resting state and with each contraction

2 Cervical Assessment

- Dilation and effacement evaluated by doing vaginal examination—also provides information about
  ○ Membrane status
  ○ Characteristic of amniotic fluid
  ○ Fetal positon
  ○ Station

2a Cervical Dilatation

- (Figure 18.2)

2b Cervical Dilatation

- To gauge dilatation, nurse places index finger and middle fingers against side of cervix to determine size of opening
- Progressive from size of fingertip to 10 cm
- Cervical effacement: Progressive thinning of cervix measured in percentage
  ○ Palpating presenting part
  ○ Portion of fetus that enters pelvis first

3 Palpating the Presenting Part

- (Figure 18.3)

SUGGESTIONS FOR CLASSROOM ACTIVITIES

Show students intrauterine pressure catheter. Have students review the institution's protocol for intrauterine pressure. Discuss internal and external fetal monitoring assessment during labor. What makes assessments different? What information is learned from each type of monitoring? Assign "Case Study: Material Assessment During Labor" activity on the Companion Website for homework.

SUGGESTIONS FOR CLINICAL ACTIVITIES

Show students intrauterine pressure catheter. Have students review the institution's protocol for internal fetal monitoring. Ask students to compare the protocol with their textbook.

LEARNING OBJECTIVE 3

Describe auscultation of fetal heart rate.

CONCEPTS FOR LECTURE

1. Vaginal examination assists in the evaluation of descent and status of membranes. *See "Skill 3-3: Auscultation of Fetal Heart Rate."*

POWER POINT LECTURE SLIDES

1 Auscultation of Fetal Heart Rate
- Location of fetal heart rate
  - Fetal heart rate heard most clearly at fetal back
  - Useful to perform Leopold's maneuvers first to locate fetal heart rate, will help determine if multiple fetuses

1a Auscultation of Fetal Heart Rate
- Assesment
  - May be intermittent
  - Found to be as effective as electronic method for fetal surveillance
- Use handheld Doppler ultrasound of fetoscope
  - When fetal heart rate is located, count for 30 seconds and multiply by two
  - Check client's pulse against fetal sounds
  - If rates are same, readjust Doppler or fetoscope
- Electronic monitoring of fetal heart rate—includes
  - Previous history of stillborn
  - Presence of complication
  - Induction of labor, preterm labor
  - Decreased fetal movement
  - Nonreassuring fetal status
  - Meconium staining of amniotic fluid
  - Trial of labor following a C-section

1b Location of Fetal Heart Rate
- (Figure 18.6)

1c Frequency of Auscultation: Assessment and Documentation

SUGGESTIONS FOR CLASSROOM ACTIVITIES

Discuss routine use of EFM, recent studies about its efficacy, and its role in nursing resource allocation. Talk about evidence-based practice. Have students review Skills 3-4: Auscultation of Fetal Heart Rate and 3-5: Electronic Fetal Monitoring on the Student CD-ROM and in the Clinical Skills Manual.

SUGGESTIONS FOR CLINICAL ACTIVITIES

Have students practice auscultation FHT by Doppler, fetoscope (where available), and EFM in the lab.

LEARNING OBJECTIVE 4

Delineate the procedure for performing Leopold's maneuvers and the information that can be obtained.

CONCEPTS FOR LECTURE

1. A complete fetal evaluation includes determining position and presentation, as well as evaluating fetal status. Leopold's maneuvers are a systematic way to evaluate the contents of the uterus by a series of four discreet palpation maneuvers. Palpation should occur between contractions to limit discomfort and facilitate identification of fetal parts.

POWERPOINT LECTURE SLIDES

 Leopold's Maneuver's
- Preparation—have laboring mother
  - Empty her bladder
  - Lie on her back with feet on bed
  - Bend Knees
- Purpose
  - Assist in determining fetal position, presentation, and lie
  - Frequent practice increases skill
- Method
  - Use universal precautions
  - Facing woman, practitioner palpates gently and deeply using palms of hands
  - One hand held steady as other explores abdomen, and then hands are switched

 Leopold's Maneuvers
- (Figure 18.5)

SUGGESTIONS FOR CLASSROOM ACTIVITIES

Include a variety of monitor strips. Discuss rate, periodic patterns, and variability. Have students review Skill 3-3: Performing Leopold's Maneuvers on the Student CD-ROM and in the Clinical Skills Manual.

SUGGESTIONS FOR CLINICAL ACTIVITIES

Assign students to an antepartum clinic where they can observe and perform Leopold's maneuvers on pregnant clients. If possible, have students use multiparous women or women with epidurals, as it is sometimes easier to palpate small parts due to frequently weaker or more relaxed abdominal muscles.

LEARNING OBJECTIVE 5

Differentiate between baseline and periodic changes in the fetal rate monitoring and describe the appearance and signficance of each.

CONCEPTS FOR LECTURE

1. Baseline rate refers to the average fetal heart rate observed during a 10-minute period of monitoring. Normal rate is 120 to 160 bpm. Baseline changes include bradycardia, tachycardia, and variability.
2. Periodic changes include accelerations, decelerations, and sinusoidal patterns.

POWERPOINT LECTURE SLIDES

 Baseline
- Normal fetal heart rate ranges from 120 to 160 bpm
  - Rate above 160 bpm is tachycardia
  - Rate below 120 bpm is termed bradycardia

Fetal Tachycardia
- Sustained rate of 161 bpm or above
- If rate is 180 bpm or above, is marked tachycardia
- Causes of fetal tachycardia
  - Early fetal hypoxia
  - Maternal fever
  - Maternal dehydration
  - Amnionitis
  - Maternal hyperthyroidism
  - Beta-sympomimetic drugs
  - Fetal anemia

- Ominous sign if tachycardia accompanied by
  - Late decelerations
  - Severe variable decelerations
  - Decreased variability

 Fetal Bradycardia
- Beat less than 110 bpm during a 10-minute period or longer
- Causes include
  - Profound hypoxia in fetus
  - Maternal hypotension
  - Prolonged umbilical cord compression
  - Fetal arrhythmias
  - Uterine hyperstimulation
  - Abruptio placentae
  - Uterine rupture
  - Vaginal stimulation in second stage of labor

 Periodic Changes
- Accelerations are transient increases in fetal heart rate normally caused by fetal movement—usually accompany uterine contractions due to fetal movement occurring in response to contractions
- Decelerations are periodic decreases in fetal heart rate from baseline—can be early, late, and variable according to time of occurrence in contraction cycle
- Early decelerations occur before onset of uterine contraction—uniform in shape, benign, and usually do not occur intervention; usually related to fetal head compression leading to vaginal stimulation

---

SUGGESTIONS FOR CLASSROOM ACTIVITIES

Review a nonreassuring tracing and explore the causes, interventions, and outcomes.

SUGGESTIONS FOR CLINICAL ACTIVITIES

Demonstrate use of the Doppler and the fetosocpe. Then, assign students to care for laboring clients with electronic fetal monitoring.

LEARNING OBJECTIVE 6

Outline steps to be performed in the systematic evaluation of fetal heart rate tracing.

CONCEPTS FOR LECTURE

1. Evaluate the uterine contraction pattern.
2. Determine the baseline fetal heart rate; determine fetal heart rate variability; and determine if a sinusoidal pattern is present.
3. Determine if there are periodic changes.

POWERPOINT LECTURE SLIDES

 Evaluate Contraction Pattern
- Nurse evaluates electronic fetal tracing by looking at pattern of uterine contraction
- Determine uterine resting tone, then assess contraction—what is frequency, duration, and intensity (if client has internal monitoring)

 Evaluate Baseline, Variability, and Sinusoidal Pattern
- Is baseline within normal limits?
- Is there tachycardia or bradycardia?

- Do you see short-term variability present or absent?
- Do you see average long-term variability? Is it absent? Minimal? Moderate? Marked?

 Periodic Changes
- Are there periodic changes?
- Do you see accelerations?
- Do they meet criteria for reactive NST?
- Are there decelerations and are they uniform in shape?
  - If uniform in shape, determine if early or late
  - Is deceleration nonuniform in shape?
  - Determine if they are variable decelerations

Suggestions for Classroom Activities

Before class, have students access information about electronic fetal monitoring from the March of Dimes Website. Use this search as a basis for discussion of nursing implications of a systematic approach to fetal monitoring.

Suggestions for Clinical Activities

During the labor and delivery rotation, ask students to do a manual palpation of contraction and a Doppler auscultation of the fetal heart rate with continuous fetal monitoring. Ask them to compare the assessment data obtained.

LEARNING OBJECTIVE 7

Identify nonreassuring fetal heart rate patterns and appropriate nursing responses.

Concepts for Lecture

1. Nonreassuring fetal heart rate patterns include severe variable decelerations, late decelerations of any magnitude, absence of variability, and prolonged deceleration.
2. Appropriate nursing responses include: notify the physician; administer maternal oxygen; turn mother to the left side; discontinue oxytocin if being administered; monitor FHR continuously; provide explanation to the mother and partner.

PowerPoint Lecture Slides

 Reassuring and Nonreassuring EFM Tracings
- Reassuring
  - Normal baseline
  - Accelerations with fetal movement
  - Present short-term variability
  - 3–5 cycles of long-term variability per minute
  - Early decels may be present
- Nonreassuring
  - Severe variable decels (FHR<70 for longer than 30–45 seconds accompanied by rising BL, slow recovery or decreasing variability)
  - Late decels of any magnitude
  - Absent variability
  - Prolonged deceleration (>60–90 seconds)
  - Severe bradycardia (FHR baseline <70)

 Types of Decelerations
- (Figure 18.11)

 Nursing Interventions for Nonreassuring FHR
- Optimize maternal positioning
- Monitor maternal v/s for hypotension and treat
- Administer IV fluids as needed
- Give supplemental oxygen if indicated
- Consider discontinuing oxytocin
- Initiate continuous monitoring

- Place internal monitors as appropriate
- Perform vaginal exam to assess for prolapsed cord or labor progress
- Assist physician with fetal blood sampling
- Prepare for expeditious birth
- Provide client and family with explanation
- Administer tocolytic as ordered

SUGGESTIONS FOR CLASSROOM ACTIVITIES

Assign students to review Table 18.4 "Guidelines for Management of Variable, Late, and Prolonged Decelerations." Have the class break into small groups to discuss priority setting with each type of deceleration. Allow time to compare results and have the group arrive at a consensus of priority interventions.

SUGGESTIONS FOR CLINICAL ACTIVITIES

Provide students the opportunity to role play therapeutic communications with clients who have a non-reassuring fetal heart rate patterns.

LEARNING OBJECTIVE 8

Discuss nursing care of the family undergoing electronic fetal monitoring.

CONCEPTS FOR LECTURE

1. Explain the use of electronic fetal monitoring (EFM).
2. Look at the mother prior to looking at the monitor.
3. Record pertinent data on the monitor strip.

POWERPOINT LECTURE SLIDES

 1 EFM Strip Initial Data Record
- Client name
- Date
- Physician or CNM's name
- Medical record number
- Gravity/parity
- EDB
- Membrane status
- Maternal vital signs

 2 Laboring Mother as Focus
- Responses from laboring mother and family can vary and be complex
- Some may feel monitoring interferes with natural process
- Focus on mother and not the device
- Be observant for cues that arise from intuition and observation
- Keep laboring mother as your central focus

 3 Ongoing Events Recorded on the EFM Strip
- Vaginal exams
- Amniotomy/ROM and results
- Vital signs
- Maternal position and position changes
- Applications of internal monitoring
- Medication administration
- Maternal behaviors (coughing, vomiting, etc.)
- Fetal scalp stimulation or blood sampling
- Oxygen administration
- Pushing
- Administration of regional block

LEARNING OBJECTIVE 9

Delineate the indications for fetal blood sampling and identify related pH values.

CONCEPTS FOR LECTURE

1. Fetal blood is sampled when a nonreassuring or confusing FHR is noted, or when acid-base information is needed.
2. Related pH values: greater than 7.25 are normal; 7.2–7.25 are borderline and require further assessment; less than 7.2 necessitate birth without delay.

POWERPOINT LECTURE SLIDES

1 Indications for Fetal Blood Sampling
  - Nonreassuring but not ominous tracing
  - Cervix > 2 cm dilated
  - Ruptured membranes
  - Presenting part at or below –2 station
  - Nonemergent situation
  - No abnormal vaginal bleedings

1a Fetal Blood Sampling Teaching
  - Teaching Highlights

2 Fetal Scalp Blood Values in Labor
  - Normal > 7.25
  - Borderline 7.20 to 7.25
  - Nonreassuring < 7.20

LEARNING OBJECTIVE 10

Describe how fetal oxygen saturation (FS_pO_2) monitoring uses pulse oximetry to monitor fetal oxygenation within the fetal blood to determine if hypoxia is occurring.

CONCEPTS FOR LECTURE

1. A fetal oxygen saturation (FS_pO_2) monitor is placed adjacent to the fetal cheek or temple and must be in constant contact with the fetal skin.

POWERPOINT LECTURE SLIDES

1 Procedure
  - Fetal oxygen saturation (FS_pO_2) monitor placed adjacent to fetal cheek or temple—must be in constant contact with fetal skin
  - Fetal oxygen saturation monitoring used when
    ○ Fetus in vertex presentation
    ○ Membranes are ruptured and cervix is at least 2 cm dilated
    ○ Fetal station is –1 or lower
    ○ Pregnancy at 36 weeks' gestation

Monitoring
- Allows labor to continue despite nonreassuring FHR tracing
- Levels of 40-70% considered reassuring
- Levels less than 30% indicate hypoxia—require immediate birth
- Levels between 30% and 40% indicate mild acidosis—require continuous monitoring and assessment

SUGGESTIONS FOR CLASSROOM ACTIVITIES

Before students come to class, assign them to check on the FDA website for information about fetal arterial oxygen saturation monitoring. Ask them to discuss potential problems that may occur with fetal arterial oxygen saturation monitoring.

SUGGESTIONS FOR CLINICAL ACTIVITIES

Ask students what equipment should be available if a laboring mother is experiencing fetal arterial oxygen saturation monitoring. Ask students to list pertinent nursing assessment and observation.

CHAPTER 19
THE FAMILY IN CHILDBIRTH: NEEDS AND CARE

RESOURCE LIBRARY

CD-ROM

Skill 4-2: Evaluating Lochia
Skill 5-1: Performing Nasal Pharyngeal Suctioning
Skill 5-2: Assigning Newborn Apgar Scores
Animation: Placental Delivery
Audio Glossary
NCLEX-RN® Review
Videos
   Fourth Stage of Labor
   Newborn Assessment

COMPANION WEBSITE

Complementary Care: Doula Information
Thinking Critically
NCLEX-RN® Review
MediaLink Applications:
   Case Study: Labor and Birth
   Care Plan Activity: Presence of Extended Family

IMAGE LIBRARY

Figure 19.1 Woman and her partner walking in the hospital during labor.
Figure 19.2 The laboring woman is encouraged to choose a comfortable position. .
Figure 19.3 The woman's partner provides support and encouragement during labor.
Figure 19.4 The nurse provides encouragement and support during pushing efforts.
Figure 19.5 Birthing positions.
Figure 19.6 A birthing sequence.
Figure 19.7 Hollister cord clamp.
Figure 19.8 To clear secretions from the newborn's nose or oropharynx, a DeLee mucus trap (shown here) or other suction device is used.

Figure 19.9 Umbilical alarm in place on a newborn infant.
Figure 19.10 Suggested method of palpating the fundus of the uterus during the fourth stage.
Figure 19.11 An adolescent mother receives breastfeeding assistance in the immediate postpartum period.

Table 19.1 Nursing Assessments in the First Stage
Table 19.3 Nursing Support of Patterned-Paced Breathing
Table 19.7 Initial Newborn Evaluation

LEARNING OBJECTIVE 1

Idenitfy the database to be created from information obtained when a woman is admitted to the birth area.

CONCEPTS FOR LECTURE

1. Information obtained during admission is used to develop a clinical pathway for the four stages of labor
   - Prenatal information.
   - Current assessments.
   - Expected teaching.
   - Nursing care expected for each stage.
   - Expected activity level.
   - Proposed comfort measures.
   - Elimination and nutritional needs.
   - Level of family involvement.

POWERPOINT LECTURE SLIDES

 Clinical Pathway for Labor
   - Information obtained during admission used to develop clinical pathway for four stages of labor
     ◦ Prenatal information
     ◦ Current assessments
     ◦ Expected teaching
     ◦ Nursing care expected for each stage
     ◦ Expected activity level
     ◦ Proposed comfort measures
     ◦ Elimination and nutritional needs
     ◦ Level of family involvement

LEARNING OBJECTIVE 2

Review the nursing care provided at admission.

CONCEPTS FOR LECTURE

1. The nursing care at admission focuses on providing an orientation to the unit and obtaining an overall physical assessment of the mother that focuses on the well-being of the mother and fetus
   - Assess the maternal vital signs and FHR.
   - Perform a vaginal exam to determine stage of cervical dilatation and state of membranes
   - Determine frequency and intensity of contractions
   - Review systems such as respiratory and neurological
   - Assess any recent symptoms experienced by the woman
   - Assess the woman's understanding of the labor process and identification of the woman's support system

POWERPOINT LECTURE SLIDES

[1] Admission
   - Nursing care at admission focuses on providing orientation to the unit and obtaining overall physical assessment of mother that focuses on well-being of mother and fetus
     ○ Assess maternal vital signs and FHR
     ○ Perform vaginal exam to determine stage of cervical dilatation and state of membranes
     ○ Determine frequency and intensity of contractions
     ○ Review systems such as respiratory and neurological
     ○ Assess any recent symptoms experienced by woman
     ○ Assess woman's understanding of labor process and identification of woman's support system

[1a] Nursing Assessments in the First Stage
   - (Table 19.1)

LEARNING OBJECTIVE 3

Discuss nursing interventions to meet the psychologic, social, physiologic, and spiritual needs of the woman during each stage of labor.

CONCEPTS FOR LECTURE

1. First stage of labor:
   - Establish rapport with the woman and support person
   - Discuss expectations of labor and delivery
   - Provide for privacy
   - Discuss individual expression of pain and discomfort
2. Second stage of labor:
   - Provide as much privacy as possible
   - Encourage woman and support person to decide who should be present at delivery
   - Provide praise and encouragement of progress

POWERPOINT LECTURE SLIDES

[1] Nursing Care in the First Stage of labor
   - Establish rapport with woman and support person
   - Discuss expectations of labor and delivery
   - Provide for privacy
   - Discuss individual expression of pain and discomfort

[1a] Woman and Her Partner
   - (Figure 19.1)

3. Third and fourth stages of labor: *Refer to Table 19.2*
   • Encourage woman and her support person to hold and look at infant as much as possible
   • Teach woman the care to be performed after the baby is delivered
   • Provide the woman with food and fluids as allowed

[2] Nursing Care in the Second Stage of labor
   • Provide as much privacy as possible
   • Encourage woman and support person to decide who should be present at delivery
   • Provide praise and encouragement of progress

[3] Nursing Care in the Third and Fourth Stages of Labor
   • Encourage woman and support person to hold and look at infant as much as possible
   • Teach woman care to be performed after baby is delivered
   • Provide woman with food and fluids as allowed

SUGGESTIONS FOR CLASSROOM ACTIVITIES

Discuss how various cultural beliefs may impact nursing assessments during the first stage of labor. Have students discuss how they would answer: "Thinking Critically: Gender Specific Care Preferences." Assign "Care Plan: Presence of Extended Family" and "Case Study: Labor and Birth" activities on the Companion Website as homework.

SUGGESTIONS FOR CLINICAL ACTIVITIES

Have students develop a care plan for the family of a laboring client. Ask students to include emotional support, comfort measures, supporting breathing techniques, and advocacy. View videos "First Stage of Labor and Transition," "Second Stage of Labor," "Third Stage of Labor," and "Fourth Stage of Labor" on the Student CD-ROM in class. Have students view animation "Placental Delivery" on the Student CD-ROM on their own.

LEARNING OBJECTIVE 4

Compare and contrast methods of promoting comfort during the first and second stages of labor.

CONCEPTS FOR LECTURES

1. Comfort measures common to the first and second stages of labor include:
   • Client anxiety reduction
   • Client education
   • Relaxation
   • Breathing patterns
   • Instruction for support person
2. Comfort measures specific to the first stage of labor:
   • Pharmacologic agents
   • Epidural
3. Comfort measures specific to the second stage of labor:
   • Effective pushing pattern
   • Rest between pushes

POWERPOINT LECTURE SLIDES

[1] Comfort Measures in Labor: First and Second Stages
   • Assist client to reduce anxiety
   • Provide information and enhance coping skills—teach about what to expect during the labor process
   • Promote relaxation techniques
   • Instruct appropriate controlled breathing pattern
   • Give instructions to woman's support person

[1a] Nursing Support of Patterned-Paced Breathing
   • (Table 19.3)

[1b] Comfortable Positions in Labor
   • (Figure 19.2)

[2] Comfort Measures During the First Stage of Labor
   • Administer pharmacologic agents as ordered by physician or certified nurse-midwife
   • Assist with placement of epidural for pain control

[2a] Partner Provides Support
   • (Figure 19.3)

[3] Comfort During the Second Stage
   • Help woman find effective pushing pattern
   • Support woman's attempts to rest between pushes

SUGGESTIONS FOR CLASSROOM ACTIVITIES

Using "MediaLink Application: Laboring Positions" on the Companion Website, discuss comfort management during labor.

SUGGESTIONS FOR CLINICAL ACTIVITIES

Demonstrate breathing techniques. Ask students to do a return demonstration of breathing techniques. Ask them what they see as important points to stress to laboring clients and their support persons.

LEARNING OBJECTIVE 5

Summarize the immediate needs of the newborn following birth.

CONCEPTS FOR LECTURE

1. Immediate care of the newborn includes:
   - Respiration
   - Warmth
   - Infection control
   - Identification

POWERPOINT LECTURE SLIDES

1 Immediate Care of the Newborn
   - Maintain respiration
   - Promote warmth
   - Prevent infection
   - Accurate identification

1a Umbilical Alarm
   - (Figure 19.9)

1b Initial Newborn Evaluation
   - (Table 19.7)

1c Clearing Newborn Secretions
   - (Figure 19.8)

SUGGESTIONS FOR CLASSROOM ACTIVITIES

- Have a class discussion about the newborn security measures practiced at clinical sites in the local community.
- Have students view the video "Newborn Assessment" and refer to "Skill 5-2: Assigning Newborn Apgar Scores" on the Student CD-ROM for review. The skill can also be found in the Clinical Skills Manual.

SUGGESTIONS FOR CLINICAL ACTIVITIES

From the Clinical Skills Manual and Student CD-ROM, incorporate "Skill 5-1: Performing Nasal Pharyngeal Suctioning" in a clinical conference. Have students practice this skill on the baby model.

LEARNING OBJECTIVE 6

Discuss the unique needs of the adolescent during birth.

CONCEPTS FOR LECTURE

1. The adolescent is unique in that she has developmental needs as well as physical needs that must be addressed.

POWERPOINT LECTURE SLIDES

1 Adolescent Mother
   - Adolescent is unique in that she has developmental needs as well as physical needs that must be addressed
   - Very young adolescent has fewer coping mechansims and less experience to draw on than older laboring mothers
     ○ Crucial to have support person
     ○ Adolescents have high risk for pregnancy and labor complications

1a Adolescent Mother
   - (Figue 19.11)

LEARNING OBJECTIVE 7

Delineate management of a precipitous birth.

CONCEPTS FOR LECTURE

1. A precipitous birth is one that occurs rapidly without a physician or certified nurse-midwife in attendance.

POWERPOINT LECTURE SLIDES

 Precipitous Birth
- Precipitous birth is one that occurs rapidly without physician or certified nurse-midwife in attendance
- Mother may fear what is going to happen and feel that everything is out of control
- Mother needs to assume comfortable position
- Nurse scrubs his or her hands if time permits
- When infant's head crowns, mother should pant
- Gentle pressure is applied against fetal head to prevent it from popping out rapidly
- Perineum is supported and head is born between contractions

CHAPTER 20
PHARMACOLOGIC PAIN RELIEF

RESOURCE LIBRARY

CD-ROM

NCLEX-RN® Review
Video: Epidural Placement
Audio Glossary

COMPANION WEBSITE

NCLEX-RN® Review
MediaLink Applications:
    Case Study: Pain Relief Therapies during Birth
    Care Plan Activity: Client with an Epidural
Thinking Critically
Complementary Care: Acupressure Information

📖 IMAGE LIBRARY

Figure 20.1 Schematic diagram showing pain pathways and sites of interruption.

Figure 20.2 The epidural space is between the dura mater and the ligamentum flavum, extending from the base of the skull to the end of the sacral canal.

Figure 20.3 Technique for lumbar epidural block.

Figure 20.5 A, Pudendal block by the transvaginal approach. B, Area of perineum affected by pudendal block.

Figure 20.6 Technique of local infiltration for episiotomy and repair.

Figure 20.7 Proper position for fingers in applying cricoid pressure until a cuffed endotracheal tube is placed by the anesthesiologist or nurse anesthetist.

Table 20.1 What Women Need to Know About Pain Relief Medications

---

LEARNING OBJECTIVE 1

Describe the use of systemic drugs to promote pain relief during labor.

CONCEPTS FOR LECTURE

1. The goal is to provide maximum pain relief with minimum risk to the mother and fetus.
2. After complete assessment, an analgesia agent is generally administered when cervical change has occurred.
3. Drugs may cause fetal respiratory depression at birth if given too late in labor. Additionally, maternal and fetal vital signs must be stable before systemic drugs may be administered.

POWERPOINT LECTURE SLIDES

 Goal of Pharmacologic Pain Relief
- Goal is to provide maximum pain relief with minimum risk to mother and fetus
- Goal is impacted by following factors
  - All systemic drugs used in labor for pain relief cross placental barrier by simple diffusion
  - Drug action in body depends on rate at which substance is metabolized by liver
  - Fetus has inadequate ability to metabolize analgesic agent

 What Women Need to Know About Pain Relief Medications
- (Table 20.1)

2 Timing of Medication
- After complete assessment, analgesic agent generally administered when cervical change has occurred—pain medication given too early may prolong labor and depress fetus

3 Nursing Management
- Drugs may cause fetal respiratory depression at birth if given too late in labor
- Maternal and fetal vital signs must be stable before systemic drugs may be administered
- Assess mother and fetus and evaluate contraction pattern before administering prescribed medications

---

SUGGESTIONS FOR CLASSROOM ACTIVITIES

Have students complete "Case Study: Pain Management in Labor" on the Companion Website. Discuss the answers with students at the beginning of the lecture.

SUGGESTIONS FOR CLINICAL ACTIVITIES

Have students review clinical protocols on their assigned units related to pain management. Ask them to find a resource on Medlineplus relating to pain management in labor. Ask them to compare and contrast the unit's protocol with the resource from Medlineplus.

LEARNING OBJECTIVE 2

Compare the major types of regional analgesia and anesthesia, including area affected, advantages, disadvantages, techniques, and nursing implications.

CONCEPTS FOR LECTURE

1. Epidural: Injection of anesthetic agent into the epidural space. Produces little or no feeling to the area from the uterus downward. Pushing during second stage of labor may be impaired due to lack of sensation. Hypotension is the most common side effect. May preload with crystalloid solution bolus. Woman may need urinary catheterization due to the loss of bladder sensation. Assess sensation motor control and orthostatic blood pressure.

2. Continuous epidural analgesia: Provides good analgesia. Produces less nausea and provides a greater ability to cough. May produce breakthrough pain, sedation, and respiratory depression. Itching and hypotension are side effects.

3. Spinal block: A local anesthetic agent is injected directly into the spinal canal. The level of anesthesia is dependent upon level of administration. May be administered higher for the cesarean birth or lower for vaginal birth. The onset of anesthesia is immediate. Side effects include maternal hypotension, which can lead to fetal hypoxia. Requires frequent blood pressure monitoring for health changes. Indwelling urinary catheter is usually needed to decrease bladder sensation and tone. Woman's legs must be protected from injury for 8 to 12 hours after birth of baby due to decreased movement and sensation.

POWERPOINT LECTURE SLIDES

1 Epidural Injection
- Injection of anesthetic agent into epidural space
- Produces little or no feeling to area from uterus downward
- Pushing during second stage of labor may be impaired due to lack of sensation
- Hypotension is most common side effect
- May preload with crystalloid solution bolus
- Woman may need urinary catheterization due to loss of bladder sensation
- Assess sensation motor control and orthostatic blood pressure

1a Technique for Lumbar Epidural Block
- (Figure 20.3)

1b Epidural Space
- (Figure 20.2)

2 Continuous Epidural Analgesia
- Provides good analgesia
- Produces less nausea and provides greater ability to cough
- May produce breakthrough pain, sedation, respiratory depression
- Itching and hypotension are side effects

4. Pudendal block: Local anesthesia is injected directly into the pudendal nerve, which produces anesthesia to the lower vagina, vulva, and perineum. Only produces pain relief at the end of labor. Has no effect on the fetus or the progress of labor. May cause hematoma, perforation of the rectum, or trauma to the sciatic nerve.

5. Local infiltration anesthesia: Local anesthesia is injected into the perineum prior to an episiotomy. Provides pain relief only for the episiotomy incision. There is no effect on maternal or fetal vital signs. Requires large amounts of local anesthetic agents.

3 Spinal Block
- Local anesthetic agent injected directly into spinal canal
- Level of anesthesia dependent upon level of administration
- May be administered higher for cesarean birth or lower for vaginal birth
- Onset of anesthesia is immediate
- Side effects include
  - Maternal hypotension, which can lead to fetal hypoxia, requiring frequent blood pressure monitoring for health changes
  - Indwelling urinary catheter usually needed due to decreased bladder sensation and tone
  - Woman's legs must be protected from injury for 8 to 12 hours after birth of baby due to decreased movements and sensation

3a Levels of Spinal Anesthesia

4 Pudendal Block
- Local anesthesia injected directly into pudendal nerve, which produces anesthesia to lower vagina, vulva, perineum
- Only produces pain relief at end of labor
- Has no effect on fetus or progress of labor
- May cause hematoma, perforation of rectum, trauma to sciatic nerve

4a Pudenal Block
- (Figure 20.5)

5 Local Infiltration
- Local anesthesia injected into perineum prior to episiotomy
- Provides pain relief only for episiotomy incision
- There is no effect on maternal or fetal vital signs
- Requires large amounts of local anesthetic agents

5a Local Infiltration
- (Figure 20.6)

SUGGESTIONS FOR CLASSROOM ACTIVITIES

Use the video "Epidural Placement" available on the Student CD-ROM to begin the lecture on regional anesthesia. Assign "Care Plan: A Woman Receiving Epidural Anesthesia" activity on the Companion Website for homework.

SUGGESTIONS FOR CLINICAL ACTIVITIES

Examine equipment used during an epidural catheter placement. Demonstrate how the laboring client is positioned.

LEARNING OBJECTIVE 3

Discuss the possible complications of regional anesthesia.

CONCEPTS FOR LECTURE

1. Regional anesthesia administered per spinal or epidural route has similar possible complications: maternal hypotension, bladder distension, inability to push during second stage of labor, severe headache with spinal anesthesia, elevated temperature with epidural anesthesia, possible neurologic damage.

POWERPOINT LECTURE SLIDES

1. Complications
   • Regional anesthesia administered per spinal or epidural route has similar possible complications
     ○ Maternal hypotension from hypovolemia or effects of anesthesia—treat with bolus of crystalloid IV fluid and notify anesthetist
     ○ Bladder distension
     ○ Inability to push during second stage of labor
     ○ Severe headache with spinal anesthesia
     ○ Elevated temperature with epidural anesthesia
     ○ Possible neurologic damage

SUGGESTIONS FOR CLASSROOM ACTIVITIES

Before class, assign students to review and complete, "Critical Thinking in Action" activity on the Student CD-ROM. Discuss answers with the students and have them come up with a care plan for this client to use for a discussion of the complications of regional anesthesia.

SUGGESTIONS FOR CLINICAL ACTIVITIES

Ask students to develop a teaching plan for a laboring mother and her family regarding complications of regional anesthesia.

LEARNING OBJECTIVE 4

Describe the nursing care related to general anesthesia.

CONCEPTS FOR LECTURE

1. The nurse should assess when the mother ate or drank last, administer prescribed premedication such as an antacid, place a wedge under the mother's right hip to displace the uterus from the vena cava, provide oxygen prior to the start of the surgery, ensure the IV access is established, and assist the anesthesiologist by applying cricoid pressure during the placement of the endotracheal tube.

POWERPOINT LECTURE SLIDES

1. Nursing Care Related to General Anesthesia
   • Nurse should
     ○ Assess when mother ate or drank last
     ○ Administer prescribed premedication such as antacid
     ○ Place wedge under mother's right hip to displace uterus and prevent vena cava compression
     ○ Provide oxygen prior to start of surgery
     ○ Ensure IV access is established
     ○ Assist anesthesiologist by applying cricoid pressure during placement of endotracheal tube

1a. Proper Position for Cuffed Endotracheal Tube
   • (Figure 20.7)

SUGGESTIONS FOR CLASSROOM ACTIVITIES

Discuss the method of action and side effects of anesthetic agents used in general anesthesia. Emphasize nursing observations and assessments of the laboring mother.

SUGGESTIONS FOR CLINICAL ACTIVITIES

Have students complete drug cards on each of the medications that may be used for "premedication" with general anesthesia. Have students compare the information they obtained on their drug cards to the protocols used on the clinical unit.

LEARNING OBJECTIVE 5

Delineate the major complications of general anesthesia.

CONCEPTS FOR LECTURE

1. Major complications of general anesthesia are fetal depression, uterine relaxation, vomiting, and aspiration.

POWERPOINT LECTURE SLIDES

[1] Major Complications
- Fetal depression
  - If mother receives general anesthesia, infant may have respiratory depression
  - Method not advocated when infant is considered high risk
- Uterine relaxation: Most general anesthetic agents cause some uterine relaxation
- Vomiting
- Aspiration: Agents may also cause vomiting and aspiration

SUGGESTIONS FOR CLASSROOM ACTIVITIES

Discuss how the nurse enhances a safe-care environment for the mother who is receiving general anesthesia.

SUGGESTIONS FOR CLINICAL ACTIVITIES

Assign students to care for a mother who has just received general anesthesia. Have students develop a problem list for a client who has received general anesthesia.

CHAPTER 21
CHILDBIRTH AT RISK

RESOURCE LIBRARY

CD-ROM

NCLEX-RN® Review
Audio Glossary
Skill 3-9: Care of the Woman with a Cord Prolapse

COMPANION WEBSITE

MediaLink Applications:
  Case Study: Client with Hemorrhage
  Care Plan Activity: Prevention of Cord Prolapse
Thinking Critically

IMAGE LIBRARY

Figure 21.1 Comparison of labor patterns.
Figure 21.2 Effects of labor on the fetal head.
Figure 21.3 Types of cephalic presentations.
Figure 21.4 Mechanism of birth in face (mentoanterior) position.
Figure 21.5 Face presentation.
Figure 21.6 Face presentation.
Figure 21.7 Breech presentation.
Figure 21.8 Transverse lie.
Figure 21.9 Twins may be in any of these presentations while in utero.
Figure 21.10 Intrapartum management of nonreassuring fetal status.

Figure 21.11 Abruptio placentae.
Figure 21.12 Classification of placenta previa.
Figure 21.13 Management of placenta previa.
Figure 21.14 Prolapse of the umbilical cord.
Figure 21.15 Knee-chest position is used to relieve cord compression during cord prolapse emergency.

Table 21.1 Causes and Sources of Hemorrhage
Table 21.2 Differential Signs and Symptoms of Placenta Previa and Abruptio Placentae
Table 21.3 Placental and Umbilical Cord Variations
Table 21.5 Tests to Determine Cause of Fetal Loss

LEARNING OBJECTIVE 1

Compare and contrast hypertonic and hypotonic labor patterns, including risk, clinical therapy, and nursing care management.

CONCEPTS FOR LECTURE

1. Hypertonic labor patterns: Characterized by increased frequency and decreased effectiveness of contraction in effacing and dilating the cervix. Usually leads to a prolonged latent phase. May cause the mother to become fatigued and have difficulty coping with the stress of labor. Pattern may cause prolonged pressure on the fetal head. Clinical therapy may involve sedation, pain medication, and bed rest. Pitocin may be given only if CPD and fetal malpresentation are ruled out. Nursing management includes decreasing environmental stimuli, decreasing anxiety, and promoting comfort.

POWERPOINT LECTURE SLIDES

1 Characteristics of Hypertonic Labor
- Increased contraction frequency
- Decreased contraction intensity
- Increased uterine resting tone
- Prolonged latent phase

1a Implications of Hypertonic Labor
- Increased discomfort due to uterine muscle cell anoxia
- Stress on coping abilities
- Prolonged labor resulting in:
  ○ Maternal exhaustion
  ○ Dehydration
  ○ Increased incidence of infection

CONCEPTS FOR LECTURE *continued*

2. Hypotonic labor patterns: Characterized by fewer than 2 to 3 contractions in a 10-minute period during the active phase of labor. The mother may experience fatigue and coping difficulties. The mother is at risk for intrauterine infection and postpartal hemorrhage. Fetus is at risk for sepsis. Clinical therapy includes assessment of adequacy of pelvic measurement and fetal maturity—the use of Pitocin or nipple stimulation once CPD and fetal malpresentation are ruled out. Nursing management includes close monitoring for signs and symptoms of infection and dehydration, and keeping vaginal exams to a minimum.

POWERPOINT LECTURE SLIDES *continued*

- Reduced uteroplacental exchange resulting in nonreassuring fetal status
- Prolonged pressure on fetal head resulting in:
  - Excessive molding
  - Caput succedaneum
  - Cephalhematoma

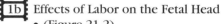 Effects of Labor on the Fetal Head
- (Figure 21.2)

 Clinical Therapy for Hypertonic Labor
- Bed rest and relaxation measures
- Pharmacologic sedation
- Oxytocin
- Amniotomy

1d Nursing Diagnoses for Hypertonic Labor
- Fatigue related to inability to relax and rest secondary to hypertonic labor pattern
- Acute pain related to woman's inability to relax secondary to hypertonic uterine contractions
- Ineffective individual coping related to ineffectiveness of breathing techniques to relieve discomfort
- Anxiety related to slow labor progress

1e Nursing Plan for Hypertonic Labor
- Provide support and encouragement
- Facilitate rest
- Administer pharmacologic agents as ordered
- Monitor maternal fatigue
- Monitor contractions and fetal status
- Institute supportive measures
  - Ambulation
  - Position changes with pillow support
  - Quiet, soothing environment
  - Touch and massage techniques
  - Personal hygiene
  - Hydrotherapy (bath or shower)
  - Relaxation exercises
  - Visualization
  - Music
- Provide information and encourage questions
  - Cause, implications, and treatment of dysfunctional labor

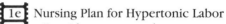 Outcomes for the Client with Hypertonic Labor
- Increased comfort
- Decreased anxiety
- Adequate coping
- More effective labor pattern

Causes of Hypotonic Labor
- Fetal macrosomia
- Multiple gestation
- Hydramnios
- Grand multiparity

 Implications of Hypotonic Labor
- Stress on coping abilities
- Prolonged labor resulting in:
  - Maternal exhaustion
  - Dehydration
  - Increased incidence of infection
- Postpartum hemorrhage due to uterine atony
- Nonreassuring fetal status due to prolonged labor pattern
- Fetal sepsis from pathogens ascending from birth canal

 Clinical Therapy for Hypotonic Labor
- Oxytocin infusion
- Nipple stimulation
- Amniotomy
- IV fluids
- Surgical birth, if needed

Active Management of Labor
- Purported benefits
  - Decreased incidence of protracted labor
  - Decreased cesarean birth rate
- Risks
  - Increased risk of infection
  - Excessive intervention
  - Increased instrument-assisted birth

 Nursing Diagnoses for Hypotonic Labor
- Acute pain related to uterine contractions secondary to dysfunctional labor
- Ineffective individual coping related to unanticipated discomfort and slow progress in labor

 Nursing Plan for Hypotonic Labor
- Frequent monitoring of vital signs, FHR, and contractions
- Assess amniotic fluid for meconium
- Monitor maternal Input & Output
- Assess bladder for distention and empty frequently
  - Encourage voiding at least q 2 hours
  - Catheterize as needed with regional block
- Minimize vaginal exams to decrease risk of infection

2f Nursing Plan for Hypotonic Labor
- Assess for signs of infection
  - Maternal fever
  - Chills
  - Foul-smelling amniotic fluid
  - Fetal tachycardia
- Provide emotional support
- Assist to cope with frustration of long labor

 2g Nursing Plan for Hypotonic Labor
- Institute supportive measures to decrease anxiety and discomfort
  - Ambulation
  - Position changes with pillow support
  - Quiet, soothing environment
  - Touch and massage techniques
  - Personal hygiene
  - Hydrotherapy (bath or shower)
  - Relaxation exercises
  - Visualization
  - Music
- Provide information and encourage questions
  - Dysfunctional labor process
  - Implications for mom and baby
  - Treatments, their disadvantages and alternatives

 2h Outcomes for the Client with Hypotonic Labor
- Woman maintains comfort during labor
- Woman understands the type of labor pattern and the treatment plan

---

SUGGESTIONS FOR CLASSROOM ACTIVITIES

- Have students research Active Management of Labor. How does AML differ between Ireland (where it originated) and the U.S. version? Is it a valuable tool? If so, what can nurses do to improve its success here?
- Discuss the role of "therapeutic rest" for prolonged prodromal labor.

SUGGESTIONS FOR CLINICAL ACTIVITIES

- Assign students to care for clients with labor dystocia. Encourage them to actively assist with comfort measures. What helped the most?
- Discuss maternal fatigue and how it related to their clients' contraction patterns.

LEARNING OBJECTIVE 2

Describe the possible impact of postterm pregnancy on the childbearing family.

CONCEPTS FOR LECTURE

1. Postterm pregnancy may result in an increased possibility of labor induction, forceps or vacuum-assisted or cesarean birth, decreased perfusion to the placenta, decreased amount of amniotic fluid and possible cord compression, meconium aspiration, macrosomia or a loss of fat and muscle mass resulting in a small-for-gestational age (SGA) newborn.

POWERPOINT LECTURE SLIDES

 1 Postterm Pregnancy
- Postterm pregnancy may result in an increased possibility of
  - Probable labor induction
  - Forceps or vacuum-assisted or cesarean birth
  - Decreased perfusion to the placenta

- ○ Decreased amount of amniotic fluid and possible cord compression
- ○ Meconium aspiration
- ○ Macrosomia or a loss of fat and muscle mass resulting in small-for-gestational age (SGA) newborn

SUGGESTIONS FOR CLASSROOM ACTIVITIES

Discuss how a postterm pregnancy impacts a newborn. Discuss the emotional implications of a postterm pregnancy for a mother.

SUGGESTIONS FOR CLINICAL ACTIVITIES

Have students review clinical protocols for postterm pregnancy, then develop a plan of care for a mother who has a postterm pregnancy.

LEARNING OBJECTIVE 3

Relate the various types of fetal malposition and malpresentation to the possible associated problems.

CONCEPTS FOR LECTURE

1. Occiput posterior position: Baby is facing up instead of down as it enters the vagina—may prolong labor. Baby is usually able to be born vaginally but may need forceps assistance to turn the baby.
2. Brow presentation: Forehead of the fetus becomes the presenting part—may cause labor to be prolonged. Cesarean birth necessary if brow presentation persists.
3. Face presentation: Face of the fetus is the presenting part—vaginal birth may be possible, but cesarean birth remains a significant possibility.
4. Breech presentation: Fetal buttock or foot/feet are the presenting part—90% of breech presentations result in cesarean birth.
5. Transverse lie: Fetal shoulder is the presenting part—fetus must be born cesarean.

POWERPOINT LECTURE SLIDES

1 Causes of Persistent OP Fetal Positioning
- Poor quality contractions
- Abnormal flexion of head
- Incomplete rotation
- Inadequate maternal pushing efforts—usually due to regional anesthesia
- Large fetus

1a Occiput Presentation
- (Figure 21.3A)

1b Implications of Persistent OP Positioning
- Prolonged labor
- Extensive perineal laceration at birth (3rd or 4th degree)
- Vaginal trauma
- Extension of midline episiotomy
- Increased fetal morbidity and mortality related to
  - ○ Prolonged labor
  - ○ Instrumental or cesarean birth

1c Clinical Therapy for Persistent OP Positioning
- Close monitoring of maternal and fetal status
- Careful assessment of labor progress
- Instrument-assisted birth as needed
- Instrument-assisted rotation to OA
- Cesarean if lack of labor progress or fetal descent indicates CPD

2 Implications of Brow Presentation
- Prolonged labor due to ineffective contractions
- Arrested fetal descent
- Cesarean birth for persistent brow presentation
- Increased risk episiotomy and extension if vaginal birth attempted

- Increased fetal mortality from cerebral and nuchal compression
- Trauma to trachea or larynx
- Facial bruising and edema
- Exaggerated fetal head molding

2a Military and Brow Presentation
- (Figure 21.3 B & C)

2b Clinical Therapy for Brow Presentation
- Monitor for conversion to face or occiput presentation
- Monitor for CPD with persistent brow presentation
- Cesarean indicated in most cases
- Mediolateral episiotomy common if vaginal birth attempted

3 Implications of Face Presentation
- Increased risk of CPD and prolonged labor
- Cesarean birth if chin is posterior
- Increased risk of infection (with prolonged labor)
- Pronounced molding of fetal head
- Facial cephalhematoma
- Edema of baby's face and throat if chin is anterior

3a Criteria for Vaginal Birth with Face Presentation
- No evidence of CPD
- Mentum anterior
- Effective labor pattern
- Reassuring FHR

3b Face Presentation
- (Figure 21.3D)

3c Mechanism of Birth in Face Position
- (Figure 21.4)

3d Face Presentation
- (Figure 21.5)

3e Clinical Therapy for Face Presentation
- Thorough assessment of fetal position/presentation
- Careful monitoring for labor progress
- Cesarean birth if mentum posterior

4 Types of Breech Presentation
- Frank
  ○ Flexion at thighs, extension at knees
  ○ Feet up by head
  ○ Buttocks present

- Complete
  - Flexion at thighs and knees
  - Feet and buttocks present
- Footling
  - Single or double
  - Extension at thighs and knees
  - Foot or feet present
- Kneeling
  - Extension at thighs, flexion at knees
  - Knees present

4a Breech Position
- (Figure 21.7)

4b Conditions Associated with Breech Presentation
- Preterm birth
- Placenta previa
- Hydramnios
- Multiple gestation
- Uterine anomalies—e.g. bicornuate uterus
- Fetal anomalies
  - Anencephaly
  - Hydrocephaly

4c Implications of Breech Presentation
- Likely cesarean birth
- Increased perinatal morbidity and mortality rates
- Increased risk of prolapsed cord
- Increased risk of cervical spinal cord injuries due to hyperextension of fetal head during vaginal birth
- Increased risk birth trauma (especially head) during any type of birth

4d Clinical Therapy for Breech Presentation
- External cephalic version (ECV) prior to labor between 36–38 weeks EGA
- Probable cesarean if version unsuccessful
- Consider alternative methods of version

5 Conditions Associated with Transverse Lie
- Grand multiparity with lax musculature
- Preterm fetus
- Abnormal uterus
- Excessive amniotic fluid
- Placenta previa
- Contracted pelvis

5a Transverse Lie
- (Figure 21.8)

5b Implications of Transverse Lie
- High risk of prolapsed cord
- Cesarean birth

5c Clinical Therapy for Transverse Lie
- Expectant management if <37 weeks EGA
- ECV at 37 weeks EGA
- Labor induction following successful version
- May attempt ECV in early labor
- Cesarean birth if version unsuccessful

SUGGESTIONS FOR CLASSROOM ACTIVITIES

Review your institution's protocols for managing fetal malpresentation. Compare these standards with AWHONN's Standards and Guidelines for Professional Nursing Practice in the Care of Women and Newborns.

SUGGESTIONS FOR CLINICAL ACTIVITIES

Discuss in post-conference the care of a laboring client who has a fetal malpresentation. Assign the students a client who has a fetal malpresentation. Have each student develop a priority problem list for this client.

LEARNING OBJECTIVE 4

Discuss the identification, management, and care of fetal macrosomia.

CONCEPTS FOR LECTURE

1. Identification of fetal macrosomia is conducted through palpation, ultrasound, and x-ray.
2. Management of fetal macrosomia involves the following: Cesarean birth; continuous fetal monitoring; notification of physician, labor dysfunction, or nonreassuring fetal status.
3. Care of the newborn with macrosomia requires assessment.
4. Care of the mother after the birth of a newborn with macrosomia requires fundal massage and close monitoring of vital signs.

POWERPOINT LECTURE SLIDES

1. Fetal Macrosomia
   - Newborn weighing more than 4500 g
   - Identification of fetal macrosomia is conducted through
     - Palpation of fetus in utero
     - Ultrasound of fetus
     - X-ray pelvimetry

2. Management of Fetal Macrosomia
   - Cesarean birth performed if fetus is greater than 4500 g
   - Continuous fetal monitoring if labor is allowed to progress
   - Requires notification of physician for early decelerations, labor dysfunction, or nonreassuring fetal status

3. Care of Newborn
   - Care of newborn with macrosomia requires assessment of newborn for
     - Cephalhematoma
     - Erb's palsy
     - Fractured clavicles

4. Care of Mother
   - Care of mother after birth of newborn with macrosomia requires
     - Fundal massage to prevent maternal hemorrhage from overstretched uterus
     - Close monitoring of vital signs

SUGGESTIONS FOR CLASSROOM ACTIVITIES

Discuss when macrosomia will occur with a pregnancy. Describe the possible complications of labor and birth with macrosomia.

SUGGESTIONS FOR CLINICAL ACTIVITIES

Ask students to review health promotion activities for a mother who has had an infant with macrosomia.

LEARNING OBJECTIVE 5

Delineate the nursing care of a woman with more than one fetus.

CONCEPTS FOR LECTURE

1. Care of the woman with more than one fetus includes frequent assessment, education of the mother, encouragement of the mother, and preparation of equipment.

POWERPOINT LECTURE SLIDES

 Multiple Gestation
- Care of woman with more than one fetus includes:
  - Frequent assessment of fetal heart tones of each fetus
  - Education of mother about signs and symptoms of preterm labor
  - Encouragement of mother to rest frequently prior to birth
  - Preparation of equipment needed to care for each individual newborn

1a Presentations in Utero
- (Figure 21.9)

SUGGESTIONS FOR CLASSROOM ACTIVITIES

With models, demonstrate various positions of twin gestations in utero. Have students develop meal plans based on multiple gestation requirements.

SUGGESTIONS FOR CLINICAL ACTIVITIES

Assign students to care for a laboring client who has multiple gestation. Have students address the psychological implications of a multiple gestation pregnancy.

LEARNING OBJECTIVE 6

Summarize the nursing care indicated for nonreassuring fetal status.

CONCEPTS FOR LECTURE

1. Nursing actions for nonreassuring fetal status include turning the woman, beginning or increasing the IV flow rate, vaginal exam, knee-chest position, discontinuing Pitocin or administering a tocolytic agent, administering oxygen, notifying physician, and obtaining additional information.

POWERPOINT LECTURE SLIDES

 Nonreassuring Fetal Status Management
- (Figure 21.10)

1a Intrauterine Resuscitation
- Corrective measures used to optimize oxygen exchange within maternal-fetal circulation
- To position:
  - Turn woman to left lateral position to treat hypotension
  - Begin or increase IV flow rate
  - Perform vaginal exam to check for cord prolapse
  - Have woman assume knee-chest position if cord prolapse is suspected
  - Discontinue Pitocin or administer a tocolytic agent to decrease contraction frequency and intensity
  - Administer oxygen
  - Notify physician
  - Obtain additional information about fetus by fetal scalp blood sampling or fetal acoustical stimulation

LEARNING OBJECTIVE 7

Compare and contrast abruptio placentae and placenta previa, including implications for the mother and fetus and nursing care.

CONCEPTS FOR LECTURE

1. Abruptio placentae is a condition in which the placenta prematurely separates from the uterine wall. It may result in severe hemorrhage; cause death to the mother, the fetus, or both; lead to clotting disorders in the mother. Nursing care involves frequent assessment of uterine tone and measurement of abdominal girth.
2. Placenta previa is a condition in which the placenta implants in the lower segment of the uterus. It may be partially or completely covering the cervical os. Bleeding occurs as the cervix begins to dilate. Bleeding may be mild to severe, depending upon how much of the placenta covers the cervical os. The fetus may develop hypoxia, anemia, or both from the bleeding episode. Nursing care involves assessing blood loss, pain, and uterine contractions. The nurse should never perform a vaginal examination if placenta previa is suspected.

POWERPOINT LECTURE SLIDES

1 Causes and Sources of Hemorrhage
   • (Table 21.1)

1a Types of Abruptio Placentae
   • Marginal
     ○ Placenta separates at its edges
     ○ Blood passes between fetal membranes and uterine wall
     ○ Blood escapes vaginally
   • Central
     ○ Placenta separates centrally
     ○ Blood trapped between placenta and uterine wall
     ○ Concealed bleeding
   • Complete
     ○ Total separation
     ○ Massive vaginal bleeding

1b Abruptio Placentae
   • (Figure 21.11)

1c Maternal Implications of Abruptio Placentae
   • Intrapartum hemorrhage
   • DIC
   • Hypofibrinogenemia
   • Ruptured uterus from overdistention
   • Fatal hemorrhagic shock
   • Postpartum complications
     ○ Vascular spasm
     ○ Intravascular clotting
     ○ Hemorrhage
     ○ Renal failure
     ○ Fatal shock

1d Differential Signs and Symptoms of Placenta Previa and Abruptio Placentae
   • (Table 21.2)

1e Fetal-Neonatal Implications of Abruptio Placentae
   • Sequelae of prematurity
   • Hypoxia
   • Anemia
   • Brain damage
   • Fetal demise

Nursing Plan for Abruptio Placentae
- Maintain two large-bore IV sites—fluids and blood products as ordered
- Monitor fetus and uterine activity electronically
  - Assess resting tone every 15 minutes
  - Assess fetal status every 15 minutes
- Monitor for signs of DIC
- Monitor Intake & Output and urine specific gravity
- Measure abdominal girth hourly, as ordered
- Assess maternal cardiovascular status frequently
  - Vital signs every 5–15 minutes
  - Skin color and pulse quality hourly
  - Measure CVP hourly, as ordered
- Review and evaluate diagnostic tests
- Prepare for cesarean, as needed
- Neonatal resuscitation, as needed
- Provide information and emotional support

 Categories of Placenta Previa
- Total: The internal os completely covered
- Partial: The internal os partially covered
- Marginal: The edge of the os covered
- Low-lying placenta: Implanted in lower segment in proximity to the os

 Classification of Placenta Previa
- (Figure 21.12)

 Implications of Placenta Previa
- Maternal psychologic stress
- Transverse lie common
- Changes in FHR
- Meconium staining
- Fetal compromise (hypoxia)
- Cesarean birth
- Neonatal anemia

Nursing Plan for Placenta Previa
- No vaginal exams!
- Objectively and subjectively assess blood loss, pain, uterine contractility
- Continuous external monitoring of FHR and uterine activity—no internal monitoring
- Monitor maternal vital signs and Intake & Output—every 5–15 minutes with active hemorrhage
- Obtain/evaluate labs
- Maintain large-bore IV access—available whole blood setup
- Verify family's ability to cope with anxiety of unknown outcome
- Provide information and emotional support
- Promote neonatal physiologic adaptation
  - Resuscitation as needed
  - Evaluate hemoglobin, cell count, erythrocyte count
  - Administer oxygen and blood as needed

SUGGESTIONS FOR CLASSROOM ACTIVITIES

Incorporate "Critical Thinking in Action" into the lecture. Have students develop a priority problem list for the client in the case study. Assign "Case Study: Client with Placental Problems" activity on the Companion Website for homework.

SUGGESTIONS FOR CLINICAL ACTIVITIES

Assign students to care for a client with abruptio placenta/placenta previa. Ask the clinical group to compare and contrast care.

LEARNING OBJECTIVE 8

Identify variations that may occur with or in the umbilical cord and insertion into the placenta.

CONCEPTS FOR LECTURE

1. Prolapse umbilical cord: Umbilical cord precedes fetal presenting part.
2. Succenturiate placenta: One or more accessory lobes of fetal villi will develop on the placenta.
3. Circumvallate placenta: A double fold of chorion and amnion form a ring around the umbilical cord on the fetal side of the placenta.
4. Battledore placenta: The umbilical cord is inserted at or near the placental margin.
5. Velamentous insertion of the umbilical cord: The vessels of the umbilical cord divide some distance from the placenta in the placental membranes.

POWERPOINT LECTURE SLIDES

1 Prolapsed Cord
- Umbilical cord precedes fetal presenting part placing pressure on cord and diminishing blood flow to fetus
- Bed rest recommended if engagement has not occurred and membranes have ruptured
- Assess for nonreassuring fetal status

1a Prolapse of the Umbilical Cord
- (Figure 21.14)

1b Relief of Cord Compression
- (Figure 21.15)

2 Succenturiate Placenta
- One or more accessory lobes of fetal villi will develop on placenta, possibly causing postpartal hemorrhage

3 Circumvallate Placenta
- Double fold of chorion and amnion form ring around umbilical cord on fetal side of placenta—increases risk of late abortion, antepartal hemorrhage, preterm labor
- May also cause IUGR, prematurity, fetal death

4 Battledore Placenta
- Umbilical cord is inserted at or near placental margin
- Leads to increased chance of preterm labor and bleeding
- May also cause prematurity and nonreassuring fetal status

5 Velamentous Insertion
- Vessels of umbilical cord divide some distance from placenta in placental membranes
- If one vessel is torn, hemorrhage occurs
- This leads to nonreassuring fetal status and/or hemorrhage in fetus

5a Placental and Umbilical Cord Variations
- (Table 21.3)

LEARNING OBJECTIVE 9

Contrast the identification, management, and nursing care of women with amniotic fluid embolus, hydramnios, and oligohydramnios.

CONCEPTS FOR LECTURE

1. Amniotic fluid embolism: Caused by a small tear in the chorion or amnion high in the uterus, which may allow amniotic fluid to enter the maternal circulatory system. Usually occurs during or after birth. The woman experiences sudden symptoms of respiratory distress leading to severe hemorrhage. This disorder is life threatening,

2. Hydramnios: In this condition, the woman has greater than 2000 mL of amniotic fluid. Associated with fetal swallowing and neurologic disorders. Also, associated with maternal gestational diabetes, Rh disorders, and multiple gestation pregnancies. Woman may experience shortness of breath and lower extremities edema. Amniocentesis may be performed to remove some of the excessive fluid. The nurse monitors the mother for complications of the amniocentesis and supports the family if fetal disorder is the cause of excess fluid.

3. Oligohydramnios: In this condition, the amount of amniotic fluid is reduced and concentrated. Often found with some renal fetal disorders, fetal postmaturity, and placental insufficiency. May cause fetal respiratory and skeletal abnormalities. May cause prolonged labor. Amnioinfusion may be used during labor to cushion the fetus and umbilical cord. The nurse must continuously monitor the labor pattern for any signs of fetal distress.

POWERPOINT LECTURE SLIDES

1 Implications of Amniotic Fluid Embolism
- Sudden onset respiratory distress
- Acute hemorrhage
- Circulatory collapse
- Cor pulmonale
- Hemorrhagic shock
- Coma and maternal death
- Fetal death if birth not immediate

1a Signs and Symptoms of Amniotic Fluid Embolism
- Dyspnea
- Cyanosis
- Frothy sputum
- Chest pain
- Tachycardia
- Hypotension
- Mental confusion
- Massive hemorrhage

1b Nursing Plan for Amniotic Fluid Embolism
- Summon emergency team
- Positive pressure oxygen delivery
- Large-bore IV
- CPR as needed
- Prepare for cesarean if birth has not occurred
- Prepare for CVP line insertion
- Administer blood

2 Implications of Hydramnios
- Maternal
  - Shortness of breath
  - Edema
  - Greatly increased cesarean rate
  - Uterine dysfunction
  - Abruptio placentae
  - Postpartum hemorrhage
- Fetal-Neonatal
  - Malformations
  - Preterm birth
  - Increased mortality rate

- Prolapsed cord
- Malpresentation

 Conditions Associated with Hydramnios
- Diabetes
- Rh sensitization
- Hydrops fetalis
- Malformations of fetal swallowing
- Neural tube defects with exposed meninges
- Anencephaly
- Cardiac anomalies
- Esophageal or duodenal atresia
- Monozygotic, monochorionic twins
- Large placenta

 Assessment Findings Suspicious for Hydramnios
- Fundal height disproportionately large for dates
- Difficulty palpating fetus and auscultating FHR
- Tense, tight abdomen on inspection
- Large spaces between fetus and uterine wall on ultrasound

 Nursing Plan with Hydramnios
- Provide information and emotional support
- Maintain absolute sterility during amniocentesis
- Collaborate with social services if fetal defect identified

 Conditions Associated with Oligohydramnios
- Postmaturity
- IUGR secondary to placental insufficiency
- Major renal malformations
  - Renal agenesis
  - Dysplastic kidneys
  - Lower urinary tract obstructive lesions

 Implications of Oligohydramnios
- Dysfunctional labor with slow progress
- Fetal deformation defects
  - Adhesions
  - Skin and skeletal abnormalities
  - Pulmonary hypoplasia
  - Dysmorphic facies
  - Short umbilical cord
- Umbilical cord compression
- Head compression

 Assessment Findings Suspicious for Oligohydramnios
- Fundal height small for dates
- Fetus easily palpated and outlined
- Fetus not ballottable
- Variable decelerations
- Reduced AFI on ultrasound

 Nursing Plan for Oligohydramnios
- Provide information and encourage questions
- Evaluate EFM tracing for variable decels or nonreassuring fetal status

- Reposition mother to relieve cord compression
- Notify clinician of signs of cord compression
- Evaluate newborn
  - Anomalies
  - Pulmonary hypoplasia
  - Postmaturity

SUGGESTIONS FOR CLASSROOM ACTIVITIES

- Show students sonograms with hydramnios and polydramnios.
- Discuss maternal mortality in the context of current societal values relating to responsibility and blame in obstetrical care. What are realistic outcomes? Who should "pay" if a woman or fetus dies from amniotic embolism? What is the nurse's role in educating the public about realistic expectations for childbirth outcomes?

SUGGESTIONS FOR CLINICAL ACTIVITIES

Ask clinical staff to show students the equipment needed for an amnioinfusion. Have students prepare a written care plan for the client with altered amniotic fluid levels.

LEARNING OBJECTIVE 10

Delineate the effects of pelvic contractures on labor and birth.

CONCEPTS FOR LECTURE

1. Labor is usually prolonged in the presence of CPD. Vaginal birth may be possible depending upon the type of CPD. The woman may increase pelvic diameter during labor by squatting, sitting, rolling from side to side, or maintaining a knee-chest position. CPD may make cesarean the only available method of birth.

POWERPOINT LECTURE SLIDES

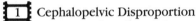 Cephalopelvic Disproportion
- Occurs when fetus is larger than pelvic diameter—clinical and x-ray pelvimetry used to determine smallest diameter through which fetal head must pass
  - Shortest AP diameter <10 cm
  - Diagonal conjugate <11.5 cm
  - Greatest transverse diameter <12 cm
- Labor usually prolonged in presence of CPD
- Vaginal birth may be possible depending upon type of CPD
- Woman may increase pelvic diameter during labor by squatting, sitting, rolling from side to side, maintaining knee-chest position, use of a labor ball—AVOID lithotomy!
- CPD may make cesarean only available method of birth

SUGGESTIONS FOR CLASSROOM ACTIVITIES

- Review fetal assessments (Chapter 18) that may be used to assess the presentation and position of the fetus when CPD is suspected.
- Have students list terminology used to describe slow labor and a small pelvis. Explore the subtext of these words and their meaning to a laboring woman. What is the nurse's role in maintaining the couple's confidence in the normalcy of childbirth?

SUGGESTIONS FOR CLINICAL ACTIVITIES

- Invite an experienced labor nurse to speak about the various positions that may be used to increase pelvic diameters in CPD.
- Have students work with laboring clients to optimize pelvic diameter. Compare labors in semi-Fowler's or lithotomy to upright positions.

LEARNING OBJECTIVE 11

Identify common complications of the third and fourth stages of labor.

CONCEPTS FOR LECTURE

1. The most common complications of the third and fourth stages of labor are retained placenta—if not expelled, the placenta must be manually removed from the uterus; lacerations—suspect when there is bright-red bleeding in the presence of a contracted uterus, usually repaired immediately after the birth of the child; placenta accreta—in this condition, the chorionic villi attach directly to the myometrium of the uterus and may result in maternal hemorrhage and failure of the placenta to separate from the uterus (may result in the need for hysterectomy at time of birth).

POWERPOINT LECTURE SLIDES

1. Retained Placenta
   - Retention of placenta beyond 30 minutes after birth
   - Occurs in 2% to 3% of all vaginal births
   - If not expelled, placenta must be manually removed from uterus—if woman does not have an epidural anesthesia in place, conscious sedation may be required

2. Lacerations
   - Lacerations suspected when bright-red bleeding in presence of contracted uterus
   - Usually repaired immediately after birth of child
   - Vaginal and perineal lacerations are categorized in terms of degrees

3. Placenta Accreta
   - Chorionic villi attach directly to myometrium of uterus
   - May result in maternal hemorrhage and failure of placenta to separate from uterus
   - May result in need for hysterectomy at time of birth
   - Incidence of placenta accreta is 10% to 25% in presence of placenta previa

SUGGESTIONS FOR CLINICAL ACTIVITIES

Have students develop a problem list (nursing diagnoses) in order of priority for common complications in the third and fourth stages of labor. Ask the clinical group to develop an expected outcome for each problem/nursing diagnosis.

LEARNING OBJECTIVE 12

Discuss perinatal loss, including etiology, diagnosis, and the nurse's role in facilitating the family's grief work.

CONCEPTS FOR LECTURE

1. Perinatal loss results from three factors: fetal factors, maternal factors, or placental or other factors.
2. Diagnosis may be made by the mother or by the physician.
3. Nursing care involves supporting the family through the grief work.

POWERPOINT LECTURE SLIDES

1. Perinatal Loss
   - Results from three factors
     - Fetal factors: Fetus has or develops disorder incompatible with life
     - Maternal factors: Mother has disorder such as diabetes or preeclampsia that creates hostile environment for fetus
     - Placental or other factors: Certain conditions such as abruptio placentae or cord accident cut off blood supply to fetus, leading to death

2 Diagnoses of Fetal Loss
- Diagnosis may be made when mother notices lack of movement in fetus or at regularly scheduled physician's visit when fetal heart tone cannot be found

2a Tests to Determine Cause of Fetal Loss
- (Table 21.5)

3 Nursing Care
- Nursing care involves supporting family through grief work
  - Assist family through labor and birth
  - Provide for woman's physical needs after birth
  - Encourage family members to express and share their thoughts and feelings about loss
  - Give family an opportunity to view, hold, name infant
  - Prepare items for family to keep to remember infant
  - Provide opportunities for religious or spiritual counseling and cultural practices
  - Visit or phone family after discharge to assist in closure
  - Make referral to appropriate perinatal loss counseling services if indicated

SUGGESTIONS FOR CLASSROOM ACTIVITIES

Bring remembrances kits to class. Discuss the significance to each aspect of the kit. Discuss resources available through the March of Dimes.

SUGGESTIONS FOR CLINICAL ACTIVITIES

Have students assist with postmortem care and assessment of a stillborn infant in the nursery. Point out ways in which the infant's dignity is maintained. Acknowledge the staff and student's feelings. Remain with the student and model behavior that supports the nurse's grieving. Discuss the importance of working through grief as nurses. Allow the students to vent their feelings at an appropriate time.

LEARNING OBJECTIVE 13

Describe the psychologic factors that may be accelerated secondary to complications during labor and birth.

CONCEPTS FOR LECTURE

1. Psychologic disorders such as depression and acute anxiety may have a profound effect on labor, particularly when complications occur that might jeopardize the mother or fetus.

POWERPOINT LECTURE SLIDES

 Psychologic Disorders
- Depression
  - Decreased ability to concentrate
  - Decreased ability to process information
  - Feeling overwhelmed
  - Hopelessness about outcome of labor
- Bipolar disorder
  - Symptoms of depression
  - Hyperexcitability if in manic phase
- Anxiety disorders
  - Chest pain
  - Shortness of breath
  - Faintness
  - Fear or terror

POWERPOINT LECTURE SLIDES *continued*

- Labor is time of mixed emotions—laboring woman with psychologic disorder may have impaired coping mechanisms and face additional emotional challenges during labor

 Nursing Implications
- Orient to new environment
- Thoroughly assess background
- Encourage appropriate coping strategies
- Maintain a safe environment
- Decrease stimulation, as needed
- Ongoing observation for objectives signs of disorder
- Use therapeutic communication and information sharing to establish rapport
- Acknowledge woman's fears, concerns, and symptoms—identify source of distress
- Use comfort measures, touch, and therapeutic communication as appropriate
- Assist in maintaining and regaining orientation to person/place/time
- Provide ongoing reassurance and information as needed
- Give pharmacologic agents as ordered for severe distress

SUGGESTIONS FOR CLASSROOM ACTIVITIES

- Review the coping techniques discussed in Chapter 8. Give examples of nontherapeutic communication during the laboring process. Ask students to react to the nontherapeutic communication.
- Have students list the expected emotional changes and behaviors of pregnancy and compare to the behaviors of women with psychologic disorders. How are they similar and what makes them different?

SUGGESTIONS FOR CLINICAL ACTIVITIES

- Have students develop teaching plans for the nursing diagnosis: Ineffective individual coping related to increased anxiety and stress during the laboring process.
- Review and have students practice therapeutic communication and touch techniques prior to interacting with clients.

CHAPTER 22
BIRTH-RELATED PROCEDURES

RESOURCE LIBRARY

CD-ROM

NCLEX-RN® Review
Video: Vacuum Extractor
Cesarean Birth Videos
Skill 3-7: Assisting with Monitoring of Women
   Undergoing Induction of Labor with Pitocin and
   Cervical Reopening Agents.

Audio Glossary

COMPANION WEBSITE

NCLEX-RN® Review
MediaLink Applications:
   Case Study: Client Undergoing Labor Induction
   Care Plan Activity: Client with Pitocin for Labor
      Augmentation
Thinking Critically

IMAGE LIBRARY

Figure 22.1 External (or cephalic) version of the fetus.

Figure 22.2 The two most common types of episiotomy are midline and mediolateral.

Figure 22.3 Application of forceps in occiput anterior (OA) position.

Figure 22.4 Vacuum extractor traction.

Figure 22.5 Uterine incisions for a cesarean birth.

LEARNING OBJECTIVE 1

Examine the methods and purpose of external and internal version.

CONCEPTS FOR LECTURE

1. An external version (cephalic version) may be done after 36 weeks' gestation to change a breech presentation to a cephalic presentation: Physician applies external manipulation to the maternal abdomen; fetal part must not be engaged; NST performed to establish fetal well-being.

2. Internal version (podalic version) is used less frequently to turn a second twin during a vaginal birth. It is used only if second fetus does not descend readily and heartbeat is not assuring.

POWERPOINT LECTURE SLIDES

1 External Version
- May be done after 36 weeks' gestation to change breech presentation to cephalic presentation
- Physician applies external manipulation to maternal abdomen
- Fetal part must not be engaged
- Reactive NST performed to establish fetal well-being
- Tocolytic given during procedure to relax the uterus

2 Internal Version
- Podalic version—used to turn second twin during vaginal birth
- Used only if second fetus does not descend readily and heartbeat is not assuring
- Physician reaches into uterus and grabs feet of fetus and pulls them down through cervix
- Tocolytic given during procedure to relax uterus

<table>
<tr><td>

SUGGESTIONS FOR CLASSROOM ACTIVITIES

Have students review literature for ECV success and complication rates. Note differences for nulliparas versus multiparas.

</td><td>

SUGGESTIONS FOR CLINICAL ACTIVITIES

Have students develop a written care plan for the client undergoing version.

</td></tr>
</table>

LEARNING OBJECTIVE 2

Discuss the use of amniotomy in current maternal-newborn care.

<table>
<tr><td>

CONCEPTS FOR LECTURE

1. There are several reasons an amniotomy (artificial rupture of the amniotic membranes) is used: To induce labor; to accelerate labor; to apply an internal fetal monitor or insert an intrauterine catheter; or when risks include a prolapsed cord and infection.

</td><td>

POWERPOINT LECTURE SLIDES

1 Purpose of Amniotomy
- Stimulate or induce labor
- Apply internal fetal or contraction monitors
- Obtain fetal scalp blood sample for pH monitoring
- Assess color and composition of amniotic fluid

</td></tr>
</table>

<table>
<tr><td>

SUGGESTIONS FOR CLASSROOM ACTIVITIES

Discuss how amniotomy aids in dilatation of the cervix. Ask students to think ahead about what complications can occur with this procedure.

</td><td>

SUGGESTIONS FOR CLINICAL ACTIVITIES

Show students an amnihook. Have them review the protocol for amniotomy on their client unit. Discuss nursing observations during the procedure with the group.

</td></tr>
</table>

LEARNING OBJECTIVE 3

Compare methods for including labor, explaining their advantage and disadvantages.

<table>
<tr><td>

CONCEPTS FOR LECTURE

1. Cervical ripening may hasten the beginning of labor or shorten the course of labor. It may cause hyperstimulation of the uterus.
2. Stripping the membranes may not induce labor—if labor is initiated, it typically begins within 48 hours—and may cause bleeding.
3. Pitocin infusion is usually effective at producing contractions. It may cause hyperstimulation of uterus.

</td><td>

POWERPOINT LECTURE SLIDES

1 Cervical Ripening
- Consists of effacement and softening of the cervix
- May be used at or near term to enhance success of and reduce time needed for labor induction when continuing pregnancy is undesirable
- May hasten beginning of labor or shorten course of labor
- May cause hyperstimulation of uterus
- Pharmacologic agents include Cytotec and prostaglandin agents—can cause uterine stimulation after insertion

2 Stripping of the Membranes
- Mechanical method: Gloved finger inserted into internal os and rotated 360 degrees twice—separating amniotic membranes lying against lower uterine segment
- Does not require monitoring or other assessments—often done as outpatient service
- May not induce labor—if labor is initiated, it typically begins within 48 hours
- May cause bleeding

</td></tr>
</table>

3 Pitocin Infusion
- Usually effective at producing contractions—may cause hyperstimulation of the uterus
- Requires small, precise dosage
- Maximum rate and dosing interval based on facility protocol, clinician order, individual situation, and maternal-fetal response
- Palpating uterus essential, unless IUPC in place
- May initially decrease blood pressure

SUGGESTIONS FOR CLASSROOM ACTIVITIES

Prior to class, assign the students "Care Plan: Client with Pitocin for Labor Augmentation Activity" on the Companion Website. Ask them to use the protocol on their assigned unit regarding Pitocin and labor induction as a resource. Discuss answers with class and ask them to compare the unit's protocol with the nursing care plan. Review "Skill 3-7: Assisting with Monitoring of Woman Undergoing Induction of Labor with Pitocin and Cervical Ripening" on the Student CD-ROM and in the Clinical Skills Manual. Assign "Case Study: Client Undergoing Labor Induction" on the Companion Website for homework.

SUGGESTIONS FOR CLINICAL ACTIVITIES

Before clinical, ask the students to complete "Thinking Critically: Determine Infusion Rate." In clinical conference, discuss the answers with the students. Ask them to list three to five key nursing assessments and observations when a client has a Pitocin infusion.

LEARNING OBJECTIVE 4

Identify at least two indications for amnioinfusion.

CONCEPTS FOR LECTURE

1. Indications for amnioinfusion include: To increase the volume of fluid in maternal oligohydramnios; to dilute moderate to heavy meconium released in utero; or to delay labor during preterm labor with premature rupture of the membranes.

POWERPOINT LECTURE SLIDES

 Amnioinfusion
- Technique by which warm, sterile normal saline or Ringer's lactate solution introduced into uterus
- Increases volume of amniotic fluid in maternal oligohydramnios
  ○ Alleviates compression on ubilical cord
  ○ Reduces FHR decelerations and fetal stress
- Dilutes moderate to heavy meconium released in utero—meconium aspiration can result in respiratory distress and pneumonia
- Delays labor during preterm labor with premature rupture of membranes

SUGGESTIONS FOR CLASSROOM ACTIVITIES

Bring an intrauterine catheter to class when discussing amnioinfusion. Discuss the procedure and nursing interventions. Ask students the following questions. Why do you have to evaluate if fluid is being adequately expelled? How do you evaluate if the fluid is being expelled?

SUGGESTIONS FOR CLINICAL ACTIVITIES

Allow students to observe an amnioinfusion. Ask them to read the clinical unit's protocol on amnioinfusion and compare it to the textbook. Discuss with the group how the protocol and text are similar and how they differ.

LEARNING OBJECTIVE 5

Describe the types of episiotomy performed and the associated nursing interventions.

CONCEPTS FOR LECTURE

1. There are two types of episiotomy used: midline and mediolateral.
2. During the episiotomy the nurse supports the woman, explaining the procedure. After delivery nursing care: Place an ice pack to the perineum; inspect the perineum frequently; instruct the woman in perineal hygiene, self-care, and comfort measures.

POWERPOINT LECTURE SLIDES

1 Episiotomy Types
- Surgical incision of perineal body to enlarge outlet—commonly used to avoid spontaneous laceration
- Two types
  - Midline: Incision begins at bottom center of perineal body and extends straight down midline to fibers
  - Mediolateral: Incision begins in midline of posterior fourchette and extends at 45 degree angle downward to right or left
- Episiotomy usually performed with regional or local anesthesia

1a Types of Episiotomy
- (Figure 22.2)

2 Nursing Care
- During procedure, provide mother with support and comfort
- Use distraction if needed—if procedure is uncomfortable, act as advocate for mother
- Document type of episiotomy in records and report to subsequent caregivers
- After procedure, provide comfort and apply ice pack
- Assess perineal area frequently—inspect every 15 minutes during first hour after birth for redness, edema, tenderness, ecchymosis, and hematomas
- Apply ice pack immediately in fourth stage
- Instruct mother in perineal hygiene and comfort measures

SUGGESTIONS FOR CLASSROOM ACTIVITIES

Discuss issues that which may predispose a client to having an episiotomy and indications for an episiotomy. Then, ask students to think about care issues in the prenatal and perinatal period that may assist in preventing episiotomy.

SUGGESTIONS FOR CLINICAL ACTIVITIES

Ask students to prepare a client handout on care after an episiotomy. Discuss handouts in clinical conference. Ask students to present this information to a postpartum client.

LEARNING OBJECTIVE 6

Summarize the indications for and risks of forceps-assisted birth.

CONCEPTS FOR LECTURE

1. Indications: Shorten the second stage of labor; assist the woman's pushing effort; help with maternal exhaustion, or when regional anesthesia impairs the woman's ability to push effectively.

POWERPOINT LECTURE SLIDES

1 Indications
- Maternal heart disease
- Maternal pulmonary adema
- Maternal infection
- Maternal exhaustion

2. Risks: Newborn bruising, edema, facial lacerations, cephalhematoma, and transient facial paralysis; woman may experience vaginal lacerations, increased bleeding, bruising, and edema.

- Fetal stress
- Premature placental separation
- Need for shorter second stage of labor
- Heavy regional block with ineffective pushing

1a Applications of Forceps
- (Figure 22.3)

2 Risks
- Newborn may experience
  - Bruising
  - Edema
  - Facial lacerations
  - Cephalhematoma
  - Transient facial paralysis
  - Cerebral hemorrhage
- Woman may experience
  - Vaginal or perineal lacerations
  - Infection secondary to lacerations
  - Increased bleeding
  - Bruising
  - Perineal edema

SUGGESTIONS FOR CLASSROOM ACTIVITIES

Assign student to research guidelines for the use of forceps on the American Academy of Pediatrics or the American College of Obstetricians and Gynecologists websites prior to class. Ask them to discuss what they have learned about the risks to the mother and fetus.

SUGGESTIONS FOR CLINICAL ACTIVITIES

Show clinical students an outlet forceps, low forceps, and midforceps. Discuss the indication for each type of forceps.

LEARNING OBJECTIVE 7

Discuss the use of vacuum extraction to assist birth.

CONCEPTS FOR LECTURE

1. The vacuum extractor assists birth by applying suction to the fetal head—but may cause cephalhematoma and increases risk for jaundice.

POWERPOINT LECTURE SLIDES

1 Vacuum Extractor
- Assists birth by applying suction to fetal head
- Should be progressive descent with first two pulls, procedure should be limited to prevent cephalhematoma—risk increases if birth not within six minutes
- Increases risk for jaundice—due to reabsorption of bruising at cup attachment site

1a Vacuum Extractor
- (Figure 22.4A)

SUGGESTIONS FOR CLASSROOM ACTIVITIES

Show the video "Vacuum Extractor" on the Student CD-ROM in class. Discuss maternal and fetal risks. If possible, show students a vacuum extractor and a vacuum extractor with a low-profile cup.

SUGGESTIONS FOR CLINICAL ACTIVITIES

Assign students to check the FDA website to read the public health advisory on the need for caution in vacuum-assisted deliveries. Ask them to discuss the precautions recommended by the FDA.

LEARNING OBJECTIVE 8

Explain the indications for cesarean birth, impact on the family unit, preparation and teaching needs, and associated nursing care.

CONCEPTS FOR LECTURE

1. Most common indications for cesarean birth are: Fetal distress, lack of labor progression, maternal infection, pelvic size disproportion, placenta previa, and previous cesarean section. Couples should be encouraged to participate in as many choices as possible concerning the surgical birth.
2. Preparation for cesarean birth requires establishing IV lines, placing an indwelling catheter, and performing an abdominal prep.
3. Teaching needs include: What to expect before, during, and after delivery; role of significant others; and interaction with the newborn.
4. Associated nursing care: Routine postpartal care including fundal checks, care of incision, monitoring Intake & Output, assessment of the respiratory system, and assessment of bowel sounds.

POWERPOINT LECTURE SLIDES

1 Indications
- Most common indications for cesarean birth
  - Fetal distress
  - Active genital herpes
  - Multiple gestation (three or more fetuses)
  - Umbilical cord prolapse
  - Tumors that obstruct birth canal
  - Lack of labor progression
  - Maternal infection
  - Pelvic size disproportion
  - Placenta previa
  - Previous cesarean section

2 Preparation
- Preparation for cesarean birth requires
  - Establishing IV lines
  - Placing indwelling catheter
  - Performing abdominal prep

3 Teaching
- Teaching needs include
  - What to expect before, during, and after delivery
  - Why it is being done
  - What sensations the woman will experience
  - Role of significant others
  - Interaction with newborn

4 Nursing Care
- Routine postpartal care including:
  - Fundal checks
  - Care of incision
  - Monitoring Intake & Output and maintaining IV access
  - Administer and teach about post-op medications
  - Assessment of respiratory system
  - Assessment of bowel sounds

4a Uterine Incisions for Cesarean Birth
- (Figure 22.5)

SUGGESTIONS FOR CLASSROOM ACTIVITIES

Show the "Cesarean Birth" videos on the Student CD-ROM in class. Discuss indications for a cesarean section. Ask students to discuss key preoperative preparation.

SUGGESTIONS FOR CLINICAL ACTIVITIES

Assign students to observe a cesarean birth. Ask the clinical group to discuss how the safety of the client can be promoted before, during, and after the procedure.

Discuss vaginal birth following cesarean birth.

CONCEPTS FOR LECTURE

1. Most common risks are: Hemorrhage, uterine rupture, infant death
2. Nursing care: Continuous EFM, internal monitoring, and IV fluid. Pitocin induction should be avoided if possible.

POWERPOINT LECTURE SLIDES

1 Vaginal Birth After Cesarean Birth
- Can occur after trial of labor in cases of nonrecurring indications for cesarean birth
- Most common risks are
  - Hemorrhage
  - Surgical injuries
  - Uterine rupture
  - Infant death or neurological complications

2 Nursing Care
- Continuous EFM
- Internal Monitoring
- IV fluids
- Avoid Pitocin if at all possible
- Classic or T uterine incision is contraindication to VBAC
- Important for nurse to support couple, explore their feelings, and provide information throughout labor

SUGGESTIONS FOR CLASSROOM ACTIVITIES

Assign students to read "Evidence-Based Nursing: Vaginal Birth After Cesarean Section," in the book. Ask the group to discuss what signs or symptoms would indicate that a vaginal birth after a C-section should not be pursued.

SUGGESTIONS FOR CLINICAL ACTIVITIES

Ask students to research vaginal birth after a cesarean birth for a media report. Have them discuss if the media report addresses a risk factor or safety concern.

CHAPTER 23
POSTPARTAL ADAPTATION AND NURSING ASSESSMENT

RESOURCE LIBRARY

⊙ CD-ROM

NCLEX-RN® Review
Skill 4-1: Assessing the Uterine Fundus Following
  Vaginal Birth
Skill 4-2: Evaluating Lochia
Skill 4-3: Postpartum Perineal Assessment
Video: Postpartum Assessment
Nursing in Action: Postpartum Assessment
Audio Glossary

COMPANION WEBSITE

NCLEX-RN® Review
MediaLink Applications:
  Case Study: Mother-Infant Bonding
  Case Study: Woman Recovering from Cesarean Birth
Thinking Critically

📖 IMAGE LIBRARY

Figure 23.1 Involution of the uterus.
Figure 23.2 The uterus becomes displaced and deviated to the right when the bladder is full.
Figure 23.3 Diastasis recti abdominis, a separation of the musculature, commonly occurs after pregnancy.
Figure 23.5 The father experiences strong feelings of attraction during engrossment.

Figure 23.6 Measurement of descent of fundus for the woman with vaginal birth.
Figure 23.7 Suggested guideline for assessing lochia volume.
Figure 23.8 Intact perineum with hemorrhoids.
Figure 23.9 Homans' sign: With the woman's knee flexed, the nurse dorsiflexes the foot.

LEARNING OBJECTIVE 1

Describe the basic physiologic changes that occur in the postpartal period as the woman's body returns to its prepregnant state.

CONCEPTS FOR LECTURE

1. The uterus is at the level of the umbilicus within a few hours after childbirth. It decreases by about one finger-breadth per day. Placental site heals by a process of exfoliation, so no scar formation occurs. Lochia flow progresses from rubra to serosa to alba.
2. Ovarian function and menstruation return in approximately 6 to 12 weeks in the nonlactating mother. Breasts begin milk production.
3. Intestines are sluggish for a few days—leading to constipation, but return to prepregnant state within a week.
4. Postpartum diuresis occurs—bladder tone is decreased, and takes approximately 6 weeks for the bladder to return to the prepregnant state. A higher than usual boggy uterus deviates to the side, usually indicating a full bladder.

POWERPOINT LECTURE SLIDES

1 Involution/Lochia
- Involution used to describe rapid reduction in size of uterus and return to prepregnant state
- Exfoliation allows for healing of placenta site and is important part of involution
- Enhanced by uncomplicated labor and birth—complete expulsion of placenta or membranes, breastfeeding, and early ambulation
- Uterus is at level of umbilicus within 6 to 12 hours after childbirth—decreases by one finger-breadth per day

5. Bradycardia is normal for the first 6 to 10 days. Hemostatic system reaches prepregnant state in 3 to 4 weeks. WBC count is often elevated. Activation of clotting factors predisposes to thrombus formation.

- Uterus rids itself of debris remaining after birth through discharge called lochia
- Lochia changes:
  - Bright red at birth
  - Rubra—dark red
  - Serosa—pink
  - Alba—white
  - Clear
- If blood collects and forms clots within uterus, fundus arises and becomes boggy (uterine atony)

1a Involution of the Uterus
- (Figure 23.1)

2 Ovulation and Menstruation/Lactation
- Return of ovulation and menstruation varies for each postpartal woman
  - Menstruation returns between 6 and 10 weeks after birth in nonlactating mother—ovulation returns within 6 months
  - Return of ovulation and menstruation in breastfeeding mother is prolonged related to length of time breastfeeding continues
- Breasts begin milk production—milk production is a result of interplay of maternal hormones

3 Elimination
- Intestines sluggish because of lingering effects of progesterone and decreased muscle tone
  - Spontaneous bowel movement may not occur for 2 to 3 days after childbirth
  - Mother may anticipate discomfort because of perineal tenderness or fear of episiotomy tearing
- Elimination returns to normal within one week
- After cesarean section, bowel tone returns in few days and flatulence causes abdominal discomfort

4 Urinary Tract
- Mother has increased bladder capacity, decreased bladder tone, swelling and bruising of tissue
- Puerperal diuresis leads to rapid filling of bladder—urinary stasis increases chance of urinary tract infection
- If fundus is higher than expected on palpation and is not in midline, nurse should suspect bladder distension

4a Uterus Becomes Displaced and Deviated to the Right When the Bladder Is Full
- (Figure 23.2)

5 Vital Signs and Blood Values
- Decreased blood volume—bradycardia rates of 50 to 70 beats per minute occur during first 6 to 10 days
- White blood cell count often elevated after delivery, activation of clotting factors predispose to thrombus formation—hemostatic system reaches nonpregnant state in 3 to 4 weeks
- Risk of thromboembolism lasts 6 weeks

SUGGESTIONS FOR CLASSROOM ACTIVITIES

Incorporate "Skill 4-1: Assessing the Uterine Fundus Following Vaginal Birth" available on the Student CD-ROM and in the Clinical Skills Manual into the lecture. Discuss how physiological adaptation of pregnancy is reversed in the postpartum period.

SUGGESTIONS FOR CLINICAL ACTIVITIES

Assist students in assessing the uterine fundus on their postpartum clients. Discuss with students the physiologic changes assessed in their postpartum clients. Have students review the "Postpartum Assessment" video on the Student CD-ROM.

LEARNING OBJECTIVE 2

Discuss the psychologic adjustments that normally occur during the postpartal period.

CONCEPTS FOR LECTURE

1. Psychologic adjustments include taking in, taking hold, maternal role attainment, and the possibility of postpartum blues.

POWERPOINT LECTURE SLIDES

 Taking In/Taking Hold
- Taking in—1 to 2 days after delivery
  - Mother is passive and somewhat dependent as she sorts reality from fantasy in birth experience
  - Food and sleep are major needs
- Taking hold—2 to 3 days after delivery
  - Mother ready to resume control over her life
  - She is focused on baby and may need reassurance

 Maternal Role Attachment
- Woman learns mothering behaviors and becomes comfortable in her new role
- Four stages to maternal role attainment
  - Anticipatory stage—during pregnancy
  - Formal stage—when baby is born
  - Informal stage—3 to 10 months after delivery
  - Personal stage—3 to 10 months after delivery

 Postpartum Blues
- Transient period of depression
  - Occurs first few days after delivery
  - Mother may experience tearfulness, anorexia, difficulty sleeping, feeling of letdown
- Usually resolves in 10 to 14 days
- Caused by:
  - Changing hormone levels
  - Psychologic adjustments
  - Unsupportive environment
  - Insecurity
  - Fatigue
  - Discomfort
  - Overstimulation

SUGGESTIONS FOR CLASSROOM ACTIVITIES

Describe the psychological adjustments of a new mother. Discuss how the nurse can assist the mother in these psychological adjustments.

SUGGESTIONS FOR CLINICAL ACTIVITIES

Ask students to determine if their assigned clients are in the "taking in" or "taking hold" stage.

LEARNING OBJECTIVE 3

Summarize the factors that influence the development of parent-infant attachment.

CONCEPTS FOR LECTURE

1. Parent-infant attachment is influenced by the involvement with the woman's own family, stability of relationships and home environment, mother's ability to trust, mother's level of self-esteem, mother's ability to enjoy herself, mother's knowledge of expectations of childbearing and childrearing, and positive reactions to the present pregnancy.

POWERPOINT LECTURE SLIDES

1 Factors that Influence Maternal-Infant Attachment
- Personal characteristics
- Involvement with the family of origin
- Relationships
- Stability of home environment
- Communication patterns
- Degree of nurturing received as child

1a Three Phases of Maternal Attachment Behavior
- Acquaintance Phase
  - Fingertip exploration
  - En face position
  - Responds verbally to sounds of infant
- Phase of mutual regulation—adjustment between needs of mother and needs of infant
- Reciprocity—mutually gratifying interaction among mother, infant, father

1b En face position

1c Father-Infant Interaction
- Engrossment
  - Sense of absorption
  - Preoccupation—interest in infant

1d The Father Experiences Strong Feelings of Attraction During Engrossment
- (Figure 23.5)

SUGGESTIONS FOR CLASSROOM ACTIVITIES

Discuss the en face position with the students. Describe engrossment in fathers and discuss ways to help them feel more involved with the new baby.

SUGGESTIONS FOR CLINICAL ACTIVITIES

Ask students to describe the benefits of the en face position with the infant of their assigned mother. Assign "MediaLink Application: Mother-Infant Bonding" activity on the Companion Website for homework.

LEARNING OBJECTIVE 4

Delineate the physiologic and psychosocial components of a normal postpartal assessment.

CONCEPTS FOR LECTURE

1. Systematic postpartal assessment includes monitoring vital signs; breast examination; assessment of fundus, incision episiotomy, and perineum; assessment of lochia in terms of type, quantity, and characteristics; assessment of bladder and bowels; and assessment of lower extremities. Psychologic assessment components include the expected phase of adjustment to parenthood; the expected level of attachment to the infant; and client education concerning self-care.

POWERPOINT LECTURE SLIDES

1 Assessment
- Assessment and client education assist in meeting needs of childbearing family—assist in detecting risk and treating possible complications
- Vital signs: Temperature elevations should last for only 24 hours

- Blood pressure is stable and pulse is initially slow, breath sound should be clear
- Easy way to remember sequence: BUBBLEHE

 Breasts, Uterus
- Assess if mother is breast- or bottle-feeding—inspect nipples and palpate for engorgement or tenderness
- Uterus
  - Determine firmness of fundus and ascertain position
  - Correlate position with approximate descent of 1 cm per day

 Bowel, Bladder, Perineum, Extremities
- Assess frequency, burning, or urgency—palpate for bladder distention
- Bowel: Assess bowel sounds, flatus, and distention
- Inspect abdominal incisions for REEDA
- Inspect the perineum for REEDA
- Assess for hemorrhoids
- Extremities
  - Assess for pedal edema, redness, and warmth
  - Check Homan's sign

 Psychological Assessment
- Focuses on mother's general attitude, feelings of competence, support systems, caregiving skill—evaluates fatigue and ability to accomplish developmental task
- Describe level of attachment to infant
- Determine mother's phase of adjustment to parenting

SUGGESTIONS FOR CLASSROOM ACTIVITIES

Use the following skills from the Student CD-ROM and Clinical Skills Manual in the lecture: "Evaluating Lochia," and "Postpartum Perineal Assessment." Assign "Case Study: Woman Recovering from Cesarean Birth" on the Companion Website for homework. .

SUGGESTIONS FOR CLINICAL ACTIVITIES

Assist students in assessing lochia on their assigned clients. Encourage them to distinguish between scant, light, moderate, and heavy. Discuss with students the "Critical Thinking in Action" case study in clinical conference.

LEARNING OBJECTIVE 5

Discuss the physical and developmental tasks that the mother must accomplish during the postpartal period.

CONCEPTS FOR LECTURE

1. The woman's physical condition returns to a nonpregnant state and she gains competence and confidence in herself as a parent.

POWERPOINT LECTURE SLIDES

 Physical and Developmental Tasks
- Following tasks must be accomplished by new mother
  - Restore physical condition
  - Develop competencies in caring for her new baby
  - Establish relationship with new baby
  - Adapt to changed lifestyle and family structure

SUGGESTIONS FOR CLASSROOM ACTIVITIES

- Discuss the developmental tasks of a new mother.
- Have students search the Web to find information concerning the Newborns' and Mothers' Health Protection Act (NMHPA). Allow time in class to discuss the implications of this legislation.

SUGGESTIONS FOR CLINICAL ACTIVITIES

- Have students observe or assist with discharge teaching, including maternal and infant care.
- Arrange for students to attend a meeting of the La Leche League or other postpartum support group. Have students note concerns expressed by the mothers, as well as the purpose and general atmosphere of the meeting. Allow time to share their observations.

CHAPTER 24
THE POSTPARTUM FAMILY: NEEDS AND CARE

RESOURCE LIBRARY

 CD-ROM

NCLEX-RN® Review
Audio Glossary

COMPANION WEBSITE

NCLEX-RN® Review
MediaLink Applications:
  Case Study: Perineal Discomfort
  Discharge Teaching Checklist
Thinking Critically

 IMAGE LIBRARY

Figure 24.1 A sitz bath promotes healing and provides relief from perineal discomfort during the initial weeks following birth.
Figure 24.2 Postpartum exercises.

Figure 24.3 The nurse provides educational information to both parents.

Table 24.5 Signs of Postpartum Complications

LEARNING OBJECTIVE 1

Relate the uses of nursing diagnoses to the findings of the "norm" postpartum assessment and analysis.

CONCEPTS FOR LECTURE

1. Nursing diagnoses focus on the normal and expected postpartal course.
2. Nursing diagnoses allow the nurse to identify expected outcomes and selected nursing interventions that will help the family meet the expected outcomes.

POWERPOINT LECTURE SLIDES

 Nursing Diagnoses
- Physiologic alterations are the basis of many postpartum diagnoses
  ○ Constipation related to fear of tearing stitches or pain
  ○ Acute pain related to perineal edema or episiotomy from birth

- Diagnoses that focus on positive aspects of childbirth and parenting
  ○ Health-seeking behaviors: Information about infant care related to expressed desire to improve parenting skills
  ○ Readiness for enhanced family coping related to successful adjustment to new baby

 Expected Outcomes and Interventions for the Family
- Once nurse completes assessments and diagnoses, can formulate expected outcomes and select nursing interventions to assist family in meeting outcomes
  ○ Outcomes formulated after nursing assessments and consultation with postpartum client and her family
  ○ Factors that could influence outcome of care should be considered

SUGGESTIONS FOR CLASSROOM ACTIVITIES

Assign students to complete "Case Study: Perineal Discomfort" activity on the Companion Website and answer the "Thinking Critically" questions in the book in advance of class. Ask students what they think may be appropriate nursing diagnoses and expected outcomes for the client in the case study.

SUGGESTIONS FOR CLINICAL ACTIVITIES

Have students assess a postpartum client and then develop a list of nursing diagnoses in order of priority.

LEARNING OBJECTIVE 2

Delineate strategies for promoting family learning during the early postpartum period.

CONCEPTS FOR LECTURE

1. The nurse should discuss desired outcomes and goals with the mother and family members.
2. The nurse should design interventions to achieve optimal health promotion.

POWERPOINT LECTURE SLIDES

1. Outcomes in the Postpartum Period
   - Nurse formulates outcomes after completing assessment and consulting with mother and family—factors influencing outcome of nursing care must be considered

2. Interventions
   - Interventions need to consider baby's schedule, as well as physical and psychologic well-being of each family member
   - Important component of care is client teaching for health promotion—teaching should be individualized and based on willingness to learn and ability of parents

---

SUGGESTIONS FOR CLASSROOM ACTIVITIES

Identify expected outcomes for the physical and psychosocial needs experienced by the mother and her family during the postpartum period.

SUGGESTIONS FOR CLINICAL ACTIVITIES

Have students develop a realistic and measurable goal for one physical and one psychosocial goal for their postpartum clients.

LEARNING OBJECTIVE 3

Discuss appropriate nursing interventions to promote maternal comfort and well-being.

CONCEPTS FOR LECTURE

1. The nurse can promote and restore maternal physical well-being by monitoring uterine status, vital signs, cardiovascular status, elimination patterns, nutritional needs, sleep and rest, and support and educational needs.
2. In addition, the postpartum woman may need medications to promote comfort, treat anemia, provide immunity to rubella, and prevent development of antigens (in the nonsensitized Rh-negative woman).

POWERPOINT LECTURE SLIDES

1. Uterine Status, VS, and CV Status
   - Monitor every 15 minutes for first hour after birth, every 30 minutes for next hour, then hourly for approximately 2 more hours, then every 8 hours or more frequently if there is bogginess, position out of midline, heavy lochia flow
   - Assess for BP within normal limits: No hypotension (not 30 mm Hg systolic or 15 mm Hg diastolic over baseline)

2. Maternal Comfort
   - Relief of perineal discomfort
     - Ice packs
     - Topical agents
     - Perineal care

- Relief of hemorrhoidal discomfort may include
  - Sitz baths
  - Topical anesthetic ointments
  - Rectal suppositories
  - Witch hazel pads

 Sitz Bath Promotes Comfort and Provides Relief
- (Figure 24.1)

 Afterpains
- Relief of afterpains
- Positioning (prone position)
- Analgesia administered an hour before breastfeeding
- Encourage early ambulation—monitor for dizziness and weakness

 Monitoring Mother's and Family's Needs
- Nurse can assist in restoration of physical well-being by
  - Assessing elimination patterns
  - Determining mother's need for sleep and rest
  - Encouraging regular diet as tolerated and increasing fluids
- Identify available support persons—involve support person and siblings in teaching as appropriate
- Determine family's knowledge of normal postpartum care and newborn care

 Medications
- Postpartum client may need medications to promote comfort, treat anemia, promote rubella, and prevent development of antigens (in nonsensitized Rh-negative woman)
- Postpartum clients should be informed about name of medication, expected action, possible side effects
- Nurse must review safety measures with medications

SUGGESTIONS FOR CLASSROOM ACTIVITIES

Identify specific pharmacologic agents used for comfort and sleep. Discuss the rationale for RhoGAM and rubella vaccine. Review the nursing implications for the previously mentioned medications. Ask students to list what the clients need to know about their prescribed medications.

SUGGESTIONS FOR CLINICAL ACTIVITIES

- Provide nursing care for client from delivery, through the recovery period, and into the postpartum period.
- Have students attend a postpartum discharge class. Have them note the questions, behaviors, and responses of the class participants.

LEARNING OBJECTIVE 4

Describe the nurse's role in promoting maternal rest and helping the mother to gradually resume an appropriate level of activity.

CONCEPTS FOR LECTURE

1. The nurse should encourage the new mother to rest when the infant rests.
2. The nurse should counsel the new mother to resume activities gradually. *Refer to Figure 24.2.*
3. The nurse recommends exercise to provide health benefits to the new mother.

POWERPOINT LECTURE SLIDES

1 Rest
- Organize nursing care to avoid frequent interruptions, educate new mother that fatigue may persist for several weeks
- Mother should be encouraged to rest when baby rests
- Mother may need to make adjustments at home and work

2 Resumption of Activities
- New mother should gradually increase activities and ambulation after birth
- She should avoid heavy lifting, excessive stair climbing, strenuous activity
- Resume light housekeeping by second week at home
- Delay returning to work until after 6-week postpartum examination

3 Exercises
- Recommend exercise to provide health benefits to new mother
- Nurse should encourage client to begin simple exercises while on nursing unit
- Inform her that increased lochia and pain may necessitate a change in her activity

SUGGESTIONS FOR CLASSROOM ACTIVITIES

Ask students to bring mats to class. Demonstrate postpartum exercises.

SUGGESTIONS FOR CLINICAL ACTIVITIES

Have students examine the educational material in the clinical area. Ask them to compare and contrast how the exercise is different for a vaginal birth and cesarean section.

LEARNING OBJECTIVE 5

Identify client teaching topics for promoting postpartal family wellness.

CONCEPTS FOR LECTURE

1. Possible reactions of siblings.
2. Resumption of sexual activity: Discuss possible temporary problems such as sleep deprivation, vaginal dryness, and lack of time together.
3. Contraception
4. Parent-Infant attachment: Help parents realize there will be both positive and negative feelings about parenthood—new parents need to understand that the infant is unique with a distinctive personality.

POWERPOINT LECTURE SLIDES

1 Reaction of Siblings
- Sibling visits reassure children their mother is well
- Father may need to hold new baby, so mother can hug older children
- Suggest to parent that bringing doll home allows older child to "care" and identify with parents

1a Sibling Acquainting with New Baby

PowerPoint Lecture Slides *continued*

2 Sexual Activity
- Sleep deprivation, vaginal dryness, and lack of time together may impact resumption of sexual activity
- Usually sexual intercourse is resumed once episiotomy has healed and lochia has stopped (about 3 weeks)
- Breastfeeding mother may have leakage of milk from nipples with sexual arousal

3 Contraception
- Information on contraception should be part of discharge planning
- Nursing staff need to identify advantages, disadvantages, risk factors, any contraindications
- Breastfeeding mothers concerned that contraceptive method will interfere with ability to breastfeed—they should be given available options

4 Parent-Infant Attachment
- Tell parents it is normal to have both positive and negative feelings about parenthood
- Stress uniqueness of each infant
- Provide time and privacy for the new family
- Include parents in nursing intervention

SUGGESTIONS FOR CLASSROOM ACTIVITIES

Describe the caretaking, perception of the baby, and support aspects of parent attachment behaviors. Ask students how nurses can support and assist parents in determining the unique needs of their infant.

SUGGESTIONS FOR CLINICAL ACTIVITIES

Ask students to review the birthing unit's teaching materials on contraception and resumption of sexual activities. Have students assess the attachment behaviors of their postpartum clients.

LEARNING OBJECTIVE 6

Compare the postpartal nursing needs of the woman who experienced a cesarean birth with the needs of a woman who gave birth vaginally.

CONCEPTS FOR LECTURE

1. The woman who experiences a cesarean birth has all the needs of the woman who had a vaginal birth: Assessment of the fundus, assessment of the breasts, perineal evaluation (may have varicose veins or hemorrhoids from pregnancy), assessment of lochia flow, and assessment of bowel and bladder.
2. After a cesarean birth, the woman needs assessment of the abdomen, incision, and bowel sounds. She should also turn, cough, and deep breathe.

POWERPOINT LECTURE SLIDES

 1 Cesarean Section Needs
- Breasts must be assessed, assess location and firmness of fundus, lochia, and incision site
- Assess foley catheter in place, color, and amount noted—bowel sounds are checked: present, decreased, or minimal

 2 Abdominal Assessment
- Cesarean birth is major abdominal surgery—if general anesthesia used, abdominal distension may cause discomfort

---

196   Chapter 24/Objective 6   © 2007 Pearson Education, Inc.

3. After a cesarean birth, the mother will have a greater need for pain medication. She will also have increased fatigue because of the surgical intervention. The mother may need encouragement to interact with the infant.

- Position client on left side, include exercises, early ambulation, avoid carbonated beverages—may need enemas and stool softeners
- Pulmonary infections may occur because of immobility and use of narcotics because of altered immune response
- Encourage turn, cough, deep breath every 2 hours while awake until she is ambulating

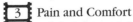 3 Pain and Comfort
- Administer analgesics within the first 24 to 72 hours—allows woman to become more mobile and active
- Comfort is promoted through proper positioning, back rubs, and oral care—reduce noxious stimuli in environment
- Encourage visits by family and newborn, which provides distraction from painful stimuli
- Encourage non-pharmacologic methods of pain relief (breathing, relaxation, and distraction)—encourage rest

3a Attachment After a Cesarean Birth
- Physical condition of mother and newborn and maternal reactions to stress, anesthesia, and medications may impact mother-infant attachment
- By second or third day, cesarean birth mother moves into "taking-hold period"
  ○ Emphasize home management and encourage mother to allow others to assume housekeeping responsibilities
  ○ Stress how fatigue prolongs recovery and may interfere with attachment process

SUGGESTIONS FOR CLASSROOM ACTIVITIES

Outline the assessment protocol for a woman who experiences a cesarean birth. Bring perineal equipment and supplies to class. Demonstrate care measures used for comfort and healing.

SUGGESTIONS FOR CLINICAL ACTIVITIES

Have students develop a priority list of the mother's needs after a cesarean birth. Demonstrate how patient-controlled analgesia equipment is "set up." Discuss what is included in patient-controlled analgesia orders.

LEARNING OBJECTIVE 7

Summarize the nursing needs of the childbearing adolescent during the postpartal period.

CONCEPTS FOR LECTURE

1. The nurse should evaluate the adolescent mother in terms of her level of maturity, available support systems, cultural background, and existing knowledge and then plan care accordingly.

POWERPOINT LECTURE SLIDES

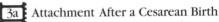 1 Adolescent Mother's Needs
- Needs depend on level of maturity, support system, cultural background
- Nurse needs to assess
  ○ Maternal-infant interaction
  ○ Roles of support people

- ○ Plans for discharge
- ○ Knowledge of childrearing
- ○ Plans for follow-up care
- Newborn examination at bedside is excellent opportunity to teach new mother about her baby—adolescent mother needs positive feedback and praise

SUGGESTIONS FOR CLASSROOM ACTIVITIES

- Include local and state resources for adolescent mothers in the lecture. Describe how these resources can be incorporated in the plan of care for an adolescent mother.
- Discuss how the adolescent mother's educational needs can be met during a pregnancy.

SUGGESTIONS FOR CLINICAL ACTIVITIES

Assign students to care for an adolescent mother on the birthing unit or to read a case study on an adolescent mother. Develop a nursing care plan addressing the needs of the adolescent mother.

LEARNING OBJECTIVE 8

Describe possible approaches to sensitive nursing care for the woman who relinquishes her newborn.

CONCEPTS FOR LECTURE

1. The mother who decides to relinquish her baby needs emotional support. She should be able to decide whether to see and hold her baby, and any special request regarding the birth should be honored.

POWERPOINT LECTURE SLIDES

 Relinquishing a Baby
- Many reasons why a woman decides she cannot parent her baby
  - ○ Emotional crisis may arise as woman attempts to resolve her concerns
  - ○ As she faces these concerns, social pressures against giving up baby
- Mother may need to complete grieving process to work through her decision—she may have made considerable adjustments to her lifestyle to give birth
- Nursing staff need to honor any special requests after birth and encourage mother to express her feelings
- Seeing newborn may assist mother in grieving process
- Some mothers may request early discharge or transfer to another unit

SUGGESTIONS FOR CLASSROOM ACTIVITIES

Invite a social worker or lawyer to speak to the class on adoption laws in your state, including the procedures to follow when caring for an infant who is to be adopted. Be sure to include local and state resources for mothers who relinquish their infants.

SUGGESTIONS FOR CLINICAL ACTIVITIES

Have students develop a nursing care plan with one physical and one psychosocial problem for a mother who relinquishes her infant.

Delineate criteria and teaching topics related to postpartum care.

CONCEPTS FOR LECTURE

1. Prior to discharge, the couple should be given any information necessary for the woman to provide appropriate self-care.
2. Parents should have a beginning skill in caring for their newborn and should be familiar with warning signs of possible complications for mother and baby.
3. Printed information is valuable in helping couples deal with questions that may arise at home.

POWERPOINT LECTURE SLIDES

1 Preparation for Discharge
- Preparation for discharge should begin when expectant mother enters birthing unit
- Mother needs to be aware of signs of postpartum complications and should be aware of her self-care needs
- Nurses should begin first by assessing knowledge and expectations of new mother and family
- Nurse should be available to answer questions and provide support to parents

1a Signs of Postpartum Complications
- (Table 24.5)

2 Infant Care
- New mother and family should know basic infant care
  - When to anticipate cord will fall off
  - Information about tub baths and immunizations
  - Family should be comfortable in feeding and handling infant, as well as safety concerns

3 Printed Information
- Nurse should review with new mother any information she has received regarding postpartum exercises, prevention of fatigue, sitz bath and perineal care, etc.—nurse should spend time with parent to determine if they have any last-minute questions before discharge
- Printed information about local agencies and support groups should be given to new family

SUGGESTIONS FOR CLASSROOM ACTIVITIES

Outline discharge teaching needs for a new mother. Include information on the family's well-being and care of the infant. Compare and contrast recommendations for postpartum education with the discharge protocols in your community's various agencies.

SUGGESTIONS FOR CLINICAL ACTIVITIES

Have students attend a breastfeeding class or an infant care class in the community. Ask students to determine the teaching styles used in the class attended.

CHAPTER 25
THE POSTPARTAL FAMILY AT RISK

RESOURCE LIBRARY

 CD-ROM

NCLEX-RN® Review
Audio Glossary

 COMPANION WEBSITE

NCLEX-RN® Review
Medialink Applications:
  Case Study: Postpartal Client
  Care Plan Activity: Postpartal Care Following
    Vaginal Birth
  Care Plan Activity: Postpartal Care Following
    Cesarean Birth
Thinking Critically
Nursing Care Plan: The Woman with a Puerperal
  Infection

IMAGE LIBRARY

Figure 25.2 Mastitis.

Table 25.2 Signs of Postpartal Hemorrhage
Table 25.3 Factors Associated with Development of Mastitis

Table 25.5 Factors Associated with Increased Risk of Thromboembolic Disease

LEARNING OBJECTIVE 1

Describe assessment of the postpartum woman for predisposing factors, onset, and signs and symptoms of various postpartum complications.

CONCEPTS FOR LECTURE

1. Predisposing factors for complications include overdistention of uterus, multiple gestation, or multiparity; rapid or prolonged labor; oxytocin induction of labor; precipitous delivery; cesarean section; PROM; or urinary catheterization.
2. Nursing assessments include frequent fundal checks and massage of fundus; frequent perineal pad checks; prevention of overdistention of the bladder; frequent vital signs assessments; assessment of Homan's sign each shift; inspection of the perineum and breasts each shift; and assessment for signs of postpartum "blues" or depression.

POWERPOINT LECTURE SLIDES

 Complications
- Common complications of the postpartal period
  - Hemorrhage
  - Infection
  - Thromboembolic disease
  - Postpartal psychiatric disorders
- Risk factors for these complications
  - Overdistention of uterus due to large baby, multiple gestation, multiparity
  - Rapid or prolonged labor
  - Oxytocin induction of labor
  - Precipitous induction of labor
  - Precipitous delivery, cesarean section
  - PROM
  - Urinary catheterization

3. Signs and symptoms of postpartum complications include postpartum hemorrhage—excessive vaginal bleeding; infection—fever, purulent discharge from vagina or incision, burning during urination, redness and pain in the breast about postpartum week; thrombophlebitis—pain and swelling in the lower extremities; and postpartum depression—feelings of overwhelming sadness and lack of desire to care for the infant.

 Nursing Assessment
- Assess fundus for signs of bogginess—note height, tone, and position of fundus
- Check vital signs, note
  - Elevated temperature
  - Elevated blood pressure
  - Elevated heart rate
  - Low blood pressure
  - Symptoms of shock
- Examine perineal pads—note
  - Amount
  - Color and odor
  - Consistency
  - Presence and size
- Assess for Homan's sign every shift

 Nursing Assessments
- Inspect perineum for
  - Edema
  - Ecchymosis
  - Pain
  - Hemorrhoids
- Inspect breasts for
  - Cracked, blistered, or bleeding nipples
  - Engorgement, red streaks, lumps, clogged milk ducts
- Check distension and displacement of bladder—discomfort voiding
- Assess for signs of depression or "baby blues"

 Signs and Symptoms
- Following signs and symptoms should be assessed for various postpartum complications
  - Hemorrhage: Vaginal bleeding, hemoglobin hematocrit, and CBC results
  - Infection: Fever, purulent discharge from vagina or incision, erythema at incision site, increased WBCs, burning during urination, redness/pain in breast about fourth postpartum week
  - Note Homan's sign, pain, tenderness, swelling in lower extremities
  - Depression: Overwhelming sadness, low self-esteem, lack of desire to care for child

---

SUGGESTIONS FOR CLASSROOM ACTIVITIES

Use the following MediaLink Application activities from the Companion Website in the lecture for discussion: "Assessment of Psychiatric Disorders," "Postpartal Hemorrhage," and "Caring for the Client with Mastitis." Assign "Care Plan: Postpartal Perineal Pain" on the Companion Website for homework.

SUGGESTIONS FOR CLINICAL ACTIVITIES

Ask the students to prepare written teaching plans with visual aids for a postpartum client that stresses the prevention of hemorrhage and infection.

LEARNING OBJECTIVE 2

Summarize the preventive measures for various complications of the postpartum period that should be incorporated into the nursing care of the postpartum woman.

CONCEPTS FOR LECTURE

1. To prevent complications, the nurse will assess the fundus for signs of bogginess; assess perineal pads for excessive bleeding; assess incisions for signs of infections; assess the bladder for signs of distension and encourage the woman to void frequently; use good handwashing techniques to prevent the transmission of infective material; assess breasts for cracking, plugged ducts, and signs of mastitis; teach the mother proper latching-on techniques and breast care; assess lower extremities for signs of thrombophlebitis, encourage early ambulation, and assess for pulmonary embolus; and assess for signs of depression.

POWERPOINT LECTURE SLIDES

 Preventive Measures
- Assess fundus for bogginess—if boggy, perform fundal massage
  - Monitor hemoglobin and hematocrit—assess for signs of anemia and avoid traumatic procedures
  - Assess perineal pads for excessive bleeding—check for clots
- Monitor for bladder distension, encourage mother to void frequently—catheterize if necessary
- Monitor woman with mediolateral episiotomies for increased bleeding
- Inspect placenta for intactness and for evidence of missing fragments
- Note if uterus is firm and if there is bleeding—this may indicate laceration

 Uterine Massage

 Infection
- Use good handwashing techniques to prevent transmission of infection
  - Assess for signs of local and systemic infections
  - Identify abnormal lab values for early intervention
- Report signs of severe infection: Foul-smelling lochia, uterine tenderness/subinvolution, severe lower abdominal pain, change in vital signs, chills, lethargy, nausea/vomiting, abdominal guarding

 Breasts
- Assess breasts for cracking, plugged ducts, signs of mastitis
- Assess for following mastitis risk factors
  - Cracked nipples
  - Poor hygiene
  - Engorgement
  - Supplemental feedings
  - Change in routine or infant feeding patterns
  - Abrupt weaning
  - Lack of proper breast support
- Demonstrate proper latch-on technique, encourage frequent feeding and position changes during feedings

 Factors Associated with Development of Mastitis
- (Table 25.3)

[1e] Lower Extremities
- Assess lower extremities for signs of thrombophlebitis, encourage early ambulation, assess for pulmonary embolus
- For clients on bed rest, turn and do range of motion exercises—use antiembolism stockings with those at risk, encourage fluids to avoid dehydration, encourage no smoking, advise against prolonged sitting or crossing legs, encourage elevation of legs while sitting

[1f] Factors Associated with Increased Risk of Thromboembolic Disease
- (Table 25.5)

[1g] Depression
- Assess woman for depression
  - Depression more severe in primiparas than in multiparas—observe for episodic tearfulness and note if mother feels overwhelmed, unable to cope, fatigued, anxious, irritable, oversensitive
- Observe new mother for objective signs of depression—listen for feelings of failure and self accusation

Suggestions for Classroom Activities

Identify the risk factors and preventive measures for postpartum hemorrhage, postpartum infection, and thromboembolic disorders. Ask students to discuss risk factors that they have seen in postpartum clients during their clinical experience. Ask students to review and answer the questions in the "Thinking Critically: Assessing Postpartal Leg Pain" feature in the book. Include a discussion of the answers in the class lecture.

Suggestions for Clinical Activities

Discuss universal precautions on the maternal-child clinical units. Have students discuss how a new mother can control infection in her home environment. Have students review client-care protocols related to thromboembolic disorders and mastitis and compare them with the recommendations in their book.

Learning Objective 3

List the causes of and appropriate nursing interventions for hemorrhage during the postpartal period.

Concepts for Lecture

1. The main causes of postpartum hemorrhage and the appropriate nursing interventions include uterine atony—perform fundal massage and check for clots; laceration of vagina and cervix (suspect if the mother is bleeding heavily in presence of firmly contracted fundus)—contact physician to suture the laceration; retained placental fragments (suspect if the client is bleeding, fundus is firm, and no lacerations are present)—thoroughly inspect placenta; and subinvolution (usually occurs 1 to 2 weeks after birth)—provide mother with discharge instructions, including information about possible complications. *Refer to Table 25.1.*

PowerPoint Lecture Slides

[1] Uterine Atony
- Lack of uterine muscle tone—caused by conditions that overdistend uterus and affect uterine contractility, and medication
- Perform fundal massage and check for clots
- Administer uterine stimulants as ordered to monitor for side effects

[1a] Laceration
- Bright red bleeding with firm uterus—suspect if mother is bleeding heavily in presence of firmly contracted fundus
- Contact physician to suture laceration

POWERPOINT LECTURE SLIDES *continued*

1b Retained Placental Fragments
- Commonly occurs when fundus is massaged prior to spontaneous placental separation
  ○ Suspect if client is bleeding with firm fundus and no laceration
  ○ Inspect fundus thoroughly after its delivery

1c Subinvolution
- Usually occurs 1 to 2 weeks after birth
  ○ Failure of uterus to return to normal size after pregnancy—lochia rubra of greater than 2 weeks duration suggests subinvolution
- Provide mother with discharge instructions and information about possible complications

1d Signs of Postpartal Hemorrhage
- (Table 25.2)

SUGGESTIONS FOR CLASSROOM ACTIVITIES

When discussing uterine atony and fundal massage, ask students to form small groups and ask them to "think ahead" about what nursing assessments need to be made with uterine atony and what equipment may be needed if the woman continues to bleed.

SUGGESTIONS FOR CLINICAL ACTIVITIES

In clinical conference, discuss delayed postpartal hemorrhage. Have students "brainstorm" about what clients need to know about this health concern prior to discharge.

LEARNING OBJECTIVE 4

Develop a nursing care plan that reflects a knowledge of etiology, pathophysiology, and current medical management for the woman experiencing postpartum hemorrhage, reproductive tract infections, urinary tract infection, mastitis, thromboembolic disease, or a postpartal psychiatric disorder.

CONCEPTS FOR LECTURE

1. Nursing care for the postpartal woman experiencing postpartum complications includes obtaining a thorough client prenatal and birth history for any predisposing factors—frequent assessment of all body systems to detect signs and symptoms of complications. These assessments include vital signs, fundal checks, lochial flow, perineum, all incisions, Homan's sign, breast and nipples, and emotional status. Discharge teaching includes ongoing medical management and self-care measures—signs and symptoms of further complications.

POWERPOINT LECTURE SLIDES

1 History
- Assess postpartum client's prenatal history and ongoing labor/birth to identify risk factors leading to postpartum complications
- Assess with knowledge that many physiologic changes of postpartum period are similar to depression
- Document specific and objective observations

1a Assessments
- Assess and document
  ○ Vital signs
  ○ Fundal checks
  ○ Lochial flow
  ○ Perineum
  ○ All incisions for REEDA
  ○ Homan's signs
  ○ Breast and nipples
  ○ Emotional status
  ○ Parent-infant attachment

1b Diagnoses
- Formulate nursing diagnoses based on
  ○ Safe and effective care environment
  ○ Physiological integrity

○ Health promotion/maintenance—self-care and health-seeking behaviors

 Nursing Care
- Observe actual and potential problems that may occur with client
- Administer appropriate treatment and medications as ordered—observe for intended impact of treatment and adverse effects
- Educate about signs of complications and needed self-care—reinforce importance of postpartum follow-up and completion of treatments and prescribed medications
- Provide client with list and phone numbers of support individuals (e.g., lactation consultant, WIC, etc.)

SUGGESTIONS FOR CLASSROOM ACTIVITIES

- Ask students to complete the NCLEX-RN® review questions on the Companion Website for homework and send them to you.
- Review "Case Study: Postpartal Thromboembolic Disease" on the Companion Website and incorporate a discharge plan on infections, hemorrhage, and thromboembolic problems. Include visual aids that may be given to the client.

SUGGESTIONS FOR CLINICAL ACTIVITIES

Ask students to discuss risk factors and potential problems of their assigned postpartum clients. Discuss the essential role of the nurse in the prevention of postpartum complications.

LEARNING OBJECTIVE 5

Evaluate the woman's knowledge of self-care measures, signs of complications to be reported to the primary healthcare provider, and measures to prevent recurrence of complications.

CONCEPTS FOR LECTURE

1. Teaching for self care includes knowledge of progress of involution; care of the breasts; prevention of infection; expected emotional changes; need for extra rest; nutritional needs; and knowledge of dosage regimens and side effects of prescribed medication. Signs and symptoms of complications include increased vaginal bleeding; fever; foul-smelling vaginal discharge; pain and/or redness in an incision; pain, redness, or swelling in the breasts and/or legs; and overwhelming feelings of sadness or inability to care for the infant.

POWERPOINT LECTURE SLIDES

 Teach for Self-Care
- Teach client normal adaptation during postpartum period: Progressive descent of fundus, no reversal of lochia—be aware of postpartum fatigue and obtain extra rest
- Teach about nutritional needs: Adequate hydration, dietary measure if anemic, nutritional needs for breastfeeding
- Mother needs to be aware of action of prescribed medications and potential side effects
- Teach about comfort measures, activity, methods to prevent fatigue, coping skills

 Signs and Symptoms
- Educate client about signs of complications prior to discharge
- Signs and symptoms of complications that should be reported to healthcare provider
  ○ Increased vaginal bleeding
  ○ Fever
  ○ Foul-smelling vaginal discharge

○ Pain and/or redness in incision
○ Pain, redness, or swelling in breasts and/or legs
• Overwhelming feelings of sadness or inability to care for infant—provide list of support organizations in the community

SUGGESTIONS FOR CLASSROOM ACTIVITIES

During the lecture, compare local healthcare facilities' postpartum instructions with information from the book.

SUGGESTIONS FOR CLINICAL ACTIVITIES

Have students develop a teaching-learning handout for a postpartum client on home self-care. Have students discuss these plans in clinical conferences. The following week in client conference, the students should be prepared to present the plan to a client preparing for discharge.

CHAPTER 26
THE PHYSIOLOGIC RESPONSES OF THE NEWBORN TO BIRTH

RESOURCE LIBRARY

CD-ROM

NCLEX-RN® Review
Skill 5-1: Performing Nasal Pharyngeal Suctioning
Audio Glossary

COMPANION WEBSITE

NCLEX-RN® Review
Case Study: Newborn Responses to Birth

IMAGE LIBRARY

Figure 26.1 Initiation of respiration in the newborn.
Figure 26.2 Transitional circulation: conversion from fetal to neonatal circulation.
Figure 26.4 Response of blood pressure (BP) to neonatal changes in blood volume.
Figure 26.5 Methods of heat loss.

Figure 26.8 Newborn stool samples.
Figure 26.9 Mother and newborn gaze at each other.
Figure 26.10 Head turning to follow movement.

Table 26.2 Normal Term Newborn Cord Blood Values
Table 26.5 Newborn Urinalysis Values

LEARNING OBJECTIVE 1

Summarize the respiratory and cardiovascular changes that occur during the transition to extrauterine life and during stabilization.

CONCEPTS FOR LECTURE

1. Newborn respiration is initated primarily by chemical and mechanical events associated with thermal and sensory stimulation.
2. Onset of respiration stimulates cardiovascular changes. Air enters the lungs, oxygen content rises in alveoli and stimulates relaxation of pulmonary arteries. This leads to decreased vascular resistance that allows complete vascular flow to the lungs.

POWERPOINT LECTURE SLIDES

1 Initiation of Respiration in the Newborn
- Production of lung fluid diminishes 2 to 4 days before labor
- 80 to 100 mL remain in the passageway of a full-term newborn
- During birth, fetal chest is compressed and squeezes fluid

1a Initiation of Respiration in the Newborn
- (Figure 26.1)

1b Chemical Stimuli
- First breath is inspiratory gasp—triggered by increased Pco_2 and decreased pH and Po_2
- Changes trigger aortic and carotid chemoreceptors—trigger brain's respiratory center
- Natural result of a normal vaginal birth

Thermal Stimuli
- Significant decrease in environmental temperature after birth
  ○ Stimulates skin nerve endings
  ○ Newborn responds with rhythmic respiration
- Excessive cooling may lead to profound depression of cold stress

 Sensory Stimuli
- Intrauterine life
  ○ Dark
  ○ Sound dampened
  ○ Fluid-filled environment
  ○ Weightless
- Newborn experiences
  ○ Light
  ○ Sounds
  ○ Effects of gravity
  ○ Abundance of tactile, auditory, and visual stimuli of birth

 Transitional Circulation
- (Figure 26.2)

 Onset of Respiration Stimulates Cardiovascular Changes
- As air enters the lungs, oxygen content rises in alveoli and stimulates relaxation of pulmonary arteries

Patent Ductus Arteriosus Closes
- With increased oxygenated pulmonary blood flow and loss of placenta, systemic blood flow increases, foramen ovale closes, and PDA begins to close
- Leads to decrease in pulmonary vascular resistance—allows complete vascular flow to lungs

 Major Changes That Occur in the Newborn Circulatory System

Suggestions for Classroom Activities

Have students complete "Case Study: Newborn Responses to Birth" on the Companion Website and discuss their answers. Review "Skill 5-1: Performing Nasal Pharyngeal Suctioning" on the Student CD-ROM and in the Clinical Skills Manual in class.

Suggestions for Clinical Activities

Rotate students through the nursery. Have students listen to a newborn's apical heart rate.

LEARNING OBJECTIVE 2

Describe how various factors affect the newborn's blood values.

CONCEPTS FOR LECTURE

1. Newborn blood values are affected by the site of the blood sample, gestational age, prenatal and/or perinatal hemorrhage, and timing of the clamping of the umbilical cord.

POWERPOINT LECTURE SLIDES

1 Blood Volume
- Blood volume of term infant estimated to be 80 mL/kg of body weight
- Varies with amount of placental transfusion received by the newborn during expulsion of placenta

1a Site of the Blood Sample
- Peripheral blood flow can be sluggish and create RBC stasis—increases RBC stasis
- Hemoglobin and hematocrit levels higher in capillary blood than in venous blood
- Blood vessels taken from venous samples are more accurate than capillary samples

1b Delayed Cord Clamping
- Blood volume increases by 50% with delayed cord clamping
- Placental vessels have 75 to 125 mL of blood at term
- Blood can transfer to newborn by holding newborn below levels of placenta and delay clamping of cord

1c Other Factors Impacting Blood Volume
- Positive association between gestational age, RBC numbers, and hemoglobin concentration
- Prenatal and perinatal hemorrhage decreases hematocrit level and can cause hypovolemia

1d Normal Term Newborn Cord Blood Values
- (Table 26.2)

SUGGESTIONS FOR CLASSROOM ACTIVITIES

Discuss physiological anemia in the newborn that is influenced by the nutritional status of the newborn. Ask students what factors impact the nutritional status of the newborn.

SUGGESTIONS FOR CLINICAL ACTIVITIES

During the clinical day, review the laboratory results of several newborns with the clinical group. Have students discuss normal and abnormal results and the related nursing implications.

LEARNING OBJECTIVE 3

Correlate the major mechanisms of heat loss in the newborn to the process of thermogenesis in the newborn.

CONCEPTS FOR LECTURE

1. Thermogenesis is achieved by: Increased basal metabolic rate, muscular activity, nonshivering thermogenesis, metabolizing of brown adipose fat.
2. Heat loss is created by: Evaporation (infant is wet from amniotic fluid and/or bath, convection, radiation, conduction.

POWERPOINT LECTURE SLIDES

1 Thermogenesis
- Nonshivering thermogenesis: Occurs when skin receptors perceive a drop in environmental temperature
- If newborn shivers, metabolic rate doubles
- Increased muscle activity

1a Thermogenesis
- BAT is primary source of heat in hypothermic newborn
  - Appears in fetus at 26 to 30 weeks
  - Increases until 2 to 5 weeks after birth

2 Methods of Heat Loss
- (Figure 26.5)

2a Heat Loss Is Created by
- Evaporation (example: wet with amniotic fluid)
- Convection (example: removed from incubator)
- Radiation (example: placing cold objects near incubator)
- Conduction (example: cold stethoscopes)

Suggestions for Classroom Activities

Newborns can chill very quickly. Bonding is encouraged in maternity nursing. Discuss with the students how the nurse can provide appropriate care and address both concerns. Assign "MediaLink Applications" exercises from the Companion Website for homework.

Suggestions for Clinical Activities

Have the students observe for examples of convection, radiation, evaporation, and conduction in the nursery.

Learning Objective 4

Explain the steps involved in the conjugation and excretion of bilirubin in the newborn.

Concepts for Lecture

1. Unconjugated bilirubin: A byproduct of the destruction of red blood cells. Bilirubin is bound to albumin. It is transferred into liver cells and bound to intracellular proteins. These proteins determine the amount of bilirubin uptake into the liver.
2. UDGPT causes unconjugated bilirubin to be attached to glucuronic acid, which produces conjugated bilirubin. This is excreted into the bile ducts, then into the common duct, and finally into the duodenum.
3. Bacteria transforms conjugated bilirubin into urobilinogen in the intestines and stercobilinogen, and it is excreted from the intestinal tract.

PowerPoint Lecture Slides

1 Conjugation of Bilirubin
- Byproduct of destruction of red blood cells—unconjugated hemoglobin
- Bilirubin bound to albumin and transferred to liver—bound to intracellular proteins

1b Conjugation of Bilirubin in Newborn

2 Conjugation of Bilirubin
- UDGPT enzyme leads to unconjugated bilirubin attached to glucuronic acid—leads to conjugated bilirubin
- Conjugated bilirubin excreted via common bile ducts into duodenum
- In intestine, bacteria transform conjugate bilirubin into urobilinogen and stercobilinogen (excreted as stone)

3 Recycling of Bilirubin
- Bilirubin can be changed back to unconjugated bilirubin—with very high beta-glucuronidase activity and delayed colonization of intestinal tract

LEARNING OBJECTIVE 5

Discuss the reasons a newborn may develop jaundice.

CONCEPTS FOR LECTURE

1. Newborns may develop jaundice because of: Accelerated destruction of fetal RBCs, impaired conjugation of bilirubin, increase bilirubin reabsorption from the intestinal tract.

POWERPOINT LECTURE SLIDES

1 Physiologic Jaundice
   - Occurs in 50% of term and 80% of preterm newborns
   - Caused by accelerated destruction of fetal RBCs and increased reabsorption of bilirubin by liver

1a Increased Amounts of Bilirubin in the Liver
   - Forceps or vacuum extraction can create more bilirubin to be handled by liver
   - Increased blood volume from delayed cord clamping with faster RBC destruction leads to increased bilirubin in blood

1b Impaired Conjugation of Bilirubin
   - Newborn does not take in calories
   - Mother may be breastfeeding
   - Defect in bilirubin excretion because of decreased GI motility—decreased oxygen to the liver

1c Increased Bilirubin Reabsorption
   - Reduced bowel motility, intestinal obstruction, or delayed passage of meconium
   - Leads to increased circulation of bilirubin in enterohepatic pathway and results in higher bilirubin levels

LEARNING OBJECTIVE 6

Describe the functional abilities of the newborn's gestational tract and liver.

CONCEPTS FOR LECTURE

1. At birth the newborn can digest most simple carbohydrates, proteins, and fats. The newborn has trouble digesting starches.
2. Meconium is passed within 24 to 48 hours after birth and then the newborn begins to have normal bowel movements.

POWERPOINT LECTURE SLIDES

1 Digestion and Absorption
   - Newborn has enough intestinal and pancreatic enzymes to digest simple carbohydrates, proteins, and fats—newborn cannot digest starch
   - By birth, newborn has experienced swallowing, gastric emptying, and propulsion

3. The newborn liver is slightly less active than the adult liver. This indicates the liver has a decreased ability to conjugate all of the bilirubin produced by the destruction of fetal RBCs. The liver plays a crucial role in iron storage, carbohydrate metabolism, and coagulation.

2. Elimination
   - Meconium is formed in utero
   - Newborn passes meconium within 48 hours—frequency of bowel movement varies

2a. Newborn Stool Samples
   - (Figure 26.8)

3. Newborn Liver
   - Slightly less active than the adult liver—may have dificulty conjugating bilirubin
   - Crucial role in iron storage: Carbohydrate metabolism (enzymes) and coagulation

SUGGESTIONS FOR CLASSROOM ACTIVITIES

Discuss typical characteristics of the newborn GI tract. Ask the class to break into small groups and discuss nursing assessments related to the GI tract. Compare group results and have the class prioritize the assessments.

SUGGESTIONS FOR CLINICAL ACTIVITIES

Have students check the different types of formula available in the nursery. Have them compare and contrast content of formulas. Ask them to research the different indications for these formulas and report results of the search.

LEARNING OBJECTIVE 7

Identify three reasons a newborn's kidneys have difficulty in maintaining fluid and electrolyte balance.

CONCEPTS FOR LECTURE

1. The following characteristics of a newborn's kidneys cause difficulty in maintaining fluid and electrolyte balance: Decreased rate of glomerular flow and limited excretion of solutes; limited tubular reabsorptions, limited ability to concentrate urine.
2. Most newborns void within 48 hours of birth.

POWERPOINT LECTURE SLIDES

1. Newborn Kidney Difficulty in Maintaining Fluid and Electrolyte Balance
   - Characteristics
     - Decreased rate of glomerular flow and limited secretion of solutes
     - Limited tubular reabsorption
     - Limited ability to concentrate urine

2. Voiding
   - 93% void by 24 hours after birth and 100% void by 48 hours after birth—initial bladder volume is 6 to 44 mL of urine
   - If newborn does not void within 48 hours, nurse should assess adequacy of fluid intake, bladder distention, restlessness, and symptoms of pain

2a. Newborn Urinalysis Values
   - (Table 26.5)

SUGGESTIONS FOR CLASSROOM ACTIVITIES

Discuss nursing observations needed when the newborn has not voided within 48 hours. Ask students to discuss how they know if the newborn's fluid intake is adequate. What are indicators of bladder distention?

SUGGESTIONS FOR CLINICAL ACTIVITIES

Have students observe the urinary function of the newborn. Ask them to document the color and odor of urine and the appearance of the diaper. Ask students to compare observations in clinical conference.

LEARNING OBJECTIVE 8

List the immunologic responses available to the newborn.

CONCEPTS FOR LECTURE

1. The newborn is unable to recognize, localize, and destroy bacteria.
2. The newborn has passive acquired immunity from the mother, which lasts from 4 weeks to 8 months.
3. The newborn begins to produce its own immunity at about 4 weeks of age.

POWERPOINT LECTURE SLIDES

1 The Newborn's Immune System
- Immune system isn't fully activated until after birth—newborn has poor hypothalamic response to pyrogens
- Fever not reliable indicator of infection—in newborn period, hypothermia is more reliable indicator of infections

2 Passive Immunity from the Mother
- Lasts 4 weeks
  - Passive acquired immunity occurs during third trimester
  - Preterm infant may be more susceptible to infection

3 Newborn's Own Immunity
- Breastfed newborn may have passive immunity from mother
- Newborns start to produce secretory IgA in the intestinal mucosa at four weeks

SUGGESTIONS FOR CLASSROOM ACTIVITIES

Signs and symptoms of infections are subtle in the newborn. With the class, develop a nursing care plan with the diagnoses of high-risk for infection. Brainstorm with the group regarding nursing assessments and interventions.

SUGGESTIONS FOR CLINICAL ACTIVITIES

Ask students to discuss 3 to 5 situations that may place the newborn at risk for infection since the immune system is not fully activated. Ask the group to develop a "consensus" regarding what nurses can teach parents about these situations.

LEARNING OBJECTIVE 9

Explain the physiologic and behavioral responses of newborns during periods of reactivity and identify possible interventions.

CONCEPTS FOR LECTURE

1. The first period of reactivity lasts 30 minutes after birth: The newborn is awake and active, appears hungry, has a strong suck; can initiate breastfeeding; vital signs are elevated. The period of inactivity to sleep lasts 30 minutes to 4 hours: The newborn is difficult to awaken; vital signs return to normal. The second period of reactivity lasts 4 to 6 hours after birth: Vital signs are variable; meconium stool is passed; newborn shows a readiness to feed.
2. The behavioral states of the newborn can be divided into the sleep state and the alert state.

POWERPOINT LECTURE SLIDES

1 First Period of Reactivity
- Period lasts about 30 minutes
- Newborn is awake and active
- Appears hungry and has a strong reflex
- Natural opportunity to start breastfeeding
- Vital signs are elevated

1a Inactivity to Sleep Phase
- After 30 minutes, newborn's activity gradually decreases
- Heart rate and respiration decrease as newborn enters sleep phase
- Will be difficult to awaken and will show no interest in sucking

1b Second Period of Reactivity
- Period of reactivity lasts 4 to 6 hours in normal newborn

- Heart and respiratory rates increase, nurse needs to be alert for apneic periods
  - Newborn passes meconium
  - Newborn sucks, roots, and swallows

 Newborn Behavior
- Sleep states: Deep or quiet sleep and active rapid eye movements (REM)
  - Length of cycle depends on age of newborn
  - Growth hormone secretion depends on regular sleep patterns
- Alert States
  - First 30 to 60 minutes after birth, many newborns display quiet alert state
  - Nurses should use alert states to encourage bonding and breastfeeding
  - Increasing wakefulness indicates maturing ability to maintain consciousness
- Subcategories include
  - Drowsy or semidozing
  - Wide awake, active awake, and crying
- Use time to facilitate feedings

Mother and Newborn Gaze at Each Other
- (Figure 26.9)

SUGGESTIONS FOR CLASSROOM ACTIVITIES

Discuss why new parents need to know about periods of reactivity and behavioral states.

SUGGESTIONS FOR CLINICAL ACTIVITIES

Students should compare periods of reactivity in infants born 12 hours apart. Have the students share their findings in clinical conference.

LEARNING OBJECTIVE 10

Describe the normal sensory perceptual abilities and behavioral states seen in the newborn period.

CONCEPTS FOR LECTURE

1. The normal sensory-perceptual abilities of the newborn are: Visual, auditory, olefactory, taste and sucking, and tactile.
2. Some of the behavioral capabilities of the newborn that assist in adaptation to extrauterine life include self-quieting ability and habituation.

POWERPOINT LECTURE SLIDES

Visual Ability
- Normal visual sensory-perceptual abilities of newborn are
  - Newborn is able to be alert, follow, and fixate on complex visual simuli for short periods of time
  - Orientation

Head Turning to Follow Movement
- (Figure 26.10)

Auditory Ability
- Normal auditory sensory-perceptual abilities of newborn are
  - Newborn able to be alert and search for appealing auditory stimulus
  - Newborn can process and respond to visual and auditory stimulation
  - Habituation

Olfactory, Taste, Suckling, Tactile
- Olfactory: Newborn able to select people by smell
- Taste and suckling: Newborn able to respond selectively to different tastes
- Newborn very sensitive to being touched, cuddled, and held
- Newborn able to attend to and interact with environment

2 Behavioral Capabilities
- Some behavioral capabilities of newborn that assist in adaptation to extrauterine life include
  - Habituation
  - Self-quieting ability

Suggestions for Classroom Activities

Differentiate between the alert and sleep states of a newborn. Ask students what they think families need to know about these states.

Suggestions for Clinical Activities

Ask students to observe newborns sleeping in the nursery. Ask them to discuss why they think newborns can sleep in a lighted and noisy environment.

CHAPTER 27
NURSING ASSESSMENT OF THE NEWBORN

RESOURCE LIBRARY

 CD-ROM

NCLEX-RN® Review
Audio Glossary

 COMPANION WEBSITE

NCLEX-RN® Review
Medialink Applications:
   Case Study: Newborn Maturity Assessment
   Care Plan Activity: Assessment of the Newborn
Thinking Critically

📖 IMAGE LIBRARY

Explain the various components of the gestational age assessment.

CONCEPTS FOR LECTURE

1. The common physical characteristics included in the gestational age assessment are skin, lanugo, sole (plantar) creases, breast tissues and size, ear form and cartilage, genitalia.
2. The neuromuscular components of gestational age scoring tools are posture, square window sign, popliteal angle, arm recoil, heel-to-toe extension, scarf signs.
3. By assessing the physical and neuromuscular components specified in the gestational age tool, the nurse determines the gestational age of the newborn and identifies the newborn as SGA, AGA, or LGA and prioritizes individual needs.

POWERPOINT LECTURE SLIDES

1 Gestational Age Assessment
- Two parts
  ○ External physical characteristics
  ○ Neurologic characteristics
- Maternal conditions, such as preeclampsia, diabetes, and maternal analgesics and anesthesia may impact certain components of gestational assessment

1a Timing and Types of Newborn Assessment
- (Table 27.1)

1b Assessment of Physical Maturity Characteristics
- Observable characteristics of newborn should be evaluated while not disturbing baby
- Gestational assessments tools examine following physical characteristics
  ○ Resting posture
  ○ Skin
  ○ Lanugo
  ○ Sole (plantar) creases
  ○ Breast tissue
  ○ Ear form and cartilage distribution
  ○ Evaluation of genitals

1c Male Genitals
- (Figure 27.6)

1d Female Genitals
- (Figue 27.7)

2 Neuromuscular Components
- Examine posture, square window sign, popliteal angle, arm recoil, heel-to-toe extension, scarf sign
- Nurse determines gestational age of newborn and identifies newborn as small for gestational age (SGA), appropriate for gestational age (AGA), or large for gestational age (LGA) and prioritizes needs

2a Square Window Sign
- (Figure 27.8)

2b Scarf Sign
- (Figure 27.9)

PowerPoint Lecture Slides *continued*

3 Classification of Newborn by Birth Weight and Gestational Age
- (Figure 27.12)

Suggestions for Classroom Activities

Assign before class, "Case Study: Newborn Maturity Assessment" from the Companion Website. Discuss answers in class with the students. If possible bring copies of the Ballard and Dubowitz rating scales to class.

Suggestions for Clinical Activities

Have students complete a gestational age assessment on a newborn. They should compare their results with that of the nursery nurse.

Learning Objective 2

Describe the normal physical and behavioral characteristics of the newborn.

Concepts for Lecture

1. Normal range for newborn vital signs include heart rate: 120 to 160 beats per minutes; respiration: 30 to 60 respirations per minutes; axillary temperature: 36.1 to 37.2°C (97.5 to 99°F); skin temperature: 36 to 36.5°C (96.8 to 97.7°F); rectal temperature, 36.6 to 37.2°C (97.8 to 99°F); blood pressure at birth: 80-60/45-40 mm Hg.
2. Normal newborn measurements include: Weight range: 2500 to 4000 g (5 lb, 8 oz to 8 lb, 13 oz), with weight dependent on maternal size and age; length range: 46 to 56 cm (18 to 22 in); head circumference range: 32 to 37 cm (12.5 to 14. 5 in)—approximately 2 cm larger than the chest circumference.
3. The newborn infant should have a head that appears large for its body. The normal newborn has a prominent abdomen, sloping shoulders, narrow hips, and rounded chest. The body appears long and the extremities short.
4. Newborns tend to stay in flexed position and will resist straightening of the extremities. Hands remain clenched. Behaviorally, the infant will sleep the majority of the time and wake for feeding. The infant should be easily consoled when upset.

PowerPoint Lecture Slides

1 Temperature
- Can be assessed by axillary skin method, continuous skin probe, rectal route—axillary temperature is preferred method
- Research indicates tympanic and digital axillary methods are accurate indicators of body temperature
- Temperature instability indicates infection

1a Axillary Temperature Measurements
- (Figure 27.16)

2 Newborn Measurements
- (Table 27.2)

2a Newborn Measurements
- Normal newborn measurements include:
  ○ Weight range: 2500 to 4000 g (5 lb, 8 oz to 8 lb, 13 oz), weight dependent on maternal size and age
  ○ Length range: 46 to 56 cm (18 to 22 in)
  ○ Head circumference range: 32 to 37 cm (12.5 to 14.5 in)

3 Head and Abdomen
- Newborn infant should have a head that appears large for its body
- Newborn has prominent abdomen, sloping shoulders, narrow hips, rounded chest—head is approximately 2 cm larger than chest circumference

4 Position and Behavior
- Newborns tend to stay in flexed position and will resist straightening
- Hands remain clenched
- Infant will sleep majority of time and wake for feeding—easily consoled when upset

SUGGESTIONS FOR CLASSROOM ACTIVITIES

Bring several newborn measurements (head, weight, and height) and growth charts to class. Have students practice graphing newborn measurements on the growth charts.

SUGGESTIONS FOR CLINICAL ACTIVITIES

Have students take vital signs and measurements on a newborn. Ask them to compare results with Table 27.4.

LEARNING OBJECTIVE 3

Summarize the components of a complete newborn assessment and the significance of normal variations and abnormal findings.

CONCEPTS FOR LECTURE

1. Basis for complete newborn assessment includes: Prenatal history, determination of gestational age, physical assessment, behavioral assessment.
2. Components of a complete newborn physical assessment include: Vital signs; weight length and head circumference; skin appearance and presence of birthmarks; examination of the head for size, appearance, symmetry, presence and status of fontanelles; hair appearance; condition and symmetry of face, eyes, and ears; appearance and condition of the nose and mouth; appearance of chest and auscultation of lungs and heart; appearance of abdomen and presence of bowel sounds; inspect umbilical stump for two arteries and one vein; appearance of appropriate genitalia; condition and patency of anus; position and condition of extremities, trunk, and spine.
3. The nurse should be knowledgeable about variations that are indicative of normal newborn responses as well as those that indicate a need for further investigation.
4. An important role of the nurse during the physical and behavioral assessments of the newborn is to teach the parents about their newborn and involve them in their baby's care. This involvement facilitates the parents' identification of their newborn's uniqueness and allays their concern.

POWERPOINT LECTURE SLIDES

1 Assessment
- Nurse includes prenatal, labor, and birthing data with assessment findings as well as gestational, behavioral, and physical assessments of newborn
- Done in first 1 to 4 hours after birth

2 Physical Assessment and Findings
- Monitor BP in cases of distress, premature birth, and anomaly
- Assess for capillary refill
- Evaluate for cold stress—notify physician of elevation or drop in temperature
- Idenitfy sleep-wake state and correlate with respiration
- Evaluate for respiratory distress

2a Weight
- Plot weight and gestational age on growth chart
- Ascertain body build of parents
- Feed infant early post birth
- Calculate fluid intake and losses
- Daily weights
- Ascertain if there is dwarfism
- Determine other signs of skeletal system adequacy

2b Posture, Skin, Hair
- Record spontaneity of motor activity and symmetry of movements
- Evaluate skin texture, turgor, pigmentation variations, and birthmarks
- Assess location and type of rash—examine for petechiae
- Examine the texture and distribution of hair
- Record size and shape of birthmarks

2c Head
- Head circumference should be 2 cm greater than chest circumference
- Assess fontanelles and sutures—observe for signs of hydrocephalus and evaluate neurologic status

2d Comparison of Cephalhematoma and Caput Succedaneum
- (Table 27.3)

Caput Succedaneum
- (Figure 27.26)

 Cephalhematoma
- (Figure 27.25)

 Face, Mouth, Eyes, and Ears
- Assess and record symmetry
- Assess for signs of Down syndrome
- Low-set ears
- Assess history for risk factors for hearing loss
- Test for Moro reflex
- Check for presence of gag, swallowing reflexes, coordinated with sucking reflex
- Check for clefts in either hard or soft palates
- Check for excessive drooling
- Check tongue for deviation, white cheesy coating

 Eyes
- Assess for PERLA (pupils equal and reactive to light and accommodation)
- Assess cornea and blink reflex
- Note true eye color does not occur before 6 months
- May have blocked tear duct
- Assess true blue sclera (osteogenic imperfecta)

 Heart and Lungs
- Assess and maintain airway
- Assess heart rate, rhythm—evaluate murmur: location, timing, and duration
  - Examine appearance and size of chest
  - Note if there is funnel chest, barrel chest, unequal chest expansion
- Assess breath sounds and respiratory efforts—evalaute color for pallor or cyanosis
- Breasts are flat with symmetric nipples—note lack of breast tissue or discharge

 Abdomen
- Abdomen appears large in relation to pelvis
  - Note increase or decrease in peristalsis
  - Note protrusion of umbilicus
- Measure umbilical hernia by palpating the opening and record
  - Note any discharge or oozing from cord
  - Note appearance and amount of vessels
- Auscultate and percuss abdomen
  - Assess for signs of dehydration
  - Assess femoral pulses
  - Note bulges in inguinal area
  - Percuss bladder 1 to 4 cm above symphysis
  - Voids within 3 hours of birth or at time of birth

 Umbilical Hernia
- (Figure 27.34)

Genitals

- Examine labia majora, labia minora, and clitoris—note size of each for gestational age assessment
- Observe for pseudomenstruation
- Inspect penis to determine whether urinary meatus is correctly positioned
- Check for phimosis
- Warm hand when inspecting scrotum
- Palpate testes separately
- Assess for hydrocele
- Note discoloration and edema (common in breech births)

 Anus

- Inspect anal area to verify that it is patent and has no fissure
- Digital exam by physician or nurse practitioner if needed
- Note passage of meconium

Extremities

- Examine extremities for gross deformities
  - Note position and condition of extremities and trunk
  - Examine more closely when infant is reluctant to move an extremity—note if there is brachial palsy or Erb-Duchenne paralysis
- Check for developmental dysplasia of the hip—perform Ortolani's maneuver or Barlow's maneuver
- Examine the back for associations with any neural tube defects

 Checking for Developmental Dysplasia of the Hip

- (Figure 27.36)

 Clubfoot

- Nurse examines feet for evidence of talipes deformity (clubfoot)
- Intrauterine positions can cause feet to appear to turn inward—"positional" clubfoot
- To determine presence of clubfoot, nurse moves foot to midline—if resists, it is true clubfoot

 Unilateral Clubfeet

 Nursing Role

- Be knowledgeable about normal newborn variations and responses that indicate further investigation
  - Respiratory distress
  - Central cyanosis
  - Thermoregulation problems
  - Dehydration
  - Imperforated anus
  - Failure to pass meconium
  - Evidence of neural tube defects
  - Evidence of need for genetic referral

4 Teaching
- During physical and behavioral assessment, identify family's need for teaching
  ○ Involve family early in care of infant
  ○ Process establishes uniqueness and allays concern
- Teaching
  ○ Feeding cues
  ○ Alert state
  ○ Cord care
  ○ Sleeping

SUGGESTIONS FOR CLASSROOM ACTIVITIES

Demonstrate physical assessment on a newborn/infant in class. Show students how they can access growth charts from nursing tools on the Companion Website. Give examples of measurements they can plot on a growth chart. Assign "Care Plan: Assessment of the Newborn" activity on the Companion Website as homework.

SUGGESTIONS FOR CLINICAL ACTIVITIES

Assign students to teach a new mother about the physical characteristics of her new infant. What do parents need to know to better meet their infant's needs?

LEARNING OBJECTIVE 4

Discuss the neurologic and neuromuscular characteristics of the newborn and the reflexes that may be present at birth.

CONCEPTS FOR LECTURE

1. Neurolgic assessment characteristics are state of alertness, resting positon, muscle tone, cry, motor activity.
2. Neuromuscular assessment characteristics are symmetric movements and strength of all extremities, head lag less than 45 degrees, ability to hold head erect briefly.
3. Normal reflexes are blink, pupillary reflex, Moro, rooting and sucking, palmar grasp, plantar grasp, stepping, Babinski, tonic neck, prone crawl, trunk incurvation.

POWERPOINT LECTURE SLIDES

1 Neurological Status
- Assessment begins with period of observation
- Observe behaviors—note:
  ○ State of alertness
  ○ Resting posture
  ○ Cry
  ○ Quality of muscle tone
  ○ Motor activity
  ○ Jitteriness
  ○ Differentiate causative factors

2 Neuromuscular Assessment
- Examine for symmetry and strength of movements
- Note head lag of less than 45 degrees
- Assess ability to hold head erect briefly

3 Reflexes
- Immature central nervous system CNS of newborn is characterized by variety of reflexes
  ○ Some reflexes are protective, some aid in feeding, others stimulate interaction
  ○ Assess for CNS integration
- Protective reflexes are blinking, yawning, coughing, sneezing, drawing back from pain
- Rooting and sucking reflexes assist with feeding

3a Moro Reflex
- (Figure 27.39)

3b Tonic Neck Reflex

3c Stepping Reflex
  • (Figure 27.43)

3d The Babinski Reflex
  • (Figure 27.42)

SUGGESTIONS FOR CLASSROOM ACTIVITIES

Before class, assign students to search the Web for information on newborn reflexes. Demonstrate neurological assessment on a newborn or "realistic" newborn model. Then, ask students to relate what they read on newborn reflexes with the instructor demonstration.

SUGGESTIONS FOR CLINICAL ACTIVITIES

Have students do a neurological assessment on a newborn. Ask them to compare their results with the normal ranges in the book.

LEARNING OBJECTIVE 5

Describe the categories of the newborn behavioral assessment.

CONCEPTS FOR LECTURE

1. The categories of the newborn behavioral assessment are: Habitation, orientation to inanimate and animate visual and auditory assessment stimuli; motor activity; frequency of alert states, state changes, color changes, activity, and peaks of activity, self quieting activity; cuddliness.

POWERPOINT LECTURE SLIDES

1 Newborn Behavioral Assessment
  • Parents may have conflicting perceptions of their newborn—nurses can help parents to identify specific behaviors of their infant
  • Observations of neonatal behaviors provide important data about well-being of newborn and individualized patterns of activity and sleep

1a Brazelton Neonatal Behavioral Assessment Scale
  • Assists in assessing newborn's state changes, temperament, individual behavior patterns
  • Assists families in learning which responses and interventions best meet need of newborn

1b Assessment
  • Assess first in quiet, softly lit room—observe for
    ○ Habitation
    ○ Orientation to inanimate and animate visual and auditory assessment stimuli
    ○ Motor activity
    ○ Frequency of alert states, state changes, color changes, peaks of activity
    ○ Self-quieting activity
    ○ Cuddliness

SUGGESTIONS FOR CLASSROOM ACTIVITIES

Discuss how information from the Brazelton Neonatal Behavioral Assessment can individualize teaching plans for parents.

SUGGESTIONS FOR CLINICAL ACTIVITIES

Ask students to observe sleep-wake patterns and to see how rapidly the newborn moves from one state to another. Ask students to document if the newborn can be consoled.

CHAPTER 28
NORMAL NEWBORN: NEEDS AND CARE

RESOURCE LIBRARY

CD-ROM

NCLEX-RN® Review
Video: Newborn Care
Skill 4-4: Assisting with Breasfeeding after Childbirth
Skill 5-1: Performing Nasal Pharyngeal Suctioning
Skill 5-3: Thermoregulation of the Newborn
Skill 10-1: Performing a Capillary Puncture
Audio Glossary

COMPANION WEBSITE

NCLEX-RN® Review
Case Study: Newborn Care
Care Plan Activity: Initial Newborn Care
Care Plan Activity: Infant Care During Transition
Thinking Critically

 IMAGE LIBRARY

Figure 28.1 Weighing of newborns.
Figure 28.2 Temperature monitoring of the newborn.
Figure 28.3 Procedure for vitamin K injection.
Figure 28.4 Injection sites.
Figure 28.5 Ophthalmic ointment.
Figure 28.6 The umbilical cord base is carefully cleansed.
Figure 28.7 Circumcision using a circumcision clamp.
Figure 28.8 Circumcision using the Plastibell.
Figure 28.9 Following circumcision, petroleum ointment may be applied to the site for the next few diaper changes.
Figure 28.10 A letter from your baby.

Figure 28.11 A father demonstrates competence and confidence in diapering his newborn daughter.
Figure 28.12 Nasal and oral suctioning.
Figure 28.13 Steps in wrapping a baby.
Figure 28.14 Infant car restraint for use from birth to about 12 months of age.
Figure 28.15 The infant teaching checklist is completed by the time of discharge.

Table 28.1 Signs of Newborn Transition
Table 28.2 Signs of Newborn Distress
Table 28.3 When Parents Should Call Their Healthcare Provider

LEARNING OBJECTIVE 1

Summarize the essential areas of information to be obtained about a newborn's birth experience and immediate postnatal period.

CONCEPTS FOR LECTURE

1. Information is gathered from the following sources on the condition of the newborn: Apgar scores, any resuscitation effort, vital signs, voiding, passage of meconium.
2. Labor and birth record: Length and course of labor, type of delivery, conditions at delivery, medications given during labor.
3. Antepartal record: Infections during pregnancy, estimated date of birth (EDB), previous pregnancies, any congenital anomalies, HIV test result.
4. Parent-newborn interaction information: Type of infant feeding desired, desire for circumcision if infant is male, support system available, whether rooming-in is desired.

POWERPOINT LECTURE SLIDES

1 Condition of the Newborn
  • Apgar scores
  • Any resuscitation effort
  • Vital signs
  • Voiding
  • Passage of meconium

1a Signs of Newborn Transition
  • (Table 28.1)

2 Labor and Birth Records
  • Length and course of labor
  • Type of delivery
  • Conditions at delivery
  • Medications given during labor

3 Antepartal Record
- Infections during pregnancy
- Estimated date of birth (EDB)
- Previous pregnancies
- Any congenital anomalies
- HIV test result

4 Parent and Newborn Interaction Information
- Type of infant feeding desired
- Desire for circumcision if infant is male
- Support system available
- Whether rooming-in is desired

SUGGESTIONS FOR CLASSROOM ACTIVITIES

Discuss the family adjustments that must be made after the birth of a newborn. Describe how parents can enhance infant attachment.

SUGGESTIONS FOR CLINICAL ACTIVITIES

Have students assist with the admission of a newborn to the nursery. Have them develop a priority nursing diagnoses list for the newborn just admitted to the nursery.

LEARNING OBJECTIVE 2

Relate the physiologic and behavioral responses of the newborn to possible interventions needed.

CONCEPTS FOR LECTURE

1. Maintenance of a clear airway and stable vital signs: The infant's cardiovascular and respiratory system are changing rapidly: the infant is dried and stimulated to breathe; free-flow oxygen is available to assist the infant's transition. Apgar score and vital signs are used to assess the infant's transition.

2. Maintenance of a neutral thermal environment: The infant is stressed by the change from the warm, moist environment of the uterus to the dry, drafty environment of the delivery room and nursery; a neutral thermal environment is needed to prevent the need for increased oxygen and calories; the newborn is dried and placed under a radiant warmer; a cap is placed on the infant's head to prevent heat loss; temperature is checked frequently and the infant is kept from drafts and open windows.

3. Prevention of hemorrhagic disease in the newborn: Newborn lacks intestinal bacterial flora, which is necessary for the production of vitamin K; prothrombin levels are low during the first few days of life; vitamin K injection is given IM quickly after birth.

POWERPOINT LECTURE SLIDES

1 Maintenance of a Clear Airway and Stable Vital Signs
- Infant's cardiovascular and respiratory system change rapidly
- Infant is dried and stimulated to breathe
- Free flow oxygen available to assist infant's transition
- Apgar score and vital signs used to assess infant's transition

2 Neutral Thermal Environment
- Infant stressed by change from warm, moist environment of uterus to dry, drafty environment of delivery room and nursery
- Neutral thermal environment needed to prevent need for increased oxygen and calories
- Newborn is dried and placed under radiant warmer
- Cap placed on infant's head to prevent heat loss
- Temperature checked frequently and infant is kept from drafts and open windows

2a Temperature Monitoring of Newborn
- (Figure 28.2)

3 Prevention of Hemorrhage
- Newborn lacks intestinal bacterial flora necessary for production of vitamin K
- Prothrombin levels low during first few days of life
- Vitamin K injection given IM quickly after birth

3a Vitamin K Injections
- (Figure 28.3)

4. Prevention of eye infection: Infant may come in contact with infected material during birth; eye prophylaxis is given to all newborns to prevent serious eye infection.
5. Assessment of neonatal distress: The nurse assesses and teaches parents signs and symptoms of respiratory distress such as tachypnea, grunting, retractions, or change in color; parents are taught use of the bulb syringe and proper positioning to prevent respiratory problems.
6. Expected periods of reactivity: The infant is usually alert for the first hour after birth; the nurse should encourage eye-to-eye contact between the infant and the parents; nurse should initiate first feedings if infant is stable.

3b Injection Sites
- (Figure 28.4)

4 Prevention of Eye Infections
- Infant may come in contact with infected material during birth
- Eye prophylaxis given to all newborns to prevent serious eye infection

4a Ophthalmic Ointment
- (Figure 28.5)

5 Assessment of Neonatal Distress
- Nurse assesses and teaches parents signs and symptoms of respiratory distress—tachypnea, grunting, retractions, change in color
- Parents taught use of bulb syringe and proper positioning to prevent respiratory problems

5a Signs of Newborn Distress
- (Table 28.2)

6 Expected Period of Reactivity
- Infant usually alert for first hour after birth
- Nurse should encourage eye-to-eye contact between infant and parents
- Nurse should initiate first feedings if infant is stable

SUGGESTIONS FOR CLASSROOM ACTIVITIES

From the Student CD-ROM, show the video "Newborn Care." Discuss key aspects of newborn care. Using the CD-ROM or Clinical Skills Manual, address "Skill 5-3: Thermoregulation of the Newborn" and review "Skill 5-1: Performing Nasal Pharyngeal Suctioning." Explain to students key aspects of this procedure and what aspects can be taught to parents.

SUGGESTIONS FOR CLINICAL ACTIVITIES

Ask students to review the clinical agency's protocols for newborns at the time of admission to the nursery (e.g., eye prophylaxis, vitamin K injection, and hepatitis immunization). Have students complete "Thinking Critically: A Newborn with Respiratory Difficulty." Discuss the answers in clinical conference.

LEARNING OBJECTIVE 3

Discuss the major nursing considerations and activities to be carried out during the first four hours after birth (admission and transitional period) and subsequent daily care.

CONCEPTS FOR LECTURE

1. Nursing interventions during the first four hours after birth include: Monitor vital signs; assess and monitor skin color; assess condition of cord; assess weight, length, and head circumference; assess extremity movement; determine gestational age classification; assess for the presence of any anomalies; identify infant and initiate security system; check for expected reflexes; assess ability to suck and swallow; bathe infant when temperature is stable; assist mother to feed as soon as infant is stable; administer necessary medications.

POWERPOINT LECTURE SLIDES

1 Nursing Interventions
- Nursing interventions during first 4 hours after birth include
  - Monitor vital signs every hour, four times daily
  - Assess and monitor skin color, including acrocyanosis
  - Assess condition of cord (note number and type of vessels)
  - Assess weight, length, head circumference
  - Assess extremity movement

2. Subsequent daily care includes: Monitor vital signs every 6 to 8 hours; assess condition of umbilical cord; initiate hearing screening if applicable; assess infant's ability to void and stool; determine if infant is feeding adequately; swaddle infant to provide for warmth; initiate necessary immunizations; initiate newborn screening tests; provide teaching to parents concerning newborn care.

 Nursing Interventions
- Determine gestational age classification
- Assess for presence of any anomalies
- Identify infant and initiate security system
- Check for expected reflexes
- Assess ability to suck and swallow
- Bathe infant when temperature is stable
- Assist mother to feed as soon as infant is stable
- Administer necessary medications

 Subsequent Daily Care
- Monitor vital signs every 6 to 8 hours
- Assess condition of umbilical cord
- Initiate hearing screening if applicable
- Assess infant's ability to void and stool
- Determine if infant is feeding adequately
- Swaddle infant to provide for warmth
- Initiate necessary immunizations
- Initiate newborn screening tests
- Provide teaching to parents concerning newborn care

SUGGESTIONS FOR CLASSROOM ACTIVITIES

Demonstrate how expected reflexes are checked on a newborn using an infant if possible or a model.

SUGGESTIONS FOR CLINICAL ACTIVITIES

From the Companion Website, have students complete "Thinking Critically: Initial Newborn Care." Discuss responses in the clinical conference.

LEARNING OBJECTIVE 4

Identify the activities that should be included in a daily care plan for a normal newborn.

CONCEPTS FOR LECTURE

1. Essential daily care includes: Assessing vital signs; assessing weight; assessing overall color; assessing intake and output; assessing and caring for umbilical cord; assessing nutritional status; assessing parent attachment; educating parents.

POWERPOINT LECTURE SLIDES

 Essential Daily Care Assessments
- Vital signs
- Weight
- Overall color
- Intake and output
- Caring for umbilical cord
- Circumcision
- Nutritional status
- Parent attachment
- Parent Education

A Letter from Your Baby
- (Figure 28.10)

SUGGESTIONS FOR CLASSROOM ACTIVITIES

Demonstrate cord care on a model. Emphasize teaching points for parents. Read "A Letter from Your Baby" in class. Ask the class what parents can learn from this letter. Assign "Case Study: Newborn Care" from the Companion Website for homework.

SUGGESTIONS FOR CLINICAL ACTIVITIES

Have students observe a circumcision in the nursery. In clinical conference, ask the students to discuss nursing responsibilities related to the circumcision.

LEARNING OBJECTIVE 5

Determine common concerns of families regarding their newborns.

CONCEPTS FOR LECTURE

1. Most parents are concerned about the immediate health of the newborn; measures taken to ensure infant safety; how to provide general infant care; how to properly feed infant.

POWERPOINT LECTURE SLIDES

[1] Common Concerns
- Most parents concerned about
  - Use of bulb syringe
  - Signs of choking
  - Positioning
  - When to call for assistance
  - Temperature maintenance
  - Holding and feeding skills—latching-on techniques if breastfeeding; bottle-feeding techniques
  - Soothing and calming techniques
  - Diapering
  - Normal void and stool patterns
  - Bathing
  - Nail care
  - Circumcision/uncircumcised penis/genital care
  - Rashes
  - Jaundice
  - Sleep-wake cycles
  - Soothing activities
  - Signs and symptoms of illness
  - Infant safety—car seats
  - Immunizations, metabolic screening

SUGGESTIONS FOR CLASSROOM ACTIVITIES

Discuss measures at local healthcare facilities to ensure newborn safety. Delineate how new parents can make a home secure for a newborn.

SUGGESTIONS FOR CLINICAL ACTIVITIES

Ask students to develop a list of community resources for car seats. Have them review the procedure for securing these car seats for parents with a need. Ask students to compare safety, weight, and height ratings for these car seats.

LEARNING OBJECTIVE 6

Describe topics and related content to be included in parent teaching on newborn and infant care.

CONCEPTS FOR LECTURE

1. Parent teaching of newborn and infant care include: Safety measures.
2. Voiding and stool characteristics and patterns.
3. Cord care.
4. Male genitalia care.
5. How to awaken infant.
6. How to quiet infant.
7. Signs of illness.

POWERPOINT LECTURE SLIDES

[1] Safety Measures
- How to properly use bulb syringe
- How to safely place infant in crib
- Watch for excessive mucus

[2] Voiding and Stool Characteristics and Patterns
- Normal color of urine and appropriate number of voidings
- Color, type, and number of expected stool—normal progression of stool changes
  - Meconium (thick, tarry, dark green)
  - Transitional stools (thin, brown to green)
  - Breastfed infant: yellow gold, soft or mushy stool

    ◦ Formula-fed infant: pale yellow, formed and pasty stools

3 Cord Care
- How to keep cord clean and dry
- How to keep diapers from irritating cord
- Normal changes of cord
- Do not give tub bath until cord falls off in 7 to 14 days
- Check cord daily for odor, oozing, and reddened areas

3a Umbilical Cord Care
- (Figure 28.6)

4 Male Genitalia Care
- If circumcised
  - Signs and symptoms of complications from circumcision
  - Care and cleaning of uncircumcised infant
  - Avoid positioning baby on his stomach
  - Check for any foul-smelling drainage or bleeding at least once a day—light, sticky, yellow drainage part of healing process
- If uncircumcised
  - Clean penis with water during diaper changes and with bath
  - Do not force foreskin back over penis

4a Circumcision Care
- (Figure 28.9)

5 How to Awaken an Infant
- Dress, undress, or bathe hands and feet of infant
- Change diaper
- Talk to infant, place in upright position
- Increase skin contact
- Hand-express milk onto baby's lips
- Stimulate rooting reflex—brush one cheek with hand or nipple

6 How to Quiet an Infant
- Move infant slowly and calmly
- Burp infant or change soiled diaper
- Swaddle infant
- Talk to or coo to infant

7 Signs of Illness
- Temperature
  - How to take temperature—axillary temperature above 38°C (100.4°F) or below 36.6°C (97.8°F)
  - Continual rise in temperature
- More than one episode of forceful or frequent vomiting over six hours
- Refusal of two feedings in a row
- Lethargy (listlessness)

- Inconsolable infant
- Discharge/bleeding from umbilical cord, circumcision, or any opening
- Two consecutive green, watery stools
- No wet diapers for 18 to 24 hours—fewer than 6 to 8 wet diapers a day
- Development of eye drainage
- Know when to call the physician

Suggestions for Classroom Activities	Suggestions for Clinical Activities
Have students develop a detailed discharge summary on the various aspects of newborn teaching.	Ask students to develop a teaching care plan for new parents on how to quiet an infant. Ask them to present their care plans to the group in clinical conference.

Learning Objective 7

Identify opportunities to individualize parent teaching and enhance each parent's abilities and confidence while providing infant care in the birthing unit.

Concepts for Lecture

1. Individualized parent teaching is best accomplished by observation and demonstration of common infant activities.

PowerPoint Lecture Slides

`1` Individualized Parent Teaching
- Individualized parent teaching best accomplished by observation and demonstration of common infant activities such as
  - Feeding
  - Bathing
  - Diaper changing
  - Cord care
  - Circumcision care
  - Handling

`1a` Father Demonstrating Diapering
- (Figure 28.11)

`1b` Other Methods to Teach
- Videotapes of selected infant care activities
- Written handouts of selected infant care activities
- Return demonstration of parents completing selected infant care activities

Suggestions for Classroom Activities	Suggestions for Clinical Activities
Discuss various cultural beliefs and how they impact baby care. Discuss how this information can enhance the nurse's ability to meet the parents' teaching needs.	Ask students to review the various teaching handouts on the unit as well as the videos. Ask them to evaluate whether a demonstration by the nursing staff would enhance the videos or teaching handouts.

Delineate the information to be included in discharge planning with the newborn's family.

CONCEPTS FOR LECTURE

1. Prior to discharge the parents are instructed in the following: General baby care.
2. Breastfeeding, if applicable.
3. Bottle-feeding, if applicable.
4. Positioning of baby; follow-up care. *Refer to Figure 28.15.*

POWERPOINT LECTURE SLIDES

1 General Baby Care
- Safety measures
- Skin and cord care
- How to detect jaundice
- Normal newborn behavior
- How to know if infant is sick and phone number of infant's healthcare provider
- How to burp and position baby
- Circumcision care of male infant

1a When Parents Should Call Their Healthcare Provider
- (Table 28.3)

2 Breastfeeding: If Applicable
- Position of baby
- Supply and demand
- Latching on and breaking suction
- Supplementing
- Care of sore nipples and engorgement
- How to express milk by hand and the use of a breast pump

3 Bottle-feeding: If Applicable
- Position for feeding
- How to prepare formula and how to clean bottles and nipples
- Determination of proper formula

4 Additional Teaching Points
- Place baby on back to sleep
- Proper use of car seats
- Remaining newborn screenings and inform about when to return if further tests are needed
- Hearing loss can occur in 1 to 3 per 1,000 infants in normal newborn population; AAP Task Force recommends screening in all obstetric units prior to discharge
- Schedule for newborn immunizations; first dose of hepatitis B vaccine should be given prior to discharge
- Appointment for infant's next visit with healthcare provider

SUGGESTIONS FOR CLASSROOM ACTIVITIES

Delineate key indicators of illness in a newborn and what parents need to know so they can report it to their healthcare provider in a timely manner. Discuss local facilities' policy on newborn hearing screening.

SUGGESTIONS FOR CLINICAL ACTIVITIES

Have students research information about the "Back to Sleep" campaign. Ask them to develop a teaching plan for new parents.

Chapter 29
Newborn Nutrition

RESOURCE LIBRARY

💿 CD-ROM

NCLEX-RN® Review
Nursing in Actions: Breastfeeding
Audio Glossary

📖 IMAGE LIBRARY

Figure 29.2 Four common breastfeeding positions.
Figure 29.3 For many mothers, the nurse's support and knowledge are instrumental in establishing successful breastfeeding.
Figure 29.4 A, C-hold. B, Mother using C-hold.
Figure 29.5 A mother helps her newborn to latch on by tickling the baby's lower lip with her nipple until the baby opens her mouth.

COMPANION WEBSITE

NCLEX-RN® Review
Thinking Critically
Case Study: Breastfeeding Client
Care Plan Activity: Breastfeeding Concerns
Actions and Effects of Selected Drugs During Breastfeeding

Figure 29.9 An infant is supported comfortably during bottle-feeding.

Table 29.3 Formula Preparation

LEARNING OBJECTIVE 1

Compare the nutritional value and composition of breast milk and formula preparations.

CONCEPTS FOR LECTURE

1. Composition of breast milk: 10% solids consisting of carbohydrates, proteins, and fats. 90% is water.
2. Breast milk has immunologic and nutritional biodegradable properties that make it the optimal food for the first year of life.
3. Most common cow milk protein-based formulas attempt to duplicate the same concentration of carbohydrates, proteins, and fats as 20kcal/oz breast milk.

POWERPOINT LECTURE SLIDES

 Composition of Breast Milk
- Breast milk is 90% water; 10% solids consisting of carbohydrates, proteins, fats, minerals, and vitamins—gender specific
- Composition can vary according to gestational age and stage of lactation
- Helps meet changing needs of baby

2 Immunologic and Nutritional Properties
- Secretory IgA, immunoglobulin found in colostrum and breast milk, has antiviral, antibacterial, antigenic-inhibiting properties
  ○ Contains enzymes and leukocytes that protect against pathogens
  ○ Composed of lactose, lipids, polyunsaturated fatty acids, amino acids, especially taurine
  ○ Cholesterol, long-chain polyunsaturated fatty acids, and balance of amino acids in breast milk help with myelination and neurologic development

2a Participating in the Breastfeeding Experience

3 Formula Preparations
- Three categories of formulas based on cow milk proteins, soy protein-based formulas, specialized or therapeutic formulas—all are enriched with vitamins, particularly vitamin D
- Most common cow milk protein-based formulas attempt to duplicate same concentration of carbohydrates, proteins, fats as 20kcal/oz of breast milk

3a Formula Preparation
- (Table 29.3)

SUGGESTIONS FOR CLASSROOM ACTIVITIES

Invite a lactation consultant to class to present information on breastfeeding.

SUGGESTIONS FOR CLINICAL ACTIVITIES

Have students attend a La Leche meeting or a breastfeeding class. In post-conference, let them report their observations regarding the type of information and support offered at the meeting.

LEARNING OBJECTIVE 2

Discuss the advantages and disadvantages of breastfeeding and formula feeding for both mother and newborn.

CONCEPTS FOR LECTURE

1. Advantages of breastfeeding: Provides immunologic protection; infants digest and absorb components of breast milk easier; provides more vitamins to infant if mother's diet is adequate; strengthens the mother-infant attachment; no additional cost; breast milk requires no preparation.
2. Disadvantages of breastfeeding: Many medications pass through to breast milk; father unable to equally participate in actual feeding of infant; mother may have difficulty being separated from infant.
3. Advantages of bottle-feeding: Provides good nutrition to infant; father can participate in infant feeding patterns.
4. Disadvantages of bottle-feeding: May need to try different formulas before finding one that is well-tolerated by the infant; proper preparation is necessary for nutritional adequacy.

POWERPOINT LECTURE SLIDES

1 Advantages of Breastfeeding
- Provides immunologic protection
- Infants digest and absorb components of breast milk easier
- Provides more vitamins to infant if mother's diet is adequate
- Strengthens mother-infant attachment
- No additional cost
- Breast milk requires no preparation

1a C-Hold
- (Figure 29.4A)

2 Disadvantages of Breastfeeding
- Many medications pass through to breast milk
- Father unable to equally participate in actual feeding of infant
- Mother may have difficulty being separated from infant

3 Bottle-Feeding Advantages
- Provides good nutrition to infant
- Father can participate in infant feeding patterns

4 Bottle-Feeding Disadvantages
- May need to try different formulas before finding one that is well-tolerated by infant
- Proper preparation necessary for nutritional adequacy

SUGGESTIONS FOR CLASSROOM ACTIVITIES

Bring to class various types of infant formula and bottles. Bring various types of breast pumps and related equipment to class. Discuss the use, advantages, and disadvantages of the different equipment. Incorporate a list of community resources on nutrition into the lecture. Discuss with students how their clients can benefit from these resources.

SUGGESTIONS FOR CLINICAL ACTIVITIES

Have students work with nursery nurses to learn more about resources for bottle-feeding and breastfeeding. Assign students to a WIC clinical. Ask them to document in a journal the different types of teaching that families receive.

LEARNING OBJECTIVE 3

Develop guidelines for helping both breast- and formula-feeding mothers to feed their newborns successfully.

CONCEPTS FOR LECTURE

1. The breastfeeding mother needs to know: How breast milk is produced; how to correctly position the infant for feeding; the procedures for feeding the infant; how to express leaking milk; how to express and store breast milk; how and when to supplement with formula; how to care for the breasts; what medications pass through the breast milk; what kind of support groups are available for breastfeeding.
2. The bottle-feeding mother needs to know: Types of formula available and how to prepare each type; the procedure for feeding the infant; how to correctly position the infant for bottle feeding; how to safely store the formula; how to safely care for bottles and nipples.

POWERPOINT LECTURE SLIDES

1 Breastfeeding Mother
- Breastfeeding mother needs to know
  - How breast milk is produced
  - How to correctly position infant for feeding
  - Procedures for feeding infant
  - How to express leaking milk
  - How to express and store breast milk
  - How and when to supplement with formula
  - How to care for breasts
  - Medications that pass through breast milk
  - Support groups for breastfeeding

1a Common Breastfeeding Positions
- (Figure 29.2A–D)

1b Latching On
- (Figure 29.5)

1c Good Breastfeeding Positions

2 Bottle-Feeding Mother
- Bottle-feeding mother needs to know
  - Types of formula available and how to prepare each type
  - Procedure for feeding infant
  - How to correctly position infant for bottle-feeding
  - How to safely store formula
  - How to safely care for bottles and nipples

2a Bottle-Feeding Position
- (Figure 29.9)

SUGGESTIONS FOR CLASSROOM ACTIVITIES

Have students review "Actions and Effects of Selected Drugs During Breastfeeding" on the Student CD-ROM. Assign students to complete "Nursing in Action: Breastfeeding" activity on the Student CD-ROM.

SUGGESTIONS FOR CLINICAL ACTIVITIES

Have students complete the "Care Plan: Breastfeeding Concerns" on the Companion Website. The class should discuss the care plan, and as a group develop priority nursing diagnoses for the care plan.

LEARNING OBJECTIVE 4

Recognize the influence of cultural values on infant care, especially feeding practices.

CONCEPTS FOR LECTURE

1. Nurse must recognize that cultural values influence infant feeding practices. Be sensitive to ethnic backgrounds of minority populations. Understand that the dominant culture in any society defines normal maternal infant feeding.

POWERPOINT LECTURE SLIDES

1 Cultural Values
- Cultural values and society influence infant feeding—different practices are not necessarily inferior
- Culture often determines specifics of breastfeeding—perception of mother's role often determines mother's comfort with breastfeeding

SUGGESTIONS FOR CLASSROOM ACTIVITIES

Incorporate developing cultural competence in the breastfeeding lecture. Discuss the impact of culture on specific feeding practices. Have students complete "Case Study: Breastfeeding Client" on the Companion Website for homework.

SUGGESTIONS FOR CLINICAL ACTIVITIES

Assign students to research different cultures and how they view breastfeeding. Have students report on their research in clinical conference.

LEARNING OBJECTIVE 5

Delineate nursing responsibilities for client education about problems the breastfeeding mother may encounter at home.

CONCEPTS FOR LECTURE

1. Nursing responsibilities include: Teach signs and symptoms of mastitis, cracked nipples, and other breastfeeding concerns (see Chapter 31); reinforce parents' understanding of the supply-demand nature of breastfeeding; help mother to find ways to get adequate rest while breastfeeding; provide information about who to contact for problems encountered at home.

POWERPOINT LECTURE SLIDES

1 Nursing Responsibilities
- Review signs and symptoms of engorgement, plugged milk ducts, mastitis
- Discuss breastfeeding preterm infant if applicable

1a Nursing Responsibilities
- Reinforce parents' understanding of supply-demand nature of breastfeeding
- Help mother find ways of getting adequate rest while breastfeeding
- Provide information about who to contact if problems occur

SUGGESTIONS FOR CLASSROOM ACTIVITIES

Discuss how prenatal and perinatal education may impact breastfeeding success.

SUGGESTIONS FOR CLINICAL ACTIVITIES

Ask students to develop a teaching plan for a working mother who plans to breastfeed.

LEARNING OBJECTIVE 6

Incorporate knowledge of newborn nutrition and normal growth patterns into parent education and infant assessment.

CONCEPTS FOR LECTURE

1. Parents need to know: Amount of formula to feed infant at each feeding and how often to feed infant; number of times per day the breastfed infant should be put to the breast; the expected weight gain of both formula- and breastfed infants; the proper diet for the breastfeeding mother.

POWERPOINT LECTURE SLIDES

 Parents Need to Know
- Amount of formula to feed infant at each feeding
- How often to feed infant
- Number of times per day breastfed infant should be put to the breast
- Expected weight gain of both formula- and breastfed infants
- Proper diet for breastfeeding mother
- Review burping, capacity of newborn stomach, positioning
- Nutritional assessment includes parental history, weight gain, growth chart percentiles, physical examination

SUGGESTIONS FOR CLASSROOM ACTIVITIES

Show students infant growth charts. Have the students plot height and weight on the charts. Demonstrate different feeding positions for bottle- and breastfeeding.

SUGGESTIONS FOR CLINICAL ACTIVITIES

Have students examine breastfeeding information and bottle-feeding information. Have them discuss how this information differs and how it is similar.

CHAPTER 30
THE NEWBORN AT RISK: CONDITIONS PRESENT AT BIRTH

RESOURCE LIBRARY

 CD-ROM

NCLEX-RN® Review
Skill 15-3: Administering a Gavage Feeding
Audio Glossary

 COMPANION WEBSITE

NCLEX-RN® Review
Case Study: Postterm Newborn
Care Plan Activity: Infant of a Diabetic Mother
Complementary Care: Infant Massage
Thinking Critically

📖 IMAGE LIBRARY

Figure 30.1 Newborn classification and neonatal mortality risk chart.

Figure 30.2 Neonatal morbidity by birth weight and gestational age.

Figure 30.3 Thirty-five-week gestational age twins.

Figure 30.4 Macrosomic infant of diabetic mother.

Figure 30.5 Postterm infant demonstrates deep cracking and peeling of skin.

Figure 30.6 A 6-day-old, 28-week gestational age, 960-g preterm infant.

Figure 30.7 Mother breastfeeding her premature infant.

Figure 30.8 Measuring gavage tube length.

Figure 30.9 Auscultation for placement of gavage tube.

Figure 30.10 Father participates in feeding experience with his premature infant.

Figure 30.11 Kangaroo (skin-to-skin) care facilitates closeness and attachment between parents and their premature infant.

Figure 30.12 Family bonding occurs when parents have opportunities to spend time with their infant.

Figure 30.13 Infant is "nested." Hand-to-mouth behavior facilitates self-consoling and soothing activities.

Figure 30.14 Nonnutritive suckling on a pacifier has a calming effect on a newborn.

LEARNING OBJECTIVE 1

Identify factors present at birth that indicates an at-risk newborn.

CONCEPTS FOR LECTURE

1. Maternal low socioeconomic level: decreased access to health care; exposure to environmental dangers, such as toxic chemicals and illicit drugs. *Refer to Figure 30.1 in the text.*
2. Preexisting maternal conditions: heart disease, diabetes, hypertension, renal disease; maternal age and parity.
3. Pregnancy complications: abruptio placentae; placenta previa; PIH.

POWERPOINT LECTURE SLIDES

 Factors That May Place an Infant at Risk at Birth
- Maternal low socioeconomic level: Decreased access to health care
- Exposure to environmental dangers
  - Toxic chemicals
  - Illicit drugs

 Preexisting Maternal Conditions
- Heart disease
- Diabetes
- Hypertension

POWERPOINT LECTURE SLIDES *continued*

- Renal disease
- Maternal age and parity

 3 Pregnancy Complications
- Abruptio placentae
- Placenta previa
- Preeclampsia

SUGGESTIONS FOR CLASSROOM ACTIVITIES

Demonstrate neonatal classification and neonatal mortality risk chart.

SUGGESTIONS FOR CLINICAL ACTIVITIES

Ask students to develop a nursing care plan for the at-risk newborn, which addresses stressful physiologic conditions and how to conserve the at-risk newborn's energy.

LEARNING OBJECTIVE 2

Compare the underlying etiologies of the physiologic complications of small-for-gestational age (SGA) newborns and preterm appropriate-for-gestational-age (Pr AGA) newborns.

CONCEPTS FOR LECTURE

1. Many of the same factors contribute to the common complications of the SGA newborn and the Pr AGA newborn: Maternal factors—grand multiparity; multiple gestation pregnancy; low socioeconomic status; poor maternal nutrition.
2. Maternal disease: Heart disease, hypertension, preeclampsia.
3. Environmental factors: Maternal use of drugs, exposure to toxins, high altitude.
4. Placental factors: Small placenta, placenta previa, abnormal cord insertions.
5. Fetal factors: Congenital infections, chromosomal syndromes.

POWERPOINT LECTURE SLIDES

1 Maternal Factors Contributing to Complications
- Grand multiparity
- Multiple gestation pregnancy
- Low socioeconomic status
- Poor maternal nutrition

2 Maternal Disease Contributing to Complications
- Heart disease
- Hypertension
- Preeclampsia

3 Environmental Factors Contributing to Complications
- Maternal use of drugs
- Exposure to toxins
- High altitude

4 Placental Factors Contributing to Complications
- Small placenta
- Placenta previa
- Abnormal cord insertions

5 Fetal Factors Contributing to Complications
- Congenital infections
- Chromosomal syndromes

SUGGESTIONS FOR CLASSROOM ACTIVITIES

Develop a list of toxins and drugs that may have adverse effects on a newborn.

SUGGESTIONS FOR CLINICAL ACTIVITIES

Have students rotate through a perinatal clinic setting to observe tests that assist in identifying at-risk newborns.

LEARNING OBJECTIVE 3

Describe the impact of maternal diabetes mellitus on the newborn.

CONCEPTS FOR LECTURE

1. Infants of diabetic mothers (IDMs) are considered at-risk and require close observation the first few hours and days of life. The most common complications of maternal diabetes mellitus are: Hypoglycemia; hypocalcemia; hyperbilirubinemia; birth trauma; polycythemia; respiratory distress syndrome; congenital birth defects—cardiac anomalies, gastrointestinal anomalies, sacral agenesis.

POWERPOINT LECTURE SLIDES

1. Characteristics of IDM Newborn
   - Macrosomic
   - Ruddy in color
   - Excessive adipose tissue
   - Large umbilical cord and placenta
   - Decreased total body water
   - Excessive fetal growth from exposure to high levels of maternal glucose

1a. Common Complications
   - Hypoglycemia
   - Hypocalcemia
   - Hyperbilirubinemia
   - Birth trauma
   - Polycythemia
   - Respiratory distress syndrome
   - Congenital birth defects: Cardiac anomalies, gastrointestinal anomalies, sacral agenesis

1b. Macrosomic Infant of Diabetic Mother
   - (Figure 30.4)

1c. Infant of Diabetic Mother
   - At risk, requires close observation first few hours to first few days
   - Infant can be small for gestational age and/or macrosomic infant

SUGGESTIONS FOR CLASSROOM ACTIVITIES

Identify which cultural groups may have a higher incidence of macrosomia.

SUGGESTIONS FOR CLINICAL ACTIVITIES

Ask students to complete "Care Plan: Infant of a Diabetic Mother" activity on the Companion Website. Discuss the case study and answers in clinical conference. Ask students to develop a list of nursing diagnoses that are a priority for a newborn of a diabetic mother.

LEARNING OBJECTIVE 4

Compare the characteristics and potential complications of the postterm newborn and the newborn with postmaturity syndrome.

CONCEPTS FOR LECTURE

1. Postterm newborn: Applies to any newborn born after 42 weeks' gestation; most are of normal size and health; large fetus may have difficult time passing through the birth canal.
2. Postmaturity syndrome, in which the fetus is exposed to poor placental function, impairs nutrition and oxygenation and has the following characteristics: Hypoglycemia; meconium aspiration; polycythemia; congenital anomalies; seizure activity; cold stress.

POWERPOINT LECTURE SLIDES

1. Postterm Newborn
   - Applies to any newborn born after 42 weeks' gestation
   - Most are of normal size and health
   - Large fetus may have difficult time passing through birth canal
   - Potential intrapartal problems
     ○ Cephalopelvic disproportion (CPD)
     ○ Shoulder dystocia

2 Postmaturity Syndrome
- Fetus exposed to poor placental function
  - Hypoglycemia
  - Asphyxia
- Impairs nutrition and oxygenation
- Has following characteristics
  - Hypoglycemia
  - Meconium aspiration
  - Polycythemia
  - Congenital anomalies
  - Seizure activity
  - Cold stress

2a Postterm Infant with Deep Cracking and Peeling of Skin
- (Figure 30.5)

SUGGESTIONS FOR CLASSROOM ACTIVITIES

Delineate which procedures may be done on a postmature infant. Discuss crucial elements of an assessment of a postmature infant.

SUGGESTIONS FOR CLINICAL ACTIVITIES

Ask students to complete "Case Study: Postterm Newborn" on the Companion Website. Ask students to discuss their answers in a clinical conference.

LEARNING OBJECTIVE 5

Discuss the physiologic characteristics of the preterm newborn that predispose each body system to various complications and are used in developing a plan of care.

CONCEPTS FOR LECTURE

1. The major problem of the preterm newborn is the variable immaturity of all systems. The degree of immaturity depends on the length of gestation. Respiratory difficulties.
2. Cardiac difficulties.
3. Temperature control difficulties.
4. Gastrointestinal difficulties.
5. Renal difficulties.
6. Reactivity and behavioral state difficulties.

POWERPOINT LECTURE SLIDES

1 Respiratory Difficulties
- Lungs are not fully mature
- Lack of surfactant causes alveoli to collapse, infant becomes hypoxic
- Incomplete development of muscular coat of pulmonary blood vessels, leads to left-to-right shunting of blood through ductus arteriosus back into lungs

2 Cardiac Difficulties
- Ductus arteriosus remains open due to low oxygen levels and low prostaglandin E levels
- Patent ductus remains open, more blood flow to lungs, increased respiratory effort, carbon dioxide retention, bounding femoral pulses

3 Temperature Control Difficulties
- Less able to produce heat because of higher ratio of body surface to body weight
- Lack of brown fat
- Thin skin, causes greater insensible water loss
- Lack of flexion increases heat loss

4 Gastrointestinal Difficulties
- Poor suck effort
- High caloric needs and limited ability to take in nutrition

- Increased basal metabolic rate and oxygen needs related to increased effort at sucking
- Increased chance of aspiration
- Decreased ability to convert amino acids
- Decreased ability to handle increased osmolarity of formula protein
- Difficulty absorbing saturated fats
- Difficulty digesting lactose
- Diminished blood flow to intestines resulting in necrotizing enterocolitis

4a Father Participates in Feeding Experience
- (Figure 30.10)

5 Renal Difficulties
- Decreased glomerular filtration rate due to decreased renal blood flow
- Inability to concentrate urine
- Decreased ability of kidney to buffer
- Delayed drug excretion time
- Spilling of glucose at lower serum glucose rate

6 Reactivity and Behavioral State Difficulties
- Delayed or lack of periods of reactivity due to poor condition of newborn
- More disorganized in sleep-wake cycle

SUGGESTIONS FOR CLASSROOM ACTIVITIES

Review the relationship of the L/S ratio and surfactant. Demonstrate on a model of fetal circulation where the patent ductus arteriosus is. Discuss how renal considerations impact drug selection in preterm infants. Describe the developmental care of the preterm infant.

SUGGESTIONS FOR CLINICAL ACTIVITIES

Ask a nursery nurse to discuss with students the equipment used to maintain a neutral thermal environment in the nursery. Have students observe reactivity periods of a preterm infant in the nursery.

LEARNING OBJECTIVE 6

Summarize the nursing assessments of and initial interventions for a newborn with selected congenital abnormalities.

CONCEPTS FOR LECTURE

1. Nursing assessments and initial interventions focus on: Respiratory.
2. Neurological. *Refer to Table 30.2.*
3. Parental involvement.

POWERPOINT LECTURE SLIDES

1 Respiratory and Nutritional Assessment
- Respiratory Assessment
  - Ability of infant to breathe
  - Maintain respiratory function
- Nutritional Assessment
  - Infant able to suck and swallow?
  - Is feeding causing respiratory distress?
  - Provide calories by breast, nipple, gastrointestinal tube, or IV

1a Measuring Gavage Tube Length
- (Figure 30.8)

1b Auscultation for Placement of Gavage Tube
- (Figure 30.9)

2 Neurological
- Is infant able to move all extremities?
- Is there a visible defect present on the spine?
- Is head circumference normal size and does it maintain normal size?
- Keep infant in prone position if necessary
- Keep defect covered with sterile saline soaks until surgery
- Keep HOB elevated if head circumference is larger than normal

3 Parental Involvement
- Assess parents' knowledge of infant's anomaly
- Keep parents informed about infant's condition
- Teach parents appropriate home care of infant

3a Family Bonding
- (Figure 30.12)

SUGGESTIONS FOR CLASSROOM ACTIVITIES

Review "Pathophysiology Illustrated: Cardiac Defects of the Early Newborn Period." Stress immediate nursing assessment measures at birth. Discuss the support that parents need if their infant has a congenital anomaly.

SUGGESTIONS FOR CLINICAL ACTIVITIES

Allow students to tour a newborn intensive care unit. Show them resources available to family members. Have students review "Skill 15-3: Administering a Gavage Feeding" on the Student CD-ROM and Clinical Skills Manual.

LEARNING OBJECTIVE 7

Explain the special care needed by an alcohol- or drug-exposed newborn.

CONCEPTS FOR LECTURE

1. Special care of the infant who was exposed to drugs or alcohol focuses on: Assessment of the mother's last drug intake and dosage; assessment of congenital anomalies and complications; assessment for signs and symptoms of withdrawal. *Refer to Table 30.3.*

POWERPOINT LECTURE SLIDES

1 Newborns with Fetal Alcohol Syndrome (FAS)
- Abnormal structural development and CNS dysfunction
- Growth deficiencies
- Distinctive facial abnormalities
- Associated anomalies

1a Risks to the Newborn of the Drug-Abusing Mother
- Respiratory distress
- Jaundice
- Congenital anomalies and growth restriction
- Behavioral abnormalities
- Withdrawal

1b Newborn Treatment
- Management of newborn complications
- Serologic tests for syphilis, HIV, and hepatitis B
- Urine drug screen
- Meconium analysis
- Social service referral
- Nutritional support

1c Care of the Drug-Dependent Newborn
- Reduce withdrawal symptoms

- Promote adequate respiration, temperature, and nutrition

[1d] Nonnutritive Sucking
- (Figure 30.14)

SUGGESTIONS FOR CLASSROOM ACTIVITIES

Demonstrate how the neonatal abstinence sheet is scored. Using "Nursing Care Plan: The Newborn of a Substance-Abusing Mother," discuss priority nursing care for the newborn of a substance-abusing mother. Discuss how fetal alcohol syndrome can be prevented.

SUGGESTIONS FOR CLINICAL ACTIVITIES

Have students present a nursing article that addresses substance abuse in pregnancy and its impact on the newborn. Encourage students to evaluate the implications for nursing care.

LEARNING OBJECTIVE 8

Relate the consequences of maternal HIV/AIDS to the management of the newborn in the neonatal period.

CONCEPTS FOR LECTURE

1. Transmission of HIV/AIDS during the perinatal and neonatal periods can occur across the placenta or through breast milk or contaminated blood. Infant of the mother who has HIV/AIDS receives the same care as all newborn infants. The nurse also includes the following aspects of care: Use standard precautions when drawing blood samples; use disposable gloves when changing diapers; protect infant from opportunistic diseases; keep newborn well-nourished to prevent failure to thrive.

POWERPOINT LECTURE SLIDES

[1] Infant of Mother with HIV/AIDS
- Infant of mother who has HIV/AIDS receives same care as all newborn infants; additionally nurse includes
  - Standard precautions when drawing blood samples
  - Disposable gloves when changing diapers
  - Skin care to prevent skin rashes
  - Protect infant from opportunistic diseases
  - Keep newborn well-nourished to prevent failure to thrive

[1a] Parents Need to Be Alert to Signs of Feeding Intolerace
- Increasing regurgitation
- Abdominal distention
- Loose stools

SUGGESTIONS FOR CLASSROOM ACTIVITIES

Discuss the opportunistic infections that may impact the newborn of a mother who has HIV/AIDS.

SUGGESTIONS FOR CLINICAL ACTIVITIES

Ask students to develop a nursing care plan for a newborn of a mother who has HIV/AIDS.

LEARNING OBJECTIVE 9

Identify the physical examination findings during the early newborn period that would make the nurse suspect congenital cardiac defects.

CONCEPTS FOR LECTURE

1. The three most common manifestations of cardiac defects are: Cyanosis; detectable heart murmur; signs of congestive heart failure.

POWERPOINT LECTURE SLIDES

[1] Manifestations of Cardiac Defects
- Three most common manifestations of cardiac defects are
  - Cyanosis
  - Detectable heart murmur
  - Signs of congestive heart failure: Tachycardia, tachypnea, diaphoresis

---

Common Cardiac Defects
- Most common cardiac defects seen in first 6 months of life
  - Left ventricular outflow obstructions
  - Hypoplastic left heart
  - Coarctation of the aorta
  - Patent ductus arteriosus
  - Transportation of great vessels
  - Tetralogy of Fallot
  - Large ventricular septal defects or atrial septal defects

SUGGESTIONS FOR CLASSROOM ACTIVITIES

Review the genetic and environmental factors that increase the risk of a congenital heart anomaly.

SUGGESTIONS FOR CLINICAL ACTIVITIES

Have students research Internet resources on congenital heart defects. In clinical conference, ask them to report on the relevancy of the congenital heart defect resource.

LEARNING OBJECTIVE 10

Explain the special care needed by newborns with an inborn error of metabolism.

CONCEPTS FOR LECTURE

1. Most infants with inborn errors of metabolism need care that centers around: Specially prepared formulas; dietary modifications; replacement hormones; continual assessment for physical abnormalities and cognitive delays. *Refer to "Pathophysiology Illustrated: Cardiac Defects of the Early Newborn Period."*

POWERPOINT LECTURE SLIDES

1 Care of Newborn with Inborn Errors of Metabolism
- Assess for signs of inborn errors of metabolism
- Carry out state-mandated newborn screening tests
- Refer parents of affected newborns to support groups
- Inform parents of centers that can provide information
  - Biochemical genetics
  - Dietary management
- Specially prepared formulas
- Replacement hormones

SUGGESTIONS FOR CLASSROOM ACTIVITIES

Before class, ask students to research what newborn screening tests are required by your state. This can be done by typing "national newborn screening" and "genetics resource center" into any search engine. Discuss newborn screening tests and resources for additional tests if required.

SUGGESTIONS FOR CLINICAL ACTIVITIES

Ask students to find out what services are offered to families of newborns with inborn errors of metabolism by the organization that handles birth to three years of age in your state or the March of Dimes. After discussing these services, ask them how they think these services will benefit the newborn.

CHAPTER 31
THE NEWBORN AT RISK: BIRTH-RELATED STRESSORS

RESOURCE LIBRARY

⊙ CD-ROM

NCLEX-RN® Review
Skill 10-1: Performing a Capillary Puncture
Nursing in Action: Infant Receiving Phototherapy
Audio Glossary

🖥 COMPANION WEBSITE

NCLEX-RN® Review
Case Study: Newborn with Jaundice
Care Plan Activity: Infection in a Newborn
MediaLink Application:
   Infant Respiratory Distress Syndrome
Thinking Critically

📖 IMAGE LIBRARY

Figure 31.1 Demonstration of resuscitation of an infant with bag and mask.
Figure 31.2 External cardiac massage.
Figure 31.3 One-day-old, 29 weeks' gestational age, 1450-g baby on respirator and in isolette.
Figure 31.5 Premature infant under an oxygen hood.
Figure 31.6 Cold stress chain of events.
Figure 31.7 Heel stick.
Figure 31.8 Potential sites for heel sticks.
Figure 31.10 Infant receiving phototherapy via overhead bilirubin lights.
Figure 31.11 Newborn on fiberoptic "bili" mattress and under phototherapy lights.
Figure 31.12 Maladaptive and adaptive parental responses during crisis period, showing unhealthy and healthy outcomes.
Figure 31.13 This 25 weeks' gestational age infant with respiratory distress syndrome may be

frightening for her parents to see for the first time due to the technology that is attached to her.
Figure 31.14 Mother of this 26 weeks' gestational age, 600-g baby begins attachment through fingertip touch.
Figure 31.15 This mother of a 35 weeks' gestational age infant with respiratory distress syndrome is spending time with her newborn and meeting the baby's need for cuddling.
Figure 31.16 Cobedding of twins facilitates delivery of care and parent interaction with healthcare members.

Table 31.1 Clinical Assessments Associated with Respiratory Distress
Table 31.3 Instructional Checklist for In-Room Phototherapy

LEARNING OBJECTIVE 1

Discuss how to identify infants in need of resuscitation and the appropriate method of resuscitation based on the labor record and observable physiologic indicators.

CONCEPTS FOR LECTURE

1. Infants at risk for resuscitation include: Nonreassuring fetal heart pattern, meconium-stained amniotic fluid and/or acidosis detected by fetal scalp sample; cardiac disease diagnosed prenatally; other congenital abnormality diagnosed prenatally; premature birth; infant of multiple pregnancy; prolonged or difficult delivery.
2. Infants at need for resuscitation: Weak cry at birth; poor respiratory effort at birth; retractions at birth.

POWERPOINT LECTURE SLIDES

▶ 1 Infants at Risk for Resuscitation
   - Nonreassuring fetal heart pattern
   - Meconium-stained amniotic fluid and/or acidosis detected by fetal scalp sample
   - Apneic episode unresponsive to tactile stimulation
   - Inadequate ventilation
   - Small for gestational age
   - Cardiac disease diagnosed prenatally

3. Resuscitation methods: Stimulation by rubbing the newborn's back; use of positive pressure to inflate the lungs; endotracheal intubation; medications: Nalaxone (Narcan) may be used to reverse effects of narcotics given to mother prior to birth.

- Other congenital abnormality diagnosed prenatally
- Premature birth
- Infant of multiple pregnancy
- Prolonged or difficult delivery

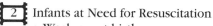 Infants at Need for Resuscitation
- Weak cry at birth
- Poor respiratory effort at birth
- Retractions at birth

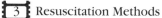 Resuscitation Methods
- Stimulation by rubbing newborn's back: Done initially to all infants
- Use of positive pressure to inflate lungs: Used if respirations are inadequate or have not been initiated
- Endotracheal intubation: Used immediately for severely premature infants, infants with known congenital anomalies, infants who do not respond to stimulation or positive pressure
- Medications: Nalaxone (Narcan) may be used to reverse effects of narcotics given to mother prior to birth

3a Demonstration of Resuscitation
- (Figure 31.1)

3b External Cardiac Massage
- (Figure 31.2)

SUGGESTIONS FOR CLASSROOM ACTIVITIES

Discuss the various procedures that may be done as part of the resuscitation of a newborn. Discuss with the students the nursing implications with each procedure.

SUGGESTIONS FOR CLINICAL ACTIVITIES

Have the clinical group locate and evaluate emergency equipment on the obstetric unit. Ask students to research and discuss neonatal advanced life support and have them correlate aspects of neonatal advanced life support with the equipment they have located.

LEARNING OBJECTIVE 2

Based on clinical manifestations, differentiate between the various types of respiratory distress (respiratory distress syndrome, transient tachypnea of the newborn, and meconiun aspirations syndrome) in the newborn and their related nursing care.

CONCEPTS FOR LECTURE

1. Respiratory distress syndrome: Lack of sufficient surfactant causes labored respirations and increased work at breathing; seen most frequently in premature newborns; nursing care involves administration of surfactant, close assessment, and supportive care if mechanical ventilation is needed. Refer to Pathophysiology Illustratred: Respiratory Distress Syndrome (RDS).

POWERPOINT LECTURE SLIDES

 Respiratory Distress Syndrome (RDS)
- Lack of sufficient surfactant causes labored respirations and increased work at breathing
- Seen most frequently in premature newborns
  - AGA
  - SGA
  - LGA

CONCEPTS FOR LECTURE *continued*

2. Transient tachypnea of the newborn (TTNB): Usually results from excess fluid in the lungs; infant breathes normally at birth but develops symptoms of respiratory distress by 4 to 6 hours of age; nursing care involves initiating oxygen therapy and restricting oral feedings until respiratory status improves.

3. Meconium aspiration syndrome: Signs and symptoms of respiratory distress beginning at birth; may depend upon the amount of meconium that is aspirated; nursing care involves vigorous and deep suctioning prior to infant taking its first breath; after initial suctioning and resuscitation efforts, nursing care involves ongoing assessment for signs and symptoms of respiratory distress and supportive care of the infant requiring mechanical ventilation or ECMO.

POWERPOINT LECTURE SLIDES *continued*

- ○ IDMs
- Nursing care involves
  - ○ Administration of surfactant
  - ○ Close assessment
  - ○ Supportive care if mechanical ventilation is needed

1a Baby on Respirator
- (Figure 31.3)

1b Clinical Assessments Associated with Respiratory Distress
- (Table 31.1)

2 Transient Tachypnea of the Newborn (TTNB)
- Usually results from excess fluid in lungs
- Infant breathes normally at birth but develops symptoms of respiratory distress by 4 to 6 hours of age
- AGA preterm and near-term infants
- Clinically can resemble RDS
- Prevalent in cesaraen-birth newborns
- Nursing care involves
  - ○ Initiating oxygen therapy—oxyhood may be required
  - ○ Intravenous fluids for fluid and electrolyte requirements
  - ○ Restricting oral feedings until respiratory status improves

2a Premature Infant Under an Oxygen Hood
- (Figure 31.5).

3 Meconium Aspiration Syndrome (MAS)
- Presence of meconium in amniotic fluid
- Fluid aspirated into tracheobronchial tree
  - ○ In utero
  - ○ During first few breaths taken by newborn
- Primarily affects
  - ○ Term
  - ○ SGA
  - ○ Postterm
  - ○ Newborns who experienced long labor

- May depend upon amount of meconium aspirated
- Nursing care involves vigorous and deep suctioning prior to infant taking its first breath
- After initial suctioning and resuscitation efforts nursing care involves
  - ○ Ongoing assessment for signs and symptoms of respiratory distress
  - ○ Supportive care of infant requiring mechanical ventilation or ECMO

3a Evaluation of Respiratory Status

LEARNING OBJECTIVE 3

Discuss selected metabolic abnormalities (including cold stress and hypoglycemia), their effects on the newborn, and the nursing implications.

CONCEPTS FOR LECTURE

1. Cold stress sets up the chain of physiologic events of hypoglycemia, pulmonary vasoconstriction, hyperbilirubinemia, respiratory distress, and metabolic acidosis.
2. Nursing interventions include: Keep infant warmed during any transport; observe for any signs of hypoglycemia; have the infant go to breast or feed early in neonatal period; assess blood glucose frequently.

POWERPOINT LECTURE SLIDES

1 Metabolic Abnormalities
- Cold stress sets up chain of physiologic events
  - Hypoglycemia
  - Pulmonary vasoconstriction
  - Hyperbilirubinemia
  - Respiratory distress
  - Metabolic acidosis

1a Cold Stress
- (Figure 31.6)

 2 Nursing Interventions
- Keep infant warmed during any transport
- Observe for any signs of hypoglycemia
- Have infant go to breast or feed early in neonatal period
- Assess blood glucose frequently

2a Hypoglycemia
- Is plasma glucose concentration at or below 40 mg/dL?
- Most common metabolic disorder in IDMs, SGA infants, preterm AGA infants
- Symptoms
  - Lethargy
  - Jitteriness
  - Poor feeding
  - Vomiting
  - Irregular respirations
  - Respiratory distress
  - Tremors, jerkiness, seizure activity
  - High-pitched cry
  - Exaggerated Moro reflex
  - Apnea
  - Hypotonia
- Hypocalcemia may concern when baby is hypoglycemic
- Monitor at-risk infants—use infant's lateral heel as preferred site

 2b Potential Sites for Heel Sticks
- (Figure 31.8)

LEARNING OBJECTIVE 4

Differentiate between physiologic and pathologic jaundice based on onset, cause, possible sequelae, and specific management.

CONCEPTS FOR LECTURE

1. Physiologic jaundice: Occurs in 50% of all newborns; appears after 24 hours of age; not visible after 10 days of age; may require phototherapy.
2. Pathologic jaundice: Usually caused by ABO or Rh incompatibility; jaundice may be present at birth; treatment begins with phototherapy but may progress to exchange transfusions; untreated hyperbilirubinemia (due to either type of jaundice) may result in neurotoxicity.

POWERPOINT LECTURE SLIDES

 1 Physiologic Jaundice
- Normal process
- Occurs during transition from intrauterine to extrauterine life
- Occurs in 50% of healthy term and 80% of preterm newborns
- Appears after 24 hours of age
- Not visible after 10 days of age
- May require phototherapy

2 Pathologic Jaundice
- Usually caused by ABO or Rh incompatibility
- Jaundice may be present at birth
- Signs of underlying illness
  - Vomiting
  - Lethargy
  - Poor feeding
  - Excessive weight loss
  - Apnea
  - Tachypnea
  - Temperature instability
- Treatment
  - Phototherapy at beginning
  - Exchange transfusions
  - Infusion of albumin
  - Drug therapy
  - Monitor for complications of kernicterus
- Untreated hyperbilirubinemia (due to either type of jaundice) may result in neurotoxicity

LEARNING OBJECTIVE 5

Explain how Rh incompatibility or ABO incompatibility can lead to the development of hyperbilirubinemia.

CONCEPTS FOR LECTURE

1. Rh incompatibility: Maternal antibodies enter the fetal circulation, then attach to and destroy fetal red blood cells; fetal system produces more RBCs; hyperbilirubinemia, anemia, and jaundice result.
2. ABO incompatibility: Mother is type O and infant is type A or B; less severe than Rh incompatibility.

POWERPOINT LECTURE SLIDES

[1] Rh Incompatibility
- Maternal antibodies enter fetal circulation
  - Attach to fetal red blood cells (RBCs)
  - Destroy fetal RBCs
- Fetal system responds
  - Produces more RBCs
  - Jaundice, anemia, and compensatory erythropoiesis result
  - Marked increase in immature RBCs (erythroblasts)

[2] ABO Incompatibility
  - Mother is blood type O
  - Infant is blood type A or B
  - May result in jaundice—not severe enough to be clinically diagnosed and treated
  - Less severe than Rh incompatibility

SUGGESTIONS FOR CLASSROOM ACTIVITIES

When discussing hemolytic disease of the newborn, discuss exchange transfusion, erythroblastosis fetalis, and hydrops fetalis.

SUGGESTIONS FOR CLINICAL ACTIVITIES

Ask each student to research hemolytic disease in the newborn and to develop a teaching brochure for expectant parents about its preventions.

LEARNING OBJECTIVE 6

Identify nursing responsibilities in caring for the newborn receiving phototherapy.

CONCEPTS FOR LECTURE

1. Nursing responsibilities for the newborn receiving phototherapy include: Expose maximum amount of skin surface for optimal therapeutic results; apply eye patches while phototherapy is in progress; assess eyes for signs/symptoms of conjunctivitis every 8 hours; frequently monitor temperature; offer infant water and formula frequently to assist in excretion of bilirubin; keep the parents informed of need for phototherapy and encourage the parents to hold and care for the infant while undergoing phototherapy.

POWERPOINT LECTURE SLIDES

[1] Nursing Responsibilities
- Expose maximum amount of skin surface for optimal therapeutic results
- Phototherapy measured every 12 hours or with daily serum bilirubin levels
- Turn lights off while blood is drawn
- Apply eye patches while phototherapy is in progress
  - Eye patches removed at least once per shift
  - Assess eyes for signs/symptoms of conjunctivitis every 8 hours
  - Allow eye contact during feeding (social stimulation)
- Frequently monitor temperature
- Offer infant water and formula frequently to assist in excretion of bilirubin
- Assess newborn skin
  - Color for jaundice
  - Bronzing
  - Developing pressure areas
- Reposition at least every 2 hours

- Keep parents informed of need for phototherapy and encourage parents to hold and care for infant while undergoing phototherapy

[1a] Infant Receiving Phototherapy
- (Figure 31.10)

[1b] Infant on a "Bili" Mattress
- (Figure 31.11)

[1c] Guidelines for Phototherapy in Hospitalized Infants

[1d] Instructional Checklist for In-Room Phototherapy
- (Table 31.3)

SUGGESTIONS FOR CLASSROOM ACTIVITIES

Ask the students to review "Nursing in Action: Infant Receiving Phototherapy" activity on the Student CD-ROM. Discuss answers in class.

SUGGESTIONS FOR CLINICAL ACTIVITIES

Ask students to develop a nursing care plan with one physical and one psychosocial nursing diagnoses for a newborn receiving phototherapy.

LEARNING OBJECTIVE 7

Discuss selected hematologic problems such as anemia and polycythemia and the nursing implications associated with each one.

CONCEPTS FOR LECTURE

1. Anemia in newborns results from prenatal blood loss, birth trauma, infection, or blood group incompatibility. Nursing assessments for signs and symptoms of anemia include recording all amounts of blood taken during laboratory testing.
2. Polycythemia may result from delayed cord clamping, twin-to-twin transfusion, or chronic intrauterine hypoxia: Nursing assessments for signs and symptoms of polycythemia.

POWERPOINT LECTURE SLIDES

[1] Anemia in Newborn
- Results from
  ○ Prenatal blood loss
  ○ Birth trauma
  ○ Infections
  ○ Blood group incompatibility
- Excessive hemolytic of RBCs usually result of blood incompatibilities but may be caused by hemolysis

[1a] Nursing Assessment
- Assess for signs of anemia (pallor)
- If blood loss acute, baby may show signs of shock such as
  ○ Capillary filling time greater than 3 seconds
  ○ Decreased pulse
  ○ Tachycardia
  ○ Low blood pressure
- Record total amount of blood drawn for all laboratory tests

[2] Polycythemia
- Blood volume and hematocrit values are increased
- More common in SGA and full-term infants
  ○ Delayed cord clamping
  ○ Maternal-fetal and twin-to-twin transfusions
  ○ Chronic intrauterine hypoxia

- Central venous hematocrit value greater than 65 to 70%
- Venous hemoglobin level greater than 22 g/dL

 Nursing Assessment
- Assess for, record, report symptoms of polycythemia
- Do initial screening of newborn's hematocrit value on admission to nursery
- Many infants asymptomatic, but as symptoms develop they are related to (and all result in poor perfusion)
  - Increased blood volume
  - Hyperviscosity of blood
  - Decreased deformability of RBCs

SUGGESTIONS FOR CLASSROOM ACTIVITIES

Discuss recombinant human erythropoietin (rEPO) in the newborn and nursing implications. Discuss iron supplementations and nursing implications. Bring examples of iron-fortified formulas to class.

SUGGESTIONS FOR CLINICAL ACTIVITIES

Ask students to research exchange transfusions in newborns on www.medlineplus.gov. Have your clinical group develop a nursing problem list in order of priority for a child receiving an exchange transfusion.

LEARNING OBJECTIVE 8

Describe the nursing assessments that would lead the nurse to suspect newborn sepsis.

CONCEPTS FOR LECTURE

1. The most common signs of newborn sepsis include: Lethargy or irritability; pallor or duskiness; hypothermia; feeding intolerance; hyperbilirubinemia; tachycardia, bradycardia, or apneic spells.

POWERPOINT LECTURE SLIDES

 Signs of Newborn Sepsis
- Subtle behavior changes
  - Infant "not doing well"
  - Lethargy or irritability
- Color changes
  - Pallor
  - Duskiness
  - Cyanosis
- "Shocky" appearance, cool, clammy skin
- Hypothermia—temperature instability
- Feeding intolerance
  - Decrease in total intake
  - Abdominal distension
  - Vomiting
  - Poor sucking
  - Lack of interest in feeding
  - Diarrhea
- Hyperbilirubinemia
- Tachycardia, bradycardia, or apneic spells

SUGGESTIONS FOR CLASSROOM ACTIVITIES

Discuss the laboratory tests that are done when sepsis is suspected in a newborn.

SUGGESTIONS FOR CLINICAL ACTIVITIES

Have students develop a nursing care plan for the infant experiencing sepsis neonatorum. As a group, discuss nursing interventions for the infant and teaching needs of the family.

LEARNING OBJECTIVE 9

Relate the consequences of selected maternally transmitted infections, such as maternal syphilis, gonorrhea, herpesvirus, and chlamydia, to the management of the infant in the neonatal period.

CONCEPTS FOR LECTURE

1. All infants receive eye prophylaxis with ophthalmic antibiotic. *Refer to Table 31.5: Neonatal Sepsis Antibiotic Therapy.* Maternal syphilis requires that the infant be isolated from other newborns and receive antibiotics at birth. Maternal herpesvirus infection requires administration of IV antiviral medications in the immediate newborn period as well as multiple cultures (skin, spinal fluid) for presence of herpesvirus.

POWERPOINT LECTURE SLIDES

 Maternal Syphilis
- Spirochetes cross placenta after 16th to 18th week of gestation
- Infant Assessment
  - Elevated cord serum IgM and FTA-ABS IgM
  - Rhinitis (snuffles)
  - Fissures on mouth corners and excoriated upper lip
  - Red rash around mouth and anus
  - Copper-colored rash over face, palms, and soles
  - Irritability
  - Generalized edema, particularly over joints
  - Bone lesions painful extremities
  - Hepatosplenomegaly, jaundice
  - Congenital cataracts
  - SGA and failure to thrive

 Nursing Management
- Initiate isolation techniques until infants have been on
- Antibiotics for 48 hours
- Administer penicillin
- Provide emotional support for parents

 Gonorrhea
- 30%–35% of newborns born vaginally to infected mothers acquire infection
- Infant assessment
  - Ophthalmia neonatorum (conjunctivitis)
  - Purulent discharge and corneal ulcerations
  - Neonatal sepsis
  - Temperature instability
  - Poor feeding response
  - Hypotonia
  - Jaundice
- Nursing management
  - Administer ophthalmic antibiotic ointment
  - Initiate follow-up referral to evaluate any loss of vision.

 Herpes Type 2
- One in 7500 births; transmitted during vaginal birth
- Infant assessment
  - Small cluster vesicular skin lesions over all the body
  - Check perinatal history for active herpes genital lesions
  - Disseminated form—DIC

○ Without skin lesions—assess for fever or subnormal temperature, respiratory congestion, tachypnea, tachycardia

 Nursing Management
- Careful handwashing
- Gown and glove isolation with linen precautions
- Administer intravenous vidarabine or acyclovir
- Initiate follow-up referral
- Encourage parental rooming-in and touching of newborn
- Show parents appropriate handwashing procedures
- Obtain cultures

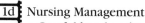 Chlamydia Trachomatis
- Acquired during passage through birth canal
- Infant assessment
  ○ Perinatal history of preterm birth
  ○ Pneumonia
  ○ Conjunctivitis
  ○ Chronic follicular conjunctivitis
- Nursing management
  ○ Instill ophthalmic erythromycin
  ○ Initiate follow-up referral

SUGGESTIONS FOR CLASSROOM ACTIVITIES

Ask students to research one of the maternally transmitted newborn infections listed in Table 31.4. Have each student give a 5-minute report on the infection that they researched. Assign "Care Plan: Infection in a Newborn" from the Companion Website for homework.

SUGGESTIONS FOR CLINICAL ACTIVITIES

Have students develop a nursing care map related to providing supportive care to an infant with sepsis. Have the clinical group discuss how a nurse can create a safe care environment for the infant with sepsis.

LEARNING OBJECTIVE 10

Describe the interventions to facilitate parental attachment with the at-risk newborn.

CONCEPTS FOR LECTURE

1. Assess the parent's level of understanding of the infant's problem. Prepare and facilitate the parents' viewing of the infant. Promote touching and facilitate parental participation in the care of the infant. Facilitate parental adjustment to the infant's special needs. *Refer to Figure 31.12.*

POWERPOINT LECTURE SLIDES

 Nurse's Role
- Assess parent's level of understanding of infant's problem
- Prepare and facilitate parents' viewing of infant
- Promote touching and facilitate parental participation in care of infant
- Facilitate parental adjustment to infant's special needs
- Parental reactions
  ○ Acute feelings of grief
  ○ Feelings of guilt and failure

 Mother Beginning Attachment
- (Figure 31.14)

Mother with Infant
- (Figure 31.15)

SUGGESTIONS FOR CLASSROOM ACTIVITIES

Discuss factors that may overwhelm parents of an at-risk infant and impact attachment. Discuss therapeutic communication techniques to use with parents. Allow time for students to role-play these techniques.

SUGGESTIONS FOR CLINICAL ACTIVITIES

Ask the clinical group to discuss how nurses can improve the self-esteem of parents of at-risk infants. Have the group discuss how culture can impact these parents.

LEARNING OBJECTIVE 11

Identify the special initial and long-term needs of parents of at-risk infants.

CONCEPTS FOR LECTURE

1. Initially, the parents need to understand the infant's problem including expected treatments. They need to understand routine well-baby care, how to perform any special procedures needed to care for the infant, referral for normal infant screening procedures, normal growth and development of infants, to have medical follow-up arranged, referral for any special equipment required at home.

POWERPOINT LECTURE SLIDES

1 Needs of Parents of At-Risk Infants
- Four psychologic tasks for coping
  - Anticipatory grief
  - Acknowldgment of maternal failure
  - Resumption of process of relating to infant
  - Understanding special needs and growth patterns
- Understand of routine well-baby care
- Understand how to perform any special procedures needed to care for infant
- Referral for normal infant screening procedures
- Understand normal growth and development of infant
- Have medical follow-up arranged
- Referral for any special equipment required at home

SUGGESTIONS FOR CLASSROOM ACTIVITIES

Discuss the role of a case manager with parents of at-risk newborns. Discuss the developmental care programs in your community. Discuss the role of the transitional care center with the parents of at-risk newborns.

SUGGESTIONS FOR CLINICAL ACTIVITIES

Ask students to research available community support agencies for families of at-risk newborns in the community. Have them report on these support agencies in a clinical conference.

CHAPTER 32
HOME CARE OF THE POSTPARTUM FAMILY

RESOURCE LIBRARY

CD-ROM

Audio Glossary
NCLEX-RN® Review

IMAGE LIBRARY

Figure 32.1 Nurse arriving for a home visit.
Figure 32.2 Various positions for holding an infant.
Figure 32.3 Babies should be placed on their backs to sleep.
Figure 32.4 When bathing the newborn, it is important to support the head.

COMPANION WEBSITE

Thinking Critically
NCLEX-RN® Review
Case Study: Follow-up with the Client at Home
Care Plan Activity: Breastfeeding Care Plan

Figure 32.5 Two basic cloth diaper shapes. Dotted lines indicate folds.
Figure 32.6 Mothers with sore nipples can leave bra flaps down after feedings to promote air drying and prevent chapping.

LEARNING OBJECTIVE 1

Discuss the components of postpartal home care.

CONCEPTS FOR LECTURE

1. The components of the postpartal home visit include: Establishing contact with the mother; identifying the purpose and goals of the visit; beginning to establish rapport with the mother; maintaining safety during the visit; assessing the mother, newborn, and family; reinforcing teaching concerning maternal and newborn care.

POWERPOINT LECTURE SLIDES

 Components of Postpartal Care
  • Establish contact with mother prior to visit
  • Identify purpose and goals of visit
  • Begin to establish rapport with mother
  • Maintain safety during visit
  • Assessment of mother, newborn, family
  • Reinforce teaching concerning maternal and newborn care

[1a] Nurse Arriving for a Home Visit
  • (Figure 32.1)

SUGGESTIONS FOR CLASSROOM ACTIVITIES

Discuss key components of the family assessment in a postpartum visit. Discuss cultural awareness and its importance in a home visit.

SUGGESTIONS FOR CLINICAL ACTIVITIES

Have students make a postpartum visit with a home health nurse. Ask them to collect data on the physical and psychosocial health of the new family.

LEARNING OBJECTIVE 2

Identify the main purposes of home visits during the postpartum period.

CONCEPTS FOR LECTURE

1. The main purposes of the home visit: Assess the status of the mother and infant; assess adaptation and adjustment of the family to the new baby; determine current informational needs; provide teaching as needed; opportunity to answer additional questions related to infant care and feeding and provide emotional support to the mother and family.

POWERPOINT LECTURE SLIDES

[1] Main Purpose of the Home Visit
- Assessment
  - Status of mother and infant
  - Adaptation and adjustment of family to new baby
- Determine current informational needs
- Teaching
  - Self-care
  - Infant care
- Opportunity to answer additional questions related to infant care and feeding
- Counseling
  - Provide emotional support to mother and family
  - Referrals

SUGGESTIONS FOR CLASSROOM ACTIVITIES

Discuss what emotional support is needed by a new family and the nurse's role in providing emotional support.

SUGGESTIONS FOR CLINICAL ACTIVITIES

Have students complete the "MediaLink Applications" activities on the Companion Website. Allow time to compare answers in class.

LEARNING OBJECTIVE 3

Summarize actions a nurse should take to ensure personal safety during a home visit.

CONCEPTS FOR LECTURE

1. Nurses need to act proactively to maintain their safety when making home visits by exercising reasonable caution and remaining alert to environmental cues.

POWERPOINT LECTURE SLIDES

[1] Nursing Actions
- Drive around neighborhood before making visit to identify potential cues to violence
- In high-risk areas, visit family during daylight hours
- Do not park in deserted or unlit areas
- Lock personal belongings in trunk of car, out of sight
- In accordance with agency policy, wear scrubs or lab coat or other uniform that identifies you as a nurse
- Pay attention to body language of anyone present, not just the client
- Be aware of personal body language and how it might be interpreted
- Leave home immediately if gun is visible and client or family member refuses to put it away
- If situation arises that feels unsafe, end the visit

SUGGESTIONS FOR CLASSROOM ACTIVITIES

Discuss violence prevention programs in your community. Describe environmental cues that indicate an unsafe environment for the nurse.

SUGGESTIONS FOR CLINICAL ACTIVITIES

Have students attend a violence prevention program at a community health facility.

LEARNING OBJECTIVE 4

Delineate aspects of fostering a caring relationship in the home.

CONCEPTS FOR LECTURE

1. Fostering a caring relationship in the home involves: genuineness and empathy; trust and rapport; regard for the mother and family.

POWERPOINT LECTURE SLIDES

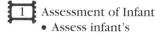 Fostering Caring Relationships
- Evidence of genuineness and empathy
- Establishment of trust and rapport
- Positive regard for mother and family
- Make appropriate referrals and follow-up plan

SUGGESTIONS FOR CLASSROOM ACTIVITIES

Discuss how the nurse can show positive regard for the family. Address weblinks on the Companion Website regarding fostering a caring relationship. Ask students what they see as important in fostering a caring relationship with clients and their families.

SUGGESTIONS FOR CLINICAL ACTIVITIES

In reflective journals, have students document when they observed caring by another student or a staff nurse.

LEARNING OBJECTIVE 5

Describe assessment and care of the newborn and reinforcement of parent teaching in the home.

CONCEPTS FOR LECTURE

1. Assess the infant's growth statistics and vital signs and observe for any signs of jaundice. Observe how the mother feeds the baby and discuss any concerns the mother may have.
2. Reinforce teaching in the following areas: Position and handling; bathing; dressing; temperature assessment; stool and urine; sleep and activity; crying; safety considerations; newborn screening and necessary immunizations.

POWERPOINT LECTURE SLIDES

1 Assessment of Infant
- Assess infant's
  - Weight
  - Length
  - Heart rate
  - Head circumference
  - Signs of jaundice
- Watch mother feed baby—discuss any concerns

 Reinforce Teaching
- Position and handling
  - Cradle hold
  - Upright position
  - Football hold
  - Side-lying position
  - Back to sleep
- Bathing
  - Every other day or twice a week
  - Sponge bath for first 2 weeks or until cord is healed—tub bath after umbilical cord healed
  - Water temperature—37.8°C (100°F)
  - Unperfumed, mild soap
  - Dry skin—apply unscented lotion or ointment, oils, or powders not recommended
- Dressing
  - T-shirt, diaper, sleeper, blanket if needed
  - Cover head when outdoors
  - Prevent sunburn
  - Launder clothes in mild soap or detergent and rinse twice

Bathing a Baby
- (Figure 32.4)

 Various Positions for Holding an Infant
- (Figure 32.2)

2c Reinforce Teaching
- Temperature assessment
  - Take temperature only when signs of illness present
  - Use acetaminophen not aspirin
- Stool and urine
  - Transitional stools
  - Breastfed infant
  - Formula-fed infant
  - 5 to 8 voids daily
- Sleep and activity—Six sleep-wake cycles after initial period of reactivity
  - Deep sleep
  - Light sleep
  - Drowsy state
  - Quiet alert state
  - Crying state
- Crying—need to be aware of reasons

 Babies Should Be Placed on Their Back
- (Figure 32.3)

 Reinforce Teaching
- Safety considerations
  - Crib safety
  - CPR classes
  - Cosleeping guidelines
  - Smoking—respiratory and fire hazzard, SIDS
- Newborn screening and necessary immunizations
  - Detect metabolic disorders, congenital hypothyroidism, sickle cell anemia
  - Obtain blood test prior to discharge
  - Hearing screening
  - Immunization schedule

Suggestions for Classroom Activities	**Suggestions for Clinical Activities**
Discuss temperature assessment and the different types available for parents to purchase.	Have students attend a baby care class. Ask them to record the types of concerns expressed by new parents, as well as the teaching methods used by the instructor.

LEARNING OBJECTIVE 6

Discuss maternal and family assessments and anticipated progress after birth.

CONCEPTS FOR LECTURE

1. Expected maternal assessments: Vital signs; weight; condition of the breasts; condition of the abdomen; elimination pattern; lochia; fundus; perineum.
2. Family assessment: Bonding; level of comfort; siblings are adjusting to the new baby; parental role adjustment; contraception.

POWERPOINT LECTURE SLIDES

 Expected Maternal Assessments
- Vital signs: Should be at prepregnancy level
- Weight: Expect weight to be near prepregnancy level at 6 weeks postpartum
- Condition of breasts
- Condition of abdomen, including healing cesarean incision if applicable
- Elimination pattern: Should return to normal by 4 to 6 weeks postpartum
- Condition of breasts

 Expected Maternal Assessments
- Lochia
  - Should progress from lochia rubra to lochia alba
  - If not breastfeeding, menstrual pattern should return at 6 weeks postpartum
- Fundus
  - Should decrease in size one finger-breadth per day after birth of baby
  - Uterus should return to normal size by 6 weeks postpartum
- Perineum: Episiotomy and lacerations should show signs of healing

 Family Assessment
- Bonding: Appropriate demonstration of bonding should be apparent
- Level of comfort: Parents should display appropriate levels of comfort with the infant
- Siblings should be adjusting to new baby
- Parental role adjustment
  - Parents should be working on division of labor
  - Changes in financial status
  - Communication changes
  - Readjustment of sexual relations
  - Adjustment to new daily tasks
- Contraception: Parents understand need to choose and use a method of contraception

SUGGESTIONS FOR CLASSROOM ACTIVITIES

On the Companion Website, under nursing tools, use the family assessment guide to supplement the lecture. Stress key points in the assessment guide that a nurse can use when making a home visit.

SUGGESTIONS FOR CLINICAL ACTIVITIES

Ask students to complete a family assessment on their assigned postpartum client.

LEARNING OBJECTIVE 7

Delineate interventions to address the common concerns of breastfeeding mothers following discharge.

CONCEPTS FOR LECTURE

1. Common concerns of the breastfeeding mother include: Nipple soreness; cracked nipples; engorgement; plugged ducts. Breastfeeding mothers are encouraged to: Nurse frequently; change the infant's position regularly; allow nipples to air dry after breastfeeding.

POWERPOINT LECTURE SLIDES

 Common Concerns of the Breastfeeding Mother
- Nipple soreness—peaks on days 3 and 6, then recedes
- Cracked nipples
- Breast engorgement
- Plugged ducts
- Effect of alcohol and medications
- Return to work
- Weaning

[1a] Breastfeeding Mothers Encouragements
- Nurse frequently
- Change infant's position regularly
- Allow nipples to air dry after breastfeeding
- Alternate breasts

SUGGESTIONS FOR CLASSROOM ACTIVITIES

Discuss the role of a lactation consultant in the hospital setting. Incorporate in the lecture a list of community resources for the breastfeeding mother. Assign "Care Plan: Breastfeeding" from the Companion Website for homework.

SUGGESTIONS FOR CLINICAL ACTIVITIES

Have students attend a La Leche League meeting or a breastfeeding class. The students should discuss the teaching strategies used by the facilitator and the content covered.

LEARNING OBJECTIVE 8

In addition to home visits, identify other types of follow-up care available to postpartal families.

CONCEPTS FOR LECTURE

1. Other types of follow-up care: Telephone calls; return visits; baby care/postpartum classes; new mother support groups.

POWERPOINT LECTURE SLIDES

 Types of Follow-Up Care
- Telephone calls—nurses must listen carefully and ask open-ended questions
- Return visits—within one week after first visit
- Telephone follow-up—within 3 days of discharge
- Baby care/postpartum classes
- New mother support groups
- Need to have a caring attitude in these activities

SUGGESTIONS FOR CLASSROOM ACTIVITIES

Discuss the role of a support group for a new mother and her family. Assign "Case Study: Follow-up with the Client at Home" from the Companion Website for homework.

SUGGESTIONS FOR CLINICAL ACTIVITIES

The Internet is used frequently for information and advice. In clinical conference, ask students what they think makes the health information reliable and of high quality for a new family.

CHAPTER 33
GROWTH AND DEVELOPMENT

RESOURCE LIBRARY

 CD-ROM

Video: Growth and Development
NCLEX-RN® Review
Audio Glossary

 COMPANION WEBSITE

Objectives
NCLEX-RN® Review
Thinking Critically
Critical Thinking: Linking Theory and Research
MediaLink Applications:
    Preparing a Preschooler for Surgery
    Developing Values in Adolescence

📖 IMAGE LIBRARY

Figure 33.1 In normal cephalocaudal growth, the child gains control of the head and neck before the trunk and limbs.

Figure 33.2 Children exposed to pleasant stimulation and who are supported by an adult will develop and refine their skills faster.

Figure 33.3 Bronfenbrenner's ecologic theory of development views the individual as interacting within five levels or systems.

Figure 33.4 Fetal alcohol syndrome.

Figure 33.5 Body proportions at various ages.

Figure 33.6 This toddler has learned to ride a Big Wheel, which he is doing right into the street.

Figure 33.7 Preschoolers continue to develop more advanced skills such as kicking a ball without falling down.

Figure 33.8 These preschoolers are participating in associative play, which means they can interact.

Figure 33.9 Jasmine is participating in dramatic play with a nurse while her mother looks on.

Figure 33.10 A, School-age children may take part in activities that require practice.

Figure 33.11 School-age girls and boys enjoy participating in sports.

Figure 33.12 The nurse can help the child and family accept and adjust to new circumstances.

Figure 33.13 Social interaction between children of same and opposite sex is as important inside the acute care setting as it is outside.

Table 33.5 Nine Parameters of Personality
Table 33.6 Patterns of Temperament

LEARNING OBJECTIVE 1

Describe major theories of development as formulated by Freud, Erikson, Piaget, Kohlberg, social learning theorists, and behaviorists.

CONCEPTS FOR LECTURE

1. Freud believed that early childhood experiences form the unconscious motivation for action later in life, and that sexual energy is centered in specific parts of the body at certain ages. Unresolved conflict at a certain stage leads to a fixation of development at that stage.

2. Erikson described eight stages of psychosocial development that occur from birth through old age. When needs are met at each stage, healthy development occurs and the individual moves on to future stages. When needs are not met, an unhealthy outcome occurs that will influence future social relationships.

3. Piaget believed that the child's view of the world is influenced largely by age, experience, and maturational

POWERPOINT LECTURE SLIDES

1 Developmental Theory: Freud
- Early childhood experiences form unconscious motivation for action later in life
- Sexual energy is centered in specific parts of the body at certain ages
- Unresolved conflict at a certain stage leads to a fixation of development at that stage

1a Freud's Stages of Development
- Oral (birth to 1 year): Derives pleasure from mouth
- Anal (1 to 3 years): Control over body secretions
- Phallic (3 to 6 years): Works out relationships with parents

ability. This theory focuses on cognitive (or intellectual) development.
4. Kohlberg developed a framework for understanding moral reasoning. He describes three levels of moral reasoning. Although he also provided age guidelines, many people never reach the highest stage of development.
5. Social learning theorists believe that children learn attitudes, beliefs, and customs through social contact with adults and other children. Children model the behavior they see, and if the behavior is positively reinforced then they tend to repeat it.
6. Behaviorists believe that behaviors can be elicited by positive reinforcement and extinguished by negative reinforcement.

- Latency (6 to 12 years): Sexual energy is at rest
- Genital (12 years to adulthood): Mature sexuality

2 Developmental Theory: Erikson
- Eight periods of psychosocial development
- Occur from birth through old age
- Two possible outcomes
  - Healthy: Move on to next stage
  - Unhealthy: Problem with future relationships

2a Erikson's Stages of Development (Pediatric)
- Trust versus mistrust (birth to 1 year)
- Autonomy versus shame and doubt (1 to 3 years)
- Initiative versus guilt (3 to 6 years)
- Industry versus inferiority (6 to 12 years)
- Identity versus role confusion (12 to 18 years)

3 Developmental Theory: Piaget
- Child's view of the world is largely influenced by
  - Age
  - Experience
  - Maturational ability
- Focuses on cognitive (or intellectual) development

3a Piaget's Stages of Development
- Sensorimotor (birth to 2 years)
- Preoperational (2 to 7 years)
- Concrete operational (7 to 11 years)
- Formal operational (11 years to adulthood)

4 Developmental Theory: Kohlberg
- Examines moral development
- Three levels of moral reasoning
- Described age guidelines—many people never reach highest stage

4a Kohlberg's Stages of Moral Development
- Preconventional (4 to 7 years)
- Conventional (7 to 12 years)
- Postconventional (12 years and older)

5 Social Learning Theorists
- Children learn attitudes, beliefs, and customs through social contact
- Children imitate behaviors they see
- If positively rewarded, they repeat behaviors
- Concept of self-efficacy—expectation that someone can produce desired event

6 Behaviorism Theories
- Applied ideas of Pavlov and Skinner to children
- Can elicit behaviors through positive reinforcement
- Can extinguish behaviors through negative reinforcement

SUGGESTIONS FOR CLASSROOM ACTIVITIES

Divide students into groups and assign each group a developmental theory. Have each group discuss how pediatric nurses can apply that particular theory to nursing practice. Have each group share their findings with the class. (HINT: Nursing applications for each developmental theory are discussed in the text after the theory is described, as well as in Table 33.3.) Assign "Critical Thinking: Linking Theory and Research" activity on the Companion Website for homework.

SUGGESTIONS FOR CLINICAL ACTIVITIES

When caring for children in the clinical setting, have students analyze a child's development using several of the theories discussed in this chapter.

LEARNING OBJECTIVE 2

Plan nursing interventions for children that are appropriate for the child's developmental stage, based on theoretical frameworks.

CONCEPTS FOR LECTURE

1. Theoretical frameworks of development help pediatric nurses guide their interventions for children based on the child's developmental stage.

POWERPOINT LECTURE SLIDES

1 Nursing Interventions: Infants
- Encourage parents to hold and stay with infant
- Provide opportunities for sucking
- Provide toys that give comfort or stimulate interest
- Pain control (trust)

1a Nursing Interventions: Toddlers
- Toilet-training procedures
  - Do not begin toilet-training in hospital
  - Accept regression during hospitalization
- Encourage independent behaviors—feeding, hygiene, dressing self
- Give short explanations
- Reward appropriate behavior

1b Nursing Interventions: Preschoolers
- Encourage parental involvement
- Provide safe versions of medical equipment for play
- Give clear explanations about illness—explain that child is not responsible for the illness
- Allow child to draw

1c Nursing Interventions: School-Age
- Provide gowns, covers, and underwear
- Explain treatments and procedures
- Encourage school work
- Encourage hobbies, favorite activities

1d Nursing Interventions: Adolescents
- Provide privacy
- Interview separately from parents when possible
- Encourage participation in care and decision-making
- Encourage peer visitation
- Provide information on sexuality

SUGGESTIONS FOR CLASSROOM ACTIVITIES

Have students complete "Case Study: Diabetic Risk Factors" on the Companion Website. Use this as a basis for class discussion on how nursing interventions would vary based on the child's development.

SUGGESTIONS FOR CLINICAL ACTIVITIES

Invite a child life specialist to speak to the students at a clinical conference about developmentally appropriate activities that pediatric nurses can use while caring for hospitalized children.

LEARNING OBJECTIVE 3

Explain contemporary developmental approaches such as temperament theory, ecologic theory, and the resilience framework.

CONCEPTS FOR LECTURE

1. Ecologic theory emphasizes the presence of mutual interactions between the child (who is unique) and various settings. Neither nature nor nurture is considered of more importance. *The levels and systems described in this theory are depicted in Figure 33.3.*

2. Temperament theory categorizes children into three patterns of temperament, which can be used to assist in adaptation of the child's environment and for a better understanding of the child. The three patterns include "easy," "difficult," and "slow-to-warm-up."

3. Resilience is the ability to function with healthy responses, even when faced with significant stress and adversity. Resiliency theory states that all individuals experience crises that lead to adaptation and development of inner strengths and the ability to handle future crises.

POWERPOINT LECTURE SLIDES

1 Ecologic Theory (Bronfenbrenner)
- Each child is unique
- Emphasizes presence of mutual interactions between child and various settings
- Neither nature nor nurture is more important
- Levels and systems

2 Temperament Theory
- Focuses on wide spectrum of behaviors in children
- How children respond to daily events
- Based on New York Longitudinal Study (1956 to present)

2a Nine Parameters of Personality
- (Table 33.5)

2b Patterns of Temperament
- (Table 33.6)

3 Resilience: Basic Ideas
- Resilience: Ability to function with healthy responses, even when faced with stress and adversity
- Protective factors
  - Provide strength
  - Examples
- Risk factors
  - Contribute to the challenge
  - Examples

3a Resiliency Theory
- All individuals experience crises that lead to adaptation and development of inner strengths
- Increases ability to handle future crises

SUGGESTIONS FOR CLASSROOM ACTIVITIES

Before class, assign students to complete "Critical Thinking: Developmental Theories and Nature Versus Nurture" activity available on the Companion Website. Use this activity as a framework when comparing traditional developmental theories to contemporary developmental theories.

SUGGESTIONS FOR CLINICAL ACTIVITIES

Assign students making home and community visits to families to explore the families' environmental systems. During post-conference, compare assessments and discuss how differences might influence children's development.

LEARNING OBJECTIVE 4

Recognize major developmental milestones for infants, toddlers, preschoolers, school-age children, and adolescents.

CONCEPTS FOR LECTURE

1. Infancy is a time of rapid growth and change. The birth weight usually doubles by about 5 months and triples by a year. *Major developmental milestones are reviewed in Tables 33.12 and 33.13.*

2. Toddlers typically display independence and negativism, and they are proud when accomplishing new things. The rate of growth slows during this time, and toddlers often have decreased food intake. By 2 years, the birth weight has usually quadrupled and the child is about one-half of the adult height. *Major developmental milestones are reviewed in Tables 33.14, 33.15, and 33.16.*

3. Preschoolers learn a great deal from the social contact they receive. They develop good language skills and tend to be very busy with projects and tasks. Physical skills and writing ability also increase. *Major developmental milestones are reviewed in Tables 33.18 and 33.20.*

4. School-age children are very industrious and begin to find activities that they enjoy and excel in. Peers are beginning to become important, and children develop a sense of achievement and self-esteem. *Major developmental milestones are reviewed in Tables 33.21 and 33.22.*

5. Adolescence marks a time of passage between childhood and adulthood, and teenagers are in a period of identity formation. Puberty occurs during this stage, as does rapid change in growth. Teenagers become interested in new activities and are less dependent on parents for transportation, and peers are important. *Major developmental milestones are reviewed in Tables 33.23 and 33.24.*

POWERPOINT LECTURE SLIDES

 Development During Infancy
- Time of rapid growth and change
- Birth weight
  - Doubles by 5 months
  - Triples by 1 year
- Begins to understand meanings of sounds and words
- By 1 year, able to feed self

 Major Developmental Milestones During Infancy
- Rolls over
- Sits up
- Stands
- Able to say 1 or 2 words
- Uses pincer grasp well

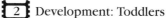 Development: Toddlers
- Typically independent and negative
- Proud of new accomplishments
- Rate of growth and food intake slows
- Birth weight quadruples by 2 years
- At 2 years, child is one-half of adult height

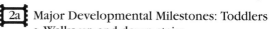 Major Developmental Milestones: Toddlers
- Walks up and down stairs
- Undresses self
- Scribbles on paper
- Kicks a ball
- Has a vocabulary of 1,000 words—uses short sentences

3 Development: Preschoolers
- Most children in daycare or school
- Increased social activities and contacts
- Language skills well-developed
- Writing ability improved
- Physical skills developed

3a Major Developmental Milestones: Preschoolers
- Uses scissors
- Rides bicycle with training wheels
- Throws a ball
- Holds a bat
- Writes a few letters
- All parts of speech are well-developed

4 Development: School-Age Children
- Very industrious
- Find activities they enjoy and excel in
- Contributes to sense of achievement, self esteem
- Peers becoming more important

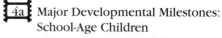 Major Developmental Milestones: School-Age Children
- Possesses reading ability
- Rides a two-wheeled bike

- Jumps rope
- Plays organized sports
- Mature use of language

5 Development: Adolescents
- Transition: End of childhood and beginning of adulthood
- Identity formation: "Who am I?"
- Puberty and rapid growth changes
- New activities
- Less dependent on parents for transportation
- Peers are important

5a Major Developmental Milestones: Adolescence
- Fine motor skills well-developed
- Gross motor skills improve due to growth spurts
- Able to apply abstract thought and analysis

SUGGESTIONS FOR CLASSROOM ACTIVITIES

Have students trace their own development from birth through adolescence, identifying as many developmental milestones as possible. For example, students can identify when they said their first words, crawled, walked, and so on. You can ask students to create a timeline or to bring in photographs of the milestones.

SUGGESTIONS FOR CLINICAL ACTIVITIES

Require students to complete an assessment of growth and development on each child they care for during their clinical rotation. This assessment can be incorporated into their care plan for that child. Have students review the "Growth and Development" video on the Student CD-ROM.

LEARNING OBJECTIVE 5

Synthesize information from several theoretical approaches to plan assessments of the child's physical growth and developmental milestones.

CONCEPTS FOR LECTURE

1. By using various developmental theories, the nurse can assess the child's growth and development holistically.

POWERPOINT LECTURE SLIDES

1 Assessing Growth and Development
- Use combination of developmental theories and assessments
- Holistic approach
- Categories of assessment
  ○ Physical growth
  ○ Cognitive development
  ○ Psychosocial development
  ○ Personality and temperament
  ○ Communication
  ○ Sexuality

SUGGESTIONS FOR CLASSROOM ACTIVITIES

Discuss assessment tools and methods that can be used to gather data from each of the categories of assessment discussed in this objective.

SUGGESTIONS FOR CLINICAL ACTIVITIES

Review communication strategies for sharing information and asking questions for each developmental stage. Use a test or procedure, such as drawing blood or starting an IV, as a common framework. Assign "Critical Thinking: Preparing a Preschooler for Surgery" activity on the Companion Website for homework.

LEARNING OBJECTIVE 6

Describe the role of play in the growth and development of children.

CONCEPTS FOR LECTURE

1. Play has often been described as the "work of childhood," and play contributes to the growth and development of children. Play can be described in terms of both social interaction and physical development of gross and fine motor skills.

POWERPOINT LECTURE SLIDES

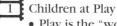 Children at Play
- Play is the "work of childhood"
- Play contributes to:
  - Cognitive growth
  - Physical development: Gross motor skills and fine motor skills
  - Social interaction

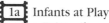 Infants at Play
- Primarily enjoy solitary play
- Others may teach infants how to play with new objects
- Progress from reacting to objects (rattle) to manipulating them
- Once they become mobile, sphere of play enlarges

 Toddlers at Play
- Increased motor skills allow new types of toys and play
- Play becomes more social, often with other toddlers—parallel play
- Imitates behavior
- Manipulating objects helps them to learn about their qualities (Example: Square block will not fit in round hole)

1c Preschoolers at Play
- Interacts with others during play
- Enjoys large motor activities
- Increased manual dexterity
- Fantasy play

1d School-Age Children at Play
- Increased physical abilities allow for wide variety of play
- Understanding of rules of a game—like for rules to be followed during play
- Cooperative play

 Adolescents at Play
- Increased maturity leads to new activities and ways to play
- Peer group becomes focus of activities
- Less reliant on parents for transportation
- Social interactions important

SUGGESTIONS FOR CLASSROOM ACTIVITIES

Ask students to think about the potential ramifications of children who are not allowed to play (such as children raised in orphanages). How is development affected?

SUGGESTIONS FOR CLINICAL ACTIVITIES

Encourage students to take children they are caring for to the hospital playroom. If the child is in isolation, have the student bring toys to the child's room. By observing children at play, the student will be able to assess many components of growth and development.

LEARNING OBJECTIVE 7

Use data collected during developmental assessments to implement activities that promote development of children and adolescents.

CONCEPTS FOR LECTURE

1. Nursing interventions should be tailored to the child's developmental stage based on data obtained from a holistic assessment.

POWERPOINT LECTURE SLIDES

1 Nursing Interventions and Development
- Assess growth and development—holistic approach
- Tailor nursing interventions based on this data

1a General Principles: Interventions and Development
- Discuss proper nutrition and feeding techniques
- Conduct health teachings and screenings based on child's age
- Encourage family to discover child's personality and temperament
- Instruct parents about expected language skills

1b General Principles: Interventions and Development
- Give parents information about normal sexual behavior of children
- Instruct school-age children about expected changes of puberty
- Give adolescents information about
  - Birth control
  - Sexually transmitted diseases

SUGGESTIONS FOR CLASSROOM ACTIVITIES

Assign students to complete the "NCLEX-RN® Review" questions available on the Student CD-ROM and Companion Website for practice.

SUGGESTIONS FOR CLINICAL ACTIVITIES

Have students develop nursing interventions based on the developmental assessment of the child.

CHAPTER 34
INFANT, CHILD, AND ADOLESCENT NUTRITION

RESOURCE LIBRARY

CD-ROM

Videos
    Anorexia Nervosa
    Breastfeeding and First Foods
    Children and Overweight
    Nutritional Status
Nursing in Action: Administering a Gavage/Tube
  Feeding
Skills 9-1 to 9-7: Growth Measurements
Skill 15-3: Administering a Gavage Feeding
NCLEX–RN® Review
Audio Glossary

COMPANION WEBSITE

Objectives
NCLEX-RN® Review
Thinking Critically
Case Study: Manage a Child's Peanut Allergy at School
Dietary Reference Intakes
Typical Daily Intake at Various Ages
MediaLink Applications:
    Growth Chart Analysis
    Diet and Culture
    Analyze Your Diet
    Fast Food Analysis
    Plan a Nutrition Teaching Session
    Vegetarian Teens: Plan a 2-Day Menu
    Youth Adolescent Questionnaire
Audio Glossary

IMAGE LIBRARY

Figure 34.1 The Food Guide Pyramid is used to provide teaching about amounts of foods recommended for daily intake.

Figure 34.2 Early childhood caries.

Figure 34.3 The baby who has developed the ability to grasp with thumb and forefinger should receive some foods that can be held in the hand.

Figure 34.4 Toddlers should sit at a table or in a high chair to eat, to minimize the chance of choking and to foster positive eating patterns.

Figure 34.5 Preschoolers learn food habits by eating with others.

Figure 34.6 The nurse accurately measures the child and then places height and weight on appropriate growth grids for the child's age and gender.

Figure 34.7 The nurse is interviewing a child about foods eaten in the last day.

Figure 34.8 Most Head Start centers participate in screening programs to identify children at risk for anemia.

Figure 34.9 Infants with failure to thrive may not look severely malnourished, but they fall well below the expected weight and height norms for their age.

Figure 34.10 This young lady began to have symptoms of anorexia at age 12 years.

Figure 34.11 This child has returned to school following surgery.

Table 34.4 Clinical Manifestations of Dietry Deficiencies/Excesses

Teaching Highlights: Foodborne Safety Guidelines

LEARNING OBJECTIVE 1

Discuss major nutritional concepts pertaining to the growth and development of children.

CONCEPTS FOR LECTURE

1. All children require nutrients in order to grow, but children with conditions such as feeding disorders, food allergies, cystic fibrosis, cerebral palsy, and diabetes have unique nutritional needs.

POWERPOINT LECTURE SLIDES

 Nutrition and Children
- All children need nutrients to grow
- Conditions with unique nutritional needs include
  - Feeding disorders
  - Food allergies

2. Nutrition monitoring should be provided throughout childhood in order to integrate dietary counseling when needed. Children now live on both ends of the spectrum of nutrition: Those who are hungry and malnourished, and those who are obese.
3. Nutrition and growth require both macronutrients and micronutrients.
4. Dietary Reference Intakes and the Food Guide Pyramid can help families gauge recommended food and caloric intake.

- ○ Cystic fibrosis
- ○ Cerebral palsy
- ○ Diabetes

2 Monitoring a Child's Nutrition
- Should occur throughout childhood
  - ○ Family finances: How they get food
  - ○ Actual diet: Vegetarian?
  - ○ Hunger
  - ○ Childhood obesity

3 Basic Concepts
- Nutrition: Taking in food and breaking it down for metabolic use
- Required products include
  - ○ Macronutrients: Carbohydrates, proteins, fats
  - ○ Micronutrients: Vitamins, minerals

4 How Much Do We Need?
- Dietary Reference Intakes
- Food Guide Pyramid

SUGGESTIONS FOR CLASSROOM ACTIVITIES

View "Nutritional Status" video on the Student CD-ROM in class.

SUGGESTIONS FOR CLINICAL ACTIVITIES

Have students identify resources in the clinical setting that can be used to help children and families make good dietary choices. These resources may include client education brochures, dietary charts, Web resources, and bulletin boards.

LEARNING OBJECTIVE 2

Describe and plan nursing interventions to meet nutritional needs for all age groups from infancy through adolescence.

CONCEPTS FOR LECTURE

1. During the first year of life, infants progress from taking a few ounces of formula to eating soft table foods. They have extremely high metabolic and growth rates, and triple their birth weight by their first birthday. Breast milk is recommended as the best source of nutrition for infants.
2. Toddlers have much slower metabolic rates than infants, and they often go for long periods of time with little or nothing to eat. Healthy snacks and meals should be provided, and toddlers usually prefer small portions of food. Toddlers should drink milk, but fruit juices should be limited. Toddlers will also begin learning how to eat with others.
3. Preschoolers and toddlers have similar diets, but preschoolers begin to see meals as a social event. They can assist in meal preparation and table setting but need close supervision around sources of heat. Preschoolers may have periods, called *food jags*, where they eat only a few foods for several days or weeks.

POWERPOINT LECTURE SLIDES

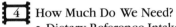 **1** Infants: Nutritional Concepts
- High metabolic and growth rates
- Triple their birth weight by 1 year of age
- Breast milk recommended
  - ○ Numerous benefits over formula
  - ○ Exclusively through first 6 months
  - ○ With supplemental food from 6 to 12 months

1a Infants: Nursing Interventions
- Promote breastfeeding in home environment
- Promote breastfeeding during hospitalization
- Prevention of dental caries
- Guidance about introducing solid foods

2 Toddlers: Nutritional Concepts
- Metabolic rate slows, so appetite decreases
- Prefer small portion sizes
- Physiologic anorexia
- Begin to learn to eat with others

CONCEPTS FOR LECTURE *continued*

4. School-age children grow gradually but eventually have a pre-adolescent growth spurt between 10 and 12 years of age. Children can prepare simple meals and should learn how to choose healthy foods. The loss of deciduous teeth begins at about 6 years of age.

5. Adolescents grow rapidly and require many calories to support growth. Many adolescents prepare much of their own food or eat fast food, and guidance about healthy food choices is important.

POWERPOINT LECTURE SLIDES *continued*

2a Toddlers: Nursing Interventions
- Guidance for parents
  - Healthy meals and snacks
  - Milk
  - Fruit juices
  - Allow for self-feeding with utensils, fingers
- Hospitalization: Allow toddler to eat with parents

3 Preschool: Nutritional Concepts
- Growth is slow and steady
- Food jags
- Meals are a social event
- Assist with food preparation, table setting

3a Preschool: Nursing Interventions
- Guidance for parents
  - Safety in the kitchen
  - Teeth brushing
  - Dentist

4 School-Age: Nutritional Concepts
- Growth is steady until pre-adolescent growth spurt occurs
- Can prepare simple meals and choose healthy foods
- Loses first tooth around 6 years of age

4a School-Age: Nursing Interventions
- Guidance for parents
  - Food choices
  - Monitor teeth brushing and flossing
- During hospitalization
  - Allow for food choices
  - Obesity risk factors: Screening

5 Adolescents
- Nutritional Concepts
  - Rapid growth requires many calories
  - Often prepare own meals or eat fast food
- Nursing interventions
  - Guidance about healthy food choices
  - Consider influence of peers

SUGGESTIONS FOR CLASSROOM ACTIVITIES

- Show the video: "Breastfeeding and First Foods," from the Student CD-ROM. Discuss barriers to breastfeeding that might be encountered by mothers.
- Assign "MediaLink Applications: Preschoolers – Plan a Nutrition Teaching Session and Vegetarian Teens – Plan a Two-Day Menu" activities from the Companion Website for homework.

SUGGESTIONS FOR CLINICAL ACTIVITIES

Have students observe the clinical area and determine how breastfeeding is promoted in the hospital. Are lactation consultants available? Are there posters on the walls from formula companies? Are new mothers given free formula to take home?

LEARNING OBJECTIVE 3

Integrate methods of nutritional assessment into nursing care of infants, children, and adolescents.

CONCEPTS FOR LECTURE

1. The nutritional status of a child can be assessed by physical measurements (growth) or by dietary intake. Growth can be measured by anthropometric measurements (weight, length, head circumference, etc.) that are then plotted on growth charts.
2. Nutritional status may also be assessed by observing some physical signs and laboratory measurements.
3. Dietary intake can be assessed by 24-hour food recall, food frequency questionnaire, dietary screening history, and food diaries.

POWERPOINT LECTURE SLIDES

1 Assessing Nutritional Status: Measurements
- Anthropometric measurements
  - Weight
  - Length and height
  - Head circumference
  - Others
- Plot on growth chart

2 Clinical Manifestations of Dietary Deficiencies/Excesses
- (Table 34.4)

2a Assessing Nutritional Status: Labs
- Hematocrit/hemoglobin
- Glucose
- Fasting insulin
- Lipids
- Liver, renal function studies

3 Assessing Dietary Intake
- 24-hour food recall
- Food frequency questionnaire
- Dietary screening history
- Food diary

SUGGESTIONS FOR CLASSROOM ACTIVITIES

Make overhead transparencies of growth charts and plot a trend of a child increasing in percentile, decreasing in percentile, and staying the same. Have students discuss possible reasons for these changes in growth over time. Assign "MediaLink Applications: Growth Chart Analysis" activity on the Companion Website as homework.

SUGGESTIONS FOR CLINICAL ACTIVITIES

Have students pick one of the four dietary intake tools discussed and administer it to their client. Examples can be found in Tables 34.5 and 34.6. Have students review Skills 9-1 through 9-7 on the Student CD-ROM and Clinical Skills Manual.

LEARNING OBJECTIVE 4

Discuss common nutritional problems of children in developed countries.

CONCEPTS FOR LECTURE

1. A significant number of children suffer from hunger due to poverty. These children may have *food insecurity*, and often suffer from malnutrition.
2. Childhood obesity is rapidly escalating due to many factors, including decreased activity, increased television viewing, high levels of dietary fat, and snacking.
3. Children are at risk for foodborne illnesses, and foodborne safety guidelines should be reinforced with families and children.
4. Children may have dietary deficiencies of iron, calcium, Vitamin D, and folic acid.

POWERPOINT LECTURE SLIDES

1 Hunger
- Directly related to poverty
- Food insecurity
- Malnutrition—signs and symptoms

2 Childhood Obesity
- Rapidly escalating—epidemic levels
- Type II diabetes now common
- Many factors involved
  - Activity levels
  - Television viewing
  - Dietary fat
  - Snacking

3 Foodborne Illnesses
  • Many mild illnesses
  • Children at greater risk for severe illness
    ○ Immature gastrointestinal system
    ○ Immature immune system

3a Common Agents Causing Foodborne Illnesses
  • *Campylobacter*
  • *Salmonella*
  • *Shigella*
  • *E. coli*
  • *Rotavirus*

3b Foodborne Safety Guidelines
  • ("Teaching Highlights: Foodborne Saftey Guidelines")

4 Common Deficiencies of Nutrients
  • Iron
  • Calcium
  • Vitamin D
  • Folic acid

SUGGESTIONS FOR CLASSROOM ACTIVITIES

• Have students locate and bring to class a recent article in the news or mass media about childhood obesity. Discuss factors relating to the increase in childhood obesity and what nurses can do to influence the problem. Assign "MediaLink Applications: Analyze Your Diet"activity on the Companion Website as homework.
• Show the video, "Children and Overweight," from the Student CD-ROM. Use this video as a way to discuss the differences between being overweight and being obese.

SUGGESTIONS FOR CLINICAL ACTIVITIES

• Students will often encounter obese children who have been admitted to the hospital for an unrelated disorder. Ask students what interventions for obesity can be accomplished during the child's admission.
• How can students teach children about preventing foodborne illnesses? Challenge students to think creatively about how to teach the four components of foodborne safety to children.

LEARNING OBJECTIVE 5

Apply the nursing process to care for children with eating disorders.

CONCEPTS FOR LECTURE

1. Children may have numerous eating disorders, including pica, failure to thrive, anorexia nervosa, bulimia, and food allergies.
2. The nursing process will be applied to discuss anorexia nervosa as a model case for children with eating disorders.

POWERPOINT LECTURE SLIDES

1 Types of Eating Disorders in Children
  • Pica
  • Failure to thrive
  • Anorexia nervosa
  • Bulimia
  • Food allergies

2 Anorexia: Background Information
  • Occurs primarily in teenage girls, young women
  • Potential causes
  • Excessive exercise, laxatives, diuretics used for weight loss
  • Clinical manifestations
  • Diagnosis and treatment

2a Assessment
  • Family history
  • Eating and exercise patterns, menstrual history

- Signs of malnutrition
- Plot height and weight on growth chart

 Diagnosis
- Imbalance nutrition—less than body requirements
- Risk for deficient fluid volume
- Risk for imbalanced body temperature
- Constipation
- Disturbed body image
- Chronic low self-esteem
- Compromised family coping

 Planning and Implementation
- Meet nutrition and fluid needs
- Administer medications
- Referrals

Evaluation
- Weight gain
- Maintenance of adequate fluid volume
- Improved self-esteem
- Intake of nutrients
- Use of counseling

SUGGESTIONS FOR CLASSROOM ACTIVITIES

Show the video, "Anorexia Nervosa," from the Student CD-ROM, before discussing the nursing plan for anorexia described above.

SUGGESTIONS FOR CLINICAL ACTIVITIES

During clinical conference, ask students to suppose they were caring for a teenager with anorexia. What are some of the challenges they might face? What would they do if a physician ordered treatments (such as nutrition through an NG tube) that the teenager refused? How can the psychiatric components of the disease be addressed in the hospital?

CHAPTER 35
PEDIATRIC ASSESSMENT

RESOURCE LIBRARY

CD-ROM

Audio Glossary
Animations:
 Otoscope Examination
 Mouth and Throat Examination
 3D Eye
 Movement of Joints
Skills 9-1 to 9-7: Growth Measurements
Skill 9-10: Blood Pressure
Skills 9-11 to 9-14: Body Temperature Measurements
Skills 9-18 and 9-19: Visual Acuity Screening
NCLEX–RN® Review

IMAGE LIBRARY

Figure 35.1 Examination of the child begins from the first contact.
Figure 35.2 Tenting of the skin associated with poor skin turgor.
Figure 35.3 Capillary refill technique.
Figure 35.4 A, Inspecting for head lice with a fine-tooth comb. B, Nits on hair.
Figure 35.5 Draw an imaginary line down the middle of the face over the nose and compare the features on each side.
Figure 35.6 External structures of the eye.
Figure 35.7 Draw an imaginary line across the medial canthi and extend it to each side of the face to identify the slant of the palpebral fissures.
Figure 35.8 The eyes of this boy with Down syndrome show a Mongolian slant.
Figure 35.9 Begin the eye muscle examination with inspection of the extraocular movements.
Figure 35.10 The cover–uncover test.
Figure 35.11 Normal fundus.
Figure 35.12 To detect the correct placement of the external ears, draw an imaginary line through the medial and lateral canthi of the eye toward the ear.
Figure 35.13 To restrain an uncooperative child, place the child prone on the examining table.
Figure 35.14 To straighten the auditory canal, pull the pinna back and up for children over 3 years of age.
Figure 35.15 Cross-section of the ear.
Figure 35.16 A, Weber test.
Figure 35.17 Technique for examining nose.

COMPANION WEBSITE

New Pediatric Blood Pressure Tables
Techniques for Assessing Selected Primitive Reflexes with Normal Findings and Their Expected Age of Occurrence
Thinking Critically
NCLEX–RN® Review
Case Study

Figure 35.18 The structures of the mouth.
Figure 35.19 Typical sequence of tooth eruption for both deciduous and permanent teeth.
Figure 35.20 The neck is palpated for enlarged lymph nodes around the ears, under the jaw, in the occipital area, and in the cervical chain of the neck.
Figure 35.21 Intercostal spaces and ribs are numbered to describe the location of findings.
Figure 35.22 The sternum and spine are the vertical landmarks used to describe the anatomic location of findings.
Figure 35.23 Two types of abnormal chest shape.
Figure 35.24 One example of a sequence for auscultation of the chest.
Figure 35.25 Indirect percussion.
Figure 35.26 Normal resonance patterns expected over the chest.
Figure 35.27 Sound travels in the direction of blood flow.
Figure 35.28 Topographic landmarks of the abdomen.
Figure 35.29 Sequence for indirect percussion of the abdomen.
Figure 35.30 Anatomic structures of the female genital and perineal area.
Figure 35.31 Palpating the scrotum for descended testicles and spermatic cords.
Figure 35.36 Does this child have legs of different lengths or scoliosis?

Figure 35.37 Inspection of the spine for scoliosis.

Figure 35.38 A, Normal palmar creases. B, Simian crease associated with Down syndrome.

Figure 35.39 Flex the infant's hips and knees so the heels are as close to the buttocks as possible.

Figure 35.40 To evaluate the child with knock-knees, have the child stand on a firm surface.

Figure 35.41 Romberg procedure.

Figure 35.42 Tests of coordination.

Figure 35.43 To assess the plantar reflex, stroke the bottom of the infant's or child's foot in the direction of the arrow.

Nursing Practice

As Children Grow: Sutures

As Children Grow: Growth and Development of Sinuses

Pathophysiology Illustrated: Tonsil Size with Infection

LEARNING OBJECTIVE 1

Describe the elements of a health history for an infant or child of different ages.

CONCEPTS FOR LECTURE

1. Client information includes the child's name, nickname, age, gender, and ethnicity. Birth date, address, phone number, and emergency contact information should be obtained as well.
2. Physiologic data includes the chief complaint, history of present illness, past medical history, current health status, and review of systems. *Tables 35.1 through 35.4 in the text are excellent references.*
3. Psychosocial data includes the family composition, socioeconomic factors, housing, school, and childcare routines. *Table 35.5 is a good reference.*
4. Developmental data includes information about the child's motor, cognitive, language, and social development.

POWERPOINT LECTURE SLIDES

1 Client Information
- Child's name, nickname
- Age, birth date
- Gender
- Ethnicity
- Address, phone number
- Emergency contact information

2 Physiologic Data
- Chief complaint: Primary problem, reason for visit
- History of present illness
- Past medical history
- Current health status
- Review of systems

3 Psychosocial Data
- Family composition
- Employment, income, financial resources
- Description of home environment
- School and/or childcare arrangements
- Recent changes in family lifestyle
- Daily routines

4 Developmental Data
- Motor development
- Cognitive development
- Language development
- Social development

SUGGESTIONS FOR CLASSROOM ACTIVITIES

Use a case study format to teach this objective, using a hypothetical child and family to model a thorough history.

SUGGESTIONS FOR CLINICAL ACTIVITIES

Early in the clinical rotation, assign students to take health histories for newly admitted clients. This works well on units that receive a lot of admissions while students are present.

LEARNING OBJECTIVE 2

Identify communication strategies to improve the quality of historical data collected.

CONCEPTS FOR LECTURE

1. Clear communication is very important, as the information collected forms the basis of many decisions. An interpreter should be used if a language barrier exists. Always be honest when answering parents' questions.
2. Techniques that help the nurse to build rapport with a family include introductions, purpose of the interview, privacy, asking open-ended questions, and asking only one question at a time. In addition, the child should be involved in the interview if his or her age is appropriate.
3. Active listening is important in order to accurately interpret the information shared during the interview.
4. Some cultures have different views about eye contact, interaction with healthcare providers, and physical touch.

POWERPOINT LECTURE SLIDES

1 Importance of Clear Communication
- Incorrect information and assumptions get passed on if communication is not clear
- Interpreters
- Always be honest

2 Strategies to Build Rapport
- Introduce self
- Explain purpose of interview
- Provide privacy
- Ask open-ended questions
- Ask one question at a time
- Involve child if age is appropriate

3 Active Listening
- Avoidance of questions
- Tone of voice—anxiety, anger, apathy, concern
- Underlying themes
- Nonverbal behavior—posture, gestures, eye contact, facial expression

4 Cultural Considerations
- Eye contact
- Interactions with healthcare providers
- Physical touch
- May say "yes" to be polite

SUGGESTIONS FOR CLASSROOM ACTIVITIES

Demonstrate the preceding communication methods to the class by role modeling the techniques with a student volunteer. It may be helpful to perform the demonstrations twice: First using closed communication techniques, then again using the open communication techniques described previously.

SUGGESTIONS FOR CLINICAL ACTIVITIES

Identify resources available in the local clinical setting for families from various cultures. What interpreting resources are available and during what hours? What accommodations for cultural food preferences and visitation patterns are allowed?

LEARNING OBJECTIVE 3

Describe the differences in sequence of the physical assessment for infants, children, and adolescents.

CONCEPTS FOR LECTURE

1. The approach and the sequence of the physical examination vary by age. Different strategies can be applied across the lifespan in order to facilitate a stress-free physical exam.

POWERPOINT LECTURE SLIDES

1 General Principles Regardless of Age
- Respect privacy and modesty
- Explain procedures before you begin them
- Involve both the child and the family

1a Newborns and Infants Younger Than 6 Months
- Usually do not resist examination
- Keep parent in sight
- Examine on table, crib
- Distraction with rattles, toys
- Sequence—flexible; auscultate when infant is quiet

1b Infants Older Than 6 Months
- Developing stranger anxiety
- Keep infant with parent
- Examine on parent's lap
- Sequence: Same as newborns

1c Toddlers
- Shy, anxious, active, cautious, wary
- Keep parent nearby
- Demonstrate assessment on parent first
- Cranial nerve assessment—make it a game
- Don't ask if you can examine toddler—answer will be "no"
- Sequence: Save instruments until the end

1d Preschoolers
- Usually cooperative if parent is nearby
- Leave undergarments on child
- Involve them in the exam—make it a game
- Assess stuffed animal first, then child
- Positive feedback
- Sequence: Based on child's preference

1e School-Age Children
- Usually willing to cooperate
- Sit on examining table
- Developing modesty—leave underwear on
- Let child listen to breath sounds, heart sounds, etc.
- Sequence: Head to toe

1f Adolescents
- Modesty is very important
- Cover parts of body not being assessed
- Unless adolescent requests parental presence, allow for privacy during exam
- Reassurance that they are developing normally
- Sequence: Head to toe

SUGGESTIONS FOR CLASSROOM ACTIVITIES

How does the developmental approach to the exam relate to the child's developmental age? For example, why does examining a stuffed animal work well with a preschool child but not well with an adolescent? Encourage students to think about the developmental tasks that children progress through.

SUGGESTIONS FOR CLINICAL ACTIVITIES

Encourage students to create a chart that highlights the differences in the sequence and approach to the physical exam as it varies by age. They can use this as a reminder when they assess children of different ages.

LEARNING OBJECTIVE 4

Modify physical assessment techniques according to the age and developmental stage of the child.

CONCEPTS FOR LECTURE

1. Health assessment begins with first meeting the child, and includes an overview of the child's appearance and behavior. Growth measurements and vital signs are taken at this point.

POWERPOINT LECTURE SLIDES

1 General Appearance
- Interaction with parent
- Behavior
- Reaction to nurse

2. Assessment techniques include inspection, palpation, auscultation, and percussion.
3. Although the physical assessment may have to be adapted based on the developmental level of the child, assessment generally proceeds from head to toe. A systematic approach prevents components of the assessment from being omitted.

1a Measurements
- Growth (plot on growth chart)
  - Height and length
  - Weight
  - Head circumference
- Vital signs

2 Assessment Techniques
- ("Nursing Practice")

3 Skin
- Color
- Bruises, lesions
- Temperature, texture
- Capillary refill time
- Edema

3a Tenting of Skin Associated with Poor Skin Turgor
- (Figure 35.2)

3b Hair
- Scalp hair: Color, distribution, cleanliness
- Hair loss
  - Tight braids
  - Skin lesions
  - Ringworm
- Body hair, pubic hair, axillary hair

3c Nits on Hair
- (Figure 35.4B)

3d Head and Face: Sutures and Fontanels
- ("As Children Grow: Sutures")

3e Head and Face
- Symmetry
- Measurement of FOC—until 3 years of age

3f Inspect Child's Face for Symmetry
- (Figure 35.5)

3g External Structures of the Eye
- (Figure 35.6)

3h Inspect Eyes for the Palpebral Slant
- (Figure 35.7)

3i Eye Spacing: Down Syndrome
- (Figure 35.8)

3j Eyes
- Color
- Pupils
- Extraocular movements
- Corneal light reflex
- Vision assessment
- Use of ophthalmoscope

3k Correct Placement of External Ears
- (Figure 35.12)

3l Ears
- Otoscope
  - Tympanic membrane
  - Techniques
- Hearing
  - Infants and toddlers
  - Preschool and older children
  - Weber test
  - Rinne test

3m Nose
- External inspection
- Patency
- Smell
- Internal inspection—use nasal speculum with otoscope

3n Sinuses: Tenderness
- ("As Children Grow: Growth and Development of Sinuses")

3o Mouth
- Lips
- Teeth
- Odors
- Gums
- Buccal mucosa
- Tongue
- Palate

3p Tonsil Size with Infection
- ("Pathophysiology Illustrated: Tonsil Size with Infecion")

3q Neck
- Inspection
- Webbing (associated with Turner's syndrome)
- Trachea midline
- Thyroid

3r Lymph Nodes Palpation
- (Figure 35.20)

3s Intercostal Spaces and Ribs
- (Figure 35.21 A and B)

3t Abnormal Chest Shape
- (Figure 35.23 A and B)

3u Chest: Feeling and Listening
- Palpation
  - Crepitus
  - Tactile fremitus
- Auscultation
  - Anterior and posterior
  - Pattern
- Percussion

Breasts
- Inspection
  - Nipple location
  - Supernumerary nipples

- Palpation—masses, nodules
- Boys—gynecomastia during puberty

 Normal Stages of Breast Development

 Heart Sounds
- Inspection and palpation: Apical impulse
- Auscultation: S1/S2, murmurs

 Heart Sounds: Listening Locations
- (Figure 35.27)

 Other Components of Heart Assessment
- Blood pressure: Compare to normals for gender and age
- Palpation of pulses

 Topographic Landmarks of the Abdomen
- (Figure 35.28)

 Abdomen: A Different Order to the Exam
- Inspection: Shape, umbilicus, abdominal movement
- Auscultation: Bowel sounds
- Percussion: Organ borders, size
- Palpation: Organs, masses, pain

 Inguinal Area
- Lymph nodes
- Masses
- Femoral pulse

 Genital Examination
- Child may feel insecure or anxious
- Young children
  - Get parent's help
  - Have parent tell child that the examination is allowed
  - Position on parent's lap
- Older children, adolescents
  - Usually prefer privacy
  - May be examined last

 Anatomic Structures of Female Genital and Perineal Area
- (Figure 35.30)

Females
- Assess pubic hair for sexual development
- Labia
- Hymen
- Vaginal discharge
- Further exam done only if abnormalities found— done by experienced provider

Males: Inspection of Genitalia
- Assess genitals and pubic hair for sexual development
- Penis—foreskin
- Scrotum
- Palpate testicles for masses, spermatic cord
- Inguinal canal
- Cremasteric reflex: Stroke inner thigh

 Anus and Rectum
- Inspect for inflammation, fissures, lesions
- Palpate lightly: Anal "wink"
- Patency of anus—newborns
- Further exam not routinely done

 Musculoskeletal System
- Inspect arms, legs, and joints for symmetry
- Palpation
- Range of motion
- Muscle strength

 Spinal Alignment: Scoliosis
- (Figure 35.36)

 Inspection of Spine for Scoliosis
- (Figure 35.37)

 Inspection of Upper Extremities
- Arms
- Hands
  - Polydactyly, syndactyly
  - Palmar creases
- Nails

 Inspection of Lower Extremities
- Hips
- Legs
- Feet

 Assessment of Nervous System: Cognitive Function
- Behavior
- Communication skills
- Memory
- Level of consciousness

 Cerebellar Function
- Balance
- Coordination
- Gait

 Reflexes
- Infants: Primitive reflexes
  - Moro
  - Palmar grasp
  - Plantar grasp
  - Placing, stepping
  - Tonic neck
- Superficial, deep tendon reflexes

LEARNING OBJECTIVE 5

Determine the sexual maturity rating of males and females based upon physical signs of secondary sexual characteristics present.

CONCEPTS FOR LECTURE

1. The age of onset of secondary sexual characteristics varies widely, but does follow a predictable pattern.
2. Females usually begin breast development between 9 and 14 years. Breast development may be asymmetric.
3. The presence, amount, and distribution of pubic hair indicates sexual development in girls. Breast development usually precedes pubic hair development, and the presence of pubic hair before age 8 is unusual.
4. Genital development and the development of pubic hair indicates sexual development in boys. Pubic hair is uncommon before age 9. Boys who have not begun showing development by age 14 should be referred for further evaluation.
5. The sexual maturity rating (SMR) is an average of the breast and pubic hair Tanner stages in females and of the genital and pubic hair stages in males.

POWERPOINT LECTURE SLIDES

1 Age of Onset of Puberty
- Varies widely
- Follows a set pattern

1a Factors Related to Age of Onset
- Race/Ethnicity (Example: African Americans have earlier onset than Caucasians)
- Environmental conditions
- Geographic location
- Nutrition (Example: Begins earlier in taller, heavier girls)

2 Breast Development
- Begins between 9 and 14 years
- May develop asymmetrically
- Abnormal (precocious) breast development:
  - Younger than 6 years in African Americans
  - Younger than 7 years in Caucasians

3 Sexual Maturity: Girls
- Based on presence, amount, and distribution of pubic hair
- Breast development usually begins before pubic hair develops
- Presence of pubic hair before age 8 is unusual

3a Stages of Female Pubic Hair Development

4 Sexual Maturity: Boys
- Pubic hair
  - Unusual before age 9
  - Goes from straight and downy to thick and curly
- Genitals
  - Penis and testicles enlarge
  - Scrotum thins out
- If no development by age 14, needs further evaluation

4a Stage of Male Genital Development

5 Sexual Maturity Rating (SMR)
- Females: Average of breast and pubic hair Tanner stages
- Males: Average of genital and pubic hair Tanner stages
- Ranges from 2 to 5 (Stage 1 is prepubertal)

SUGGESTIONS FOR CLASSROOM ACTIVITIES

Ask students what they would say to a school-age child or adolescent who was concerned about his or her sexual development.

SUGGESTIONS FOR CLINICAL ACTIVITIES

Discuss methods the nurse can employ to make genital examination less anxious for children of various ages. How does the approach for a preschooler differ from that of an adolescent?

LEARNING OBJECTIVE 6

Recognize at least five important signs of a serious alteration in health condition that require urgent nursing intervention.

CONCEPTS FOR LECTURE

1. The physical assessment usually offers important findings about a child's health condition. Assessment findings may be subtle or obvious. Continuous monitoring and reassessment to identify trends are critical in identifying serious changes in the child's status.

POWER POINT LECTURE SLIDES

1 ABC's
- Airway and breathing
  - Respiratory rate
  - Work of breathing
  - Oxygen saturation
  - Change in level of consciousness—brain needs oxygen
- Circulation
  - Heart rate—bradycardia, tachycardia
  - Perfusion—skin characteristics, pulses, capillary refill, end-organ perfusion (kidneys, liver, brain)

1a Neurological
- Change in level of consciousness
- Seizures
- Change in pupil reactivity

1b Gastrointestinal
- Rapidly expanding abdomen
- Sudden change in bowel sounds
- Blood: Occult or frank

1c Genitourinary
- Signs of renal failure
- No response to diuretics
- Diminishing urine output

1d Skin
- Sudden rash—drug reactions
- Signs of infection
- Purpura

SUGGESTIONS FOR CLASSROOM ACTIVITIES

Discuss as a class the general principles that nurses should follow when working with a child who has a sudden change in his or her health status.

SUGGESTIONS FOR CLINICAL ACTIVITIES

Locate emergency equipment in the clinical setting. If possible, have students practice handling the equipment (Examples: Connecting an Ambu-bag to oxygen supply, bagging a child, etc.).

CHAPTER 36
SOCIAL AND ENVIRONMENTAL INFLUENCES ON THE CHILD

RESOURCE LIBRARY

 CD-ROM

Videos:
   Extreme Sports
   Violence in the Media
   Identifying Child Abuse
   Smoking and Smoking Cessation
   Identifying Youth Who Abuse Drugs and Alcohol
Audio Glossary
NCLEX-RN® Review
Objectives
Critical Thinking

📖 IMAGE LIBRARY

Figure 36.1 The special relationship between a father about to be deployed in the military and his young daughter is clear.
Figure 36.2 Most children will spend time in childcare settings.
Figure 36.3 Approximately 70% of children have tried smoking by their high school years.
Figure 36.4 Methamphetamine is a popular drug because it can be manufactured with items that are available to the lay public.

🌐 COMPANION WEBSITE

MediaLink Applications:
   Develop a Teaching Plan: Individualized Sport
   Music and Violence

Figure 36.5 Physical inactivity is a growing problem among children and can contribute to poor health.
Figure 36.6 What protective gear should children use for skateboarding?
Figure 36.7 Talk openly with adolescents about their health and teach them to avoid health risks connected with tattoos and piercing.
Figure 36.8 Therapeutic strategies with young children involve various methods of communication, such as dramatic play and art.

LEARNING OBJECTIVE 1

Identify major social and environmental factors that influence the health of children and adolescents.

CONCEPTS FOR LECTURE

1. Many social and environmental factors influence children's health. Most morbidity is related to preventable causes, such as car crashes, fires, drowning, and homicides. Mental disorders and pregnancy are common reasons for adolescents to be admitted to the hospital.

POWERPOINT LECTURE SLIDES

1 Social and Environmental Factors that Influence Health of Children
- Many causes of death are preventable
  - Car crashes
  - Fires
  - Drowning
  - Homicide

1a Social Factors Relating to Adolescents
- Same as children
- Others
  - Pregnancy
  - Mental health disorders

1b Additional Factors to Consider
- Poverty
- Stress

- Family structure
- Child care
- Substance abuse
- Physical inactivity
- Violence/abuse

SUGGESTIONS FOR CLASSROOM ACTIVITIES	SUGGESTIONS FOR CLINICAL ACTIVITIES
Assign students to develop parent or child teaching plans focused on stress management for children of various ages. Compare stress risks and strategies for different age groups.	Determine the causes of death for children in the local community. Do they coincide with national statistics? What social and environmental factors do local experts believe have the greatest impact on children's health?

LEARNING OBJECTIVE 2

List external influences that affect child and adolescent health.

CONCEPTS FOR LECTURE

1. External influences that affect child and adolescent health include poverty, stress, family structure, school and child care, community, and culture.

POWERPOINT LECTURE SLIDES

1 External Influences that Affect Health
- Poverty
- Stress
- Family structure
- School and child care
- Community
- Culture

1a Poverty
- One in six children is poor
- Poor children are more likely to
  - Have unmet health needs
  - Have trouble with school
  - Become teen parents
  - Experience multiple health problems

1b Consequences of Poverty
- Inadequate, unsafe housing
- Lack of nutritious food
- Malnutrition
- Homelessness—children comprise one-third of the homeless population

1c Stress
- How do children manifest stress?
  - Behavior regresses
  - Trouble sleeping
  - Hyperactive behavior
  - Gastrointestinal symptoms
  - Crying
  - Withdrawal from normal activities

1d Stressful Events for Children
- Moving to new home or school
- Marital difficulties in the family
- Abuse
- Parent deployed in the military

- Parental expectations for achievement too high
  - Sports and extracurricular activities
  - School

1e Consequences of Stress on Health
- Frequent respiratory illnesses
- Frequent gastrointestinal illnesses
- Increased risk for injury
- Long-term effects
  - Hypertension
  - Stroke
  - Heart attack

1f Family Structure
- Considerations
  - Number of parents present
  - Number of parents working
  - Number of siblings
  - Presence of extended family for support
  - Divorce
- Effects on health
  - Financial effect of family structure
  - Stress

1g School and Child Care
- Health activities in schools
  - Screening programs (hearing, vision, scoliosis)
  - Presence of school nurses
  - Teaching of health-related material (hygiene, nutrition, etc.)
- Chronic illness in schools
- Child care—incorporates health into care

1h Community
- May support child's development
- May expose child to hazards
- Sidewalks
- Air quality
- Quality of housing (lead exposure)
- Gangs, drug activity

1i Culture
- Immigrants
- Language acquisition
- Culture shock
- Health practices

SUGGESTIONS FOR CLASSROOM ACTIVITIES

During class, have students read "Evidence-Based Nursing: Homelessness from the Viewpoint of Children," located in the book. Incorporate the findings from this study into the discussion about homelessness.

SUGGESTIONS FOR CLINICAL ACTIVITIES

Students will likely care for children and families who are homeless or live in poverty. Have students identify local community resources to which they can refer families.

LEARNING OBJECTIVE 3

Apply the ecological model and resilience theory to assessment of the social and environmental factors in children's lives.

CONCEPTS FOR LECTURE

1. The ecological model views the child and the environment as interacting forces. Children influence the systems around them, and the systems in turn influence the child.
2. Resilience theory examines risk and protective factors in the child's environment.

POWERPOINT LECTURE SLIDES

1 Ecological Model
- Described by Bronfenbrenner
- Views child and environment as interacting forces
- Both the child and the environment influence each other
- Example
  ◦ Workplace does not provide health insurance
  ◦ Result: Lack of access to health care

1a Five Levels of Ecological Model
- Microsystem
- Mesosystem
- Exosystem
- Macrosystem
- Chronosystem

2 Resilience Theory
- Examines risk and protective factors
- May be modified to improve health

2a Examples of Risk Factors
- Lack of health insurance
- Lack of primary care provider
- Lack of immunizations

2b Examples of Protective Factors
- Availability of parent to stay with child
- Child readily adapts to new situations
- Extended family nearby for support

SUGGESTIONS FOR CLINICAL ACTIVITIES

When students are completing care plans for children and families they have cared for, have them incorporate the ecological model into their care plan. This encourages students to consider the effect of various systems on the child's health status.

LEARNING OBJECTIVE 4

Examine the effects of substance use, physical activity, and other lifestyle patterns on health.

CONCEPTS FOR LECTURE

1. Tobacco use is the most preventable cause of adult death in the United States. Most adults begin smoking during their teenage years.
2. Substance abuse occurs in children and adolescents of all socioeconomic levels and is a growing health problem.
3. Physical inactivity reflects our society's lifestyle. Children have become increasingly sedentary, which has led to a rise in childhood obesity.

POWERPOINT LECTURE SLIDES

1 Tobacco Use
- Most preventable cause of adult death in the United States
- Usual age for first cigarette: 9 to 14 years
- 80% of adults begin smoking before age 18
- Consequences of tobacco use
  ◦ Cardiovascular disease
  ◦ Cancer
  ◦ Chronic lung disease
  ◦ Low birth weight

4. Other lifestyle patterns that can influence the health of children and adolescents include the use of protective equipment, body art, and sexual orientation.

1a Characteristics that Increase Likelihood of Tobacco Use
- Increasing age
- Male gender
- Ethnic group
- Ease of obtaining tobacco products
- Smoking among family members

2 Substance Abuse
- Occurs in all socioeconomic levels
- Growing health problem
  - Alcohol
  - Cocaine
  - Crack
  - Heroin
  - Over-the-counter medication abuse

2a Why Do Children Try Drugs?
- Maladaptive coping response to stress
- Family members or peers use drugs
- Low self-esteem

2b Health Consequences of Substance Abuse
- Dependence
- Weight loss
- Chronic fatigue, malaise
- Respiratory symptoms
- Suicide, homicide
- Accidental overdose

3 Physical Inactivity
- Children are increasingly sedentary
  - TV, video games, computers
  - Less time for PE in schools
  - Less participation in outdoor activities, sports
- Dramatic rise in childhood obesity
  - Sedentary lifestyle
  - Increased intake of snacks, calories

3a Sedentary Versus Active Lifestyles
- (Figure 36.5)

3b Health Consequences of Obesity
- Type II diabetes—long-term consequences
- Social issues

4 Use of Protective Equipment
- Sports that require protective equipment to prevent injury:
  - Rollerblading
  - Skateboarding
  - Hockey
  - Football
  - Baseball
  - Skiing

4a What Protective Gear Is Required?
- (Figure 36.6)

Other Protective Equipment
- Seat belts
- Car seats/booster seats
- Helmets

 Body Art
- Tattoos
- Piercings
- Health risks
  - Infections (skin pathogens)
  - Hepatitis B and C; HIV
  - Branding or scarification

 Sexual Orientation
- Most teens feel attraction to the opposite sex
- Other lifestyles
  - Homosexuality
  - Bisexuality
  - Transgender
- Health risks
  - Rejection by family or peers
  - Harassment
  - Assault
  - Suicide
  - Sexually transmitted diseases

SUGGESTIONS FOR CLASSROOM ACTIVITIES

- In class, view the videos on "Smoking and Smoking Cessation" and "Identifying Youth Who Abuse Drugs and Alcohol Use." Invite a substance abuse counselor to class to discuss adolescent patterns of drug and alcohol use and abuse.
- Watch the video "Extreme Sports" available on the Student CD-ROM and assign "MediaLink Applications: Develop a Teaching Plan: Individualized Sport" activity for students to complete in-class. Allow time to discuss answers.

SUGGESTIONS FOR CLINICAL ACTIVITIES

Role play with students how they might approach a teenager who is engaging in one or more of the behaviors discussed in this objective.

LEARNING OBJECTIVE 5

Plan nursing interventions for children who experience violence.

CONCEPTS FOR LECTURE

1. Potential sources of violence involving children include violence in the media, abuse, homicide, terrorist attacks, and wars.
2. There are many nursing interventions that can be applied to children experiencing violence. *Tables 36.7 and 36.8 are helpful references.*

POWERPOINT LECTURE SLIDES

 Sources of Violence
- Media (TV, movies, computer games)
- Abuse
- Homicide
- Terrorism
- War
- Bullying

Nursing Interventions
- Firearm safety
- Limit exposure to violent media

- Allow children to reflect on feelings about terrorism, war—drawings, art therapy
- Provide information

2a Nursing Interventions for Bullying at School
- Inform students that bullying is not tolerated
- Ensure adult supervision of hallways and playgrounds
- Teach children to report bullying
- Be alert for behavior changes
- Be aware of risk factors and assessment questions

SUGGESTIONS FOR CLASSROOM ACTIVITIES

During class, show the video "Violence in the Media," available on the Student CD-ROM. Use this as a basis for the discussion about violence. Assign students to complete "Critical Thinking: Music and Violence" activity on the Companion Website for homework.

SUGGESTIONS FOR CLINICAL ACTIVITIES

Ask students to pay attention to the types of TV shows, movies, and computer games that children watch and play in the hospital setting. Many times these activities contain excessive violence, which provides the nurse an opportunity to address the issue with the child and family.

LEARNING OBJECTIVE 6

Explore the nursing role in prevention and treatment of child abuse and neglect.

CONCEPTS FOR LECTURE

1. Abuse is a relatively common form of violence inflicted on children, and can involve neglect, physical abuse, emotional abuse, or sexual abuse. The most common perpetrator of abuse is the parent or guardian of the child. There are numerous risk factors that are associated with abusive behavior.
2. Prevention and treatment of abuse center on promotion of parenting skills, detection of abuse, and reporting.

POWERPOINT LECTURE SLIDES

1 Types of Abuse
- Physical abuse
- Neglect
- Emotional abuse
- Sexual abuse

1a Who Typically Abuses Children?
- Parent
- Guardian
- Boyfriend of child's mother

1b Risk Factors Associated with Abuse
- Drug addiction, alcoholism
- Low self-esteem
- Poor impulse control
- Prior history of abuse
- Marital or environmental stressors
- Social isolation
- Unrealistic expectations for the child

2 Prevention of Abuse
- Promotion of parenting skills
- Let parents know it is okay to walk away from a crying baby
- Be aware of risk factors

Abuse Detection and Management
- Be alert for physical and emotional signs and symptoms
- Prevent further injury
- Believe the child
- Reporting requirements
- Objective documentation
- Treat any physical symptoms or injuries
- Refer for further emotional support

SUGGESTIONS FOR CLASSROOM ACTIVITIES

During the discussion of this objective, view the video, "Identifying Child Abuse," available on the Student CD-ROM.

SUGGESTIONS FOR CLINICAL ACTIVITIES

Invite a social worker from your local child protection services department to talk with the students about detections of child abuse and reporting requirements for nurses.

CHAPTER 37
HEALTH PROMOTION AND HEALTH MAINTENANCE FOR THE INFANT AND YOUNG CHILD

RESOURCE LIBRARY

CD-ROM

Videos:
  Temper Tantrums
  Making the Pacifier Decision
NCLEX-RN® Review
Audio Glossary

📖 IMAGE LIBRARY

Figure 37.1 A, The nurse is providing a health supervision visit in the child's home after discharge from the hospital for an acute illness. B, A nurse is providing information to a child visiting a mobile healthcare van.

Figure 37.2 The nurse plays many roles in providing health promotion and health maintenance for children.

Figure 37.3 Follow all directions for performing the Denver II assessment and for interpreting responses.

Figure 37.5 This 18-month-old toddler is having a blood screening test to detect iron deficiency anemia.

Figure 37.6 The nurse begins assessment of the infant's family when they are seen in the waiting room and called in for care.

🌐 COMPANION WEBSITE

NCLEX-RN® Review
MediaLink Applications:
  Case Study: Domestic Violence

Figure 37.7 Weighing and measuring length during health supervision visits provides important information about the child's nutrition and general development.

Figure 37.8 Interactions between the parent and infant provide clues to mental health.

Figure 37.9 The approach to examination of the toddler or preschooler is important in order to elicit cooperation.

Figure 37.10 This toddler enjoys motor activity that uses large muscle groups.

Table 37.2 Nutrition Teaching for Health Promotion and Health Maintenance Visits

LEARNING OBJECTIVE 1

Define health promotion and health maintenance.

CONCEPTS FOR LECTURE

1. *Health promotion* refers to activities that increase well-being or enhance wellness or health. *Health maintenance* refers to activities that preserve a person's present state of health and that prevent disease or injury occurrence.

POWERPOINT LECTURE SLIDES

[1] What Is Health?
- WHO definition
  - State of complete physical, mental, and social well-being
  - Not merely absence of disease or illness
- Health is dynamic and changes often

[1a] What Is Health Promotion?
- Activities that increase well-being and enhance wellness or health
- Examples
  - Good nutrition
  - Physical activity
  - Oral health

1b What Is Health Maintenance?
- Activities that preserve a person's present state of health
- Prevents disease or injury occurrence
- Examples
  - Developmental screening
  - Immunizations
  - Preventing injury (safety hazards)

SUGGESTIONS FOR CLASSROOM ACTIVITIES

To help students understand the difference between health promotion and health maintenance, list several examples of each concept on the chalkboard. Have students identify which examples fit with each concept.

LEARNING OBJECTIVE 2

Describe how health promotion and health maintenance are addressed by partnering with families during health supervision visits.

CONCEPTS FOR LECTURE

1. Health promotion and health maintenance are integrated into healthcare visits. Nurses partner with families during these visits by involving the family during the information gathering part of the visit.

POWERPOINT LECTURE SLIDES

1 Health Promotion
- Health supervision visits
  - Integrate health promotion and health maintenance
  - Done throughout child's life
- Partnering with families
  - Have care provider give information about the child
  - Ask questions
  - Incorporate answers into the rest of the visit

SUGGESTIONS FOR CLASSROOM ACTIVITIES

Ask the class how they might collect an accurate health history during a health supervision visit if a relative who did not know the child well brought the child to the visit.

LEARNING OBJECTIVE 3

Describe the components of a health supervision visit.

CONCEPTS FOR LECTURE

1. Key assessments that are completed during health supervision visits include growth and development, physical activity, oral health, mental and spiritual health, and relationships.
2. Disease screening and injury prevention strategies are important components of health supervision visits.

POWERPOINT LECTURE SLIDES

1 Areas to Assess During Health Supervision Visits
- Growth and development
- Physical activity
- Oral health
- Mental and spiritual health
- Relationships

1a Growth and Development
- Plot height, weight, and body mass on growth chart

- Important to look at trends too—sudden increase or decrease on growth chart from visit to visit
- Denver II developmental screening tool

1b Nutrition
- Discuss proper foods for child's age
- Ask what child is eating
- Ask parents what questions they have about child's eating patterns—use this as basis for further interventions

1c Physical Activity
- Ask about frequency of physical activity
- Ask about favorite activities
  ○ Sports
  ○ Watching TV
  ○ Playing computer games
- Physical activity should be encouraged at all ages

1d Oral Health
- Prevention of caries
- Brushing and flossing teeth
- Referral to dentist as needed

1e Mental and Spiritual Health
- Mood
- Child temperament
- Stressors and how child manages stress
- Signs of depression, anxiety, abuse, neglect

1f Relationships
- Family
- Other children
- Family friends
- Peers
- School
- Larger community

2 Disease Screenings and Prevention
- Immunizations
- Screening for various diseases, such as
  ○ Anemia
  ○ Lead poisoning
  ○ Metabolic disorders

2a Injury Prevention Strategies
- Discuss how parents can maintain a safe environment
- Based on child's age and highest risk for injury

SUGGESTIONS FOR CLASSROOM ACTIVITIES

- Create profiles of young children in different age groups. List which tasks on the Denver II developmental screening tool the children can and cannot do (it is helpful to have profiles of both normal and delayed children). Have students practice calculating the child's age and indicating which tasks that child can and cannot do on the Denver tool. You can also discuss how the screening tool is interpreted.
- Show the video, "The Importance of Physical Activity," available on the Student CD-ROM, as you discuss the topic of physical activity assessment.

SUGGESTIONS FOR CLINICAL ACTIVITIES

In order to help students become proficient at using growth charts, require them to plot the height, weight, and body mass index of each child they care for during their clinical rotation.

LEARNING OBJECTIVE 4

Explore the nurse's role in providing health promotion and health maintenance for the infant and young child.

CONCEPTS FOR LECTURE

1. The nurse can integrate six concepts into the care of children during health maintenance visits.

POWERPOINT LECTURE SLIDES

1. Partnering with Families: Six Concepts
   - Build effective partnership with the family
   - Foster family-centered communication
   - Focus on health promotion and health maintenance
   - Manage time well
   - Educate families during "teachable moments"
   - Advocate for child health issues

SUGGESTIONS FOR CLASSROOM ACTIVITIES

Lead students in a discussion of how the six concepts described in this objective can be applied to actual practice.

LEARNING OBJECTIVE 5

Describe the general observations made of infants and their families as they come to the pediatric healthcare home for health supervision visits.

CONCEPTS FOR LECTURE

1. The nurse can gather much information by observing the child and family interact in the waiting room and examination room.

POWERPOINT LECTURE SLIDES

1. Observing the Child and Family
   - Assessment begins when you first see the child and family
     - Waiting room
     - Examination room

1a. Questions to Ask
   - Do child and parent have close physical contact, eye contact, and vocalization during visit?
   - Does baby respond to eye contact, movement, and vocalizations by the nurse?
   - Do parents appear relaxed or stressed?

- Does child behave as expected for age and situation?
- Is parent able to effectively handle child being seen as well as any other siblings present?

 1b Assessment of a Family
- (Figure 37.6)

SUGGESTIONS FOR CLASSROOM ACTIVITIES	SUGGESTIONS FOR CLINICAL ACTIVITIES
When showing Figure 37.6, ask the students what observations the nurse could make if he or she saw this family in the waiting room. What further questions would they want to follow up on?	Arrange for students to work with a pediatric nurse practitioner who cares for preschoolers and toddlers and their parents in the office setting. Have the student call the child and parents into the exam room. In post-conference, have students discuss findings regarding their observations.

LEARNING OBJECTIVE 6

Describe the areas of assessment and intervention for health supervision visits of infants and young children—growth and developmental surveillance, nutrition, physical activity, oral health, mental and spiritual health, family and social relations, disease prevention strategies, and injury prevention strategies.

CONCEPTS FOR LECTURE

1. Because infants grow and change rapidly, health supervision visits occur frequently during this developmental stage.

POWERPOINT LECTURE SLIDES

1 Growth and Development
- Measure and plot length, weight, and FOC—watch for changes in percentile
- Physical assessment
- Development
  - Screening tool
  - General observations and questions
  - Referral if not meeting milestones

1a Nutrition
- Infant will triple birth weight by 1 year of age
- Determine formula or breast milk
- Eating patterns
- Guidance about food choices

1b Nutrition Teaching for Health Promotion and Health Maintenance Visits
- (Table 37.2)

1c Physical Activity
- Needed to develop fine and gross motor skills
- Appropriate toys for infants
- Allow opportunities for activity

1d Oral Health
- Inspect infant's mouth
- Usually has 2 teeth by 6 months of age
- Wipe gums with soft moist gauze daily
- Brush teeth

Mental and Spiritual Health
- Goals
  - Infant feels secure
  - Environment is nurturing
- Discuss stranger anxiety
- Discuss separation anxiety
- Discuss self-regulation

 Relationships
- Family is primary relationship
- Encourage daily play
- Let parents know that it is okay to take breaks if infant is frustrating them

Disease Prevention Strategies
- Immunizations
- When to call the physician
- Screenings
  - Anemia
  - Vision and hearing
- Minimize environmental smoke
- Infant sleeps on back (SIDS prevention)

Injury Prevention Strategies
- Car seats
- Choking hazards
- Home environment
- Homes infants visit
  - Friends
  - Relatives

SUGGESTIONS FOR CLASSROOM ACTIVITIES

Before class, assign students to complete the activity "MediaLink Applications: Safety-Proofing for Baby," available on the Companion Website. Use this activity as a framework for discussing injury prevention with infants.

SUGGESTIONS FOR CLINICAL ACTIVITIES

Arrange for students to rotate through a pediatric clinic that performs health supervision visits for infants and toddlers.

LEARNING OBJECTIVE 7

Plan health promotion and health maintenance strategies employed during health supervision visits of infants and young children.

CONCEPTS FOR LECTURE

1. Health promotion and health maintenance strategies are routinely employed during health supervision visits.

POWERPOINT LECTURE SLIDES

 Strategies to Promote Health During Health Supervision Visits
- Explain procedures and purpose of procedures to parents
- Allow parents to help during exam
- Encourage parents to ask questions
- Encourage parents to share general perceptions of the child
- What to expect at the next visit

LEARNING OBJECTIVE 8

Apply the nursing process in assessment, diagnosis, goal setting, intervention, and evaluation of health promotion and health maintenance activities for the infant and young child.

CONCEPTS FOR LECTURE

1. The nursing process can be applied to health promotion and health maintenance activities.

POWERPOINT LECTURE SLIDES

1 Nursing Process Related to Health Promotion
- Assessment
- Diagnosis
- Planning and implementation
- Evaluation

1a Assessment
- Growth and development
- Expected feeding changes
- Complete assessment

1b Diagnosis
- Interrupted breastfeeding
- Compromised family coping
- Risk for altered parent/child attachment
- Sleep pattern disturbance
- Risk for infection
- Risk for injury
- Risk for altered growth and development

1c Planning and Implementation
- Establish trust
- Share information
- Administer immunizations—discuss side effects, comfort measures
- Perform screenings
- Child and family teaching

1d Evaluation
- Parents can state common safety hazards
- Infant demonstrates normal growth and development
- Infant remains free of disease and injury

LEARNING OBJECTIVE 9

Recognize the importance of family in infant and child health care, and include family assessment in each health supervision visit.

CONCEPTS FOR LECTURE

1. Because the family is viewed as the expert about the child, it is critical to involve the family in each health supervision visit.

POWERPOINT LECTURE SLIDES

1 Involving the Family
- Family is the constant in the child's life
- Family is the expert about the family
- Must be involved in health supervision visits

1a. At Each Visit: Family Assessment
- Interview family about developmental status of child
- Observe family interaction
- Discuss parental concerns

SUGGESTIONS FOR CLASSROOM ACTIVITIES

Invite parents to speak to the class about their experiences with health supervision visits.

LEARNING OBJECTIVE 10

State components of growth and development surveillance needs for toddlers and preschoolers.

CONCEPTS FOR LECTURE

1. It is important to monitor growth during the toddler and preschool years, as it is a primary way of evaluating nutritional status. Changes in growth may also be red flags for endocrine or cardiac disorders.
2. Meeting developmental milestones indicates that toddlers and preschoolers are developing normally.

POWERPOINT LECTURE SLIDES

1. Growth Monitoring
- Weight
- Height—once standing, use stadiometer to measure height
- Body mass index (BMI)

1a. Why We Still Monitor Growth
- Indicates nutritional status
- Changes may be red flags for
  - Endocrine diseases
  - Cardiac diseases
- Consider gene pool child came from—parental height, weight, BMI

2. Developmental Screening
- Look for developmental milestones
- Use a tool (Denver II)
- Suggest toys that may encourage development

SUGGESTIONS FOR CLASSROOM ACTIVITIES

Ask students to think of endocrine and cardiac disorders that could affect the growth of a toddler or preschooler. Would they expect the growth to decrease or increase?

SUGGESTIONS FOR CLINICAL ACTIVITIES

Many families do not participate in health supervision visits, and their only opportunity to receive health promotion is when the child is hospitalized. Identify local resources that the nurse could refer families to in order to receive free or low-cost health supervision visits.

LEARNING OBJECTIVE 11

Describe the nutrition, physical activity, and oral health needs of toddlers and preschoolers.

CONCEPTS FOR LECTURE

1. Good nutrition fosters normal growth, promotes development, and helps prevent disorders such as anemia, tooth decay, and immune dysfunction. Parents often have concerns about toddlers' food intake, as toddlers often consume small amounts of food. *Table 37.7 is a good reference*.

POWERPOINT LECTURE SLIDES

1. Good Nutrition
- Fosters normal growth
- Promotes development
- Prevents disorders such as
  - Anemia
  - Tooth decay
  - Immune dysfunction

2. Toddlers require physical activity to encourage further motor development. Preschoolers will begin to become more coordinated with movement.
3. Oral health is important for toddlers and preschoolers as they are at risk for early childhood caries, which can cause speech delays and pain.

1a Toddlers and Food
- Transition from bottle to cup
- Food takes on a social component now
- Parents worry about toddler's lack of appetite
- Develops food preferences and dislikes
- Choking hazards
- Limit juice, colas, high-fat foods

2 Physical Activity
- Increases fine and gross motor skills (mostly toddlers)
- Increases coordination (preschoolers)
- Examples
  - Hop
  - Run
  - Skip
  - Throw a ball
  - Push and pull objects

2a Encouraging Physical Activity
- Assess child's patterns of activity
- Determine favorite activities
- Limit TV time if needed
- Safety issues

3 Oral Health
- Risk for early childhood caries
  - Speech delays
  - Pain
- By 2 years, child has full set of 20 primary teeth—will begin loosing teeth around age 6

3a Oral Health Promotion
- Assess condition and number of teeth
- Determine if child has had a dental examination
- Assess if water source contains fluoride
- Review oral hygiene

SUGGESTIONS FOR CLASSROOM ACTIVITIES

Have the class brainstorm creative ways to encourage physical activity and oral hygiene in toddlers and preschoolers.

SUGGESTIONS FOR CLINICAL ACTIVITIES

Many of the health promotion topics discussed in this objective could be applied in the hospital setting as well. For example, toddlers and preschoolers in the hospital could be screened for caries. Encourage students to include these aspects of health promotion in their care of the hospitalized child.

LEARNING OBJECTIVE 12

Integrate pertinent mental health care into health supervision visits for young children.

CONCEPTS FOR LECTURE

1. Fostering a positive self-image is important to the young child's mental health. Common mental health concerns in this age group include nightmares, temper tantrums, and daily stressors.

POWERPOINT LECTURE SLIDES

1 Mental Health Issues and Concerns
- Assessment of child and family
  - What is a typical day like?
  - Observe communication patterns

○ Self-esteem: Related to tasks child can do (Example: brush teeth independently)

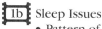 Self-Regulation
- Controls
  ○ Anger
  ○ Desire for objects or food
  ○ Other behaviors
- Child must learn to control and regulate self—positive discipline

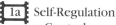 Sleep Issues
- Pattern of sleep
- Where child sleeps
- Nightmares
- Night terrors

SUGGESTIONS FOR CLASSROOM ACTIVITIES

While discussing self-regulation, show the video "Temper Tantrums," available on the Student CD-ROM.

LEARNING OBJECTIVE 13

Synthesize data about the family and other social relationships to promote and maintain the health of toddlers and preschoolers.

CONCEPTS FOR LECTURE

1. Toddlers and preschoolers make great strides in relationships and socialization, which are often expressed through play. One of the major goals during this age is to learn to be separate from parents.

POWERPOINT LECTURE SLIDES

 Toddlers and Relationships
- Enjoy playing with other children
- Play "side by side," not cooperatively
- Will play with adults

1a Preschoolers and Relationships
- Play cooperatively with other children ("house")
- Improving language skills
- Like to help with tasks
  ○ Setting table
  ○ Picking up toys

1b Separation
- Toddlers and preschoolers must learn to be away from parents
- Must learn that parent will return
- Parents may feel guilty for leaving
- Strategy: Allow child to keep a familiar object with them

SUGGESTIONS FOR CLASSROOM ACTIVITIES

Ask students to think of other issues that may affect the relationships of toddlers and preschoolers.

SUGGESTIONS FOR CLINICAL ACTIVITIES

Have students visit the playroom at the hospital to observe children playing "side by side" and cooperatively.

LEARNING OBJECTIVE 14

Plan assessment and interventions appropriate for health promotion and health maintenance during health supervision visits of toddlers and preschoolers.

CONCEPTS FOR LECTURE

1. During health supervision visits, the nurse assesses the child and follows through with specific interventions that are appropriate to that child and family.

POWERPOINT LECTURE SLIDES

 Assessment
- Complete assessment
  - ○ Growth and development
  - ○ Nutrition
  - ○ Physical activity
  - ○ Oral health
  - ○ Mental health
  - ○ Relationships
- Focus on developmental milestones

 Interventions
- Guidance related to toilet training
- Administer immunizations
- Provide screenings
- Discuss common safety hazards and injury prevention
- Reinforce need for continued health supervision visits
- Allow time for questions

SUGGESTIONS FOR CLASSROOM ACTIVITIES

Review the most current immunization schedule with students and discuss practical methods to decrease the trauma of receiving injections.

CHAPTER 38
HEALTH PROMOTION AND HEALTH MAINTENANCE FOR THE OLDER CHILD AND ADOLESCENT

RESOURCE LIBRARY

CD-ROM
Video: Teen Mental and Spiritual Health
NCLEX-RN® Review
Audio Glossary

IMAGE LIBRARY

Figure 38.1 This school-age child is receiving teaching from the nurse about food choices.
Figure 38.2 Everyone needs to be physically active.
Figure 38.3 School-age children often enjoy hikes with family, clubs, or other groups.
Figure 38.4 A student with diabetes is showing the school nurse how she programs her insulin pump.
Figure 38.5 This boy is learning about the effects of smoking on the body through the concrete experience of examining a model of the lungs.

COMPANION WEBSITE
NCLEX-RN® Review
MediaLink Applications:
  Develop a Teaching Plan: Smoking Education
  Case Study: Immunization Update

Figure 38.6 Parents often accompany teens with a healthcare problem in for the examination.
Figure 38.7 This teen girl is an avid "boarder."
Figure 38.8 Teens often become associated with causes.
Figure 38.9 Adolescents often drive motorized vehicles and may be at risk for injury if not properly prepared or protected.

LEARNING OBJECTIVE 1

Apply knowledge of school-age growth and development to identify needed assessment of nutrition and physical activity.

CONCEPTS FOR LECTURE

1. Key concepts related to nutrition in school-age children are independence and formation of long-term feeding habits. Assessment includes measurement of height, weight, body mass index (BMI), and observations about nutritional status.
2. Physical activity during childhood is critical to developing lifelong exercise habits. There are numerous benefits to exercise and physical activity during childhood.

POWERPOINT LECTURE SLIDES

1 Nutrition and the School-Age Child
- Increasingly independent with food choices
  - Strong likes and dislikes
  - May prepare own food
  - May have access to vending machines
- Forming lifelong feeding habits
  - Healthy food choices
  - Risk for obesity

 Assessment Parameters: Measurements
- Height
- Weight
- Body mass index (BMI)
- Plot on growth chart to determine percentiles
- Growth spurts

POWERPOINT LECTURE SLIDES *continued*

 1b Physical Assessment
- Condition of
  - Skin
  - Hair
  - Nails
- Ask questions about diet, food preferences, eating patterns

 1c Nutrition: Teaching Points with Families
- Eating patterns are hard to change—tackle one at a time
- Healthy snacks
- Increase calcium intake
- Limiting carbonated drinks

 2 Physical Activity and School-Age Children
- Refining skills such as
  - Hand-eye coordination
  - Muscular strength
  - Agility
  - Speed
- Examples of activities
  - Team sports
  - Individual activities

 2a Benefits of Activity
- Socialization
- Positive sense of accomplishment and self-esteem
- Weight control
- Increasing physical ability

2b Assessment of Physical Activity
- Physical activity patterns of parents
- Ask about amount of activity child does
  - Physical education during school
  - May be limited due to budget cuts
- Suggest activities child and family can do together
- Discuss protective equipment

SUGGESTIONS FOR CLASSROOM ACTIVITIES

It can be very difficult for children and families to change eating habits. During the class discussion, role-play a scenario with students where you pretend to be a school-age child and a student pretends to be the nurse. Ask the student to suggest ways for you to increase calcium intake, limit carbonated beverages, and eat healthier snacks.

SUGGESTIONS FOR CLINICAL ACTIVITIES

When students are caring for a hospitalized school-age child, have the students include nutrition and physical activity assessments in their overall assessment of the child and family.

LEARNING OBJECTIVE 2

State components of self-concept for school-age children.

CONCEPTS FOR LECTURE

1. The major components of self-concept include a sense of accomplishment, positive self-esteem, body image, and sexuality. The school-age years are an important time for the development of a child's self-concept.

POWERPOINT LECTURE SLIDES

 Self-Concept: What Is It?
- The mental idea that one has of the self
- School-age years are an important time for development of self-concept
- Components of self-concept
  ○ Self-esteem and sense of accomplishment
  ○ Body image
  ○ Sexuality

 Self-Esteem and Sense of Accomplishment
- Feelings and beliefs about competence
- Worth as an individual
- Ability to meet challenges
- Learn from success and failure
- Sense of accomplishment
  ○ What is child good at?
  ○ Physical activities
  ○ School performance

 Body Image
- The idea that one forms about one's body
- Look at child's appearance and dress
  ○ Clean and neat?
  ○ Appears insecure?
  ○ Posture?
  ○ Dress appropriate for age?
- Ask parents if they have concerns about child's body image

 Sexuality
- Person's view of self as a sexual being
- School-age children
  ○ Have many misconceptions about the bodies of men and women, sexual intercourse, and reproduction
  ○ May begin to ask questions
  ○ Questions should be answered truthfully and fully
  ○ Children typically learn about sex through the media

 Puberty and the School-Age Child
- Girls may have bodily changes as early as 9 or 10 years of age
- Boys generally begin about 2 years later than girls

SUGGESTIONS FOR CLASSROOM ACTIVITIES

Children often get information about sexuality through the media. Show clips of TV shows, movies, or advertisements that children may see on TV and discuss the information that children may receive from these programs. Prime-time TV and day-time talk shows are a good source of media for this activity.

SUGGESTIONS FOR CLINICAL ACTIVITIES

Assessing a child's self-esteem is an important component of the holistic assessment. Encourage students to use the questions discussed in "Teaching Highlights: Evaluating and Fostering Self-Esteem," during their care of hospitalized children.

LEARNING OBJECTIVE 3

Describe the growing importance of peers in planning teaching strategies with school-age children.

CONCEPTS FOR LECTURE

1. The school-age child begins to understand that peers are important and may begin to feel the effects of peer pressure.
2. Teaching strategies must appeal to the group as a whole, and educational methods must be varied and interesting.

POWERPOINT LECTURE SLIDES

1 School-Age Children and Peers
- Begin to understand that peers are important
- Generally want to be liked and accepted by peers
  - Usually begins by 8 to 9 years of age
  - May lead to risk-taking behaviors

1a Assessing the Impact of Peers
- Ask child
  - What things friends try to get them to do that they know they should not do
  - If the child has tried smoking or alcohol
- Asking these questions when parents are not present may increase the child's honesty

2 Teaching Strategies for School-Age Children
- Must appeal to group as a whole—children are used to learning in a group setting from school
- Must use interesting and varied teaching methods—examples

SUGGESTIONS FOR CLASSROOM ACTIVITIES

Have students design a brief educational activity for school-age children using the basic principles described in this objective.

SUGGESTIONS FOR CLINICAL ACTIVITIES

Role play with students—how they might ask questions of a school-age child to determine the impact of peers in the child's life.

LEARNING OBJECTIVE 4

Use knowledge of the major injury risks of school-age children to plan nursing interventions that contribute to their prevention.

CONCEPTS FOR LECTURE

1. Injuries are a common cause of morbidity and mortality among school-age children, and injury prevention efforts should focus on the most common sources of injury. Children are at risk for injuries from firearms, sport activities, motor vehicle crashes, and bicycle accidents. *Table 38.3 is a good reference for this content*.

POWERPOINT LECTURE SLIDES

1 Injuries and School-Age Children
- Common source of morbidity and mortality
- Children have more independence
- May engage in activities unsupervised

1a Examples of Sources of Injuries
- Firearms
- Motor vehicle crashes
  - Seat belt use
  - Booster seats
- Bicycle accidents; helmet use
- Sports injuries—protective gear
- Common theme: Most of these injuries are preventable

SUGGESTIONS FOR CLASSROOM ACTIVITIES

During class, have students read "Evidence-Based Nursing: Bicycle Helmet Effectiveness and Use" and "Evidence-Based Practice: Bicycle Helmet Effectiveness and Use." Have the class discuss the "Critical Thinking" questions at the end of the activity.

SUGGESTIONS FOR CLINICAL ACTIVITIES

Determine what local resources exist to promote injury prevention among children. For example, many hospitals partner with Safe Kids to develop injury prevention programs. If these resources are available locally, have students attend an activity designed to prevent injuries in children (examples: car seat fitting, bicycle safety program, assessment of home for safety issues, etc.).

LEARNING OBJECTIVE 5

Identify the major health concerns of the adolescent years.

CONCEPTS FOR LECTURE

1. The major health concerns of adolescents include school performance, sexual issues, body image issues, and the need for independence.

POWERPOINT LECTURE SLIDES

1 Adolescents and Health
- Adolescents are seen sporadically for health care—visits are still recommended yearly
- Usually healthy
- Do not require immunizations as often
- Typical reasons for visit to healthcare provider
  ○ Minor illness
  ○ Birth control
  ○ Sports examination

1a Major Health Concerns of Adolescents
- School performance
- Sexual issues
- Body image issues
- Need for independence

SUGGESTIONS FOR CLASSROOM ACTIVITIES

Before class, assign students to complete "Case Study: Immunization Update," available on the Companion Website. Use this activity as a basis for discussing typical reasons that adolescents visit a healthcare provider.

SUGGESTIONS FOR CLINICAL ACTIVITIES

Have students assist with sports examinations for adolescents. This activity works best for summer classes since the majority of sports examinations are done in the late summer before classes begin.

LEARNING OBJECTIVE 6

Apply communication skills to interactions with adolescents and their families.

CONCEPTS FOR LECTURE

1. Adolescents need their parents for guidance and reassurance as the teenager strives to gain independence. Adolescents commonly strike out at parents, test limits, and have conflicts with their parents. There are several communication skills that can be used to promote positive interactions between adolescents and their families.

POWERPOINT LECTURE SLIDES

1 Adolescents and Parents
- Adolescents are trying to gain independence
- Teens still need parents for guidance and reassurance
- Adolescents may
  ○ Strike out at parents
  ○ Test limits
  ○ Have conflicts with parents

1a Communication Strategies for Teens and Parents
- Assist parents in understanding that adolescent is striving for independence

- Reassure adolescent that parent is trying to provide guidance
- Encourage parents to reward positive behaviors
- Encourage adolescent to discuss specific issues rather than global subjects
- Respectful communication
- Others?

SUGGESTIONS FOR CLASSROOM ACTIVITIES

- Have students provide examples of the communication strategies discussed in this objective.
- Have students role play how the communication strategies described can be applied. Have one or two students play the role of the parents and another student play the role of the adolescent. This activity works better if you provide the students with cue cards about what the situation is and what you would like their responses to be.

SUGGESTIONS FOR CLINICAL ACTIVITIES

Invite a social worker or child-life specialist from the hospital to speak with students during clinical conference about communication strategies for adolescents and parents.

LEARNING OBJECTIVE 7

Apply assessment skills to plan data gathering methods for nutrition, physical activity, and mental health status of youth.

CONCEPTS FOR LECTURE

1. Nutrition can be a challenge for many adolescents, as they often have poor diets. Weight changes may also be a concern. After assessing nutritional status, the nurse can suggest several ways to promote a healthy diet.
2. Physical activity tends to decrease during adolescence, especially among girls. Promoting physical activity is important, as it sets up habits for lifelong exercise and activity.
3. Adolescents often have challenges with mental health issues, which are closely linked to developmental tasks such as independence, forming close relationships, gaining confidence, and setting goals for the future.

POWERPOINT LECTURE SLIDES

1 Nutrition and the Adolescent
- Need well-balanced diet to support growth and immune function
- Teens often do not eat well
  ○ Lead busy lives
  ○ Like high-fat, high-calorie foods
- May be dieting to achieve weight loss
- Family may not have financial resources to buy healthy foods

1a Nutritional Assessment
- Plot height, weight, and BMI on growth chart
- Ask if they have concerns about weight
- Discuss usual meal routines and favorite foods

1b Promoting Healthy Nutrition
- Five fruits and vegetables daily
- Whole grain products
- Eating three meals a day (don't skip breakfast)
- How to plan menus
- Limiting high-fat, high-calorie foods

2 Physical Activity and the Adolescent
- Physical activity levels decrease during adolescence, especially among girls
  ○ Only 30% to 60% of teens report daily vigorous activity
  ○ Only 19% of 12th graders regularly attend PE class at school
- Assess physical activity levels and favorite activities during health visits
  ○ Sports
  ○ Other activities

Promoting Physical Activity
- Suggest one thing they can do every day that increases activity levels
  - Walking the dog
  - Take the stairs instead of the elevator
  - Ride their bicycle to school
- Suggesting peer group activities is helpful

 Adolescents and Mental Health
- Mental health linked to
  - Gaining independence
  - Forming close relationships
  - Becoming confident in accomplishments
  - Setting goals for the future

Assessing Mental Health Status
- Ask what the teen is proud of
- Ask what the teen is disappointed in
- Ask about body image
- Ask about sexual activity
  - Ask directly if they have had intercourse
  - Focus on birth control, prevention of STD's

SUGGESTIONS FOR CLASSROOM ACTIVITIES

Before discussing mental health during adolescence, show the video, "Teens and Mental Health," available on the Student CD-ROM. Use this video as a basis for the discussion.

SUGGESTIONS FOR CLINICAL ACTIVITIES

When caring for a hospitalized adolescent, have students note what the adolescent is eating on his or her meal tray. This can often open the door for a discussion about health nutrition during adolescence.

LEARNING OBJECTIVE 8

Intervene with adolescents by integrating activities to promote health and to prevent disease and injury.

CONCEPTS FOR LECTURE

1. Although most adolescents are generally healthy, there are several screening tests that should be performed during adolescence.
2. Injury is the greatest health hazard for adolescents, so injury prevention is a critical topic to discuss during health visits with adolescents. *Tables 38.6 and 38.7 are good references for this content.*

POWERPOINT LECTURE SLIDES

 Disease Prevention During Adolescence
- Most adolescents are generally healthy
- Screening tests during adolescence
  - Scoliosis
  - Anemia
  - Sexually transmitted diseases
  - Vision and hearing
  - Blood pressure
  - Urinalysis
  - Pap smear, breast exam
  - Screening tests for sexually active teens

 Disease Prevention Assessments
- Smoking
- Depression
- Stress
- Alcohol or other substance use
- Immunization status
- Testicular, breast exams
- Prevention of skin cancer
  - Sunscreen use
  - Limiting exposure
  - Tanning beds

POWERPOINT LECTURE SLIDES *continued*

 2 Injury Prevention During Adolescence
- Injury is greatest health hazard for adolescents
- Driving and motor vehicle collisions
  - Easily distracted
  - Little experience with maneuvering a car
  - Drinking and driving
  - Driving while tired
  - Use of restraint devices

2a Other Sources of Injury
- Four-wheelers
- Watercraft: boats, jet skis
- Power tools
- Firearms
- Fires
- Sports
- Abuse

SUGGESTIONS FOR CLASSROOM ACTIVITIES

Before class, assign students to complete the activity, "MediaLink Applications: Smoking Education," available on the Companion Website. Use this activity as a framework for discussing disease prevention among adolescents.

SUGGESTIONS FOR CLINICAL ACTIVITIES

Have students identify resources available in the local clinical setting that can be used to teach adolescents about disease and injury prevention strategies.

CHAPTER 39
NURSING CONSIDERATIONS FOR THE CHILD AND FAMILY IN THE COMMUNITY

RESOURCE LIBRARY

 CD-ROM

Videos:
  Disaster Preparedness
  EMS for Children
Audio Glossary
NCLEX-RN® Review

 COMPANION WEBSITE

MediaLink Applications:
  Identify Health Issues in Childcare Settings
  Develop an Individualized Health Plan (IHP)
  Complete an Emergency Information
    Form (EIF)
School Policy Review
Teaching Plans:
  Disasters and the Family with an Infant
  Disasters and the Family with a Child
  Disasters and the Child Assisted by Technology
Thinking Critically
NCLEX-RN® Review
Case Study

📖 IMAGE LIBRARY

Figure 39.1 A visit to the home when all family members are present provides the best information for completion of an assessment tool such as the Home Observation for Measurement of the Environment (HOME).

Figure 39.2 Nurses carefully assess children in the office setting who present with an acute care illness.

Figure 39.3 The school is often the setting for screening tests of large groups of students to identify those that may have a problem that interferes with learning.

Figure 39.4 Assess the childcare center's environment for safety hazards.

Figure 39.5 Nurses provide both short-term and long-term services to families in the home setting.

Figure 39.6 Children with chronic conditions may have a visible or nonvisible health condition, or

nonvisible until an acute episode of their condition makes the condition visible.

Figure 39.7 Nurses often assume a larger role in working with children and families with a chronic health condition, and educating the family to manage diabetes type 1 is an important role of this pediatric nurse, who is also a certified diabetes educator.

Figure 39.8 Because some children need medications or other therapies during school hours, the parents and child, school nurse, teacher, and school administrators develop a plan to manage the child's condition during school hours.

Figure 39.9 Daily caregiving demands of the child who is medically fragile continue 24 hours a day, 7 days a week.

LEARNING OBJECTIVE 1

List the categories of family strengths that help families cope with stressors.

CONCEPTS FOR LECTURE

1. All families experience stressors, which can be positive or negative.
2. Family strengths are the relationships and processes that support and protect families during times of adversity and change. *Refer to Table 39.1 during this discussion.*

POWERPOINT LECTURE SLIDES

 Family Stressors
  • All families experience stressors
  • Stressors can be viewed as
    ○ Positive
    ○ Negative

- Varies based on individual family's situation
- Families respond to stressors—interactions may change as a result

1a Examples of Positive Family Stressors
- Birth of a child
- Starting school
- Acceptance into college

1b Examples of Negative Family Stressors
- Serious illness or chronic health condition
- Financial hardship
- Relationship concerns

2 Family Strengths
- Relationships and processes that support and protect families during times of adversity and change
- Help maintain family cohesion

2a Four Types of Family Strengths
- Individual or family traits (optimism, resilience)
- Individual or family assets (finances)
- Individual or family capabilities, skills, and competencies—problem-solving
- Motivation

2b Resilient Families
- "Bounce back" from stressors and challenges
- Gain sense of competence, which makes them more resilient

2c Characteristics of the Resilient Family
- Balancing illness with other family needs
- Forming collaborative relationships with providers
- Communication skills
- Flexibility and commitment
- Positive meaning to the situation
- Coping and problem-solving

2d Why Focus on Family Strengths?
- Nurse can use these strengths to develop rapport with family
- Validate family members' emotions
- Increase resilience, management of the problem

SUGGESTIONS FOR CLASSROOM ACTIVITIES

Ask students whether they consider their own families to be "resilient." Why or why not?

SUGGESTIONS FOR CLINICAL ACTIVITIES

Families in the hospital setting are often facing stressors. What strategies can the nurse use in the clinical setting to help families cope with these stressors and encourage resilience?

LEARNING OBJECTIVE 2

Describe the advantages of using a family assessment tool.

CONCEPTS FOR LECTURE

1. Family assessment tools can be used to collect important information about family functioning, nurturing, problem solving, and communication. There are several family assessment tools available. *The Family APGAR Questionnaire is located in Table 39.2 of the text*.

POWERPOINT LECTURE SLIDES

 Family Assessment Tools Collect Information About
- Family functioning
- How family nurtures its members
- Coping strategies
- Stressors
- Problem solving and communication

1a Examples of Family Assessment Tools
- Family APGAR: Five-item screening questionnaire
- HOME inventory
  - Measures stimulation and support available to children
  - Interview and observation of home environment
  - 45 to 90 minutes
- Friedman family assessment tool: Collects data about relationships, functioning, strengths, and problems

---

SUGGESTIONS FOR CLASSROOM ACTIVITIES

After discussing the available family assessment tools, have students discuss the pros and cons of each tool. What setting is most appropriate for each tool? What information does each tool provide the nurse?

SUGGESTIONS FOR CLINICAL ACTIVITIES

Assign students to complete a family assessment using one of the tools discussed in the book. This assessment could occur during clinical care of a hospitalized family, or it could occur in an outpatient or community setting.

LEARNING OBJECTIVE 3

List the variety of community healthcare settings where nurses provide health services to children.

CONCEPTS FOR LECTURE

1. Children receive most of their health care in community settings, and there continues to be a shift to care for children outside of the hospital setting.

POWERPOINT LECTURE SLIDES

1 Community Settings
- Children receive most of their health care in community settings
  - Child care centers
  - Schools
  - Camps
  - Physician's office
  - Hospital or public health clinics
  - Homeless shelters
  - The home

1a Trends in Healthcare Delivery
- Hospital to community shift
- Shorter stays in the hospital

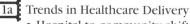

- Home health services
  - Long-term IV antibiotics
  - Home dialysis
  - Technological advances

SUGGESTIONS FOR CLASSROOM ACTIVITIES

Discuss potential pros and cons of the shift in caring for children in the community rather than in the hospital.

SUGGESTIONS FOR CLINICAL ACTIVITIES

Identify local settings where children potentially receive health care. Determine if RNs provide that care (for example, are there RNs in every school in your community, or do RNs supervise several schools).

LEARNING OBJECTIVE 4

Describe the role of the nurse in each identified healthcare setting.

CONCEPTS FOR LECTURE

1. Nurses working in the office or healthcare center setting coordinate the healthcare needed by the child with all other healthcare settings.
2. Nurses working in the school setting focus on promoting health and safety and providing direct care to ill and injured children.
3. Nurses working in childcare settings often serve as consultants in the development of policies. They also train staff and monitor health practices in the setting.
4. Nurses working in the home health setting often care for (or assist families who care for) medically fragile children. They also assess the home environment and assist families in planning for emergencies.

POWERPOINT LECTURE SLIDES

1 Nurses in Office or Healthcare Center Setting
- Coordinate care
- Triage based on severity of illness
- Assessment and physical exam
- Screening tests
- Immunizations, health promotion
- Link families to community resources
- Maintain safe environment

2 Nurses in School Setting
- Promote health and safety
- Infection control
- Direct care for ill or injured children
- Screening
- Administering medications
- Crisis intervention/support services
- Facilitating return to school after illness or surgery

3 Nurses in Childcare Settings
- Help develop policies regarding health and safety
- Train staff
- Monitor and promote health practices
- Infection control
- Emergency care planning

4 Nurses in Home Health Settings
- Care of medically fragile children—teaching families how to care for these children
- Assess home environment
- Emergency preparedness

SUGGESTIONS FOR CLASSROOM ACTIVITIES

There are numerous MediaLink Applications activities available on the Companion Website that can augment the discussion of this objective, including:

- Review a clinic or office setting and identify potential hazards to young children. Develop a plan to improve the safety of the office or clinic setting.
- Provide health education in the schools
- Identify health issues in childcare settings
- Complete an emergency information form (EIF)
- Assist parents with case management
- Create a family disaster plan: Family with an Infant, Family with a School-age Child, Child Assisted by Technology

SUGGESTIONS FOR CLINICAL ACTIVITIES

Arrange for students to rotate through some of the community settings described in this objective as part of their clinical rotation.

LEARNING OBJECTIVE 5

Describe the responses of children to disasters by developmental stage.

CONCEPTS FOR LECTURE

1. Children are particularly vulnerable during a disaster, both in their physical ability to escape and in their psychological vulnerability.
2. Children have different responses to disasters based on their developmental age. *Table 39.3 is a good reference.*

POWERPOINT LECTURE SLIDES

1 Vulnerabilities of Children During Disasters
- Physical and cognitive level
  - May limit ability to escape
  - May become separated from family
- Psychological vulnerabilities
  - Fewer coping skills and limited understanding
  - Fear and anxiety
  - May believe TV reports are new events each time they are replayed

1a Emergency Needs of Children During Disasters
- More vulnerable to agents absorbed through the skin
- May be unable to escape danger—may not follow instructions during evacuation
- Parents may become incapacitated
- Cannot distinguish between reality and fantasy
- May fear emergency personnel in protective suits or hoods

2 Developmental Responses: Toddlers/Preschoolers
- Reaction reflects that of parents
- Regressive behaviors
- Decreased appetite, vomiting, diarrhea
- Sleep disorders
- Re-enactment by play
- Post-traumatic stress disorder (PTSD)

2a Developmental Responses: School Age
- Fear, anxiety
- Increased hostility
- Somatic complaints
- Sleep disorders
- School problems
- PTSD

Developmental Responses: Preadolescents
- Hostility
- Somatic complaints
- Eating disorders
- Rebellion
- Interpersonal difficulties
- PTSD

 Developmental Responses: Adolescents
- Rebellion, behavior problems
- Somatic complaints
- Sleep, eating disorders
- Lack of concentration
- Decreased interest in social activities, hobbies
- PTSD

SUGGESTIONS FOR CLASSROOM ACTIVITIES

In many recent disasters, infants and young children have been separated from their families. Discuss strategies that nurses can use to prevent this from happening.

SUGGESTIONS FOR CLINICAL ACTIVITIES

Explore the possibility of students signing up as volunteers with the local chapter of the Red Cross and completing basic disaster training. In the event of an actual local disaster, students would then be able to directly provide care to those affected.

LEARNING OBJECTIVE 6

Define the child with a chronic condition by categories of impairments.

CONCEPTS FOR LECTURE

1. A chronic condition is a condition that is expected to last 3 months or more. These conditions can be categorized based on the limitations imposed by each. These children receive most of their health care in the community.

POWERPOINT LECTURE SLIDES

 Chronic Conditions
- Expected to last more than 3 months at time of diagnosis
- Receive most of health care in the community

 Categories of Chronic Conditions
- Limitations in function that would typically be expected
- Disfigurement
- Dependency on medications or diet to control condition
- Dependency on medical technology
- Need more medical care than children of same age
- Require ongoing treatments at home or school

 Impact of Chronic Illness on Health Care
- 12.8% of children with special needs consume 45% of all pediatric healthcare costs

SUGGESTIONS FOR CLASSROOM ACTIVITIES

What impact does having a child with a chronic condition have on a family? What stressors does it bring about? Relate this discussion back to the material discussed in Objective 1 about family functioning and stressors.

SUGGESTIONS FOR CLINICAL ACTIVITIES

Many children with chronic illnesses are followed in outpatient clinics based in hospitals. Assign students to rotate through these clinics if possible.

LEARNING OBJECTIVE 7

List the skills and knowledge needed by the nurse to effectively care for the child with a chronic condition in the community.

CONCEPTS FOR LECTURE

1. Nurses in the community who work with children and families with chronic illnesses need a wide variety of skills in order to provide quality care.

POWERPOINT LECTURE SLIDES

[1] Skills and Knowledge Nurses Need
- Knowledge of pathophysiology, trajectory of disease
- Knowledge of child and family reactions to stress of disease
- Ability to work with the family
- Ability to provide culturally sensitive care
- Good assessment skills

[1a] Skills and Knowledge Nurses Need
- Good communication skills
- Ability to collaborate with other professionals
- Knowledge of local resources/referrals
- Ability to identify dysfunctional family

SUGGESTIONS FOR CLASSROOM ACTIVITIES

After reviewing the list of skills in this objective, ask students which skills they think are the easiest to develop. Which ones are the most difficult?

SUGGESTIONS FOR CLINICAL ACTIVITIES

When students are rotating through community-based sites, have them ask nurses which skills they believe are the most critical to have when caring for children and families with chronic illnesses.

LEARNING OBJECTIVE 8

Describe nursing interventions to support the child with a chronic condition's transition to school and adult living.

CONCEPTS FOR LECTURE

1. Nurses can do several things that provide support for families who are transitioning a child with a chronic condition to school or to adult living.

POWERPOINT LECTURE SLIDES

[1] Transition to School
- Assist family in understanding the role of the teacher—educational role
- Educate teachers and staff about unique needs of the child (Example: Hypoglycemia symptoms)
- Provide instruction about medical equipment child uses (Example: Insulin pump)
- Supervise healthcare aides

[1a] Transition to Adult Living
- Identify adult-oriented healthcare services for the family
- Help family explore alternative living arrangements
- Provide referrals to agencies who can assist with workplace skills

SUGGESTIONS FOR CLASSROOM ACTIVITIES

Before this class, assign students to complete the activity "MediaLink Applications: Develop an Individualized Health Plan (IHP): Child with a Chronic Condition Entering School," located on the Companion Website.

SUGGESTIONS FOR CLINICAL ACTIVITIES

Identify local resources in the clinical setting that can be used to help families transition to school or to adult living.

LEARNING OBJECTIVE 9

Discuss the family's role in care coordination.

CONCEPTS FOR LECTURE

1. Families play a major role in coordinating the care of children with chronic illnesses, including determining responsibility for who cares for the child and increased financial expenses. Over time, the family becomes the expert caregivers for their child.

POWERPOINT LECTURE SLIDES

1 Family Role in Care Coordination
- Who will care for the child?
  - Responsibility
  - Knowledge of medicines, equipment, treatments
  - Transport to and from appointments
  - Respite care

1a Family Role in Care Coordination
- Financial impact
  - Increased out-of-pocket expenses
  - One parent may quit job to care for child
  - Insurance issues
- Primary caregivers
- Over time, family becomes the expert about that child

SUGGESTIONS FOR CLASSROOM ACTIVITIES

Invite a family who cares for a child with a chronic illness in the home setting to speak to your class about their experiences.

SUGGESTIONS FOR CLINICAL ACTIVITIES

When caring for a family who has a child with a chronic illness, encourage the student to explore how the family copes with the child's care in the home setting. Also, the student should assess the possible need for respite care.

CHAPTER 40
NURSING CONSIDERATIONS FOR THE HOSPITALIZED CHILD

RESOURCE LIBRARY

 CD-ROM

Video: Treatment Room
Skill 10-4: Performing a Venipuncture
Skill 11-1: Administering an Oral Medication
Skill 11-2: Administering an Intramuscular
  Injection
Skill 11-4: Administering an Intravenous
  Medication
Skill 11-12: Using a Metered Dose Inhaler (MDI)
NCLEX-RN® Review
Audio Glossary

COMPANION WEBSITE

NCLEX-RN® Review
MediaLink Applications:
  Communication Strategy: Preparing a Toddler for
    Venipuncture
  Case Study: Preparing an Adolescent for Surgery
  Care Plan: Preparing a School-Age Child for Surgery
Audio Glossary

IMAGE LIBRARY

Figure 40.1 Allowing the child to dress up as a doctor or a nurse helps prepare the child for hospitalization.

Figure 40.2 The child's anxiety and fear often will be reduced if the nurse explains what is going to happen and demonstrates how the procedure will be done by using a doll.

Figure 40.3 Jasmine's parents are taking the time to prepare her for hospitalization by reading a book recommended by the nurse.

Figure 40.4 The nurse is monitoring a young child who is in a short-stay unit for treatment of dehydration and fever.

Figure 40.5 Rehabilitation units provide an opportunity for the child to relearn tasks like walking and climbing stairs.

Figure 40.6 A, Volunteers such as this foster grandmother can provide stimulation and nurturing to help young children adapt to lengthy hospitalizations. B, Child life specialists plan activities for young children in the hospital to facilitate play and stress reduction.

Figure 40.7 The nurse can use a simple gender-specific outline drawing of a child's body to encourage children to draw what they think about their medical problem.

Figure 40.8 A child life specialist works with children being treated for cancer.

Figure 40.9 Hospitals may have pet therapy from specially trained animals to provide comfort and distraction during healthcare.

Figure 40.10 A, Age-appropriate play will help the child adjust to hospitalization and care. B, Having the child play with dolls that have "disabilities" similar to his or her own will help the child adjust.

Figure 40.11 Having interaction with other hospitalized adolescents and maintaining contact with friends outside the hospital are very important so that the teenager does not feel isolated and alone.

Figure 40.12 Shriners Hospital in Spokane, Washington, has a special classroom and teacher for children undergoing a lengthy hospital stay, enabling them to remain current with their schoolwork.

Figure 40.13 This child has just undergone surgery and is in the PICU.

Figure 40.14 This child with chronic medical problems is being cared for at home.

LEARNING OBJECTIVE 1

Discuss the child's understanding of health and illness according to the child's psychosocial and developmental levels.

CONCEPTS FOR LECTURE

1. Children have a different understanding of health and illness than adults. The child's understanding of illness and hospitalization is based primarily on the cognitive ability at different developmental stages and on previous experiences with healthcare professionals.
2. The nurse can classify a child's expected understanding of health and illness based on his or her age.

POWERPOINT LECTURE SLIDES

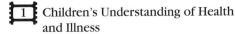 Children's Understanding of Health and Illness
- Different than adults
- Based primarily on
  - Cognitive ability at different developmental stages
  - Previous experiences with healthcare professionals

2 Infants
- By 6 months—realize they are separate beings
- Can identify primary caregivers
  - May feel anxious with strangers
  - Separation anxiety
- If left alone, hospitalization can be more traumatic—encourage parents to stay with infant
- Can sense parent's anxiety

2a Toddlers and Preschoolers
- Begin to understand illness but not its cause
- Magical thinking; "bad behavior, animal, etc. made me sick"
- Knows names and locations of some body parts—usually those that can be seen
- Separation from parents is major stressor
- Fear bodily mutilation
  - Demonstrate on dolls first
  - Band-aids

2b School-Age Children
- More realistic understanding of illness
- Like models, drawings as part of explanation
- Understands more about body parts—heart, lungs, bones
- Less fear of separation, as they know parent will return
- Fears: Pain, stitches, disfigurement

2c Adolescents
- Good understanding of illness and body
- Worry about body image
- Establishing self-identity—allow choices and control when possible
- Major stressors of hospitalization—separation from peers, home, and school

SUGGESTIONS FOR CLASSROOM ACTIVITIES

Divide the class into four groups, one for each developmental level of the child. Based on their knowledge of how children understand health and illness, have each group identify three techniques the nurse could use when caring for the child in the hospital. Have each group share their ideas with the class.

SUGGESTIONS FOR CLINICAL ACTIVITIES

Suggest that students make small index cards for each developmental group (infants, toddlers, etc.) on which they list the expected understanding of health and illness and techniques to use with that group. When they care for a child, they have a ready reference in their pocket that helps them incorporate developmentally appropriate interventions into their nursing care.

LEARNING OBJECTIVE 2

Recognize the effect of hospitalization on the child and family.

CONCEPTS FOR LECTURE

1. Hospitalization disrupts a family's usual routines. Parental roles may be altered, and family members may be anxious or fearful.
2. The siblings of a hospitalized child may receive less attention than usual and may feel anxious, guilty, or jealous. *See "Teaching Highlights: Strategies for Assisting the Sibling of a Hospitalized Child" for details.*

POWERPOINT LECTURE SLIDES

[1] Effect of Hospitalization on Family
- Disrupts usual routines
  - Changes in who is at home with siblings
  - Changes in who is working
- May be anxious or fearful
  - Severity of illness
  - Watching child suffer pain

[1a] What Can Nurses Do?
- Tailor care to family's needs and preferences
- Honest and open communication
- View parent as the expert about the child
- Respect cultural practices

[2] Effects on Siblings
- Less attention from parents
- May fantasize about illness or injury
- May fear ill child will die
- Guilt, insecurity, anxiety, jealousy
- Behavioral or school problems
- Nursing strategies

SUGGESTIONS FOR CLASSROOM ACTIVITIES

Invite a panel of parents whose children have been hospitalized to speak to the class. Ask the parents to discuss how the child's hospitalization affected their family, and what nursing interventions were helpful in that situation.

SUGGESTIONS FOR CLINICAL ACTIVITIES

Invite a child life specialist to clinical conference to discuss strategies to help siblings cope with hospitalization.

LEARNING OBJECTIVE 3

Assess the family's risk and protective factors that will influence adaptation to hospitalization.

CONCEPTS FOR LECTURE

1. Completing a family assessment is critical when developing a plan of care for the child. *Refer to Table 40.5 during this objective.*

POWERPOINT LECTURE SLIDES

[1] Family Assessment: Considerations
- Financial resources
  - Consider time off from work
  - Cost of travel, staying with child
- Access to health care
- Availability of community services
- Cultural considerations

1a Family Assessment: Communication
- Family dynamics
- Quality of communication
- Methods of handling problems
- Sources of strength

1b Family Assessment: Support
- Prior methods of coping—were they helpful?
- Support groups
- Referral to outside agencies

SUGGESTIONS FOR CLASSROOM ACTIVITIES

Create profiles of families with different strengths and challenges. Divide students into groups and have them list various factors with each family that would require further family assessment.

SUGGESTIONS FOR CLINICAL ACTIVITIES

When students are caring for a child, have them complete a family assessment as part of their plan of care.

LEARNING OBJECTIVE 4

Identify several types of hospital units and the needs that children and families have in each unit.

CONCEPTS FOR LECTURE

1. Because children admitted to various hospital units are in different phases of illness, the needs of the child and family vary from unit to unit.

POWERPOINT LECTURE SLIDES

1 Emergency Department (ED)
- Visit to ED is usually unexpected
- Parents usually frightened, insecure—allow them to stay with child
- Need honest, accurate information—repeat information frequently
- Family presence during resuscitations, invasive procedures

1a Intensive Care
- Child's prognosis may be guarded, uncertain
- Parents may be anxious
- Hi-tech equipment
- Many people in and out of child's room
- Parents need
  - To be with their child
  - Honest, accurate information
  - Encouragement to touch or hold child

1b Preoperative and Postoperative Units
- Allow parent to stay with child until surgery begins
- Need orientation to unit
  - Where they can stand or sit
  - What equipment they need to wear (gowns, masks, etc.)
- Explain equipment

1c Short-Stay Units
- Used for many procedures and minor surgeries
- Benefits
  - Lessens disruption of family patterns
  - Cost effective

- Parent will provide much of child's care at home
  - Teaching
  - Resources available
  - Follow-up care

 Children in Isolation During Hospitalization
- Have limited contact with other children—may lack stimulation
- Encourage family to visit—discuss use of gowns, gloves, and masks
- Explain rationale for isolation

 Rehabilitation Units
- Ongoing care and recovery after acute illness
- Goals of rehabilitation
  - Help child with physical or mental challenges
  - Reach fullest potential
  - Promote developmentally appropriate skills
- Family involvement is critical

SUGGESTIONS FOR CLASSROOM ACTIVITIES

Before class, assign students to complete "Case Study: Preparing an Adolescent for Surgery," available on the Companion Website. Use this as a basis for discussing the preoperative and postoperative unit.

SUGGESTIONS FOR CLINICAL ACTIVITIES

As students care for and observe care of children in various settings, discuss the needs of parents and children in each of the units discussed in this objective.

LEARNING OBJECTIVE 5

Identify methods that the child and family use to adapt to hospitalization.

CONCEPTS FOR LECTURE

1. Methods that are used to help the child and family adapt to hospitalization include child life programs, rooming in, therapeutic play, and therapeutic recreation.

POWERPOINT LECTURE SLIDES

 Methods to Promote Adaptation to Hospitalization
- Child life programs
- Rooming in
- Therapeutic play
- Therapeutic recreation

 Child Life Programs
- Age-appropriate play
- Preparation for procedures
- Focus on emotional needs of child
- Support family in providing child's care

 Rooming In
- Parent stays in child's room and helps provide care
- Accommodations vary (cots, day beds, etc.)
- Collaboration between nurse and parent is important

 Therapeutic Play
- "Play is the work of childhood"
- Often a collaborative effort between nurses, child life therapists, and parents

Therapeutic Recreation
- Used with adolescents
- Focus on contact with peers
- Parties, games, movies, etc.

LEARNING OBJECTIVE 6

Describe types of therapeutic play and recreation used with hospitalized children.

CONCEPTS FOR LECTURE

1. The stress of illness and hospitalization increases the value of play. Specific play activities are based upon the child's level of development. *It may be helpful to refer to Table 40.8.*

POWERPOINT LECTURE SLIDES

1 Purposes of Play
- Facilitates normal development
- Helps child
  ○ Learn about health care
  ○ Express anxieties
  ○ Work through feelings
- Achieve control

1a Types of Play
- Therapeutic play
  ○ Helps assess knowledge of illness or injury
  ○ Child draws body
  ○ Child makes up a story
- Dramatic play—acts out experience of health care

1b Toddlers
- Helps them release tension
- Playing peek-a-boo, hide-and-seek
- Read books and stories
- Dolls
- Building blocks
- Safe hospital equipment (stethoscopes, syringes without needles)

1c Preschoolers
- Outline of body
- Playing with safe hospital equipment
- Crayons and coloring
- Puppets, play dough
- Pet therapy

1d School-Age Children
- Child may regress with hospitalization
- Collecting objects
- Games, books, schoolwork, crafts, computers

1e Adolescents
- Therapeutic recreation
- Focus on peers
- Telephone contact
- Examples
  ○ Pizza parties
  ○ Video games
  ○ Movie night

SUGGESTIONS FOR CLASSROOM ACTIVITIES

Bring examples of hospital equipment to the lecture and discuss which types of equipment are safe for children to play with and which ones are not.

SUGGESTIONS FOR CLINICAL ACTIVITIES

Role model age-appropriate play for students using toys found in the clinical setting.

LEARNING OBJECTIVE 7

Use knowledge of child and family response to hospitalization to plan nursing interventions to facilitate coping with hospitalization.

CONCEPTS FOR LECTURE

1. There are numerous nursing interventions that can help children and families cope with hospitalization.

POWERPOINT LECTURE SLIDES

`1` Nursing Interventions
- Base interventions around child's understanding of health and illness
- Assess family for strengths and challenges
- Collaborate with child life
- Encourage rooming in
- Therapeutic play

`1a` Nursing Interventions
- Meet educational needs of school-age children
- Preparation for procedures
- Consider parent the expert about the child

SUGGESTIONS FOR CLASSROOM ACTIVITIES

Create a case study of a child who is hospitalized and use it as a framework to discuss the various nursing interventions that could be used during his or her hospitalization.

SUGGESTIONS FOR CLINICAL ACTIVITIES

When students are completing their plan of care for a child they have cared for, require them to include interventions that help children and families cope with hospitalization. Assign "Care Plan: Preparing a School-Age Child for Surgery" from the Companion Website for homework.

CHAPTER 41
THE CHILD WITH A LIFE-THREATENING CONDITION AND END-OF-LIFE CARE

RESOURCE LIBRARY

CD-ROM

Videos
  Involving Family in NICU Setting
  Presenting Bad News to Families
  Parental Reactions to Death of a Child
Audio Glossary
NCLEX-RN® Review

COMPANION WEBSITE

MediaLink Applications:
  Case Study: Newborn in NICU with
    Bronchopulmonary Dysplasia
  Care Plan: Adolescent in PICU for a Brain Injury
  Case Study: Loss of a Schoolmate
  Family-Centered Care Plan: Death of a Child
  Helping Families Grieve
  Preparing the Family for Hospice
  Complementary Care: Use of Music Therapy
    in Grief
  Grief Resources for Nurses
Thinking Critically
NCLEX-RN® Review

IMAGE LIBRARY

Figure 41.1 Jooti feels pain, hears noises, has her sleep disrupted, and has limited mobility because of all the equipment attached to her.

Figure 41.2 By their very nature, PICUs are ominous and sterile.

Figure 41.3 In times of crisis, everyone likes to know that someone is in charge and who that person is.

Figure 41.4 During the sibling's visit to the ill child, it is important to talk with the sibling and answer

any questions in an honest manner at a level the child can understand.

Figure 41.5 It is important that parents and siblings feel comfortable communicating with the seriously ill child.

Figure 41.6 The toddler with a life-limiting condition recognizes that he feels bad and that routines are different.

Figure 41.7 Nurses need to express grief in a supportive environment after a child's death.

LEARNING OBJECTIVE 1

Describe the child's responses to having a life-threatening illness or injury by developmental level.

CONCEPTS FOR LECTURE

1. Because children of various ages are at different stages of development, their responses to illness and injury vary. *Table 41.1 summarizes this information.*

POWERPOINT LECTURE SLIDES

 Child's Response to Injury or Illness—Varies by Developmental Stage
  • Infants: Developmental issues
    ○ Separation anxiety
    ○ Stranger anxiety
    ○ Painful, invasive procedures
    ○ Immobilization
    ○ Sleep deprivation
    ○ Sensory overload

1a Infants: Response to Illness
- Sleep-awake cycle disrupted
- Feeding routines disrupted
- Displays excessive irritability

1b Toddlers: Developmental Issues
- Separation anxiety
- Loss of self-control
- Immobilization
- Painful, invasive procedures
- Bodily injury or mutilation
- Fear of the dark

1c Toddlers: Response to Illness
- Frightened if forced to lie supine
- Associates pain with punishment
- Wonders why parents don't come to the rescue

1d Preschoolers: Developmental Issues
- Separation anxiety—fear of abandonment
- Loss of self-control
- Bodily injury or mutilation
- Painful, invasive procedures
- Fear of ghosts, monsters, and the dark—rich fantasy world

1e Preschoolers: Response to Illness
- Difficulty separating reality from fantasy
- Fears ghosts, monsters
- Fears body parts will leak out when skin is not intact—band-aids
- Fears that tubes are permanent
- Demonstrates withdrawal, aggression, regression

1f School-Age Children: Developmental Issues
- Loss of control
- Loss of privacy and control over bodily functions
- Bodily injury
- Painful, invasive procedures
- Fear of death

1g School-Age Children: Responses
- Increased sensitivity to environment
- Detailed recall of events

1h Adolescents: Developmental Issues
- Loss of control
- Fear of altered body image, disfigurement, disability, or death
- Separation from peer group
- Loss of privacy and identity

1i Adolescents: Responses
- Denial
- Regression
- Withdrawal
- Intellectualization
- Projection
- Displacement

LEARNING OBJECTIVE 2

Discuss the responses of parents and siblings when the child has a life-threatening illness or injury.

CONCEPTS FOR LECTURE

1. Parents typically respond to a life-threatening illness in their child by displaying emotions such as shock, disbelief, anger, and guilt. *Table 41.2 is a good reference.*
2. Siblings of a critically ill child often may feel resentment or anger towards the ill child. Normal family routines are altered, and the siblings may feel ignored and forgotten.

POWERPOINT LECTURE SLIDES

1 Parental Response to Life-Threatening Illness in a Child
- Display many emotions
- Typically go through stages
- Depends on previous experience with child's illness

1a Shock and Disbelief
- Universal reaction
- Loss of control
- Can last for days

1b Anger and Guilt
- Anger at themselves, providers, other people, child
- May be angry at God
- Guilt
  - "If only I hadn't ..."
  - "If I had brought him in sooner ..."

1c Deprivation and Loss
- Loss of parental care-taking role
- May feel helpless or worthless
- Self-esteem may decrease

1d Anticipatory Waiting
- Occurs after stabilization when survival seems likely
- "Life suspended in time"
- Need for accurate information, contact with staff

1e Readjustment or Mourning
- Readjustment: Child recovers, improves, or prepares for transfer
- Mourning
  - Child dies or faces long-term recovery
  - Grief stages begin all over again

2 Response of Siblings to Critical Illness
- Left out, forgotten, neglected
- Day-to-day family routines change
- Jealousy, resentment, anger
- Regression
- May fear becoming ill themselves
- Should be encouraged to visit (child life involvement)

SUGGESTIONS FOR CLASSROOM ACTIVITIES

- Show the video "Involving Family in NICU Setting," available on the Student CD-ROM. Ask the class how the nursing staff can involve the family in the critical-care setting.
- Clip out various obituaries from the local paper from children who have died. Based on the message and tone, have the students identify what stage of grief the family was in when they wrote the obituary.

SUGGESTIONS FOR CLINICAL ACTIVITIES

Identify resources available that the bedside nurse in the local clinical setting can use to help support families and siblings during times of stress. Examples include social workers, chaplains, child life specialists, case managers, therapists, and advanced practice nurses.

LEARNING OBJECTIVE 3

Describe the coping mechanisms used by the child and family in response to stress.

CONCEPTS FOR LECTURE

1. Children and adults use various methods to cope with illness and injury within the family.

POWERPOINT LECTURE SLIDES

1 Coping: What Is It?
- Cognitive and behavioral responses
- Manage specific internal and external demands
- Enables person to solve problems
- Enables person to respond emotionally to the situation

1a Coping Mechanisms: Children
- Regression
- Return to an earlier behavior
- Denial
- Repression (involuntary forgetting)
- Postponement
- Bargaining
- May mirror the parents' responses and behaviors

1b Factors that Influence Coping in Children
- Temperament
- Previous coping experiences
- Previous experiences with illness
- Availability of support systems

1c Coping Mechanisms: Families
- Irritability
- Crying
- Hostility
- Withdrawal

SUGGESTIONS FOR CLASSROOM ACTIVITIES

Ask students to share examples of the coping mechanisms discussed in this objective.

SUGGESTIONS FOR CLINICAL ACTIVITIES

When caring for hospitalized children, remind students to be alert for coping mechanisms that children may be using. Discuss ways the nurse can allow the child to use these coping mechanisms.

LEARNING OBJECTIVE 4

Develop a nursing care plan for the child with a life-threatening illness or injury.

CONCEPTS FOR LECTURE

1. The nursing care of the child with a life-threatening illness or injury includes reducing anxiety, relieving powerlessness, and treating pain. *"Nursing Care Plan: The Child Coping with a Life-Threatening Illness or Injury" provides details about these interventions.*

POWERPOINT LECTURE SLIDES

- **1** Nursing Care of the Child with a Life-Threatening Illness
  - Reducing anxiety
  - Relieving powerlessness
  - Treating pain

- **1a** Anxiety: Interventions
  - Encourage parents to remain at bedside
  - Talk with the child
  - Avoid discussions the child should not hear
  - Preparation for procedures
  - Support personnel
  - Blankets, pictures, familiar toys
  - Primary nursing model

- **1b** Powerlessness: Interventions
  - Choices when possible
  - Allow self-care
  - Provide routines
  - Encourage play
  - Provide means of communication—word board
  - Issues with restraints

- **1c** Pain: Interventions
  - Pain assessment—proper pain scale based on development/age
  - Analgesics
  - Diversional activities

SUGGESTIONS FOR CLASSROOM ACTIVITIES

Discuss how nurses can help children maintain routines while the child is hospitalized.

SUGGESTIONS FOR CLINICAL ACTIVITIES

Identify pain scales that are used in the local clinical setting to assess pain in children of various ages.

LEARNING OBJECTIVE 5

Identify the physiologic and psychologic changes that occur in the dying child.

CONCEPTS FOR LECTURE

1. The human body goes through many physiological changes as it dies. *"Clinical Manifestations: The Dying Child," reviews these changes in detail.*
2. Children usually do not have the same fears about dying that adults do. Children are often more fearful of abandonment than death and are typically aware that they are dying even if no one has told them.

POWERPOINT LECTURE SLIDES

- **1** Physiologic Changes with Death
  - Predictable changes occur
  - Rate at which they occur may vary

- **1a** Cardiovascular System
  - Changes in heart rate, blood pressure—decreases cardiac output
  - Decreased perfusion
  - Diaphoresis
  - Cool, clammy skin
  - Mottling skin

- **1b** Respiratory System
  - Pulmonary congestion due to decreased cardiac output

- Tachypnea
- Hypoxia
- Air hunger
- Cheyne-Stokes breathing
- Secretions accumulate—"death rattle"

1c Neurological System
- Decreased level of consciousness
  - Acidosis
  - Decreased cerebral perfusion
  - Hypoxemia
- Agitation, restlessness, confusion
- Visions, hallucinations
- Hearing and vision usually the last senses to go

1d Musculoskeletal System
- Muscle weakness and fatigue
- Difficulty swallowing
- May be unable to
  - Position self
  - Cough or clear secretions
  - Get to a toilet

1e Renal System
- Decreased kidney perfusion
- Decreased urine output
- Sphincters relax—urinary incontinence may occur

1f Gastrointestinal System
- Decreased oral intake/anorexia
- Sphincters relax—bowel incontinence may occur

2 Psychological Issues with Death
- Children do not fear death like adults do
- Children do fear abandonment and separation from parents
- Usually aware of death process even if no one has told them

SUGGESTIONS FOR CLASSROOM ACTIVITIES

As you discuss the clinical manifestations of death, discuss common interventions used to promote comfort during death. For example, air hunger may be treated with opioids, head of bed elevation, and increased airflow in the room.

SUGGESTIONS FOR CLINICAL ACTIVITIES

Have students role play how they would talk to a dying child. Refer to Table 41.5 for specific strategies.

LEARNING OBJECTIVE 6

Develop a nursing care plan to provide family-centered care for the dying child and the family.

CONCEPTS FOR LECTURE

1. Nursing interventions appropriate for the family with a dying child include providing physical comfort for the child, providing emotional comfort, maintaining family functioning, and promoting cultural values. *Table 41.6 and Table 41.7 are helpful references.*

POWERPOINT LECTURE SLIDES

1 Interventions for the Dying Child and the Family
- Physical comfort
  - Pain medications
  - Nonpharmacologic methods
- Emotional comfort
- Decision-making

- Support group referral
- Family presence at time of death
- Preparations for death
- Involve whole family, siblings

 Cultural Considerations
- Beliefs about death
- Postmortem care

SUGGESTIONS FOR CLASSROOM ACTIVITIES

There are numerous resources that can be used to augment this objective:

- Videos on the Student CD-ROM: "Presenting Bad News to Families" and "Parental Reactions to Death of a Child."
- Companion Website activities: "MediaLink Applications: Helping Families Grieve," "Critical Thinking: Preparing the Family for Hospice," "Complementary Care: Use of Music Therapy in Grief."

SUGGESTIONS FOR CLINICAL ACTIVITIES

If there is a local support group for bereaved parents, arrange for students to observe a meeting.

LEARNING OBJECTIVE 7

Describe the development of the child's concept of death.

CONCEPTS FOR LECTURE

1. Children have varying concepts of death that are based on their developmental level, including whether death is permanent and whether there is a connection between illness and death. *Table 41.8 is a helpful reference*.

POWERPOINT LECTURE SLIDES

1 Infant's Concept of Death
- No concept of death
- May sense caregivers are tense
- May sense that routines are altered

1a Toddler's Concept of Death
- Cannot distinguish fact from fantasy
- No understanding of true concept of death
- Senses separation
- Equates death to separation or abandonment

1b Preschooler's Concept of Death
- Believes death is temporary
- Believes dead person can come back to life— "magical thinking"
- Believes bad thoughts cause death
- Has beginning concept of death—death of plants, animals

1c School-Age Child's Concept of Death
- More realistic understanding of death
- By 8 to 10 years, knows death is permanent and irreversible
- Knows that people can die from internal and external causes
- Believes that death is universal
- May have exaggerated concerns about death

Adolescent's Concept of Death
- Capable of understanding death
- Understands the connection between illness and death
- May feel invincible
- Understands that death impacts other people deeply

SUGGESTIONS FOR CLASSROOM ACTIVITIES

Before class, assign students to review "Care Plan: Death of a Child" activity available on the Companion Website. During class, ask students how the various interventions discussed in that care plan relate to the child's concept of death at various ages.

SUGGESTIONS FOR CLINICAL ACTIVITIES

Have students identify resources in the clinical setting that may be used to support children and families nearing death. These materials may include written materials, art materials, handprints or footprints, and so on.

LEARNING OBJECTIVE 8

Describe the responses of nurses caring for children who die.

CONCEPTS FOR LECTURE

1. Caring for dying children is very stressful, and it is natural for nurses to feel a sense of loss and grief when a child dies.

POWERPOINT LECTURE SLIDES

 Nurses' Responses to Death of a Child
- Feels sense of loss, grief
- Deeper loss when nurse has cared for child for a long time
- Feelings of helplessness
- May distance self from family
- Reluctant to form close connections with other children in the unit
- If nurse has his or her own children, reaction to death may be intense

 Sharing Grief and Feelings: Importance of Support
- (Figure 41.7)

SUGGESTIONS FOR CLASSROOM ACTIVITIES

Invite a panel of pediatric nurses to attend class and discuss how they cope with the death of children that they care for. This panel works best when there is a wide range of nurses represented: men, women, critical care nurses, acute care nurses, and so on. Have the students prepare one or two questions in advance to ask the panel.

SUGGESTIONS FOR CLINICAL ACTIVITIES

Many hospitals have formal support programs for staff when a child dies. If such a program exists in your clinical setting, arrange for the facilitator to come to a clinical conference to discuss self-care actions that nurses can use when children they are caring for die.

CHAPTER 42
PAIN ASSESSMENT AND MANAGEMENT IN CHILDREN

RESOURCE LIBRARY

⊙ CD-ROM

NCLEX-RN® Review
Animation: Morphine
Video
  Pain Management Kit
  Pain Perception
Nursing in Action: Administering Patient-Controlled
  Analgesia
Nursing in Action: Sedation Monitoring
Postoperative Pain Flow Chart
Audio Glossary
Skill 13-1 Selected Pediatric Pain Scales
Skill 13-2 Patient-Controlled Analgesia
Skill 13-3 Monitoring Sedation
Skill 13-4 Local Pain Blocks

📖 IMAGE LIBRARY

Figure 42.1 Neonatal characteristic facial
responses to pain include bulged brow, eyes
squeezed shut, furrowed nasolabial creases,
open lips, pursed lips, stretched mouth, taut
tongue, and a quivering chin.
Figure 42.2 Use the Oucher Scale that is the best
match for the ethnicity of the child.
Figure 42.3 The Faces Pain Rating Scale is valid and
reliable in helping children to report their level of
pain.

🌐 COMPANION WEBSITE

NCLEX-RN® Review
Case Study
Thinking Critically
MediaLink Applications:
  Managing Light Sedation
  Calculating Opioid Dosage
  Postoperative Pain Assessment
Complementary Care: Hypnotherapy for Children

Figure 42.6 When painful procedures are planned,
use EMLA cream to anesthetize the skin where the
painful stick will be made.

Table 42.2 Physiologic Consequences of Unrelieved
Pain in Children
Table 42.9 NSAIDs and Recommended Doses for
Children and Adolescents
Table 42.10 Characteristics of Light and Deep
Sedation

LEARNING OBJECTIVE 1

Describe the physiologic and behavioral consequences of pain in children.

CONCEPTS FOR LECTURE

1. Many beliefs about children and pain are outdated. We
now know that neonates do feel pain, infants can
remember pain, parents rarely exaggerate their child's
pain, and that children rarely get addicted to pain medication. Although children heal from surgery faster
than adults, they still experience the same amount of
pain. *See Table 42.1 for details.*
2. The clinical manifestations of pain can be seen both
physiologically and behaviorally.
3. Short-term consequences of pain include respiratory
changes, neurologic changes, and metabolic changes.
Long-term consequences of pain are not well-known.

POWERPOINT LECTURE SLIDES

1 Outdated Beliefs About Children's Pain
  • Neonates feel pain
  • Infants remember pain episodes
  • Parents rarely exaggerate child's pain level
  • Children rarely become addicted to pain
    medications
  • Children experience same pain post-op as adults

2 Clinical Manifestations of Pain: Physiologic
  • Tachycardia
  • Tachypnea

- Hypertension
- Pupil dilation
- Pallor
- Increased perspiration
- Secretion of catecholamines, adrenocorticoid hormones

2a Clinical Manifestations of Pain: Behavioral
- Short attention span
- Irritability
- Facial grimacing, biting or pursing lips
- Protecting the painful area
- Drawing up knees
- Lethargic, withdrawn
- Sleep disturbances

2b Neonatal Characteristic Facial Responses to Pain
- (Figure 42.1)

3 Physiologic Consequences of Unrelieved Pain in Children
- (Table 42.2)

3a Consequences of Pain: Long-term
- Not well-known at this time

SUGGESTIONS FOR CLASSROOM ACTIVITIES

Ask students to think back to their own childhood. Can they recall a time when they had severe pain? What was the cause? How was it treated? Do they believe that it affected them?

SUGGESTIONS FOR CLINICAL ACTIVITIES

During the clinical day, find an infant whom the students can examine. Have them state what physiologic and behavioral indicators they would look for to determine if the child is experiencing pain.

LEARNING OBJECTIVE 2

Select an appropriate tool to assess the pain of infants and children in each age group.

CONCEPTS FOR LECTURE

1. There are numerous tools available to assess pain in infants and children. The appropriate tool varies by age.
2. An appropriate tool for measuring pain in neonates is the Neonatal Infant Pain Scale (NIPS). *See Table 42.5.*
3. For infants, the NIPS or the FLACC Behavioral Pain Assessment Scale may be used. *See Tables 42.5 and 42.6.*
4. Toddlers may be able to self-report pain, but they cannot be given more than three choices on a pain scale (such as none, some, a lot).
5. Once children can understand rank and order, they can use a numerical scale to report pain. Examples of self-report pain scales include the Faces Pain Rating Scale and the Oucher Scale.
6. By about the age of 8, children can also describe pain in more detail (such as sharp, dull, aching, etc.).

POWERPOINT LECTURE SLIDES

1 Tool Used to Assess Pain
- Appropriate tool is based on age of child
- Scales provide only an indirect estimate of child's pain
- Some rely only on observation, others involve the child

2 Neonates: Pain Assessment Tools
- NIPS

3 Infants: Pain Assessment Tools
- NIPS
- FLACC

4 Toddlers: Self-Report
- Can usually understand concept of "more or less"
- Only give 3 choices on pain scale—none, some, a lot

5. Using a Numerical Scale to Report Pain
- Child must understand rank and order
  - "Which number is larger, 5 or 9?"
  - Understands smaller to bigger amounts using blocks or pieces of paper
- Examples: Faces Pain Rating Scale, Oucher Scale, Poker Chip Scale

6. School-Age Children, Adolescents
- By about age 8, can describe pain in more detail and give its location
  - Dull
  - Aching
  - Sharp
  - Burning
  - Many others

SUGGESTIONS FOR CLASSROOM ACTIVITIES

During the discussion on pain scales, go to the Oucher Scale Website (see Weblinks on the Companion Website, www.oucher.org). Briefly discuss the importance of using a tool that has been tested for reliability and validity. Ask students why it is important for the Oucher Scale to be available for multiple ethnicities.

SUGGESTIONS FOR CLINICAL ACTIVITIES

Have students review "Skill 13-1: Selected Pediatric Pain Scales," from the Student CD-ROM and Clinical Skills Manual before attending clinical conference.

LEARNING OBJECTIVE 3

Describe the nursing assessment and management for a child receiving an opioid analgesic.

CONCEPTS FOR LECTURE

1. Opioid analgesics are commonly given for severe pain, such as after surgery or a severe injury. They may be administered by the oral, subcutaneous, intramuscular, rectal, and intravenous routes, although the oral and intravenous routes are preferred for children.
2. Dosage of analgesics in children is always weight-based *Refer to Table 42.7 for oral and IV dosing of common opioids.* Common side effects of opioids include sedation, nausea, vomiting, constipation, and itching. Less common complications include respiratory depression, cardiovascular collapse, and addiction.
3. Pain relief should be provided around the clock, as delays in giving analgesics increase the chances of breakthrough pain. Patient-controlled analgesia (PCA) may be used with children, especially in the first 48 hours after surgery.
4. Withdrawal may occur when opioids have been given for an extended period of time.

POWERPOINT LECTURE SLIDES

1. Opioid Analgesics
- Used to treat severe pain
- Preferred routes: oral, intravenous

2. Dosing of Opioids
- Always weight-based
- Equianalgesic dosing

2a. Common Side Effects
- Sedation
- Nausea, vomiting
- Constipation
- Itching

2b. Less Common Complications
- Respiratory depression
- Cardiovascular collapse
- Addiction

3. Timing of Opioids
- Should be given around the clock when needed
- Delays increase breakthrough pain
- Patient-controlled analgesia (PCA)

4. NSAIDs and Recommended Doses for Children and Adolescents
- (Table 42.9)

SUGGESTIONS FOR CLASSROOM ACTIVITIES

- When discussing opioids, show the animation "Morphine," from the Student CD-ROM. The video provides a visual about how opioids act to treat pain.
- Before discussing patient-controlled analgesia, review "Skill 13-2: Patient-Controlled Analgesia," from the Student CD-ROM and Clinical Skills Manual.

SUGGESTIONS FOR CLINICAL ACTIVITIES

Role play with students about what they would do if a child receiving opioids suffered from respiratory depression. What equipment and medications would they need? What actions would be the first priority? Refer to "Nursing Practice 42.1," "Nursing Practice 42.2," and "Nursing Practice 42.3," for details

LEARNING OBJECTIVE 4

Explain the rationale for the effectiveness for nonpharmacologic (complementary) methods of pain control.

CONCEPTS FOR LECTURE

1. The Gate Control Theory helps explain why complementary pain management techniques are effective in helping to control pain. *Refer to "Pathophysiology Illustrated: Pain Perception" when discussing this theory*.
2. Methods of nonpharmacologic interventions include distraction, cutaneous stimulation, sucrose solution, electroanalgesia, guided imagery, relaxation, hypnosis, and heat or cold application.

POWERPOINT LECTURE SLIDES

1 Gate Control Theory
- Stimulation by nonpainful touch and pressure stimulates larger A-delta fibers
- Causes dorsal horn of spinal cord to "close the gate"
- Result is decreased transmission of pain impulses to the brain

2 Nonpharmacologic Methods
- Distraction
- Cutaneous stimulation
- Sucrose solution
- Electroanalgesia
- Guided imagery
- Relaxation
- Hypnosis
- Application of heat/cold

SUGGESTIONS FOR CLASSROOM ACTIVITIES

Have students read "Complementary Care: Hypnotherapy for Children." Ask students if they have ever seen hypnotherapy used in the hospital setting. If a parent requested this option, what could the nurse do to advocate for hypnotherapy?

SUGGESTIONS FOR CLINICAL ACTIVITIES

During clinical conference, have students discuss how parents can help children cope with pain. Interventions vary by age. "Teaching Highlights: Helping a Child Cope With Pain" is a good reference for this discussion.

LEARNING OBJECTIVE 5

Assess children of different ages with acute pain and develop a nursing care plan that integrates pharmacologic interventions and developmentally appropriate nonpharmacologic (complementary) therapies.

CONCEPTS FOR LECTURE

1. The nursing process can be applied as a framework for working with children of all ages who are experiencing acute pain. *"Nursing Care Plan: The Child with Postoperative Pain" is a good reference for this discussion*.

POWERPOINT LECTURE SLIDES

1 Assessment
- Assess physiologic and behavioral signs
- Use an age-appropriate tool to assess pain
- Consider external factors
  ◦ Tightness of cast, dressings
  ◦ Positioning in bed

Diagnosis
- Acute pain
- Anxiety
- Sleep pattern disturbance
- Ineffective therapeutic regimen management
- Ineffective breathing pattern
- Risk for constipation

 Planning and Implementation
- Pharmacologic interventions
- Nonpharmacologic (complementary) interventions

1c Evaluation
- Pain management is effective in improving comfort
- Age-appropriate nonpharmacologic interventions increase comfort

---

SUGGESTIONS FOR CLASSROOM ACTIVITIES

Approach this care plan using a case study format. Suggestions may be found on the Companion Website: "MediaLink Applications: Managing Light Sedation," and "MediaLink Applications: Calculating Opioid Dosage." This helps students apply the nursing process to a realistic case.

SUGGESTIONS FOR CLINICAL ACTIVITIES

Before clinical conference, have students complete "Critical Thinking: Postoperative Pain Assessment" activity from the Companion Website. Compare their answers to the process or protocol used in the actual hospital. If there is no written protocol or order set in place, discuss the benefits of such a protocol for making care more consistent and increasing nursing autonomy.

LEARNING OBJECTIVE 6

Develop a nursing care plan for assessing and monitoring the child having sedation and analgesia for a medical procedure.

CONCEPTS FOR LECTURE

1. Pain control should be provided for children undergoing both major and minor procedures. The anticipation of the procedure can be very anxiety-provoking for the child, and poor pain control during prior procedures can lead to a very uncooperative child.
2. Topical anesthetics can be used to prevent pain for minor procedures such as venipuncture and IV starts.
3. Sedation is used during major medical procedures, with the goal being to provide both analgesia and anxiolysis.
4. Nursing responsibilities for the child receiving sedation involves considerations about timing of drug administration, as well as monitoring during the procedure.

POWERPOINT LECTURE SLIDES

1 Medical Procedures
- Pain control should be provided even for minor procedures
- Anticipation of procedure causes anxiety and distress
- Child may be uncooperative if severe pain has been experienced during prior procedures

2 Minor Procedures
- Topical anesthetics
  - EMLA: 60-minute absorption time
  - ELA-MAX: 30-minute absorption time
  - Vapocoolant sprays: Instantaneous
  - Intradermal lidocaine: Less than a minute (buffer with sodium bicarbonate to lessen stinging)

2a EMLA Application
- (Figure 42.6)

3 Major Procedures
- Sedation: Two goals
  - Analgesia
  - Anxiolysis

Drugs Used for Sedation
- Benzodiazepines
  - Diazepam (Valium)
  - Midazolam (Versed)
  - Lorazepam (Ativan)
- Hypnotics/barbiturates
  - Thiopental
  - Pentobarbital

 Drugs Used for Sedation
- Ketamine
- Propofol (Diprivan)
- Analgesics: Fentanyl

 Characteristics of Light and Deep Sedation
- (Table 42.10)

 Considerations of Drug Administration
- Allow enough time for drug to take effect
- Administer drugs by a nonpainful route when possible
- Avoid delays in performing procedure
- Document results of pain management

 Monitoring During Sedation
- Airway is patent
- Respiratory effort, color, vital signs
- Pulse oximetry
- Level of consciousness

SUGGESTIONS FOR CLASSROOM ACTIVITIES

Before students come to class, assign them to review "Skill 13-3: Monitoring Sedation" from the Student CD-ROM and Clinical Skills Manual. Use this as a basis for discussion.

SUGGESTIONS FOR CLINICAL ACTIVITIES

Discuss the concept of "thinking ahead." For example, if a child is receiving light sedation, what equipment should be available in the event that the child progresses into deep sedation? What interventions should occur? What medications would be administered? By thinking through these potential problems before they occur, students can be better prepared to deal with them if they actually occur.

CHAPTER 43
THE CHILD WITH ALTERATIONS IN FLUID, ELECTROLYTE, AND ACID-BASE BALANCE

RESOURCE LIBRARY

 CD-ROM

Acid-Base Balance Animation
Audio Glossary
NCLEX-RN® Review

 COMPANION WEBSITE

Case Study: Dehydration and Fluid Calculation
Care Plan: Hyponatremic Dehydration in Breastfeeding

MediaLink Applications:
  Care Plan: Infant Feeding
  Formula Preparation at a Home Visit
  Identifying Intravenous Fluids
  Interpreting Blood Gases
  Understanding School-Age Athletes and Fluid Needs
Audio Glossary
NCLEX-RN® Review

📖 IMAGE LIBRARY

Figure 43.1 The major body fluid compartments.

Figure 43.2 Normal routes of fluid excretion from infants and children.

Figure 43.3 Use of an overhead warmer or phototherapy increases insensible fluid excretion through the skin, thus increasing the fluid intake needed.

Figure 43.4 The use of a volume control device with an intravenous saline solution is important to prevent a sudden extracellular fluid volume overload.

Figure 43.5 If isotonic fluid containing sodium is given too rapidly or in too great an amount, an extracellular fluid volume excess will develop.

Figure 43.6 This infant with congenital heart disease has signs of generalized edema.

Figure 43.7 Edematous tissue is easily damaged.

Figure 43.8 A, Water balance is maintained by the simple passage of molecules from greater to lesser concentration across cell membranes. B, Sodium levels are maintained by an active transport system, the sodium-potassium pump, which moves these electrolytes across cell membranes in spite of their concentration.

Figure 43.9 Because this child has a nasogastric tube in place, it is important to monitor his potassium levels.

Figure 43.10 This child may develop respiratory acidosis or respiratory alkalosis.

Figure 43.11 This child, who has muscular dystrophy, uses a "turtle" respirator at home to assist with breathing.

Figure 43.12 With any postoperative or immobilized child, it is important to monitor urine output to detect oliguria.

Figure 43.13 Teaching parents to use safety latches on cabinets to keep aspirin away from small children can help prevent one cause of metabolic acidosis.

Table 43.1 Electrolyte Concentrations in Body Fluid Compartments

Table 43.12 Risk Factor Assessment for Fluid Imbalances

Table 43.13 Risk Factor Assessment for Electrolyte Imbalances

Pathophysiology Illustrated: Pottassium Ions.

Pathophysiology Illustrated: Buffer Responses to Acid and Base.

Pathophysiology Illustrated: The Bicarbonate Buffer System.

Pathophysiology Illustrated: The Kidneys and Metabolic Acids.

LEARNING OBJECTIVE 1

Describe normal fluid and electrolyte status for children at various ages.

CONCEPTS FOR LECTURE

1. Fluid and electrolytes are highly regulated in the human body. A basic vocabulary is necessary to discuss the location and flow of fluids in the body.
2. Neonates and young infants have a proportionately larger extracellular fluid volume than older children and adults, and they are vulnerable to dehydration.
3. Infants and children under age 2 lose a greater proportion of fluid each day than older children and adults. This makes them more dependent on adequate intake. Older children are also at risk for dehydration during exercise.
4. Health conditions that make infants and young children vulnerable to fluid deficits include increased respiratory rate during illness, fever, vomiting and diarrhea, and certain medical treatments.

POWERPOINT LECTURE SLIDES

1 Basic Vocabulary
- Body fluid
- Sensible water loss
- Insensible water loss
- Intracellular fluid
- Extracellular fluid
- Intravascular fluid
- Interstitial fluid

1a Electrolyte Concentrations in Body Fluid Compartments
- (Table 43.1)

2 Neonates and Young Infants
- Vulnerable to dehydration: Why?
  - Larger extracellular fluid volume than children and adults
  - High daily fluid requirement
  - Little fluid volume reserve

3 Infants and Children Less Than 2 Years
- Lose a greater proportion of fluid daily than older children and adults—makes them more dependent on adequate intake
- Greater amount of skin surface proportionately—increased insensible losses
- High metabolic and respiratory rates—increased insensible losses

3a Older Children
- High metabolic and respiratory rates; increased insensible losses
- Dehydrate easily during physical exercise, especially in hot weather

4 Health Conditions That Make Infants and Children Vulnerable to Fluid Deficits
- Increased respiratory rate during illness
- Fever
- Vomiting
- Diarrhea
- Drainage tubes (fluid loss)
- Phlebotomy
- Phototherapy (newborns)

SUGGESTIONS FOR CLASSROOM ACTIVITIES

Before class, assign students to complete the activity, "MediaLink Applications: Understanding School-Age Athletes and Fluid Needs," available on the Companion Website. Use this as a framework for discussing why children are at risk for dehydration during exercise.

SUGGESTIONS FOR CLINICAL ACTIVITIES

Have students identify conditions in the child they are caring for, as well as medical treatments or procedures, that increase the child's risk for dehydration. Have students complete "Care Plan: Hyponatremic Dehydration in Breastfeeding" and "MediaLink Application: Infant Feeding" activites as review from the Companion Website.

LEARNING OBJECTIVE 2

Identify regulatory mechanisms for fluid and electrolyte balance.

CONCEPTS FOR LECTURE

1. Conservation of fluid and electrolytes is primarily achieved through the kidney. Since infants and young children have immature kidneys, they are less able to conserve fluids and electrolytes.
2. Aldosterone causes the body to retain sodium and water. Antidiuretic hormone (ADH) causes the body to retain water.

POWERPOINT LECTURE SLIDES

1 Conservation of Fluids and Electrolytes
- Primarily regulated through the kidney (example: too much fluid or electrolytes present—kidneys removes excess via urine)
- Infants and young children
  - Immature kidneys
  - Poor conservation mechanism
  - Don't concentrate urine well
  - Risk for electrolyte imbalance—dehydration

1a Electrolyte Regulation: Infants and Young Children
- Poorly regulate
  - Sodium
  - Calcium
- Weaker transport system for ions and bicarbonate—greater risk for acidosis, acid-base disturbance

2 Role of Hormones in Fluid Balance
- Monitor fluid status by stretch receptors, chemoreceptors (osmolality)
- Aldosterone: Sodium and water retention
- Antidiuretic hormone (ADH): Water retention

SUGGESTIONS FOR CLASSROOM ACTIVITIES

When explaining the regulation of electrolytes and fluid balance, use examples that students can relate to. For example, ask them what their urine would look like if they had been febrile and vomiting for a day. Questions such as "How did your body know to concentrate your urine?" and "Would you expect the sodium level to be low, normal, or high in that urine?" can help them understand the physiology of the process.

SUGGESTIONS FOR CLINICAL ACTIVITIES

When caring for children with fluid and electrolyte imbalances, review laboratory tests that can help determine the degree of dehydration and the response to therapy.

CONCEPTS FOR LECTURE

1. Dehydration is one of the most common conditions during childhood, and there are three classifications of dehydration: isotonic, hypotonic, and hypertonic. Treatment is aimed at restoring fluid status. *"Nursing Care Plan: Mild or Moderate Dehydration" and "Nursing Care Plan: Severe Dehydration" can be used to augment the discussion.*

2. Extracellular fluid volume excess develops when there is too much fluid in the vascular and interstitial compartment. This may be caused by disease or by excessive IV fluid administration. Therapy focuses on treating the underlying cause and administration of diuretics.

3. Electrolytes are tightly regulated by the body, and are normally gained and lost in equal amounts in order to maintain a balance. Serum values only reflect the level of the electrolyte in the blood, and do not reflect the concentration of the electrolyte in other body compartments. Electrolyte abnormalities are reviewed in the corresponding slides.

POWERPOINT LECTURE SLIDES

1 Dehydration: Three Types
- Isotonic
  - Loss of sodium and water is equal
  - Serum sodium is normal
- Hypotonic
  - More sodium is lost than water
  - Serum sodium is low
- Hypertonic
  - More water is lost than sodium
  - Serum sodium is high

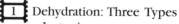 **1a** Etiology of Dehydration in Children
- Diarrhea (5 million deaths from dehydration worldwide)
- Vomiting—nasogastric tubes
- Hemorrhage
- Burns

1b Pathophysiology of Dehydration
- Initial dehydration (first 3 days)
  - Most of fluid loss (80%) is from extracellular fluid compartment
  - 20% is from intracellular fluid compartment

1c Treatment of Dehydration
- Oral rehydration solutions
- Intravenous fluid replacement
  - Choice of fluid
  - Amount of fluid
- Frequent monitoring and reassessment
- Weight
- Labs

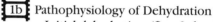 **2** Extracellular Fluid Volume Excess—Edema
- Excess fluid in the intravascular and interstitial compartments
- Etiology
  - Excessive IV fluid administration
  - Tumors that secrete aldosterone
  - Congestive heart failure
  - Liver failure
  - Nephrotic syndrome
  - Burns
  - Renal failure

2a Treatment
- Treat the underlying disease process
- Administer diuretics
- Monitor intake and output, weight
- Use small IV fluid bags and pumps to regulate IV rate flow for children
- Skin care for edematous areas

 3 Electrolyte Abnormalities
- Electrolytes in usually equals electrolytes out

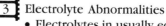

- Body maintains balance unless disease state occurs
- Blood levels measure serum electrolytes only—may vary in other fluid compartments

3a Sodium
- Reflect osmolality of body fluids
- Sodium balance and water balance are closely tied
- Most abundant extracellular ion

3b Hypernatremia
- Body fluids are too concentrated—more sodium than water
- Causes: Decreased water intake or increased solute intake—diabetes insipidus
- Treatment
  - Fluid replacement
  - Treat underlying cause

3c Hyponatremia
- Body fluids are too dilute—more water than sodium
- Causes: Water intoxication, diluted formula, SIADH
- Complications: Cerebral edema, seizures
- Treatment: Replace sodium

3d Potassium
- Most abundant intracellular ion
- Essential electrolyte
- Can shift in and out of cells
- Excreted primarily by urine, but also in sweat, feces

3e Potassium Ions
- ("Pathophysiology Illustrated: Potassium Ions")

3f Hyperkalemia
- Excess potassium in the blood
- Causes
  - Increased potassium intake (oral, IV)
  - Shift of potassium out of cells into interstitial fluid (massive cell death, old transfused blood, acidosis)
  - Decreased potassium excretion (renal failure)
- Treatment
  - Treat underlying cause
  - Cation exchange resin (Kayexalate)
  - Dialysis

3g Hypokalemia
- Decreased potassium in the blood
- Causes
  - Decreased potassium intake (NPO status, IV fluids)
  - Shift of potassium into cells (alkalosis, insulin therapy)
  - Increased potassium excretion (diuretics, diarrhea, others)
- Treatment
  - Replacement (IV or oral)
  - Treat underlying cause

Calcium
- Most abundant mineral in the body
- Involved in
  - Muscle and nerve function
  - Bone strength
  - Hormone secretion
  - Blood clotting

 Hypercalcemia
- Excess of calcium in the plasma
- Most of calcium is stored in bones
- Causes
  - Increased calcium intake
  - Shift of calcium from bones to extracellular fluid (hyperparathyroidism, prolonged immobility)
- Treatment:
  - Furosemide (Lasix) increases calcium excretion
  - Glucocorticoids decrease absorption
  - Phosphate (binds with calcium)
  - Dialysis

 Hypocalcemia
- Serum deficit of calcium
- Most of calcium stored in bones
- Causes
  - Decreased intake of vitamin D and/or calcium
  - Hyperphosphatemia
  - DiGeorge syndrome
- Treatment
  - Treat underlying cause
  - Replace calcium (oral or IV)
  - Vitamin D

 Magnesium
- Necessary for enzyme function, nerve function
- Absorbed in ileum
- Present mostly in the cells and bones—small amount in extracellular fluid
- Excreted in urine, sweat, and feces

 Hypermagnesemia
- Excess magnesium in blood
- Causes
  - Renal failure
  - Excess magnesium intake (IV)
- Treatment:
  - Diuresis
  - Dialysis

3m Hypomagnesemia
- Decreased magnesium in blood
- Causes
  - Malnutrition, decreased intake
  - Chronic diarrhea
  - Prolonged suctioning
- Treatment
  - Treat underlying cause
  - Replacement

LEARNING OBJECTIVE 4

Describe acid-base balance and recognize disruptions common in children.

CONCEPTS FOR LECTURE

1. The body tightly controls acid-base balance through several mechanisms, including the use of buffers, exhalation of carbon dioxide, and the excretion of metabolic acids.
2. Blood gases are used to evaluate the acid-base status.
3. The four major types of acid-base imbalance include respiratory acidosis, respiratory alkalosis, metabolic acidosis, and metabolic alkalosis.

POWERPOINT LECTURE SLIDES

1 Acid-Base Balance
- Tightly regulated
- Balance of acids (hydrogen) and bases (bicarbonate)
- Enzymes and cells operate in a very narrow range of pH

1a Normal pH Varies by Age
- Slightly basic
- Infants: 7.36 to 7.42
- Children: 7.37 to 7.43
- Adolescents: 7.35 to 7.41

1b Types of Acids in the Body
- Carbonic acid
  - Carbon dioxide and water
  - Lungs excrete carbon dioxide
- Metabolic (noncarbonic) acids
  - Pyruvic acid
  - Sulfuric acid
  - Lactic acid
  - Hydrochloric acid
  - Can be neutralized by buffers in body fluids
  - Can be excreted by the kidneys

1c Buffers
- Binds hydrogen ions when there are too many
- Releases hydrogen ions when there are not enough
- Types of buffers
  - Bicarbonate
  - Protein
  - Hemoglobin
  - Phosphate
- Once buffers are saturated, kidney excretes acids

1d Buffer Responses to Acid and Base
- ("Pathophysiology Illustrated: Buffer Responses to Acid and Base")

1e The Bicarbonate Buffer System
- ("Pathophysiology Illustrated: The Bicarbonate Buffer System")

1f Role of the Lungs
- Excrete excess carbonic acid from body
- Faster and deeper breathing rate equals more carbonic acid excreted

- Indirect measure of carbonic acid is P_{CO_2}
- Chemoreceptors monitor P_{CO_2} and pH of the blood—respiratory rate is adjusted to compensate

1g Role of the Kidneys
- Excrete metabolic acids in two ways
  - Reabsorb bicarbonate
  - Form new bicarbonate

1h The Kidneys and Metabolic Acids
- ("Pathophysiology Illustrated: The Kidneys and Metabolic Acids")

2 Blood Gases
- Evaluate acid-base status
- Traditionally arterial (but can be venous or capillary)
- P_{CO_2} reflects carbonic acid status (respiratory)
- Bicarbonate reflects metabolic acid status

3 Four Types of Acid-Base Imbalance
- Respiratory acidosis
- Respiratory alkalosis
- Metabolic acidosis
- Metabolic alkalosis

3a Respiratory Acidosis
- Accumulation of carbon dioxide in blood
- Cause: Anything that interferes with ability of lungs to excrete carbon dioxide—examples

3b Respiratory Alkalosis
- Too little carbon dioxide in blood
- Cause: Hyperventilation
  - Anxiety
  - Pain
  - Fever
  - Aspirin toxicity
  - Sepsis
  - Mechanical overventilation

3c Metabolic Acidosis
- Excess of any acid other than carbonic acid in the blood
- Causes
  - Excess accumulation of acid
  - Excess loss of bicarbonate
  - Examples
- Compensation occurs by increasing respiratory rate, depth

3d Metabolic Alkalosis
- Too few metabolic acids in the blood
- Causes
  - Gain of bicarbonate
  - Excess loss of acid
  - Examples
- Compensation occurs by decreasing respiratory rate, depth

LEARNING OBJECTIVE 5

Analyze assessment findings to recognize fluid-electrolyte problems and acid-base imbalance in children.

CONCEPTS FOR LECTURE

1. A strategy for assessing children at risk for fluid and electrolyte imbalances is to perform a rapid risk assessment to see which factors are present. *This strategy is reviewed in Tables 43.12 and 43.13.*

2. Further assessment for fluid imbalances includes assessing weight changes, vascular volume interstitial volume, and cerebral function. Further assessment of electrolyte imbalance includes assessing serum electrolyte levels, skeletal muscle strength, neuromuscular excitability, gastrointestinal tract function, and cardiac rhythm. *Tables 43.14 and 43.15 provide more details that may be useful references during the lecture.*

3. Assessment findings with acid-base imbalances vary depending upon the particular imbalance.

POWERPOINT LECTURE SLIDES

1 Risk Factor Assessment for Fluid Imbalances
- (Table 43.12)

1a Risk Factor Assessment for Electrolyte Imbalances
- (Table 43.13)

2 Further Assessment: Fluid Imbalance
- Weight changes
- Vascular volume
- Interstitial volume
- Cerebral function

2a Further Assessment: Electrolyte Imbalance
- Serum electrolyte levels
- Skeletal muscle function/strength
- Neuromuscular excitability
- Gastrointestinal tract functioning
- Cardiac rhythm
- Cerebral function

3 Assessment Findings: Respiratory Acidosis
- Central nervous system depression
  - Lethargy
  - Confusion
  - Headache
  - Increased intracranial pressure
- Tachycardia
- Cardiac arrhythmias

3a Assessment Findings: Respiratory Alkalosis
- Neuromuscular irritability
- Paresthesias in extremities, around mouth
- Muscle cramping
- Dizziness
- Confusion

3b Assessment Findings: Metabolic Acidosis
- Signs of respiratory compensation
  - Increased rate and depth of respirations
  - "Kussmaul" respirations
- Decreased peripheral vascular resistance and hypotension
- Cardiac arrhythmias
- Pulmonary edema
- Hypoxia
- Confusion
- Drowsiness

Assessment Findings: Metabolic Alkalosis
- Signs of respiratory compensation—decreased rate and depth of respirations
- Signs of hypokalemia
- Neuromuscular irritability
- Cramping
- Paresthesia
- Tetany
- Weakness, lethargy, confusion
- Seizures
- Can progress to coma if untreated

SUGGESTIONS FOR CLASSROOM ACTIVITIES

To help students differentiate among various fluid, electrolyte, and acid-base assessment findings, create case studies of children with findings indicative of an imbalance. Challenge the class to identify the imbalance based upon the assessment findings you describe. You can also create a game out of this activity to make it competitive.

SUGGESTIONS FOR CLINICAL ACTIVITIES

Identify equipment in the clinical setting that is used in the monitoring and/or assessment of fluid, electrolyte, and acid-base imbalances (examples: scale, cardiac monitor, end-tidal carbon dioxide monitor, reflex hammer, etc.)

LEARNING OBJECTIVE 6

Describe appropriate nursing interventions for children experiencing fluid-electrolyte problems and acid-base imbalance.

CONCEPTS FOR LECTURE

1. Nursing interventions for children with fluid, electrolyte, and acid-base imbalances focus on correcting the underlying cause, monitoring for complications and response to therapy, and providing teaching to children and families.

POWERPOINT LECTURE SLIDES

 Nursing Interventions: Dehydration
- Prevent dehydration
- Provide oral rehydration fluids
- Monitor intravenous fluid administration
- Monitor response to therapy
- Teaching

 Nursing Interventions: Fluid Volume Excess
- Monitor weight
- Skin care
- Correct underlying cause
- Monitor response to therapy
- Teaching

1b Nursing Interventions: Hypernatremia
- Monitor sodium level, intake and output, urine specific gravity
- Assess level of consciousness
- Consider underlying cause
- Teaching
- Prevention in the hospital setting—free water with tube feedings

1c Nursing Interventions: Hyponatremia
- Monitor sodium level, intake and output
- ADH levels
- Formula preparation—dilution?
- Monitor level of consciousness
- Seizure precautions

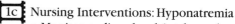

- Prevention in the hospital setting
  - Use normal saline rather than sterile water for irrigations
  - Avoid tap water enemas

1d Nursing Interventions: Hyperkalemia
- Stop any potassium-containing fluids from infusing
- Administer medications
  - Glucose and insulin
  - Bicarbonate
  - Calcium
  - Kayexalate
- Monitor cardiopulmonary status
- Prevention in the hospital setting
  - Risk increases with use of old blood for transfusion
  - IV fluids that contain potassium
  - Don't give potassium-containing fluids to a child who has oliguria or anuria

1e Nursing Interventions: Hypokalemia
- Ensure adequate potassium intake
- If child is taking digitalis, hypokalemia potentiates digitalis toxicity—assess for nausea, vomiting, bradycardia
- Cardiac monitoring
- Potassium replacement (oral or IV)

1f Nursing Interventions: Hypercalcemia
- Encourage fluid intake
- Increase mobility
- Avoid calcium-rich foods, calcium supplements
- Avoid vitamin D supplements

1g Nursing Interventions: Hypocalcemia
- Calcium replacement (oral or IV)—never given IM: Causes tissue necrosis
- Calcium supplementation
- Teaching

1h Nursing Interventions: Hypermagnesemia
- Monitor serum levels, blood pressure, reflexes
- Monitor for cardiac arrhythmias
- Avoid magnesium-containing substances
  - Dietary sources
  - Medication (milk of magnesia)
  - Sea salt
- Diuresis
- Dialysis

1i Nursing Interventions: Hypomagnesemia
- Monitor reflexes, cardiac functioning, muscle cramps
- Replace magnesium (oral, IM, or IV)
- Increase magnesium in diet—food choices
- Teaching

Nursing Interventions: Respiratory Acidosis
- Treat underlying cause
- Positioning
- Suctioning
- Medications—bronchodilators
- Monitor blood gases

Nursing Interventions: Respiratory Alkalosis
- Decrease respiratory rate and depth
  - Calming techniques
  - Stress management
- Pain control
- Monitor blood gases

Nursing Interventions: Metabolic Acidosis
- Allow for respiratory compensation—positioning
- Administer medications
- Treat underlying cause
- Monitor blood gases
- Assess level of consciousness
- Observe for nausea, vomiting, neuromuscular irritability
- Consider sources for acid loss (vomiting, diarrhea, NG tube)—treat underlying cause
- Monitor blood gases

SUGGESTIONS FOR CLASSROOM ACTIVITIES

For each electrolyte imbalance, have students draw a concept map that links the pathophysiology of the imbalance to the signs and symptoms, treatment, and nursing interventions. By understanding these linkages, students will better understand the monitoring and treatment of these imbalances.

SUGGESTIONS FOR CLINICAL ACTIVITIES

When caring for children with fluid and electrolyte imbalances, have students identify complications that could be life-threatening (e.g., shock, arrhythmias, seizures, etc.). Discuss the monitoring and treatment of these imbalances with the students.

CHAPTER 44
THE CHILD WITH ALTERATIONS IN IMMUNE FUNCTION

RESOURCE LIBRARY

CD-ROM

Animations:
 HIV Infection/Transmission
 Methotrexate
Video:
 AIDS/HIV
Audio Glossary
NCLEX-RN® Review

IMAGE LIBRARY

Figure 44.1 This nurse is disposing of a needle and syringe in a biohazard container, a necessary practice to avoid the transmission of HIV through needle sticks with contaminated needles.

Figure 44.2 The physical therapist uses hydrotherapy to help maintain joint function in a child who has juvenile rheumatoid arthritis.

Figure 44.3 Results of intradermal skin testing on the forearm.

Figure 44.4 The school nurse is teaching a parent and a teacher about the correct use of the EpiPen, which

COMPANION WEBSITE

MediaLink Applications:
 Case Study: Toddler with HIV
 Case Study: Postexposure Management
  of Needlestick Injuries
Audio Glossary
NCLEX-RN® Review

is being maintained at home and at school in case of allergic reaction in a child who has peanut allergy.

Table 44.1 Classes of Immunoglobulins
Table 44.6 Characteristic Findings in Children with Allergies
Table 44.7 Measures to Protect Latex Allergy
Table 44.8 Sources of Latex in Hospital, Home, and Community with Recommended Alternatives

Pathophysiology Illustrated: Primary Immune Response.

LEARNING OBJECTIVE 1

Describe the structure and function of the immune system and apply that knowledge to the care of children with immunological disorders.

CONCEPTS FOR LECTURE

1. The primary function of the immune system is to recognize foreign substances in the body and to eliminate these foreign substances as efficiently as possible.

2. Antibodies are found in serum, body fluids, and certain tissues. Antibodies are a type of protein called immunoglobulins, of which there are five types.

3. The primary immune response occurs once an antigen invades the body and antibodies are reactive to specific antigens. This is the primary response and occurs within 3 days. Once the antigen has been encountered, secondary immune response occurs (usually within 24 hours) after each subsequent encounter.

POWERPOINT LECTURE SLIDES

1 Immune System: Function
 • Recognize self from non-self
 • Eliminate foreign substances efficiently
 • Immunity is either
  ○ Natural
  ○ Acquired
 • Antibodies trigger the immune response

2 Structure of the Immune System
 • Antibodies
  ○ Found in serum, body fluids, and certain tissues
  ○ Type of protein called immunoglobulins (five types)

- Antigens
  - Work against antibodies
  - "Trigger" for immune response
- White blood cells
- Lymphoid tissue
- Not fully developed until age 6

 Classes of Immunoglobulins
- (Table 44.1)

 Immune Response
- Primary
  - Occurs after antigen invades body
  - Antibodies are reactive to specific antigens
  - Occurs within 3 days
- Secondary
  - Subsequent encounter with an antigen
  - Triggers memory cells in immune system
  - Result is faster response—about 24 hours

 Primary Immune Response
- ("Pathophysiology Illustrated: Primary Immune Response")

SUGGESTIONS FOR CLASSROOM ACTIVITIES

When discussing immune response, use the analogy of a war, including soldiers (antibodies), the enemy (antigens), supply lines (vasodilation), and so on.

SUGGESTIONS FOR CLINICAL ACTIVITIES

Discuss why newborns and young children are more at risk for infection than older children and adults.

LEARNING OBJECTIVE 2

Explain the differences between active and passive immunity.

CONCEPTS FOR LECTURE

1. Active immunity is acquired and consists of both humoral (antibody-mediated) and cell-mediated immunity. The body must make antibodies in response to an antigen. This is the type of immunity that most immunizations bring about.

2. Passive immunity refers to antibodies that are produced in another human or animal host and that are given to a child to confer immediate immunity. Immunoglobulins (such as IVIG) are an example of passive immunity.

POWERPOINT LECTURE SLIDES

 Active Immunity
- Acquired immunity
  - Humoral (antibody-mediated)
  - Cell-mediated
- Body makes antibodies in response to antigens—immunizations

 Passive Immunity
- Antibodies are produced in another human or animal host
- Given to child to confer immediate immunity
- Example: immunoglobulins (IVIG)
- Maternal antibodies passed through breast milk

SUGGESTIONS FOR CLASSROOM ACTIVITIES

Assign groups of students specific viral or bacterial disease processes. Have the group present whether immunity to that disease would be active or passive or if it is possible to develop immunity to that specific disease.

SUGGESTIONS FOR CLINICAL ACTIVITIES

Identify the reason for admission and include in the student's discussion of their client if the disease could have been prevented from immunity. If the disease could have been prevented, discuss if it would have been from active or passive immunity.

LEARNING OBJECTIVE 3

Identify infection control measures to prevent the spread of infection in children with an immunodeficiency.

CONCEPTS FOR LECTURE

1. There are numerous nursing interventions that can be used to prevent infection in children with an immunodeficiency, including handwashing, standard and transmission-based precautions, sterile technique, and avoiding contact with infected individuals.

POWERPOINT LECTURE SLIDES

1 Prevention of Infection in Immunosuppressed Children
- Handwashing
- Standard precautions—transmission-based precautions
- Sterile technique for procedures
- Negative pressure room
- Avoid contact with infected people

1a Prevention of Infection
- Live virus vaccines
  - Virus may shed and infect child
  - Caution with family members, close contacts receiving vaccine
- Food and items entering child's room—plants and flowers
- Maintain skin integrity
- Encourage adequate fluid and nutrition

SUGGESTIONS FOR CLASSROOM ACTIVITIES

Have students list which vaccines are live virus vaccines and which ones are not.

SUGGESTIONS FOR CLINICAL ACTIVITIES

Review the equipment available in the local clinical setting that can be used to prevent transmission of infection.

LEARNING OBJECTIVE 4

Develop a nursing care plan in partnership with the family for a child with human immunodeficiency virus (HIV).

CONCEPTS FOR LECTURE

1. Prevention of the spread of HIV is important, especially for neonates whose mothers have HIV. Proper disposal of used needles and using standard precautions can also help prevent spreading HIV.
2. Prevention of further infection is important for children with HIV. Interventions include frequent handwashing, limiting exposure to infected people, and following a modified immunization schedule.
3. Promote adherence to the medication regimen, as nonadherence may result in increased morbidity and mortality.
4. Children with AIDS are at risk for pneumonia, so promotion of respiratory function is important in preventing infections.

POWERPOINT LECTURE SLIDES

1 Prevention of Spread of HIV: Status Known
- Neonates
  - Avoid fetal scalp electrodes during labor
  - Bathe infant immediately after delivery
  - Delay heel-sticks and injections until after bath
  - Encourage formula feeding (HIV transmitted via breast milk)

1a Prevention of Spread of HIV: Status Unknown
- Standard precautions
- Prevention of needle-stick injuries
  - Protective needles, IVs, scalpels, etc.
  - Mandated to prevent injury to healthcare workers

5. Children with AIDS are at risk for failure to thrive. Adequate nutritional intake can be promoted by encouraging parents to provide nutritious meals and supplementing vitamins.
6. Emotional support should be provided to both the family and the child. Although the survival and long-term outlook for children with HIV has greatly improved, there is still a social stigma involved with the disease.

2 Prevention of Infection in Children with HIV
- Frequent handwashing
- Limit exposure to ill people
- Modified immunization schedule
- Annual TB skin tests
- Prevention of sexually transmitted disease (adolescents)

3 Importance of Taking Medications
- Number and cost of medications can be overwhelming
- Nonadherence may result in increased morbidity and mortality
- Why kids might not take medications:
  - Taste or texture
  - Difficulty swallowing pills
  - Side effects—nausea, rashes

3a Strategies to Improve Medication Adherence
- Education about purpose of medication
- Benefits of adhering to regimen
- Positive reinforcement
- Discuss family's individual situation

4 Promote Respiratory Function
- At risk for pneumonia
- Cough and deep breathe every 2 to 4 hours
- Rest periods to conserve energy

5 Maintain Adequate Nutrition
- At risk for failure to thrive
- Healthy foods
- Vitamins (antioxidants)
- Diarrhea is common
- *Candida* infections are common—may inhibit appetite due to oral lesions

6 Provide Emotional Support
- Other family members may also be infected
- Stigma of disease
- Privacy
- May have fears or misconceptions about current status of disease treatment and survival

SUGGESTIONS FOR CLASSROOM ACTIVITIES

- During the discussion on HIV, show the animation, "HIV Infection/Transmission," and the video, "AIDS/HIV," available on the Student CD-ROM.
- Before class, assign students to complete "Case Study: Postexposure Management of Needlestick Injuries," available on the Companion Website, as a basis for discussion.

SUGGESTIONS FOR CLINICAL ACTIVITIES

Assign students to the infectious disease clinic to observe the outpatient management of children with HIV and AIDS.

LEARNING OBJECTIVE 5

Describe nursing management for the child with systemic lupus erythematosus or juvenile rheumatoid arthritis.

CONCEPTS FOR LECTURE

1. Systemic lupus erythematosus (SLE) and juvenile rheumatoid arthritis (JRA) are both chronic autoimmune disorders. SLE involves the deposition of antigen-antibody complexes into connective tissue, triggering an inflammatory response. Small blood vessels, glomeruli, joints, spleen, and heart valves are commonly affected. JRA involves the joints and is characterized by decreased mobility, swelling, and pain.

2. Nursing interventions that are common to both diseases include promoting adequate nutrition, managing flare-ups, managing side effects of medication, promoting rest and comfort, and providing emotional support.

3. Nursing interventions specific to SLE include promoting skin integrity, preventing infection, and maintaining fluid balance.

4. Nursing interventions specific to JRA include promoting improved mobility.

POWERPOINT LECTURE SLIDES

1 Systemic Lupus Erythematosus (SLE)
- Chronic autoimmune disorder
- Unknown etiology
  - Possible genetic component
  - Environmental trigger?
- Antigen-antibody complexes deposited in connective tissue
- Inflammatory response results
- Small blood vessels, glomeruli, joints, spleen, heart valves affected

1a Juvenile Rheumatoid Arthritis (JRA)
- Chronic autoimmune disorder
- Characterized by
  - Joint inflammation
  - Decreased mobility
  - Swelling
  - Pain

2 Nursing Interventions Common to SLE and JRA
- Promote adequate nutrition
- Assist in avoidance of flare-ups
- Manage side effects of medication
  - Methotrexate
  - Other medications
- Promote rest and comfort
- Provide emotional support

3 Nursing Interventions Specific to SLE
- Promote skin integrity—rash predisposes to infection
- Prevent infection
- Maintain fluid balance—due to renal involvement

4 Nursing Interventions Specific to JRA
- Promote improved mobility
  - Physical therapy
  - Range-of-motion exercises
- Prevent infection if child is on immunosuppressive drugs

SUGGESTIONS FOR CLASSROOM ACTIVITIES

Methotrexate is commonly used to treat both SLE and JRA. Show the animation "Methotrexate" available on the Student CD-ROM and discuss how the drug modulates these disease processes.

SUGGESTIONS FOR CLINICAL ACTIVITIES

Attend a local support group, clinic, or active Web chat for children with chronic inflammatory disease such as SLE or JRA.

LEARNING OBJECTIVE 6

Describe exposure prevention measures for the child with latex allergy.

CONCEPTS FOR LECTURE

1. Latex allergy is increasingly common, as sources of latex products have risen in the past few years. Healthcare workers and clients are at risk. *Table 44.8 is a good reference*. Symptoms of latex allergy range from mild topical reactions to full anaphylaxis.
2. Exposure to latex must be prevented in a child with known latex allergies. This involves removing all sources of latex from the child's environment, as well as teaching parents what to do in case of a reaction.

POWERPOINT LECTURE SLIDES

 Latex Allergy
- Increasingly common
- Who has it?
  - 10% of healthcare workers
  - 50% of children with spina bifida
  - 34% of children with three or more surgeries
- What is it?
  - An IgE-mediated response
  - Develops after repeated exposure to latex
- Sources of latex

 Symptoms of Latex Allergy: A Range
- Topical reaction
  - Red, inflamed skin
  - Blisters on skin
- Systemic reaction
  - Itchy eyes
  - Wheezing
  - Anaphylaxis

 Measures to Protect Latex Allergy
- (Table 44.7)

 Preventing Exposure to Latex in Children with Known Latex Allergy
- Environment must be free of latex
  - Must know which household and community products contain latex
  - School and community sources of latex
- Medic alert bracelet is encouraged
- Discuss how to detect and treat a reaction— EpiPen may be prescribed for severe reactions

SUGGESTIONS FOR CLASSROOM ACTIVITIES

Using Table 44.8, have students make a list of latex-containing products that are in their own houses. This will help to increase their awareness of various products that contain latex.

SUGGESTIONS FOR CLINICAL ACTIVITIES

Have students search the clinical unit for products that contain latex. Many hospitals have adopted a latex-free environment. If so, have students identify various sources of latex that families may bring to the hospital (e.g., latex balloons, home feeding nipples, home pacifiers, etc.)

LEARNING OBJECTIVE 7

Apply nursing interventions and prevention measures for the child experiencing other hypersensitivity reactions.

CONCEPTS FOR LECTURE

1. Many children have allergies, and allergic reactions can range from mild to severe. Allergens are substances that trigger a reaction and can be inhaled, ingested, or absorbed.

POWERPOINT LECTURE SLIDES

Allergies and Children
- Very common
- Common allergens
  - Medications
  - Animal dander
  - Dust

2. There are several nursing interventions that should be implemented for the child with hypersensitivity reactions, including careful assessment, teaching how to minimize or prevent exposure, and allergy-proofing the home.

- ○ Mites
- ○ Mold
- ○ Plants
- ○ Foods (nuts, seafood, egg whites)
- Reactions can be mild or severe—local or systemic

1a Characteristic Findings in Children with Allergies
- (Table 44.6)

2 Nursing Care for the Child with Hypersensitivity Reactions
- Thorough assessment
  - ○ Focus on symptoms: Continuous or intermittent?
  - ○ How long do episodes last?
  - ○ Variations in symptoms?
  - ○ Close attention to skin, GI tract

2a Nursing Interventions
- Skin testing for allergies—goal is to identify the allergen
- Treat the symptoms
- Discuss minimizing or avoiding exposure to allergens
- Discuss emergency treatment of future reactions

2b Allergy-Proofing the Home
- Pets
  - ○ Recommend removal of pet
  - ○ Frequent baths may decrease dander
- Frequent dusting of house
- Eliminate carpeting
- Eliminate cigarette smoke
- Fabrics and pillows should be hypoallergenic and frequently cleaned
- Air filters

SUGGESTIONS FOR CLASSROOM ACTIVITIES

Before class, assign students to gather information about how to "allergy-proof" a home. Use their findings to augment the discussion of the topic during the lecture.

SUGGESTIONS FOR CLINICAL ACTIVITIES

Assign students to spend a day in an allergy clinic or office. The students may observe different types of testing and education for specific allergies. The student could provide a detailed case report of a child observed that day.

CHAPTER 45
THE CHILD WITH INFECTIOUS AND COMMUNICABLE DISEASES

RESOURCE LIBRARY

CD-ROM

Skill 9-11: Oral Route (Body Temperature)
Skill 9-12: Axillary Route (Body Temperature)
Skill 9-13: Rectal Route (Body Temperature)
Skill 9-14: Tympanic Route (Body Temperature)
NCLEX-RN® Review
Audio Glossary

COMPANION WEBSITE

NCLEX-RN® Review
MediaLink Applications:
   Care Plan: Develop an Immunizations Schedule:
     Infant with HIV, Healthy Infant, Preschooler
   Immunizations and Older Children
   Vaccine Administration Record
   Immunization FAQ
   Case Study: Reporting an Adverse Vaccine Event
   Bioterrorism Preparedness
Thinking Critically
Vaccine Safety Information
Immunization Safety Research
Catch-Up Schedule for Immunizations
Audio Glossary

IMAGE LIBRARY

Figure 45.1 Infectious diseases are easily transmitted in settings such as childcare centers where children handle common objects.

Figure 45.2 Proper handwashing is one of the most effective measures in preventing transmission of microorganisms.

Figure 45.3 Give immunizations quickly and efficiently.

Pathophysiology Illustrated: The Chain of Infection.

LEARNING OBJECTIVE 1

Describe the reasons why children are more vulnerable than adults to infectious and communicable diseases.

CONCEPTS FOR LECTURE

1. Infants are particularly vulnerable to diseases for several reasons. Their immune systems are not fully mature at birth. The antibodies that are passively acquired from their mothers have limited protection, and this protection further decreases over time. Finally, infants have incomplete disease protection until they receive immunizations.

2. Children get exposed to diseases through interactions with other children and adults. This exposure to illness allows them to naturally develop antibodies to these diseases, which prevents subsequent infections from the same organism.

3. Many behaviors of children contribute to the ease with which infections are transmitted, including poor hygiene and handwashing.

POWERPOINT LECTURE SLIDES

1 Why are Infants Vulnerable to Infectious Disease?
- Immune system is not mature at birth
- Passively acquire antibodies from mother
  - Protection is limited
  - Protection fades after birth
- Have not received immunizations yet, so protection is incomplete

2 Why Does It Seem Like Kids Are Always Sick?
- Children get exposed to diseases through contact with others
- Allows them to develop natural antibodies to diseases
- Prevents subsequent infections with the same organism

3 Behaviors of Children that Contribute to Disease Transmission
- Poor hygiene, leaking diapers (fecal-oral route)
- Poor handwashing (fecal-oral, contact routes)
- Don't blow their nose often (nasal secretions)
- Daycare staff may not use proper handwashing techniques

SUGGESTIONS FOR CLASSROOM ACTIVITIES

Discuss how the nurse can help children and families learn how to prevent disease transmission. "Teaching Highlight 45.1: Reducing the Transmission of Infection," can be used to generate ideas for the discussion.

SUGGESTIONS FOR CLINICAL ACTIVITIES

Hospitalized children often do not wash their hands after toileting or before eating. Discuss the importance of teaching children proper handwashing techniques, as well as how the nurse can teach these techniques during hospitalization.

LEARNING OBJECTIVE 2

Describe the process of infection and modes of transmission.

CONCEPTS FOR LECTURE

1. An infectious disease is any communicable disease caused by microorganisms that are commonly transmitted from one person to another, or from an animal to a person. A communicable disease is an illness directly or indirectly transmitted from one person or animal to another by contact with body fluids, contaminated items, or by vectors (such as ticks, mosquitoes, etc.).
2. For a communicable disease to occur, three links need to be present: an infectious agent or pathogen, an effective means of transmission, and a susceptible host. The pathogen must also have a suitable reservoir, or habitat, that can be living or nonliving. Transmission may be direct or indirect.
3. Infection control aims to interrupt the chain of transmission, or eliminate either the reservoir or the habitat.

POWERPOINT LECTURE SLIDES

1 Definitions Regarding Infections
- Infectious disease
- Communicable disease
- Vectors

2 The Chain of Infection
- ("Pathophysiology Illustrated: The Chain of Infection")

2a Modes of Transmission
- Direct: Physical contact between source of infection and new host
- Indirect: Pathogens survive outside humans before causing infection

3 Infection Control Goals
- Interrupt transmission (example: isolation of infected person)
- Eliminate reservoir or habitat (example: spray insecticide on mosquitoes carrying West Nile Virus)

SUGGESTIONS FOR CLASSROOM ACTIVITIES

When discussing the chain of infection, use influenza as an example. Most students have had influenza and can relate the disease to the concepts discussed.

SUGGESTIONS FOR CLINICAL ACTIVITIES

Discuss how infection control methods commonly used in the hospital affect the chain of infection. Specifically, why do different pathogens have different infection control methods (such as contact versus droplet)?

LEARNING OBJECTIVE 3

Explain the role that vaccines play in reduction and elimination of infectious and communicable diseases.

CONCEPTS FOR LECTURE

1. Vaccines introduce an antigen into the body. An antigen is a foreign substance that triggers an immune response, and an antibody is a protein produced by the body in response to the antigen.
2. Active immunity occurs when antibody production is stimulated without causing clinical disease. The body must have the ability to make antibodies for immunity to occur. Passive immunity can be induced with antibodies produced in another human or animal host.
3. Many diseases have been nearly eliminated or significantly decreased due to vaccinations.
4. Types of vaccines used in the United States include killed virus vaccines, toxoids, live virus vaccines, recombinant forms, and conjugated forms.
5. The schedule for vaccination is routinely updated and is available on the CDC Website. *For the 2005 recommendations, refer to Table 45.1. Supplemental immunizations for certain children are summarized in Table 45.2.*
6. There are numerous barriers to vaccination, including limited access to health care, inadequate education about the importance of vaccination, and religious prohibitions. An increasing number of parents are choosing not to vaccinate their children, which could have a significant impact on the health of their own child and other children in the community.

POWERPOINT LECTURE SLIDES

1 Vaccines: Basic Concepts
- Vaccines: Introduce antigens into the body
- Antigen: Foreign substance—triggers immune response
- Antibody: Protein made by the body in response to antigen

2 Types of Immunity
- Active: Body makes antibodies without presence of clinical disease (example: tetanus vaccine)
- Passive: Antibodies made by another human or animal and given to another person—does not confer long-term immunity (example: tetanus immunoglobulin)

3 Diseases Decreased by Vaccination
- Measles, mumps, rubella
- Polio
- Whooping cough (pertussis)
- Diphtheria
- Smallpox
- *Haemophilus influenzae* type B (Hib)
- Hepatitis B
- Chickenpox (varicella)

4 Types of Vaccines
- Killed virus vaccine (inactivated polio)
- Toxoid (tetanus toxoid)
- Live virus vaccine (measles, varicella)
- Recombinant form (hepatitis B, pertussis)
- Conjugated form (Hib)

5 Vaccination Schedule
- Routinely updated
- Available on CDC Website
- Supplemental vaccines
- Catch-up schedule

6 Barriers to Vaccination
- Economic factors
- Limited access to health care
- Clinic only open during working hours
- Parent does not understand importance of vaccines
- Religious prohibition

6a Reasons Why Parents Do Not Vaccinate Kids
- Concern that vaccine is dangerous (autism, SIDS)
- Vaccine might not fully prevent disease
- Does not want government to monitor vaccination status
- The disease is not a threat anymore
- Side effects from vaccine do not justify benefit
- Belief that they can control child's susceptibility to disease

Distribute copies of the latest vaccination schedule to the class (or, have them download their own copy from the CDC Website). Using different ages, ask what immunizations the child would receive if he or she presented to the clinic. After the students understand how to interpret the chart, have them determine how to catch a child up on missed vaccines. Resources for these activities are located on the Companion Website, including, "MediaLink Applications: Catch-Up Schedule for Immunizations," "MediaLink Applications: Develop an Immunization Schedule - Infant with HIV," "MediaLink Applications: Immunizations and Older Children," and "MediaLink Applications: Vaccine Administration Record."

An 8-year-old child comes in for an appendectomy, and while taking the health history the parent states that the child has never received any immunizations. How might the nurse further explore this issue with the parent? Use PowerPoint slides 6 and 6a in this chapter to develop the scenario, as well as "FAQ About Immunizations," located on the Companion Website.

LEARNING OBJECTIVE 4

Develop a nursing care plan for children of all ages needing immunizations.

CONCEPTS FOR LECTURE

1. Assessment and diagnosis by the nurse are the first steps in the care of a child needing immunizations. *"Nursing Care Plan: The Child Needing Immunizations," and Table 45.3 are good references.*
2. Planning involves advocating for immunization, informing parents about side effects, and obtaining consent.
3. Implementation includes administration of the vaccine, as well as documentation. Adverse events must be reported by law—*refer to Table 45.4.*
4. Evaluation serves as a way for the nurse to verify that nursing care was complete and thorough.

POWERPOINT LECTURE SLIDES

1 Assessment
- Examine immunization record
- Consult catch-up schedule if child is behind
- Make full use of opportunities to vaccinate
- Minor illness or fever is not a contraindication to vaccination
- Ask about past reactions to vaccines, pregnancy, allergy to vaccine components (eggs, neomycin, gelatin)

1a Diagnosis
- Risk for infection
- Knowledge deficit
- Risk for injury
- Risk for impaired skin integrity
- Ineffective health maintenance

2 Planning
- Advocate for immunization
- Inform parents of possible side effects
- Provide written and verbal information
- Obtain consent

3 Implementation
- Be efficient, but support child
- Longer needle used to ensure IM (not SQ) administration
- Do not lie—the immunization *will* hurt
- Give injections in multiple extremities if needed
- Allow parent to comfort child

3a Documenting the Immunization
- Required elements
  ○ Date of administration
  ○ Vaccine given
  ○ Manufacturer, lot number, and expiration date

PowerPoint Lecture Slides *continued*

   ○ Site and route of administration
   ○ Name, title, and address of nurse administering vaccine
   • Give parent immunization record to keep
   • Provide guidelines for managing mild reactions at home
   • Report any adverse events

 Evaluation
   • Parent fully informed and consent to immunization
   • Immunizations are appropriate for child's age
   • Parents are prepared to manage mild reactions at home

SUGGESTIONS FOR CLASSROOM ACTIVITIES

Have students review "MediaLink Applications: Reporting an Adverse Vaccine Event," located on the Companion Website. Use the case study as a stimulus for discussion during this objective.

SUGGESTIONS FOR CLINICAL ACTIVITIES

Children are often extremely fearful of immunizations, and have often had negative experiences with prior immunizations. During clinical conference, have students read "Evidence-Based Nursing 45.1: Nursing Care During Immunizations." Use "Thinking Critically" at the end to stimulate discussion about how to reduce children's pain and anxiety during immunizations.

LEARNING OBJECTIVE 5

Recognize common infectious and communicable diseases.

CONCEPTS FOR LECTURE

1. Infectious and communicable diseases that may be seen during childhood (*summarized in Table 45.5*) include chickenpox, coxsackievirus, diphtheria, fifth disease, *Haemophilus influenzae* type B, influenza, measles, mononucleosis, mumps, pertussis, pneumococcus, poliomyelitis, roseola, rubella, streptococcus A, and tetanus.
2. Infectious diseases that are commonly transmitted by insect or animal hosts (*summarized in Table 45.6*) include Lyme disease, malaria, rabies, Rocky Mountain Spotted Fever, and West Nile Virus.

POWERPOINT LECTURE SLIDES

 Chickenpox (varicella)
   • Agent: Varicella-zoster
   • Transmission: Airborne, direct contact
   • Systemic manifestations: Fever, malaise, headache, abdominal pain
   • Skin manifestations: Clear, fluid-filled vesicles all over the body
   • Treatment: Supportive
   • Nursing: Isolation, symptom management

 Chickenpox
   • (Unnumbered Figure 45.1)

 Coxsackievirus (Herpangina; Hand, Foot, and Mouth Disease)
   • Agent: *Coxsackievirus A16, Enterovirus 71*
   • Transmission: Fecal-oral and respiratory routes
   • Systemic manifestations: Fever, sore throat
   • Skin manifestations
      ○ Herpangina: Papulovesicular lesions in pharynx only
      ○ Hand, foot, and mouth disease: Papulovesicular lesions on inside of cheek, gums, tongue, as well as hands and feet
   • Treatment: Supportive
   • Nursing: Isolation, topical lotions, cool drinks

1c Diphtheria
- **Agent:** *Corynebacterium diphtheriae*
- Transmission: Contact with nasal or eye discharge
- Systemic manifestations: Fever, anorexia, rhinorrhea, cough, stridor
- Skin manifestations: Tonsils, pharynx covered in thick, bluish-white patch
- Treatment: Antibiotics, IV antitoxin
- Nursing: Isolation, monitor for respiratory distress, administer antibiotics

1d Erythema Infectiosum (Fifth Disease)
- Agent: Human *parvovirus B19*
- Transmission: Respiratory secretions and blood
- Systemic manifestations: Flu-like illness
- Skin manifestations: Fiery-red rash on cheeks ("slapped face" appearance)—maculopapular rash on trunk and limbs
- Treatment: Supportive
- Nursing: Isolation, fever control, antipruritics, soothing baths (oatmeal)

1e Characteristic Facial Rash of Erythema Infectiosum (Fifth Disease)
- (Unnumbered Figures 45.2A and B)

1f *Haemophilus Influenzae* Type B
- Agent: *H. influenzae* bacteria (several serotypes exist)
- Transmission: Direct contact or droplet inhalation
- Systemic manifestations: Viral upper respiratory tract infection that invades bloodstream—may cause meningitis, epiglottitis, pneumonia, or sepsis
- Skin manifestations: None specific
- Treatment: Antibiotics
- Nursing: Isolation, prophylaxis for close contacts, antipyretics

1g Influenza
- **Agent:** *Orthomyxoviridae*, types A and B
- Transmission: Aerosolized particles, direct contact with secretions
- Systemic manifestations: Fever, chills, malaise, headache, nausea, and vomiting
- Skin manifestations: None specific
- Treatment: Supportive—antivirals for children at risk for complications
- Nursing: Isolation, prevent dehydration, comfort

1h Measles (Rubeola)
- Agent: *Morbillivirus*
- Transmission: Airborne, droplet, and contact
- Systemic manifestations: High fever, conjunctivitis, cough, anorexia, malaise

- Skin manifestations: Koplik spots on buccal mucosa—red, blotchy, maculopapular rash (face, trunk, limbs)
- Treatment: Supportive—antibiotics for secondary infections
- Nursing: Isolation, antipyretics, antitussives, monitor respiratory status

1i Koplik Spots on Oral Mucosa, Fifth Day of Rash
- (Unnumbered Figure 45.4)

1j Measles, Third Day of Rash
- (Unnumbered Figures 45.3A and B)

1k Mononucleosis
- Agent: Epstein-Barr virus
- Transmission: Direct contact with secretions
- Systemic manifestations: Malaise, headache, fatigue, fever, lymphadenopathy—weakness and lethargy may persist for months
- Skin manifestations: None specific
- Treatment: Supportive
- Nursing: Antipyretics, bed rest during acute phase

1l Mumps (Parotitis)
- Agent: *Rubulavirus*
- Transmission: Contact with respiratory secretions
- Systemic manifestations: Malaise, fever, pain with chewing, parotid gland swelling
- Skin manifestations: None specific
- Treatment: Supportive—disease is usually self-limiting
- Nursing: Isolation, comfort

1m Mumps with Diffuse Lymphedema on the Neck
- (Unnumbered Figures 45.5A and B)

1n Pertussis (Whooping Cough)
- Agent: *Bordetella pertussis*
- Transmission: Respiratory droplets—direct contact with secretions
- Systemic manifestations: Runny nose, fever, mild cough that becomes more severe at night—infants do not manifest the "whooping" sound
- Skin manifestations: None specific
- Treatment: Antibiotics, steroids, supportive care
- Nursing: Isolation, monitor respiratory status, dehydration

1o Pneumococcal Infection
- Agent: *Streptococcus pneumoniae*
- Transmission: Respiratory secretions, droplet
- Systemic manifestations: Related to area of infection (otitis, sinusitis, bacteremia, pneumonia, meningitis)
- Skin manifestations: None specific

- Treatment: Antibiotics (many resistant strains exist)
- Nursing: Isolation, antipyretics, encourage fluids

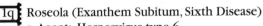 Poliomyelitis
- Agent: Poliovirus
- Transmission: Fecal-oral, possibly respiratory
- Systemic manifestations: May be mild or severe—CNS symptoms, respiratory weakness, paralysis
- Skin manifestations: None specific
- Treatment: Supportive
- Nursing: Monitor respiratory status, comfort

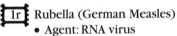 Roseola (Exanthem Subitum, Sixth Disease)
- Agent: Herpesvirus type 6
- Transmission: Possibly respiratory secretions of healthy individuals
- Systemic manifestations: High fever for 3 to 8 days, otherwise no symptoms
- Skin manifestations: Pale pink, maculopapular rash (trunk, face, neck, limbs)
- Treatment: Supportive—disease usually self-limiting
- Nursing: Rarely hospitalized—fever control

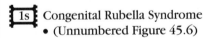 Rubella (German Measles)
- Agent: RNA virus
- Transmission: Droplet or direct contact
- Systemic manifestations: Low-grade fever, headache, malaise, anorexia
- Skin manifestations: Pink, nonconfluent, maculopapular rash
- Treatment: Supportive—disease usually mild
  Major risk for fetus if mother infected during first trimester
- Nursing: Isolation, especially from pregnant women—comfort measures

1s Congenital Rubella Syndrome
- (Unnumbered Figure 45.6)

 Streptococcus A
- Agent: Group A streptococci (GAS)
- Transmission: Contact with respiratory secretions—direct contact
- Systemic manifestations: Pharyngeal (sore throat, fever)
- Skin manifestations: Pyodermal (impetigo)—honey-colored lesions
- Treatment: Antibiotics—uncomplicated impetigo treated topically
- Nursing: Usually cared for at home—fever management, warm fluids

1u Tetanus
- Agent: *Clostridium tetani* or tetanus bacillus
- Transmission: Via wounds in the skin

- Systemic manifestations: Neck or jaw stiffness, facial spasms, prolonged muscle contraction
- Skin manifestations: None specific
- Treatment: Tetanus immune globulin— respiratory monitoring and ventilation
- Nursing: Wound care, monitor respiratory status, hydration

 Lyme Disease
- Agent: *Borrelia burgdorferi*, a spirochete
- Transmission: Tick bite (infected spirochete transmitted when tick draws blood)
- Systemic manifestations: Malaise, headache, mild fever, joint aches
- Skin manifestations: Red, "bulls-eye" rash around tick bite
- Treatment: Antibiotics
- Nursing: Discuss prevention of tick bites and proper tick removal—treatment usually occurs at home, rest and completion of antibiotics

 Lyme Disease
- (Unnumbered Figure 45.8)

 Malaria
- Agent: *Plasmodium* (four species exist)
- Transmission: Via infected female mosquito bite
- Systemic manifestations: Malaise, headache, vomiting, diarrhea, high fever spike every 48 to 72 hours
- Skin manifestations: None specific
- Treatment: Fluid replacement, antipyretics, anemia management, chloroquine treats most species of the parasite
- Nursing: Standard precautions—monitor fluid intake, signs of worsening illness (confusion, seizures, shock), antipyretics

 Rabies (Hydrophobia)
- Agent: *Rhabdoviridae* (two types—one in dogs, one in wildlife)
- Transmission: Infected saliva from bite of rabid animal
- Systemic manifestations: Long incubation period—headache, fever, malaise, difficulty swallowing (leads to hydrophobia)—untreated, leads to coma and death
- Skin manifestations: None specific
- Treatment: Human rabies immune globulin for passive immunity—rabies vaccine for active immunity
- Nursing: Administration of vaccine and education about side effects

 Rocky Mountain Spotted Fever
- Agent: *Rickettsia rickettsii*
- Transmission: Transmitted by infected ticks
- Systemic manifestations: May be mild (malaise, fever) to severe (encephalitis, shock)

- Skin manifestations: Maculopapular rash (extremities, then trunk)
- Treatment: Doxycycline
- Nursing: Prevention of tick bites—standard precautions, administer antibiotics, monitor for worsening symptoms

2e Rocky Mountain Spotted Fever
- (Unnumbered Figure 45.9)

2f West Nile Virus
- Agent: Arbovirus
- Transmission: Infected wild birds—mosquito carries virus from bird to human via bite
- Systemic manifestations: Most are asymptomatic—about 20% have flu-like symptoms and 1% have severe neurologic illness
- Skin manifestations: None specific
- Treatment: Supportive
- Nursing: Standard precautions—prevention of mosquito bites

SUGGESTIONS FOR CLASSROOM ACTIVITIES

Before class, divide students into groups and have each group be responsible for briefly presenting each infectious disease discussed in this chapter. Encourage them to locate pictures of the diseases, as the skin patterns are very important in the recognition of the disease.

SUGGESTIONS FOR CLINICAL ACTIVITIES

It is difficult to remember the isolation requirements for each of these infectious diseases. Identify resources available in the clinical setting that nurses can refer to for specific information about these diseases.

LEARNING OBJECTIVE 6

Develop a nursing care plan for a child with a common infectious disease.

CONCEPTS FOR LECTURE

1. The nursing process can be applied to children with infectious diseases.

POWERPOINT LECTURE SLIDES

1 Assessment
- Hydration status, fluid intake
- Vital signs, including fever
- Comfort level
- Appetite
- Rash
- Toxic appearance (lethargy, poor perfusion, changes in respiratory pattern)

1a Diagnosis
- Hyperthermia
- Risk for deficient fluid volume
- Impaired skin integrity
- Impaired oral mucous membranes
- Ineffective therapeutic regimen management

Planning and Implementation
- Most children cared for at home—some hospitalized
- Isolation to prevent spread of infection
- Wipe down toys, flat surfaces
- Treatment of fever
- Encourage fluid intake
- Involve parents

 Evaluation
- Opportunities to spread infection are minimized
- Fever is effectively managed
- Antibiotics, if ordered, are given fully

SUGGESTIONS FOR CLASSROOM ACTIVITIES

Assign students to complete this objective before class and bring the care plan with them to class. Have students trade care plans and critique each other's work.

SUGGESTIONS FOR CLINICAL ACTIVITIES

During clinical conference, discuss nonpharmacologic strategies for managing fever in children.

CHAPTER 46
THE CHILD WITH ALTERATIONS IN EYE, EAR, NOSE, AND THROAT FUNCTION

RESOURCE LIBRARY

 CD-ROM

Animations:
  Ear Abnormalities
  Middle Ear Dynamics
Videos:
  3D Eye/Eye Anatomy
  3D Ear/Ear Anatomy
  Otitis Media
Nursing in Action:
  Eye, Ear, and Nose Medication Administration
  Obtaining a Sample for Throat Culture
Skills 9-18 to 9-19: Visual Acuity Screening
Skill 10-15: Obtaining a Sample for Throat Culture
Audio Glossary
NCLEX-RN® Review

COMPANION WEBSITE

MediaLink Applications:
  Plan Interventions for Visual Disorders
  Early Identification and Intervention for Hearing
    Loss
  Neonate Screening and the Law
  Plan a Vision Screening Program
  Case Study: Otitis Media
Thinking Critically
NCLEX-RN® Review
Audio Glossary

IMAGE LIBRARY

Figure 46.1 Acute conjunctivitis.
Figure 46.2 This premature infant in the neonatal intensive care unit is receiving artificial ventilation, a risk factor for retinopathy of prematurity.
Figure 46.3 This child needs ongoing developmental assessment and a comprehensive individualized education plan.
Figure 46.4 Acute otitis media is characterized by pain and a red, bulging, nonmobile tympanic membrane.
Figure 46.5 Otitis media with effusion is noted on otoscopy by fluid line or air bubbles.
Figure 46.6 This young child is pulling at the ear and acting fussy, two important signs of otitis media.

Figure 46.7 Listening to loud music with headphones or at rock concerts is a frequent cause of hearing loss among teenagers and young adults.
Figure 46.8 Newborn hearing screening is an effective tool in diagnosing some causes of hearing impairment very early in life.
Figure 46.9 This child with a hearing impairment and tracheostomy is communicating by means of American Sign Language.

As Children Grow: Eustachian Tube.

LEARNING OBJECTIVE 1

Describe abnormalities of the eyes, ears, nose, throat, and mouth in children.

CONCEPTS FOR LECTURE

1. Common eye abnormalities in children include conjunctivitis, cellulitis, visual disorders, and injuries to the eye.
2. Common ear abnormalities in children include otitis media, otitis externa, and hearing impairment.

POWERPOINT LECTURE SLIDES

 Eye Abnormalities in Children
  • Conjunctivitis
  • Cellulitis
  • Visual disorders
  • Injuries to the eye

3. Common disorders of the nose, throat, and mouth include epistaxis, nasopharyngitis, sinusitis, tonsillitis, and trauma to the mouth and teeth.

 Conjunctivitis
- Inflammation of the conjunctiva
  - Clear membrane
  - Lines inside of lid and sclera
- Caused by
  - Viruses
  - Bacteria
  - Allergy
  - Trauma
  - Irritants

 Acute Conjunctivitis
- (Figure 46.1)

 Conjunctivitis
- Symptoms
  - Itching, burning
  - Mucopurulent discharge
  - Crusty eyelids
  - Pink sclera
  - No loss of vision
- Treatment
  - Bacterial: Antibiotics
  - Viral: Comfort measures
  - Allergen: Antihistamines, mast-cell stabilizers

 Cellulitis (Periorbital)
- Infection of eyelid and surrounding tissues
- Usually bacterial
- Symptoms
  - Swollen, tender, red/purple eyelid
  - Restricted, painful eye movement
  - Fever
- Treatment: Antibiotics (IV)

 Visual Disorders
- Concept of binocularity
  - Eyes move and function together
  - Helps brain interpret images
- Diagnosis and treatment of visual disorders—prompt treatment prevents loss of visual acuity

 Types of Visual Disorders
- Hyperopia (farsightedness)
- Myopia (nearsightedness)
- Astigmatism
- Strabismus
- Amblyopia
- Cataracts
- Glaucoma
- Color blindness
- Retinopathy of prematurity

1g Eye Injuries
- Common in all children ages 9 to 11, and boys ages 11 to 15
- Causes: Sports, darts, fireworks, BB guns, burns
- Treatment
  ○ Prevention
  ○ Medical, surgical treatments

2 Ear Abnormalities in Children
- Otitis media
- Otitis externa
- Hearing impairment

2a Otitis Media
- Inflammation with or without infection of the middle ear
- Nearly all children have by age 7
- Peak incidence: First 2 years of life
- Cause: Eustachian tube dysfunction

2b Changes in Eustachian Tube with Growth
- ("As Children Grow: Eustachian Tube")

2c Otitis Media
- Symptoms
  ○ Ear pain (tugging on ear)
  ○ Redness of tympanic membrane
  ○ Middle ear effusion

2d Acute Otitis Media: Tympanic Membrane
- (Figure 46.4)

2e Otitis Media with Effusion
- (Figure 46.5)

2f Otitis Media: Characteristic Ear Pulling
- (Figure 46.6)

2g Otitis Media: Treatment
- Current recommendations about antibiotic use
- Delayed treatment
- Myringotomy

2h Otitis Externa
- Inflammation of skin and soft tissues of the ear
- "Swimmer's ear"
- Irritated canal easily infected
- Symptoms: Pain, itching, swelling
- Treatment: Cleansing, antibiotic drops, steroid drops

2i Hearing Impairment
- Affects about 1 million children in the United States

- Defined by severity
- Causes
  - Genetic
  - Environmental
  - Unknown causes

 Hearing Impairment
- Symptoms
  - Hearing loss picked up on screening
  - Delayed language development
- Treatment
  - Early identification
  - Cochlear implants
  - Hearing aids
  - Some forms are not treatable

 Disorders of the Nose, Throat, and Mouth
- Epistaxis
- Nasopharyngitis
- Sinusitis
- Pharyngitis
- Tonsillitis
- Mouth ulcers
- Trauma to the mouth and teeth

 Epistaxis (Nosebleed)
- Common in school-aged children, especially boys
- Anterior nares most common site
- Causes: Nosepicking, foreign bodies, low humidity
- Treatment
  - Keep upright, head tilted forward
  - Squeeze nares shut for 10 to 15 minutes
  - If not successful, local vasoconstrictors may be used
  - Cauterizers, nasal packing

 Nasopharyngitis
- "Common cold"
- Inflammation and infection of nose and throat
- Causes: Bacteria, viruses (over 200)
- Treatment
  - Nose drops
  - Humidify room
  - Antipyretics

 Sinusitis
- Inflammation of one or more of the paranasal sinuses
- Symptoms: Facial pain, headache, fever
- Treatment: Antibiotics commonly used
- Chronic sinusitis: refer to specialist

 Pharyngitis
- Infection of the pharynx and tonsils
- Rare in children less than 1 year—common at 4 to 7 years
- Causes: 80% viral, 20% bacterial (strep throat)
- Symptoms: sore throat, exudate, low-grade fever

- Treatment
  - Bacterial: Antibiotics
  - Viral: Comfort care

 Tonsillitis
- Infection and hypertrophy of the palatine tonsils
- Causes: Viral, bacterial
- Symptoms: Breathing and swallowing difficulties
- Treatment
  - Antibiotics
  - Tonsillectomy

 Trauma to the Mouth and Teeth
- Causes: Injuries, sports
- Symptoms: Bleeding, dental damage
- Treatment
  - Control bleeding
  - Transport to emergency room or emergency dentist

SUGGESTIONS FOR CLASSROOM ACTIVITIES

There are numerous animations and videos available to augment your discussion of this objective, including:

- Animations on the Student CD-ROM: "Ear Abnormalities," "Eye Abnormalities," and "Middle Ear Dynamics."
- Videos on the Student CD-ROM: "3D Ear/Ear Anatomy," "3D Eye/Eye Anatomy," and "Otitis Media."
- Have students complete the activity on the Companion Website "Case Study: Otitis Media."

SUGGESTIONS FOR CLINICAL ACTIVITIES

Many of the preceding disorders are most commonly diagnosed in the outpatient setting. Consider assigning students to an outpatient acute care clinic or a pediatrician's office in order to give them the opportunity to observe and care for children with these disorders.

LEARNING OBJECTIVE 2

Plan for screening programs and identification of children with vision and hearing abnormalities.

CONCEPTS FOR LECTURE

1. Early identification of vision and hearing deficits through screening is critical in order to prevent further vision and hearing loss.

POWERPOINT LECTURE SLIDES

 Importance of Vision and Hearing Screening
- Early identification
- Earlier treatment
- Prevent further loss of vision or hearing

 Strategies for Vision Screening
- Screening can be done at any age
- Most schools mandate vision screening
- Assessment
  - Eye symmetry, movement
  - Ability to follow objects
  - Age-appropriate visual acuity test

 Strategies for Hearing Screening
- Screening can be done at any age
- All newborns should be screened in the newborn nursery before discharge
- Assess hearing and speech development at all well-child visits

SUGGESTIONS FOR CLASSROOM ACTIVITIES

There are several activities on the Companion Website that can be used to expand the student's thinking about screening programs. These include:

- MediaLink Applications: Early Identification and Intervention for Hearing Loss"
- MediaLink Applications: Neonate Screening and the Law"
- Critical Thinking: Plan a Vision Screening Program

SUGGESTIONS FOR CLINICAL ACTIVITIES

Assign students to work with a school nurse at a local elementary school and have the students assist with vision and hearing screenings. Recommend that students review Skills 9-17 through 9-19, "Visual Acuity Screening" available on the Student CD-ROM and in the Clinical Skills Manual before attending the screenings.

LEARNING OBJECTIVE 3

Plan nursing care for children with vision or hearing impairments.

CONCEPTS FOR LECTURE

1. Nursing interventions for children with vision impairment include encouraging the use of all senses, promoting socialization, and encouraging normality.
2. Nursing interventions for children with hearing impairment include techniques for communicating with deaf children, awareness of hearing aids used by children, and facilitating interpreters.

POWERPOINT LECTURE SLIDES

1 Nursing Interventions: Vision Impairment
- Encourage use of all senses
- Promote socialization
- Encourage physical contact (hug, stroke, etc.)
- Call child's name when entering or leaving the room
- Describe all procedures before they are done
- Describe foods and location on tray

1a Additional Interventions
- Blind children tend to have blank stares and faces, but still feel emotion—encourage other ways to signify feelings (touch on arm = smile)
- Give child age-appropriate tasks
- Encourage contact with peers as child grows older, including games and sports

2 Nursing Interventions: Hearing Impairment
- Communicating with a deaf child who reads lips
  - Get child's attention
  - Position your face 3 to 6 feet away from the child's face
  - Make sure room is well lit
  - Speak slowly

2a Additional Interventions
- Become familiar with the different types of hearing aids
- Child may speak, but speech may be difficult to understand
- Facilitate availability of interpreters for sign language
- Help parents meet child's educational needs

SUGGESTIONS FOR CLASSROOM ACTIVITIES

Before class, assign students to complete the activity, "MediaLink Applications: Plan Interventions for Visual Disorders," available on the Companion Website. Use this activity as a basis for discussing nursing interventions for children with visual impairments.

SUGGESTIONS FOR CLINICAL ACTIVITIES

Ask a sign language interpreter or audiologist to attend a clinical conference in order to discuss practical interventions for children with hearing impairments.

Learning Objective 4

Use latest recommendations when implementing care and teaching for children with abnormalities of eyes, ears, nose, throat, and mouth.

Concepts for Lecture

1. Because so many children are affected by disorders of the eyes, ears, nose, throat, and mouth, recommendations regarding identification and treatment are routinely updated. Nurses are in a unique position to implement and educate families about these recommendations.

PowerPoint Lecture Slides

1 Screening Programs
- Importance of routine screening
- Vision
- Hearing

1a Teachable Moments for Parents
- Correct use of eyeglasses
- Correct use of hearing aids
- Correct use of medications

1b Antibiotics: To Use or Not To Use
- Sinus infections
- Ear infections
- Issue of drug-resistant bacteria
- Recommendations from the American Academy of Pediatrics

1c Cochlear Implants
- Risks
- Benefits
- Recommendations

Suggestions for Classroom Activities

During class, have students read "Evidence-Based Nursing: Otitis Media." Use the critical thinking questions to have a discussion about how nurses could teach parents about this information as a preventive method.

Suggestions for Clinical Activities

While in the clinical setting, encourage students to talk with physicians about their views regarding the use of antibiotics to treat otitis media.

Learning Objective 5

Integrate preventive and treatment principles when implementing care for children related to eyes, ears, nose, and throat.

Concepts for Lecture

1. Many injuries to the eyes, ears, nose, throat, and mouth are preventable. Common prevention strategies are reviewed.

PowerPoint Lecture Slides

1 Prevention of Eye Injuries
- Protective eyewear
  - Sports
  - School projects
  - Yard work
- Awareness of activities that can injure the eye

1a Prevention of Ear Injuries and Hearing Loss
- Injuries
  - Awareness of objects that can get stuck in ear (toddlers)
  - Sharp objects that can penetrate tympanic membrane
- Hearing loss
  - Loud music with and without headphones
  - Ear protection when exposed to loud noise

1b Prevention of nose, throat, and mouth injuries
- Mouth guards when playing sports
- Awareness of objects that can get stuck in the nose (toddlers)

Suggestions for Classroom Activities

Remind students that any organic object that is stuck in the ear or nose will expand due to the moisture present in the cavity. You can demonstrate this in class by taking a pea, peanut, or other common object and placing it in a glass of water. Students will note that it swells and expands over time.

Suggestions for Clinical Activities

Assign students to observe in the pediatric emergency room, where many injuries to the eyes, ears, nose, and throat are seen.

CHAPTER 47
THE CHILD WITH ALTERATIONS IN RESPIRATORY FUNCTION

RESOURCE LIBRARY

CD-ROM

Animations
  CO$_2$ and O$_2$ Transport
  Gas Exchange
Videos
  Pediatric Respiratory Emergency Management
  SIDS
Skill 11-12: Using a Metered Dose Inhaler
Skill 14-2: Oxygen Saturation: Pulse Oximetry
Skill 14-5: Peak Expiratory Flow Meter
Skill 14-11: Tracheostomy Care
Skill 14-25: Performing Chest Physiotherapy/Postural
  Drainage
NCLEX-RN® Review
Audio Glossary

COMPANION WEBSITE

Thinking Critically
MediaLink Applications:
  Teaching Plan: Metered Dose Inhaler
  Teaching Plan: Discharge Instructions for a Child
    with a Tracheostomy Tube
  Nursing Care Plan: The Child with Cystic Fibrosis
NCLEX-RN® Review
Audio Glossary

IMAGE LIBRARY

Figure 47.1 An aspirated foreign body (coin) is clearly visible in the child's trachea on this chest x-ray.

Figure 47.2 The phrase "thumb sign" has been used to describe this enlargement of the epiglottis.

Figure 47.3 Many children with BPD are cared for at home, with the support of a home care program to monitor the family's ability to provide airway management, oxygen, and ventilator support.

Figure 47.4 Acute exacerbations of asthma may require management in the emergency department.

Figure 47.5 Medications given by aerosol therapy allow children the freedom to play and entertain themselves.

Figure 47.6 Cystic fibrosis is an inherited autosomal recessive disorder of the exocrine glands, so it is not uncommon to see siblings with it such as this brother and sister.

Figure 47.7 Digital clubbing.

Figure 47.8 This 6-month-old girl is being evaluated for cystic fibrosis using the sweat test.

Figure 47.9 Postural drainage can be achieved by clapping with a cupped hand on the chest wall over the segment to be drained to create vibrations that are transmitted to the bronchi to dislodge secretions.

Table 47.2 Risk Factors for Sudden Infant Death Syndrome (SIDS)

Table 47.15 Medications Used to Treat Cystic Fibrosis

As Children Grow: Airway Development.

As Children Grow: Trachea Position.

Pathophysiology Illustrated: Airway Diameter.

Pathophysiology Illustrated: Retraction Sites.

Pathophysiology Illustrated: Airway Changes with Croup.

Pathophysiology Illustrated: Pneumothorax.

Video on CD-ROM: Pediatric Respiratory Emergency Management.

LEARNING OBJECTIVE 1

Describe unique characteristics of the pediatric respiratory system anatomy and physiology and apply that information to the care of children with respiratory conditions.

CONCEPTS FOR LECTURE

1. A child's respiratory tract continues to grow and change until about 12 years of age. There are significant differences between the adult and pediatric airway.
2. The child's upper airway is short and narrow, which increases the potential for obstruction. A child's little finger is a good estimate for the diameter of his or her airway size. There is an inverse relationship between airway diameter and resistance: The narrower the airway is, the greater the airway resistance.
3. The child's lower airway also develops throughout childhood. The alveoli change size and shape and increase in number until puberty. This increases the area available for gas exchange. Smooth muscles of the bronchi and bronchioles develop during the first year of life. Until children are about 6 years of age, the intercostals muscles are immature and the diaphragm is the primary muscle used for ventilation. The cartilaginous ribs are very flexible, which causes retractions that worsen during respiratory distress.

POWERPOINT LECTURE SLIDES

1 Growth and the Respiratory System
- Child's respiratory tract grows until about age 12

2 Upper Airway
- Short and narrow when compared to adult airway
- Child's little finger estimates his or her airway diameter

2a Airway Development
- ("As Children Grow: Airway Development")

2b Trachea Position
- ("As Children Grow: Trachea Position")

2c Airway Diameter
- Inverse relationship between airway diameter and airway resistance
- ("Pathophysiology Illustrated: Airway Diameter")

2d Upper Airway: Newborns
- Until 4 weeks of age, obligatory nose breathers
- Nasal patency is critical

3 Lower Airway
- Alveoli change size and shape, increase in number
  - Continues until puberty
  - Increases area available for gas exchange
- Smooth muscles of bronchi and bronchioles
  - Develop during first year of life
  - Until developed, less able to trap invaders

3a Lower Airway
- Intercostal muscles immature—diaphragm primary muscle used to breathe
- Ribs are primarily cartilage and are very flexible—retractions seen, especially during respiratory distress

3b Retractions
- ("Pathophysiology Illustrated: Retraction Sites")

SUGGESTIONS FOR CLASSROOM ACTIVITIES

Show the animation of CO_2 and O_2 transport from the Student CD-ROM. How are infants able to sustain life-sustaining gas exchange if they have fewer alveoli than adults?

SUGGESTIONS FOR CLINICAL ACTIVITIES

Endotracheal tubes (ETTs) closely estimate the size of a child's airway. Visit the emergency department, pediatric intensive care unit, or pediatric operating room to view the various sizes of ETTs available. This gives students a visual reference to the size of a child's airway.

LEARNING OBJECTIVE 2

Describe the different respiratory conditions and injuries that can cause respiratory distress in infants and children.

CONCEPTS FOR LECTURE

1. Conditions that can cause respiratory distress in children can be divided into two categories: acute and chronic.
2. Common causes of acute respiratory distress include foreign-body aspiration, apnea, apparent life-threatening event (ALTE), obstructive sleep apnea (OSA), sudden infant death syndrome (SIDS), croup, epiglottitis, bacterial tracheitis, bronchitis, bronchiolitis, pneumonia, and tuberculosis.
3. Common chronic respiratory conditions include bronchopulmonary dysplasia (BPD), asthma, and cystic fibrosis.
4. Injuries of the respiratory system include smoke inhalation, blunt chest trauma, and pneumothorax.
5. All of the above conditions may lead to respiratory failure, which occurs when the body can no longer maintain effective gas exchange.

POWERPOINT LECTURE SLIDES

1 Conditions Causing Respiratory Distress
- Acute
  - Generally reversible
  - Vary in severity
- Chronic
  - Generally irreversible
  - Characterized by exacerbations and remissions

2 Acute Disorders of the Respiratory System
- Foreign-body aspiration (FBA)
  - Inhalation of any object into the respiratory tract
  - Food (nuts, popcorn, hot dogs), toys, coins, latex balloons common
  - Right lung is most common site of obstruction
  - Clinical manifestations

2a Aspirated Foreign Body Visible in Child's Trachea
- (Figure 47.1)

2b FBA: Therapy
- (Video on CD-ROM: "Pediatric Respiratory Emergency Management")

2c Apnea
- No breathing for more than 20 seconds—compare to periodic breathing
- May cause cyanosis, pallor, hypotonia, or bradycardia

2d Apparent Life-Threatening Event (ALTE)
- Apnea plus
  - Color change
  - Limp muscle tone
  - Choking or gagging
- Most common in infants younger than 4 months
- May occur during sleep or feeding

2e ALTE: Is It SIDS?
- There is different pathophysiology
- ALTE may or may not have a cause
  - Gastroesophageal reflux
  - Seizures
  - Cardiac arrhythmias
  - Metabolic or endocrine problems
- Interventions

2f Obstructive Sleep Apnea (OSA)
- Airway obstruction (partial or complete) during sleep
- Peaks between 2 to 6 years of age due to enlarged tonsils and adenoids—may be associated with obesity
- Diagnosis by polysomnography
- Treatments

2g Sudden Infant Death Syndrome (SIDS)
- Unexpected death of child younger than 1 year
- Diagnosed at autopsy based on clinical findings
- May be due to brain structure defect

2h Risk Factors for Sudden Infant Death Syndrome (SIDS)
- (Table 47.2)

2i Croup
- Broad term of upper airway illnesses—examples
- Affect large numbers of children

2j Laryngotracheobronchitis (LTB)
- Type of croup illness
- ("Pathophysiology Illustrated: Airway Changes with Croup")

2k LTB
- Usually viral cause
- Most common: 3months to 4 years of age
- Signs: Tachypnea, stridor, seal-like barking cough
- Treatment

2l Epiglottitis
- Inflammation of the epiglottis
- Potentially life-threatening
- Usually caused by *H. influenzae* type B (Hib)—Hib vaccination now required for children
- Signs and symptoms: Fever, drooling, difficulty swallowing

2m Lateral Neck X-ray
- (Figure 47.2)

2n Epiglottitis: Interventions
- Avoid inspecting mouth or throat
- Allow child to maintain position of comfort
- Treatment

2o Bacterial Tracheitis
- *S. aureus* (most common) infection of the upper trachea
- Signs and symptoms: Fever, cough, stridor, purulent secretions
- Treatment

2p Bronchitis
- Unusual in childhood
- Symptoms: coarse, hacking cough that is worse at night
- Treatment

2q Bronchiolitis
- RSV and other viruses are main cause
- Pathophysiology
- Symptoms: Nasal symptoms, cough, fever, wheezing, tachypnea, retractions, decreased activity level, decreased oral intake, dehydration
- Treatment

Pneumonia
- Inflammation or infection of bronchioles and alveoli
- Viral, mycoplasmal, bacterial sources
- Pathophysiology
- Symptoms: Fever, rhonchi, crackles, wheezes, cough, dyspnea, tachypnea, restlessness, decreased breath sounds
- Treatment

 Tuberculosis (TB)
- Caused by *M. tuberculosis*
- Pathophysiology
- Symptoms: Cough, weight loss, fever, night sweats
- Treatment

 Chronic Disorders of the Respiratory System
- Bronchopulmonary dysplasia (BPD)
  - Results from acute respiratory disease during neonatal period
  - Most common in very premature infants
  - Triggers: Positive pressure ventilation, oxygen
  - Symptoms: Persistent signs of respiratory distress
  - Treatment

 Asthma
- Inflammation and hyper-responsiveness of airway
- Leads to obstruction
- Most common chronic illness among children
- Pathophysiology
- Symptoms:
  - Cough
  - Wheezing
  - Dyspnea
  - Use of accessory muscles
- Treatment

 Cystic Fibrosis (CF)
- Inherited autosomal recessive disorder
- Pathophysiology
- Symptoms: Meconium ileus (infants), fatty stools, chronic cough, frequent infections, poor weight gain, voracious appetite, delayed onset of puberty

 Mechanisms of Injury
- Smoke inhalation
  - Directly injures airway and lung tissue
  - Smoke, heat, carbon monoxide, chemicals
  - Symptoms: Singed nasal hair, soot near mouth/nose, stridor
  - Treatment

4a Blunt Chest Trauma
- Usually result of motor vehicle crash
- Pliable chest wall doesn't protect underlying organs well
- Pulmonary contusion may result, as well as pneumothorax

4b Pneumothorax
  • ("Pathophysiology Illustrated: Pneumothorax")

5 Consequences of Respiratory Distress
  • May lead to respiratory failure, which can be fatal if not treated promptly

SUGGESTIONS FOR CLASSROOM ACTIVITIES

• There are numerous disorders discussed in this chapter. Have students group together in pairs and assign each pairing a brief overview of a disorder to present to the whole class.
• Bring various items to class that are often associated with foreign-body aspiration and pass them around during the discussion on FBA. Remind students how to estimate the size of a child's airway.
• Provide copies of line drawings of the basic pediatric airway. Divide students into groups and have them sketch in a drawing representing the pathophysiology of a respiratory disease. Have groups share their results with the class.

SUGGESTIONS FOR CLINICAL ACTIVITIES

• Have students role-play what to do in the event of a respiratory arrest. Correct use of a mask and Ambu-bag can be reviewed.
• Many clients with respiratory disorders are monitored with pulse oximeters. Discuss the limitations of pulse oximetry as a monitoring device. Students may review "Skill 14-2: Oxygen Saturation: Pulse Oximetry" located on the Student CD-ROM and in the Clinical Skills Manual.
• Ask students to compare the differences in respiratory diseases between children and adults. For example, how is pneumonia in an infant different from pneumonia in an adult? What needs to be monitored? How is it treated?

LEARNING OBJECTIVE 3

Assess the child's respiratory signs and symptoms to distinguish between mild, moderate, and severe respiratory distress and describe the appropriate nursing care for each level of severity.

CONCEPTS FOR LECTURE

1. Respiratory distress can lead to respiratory failure if it is not recognized and treated promptly. *Refer to Table 47.7 and "Clinical Manifestations: Respiratory Failure and Imminent Respiratory Arrest" during this part of the lecture.*
2. Mild respiratory distress has signs that indicate the child is attempting to compensate.
3. Moderate respiratory distress marks the beginning of initial decompensation.
4. Severe respiratory distress signals that respiratory arrest is imminent.

POWERPOINT LECTURE SLIDES

1 Respiratory Failure
  • Body can no longer maintain effective gas exchange
  • Process begins at alveoli
  • Results in hypoxemia and hypercapnia

2 Mild Respiratory Distress: Attempting to Compensate
  • Signs and symptoms
    ○ Restlessness
    ○ Tachypnea
    ○ Tachycardia
    ○ Diaphoresis
  • Nursing interventions

3 Moderate Respiratory Distress: Early Decompensation
  • Signs and symptoms
    ○ Nasal flaring
    ○ Retractions
    ○ Grunting, wheezing
    ○ Anxiety, irritability, mood changes, confusion
    ○ Hypertension
  • Nursing interventions

4 Severe Respiratory Distress: Respiratory Failure/Imminent Arrest
- Signs and symptoms
  - Dyspnea
  - Bradycardia
  - Cyanosis (note that cyanosis is a late sign)
  - Stupor, coma
- Nursing interventions

SUGGESTIONS FOR CLASSROOM ACTIVITIES

Demonstrate each of the three degrees of respiratory distress described and have students identify which phase of distress you are in. Then have them identify nursing interventions that are appropriate for each level.

SUGGESTIONS FOR CLINICAL ACTIVITIES

Discuss medications commonly used to treat respiratory diseases in children. Administration and monitoring may be discussed. *Table 47.13 as well as "Drug Guide: Albuterol," offer a good place to start.*

LEARNING OBJECTIVE 4

Develop a nursing care plan for a child with common acute respiratory conditions.

CONCEPTS FOR LECTURE

1. For this objective, bronchopulmonary dysplasia (BPD) will serve as the model nursing care plan for acute respiratory conditions. *Students may also refer to "Nursing Care Plan: The Child with Bronchiolitis"*

POWERPOINT LECTURE SLIDES

1 Background
- Etiology: RSV, other viruses
- Pathophysiology
- Clinical manifestations
  - Nasal symptoms, cough, fever, wheezing, tachypnea, retractions
  - Less playful, decreased oral intake
  - Dehydration
- Diagnosis: ELISA test on nasal wash specimen
- Treatment: Supportive

 1a Assessment
- Airway
- Respiratory function
- Sequential monitoring: Getting better or getting worse

 1b Diagnosis
- Ineffective breathing pattern
- Activity intolerance
- Risk for deficient fluid volume
- Anxiety (child and parent)

 1c Planning and Implementation
- Maintain respiratory function
- Hydration
- Reduce anxiety
- Prepare for home care

 1d Evaluation
- The child returns to respiratory baseline within 48 to 72 hours
- Hydration status is maintained
- Parents and child show decreasing anxiety

LEARNING OBJECTIVE 5

Develop a nursing care plan for the child with a chronic respiratory condition.

CONCEPTS FOR LECTURE

1. For this objective, cystic fibrosis (CF) will serve as the model nursing care plan for chronic respiratory conditions. *Students may also refer to "Nursing Care Plan: The Child with Cystic Fibrosis," located on the Companion Website, as well as Tables 47.14 and 47.15.*

POWERPOINT LECTURE SLIDES

1 Background: Cystic Fibrosis (CF)
- Inherited autosomal recessive disorder
- Pathophysiology
- Clinical manifestations
  - Thick, sticky mucus
  - Meconium ileus (infants)
  - Frothy, foul, fatty stools that float ("4 Fs")
  - Chronic moist, productive cough—frequent infections
  - Poor weight gain, voracious appetite
  - Short stature, delayed onset of puberty

1a Cystic Fibrosis Evaluation
- Diagnosis: Sweat test—DNA
- (Figure 47.8)

1b Treatment
- Medications
- Prevent infections
- Optimize nutrition

1c Medications Used to Treat Cystic Fibrosis
- (Table 14.15)

1d Assessment
- Symptoms of respiratory infection
- Close attention to breath sounds, cough
- Cyanosis, clubbing
- Growth (plot on growth chart)
- Signs of malnourishment
- Stooling pattern
- Coping, day-to-day issues

1e Diagnosis
- Ineffective airway clearance
- Risk for infection
- Imbalanced nutrition: Less than body requirements
- Parental role conflict

Planning and Implementation
- Provide respiratory therapy
- Administer medications and meet nutritional needs
- Provide psychosocial support
- Discharge planning and home teaching

 Evaluation
- Child and family able to provide daily pulmonary care
- Child and family develop a schedule and routine that fits into family and school activities
- Child consumes adequate calories and pancreatic enzymes to support growth

---

SUGGESTIONS FOR CLASSROOM ACTIVITIES

Have students make a list of all the daily required medications and respiratory treatments required for a child with CF. How much time would a family need to allow to complete all the treatments each day?

SUGGESTIONS FOR CLINICAL ACTIVITIES

Students often find the psychosocial component of chronic illness difficult to approach with a child and family. When a student has a client with CF, role-play methods the student can use to address the psychosocial issues surrounding this chronic illness with the child and family.

CHAPTER 48
THE CHILD WITH ALTERATIONS IN CARDIOVASCULAR FUNCTION

RESOURCE LIBRARY

CD-ROM

Animations
  Blood Pressure
  Congenital Heart Defects
  Digoxin
  Heart Sounds
Skill 9-10: Blood Pressure
Skill 15-2: Inserting and Removing a Nasogastric Tube
Skill 10-6: Blood Gases
Audio Glossary
NCLEX-RN® Review

COMPANION WEBSITE

MediaLink Applications:
  Nursing Care Plan: Pediatric Heart Transplant
  Case Study: Newborn after Heart Surgery
  Teaching Plan: Infective Endocarditis Prophylaxis
  Teaching Plan: Healthy Heart Curricula
Thinking Critically
NCLEX-RN® Review
Audio Glossary

IMAGE LIBRARY

Figure 48.1 Jooti is receiving intravenous fluids and oxygen.

Figure 48.2 Infants with cardiac conditions often require supplemental feedings to provide sufficient nutrients for growth and development.

Figure 48.3 A child with atrial septal defect repair. Surgery is performed with this type of defect to prevent pulmonary artery hypertension.

Figure 48.4 A, This infant is cyanotic due to a heart defect that reduces pulmonary blood flow.
B, Clubbing of the fingers in an older child is one manifestation of a heart defect that reduces pulmonary blood flow.

Figure 48.5 A young child with an uncorrected or partially corrected defect that reduces pulmonary blood flow may squat (assumes a knee–chest position) to reduce systemic blood flow return to the heart.

Figure 48.6 Anatomic location of the modified Blalock-Taussig and Glenn shunts for palliative procedures.

Figure 48.7 This child shows many of the signs of the acute stage of Kawasaki disease.

Table 48.1 Drugs Used to Treat Congestive Heart Failure

Pathophysiology Illustrated: Hypovolemic Shock.
Pathophysiology Illustrated: Septic Shock.
Pathophysiology Illustrated: Cardiogenic Shock.

LEARNING OBJECTIVE 1

Describe the anatomy and physiology of the cardiovascular system focusing on the flow of blood and action of the heart valves.

CONCEPTS FOR LECTURE

1. Significant cardiovascular changes occur as newborns transition from intrauterine to extrauterine life.
2. In order to understand the anatomy and pathophysiology of congenital heart defects, it is very important to understand the normal anatomy of the heart.

POWERPOINT LECTURE SLIDES

 Transition to Extrauterine Life
- Systemic vascular resistance increases
- Foramen ovale closes
- Ductus arteriosus constricts—closes within 10 to 15 hours of birth
- Left ventricle enlarges due to increased pressure

CONCEPTS FOR LECTURE *continued*

3. Normal vital signs change during childhood. For example, normal blood pressure starts low during infancy and rises as the child grows.
4. Infants have very little reserve in terms of oxygenation and cardiac output. Infants and children respond to severe hypoxemia with bradycardia—thus, bradycardia is a significant warning sign of impending cardiac arrest.

POWERPOINT LECTURE SLIDES *continued*

`2` Normal Heart
  - Blood flow
  - Valves

`3` Changes in Vital Signs
  - Heart rate: High to low—high heart rate to keep up with metabolic demands
  - Blood pressure: Low to high—increases as heart develops

`4` Oxygenation
  - Pulse oximetry: Amount of oxygen available for tissue delivery
  - Normal versus hypoxic levels
  - Response to chronic hypoxia: Polycythemia

`4a` Cardiac Functioning
  - Little cardiac reserve during infancy
  - Cardiac output (CO) depends on heart rate
    - CO = HR x SV
    - Infants can't vary SV so they increase HR to increase CO

SUGGESTIONS FOR CLASSROOM ACTIVITIES

- Have students pretend that they are a single red blood cell, and have them make a list of how they travel through the body. This helps students to visualize the cardiovascular system in a different way than just by looking at a picture.
- Use the animation "Normal Heart Hemodynamics," available on the Student CD-ROM, to help students visualize the changes that occur during the newborn period.

SUGGESTIONS FOR CLINICAL ACTIVITIES

Discuss how interventions for bradycardia differ in children compared to adults, and how hypoxia relates to bradycardia.

LEARNING OBJECTIVE 2

Recognize the signs of congestive heart failure in an infant and child.

CONCEPTS FOR LECTURE

1. Congestive heart failure (CHF) occurs when cardiac output cannot keep up with the body's circulatory and metabolic demands. CHF may result from congenital heart defects, problems with heart contractility, and disease processes that require high cardiac output. CHF may also result from acquired heart diseases such as cardiomyopathy or Kawasaki disease.
2. Early signs of CHF in infants include tiring during feeding, weight loss, diaphoresis, and frequent infections. Early signs of CHF in children include exercise intolerance, dyspnea, abdominal pain, and peripheral edema. Late signs of CHF include tachypnea and other respiratory symptoms, tachycardia, and cardiomegaly. *"Clinical Manifestations: Congestive Heart Failure" is a good reference for this topic.*

POWERPOINT LECTURE SLIDES

`1` Congestive Heart Failure (CHF)
  - Occurs when cardiac output cannot keep up with circulatory or metabolic demands
  - Congenital heart defects
  - Decreased heart contractility
  - Disease processes that require high cardiac output
    - Severe anemia
    - Acidosis
    - Respiratory disease
  - Acquired diseases
    - Cardiomyopathy
    - Kawasaki disease

`1a` Congenital Heart Defects and CHF
  - Volume overload on heart due to increased pulmonary circulation

- Obstructive defects that increase workload on heart
- CHF may be unilateral or bilateral

☐2☐ Early Signs of CHF: Infants
- Tiring during feeding
- Weight loss (or lack of weight gain)
- Diaphoresis
- Frequent infections

☐2a☐ Early Signs of CHF: Children
- Exercise intolerance
- Dyspnea
- Abdominal pain
- Peripheral edema

☐2b☐ Late Signs of CHF
- Respiratory symptoms
  ○ Tachypnea, nasal flaring, retractions
  ○ Cough, crackles
- Tachycardia
- Generalized fluid overload
- Cardiomegaly

SUGGESTIONS FOR CLASSROOM ACTIVITIES

Show the animation, "Congenital Heart Defects," available on the Student CD-ROM. This helps illustrate the relationship between CHF and congenital heart defects.

SUGGESTIONS FOR CLINICAL ACTIVITIES

When caring for a child at risk of CHF, discuss specific signs and symptoms that should be assessed and monitored based on the child's age. Compare these signs and symptoms to those of adults with CHF.

LEARNING OBJECTIVE 3

Develop a nursing care plan for a child with congestive heart failure.

CONCEPTS FOR LECTURE

1. Assessment of the infant or child with CHF includes a head-to-toe physical assessment, as well as assessing the psychosocial and developmental aspects. *Refer to Table 48.2 for details regarding assessment.*
2. Nursing diagnoses may include decreased cardiac output, increased fluid volume, risk for impaired skin integrity, imbalanced nutrition, and compromised family coping. Refer to *"Nursing Care Plan: The Child Hospitalized with Congestive Heart Failure" for details.*
3. Planning and implementation include administration of medications, maintaining oxygenation, promoting rest, fostering development, providing adequate nutrition, and providing support and discharge teaching.
4. Evaluation is completed to assess the effectiveness of interventions.

POWERPOINT LECTURE SLIDES

☐1☐ Assessment
- Physical
- Psychosocial
- Developmental

☐2☐ Diagnosis
- Decreased cardiac output
- Increased fluid volume
- Risk for impaired skin integrity
- Imbalanced nutrition
- Compromised family coping

☐3☐ Drugs Used to Treat Congestive Heart Failure
- (Table 48.1)

☐3a☐ Planning and Implementation
- Maintain oxygenation and myocardial function
- Promote rest
- Foster development
- Provide adequate nutrition

- Provide emotional support
- Discharge planning and teaching

 4 Evaluation
  - Cardiac output sufficient to meet demands
  - Oxygenation is adequate
  - Intake and output are balanced
  - Child demonstrated weight gain
  - Evidence of decreased anxiety

Suggestions for Classroom Activities

When discussing medications used to treat CHF, show the animation "Digoxin," located on the Student CD-ROM. This helps students visualize the action of the drug.

Suggestions for Clinical Activities

Have students discuss how to administer digoxin, including monitoring of blood levels and other associated labs, dosing, assessment of the child, and signs of toxicity.

Learning Objective 4

Describe the pathophysiology associated with congenital heart defects with increased pulmonary circulation, decreased pulmonary circulation, and obstructed systemic blood flow.

Concepts for Lecture

1. Congenital heart defects that increase pulmonary blood flow include patent ductus arteriosus, atrial septal defect, ventricular septal defect, and atrioventricular canal defect. *Refer to Table 48.6 for details.*
2. Congenital heart defects that decrease pulmonary blood flow include pulmonic stenosis, tetralogy of Fallot, and pulmonary or tricuspid atresia. *Refer to Table 48.7 for details.*
3. Mixed congenital heart defects include transposition of the great arteries (TGA), truncus arteriosis, and total anomalous pulmonary venous return (TAPVR). Infant survival is dependent upon the mixing of systemic and pulmonary blood. *Refer to Table 48.8 for details.*
4. Obstructive congenital heart defects include aortic stenosis (AS), coarctation of the aorta (COA), and hypoplastic left heart syndrome (HLHS). *Refer to Table 48.9 for details.*

PowerPoint Lecture Slides

1 Defects That Increase Pulmonary Blood Flow
  - Patent ductus arteriosus (PDA)
  - Atrial septal defect (ASD)
  - Ventricular septal defect (VSD)
  - Atrioventricular canal defect (AV Canal)
  - If untreated, pulmonary overcirculation leads to CHF, pulmonary hypertension, and eventually death

1a PDA
  - Persistent fetal circulation
  - Very common in preterm infants
  - Can be closed with medication, devices, or surgery
  - Prognosis is good

1b ASD
  - Opening in atrial septum that permits left-to-right shunting of blood
  - Opening may be small or large
  - Very common heart defect
  - Closure: Spontaneous, devices, or surgery
  - Prognosis good if ASD is closed

1c VSD
  - Opening in ventricular septum permits left-to-right shunting of blood
  - Most common heart defect
  - Closure: Small VSDs may close spontaneously—surgery
  - Prognosis: High risk if repair needed in first few months of life

1d AV Canal
- ASD + VSD + tricuspid and mitral valve defects
- Associated with Down syndrome
- Repair: Surgical
- Prognosis: Mitral valve insufficiency and arrhythmias are common

2 Defects That Decrease Pulmonary Blood Flow
- Pulmonic stenosis (PS)
- Tetralogy of Fallot (TOF)
- Pulmonary or tricuspid atresia
- All increase the workload on the heart and can lead to CHF

2a PS
- Narrowing of pulmonary valve (or area above/below valve)
- Second most common heart defect
- Repair: Dilate with balloon or surgical valvotomy
- Prognosis is good with repair

2b TOF
- Four defects: PS, right ventricular hypertrophy, VSD, overriding aorta
- Elevated right heart pressure causes right-to-left shunt
- Repair: Surgical
- Prognosis: Improved quality of life—may have right ventricular dysfunction

2c Pulmonary or Tricuspid Atresia
- Right side of heart or tricuspid valve not developed
- PDA provides blood to pulmonary artery and foramen ovale provides blood to left side of heart
- Repair: Surgical (prostaglandin E1 given to maintain PDA pre-op)
- Prognosis: Right ventricular dysfunction is common

3 Mixed Defects
- Transposition of the great arteries (TGA)
- Truncus arteriosus
- Total anomalous pulmonary venous return (TAPVR)
- Infant survival is dependent on mixing of systemic and pulmonary blood

3a TGA
- Parallel circulation—life-threatening at birth
- Mixing can occur via PDA, patent foramen ovale (PFO), ASD, or VSD
- Correction
  - Prostaglandin E1 to maintain PDA
  - Balloon atrial septostomy to enlarge PFO (creates ASD)
  - Surgical repair, usually within first week of life
- Prognosis: Pulmonary and aortic stenosis, coronary artery obstruction may occur—5-year survival is 82%

Truncus Arteriosus
- Single large vessel empties both ventricles
- Uncommon heart defect
- Repair: Surgical
- Prognosis: Improving—long-term is unknown

 TAPVR
- Pulmonary veins empty into right atrium instead of left atrium
- Foramen ovale allows oxygenated blood to move from the right atrium to the left atrium
- Repair
  - Prostaglandin E1 to maintain PDA
  - Balloon atrial septostomy to enlarge PFO into an ASD
  - Surgical repair
- Prognosis: Generally good

 Defects that Obstruct Systemic Blood Flow
- Aortic stenosis (AS)
- Coarctation of the aorta (COA)
- Hypoplastic left heart syndrome (HLHS)
- Increase workload on one or both ventricles of the heart, leading to CHF if untreated

 AS
- Narrowed aortic valve obstructs blood flow
- Repair
  - Dilate valve with balloon
  - Surgical valvuloplasty or valve replacement
- Prognosis: May need repeated valve replacements or dilations as child grows—sudden death can occur

 COA
- Aorta narrows, usually near the ductus, obstructing blood flow
- Common defect
- Four-extremity blood pressures
  - Blood pressure higher in arms than legs
  - Weak femoral or pedal pulses
- Repair: Dilate with balloon or surgical repair
- Prognosis: Persistent hypertension is common—aorta can stenose at surgical site

HLHS
- Absence of mitral and aortic valves, abnormally small aorta
- Very severe heart defect
- Prostaglandin E1 to maintain PDA
- Treatment options
  - Comfort care
  - Norwood procedure (three-staged palliation)
  - Heart transplantation
  - Pros and cons of each option

HLHS: Prognosis
- Without surgery, death within days

- Norwood procedure
  - ○ Survival rates improving
  - ○ First stage has highest mortality
  - ○ Long-term survival unknown
- Transplantation
  - ○ 63% of infants waiting for donor heart die while waiting
  - ○ Lifespan of transplanted heart
  - ○ Immunosuppression required

SUGGESTIONS FOR CLASSROOM ACTIVITIES

Many students learn by seeing and doing so have the students create these heart defects. After dividing them into groups, distribute blank paper, colored markers, and Play-Dough. Assign each group to either draw or sculpt (using Play-Dough) a heart defect and then present it to the class. Hint: Use red for oxygenated blood, blue for deoxygenated blood, and purple for mixed blood. Red and blue Play-Dough can be mixed together to create purple.

SUGGESTIONS FOR CLINICAL ACTIVITIES

Identify teaching resources available in the clinical setting for use in teaching children and families about different congenital heart defects.

LEARNING OBJECTIVE 5

Develop a nursing care plan for the infant with a congenital heart defect cared for at home prior to corrective surgery.

CONCEPTS FOR LECTURE

1. The nursing care plan can be applied to families caring at home for children who are awaiting corrective surgery. *Refer to "Nursing Care Plan: The Child with Congestive Heart Failure Being Cared For at Home" for details.*

POWERPOINT LECTURE SLIDES

 Assessment
- Growth is critical
- Nutritional intake
- Psychosocial considerations

 Diagnosis
- Excess fluid volume
- Ineffective infant feeding pattern
- Risk for infection
- Interrupted family processes

 Planning and Implementation
- Administer medications
- Promote rest, nutrition, and growth
- Maintain metabolic demands and oxygenation
- Provide emotional support

 Provide Education Regarding Home Care
- Feeding strategies—may require nasogastric tube feedings
- Prevent infectious diseases
  - ○ Handwashing
  - ○ Minimize exposure
  - ○ RSV prophylaxis
- When to notify physician
  - ○ Fever
  - ○ Poor feeding
  - ○ Vomiting, diarrhea

PowerPoint Lecture Slides *continued*

 Evaluation
- Adequate nutritional intake
- Child maintains growth pattern
- Child receives immunizations as required

SUGGESTIONS FOR CLASSROOM ACTIVITIES

Challenge students to think about the relationship between growth and congenital heart defects. Why is growth so challenging for infants with heart defects? Why is it so important for growth to occur? How does growth relate to the timing and potential success of their surgery?

SUGGESTIONS FOR CLINICAL ACTIVITIES

Have students develop a teaching plan for the family who will care for a child at home who is awaiting corrective surgery. Include "Skill 15-2: Inserting and Removing a Nasogastric Tube" and "Skill 15-3: Administering a Gavage Feeding" available on the Student CD-ROM and Clinical Skills Manual if the family will be performing these procedures at home.

LEARNING OBJECTIVE 6

Develop a nursing care plan for the child undergoing open-heart surgery.

CONCEPTS FOR LECTURE

1. Assessment of the infant or child who has undergone surgical repair includes a head-to-toe physical assessment, as well as assessing the psychosocial and developmental aspects. *Refer to Table 48.2 for details regarding assessment.*
2. Nursing diagnoses may relate to pain, breathing, fluid volume, and infection.
3. Planning and implementation include pain management, promoting respiratory function, managing fluids and nutrition, encouraging activity, and planning for discharge. Home teaching is also important.
4. Evaluation is completed to assess the effectiveness of interventions.

POWERPOINT LECTURE SLIDES

 Assessment
- Head-to-toe assessment
- Incision site
- Tissue perfusion
  - Capillary refill, pulses, warmth
  - Brain: Level of consciousness
  - Kidneys: Urine output
- Pain

 Nursing Diagnosis
- Ineffective breathing pattern
- Acute pain
- Risk for imbalanced fluid volume
- Risk for infection

 Planning and Implementation
- Pain management
- Promote respiratory function
- Manage fluids and nutrition
- Encourage activity
- Plan for discharge

 Home Teaching Points
- Risk for post-traumatic stress disorder
- Encourage normality
- Infective endocarditis risk and prophylaxis

 Evaluation
- Pain is effectively managed
- Full lung expansion is maintained
- Incision is healing without signs of infection
- Catch-up growth occurs over months to years

LEARNING OBJECTIVE 7

Identify heart diseases acquired during childhood and how they differ from congenital defects.

CONCEPTS FOR LECTURE

1. Rheumatic fever is an inflammatory disorder of the connective tissue that follows an initial infection by some strains of group A beta-hemolytic streptococci. The heart, joints, brain, and skin tissues are affected.
2. Infective endocarditis is an inflammation of the lining, valves, and arterial vessels of the heart. It may be caused by bacterial, enterococci, and fungal infections. Valvular damage from the infection may result in congestive heart failure.
3. Kawasaki disease is an acute systemic inflammatory illness that is the leading cause of acquired heart disease in children. The etiology is unknown, although it is believed that there is an infectious trigger in genetically predisposed children. The disease affects the small- and medium-sized arteries, including the coronary arteries.

POWERPOINT LECTURE SLIDES

 Rheumatic Fever
- Definition
- Etiology: Group A beta-hemolytic streptococci
- Clinical manifestations
  - Heart
  - Joints
  - Brain
  - Skin

 Rheumatic Fever: Treatment
- Antibiotics to eradicate strep infection
- Aspirin to treat carditis, inflammation
- Steroids
- Long-term antibiotic prophylaxis
- Most children recover fully

 Rheumatic Fever: Nursing Management
- Prevention (throat cultures, completion of antibiotic regimen)
- Monitor temperature
- Bed rest
- Administer medications
- Home teaching

 Infective Endocarditis
- Definition
- Risk factors
  - Congenital heart defect
  - Rheumatic heart disease
  - Central venous catheters
- Etiology: Bacteria, enterococci, or fungi
- Clinical manifestations
  - Fever
  - Fatigue, muscle aches
  - New or changing murmur
  - Signs of congestive heart failure

 Infective Endocarditis: Treatment
- Antibiotics, antifungals—2- to 8-week therapy
- Treat congestive heart failure if present
- Assess valve damage—surgical valve replacement may be needed

POWERPOINT LECTURE SLIDES *continued*

2b Infective Endocarditis: Nursing Management
- Administer medications—blood levels for some antibiotics
- Monitor for signs of congestive heart failure, embolism
- Promote developmental activities

3 Kawasaki Disease
- Definition
- Leading cause of acquired heart disease in children
- Etiology: Unknown—thought to be an infectious trigger in genetically predisposed children
- Clinical manifestations
  - Three stages of illness
  - Fever
  - Conjunctival hyperemia
  - Cervical lymph node enlargement
  - Cracking skin (lips, fingers, toes)
  - Coronary artery aneurisms

3a Signs of Acute Stage of Kawasaki Disease
- (Figure 48.7)

3b Kawasaki Disease: Treatment
- Intravenous immunoglobulin
- Aspirin
  - Anti-inflammatory dose initially
  - Antiplatelet dose after fever decreases
- Monitor for coronary artery aneurisms

3c Kawasaki Disease: Nursing Management
- Administer medications
- Promote comfort
- Home teaching

SUGGESTIONS FOR CLASSROOM ACTIVITIES

Use the animation on the Student CD-ROM, "Heart Sounds," to discuss how heart murmurs may appear or change in the presence of infective endocarditis.

SUGGESTIONS FOR CLINICAL ACTIVITIES

Aspirin always comes in tablet, or solid, form. Have students demonstrate how they would administer aspirin to a toddler with Kawasaki disease.

LEARNING OBJECTIVE 8

Describe the pathophysiology of hypovolemic shock, distributive shock, and cardiogenic shock.

CONCEPTS FOR LECTURE

1. Hypovolemic shock occurs when there is inadequate tissue and organ perfusion resulting from a loss of fluid in the intravascular compartment.
2. Distributive shock (also known as maldistributive shock) occurs when the blood volume is inadequately distributed, usually resulting from a decrease in systemic vascular resistance.

POWERPOINT LECTURE SLIDES

1 Hypovolemic Shock
- Definition
- Causes of decreased intravascular blood volume
  - Hemorrhage
  - Plasma loss from burns, nephrotic syndrome, or sepsis
  - Fluid and electrolyte loss from dehydration, diabetic ketoacidosis, or diabetes insipidus

3. Cardiogenic shock occurs when the heart fails to maintain adequate cardiac output and tissue perfusion.

1a Hypovolemic Shock: Pathophysiology
  • ("Pathophysiology Illustrated: Hypovolemic Shock")

1b Hypovolemic Shock
  • Clinical manifestations
  • Clinical therapy
  • Nursing management

2 Distributive Shock (Maldistributive Shock)
  • Definition
  • Causes of decreased systemic vascular resistance
    ○ Anaphylaxis
    ○ Sepsis
    ○ Spinal cord injury

2a Distributive Shock: Pathophysiology
  • ("Pathophysiology Illustrated: Septic Shock")

2b Distributive Shock
  • Three phases
    ○ Compensated
    ○ Uncompensated
    ○ Refractory
  • Clinical manifestations
  • Clinical therapy

3 Cardiogenic Shock
  • Definition
  • Causes of poor cardiac output
    ○ Congestive heart failure
    ○ Cardiovascular surgery
    ○ Severe obstructive congenital heart disease
    ○ Arrhythmias

3a Cardiogenic Shock: Pathophysiology
  • ("Pathophysiology Illustrated: Cardiogenic Shock")

3b Cardiogenic Shock
  • Clinical manifestations
  • Clinical therapy

SUGGESTIONS FOR CLASSROOM ACTIVITIES

Divide students into three groups and provide each group with a blank overhead transparency and colored markers. Have them draw a concept map showing the pathophysiology of one of the three types of shock discussed above. Share the concept maps with the entire class.

SUGGESTIONS FOR CLINICAL ACTIVITIES

While caring for a child with shock, discuss how laboratory values can reflect end-organ perfusion. Examples include liver function tests, BUN and creatinine, and lactate levels.

CHAPTER 49
THE CHILD WITH ALTERATIONS IN HEMATOLOGIC FUNCTION

RESOURCE LIBRARY

CD-ROM

Animations:
   Circulatory System
   Types of Blood Cells
   Sickle Cell Anemia
Nursing in Action: Administering Blood or Blood
   Products
Audio Glossary
NCLEX-RN® Review

IMAGE LIBRARY

Figure 49.1 Types of blood cells.
Figure 49.2 In iron deficiency anemia, red blood
cells appear hypochromic as a result of decreased
hemoglobin synthesis.
Figure 49.3 Many of these red blood cells show an
elongated crescent shape characteristic of sickle cell
anemia.
Figure 49.4 Red blood cell appearance in
b–thalassemia.

COMPANION WEBSITE

MediaLink Applications:
   Ethical Considerations: Hemophilia
   Hematopoietic Stem Cell Transplantation (HSCT)
Care Plan: A School-Age Child with Hemophilia
Case Study: An Adolescent in Sickle Cell Crisis
Thinking Critically
NCLEX-RN® Review
Audio Glossary

Figure 49.5 The child undergoing bone marrow
transplantation is hospitalized in a special unit while
receiving chemotherapy before the transfusion.

Table 49.2 White Blood Cells and Their Functions
Pathophysiology Illustrated: Sickle Cell Anemia

LEARNING OBJECTIVE 1
Describe the function of red blood cells, white blood cells, and platelets.

CONCEPTS FOR LECTURE

1. Red blood cells transport oxygen from the lungs to the
   tissues, and return carbon dioxide back to the lungs.
2. White blood cells are composed of five different types
   of cells, with functions primarily involved in immunity,
   phagocytosis, and inflammation. White blood cells
   essentially aid in protecting the body.
3. Platelets function as part of the clotting cascade to
   stop bleeding.

POWERPOINT LECTURE SLIDES

1 Types of Blood Cells
   • (Figure 49.1)

1a Red Blood Cells (RBCs)
   • Most abundant cells in the blood
   • Erythropoiesis: Process of forming new RBCs
   • Any condition that causes tissue hypoxia triggers
     new RBCs to form
   • Formed in bone marrow
   • Function
   • Carry oxygen from lungs to tissues
   • Return carbon dioxide to lungs

1b Red Blood Cells: Terms
   • Polycythemia: Above-average increase in RBCs
   • Anemia: Reduction of number of RBCs
   • Newborns—higher levels of RBCs at birth

2 White Blood Cells (WBCs)
   • Also known as leukocytes
   • Formed in bone marrow and lymph tissue

- Mobile: Move around the body
- Part of body's protective system
- Five types of WBCs, each with a distinct function

2a White Blood Cells and Their Functions
  - (Table 49.2)

3 Platelets
  - Also known as thrombocytes
  - Function: Help stop bleeding
  - Formed in bone marrow and stored in spleen
  - Requires clotting factors and vitamin K to form clot—newborns (vitamin K injection at birth)

SUGGESTIONS FOR CLASSROOM ACTIVITIES

Show the following animations when discussing the functions of red blood cells, white blood cells, and platelets:

- "Circulatory System"
- "Types of Blood Cells"

Both animations are available on the Student CD-ROM.

SUGGESTIONS FOR CLINICAL ACTIVITIES

Many hospitalized children have a complete blood count (CBC) performed during their illness. Have students analyze the lab results and discuss abnormal values and significant normal values. Students can also discuss the various ranges of normal lab values based on the age of the child (for example, a normal WBC of a newborn versus an adolescent).

LEARNING OBJECTIVE 2

Discuss the pathophysiology and clinical manifestations of the major disorders of red blood cells affecting the pediatric population.

CONCEPTS FOR LECTURE

1. Iron-deficiency anemia is the most common type of anemia and the most common nutritional deficiency in children. Infants and children who are malnourished or who do not have adequate iron intake are at risk, as well as children who have chronic blood loss. Clinical manifestations include pallor, fatigue, and irritability.

2. Normocytic anemia occurs as a result of numerous inflammatory and infectious conditions. Clinical manifestations are similar to iron-deficiency anemia, although hepatomegaly and splenomegaly may also be present.

3. Sickle-cell anemia is a hereditary condition in which normal hemoglobin is partly or completely replaced with abnormal hemoglobin S (Hgb S). Clinical manifestations occur primarily due to vaso-occlusion.

4. The thalassemias are a group of inherited blood disorders with anemia due to impaired hemoglobin synthesis. Clinical manifestations are usually detected in infancy, and include pallor, failure to thrive, hepatosplenomegaly, and severe anemia.

POWERPOINT LECTURE SLIDES

1 Iron-Deficiency Anemia
  - Most common type of anemia in children
  - Most common nutritional deficiency in children
  - Can occur due to
    - Blood loss (acute or chronic)
    - Increased demand for blood production
    - Poor nutritional intake
    - 9% to 11% of adolescent females have anemia, primarily due to menorrhagia

1a Iron-Deficiency Anemia
  - Clinical manifestations (short-term)
    - Pallor
    - Fatigue
    - Irritability
  - Clinical manifestations (long-term)
    - Nail-bed deformities/clubbing
    - Growth retardation
    - Developmental delay
    - Tachycardia
    - Systolic heart murmur
  - Diagnosis: Labs
  - Treatment: Iron supplementation, dietary changes

2 Normocytic Anemia
- RBCs are decreased in number but are normal size
- Usually occurs as a result of underlying condition
  - Infections (sepsis, meningitis)
  - Inflammation (arthritis, cancer)
  - Hemorrhage
- Clinical manifestations
  - Similar to iron-deficiency anemia
  - Hepatomegaly and splenomegaly may be present too
- Treatment: Treat underlying cause

3 Sickle-Cell Anemia
- Hereditary disease
- Normal hemoglobin is partly or completely replaced by abnormal hemoglobin S (Hgb S)—shape of Hgb S: Sickle
- Primarily occurs in African Americans—Mediterranean descent as well
- Carriers versus active disease

3a Sickle-Cell Anemia: Pathophysiology
- A trigger causes cells to sickle
  - Fever
  - Dehydration
  - Stress
  - Hypoxia
  - Infection
- Once sickled, cells occlude blood vessels
  - Causes local tissue ischemia and infarction
  - Eventually damages tissues and organs
- Spleen is clogged with sickled cells and children are functionally asplenic—at risk for infection
- Sickled cells can resume normal shape when rehydrated and reoxygenated

3b Pathophysiology Illustrated: Sickle Cell Anemia
- ("Pathophysiology Illustrated: Sickle Cell Anemia")

3c Sickle-Cell Anemia: Clinical Manifestations
- Fetal hemoglobin present until 4 to 6 months—usually asymptomatic until fetal hemoglobin is gone
- Vaso-occlusive crises
- Splenic sequestration
- Aplastic crises

3d Sickle-Cell Anemia: Diagnosis and Treatment
- Diagnosis: Newborns are screened for disease at birth
- Treatment
  - No cure
  - Prevention of triggers
  - Supportive care during crises
  - Immunizations

Thalassemias
- Group of inherited blood disorders
- Hemoglobin synthesis is impaired
- Anemia can be mild or severe
- Types of thalassemia
  - Thalassemia minor (trait): Mild anemia
  - Thalassemia intermedia: Severe anemia
  - Thalassemia major: Requires transfusion

 Thalassemias
- Pathophysiology
  - Defective synthesis of RBCs (beta chain)
  - Structurally impaired RBCs
  - Shortened lifespan of RBCs
- Clinical manifestations (usually detected in infancy)
  - Pallor
  - Failure to thrive
  - Hepatosplenomegaly
  - Severe anemia (less than 6 g/dL)

Thalassemias
- Diagnosis
  - Hemoglobin electrophoresis
  - Decreased hemoglobin, hematocrit, reticulocytes
- Treatment
  - Supportive: Goal is to maintain normal hematocrit levels
  - Blood transfusions
- At risk for iron overload due to frequent transfusions

Suggestions for Classroom Activities

Demonstrate the concept of vaso-occlusion during sickle-cell disease with a piece of paper and an empty paper towel roll. Wad up the paper (normal RBC) into a tight ball and drop it through the paper towel roll (blood vessel). It passes through easily. Now shape the ball into a sickled cell, and note that it does not pass through the paper towel roll easily. Therefore, the distal tissues do not receive oxygen, leading to ischemic pain characteristic of the disease. You can also show the animation, "Sickle Cell Anemia," available on the Student CD-ROM.

Suggestions for Clinical Activities

It is common for the hospitalized child to have anemia. Discuss the possible reasons for a hospitalized child to become anemic. Have students identify iron-rich foods that children might eat.

LEARNING OBJECTIVE 3

Discuss the pathophysiology and clinical manifestations of the major disorders of white blood cells affecting the pediatric population.

Concepts for Lecture

1. Aplastic anemia is a failure of the bone marrow stem cells to produce all types of blood cells. Clinical manifestations include anemia, neutropenia, thrombocytopenia, infection, fatigue, and tachycardia.

PowerPoint Lecture Slides

 Aplastic Anemia
- Bone marrow does not produce all types of blood cells (pancytopenia)
  - RBCs
  - WBCs
  - Platelets

- May be congenital or acquired
- Symptoms related to degree of bone marrow failure

 Aplastic Anemia: Clinical Manifestations
- Anemia
- Neutropenia
- Thrombocytopenia
- Infection
- Fever
- Fatigue
- Tachycardia

1b Aplastic Anemia: Treatment
- Congenital
  - Bone marrow transplant
  - Poor prognosis
- Acquired
  - Immunosuppressive drug therapy
  - Bone marrow transplant

SUGGESTIONS FOR CLASSROOM ACTIVITIES

Have students draw a concept map indicating how the clinical manifestations of aplastic anemia are related to the pathophysiology of the disease process.

SUGGESTIONS FOR CLINICAL ACTIVITIES

Children with aplastic anemia often receive transfusions of blood products. Have students review this skill by completing "Nursing in Action: Administering Blood or Blood Products" activity available on the Student CD-ROM.

LEARNING OBJECTIVE 4

Discuss the pathophysiology and clinical manifestations of the major disorders of platelets affecting the pediatric population.

CONCEPTS FOR LECTURE

1. Hemophilia, an X-linked recessive trait, is a group of disorders that occurs primarily in males and causes a deficiency of specific clotting factors. Clinical manifestations include mild to severe bleeding, bleeding into joint spaces, and bleeding from minor trauma.
2. Von Willebrand disease is a hereditary bleeding disorder that occurs in both men and women. Von Willebrand factor, which plays a necessary role in platelet adhesion, is deficient. Classic symptoms include easy bruising and epistaxis. Teenage girls may have menorrhagia.
3. Disseminated intravascular coagulation (DIC) is an acquired, abnormal activation of the clotting system that results in widespread clot formation throughout the body. After clotting factors have been used up, bleeding occurs. DIC is usually the result of other serious illnesses and common symptoms include bleeding and oozing, shock, and vessel thrombosis.

POWERPOINT LECTURE SLIDES

1 Hemophilia
- X-linked recessive trait
  - Genes for clotting factors VIII and IX are on the X chromosome
  - Woman carrier has 50% chance of transmitting disease to her sons
  - One-third of cases have no family history and are a new mutation
- Disease occurs primarily in males
- Female carriers usually do not manifest symptoms of disease—may have prolonged bleeding during dental work or surgery

 Hemophilia: Clinical Manifestations
- Mild to severe bleeding tendencies
- Asymptomatic until 6 months of age—mobility (minor trauma occurs)
- Hemarthrosis (bleeding into joint spaces)
  - Pain
  - Tenderness
  - Decreased range of motion

4. Idiopathic thrombocytopenic purpura (ITP) is a disorder where the spleen destroys the body's platelets. Platelet production in the bone marrow is normal. ITP is the most common bleeding disorder in children. Clinical manifestations include multiple bruises, petechiae, epistaxis, and blood in the urine or stool.

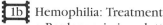

- Bruise easily
- Nosebleeds
- Hematuria

1b Hemophilia: Treatment
- Replace missing clotting factors
- DDAVP: 2- to 4-fold increase in factor VIII activity
- Gene therapy being explored for the future
- Near-normal life expectancy

2 Von Willebrand Disease
- Genetic disease (autosomal dominant transmission)
- Affects men and women
- Deficiency of von Willebrand factor—necessary for platelet adhesion

2a Von Willebrand Disease: Symptoms
- Easy bruising
- Epistaxis
- Gingival bleeding
- Increased bleeding with lacerations
- Teenage girls: Menorrhagia

2b Von Willebrand Disease: Treatment
- Infusion of von Willebrand protein concentrate
- DDAVP may also be given
- Prognosis is good
- Life expectancy is normal

3 Disseminated Intravascular Coagulation (DIC)
- Life-threatening
- Triggered by serious illness (hypoxia, shock, cancer, etc.)
- Abnormal activation of clotting system
- Widespread clots throughout the body
- As clotting factors are used up, bleeding then occurs

3a DIC: Clinical Manifestations
- Bleeding and oozing from
  - Nose
  - Mouth
  - Percutaneous lines
  - Puncture wounds, etc.
- Shock
- Hypotension
- Vascular thrombosis
- Impaired tissue perfusion

3b DIC: Treatment
- Treat the underlying cause
- Replace depleted clotting factors, fibrinogen, and platelets
- Heparin—prevents further thrombosis

4 Idiopathic Thrombocytopenic Purpura (ITP)
- Spleen destroys platelets
- Bone marrow production of platelets is normal
- When destruction exceeds production, platelet count decreases and bleeding occurs

- Most common bleeding disorder in children
- Peak age: 2 to 10 years
- Usually follows a viral illness (immune trigger)

 4a ITP: Clinical Manifestations
- Multiple bruises
- Petechiae
- Purpura
- Bleeding from gums or nose
- Blood in urine or stool

4b ITP: Treatment
- Corticosteroids
- Intravenous immunoglobulins
- About half of children have complete remission
- If no response to medications after 6 months to a year, splenectomy

SUGGESTIONS FOR CLASSROOM ACTIVITIES

Consider assigning the following activities available on the Companion Website before class and using them as a basis for discussion:

- "Critical Thinking: Ethical Considerations: Hemophilia"
- "Care Plan: A School-Age Child with Hemophilia"

SUGGESTIONS FOR CLINICAL ACTIVITIES

Monitor the operating room schedule and when a child is scheduled for splenectomy secondary to ITP, assign a student to observe the procedure.

LEARNING OBJECTIVE 5

Describe the nursing management and collaborative care of a child with a hematologic disorder.

CONCEPTS FOR LECTURE

1. The nursing management and collaborative care of hematologic disorders can be characterized in three groups: red blood cell disorders, white blood cell disorders, and clotting disorders.
2. Since hematologic disorders can be acute or chronic, there are a wide variety of medical and psychosocial issues that the family and child face. A team approach is the most effective method to support the family.

POWERPOINT LECTURE SLIDES

 1 Nursing Management: Red Blood Cell Disorders
- Prepare child for frequent blood tests
- Administer and monitor transfusions
- Provide for periods of rest
- Encourage food with a high iron content
- Anemia screening

1a Nursing Management: White Blood Cell Disorders
- Prevent infection
  - Frequent handwashing
  - Limit child's contact with anyone displaying signs and symptoms of infection
- Prevent bleeding
- Administer and monitor transfusions

1b Nursing Management: Clotting Disorders
- Prevent and control bleeding episodes—limit invasive procedures
- Limit joint involvement
- Avoid use of aspirin products

2 Collaborative Care
- Hematologic diseases can be acute or chronic
- Require extensive support of child and family
- Team approach

LEARNING OBJECTIVE 6

Discuss nursing implications for a child receiving hematopoietic stem cell transplantation (HSCT).

CONCEPTS FOR LECTURE

1. Hematopoietic stem cell transplantation (HSCT), also known as bone marrow transplantation, is a treatment used for diseases such as severe combined immunodeficiency syndrome, aplastic anemia, and leukemia. Stem cells exist primarily in the bone marrow but also circulate in the peripheral blood. There are three types of bone marrow transplant: autologous, isogeneic, and allogeneic.

2. Nursing management for the child with HSCT includes prevention of infection, controlling bleeding, maintaining adequate nutrition and hydration, monitoring for signs of rejection, and providing emotional support to the child and family.

POWERPOINT LECTURE SLIDES

1 Hematopoietic Stem Cell Transplantation (HSCT)
- Also known as bone marrow transplant (BMT)
- Used to treat
  - Severe combined immunodeficiency syndrome
  - Aplastic anemia
  - Leukemia
- Stem cells exist primarily in bone marrow—also present in peripheral blood and cord blood

1a Three Types of BMT
- Autologous: Child's own cells are taken, stored, and reinfused after chemotherapy
- Isogeneic: Cells are taken from an identical twin
- Allogeneic: Donor (usually a sibling) has compatible blood and donates cells to child

1b Process of BMT
- Chemotherapy and/or total body irradiation
  - Goal: Destroy circulating blood cells and diseased bone marrow
  - Lasts 4 to 12 days
  - Child is at high risk for infection
- Child transfused with donor cells
- If successful, cells implant in the bone and begin to grow
  - Takes 2 to 4 weeks for donor cells to proliferate and mature
  - High risk for infection
- Result: Healthy bone marrow capable of making new cells

2 Nursing Management of BMT
- Prevent infection
  - Protective isolation
  - Avoid fresh fruit and flowers
- Control bleeding
  - Limit invasive procedures
  - No intramuscular injections or rectal temperatures
  - Maintain pressure on any injection site for at least 5 minutes
  - Transfuse with red blood cells or platelets as needed

POWERPOINT LECTURE SLIDES *continued*

2a Nursing Management
- Maintain adequate nutrition and hydration
  - Implement TPN as needed
  - Provide frequent, small meals
- Monitor for signs of rejection
  - Assess temperature frequently
  - Assess skin and GI system for signs and symptoms of graft versus host disease (GVHD)
- Provide emotional support to child and family

SUGGESTIONS FOR CLASSROOM ACTIVITIES	**SUGGESTIONS FOR CLINICAL ACTIVITIES**
Before class, assign students to complete the activity, "MediaLink Applications: Hematopoietic Stem Cell Transplantation," located on the Companion Website. Use this as a framework for discussing this objective.	• If a bone marrow transplant unit is available in the local clinical setting, assign students to observe there. • Review with students what is meant by "protective isolation," and how this type of isolation differs from traditional isolation.

CHAPTER 50
THE CHILD WITH ALTERATIONS IN CELLULAR GROWTH

RESOURCE LIBRARY

 CD-ROM

Videos:
  Cancer Overview
  Leukemia
Audio Glossary
NCLEX-RN® Review

 COMPANION WEBSITE

Objectives
Drug Guide: Methotrexate
Commonly Used Chemotherapy Drug
  Combinations
MediaLink Applications:
  Exploring the Controversy: Stem Cell
    Transplantation
  Life with Leukemia: A Teen in Transition
Case Study: Teen with Ewing's Sarcoma
NCLEX-RN® Review

IMAGE LIBRARY

Figure 50.1 Percentage of primary tumors by site of origin for different age groups.

Figure 50.2 Computed tomography (CT) can be a frightening procedure for children.

Figure 50.3 Chemotherapy protocol.

Figure 50.4 One of the most common threats to a child's body image at any age is hair loss induced by chemotherapy.

Figure 50.5 The child with cushingoid changes frequently has a rounded face and prominent cheeks.

Figure 50.6 The child with cancer depends on parents and family members to provide support.

Figure 50.7 Survivors of childhood cancer.

Figure 50.8 A child in a pediatric oncology clinic giving injections to a doll.

Figure 50.9 A vascular access device allows chemotherapeutic agents to be administered without the need for repeated "sticks" to the child.

Nursing Practice: Laboratory Values in Leukemia

Pathophysiology Illustrated: Brain Tumors
Pathophysiology Illustrated: Hodgkin's Disease

LEARNING OBJECTIVE 1

Describe the incidence, known etiologies, and common clinical manifestations of cancer.

CONCEPTS FOR LECTURE

1. In children under 15 years of age, cancer is the leading cause of disease-related death. However, mortality rates have improved and continue to improve. The overall survival rate for childhood cancer is 80%. *Refer to Figure 50.1 to compare the most common forms of childhood cancers among children of different age groups.*

POWERPOINT LECTURE SLIDES

1 Incidence of Childhood Cancer
  • Leading cause of disease-related death in kids younger than 15 years
  • Mortality rates continue to improve
  • Overall survival is 80%, but depends on age and cancer type
  • Primary tumor site varies by age

2. The etiology of childhood cancer can be conceptually broken down into three categories: (1) external stimuli that cause genetic mutations, (2) immune system and gene abnormalities, and (3) chromosomal abnormalities.

3. Although some types of childhood cancer manifest no symptoms until the cancer is advanced, there are several warning signs of childhood cancer. However, many of these symptoms are nonspecific, and are commonly seen with routine childhood illnesses.

 Etiology of Childhood Cancer: Three Categories
- External stimuli that cause genetic mutations
- Immune system and gene abnormalities
- Chromosomal abnormalities

2a External Stimuli that Cause Genetic Mutations (Carcinogens)
- Diethylbesterol
- Steroids
- Chemotherapy agents
- Immunosuppressants
- Radiation exposure
- Ultraviolet radiation from the sun (skin cancer)

2b Immune System and Gene Abnormalities
- Immune surveillance
- Diseases that affect the immune system
- Viruses
- Familial genetic abnormalities

2c Chromosomal Abnormalities
- Some chromosomal abnormalities linked to increase cancer risk
  - Downs syndrome and leukemia
  - Chromosome 11 abnormalities and Wilms' tumor

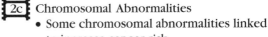 Common Presenting Symptoms of Childhood Cancer
- Pain
- Cachexia
- Anemia
- Infection
- Bruising
- Neurologic symptoms
- Palpable mass

SUGGESTIONS FOR CLASSROOM ACTIVITIES

- At the beginning of this class, show the video "Cancer Overview," (available on the Student CD-ROM) as an introduction to the topic of childhood cancer.
- Using "Teaching Highlights: Ways to Decrease the Incidence of Cancer in Children," discuss actions nurses can take to educated children and families about the prevention of cancer.

SUGGESTIONS FOR CLINICAL ACTIVITIES

Determine the incidence of various types of childhood cancer in your local setting. Do the local patterns of cancer match the national patterns described in the text? Where do children go for treatment? What kinds of treatment are available locally?

LEARNING OBJECTIVE 2

Synthesize information about diagnostic tests and clinical therapy for cancer to plan comprehensive care for children undergoing these procedures.

CONCEPTS FOR LECTURE

1. Common diagnostic tests for childhood cancer include complete blood counts, bone marrow aspiration, lumbar puncture, and imaging studies. *Refer to Table 50.1 for key points.*
2. Clinical therapy for childhood cancer is complex. Cancer is treated with one or a combination of therapies, including surgery, chemotherapy, radiation, biotherapy, and bone marrow/stem-cell transplantation. The choice of treatment is determined by the type of cancer, its location, and the degree of metastasis.

POWERPOINT LECTURE SLIDES

1 Common Diagnostic Tests for Childhood Cancer
- Laboratory tests
- Imaging studies

1a Laboratory Tests
- Blood work
  - Complete blood count
  - Electrolytes
  - Liver function test
  - Absolute neutrophil count (ANC)
- Bone marrow aspiration/biopsy
- Lumbar puncture

1b Imaging Studies
- Computed tomography (CT)
- Magnetic resonance imagine (MRI)
- Ultrasound
- Nuclear medicine scans
- Positron emission tomography (PET)

1c Purpose of Diagnostic Tests
- Identify source of cancer (primary site)
- Determine if cancer has metastasized
- Stage cancer

2 Clinical Therapy for Cancer: Options
- Surgery
- Chemotherapy
- Radiation
- Biotherapy
- Bone marrow/stem cell transplantation

2a Considerations in Choice of Therapy
- Type of cancer
- Location
- Degree of metastasis
- Goal of therapy
  - Curative
  - Supportive
  - Palliative

2b Surgery
- Remove or debulk tumor
- May determine stage and type of cancer
- Example: Wilms' tumor

2c Chemotherapy
- Drugs that kill both normal and cancerous cells
- Timed for maximum cellular destruction
- Different drugs work on different phases of cell growth
- Example: Leukemia

2d Radiation
- Energy destroys DNA and cell

- Used for local and regional control of cancer—may be used in combination with surgery and chemotherapy
- May be curative or palliative
- Example: Hodgkin's disease

 Biotherapy
- Uses parts of the body already programmed to destroy cells to target cancer cells
- Most are new or still under investigation
  - Antibodies that are specific to certain cancers
  - Vaccines that help the body fight cancer
  - Interferon
  - Tumor necrosis factor (TNF)

 Bone Marrow/Stem-Cell Transplant
- Goal: Kill cancer with chemotherapy or radiation, then resupply the body with stem cells
- Sources of stem cells
  - Child's own bone marrow (autologous transplant)
  - Compatible donor (allogenic transplant)
- Umbilical cord blood

 Complementary Therapies
- Nutritional supplements
- Herbal supplements
- Touch therapy
- Mind/body interventions

 Palliative Care
- Goal is to provide comfort and emotional support
- Address pain, dyspnea, nutrition, elimination, and fatigue
- Palliative care team offers holistic approach

SUGGESTIONS FOR CLASSROOM ACTIVITIES

- Before class, assign students to review "Commonly Used Chemotherapy Drug Combinations," available on the Companion Website. Use this information, along with "Pathophysiology Illustrated: Chemotherapy Drug Action," and Table 50.2 to discuss a sample chemotherapy treatment plan.
- Discuss the pros and cons of using umbilical blood as a source of stem cells. Refer to "MediaLink Applications: Stem Cell Transplatation" activity available on the Companion Website.

SUGGESTIONS FOR CLINICAL ACTIVITIES

- Assign students to the pediatric imaging department to observe the diagnostic studies that may be used in diagnosing or treating childhood cancers.
- Discuss the difference in the automated versus manual differential of the complete blood count. Assign students to observe these laboratory analyses in the hospital laboatory.

LEARNING OBJECTIVE 3

Integrate information about oncologic emergencies into plans for monitoring all children with cancer.

CONCEPTS FOR LECTURE

1. Oncologic emergencies can be organized into three groups: metabolic, hematologic, and those involving space-occupying lesions.

POWERPOINT LECTURE SLIDES

 Oncologic Emergencies: Three Groups
- Metabolic
- Hematologic
- Space-occupying lesions

CONCEPTS FOR LECTURE *continued*

2. Metabolic emergencies result from the lysis of tumor cells, a process called tumor lysis syndrome. Septic shock and hypercalcemia are also considered metabolic emergencies.
3. Hematologic emergencies result from bone marrow suppression or hyperleukocytosis.
4. Space-occupying lesions occur when rapid tumor growth causes compression, resulting in increased pressure or obstruction.

POWERPOINT LECTURE SLIDES *continued*

 Metabolic Emergencies: Tumor Lysis Syndrome
- Results from lysis of tumor cells
- Cell lysis results in release of
  - Uric acid
  - Potassium
  - Phosphate
  - Calcium
- Serum sodium levels may decrease

2a Tumor Lysis Syndrome
- Most common in
  - Burkitt's lymphoma
  - Acute lymphocytic leukemia
- Lab studies

 Other Metabolic Emergencies
- Septic shock
  - Risk factor: Immunosuppression
  - Symptoms
  - Management
- Hypercalcemia
  - Occurs when bone is destroyed, releasing calcium
  - Management

3 Hematologic Emergencies: Bone Marrow Suppression
- Results in anemia and thrombocytopenia
- Hemorrhage then occurs
  - Gastrointestinal bleeding
  - Strokes
  - Disseminated intravascular coagulation (DIC)
- Treatment

3a Hematologic Emergencies: Hyperleukocytosis
- High numbers of leukemic blast cells
- Infiltrate and obstruct small blood vessels
- Treatment

4 Space-Occupying Lesions
- Rapid tumor growth may cause
  - Spinal cord compression
  - Increased intracranial pressure
  - Brain herniation
  - Seizures
  - Hepatomegaly
  - Superior vena cava syndrome
- Treatment

SUGGESTIONS FOR CLASSROOM ACTIVITIES

To illustrate the concept of space-occupying lesions, bring a balloon and a cardboard box to class. Cut a small hole in the cardboard box and place the end of balloon through the hole. As you blow up the balloon, explain that the balloon represents the rapidly expanding tumor growth, which can then compress surrounding tissue (as in the spinal cord or superior vena cava) or increase pressure (as in intracranial pressure).

SUGGESTIONS FOR CLINICAL ACTIVITIES

Assign students to the pediatric oncology unit and have them discuss the management of hematologic emergencies with nurses who work on the unit.

LEARNING OBJECTIVE 4

Recognize the most common solid tumors in children, describe their treatment, and plan comprehensive nursing care.

CONCEPTS FOR LECTURE

1. Brain tumors are the most common solid tumors in children. The cause of most brain tumors is unknown. These tumors manifest by behavioral or nervous system changes that occur either rapidly or more slowly and subtly. Although treatment varies with the type of tumor, surgery, radiation, and chemotherapy are typically used. Nursing management focuses on coordination of care, postoperative care, administering medications, and monitoring for complications.

2. Neuroblastoma is a smooth, hard, nontender mass that can occur anywhere along the sympathetic nervous system chain. Common locations include the abdominal, adrenal, thoracic, and cervical areas. Clinical manifestations depend upon the location of the mass. Surgery, followed by chemotherapy, is usually the therapy of choice. Nursing management includes postoperative care, medication administration, and teaching.

3. Wilms' tumor (also known as nephroblastoma) is a common intrarenal tumor. The tumor is usually asymptomatic, although a mass may be present. Therapy involves surgery and chemotherapy or radiation therapy. Nursing management focuses on postoperative care and chemotherapy monitoring and administration.

4. Bone tumors include osteosarcoma and Ewing's sarcoma. Osteosarcoma is a rare malignant bone tumor primarily seen in adolescent boys. Ewing's sarcoma is a small malignant tumor that involves the shaft of the long bones. Clinical manifestations include pain, swelling, and some laboratory abnormalities. Nursing management includes postoperative care and monitoring. Children who have had limbs amputated often have concerns regarding body image.

POWERPOINT LECTURE SLIDES

1 Brain Tumors
- Most common solid tumor in children
- Etiology unknown

1a Pathophysiology Illustrated: Brain Tumors
- ("Pathophysiology Illustrated: Brain Tumors")

1b Brain Tumors: Clinical Manifestations
- May be rapid or slow and subtle
- Include behavioral and/or nervous system changes
- Common symptoms
  - Headache
  - Nausea and/or vomiting
  - Dizziness
  - Change in vision or hearing
  - Fatigue
  - Slight incoordination

1c Brain Tumors: Therapy
- Diagnosed with various imaging studies
- Treatment depends on type of tumor
  - Surgery
  - Radiation (not used for kids under 3 years)
  - Chemotherapy (given intrathecally due to blood-brain barrier)

1d Brain Tumors: Nursing Management
- Coordinate care
- Monitor neurologic status
- Postoperative care
- Administer medications
- Monitor for complications
  - Increased intracranial pressure
  - Seizures
  - Diabetes insipidus (DI)
- Discharge planning and home teaching

2 Neuroblastoma
- Smooth, hard, nontender mass
- Occurs anywhere along the sympathetic nervous system chain
- Common locations
  - Abdomen
  - Thoracic area
  - Adrenal area
  - Cervical area

2a Neuroblastoma: Clinical Manifestations
- Depends upon location of mass
- Retroperitoneal mass
  - Altered bowel or bladder function
  - Weight loss
  - Abdominal distention
  - Enlarged liver

- Mediastinal mass
  - Dyspnea
  - Infection

 Neuroblastoma
- Therapy
  - Surgical removal of mass
  - Follow with chemotherapy—multiple drugs used
  - Radiation used occasionally
- Nursing management
  - Postoperative care
  - Administer medications
  - Child and family teaching

 Wilms' Tumor (Nephroblastoma)
- Intrarenal tumor
- Common abdominal tumor
- Most common age: 2 to 5 years

 Wilms' Tumor: Clinical Manifestations
- Usually asymptomatic; hypertension may occur due to renin release
- Mass may be noticed by parent
  - Firm, lobulated mass
  - Located to one side of the midline of the abdomen

 Wilms' Tumor: Therapy
- Surgery
  - Remove affected kidney
  - Look for metastasis
- Chemotherapy—with or without radiation therapy

 Wilms' Tumor: Nursing Management
- Postoperative care
- Chemotherapy
  - Administration
  - Monitoring

 Bone Tumors
- Osteosarcoma
  - Rare, malignant bone tumor
  - Occurs primarily in adolescent boys
- Ewing's sarcoma
  - Small, malignant tumor
  - Occurs in shaft of long bones (femur, tibia, etc.)
  - May occur in any bone

 Bone Tumors: Clinical Manifestations
- Pain
- Swelling
- Lab abnormalities

Bone Tumors: Therapy
- Osteosarcoma
  - Limb-salvage or amputation surgery
  - Aggressive chemotherapy
  - Metastasis is common

- Ewing's sarcoma
  - ◦ Chemotherapy to reduce tumor size
  - ◦ Surgery: limb-salvage most common
  - ◦ Follow-up chemotherapy
  - ◦ Metastasis is common

 Bone Tumors: Nursing Management
- Postoperative care and monitoring
- Body image concerns
  - ◦ Prosthesis
  - ◦ Support group, other adolescents with amputations
  - ◦ School access

SUGGESTIONS FOR CLASSROOM ACTIVITIES

Before class, assign students to review the "Case Study: Teen with Ewing's Sarcoma" located on the Companion Website. Use the case study as a basis for discussion about nursing management of adolescents with bone tumors.

SUGGESTIONS FOR CLINICAL ACTIVITIES

Find out if a support group exists locally for children who have had limbs amputated. If it does, assign students to attend the group. If it does not exist, students could help facilitate such a group.

LEARNING OBJECTIVE 5

Plan care for children and adolescents of all ages who have a diagnosis of leukemia.

CONCEPTS FOR LECTURE

1. Leukemia, characterized by an abnormal proliferation of white blood cells, is the most common form of pediatric cancer. The two most common forms of leukemia are acute lymphoblastic leukemia (ALL) and acute myelogenous leukemia (AML).
2. The pathophysiology of leukemia involves a large number of immature white blood cells that replace normal white blood cells. This leaves the body vulnerable to infection, and eventually results in anemia and thrombocytopenia.
3. Clinical manifestations are directly related to the pathophysiology of the disease process. In addition, symptoms may be related to infiltration and the resulting mass and pressure effect.
4. Leukemia is diagnosed based on blood counts and bone marrow aspiration. Therapy involves radiation and chemotherapy. The most important prognostic indicator is the initial leukocyte count: The higher it is upon a diagnosis, the worse the prognosis.
5. Nursing management focuses on assessment, diagnosis, planning and implementation, and evaluation.

POWERPOINT LECTURE SLIDES

 Leukemia
- Most common form of childhood cancer
- Abnormal proliferation of white blood cells (WBCs)
- Two main types
  - ◦ Acute lymphoblastic leukemia (ALL)
  - ◦ Acute myelogenous leukemia (AML)

Pathophysiology
- Stem cells in bone marrow produce large number of WBCs
- These WBCs are immature and do not function normally
- They replace normal WBCs
- Risk for infection increases
- Red blood cells and platelets are replaced
- Results: anemia, thrombocytopenia, immunosuppression

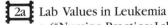 Lab Values in Leukemia
- ("Nursing Practice: Laboratory Values in Leukemia")

Clinical Manifestations
- Fever
- Pallor
- Overt signs of bleeding
- Lethargy, malaise
- Joint or bone pain
- Enlarged liver, spleen, lymph nodes

Clinical Manifestations: Infiltration
- Central nervous system: Cells mass and put pressure on nerves
  - Headache
  - Vomiting
  - Papilledema
- Testicles—painless enlargement of testicle
- Spinal cord
- Bone marrow

 Diagnosis
- Blood counts
  - Anemia
  - Thrombocytopenia
  - Neutropenia
- Bone marrow aspiration—immature lymphoblasts

 Therapy
- Radiation and chemotherapy
- Four phases
  - Induction
  - Consolidation
  - Delayed intensification
  - Maintenance

 Prognosis
- Prognosis generally better than in the past
- Favorable factors
  - Age of onset is 2 to 10 years
  - Initial hemoglobin less than 10 g/dL
  - Rapid response to chemotherapy
- Most important indicator is initial WBC count—the higher it is at diagnosis, the worse the prognosis
- 10% relapse within 1 year after treatment

 Nursing Assessment
- Signs of bruising, bleeding, or infection
- Renal function
- Mucosal sores in mouth
- Central nervous system infiltration
  - Decreased level of consciousness
  - Irritability
  - Vomiting
  - Lethargy

 Nursing Diagnosis
- Imbalanced nutrition, less than body requirements
- Risk for infection
- Risk for injury
- Activity intolerance
- Pain
- Disturbed sleep pattern
- Anxiety

 Planning and Implementation
- Prevent infection
- Skin and mouth care

- Attention to renal function
- Monitor IV site for extravasation
- Red blood cell, platelet administration
- Chemotherapy administration
- Psychosocial interventions

5c Evaluation: Expected Outcomes
- Prevention of infections
- Adequate hydration
- Normal urine output
- Normal blood values
- Adaptation to illness

SUGGESTIONS FOR CLASSROOM ACTIVITIES

At the beginning of this portion of the class, show the video "Leukemia," located on the Student CD-ROM. Use this video as an introduction to this topic.

SUGGESTIONS FOR CLINICAL ACTIVITIES

Ask a child and family with leukemia to talk with students during a clinical conference about what it is like to live with the disease and what hospitalizations are like. As an alternative, use the "MediaLink Applications: Life with Leukemia: A Teen in Transition," activity available on the Companion Website, as a basis for the discussion.

LEARNING OBJECTIVE 6

Recognize the most common soft-tissue tumors in children, describe their treatment, and plan comprehensive care.

CONCEPTS FOR LECTURE

1. Soft-tissue tumors include Hodgkin's disease, non-Hodgkin's lymphoma, rhabdomyosarcoma, and retinoblastoma.
2. Hodgkin's disease is a disorder of the lymphoid system that occurs most commonly in adolescent boys. The main symptom is a nontender, firm lymph node that is usually in the supraclavicular or cervical nodes. After diagnosis via lymph node biopsy, therapy includes chemotherapy and radiation.
3. Non-Hodgkin's lymphoma is a malignant tumor of the lymphoreticular system. It is the third most common group of malignancies in children (following leukemia and brain tumors). Children usually present with fever and weight loss, as well as enlarged lymph nodes. Chemotherapy is the primary form of therapy.
4. Rhabdomyosarcoma occurs most often in the muscles of the eyes and neck, although it can occur in other muscles as well. Clinical manifestations vary based on the tumor site. The tumor is removed via surgery, and therapy then focuses on chemotherapy and radiation.
5. Retinoblastoma is an intraocular malignancy of the retina that may be bilateral or unilateral. A white pupil (leukokoria) is the main clinical sign. Radiation, chemotherapy, and surgery are all typical therapies, and the eye may be surgically removed.

POWERPOINT LECTURE SLIDES

1 Soft-Tissue Tumors
- Hodgkin's disease
- Non-Hodgkin's lymphoma
- Rhabdomyosarcoma
- Retinoblastoma

2 Hodgkin's disease
- Disorder of lymphoid system
- Arises from single lymph node or group of lymph nodes
- Peak occurrence in adolescent boys

2a Pathophysiology Illustrated: Hodgkin's Disease
- ("Pathophysiology Illustrated: Hodgkin's Disease")

2b Hodkin's Disease: Clinical Manifestations
- Main symptom:
  ○ Nontender, firm lymph node
  ○ Usual location: supraclavicular or cervical nodes
- Other symptoms seen with aggressive disease process:
  ○ Fever
  ○ Night sweats
  ○ Weight loss
- Diagnosis: Lymph node biopsy

2c Hodkin's Disease: Therapy
- Chemotherapy—four-drug combination used
- Radiation often used
- Bone marrow transplant

Non-Hodgkin's Lymphoma
- Three subtypes
- Third most common form of cancer in kids—after leukemia, brain tumor
- Malignant tumor of the lymphoreticular system—internal framework of the lymph system

 Non-Hodgkin's Lymphoma: Clinical Manifestations
- Fever
- Weight loss
- Enlarged, nodular lymph nodes
- Diagnosis
  - CBC, other labs
  - Bone marrow aspiration
  - Imaging studies
  - Tissue biopsy

 Non-Hodgkin's Lymphoma: Therapy
- Chemotherapy
- Radiation not used commonly
- Surgery
  - Tissue biopsy
  - Treat complications caused by tumor

 Rhabdomyosarcoma
- Common sites
  - Muscles around the eyes
  - Muscles in the neck
- Less common sites
  - Abdomen
  - Genitourinary tract
  - Extremities

 Rhabdomyosarcoma: Clinical Manifestations
- Depends upon tumor site
- Eyes
  - Swelling
  - Ptosis
  - Visual disturbances

 Rhabdomyosarcoma: Eye Characteristics

 Rhabdomyosarcoma: Therapy
- Surgical removal of tumor
- Radiation
- Chemotherapy

5 Retinoblastoma
- Intraocular malignancy of the retina
- Bilateral or unilateral
- May be inherited
- Main clinical sign: White pupil (leukokoria)

5a Retinoblastoma: Leukokoria

5b | Retinoblastoma: Therapy
- Radiation
- Chemotherapy
- Surgery—eye may be removed

SUGGESTIONS FOR CLASSROOM ACTIVITIES

Divide students into groups and have each group draw (on an overhead transparency or a large piece of paper from a flip chart) a basic sketch of a child with one of the soft-tissue tumors described above. They should include depictions of each clinical manifestation on their sketch. Have the rest of the class guess which disease process has been drawn and use this as the basis for the rest of the objective.

SUGGESTIONS FOR CLINICAL ACTIVITIES

Assign students to observe in an outpatient pediatric chemotherapy clinic. Students should have the opportunity to interact with many children with soft-tissue tumors.

LEARNING OBJECTIVE 7

Describe the impact of cancer survival on children and use this information to plan for ongoing physiological and psychosocial care in the children's futures.

CONCEPTS FOR LECTURE

1. The diagnosis of "cancer" can be devastating, and children often react differently to the diagnosis than their parents do.
2. Psychosocial assessment focuses on body image, stress and coping abilities, support systems, and developmental level.
3. There can be many long-term physiologic effects of therapies used to treat cancer.

POWERPOINT LECTURE SLIDES

1 | Cancer Diagnosis: Reaction of Parents
- Disbelief, shock
- Must gather resources, make treatment decisions
- Travel often required for treatment
- Financial strain, potential job loss
- Adaptation

1a | Cancer Diagnosis: Reaction of Child
- Depends upon child's age
- Infants and toddlers: Limited understanding
- Preschooler: May believe they caused illness
- School-age: Improved understanding, like to talk about it
- Adolescent: Like to talk with other adolescents

2 | Psychosocial Assessment: Areas of Focus
- Body image
- Stress and coping
- Support systems
- Developmental level

3 | Potential Long-term Effects of Surgery
- Adhesions (can lead to intestinal obstruction)
- Visual impairment
- Neurologic changes
- Sterility

3a | Potential Long-Term Effects of Radiation
- Impairs growth of bones and teeth—can lead to scoliosis, dental problems
- Hypothyroidism
- Delayed puberty, sterility
- Secondary cancers

Potential Long-Term Effects of Chemotherapy
- Cardiomyopathy
- Lung, renal toxicity
- Neurologic changes
- Infertility
- Hearing loss, vision changes

SUGGESTIONS FOR CLASSROOM ACTIVITIES

Invite a social worker, case manager, or child life specialist who works with children and families with cancer to speak to the class about the effects the cancer diagnosis has on families.

SUGGESTIONS FOR CLINICAL ACTIVITIES

Students are often hesitant to assess and plan interventions in the psychosocial realm. When caring for these children, have students write three age-appropriate questions that they can use with the child and his or her family to encourage discussion about psychosocial issues.

CHAPTER 51
THE CHILD WITH ALTERATIONS IN GASTROINTESTINAL FUNCTION

RESOURCE LIBRARY

CD-ROM

Skills 15-3: Administering a Gavage Feeding
Skill 16-3: Changing the Dressing for an Infant with an Ostomy
Skill 16-4: Changing an Ostomy Pouch for an Infant or Child
Animations:
  Lead Poisoning
Videos:
  Activated Charcoal
  Digestive System
  Stool Toileting: Refusals and Rewards
Nursing in Action: Changing an Ostomy Pouch
Audio Glossary
NCLEX-RN® Review

COMPANION WEBSITE

Thinking Critically
Case Study: The Child with Cleft Palate
Care Plan: Managing Emesis in Pediatric Conditions
NCLEX-RN® Review
Case Study

IMAGE LIBRARY

Figure 51.1 A, Unilateral cleft lip. B, Bilateral cleft lip.
Figure 51.2 A, Repaired unilateral cleft lip. B, Repaired bilateral cleft lip.
Figure 51.3 A gastrostomy tube is used to feed the child with a gastrointestinal disorder such as esophageal atresia.
Figure 51.5 The newborn with gastroschisis has abdominal contents located outside the abdominal wall.
Figure 51.6 The umbilical hernia of the newborn usually closes as the muscles strengthen in later infancy and childhood.

Figure 51.7 Nursing strategies to address altered perceptions of body image and increased feelings of dependence are important when working with adolescents who have ostomies.
Figure 51.8 The child with celiac disease commonly shows failure to grow and wasting of extremities.

Pathophysiology Illustrated: Esophageal Atresia and Tracheoesophageal Fistula
Pathophysiology Illustrated: Pyloric Stenosis
Pathophysiology Illustrated: Viral Hepatitis

LEARNING OBJECTIVE 1
Describe the general function of the gastrointestinal system.

CONCEPTS FOR LECTURE

1. General functions of the gastrointestinal system include ingestion, digestion, and absorption of fluids and nutrients; metabolism of needed nutrients; and excretion of waste products.

POWERPOINT LECTURE SLIDES

 Functions of Gastrointestinal (GI) System
  • Ingestion, digestion, and absorption of fluids and nutrients
  • Metabolism of needed nutrients
  • Excretion of waste products

---

2. The gastrointestinal tract, while structurally complete at birth, undergoes changes as the infant grows and develops in order to make it functionally mature.

 General Principles of GI Illnesses
- Can result from:
  ○ Congenital defect
  ○ Acquired disease
  ○ Infection
  ○ Injury
- All gastrointestinal illnesses affect nutrient absorption
  ○ Short term
  ○ Long term (growth delay)

 Development of the GI Tract
- Before birth, placenta provides nutrients and waste
- GI tract structurally complete at birth but is immature
- Sucking is a reflex until 6 weeks of age, then it is voluntary

2a Changes in GI Tract with Time
- Stomach capacity increases
- Intestinal motility increases
- Enzyme secretion increases
- Liver matures over first year of life
- By age 2: Three meals a day—excretory control

SUGGESTIONS FOR CLASSROOM ACTIVITIES

As an introduction to this topic, show the animation "Digestive System," available on the Student CD-ROM.

SUGGESTIONS FOR CLINICAL ACTIVITIES

Ask students how they would explain the basic functions of the gastrointestinal tract to children of various ages. They can use these concepts when they teach children and families during their clinical rotations.

LEARNING OBJECTIVE 2

Discuss the pathophysiological processes associated with specific gastrointestinal disorders in the pediatric population.

CONCEPTS FOR LECTURE

1. Structural defects occur when the growth and development of fetal structures are interrupted during the first trimester. Examples of structural defects include cleft lip and palate, esophageal atresia with tracheoesophageal fistula, and pyloric stenosis.
2. Intussusception is one of the most frequent causes of intestinal obstruction in infancy and occurs when one portion of the intestine prolapses and telescopes into itself.
3. The two major abdominal wall defects common in children include omphalocele and gastroschisis. Omphalocele tends to be associated with other congenital anomalies, while gastroschisis tends to be an isolated defect.

POWERPOINT LECTURE SLIDES

1 Structural GI Defects
- Growth and development of GI tract interrupted in first trimester
- Affect one or more areas
- Atresia: Absence or closure of a normal body orifice
- Malposition
- Nonclosure

1a Structural Defects
- Cleft lip and palate
- Esophageal atresia with tracheoesophageal fistula
- Pyloric stenosis

4. Anorectal malformations are common congenital anomalies and can range from minor to complex. Anorectal malformations may occur in isolation or may be associated with other congenial defects.

5. A hernia is a protrusion of an organ or part of an organ through the muscle wall of the cavity that normally contains it. Diaphragmatic hernia and umbilical hernia are two types of hernias seen in children, although inguinal hernias are the most common *(Note: Inguinal hernias are covered in Chapter 52).*

6. Gastroesophageal reflux (GER), Hirschsprung disease, gastroenteritis, and constipation are disorders of motility. GER affects about half of all children, although only a small portion will go on to develop gastroesophageal reflux disease.

7. Inflammatory disorders are reactions of specific tissues of the GI tract to trauma caused by injuries, foreign bodies, chemicals, microorganisms, or surgery. Disorders in this category include appendicitis, peptic ulcers, necrotizing enterocolitis, Meckel's diverticulum, and inflammatory bowel disease.

8. Celiac disease, lactose intolerance, and short bowel syndrome represent three types of malabsorption disorders, defined by the lack of digestion or absorption of nutrients.

9. Hepatic disorders include biliary atresia and hepatitis. Children are most likely to get hepatitis A or hepatitis B. Biliary atresia is the most common pediatric liver disease necessitating transplant.

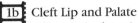

1b Cleft Lip and Palate
- Occur singly or in combination
- Maxillary processes fail to fuse
- Multifactorial cause suspected
  - Environment
  - Genetics
  - Folate

1c Unilateral Cleft Lip
- (Figure 51.1A)

1d Bilateral Cleft Lip
- (Figure 51.1B)

1e Esophageal Atresia and Tracheoesophageal Fistula (TEF)
- Esophagus and trachea do not develop as parallel tracts
- Esophagus ends as either
  - Blind pouch
  - Connected to trachea by a fistula

1f Esophageal Atresia and TEF: Pathophysiology
- ("Pathophysiology Illustrated: Esophageal Atresia and Tracheoesophageal Fistula")

1g Pyloric Stenosis
- Hypertrophic obstruction of the pyloric sphincter
- Occurs in boys more than girls
- Hypertrophy of pyloric sphincter results in
  - Obstruction of sphincter
  - Inability to move food from stomach to duodenum
  - Vomiting and dehydration

1h Pyloric Stenosis: Pathophysiology
- ("Pathophysiology Illustrated: Pyloric Stenosis")

2 Intussusception
- One portion of the intestine prolapses and then invaginates (or, "telescopes") into itself
- Results in
  - Obstructed blood flow
  - Ischemia and necrosis
  - Hemorrhage, perforation if untreated
- Frequent cause of intestinal obstruction
- Most cases occur in boys ages 3 months to 6 years

3 Abdominal Wall Defects
- Omphalocele
  - Congenital malformation
  - Intra-abdominal contents herniate through umbilical cord
  - Covered with peritoneal membrane
  - Often associated with other anomalies
- Gastroschisis
  - Abdominal organs herniate through abdominal wall
  - Not covered with peritoneal membrane

3a Omphalocele

3b Gastroschisis
- (Figure 51.5)

4 Anorectal Malformations
- Common congenital defects
- Minor to complex
- Occur in isolation or with other defects—VACTERL
- Types
  - Anal stenosis
  - Anal atresia
  - Imperforate anus

5 Hernias
- Protrusion of an organ through the muscle wall of the cavity that normally contains it
- Types
  - Inguinal
  - Diaphragmatic
  - Umbilical

5a Diaphragmatic Hernia
- Abdominal contents protrude into lung cavity through the diaphragm
- Foramen of Bochdalek is most common location—left side of diaphragm
- Life-threatening problem

5b Umbilical Hernia
- Results from weak or imperfectly closed umbilical ring; diastasis recti
- Occurs in 1 out of 6 children
- 10 times more common in African-American children than white children

5c Umbilical Hernia
- (Figure 51.6)

6 Disorders of Motility
- Gastroesophageal reflux
- Hirschsprung disease

6a Gastroesophageal Reflux (GER)
- Affects half of all children
- Lower esophageal sphincter relaxes
  - Allows passive regurgitation of stomach contents into esophagus
  - May also enter airway (aspiration)

6b Gastroesophageal Reflux Disease (GERD)
- Serious manifestation of GER
- Characterized by
  - Poor weight gain
  - Esophagitis
  - Persistent respiratory symptoms
- Requires treatment

6c Hirschsprung Disease
- Congenital aganglionic megacolon
- Congenital anomaly
- Portion of large intestine lacks parasympathetic innervation
- Results in
  - Inadequate motility
  - Obstruction of the intestine

6d Gastroenteritis (Acute Diarrhea)
- Inflammation of stomach and intestines
  - Fluid, electrolyte loss
  - Dehydration
- May be acute or chronic
- Nausea, vomiting, diarrhea

6e Constipation
- Decrease in frequency of stools
- Formation of hard stools
- Liquid stool oozing past hard, dry stool
- May be caused by underlying disease, diet, or psychologic factors

7 Inflammatory Diseases
- Reactions of tissue in the GI tract to trauma caused by
  - Injuries
  - Foreign bodies
  - Chemicals
  - Microorganisms
  - Surgery
- May be acute or chronic

7a Inflammatory Diseases in Childhood
- Appendicitis
- Peptic ulcers
- Necrotizing enterocolitis
- Meckel's diverticulum
- Inflammatory bowel disease

7b Appendicitis
- Inflammation of vermiform appendix
- Occurs most often in adolescent boys—can occur in any age
- Pathophysiology: Obstruction of appendiceal lumen—may perforate or rupture as pressure increases

7c Peptic Ulcer
- Erosion of muscle tissue in stomach or duodenum
- Etiology: *H. pylori*
- May bleed or perforate if untreated

7d Necrotizing Enterocolitis
- Potentially life-threatening
- Affects neonates, especially premature babies
- Intestinal ischemia

- Bacterial or viral infection
- Inflammation and dilation of bowel
- Gas accumulates in bowel (may perforate)

 Meckel's Diverticulum
- Omphalomesenteric duct fails to atrophy
- Outpouching of ileum remains
  - Pouch secretes acid
  - Result: Irritation, ulceration
- Usually diagnosed by age 2
- If untreated, may lead to perforation or peritonitis

 Inflammatory Bowel Disease
- Crohn's disease
  - Chronic, inflammatory process involving mucosa and submucosa
  - Occurs randomly in GI tract
  - Fistulas and ulcers common
- Ulcerative colitis
  - Inflammation of mucosa only
  - Diarrhea, abdominal pain, cramping

 Malabsorption Disorders
- Cannot digest or absorb nutrients in diet
- Celiac disease
- Lactose intolerance
- Short bowel syndrome

 Celiac Disease
- Gluten-sensitive enteropathy—genetic predisposition
- Intolerance for gluten—protein found in wheat, barley, oats, and rye
- Results in accumulation of glutamine, which is toxic to intestinal mucosa
  - Damages villi
  - Long-term risk of GI tract cancers

 Celiac Disease: Failure to Thrive
- (Figure 51.8)

 Lactose Intolerance
- Inability to digest lactose—disaccharide found in milk, dairy products
- Congenital or acquired lactase deficiency
- Result: Diarrhea

 Short Bowel Syndrome
- Intestine is shortened, usually from bowel resection
- Decreased surface area for nutrient absorption
- Results
  - Watery diarrhea
  - Fluid, electrolyte imbalances
  - Poor growth, malnutrition
  - Vitamin, nutrient loss

Hepatic Diseases
- Biliary atresia
- Hepatitis

 Biliary Atresia
- Closure or absence of bile duct
- Bile cannot flow from liver into duodenum
- Results in
  - Cholestasis
  - Fibrosis
  - Cirrhosis
  - Death
- Cause is unknown

 Hepatitis
- Inflammation of liver due to viral infection
- Acute or chronic
- Children most likely to get hepatitis A or B
  - Hepatitis A: Fecal-oral route—acute
  - Hepatitis B: Blood/body secretion—chronic

Hepatitis: Pathophysiology
- ("Pathophysiology Illustrated: Viral Hepatitis")

Suggestions for Classroom Activities

Use a long, cylindrical balloon to illustrate the pathophysiology of intussusception. After the balloon is lightly inflated, use your finger to push one end of it into the lumen, mimicking what happens in the intestine during intussusception.

Suggestions for Clinical Activities

Many gastrointestinal disorders in childhood are treated surgically. When possible, assign students to observe in the pediatric operating room the surgical correction and treatment of these disorders.

Learning Objective 3

Identify signs and symptoms that may indicate a disorder of the gastrointestinal system.

Concepts for Lecture

1. Signs and symptoms of gastrointestinal illnesses tend to be nonspecific and overlap from disease to disease.

PowerPoint Lecture Slides

 Signs and Symptoms of GI Disorders
- Inability to gain weight or weight loss
- Vomiting
- Diarrhea
- Constipation
- Lack of energy—lethargy
- Abdominal distention
- Abdominal tenderness

 Signs and Symptoms of Specific Disorders
- Pyloric stenosis—projectile vomiting
- Intussusception—currant jelly stools
- GERD
- Hirshsprung disease
- Appendicitis
- Meckel's diverticulum
- Hepatic disorders

SUGGESTIONS FOR CLASSROOM ACTIVITIES

- For each gastrointestinal disease described in the chapter, have students make a list of signs and symptoms that are different from the general symptoms described previously. This can help them learn how to differentiate these diseases.
- Bring a jar of currant jelly purchased from a grocery store to illustrate the type of stools that may be seen in children with intussusception. Have students view the video "Stool Toileting: Refusals and Rewards" on the Student CD-ROM.

SUGGESTIONS FOR CLINICAL ACTIVITIES

Demonstrate how to perform an abdominal exam on children of different ages. For example, students often have difficulty performing exams on infants and toddlers who cannot describe symptoms of pain. Strategies and tips for assessing young children can be discussed.

LEARNING OBJECTIVE 4

Describe nursing management and plan care for disorders of the gastrointestinal system.

CONCEPTS FOR LECTURE

1. There are several components of general nursing care that should be done for any child with a gastrointestinal disorder.
2. Nursing management of common gastrointestinal disorders includes the general principles described previously, as well as actions specific to each disease process.

POWERPOINT LECTURE SLIDES

1 General Principles of Nursing Care: GI Disorders
- Assess abdominal girth
- Assess bowel sounds
- Begin oral feeding with frequent, small feedings of clear liquids—advance diet as tolerated

1a General Principles
- Assess location and type of pain child is experiencing
- Assess for nausea, vomiting
- Determine stool pattern
- Monitor intake and output

2 Cleft Lip and Palate
- Emotional support
- Postoperative care
- Long-term care and follow-up

2a Esophageal Atresia and TEF
- Detection
- Preparation for surgery
- Feeding regimen

2b Pyloric Stenosis
- Rehydration
- Correction of electrolyte imbalances
- Postoperative care
- Feeding regimen

2c Intussusception
- Fluid and electrolyte balance
- Postoperative care
- Nasogastric tube patency
- Feeding regimen

2d Hirschsprung Disease
- Bowel regimen pre-op
- Post-op care
- Colostomy teaching

2e Appendicitis
- Pain control
- Hydration
- Emotional support
- Monitor for infection
- Prevent respiratory complications

 2f Crohn's Disease and Ulcerative Colitis
- Body image
- Dietary changes
- TPN

 2g Gastroenteritis
- Fluids and electrolytes
- Infection control
- Oral rehydration—intravenous if not tolerated
- Skin care

 2h Celiac Disease
- Dietary counseling (involve dietitian)
  - Products to avoid
  - Cost factors
  - Age considerations

SUGGESTIONS FOR CLASSROOM ACTIVITIES

- Have the class read "Evidence-Based Nursing: Postoperative Feeding Methods Following Pyloromyotomy in Infants," and use the critical thinking questions as a basis for discussion of the nursing care of the infant with pyloric stenosis.
- Before class, assign students to complete "Case Study: Care of the Child with Cleft Palate," available on the Companion Website. Use this case study as a basis for discussing the nursing care of children with this disorder.

SUGGESTIONS FOR CLINICAL ACTIVITIES

Assign students to observe in a pediatric outpatient gastrointestinal clinic to gain exposure to how these disorders are monitored and treated throughout the child's life.

LEARNING OBJECTIVE 5

Analyze developmentally appropriate approaches for nursing management of gastrointestinal disorders in the pediatric population.

CONCEPTS FOR LECTURE

1. The principles of growth and development should be applied in the nursing management of children across the lifespan with gastrointestinal disorders.

POWERPOINT LECTURE SLIDES

 1 Growth and Developmental Considerations: Diet
- Facilitate breastfeeding in infants with structural defects
- Instruct parents in the use of thickening agents for GER and GERD
- Assist parents in making decisions about age-appropriate food choices for disorders that have special diets
  - Hepatitis
  - Celiac disease
  - Crohn's disease
  - Ulcerative colitis

1a Growth and Developmental Considerations: Ostomies
- Encourage children with ostomies to take responsibility for their own care
- Body image concerns

1b Growth and Developmental Considerations: Body Image
- Steroids (side effects)
- Ostomies
- Central venous catheters for TPN
- Short stature
- Delayed onset of puberty

SUGGESTIONS FOR CLASSROOM ACTIVITIES

Divide the class to represent the four age groups (infant, toddler, child, adolescent). Give them a handout with three gastrointestinal disorders that span a lifetime. Have each group decide what would be the appropriate nursing care based on each age group. Tell them to include play, safety, education, and nursing interaction.

SUGGESTIONS FOR CLINICAL ACTIVITIES

Assign students to shadow a dietitian in order to learn how to address the dietary aspects of pediatric gastrointestinal disorders.

LEARNING OBJECTIVE 6

Discuss nursing management of the child with an injury (trauma or ingestion of injurious agent) to the gastrointestinal system.

CONCEPTS FOR LECTURE

1. In children, the majority of abdominal trauma is blunt trauma sustained in motor vehicle crashes, auto-pedestrian accidents, and abuse. Nursing care focuses on monitoring the child's status, as well as providing interventions as needed.

2. Poisoning is a common occurrence in pediatrics, and most poisonings occur in the home. Young children, ages 1 to 4, are at the highest risk for poisoning. Prevention of poisoning by assessing the home for potentially toxic substances is important.

3. Foreign objects are most likely to be ingested by children who are 6 months to 3 years of age. Common objects ingested include coins, pins, toys, batteries, and bones from food.

4. The removal of lead from paint has significantly decreased the incidence of lead poisoning; however, children who live in older houses remain at risk for lead poisoning.

POWERPOINT LECTURE SLIDES

1 Abdominal Trauma in Children
- Blunt trauma (85%)
  - Motor vehicle crashes
  - Auto-pedestrian
  - Abuse
- Mechanism of injury can predict actual injury

1a Abdominal Trauma: Nursing Assessment
- Clinical manifestations:
  - Pain, guarding
  - Abdominal distention
  - Decreased or absent bowel sounds
  - Nausea and/or vomiting
  - Hypotension
  - Shock

1b Abdominal Trauma: Nursing Management
- Post-op and monitoring
  - Fluid, blood replacement
  - Frequent vital signs
  - Intake and output monitoring
- Emotional support—parents may feel guilty

- Prevention
  - Protective gear (helmets, pads)
  - Car seats

 Poisoning
- Common in children
- Most common age: 1 to 4 years
- Most poisonings occur in the home; sources of toxins
- Role of Poison Control Center

 Poisoning: Nursing Management
- Immediate care in emergency room
  - Prevent further absorption of poison
  - Reverse effects
  - Enhance elimination
- Further care
  - Emotional support
  - Prevent recurrence

 Ingestion of Foreign Objects
- Most common in children ages 6 months to 3 years
- Most common objects:
  - Coins (27% to 70% of cases)
  - Pins
  - Toys
  - Batteries
  - Bones from food

 Ingestion of Foreign Objects: Nursing Management
- Detection; symptoms: Drooling, dysphagia, coughing, wheezing
- Assist with endoscopic exam and/or removal
- Prevent recurrence

 Lead Poisoning
- Source of lead: Paint (before mid-1970s); dust, chips, contaminated soil
- Older houses may still have lead-based paint
- Effects of lead in body (highest risk in children less than 7 years)
  - Impaired mental function
  - Decreased IQ
  - Impaired hearing
  - Delayed growth

4a Lead Poisoning: Detection
- Routine screening with well-child visits
  - Questionnaire to determine risk level
  - Blood level

4b Lead Poisoning:
- Interventions
  - Removal of lead from child's environment
  - Chelation therapy—binds lead, enhances excretion
  - Follow-up blood levels

- Lead Poisoning: Nursing Management
  - Screening
  - Education
  - Follow-up

SUGGESTIONS FOR CLASSROOM ACTIVITIES

When discussing poisoning, show the video "Activated Charcoal" and the animation "Insider's View: Effects of Lead on the Body," both of which are available on the Student CD-ROM.

SUGGESTIONS FOR CLINICAL ACTIVITIES

Assign students to observe in the pediatric emergency room, and discuss the role of the emergency room staff when a child presents with suspected poisoning.

CHAPTER 52
THE CHILD WITH ALTERATIONS IN GENITOURINARY FUNCTION

RESOURCE LIBRARY

 CD-ROM

Animations/Videos:
  Circumcision
  Renal Function
  Furosemide (Drug Animation)
  Sexually Transmitted Infections
Skill 16-1: Performing a Urinary Catheterization
NCLEX-RN® Review
Audio Glossary

COMPANION WEBSITE

NCLEX-RN® Review
Thinking Critically
Case Study
Audio Glossary
MediaLink Application:
  Care Plan: A School-Age Child with Enuresis
  Case Study: A Child with Chronic Kidney Failure
  Care Plan: A Child with Kidney Failure
  Care Plan: A Child with Nephrotic Syndrome

📖 IMAGE LIBRARY

Figure 52.1 The kidneys are located between the twelfth thoracic (T12) and third lumbar (L3) vertebrae.

Figure 52.2 This child has bladder exstrophy, noted by extrusion of the posterior bladder wall through the lower abdominal wall.

Figure 52.3 Hypospadias and epispadias.

Figure 52.4 This boy has generalized edema, a characteristic finding in nephrotic syndrome.

Figure 52.5 A color wheel, such as the one shown here, can be used as a guide in standardizing descriptions of urine color.

Figure 52.6 This child is undergoing hemodialysis.

Clinical Manifestations: Acute versus Chronic Renal Failure

Pathophysiology Illustrated: Obstruction Sites in the Urinary System

Pathophysiology Illustrated: Acute Renal Failure

LEARNING OBJECTIVE 1

Describe the pathophysiologic processes associated with genitourinary disorders in the pediatric population.

CONCEPTS FOR LECTURE

1. Enuresis is repeated involuntary voiding by a child old enough that bladder control is expected, usually about 5 to 6 years of age. Enuresis can result from neurologic or congenital structural disorders, illness, or stress. Treatment includes bladder training, fluid restriction, enuresis alarms, and medication. *See "Nursing Practice: Questions to Ask When Taking an Enuresis History"*

POWERPOINT LECTURE SLIDES

1 Enuresis
  • Definition
  • Potential causes
  • Neurologic or congenital structural disorders
  • Illness (diabetes, renal insufficiency)
  • Stress

1a Enuresis Treatments
  • Bladder training
  • Fluid restriction
  • Enuresis alarms
  • Medications
    ○ Imipramine
    ○ Desmopressin

---

2. Nephrotic syndrome is a clinical state characterized by edema, massive proteinuria, hypoalbuminemia, hypoproteinemia, hyperlipidemia, and altered immunity. Generalized edema of the extremeties, abdomen, and genitals usually prompts parents to seek treatment, which includes steroids, albumin, and diuretics. *Refer to "Drug Guide: Prednisone" for details.*

3. Renal failure is classified as acute or chronic. Acute renal failure usually occurs suddenly (days to weeks) and may be reversible, where chronic renal failure occurs over months to years and is usually not reversible. Diagnostic tests and clinical manifestations between the two vary. Hyperkalemia is the most life-threatening complication of renal failure.

4. Polycystic kidney disease (PKD) is a genetic disorder where cystic sacs form in the collecting ducts of the kidneys. Eventually, urinary flow is obstructed. Severe forms of PKD may cause renal failure shortly after birth, whereas less severe forms of PKD may not cause symptoms until later in the child's life.

5. Hemolytic-uremic syndrome (HUS) is an acute renal disease characterized by hemolytic anemia, thrombocytopenia, and acute renal failure. The most common cause is a toxin produced by *E. coli* 0157:H7 that is often found in undercooked ground beef. Most children recover from the disease, but some may go on to develop chronic renal failure.

6. Acute postinfectious glomerulonephritis (APIGN) is an inflammation of the glomeruli of the kidneys, and is triggered by deposition of antigen-antibody complexes in the glomeruli. The most common organism that triggers this response is Group A streptococcal infections of the skin and pharynx. Treatment is symptomatic, and most children recover within a few weeks.

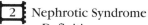

2 Nephrotic Syndrome
- Definition
- Variations: primary, secondary, congenital
  - Most common (80%): Minimal change nephrotic syndrome
- Pathophysiology

2a Nephrotic Syndrome: Clinical Manifestations
- (Figure 52.2)

2b Nephrotic Syndrome: Treatments
- Corticosteroid (prednisone): Decreases proteinuria
- Albumin and diuretics: reduce edema
- ACE inhibitor: decreases protein excretion

3 Renal Failure: Acute versus Chronic
- ("Clinical Manifestations: Acute versus Chronic Renal Failure")

3a Acute Renal Failure: Pathophysiology
- ("Pathophysiology Illustrated: Acute Renal Failure")

3b Chronic Renal Failure
- Occurs over time
- Results in
  - Uremia
  - Anemia
  - Hypertension
  - Metabolic acidosis
  - Hyperphosphatemia and/or hypocalcemia

4 Polycystic Kidney Disease (PKD)
- Genetic disorder
- Varies in severity
- Pathophysiology
- Treatment is supportive

5 Hemolytic-Uremic Syndrome (HUS)
- Triad of symptoms
  - Hemolytic anemia
  - Thrombocytopenia
  - Acute renal failure
- Source: Toxin of *E. coli* 0157:H7
  - Potential sources of *E. coli*

5a HUS: Treatment
- Antihypertensives
- Fluid restriction
- Diet (low protein, potassium, sodium, phosphorus)
- Antibiotics are controversial
- Antidiarrheal agents contraindicated

6 Acute Postinfectious Glomerulonephritis (APIGN)
- Definition
- Common cause: Group A Beta-streptococcus
- Pathophysiology
- Treatment supportive—most recover

Suggestions for Classroom Activities

- Before class, create a list of assessment data and laboratory values typical for a client with one of the renal disorders described previously. Challenge the students to analyze the data and determine which disease the client has. By creating several different scenarios, students can learn to differentiate these disorders. (Hint: refer to Table 52.4 to help students during this exercise.)
- Furosemide is a common diuretic used in several of the previously mentioned conditions. Show the animation "Furosemide" available on the Student CD-ROM. Ask students to identify why hypokalemia is a common side effect of furosemide. Discussion about the onset of action, duration, and monitoring of the client on diuretics is also appropriate
- When discussing acute postinfectious glomerulonephritis (APIGN) during lecture, show the animation "Renal Function" available on the Student CD-ROM. This brief animation shows students exactly where the glomeruli are located, and you can point out that the antigen-antibody complexes that "clog up" the glomeruli are carried through the blood.

Suggestions for Clinical Activities

- When students are caring for a client with one of the previously mentioned disorders, have them compare how the client presented with the description in the text. Was the client's presentation classic or atypical?
- Ask students how they would perform teaching for parents regarding prevention of HUS. Have them identify other foods besides uncooked ground beef that can cause HUS.

Learning Objective 2

Discuss the nursing management of a child with a structural defect of the genitourinary system.

Concepts for Lecture

1. Bladder exstrophy occurs when the posterior bladder wall extrudes through the lower abdominal wall. Preoperative nursing care includes prevention of infection and trauma to the exposed bladder. Post-op care includes immobilization to promote pelvic closure, wound care, pain control, and monitoring of renal function.
2. Hypospadias and epispadias are congenital anomalies involving the abnormal location of the urethral meatus in males. After surgical repair, nursing priorities include pain management, monitoring urine output, and monitoring of the urinary stent (if present).

PowerPoint Lecture Slides

1 Bladder Exstrophy
- (Figure 52.2)

1a Bladder Exstrophy: Nursing Management
- Pre-op: Protect bladder and surrounding tissue—prevent infection
- Post-op:
  - Immobilize pelvis to promote healing
  - Wound and skin care
  - Pain management
  - Monitoring renal function

2 Hypospadias and Epispadias
- (Figure 52.3)

3. Obstructive uropathies—congenital abnormalities that interfere with urine flow—include ureteropelvic junction (UPJ) obstruction and posterior urethral valves. Prune-belly syndrome is a congenital defect in which the abdominal musculature does not develop. The end result of these defects is hydronephrosis, which leads to renal failure if left untreated.

4. Phimosis occurs when the foreskin over the glans penis cannot be pulled back, usually due to infection or adhesions. Treatment includes betamethasone cream or circumcision.

5. Cryptorchidism (undescended testes) occurs when one or both testes fail to descend through the inguinal canal into the scrotum. Surgical correction is carried out by 1 year of age to prevent complications of uncorrected cryptorchidism, which include infertility and malignancy. Surgery is usually done on an outpatient basis, and discharge teaching is a nursing priority.

6. Inguinal hernia occurs when abdominal tissue—usually bowel—extends into the inguinal canal. Incarceration describes a hernia that cannot be reduced and has impaired circulation, which is a medical emergency. Surgical correction is usually an outpatient procedure, and nursing management involves discharge teaching, pain control, and wound care.

7. Testicular torsion is an emergency condition in which the testis suddenly rotates on its spermatic cord, cutting off its blood supply. Surgery must be done within 4 to 6 hours in order to restore blood supply to the testis. Since the child often goes home within a few hours of the surgery, nursing care is focused on discharge teaching.

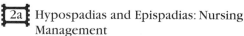

2a Hypospadias and Epispadias: Nursing Management
- Pre-op: Circumcision is contraindicated
- Post-op:
  - May be day surgery procedure, or may be admitted
  - Pain management
  - Monitor urine output
  - Stent may be present to maintain urethral patency—monitor urine output and stent patency and prevent child from removing stent

3 Obstructive Uropathies
- Congenital anomalies that interfere with urine flow
- All result in hydronephrosis and eventually chronic renal failure
  - Ureteropelvic junction (UPJ) obstruction
  - Posterior urethral valves (PUVs)
  - Prune-belly syndrome

3a Obstructive Uropathies
- ("Pathophysiology Illustrated: Obstruction Sites in the Urinary System")

3b Obstructive Uropathies: Post-op Nursing Management
- Monitor intake and output
- Observe for signs of urinary retention
- Monitor any stents or catheters for patency
- Dressing changes/wound care

4 Phimosis
- Definition
- Management involves teaching regarding treatments
- Medical: Betamethasone cream
- Surgical: Circumcision

5 Cryptorchidism
- Definition
- Risk of testicular cancer increased
- Treatment is surgical correction (orchiopexy)
  - Usually discharged on day of surgery
  - Nursing care involves pain control and discharge teaching

6 Inguinal Hernia
- Definition
- Risk of incarceration
- Post-op nursing care:
  - Pain management
  - Wound care
  - Discharge teaching

7 Testicular Torsion
- Definition
- Medical emergency: 4 to 6 hour window to restore blood flow to testis
- Usually discharged home within hours after surgery
- Discharge teaching
  - Pain management
  - Wound/incision care
  - Avoid heavy lifting

SUGGESTIONS FOR CLASSROOM ACTIVITIES

- After discussing phimosis, show the video "Circumcision" on the Student CD-ROM. The video discusses the purpose of circumcision, as well as cultural and geographic variations in the practice. After viewing the video, have students discuss factors that families might consider in deciding whether or not to circumcise a newborn baby boy.
- Ask students to pretend that they are working in a clinic when a 12-year-old boy arrives vomiting and with abdominal pain. During his intake interview, he reveals to the nurse that he is also having pain "down there." The pain started about 4 or 5 hours ago, but he was too embarrassed to tell his mother. The nurse suspects that he may have testicular torsion. Have students role-play how they would deal with this client. Key points include providing privacy during the examination, thorough assessment, and urgent referral to the emergency department. The client may have questions about fertility and the surgical procedure to correct testicular torsion that can be worked into the scenario.

SUGGESTIONS FOR CLINICAL ACTIVITIES

When a student is caring for a patient who has had urological surgery, have the student draw the urinary system before and after the surgery. Include any drains, stents, or catheters that are present. Discuss the purpose of each of these tubes, as well as the expected output from each tube. Many students are visual learners, and drawing this "map" of their client can increase their understanding of both the pathophysiology and the treatment.

LEARNING OBJECTIVE 3

Develop a nursing care plan for the child with a urinary tract infection.

CONCEPTS FOR LECTURE

1. Urinary tract infections (UTIs) can either be acute or chronic and can occur anywhere along the urinary tract. This includes the upper urinary tract (pyelonephritis involving the kidneys and ureters) and lower urinary tract (cystitis involving the bladder and/or urethra).
2. UTIs are very common in children. Males have higher rates of structural defects of the urinary tract, leading to higher rates in males versus females during the newborn and infancy stage. Girls have higher rates after infancy due to the shorter female urethra and its proximity to the anus, which increases exposure to fecal bacteria.

POWERPOINT LECTURE SLIDES

1 Nursing Care Plan Development
- Urinary tract infections (UTIs)
  - Acute
  - Chronic

2 Assessment
- Physiologic
- Psychosocial

3 Diagnosis
- Impaired urinary elimination
- Risk for disproportionate growth
- Urinary retention
- Ineffective therapeutic regimen management
- Risk for deficient fluid volume

CONCEPTS FOR LECTURE *continued*

3. Most UTIs are caused by *E.coli*, especially if this is the child's first UTI. Other causative agents are possible.

4. Symptoms of UTI in newborns are nonspecific, including fever, failure to thrive, poor feeding, vomiting and diarrhea, strong-smelling urine, and irritability. After the toddler years, symptoms of UTIs are similar to those of adults. About 40% of UTIs are asymptomatic. *Refer to "Teaching Highlights: Prevention of Urinary Track Infections."*

5. Antibiotics are the treatment of choice. Follow-up cultures should be sterile and may be monitored up to one year.

POWERPOINT LECTURE SLIDES *continued*

4 Planning and Implementation
  - Administering medications
  - Rehydration
  - Monitoring renal function
  - Teaching: Prevention of future UTIs

5 Evaluation
  - Expected outcomes
    ◦ Child increases fluid intake and number of times voiding each day.
    ◦ Future UTIs are prevented

SUGGESTIONS FOR CLASSROOM ACTIVITIES

Divide students into groups of 4 to 6 and have each group develop the nursing care plan for a child with a UTI. Have them write their answers on an overhead transparency. Compare the various care plans and discuss differences among the various groups. In addition to correcting errors or omissions, this activity allows students to see the variations in how nursing care is prioritized.

SUGGESTIONS FOR CLINICAL ACTIVITIES

Discuss various methods for obtaining urine specimens in children of different ages (infants, toddlers, school age, adolescents). Encourage students to review "Skill 16-1: Performing a Urinary Catheterization" on the Student CD-ROM and in the Clinical Skills Manual. Discuss the differences in catheterizing children versus adults.

LEARNING OBJECTIVE 4

Describe the growth and developmental issues for the child with chronic renal failure.

CONCEPTS FOR LECTURE

1. Children with chronic renal failure often have delayed physical growth and maturation due to the effects of uremia on hormones. Puberty is often delayed.

2. While chronic renal failure in and of itself is not associated with developmental delays, children with the disease may have difficulty with social adjustment and success in school. Screening the younger child with appropriate developmental screening tests, such as the Denver II, should be a part of the child's assessment.

3. Chronic renal failure presents many challenges for the child and family, including coping with altered body image, short stature, delayed onset of puberty, and possible physical side effects of medications. If the child is receiving hemodialysis, he or she may miss significant time in school.

POWERPOINT LECTURE SLIDES

1 Chronic Renal Failure: Effects on Growth
  - Growth often delayed
  - Puberty often delayed
  - Uremic environment affects hormones

2 Developmental Concerns
  - Screen with Denver II
  - May have difficulty with social coping, success in school

3 Psychosocial Challenges
  - Altered body image
    ◦ Short stature
    ◦ Delayed onset of puberty
    ◦ Possible side effects of medication
    ◦ Being "different" from peers (presence of catheter, special diet, etc.)
    ◦ Restrictions on physical activity

3a Challenges with Schooling
  - May miss school often, especially if on hemodialysis
  - Uremia decreases cognition and affects ability to concentrate
  - Strategies
    ◦ Encourage promotion in age-appropriate activities

- ○ Attendance at school is important—may need alternative schooling arrangements
- ○ Promote child's self-worth and self-esteem
- ○ Adolescents: Slowly move towards greater self-care

SUGGESTIONS FOR CLASSROOM ACTIVITIES

- Invite a family who has a child with chronic renal failure to attend your class. Have students prepare one or two questions to ask the family. Allow the parents and the child (if age is appropriate) to share the child's story regarding renal failure and dialysis. The family will likely discuss many of the concepts in this objective.
- Divide students into groups of 4 to 6 people. Have each group read "Evidence-Based Nursing: Living with End-Stage Renal Disease," then have each group list three things they would consider in the future when working with children and families coping with ESRD.

SUGGESTIONS FOR CLINICAL ACTIVITIES

When taking care of a child or adolescent with chronic renal failure, discuss the concept of nonadherence with the student. Novice students often assume that all clients adhere to the prescribed treatment, and students may become judgmental when this does not occur. If nonadherence was the reason for admission (e.g., missed dialysis treatments, not taking medications, etc.), discuss strategies that the nurse can use to improve adherence.

LEARNING OBJECTIVE 5

Outline a plan to meet the fluid and dietary restrictions of a child with a renal disorder.

CONCEPTS FOR LECTURE

1. The type of diet prescribed for the child depends on the pathophysiology of the renal disorder.
2. Growth in children with renal disorders is important, and most diets include high amounts of calories and protein. The protein intake must be balanced with the azotemia, as BUN and creatinine will rise with high protein intake.
3. In the presence of renal failure, sodium, potassium, and phosphorus are often restricted. Normal, healthy kidneys control sodium balance through fluid balance, and remove excess potassium and phosphorus from the body through the urine. During renal failure, these three electrolytes tend to accumulate.
4. The renal dietitian is a powerful ally for the nurse who is caring for a child with a renal disorder.

POWERPOINT LECTURE SLIDES

1 Fluid and Dietary Restrictions for Renal Disorders
- Type of diet depends on the pathophysiology of the disease

1a Nephrotic Syndrome
- Diet: Normal—protein loss will be replaced by IV albumin
- "No added salt" during corticosteroid treatment—total body sodium is elevated
- Fluid intake: Normal unless edema is severe

1b Hemolytic-Uremic Syndrome (HUS)
- Diet: High-calorie, high-carbohydrate
  - ○ Protein may be restricted
  - ○ Sodium, potassium, phosphorus restricted
- Fluids: Restricted

1c Acute Postinfectious Glomerulonephritis (APIGN)
- Diet
  - ○ Protein: Restricted if azotemia is severe
  - ○ Electrolytes: Sodium, potassium may be restricted
- Fluids: Degree of edema determines fluid restriction

2 Acute Renal Failure (ARF)
- Diet
  - ○ Protein: Increased due to high metabolic rate during ARF

○ Electrolytes: Sodium, potassium, phosphorus may be restricted
- Fluids: Restricted during oliguria—may need adjustment based on weight, serum sodium levels, fever, and urine output

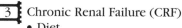 Chronic Renal Failure (CRF)
- Diet
  ○ Children must continue to grow, which requires protein and carbohydrates—protein intake, growth, and weight are carefully monitored, especially in infants and young children
  ○ Electrolytes: Sodium, potassium, phosphorus may be restricted
- Fluids: May be restricted, depending on weight, presence of urine output, and type of dialysis child receives

Strategies
- Foods may be supplemented to increase protein, calories
- If the child cannot take in enough calories by mouth, options include
  ○ Nasogastric tube and feedings
  ○ Gastrostomy tube and feedings
  ○ Parenteral nutrition
- Renal dietitian is key

SUGGESTIONS FOR CLASSROOM ACTIVITIES

Divide students into groups of 4 to 6 people. Ask them to make a list of the foods they ate the day before. Have them refer to Table 52.7. Have them cross through any foods that they could not eat if they were on a diet that restricted sodium, potassium, and phosphorus. Students will discover that the electrolyte-restricted diet is very bland and extremely difficult to follow. This can give them insight into the challenges these clients face.

SUGGESTIONS FOR CLINICAL ACTIVITIES

Have students explore the clinical setting for resources regarding the renal diet. For example, if they had a patient who was on a low-sodium, low-potassium, and low-phosphorus diet, how would they evaluate the food tray before taking it into the patient's room? Resources regarding foods high in these electrolytes can be found in many places in the clinical setting: textbooks, client education materials, the dietary office, the World Wide Web, and the dialysis clinic.

LEARNING OBJECTIVE 6

Develop a nursing care plan for the child with acute and chronic renal failure on dialysis.

CONCEPTS FOR LECTURE

1. Although there are differences, acute and chronic renal failure have many parallels regarding nursing care.

POWERPOINT LECTURE SLIDES

 Assessment
- ("Clinical Manifestations: Acute versus Chronic Renal Failure")

Diagnosis: ARF
- Ineffective renal tissue perfusion
- Excess fluid volume
- Imbalanced nutrition: Less than body requirements

- Risk for infection
- Compromised family coping

[1b] Diagnosis: CRF
- Delayed growth and development
- Impaired social interaction
- Activity intolerance
- Ineffective therapeutic regimen management
- Disturbed body image

[1c] Planning and Implementation
- Prevent complications
- Maintain fluid balance
- Administer medications
- Meet nutritional needs
- Prevent infection
- Provide emotional support
- Discharge planning/home care teaching

[1d] Evaluation
- Fluid status, electrolytes, and acid-base status balanced
- Nutritional needs met
- Child acquires no secondary infections

SUGGESTIONS FOR CLASSROOM ACTIVITIES

Ask the students to refer to "Delivering Cultural Competence: Reducing Sodium in the Asian Child's Diet." Identify unique characteristics of the diet of cultures present in your community that may present challenges for the child with renal failure. For example, the Hispanic diet often includes cheese, tomatoes, and beef—all of which could be restricted due to electrolyte content. If time allows, students can then propose alternatives that could be suggested to clients. Assign "Care Plan: A Child with Kidney Failure" activity for homework.

SUGGESTIONS FOR CLINICAL ACTIVITIES

When students are caring for a child with chronic renal failure, ask them to draw a concept map to relate the pathophysiology of the disease with the medications and the labs. For example, students can visually relate the following points: During renal failure, the kidneys do not produce erythropoietin, which leads to anemia. This is treated with synthetic erythropoietin, which is monitored by the hemoglobin and hematocrit, as well as the reticulocyte count. Since chronic renal failure is a disease with complex pathophysiology, multiple medications, and numerous labs, the concept map can help students make connections that might otherwise be overlooked.

LEARNING OBJECTIVE 7

List psychosocial issues for children of different ages who have surgery on the genitourinary system.

CONCEPTS FOR LECTURE

1. Infants who have had genitourinary surgery may have issues with bonding and trust if their basic needs are not met.
2. Toddlers and school-age children who have had genitourinary surgery may not achieve urinary continence. This can lead to issues with self-esteem and self-confidence.

POWERPOINT LECTURE SLIDES

[1] Infants
- Bonding with parents
- Trust learned through basic needs being met
  - Food
  - Bathing
  - Wound care

[2] Toddlers and School-Age Children
- Self-esteem
- Self-confidence

CONCEPTS FOR LECTURE *continued*

3. Adolescents who have had genitourinary surgery may also have issues with self-esteem and self-confidence. They may have difficulty achieving sexual identity and may have concerns about fertility and sexual function. Children who have uncomplicated genitourinary surgery or who have no loss of function or continence are less likely to have psychosocial issues than children who have complicated repairs with residual defects.

POWERPOINT LECTURE SLIDES *continued*

 Adolescents
- Self-esteem
- Self-confidence
- Concerns about sexuality, fertility
- Difficulty achieving sexual identity

SUGGESTIONS FOR CLASSROOM ACTIVITIES

Have students role-play how they would approach children with the preceding psychosocial issues. For infants and toddlers, one student can be the parent and the other can be the nurse. For adolescents, one student can be the adolescent and the other can be the nurse. Teaching points include close attention to body language, asking open-ended questions, and developing a trusting therapeutic relationship.

SUGGESTIONS FOR CLINICAL ACTIVITIES

Have students consult with a child life specialist in the clinical setting. Ask the student to make a list of three strategies for dealing with psychosocial issues in each age group. These can be shared during clinical conference.

CHAPTER 53
THE CHILD WITH ALTERATIONS IN NEUROLOGIC FUNCTION

RESOURCE LIBRARY

 CD-ROM

Animations
   3-D Brain and Brainstem
   Coup-contrecoup Injury
   Diazepam
Videos:
   Seizure Disorders
   Living with Spina Bifida
Skill 9-5: Head Circumference
Skill 14–2: Oxygen Saturation: Pulse Oximetry
Skill 15–2: Inserting and Removing a Nasogastric Tube
Audio Glossary
NCLEX-RN® Review

 COMPANION WEBSITE

Complementary Care: Music Therapy for Special
   Needs Children
Thinking Critically
Case Study: Post-Concussion for Return to
   Competitive Play
Critical Thinking: Traumatic Brain Injury Death
   Prevention
NCLEX-RN® Review
Case Study

📖 IMAGE LIBRARY

Figure 53.1 Transverse section of the brain and spinal cord.

Figure 53.2 A, Decorticate posturing, characterized by rigid flexion, is associated with lesions above the brainstem in the corticospinal tracts. B, Decerebrate posturing, distinguished by rigid extension, is associated with lesions of the brainstem.

Figure 53.3 Pupil findings in various neurologic conditions with altered consciousness.

Figure 53.4 A child who has a seizure when standing should be gently assisted to the floor and placed in a side-lying position.

Figure 53.5 The child with bacterial meningitis assumes an opisthotonic position, with the neck and the head hyperextended, to relieve discomfort.

Figure 53.6 To test for Kernig sign, raise the child's leg with the knee flexed.

Figure 53.7 To test for Brudzinski sign, flex the child's head while in a supine position.

Figure 53.8 In communicating hydrocephalus, an excessive amount of cerebrospinal fluid accumulates in the subarachnoid space, producing the characteristic head enlargement seen here.

Figure 53.9 A ventriculoperitoneal shunt, commonly used to treat children with hydrocephalus, is usually placed at 3 to 4 months of age.

Figure 53.10 Lumbosacral myelomeningocele is caused by a neural tube defect that results in incomplete closure of the vertebral column.

Figure 53.11 Help determine the best assistive device for the child to gain the most independence for mobilizing and to promote development.

Figure 53.12 In craniosynostosis, the head shape is dependent upon which sutures are involved.

Figure 53.13 A child having a baclofen pump filled.

Figure 53.14 A child with cerebral palsy has abnormal muscle tone and lack of physical coordination.

Figure 53.15 Mechanics of injury to the spinal cord.

Figure 53.16 Splints are often used to prevent contractures, thus maintaining optimal functioning of the child's hands or feet.

Table 53.1 Summary of Anatomic and Physiologic Differences Between Children and Adults

Table 53.3 Glasgow Coma Scale for Assessment of Coma in Infants and Children

Table 53.6 Anticonvulsants Used to Treat Seizure Disorders

Table 53.7 Stages of Reye Syndrome

Growth and Development: Cues in the Glasgow Coma Scale Assessment

LEARNING OBJECTIVE 1

Describe the anatomy and physiology of the neurologic system.

CONCEPTS FOR LECTURE

1. The basic structures of the neurologic system are the brain, spinal cord, and the nerves. Due to anatomic differences, children are at risk for different injuries to the central nervous system than adults.
2. The nervous system is immature at birth, and continues to develop during the first 4 years of life.

POWERPOINT LECTURE SLIDES

1 Basic Structures of the Neurologic System
- Brain
- Spinal cord
- Nerves

1a Transverse Section of the Brain and Spinal Cord
- (Figure. 53.1)

1b Summary of Anatomic and Physiologic Differences Between Children and Adults
- (Table 53.1)

2 Developmental Considerations
- Nervous system complete but immature at birth
- Infant born with all nerves he or she will have
- Myelination of nerves incomplete until age 4
- Development proceeds in cephalocaudal direction

SUGGESTIONS FOR CLASSROOM ACTIVITIES

While discussing the anatomy of the nervous system, use the animation "3-D Brain and Brainstem" available on the Student CD-ROM

SUGGESTIONS FOR CLINICAL ACTIVITIES

While in the clinical setting, locate CAT scans of the head. Identify anatomic structures that are visible on the CAT scans.

LEARNING OBJECTIVE 2

Describe the nursing assessment process and tools used for infants and children with altered levels of consciousness and other neurologic conditions.

CONCEPTS FOR LECTURE

1. Level of consciousness (LOC) is one of the most important indicators of neurologic dysfunction. It is important to understand the differences in the terms used to describe LOC.
2. Decline of a child's LOC follows a sequential pattern of deterioration. Close assessment and monitoring helps detect changes in the child's status. The Glasgow Coma Scale (GCS) is a tool that aims to quantify the child's LOC.

POWERPOINT LECTURE SLIDES

1 Level of Consciousness (LOC)
- Most important indicator of neurologic dysfunction
- Describing LOC
  - Conscious versus unconscious
  - Alertness: Ability to react to stimuli
  - Cognitive power: Processing of data

1a Levels of LOC
- Confusion
- Delirium
- Obtunded
- Stupor
- Coma

Causes of Altered LOC
- Trauma and/or injury
- Hypoxia
- Infection
- Poisoning
- Seizures
- Endocrine or metabolic disturbances
- Electrolyte or acid-bases imbalance
- Congenital structural defect

 Assessment of LOC: Monitoring
- Responsiveness to environment or stimuli
- Pupil size and reactivity
- Movement of extremities
- Ability to maintain an airway
- Changes in vital signs
- Changes in breathing patterns
- Status of the cranial nerves

 Deterioration of LOC: A Sequential Pattern
- Awake and alert—responds appropriately
- Slight disorientation to time, place, or person
- Restless, fussy, or irritable
- Drowsy but responds to loud commands, painful stimuli
- Nonpurposeful response
- Posturing
- No response

 Tools to Quantify LOC: Glasgow Coma Scale (GCS)
- Allows for comparison and tracking of LOC
- Pediatric criteria take into account child's developmental age

 Glasgow Coma Scale for Assessment of Coma in Infants and Children
- (Table 53.3)

GCS: Developmental Considerations
- ("Growth and Development: Cues in the Glasgow Coma Scale Assessment")

SUGGESTIONS FOR CLASSROOM ACTIVITIES

Have a student volunteer to act out the changes that a child goes through as LOC decreases.

SUGGESTIONS FOR CLINICAL ACTIVITIES

Have students practice assessing LOC using the Glasgow Coma Scale on children of various ages.

LEARNING OBJECTIVE 3

Differentiate between the signs of infants and children with epilepsy and status epilepticus, and describe appropriate nursing management for each condition.

CONCEPTS FOR LECTURE

1. Children may have a wide variety of seizures, although the most common type is tonic-clonic seizures. *Refer to "Clinical Manifestations: Seizures" for details.*
2. The main distinguishing factor between epilepsy and status epilepticus is the length of the seizure.
3. The basic nursing interventions for epilepsy and status epilepticus are similar and are focused on stopping the seizure and keeping the child safe. Children with status epilepticus will require more aggressive measures to stop their seizures, and may need airway management as well.

POWERPOINT LECTURE SLIDES

1 Type of Seizures in Children
- Partial seizures
  - Complex
  - Simple
- Tonic-clonic (most common)
- Absence
- Myoclonic
- Infantile spasms
- Akinetic and/or atonic seizures

2 Epilepsy versus Status Epilepticus
- Epilepsy—seizure lasts seconds to minutes
- Status epilepticus
  - Seizure lasts more than 30 minutes
  - Or, series of small seizures during which consciousness is not regained

3 Nursing Interventions for All Seizures
- History
- Details of seizure
  - Onset, length
  - Aura
  - Loss of consciousness
- Seizure may be brief, self-limiting
- Protect child from harming self

3a Anticonvulsants Used to Treat Seizure Disorders
- (Table 53.6)

3b Interventions for Status Epilepticus
- Airway management
- Suction excess secretions
- Administer oxygen
- Monitor vital signs and neurologic status
- Establish intravenous access
- If hypoglycemic, administer glucose
- Additional medications

3c Long-Term Management of Seizures
- Most are treated with monotherapy medication—successful in 60% to 70% of children
- Ketogenic diet
- Family teaching
  - Management of seizure at home, school
  - Blood levels may be needed to monitor anticonvulsant dosing

In order to introduce the topic of seizures, show the video "Seizure Disorders," available on the Student CD-ROM, at the beginning of this objective.

SUGGESTIONS FOR CLINICAL ACTIVITIES

When students are caring for children with seizure disorders, discuss the concept of "seizure precautions," as well as the rationale for the required equipment that is at the child's bedside. Review initial interventions the student should begin if the child has a seizure.

LEARNING OBJECTIVE 4

Differentiate between signs of bacterial meningitis, viral meningitis, encephalitis, Reye syndrome, and Guillain-Barré syndrome in infants and children.

CONCEPTS FOR LECTURE

1. Bacterial meningitis is characterized by fever, lethargy, vomiting, headache, and nuchal rigidity. Children with meningococcal meningitis also have a hemorrhagic rash.
2. The symptoms of viral meningitis are similar to those of bacterial meningitis. Viral meningitis is less severe than bacterial meningitis, and symptoms tend to be less intense.
3. Encephalitis is an inflammation of the brain usually caused by a viral infection. Meningeal irritation may be present in addition to a wide variety of neurologic symptoms.
4. Reye syndrome is an acute encephalopathy that is commonly associated with the use of aspirin and a mild viral infection.
5. Guillain-Barré syndrome is characterized by deteriorating motor function and paralysis that progresses in an ascending pattern.

POWERPOINT LECTURE SLIDES

1 Bacterial Meningitis
- Inflammation of the meninges
- Newborns and infants at greatest risk
- Higher morbidity and mortality than viral meningitis
- Common bacterial causes
  - *Haemophilus influenzae* type B
  - *Neisseria meningitides*
  - *Streptococcus pneumoniae*
  - Group B *Streptococcus*

1a Bacterial Meningitis: Signs and Symptoms (Infants)
- Fever
- Changes in feeding pattern
- Vomiting, diarrhea
- Anterior fontanelle bulging or flat
- Alert, restless, lethargic, or irritable
- Difficult to console

1b Bacterial Meningitis: Signs and Symptoms (Children)
- Fever
- Confusion, delirium, irritable, lethargic
- Vomiting
- Muscle or joint pain
- Hemorrhagic rash (meningococcal meningitis)
- Meningeal irritation
  - Headache
  - Photophobia
  - Nuchal rigidity

1c Opisthotonic Position
- (Figure 53.5)

1d Testing for Kernig Sign
- (Figure 53.6)

1e Testing for Brudzinski Sign
- (Figure 53.7)

Progression of Symptoms
- Seizures
- Apnea
- Cerebral edema
- Subdural effusion
- Hydrocephalus
- Disseminated intravascular coagulation (DIC)
- Shock
- Increased intracranial pressure

 Bacterial Meningitis: Treatment
- Labs and cultures (blood, urine, cerebrospinal fluid)
- Intravenous antibiotics
- Steroids, anticonvulsants, antipyretics
- IV fluids, fluid resuscitation
- May be left with severe neurologic deficits

 Viral (Aseptic) Meningitis
- Inflammatory response of meninges
- Most common cause: Enterovirus
- Child not as ill-appearing as child with bacterial meningitis

 Viral Meningitis: Signs and Symptoms
- Irritable or lethargic—general malaise
- Fever
- Headache
- Photophobia
- Upper respiratory symptoms
- Positive Kernig and Brudzinski signs—indicate meningeal irritation
- Seizures are rare

 Viral Meningitis: Treatment
- Labs and cultures (blood, urine, cerebrospinal fluid)
- Intravenous antibiotics until cultures are negative—treat as bacterial meningitis until proven otherwise
- Treatment of symptoms is supportive
- Symptoms usually resolve in 3 to 10 days
- Neurologic deficits are uncommon

 Encephalitis
- Inflammation of the brain
- Meninges may be inflamed as well
- Viruses most common cause (herpes simplex type 1)

Encephalitis: Signs and Symptoms
- Depend on causative organism
- Classic presentation:
  - Acute onset of febrile illness
  - Neurologic signs (disoriented, confused)
  - Severe headache, nausea, vomiting
  - Meningeal signs
  - Seizures

3b Encephalitis: Treatment
- Diagnosis by history, lab findings
- Acyclovir (for herpes infections)
- Supportive care
- Many children left with severe neurologic deficits

4 Reye Syndrome
- Acute encephalopathy
- Associated with use of aspirin and a mild viral illness
- With decreased aspirin use, condition is now rare
- Condition develops over five stages

4a Stages of Reye Syndrome
- (Table 53.7)

4b Reye Syndrome: Treatment
- Diagnosis by history, lab findings
- Treatment is supportive
- Often require treatment for increased intracranial pressure
- Mortality is high

5 Guillain-Barré Syndrome
- Acute inflammatory demyelinating polyneuropathy
- Motor function deteriorates, causing paralysis
- Ascending pattern (legs to head)
- Cause: Autoimmune response to infectious organism

5a Guillain-Barré Syndrome: Signs and Symptoms
- History of infectious illness about 10 days prior to onset of symptoms
- Infants: Severe hypotonia, respiratory distress, poor feeding
- Children
  - Progressive symmetric weakness
  - Legs to upper extremities, head
  - Difficulty swallowing
  - Respiratory failure

5b Guillain-Barré Syndrome: Treatment
- Supportive care for respiratory failure
- Intravenous immunoglobulin (IVIG)
- Plasmapheresis
- Condition is rarely fatal

SUGGESTIONS FOR CLASSROOM ACTIVITIES

To help students differentiate between these disease processes, create case studies of children that display the common signs and symptoms of each disease process and have students determine which disease the child has based on the signs and symptoms you describe.

SUGGESTIONS FOR CLINICAL ACTIVITIES

Lumbar punctures are commonly used with these disorders as a part of the diagnostic workup. Review the nurse's role in assisting with the lumbar puncture and discuss positioning of the child after the procedure is completed. If possible, have students assist with lumbar punctures.

LEARNING OBJECTIVE 5

Describe the nursing care for the child with myelodysplasia and hydrocephalus.

CONCEPTS FOR LECTURE

1. Pre-op nursing care for children with myelodysplasia is focused on protecting the meningocele, while post-op care is focused on monitoring for signs of infection, hydrocephalus, and increased intracranial pressure.
2. Nursing care for the child with hydrocephalus includes positioning, and monitoring for signs of shunt malfunction, infection, and increased intracranial pressure.

POWERPOINT LECTURE SLIDES

- **[1]** Myelodysplasia: Pre-op Nursing Care
  - Cover sac with sterile dressing (warm saline)
  - Monitor for CSF leakage
  - Place infant in prone position with knees slightly flexed
  - Assess bowel, bladder function
  - Monitor for signs of infection
  - Feed with head turned to one side
  - Avoid latex products

- **[1a]** Myelodysplasia: Post-op Nursing Care
  - Monitor for wound healing
  - Monitor for signs of infection
  - Monitor for signs of hydrocephalus, increased ICP
  - Place in prone or side-lying position
  - Measure head circumference daily
  - Assess intake and output
  - Avoid latex products

- **[2]** Hydrocephalus: Nursing Care
  - Measure head circumference daily
  - Observe for signs of increased ICP
  - Neurologic assessment
  - Signs of shunt malfunction
  - Positioning: Usually supine—head of bed is raised gradually

- **[2a]** General Nursing Care: Reminders
  - Provide emotional support to child, parents
  - Teaching about medications
  - Teaching about signs of shunt malfunction

SUGGESTIONS FOR CLASSROOM ACTIVITIES

At the beginning of this objective, show the video "Living with Spina Bifida," available on the Student CD-ROM, as a way to introduce this disorder.

SUGGESTIONS FOR CLINICAL ACTIVITIES

Assign students to observe in the operating room to observe a myelomeningocele repair or a shunt insertion/revision.

LEARNING OBJECTIVE 6

Describe the focus of community-based nursing care for the child with cerebral palsy.

CONCEPTS FOR LECTURE

1. Cerebral palsy is commonly caused by congenital, hypoxic, ischemic, or infectious insults to the central nervous system. Very premature infants are at high risk for developing cerebral palsy.
2. Nurses in the community play a critical role in coordinating care for the child with cerebral palsy.

POWERPOINT LECTURE SLIDES

- **[1]** Cerebral Palsy (CP): Background Information
  - Cerebral palsy caused by insult to central nervous system
    - Congenital
    - Hypoxic
    - Ischemic
    - Infectious
  - Very premature infants at high risk
  - Birth asphyxia accounts for only 9% of cases

POWERPOINT LECTURE SLIDES *continued*

2 Nurses in the Community: Care of the Child with CP
- Continuous support
- Coordination of care—referrals
- Working with schools to individualize education plan
- Adaptive devices
- Transition to adult living

SUGGESTIONS FOR CLASSROOM ACTIVITIES	SUGGESTIONS FOR CLINICAL ACTIVITIES
Invite a family who has a child with cerebral palsy to speak to the class about how nurses can provide optimal care for these children in the community setting.	If there are facilities that care for children with cerebral palsy in the community, assign students to observe nurses working in the facility.

LEARNING OBJECTIVE 7

Distinguish between the assessment findings of the child with a mild, moderate, or severe traumatic brain injury.

CONCEPTS FOR LECTURE

1. Brain injury can be classified into three categories: mild, moderate, and severe. Assessment findings differ among these three groups. *"Clinical Manifestations: Clinical Manifestations of Traumatic Brain Injury by Severity" is the primary reference for this objective.*

POWERPOINT LECTURE SLIDES

1 Classification of Brain Injury
- Mild
- Moderate
- Severe

1a Assessment Findings: Mild Brain Injury
- No loss (or very brief loss) of consciousness
- Mild headache that will not go away with medications
- Memory problems
- Fatigue and irritability
- Change in appetite
- Changes in school performance
- Sensitivity to lights and sounds

1b Assessment Findings: Moderate Brain Injury
- Glasgow Coma Scale: 9 to 12
- Loss of consciousness
- Headache
- Nausea and vomiting
- Amnesia for 1 to 24 hours

1c Assessment Findings: Severe Brain Injury
- Glasgow Coma Scale: less than 8
- Amnesia for more than 24 hours
- Signs of increased ICP
- Prolonged period of unconsciousness

SUGGESTIONS FOR CLASSROOM ACTIVITIES	SUGGESTIONS FOR CLINICAL ACTIVITIES
The signs and symptoms of brain injury are directly related to the mechanism of injury. To illustrate this concept, use the animation "Coup-contracoup Injury" available on the Student CD-ROM.	Visit the radiology department to locate CAT scans of children with head injuries of varying severity. What radiographic abnormalities are present in each type of head injury?

LEARNING OBJECTIVE 8

Contrast the appropriate initial nursing management for mild and severe traumatic brain injury.

CONCEPTS FOR LECTURE

1. Nursing management of mild brain injury involves monitoring level of consciousness and instructing parents on home monitoring parameters.
2. Nursing management of severe brain injury includes stabilization of vital signs, frequent monitoring, administering medications, and supporting the family.

POWERPOINT LECTURE SLIDES

1 Nursing Management: Mild Brain Injury
- Monitor level of consciousness
- Signs of increased ICP
- Home teaching
- Restrictions on activities
- May take 6 weeks for full healing—may affect school performance

2 Nursing Management: Severe Brain Injury
- Airway, breathing, and circulation; hyperventilation—prolonged use causes cerebral ischemia
- Assess neurologic status frequently
- Elevate head of bed 30 degrees if no neck injury present
- Keep head midline to promote venous drainage
- Minimal stimulation
- Monitor vital signs, intake and output, and intracranial pressure
- Skin care, range of motion

2a Medications Common with Severe Brain Injury
- Diuretics (furosemide, mannitol)
- Ophthalmic lubricants to protect cornea
- Stool softeners
- Sedatives, paralytics if needed

2b Other Interventions
- Support family
- Coordination of care
- Planning for discharge or rehabilitation
- Prevention of injuries

SUGGESTIONS FOR CLASSROOM ACTIVITIES

Before class, assign students to complete the exercise "Critical Thinking: Traumatic Brain Injury Death Prevention," available on the Companion Website. Use this activity to frame the discussion about prevention of brain injuries. Assign "Case Study: Post-Concussion for Return to Competitive Play" activity on the Companion Website for homework.

SUGGESTIONS FOR CLINICAL ACTIVITIES

Assign students to observe or care for clients in the pediatric ICU, where many children with severe brain injury are cared for. In addition, consider assigning students to a pediatric rehabilitation hospital in order to see the long-term care required for many of these children.

CHAPTER 54
THE CHILD WITH ALTERATIONS IN COGNITIVE AND MENTAL HEALTH FUNCTION

RESOURCE LIBRARY

 CD-ROM

Videos:
  ADD/ADHD
  Down Syndrome
Audio Glossary
NCLEX-RN® Review

 COMPANION WEBSITE

Thinking Critically
Case Study: Calculating SSRI Dosage
Critical Thinking: Females and Post-traumatic
  Stress Disorder
Nursing Practice: Putting National Mental Health
  Goals into Community Practice
MediaLink Applications:
  Help Families to Evaluate Mental Health
    Information on the Internet
NCLEX-RN® Review
Case Study

IMAGE LIBRARY

Figure 54.1 "Me."
Figure 54.2 "Self-Portrait."
Figure 54.3 "An Activity."
Figure 54.4 "A Family Activity."
Figure 53.3. This drawing depicts a recurring incident of physical and emotional abuse by his mother's live-in boyfriend.
Figure 54.5 This child with autism sits stiffly in the chair and engages in rhythmic rocking behavior.
Figure 54.6 The psychologist uses play therapy to help Cassandra reenact her car crash.

Figure 54.7 This nurse conducts a group therapy session for children who have experienced traumatic events and have resulting anxiety disorders.
Figure 54.8 Physical therapy is an important component of medical management for many children who are mentally retarded.

Clinical Manifestations: Various Learning Disabilities

LEARNING OBJECTIVE 1

Define mental health and describe major mental health disruptions in childhood.

CONCEPTS FOR LECTURE

1. Mental health is foundational to a sense of personal well-being. It involves the successful engagement in activities and relationships and the ability to adapt to and cope with change.
2. The major mental health disruptions in childhood include pervasive developmental disorders, attention deficit and attention deficit hyperactivity disorder, mood disorders, anxiety disorders, tic disorders, and schizophrenia.

POWERPOINT LECTURE SLIDES

1 Mental Health
   • What is it?
   • Children often don't receive mental health services early—leads to increased rates of hospitalizations
   • National Goals for Mental Health

2 Mental Health Disorders in Childhood
   • Pervasive developmental disorders
   • Attention deficit and attention deficit hyperactivity disorders (ADD and ADHD)

- Mood disorders
- Anxiety disorders
- Tic disorders
- Schizophrenia

 Pervasive Developmental Disorders
- Begin in early childhood
- Affect 12% to 16% of children
- Impaired social interactions and communication
- Restricted interests, activities, and behaviors
- Includes autism, Asperger syndrome

 ADD/ADHD
- Affects 4% to 12% of children, boys more than girls
- Can affect adolescents and adults
- Central nervous system processing is altered
- Inappropriate behaviors involving attention

 Mood Disorders
- Depression
  - Only recently recognized in children
  - Affects 2% of children before puberty
  - Affects 4% to 8% of adolescents
- Bipolar disorder
  - Extreme changes in mood
  - Affects about 1% of children
  - Average age of onset: 11 years

 Anxiety Disorders
- Large group of disorders
- Characterized by feelings of worry and uncertainty
- Generalized anxiety disorder
- Separation anxiety disorder
- Panic disorder
- Obsessive-compulsive disorder
- School phobia
- Post-traumatic stress disorder
- Others

 Tic Disorders
- Sudden, rapid, recurrent, nonrhythmic, brief motor movements or vocalizations
- Worsen during stress or tiredness
- Range from mild to severe

 Schizophrenia
- Relatively rare in children
- Prevalence increases after puberty

SUGGESTIONS FOR CLASSROOM ACTIVITIES

- Before class, assign students to complete the "Media-Link Applications: Nursing Practice—Putting National Mental Health Goals into Community Practice" activity located on the Companion Website. Use this information as a background for discussing mental health initiatives during childhood.
- Show the video, "ADD/ADHD," located on the Student CD-ROM as an introduction to the topic.

SUGGESTIONS FOR CLINICAL ACTIVITIES

Assign students to observe in the mental health or psychiatric unit of the hospital in order to observe pediatric patients with these disease processes.

LEARNING OBJECTIVE 2

Discuss the clinical manifestations of the major mental health disorders of childhood and adolescence.

CONCEPTS FOR LECTURE

1. The clinical manifestations of major mental health disorders of childhood vary by disease. Most of these disorders have a range of symptoms from mild to severe.

POWERPOINT LECTURE SLIDES

1 Clinical Manifestations: Pervasive Developmental Disorders
- Impaired social interaction and communication
- Restricted interests, social activities, and behaviors
- Usually apparent by age 3
- Rigid, obsessive behavior

1a Clinical Manifestations: ADD/ADHD
- Decreased attention span
- Impulsiveness
- Increased motor activity
- Difficulty completing tasks
- May be shunned or teased by other children

1b Clinical Manifestations: Mood Disorders
- Declining school performance
- Withdrawal from social activities
- Appetite and sleep disturbances
- Somatic complaints (headaches)
- Decreased energy levels
- Sadness, hopelessness

1c Clinical Manifestations: Anxiety Disorders
- Restlessness
- Poor concentration
- Irritability
- Sleep disturbances
- Uneasiness in unfamiliar surroundings
- Ritualistic thoughts and actions

1d Clinical Manifestations: Tic Disorders
- Brief motor movements or vocalizations that are
  - Sudden
  - Rapid
  - Nonrhythmic
  - Brief

1e Clinical Manifestations: Schizophrenia
- Social withdrawal
- Impaired social relationships
- Flat affect
- Regression
- Hallucinations

SUGGESTIONS FOR CLASSROOM ACTIVITIES

Act out the clinical manifestations of various mental health conditions, and see if the class can determine which disorder you are depicting. Then, discuss the clinical manifestations in more detail.

SUGGESTIONS FOR CLINICAL ACTIVITIES

Students often find it helpful for the instructor to review terms used to describe mental health conditions objectively in the clinical setting.

LEARNING OBJECTIVE 3

Plan for nursing management of children and adolescents with mental health disruptions in the hospital and community settings.

CONCEPTS FOR LECTURE

1. Overarching nursing management principles can be applied in the management of children with mental health disorders in both the hospital and the community.
2. Each mental health disorder has a unique set of nursing interventions that are helpful in working with children with that disorder.

POWERPOINT LECTURE SLIDES

 1 Overarching Principles: Hospitalized Children
- Assess current level of functioning
- Continue prescribed treatments and medications if possible
- Ensure that dangerous objects are out of reach, and child is directly supervised
- Assess potential for self-harm

1a Overarching Principles: Community Settings
- Conduct ongoing assessment of level of functioning
- Provide individual and group therapy sessions
- Refer families to mental health resources and support groups

 2 Nursing Management: Pervasive Developmental Disorders
- Stabilize environmental stimuli
- Provide supportive care
- Enhance communication
- Maintain safe environment
- Provide anticipatory guidance

 2a Nursing Management: ADD/ADHD
- Administer medications
- Minimize environmental distractions
- Implement behavior management plans
- Provide emotional support
- Promote self-esteem

2b Nursing Management: Mood Disorders
- Administer medications
- Provide supportive care
- Encourage discussion of feelings
- Promote effective coping skill use
- Provide activities to promote social interaction
- Ensure adequate nutritional intake

 2c Nursing Management: Anxiety Disorders
- Initiate behavioral and cognitive therapy
- Conduct group therapy sessions
- Teach relaxation, guided imagery
- Identify resources and funding

 2d Nursing Management: Schizophrenia
- Physical safety
- Administer medications
- Monitor for side effects from medications
- Psychological care

SUGGESTIONS FOR CLASSROOM ACTIVITIES

Many families seek out health information on the Internet; however, information on Websites may or may not be accurate. To encourage students to think about this issue, assign them to "MediaLink Applications: Help Families to Evaluate Mental Health Information on the Internet," located on the Companion Website.

SUGGESTIONS FOR CLINICAL ACTIVITIES

Have students attend an outpatient support group for children and families with the disorders described previously in this chapter.

LEARNING OBJECTIVE 4

Describe characteristics of common cognitive disorders of childhood.

CONCEPTS FOR LECTURE

1. Cognitive disorders can range from behaviors displayed in school to physical signs that are visible at birth. There is a wide array of cognitive disorders ranging from mild to severe. The text focuses on learning disabilities and mental retardation.
2. Learning disabilities are a common problem in childhood, affecting about 5% of schoolchildren. The brain cannot receive or process information in the normal manner, causing difficulty in areas such as reading, writing, math, or understanding oral information. The child's IQ is usually normal.
3. Mental retardation is a significant limitation in intellectual functioning and adaptive behavior. It begins in childhood, and the IQ is usually less than 70 to 75. Common syndromes associated with mental retardation include Down syndrome, fragile X syndrome, and fetal alcohol syndrome.

POWERPOINT LECTURE SLIDES

 1 Cognitive Disorders
- Wide array occur, ranging from mild to severe
- Difficulties in school
- Physical signs visible at birth

 2 Learning Disabilities
- Common in childhood
- Affect about 5% of children
- Brain cannot receive or process information normally
- Can involve reading, writing, math, or understanding oral information
- IQ is usually normal

 2a Types of Learning Disabilities
- ("Clinical Manifestations: Various Learning Disabilities")

Mental Retardation
- Significant limitation in
  - Intellectual functioning
  - Adaptive behavior
- Begins before age 18
- IQ is usually less than 70 to 75

 Syndromes Associated with Mental Retardation
- Down syndrome
- Fragile X syndrome
- Fetal alcohol syndrome

 Down Syndrome
- Incidence: 1 in 1,000 infants
- At risk for cardiac defects, leukemia, hearing loss, thyroid disease
- Clinical manifestations
  - Hypotonia
  - Epicanthial eye folds
  - Simian crease on palm
  - Flat nose
  - Wide, short neck
  - Mental retardation

 Fragile X Syndrome
- Genetic anomaly on X chromosome
- Protein necessary for normal brain development is missing
- Clinical manifestations
  - Long face with prominent jaw and large ears
  - Strabismus
  - Aggressive behaviors
  - Mental retardation

Fetal Alcohol Syndrome
- Caused by effect of alcohol on developing fetus
- Clinical manifestations
  - Failure to thrive
  - Flat midface with low nasal bride
  - Poor coordination
  - Poor impulse control
  - Low normal IQ to mental retardation

 Mental Retardation: General Concepts
- Mild to severe
- IQ is not as important as functional assessment
  - Motor movement
  - Language
  - Adaptive behavior
- Achieve developmental milestones slowly

SUGGESTIONS FOR CLASSROOM ACTIVITIES

Show the video, "Down Syndrome," available on the Student CD-ROM, to illustrate the characteristics of this syndrome during the lecture.

SUGGESTIONS FOR CLINICAL ACTIVITIES

When caring for children with one of the syndromes that is associated with mental retardation, have students practice the concept of the "functional assessment" described previously.

LEARNING OBJECTIVE 5

Plan nursing management for children with cognitive disorders.

CONCEPTS FOR LECTURE

1. Nursing management for children with mental retardation focuses on early screening and detection, referral to intervention and support programs, and partnering with parents during hospitalization.
2. Nursing management for children with learning disabilities focuses on early detection, referral, goal setting, and promotion of self-esteem.

POWERPOINT LECTURE SLIDES

1 Nursing Management of Mental Retardation
- Early detection and screening
  - Developmental milestones
  - Denver II developmental screening test

1a Nursing Management of Mental Retardation
- Provide emotional support and information
  - Loss of perfect child
  - Support groups
  - Honest information
- Maintain safe environment
  - Physical safety
  - Safety with strangers

1b Nursing Management of Mental Retardation
- Promote adaptive functioning
- Allow home routine during hospitalization
  - Self-care routines
  - Medication schedules
  - Medication administration techniques
  - Interventions (suctioning, feeding, etc)

2 Nursing Management of Learning Disabilities
- Early detection
- Referral to school or testing resource
- Plan for learning needs
- Establish goals
- Promote self-esteem

SUGGESTIONS FOR CLASSROOM ACTIVITIES

Have the class take a few minutes to read "Evidence-Based Nursing: Family Needs During Hospitalization for Mental Health Care." Use the critical thinking questions at the end to discuss the needs families express during hospitalization. How might these needs differ from families of children with chronic illness (e.g., the family with a child who is mentally retarded)?

SUGGESTIONS FOR CLINICAL ACTIVITIES

Discuss practical strategies students can use to negotiate hospital care routines with the family of a child who is mentally retarded. Discuss the benefits to partnering with the family in this situation.

LEARNING OBJECTIVE 6

Establish and evaluate expected outcomes of care for the child with a cognitive disorder.

CONCEPTS FOR LECTURE

1. The expected outcomes of nursing care depend on the child's needs and developmental level.
2. Early outcomes focus on the understanding of the diagnosis, while later outcomes focus on the child's skills, as well as utilization of resources in the community.

POWERPOINT LECTURE SLIDES

 Expected Outcomes of Nursing Care
- Depend on
  - Child's needs
  - Child's developmental level
  - Others factors

[2] Outcomes
- Early outcomes
  - Understanding of child's diagnosis
  - Specific physical and developmental needs of the child
- Later outcomes
  - Child's communication skills
  - Child's self-care skills
  - Utilization of community and educational resources

SUGGESTIONS FOR CLASSROOM ACTIVITIES

Ask the class how they would evaluate the outcomes described in this objective. Discuss as a group the nursing evaluation of a child in the school with a cognitive disorder. What can be done to enhance the achievement of these goals by the nurse? What community organizations are available to help?

SUGGESTIONS FOR CLINICAL ACTIVITIES

Have students identify local resources in their community that might be helpful for families who have children with mental retardation.

CHAPTER 55
THE CHILD WITH ALTERATIONS
IN MUSCULOSKELETAL FUNCTION

RESOURCE LIBRARY

CD-ROM

Animation: Muscle Physiology
NCLEX-RN® Review
Audio Glossary

COMPANION WEBSITE

NCLEX-RN® Review
Thinking Critically
Case Study: Fracture Assessment
Care Plan: Home Care of an Infant in a Spica Cast
Audio Glossary

IMAGE LIBRARY

Figure 55.1 The parts of long bones.
Figure 55.2 Metatarsus adductus is characterized by convexity (curvature) of the lateral border of the foot.
Figure 55.3 This girl has a long leg cast, which was applied after surgery to correct her clubfoot deformity.
Figure 55.4 A, Genu valgum, or knock-knees.
Figure 55.5 The asymmetry of the gluteal and thigh fat folds is easy to see in this child with developmental dysplasia of the hip.
Figure 55.6 The most common treatment for DDH in a child under 3 months is a Pavlik harness.
Figure 55.7 For infants older than 3 months of age, skin traction is commonly used for treatment of DDH.
Figure 55.8 Although the Toronto brace may seem formidable for a child to wear, you can see by this photograph that, as usual, children adapt quite well to it.

Figure 55.9 A child may have varying degrees of scoliosis.
Figure 55.10 This boy from Kenya had surgery to correct severe kyphosis and scoliosis, caused by tuberculosis of the spine.
Figure 55.11 Since the leg muscles of children with muscular dystrophy are weak, these children must perform the Gowers' maneuver to raise themselves to a standing position.
Figure 55.12 This young boy with muscular dystrophy needs to receive tube feedings and home nursing care.
Figure 55.13 The Salter-Harris classification system is based on the angle of the fracture in relation to the epiphysis.

Pathophysiology Illustrated: Clubfoot
Pathophysiology Illustrated: Slipped Epiphysis

LEARNING OBJECTIVE 1

Describe pediatric variations in the musculoskeletal system.

CONCEPTS FOR LECTURE

1. The skeletal system continues to grow and mature throughout childhood. Growth takes place at the epiphyseal plates, which are located near the ends of the bones. In addition, the bones of children are porous and less dense than those of adults, making them more likely to bend, buckle, and break. However, bones tend to heal quickly due to rapid bone growth.

POWERPOINT LECTURE SLIDES

 Skeletal System: Growth
  • Ends of long bones (epiphyses) remain cartilaginous—growth occurs here
  • Skeletal maturation: About 20 years of age
  • Calcium is needed for new bone growth

1a Parts of Long Bones
  • (Figure 55.1)

2. Unlike the skeletal system, the muscular system is almost completely formed at birth. Muscles increase in length and circumference but not in number. Until puberty, both ligaments and tendons are stronger than bone. As a result, fractures are sometimes mistaken for sprains.

 Bones: Injury
- Bones of children very porous and less dense than adults
- Injury to epiphyseal plate can impact future growth
- Bones can bend, buckle, and break
- Rapid growth allows for rapid healing

 Bones: Functional Changes
- Curvature of spine changes as child holds head up, stands
- Failure of spine to change results in abnormal spine curvature
  - Kyphosis
  - Lordosis

 Muscular System
- Completely formed at birth
- Muscles increase in length and circumference but not in number
- Ligaments and tendons
  - Stronger than bones until puberty occurs
  - Tendons grow in length and fibrous tissue as mechanical pressure is placed on them

 Muscular System: Injury
- Fractures may be mistaken for sprains
  - Sprain: Torn ligament
  - Caused by twisting or trauma to joint

SUGGESTIONS FOR CLASSROOM ACTIVITIES

Use the animation: "Muscle Physiology," available on the Student CD-ROM, to review how muscles work. This concept is important in order to understand disease processes that affect the musculoskeletal system.

SUGGESTIONS FOR CLINICAL ACTIVITIES

Examine x-rays of children of different ages. Look for the differences in bone size, as well as the epiphyseal plate.

LEARNING OBJECTIVE 2

Plan nursing care for children with structural deformities of foot, hip, and spine.

CONCEPTS FOR LECTURE

1. Structural disorders of the feet and legs include metatarsus adductus, clubfoot, genu varum, and genu valgum.
2. Structural disorders of the hip include hip dysplasia, Legg-Calve-Perthes disease, and slipped capital femoral epiphysis.
3. Structural disorders of the spine include scoliosis, torticollis, kyphosis, and lordosis.

POWERPOINT LECTURE SLIDES

 Metatarsus Adductus
- Most common congenital foot disorder
- Forefoot turns inward ("intoeing")
- Probable cause: Genetic; intrauterine positioning
- Treatment: Exercise, casting, braces, orthopedic shoes

 Metatarsus Adductus Characteristics
- (Figure 55.2)

1b Metatarsus Adductus: Nursing Care
- Parental teaching
  - Condition is correctable
  - How to exercise foot
  - Cast care if child requires casting

1c Clubfoot
- Congenital anomaly: Foot is twisted—involves muscles, bones, and tendons
- Occurs in boys more than girls—bilateral in half of cases
- Cause unknown—many theories
- Treatment
  - Cannot be corrected by exercise
  - Serial casting if done early
  - Surgical correction (3 to 12 months of age)

1d Clubfoot
- ("Pathophysiology Illustrated: Clubfoot")

1e Clubfoot: Nursing Care
- Provide emotional support
- Cast and brace care
- Postsurgical care
- Home care teaching

1f Genu Varum and Genu Valgum
- Genu varum: "Bowlegs," Blount's disease, rickets
- Genu valgum: "Knock-knees"
- Normal unless persists beyond 4 to 5 years of age
- Treatment: Braces, surgery

1g Genu Valgum and Genu Varum
- (Figure 55.4)

1h Genu Varum and Genu Valgum: Nursing Care
- Parental reassurance if child is less than 4 years of age
- Parental teaching—brace wear

2 Developmental Dysplasia of the Hip (DDH)
- Femoral head and acetabulum improperly aligned
- May include hip instability, dislocation, subluxation, or dysplasia
- Occurs in girls more than boys—unilateral in 80% of cases
- Cause: Unknown—genetic factors likely

2a Asymmetry of Gluteal and Thigh Fat Folds
- (Figure 55.5)

2b DDH: Treatment
- Pavlik harness (younger than 3 months of age)
- Skin traction (older than 3 months of age)
- Spica cast, surgery (older than 18 months of age)

2c DDH: Pavlik Harness
- (Figure 55.6)

2d DDH: Skin Traction
- (Figure 55.7)

2e DDH: Nursing Care
- Assessment of hip during well-child visits
- Nursing care depends on the treatment
  - Maintain traction
  - Provide cast care
  - Prevent complications from immobility

2f Legg-Calve-Perthes Disease
- Avascular necrosis of the femoral head—blood supply to femoral epiphysis is interrupted
- Occurs in boys more than girls
- Average age of onset: 7 years
- Cause unknown—may be genetic or coagulation system disorder
- Occurs in four distinct stages of 1 to 4 years
- Treatment: Traction, casting, bracing—goal is to keep hip abducted

2g Legg-Calve-Perthes Disease: Toronto Brace
- (Figure 55.8)

2h Legg-Calve-Perthes Disease: Nursing Care
- Assessment: Hip discomfort plus limp—pain
- Promote normal growth and development
- Brace care

2i Slipped Capital Femoral Epiphysis (SCFE)
- Femoral head displaced from femoral neck
- Occurs during adolescent growth spurt
- Occurs in boys more than girls
- Cause: Unknown—likely related to obesity, endocrine disorders
- Symptoms: Acute or chronic—limp, pain, loss of hip motion

2j SCFE: Pathophysiology
- ("Pathophysiology Illustrated: Slipped Epiphysis")

2k SCFE: Treatment and Nursing Care
- Treatment: Surgical most common
- Address obesity if present
- Provide emotional support
- Home care teaching

3 Scoliosis
- Lateral *S*- or *C*-shaped curvature of the spine
- More than 10 degrees is abnormal

- Types
  - Idiopathic (most common)
  - Congenital
  - Acquired
  - Most common in girls around adolescent growth spurt

 Degrees of Scoliosis
- (Figure 55.9)

 Scoliosis: Causes
- Idiopathic—cause unknown
- Congenital
  - Related to spinal structure
  - Examples: Spina bifida, cerebral palsy, muscular dystrophy
- Acquired: Injury to spinal cord

 Scoliosis: Treatment
- Observation, serial x-rays
- Mild (10 to 20 degree curve): Exercise
- Moderate (20 to 40 degree curve): Brace (worn 23 hours a day)
- Severe (greater than 40 degree curve): Surgery (spinal fusion)

 Scoliosis: Nursing Care
- Screening (usually during fifth and seventh grades)
- Promote acceptance of care plan
- Post-op care
- Home care teaching

Torticollis
- Head tilt caused by rotation of the spine
- Treatment
  - Stretching exercises
  - Surgical correction

Kyphosis and Lordosis
- Kyphosis: Convex curvature of spine ("hunchback"): Treatment—exercise, bracing, surgery
- Lordosis: Concave curvature of spine ("swayback"): Treatment—exercise, postural awareness

---

SUGGESTIONS FOR CLASSROOM ACTIVITIES

Due to the high incidence of scoliosis in girls, it is common for several students in a class to have scoliosis. Ask the class if anyone is willing to share how the condition is monitored and treated.

SUGGESTIONS FOR CLINICAL ACTIVITIES

Have students screen adolescent clients for scoliosis.

LEARNING OBJECTIVE 3

Recognize signs and symptoms of infectious musculoskeletal disorders and refer for appropriate care.

CONCEPTS FOR LECTURE

1. Osteomyelitis is an infection of the bone that may be acute or chronic, and treatment involves antimicrobial therapy.
2. Skeletal tuberculosis and septic arthritis occur infrequently in children. *Refer to "Clinical Manifestations: Skeletal Tuberculosis and Septic Arthritis" for a summary.*

POWERPOINT LECTURE SLIDES

1 Osteomyelitis
- Infection of the bone, usually a long bone in lower extremity
- Acute or chronic
- Occurs at any age—boys more than girls (due to trauma)
- Cause: Microorganism, usually bacterial
- Symptoms: Pain, swelling, decreased mobility, fever
- Treatment: Antimicrobials (oral or IV) for 3 to 6 weeks

1a Osteomyelitis: Nursing Care
- Immunization status (tetanus)
- Obtain cultures and blood work
- Administer fluids and medications
- Protect from spread of infection
- Encourage well-balanced diet
- Home care teaching—considerations for home IV therapy

2 Skeletal Tuberculosis
- Rare infection that affects spine and other joints
- Antimicrobial therapy

2a Septic Arthritis
- Joint infection
- Most common sites: Knee, hip, ankle, elbow
- Joint drained via aspiration, then IV antibiotics for 3 to 4 weeks

SUGGESTIONS FOR CLASSROOM ACTIVITIES

Discuss why long-term IV antibiotics are required to treat infections involving bones and joints. What makes these infections different from a lung or ear infection?

SUGGESTIONS FOR CLINICAL ACTIVITIES

If a child will require long-term home IV antimicrobial therapy, have students identify local resources available in their community to achieve this therapy. For example, are parents taught to administer the antibiotics themselves, or do nurses make home visits? What kinds of long-term IV access are available, and what are the risks of these devices?

LEARNING OBJECTIVE 4

Partner with families to plan care for children with musculoskeletal conditions that are chronic or require long-term care.

CONCEPTS FOR LECTURE

1. Achondroplasia (dwarfism) is a genetic condition where the head and torso are normal, but the arms and legs are short in size. There is no treatment for this disorder so nursing care focuses on helping families develop a positive self-image for the child.

POWERPOINT LECTURE SLIDES

1 Achondroplasia (Dwarfism)
- Genetic condition
- Head, torso are normal size—arms and legs are short
- Treatment: None (gene therapy in the future)— limb lengthening may be palliative

2. Marfan syndrome is a genetic condition that involves the connective tissue. There are cardiac, skeletal, and respiratory manifestations of the disease. Although there are no specific treatments, surgery may be done to prevent dissection of the aorta, which is the major cause of death.

3. Osteogenesis imperfecta, also known as brittle bone disease, is a collagen disorder. These children have frequent fractures, as well as other physical symptoms. Management is focused on preventing fractures and deformities.

4. Muscular dystrophy refers to a group of inherited diseases characterized by muscle fiber degeneration and muscle wasting. They are all terminal disorders, although the progression varies from a few years to many years. Nursing care focuses on the parent and the child, and includes promoting independence and mobility, emotional support, and acceptance of the disease process.

- Nursing care
  - Genetic counseling for parents
  - Positive self-image
  - Modifications to adjust for size

2 Marfan Syndrome
- Genetic condition that affects the connective tissue
- Common problems
  - Cardiac: Mitral valve prolapse, aortic regurgitation, and abnormal aortic root dimensions
  - Skeletal: Pectus excavatum, long arms and digits, scoliosis, elongated head, high arched palate
  - Ocular: Lens subluxation
  - Respiratory: Pneumothorax

2a Marfan Syndrome: Treatment
- None specific
- Surgery to prevent aortic dissection (most common cause of death)

2b Marfan Syndrome: Nursing Care
- Identification of disease
- Monitoring
- Surgical care
- Genetic counseling
- Medication management

3 Osteogenesis Imperfecta
- "Brittle bone disease"
- Genetic condition affecting collagen production
- Manifestations
  - Frequent fractures
  - Blue sclerae
  - Thin, soft skin
  - Short stature

3a Osteogenesis Imperfecta: Treatment
- Fracture prevention, treatment
- Prevention of deformity
- Maximize mobility
- Support for family, child

4 Muscular Dystrophy
- Group of inherited diseases—Duchenne most common
- Muscle fibers degenerate
- Onset varies (birth to late in life)
- Progression varies (few years to many years)
- All are terminal

4a Muscular Dystrophy: Treatment
- None specific
- Gene therapy in the future?
- Preserve muscle function: Steroids, deflazacort
- Prevent complications (infection, spinal deformities)

4b Muscular Dystrophy: Nursing Care
 • Promote independence and mobility
 • Psychosocial support and acceptance
 • Referral to resources for support

SUGGESTIONS FOR CLASSROOM ACTIVITIES

It is likely that Abraham Lincoln had Marfan syndrome. Show pictures of Lincoln when discussing the physical manifestations of the disease process.

SUGGESTIONS FOR CLINICAL ACTIVITIES

During clinical conference, discuss possible complications of muscular dystrophy that may require children to be admitted to the hospital. Discuss how the nurse can offer psychosocial support to these children and families.

LEARNING OBJECTIVE 5

Plan nursing interventions to promote safety and developmental progression in children who require braces, casts, traction, and surgery.

CONCEPTS FOR LECTURE

1. Nursing care of children who require braces, casts, traction, and surgery varies by age. *Resources available in the text include Tables 55.2, 55.4, and 55.5, as well as "Teaching Highlights: Care of the Child with a Cast" and "Teaching Highlights: Guidelines for Brace Wear".*

POWERPOINT LECTURE SLIDES

1 Care of the Child in a Cast
 • Elevation
 • Drainage, bleeding
 • Neurovascular checks—pulses, capillary refill, warmth, edema
 • Itching

1a Care of the Child in a Brace
 • Brace should be comfortable
 • Skin care
 • Wear clothes beneath brace

1b Care of the Child in Traction
 • Types of traction
   ○ Skin
   ○ Dunlop
   ○ Bryant
   ○ 90-90
   ○ Skeletal
   ○ Halo
   ○ Russell

1c Post-Surgical Care: External Fixator
 • Neurovascular checks
 • Pin care
 • Drainage

SUGGESTIONS FOR CLASSROOM ACTIVITIES

Before class, have students access the Companion Website and review, "Care Plan: Home Care of an Infant in a Spica Cast." Use this as a basis to discuss developmental considerations for children requiring casts.

SUGGESTIONS FOR CLINICAL ACTIVITIES

Review the signs and symptoms of compartment syndrome when discussing care of the child in a cast. If a child is displaying these signs and symptoms, discuss the appropriate actions the nurse should take. "Clinical Manifestations: Compartment Syndrome" is a good resource.

LEARNING OBJECTIVE 6

Provide nursing care for fractures, including teaching for injury prevention and nursing implementations for the child who has sustained a fracture.

CONCEPTS FOR LECTURE

1. Fractures can occur at any age, and may result from direct trauma to bones or from diseases that weaken the bone. *Refer to "Pathophysiology Illustrated: Classification and Types of Fractures" for details regarding types of fractures.* Nursing care focuses on maintaining proper alignment, monitoring neurovascular status, pain control, and discharge teaching.

2. Sports injuries are a common cause of fractures in children. *Refer to Table 55.6.* Many sports injuries can be prevented.

POWERPOINT LECTURE SLIDES

1 Fractures
- Occur at any age
- Result from trauma to bones or diseases that weaken bones
- Types
- Signs and symptoms
- Treatment: Closed versus open reduction

1a Fractures: Nursing Care
- Maintain proper alignment
- Monitor neurovascular status
- Pain control
- Promote mobility
- Discharge teaching

2 Sports Injuries
- Most common type of injury in youths 13 to 19 years
- Football, wrestling, soccer, gymnastics

2a Risk Factors for Injury in Childhood
- Vulnerability of growth plates
- Increased joint mobility leads to joint injuries
- Softer bones lead to fractures
- Lack of experience, training
- Not wearing protective gear
- Impatience with healing process

2b Prevention of Injury
- Proper training and instruction
- Protective gear
- Supervision
- Warm up before activity

SUGGESTIONS FOR CLASSROOM ACTIVITIES

Before class, assign students to access "Case Study: Fracture Assessment" located on the Companion Website. Use this as a basis for discussion regarding management of fractures during childhood.

SUGGESTIONS FOR CLINICAL ACTIVITIES

Demonstrate methods to assess neurovascular status in infants and toddlers. How do these methods vary from older children?

CHAPTER 56
THE CHILD WITH ALTERATIONS IN ENDOCRINE FUNCTION

RESOURCE LIBRARY

 CD-ROM

Animations:
  Physiology of Diabetes
  Responding to Hypoglycemia
Video
  Adolescent Diabetes and Quality of Life
Skills 9-1 through 9-7
NCLEX-RN® Review
Audio Glossary

 COMPANION WEBSITE

Objectives
NCLEX-RN® Review
Case Study: Diabetic Risk Factors
Thinking Critically
Case Study: Child with Type 1 Diabetes Returning
  to Elementary School
MediaLink Applications:
  Identify Strategies to Help Girls Understand Early
    Pubertal Development
  Develop a Peer Strategy: Child with Inborn Errors
    of Metabolism and Diet

IMAGE LIBRARY

Figure 56.1 Major organs and glands of the endocrine system.
Figure 56.2 Feedback mechanism in hormonal stimulation of the gonads during puberty.
Figure 56.3 Exophthalmos and an enlarged thyroid in an adolescent with Graves disease.
Figure 56.4 Newborn girl with ambiguous genitalia.
Figure 56.5 Conventional therapy.
Figure 56.6 This mother is being taught how to test her child's blood glucose level.
Figure 56.7 Insulin injection sites.

Figure 56.8 This girl is old enough to understand the need to take glucose tablets or another form of a rapidly absorbed sugar when her blood glucose level is low.
Figure 56.9 Acanthosis nigricans.
Figure 56.10 What characteristic physical manifestations of Turner syndrome can you identify in this girl?

Clinical Manifestations: Diabetes Insipidus

LEARNING OBJECTIVE 1

Identify the function of important hormones of the endocrine system.

CONCEPTS FOR LECTURE

1. The endocrine system controls the cellular activity that regulates growth and metabolism. Hormones are chemical messengers in the body. Several important hormones are reviewed in the text, including gonadatropin-releasing hormone, growth hormone, antidiuretic hormone, thyroid and parathyroid hormones, and insulin. *Table 56.1 provides an overview of additional hormones in the body.*

POWERPOINT LECTURE SLIDES

1 Endocrine System
  • Controls cellular activity that regulates growth and metabolism
  • Glands secrete hormones
  • Hormones are chemical messengers
  • Messages are received by cells

1a Functions of the Endocrine System
  • Differentiate reproductive system in the fetus
  • Regulate growth and development throughout childhood

- Enable sexual reproduction (puberty)
- Maintenance of homeostasis

 Overview of Hormone Functions
- Gonadatropin-releasing hormone—stimulates anterior pituitary to produce LH, FSH
- Growth hormone—regulates bone and tissue growth
- Antidiuretic hormone—regulates water reabsorption in kidneys

 Overview of Hormone Functions
- Thyroid hormone—regulates metabolism
- Parathyroid hormone—regulates calcium balance
- Insulin—regulates glucose uptake into cells

SUGGESTIONS FOR CLASSROOM ACTIVITIES

When introducing the endocrine system, use the animation "Hormone Regulation and Secretion Animation" available on the Student CD-ROM to illustrate the physiology of the endocrine system.

SUGGESTIONS FOR CLINICAL ACTIVITIES

When students are caring for a child with an endocrine dysfunction, have the student draw the regulatory pathway for that hormone. This exercise will help the student understand the pathophysiology of the disease, as well as diagnostic tests, signs and symptoms, and medications used to treat the disease.

LEARNING OBJECTIVE 2

Identify signs and symptoms that may indicate a disorder of the endocrine system.

CONCEPTS FOR LECTURE

1. There are general "red flags" that may indicate a disorder of the endocrine system. These symptoms can be grouped into categories that include growth, metabolism, mental retardation, and sexual development.

POWERPOINT LECTURE SLIDES

 Red Flags That May Indicate Endocrine Disease
- Four categories
  - Growth
  - Metabolism
  - Mental retardation
  - Sexual development

 Growth
- Delayed growth: Short stature—growth hormone deficiency
- Rapid growth: Tall stature—hyperpituitarism (rare in children)

 Metabolism
- Increased urine output—diabetes, diabetes insipidus
- Polydipsia, polyphagia, weight loss—diabetes
- Changes in sleep pattern, weight, energy level—thyroid disease
- Failure to thrive—inborn errors of metabolism

 Mental Retardation
- Congenital hypothyroidism
- Inborn errors of metabolism

1d Sexual Development
- Precocious puberty
- Delayed pubertal development

SUGGESTIONS FOR CLASSROOM ACTIVITIES

Before class, assign students to complete the activity "MediaLink Applications: Identify Strategies to Help Girls Understand Early Pubertal Development" available on the Companion Website.

SUGGESTIONS FOR CLINICAL ACTIVITIES

Invite a pediatric endocrinologist to speak to the group during a clinical conference and ask him or her to discuss ways that nurses can identify children at risk for endocrine disorders.

LEARNING OBJECTIVE 3

Describe differences in pathophysiology between primary and nephrogenic diabetes insipidus.

CONCEPTS FOR LECTURE

1. There are two forms of diabetes insipidus (DI): primary and nephrogenic. Both forms have similar symptoms, including polyuria and polydipsia. Due to differences in pathophysiology, primary DI responds to vasopressin with a decrease in urine output; however, nephrogenic DI does not respond to vasopressin.

POWERPOINT LECTURE SLIDES

1 Antidiuretic Hormone (ADH)
- Secreted by posterior pituitary gland
- Regulates water balance
  - Tubules of kidney respond to ADH
  - Plasma osmolarity
- More ADH = water retention, decreased urine output
- Less ADH = increased urine output
- ADH is also known as vasopressin

1a Two Types of DI
- Primary DI (also known as central DI, true DI)
- Nephrogenic DI (also known as familial DI)

1b Etiology of DI
- Primary DI
  - Brain tumor
  - Central nervous system infection or trauma
- Nephrogenic DI
  - Drug toxicity
  - Genetic

1c Symptoms of DI
- ("Clinical Manifestations: Diabetes Insipidus")

1d Differences in Pathophysiology
- Primary DI: Lack of ADH secretion
- Nephrogenic DI: Kidneys do not respond to ADH

1e Diagnosis of DI
- Water deprivation test
- Tests kidney's responsiveness to vasopressin

1f Treatment of DI
- Primary DI—DDAVP
- Nephrogenic DI
  - Thiazide diuretics (promote sodium excretion, water reabsorption)
  - High fluid intake diet
  - Monitoring of electrolytes

SUGGESTIONS FOR CLASSROOM ACTIVITIES

A way to remember the pathophysiology of DI is "high and dry." The sodium levels are high and the intravascular fluid status is dehydrated (or "dry").

SUGGESTIONS FOR CLINICAL ACTIVITIES

Contact the office of a pediatric endocrinologist or pediatric nephrologist and ask if there are any water deprivation tests scheduled during your clinical rotation. If so, arrange to have students observe this diagnostic test.

LEARNING OBJECTIVE 4

Identify all conditions for which short stature is a sign.

CONCEPTS FOR LECTURE

1. Numerous disorders have short stature as a finding. For this reason, it is important for nurses to know how to plot a child's height on a growth chart.

POWERPOINT LECTURE SLIDES

1 Short Stature: Conditions
- Growth hormone deficiency
- Familial short stature
- Hypothyroidism
- Turner syndrome
- Constitutional growth delay

1a Short Stature: Conditions
- Chronic renal failure
- Inborn error of metabolism
- Severe cardiac, pulmonary, or gastrointestinal disease

SUGGESTIONS FOR CLASSROOM ACTIVITIES

Based on their knowledge of pathophysiology, challenge the class to explain why short stature is a sign of the conditions discussed in this objective.

SUGGESTIONS FOR CLINICAL ACTIVITIES

During clinical time, have students measure the height of various children and plot the results on a growth chart.

LEARNING OBJECTIVE 5

Develop a nursing care plan for each type of acquired metabolic disorder.

CONCEPTS FOR LECTURE

1. The nursing care of children with acquired metabolic disorders includes teaching children and families about the disorder, administering medications, and carrying out diagnostic tests. Some children are at risk for fluid and electrolyte imbalances and require monitoring, dietary changes, and fluid and electrolyte replacement. Children who have alterations in body image may need support to develop a positive self-image.

POWERPOINT LECTURE SLIDES

1 Diabetes Insipidus
- Monitor intake and output
- Replace fluids (oral or IV)
- Administer DDAVP
- Home teaching for monitoring, medication use, diet

1a SIADH
- Seizure risk due to hyponatremia
  ○ Seizure precautions
  ○ Monitor sodium levels, level of consciousness
- Monitor intake and output
- Laboratory monitoring
- Fluid restriction

1b Hyperpituitarism
- Teach child and family about disorder
- People may assume child is older than he or she actually is

- Emotional support
- Pre- and post-op care if pituitary adenoma is removed surgically

1c Precocious Puberty
- Teach child and family about disorder
- Hormonal medication treatment—cost
- Body image
- Pre- and post-op care if hypothalamic tumor is removed

1d Hyperthyroidism
- Teach child and family about disorder—others in family may have disorder too
- Promote rest
- Provide emotional support
- Increased caloric intake
- Pre- and post-op care as needed

1e Hyperparathyroidism
- Fluid and electrolyte monitoring/replacement
- Post-op care
  - Monitor for respiratory distress
  - Risk for airway obstruction
  - Risk for infection
- Monitor calcium, phosphorus levels

1f Adrenal Insufficiency (Addison Disease)
- Teach child and family about disorder
- Administer replacement hormones
  - Hydrocortisone
  - Fludrocortisone
- Home medication-use teaching
- Risk of acute episodes

1g Pheochromocytoma
- Pre- and post-op teaching and care
- Monitoring of vital signs, blood pressure
- Administer antihypertensives
- Need for long-term, follow-up care

SUGGESTIONS FOR CLASSROOM ACTIVITIES	**SUGGESTIONS FOR CLINICAL ACTIVITIES**
Divide the class into groups and have each group briefly present the disorder and associated nursing care to the class.	Assign students to post-op units where many children with these disorders are cared for after surgery.

LEARNING OBJECTIVE 6

Develop a family education plan for the child that needs lifelong cortisol replacement.

CONCEPTS FOR LECTURE

1. Families with children who require lifelong cortisol replacement need education about medication administration, as well as knowledge of the symptoms of acute adrenal insufficiency.

POWERPOINT LECTURE SLIDES

1 Medication Administration
- Administer early in the morning or every other day
  - Mimics normal diurnal pattern
  - Minimizes side effects

- Give oral dose at mealtimes or with antacids to minimize gastric upset
- Liquid formulations are very bitter
- Injectable formulations: Use when child is ill—has vomiting
- Failure to give medication can cause adrenal insufficiency

1a Signs of Adrenal Insufficiency
- Irritability, headache, confusion, restlessness
- Nausea and vomiting, diarrhea
- Abdominal pain
- Fever
- Loss of appetite
- If untreated, shock

1b Other Teaching Points
- Inform all healthcare providers of child's condition and medication use
- Wear medical alert bracelet

SUGGESTIONS FOR CLASSROOM ACTIVITIES

Challenge students to explain the pathophysiology of the signs of adrenal insufficiency.

SUGGESTIONS FOR CLINICAL ACTIVITIES

Have students determine what teaching materials are available in the local clinical setting to use with children and families who require lifelong cortisol replacement.

LEARNING OBJECTIVE 7

Distinguish between the nursing care of the child with Type 1 and Type 2 diabetes.

CONCEPTS FOR LECTURE

1. Nursing care of the child with Type 1 diabetes focuses on monitoring blood glucose, education, medication administration, and teaching. The family also needs to understand the underlying pathophysiology of the condition.
2. Nursing care of the child with Type 2 diabetes includes monitoring blood glucose, education, and teaching. Medications usually include oral hypoglycemics—insulin may or may not be needed. Children with Type II diabetes who are overweight should be encouraged to lose weight.

POWERPOINT LECTURE SLIDES

1 Type 1 Diabetes: Underlying Pathophysiology
- Autoimmune response (genetic, environmental trigger)
- Beta cells of pancreas are destroyed
- Little to no insulin is produced by the body
- Lifelong insulin replacement is needed

1a Nursing Care: Type I Diabetes
- Education about disease
- Monitoring blood glucose frequently
- Administer insulin
  - Insulin pump
  - Different types of insulin
- Dietary modifications
- Symptoms of hypoglycemia, hyperglycemia
- Sick day rules
- Emotional support (chronic illness)

2 Type 2 Diabetes: Underlying Pathophysiology
- Pancreas may not secrete enough insulin—insulin secretory defect
- Cells may be resistant to insulin that is secreted—insulin resistance
- Major risk factor: Obesity—80% of children with Type 2 diabetes are obese

POWERPOINT LECTURE SLIDES *continued*

 Nursing Care: Type 2 Diabetes
- Education about disease and benefits of weight loss
- Monitoring blood glucose and blood pressure
- Assess diet and activity pattern
  - Medication administration
  - Oral hypoglycemics
- Insulin
- Symptoms of hypoglycemia, hyperglycemia
- Emotional support

SUGGESTIONS FOR CLASSROOM ACTIVITIES

- Before class, assign students to complete "Case Study: Child with Type 1 Diabetes Returning to Elementary School," available on the Companion Website. Use this case study as a framework for discussing the transition from the acute care setting to the home environment.
- Ask the class which is more dangerous for a child with Type 1 diabetes: hypoglycemia or hyperglycemia. Discuss the differences between the two conditions and the acute treatment of each.

SUGGESTIONS FOR CLINICAL ACTIVITIES

- Assign students to observe in an outpatient clinic that follows children with diabetes. Students can then compare and contrast these two different disease processes.
- When caring for a child with diabetes, review the age-appropriate signs and symptoms of hypoglycemia with the student. Discuss how hypoglycemia might be treated with that particular child.

LEARNING OBJECTIVE 8

Develop a nursing care plan for the child with an inherited metabolic disorder.

CONCEPTS FOR LECTURE

1. Children with inherited metabolic disorders often require special diets to manage their condition. Medication may be administered in some conditions (such as congenital hypothyroidism). Parents often need support and encouragement.

POWERPOINT LECTURE SLIDES

 Nursing Care of the Child with Inherited Metabolic Disorders
- Detection—mandatory screening (Example: Hypothyroidism)
- Dietary modifications
  - Inborn errors of metabolism
  - Special formulas
  - Consult dietitian

Nursing Care of Child with Inherited Metabolic Disorders
- Support for family and child
- Lifelong follow-up required

SUGGESTIONS FOR CLASSROOM ACTIVITIES

Before class, assign students to complete the activity: "MediaLink Applications: Develop a Peer Strategy: Child with Inborn Errors of Metabolism and Diet," available on the Companion Website. Use this activity as a framework to discuss this objective in class.

SUGGESTIONS FOR CLINICAL ACTIVITIES

Invite a dietitian to speak with the students during a clinical conference regarding the various formulas and dietary modifications required for children with congenital metabolic disorders.

CHAPTER 57
THE CHILD WITH ALTERATIONS IN SKIN INTEGRITY

RESOURCE LIBRARY

CD-ROM

Animations:
  Integumentary Repair
  Layers of the Skin
Nursing in Action: Topical Medication: Burn
  Wound Care
Skill 13-3: Sedation Monitoring
Skill 16-1: Performing a Urinary Catheterization
Audio Glossary
NCLEX-RN® Review

COMPANION WEBSITE

Thinking Critically
  Care Plan: Atopic Dermatitis
MediaLink Applications:
  Adolescents and Acne Management
  Develop a Community Education Program:
    Dog Bite Reduction
  Scald Burn Reduction in Children
NCLEX-RN® Review
Case Study

IMAGE LIBRARY

Figure 57.1 Layers of the skin with accessory structures.
Figure 57.2 Diaper dermatitis.
Figure 57.3 Seborrheic dermatitis.
Figure 57.4 Chronic eczema.
Figure 57.5 Pustular acne can have a significant effect on an adolescent's self-esteem.
Figure 57.6 Bullous impetigo.
Figure 57.7 Characteristic appearance of cellulitis.
Figure 57.8 Thrush, an acute pseudomembranous form of oral candidiasis, is a common fungal infection in infants and children.
Figure 57.9 Diffuse scabies in an infant.
Figure 57.10 Thermal (scald) burns are the most common burn injury in infancy.

Figure 57.11 Electrical burn caused by biting on electrical cord.
Figure 57.12 Lund and Browder chart for determining percentage of body surface areas in pediatric burn injuries.
Figure 57.13 A, Trans-Cyte, a temporary skin substitute, prior to application. B, Application of Trans-Cyte after debridement of a scald burn.

Table 57.2 Distribution of Lesions by Type of Allergen
Table 57.6 Classification of Burn Severity in Chiidren

LEARNING OBJECTIVE 1

Identify the characteristics of different skin lesions by their cause, including those caused by irritants, drug reactions, mites, infection, and injury.

CONCEPTS FOR LECTURE

1. The characteristics of skin lesions vary based on their cause.

POWERPOINT LECTURE SLIDES

1 Irritant Skin Lesions
  • Papulovesicular lesions
  • Very pruritic
  • Erythematous
  • Well-circumscribed

1a Drug Reactions
- Erythematous macules and papules
- Pruritic
- Urticaria

1b Mites
- Intense pruritis
- Papular, pustular, and vesicular lesions

1c Infection
- Edema
- Erythema
- Papular and vesicular lesions

1d Injuries
- Pressure ulcers and burns
  - Loss of tissue in stages
  - Begins with epidermis
- Animal bites—puncture wounds

SUGGESTIONS FOR CLASSROOM ACTIVITIES

Divide students into groups and provide each group with a set of colored pencils and a blank piece of paper. Have each group draw one of the lesions described previously, including the common characteristics of that lesion. Share each group's drawing with the class.

SUGGESTIONS FOR CLINICAL ACTIVITIES

When a student is caring for a child with a skin lesion, review the proper terminology used for documentation. Students often have difficulty describing what they are seeing.

LEARNING OBJECTIVE 2

Describe the stages of wound healing.

CONCEPTS FOR LECTURE

1. There are three distinct stages in wound healing: inflammation, reconstruction (or epithelialization), and maturation (or remodeling). *Refer to "Pathophysiology Illustrated: Phases of Wound Healing" for graphic representations of these stages.*

POWERPOINT LECTURE SLIDES

1 Stages in Wound Healing
- Inflammation
- Reconstruction (or epithelialization)
- Maturation

1a Inflammation
- Lasts 3 to 5 days
- Prepares the site for repair
- Clot forms (red blood cells, fibrin, and platelets)
- Vasodilation occurs
  - Allows white blood cells to travel to the injury
  - White blood cells ingest bacteria and debris

1b Reconstruction (or Epithelialization)
- Lasts from 5 days to 4 weeks, depending on extent of injury
- Blood flow reestablished by capillaries
- Enzymes debride area and dissolve clot
- Wound edges grow towards each other—collagen, fibroblasts, granulation tissue
- Epithelial cells form over the site

1c Maturation (or Remodeling)
- Lasts for months to years
- Collagen produces a scar
- Keloids

SUGGESTIONS FOR CLASSROOM ACTIVITIES

Use the animation "Integumentary Repair" located on the Student CD-ROM to give students a visual representation of this process during the lecture.

SUGGESTIONS FOR CLINICAL ACTIVITIES

Have students discuss how the stage of wound healing their client is in impacts their nursing care.

LEARNING OBJECTIVE 3

Identify the skin conditions that have a hereditary cause or hereditary predisposition.

CONCEPTS FOR LECTURE

1. Two skin conditions that have a hereditary cause or predisposition include contact dermatitis and atopic dermatitis (eczema).
2. Contact dermatitis is an inflammation of the skin that occurs in response to direct contact with an allergen or irritant. Common irritants include soaps, detergents, fabric softeners, lotions, urine, and stool. Common allergens include poison ivy, neomycin, nickel, fragrances, and latex.
3. Atopic dermatitis (eczema) is a chronic, superficial inflammatory skin disorder characterized by intense pruritis. It affects infants, children, and adolescents. Those who will have the disorder usually develop it early in life. Eczema is characterized by red patches with exudates and crust.

POWERPOINT LECTURE SLIDES

1 Hereditary Skin Conditions
- Contact dermatitis
- Atopic dermatitis (eczema)

2 Contact Dermatitis
- Inflammation of the skin
- Occurs in response to direct contact with
  - An allergen
  - An irritant
- Very common in infants and children

2a Contact Dermatitis: Irritants
- External irritant
- Inflammatory response occurs, but no immune response
- Common irritants
  - Soaps, detergents, fabric softeners
  - Bleach
  - Lotion
  - Urine or stool

2b Contact Dermatitis: Allergens
- Antigen absorbed from skin triggers immune response
- Common allergens
  - Poison ivy, poison oak
  - Neomycin
  - Nickel
  - Fragrances
  - Latex

2c Contact Dermatitis: Symptoms
- Erythema, edema, pruritis, vesicles
- Bullae that rupture, ooze, and crust
- Rash limited to contact area
- Develops within hours of exposure
- Peak in 3 to 5 days
- Resolve in 3 to 4 weeks

2d Distribution of Lesions
- (Table 57.2)

2e Contact Dermatitis: Treatment
- Remove offending agent!
- Calamine lotion
- Antihistamines
- Steroids (topical versus oral)

Atopic Dermatitis (Eczema)
- Chronic, superficial inflammatory skin disorder
- Affects up to 20% of school-age children
- 75% of those who have the condition develop it during infancy
- Etiology unknown
  ○ Genetic predisposition plus trigger
  ○ Immune disorder

 Atopic Dermatitis: Symptoms
- Red patches with vesicles, exudates, and crust
- Scaling with erythema and excoriation
- Lichenification
- Face, upper arms, back, thighs, hands, feet

 Chronic Eczema
- (Figure 57.4)

 Atopic Dermatitis: Treatment
- No cure
- Goals:
  ○ Hydrate and lubricate skin
  ○ Reduce pruritis
  ○ Minimize inflammatory changes
  ○ Reduce flare-ups

Atopic Dermatitis: Treatment
- Wet compresses ("wet on wet")
- Occlusive ointments after bathing
- Moisturizing ointments
- Topical steroids
- Antibiotics
- Immunomodulators (Example: Tacrolimus)

SUGGESTIONS FOR CLASSROOM ACTIVITIES

Before class, assign students to review the "Care plan: Atopic Dematitis" located on the Companion Website. Use this care plan as a basis for discussing the disease process.

SUGGESTIONS FOR CLINICAL ACTIVITIES

Discuss the concept of "latex precautions." Which children are at high risk for latex allergies? Which products available in the local clinical setting contain latex? Have students survey packaging in the supply room to determine if products containing latex are available.

LEARNING OBJECTIVE 4

Describe a nursing care plan for a child with alterations in skin integrity, including dermatitis, infectious disorders, and infestations.

CONCEPTS FOR LECTURE

1. The nursing model can be applied to create a nursing care plan for the child with alterations in skin integrity, including assessment, diagnosis, planning and implementation, and evaluation.

POWERPOINT LECTURE SLIDES

 Assessment
- Thorough history
  ○ Allergy
  ○ Environmental or dairy factors
  ○ Past exacerbations
- Distribution and type of lesions
- Effect on sleeping pattern, quality of life

POWERPOINT LECTURE SLIDES *continued*

 Diagnosis
- Impaired tissue integrity
- Disturbed sleep pattern
- Risk for infection
- Chronic low self-esteem
- Ineffective therapeutic regimen management

 Planning and Implementation
- Eliminate allergens from environment
- Cleanse skin as ordered
- Apply topical medications
- Cool soaks as ordered
- Treat clothing, linens, and toys (infestations only)
- Keep fingernails clipped short

Evaluation
- Identify triggers and eliminate them
- Itching is controlled
- Infection does not develop

SUGGESTIONS FOR CLASSROOM ACTIVITIES

Bring pictures of various skin conditions and ask students how they would describe the distribution and type of lesions in the picture you are showing.

SUGGESTIONS FOR CLINICAL ACTIVITIES

Consider assigning students to an outpatient dermatology office that treats pediatric clients.

LEARNING OBJECTIVE 5

Develop an education plan for adolescents with acne to promote self-care.

CONCEPTS FOR LECTURE

1. Acne is a chronic inflammatory disorder that is the most common skin disorder in the pediatric population.
2. Clinical therapies for acne include topical keratolytics, topical antibiotics, topical retinoids, oral antibiotics, and oral isotretinoin.
3. Education for the adolescent with acne focuses on triggers of acne, skin cleansing routines, medications, and side effects. Psychologic support should also be considered. *Refer to "Nursing Care Plan: The Adolescent with Acne."*

POWERPOINT LECTURE SLIDES

 Acne
- Chronic inflammatory disorder of the hair follicles
- Face and trunk
- Most common skin disorder in pediatrics
- Triggers
  - Adolescents: Androgen production, sebum overproduction
  - Neonates: Response to maternal androgens

 Acne: Clinical Therapies
- Topical
  - Keratolytics (Example: Benzoyl peroxide)
  - Antibiotics
  - Retinoids (Example: Tretinoin)
- Oral:
  - Antibiotics
  - Isotretinoin (Accutane)
- Others

 Education Plan: Triggers of Acne
- Acne does not have a dietary cause
- Excessive perspiration and emotional stress increase acne
- Skin cleansing routines

Education Plan: Medications
- Medication administration
- Side effects
- Precautions
  ○ Contraception
  ○ Sun exposure

3b Education Plan: Psychosocial Considerations
- Body image
- Self-esteem
- Peer relationships
- Assess: Refer for counseling if needed

SUGGESTIONS FOR CLASSROOM ACTIVITIES

Before class, assign students to complete the "Media-Link Applications: Adolescents and Acne Management," activity located on the Companion Website. Use this as a basis for discussing this objective.

SUGGESTIONS FOR CLINICAL ACTIVITIES

Discuss typical topical and systemic medications used to treat acne, as well as the precautions that must be followed while adolescents take these medications.

LEARNING OBJECTIVE 6

Describe the process to measure the extent of burns and burn severity in children.

CONCEPTS FOR LECTURE

1. Burns are a common type of injury in pediatrics. There are four types of burns, including thermal, chemical, electrical, and radioactive. Children are at risk for different types of burns based on their developmental age.

2. Burns are classified by their depth, percentage of body surface area affected, and the involvement of specific body parts. *Refer to "Pathophysiology Illustrated: Classification of Burns by Depth."*

POWERPOINT LECTURE SLIDES

1 Burns: Background
- Common injury in pediatrics
- Four types of burns
  ○ Thermal
  ○ Chemical
  ○ Electrical
  ○ Radioactive

1a Burn Risk: Developmental Considerations
- Infants: Scalds, house fires
- Toddlers: Pull hot liquids on themselves
- Preschool: Scalds, contact with hot appliances
- School-age: Playing with matches, combustion experiments
- Adolescents: Accidental or risk-taking behaviors

2 Classification of Burns: Based On
- Depth of injury
- Percentage of body surface area affected
- Involvement of specific body parts

2a Depth of Injury
- Superficial
- Partial thickness
- Full thickness

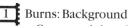 Lund and Browder Chart: Percentage of Body Surface Area Affected
- (Figure 57.2)

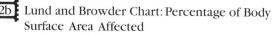

Involvement of Specific Body Parts
- Face
- Hands
- Feet
- Perineal area
- Circumferential burns

2d Burn Severity in Children
- (Table 57.6)

SUGGESTIONS FOR CLASSROOM ACTIVITIES

Before class, assign students to complete the activity, "MediaLink Applications: Develop an Education Program to Reduce Potential for Burns in Young Children," located on the Companion Website.

SUGGESTIONS FOR CLINICAL ACTIVITIES

Using scenarios that you create, have students practice using the Lund and Brower chart to determine the percentage of a child's body that has been burned.

LEARNING OBJECTIVE 7

Develop a nursing care plan for the child with a full thickness burn injury.

CONCEPTS FOR LECTURE

1. Assessment of the child with full thickness burns includes airway assessment, breathing, and circulation; history and type of burn; possibility of other injuries; pain assessment, and close attention to fluid status. The burn should be consistent with the history, as about 10% of burns in children are due to child abuse.
2. Diagnosis helps guide nursing interventions. *Refer to "Nursing Care Plan: The Child with a Major Burn Injury" for detailed interventions.*
3. Evaluation is done to determine the effectiveness of nursing interventions.

POWERPOINT LECTURE SLIDES

1 Assessment
- Airway, breathing, circulation
- History and type of burn—10% of burns are due to child abuse
- Other injuries (falls, explosion)
- Pain assessment
- Fluid status

1a Burns Injuries Associated with Child Abuse

2 Diagnosis
- Acute pain
- Risk for infection
- Risk for deficient fluid volume
- Ineffective tissue perfusion
- Ineffective breathing pattern

2a Planning and Implementation
- Burn care
  - Dressing changes
  - Hydrotherapy
  - Antibiotic therapy
  - Skin grafting
- Pain management
- Prevent complications
- Provide emotional support

3 Evaluation
- Adequate pain relief
- Free from infection
- Adequate urine output
- Adequate perfusion
- Improvement in breathing pattern

<table>
<tr>
<td>

SUGGESTIONS FOR CLASSROOM ACTIVITIES

Before class, assign students to complete the "Nursing in Action: Topical Medication: Burn Wound Care" activity located on the Student CD-ROM. Use this as a framework for discussion about nursing care of the child with a major burn.

</td>
<td>

SUGGESTIONS FOR CLINICAL ACTIVITIES

Assign students to observe in a burn unit. If a burn unit is not available in your clinical setting, see if the physical therapy department treats burn clients on an outpatient basis and assign students to observe those treatments.

</td>
</tr>
</table>

LEARNING OBJECTIVE 8

Identify preventive strategies to reduce the risk of injury from bites and stings.

<table>
<tr>
<td>

CONCEPTS FOR LECTURE

1. There are numerous prevention strategies to prevent bites and stings from insects.

</td>
<td>

POWERPOINT LECTURE SLIDES

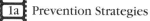 Prevention of Insect Bites and Stings
- Know the insects common in your locale
- Teach children to avoid dangerous insects
- Apply a commercial insect repellant—DEET: Precautions

1a Prevention Strategies
- Inspect skin for ticks after playing outside
- Wear long pants and sleeves to avoid tick bites
- Stay calm when near stinging insets
- Avoid eating sweetened foods and beverages when outside
- Treat pets for fleas and ticks

</td>
</tr>
</table>

<table>
<tr>
<td>

SUGGESTIONS FOR CLASSROOM ACTIVITIES

If you would like to have students think about prevention of dog bites, assign them to complete the "Critical Thinking: Develop a Community Education Program: Dog Bite Reduction" located on the Companion Website.

</td>
<td>

SUGGESTIONS FOR CLINICAL ACTIVITIES

Consider discussing the following questions while in the clinical setting: What are some of the serious clinical consequences of bites and stings? What diseases can be transmitted by insects? How can prevention strategies be communicated to parents?

</td>
</tr>
</table>

NCLEX-RN® TEST QUESTIONS

CHAPTER 1

1.1 A nurse is examining different nursing roles. Which of the following best illustrates an advanced practice nursing role?
a. A registered nurse who is the manager of a large obstetrical unit.
b. A registered nurse who is the circulating nurse at surgical deliveries (cesarean sections).
c. A clinical nurse specialist working as a staff nurse on a mother–baby unit.
d. A clinical nurse specialist with whom other nurses consult for her expertise in caring for high-risk infants.

Answer: d
Rationale: A clinical nurse specialist with whom other nurses consult for expertise in caring for high-risk infants would define an advanced practice nursing role. They have specialized knowledge and competence in a specific clinical area, and are master's-prepared. A registered nurse who is the manager of a large obstetrical unit or one who is a circulating nurse at surgical deliveries (cesarean sections) is defined as a professional nurse, and has graduated from an accredited program in nursing and completed the licensure examination. A clinical nurse specialist working as a staff nurse on a mother–baby unit might have the qualifications for an advanced practice nursing staff but is not working in that capacity.
Assessment
Safe, Effective Care Environment
Analysis

1.2 The major focus of the nurse practitioner is on:
a. leadership.
b. physical and psychosocial clinical assessment.
c. independent care of the high-risk, pregnant client.
d. tertiary prevention.

Answer: b
Rationale: Physical and psychosocial clinical assessment is the major focus of the nurse practitioner (NP) who provides care in many different clinical settings. Leadership might be a quality of the NP, but it is not the major focus. NPs cannot provide independent care of the high-risk pregnant client but must work under a physician's supervision. The NP cannot do tertiary prevention as a major focus.
Assessment
Safe, Effective Care Environment
Application

1.3 The role of certified nurse–midwife (CNM) is to: (Select all that apply.)
a. be prepared to manage independently the care of women at low risk for complications during pregnancy and birth.
b. give primary care for high-risk clients who are in hospital settings.
c. give primary care for healthy newborns.
d. obtain a physician consultation for any technical procedures at delivery.
e. be educated in two disciplines of nursing.

Answers: a, c, e
Rationale: A CNM is prepared to manage independently the care of women at low risk for complications during pregnancy and birth and the care of healthy newborns. The CNM is educated in the disciplines of nursing and midwifery. CNMs cannot give primary care for high-risk clients who are in hospital settings. The physician provides the primary care. The CNM does not need to obtain a physician consultation for any technical procedures at delivery.
Planning
Safe, Effective Care Environment
Application

1.4 During the hospital admission process, the child's parent receives information about the pediatric unit's goals, including the statement that the unit practices "family-centered care." The parent asks why that should be important. The nurse would respond that in the "family-centered care" paradigm, the:
a. mother is the principal caregiver in each family.
b. child's physician is the key person in assuring the health of a child is maintained.

Answer: c
Rationale: The foundation for the development of trusting relationships and partnerships with families is the recognition that the family is the principal caregiver, knows the unique nature of each individual child best, plays the vital role of meeting the child's needs, and is responsible for ensuring each child's health. Culturally competent care recognizes that both matriarchal and patriarchal households exist. The physician is not present during the day-to-day routines in a child's life.
Planning
Health Promotion and Maintenance
Application

c. family serves as the constant influence and continuing support in the child's life. d. father is the leader in each home; thus, all communications should include him.	
1.5 Despite the availability of State Children's Health Insurance Programs (SCHIPs), many eligible children are not enrolled. The nursing intervention that can best help eligible children to become enrolled is: a. assessment of the details of the family's income and expenditures. b. case management to limit costly, unnecessary duplication of services. c. advocacy for the child by encouraging the family to investigate its SCHIP eligibility. d. education to the family about the need for keeping regular well-child visit appointments.	Answer: c Rationale: In the role of an advocate, a nurse will advance the interests of another by suggesting the family investigate its SCHIP eligibility. Financial assessment is more commonly the function of a social worker. The case management activity mentioned will not provide a source of funding, nor will the educational effort described. Implementation Health Promotion and Maintenance Application
1.6 The telephone triage nurse at a pediatric clinic knows each call is important. However, recognizing that infant deaths are most frequent in this group, the nurse must be extra attentive during the call from the parent of an infant: a. less than 3 weeks old. b. of an American Indian family. c. of a non-Hispanic black family. d. between 6 and 8 months old.	Answer: a Rationale: Almost two-thirds of all infant deaths occur during the first 28 days after birth. This category has a higher risk of death than the other categories listed (American Indian family, non-Hispanic black family, and infant age between 6 and 8 months old). Implementation Health Promotion and Maintenance Application
1.7 A nurse is providing anticipatory guidance to a group of parents of children in the infant-to-preschool age group. After reviewing statistics on the most common cause of death in this age group, the nurse would include information about prevention of: a. cancer by reducing the use of pesticides in the home. b. accidental injury including pool and traffic accidents. c. heart disease by incorporating heart-healthy foods into the child's diet. d. pneumonia by providing a diet high in vitamin C from fruits and vegetables.	Answer: b Rationale: Unintentional injuries were the most common cause of death in 2000 for children between the ages of 1 and 4 years old. Other major causes of death for this age group included cancer, heart disease, and pneumonia. Implementation Safe, Effective Care Environment Application
1.8 The maternity nurse's best defense against an accusation of malpractice or negligence is that the nurse: a. followed the physician's written orders. b. met the Association of Women's Health, Obstetric and Neonatal Nurses (AWHONN) standards of practice.	Answer: b Rationale: Meeting the AWHONN standards of practice would cover the maternity nurse against an accusation of malpractice or negligence because the standards are rigorous and cover all bases of excellent nursing practice. Following the physician's written orders or acting on the advice of the nurse manager are not enough to defend the nurse from accusations because the orders and/or advice may be wrong or unethical. Being a certified nurse midwife or nurse practitioner

c. is a certified nurse midwife or nurse practitioner. d. was acting on the advice of the nurse manager.	does not defend the nurse against these accusations if she does not follow the AWHONN standards of practice. Planning Safe, Effective Care Environment Application
1.9 A nurse is working with pediatric clients in a research facility. The nurse recognizes that federal guidelines are in place, which delineate that pediatric clients must give consent for participation in research trials. Based on the client's age, the nurse would seek assent from which child? (Select all that apply.) a. A precocious 4-year-old starting as a cystic fibrosis research study participant. b. A 7-year-old leukemia client electing to receive a newly developed trial medication. c. A 10-year-old starting in an investigative study for clients with precocious puberty. d. A 13-year-old client beginning participation in a research program for ADHD treatments.	Answers: b, c, d Rationale: Federal guidelines mandate that research participants 7 years old and older must receive developmentally appropriate information about healthcare procedures and treatments, and give assent. Planning Psychosocial Integrity Application
1.10 A 12-year-old pediatric client is in need of surgery. The healthcare member who is legally responsible for obtaining informed consent for an invasive procedure is: a. the nurse. b. the physician. c. the unit secretary. d. the social worker.	Answer: b Rationale: Informed consent is legal preauthorization for an invasive procedure. It is the physician's legal responsibility to obtain this because it consists of an explanation about the medical condition, a detailed description of treatment plans, the expected benefits and risks related to the proposed treatment plan, alternative treatment options, the client's questions, and the guardian's right to refuse treatment. Planning Safe, Effective Care Environment Application
1.11 A nurse who tells family members the sex of a newborn baby without first consulting the parents would be considered having committed: a. a breach of privacy. b. negligence. c. malpractice. d. a breach of ethics.	Answer: a Rationale: A breach of privacy would have been committed in this situation, because it violates the right to privacy of this family and the right to privacy is the right of a person to keep his or her person and property free from public scrutiny (even other family members). Negligence and malpractice are punishable legal offenses and are more serious. A breach of ethics would not apply to this situation. Implementation Safe, Effective Care Environment Application
1.12 According to the 1973 Supreme Court decision in *Roe v. Wade*, abortion is legal if induced: a. at a federally funded clinic. b. before the period of viability. c. to provide tissue for therapeutic research. d. at a military hospital overseas.	Answer: b Rationale: Abortion can be performed legally until the period of viability; after viability, the rights of the fetus take precedence. Whether at a federally funded clinic or at a military hospital overseas, abortion can be provided legally if under U.S. laws. Abortion cannot be used to provide tissue for therapeutic research. Planning Safe, Effective Care Environment Application

1.13 A nurse is relating information to a client about the Human Genome Project. Which of the following best characterizes the activity of the Human Genome Project? a. cloning. b. genetic mapping. c. genetic manipulation. d. gamete intrafallopian transfer.	Answer: b Rationale: Genetic mapping is what the Human Genome Project has completed on human genetic material. It has nothing to do with cloning or genetic manipulation. Gamete intrafallopian transfer is a form of assisted reproductive technology. Assessment Safe, Effective Care Environment Analysis
1.14 Which of the following families might find cord blood banking to be especially useful? a. a family with a history of leukemia. b. a family with a history of infertility. c. a family that wishes to select the sex of a future child. d. a family that wishes to avoid a future intrauterine fetal surgery.	Answer: a Rationale: Families with a history of leukemia might find cord blood banking useful because cord blood, like bone marrow and embryonic tissue, contains regenerative stem cells, which can replace diseased cells in the affected individual. A family with a history of infertility, or one that wishes to select the sex of a future child or avoid a future intrauterine surgery, would not be helped by cord blood banking. Planning Physiological Integrity Analysis
1.15 Which of the following practices characterize the basic competencies related to evidence-based practice? (Select all that apply.) a. clinical practice supported by good evidence. b. clinical practice supported by intuitive evidence. c. clinical practice supported by data. d. clinical practice that promotes quality. e. clinical practice that provides a useful approach to problem solving.	Answers: a, c, d, e Rationale: Supported by good evidence and data, promotes quality, and provides a useful approach to problem solving are the hallmark characteristics of the basic competencies related to evidence-based practice. Clinical practice supported by intuitive evidence does not provide valid evidence and data for the proper actions. Assessment Safe, Effective Care Environment Analysis

CHAPTER 2

2.1 A 7-year-old client tells you that, "grandpa, mommy, daddy, and my brother live at my house." The nurse identifies this family type as: a. binuclear. b. extended. c. gay and lesbian. d. traditional.	Answer: b Rationale: An extended family contains a parent or a couple who share the house with their children and another adult relative. A binuclear family includes the divorced parents who have joint custody of their biologic children, while the children alternate spending varying amounts of time in the home of each parent. A gay or lesbian family is comprised of two same-sex domestic partners; they might or might not have children. The traditional nuclear family consists of an employed provider parent, a homemaking parent, and the biologic children of this union. Assessment Health Promotion and Maintenance Application
2.2 A nurse is performing a family assessment. A father and mother who work are considered what type of family? a. a traditional nuclear family. b. a dual-career/dual-earner family. c. an extended family. d. an extended kin family.	Answer: b Rationale: A dual-career/dual-earner family is characterized by both parents working, by either choice or necessity. The traditional nuclear family is defined as a husband/provider, a wife who stays home, and children. An extended family is defined as couples who share household and childrearing responsibilities with parents, siblings, or other relatives. An extended kin family is a specific form of an extended family. Assessment Health Promotion and Maintenance Application

2.3 A nurse is comparing several different families' developmental stages. What serves as a marker for a family's developmental stage according to Duvall? a. the youngest child's age. b. the mother's age. c. the oldest child's age. d. the father's age.	Answer: c Rationale: The oldest child's age serves as a marker for the family's developmental stage, except in the last two stages, when children are no longer present. The mother's age, the youngest child's age, and the father's age are not markers, according to Duvall. Assessment Health Promotion and Maintenance Analysis
2.4 The nurse is caring for a postpartal client who is of Hmong descent and immigrated to the United States five years ago. The client asks for the regular hospital menu because she likes American food. The nurse assesses this response to be related to which of the following cultural concepts? a. acculturation. b. ethnocentrism. c. enculturation. d. stereotyping.	Answer: a Rationale: Acculturation (assimilation) is the correct assessment because she adapted to a new cultural norm in terms of food choices. Ethnocentrism refers to a social identity that is associated with shared behaviors and patterns. Enculturation is when culture is learned and passed on from generation to generation and often happens when a group is isolated. Stereotyping is assuming that all members of a group have the same characteristics. Assessment Health Promotion and Maintenance Application
2.5 A home health nurse has set up a home visit with a Korean couple in order to follow up on their jaundiced 4-day-old baby, who was discharged home yesterday. Considering family power structure what family members might the nurse expect to see in the home? a. just the parents. b. the grandmother. c. the grandfather and parents. d. the godparents.	Answer: c Rationale: The grandfather is the family member who plays a key role in decision making and who is likely to be present in this situation. Asians traditionally revere their elders and their wisdom. Just the parents, the grandmother, or the godparents would not have the last word in decision making for this family. Implementation Health Promotion and Maintenance Analysis
2.6 A woman of Korean descent has just given birth to a son. Her partner wishes to give her sips of hot broth from a thermos they brought with them. They have refused your offer of ice chips or other cold drinks for the client. The nurse should: a. explain to the client that she can have the broth if she will also drink cold water or juice. b. encourage the partner to feed the client sips of their broth. Ask if the client would like you to bring her some warm water to drink as well. c. explain to the couple that food can't be brought from home, but that the nurse will make hot broth for them. d. encourage the client to have the broth, after the nurse takes it to the kitchen and boils it first.	Answer: b Rationale: Encouraging the partner to feed the client sips of their broth and asking if the client would like you to bring her some warm water to drink are approaches that show cultural sensitivity. The equilibrium model of health, based on the concept of balance between light and dark, heat and cold, is the foundation for this belief and practice. Explaining to the client that she can have broth if she will drink cold water or juice first does not show cultural sensitivity and does not respect the client's beliefs. Explaining to the couple that food can't be brought from home but that you will make hot broth for them and encouraging the client to have broth after you take it to the kitchen and boil it first are both incorrect responses. Implementation Health Promotion and Maintenance Application

2.7 The nurse is working with a child whose religious beliefs differ from the general population. The best nursing intervention to use to meet the specific spiritual needs of this child and family is to:

a. ask "How does the child's and family's religious/spiritual beliefs impact their practices for health and illness?"

b. show respect while allowing time and privacy for religious rituals.

c. ask, "What do you think caused the child's illness?"

d. identify healthcare practices forbidden by religious or spiritual beliefs.

Answer: b
Rationale: Showing respect while allowing time and privacy for religious rituals is an intervention. The other three items may be part of the spiritual assessment process.
Implementation
Psychosocial Integrity
Application

2.8 The nurse is working with a child newly enrolled into an English-as-a-second-language class. The nurse wants to teach the child about the importance of handwashing before meals and of not eating food dropped on the exam room floor. The best way to assimilate the nurse's cultural values about hygienic nutrition is to:

a. have the nurse model proper handwashing before examining the child and throw out the dropped cookie.

b. provide written materials in English about hygiene and diet for the client to take home.

c. have the child repeat his interpretation of the information that was taught.

d. schedule a medical interpreter to accompany the client to his next visit.

Answer: c
Rationale: Assimilation is described as adopting and incorporating traits of the new culture within one's practices. Information must be understood before it is assimilated. The purpose of modeled behavior may be misunderstood if it is not accompanied by an explanation. In working with families with limited English proficiency, it is optimal to have a medical interpreter present for the entire visit. When an interpreter is not available, asking the client to repeat her understanding of what was taught reveals how concepts were understood. Written materials in English hold minimal value for clients with limited understanding. When teaching has been done, the nurse has a responsibility to assess client understanding; thus, an interpreter at the next visit will not help the nurse or the client now.
Implementation
Health Promotion and Maintenance
Analysis

2.9 The charge nurse is reviewing the care plans written by the unit's staff nurses. The charge nurse recognizes that the NANDA nursing diagnosis most likely to be construed as culturally biased and possibly offensive is:

a. Fear related to separation from support system during hospitalization.

b. Spiritual Distress related to discrepancy between beliefs and prescribed treatment.

c. Interrupted Family Processes related to a shift in family roles secondary to demands of illness.

d. Noncompliance related to impaired verbal communication secondary to recent immigration from non-English-speaking area.

Answer: d
Rationale: The phrase "impaired verbal communication" might be offensive because speaking a different language is not equivalent to being impaired, and noncompliance does not stem from misunderstanding. The other options seek to explain how the culturally sensitive nurse can partner with the families more effectively.
Diagnosis
Psychosocial Integrity
Analysis

2.10 During the assessment, the nurse notices that a black baby has a darker and slightly bluish-hued patch about 5 cm by 7 cm on the buttocks and lower back. What is the nurse's next action?

a. Call the Department of Social Services (DSS) to report this sign of abuse.

b. Confer with the physician about the possibility of a bleeding tendency.

c. Ask the mother about the cause of the bruise.

d. Chart the presence of a Mongolian spot.

Answer: d
Rationale: The nurse will chart the presence of a Mongolian spot, such as is observed in races with dark skin tones. The nurse who calls the DSS to report this patch as a sign of abuse will reveal ignorance in culturally competent assessments and possibly provoke harassment of the family. Similarly, if choosing to confer with the physician, the nurse will reveal ignorance in culturally competent assessments. Asking the mother about the cause of the bruise reveals cultural ignorance in a less damaging manner than calling DSS.
Assessment
Physiological Integrity
Application

2.11 A nurse is working in a clinic where children from several cultures are seen. As a first step toward the goal of personal cultural competence, the nurse will:

a. enhance cultural skills.

b. gain cultural awareness.

c. seek cultural encounters.

d. acquire cultural knowledge.

Answer: b
Rationale: Campinha-Bacote's theory of cultural competence (1999, 2002) sees the healthcare professional in a state of ever-increasing cultural competence. One begins by gaining cultural awareness or by gaining an effective and cognitive self-awareness of personal world-view biases, beliefs, etc. Another early step, acquiring cultural knowledge, includes studying information about the beliefs, biological variations, and favored treatments of specific cultural groups. Ways to enhance cultural skill include learning a prevalent language or learning how to recognize health-manifesting skin color variations in different races. During daily interactions with clients from diverse backgrounds, these cultural encounters allow the nurse to appreciate the uniqueness of individuals from varying backgrounds.
Planning
Psychosocial Integrity
Application

2.12 The dramatic increase in complementary and alternative therapies that began in the final decade of the twentieth century probably was the result of which of the following factors? Select all that apply.

a. the advent of the Internet.

b. the use of traditional Western medicine for treatment.

c. increased consumer awareness of the limitations of conventional medicine.

d. increased international travel.

e. increased media attention.

Answers: a, c, d, e
Rationale: The advent of the Internet, along with increased consumer awareness of the limitations of the current conventional medicine and increased international travel, has received increased media attention. The use of traditional Western medicine for treatment often has stopped the use of complementary therapies and forced clients to hide the fact they use them from their healthcare providers.
Assessment
Health Promotion and Maintenance
Application

2.13 Complementary and alternative therapies have many benefits for the childbearing family and others. However, many of these remedies have associated risks. Which of the following situations would be considered a risk? Select all that apply.

a. getting a massage from a licensed massage therapist for back pain, prescribed by the primary caregiver.

b. trying out a homeopathic medicine from a friend to reduce swelling in the legs.

c. getting a chiropractic treatment for low back pain due to discomforts of

Answers: b, c, d
Rationale: Trying out a homeopathic medicine from a friend to reduce swelling in your legs, getting a chiropractic treatment for low back pain due to discomforts of pregnancy without telling the primary healthcare provider, and taking an herbal preparation suggested by a health food store worker for treatment of leg pain are all risk factors when considering these therapies. Lack of standardization, lack of regulation and research to substantiate their safety and effectiveness, and inadequate training and certification of some healers make some therapies risky. Joining a group that practices Tai Chi weekly to help with physical fitness and movement and getting a massage from a licensed massage therapist for back pain and prescribed by the primary caregiver are all perfectly good uses of complementary therapies.

pregnancy without telling the primary healthcare provider. d. taking an herbal preparation suggested by a health food store worker for treatment of leg pain. e. joining a group that practices Tai Chi weekly to help with physical fitness and movement.	Assessment Safe, Effective Care Environment Application
2.14 A pregnant client is interested in the use of herbs during her pregnancy. There are basic principles the nurse should follow in advising the client. Which of the following would not be considered a basic principle? a. avoid the use of any herbs during the first trimester. b. avoid highly concentrated extracts of herbs. c. avoid the use of any herbs throughout pregnancy. d. consult with your healthcare provider before taking any herbs, even as teas.	Answer: c Rationale: Avoiding the use of any herbs throughout her pregnancy is not necessary. Many herbal preparations can be used after the first trimester if the basic principles found in the other answers are followed. Avoid the use of any herbs during the first trimester, avoid the use of highly concentrated extracts of herbs, and consult with your healthcare provider before taking any herbs, even as teas, are the basic principles in advising. Planning Safe, Effective Care Environment Application
2.15 A nurse is reviewing research related to use of complementary and alternative therapies medicine. The nurse discovers that the people most likely to use complementary and alternative therapies medicine are: a. affluent middle-aged men. b. affluent middle-aged women. c. elderly women who are middle class. d. females in their twenties who are middle class.	Answer: b Rationale: Research suggests that middle-aged women who are affluent use complementary medicine most often. Elderly women who are middle class, women in their twenties who are middle class, and middle-aged men who are affluent use complementary therapies less. Eighty percent of all people who do use them also use conventional medicine. Assessment Safe, Effective Care Environment Analysis

CHAPTER 3

3.1 A school nurse is teaching a health class to middle school children. The nurse explains that the follicle-stimulating hormone (FSH) and luteinizing hormone (LH) are secreted by the: a. hypothalamus. b. ovaries and testes. c. posterior pituitary. d. anterior pituitary.	Answer: d Rationale: The anterior pituitary secretes FSH and LH, which are primarily responsible for maturation of the ovarian follicle. The hypothalamus secretes gonadotropin-releasing hormone to the pituitary gland in response to signals from the central nervous system. The ovaries secrete the female hormone of estrogen and progesterone, and the testes secrete testosterone. The posterior pituitary gland secretes oxytocin and antidiuretic hormone. Implementation Health Promotion and Maintenance Analysis
3.2 A pregnant adolescent asks the nurse, "Why does the physician call measuring my uterus 'a fundal height'?" The nurse's answer is based on the fact that the fundus of the uterus is located: a. between the internal cervical os and the endometrial cavity. b. in the elongated portion where the fallopian tubes enter. c. in the lower third area. d. in the uppermost (dome-shaped top) portion.	Answer: d Rationale: The rounded uppermost (dome-shaped top) portion of the uterus that extends above the points of attachment of the fallopian tubes is called the fundus. The isthmus is that portion of the uterus between the internal cervical os and the endometrial cavity. The elongated portion where the fallopian tubes enter the uterus is called the cornua, and the lower third of the uterus is called the cervix or neck. Implementation Health Promotion and Maintenance Application

3.3 A nurse teaches newly pregnant clients that if an ovum is fertilized and implants in the endometrium, the hormone the fertilized egg begins to secrete is: a. estrogen. b. human chorionic gonadotropin (hCG). c. progesterone. d. luteinizing.	Answer: b Rationale: When the ovum is fertilized and implants in the endometrium, the fertilized egg begins to secrete human chorionic gonadotropin (hCG) hormone to maintain the corpus luteum. Estrogen and progesterone are ovarian hormones and luteininzing hormone is excreted by the anterior pituitary. Implementation Health Promotion and Maintenance Application
3.4 A woman has been unable to complete a full-term pregnancy because the fertilized ovum fails to implant in the uterus. This is most likely due to a lack of which hormone? a. estrogen. b. progesterone. c. FSH. d. LH.	Answer: b Rationale: Progesterone decreases uterine motility and contractility; thus a lack of progesterone will affect the ability of the uterus to be prepared for implantation after the ovum is fertilized. Estrogen is incorrect because it primarily assists in maturation of the ovarian follicles and causes endometrial mucosa to proliferate. FSH and LH are hormones secreted by the pituitary gland. Diagnosis Health Promotion and Maintenance Analysis
3.5 The vascularity of the uterus increases and the endometrium becomes prepared for a fertilized ovum in which phase of the menstrual cycle? a. menstrual. b. proliferative. c. secretory. d. ischemic.	Answer: b Rationale: The proliferative phase refers to the buildup of the endometrium as blood supply and uterine size is increased. The menstrual phase refers to the cyclic uterine bleeding in response to hormonal changes. The secretory phase occurs after ovulation and the ischemic phase occurs if fertilization does not occur. Assessment Health Promotion and Maintenance Application
3.6 A woman is experiencing mittelschmerz and increased vaginal discharge. Her temperature has increased by 0.6°C (1.0°F) for the past 36 hours. This most likely indicates that: a. menstruation is about to begin. b. ovulation will occur soon. c. ovulation has occurred. d. she is pregnant and will not menstruate.	Answer: c Rationale: Signs that ovulation has occurred include: pain associated with rupture of the ovum (mittelschmerz), increased vaginal discharge, and a temperature increase of 0.6°C for the past 36 hours. A temperature increase does not occur when menstruation is about to begin or before ovulation has occurred. She is pregnant and will not menstruate is incorrect because this can only be detected through testing the urine for the presence of human chorionic gonadotropin hormone. Diagnosis Health Promotion and Maintenance Analysis
3.7 The client shows an understanding of the pelvic cavity divisions by stating: a. "The true pelvis is made up of the sacrum, coccyx, and the innominate bones." b. "The false pelvis consists of the inlet, the pelvic cavity, and the outlet." c. "The true pelvis is the portion above the pelvic brim." d. "The relationship between the false pelvis and the fetal head is of paramount importance."	Answer: a Rationale: The true pelvis is made up of the sacrum, coccyx, and innominate bones and represents the bony limits of the birth canal. It's the true pelvis that consists of the inlet, the pelvic cavity, and the outlet not the false pelvis. The false pelvis is the portion above the pelvic brim. It is, therefore, the relationship between the true pelvis (not the false) and the fetal head that is of paramount importance. Evaluation Health Promotion and Maintenance Application

3.8 When planning care for a client who has undergone an episiotomy, it would be important to include a goal that addresses the need for pain relief of the:
a. mons pubis.
b. perineum.
c. labia minora.
d. hymen.

Answer: b
Rationale: The perineum is the superficial area between the anus and vagina, and this tissue is often the site of an episiotomy or lacerations during childbirth. The mons pubis refers to the soft mound overlying the pubic bone and is not involved in an episiotomy. The labia minora are the inner folds of the vagina and the hymen, if present, is a thin elastic collar of tissue that surrounds the vaginal opening. Neither of these is cut in an episiotomy.
Planning
Physiological Integrity
Application

3.9 The normal position of the uterus within the body cavity is:
a. anteflexed.
b. retroflexed.
c. retroverted.
d. anteverted.

Answer: d
Rationale: Anteverted is the normal position of the uterus as the uterus bends forward forming a sharp angle with the vagina. Retroflexed, or bending backward, retroverted and anteflexed, or not flexed, are not normal uterine positions within the body cavity.
Assessment
Health Promotion and Maintenance
Comprehension

3.10 The nurse explains to the client that the obstetric conjugate measurement is important because:
a. the size of this diameter determines whether the fetus can move down into the birth canal in order for engagement to occur.
b. this measurement determines the shape of the inlet.
c. the fetus passes under it during birth.
d. this determines the tilt of the pelvis.

Answer: a
Rationale: The obstetric conjugate extends from the middle of the sacral promontory to an area approximately 1 cm below the pubic crest. The fetus passes through the obstetric conjugate, and the size of this diameter determines whether the fetus can move down into the birth canal in order for engagement to occur. The transverse diameter is the largest diameter of the inlet and helps determine its shape. The fetus passes under the pubic arch, which is part of the pelvic outlet. A change in the lumbar curve can increase or decrease the tilt of the pelvis.
Implementation
Health Promotion and Maintenance
Application

3.11 A school nurse, teaching a health class to adolescent males, explains that spermatozoa become motile and fertile during the 2 to 10 days they are stored in the:
a. epididymis.
b. vas deferens.
c. prostate gland.
d. urethra.

Answer: a
Rationale: The epididymis provides a reservoir where maturing spermatozoa become both motile and fertile. The spermatozoa remain in the epididymis for 2 to 10 days. The vas deferens connects the epididymis with the prostate. The prostate gland secretes a fluid that protects the sperm from the acidic environment of the vagina. The urethra is the passageway for both urine and semen.
Implementation
Health Promotion and Maintenance
Application

3.12 Based on the anatomy of the male external genitalia, which of the following is the most logical cause of inability to achieve erection?
a. weakness or atrophy of the penile muscles.
b. poor circulation to the penis.
c. an undescended testicle.
d. decreased functioning of the seminiferous tubules.

Answer: b
Rationale: Poor circulation to the penis is the most logical cause because the penis becomes erect as result of innervation from the pudendal nerve, causing its blood vessels to become engorged. Weakness or atrophy of the penile muscle, an undescended testicle, and decreased function of the seminiferous tubules do not play a primary role in the inability to achieve erection.
Diagnosis
Health Promotion and Maintenance
Application

3.13 A man who has had a vasectomy becomes functionally sterile because the sperm: a. are no longer being produced. b. are no longer motile and fertile. c. cannot reach the outside of the body. d. cannot penetrate an ovum.	Answer: c Rationale: Sperm cannot reach the outside of the body in a man who has a vasectomy. The main function of the vas deferens, which is ligated in a vasectomy, is to squeeze the sperm from their storage site into the urethra. Sperm are no longer being produced is false because the sperm are produced in the seminiferous tubules in the testes and are not affected by a vasectomy. Sperm cannot penetrate an ovum is true, but only because they cannot reach the outside of the body due to the ligation. Sperm are no longer motile and fertile is not true because a vasectomy does not affect motility or fertility of sperm. Assessment Health Promotion and Maintenance Application
3.14 The uterine ligaments support and stabilize the various reproductive organs. Which of the following are true statements about the individual ligaments? Select all that apply. a. The infundibulopelvic ligaments suspend and support the uterus. b. The broad ligament keeps the uterus centrally placed. c. The uterosacral ligaments contribute to the pain of dysmenorrhea (painful menstruation). d. The ovarian ligaments anchor the ovary to the uterus. e. The cardinal ligaments prevent uterine prolapse and support the upper vagina.	Answers: b, c, d, e Rationale: The broad ligament keeps the uterus centrally placed, the uterosacral ligaments contribute to the pain of dysmenorrhea (painful menstruation), the ovarian ligaments anchor the ovary to the uterus, and the cardinal ligaments prevent uterine prolapse and support the upper vagina. The infundibulopelvic ligaments suspend and support the ovaries not the uterus. Assessment Health Promotion and Maintenance Application
3.15 Place the phases of the uterine (menstrual) cycle in order beginning with the end of the menstrual phase. (Write your answer in the space below.) a. ischemic phase b. proliferative c. secretory	Answer: b, c, a Rationale: After the menstrual phase ends, the proliferative phase begins when the endometrial glands enlarge. The secretory phase follows. If fertilization does not occur, the ischemic phase begins. Assessment Health Promotion and Maintenance Application

CHAPTER 4

4.1 A client asks her nurse "Is it okay for me to take a tub bath during the heavy part of my menstruation?" The correct response by the nurse is: a. "Tub baths are contraindicated during menstruation." b. "You should shower and douche daily instead." c. "Either a bath or a shower is fine at that time." d. "You should bathe and use a feminine deodorant spray during menstruation."	Answer: c Rationale: Bathing, whether it is a tub bath or shower, is as important (if not more so) during menses as at any other time. Douching should be avoided during menstruation. Feminine deodorant sprays are unnecessary. Implementation Physiological Integrity Application

4.2 When taking a sexual history from a client, the nurse should:

a. ask questions that the client can answer with a "yes" or "no".
b. ask mostly open-ended questions.
c. have the client fill out a comprehensive questionnaire and review it after the client leaves.
d. try not to make much direct eye contact.

Answer: b
Rationale: Open-ended questions are often useful in eliciting information. "Yes" or "no" answers will not provide the necessary information. It is helpful to use direct eye contact as much as possible, unless culturally unacceptable. Filling out a questionnaire is not appropriate.
Assessment
Health Promotion and Maintenance
Application

4.3 A client comes to the clinic complaining of severe menstrual cramps. She has never been pregnant, has been diagnosed with ovarian cysts, and has had an intrauterine device (IUD) for two years. The most likely cause for the client's complaint is:

a. primary dysmenorrhea.
b. secondary dysmenorrhea.
c. menorrhagia.
d. hypermenorrhea.

Answer: b
Rationale: Secondary dysmenorrhea is associated with pathology of the reproductive tract and usually appears after menstruation has been established. Conditions that most frequently cause secondary dysmenorrhea include ovarian cysts and the presence of an intrauterine device. Primary dysmenorrhea is defined as cramps without underlying disease. Menorrhagia is excessive, profuse flow. Hypermenorrhea is an abnormally long menstrual flow.
Assessment
Health Promotion and Maintenance
Analysis

4.4 A teaching plan for a client with premenstrual syndrome (PMS) should include a recommendation to restrict her intake of:

a. high-starch foods such as potatoes and spaghetti.
b. chicken, eggs, and fish.
c. breads, cereals, and beans.
d. coffee, colas, and chocolate cake.

Answer: d
Rationale: A client with PMS is advised to restrict her intake of foods containing methylxanthines such as chocolate, cola, and coffee. She should increase her intake of complex carbohydrates and proteins.
Planning
Physiological Integrity
Application

4.5 In using the natural method of contraception, the nurse should instruct the client to begin counting the first day of her cycle as:

a. the day her menstrual period ceases.
b. the first day after her menstrual period ceases.
c. the first day of her menstrual period.
d. the day of ovulation.

Answer: c
Rationale: The first day of menstruation is the first day of the cycle. The other answers are not indicators of the first day of the cycle.
Implementation
Health Promotion and Maintenance
Application

4.6 How is the cervical mucus method of contraception different from the calendar (rhythm) method? The cervical mucus method:

a. is more effective for women with irregular cycles.
b. is free, safe, and acceptable to women of many religions.
c. provides an increased awareness of the body.
d. requires no artificial substances or devices.

Answer: a
Rationale: The cervical mucus method can be used by women with irregular cycles. The other choices apply to both methods.
Evaluation
Health Promotion and Maintenance
Application

4.7 A client who wants to use the vaginal sponge as a method of contraception shows that she understands the appropriate usage with which of the following statements? a. "I need to use a lubricant prior to insertion." b. "I need to add spermicidal cream prior to intercourse." c. "I need to moisten it with water prior to use." d. "I need to leave it in no longer than 6 hours."	Answer: c Rationale: To activate the spermicide in the vaginal sponge, it must be moistened thoroughly with water. Lubricant and spermicidal cream are not needed. The sponge can remain in place for 24 hours. Evaluation Health Promotion and Maintenance Application
4.8 The nurse at the family planning clinic has done some teaching on oral contraceptives in the waiting room. The nurse knows that the teaching has been effective when one of the clients responds: a. "I can't take 'the pill' if I'm over 30." b. "I can take 'the pill,' even though I smoke heavily." c. "My periods will become slightly heavier when I take 'the pill'." d. "I can't take 'the pill' if I have gallbladder disease."	Answer: d Rationale: Oral contraceptive is contraindicated in women with gallbladder disease and those who smoke heavily. There is not an age specification. Menstrual flow is decreased with the use of oral contraceptives. Evaluation Physiological Integrity Application
4.9 A client who is 36 years old, weighs 200 pounds, is monogamous, and does not smoke desires birth control. The nurse understands that which of the following is inappropriate for this client? a. intrauterine device. b. vaginal sponge. c. combined oral contraceptives. d. transdermal hormonal contraception.	Answer: d Rationale: Transdermal hormonal contraception is contraindicated due to her obesity. This client may use an intrauterine device, the vaginal sponge, or combined oral contraceptives. Diagnosis Health Promotion and Maintenance Analysis
4.10 Which client would not be a good candidate for Depo-Provera (DMPA)? a. one who wishes to get pregnant within three months. b. a nursing mother. c. one with a vaginal prolapse. d. one who weighs 200 pounds.	Answer: a Rationale: Return of fertility after the use of Depo-Provera takes an average of nine months. A nursing mother can use Depo-Provera. Obesity and vaginal prolapse do not prevent the use of Depo-Provera. Implementation Physiological Integrity Application
4.11 A couple asks the nurse what would be the safest method of sterilization. The nurse should reply, "Generally, the safest method of permanent sterilization would be a: a. laparotomy tubal ligation." b. laparoscopy tubal ligation." c. minilaparotomy." d. vasectomy."	Answer: d Rationale: Vasectomy is a relatively minor procedure. The other choices are all female sterilization procedures that involve more risks. Implementation Health Promotion and Maintenance Application

4.12 When a woman who has been raped is admitted to the emergency room, which nursing intervention has priority? a. explain exactly what will need to be done to preserve legal evidence. b. assure the woman that everything will be all right. c. create a safe, secure atmosphere for her. d. contact family members.	Answer: c Rationale: The first priority in caring for a survivor of a sexual assault is to create a safe, secure atmosphere. The other interventions would not take priority over safety at this time. Planning Safe, Effective Care Environment Analysis
4.13 A menopausal woman tells her nurse that she experiences discomfort from vaginal dryness during sexual intercourse, and asks, "What should I use as a lubricant?" The nurse should recommend: a. petroleum jelly. b. a water-soluble lubricant. c. body cream or body lotion. d. less-frequent intercourse.	Answer: b Rationale: A water-soluble jelly should be used. Petroleum jelly, body creams, and body lotions are not water-soluble. Less-frequent intercourse is an inappropriate response. Implementation Physiological Integrity Application
4.14 When teaching a woman about the use of a diaphragm, it is important to instruct her that the diaphragm should be rechecked for correct size: a. every five years routinely. b. when weight gain or loss beyond five pounds has occurred. c. after each birth. d. only after significant weight loss.	Answer: c Rationale: The diaphragm should be rechecked for correct size after each childbirth and whenever a woman has gained or lost 10 pounds or more. Implementation Health Promotion and Maintenance Application
4.15 A nurse is providing a client with instructions regarding breast self-examination (BSE). Which of the following statements by the client would indicate that the teaching has been successful? Select all that apply. a. "I should perform BSE one week prior to the start of my period." b. "When I reach menopause, I will perform BSE every two months." c. "Knowing the texture of my breasts is important." d. "I should inspect my breasts while standing with my arms down at my sides." e. "I should inspect my breasts while in a supine position with my arms at my sides."	Answers: c, d Rationale: A woman who knows the texture and feel of her own breasts is far more likely to detect changes that develop. The breasts should be inspected while standing with arms at sides. Supine is not a correct position. BSE should be performed one week after the start of each menstrual period. BSE should be performed monthly, on the same day each month, during menopause. Evaluation Health Promotion and Maintenance Application

5.1 In teaching women about ways of preventing toxic shock syndrome (TSS), it is important for the nurse to know that women at increased risk are those who:
a. use high-absorbency tampons.
b. use an IUD.
c. use oral contraception.
d. have multiple sexual partners.

Answer: a
Rationale: The use of super-absorbent tampons and occluding the cervical os with a contraceptive during menses increase the risk of TSS. Using an IUD, oral contraceptive, or having multiple sexual partners does not increase the risk of TSS.
Planning
Health Promotion and Maintenance
Analysis

5.2 A nonpregnant client reports a fishy smelling, thin, white, watery vaginal discharge. She is diagnosed with bacterial vaginosis (BV). The nurse would be expecting to administer:
a. penicillin G (Bicillin) 2 million units IM one time.
b. zithromax (Azithromycin) 1 mg po bid for 2 weeks.
c. doxycycline (Vibramycin) 100 mg po bid for a week.
d. metronidazole (Flagyl) 500 mg po bid for a week.

Answer: d
Rationale: The nonpregnant woman who is diagnosed with bacterial vaginosis (BV) is treated with metronidazole (Flagyl) 500 mg orally twice a day for seven days. Penicillin, zithromax, and doxycycline are not used to treat BV.
Planning
Physiological Integrity
Analysis

5.3 The client being given discharge instructions with a diagnosis of vulvovaginal candidiasis (VVC) demonstrates understanding when she states:
a. "I need to apply the miconazole (Monistat) for 10 days."
b. "I need to douche daily."
c. "I need to add yogurt to my diet."
d. "I need to wear nylon panties."

Answer: c
Rationale: Yogurt helps prevent recurrence. Douching daily, wearing nylon panties, and applying miconazole for 10 days do not prevent or assist in treating vulvovaginal candidiasis.
Evaluation
Health Promotion and Maintenance
Application

5.4 The physician has prescribed metronidazole (Flagyl) for a woman diagnosed with trichomoniasis. The nurse's instructions to the woman should be:
a. "Both partners must be treated with the medication."
b. "Alcohol does not need to be avoided while taking this medication."
c. "It will turn your urine orange."
d. "It may produce drowsiness."

Answer: a
Rationale: Both partners should be treated with the medication. Alcohol should be avoided. Metronidazole does not turn the urine orange or cause drowsiness.
Implementation
Physiological Integrity
Application

5.5 The couple demonstrates understanding of the consequences of not treating chlamydia when they state:
a. "She could become pregnant."
b. "She could have severe vaginal itching."
c. "He could get an infection in the tube that carries the urine out."
d. "It could cause us to develop a rash."

Answer: c
Rationale: Chlamydia is a major cause of nongonococcal urethritis (NGU) in men. It does not cause a woman to become pregnant, vaginal itching, or a rash.
Evaluation
Health Promotion and Maintenance
Application

5.6 Which of the following clients should be treated with ceftriaxone (Rocephin) IM and doxycycline (Vibramycin) orally? a. a pregnant client with gonorrhea and yeast infection. b. a nonpregnant client with gonorrhea and chlamydia. c. a pregnant client with syphilis. d. a nonpregnant client with chlamydia and trichomoniasis.	Answer: b Rationale: This combined treatment provides dual treatment for gonorrhea and chlamydia because the two infections frequently occur together. The other choices are incorrect. Implementation Physiological Integrity Application
5.7 Which of the following statements by the client verifies correct knowledge about vaginal herpes? a. "I should douche daily to prevent infection." b. "I may have another breakout during my period." c. "I am more likely to develop cancer of the cervix." d. "I should use sodium bicarbonate on the lesions to relieve discomfort."	Answer: b Rationale: Menstruation seems to trigger recurrences of herpes. Burow's (aluminum acetate) solution relieves discomfort, not sodium bicarbonate. Douches do not prevent infection. There is no relation to herpes and cancer of the cervix. Evaluation Health Promotion and Maintenance Application
5.8 A client comes in complaining of wart-like lesions on the vulva, painful wrist and finger joints, and a chronic and hoarse sore throat. The appropriate treatment would be: a. penicillin G (Bicillin) IM b. acyclovir (Zovirax) po c. ceftriaxone (Rocephin) IM d. azithromycin (Zithromax) po	Answer: a Rationale: The symptoms are the result of syphilis. Syphilis is treated with penicillin G administered intramuscularly. Acyclovir, ceftriaxone, and azithromycin are not used to treat syphilis. Implementation Physiological Integrity Application
5.9 The nurse walks in to find the client crying after the physician informed her of her diagnosis of human papillomavirus (HPV). Which of the following statements by the nurse conveys an attitude of acceptance towards the client with a sexually transmitted infection? a. "Don't worry about it. In a few weeks, with treatment, the lesions will disappear." b. "You seem upset. I'll get the doctor." c. "You seem upset. Can I help answer any questions?" d. "I think you need to see a therapist."	Answer: c Rationale: The nurse's attitude of acceptance and matter-of-factness conveys to the woman that she is still an acceptable person who happens to have an infection. The other statements are not conveying acceptance, they are ignoring the needs of the client. Implementation Psychosocial Integrity Application
5.10 The nurse obtains a health history from the following clients. To which one should she give priority for teaching about cervical cancer prevention? a. age 30, treated for PID. b. age 25, monogamous. c. age 20, pregnant. d. age 27, uses a diaphragm.	Answer: a Rationale: Exposure to sexually transmitted infections increases risk of abnormal cell changes and cervical cancer. Pregnancy, use of a diaphragm, and practicing monogamy do not increase risks of cervical cancer. Planning Health Promotion and Maintenance Analysis

5.11 The client gives correct information regarding ways to prevent a recurrence of her urinary tract infection when she states: a. "I should wipe from back to front after urination." b. "I should urinate when I feel the urge." c. "I should try to restrict my intake of fruits." d. "I should use a diaphragm."	Answer: b Rationale: Retention overdistends the bladder and can lead to infection. Wiping from back to front after urination may transfer bacteria from the anorectal area to the urethra. Organic acids from fruits inhibit bacterial growth. The use of a diaphragm does not prevent recurrence of a urinary tract infection. Evaluation Physiological Integrity Application
5.12 A nurse is assessing a pregnant client for right-sided flank pain. The nurse explains to the client that this type of pain is a common symptom of pyelonephritis in the pregnant client because of: a. temporary suspension of urine output. b. nausea and vomiting. c. the position of the uterus in the abdomen. d. a colicky large intestine.	Answer: c Rationale: The right side is almost always involved if the woman is pregnant because the large bulk of intestines to the left pushes the uterus to the right. Temporary suspension of urine output, and nausea and vomiting, are symptoms from the pyelonephritis. A colicky large intestine is an incorrect response. Implementation Physiological Integrity Application
5.13 A client is hospitalized for pelvic inflammatory disease. Which of the following nursing interventions would have priority? a. encourage oral fluids. b. administer cefotetan IV. c. enforce bed rest. d. remove IUD if present.	Answer: b Rationale: Administration of medications to treat the disease is priority. Bed rest and encouraging oral fluids are not a priority. Removal of the IUD is not a nursing intervention. Planning Physiological Integrity Application
5.14 The nurse interviews a 28-year-old client with a new medical diagnosis of endometriosis. Which of the following questions are most appropriate? Select all that apply. a. "Are you having hot flashes?" b. "Are you experiencing pain during intercourse?" c. "Is a discharge present?" d. "Are you having pain during your period?" e. "Have you noticed any skin rashes?" f. "Do you have any children?"	Answers: b, d, f Rationale: The primary symptoms of endometriosis include dysmenorrhea, dyspareunia, and infertility. Hot flashes, a discharge, and skin rashes are not symptoms of endometriosis. Assessment Physiological Integrity Application
5.15 A nurse is taking care of a client after an abdominal hysterectomy. A priority nursing diagnosis in the early post-operative period would be: a. acute pain. b. powerlessness. c. hyperthermia. d. constipation.	Answer: a Rationale: Pain is a concern when an abdominal hysterectomy is performed. Powerlessness, hyperthermia, and constipation would have lower priorities immediately after surgery. Diagnosis Physiological Integrity Application

6.1 An infertile couple confides in the nurse at the infertility clinic that they feel overwhelmed with the decisions facing them. Which of the following nursing strategies would be most appropriate?
a. refer them to a marriage counselor.
b. provide them with information and instructions throughout the diagnostic and therapeutic process.
c. express concern and caring.
d. inquire about the names they have chosen for their baby.

Answer: b
Rationale: The nurse can provide comfort to couples by offering a sympathetic ear, a nonjudgmental approach, and appropriate information and instruction throughout the diagnostic and therapeutic process. Expressing concern, inquiring about names, and referring the couple to a counselor are not appropriate.
Planning
Health Promotion and Maintenance
Application

6.2 The nurse is reviewing assessment data from several different male clients. Which one should receive information about causes of infertility?
a. circumcised client.
b. client with a history of premature ejaculation.
c. client with a history of measles at age 12.
d. client employed as an engineer.

Answer: b
Rationale: Premature ejaculation is a possible cause of infertility. Circumcision, having the measles, and being an engineer do not affect fertility.
Planning
Health Promotion and Maintenance
Analysis

6.3 A nurse is reviewing the basal body temperature method with a couple. Which of the following statements would indicate that the teaching has been successful?
a. "I have to go buy a special type of thermometer."
b. "I need to wait five minutes after smoking a cigarette before I take my temperature."
c. "I need to take my temperature before I get out of bed in the morning."
d. "I need to take my temperature for at least two minutes every day."

Answer: c
Rationale: The woman takes her temperature for five minutes every day before arising and before starting any activity, including smoking. The temperature can be taken with a standard oral or rectal thermometer.
Evaluation
Health Promotion and Maintenance
Analysis

6.4 The nurse is planning to teach couples factors that influence fertility. Which of the following should not be included in the teaching plan?
a. sexual intercourse should occur four times a week.
b. get up to urinate one hour after intercourse.
c. do not douche.
d. institute stress reduction techniques.

Answer: a
Rationale: Intercourse should occur one to three times per week at intervals of no less than 48 hours. Urinating one hour after intercourse, not douching, and stress reduction techniques should be included in the teaching plan.
Planning
Health Promotion and Maintenance
Application

6.5 A client calls the urologist's office to receive instructions about semen analysis. The nurse instructs the client to:

a. avoid sexual intercourse 24 hours prior to obtaining a specimen.
b. use a latex condom to collect the specimen.
c. expect that a repeat test may be required.
d. expect a small sample.

Answer: c
Rationale: A repeat semen analysis may be required to adequately assess the man's fertility potential. The specimen is collected after 2 to 3 days of abstinence, usually by masturbation. Regular condoms should not be used, due to spermicidal agents that they contain. A small sample is not an appropriate instruction.
Implementation
Health Promotion and Maintenance
Application

6.6 A client calls the fertility clinic to schedule a laparoscopy. The nurse instructs the client to:

a. stay on bed rest 48 hours after procedure.
b. expect to have shoulder and arm pain.
c. purchase a rectal tube to relieve the gas.
d. lay on her back to relieve the gas pain.

Answer: d
Rationale: Assuming a supine position may help to relieve discomfort caused by remaining gas. Normal activities can be resumed after 24 hours. The client may experience shoulder and chest pain caused by gas in the abdomen. Insertion of a rectal tube is not an intervention expected of the client.
Implementation
Health Promotion and Maintenance
Application

6.7 The physician has prescribed the medication Clomid (clomiphene citrate) for a client with infertility. The nurse's instructions to the woman should be:

a. "Have sexual intercourse every day for one week, starting five days after completion of medication."
b. "Take a pregnancy test before restarting medication."
c. "Contact the doctor if visual disturbances occur."
d. "Discontinue the medication if hot flashes occur."

Answer: c
Rationale: Contact the doctor if visual disturbances occur because the medication may have to be discontinued. Sexual intercourse should occur every other day. If a woman does not have a period, she must be checked for the possibility of pregnancy. If hot flashes occur, relief can be obtained without discontinuing medication.
Implementation
Physiological Integrity
Application

6.8 The nurse at the fertility clinic instructs a couple on the Huhner test. The nurse knows that the teaching has been effective when they state:

a. "We must have sexual intercourse one day prior to the menstrual cycle."
b. "This test removes the spontaneity from our sex lives."
c. "The specimen is collected in a sterile cup."
d. "This test counts the number of sperm my husband produces."

Answer: b
Rationale: The focus of the postcoital exam is on the timing of intercourse. The Huhner test is performed one or two days before the expected date of ovulation. The specimen is collected into a 10 ml syringe. The motility of the sperm is evaluated.
Evaluation
Physiological Integrity
Analysis

6.9 A client and her husband have contacted their physician about fertility problems. At the initial visit, the nurse instructs them on the infertility workup. Which of the following statements by the client would indicate that the instructions have been successful?

a. "The first test that we need to schedule is a semen analysis."
b. "We need to schedule the Huhner test first."
c. "We need to schedule an appointment with the social worker in order to adopt."
d. "We need to schedule an appointment with a counselor."

Answer: a
Rationale: A semen analysis is one of the first diagnostic tests prior to doing invasive procedures. The Huhner test would not be done first. Scheduling to meet with a social worker would not be done after the initial visit. A counselor visit is not part of the infertility workup.
Evaluation
Health Promotion and Maintenance
Analysis

6.10 During the initial visit with the nurse at the fertility clinic, the client asks what effect cigarette smoking has on the ability to conceive. The nurse's best response is:

a. "Smoking has no effect."
b. "Only if you smoke more that one pack a day will you experience difficulty."
c. "After your first semen analysis, we will determine if there will be any difficulty."
d. "Smoking can affect sperm motility."

Answer: d
Rationale: Cigarette smoking may depress sperm motility. The other responses are incorrect.
Implementation
Health Promotion and Maintenance
Application

6.11 A male client visits the infertility clinic for the results of his comprehensive exam. The exam indicated oligospermia. The client asks the nurse which procedure would assist him and his wife to conceive. The nurse's best response is: (Select all that apply.)

a. "You may want to consider adoption."
b. "An option you may consider is in vitro fertilization."
c. "Surrogacy may be your best option."
d. "Many couples utilize therapeutic husband insemination."
e. "The GIFT procedure has had much success."

Answers: b, d
Rationale: Therapeutic husband insemination is generally indicated for such seminal deficiencies as oligospermia. The in vitro fertilization procedure is used in cases in which infertility has resulted from male infertility. Adoption and surrogacy are not immediate options. The GIFT procedure is not an immediate option.
Implementation
Health Promotion and Maintenance
Application

6.12 A 58-year-old father and a 45-year-old mother gave birth to a baby boy two days ago. The nurse assesses a single palmar crease and low-set ears on the newborn. The nurse plans to counsel the couple about which of the following chromosomal abnormality?

a. trisomy 13.
b. trisomy 18.
c. trisomy 21.
d. trisomy 26.

Answer: c
Rationale: A single palmar crease and low-set ears are characteristics of trisomy 21 (Down syndrome). They are not characteristics of trisomy 13 and trisomy 18. Trisomy 26 is not a chromosomal abnormality.
Planning
Psychosocial Integrity
Application

6.13 A newborn has been diagnosed with a disorder that occurs through an autosomal recessive inheritance pattern. The parents ask the nurse "Which of us passed on the gene that caused the disorder?" The nurse responds: a. the female. b. the male. c. neither. d. both.	Answer: d Rationale: In an autosomal recessive inherited disorder, both parents are carriers of the abnormal gene. It is not a sex-linked disorder or an abnormal chromosome disorder. Implementation Health Promotion and Maintenance Application
6.14 A nurse counsels a couple on sex-linked disorders. Both are carriers of the disorder. They ask the nurse how this disorder will affect any children they may have. The nurse's best response is: a. "If you have a daughter, she will not be affected." b. "Your son will be affected, since the father has the disorder." c. "There is a 25% chance that your son will have the disorder, since the mother has the disorder." d. "There is a 50% chance that your son will be a carrier only."	Answer: d Rationale: There is a 50% chance that a carrier mother will pass the normal gene to each of her sons, who will be unaffected. There is a 50% chance that a carrier mother will pass the abnormal gene to each of her sons, who will be affected. Fathers affected with a sex-linked disorder cannot pass the disorder to their sons, but all their daughters become carriers of the disorder. There is a 50% chance that a carrier mother will pass the abnormal gene to each of her daughters, who will become carriers. Implementation Health Promotion and Maintenance Application
6.15 The nurse is reviewing prenatal assessment data for several clients. Which one would be most likely to receive a genetic amniocentesis? a. 25-year-old primipara. b. 40-year-old primipara. c. 30-year-old multipara. d. 28-year-old conceived after taking fertility drugs.	Answer: b Rationale: Women age 35 or older are at greater risk for having children with chromosomal abnormalities and would likely be receiving a genetic amniocentesis. The 25-year-old primipara, 30-year-old multipara, or the 28-year-old who conceived after taking fertility drugs would not be as likely to receive a genetic amniocentesis. Assessment Health Promotion and Maintenance Analysis

CHAPTER 7

7.1 In order for fertilization to occur, what portion of the sperm must enter the ovum? a. the entire sperm. b. only the head. c. only the tail. d. either the head or the tail.	Answer: b Rationale: Only the head of the sperm enters the ovum in a twofold process known as capacitation and acrosomal reaction. The entire sperm, only the tail, and either the head or the tail are incorrect due to the above reason. Assessment Health Promotion and Maintenance Analysis
7.2 The cell division process that results in two identical cells, each with the same number of chromosomes as the original cell, is called: a. meiosis. b. mitosis. c. oogenesis. d. gametogenesis.	Answer: b Rationale: Mitosis is the process of cell division described. Meiosis is a process of cell division leading to the development of eggs and sperm. Oogenesis is the process by which female gametes, or ova, are produced. Gametogenesis is the process by which germ cells are produced. Assessment Health Promotion and Maintenance Analysis

7.3 Once the ovum has entered the fallopian tube, which of the following facilitates movement of the ovum through the fallopian tube and toward the uterus? a. estrogen-induced tubal peristalsis. b. progesterone-induced cervical mucus changes. c. motions of the fallopian fimbriae. d. movements of the corona radiata of the ovum.	Answer: a Rationale: Estrogen-induced tubal peristalsis helps move the ovum through the tube, as the ovum has no inherent power of movement. Progesterone-induced cervical changes also can aid in ovum transport but are not the primary mover. Motions of the fallopian fimbriae occur as the ovum is released at ovulation but do not facilitate the movement through the fallopian tube. Movements of the corona radiata of the ovum surround the zona pellucida, and since the ovum has no inherent power of movement, it does not facilitate movement through the fallopian tube. Assessment Health Promotion and Maintenance Analysis
7.4 When evaluating information taught about conception and fetal development, the client verbalizes understanding about transportation time of the zygote through the fallopian tube and into the cavity of the uterus with which statement? a. "It will take at least 3 days for the egg to reach the uterus." b. "It will take 8 days for the egg to reach the uterus." c. "It will only take 12 hours for the egg to go through the fallopian tube." d. "It will take 18 hours for the fertilized egg to implant in the uterus."	Answer: a Rationale: "It will take at least 3 days for the egg to reach the uterus" is the correct statement. The other statements—"It will take 8 days for the egg to reach the uterus," "It will only take 12 hours for the egg to go through the fallopian tube," and "It will take 18 hours for the fertilized egg to implant in the uterus"—all are incorrect interpretations of the information on conception. Evaluation Health Promotion and Maintenance Application
7.5 If only a small volume of sperm is discharged into the vagina, an insufficient amount of enzymes may be released when they encounter the ovum. In that case, pregnancy would probably not result because: a. peristalsis of the fallopian tube would decrease, making it difficult for the ovum to enter the uterus. b. the block to polyspermy (cortical reaction) would not occur. c. the fertilized ovum would be unable to implant in the uterus. d. sperm would be unable to penetrate the zona pellucida of the ovum.	Answer: d Rationale: Sperm would be unable to penetrate the zona pellucida of the ovum because it takes hundreds of acrosomes (the result of the acrosomal reaction) to rupture and release enough hyaluronic acid to clear the way for a single sperm to penetrate the ovum's zona pellucida successfully. "Peristalsis of the fallopian tube would decrease, making it difficult for the ovum to enter the uterus" is an incorrect statement. "The block to polyspermy (cortical reaction) would not occur" is incorrect because a block to polyspermy indicates the ovum has been penetrated by a fertilizing sperm. The fertilized ovum would be unable to implant in the uterus because fertilization is unlikely to occur with a low sperm count. Assessment Health Promotion and Maintenance Analysis
7.6 Which of the following would be typical of a fetus at 20 weeks? (Select all that apply.) a. The fetus has a body weight of 435 to 465 g. b. The fetus actively sucks and swallows amniotic fluid. c. The kidneys begin to produce urine. d. Nipples appear over the mammary glands. e. Lanugo covers the entire body.	Answers: a, b, d, e Rationale: A fetus at 20 weeks has a body weight of 435 to 465 g, can actively suck and swallow amniotic fluid, has nipples that appear over the mammary glands, and has lanugo that covers the entire body. Kidneys begin to produce urine between 9 and 12 weeks' gestation. Assessment Health Promotion and Maintenance Analysis

7.7 At her first prenatal visit, a woman and the nurse are discussing fetal development. The client asks, "When will my baby actually have a heartbeat?" The nurse should reply, "The heartbeat of an embryo is distinguishable by week number _____ of development."

Answer: 4
Rationale: The fourth week is when the tubular heart is beating at a regular rhythm and pushing its own primitive blood cells through the main blood vessels.
Implementation
Health Promotion and Maintenance
Application

7.8 A woman is seven months pregnant, and has come to the obstetrical clinic for a routine prenatal examination. During the assessment, the nurse hears a soft blowing sound above the mother's symphysis pubis. The rate of sound is synchronous with the mother's heartbeat. The nurse identifies this as:

a. a normal sound called funic soufflé.
b. a normal sound called uterine soufflé.
c. an abnormal sound representing an aortic aneurysm.
d. an abnormal sound representing a false knot in the cord.

Answer: b
Rationale: The normal sound called uterine soufflé is timed precisely with the mother's pulse and is heard over the mother's pubis during the last months of pregnancy. The normal sound called funic soufflé is synchronous with the fetal heartbeat and fetal blood flow through the umbilical arteries. An abnormal sound representing an aortic aneurysm and an abnormal sound representing a false knot in the cord are incorrect assessments of this sound.
Diagnosis
Health Promotion and Maintenance
Analysis

7.9 The placenta produces hormones that are vital to the function of the fetus. Which hormone is primarily responsible for the maintenance of pregnancy past the eleventh week?

a. human chorionic gonadotropin (hCG).
b. human placental lactogen (hPL).
c. estrogen.
d. progesterone.

Answer: d
Rationale: Progesterone is primarily responsible for maintenance of pregnancy past the eleventh week because it decreases the contractility of the uterus, thus preventing uterine contractions from causing spontaneous abortion. Human chorionic gonadotropin (HCG) begins to decrease as placental hormone production increases. Human placental lactogen (hPL) stimulates certain changes in the mother's metabolic processes and can be detected by 4 weeks after conception. Estrogen secreted by the placenta is in the form of estriol and cannot be synthesized by the placenta alone.
Assessment
Health Promotion and Maintenance
Analysis

7.10 During a prenatal examination, a client asks, "How does my baby get air?" The nurse would give correct information by saying:

a. "The lungs of the fetus carry out respiratory gas exchange in utero."
b. "The placenta assumes the function of the fetal lungs by supplying oxygen and allowing the excretion of carbon dioxide into your bloodstream."
c. "The blood from the placenta is carried through the umbilical artery, which penetrates the abdominal wall of the fetus."
d. "The fetus is able to obtain sufficient oxygen due to the fact that your hemoglobin concentration is 50% greater during pregnancy."

Answer: b
Rationale: The placenta assumes the function of the fetal lungs by supplying oxygen and allowing the excretion of carbon dioxide into your bloodstream would be the correct information. "The lungs of the fetus carry out respiratory gas exchange in utero" is incorrect because most of the blood supply bypasses the fetal lungs, since they do not carry out respiratory gas exchange. "The blood from the placenta is carried through the umbilical artery, which penetrates the abdominal wall of the fetus" is incorrect because blood is carried through the umbilical vein. "The fetus is able to obtain sufficient oxygen due to the fact that your hemoglobin concentration is 50% greater during pregnancy" benefits the mother for future blood loss in birth.
Implementation
Health Promotion and Maintenance
Application

7.11 The fetus is wrinkled, covered with vernix, opens and closes eyelids, and has physiologically immature lungs that would sufficiently provide gas exchange. What gestational age is this fetus?
a. 23 weeks.
b. 25 weeks.
c. 30 weeks.
d. 34 weeks.

Answer: b
Rationale: Twenty-five weeks is the gestational age of the fetus in the description. At 23 weeks, the fetal skin is reddish and wrinkled, and eyes are still closed. At 30 weeks, the fetus gains weight and has rhythmic breathing movements. At 34 weeks, the fetus has less wrinkled skin and lanugo begins to disappear.
Assessment
Health Promotion and Maintenance
Analysis

7.12 In evaluating the effect of prior teaching regarding functions of the amniotic fluid, the nurse recognizes that more teaching is required when the client states:
a. "The fluid helps cushion the baby against harm."
b. "The fluid helps maintain environmental temperature."
c. "The fluid aids in musculoskeletal development."
d. "The fluid is responsible for oxygen exchange."

Answer: d
Rationale: "The fluid is responsible for oxygen exchange" would require more teaching because the oxygen exchange is facilitated by the placenta circulation. The fluid does help cushion the baby against harm, helps maintain environment temperature, and aids in musculoskeletal development by allowing freedom of movement.
Evaluation
Health Promotion and Maintenance
Application

7.13 A pregnant woman tells the midwife, "I've heard that if I eat certain foods during my pregnancy, the baby will be a boy." The nurse's response should explain that this is a myth, and that the sex of the baby is determined at the time of:
a. ejaculation.
b. fertilization.
c. implantation.
d. differentiation.

Answer: b
Rationale: Fertilization is the time when the sex of the zygote is determined. Ejaculation is the release of sperm from the male. Implantation refers to the implanting of the fertilized ovum in the uterine endometrium. Differentiation refers to a cell division process.
Implementation
Health Promotion and Maintenance
Application

7.14 The process of implantation is characterized by which of following processes? (Select all that apply.)
a. The trophoblast attaches itself to the surface of the endometrium.
b. The most frequent site of attachment is the lower part of the anterior uterine wall.
c. Between 7 and 10 days, the zona pellucida disappears and the blastocyst implants itself in the uterine lining.
d. The lining of the uterus thins below the implanted blastocyst.
e. The cells of the trophoblast grow down into the uterine lining, forming the chorionic villi.

Answers: a, c, e
Rationale: During implantation, the trophoblast attaches itself to the surface of the endometrium, and between 7 and 10 days, the zona pellucida disappears and the blastocyst implants itself in the thickened uterine lining. The cells of the trophoblast grow down into the thickened lining forming the chorionic villi. The most frequent site of attachment is not the lower part of the anterior wall, but rather the upper part of the posterior uterine wall. The lining of the uterus thickens, rather than thins, below the implanted blastocyst.
Assessment
Health Promotion and Maintenance
Analysis

7.15 Prenatal influences on the intrauterine environment include which of the following? (Select all that apply.)
a. the use of saunas or hot tubs.
b. the use of drugs.
c. the quality of the sperm or ovum.
d. maternal nutrition.
e. vitamins and folic acid.

Answers: a, b, d, e
Rationale: The use of saunas or hot tubs is associated with maternal hyperthermia. The use of drugs can have teratogenic effects. Maternal nutrition, if deficient, can cause damage to the fetus. Vitamins and folic acid taken prior to and during the pregnancy can have beneficial effects. The quality of the sperm or ovum will affect embryonic development but not necessarily affect the intrauterine environment.
Assessment
Safe, Effective Care Environment
Application

8.1 A primigravida is admitted to the labor unit with contractions every 7–8 minutes. She is 3 cm dilated, 70% effaced, and 0 station. She is very anxious, having difficulty coping with contractions, and states she did not attend prenatal classes. Which of the following would be the most effective nursing intervention?

a. Instruct the client in abdominal breathing and progressive relaxation.
b. Instruct the client in patterned paced breathing and touch relaxation.
c. Instruct the client in pelvic tilt and pelvic rock exercises.
d. Call the physician and request a sedative.

Answer: a
Rationale: Abdominal breathing and progressive relaxation assist the client in relaxing and allow the uterine muscles to work more efficiently. Patterned paced breathing and touch relaxation are exercises taught in childbirth preparation classes and involve the use of a partner. Pelvic tilt and rock exercises are body-conditioning exercises. Providing sedatives would not allow the client to participate actively in the process.
Implementation
Health Promotion and Maintenance
Application

8.2 While teaching a preconception class, the nurse includes which of the following recommendations to decrease the risk of neural tube defects?

a. 500 mg vitamin C every day.
b. 0.4 mg folate every day.
c. 1500 mg calcium every day.
d. 600 mg vitamin A every day.

Answer: b
Rationale: Folic acid supplementation prior to conception is recommended since this decreases the risk of neural tube defects. The other nutrients do not decrease the risk of neural tube defects.
Implementation
Health Promotion and Maintenance
Application

8.3 An expectant couple desires to determine compatibility with a care provider. They ask the nurse for assistance. Which of the following questions should be addressed first?

a. "Can my children attend the birth?"
b. "If I have a cesarean birth, can my husband attend?"
c. "What is your philosophy of birth?"
d. "What percentage of your clients has episiotomies?"

Answer: c
Rationale: A thorough understanding of the provider's philosophy is essential to determining compatibility. Children attendance, a husband's presence for a cesarean birth, and episiotomy percentages are complements of the provider's philosophy.
Implementation
Safe, Effective Care Environment
Analysis

8.4 The nurse is assisting an expectant couple in developing a birth plan. Which of the following instructions would the nurse include in the teaching plan?

a. The birth plan includes only client choices and does not take into account standard choices of the healthcare provider.
b. The birth plan allows the client to make choices about the birth process; however, these choices cannot be altered.
c. The birth plan is a legally binding contract between the client and the healthcare provider.
d. The birth plan is a communication tool between the client and the healthcare provider.

Answer: d
Rationale: The birth plan is used as a tool for communication among the expectant parents, the healthcare provider, and the healthcare professionals at the birth setting. It is not a legal document. The written plan identifies options that are available; thus, it can be altered.
Planning
Safe, Effective Care Environment
Application

8.5 The nurse is teaching a class to prenatal clients about the benefits of a doula. Which statement by a client demonstrates the need for further teaching? a. "The doula will deliver the baby." b. "The doula will assist with the birth." c. "The doula will provide guidance and encouragement." d. "The doula will attend to my comfort needs."	Answer: a Rationale: The doula is trained to assist with births, but she does not deliver the baby. The doula offers guidance and encouragement and attends to the many comfort needs of the laboring mother and her family. Evaluation Psychosocial Integrity Analysis
8.6 A couple would like their 5-year-old to attend the birth. Which statement by the nurse would assist in the plan of care for the 5-year-old? a. "You should let your child stay home because you will be focusing on the birth." b. "Children under 12 are not allowed to be present at the birth." c. "You should bring someone who can tend only to any specific needs of your child." d. "Bring some toys to keep you child occupied."	Answer: c Rationale: A sibling should have his or her own support person whose primary responsibility is to take care of the child's needs. Children are allowed to be present at births. Preparing the child on what to expect is beneficial. Planning Psychosocial Integrity Application
8.7 The nurse is planning for an adolescent parenting class. Which topics would be a priority for the nurse to include in the adolescent class? (Select all that apply.) a. sexuality in pregnancy. b. newborn care. c. birth settings. d. health dangers for the baby. e. how to be a good parent.	Answers: b, d, e Rationale: Areas of concern for teens focus on how to be a good parent, how to care for the new baby, and health dangers to the baby. Sexuality in pregnancy and birth settings are not a priority. Planning Health Promotion and Maintenance Analysis
8.8 During a breastfeeding class, the nurse discusses ways to include the father in the breastfeeding process. The nurse knows further teaching is necessary when a prospective father states: a. "I can feed the baby a bottle." b. "I can burp the baby between breasts." c. "I can rock the baby to sleep after breastfeeding." d. "When the baby wakes up, I can bring the baby to her mother."	Answer: a Rationale: Feeding the baby a bottle is not an option. Breastfeeding has to be established. To include the father in the breastfeeding process include: bringing the baby to the mother for feedings, burping the baby between breasts and/or after feeding, and rocking the baby back to sleep. Evaluation Psychosocial Integrity Analysis
8.9 Parents planning on a vaginal birth after a cesarean birth (VBAC) should prepare: a. exclusively for a vaginal delivery. b two birth plans: one for vaginal and one for cesarean. c for a long labor. b. for a short labor.	Answer: b Rationale: In the care of vaginal birth after cesarean birth (VBAC), two birth plans should be prepared: one for vaginal delivery and one for cesarean birth. Preparing exclusively for a vaginal delivery will decrease a parent's sense of control over the birth experience if a cesarean needs to be performed. The length of labor (short or long) cannot be determined for a VBAC delivery. Planning Health Promotion and Maintenance Application

8.10 An expectant mother asks a nurse, "Why do I need to learn breathing patterns I can use during labor?" The nurse relates to the client that the primary reason for using controlled breathing patterns during labor is to: a. promote adequate oxygen to the laboring mother and the baby. b. keep the laboring mother distracted. c. keep the laboring mother awake. d. involve the partner in the birth process.	Answer: a Rationale: Breathing techniques help keep the mother and her unborn baby adequately oxygenated. Breathing techniques are not intended to distract the laboring mother but to focus her attention. They are not done to keep the laboring mother awake or to involve the partner in the birth process. Assessment Physiological Integrity Analysis
8.11 A couple discusses their childbirth preparation options with the nurse. They want the father to be actively involved, and for the expectant mother to avoid medications during the birthing process. The nurse's best response is: a. "The hospital will follow your wishes." b. "The Leboyer method will provide what you want." c. "The Bradley method will provide your needs." d. "The Lamaze method will be easy to follow."	Answer: c Rationale: The Bradley method is referred to as partner- or husband-coached natural childbirth. The Lamaze method involves the breathing technique that facilitates delivery by relaxing at the proper time. The Leboyer method emphasizes the provision of a gentle and peaceful environment for the birth process. The hospital method is not an option for preparation. Planning Health Promotion and Maintenance Application
8.12 A client states she is not interested in Lamaze classes because she is single and does not want to have natural childbirth. The nurse's best response would be: a. "Lamaze classes promise painless childbirth. If you learn their methods, your pain is minimal." b. "Lamaze classes can teach you relaxation methods and also the benefits and risks of pain relief methods. This assists you in making the best decision for you." c. "You are very nervous. I think these classes would be best for you." d. "Lamaze classes are geared toward couples. You may want to find a different class."	Answer: b Rationale: Lamaze teaches relaxation methods by utilizing patterned breathing. Those who are able to use the method require little if any anesthesia during delivery. The other choices are inappropriate. Planning Health Promotion and Maintenance Application
8.13 What content would be appropriate for a nurse to include in an early pregnancy class? a. the father's role in breastfeeding. b. purchasing of a car seat. c. how to care for an episiotomy. d. methods to cope with stress.	Answer: d Rationale: Coping with stress is a topic appropriate for an early pregnancy class. The father's role in breastfeeding is a topic for a breastfeeding class. Purchasing a car seat and episiotomy care are topics that are appropriate for later classes (second and third trimesters). Planning Health Promotion and Maintenance Application

8.14 A nurse conducts a class on relaxation exercises. Which couple is demonstrating the appropriate technique for touch relaxation?

a. The expectant mother relaxes muscles in response to her partner's touch.
b. The expectant mother relaxes one muscle group at a time as her partner observes.
c. The expectant mother and her partner perform light abdominal stroking.
d. The expectant mother relaxes the rest of the body while tensing a specific muscle under the direction of her partner.

Answer: a
Rationale: Touch relaxation increases cooperation and teamwork between the woman and her coach during labor. Progressive relaxation relaxes one muscle group at a time. Effleurage involves performing light abdominal stroking. Disassociation relaxation involves relaxing the rest of the body while tensing a specific muscle group.
Evaluation
Physiological Integrity
Analysis

8.15 During a preconception counseling meeting with the nurse, a couple asks what changes they will need to make to their lifestyle. The nurse's best response is:

a. "You can no longer use over-the-counter medications."
b. "Your partner will have to give up smoking."
c. "Start taking a multivitamin now."
d. "You should stop exercising until you see the doctor."

Answer: c
Rationale: It is important prior to conception to have adequate amounts of nutrients, particularly folic acid. A woman should avoid areas where secondhand smoke is common. A woman who uses over-the-counter medications needs to discuss their usage with her doctor. A regular exercise program should be established at least three months prior to becoming pregnant.
Planning
Health Promotion and Maintenance
Application

CHAPTER 9

9.1 A client with a normal prepregnancy weight asks why she has been told to gain 25 to 35 pounds during her pregnancy, but her underweight friend was told to gain more weight. The nurse should tell the client that recommended weight gain during pregnancy should be:

a. 25 to 35 pounds, regardless of a client's prepregnant weight.
b. more than 25 to 35 pounds for an overweight woman.
c. more than 25 to 35 pounds for an underweight woman.
d. the same for a normal weight woman as for an overweight woman.

Answer: c
Rationale: Prepregnant weight determines the recommended weight gain during pregnancy. Underweight women are encouraged to gain the amount of weight needed to bring them to normal body plus 25 to 35 pounds. Women of normal weight should gain 25 to 35 pounds during pregnancy for optimal fetal outcome. Overweight women should gain 15 to 25 pounds during pregnancy.
Implementation
Health Promotion and Maintenance
Application

9.2 The nurse has received a phone call from a multigravida, who is 21 weeks pregnant and has not felt fetal movement yet. The best action for the nurse to take would be to:

a. reassure the client that this is a normal finding in multigravidas.
b. suggest that she should feel for movement with her fingertips.
c. schedule an appointment for her with her physician for that same day.
d. tell her gently that her fetus is probably dead.

Answer: c
Rationale: Quickening, or fetal movement, usually is detected by the pregnant woman at 18 to 20 weeks' gestation. Women who have been pregnant previously may feel fetal movement earlier in pregnancy than those who have never been pregnant. Not feeling fetal movement by 21 weeks indicates that the client's due date is not accurate or that the fetus has died in utero. The client should therefore see her physician. Telling the client that the fetus may have died in utero, before having confirmation of this fact, is nontherapeutic.
Planning
Health Promotion and Maintenance
Application

9.3 A woman telephones the clinic to say that it has been six weeks since her last menstrual period, but a home pregnancy test run today was negative. She asks, "Do you think I could be pregnant?" After determining that the test was performed correctly, the nurse's best reply would be:

a. "Probably not. These tests rarely give a false-negative result."
b. "You might be. If you haven't started your period in one week, you should repeat the test and call the clinic again."
c. "You probably are. There are a lot of false-negative results with these tests."
d. "You may have an ectopic pregnancy. You should be seen by a doctor in the next few days."

Answer: b
Rationale: Current home pregnancy tests are quite accurate when used correctly. Some can detect pregnancy as early as the first day of the missed period. If a woman has delayed menses and suspects pregnancy, but the home pregnancy test is negative, she should wait one week and repeat the home test.
Implementation
Health Promotion and Maintenance
Application

9.4 The nurse understands that a client's pregnancy is progressing normally when which of the following physiologic changes are documented on the prenatal record of a woman at 36 weeks' gestation? Select all that apply.

a. The joints of the pelvis have relaxed, causing hip pain.
b. The cervix is firm and purplish-blue in color.
c. The uterine fundus is at a height of 35 cm above the pubic symphysis.
d. Gastric emptying time is prolonged, and the client complains of gas and bloating.
e. Supine hypotension creating dizziness occurs when the client lies on her back.

Answers: a, c, d, e
Rationale: The pregnancy hormone relaxin creates softening of the ligaments, which in turn can lead to hip or pubic symphysis pain in late pregnancy. Cervical changes during pregnancy include softening and purplish-blue discoloration. The growing fetus causes an enlargement of the uterus; from 20 weeks until delivery, the fundal height measured in cm should be within 2 to 3 of the number of actual weeks of gestation. Gas and bloating are seen as the increased progesterone level causes smooth muscle relaxation, resulting in delayed gastric emptying and slowed peristalsis. Supine hypotension occurs when the fetus compresses the vena cava against the vertebrae when the mother is supine.
Evaluation
Health Promotion and Maintenance
Analysis

9.5 A client calls a prenatal clinic stating: "I have nausea in the morning, I am late with my menstrual cycle, and I am feeling really fatigued." The nurse explains to the client that these symptoms are:

a. subjective or presumptive signs of pregnancy, but not diagnostic.
b. objective or probable signs of pregnancy, but not diagnostic.
c. diagnostic or positive signs of pregnancy.
d. signs of an ectopic pregnancy.

Answer: a
Rationale: Subjective (presumptive) changes of pregnancy are the symptoms the woman experiences and reports. Nausea in the morning, a missed menstrual cycle, and fatigue are subjective (presumptive) signs, but cannot be considered proof of pregnancy. Objective or probable changes are signs that an examiner can perceive. They include changes in the pelvic organs, enlargement of the abdomen, changes in the pigmentation of the skin, etc. However, these changes are not considered to be proof of pregnancy. The positive signs of pregnancy are completely objective and cannot be confused with a pathologic state. The fetal heartbeat detected by an electronic Doppler is a positive sign of pregnancy. The symptoms described would not be indicative of an ectopic pregnancy.
Diagnosis
Health Promotion and Maintenance
Analysis

9.6 It is one week before a pregnant client's due date. The nurse notes on the chart that the client's pulse rate was 74 to 80 before pregnancy. Today, the client's pulse rate at rest is 90. The nurse

Answer: a
Rationale: The pulse rate will increase 10 to 15 beats per minute during pregnancy due to the increased blood volume during pregnancy.
Assessment
Health Promotion and Maintenance
Application

---

should take which of the following actions?
a. chart the findings.
b. notify the physician of tachycardia.
c. prepare the client for an electrocardiogram (EKG).
d. prepare the client for transport to the hospital.

9.7 A pregnant client, at 16 weeks' gestation, has a hematocrit of 35%. Her prepregnancy hematocrit was 40%. Which of the following statements by the nurse best explains this change?
a. "Because of your pregnancy, you're not making enough red blood cells."
b. "Because your blood volume has increased, your hematocrit count is lower."
c. "This change may indicate a serious problem that might harm your baby."
d. "You're not eating enough iron-rich foods like meat."

Answer: b
Rationale: The increase in plasma volume during pregnancy averages about 50% and because the plasma volume increase (50%) is greater than the erythrocyte increase (30%), the hematocrit, which measures the concentration of red blood cells in the plasma, decreases slightly. The pregnancy would not cause a decrease in the production of red blood cells. This is referred to as physiologic anemia of pregnancy and is not harmful to the fetus. It does not mean that the woman is not getting adequate iron.
Implementation
Health Promotion and Maintenance
Application

9.8 A client complains that during her first months of pregnancy, "It seems like I have to go to the bathroom every five minutes." The nurse relates to the client that this is because:
a. the client probably has a urinary tract infection.
b. bladder capacity increases throughout pregnancy.
c. the growing uterus puts pressure on the bladder.
d. some women are very sensitive to body function changes.

Answer: c
Rationale: The bladder is compressed by the growing uterus throughout pregnancy. Increased pressure begins early in the first trimester, when the uterus is still located in the pelvis. During the second trimester, the uterus rises into the abdomen, and bladder pressure is decreased. However, late in the third trimester, when the fetal presenting part descends, an even greater increase in bladder pressure is created.
Diagnosis
Health Promotion and Maintenance
Application

9.9 A client, who is in the second trimester of pregnancy, tells the nurse that she has developed a darkening of the line in the midline of her abdomen from the symphysis pubis to the umbilicus. Which of the following are other expected changes during pregnancy that she may also notice?
a. lightening of the nipples and areolas.
b. reddish streaks called striae on her abdomen.
c. a decrease in hair thickness.
d. small purplish dots on her face and arms.

Answer: b
Rationale: Reddish streaks called striae or stretch marks often appear on the abdomen of pregnant women. Increased estrogen levels cause a number of skin changes during pregnancy, including chloasma (a darkening of the skin on the face) and increased pigmentation of the nipples and areolas. A greater percentage of hair follicles go into the dormant phase, resulting in less hair shedding, which is perceived as thickening of the hair. Although raised red spots on the skin (spider nevi) are a normal finding, petechiae are not.
Assessment
Health Promotion and Maintenance
Analysis

9.10 A prenatal educator is asking a partner about normal psychological adjustment of an expectant mother during the second trimester of pregnancy. Which of the following answers by the partner would indicate a typical expectant mother's response to pregnancy?

Answer: b
Rationale: Psychologic adjustment to pregnancy is as significant as the physiologic changes. In the first trimester, pregnant women tell their partners of the pregnancy, explore their relationship with their mother and think about their own role as a mother, might fear miscarriage, and might feel ambivalence or anxiety about the pregnancy and the changes to their life that a child will bring. The second trimester brings increased introspection and consideration of how she will parent. She might begin to get furniture and clothing as concrete preparation, and as quickening is experienced, the fetus becomes real and is incorporated into the sense of self.

a. "She is very body-conscious and hates every little change." b. "She daydreams about what kind of parent she is going to be." c. "I haven't noticed anything. I just found out she was pregnant." d. "She has been having dreams at night about misplacing the baby."	The third trimester brings insomnia and physical discomfort from body changes, and preparation for childbirth; the needs of the newborn is undertaken, and excitement is often felt as the due date gets closer, but dreams of misplacing the baby or being unable to get to the baby are common. Evaluation Health Promotion and Maintenance Analysis
9.11 At a second-trimester prenatal visit, a married couple are discussing their new roles as parents with the nurse. The father comments that he really wants to be a good father to their new baby. The nurse should explain that in developing the fatherhood role, the most important thing is to: a. participate actively in as many aspects of childbearing and childrearing as possible. b. identify a father he admires and try to develop a fathering role similar to that. c. decide with his partner on a fathering role that is mutually agreeable to both of them. d. begin by examining the basic pattern of fathering that his father used with him.	Answer: c Rationale: A mutually developed fathering role will reduce anxiety and miscommunication. Participation in childrearing and especially childbearing is culturally determined, and may not be viewed as desirable. Fathering may be imitated from either one's own father or another father that is admired, but discussion and consensus on the tasks the father will take on will prevent miscommunication and promote family cohesiveness. Planning Health Promotion and Maintenance Application
9.12 The 20-year-old client at 10 weeks' gestation is preparing for her first prenatal visit. She confides: "This pregnancy was unplanned. I'm not sure if I want to be pregnant or not. I haven't even told my boyfriend I'm pregnant. And I haven't decided if I'm going to continue the pregnancy." Which of the following statements should the nurse make next? a. "It's really unusual for a pregnant woman to feel this way early in the pregnancy." b. "These thoughts are because your mother died when you were 4 years old." c. "You should go to a pregnancy support group to be a good mother." d. "It's common to feel ambiguous about pregnancy in the first trimester."	Answer: d Rationale: Ambivalence towards the pregnancy is very common in the first trimester. Fathers might not be told immediately about the diagnosis of pregnancy. Uncertainty about the quality of parenting that one can provide is often experienced, especially prior to quickening (when the fetus becomes more real to the client). Clients become more introspective, and explore what it means to be a mother. Fantasies about miscarriage and what the baby will look like are common. Evaluation Health Promotion and Maintenance Application
9.13 The partner of a pregnant client at 16 weeks' gestation accompanies her to the clinic. The partner tells you that the baby just doesn't seem real to him, and he's having a hard time relating to his partner's fatigue and food aversions. Which of the following statements would be best for the nurse to make? a. "If you would concentrate harder, you'd be aware of the reality of this pregnancy."	Answer: d Rationale: Ambivalence is common among partners, especially prior to their either seeing the baby on ultrasound or feeling the baby kick and move. Kicking and ultrasound visualization are concrete evidence of the baby's existence, and often are turning points in acceptance for partners. The ambivalence and disbelief occur across all socioeconomic groups, in both partners who were fathered well and those who grew up without a father. It is not indicative of psychological pathology. Implementation Health Promotion and Maintenance Application

b. "My husband had no problem with this. What was your childhood like?"

c. "You may need professional psychological counseling. Ask your physician."

d. "Many men feel this way. Feeling the baby move will help make it real."

9.14 The nurse is caring for a pregnant client who speaks little English. Which of the following actions should the nurse take to make certain that the client understands the plan of care?

a. Write all of the instructions down and send them home with the client.

b. Obtain a medical interpreter of the language the client speaks.

c. Ask a housekeeper who speaks this language to interpret.

d. Use gestures and facial expressions to get the plan across.

Answer: b
Rationale: Women of all cultures and all language backgrounds deserve quality prenatal care. When working with a woman who speaks little or no English, a trained medical interpreter should be obtained. Using family members, friends, or other staff to interpret may be problematic because few people understand medical terminology, and it can lead to confidentiality issues. Writing English is not helpful, because verbal fluency usually develops before written fluency in language learners.
Implementation
Health Promotion and Maintenance
Application

9.15 A client, who is in her fourteenth week of pregnancy, is in the clinic for a prenatal visit. Her mother also is present. The grandmother-to-be states that she is quite uncertain about how she can be a good grandmother to this baby because she works full-time, and her own grandmother was retired and was always available when needed by a grandchild. The best response to this concern would be:

a. "Don't worry. You'll be a wonderful grandmother. It will all work out fine."

b. "Grandmothers are supposed to be available. You should retire from your job."

c. "As long as there is another grandmother available, you don't have to worry."

d. "What are your thoughts on what your role as grandmother will include?"

Answer: d
Rationale: As society has changed to encourage a more active lifestyle in the aging population, the role of grandparents has also changed. Grandparenting can take many forms. Some grandparents are young and employed full-time, while others are retired and have more free time. Encouraging open communication between grandparents-to-be and the parents-to-be can avoid miscommunication in expectations. Grandparenting classes are one way that these roles can be explored. It is important to avoid clichés and placing guilt on clients to promote effective therapeutic communication.
Implementation
Health Promotion and Maintenance
Application

CHAPTER 10

10.1 Which of the following pieces of information that the nurse obtains from a pregnant client would indicate this client is at risk for preterm labor?

a. The client smokes two packs of cigarettes per day and delivered her last child at 34 weeks.

b. The client has group B streptococcus in her urine, and is primiparous.

c. The client had congenital hip dysplasia as a child and is 15 pounds overweight.

d. The client lives in a second-floor apartment without stairs and walks to work.

Answer: a
Rationale: Smoking is a risk factor for preterm birth and low birth weight. Nicotine is a vasoconstrictor, and causes the arterioles in the placenta and the uterus to constrict, decreasing blood flow to the uterine musculature as well as the fetus. During and after smoking a cigarette, both the maternal and fetal oxygen saturation drop, and the carbon monoxide found in cigarette smoke also will decrease fetal oxygenation. The presence of group B streptococcus puts the newborn at risk for sepsis after delivery. Neither hip dysplasia nor being 15 pounds overweight predisposes a woman to developing preterm labor. Walking is considered moderate-intensity exercise and is a healthy practice during pregnancy.
Diagnosis
Health Promotion and Maintenance
Analysis

10.2 A woman tells the clinic nurse that her last normal menstrual period was September 8. You would calculate her due date to be: _____. (Use format month-day numerically, i.e., January 1 would be 01-01.)	Answer: 06-15 Rationale: Using Naegele's rule, you take the first day of the last menstrual period, subtract three months, and add seven days. Subtracting three months from September is June, adding seven days to the eighth is the fifteenth. Diagnosis Health Promotion and Maintenance Application
10.3 What is the best method for the nurse to use to teach a client from Mexico who speaks primarily Spanish and a little English? a. Ask the client's husband to repeat the information. b. Provide written materials in English for the client to take home. c. Have the client repeat what her understanding is of the information. d. Schedule a medical interpreter to accompany the client on her next visit.	Answer: c Rationale: When working with clients who have limited English proficiency, it is optimal to have a medical interpreter present for the entire visit. If this is not possible, asking the client to repeat her understanding of what was taught to her will tell the nurse what information was learned. Written materials in English are of little value to someone who doesn't understand the language. Asking the husband what he understands will assess the husband's learning. When teaching has been done, the nurse has a responsibility to make certain that the client has understood; thus, an interpreter at the next visit will not help the nurse or the client now. Evaluation Health Promotion and Maintenance Application
10.4 A woman gave birth to her first pregnancy, a fetus at 18 weeks' gestation, last week. She is in the clinic for follow-up, and notices that her chart states she has had 1 abortion. The client is upset over the use of this word. How can the nurse best explain this terminology to the client? a. "Abortion is the medical term for all pregnancies that end before 28 weeks." b. "Abortion is the word we use when someone has miscarried." c. "Abortion is how we label babies born in the second trimester." d. "Abortion is what we call all babies who are born dead."	Answer: a Rationale: Abortions are fetal losses prior to the onset of the third trimester and include elective induced (medical or surgical) abortions, ectopic pregnancies, and spontaneous abortions or miscarriages. Implementation Health Promotion and Maintenance Application
10.5 The clinic nurse is compiling informational data for a yearly report. Which following client would be classified as a primigravida? a. a client at 18 weeks' gestation who had a spontaneous loss at 12 weeks. b. a client at 13 weeks' gestation who had an ectopic pregnancy at 8 weeks. c. a client at 14 weeks' gestation who has a 3-year-old daughter at home. d. a client at 15 weeks' gestation who has never been pregnant before.	Answer: d Rationale: *Primigravida* can be broken down into the Latin roots: *primi* (prime, or first) and *gravida* (pregnancy). A pregnant woman who has had a pregnancy end before 20 weeks is considered a primipara. A pregnant woman who has been pregnant before is called a multigravida. Assessment Health Promotion and Maintenance Analysis
10.6 When giving her obstetrical history, your pregnant client tells you that she has had two prior pregnancies. She has a miscarriage with the first pregnancy at 8 week. The second pregnancy was twin girls who were born at 34 weeks, but died 3 days later.	Answer: a Rationale: Gravida refers to the total number of pregnancies. Para refers to the number of births that occurred after 20 weeks gestation, regardless if the deliveries were born alive or stillborn, and also regardless of whether the children are still living. This client is in her third pregnancy, making her a gravida 3. She had one delivery after 20 weeks—her twins, at 34 weeks. A multi-fetal gestation like twins or triplets or higher is considered one pregnancy and one delivery.

The nurse should record that the client is: a. gravida 3 para 1. b. gravida 3 para 0. c. gravida 3 para 2. d. gravida 2 para 3.	Assessment Health Promotion and Maintenance Application
10.7 A 25-year-old primigravida is 20 weeks pregnant. At the clinic, her nurse obtains the following vital signs. Which of these findings would necessitate notifying a doctor immediately? a. pulse regular at 88/min. b. rhonchi in both bases. c. temperature 37.4°C (99.3°F). d. blood pressure 130/78.	Answer: b Rationale: The respiratory rate in pregnancy increases slightly to 16 to 24/min, and the inspiratory phase is longer than in a nonpregnant state, but vesicular sounds are expected. Any adventitious breath sounds are abnormal. The pulse will increase 10 to 15 beats/min during pregnancy, with 60 to 90 beats/min being the normal range. A blood pressure of less than 135/85 is considered normal. Temperature norms in pregnancy are slightly higher due to fetal metabolism: 36.2° to 37.6°C (98° to 99.6°F). Diagnosis Health Promotion and Maintenance Analysis
10.8 The primigravida at 22 weeks' gestation has a fundal height palpated slightly below the umbilicus. Which of the following statements would best describe to the client why she needs to be seen by a physician today? a. "Your baby is growing too much and getting too big." b. "Your uterus might have an abnormal shape." c. "The position of your baby can't be felt." d. "Your baby might not be growing enough."	Answer: d Rationale: The fundal height at 20 weeks should be about even with the umbilicus. At 22 weeks, the fundus should be above the umbilicus. A 22 weeks' gestation with a fundal height below the umbilicus may indicate fetal death in utero. Uterine shape can be assessed only with diagnostic imaging techniques such as ultrasound or CT scan. The position of the baby is not noted until 36 weeks gestation because as the presenting part descends into the pelvis in preparation for labor, it is important that the fetus be in a vertex presentation. Evaluation Health Promotion and Maintenance Application
10.9 The clinic nurse is assisting with an initial prenatal assessment. The following findings are present: Spider nevi present on lower legs; dark pink, edematous nasal mucosa; mild enlargement of the thyroid gland; mottled skin and pallor or palms and nail beds; heart rate 88 with murmur present. What is the best action for the nurse to take based on these findings? a. Document the findings on the prenatal chart. b. Have the physician see the client today. c. Instruct the client to avoid direct sunlight. d. Analyze previous thyroid hormone lab results.	Answer: b Rationale: Mottling of the skin is indicative of poor oxygenation and a circulation problem. Skin and nail bed pallor can indicate either hypoxia or anemia. These abnormalities must be reported to the physician immediately. Spider nevi are common in pregnancy due to the increased vascular volume and high estrogen levels. Nasal passages can be stuffy during pregnancy from edema, caused by increased estrogen levels. The thyroid gland increases in size during pregnancy due to hyperplasia. Implementation Health Promotion and Maintenance Analysis
10.10 Which of the following would be part of a routine physical assessment for a second-trimester primiparous client whose prenatal care began in the first trimester and is ongoing? a. measurement of the diagonal conjugate. b. hepatitis B screening (HbsAg). c. fundal height measurement. d. complete blood count.	Answer: c Rationale: At each prenatal visit, the blood pressure, pulse, and weight are assessed and the size of the fundus is measured. Fundal height should be increasing with each prenatal visit. Pelvic measurements are usually done at the initial prenatal appointment. Hepatitis B screening, complete blood count or hemoglobin and hematocrit plus platelet count are done at the initial prenatal appointment. Assessment Health Promotion and Maintenance Application

10.11 A nurse, examining a prenatal client, recognizes that a lag in progression of measurements of fundal height from month to month and week to week may signal: a. intrauterine growth restriction. b. twin pregnancy. c. polyhydramnios. d. breech position.	Answer: a Rationale: A lag in progression of measurements of fundal height from month to month and week to week may signal intrauterine growth restriction (IUGR). A sudden increase in fundal height may indicate twins or polyhydramnios (excessive amount of amniotic fluid). Breech position would still have a normal fundal height measurement. Assessment Health Promotion and Maintenance Analysis
10.12 A client comes to the clinic stating that her menstrual period regularly occurs every 32 days for 4 days. On what day during her cycle is ovulation most likely to occur? Write your answer in the space below.	Answer: 18 Rationale: The first day of bleeding is the first day of the menstrual cycle. Ovulation occurs 14 days prior to the onset of bleeding. In a 32-day cycle, ovulation would occur on the eighteenth day. Implementation Health Promotion and Maintenance Application
10.13 The primiparous client has completed her first prenatal clinic appointment. She is asking how often prenatal visits will be done if everything remains normal and she develops no complications. Which of the following statements best answers her question? "Prenatal visits are scheduled: a. every 2 weeks for the first 28 weeks, then every week." b. every 4 weeks until 30 weeks, every 3 weeks until 36 weeks, then every week." c. every 4 weeks until 28 weeks, every 2 weeks until 36 weeks, then every week." d. every 4 weeks until 30 weeks, then every other week."	Answer: c Rationale: Normal prenatal exams are scheduled every 4 weeks until 28 weeks, every 2 weeks until 36 weeks, and then every week until delivery. Clients at high risk and those experiencing complications will be seen more frequently. Implementation Health Promotion and Maintenance Application
10.14 While completing the medical and surgical history during the initial prenatal visit, the 16-year-old primigravida interrupts with "Why are you asking me all these questions? What difference does it make?" Which of the following statements would best answer the client's questions? "We ask these questions: a. to detect anything that happened in your past that might affect the pregnancy." b. to see if you can have prenatal visits less often than most clients." c. to make sure that our paperwork and records are complete and up to date." d. to look for any health problems in the past that might affect your parenting."	Answer: a Rationale: The medical and surgical histories of a new prenatal client must be accurate and complete to detect conditions that may be exacerbated during pregnancy or delivery, to ensure safety of both the mother and the fetus. Prenatal visits follow a set schedule for normal clients without complications. Paperwork is a lower priority than client care. The psychological history of a client, not the medical or surgical histories, may indicate potential problems with parenting. Implementation Health Promotion and Maintenance Application

10.15 The pregnant client at 16 weeks has just been told that she has a positive hepatitis B screen. She understands what this means if she states:
a. "I have hepatitis B, which I could pass on to my baby."
b. "I am anemic and should eat more iron-rich foods."
c. "My blood pressure is high, and it is affecting my baby."
d. "I have a rare blood type, and the baby could have it, too."

Answer: a
Rationale: A positive hepatitis B surface antigen (HbsAg) indicates that the client is infectious and could transmit the infection to the fetus through contact with blood and body fluids during labor and birth. Infants born to mothers with a positive HbsAg are given hepatitis B immune globulin immediately after delivery.
Evaluation
Health Promotion and Maintenance
Analysis

CHAPTER 11

11.1 A client in her third trimester of pregnancy reports frequent leg cramps. What strategy would be most appropriate for the nurse to suggest?
a. point the toes of the affected leg.
b. increase intake of protein-rich foods.
c. limit her activity for several days.
d. flex the foot to stretch the calf.

Answer: d
Rationale: Leg cramps are a common problem in pregnancy, resulting from an imbalance in the calcium–phosphorus ration; pressure on nerves or decreased circulation in the legs from the enlarged uterus; or fatigue. Leg cramps are exacerbated by pointing the toes. Dorsiflexing the foot will allow stretching of the calf muscles and will help relieve the cramps.
Implementation
Health Promotion and Maintenance
Application

11.2 A pregnant client who swims three to five times per week asks the nurse if she should stop this activity. What is the appropriate nursing response?
a. "You should decrease the number of times you swim per week."
b. "Continuing your exercise program would be beneficial."
c. "You should discontinue your exercise program immediately."
d. "You should consider a less strenuous type of exercise."

Answer: b
Rationale: Thirty minutes of moderate-intensity exercise daily is recommended for pregnant women. Women who exercise regularly have better muscle tone, self-image, bowel function, energy levels, sleep, and postpartum recovery than do those who are sedentary.
Implementation
Health Promotion and Maintenance
Application

11.3 To promote self-care, the nurse should help the pregnant client understand that nausea may be relieved by:
a. the intake of spicy foods.
b. avoiding eating until two hours after rising.
c. eating small, frequent meals.
d. avoiding carbonated beverages.

Answer: c
Rationale: Nausea occurs in 70 to 85% of pregnant women, most commonly in the first trimester. Nausea can be exacerbated by ketosis, fatigue, and certain foods, such as those containing caffeine or spices. Eating dry carbohydrates prior to rising and avoiding severe hunger by eating small, frequent meals throughout the day can help to prevent or decrease the severity of the nausea. Ginger can be helpful, as can "sea-bands" (which stimulate acupressure points at the wrists). Occasionally, medications are required to prevent dehydration and weight loss.
Implementation
Health Promotion and Maintenance
Application

11.4 Which method of travel would be most appropriate for a client in her twenty-fifth week of pregnancy?
a. automobile.
b. airplane.
c. train.
d. This client should not travel.

Answer: c
Rationale: In the latter half of pregnancy, frequent movement is recommended for pregnant women, both to increase comfort and to decrease venous pooling, which can lead to thrombophlebitis. The train allows the most movement for the traveling pregnant woman.
Planning
Health Promotion and Maintenance
Application

11.5 Which of the following statements, if made by a pregnant client, indicates that she understands health promotion during pregnancy?
a. "I lie down after eating to relieve heartburn."
b. "I try to limit my fluid intake to three or four glasses each day."
c. "I elevate my legs while sitting at my desk."
d. "I am avoiding exercise to stay well rested."

Answer: c
Rationale: Health promotion includes actions to take and avoid during pregnancy for optimal health. Heartburn is gastroesophageal reflux and will be exacerbated by lying down. At least 8 to 10 glasses of fluids should be consumed each day to maintain the increased blood volume of pregnancy. Elevating the legs can help decrease lower leg edema. Regular mild to moderate exercise has many benefits for pregnant women.
Evaluation
Health Promotion and Maintenance
Analysis

11.6 The pregnant client has asked the nurse what kinds of medications cause birth defects. Which statement would best answer this question?
a. "Birth defects are very rare. Don't worry; your doctor will watch for problems."
b. "Some medications that are used for conditions like seizures can cause birth defects."
c. "Too much vitamin C is one of the most common issues, but is avoidable."
d. "Almost all medications will cause birth defects in the first trimester."

Answer: b
Rationale: Teratogens are substances that cause birth defects. Alcohol is one example, as are Coumadin (warfarin) and Accutane (isotretinoin). The greatest risk is during the first trimester, but not all medications are teratogenic. Those medications with clear evidence of teratogenicity are classified in Pregnancy Category X, and should be avoided when conception is being attempted and during the first trimester.
Implementation
Health Promotion and Maintenance
Application

11.7 A Navajo client who is 36 weeks pregnant meets with the medicine man frequently. The nurse understands this to mean the client:
a. needs spiritual direction.
b. does not trust her physician.
c. will not adapt to mothering well.
d. is extremely fearful of labor and birth.

Answer: a
Rationale: As a result of the introspection that develops, pregnant women often will seek spiritual guidance from their preferred spiritual leader. This does not indicate any type of pathology. The nurse has a professional responsibility to promote spiritual well-being of her clients. Understanding the belief systems of the client population will facilitate intercultural communication, and will help the nurse provide appropriate information using appropriate teaching methods.
Diagnosis
Health Promotion and Maintenance
Application

11.8 A 43-year-old client has just had a positive pregnancy test. She cries and states, "I just don't know what I'll do. I can't be pregnant." Which of the following nursing diagnoses would be the most appropriate?
a. Decisional conflict related to unexpected pregnancy.
b. Knowledge deficit related to advanced maternal age.
c. Depression related to unexpected pregnancy.
d. Self-esteem disturbance related to advanced maternal age.

Answer: a
Rationale: An unplanned pregnancy at any age is often a life-changing event for the client. Women over the age of 35 have a higher incidence of pregnancy complications. Depression can occur, but we do not have enough client data to indicate that this client is depressed. Self-esteem can be affected by a pregnancy at this age, as peers may be becoming grandparents, and if the client has other children, they may be nearing adulthood.
Diagnosis
Health Promotion and Maintenance
Application

11.9 A 38-year-old client in her second trimester states she desires to begin an exercise program to decrease her fatigue. Which of the following would be the most appropriate nursing response?

Answer: a
Rationale: Mild to moderate exercise during pregnancy is healthy for moms and babies. The increased stamina that correlates with physical fitness can help decrease fatigue in pregnancy, but the second trimester will bring fatigue, as fetal metabolism creates demands on the maternal system. The age of 38 is not too old

a. "Fatigue should resolve in the second trimester, but walking daily might help."
b. "Avoid a strenuous exercise regimen at your age. Drink coffee TID."
c. "Avoid an exercise regime due to your pregnancy. Try to nap daily."
d. "Fatigue will increase as pregnancy progresses, but jogging daily may help."

to begin an exercise routine, but during pregnancy, a client should not begin a new type of extremely strenuous or high-impact activity. Those clients who have regularly engaged in strenuous or high-impact activities prior to pregnancy can continue that practice unless pregnancy complications that contraindicate exercise develop.
Implementation
Health Promotion and Maintenance
Application

11.10 A Chinese woman who is 16 weeks pregnant states that ginseng and bamboo leaves help to reduce her anxiety. Which nursing strategy is most appropriate?
a. Advise the client to avoid the use of all herbs.
b. Assess the amount and frequency with which the client is using the remedy.
c. Tell the client that her remedies have no scientific foundation.
d. Assess where the client obtains her remedy and investigate the source.

Answer: b
Rationale: Use of herbs is a common alternative healthcare practice for many women. Pregnant women are often told of "secret family recipes" for avoiding or minimizing the discomforts of pregnancy. Because some herbs have negative effects on pregnancy, using a reliable reference to determine the actions of the herbs can educate both the nurse and the client.
Implementation
Health Promotion and Maintenance
Application

11.11 Which client statement, if made in the first trimester of pregnancy, would indicate a need for further education? Select all that apply.
a. "I have to use an astringent mouthwash daily."
b. "I am sleeping with a cool mist vaporizer by my bed."
c. "Now all I wear is all-cotton underwear."
d. "I'm making sure I eat vegetables every day."
e. "I quit taking all medications and vitamins yesterday."

Answers: a, e
Rationale: Periodontal disease during pregnancy is a risk factor for preterm labor and low-birth-weight infants. Dental care is recommended during pregnancy. Extractions, fillings, and surgery can be done under local anesthesia during pregnancy, preferably during the second trimester. Pregnant women should tell their dentists that they are pregnant to avoid exposure to teratogens like x-rays. Although the risk of teratogenicity is something to consider with medications, some medications (such as antidepressants and antiseizure medications) either must be tapered off (such as SSRIs) or should not be discontinued during pregnancy. Increasing the fruit and vegetable intake is good nutrition during pregnancy, but vitamins (especially folic acid) often are prescribed during the first trimester. Increasing the humidity of the home can ease the nasal stuffiness of pregnancy. Cotton underwear is found to be most comfortable during pregnancy due to the increased perineal perspiration and vaginal secretions; cotton panties also help decrease the incidence of vaginal yeast infections.
Diagnosis
Health Promotion and Maintenance
Analysis

11.12 Which method should the nurse use to explain the importance of fetal activity assessment to the client?
a. daily phone calls to the client at work or home.
b. review the client's written record of fetal movement.
c. demonstrate the use of the written fetal movement record.
d. explain the fetal movement counting method to the client.

Answer: b
Rationale: Clients should be instructed to begin counting fetal movement between 24 to 28 weeks. A fetus that has been active and has a sudden decrease in movements may be conserving energy due to hypoxia. Movements are counted in a specified time period, such as for one hour after each meal, or beginning with arising in the morning. Writing down the count is more accurate than the client simply remembering. When the nurse examines this written record the client has kept, it reinforces the importance of the record, and improves the likelihood of continued record keeping.
Planning
Health Promotion and Maintenance
Application

11.13 The nurse teaches the pregnant client that positions for sexual intercourse may need modification during later pregnancy. An appropriate position for intercourse during the third trimester is: a. lithotomy. b. fowler's. c. supine. d. side-lying.	Answer: d Rationale: As the abdomen increases in girth during later pregnancy, changes in position may need to be utilized to achieve sexual activity. Side-lying reduces pressure on the abdomen, and avoids supine hypotension. Implementation Health Promotion and Maintenance Application
11.14 The pregnant client in her second trimester states, "I didn't know my breasts would become so large. How do I find a good bra?" The best answer for the nurse to make would be: a. "Avoid cotton fabrics and get an underwire bra; they fit everyone best." b. "Just buy a bra one cup size bigger than usual, and it will fit." c. "Look for wide straps and cups big enough for all of your breast tissue." d. "There isn't much you can do for comfort. Try not wearing a bra at all."	Answer: c Rationale: Breast enlargement can create discomfort, first as the prepregnancy bra becomes too small and later from the increased weight of the breasts (an average of 1 to 1.5 pounds per breast). To obtain maximum comfort, instruct the client to get a bra that fits well with wide, non-stretch straps, a cup big enough to hold all of the breast tissue, and a band that will expand as the rib cage circumference increases during late pregnancy. Cotton is a comfortable fabric due to increased perspiration during pregnancy. Implementation Health Promotion and Maintenance Application
11.15 The primiparous client has told the nurse that she is afraid she will develop hemorrhoids during pregnancy because her mother did. Which of the following statements would be best for the nurse to make? a. "It is not unusual for women to develop hemorrhoids during pregnancy." b. "Most women don't have any problem until after they've delivered." c. "If you mother had hemorrhoids, you will get them too. Get used to the idea." d. "If you get hemorrhoids, you probably will need surgery to get rid of them."	Answer: a Rationale: Hemorrhoids are anal varicose veins. The increased weight of the gravid uterus, combined with constipation, can result in the varicosities prolapsing. Many pregnant women will develop hemorrhoids either during pregnancy or after delivery from the pushing efforts of the second stage of labor. Topic relief agents such as Preparation H or Tucks pads can provide relief of the itching and burning sensations. Although there is a familial tendency to develop varicosities, including hemorrhoids, a family history does not automatically mean that a client will develop the condition. Most hemorrhoids will resolve spontaneously and will not require surgical intervention. Implementation Health Promotion and Maintenance Application

CHAPTER 12

12.1 A client presents to the antepartum clinic with a history of a 20-pound weight loss. Her pregnancy test is positive. She is concerned about gaining the weight back and asks the nurse if she can remain on her diet. The nurse's best response would be: a. "As long as you supplement your diet with the prenatal vitamin, the amount of weight you gain in pregnancy is not significant."	Answer: b Rationale: Supplementation with vitamins is important, but so is maintaining weight gain within the respected parameters. Good nutrition is essential for the health and well-being of the mother and the fetus. Adequate weight gain is an indicator of adequate nutrition. Child neglect can apply only after the child has been born. Weight gain during pregnancy typically is not water-related except with disease processes. Excess weight gain can be difficult to lose. Implementation Physiological Integrity Application

b. "I understand that gaining weight after such an accomplishment must not look attractive, but weight gain during pregnancy is important for proper fetal growth."
c. "Dieting during pregnancy is considered child neglect."
d. "Excessive weight gain in pregnancy is due to water retention, so weight loss following birth will not be an issue."

12.2 A pregnant client who follows a strict vegan diet asks the nurse to assist her with her diet. The nurse will want to assess intake of which nutrient? a. iron. b. vitamin C. c. vegetables. d. fruits.	Answer: a Rationale: Vegans do not eat meat or meat byproducts, and consequently tend to have low iron levels. It is difficult for vegan clients to have adequate intakes of iron and proteins prior to pregnancy. This problem increases with the pregnancy and the infant's needs for iron stores. Vegans tend to eat adequate amounts of fruits and vegetables, hence they have adequate vitamin C intake. Assessment Physiological Integrity Application
12.3 A pregnant client who is a vegetarian asks the nurse for assistance with her diet. What instruction would the nurse give? a. "Protein is important; therefore, the addition of one serving of meat is necessary." b. "Complete proteins are found in vegetable products." c. "A daily supplement of 4 mg vitamin B_{12} is important." d. "The high fiber in a vegetarian diet is dangerous for pregnant women."	Answer: c Rationale: The lack of meat and meat byproducts requires the client to take a dietary supplement of vitamin B_{12}. Vegetarians do not eat meat or meat byproducts, and the nurse cannot force this issue. Vegetables must be combined with other appropriate foods to form complete proteins. The high fiber found in vegetarian diets actually is good for the pregnant woman whose GI tract has slowed down. Implementation Health Promotion and Maintenance Application
12.4 The pregnant client cannot tolerate milk or meat. What would the nurse recommend to the client to assist in meeting protein needs? a. wheat bread and pasta. b. ice cream and peanut butter. c. eggs and tofu. d. beans and potatoes.	Answer: c Rationale: Wheat bread and pasta are not a source of complete protein. Ice cream is a milk byproduct and would not be tolerated by this client. Beans and potatoes would not provide the client with adequate protein. The best selection of food choices that are nondairy and complete proteins alone are eggs and tofu. Implementation Physiological Integrity Application
12.5 In early pregnancy class the nurse emphasizes the importance of 8 to 10 glasses of fluid per day. How many of these should be water? a. 1 to 2. b. 2 to 4. c. 4 to 6. d. 8 to 10.	Answer: c Rationale: Women need 8 to 10 glasses of fluid each day. Limits should be placed on the consumption of caffeine and sodas. The client should consume 4 to 6 glasses of water per day to supply the pregnant client and the fetus with adequate fluid. Less than 4 glasses is not an adequate intake of water. If the client is consuming all 8 to 10 glasses of fluids in the form of water, she is not getting adequate intake of calcium and fruit juices. Implementation Health Promotion and Maintenance Application

12.6 A teenage pregnant client is diagnosed with iron-deficient anemia. Which nutrient should the nurse encourage to increase iron absorption? a. vitamin A. b. vitamin C. c. vitamin D. d. vitamin E.	Answer: b Rationale: Vitamin C is known to enhance the absorption of iron from meat and non-meat sources. While vitamins A, D, and E are good for the body, they do not promote the absorption of iron. Planning Physiological Integrity Application
12.7 Niacin intake should increase during pregnancy. Which of the following foods would the nurse suggest to increase intake of niacin? a. fish. b. apples. c. broccoli. d. lettuce.	Answer: a Rationale: Sources rich in niacin include meats, fish, and enriched grains. Apples, broccoli, and lettuce will provide sources of other vitamins; however, they do not contain significant niacin. Planning Physiological Integrity Application
12.8 Zinc intake should increase during pregnancy. Which of the following foods would the nurse suggest to increase intake of zinc? a. shellfish. b. bananas. c. pears. d. cabbage.	Answer: a Rationale: Zinc is found in greatest concentration in meats and meat byproducts. Also, enriched grains tend to be higher in zinc. Bananas, pears, and cabbage are high in other nutrients but do not have significant levels of zinc. Planning Physiological Integrity Application
12.9 A pregnant client who is of normal prepregnancy weight is now 30 weeks pregnant. She asks the nurse what is appropriate weight gain. The nurse's best response is: a. "Twenty-five to thirty-five pounds." b. "Thirty to forty pounds." c. "Seventeen to eighteen pounds." d. "Less than fifteen pounds."	Answer: a Rationale: Optimum ranges of weight gain are: underweight woman, 28 to 40 lb; normal-weight woman, 25 to 35 lb.; overweight woman, 15 to 25 lb; and obese woman, less than 15 lb. Therefore an appropriate weight gain for a normal weight woman would be 25 to 35 pounds. Implementation Health Promotion and Maintenance Application
12.10 A pregnant client confides to the nurse that she is eating laundry starch daily. The nurse should assess the client for: a. alopecia. b. weight loss. c. iron-deficiency anemia. d. fecal impaction.	Answer: c Rationale: The ingestion of non-nutritive food sources is called pica. The eating of these non-nutritive substances has been found to interfere with the absorption of iron. These clients typically do not lose weight because they have been participating in this lifestyle prior to pregnancy. The clients might show lack of hair luster, but they do not experience alopecia. The clients may experience more constipation than non-pica clients; however, they do not become impacted. Assessment Physiological Integrity Application
12.11 In order to accurately assess a pregnant client's food intake, the nurse would: a. assess laboratory values. b. ask her to complete a 24-hour dietary recall. c. observe for clinical signs of malnutrition. d. ask about her cooking facilities.	Answer: b Rationale: A 24-hour recall is the only method listed that assesses the client's food intake. Laboratory values and clinical signs of malnutrition provide information only on the nutritional status of the client. Cooking facilities are not related to food intake. Implementation Health Promotion and Maintenance Application

12.12 When preparing nutritional instruction, which of the following pregnant clients would the nurse consider highest-priority? a. 30-year-old G2. b. 22-year-old primigravida. c. 35-year-old G4. d. 15-year-old nulligravida.	Answer: d Rationale: Adolescent clients typically are still in their own growth cycle. Suddenly, they have to supply nutrition for themselves and the fetus. This places them at highest risk for malnutrition for themselves and their infant. The 22-year-old, the 30-year-old, and the 35-year-old have completed their growth cycles, and their bodies can focus on diverting the nutritional needs to the fetus. Planning Safe, Effective Care Environment Analysis
12.13 The pregnant client states she does not want "to take all these supplements." What recommendation could the nurse make for the client? Select all that apply. a. "Folic acid has been found to be essential for minimizing the risk of neural tube defects." b. "You do not have to take these supplements if you think you are healthy enough." c. "Most women do not have adequate intake of iron prepregnancy, and the iron needs increase with pregnancy." d. "These medications do the same thing. I will call your physician to cancel one of your medications."	Answers: a, c Rationale: Research has shown such a strong correlation between decreased folic acid/folate intake and the risk of neural tube defects that all women thinking of becoming pregnant are encouraged to begin taking a 400 mcg supplement two months before attempting conception. Iron is essential because most pregnant women do not have adequate intake of iron before pregnancy. The client must take both supplements. Planning Health Promotion and Maintenance Application
12.14 The postpartal client has been home for a week following a vaginal delivery with a first-degree tear. The nurse is preparing for a home visit. The nurse would need to assess for: a. dietary intake of fiber and fluids. b. dietary intake of folic acid and prenatal vitamins. c. return of the hemoglobin and hematocrit to baseline. d. return of protein and albumin to predelivery levels.	Answer: a Rationale: This mother needs to avoid the risk of constipation. She might be hesitant to have a bowel movement due to perceived pain from the vaginal tear. It will take several months for the laboratory levels to return to normal. Dietary intake of prenatal vitamins is important, but not folic acid. Planning Health Promotion and Maintenance Application
12.15 The breastfeeding mother is concerned about the decreased production of milk. The nurse knows further teaching is needed based on which statement? a. "I am drinking a minimum of 8 to 10 glasses of liquid a day." b. "I have started cutting back on my protein intake." c. "At least three times a day, I am drinking a glass of milk." d. "I try to take a nap in the morning and afternoon when the baby is sleeping."	Answer: b Rationale: The breastfeeding mother must consume a minimum of 8 to 10 glasses of liquid per day, with an increase in her protein and calcium intake. It has also been found that adequate rest is necessary for the body to maintain its production of milk. The decreased intake of protein will decrease milk production. Evaluation Health Promotion and Maintenance Analysis

13.1 A 16-year-old is making her first prenatal visit to the clinic in her fourth month of pregnancy. The nurse's first responsibility would be to:
a. contact the social worker.
b. develop a trusting relationship.
c. schedule the client for prenatal classes.
d. teach the client about proper nutrition.

Answer: b
Rationale: The most important goal for the nurse caring for a pregnant adolescent is to be open-minded and nonjudgmental to foster trust between the adolescent and the nurse. Through a trusting relationship, the nurse can provide counseling and education to the mother-to-be, both about her body and the fetus. Although nutrition is an important physiologic need, without a trusting relationship, little teaching will occur, as the teen will often "tune out" adults she does not trust. A social worker might be able to provide assistance with financial program eligibility, support groups, or obtaining baby items such as furniture and car seats. Prenatal classes specifically designed for teen moms and attended by only teen moms facilitate both learning and support for the teens.
Planning
Health Promotion and Maintenance
Application

13.2 A pregnant adolescent client states that it is important not to have a baby that weighs too much. She states this has been her rationale for limiting calories. Her weight has decreased from 110 pounds to 106 pounds. Which of the following nursing diagnoses would have priority?
a. Knowledge Deficit related to fetal development.
b. Altered Nutrition: less than body requirements related to poor eating habits.
c. Body Image disturbance related to situational crisis.
d. Anxiety related to unanticipated pregnancy.

Answer: b
Rationale: Teens might not understand the physiology behind the profound body changes of pregnancy. Pregnant adolescents are just adapting to a new body image created by the changes of puberty, when the pregnancy produces rapid and substantial body changes. The desire to maintain a socially desirable figure can lead to nutritional deficits. The first role of the nurse is to explain why food is important to the growing fetus, specifying how each food group will help the fetus develop. Next, the nurse must assist the pregnant adolescent to plan foods that she likes to eat from each food group. Anticipatory guidance in the body changes that will take place will assist the adolescent's adjustment to them. Although many teens are anxious, this teen is expressing a direct nutritional deficit.
Diagnosis
Health Promotion and Maintenance
Analysis

13.3 A 14-year-old is brought to the clinic by her mother. The teen is determined to be about 28 weeks pregnant. The mother states, "We knew she was gaining weight, but she said she couldn't be pregnant." The nurse understands that this typical behavior is:
a. low self-esteem.
b. anger.
c. denial.
d. ignorance.

Answer: c
Rationale: Denial is a coping mechanism used to maintain psychological stability when confronting something negative or emotionally difficult. Parents of pregnant adolescents usually do not want their child to be pregnant at that age, and so denial may be experienced. Teens may become pregnant in part because of low self-esteem, believing themselves not worthy or important. Anger will often manifest as loud or negative speech, which may include blaming or shaming. The parents may be ignorant of their child's sexual activity, but when faced with weight gain, they denied pregnancy could be the cause of the change.
Diagnosis
Psychosocial Integrity
Application

13.4 Which of the following statements from the mother of a pregnant 13-year-old would be an expected response?
a. "We had such high hopes for you."
b. "But she was always an easygoing child."
c. "I told you that boy was up to no good."
d. "This is just one of those things that happen."

Answer: a
Rationale: When an adolescent pregnancy is first revealed to the teen's mother, the result is often anger, shame, or disappointment. The degree of negative response will be determined by the age of the teen, the family expectations for the teen, and presence or absence of other teen pregnancies in the family or support network. In early adolescents, the teen's mother frequently accompanies her daughter to prenatal examinations. The role of the nurse is to facilitate communication between mother and daughter and provide education for both.
Evaluation
Psychosocial Integrity
Application

13.5 The nurse seeks to involve the adolescent father in the prenatal care of his girlfriend. The rationale for this nursing strategy includes:
a. increasing the self-care behaviors of the pregnant teen.
b. avoiding conflict between the adolescent father and pregnant teenager.
c. increasing the confidence of the pregnant teenager.
d. avoiding legal action by the adolescent father's family.

Answer: a
Rationale: The nurse first must explore what the relationship is between the pregnant teen and the father. Relationships between adolescents tend to be short-lived, and pregnancy is an added stressor for the couple. If the client desires the participation of her partner, the nurse should provide education and support appropriate to the age, knowledge, and developmental level of the adolescent father. Involving the partner of a pregnant adolescent helps the mom-to-be feel more confident in her decision making and improves her self-confidence and self-esteem, which in turn will improve positive self-care behaviors.
Planning
Health Promotion and Maintenance
Application

13.6 The 19-year-old pregnant woman begins a job to "save money for the baby." The nurse understands this statement to demonstrate what?
a. striving for gaining autonomy and independence.
b. completed development of a sense of identity.
c. needing attainment of a sense of achievement.
d. having developed an intimate relationship.

Answer: a
Rationale: There are several developmental tasks during adulthood: gaining confidence in one's sexuality, developing intimate relationships, gaining independence and autonomy, and developing a sense of identity and sense of achievement. Having a job is how most teens develop financial independence and autonomy.
Diagnosis
Health Promotion and Maintenance
Analysis

13.7 Which statement would a pregnant teenager at her initial prenatal examination be most likely to make? (Select all that apply.)
a. "I didn't know I could get pregnant the first time I had sex."
b. "Several of my friends go to clinics to get contraception."
c. "It's no big deal; two of my best friends have babies, too."
d. "I was 13 years old when I had sex the first time."
e. "My family and my boyfriend are really happy and supportive."

Answers: a, c, d
Rationale: There are several contributing factors for the United States' having a higher adolescent pregnancy rate than any other developed nation in the world. These factors include lack of knowledge about conception, difficulty accessing contraception, decreased social stigma of being a young and single mother, younger age at onset of sexual activity, poverty, and early childhood sexual abuse. Lack of support from the partner and parents is common, especially when the pregnancy is first diagnosed and disclosed.
Assessment
Health Promotion and Maintenance
Application

13.8 After assessing the data obtained from a pregnant teenager and her family, the nurse assigns the diagnosis of "Family Coping, ineffective related to unanticipated pregnancy." Which of the following goals would be appropriate?
a. The teenager and family will participate in discussions regarding pregnancy.
b. The teenager and family will develop skills for parenting the infant.
c. The teenager and family will develop a trusting relationship with the healthcare providers.
d. The teenager and family will develop self-care skills for the pregnancy.

Answer: a
Rationale: Communication between family members is essential for them to understand each other's viewpoints. Joining into a discussion facilitated by the nurse will help begin the communication process for the family. Once communication has been established, making plans for the future can take place, which in turn promotes family coping. Taking care of oneself or a newborn physically will not necessarily lead to family coping. And although trust in the healthcare providers is essential for the teen to accept teaching and have effective communication with the providers, this is an individual intervention aimed only at the pregnant teen, and not at the entire family.
Planning
Psychosocial Integrity
Analysis

13.9 Appropriate nursing strategies for the nursing diagnosis "Family Coping, ineffective related to unanticipated adolescent pregnancy" would include:

a. assess the support network of the client and family.
b. assess parenting skills of client and father of the baby.
c. discuss fears and concerns of the body image.
d. discuss the importance of regular prenatal care.

Answer: a
Rationale: Once the nursing diagnosis of "Family Coping, ineffective related to unanticipated pregnancy" is made, the next step for the nurse is to plan how to facilitate improving the family's coping. Coping with an unanticipated pregnancy is a complex psychosocial task, which requires communication, complete understanding of the situation, and the ability to make plans for the future, which includes the pregnancy. Only after the family has adjusted to the idea of this pregnancy is it appropriate to begin teaching parenting skills. Body image concerns and prenatal care are individual and personal issues for the pregnant adolescent, not the family.
Planning
Health Promotion and Maintenance
Application

13.10 Which of the following is critical for an effective adolescent pregnancy prevention program to include?

a. role models from similar cultural and racial backgrounds.
b. planning executed by the planner and organizer only.
c. short-term, informal programs available twice per year.
d. focus on the expectations of the adolescents' parents.

Answer: a
Rationale: The National Campaign to Prevent Teen Pregnancy's task forces found that the programs most effective at preventing teen pregnancy include adolescents in the planning of activities, are both long-term and intensive, focus on adolescent males and not just females, and provide models from similar cultural and racial backgrounds as the participants.
Planning
Health Promotion and Maintenance
Application

13.11 During the initial prenatal visit, the pregnant teenager states that she does not know how she got pregnant. The nurse can help to educate her regarding anatomy by:

a. allowing her to witness a pelvic exam on another teenager.
b. encouraging her to ask her mother abut the physiology of pregnancy.
c. including anatomic models and drawings in the teaching session.
d. discussing the process of fetal development with the client.

Answer: c
Rationale: Lack of knowledge about conception is common in pregnant teens. To teach the client about anatomy and physiology, as well as to dispel myths she may hold, the nurse should use appropriate medical terminology and refer to models, pictures, and drawings. Offering the client a mirror during the pelvic exam is also helpful. One client is not allowed to be present during another client's visit or exam due to privacy issues and HIPAA. Her mother might not have accurate information or might be uncomfortable discussing these issues with her teen daughter. While fetal development is important to understand, discussing it now does not address the client's stated concern.
Planning
Health Promotion and Maintenance
Application

13.12 In order to give the pregnant adolescent a role in her prenatal care, the nurse could allow her to:

a. choose the type of prenatal vitamin she takes.
b. measure and record her weight at each visit.
c. choose the schedule of her prenatal visits.
d. decide if she wants her labor to be induced.

Answer: b
Rationale: Prenatal vitamins are prescribed by the certified nurse, midwife, or the physician. Many formulations exist, and some may not be indicated for this client due to her nutritional practices and lab results. In addition, if the client is a member of a Health Maintenance Organization, only certain medications (including prenatal vitamins) are accepted for coverage. Having the client weigh herself and record her weight involves her in the prenatal care. Prenatal visit schedules are set to detect developing complications of pregnancy. Induction of labor is a medical decision and should not be taken lightly.
Planning
Health Promotion and Maintenance
Application

13.13 Which of the following statements, if made by the pregnant adolescent, indicates that she understands her increased risk of physiologic complications during pregnancy?

Answer: c
Rationale: Pregnant adolescents are at high risk for complications such as pregnancy-induced hypertension, anemia, preterm birth, low-birth-weight infants, and fetal harm from cigarette smoking, alcohol consumption, or the use of street drugs. Early and regular prenatal care is the best intervention to prevent complications or to detect them early, to minimize the harm to both the teen and her fetus.

a. "It's no big deal that I started prenatal care in my seventh month." b. "My anemia and eating mostly fast food are not important." c. "I need to take good care of myself so my baby doesn't come early." d. "My smoking and using crack cocaine won't harm my baby."	Evaluation Health Promotion and Maintenance Analysis
13.14 The nurse is preparing an in-service presentation for a group of middle school nurses. Which statements, if made by the nurse, would indicate that the nurse understands the role of culture in adolescent pregnancy? (Select all that apply.) a. "Eighty-five percent of teen mothers are middle class, and give birth to gain adult status." b. "Teens who have a lot of time without adult supervision are more sexually active." c. "Although the rate has dropped, teens of color are more likely to become pregnant." d. "Young teens who have a child are more likely to have another while still a teen." e. "Most pregnant teens do not have any relatives who had their first child as teens."	Answers: b, c, d Rationale: When teens in poverty become pregnant, they are more likely to maintain the pregnancy and view the birth as a way to be seen as an adult. Middle-class teens are more likely to have future education and career goals, use contraception, and seek therapeutic abortion if they become pregnant. The pregnancy rate for African-American teens age 15 to 17 has dropped by 15%, but Hispanic- and African-American teens have a disproportionately large number of adolescent births. Teens who participate in after-school activities are less likely to be sexually active, and therefore have fewer pregnancies. Conversely, teens who spend more time without adult supervision are more likely to be sexually active and to become pregnant. When the first birth occurs in the early teen years, the next birth also is likely to occur prior to adulthood. Having a mother or a sister who had her first child during adolescence is a risk for a teen to become pregnant. Planning Health Promotion and Maintenance Application
13.15 The nurse who is counseling a group of middle school girls on pregnancy avoidance should include which of the following statements? a. "Although sexuality is common in the media, your peer pressure to have sex is not an important factor." b. "It has become far less acceptable to give birth during your teenage years than it used to be." c. "Although condom use is growing, there is still an increasing rate of STDs among teens." d. "You have learned enough from your friends and families to understand how pregnancy occurs."	Answer: c Rationale: Images of sexuality are common in American society: in music lyrics and videos, in advertising, in television shows and movies. Peer pressure to have sex is also common and is a strong influence on when a teen becomes sexually active. Society has become more accepting of teen pregnancy, and there are fewer stigmas attached to being a young mother. Condom use is increasing, but the rate of STD infections, including HIV, is also rising. Formal education of the physiology of the body and conception will decrease the myths and misunderstandings that abound among teens and undereducated adults. Implementation Health Promotion and Maintenance Application

CHAPTER 14

14.1 A newly diagnosed type 1, well-controlled, insulin-dependent diabetic is at 20 weeks' gestation. She asks the nurse how her diabetes will affect her baby. The best explanation would include: a. "Your baby may be smaller than average at birth." b. "Your baby will probably be larger than average at birth."	Answer: b Rationale: The infant produces excessive amounts of insulin—hyperinsulinism. This affects the infant in that he utilizes the glucose in the bloodstream, stimulating growth—macrosomia. Poorly controlled type I diabetics who have developed vascular problems will have infants who are small for gestational age (SGA) due to placental insufficiency. The demands of pregnancy will make it difficult for the best of clients to control blood sugars on a regular basis. Within minutes of delivery, the baby of a type 1 diabetic can begin to have blood sugar problems.

c. "As long as you control your blood sugar, your baby will not be affected at all." d. "There are no effects until about two hours after birth, when your baby might have low blood sugar."	Implementation Physiological Integrity Application
14.2 The pregnant client has a history of rheumatic heart disease as a child, with residual effects. She is concerned for her health and the safety of the pregnancy. The client asks the nurse, "When am I most likely to experience problems related to my heart condition?" The nurse's best response is: a. 12 to 16 weeks' gestation. b. 20 to 24 weeks' gestation. c. 28 to 32 weeks' gestation. d. 36 to 40 weeks' gestation.	Answer: c Rationale: Blood volume has reached its maximum amount between 28 and 32 weeks. Before 28 weeks, the blood volume has increased only slightly. After about 32 weeks, the blood volume has stabilized. The cardiac system will be most affected when the volume is rising sharply to its maximum amount, which would be 28 to 32 weeks. Implementation Physiological Integrity Application
14.3 A 26-year-old multipara is 26 weeks pregnant. Her previous births include two large-for-gestational-age babies and one unexplained stillbirth. Which tests would the nurse anticipate as being most definitive in diagnosing gestational diabetes? a. a 50 g, one-hour glucose screening test. b. a single fasting glucose level. c. a 100 g, one-hour glucose tolerance test. d. a 100 g, three-hour glucose tolerance test.	Answer: d Rationale: All women get the initial 50 g of glucose and a one-hour screening. However, a client with a history of LGA infants or gestational diabetes will be given the 100 g of glucose and the three-hour glucose tolerance test. A single fasting glucose level is not an adequate indicator of the glucose level in relation to food, nor is the 100 g and a one-hour tolerance test. Assessment Physiological Integrity Analysis
14.4 A 26-year-old multigravida is 28 weeks pregnant. She has developed gestational diabetes. She has a program of regular exercise, which includes walking, bicycling, and swimming. What instructions should be included in a teaching plan for this client? a. Exercise either just before meals or wait until two hours after a meal. b. Carry hard candy (or other simple sugar) when exercising. c. If your finger stick shows less than 120 mg/dL, ingest 20 g of carbohydrate. d. If your finger stick shows more than 120 mg/dL, drink a glass of whole milk or other source of carbohydrate.	Answer: b Rationale: Clients are encouraged to continue any exercise programs in which they already are involved. They are encouraged to keep hard candy (simple sugar) with them at all times, just in case the exercise induces hypoglycemia. It is best to exercise just after a meal, in order to utilize the glucose. A finger stick of 120 mg/dL is considered to be at the high end of normal, therefore, such clients need no additional carbohydrate intake. Planning Physiological Integrity Application
14.5 A woman is 34 weeks pregnant. When she comes for an early-morning clinic visit, she mentions that she did not have time to eat breakfast. Results of her urine specimen show a small amount of ketones to be present. This most likely indicates: a. normal pregnancy-induced changes in carbohydrate metabolism. b. a asymptomatic urinary tract infection.	Answer: a Rationale: When the pregnant client has been fasting for a period of time, the fetus is utilizing the client's glucose stores, and fat is broken down, resulting in a slight elevation in ketones. A client with gestational diabetes and a diet high in fat would have a much higher level of ketones broken down. Ketones are the byproduct of fat breakdown, and would not be present in the client with a urinary tract infection.

c. the early onset of gestational diabetes. d. that her diet is high in fats.	Diagnosis Physiological Integrity Analysis
14.6 A 21-year-old is 12 weeks pregnant with her first baby. She has cardiac disease, class III, as a result of having had childhood rheumatic fever. During a prenatal visit, the nurse reviews the signs of cardiac decompensation with her. The nurse will know that the client understands these signs and symptoms if she states, "I would notify my doctor if I have: a. a pulse rate increase of 10 beats per minute." b. breast tenderness." c. mild ankle edema." d. a frequent cough."	Answer: d Rationale: With the increased workload of the heart with pregnancy and the increase in blood volume, this client is at risk for developing congestive heart failure. This would result in the frequent cough. The majority of pregnant clients will develop breast tenderness, and the heart rate will increase. The client with rheumatic heart disease will have a much higher pulse rate. Also, the client with rheumatic heart disease who develops congestive heart failure would have severe ankle edema. Evaluation Physiological Integrity Analysis
14.7 A 26-year-old multipara is 24 weeks pregnant. Her previous births include two large-for-gestational-age babies and one unexplained stillbirth. With this history, what assessment should be made in order to identify her most probable pregestational problem? a. breath sounds. b. hemoglobin and hematocrit. c. urine and blood glucose. d. urine for bacteria.	Answer: c Rationale: Large-for-gestational-age (LGA) babies typically result from the high levels of glucose. If the glucose levels rise above the renal threshold, the glucose will spill into the urine. Therefore, it is important to monitor glucose levels if the client has a history of LGA babies. The client's breath sounds will have no effect on size or stillbirths. If the client is anemic, this could result in a baby who is small for gestational age, not large for gestational age. Bacteria in the urine will result in a urinary tract infection, leading to the potential for preterm labor, but not large for gestational age or stillbirth. Assessment Health Promotion and Maintenance Application
14.8 A client is 12 weeks pregnant with her first baby. She has cardiac disease, class III. She states that she had been taking sodium warfarin (Coumadin), but her physician changed her to heparin. She asks the nurse why this was done. The nurse's response should be: a. "Heparin may be given by mouth, while Coumadin must be injected." b. "Heparin is safer because it does not cross the placenta." c. "They are the same drug, but heparin is less expensive." d. "Coumadin interferes with iron absorption in the intestines."	Answer: b Rationale: Heparin is safest for the client to take because it does not cross the placental barrier. Heparin is an injectable and Coumadin is a pill. Heparin does not cost less. Coumadin does not interfere with iron absorption in the intestines. Implementation Physiological Integrity Application
14.9 A 21-year-old woman is 12 weeks pregnant with her first baby. She has cardiac disease, class III, as a result of having had childhood rheumatic fever. Which planned activity would indicate to the nurse that the client needs further teaching? a. "I will be sure to take a rest period every afternoon."	Answer: d Rationale: Because of the class III of the heart disease, this client is encouraged to get adequate rest. With the slightest of exertion, her heart rate will rise, and she will become symptomatic. Therefore, she should not establish a new exercise program. Childbirth classes would be helpful for the client, as long as she is aware not to overexert herself. Travel during the pregnancy would be based upon the tolerance of the client. However, a trip to Disney World would involve a large amount of activity and would stress the pregnancy.

b. "I would like to take childbirth education classes in my last trimester." c. "I will have to cancel our trip to Disney World." d. "I am going to start my classes in water aerobics starting next week."	Evaluation Physiological Integrity Analysis
14.10 A pregnant woman is married to an intravenous drug user. She had a negative HIV screening test just after missing her first menstrual period. What would indicate that the client needs to be retested for HIV? a. a hemoglobin of 11 g/dL and a rapid weight gain. b. elevated blood pressure and ankle edema. c. shortness of breath and frequent urination. d. unusual fatigue and recurring candida vaginitis.	Answer: d Rationale: The client who is HIV positive would have a suppressed immune system and would experience symptoms of fatigue and an opportunistic infection such as candida vaginitis. The client would be anemic and anorexic, with a decrease in blood pressure and no ankle edema. Shortness of breath and frequent urination are not signs of a need to retest for HIV. Diagnosis Health Promotion and Maintenance Analysis
14.11 A woman is 32 weeks pregnant. She is HIV positive but asymptomatic. What would be important in managing her pregnancy and delivery? a. an amniocentesis at 30 and 36 weeks. b. weekly nonstress testing beginning at 32 weeks' gestation. c. application of a fetal scalp electrode as soon as her membranes rupture in labor. d. administration of intravenous antibiotics during labor and delivery.	Answer: b Rationale: Clients who are HIV positive are considered high-risk pregnancies; therefore, beginning at about 32 weeks, these clients have weekly nonstress tests to assess for intrauterine growth retardation (IUGR). All invasive procedures are avoided that would expose the uninfected infant to the HIV virus. Antibiotics would be ineffective for either the mother or the infant who is HIV positive. Planning Physiological Integrity Application
14.12 A 20-year-old woman is at 28 weeks' gestation. Her prenatal history reveals past abuse of drugs, and urine screening indicates that she has recently used heroin. The nurse should recognize that the woman is at increased risk for: a. erythroblastosis fetalis. b. diabetes mellitus. c. abruptio placentae. d. pregnancy-induced hypertension.	Answer: d Rationale: Women who use heroin are at risk for poor nutrition, anemia, and pregnancy-induced hypertension or preeclampsia. Abruptio placentae is seen more commonly in cocaine/crack use. Diabetes is an endocrine disorder that is unrelated to drug use/abuse. Erythroblastosis fetalis is secondary to physiological blood disorders such as Rh incompatibility. Assessment Physiological Integrity Analysis
14.13 A woman's history and appearance suggest drug abuse. The nurse's best approach would be to: a. ask the woman directly, "Do you use any street drugs?" b. ask the woman if she would like to talk to a counselor. c. ask some questions about over-the-counter medications and avoid the mention of illicit drugs. d. explain how harmful drugs can be for her baby.	Answer: a Rationale: The best method of dealing with the client that the nurse suspects of using drugs is to be direct and ask the question in a direct fashion without prejudice, bias, or negative body language. Lack of judgmental attitudes/body language typically results in honest answers. It is the responsibility of the nurse to question the client and not avoid the issue. Finally, when talking to clients in a therapeutic manner, it is important not to be threatening with the information nor judgmental in the responses—such as stating the drugs will harm the baby. Implementation Psychosocial Integrity Application

14.14 The client has just been diagnosed as a diabetic. The nurse who has been teaching knows the teaching was effective when the client says:
a. "Ketones in my urine mean that my body is using the glucose appropriately."
b. "I should be urinating frequently and in large amounts to get rid of the extra sugar."
c. "My pancreas is making enough insulin, but my body isn't using it correctly."
d. "I may be hungry frequently because the sugar isn't getting into the tissues the way it should."

Answer: d
Rationale: The client who understands the disease process is aware that if the body is not getting the glucose it needs, the message of hunger will be sent to the brain. Ketones are produced when fat is being utilized for glucose, and this is not a desirable response. Frequent urination is an indication of glucose above the renal threshold, and is not a good indicator of diabetic stability. Diabetes is a result of lack of insulin production. If the insulin is being produced, the body will utilize it.
Evaluation
Physiological Integrity
Analysis

14.15 During the history, the client admits to being HIV positive and knowing she is about 16 weeks pregnant. Which statements made by the client indicate an understanding of the plan of care both during the pregnancy and postpartally? (Select all that apply.)
a. "I will take my Zidovudine (ZVD) at the same time every day."
b. "During labor and delivery, I can expect the Zidovudine (ZVD) to be given in my IV."
c. "After delivery, the dose of Zidovudine (ZVD) will be doubled to prevent further infection."
d. "My baby will be started on Zidovudine (ZVD) within 12 hours of delivery."

Answers: a, b, d
Rationale: All HIV-positive clients are begun on a three-part therapy after the first trimester. The initial treatment is ZVD orally every day. It is recommended, to keep the level consistent, that dosages be taken consistently. During the labor and delivery process, the doses will be given intravenously. Finally, within 8 to 12 hours after delivery, the infant is begun on ZVD and kept on the medication a minimum of six weeks. The mother will continue with her oral dosage of ZVD after delivery just as prior to delivery.
Evaluation
Physiological Integrity
Analysis

CHAPTER 15

15.1 A 19-year-old woman is expecting her first baby. During the nursing interview, the woman reports that she has been sexually active for three years. Two years ago, she had gonorrhea, which progressed to pelvic inflammatory disease (PID). Prenatal lab tests show that her hemoglobin value is 11.5 g/dL. Which item from this history data indicates that the client is at risk for an ectopic pregnancy?
a. anemia.
b. sexual activity since age 17.
c. gonorrhea.
d. pelvic inflammatory disease (PID).

Answer: d
Rationale: The client is at risk for ectopic pregnancy when there has been damage to the fallopian tubes. Examples of physiological problems that can cause tissue damage/scarring are pelvic inflammatory disease (PID), history of tubular pregnancy, endometriosis, and congenital tubular anomalies.
Evaluation
Health Promotion and Maintenance
Analysis

15.2 A pregnant woman at 16 weeks' gestation is diagnosed with hyperemesis gravidarum. She has been admitted to the floor from the emergency department. Which nursing diagnosis would receive priority for the nurse planning care?

Answer: a
Rationale: The newly admitted client with hyperemesis gravidarum has been experiencing excessive vomiting and is in a fluid volume deficit state. Because no preexisting cardiac condition is present, the body has compensated for this fluid loss. The risk for injury is present due to the symptoms of fluid volume deficit, however, it is not the priority. The nutrition status of the client is compromised,

a. Fluid Volume Deficit b. Decreased Cardiac Output c. Risk for Injury d. Alteration in Nutrition: less than body requirements	however, until we correct the emesis and the fluid volume status. The nutritional status will not be affected. Planning Safe, Effective Care Environment Application
15.3 A woman is experiencing preterm labor. The client asks why she is on betamethasone (Celestone). The best response by the nurse would be: a. "This medication will halt the labor process, until the baby is more mature." b. "This medication will relax the smooth muscles in the infant's lungs so that, if born early, it can breathe." c. "This medication has been found to be effective in stimulating lung development in the preterm infant." d. "This medication is an antibiotic that will help resolve your urinary tract infection, which has led to your preterm labor."	Answer: c Rationale: Betamethasone (Celestone) has been found to induce pulmonary maturation, and thereby decrease the risk of respiratory problems in the preterm infant. It has no effect on the labor process, or on the smooth muscles in the lungs. This medication is not an antibiotic and, therefore, will not help resolve a UTI. Implementation Physiological Integrity Application
15.4 A woman is being treated for preterm labor with magnesium sulfate. The nurse is concerned that the client is in early drug toxicity. What assessment finding by the nurse indicates early magnesium sulfate toxicity? a. patellar reflexes decrease to a weak +1. b. complaints by the client of feeling flushed and warm. c. respiratory rate decrease to 14. d. fetal heart rate of 120.	Answer: a Rationale: Early signs of magnesium sulfate toxicity are related to a decrease in deep tendon reflexes. Late signs of toxicity are a respiratory rate less than 12, urine output less than 30 cc/hr, and confusion. Magnesium typically has no effect on fetal heart rate. The peripheral vasodilation will cause flushing and a feeling of warmth—this is a side effect, not a toxic effect. Assessment Physiological Integrity Application
15.5 A woman has had her hydatidiform mole (molar pregnancy) evacuated, and is prepared for discharge. The nurse should make certain that the client understands that it is essential that she: a. not become pregnant for at least one year. b. receive RhoGAM with her next pregnancy and birth. c. have her blood pressure checked weekly for the next 30 days. d. seek genetic counseling with her partner before the next pregnancy.	Answer: a Rationale: Hydatidiform mole (molar pregnancy) is the result of an empty ovum being fertilized or two sperm fertilizing one egg. For one year after the pregnancy, hCG levels are monitored to assess for carcinoma growth. Clients are advised not to get pregnant due to potential confusion as to tumor growth or pregnancy. There is no indication for the administration of RhoGam. There is no indication of blood pressure problems or pre-eclampsia. This is not a genetic defect that genetic counseling could/would resolve. Planning Physiological Integrity Application
15.6 A clinic nurse is planning when to administer Rh immune globulin (RhoGAM) to an Rh-negative pregnant client. When should the first dose of Rh immune globulin (RhoGAM) be administered? a. after the birth of the infant. b. 1 month postpartum. c. during labor. d. at 28 weeks' gestation.	Answer: d Rationale: Since transplacental hemorrhage is possible during pregnancy, an antibody screen is performed on an Rh-negative woman at 28 weeks' gestation. If she has no antibody titer, she is given an IM injection of 300 mcg Rh immune globulin (RhoGAM). During labor, after birth, and 1 month postpartum would be too late for the first dose of RhoGAM if transplacental hemorrhage that is possible during pregnancy has occurred. A second dose, however, is given after birth during the postpartum period. Planning Health Promotion and Maintenance Application

15.7 During a prenatal exam a client expresses several psychosomatic symptoms and has several vague complaints. What could these behaviors indicate?

a. abuse.
b. mental illness.
c. depression.
d. nothing, they are normal.

Answer: a
Rationale: Chronic psychosomatic symptoms and vague complaints can be indicators of abuse. They are not indicators of mental illness or depression. The first step toward helping the battered woman is to identify her so these signs should not be discounted as normal.
Assessment
Psychosocial Integrity
Analysis

15.8 A woman is 10 weeks pregnant. Her initial prenatal laboratory screening test for rubella showed an antibody titer of less than 1:6. The woman calls the clinic and tells the nurse that she has been exposed to measles. The nurse's best response is:

a. "Since you are in your first trimester of pregnancy, this is not likely to be a problem."
b. "Would you like to see a counselor to talk about your options for the remainder of your pregnancy?"
c. "You should come to the clinic in the next day or two for further evaluation."
d. "You need to have a rubella vaccination immediately. Can you get a ride to the clinic today?"

Answer: c
Rationale: Exposure to rubella in the first trimester has the greatest risk for causing congenital anomalies. Clients are not vaccinated during the pregnancy. So the best advice for the client would be to come to the clinic in the next day or two to talk with the nurse and physician about her options. It is nontherapeutic to send them to a counselor.
Implementation
Health Promotion and Maintenance
Application

15.9 A pregnant client has been identified as being at risk for preterm labor. The nurse knows the client understands signs of preterm labor when she states, "I may be in labor if I:

a. have breast tenderness."
b. have uterine contractions that occur every 10 minutes (or more frequently) for 1 hour."
c. feel the baby move more than 3 times in an hour."
d. have some morning nausea."

Answer: b
Rationale: When a pregnant client is at risk for preterm labor, she should know that if contractions occur every 10 minutes (or more frequently) for 1 hour she should telephone her physician or certified nurse-midwife and make arrangements to be checked for ongoing labor. Breast tenderness, feeling 3 fetal movements in an hour, and nausea in the morning are all normal findings of pregnancy and do not indicate labor is occurring.
Evaluation
Health Promotion and Maintenance
Analysis

15.10 The nurse has the following assessment findings on a client with preeclampsia: blood pressure 158/100; urinary output 50 mL/hour; lungs clear to auscultation; urine protein 1+ on dipstick; edema of the hands, ankles, and feet. On the next hourly assessment, which of the following new assessment findings would be an indication of worsening of the preeclampsia?

a. blood pressure 158/104.
b. urinary output 20 mL/hour.
c. reflexes 2+.
d. platelet count 150,000.

Answer: b
Rationale: The decrease in urine output is an indication of decrease in GFR, which indicates a loss of renal perfusion. The blood pressure has not had a significant rise, the reflexes are normal at 2+, and the platelet count is normal, though at the lower end. The assessment finding most abnormal and life-threatening is the urine output change.
Assessment
Physiological Integrity
Analysis

15.11 A woman is 16 weeks pregnant. She has had cramping, backache, and mild bleeding for the past three days. Her physician determines that her cervix is dilated to two centimeters, with 10% effacement, but membranes are still intact. She is crying, and says to the nurse, "Is my baby going to be okay?" In addition to acknowledging the client's fear, the nurse should also say:

a. "Your baby will be fine. We'll start an IV, and get this stopped in no time at all."
b. "Your cervix is beginning to dilate. That is a serious sign. We will continue to monitor you and the baby for now."
c. "You are going to miscarry. But you should be relieved, because most miscarriages are the result of abnormalities in the fetus."
d. "I really can't say. However, when your physician comes, I'll ask her to talk to you about it."

Answer: b
Rationale: A cerclage can be performed in the first trimester and early into the second trimester. Many interventions can be attempted to prevent further dilation and effacement. This is a serious situation. The client should not be offered false hope of everything being fine. The nurse should avoid justification of the miscarriage. The nurse should not defer the conversation to someone else (i.e., the physician).
Implementation
Psychological Integrity
Application

15.12 A woman is 30 weeks pregnant. She has come to the hospital because her membranes have ruptured. Based on this information, which nursing diagnosis could be made for the mother? Risk for:

a. impaired gas exchange.
b. infection.
c. ineffective individual coping.
d. fluid volume deficit.

Answer: b
Rationale: Because of the rupture of membranes and the preterm status, an attempt will be made to mature the fetal lungs and maintain the pregnancy for as long as possible. Therefore, the greatest risk is for infection. This client is not at risk for fluid volume deficit or impaired gas exchange. There is not enough information to determine how she is coping.
Diagnosis
Physiological Integrity
Application

15.13 A woman is hospitalized with severe preeclampsia. The nurse is meal planning with the client. The nurse should encourage a diet that is high in:

a. sodium.
b. carbohydrates.
c. protein.
d. fruits.

Answer: c
Rationale: The client who experiences preeclampsia is losing protein. While it is important that she have adequate intake of carbohydrates and fruits, she needs to limit her intake of sodium and increase her intake of high-protein foods.
Planning
Physiological Integrity
Application

15.14 The nurse is assessing a client who has severe preeclampsia. The assessment finding that should be reported to the physician is:

a. 1+ proteinuria.
b. platelet count of 20,000.
c. urine output of 50 mL per hour.
d. 2+ DTRs.

Answer: b
Rationale: The client could be experiencing HELLP syndrome (hemolysis, elevated liver enzymes, and low platelet count). This condition is sometimes associated with severe preeclampsia, and women who experience this multiple-organ-failure syndrome have high morbidity and mortality rates. A platelet count less than 20,000 is critically low. The DTRs of 2+ are normal, and the urine output of >30 cc/hour is normal. The 1+ spilling of protein is abnormal, but this is acceptable for a client with preeclampsia.
Assessment
Physiological Integrity
Application

15.15 The pharmacy sends 500 cc of NS with 40 grams of magnesium sulfate. The order is for the medication to infuse at 2 grams per hour. The nurse would set the pump at _____ cc/hr.

Answer: 25
Rationale: If there are 40 grams per 500 cc, then there are 2 grams for every 25 cc. To infuse 2 grams in an hour, the pump would have to be set at 25 cc/hr.
Implementation
Physiological Integrity
Application

16.1 A woman is at 32 weeks' gestation. Her fundal height measurement at this clinic appointment is 26 centimeters. After reviewing her ultrasound results, the healthcare provider asks the nurse to schedule the client for a series of sonograms to be done every two weeks. The nurse should make sure that the client understands that the main purpose for this is to:
a. assess for congenital anomalies.
b. evaluate fetal growth.
c. determine fetal presentation.
d. rule out a suspected hydatidiform mole.

Answer: b
Rationale: A person who is at 32 weeks' gestation should measure 32 cm of fundal height. When a discrepancy between fundal height and measurement exists, the purpose of serial ultrasounds is to monitor fetal growth. Assessment of anomalies or of fetal presentation, or ruling out a hydatidiform mole, would require only one ultrasound.
Implementation
Health Promotion and Maintenance
Application

16.2 In assisting with an abdominal ultrasound procedure for determination of fetal age, the nurse:
a. asks the woman to sign an operative consent form prior to the procedure.
b. has the woman empty her bladder before the test begins.
c. assists the woman into a supine position on the examining table.
d. instructs the woman to eat a fat-free meal two hours before the scheduled test time.

Answer: c
Rationale: Clients are placed in a supine position on the table. Abdominal ultrasounds are not invasive procedures, and do not require a consent form. The recommendation is that the client has a full bladder to help elevate the uterus out of the pelvic cavity for better visualization. Dietary intake is not relevant to the ultrasound.
Implementation
Physiological Integrity
Application

16.3 Each of the following pregnant women is scheduled for a 14-week antepartal visit. In planning care, the nurse would give priority teaching on amniotic fluid alpha-fetoprotein (AFP) screening to which client?
a. 28-year-old with history of rheumatic heart disease.
b. 18-year-old with exposure to HIV.
c. 20-year-old with a history of preterm labor.
d. 35-year-old with a child with spina bifida.

Answer: d
Rationale: Alpha-fetoprotein (AFP) is elevated in multigestational pregnancies and in pregnancies with neural tube defects such as spina bifida and Down syndrome. The 35-year-old is considered to be of advanced maternal age and is at risk for having a child with Down syndrome. With the past history of a child with spina bifida, she would be highly encouraged to have the AFP screening. The client with rheumatic heart disease would need to be monitored for pregnancy and the stressors it places on the client. The client with HIV screening needs HIV testing and protection education. The client with a history of preterm labor needs education on prevention and signs and symptoms of preterm labor.
Planning
Safe, Effective Care Environment
Analysis

16.4 A woman at 28 weeks' gestation is asked to keep a fetal activity diary and to bring the results with her to her next clinic visit. One week later, she calls the clinic and anxiously tells the nurse that she has not felt the baby move for over 30 minutes. The most appropriate initial comment by the nurse would be:
a. "You need to come to the clinic right away for further evaluation."
b. "Have you been smoking?"
c. "When did you eat last?"
d. "Your baby may be asleep."

Answer: d
Rationale: Lack of fetal activity for 30 minutes typically is insignificant and only means the infant is sleeping. After meals, typically an infant is active and moving. Smoking also typically will stimulate the infant. The mother would need to come to the clinic only if there had been no fetal activity for several hours. If the mother truly is concerned, in 30 minutes, she could eat a complex carbohydrate snack. This would stimulate the infant, and the mother should have fetal activity. But at present, this is an indicator the infant is sleeping.
Implementation
Health Promotion and Maintenance
Application

16.5 At 32 weeks' gestation, a woman is scheduled for a second nonstress test (in addition to the one she had at 28 weeks' gestation). Which response by the client would indicate an adequate understanding of this procedure?

a. "I can't get up and walk around during the test."
b. "I'll have an IV started before the test."
c. "I must avoid drinks containing caffeine for 24 hours before the test."
d. "I need to have a full bladder for this test."

Answer: a

Rationale: The purpose of the nonstress test is to determine the results of movement on fetal heart rate. The client will have to lie still on her side during the procedure. There is no IV needed to administer medications. Caffeine might cause the infant to be more active and cause the test to go quicker. Clients usually are asked to have their bladders full only for ultrasounds.

Evaluation
Physiological Integrity
Analysis

16.6 During a nonstress test, the nurse notes that the fetal heart rate decelerates about 15 beats during a period of fetal movement. The decelerations occur twice during the test and last 20 seconds each. The nurse realizes these results will be interpreted as:

a. a negative test.
b. a reactive test.
c. a nonreactive test.
d. an equivocal test.

Answer: c

Rationale: Nonstress tests are scored as either reactive or nonreactive. A reactive stress test has the expected results of an increase in heart rate of 15 beats per minutes for 15 seconds or more. In a nonreactive stress test, the reactivity criteria are not met. Since this client experienced a deceleration during the test, this is considered nonreactive.

Diagnosis
Physiological Integrity
Analysis

16.7 A pregnant woman is having a nipple-stimulated contraction stress test. Which result indicates hyperstimulation?

a. The fetal heart rate decelerates when three contractions occur within a 10-minute period.
b. The fetal heart rate accelerates when contractions last up to 60 seconds.
c. There are more than five fetal movements in a 10-minute period.
d. There are more than three uterine contractions in a 6-minute period.

Answer: d

Rationale: Hyperstimulation is characterized by contractions closer than or equal to every 6 minutes or lasting longer than 90 seconds. Decelerations are considered a positive contraction stress test. The acceleration of the heart rate and the fetal movement are considered a negative contraction stress test.

Assessment
Physiological Integrity
Analysis

16.8 Which response would indicate that a client clearly understands the risks of an amniocentesis?

a. "I might go into labor early."
b. "It could produce a congenital defect in my baby."
c. "Actually, there are no real risks to this procedure."
d. "The test could stunt my baby's growth."

Answer: a

Rationale: Amniocentesis has the potential for causing preterm labor, along with other complications, such as infection or bleeding. Congenital effects are the result of heredity or medications. Growth retardation most commonly is associated with heredity or poor nutrition.

Evaluation
Physiological Integrity
Analysis

16.9 The nurse knows that a lecithin/sphingomyelin (L/S) ratio finding of 2:1 on amniotic fluid means:

a. fetal lungs are still immature.
b. the fetus has a congenital anomaly.
c. fetal lungs are mature.
d. the fetus is small for gestational age.

Answer: c

Rationale: A 2:1 L/S ratio indicates that the risk of respiratory distress syndrome (RDS) is very low and that the fetus' lungs are mature. Early in pregnancy, the sphingomyelin concentration in amniotic fluid is greater than the concentration of lecithin, and so the L/S ratio is low if the fetus' lungs are immature, which is not the case in this instance. The L/S ratio isn't a measurement for congenital anomalies or size of the fetus.

Assessment
Physiological Integrity
Application

16.10 Which client has indications that most warrant fetal monitoring in the third trimester?

a. gravida 4, para 3, 39 weeks, with a history of one spontaneous abortion at 8 weeks.
b. gravida 1, para 0, 40 weeks, with a history of endometriosis and a prior appendectomy.
c. gravida 3, para 2, with a history of gestational diabetes controlled by diet.
d. gravida 2, para 1, 36 weeks, with hypertension disorder of pregnancy.

Answer: d
Rationale: The preterm client with a pregnancy-associated disorder needs close monitoring for preterm labor onset or the need to induce preterm labor. The client with the spontaneous abortion would have needed to be monitored in the first trimester. The client with endometriosis and appendectomy would have been a concern with conception. The client with a history of gestational diabetes controlled by diet would need maternal monitoring and fetal monitoring if she developed gestational diabetes again.
Planning
Health Promotion and Maintenance
Analysis

16.11 A type I diabetic who is at 32 weeks' gestation is having a nonstress test for fetal well-being since she has been having problems with glucose control. Which meets the criteria for her test to be considered reactive?

a. fetal heart rate baseline of 150 with two accelerations to 160 for 10 seconds within 20 minutes.
b. fetal heart rate baseline of 140 with one acceleration to 160 for 15 seconds within 30 minutes.
c. fetal heart rate baseline of 140 with two accelerations to 155 for 15 seconds within 20 minutes.
d. fetal heart rate baseline of 130 with two accelerations to 140 for 15 seconds within 20 minutes.

Answer: c
Rationale: Nonstress tests are scored as either reactive or nonreactive. A reactive stress test has the results expected of two episodes of fetal movement, resulting in an increase in heart rate of 15 beats per minutes for 15 seconds or more within 20 minutes. In a nonreactive stress test, the reactivity criteria are not met. Answer a is an increase of only 10 beats per minutes. A fetal heart rate baseline of 140 with one acceleration to 160 for 15 seconds within 30 minutes is an increase of 20 beats per minutes for 15 seconds, but the time is 30 minutes. A fetal heart rate baseline of 130 with two accelerations to 140 for 15 seconds within 20 minutes is an increase of 20 beats per minutes. A fetal heart rate baseline of 140 with two accelerations to 155 for 15 seconds within 20 minutes is perfect: 15 beats per minutes for 15 seconds in 20 minutes.
Assessment
Physiological Integrity
Analysis

16.12 The client is having a nonstress test the next day. Which instructions should the nurse give to the client?

a. "Be sure to come in with a full bladder."
b. "Remember not to eat anything before the test."
c. "You will feel some contractions during the test."
d. "The test should last no longer than 30 minutes."

Answer: d
Rationale: The nonstress test requires that the client lie on her side for a minimum of 20 minutes. This client would find a full bladder distressing. Eating prior to coming for the test might help in that the infant will be stimulated from the glucose. Contractions during the test would be a contraction stress test.
Implementation
Physiological Integrity
Application

16.13 A client at 37 weeks' gestation has a mildly elevated blood pressure. Her antenatal testing demonstrates a fetal heart rate baseline of 150 with three contractions in 10 minutes, no decelerations, and accelerations four times in one hour. This test would be considered a:

a. positive nonstress test.
b. negative contraction stress test.
c. positive contraction stress test.
d. negative nonstress test.

Answer: b
Rationale: The fact that the contractions are present rules out the nonstress test. The desired result is a negative contraction stress test; this means that there are three contractions in 10 minutes, without decelerations. A positive contraction stress test is undesirable because the fetus is experiencing decelerations with over half the contractions.
Assessment
Physiological Integrity
Analysis

16.14 Out of all the clients who have been scheduled to have a biophysical profile, the nurse would clarify the order for which client?
a. a gravida with intrauterine growth restriction.
b. a gravida with mild hypertension of pregnancy.
c. a gravida who is post-term.
d. a gravida who complains of decreased fetal movement for two days.

Answer: b
Rationale: The biophysical profile is used when there is a risk of placental and/or fetal compromise. The gravida with mild hypertension will need to be monitored more closely throughout the pregnancy but is not a candidate at present for a biophysical profile. The infant who has intrauterine growth problems and who is post-term might be compromised due to placental insufficiency. The gravida who is experiencing decreased fetal movement for two days needs assessment of the placenta and the fetus.
Implementation
Physiological Integrity
Application

16.15 The nurse is preparing the client for an amniocentesis. The ultrasound shows the fetus to be positioned as in the picture. At what site would the nurse prep the client for the amniocentesis?

Answer: c
Rationale: The amniocentesis would be performed where the largest pocket of fluid could be found. The bladder should be empty to avoid perforating it with the needle. The insertion site would be away from the placenta and the fetus.
Implementation
Physiological Integrity
Application

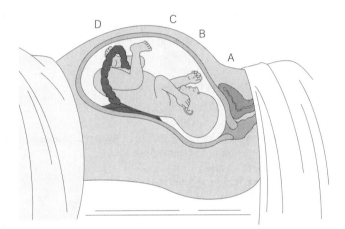

CHAPTER 17

17.1 A client is admitted to the labor and delivery unit with contractions that are regular, 2 minutes apart, and lasting 60 seconds. She reports that she had bloody show earlier that morning. A vaginal exam reveals that her cervix is 100 percent effaced and 8 cm dilated. The nurse interprets this to indicate the client is in which phase of labor?
a. active.
b. latent.
c. transition.
d. fourth.

Answer: c
Rationale: The transition phase begins with 8 cm of dilatation, and is characterized by contractions that are closer and more intense. Active and latent are not correct because dilatation is less than 8 cm, and contractions are less frequent and are of shorter duration. Fourth is not right because the fourth phase does not exist. The fourth stage occurs after delivery of the placenta.
Assessment
Health Promotion and Maintenance
Application

17.2 The midwife performs a vaginal exam and determines that the fetal head is at a −2 station. As the nurse, you know that birth:
a. is imminent.
b. is likely to occur in 1 to 2 hours.
c. will occur later in the shift.
d. is difficult to predict.

Answer: d
Rationale: A −2 station means that the fetus is 2 cm above the ischial spines. With the infant's head being that high in the pelvis, it is difficult to predict when birth will occur. For birth to be imminent, the head more likely would be at a +2 station.
Assessment
Health Promotion and Maintenance
Application

17.3 A clinic nurse is preparing diagrams of pelvic shapes. Which pelvic shapes are considered least adequate for childbirth? (Select all that apply.) a. android. b. anthropoid. c. gynecoid. d. platypelloid.	Answers: a, b, d Rationale: The gynecoid pelvis is the most common female pelvis, and all of its diameters are adequate for childbirth. The other pelvis types are not consistent with adequacy for childbirth. Assessment Health Promotion and Maintenance Application
17.4 When comparing the similarities between the anterior and posterior fontanelles of a newborn, it can be said that both: a. are approximately the same size. b. close within 12 months of birth. c. are used in labor to identify station. d. allow for molding of the head.	Answer: d Rationale: The anterior fontanelle measures approximately 2×3 cm, and closes around the eighteenth month. The posterior fontanelle is much smaller, and closes between 8 and 12 weeks after birth. In labor, the presenting part is used to identify station, not the fontanelles. Assessment Health Promotion and Maintenance Analysis
17.5 A nurse is aware that labor and birth will most likely proceed normally when the fetal position is: a. occiput posterior. b. mentum anterior. c. occiput anterior. d. mentum posterior.	Answer: c Rationale: The most common fetal position is occiput anterior. When this position occurs, labor and birth are likely to proceed normally. Positions other than occiput anterior are more frequently associated with problems during labor; therefore, they are called malpositions. Assessment Health and Maintenance Analysis
17.6 In order to identify the duration of a contraction, the nurse would: a. start timing from the beginning of one contraction to the completion of the same contraction. b. time between the beginning of one contraction to the beginning of the next contraction. c. palpate for the strength of the contraction at its peak. d. time from the beginning of the contraction to the peak of the same contraction.	Answer: a Rationale: Duration is measured from the beginning of a contraction to the completion of the same contraction. Implementation Health Promotion and Maintenance Application
17.7 The labor nurse would not encourage a mother to bear down until after the cervix is completely dilated in order to prevent which of the following? (Select all that apply.) a. maternal exhaustion. b. cervical edema. c. tearing and bruising of the cervix. d. enhanced perineal thinning.	Answers: a, b, c Rationale: If the cervix is not completely dilated, cervical edema, tearing and bruising of the cervix, and maternal exhaustion can occur. Implementation Health Promotion and Maintenance Application
17.8 A primigravida client calls the labor and delivery floor and tells the nurse that she is 39 weeks pregnant, and that over the last 4 or 5 days she has noticed that although her breathing has become easier, she is having leg cramps, a slight amount of edema in her lower legs, and an increased amount of vaginal secretions. The nurse tells the	Answer: b Rationale: Lightening describes the effect occurring when the fetus begins to settle into the pelvic inlet. Quickening is the first movement the mother feels. Dilation describes the increase in size of the cervical os. Braxton Hicks contractions occur before the onset of labor. Assessment Health Promotion and Maintenance Application

client that she has experienced what is commonly called: a. quickening. b. lightening. c. dilation. d. Braxton Hicks contractions.	
17.9 A client who is having false labor most likely would have which of the following? (Select all that apply.) a. contractions that do not intensify while walking. b. an increase in the intensity and frequency of contractions. c. progressive cervical effacement and dilatation. d. pain in the abdomen that does not radiate.	Answers: a, d Rationale: True labor results in progressive dilation, increased intensity and frequency of contractions, and pain in the back that radiates to the abdomen. True labor contractions intensify while walking. Assessment Health Promotion and Maintenance Application
17.10 While caring for a labor client, you notice during a vaginal exam that the baby's head has internally rotated. What would you expect the next set of cardinal movements for a baby in a vertex presentation to be? a. flexion, extension, restitution, external rotation, expulsion. b. expulsion, external rotation, restitution. c. restitution, flexion, external rotation, expulsion. d. extension, restitution, external rotation, expulsion.	Answer: d Rationale: The fetus changes position in the following order: descent, engagement, flexion, internal rotation, extension, restitution, external rotation, expulsion. Assessment Health Promotion and Maintenance Application
17.11 A client is admitted to the labor unit with contractions 1.5 to 2 minutes apart lasting 60 to 90 seconds. The client is apprehensive and irritable. This client is most likely in what phase of labor? a. active. b. transition. c. latent. d. second.	Answer: b Rationale: During the transition phase of labor contractions have a frequency of about every 1.5 to 2 minutes with a duration of 60 to 90 seconds. The woman may become apprehensive and irritable during this stage. The latent phase is characterized by mild contractions progressing from a frequency of 10 to 20 minutes to 5 to 7 minutes. In the latent stage, the woman is excited labor has begun. The active phase is characterized by contractions every 2 to 3 minutes; there is a sense of fear of loss of control during this phase, but it's not as pronounced as in the transition stage. The second stage is the pushing stage, and the woman may feel relieved that the birth is near and she can push. The second stage is not a phase of labor. Assessment Health Promotion and Maintenance Analysis
17.12 During the fourth stage of labor, your client's assessment includes a BP of 110/60, pulse 90, and the fundus is firm midline and halfway between the symphysis pubis and the umbilicus. You would: a. turn her onto her left side. b. place the bed in Trendelenburg position. c. massage the fundus. d. continue to monitor.	Answer: d Rationale: During the fourth stage of labor, the mother experiences a slight drop in blood pressure and a slightly increased pulse. Trendelenburg or a left lateral position is not necessary with a BP of 110/60 and a pulse of 90. The uterus should be midline and firm; massage is not necessary. Because this is a normal scenario for the fourth stage, monitoring is the only action necessary. Evaluation Health Promotion and Maintenance Application

17.13 How would the nurse best analyze the results from a client's sonogram that show the fetal shoulder as the presenting part? a. breech, transverse. b. breech, longitudinal. c. military, longitudinal. d. vertex, transverse.	Answer: a Rationale: A shoulder presentation is one type of breech presentation and is also called a transverse lie. Assessment Health Promotion and Maintenance Analysis
17.14 A primigravida client arrives in the labor and delivery unit and describes her contractions as occurring every 10 to 12 minutes, lasting 30 seconds. She is smiling and very excited about the possibility of being in labor. On exam, her cervix is dilated 2 cm, 100% effaced, and is a −2 station. Which of the following best describes this labor? a. second phase. b. latent phase. c. active phase. d. transition phase.	Answer: b Rationale: The latent phase of labor starts with the beginning of regular mild contractions. The mother is talkative and excited and has minimal cervical changes. During the active phase, the woman's cervix dilates from 3 to 4 cm to 8 cm, and the mother has an increasing level of anxiety. During transition, the cervix dilates from 8 to 10 cm, and the mother becomes restless. There is no phase of labor that is identified as the second phase. Assessment Health Promotion and Maintenance Analysis
17.15 A laboring client is beginning to hyperventilate. The nurse recognizes this could result in: a. respiratory alkalosis. b. metabolic alkalosis. c. respiratory acidosis. d. metabolic acidosis.	Answer: a Rationale: With hyperventilation there is a fall in $PaCO_2$ and respiratory alkalosis results. Metabolic alkalosis would not occur with hyperventilation. Respiratory acidosis may occur as a woman's $PaCO_2$ levels rise during the second stage of labor. By the end of the first stage, a mild metabolic acidosis may have developed, not because of hyperventilation, but because of compensation to the respiratory alkalosis. Diagnosis Physiological Integrity Analysis

CHAPTER 18

18.1 After several hours of labor, the electronic fetal monitor (EFM) shows repetitive variable decelerations in the fetal heart rate. You would interpret the decelerations to be consistent with: a. breech presentation. b. uteroplacental insufficiency. c. comprehension of the fetal head. d. umbilical cord comprehension.	Answer: d Rationale: Variable decelerations occur when there is umbilical cord compression. Early decelerations occur with fetal head compression, and uteroplacental insufficiency causes late decelerations. Breech presentations by themselves do not cause decelerations. Assessment Health Promotion and Maintenance Application
18.2 The nurse has just palpated a laboring woman's contractions and compares the consistency with that of the forehead. The intensity of these contractions would be identified as: a. mild. b. moderate. c. strong. d. weak.	Answer: c Rationale: Mild contractions are similar to the consistency of the nose, moderate are similar to the chin, and strong are similar to the forehead. Weak contractions are not identified. Assessment Health Promotion and Maintenance Application
18.3 During maternal assessment the nurse determines the fetus to be in a left occiput anterior (LOA) position. Auscultation of the fetal heart rate should begin in the: a. right upper quadrant. b. left upper quadrant.	Answer: d Rationale: The fetal heart rate is best heard at the fetal back. In a cephalic presentation, the heart rate is heard in the lower quadrants. Because this fetus has been identified as being on the mother's left side, the heart tones should be on the mother's left lower quadrant. Assessment Health Promotion and Maintenance

c. right lower quadrant. d. left lower quadrant.	Application
18.4 A laboring maternal client asks the nurse, "Why does the physician want to use an intrauterine pressure catheter (IUPC) during my labor?" The nurse would be accurate in explaining that the best rationale for using an IUPC is: a. the IUPC can be used throughout the birth process. b. a tocodynamometer is subject to artifacts. c. the IUPC provides more accurate data than the tocodynamometer. d. the tocodynamometer can only be used after the cervix is dilated 2 cm.	Answer: c Rationale: The IUPC, inserted only after membranes have ruptured, provides accurate measurement of uterine contraction intensity. Internal electronic monitoring is used when it is imperative to have accurate intrauterine pressure readings to evaluate the stress on the uterus. A tocodynamometer is used for external monitoring. External monitoring provides a continuous recording of the frequency and duration of uterine contractions and is noninvasive. However, it does not accurately record the intensity of the uterine contraction. The tocodynamometer can be used at any time; it is not related to cervix dilatation and if used correctly is not subject to artifact. Planning Health Promotion and Maintenance Application
18.5 Before performing Leopold's maneuvers, the nurse would: (Select all that apply.) a. have the client empty her bladder. b. place the client in Trendelenburg position. c. have the client lie on her back with her feet on the bed and knees bent. d. turn the client to her left side.	Answers: a, c Rationale: Before performing Leopold's maneuvers the nurse instructs the client to empty her bladder. This prevents pressure on the bladder and the fetal structures are more easily palpated when the bladder is empty. The second step is to have the client lie on her back with her feet on the bed and knees bent. Placing the client in Trendelenburg or on her left side is not consistent with accurately performing Leopold's maneuver. Implementation Health Promotion and Maintenance Application
18.6 A nurse is analyzing several fetal heart rate patterns. The pattern that would be of most concern to the nurse would be: a. moderate long-term variability. b. early decelerations. c. late decelerations. d. accelerations.	Answer: c Rationale: Late decelerations are caused by uteroplacental insufficiency. The late deceleration pattern is considered a nonreassuring sign. Moderate long-term variability is a reassuring sign that the fetus is not suffering from cerebral asphyxia. Early decelerations occur before the onset of the uterine contraction. Early deceleration is usually considered to be benign. Accelerations are thought to be a sign of fetal well-being. Assessment Health Promotion and Maintenance Analysis
18.7 The nurse auscultates the FHR and determines a rate of 112 bpm. Which of the following actions is appropriate? a. Inform the maternal client that the rate is normal. b. Reassess the FHR in five minutes because the rate is low. c. Report the FHR to the doctor immediately. d. Turn the maternal client on her side and administer oxygen.	Answer: a Rationale: A fetal heart rate of 112 bpm falls within the normal range of 110 to 160 bpm so there is no need to inform the doctor, reposition the client, or reassess later. Implementation Health Promotion and Maintenance Application
18.8 The fetal heart rate pattern associated with abruptio placentae, uterine hyperstimulation, umbilical cord compression, and maternal hypotension is known as fetal: a. sinusoidal pattern. b. variable deceleration. c. tachycardia. d. bradycardia.	Answer: d Rationale: Causes of fetal bradycardia include: fetal hypoxia, maternal hypotension, prolonged umbilical cord compression, fetal arrhythmia, uterine hyperstimulation, abruptio placentae, uterine rupture, and vagal stimulation. A fetal sinusoidal pattern is associated with Rh isoimmunization, fetal anemia, and fetal hypoxia. Variables result from maternal drugs, hypoxia, and fetal sleep. Tachycardia is associated with hypoxia, maternal fever, or maternal hyperthyroidism. Diagnosis Health Promotion and Maintenance Application

18.9 The nurse is analyzing a maternal client's fetal heart rate (FHR) monitor strip. The nurse notes that some early decelerations are present. The nurse explains to the client that early decelerations are most often related to:
a. umbilical cord compression.
b. fetal head compression.
c. uteroplacental insufficiency.
d. fetal hypoxia.

Answer: b
Rationale: Uteroplacental insufficiency results in late decelerations. Cord compression results in variable decelerations. Hypoxia results in decreased variability.
Implementation
Health Promotion and Maintenance
Analysis

18.10 Upon assessing the FHR tracing, the nurse determines that there is increased variability. The increased variability would be caused by which of the following? (Select all that apply.)
a. early mild hypoxia.
b. fetal stimulation.
c. alterations in placental blood flow.
d. fetal sleep cycle.

Answers: a, b, c
Rationale: Fetal sleep cycle is the only one of the four selections that does not cause increased variability.
Assessment
Health Promotion and Maintenance
Application

18.11 Which of the following fetal pH values during labor are considered nonreassuring? (Select all that apply.)
a. 7.15 and below.
b. 7.15 to 7.20.
c. 7.20 to 7.25.
d. 7.25 and above.

Answers: a, b
Rationale: Values below 7.20 are nonreassuring. Values of 7.20 to 7.25 are borderline. Values above 7.25 are considered normal.
Assessment
Physiological Integrity
Analysis

18.12 A fetus that is not in any stress would respond to a fetal scalp stimulation test by showing which of the following changes on the monitor strip?
a. late decelerations.
b. early decelerations.
c. accelerations.
d. increased long-term variability.

Answer: c
Rationale: A fetus that is not experiencing stress responds to scalp stimulation with an acceleration of the FHR. Late decelerations indicate uteroplacental insufficiency, early decelerations are indicative of head compression, and increased long-term variability is a parameter assessed when there is the presence of a questionable FHR pattern because long-term variability, when normal, can indicate that the fetus is not suffering from cerebral asphyxia.
Assessment
Health Promotion and Maintenance
Application

18.13 After noting meconium-stained amniotic fluid, fetal heart rate decelerations, and a fetal blood pH of 7.20, the physician diagnoses a severely depressed fetus. The appropriate nursing action at this time would be to:
a. increase the mother's oxygen rate.
b. turn the mother to the left lateral position.
c. prepare the mother for a forceps or cesarean birth.
d. increase the intravenous infusion rate.

Answer: c
Rationale: Meconium-stained fluid, heart rate decelerations, and a pH of 7.20 are all indications that delivery must be done without delay. Position change to the left side, use of oxygen, and increasing the IV rate are not nursing actions that would change the status of the severely depressed fetus.
Implementation
Physiological Integrity
Application

18.14 A nurse is analyzing fetal cord blood results. If the fetal blood pH is less than 7.25 the nurse can conclude that the fetus was:
a. acidotic and hypoxic.
b. alkalotic and hypoxic.
c. well oxygenated.
d. alkalotic but well oxygenated.

Answer: a
Rationale: Normal fetal blood pH should be above 7.25. Lower levels indicate acidosis and hypoxia.
Assessment
Physiological Integrity
Analysis

18.15 Persistent early decelerations on the fetal monitoring strip are noted. The nurse's first action would be to:
a. turn the mom on her left side and give oxygen.
b. check for prolapsed cord.
c. do nothing. This is a benign pattern.
d. prepare for immediate forceps or cesarean delivery.

Answer: c
Rationale: Early decelerations are considered benign, and do not require any intervention. Whereas, variable or late decelerations would require intervention.
Implementation
Health Promotion and Maintenance
Application

CHAPTER 19

19.1 The client presents to labor and delivery stating that her water broke 2 hours ago. Barring any abnormalities, how often would the nurse expect to take the client's temperature?
a. every hour.
b. every 2 hours.
c. every 4 hours.
d. every shift.

Answer: b
Rationale: Maternal temperature is taken every 4 hours unless it is above 37.5°C. If elevated, it is taken every hour.
Assessment
Physiological Integrity
Application

19.2 The laboring client presses the call light and reports that her water has just broke. The nurse's first action would be to:
a. check fetal heart tones.
b. encourage the mother to go for a walk.
c. change bed linen.
d. call the physician.

Answer: a
Rationale: Fetal heart tones should be checked after rupture of the membranes to assess for cord compression. The bed linen can be changed after assessing the heart rate. The physician does not need to be called after rupture of the membranes unless there is a change in status of the fetus or client. If the presenting part is not engaged, the laboring client should not be allowed to walk because there is a risk of cord prolapse once the membranes have ruptured.
Implementation
Health Promotion and Maintenance
Application

19.3 Of the most frequent responses to pain, which of the following is most likely to impede your client's progress in labor?
a. increased pulse.
b. elevated blood pressure.
c. muscle tension.
d. increased respirations.

Answer: c
Rationale: Increased pulse, respiration, and blood pressure all are manifestations of pain but do not impede labor.
Assessment
Health Promotion and Maintenance
Application

19.4 Why is it important for the nurse to assess the bladder regularly and encourage the laboring client to void every two hours?
a. A full bladder impedes oxygen flow to the fetus.
b. Frequent voiding prevents bruising of the bladder.
c. Frequent voiding encourages sphincter control.
d. A full bladder can impede fetal descent.

Answer: d
Rationale: A full bladder can impede the descent of the fetus. Frequent voiding or catheterization allows for quicker descent. Frequent voiding has nothing to do with sphincter control or bruising of the bladder. Oxygen flow to the fetus is not impacted by a full bladder.
Implementation
Health Promotion: Prevention and Early Detection
Application

19.5 The laboring client is complaining of tingling and numbness in her fingers and toes, dizziness, and spots before her eyes. The nurse recognizes that these are clinical manifestations of:
a. hyperventilation.
b. seizure auras.
c. imminent birth.
d. anxiety.

Answer: a
Rationale: These symptoms all are consistent with hyperventilation. Anxiety, imminent birth, and seizure auras do not have these types of symptoms.
Assessment
Physiological Integrity
Analysis

19.6 Upon delivery of the newborn, the nursing intervention that most promotes parental attachment is: a. placing the newborn under the radiant warmer. b. placing the newborn on the maternal abdomen. c. allowing the mother a chance to rest immediately after delivery. d. taking the newborn to the nursery for the initial assessment.	Answer: b Rationale: Placing the baby on the maternal abdomen promotes attachment and bonding, and gives the mother a chance to interact with her baby immediately. Removing the baby from the mother does not promote interaction. Implementation Health Promotion: Growth and Development Application
19.7 At one minute after birth, the infant has a heart rate of 100 bpm and is crying vigorously. His limbs are flexed, his trunk is pink, and his feet and hands are cyanotic. The infant cries easily when the soles of his feet are stimulated. The appropriate Apgar score would be _____.	Answer: 9 Rationale: Two points each are scored in the categories of heart rate, respiratory effort, muscle tone, and reflex irritability. One point is scored in the category of skin color. The total Apgar would be 9. Assessment Health Promotion and Maintenance Application
19.8 Before applying a cord clamp, the nurse assesses the umbilical cord for the presence of vessels. The expected finding is: a. one artery, one vein. b. two arteries, one vein. c. two veins, one artery. d. two veins, two arteries.	Answer: b Rationale: Two arteries and one vein are present in a normal umbilical cord. Assessment Health Promotion and Maintenance Analysis
19.9 As compared with admission considerations for an adult woman in labor, the nurse's priority for an adolescent in labor would be to assess: a. cultural background. b. plans for keeping the infant. c. support persons. d. developmental level.	Answer: d Rationale: Cultural background and support person(s) are important to planning anyone's care. Before considering these areas, it is important to identify the adolescent's level of development so that a plan of care is consistent with the adolescent's abilities. Knowing the adolescent's level of development is also important when planning nursing care for the adolescent who is keeping her infant. Assessment Psychosocial Integrity Analysis
19.10 Breathing techniques used in labor provide which of the following? (Select all that apply.) a. a form of anesthesia. b. a source of relaxation. c. an increased ability to cope with contractions. d. a source of distraction.	Answers: b, c, d Rationale: When used correctly, breathing techniques can increase the woman's pain threshold, permit relaxation, enhance the ability to cope with contractions, provide a sense of control, and allow the uterus to function more effectively. Breathing techniques do not provide a form of anesthesia. Evaluation Health Promotion and Maintenance Application
19.11 Oxytocin 20 units was given to your client at the time of the delivery of the placenta. This was done primarily to: a. contract the uterus and minimize bleeding. b. decrease breast milk production. c. decrease maternal blood pressure. d. increase maternal blood pressure.	Answer: a Rationale: Oxytocin is given to contract the uterus and minimize bleeding. Oxytocin does not have an effect on maternal blood pressure or breast milk production. Implementation Physiological Integrity Application

19.12 Two hours after delivery a client's fundus is boggy and has risen to above the umbilicus. The first action the nurse would take is to: a. massage the fundus until firm. b. express retained clots. c. increase the intravenous solution. d. call the physician.	Answer: a Rationale: Massage of the uterus has to occur before the expression of retained clots. The physician does not need to be notified until either the uterus does not respond to massage or the bleeding does not decrease. Implementation Health Promotion and Maintenance Application
19.13 An expectant father has been at the bedside of his laboring partner for more than 12 hours. An appropriate nursing intervention would be to: a. insist he leave the room for at least the next hour. b. tell him he is not being as effective as he was and needs to let someone else take over. c. offer to remain with his partner while he takes a break. d. suggest that the client's mother may be of more help.	Answer: c Rationale: Support persons frequently are reluctant to leave the laboring woman to take care of their own needs. Offering to stay with the woman so that he can take a break reassures the support person that the woman will be well cared for in his absence. Insisting that the father leave, telling him that he is ineffective, or suggesting the client's mother take his place does not reassure him about the care the woman will receive in his absence. Implementation Health Promotion and Maintenance Application
19.14 A client's labor has progressed so rapidly that a precipitous birth is occurring. The nurse should: a. go to the nurse's station and immediately call the physician. b. run to the delivery room for an emergency birth pack. c. stay with the client and ask for auxiliary personnel for assistance. d. try to delay the delivery of the infant's head until the physician arrives.	Answer: c Rationale: If birth is imminent, the nurse must not leave the client alone. The nurse can direct auxiliary personnel to contact the physician and retrieve the emergency birth pack. The nurse should not hold the infant's head back from delivering, but should apply gently pressure against the head to prevent it from popping out rapidly. Implementation Health Promotion and Maintenance Application
19.15 A client delivered 30 minutes ago. Which postpartal finding should the nurse continue to monitor closely? a. a soaked perineal pad since the last 15-minute check. b. an edematous perineum. c. a client with tremors. d. a fundus located at the umbilicus.	Answer: a Rationale: A soaked perineal pad contains approximately 100 ml of blood. If the perineal pad becomes soaked in a 15-minute period, continuous observation is necessary. An edematous perineum, a client with tremors, and a fundus located at the umbilicus are normal postpartal findings. Evaluation Health Promotion and Maintenance Analysis

CHAPTER 20

20.1 A client has just been admitted for labor and delivery. She is having mild contractions every 15 minutes lasting 30 seconds. The client wants to have a medication-free birth. When discussing medication alternatives, the nurse should be sure the client understands that: a. in order to respect her wishes, no medication will be given. b. pain relief will allow a more enjoyable birth experience. c. the use of medications allow the client to rest and be less fatigued. d. maternal pain and stress can have a more adverse effect on the fetus than a small amount of analgesia.	Answer: d Rationale: While pain relief can lead to a more enjoyable experience and allow the mother to be less fatigued, it might be the view of the nurse and not the mother. It is important to respect the client's wishes when possible. The decision not to medicate should be an informed one, and it is possible that the client does not know about the effects pain and stress can have on the fetus. Once the effects are explained, it is still the client's choice whether to receive medication. Planning Physiological Integrity Application

20.2 After receiving nalbuphine hydrochloride (Nubain), a woman's labor progresses rapidly and the baby is born less than one hour later. The baby shows signs of respiratory depression. Which medication should the nurse be prepared to give to the newborn? a. fentanyl (Sublimaze). b. butorphanol tartrate (Stadol). c. naloxone (Narcan). d. pentobarbital (Nembutal).	Answer: c Rationale: Narcan is the only choice that is an opiate antagonist, which would reverse the effects of the Nubain. Implementation Physiological Integrity Application
20.3 After administration of an epidural anesthetic to a client in active labor, it is most important to assess the client immediately for: a. hypotension. b. headache. c. urinary retention. d. bradycardia.	Answer: a Rationale: The most common complication of an epidural is maternal hypotension. A headache, urinary retention, and bradycardia could be seen with spinal anesthesia. Assessment Physiological Integrity Application
20.4 A laboring client has received an order for epidural anesthesia. In order to prevent the most common complication associated with this procedure, the nurse would expect to do which of the following? a. observe fetal heart rate variability. b. rapidly infuse 500 to 1000 ml of intravenous fluids. c. place the client in a right lateral position. d. teach the client appropriate breathing techniques.	Answer: b Rationale: Administering a fluid bolus prior to an epidural generally prevents maternal hypotension, which is the most common disadvantage to the procedure. Planning Physiological Integrity Application
20.5 Which of the following are common side effects of epidural anesthesia? (Select all that apply.) a. elevated maternal temperature. b. urinary retention. c. nausea. d. long-term back pain.	Answers: a, b, c Rationale: Elevated temperature, urinary retention, and nausea all are potential side effects. Long-term back pain should not be the result of an epidural. Assessment Physiological Integrity Application
20.6 Prior to receiving lumbar epidural anesthesia, the nurse would anticipate placing the laboring client in which of the following positions? a. on her right side in the center of the bed, with her back curved. b. lying prone, with a pillow under her chest. c. on her left side, with the bottom leg straight and the top leg slightly flexed. d. sitting on the edge of the bed, with her back slightly curved and her feet on a stool.	Answer: d Rationale: Sitting on the edge of the bed with the back slightly curved and the feet on a stool allows the epidural spaces to be accessed easier. None of the other positions is consistent with access to the epidural spaces. Planning Physiological Integrity Application

20.7 A client is having contractions that are lasting 20 to 30 seconds and occurring every 8 to 20 minutes. The client is requesting something to help relieve the discomfort of contractions. The nurse should suggest:
a. a mild analgesic be administered.
b. an epidural.
c. a local anesthetic block.
d. nonpharmacological methods for pain relief.

Answer: d
Rationale: The client does not have an established labor pattern and analgesics or epidurals given for pain relief may prolong labor or stop the process. A local anesthetic block is given during the delivery of the baby to numb the perineal area. For this pattern of labor nonpharmacological methods for pain relief should be suggested. These can include: back rubs, showers, whirlpools, and the application of cool cloths.
Planning
Physiological Integrity
Application

20.8 Narcotic analgesia is administered to a laboring mother at 10:00 A.M. The infant is delivered at 12:30. The nurse would expect the narcotic analgesia to do which of the following?
a. be used in place of preoperative sedation.
b. result in neonatal respiratory depression.
c. prevent the need for anesthesia with an episiotomy.
d. enhance uterine contractions.

Answer: b
Rationale: Analgesics do not enhance uterine contractions and do not take the place of preoperative sedation. Local anesthetic is needed for an episiotomy. Because analgesics can last for more than three hours, the newborn is at risk for respiratory depression.
Evaluation
Physiological Integrity
Analysis

20.9 Two hours after an epidural infusion has begun, a client complains of itching on the face and neck. The nurse should:
a. remove the epidural catheter and place a Band-Aid at the injection site.
b. offer the client a cool cloth and let her know the itching is temporary.
c. recognize this is a common side effect and follow protocol for administration of diphenhydramine (Benadryl).
d. call the anesthesia care provider to re-dose the epidural catheter.

Answer: c
Rationale: Itching is a side effect of the medication used for an epidural infusion. Using a cool cloth or removing the epidural catheter does not address the side effects of the medication. The anesthesia care provider would not re-dose, as that would continue or worsen the effects of the medication. Benadryl is given to counteract the effects of the medication.
Implementation
Physiological Integrity
Application

20.10 A nurse is checking the doctor's orders for a postpartum client. The doctor has written for the client to be on bedrest for 6 to 12 hours. The nurse knows this is an appropriate order if the client had which type of anesthesia?
a. spinal.
b. pudendal.
c. general.
d. epidural.

Answer: a
Rationale: Keeping the postpartum client in bed for 6 to 12 hours after receiving a spinal is thought to decrease the risk of headache and allow sensation to return to extremities before ambulating.
Evaluation
Physiological Integrity
Analysis

20.11 Toward the end of the first stage of labor, a pudendal block is administered transvaginally. The nurse anticipates the client's care to include:
a. monitoring for hypotension every 15 minutes.
b. monitoring FHR every 15 minutes.
c. monitoring for bladder distention.
d. no additional assessments.

Answer: d
Rationale: Because a pudendal block is done using a local anesthetic, there is no need for any additional monitoring of the mom or fetus.
Planning
Physiological Integrity
Application

20.12 An analgesic medication has been administered intramuscularly to a client in labor. The nurse would evaluate the medication as effective if:
a. the client dozes between contractions.
b. the client is moaning with contractions.
c. the contractions decrease in intensity.
d. the contractions decrease in frequency.

Answer: a
Rationale: Increasing pain interferes with the mother's ability to cope. Analgesics decrease discomfort and increase relaxation. While the intensity and frequency of the contractions may be affected, the intent is to help the mother cope.
Evaluation
Physiological Integrity
Analysis

20.13 A primigravida dilated to 5 cm has just received an epidural for pain. She complains of feeling lightheaded and dizzy within 10 minutes after the procedure. Her blood pressure before the procedure was 120/80 and is now 80/52. In addition to the bolus of fluids she has been given, which medication is preferred to use to increase her BP?
a. epinephrine.
b. terbutaline.
c. ephedrine.
d. epifoam.

Answer: c
Rationale: Ephedrine is the medication of choice to increase maternal blood pressure. Epinephrine is used to relieve bronchospasm or during anaphylactic reactions. Terbutabline is used as a tocolytic and epifoam is a topical anesthetic.
Implementation
Physiological Integrity
Analysis

20.14 A cesarean section is ordered for your client. Because she is to receive general anesthesia, the primary danger the nurse is concerned with is:
a. fetal depression.
b. vomiting.
c. maternal depression.
d. uterine relaxation.

Answer: a
Rationale: A primary danger of general anesthesia is fetal depression. The depression in the fetus is directly proportional to the depth and duration of the anesthesia.
Diagnosis
Physiological Integrity
Application

20.15 A client received an epidural anesthesia during the first stage of her labor. The epidural is discontinued immediately after delivery. This client is at increased risk for which of the following during the fourth stage of labor?
a. nausea.
b. bladder distention.
c. uterine atony.
d. hypertension.

Answer: b
Rationale: The epidural is discontinued after delivery, decreasing the likelihood of nausea. Bladder distention may be a result of decreased bladder sensation in the fourth stage. Hypotension, not hypertension, is an early side effect of epidurals. Uterine atony is not the result of an epidural.
Assessment
Physiological Integrity
Application

CHAPTER 21

21.1 A woman has been having contractions since 4 A.M. At 8 A.M., her cervix is dilated to 5 cm. Contractions are frequent and mild to moderate in intensity. Cephalopelvic disproportion (CPD) has been ruled out. After giving the mother some sedation so she can rest, the nurse would anticipate preparing for:
a. oxytocin induction of labor.
b. amnioinfusion.
c. increased intravenous infusion.
d. cesarean section.

Answer: a
Rationale: Hypertonic labor patterns result in frequent ineffectual contractions that exhaust the mother. Sedation is used to let the mother rest and stop the ineffective contractions. If sedation does not stop the ineffective contractions, oxytocin may be used to establish more effective contractions. Increasing the IV infusion and amnioinfusion are not methods that would change the ineffective labor pattern. Since CPD has been ruled out, a cesarean section is not anticipated.
Planning
Physiological Integrity
Application

21.2 Which of the following places a mother at risk for developing disseminating intravascular coagulation (DIC)? a. diabetes mellitus. b. abruptio placentae. c. cesarean delivery. d. multiparity.	Answer: b Rationale: Damage to the uterine wall results from an abruptio placentae. This damage results in release of thromboplastin into the maternal blood supply, and triggers the development of DIC. Diabetes, cesarean delivery, and multiparity do not cause the same release of thromboplastin that triggers DIC. Assessment Physiological Integrity Application
21.3 A client, in her thirty-second week of pregnancy, is admitted with painless vaginal bleeding. Placenta previa has been confirmed by ultrasound. What should be included in the nursing plan of care for this client? (Select all that apply.) a. no vaginal exams. b. encourage activity. c. no intravenous access until labor begins. d. evaluate fetal heart rate with an external monitor. e. monitor blood loss, pain, and uterine contractility.	Answers: a, d, e Rationale: Expectant management of placenta previa, when the pregnancy is less than 37 weeks' gestation, includes: no vaginal exams, bedrest with bathroom privileges as long as there is no bleeding, monitoring blood loss, pain and uterine contractility, evaluating FHR with an external monitor, monitoring maternal vital signs, laboratory evaluation of hemoglobin, hematocrit, Rh factor and urinalysis, intravenous fluids, and two units of blood available. Therefore, activity should not be encouraged, and an intravenous access would be initiated before labor begins. Planning Physiological Integrity Application
21.4 A primigravida is admitted to the birth setting in early labor. She is 3 cm dilated, −2 station, with intact membranes and FHR of 150 bpm. Her membranes rupture spontaneously, and the FHR drops to 90 bpm with variable decelerations. The initial response from the nurse would be to: a. perform a vaginal exam. b. notify the physician. c. place the client in a left lateral position. d. administer oxygen at 2 L per nasal cannula.	Answer: a Rationale: A drop in fetal heart rate accompanied by variable decelerations is consistent with a prolapsed cord, and a vaginal exam is the best way to confirm. The vaginal exam should be done before notification of the physician. Oxygen and positioning will not relieve the decreased heart rate if the cord is compromised. Assessment Physiological Integrity Application
21.5 A woman is in active labor. The nurse determines that the fetus's position is occiput posterior. Which nursing diagnosis will apply to this woman's care if the occiput-posterior position becomes persistent? a. acute pain. b. risk for injury. c. impaired gas exchange. d. fluid volume deficit.	Answer: a Rationale: Acute pain is the diagnosis that will apply to this woman. Back pain is experienced during persistent occiput posterior position because the fetal occiput compresses the sacral nerves. Risk for injury is an appropriate diagnosis if the labor is progressing quickly or precipitously. Impaired gas exchange occurs when there is an interruption in umbilical blood, often secondary to compression of the cord. Fluid volume deficit would be an appropriate diagnosis if there was risk of excessive bleeding. Diagnosis Physiological Integrity Application
21.6 A woman has been in labor for 16 hours. Her cervix is dilated to 3 cm and is 80% effaced. The fetal presenting part is not engaged. The nurse would suspect: a. breech malpresentation. b. fetal demise. c. cephalopelvic disproportion (CPD). d. abruptio placentae.	Answer: c Rationale: Neither a breech presentation nor a fetal demise will prevent the presenting part from becoming engaged. An abruptio placentae has specific complications; however, it will not prevent engagement of the presenting part. Diagnosis Physiological Integrity Application

21.7 After delivery of the neonate, it is determined that there is a placenta accreta. Which of the following interventions should the nurse anticipate being carried out?
a. 2 L oxygen by mask.
b. intravenous antibiotics.
c. intravenous oxytocin.
d. hysterectomy.

Answer: d
Rationale: In placenta accreta, the placenta adheres in varied amounts to the myometrium. Use of oxygen, antibiotics, or oxytocin will not assist in the separation of the placenta. If hemorrhage occurs or the placenta fails to separate, the mom may need a hysterectomy.
Planning
Physiological Integrity
Analysis

21.8 A laboring multipara is having intense uterine contractions with hardly any uterine relaxation between contractions. Vaginal examination reveals rapid cervical dilation and fetal descent. The nurse should:
a. notify the physician of these findings.
b. place the woman in knee-chest position.
c. turn off the lights to make it easier for the woman to relax.
d. assemble supplies to prepare for a cesarean birth.

Answer: a
Rationale: This client is exhibiting manifestations of a precipitous birth. The best action by the nurse is to notify the physician and prepare for delivery. Placing the woman in a knee-chest position may be needed if the fetus is in a persistent occiput posterior position and labor is arrested. At this stage of labor, as described, turning the lights off so relaxation is enhanced would not be appropriate. There isn't any indication of fetal distress so preparing for a cesarean is also not appropriate.
Implementation
Physiological Integrity
Application

21.9 A nurse is comparing advantages of using active management of labor (AMOL) with a less interventional approach. The nurse knows that the goal of AMOL is:
a. preventing protracted labor and arrest of progress.
b. preventing infection from prolonged rupture of membranes.
c. detecting and intervening in cases of precipitous labor.
d. relieving the anxiety and fear accompanying labor.

Answer: a
Rationale: AMOL is identified as a preventative treatment that reduces the chance for protracted labor and decreases the cesarean birth rate.
Planning
Physiological Integrity
Analysis

21.10 A woman has just given birth. During labor, the fetus was in a brow presentation, but after a prolonged labor, the fetus converted to face presentation, and was delivered vaginally with forceps assist. The nurse should explain to the parents that:
a. the infant will need to be observed for meconium aspiration.
b. facial edema and head molding will subside in a few days.
c. the infant will have prophylactic antibiotics.
d. breastfeeding will need to be delayed for a day or two.

Answer: b
Rationale: There is no reason to delay breastfeeding or to place the infant on antibiotics. There is no mention of meconium-stained fluid that would cause the nurse to assess for meconium aspiration.
Implementation
Health Promotion and Maintenance
Application

21.11 A client is admitted to labor and delivery with a history of ruptured membranes for two hours. This is her sixth delivery; she is 40 years old, and smells of alcohol and cigarettes. This client is at risk for:
a. gestational diabetes.
b. placenta previa.

Answer: c
Rationale: Abruptio placentae is associated with excessive intrauterine pressure and can be caused by alcohol and cigarette use, increased age, and increased parity.
Evaluation
Health Promotion and Maintenance
Analysis

c. abruptio placentae.
d. placenta accreta.

21.12 A nurse is caring for a client with hydramnios. The nurse will watch for: a. maternal chest pain, dyspnea, tachycardia, and hypotension. b. newborn congenital anomalies. c. newborn postmaturity and renal malformations. d. maternal prolonged labor.	Answer: b Rationale: Chest pain, dyspnea, tachycardia, and hypotension are symptoms of amniotic embolism. Postmaturity and renal malformations occur with oligohydramnios. Prolonged labor occurs with cephalopelvic disproportion. Assessment Health promotion and maintenance Application
21.13 A pregnant client in her second trimester is complaining of spotting. Causes for spotting in the second trimester are diagnosed primarily through the use of a(n): a. nonstress test. b. vibroacoustic stimulation test. c. ultrasound. d. contraction stress test.	Answer: c Rationale: Nonstress, contraction stress test, and vibroacoustic stimulation are used to identify the well-being of the fetus. Ultrasound is a noninvasive way to identify the location of the placenta. Assessment Health Promotion and Maintenance Application
21.14 A client has been admitted to the labor unit with a known fetal demise. The nurse should place the client in a room that is: a. close to the nurse's station. b. private, away from other laboring women. c. by the delivery room. d. by the postpartum unit.	Answer: b Rationale: The couple with a known fetal demise should be placed in a private room farthest away from other laboring women. Close to the nurse's station, by the delivery room, and by the postpartum unit would place the client in close proximity to women who are delivering healthy newborns. This would not be therapeutic for a client who has a known fetal demise. Planning Health Promotion and Maintenance Application
21.15 A couple requests to see their stillborn infant. The nurse should prepare the infant by: (Select all that apply.) a. wrapping him/her in a blanket. b. removing all blankets from the infant. c. placing a hat on the infant. d. removing any identification from the infant. e. placing a diaper on the infant.	Answers: a, c Rationale: Wrapping the infant in a blanket and applying a hat will allow the parents an opportunity to view the infant before seeing any defects or extensive bruising. Most parents will eventually remove the covering to inspect the infant, however, applying a covering allows them time to adjust to the appearance at their own pace. Removing blankets or identification from the infant would not be appropriate. Placing a diaper on the infant is not necessary. Implementation Psychosocial Integrity Application

CHAPTER 22

22.1 Your client tells you that she has come to the hospital so that her baby's position can be changed. You would begin to organize the supplies needed to do which of the following procedures? a. a version. b. an amniotomy. c. Leopold's maneuver. d. a ballottement.	Answer: a Rationale: Amniotomy is the artificial rupture of membranes. Leopold's maneuver is a series of steps done to determine fetal position. Ballottement occurs when the fetus floats away and then returns to touch an examiners hand during vaginal exam. Planning Physiological Integrity Application

22.2 A woman has been admitted for an external version. She has completed an ultrasound exam and is attached to the fetal monitor. Prior to attempting the procedure, terbutaline will be given in order to:
a. provide analgesia.
b. relax the uterus.
c. induce labor.
d. prevent hemorrhage.

Answer: b
Rationale: Terbutaline is a tocolytic with the purpose of relaxing the uterus. Terbutaline has no analgesic effect, does not induce labor, and does not prevent hemorrhage.
Planning
Physiological Integrity
Application

22.3 A laboring client's obstetrician has suggested amniotomy as a method for inducing labor. Which of the following assessments must be made just before the amniotomy is performed?
a. maternal temperature, BP, and pulse.
b. estimation of fetal birth weight.
c. fetal presentation, position, and station.
d. biparietal diameter.

Answer: c
Rationale: The most important assessment is for fetal presentation, position, and station. Fetal presentation and position must be known in order to decide if vaginal delivery is possible. Station is important because if the fetal head is not engaged, a prolapsed cord is a risk. Maternal vitals, birth weight, and biparietal diameter do not affect the decision to perform an amniotomy.
Assessment
Health Promotion and Maintenance
Application

22.4 After inserting prostaglandin gel for cervical ripening, the nurse should:
a. apply an internal fetal monitor.
b. insert an indwelling catheter.
c. withhold oral intake and start intravenous fluids.
d. place the client in a supine position with a right hip wedge.

Answer: d
Rationale: An internal fetal monitor cannot be applied until adequate cervical dilatation has occurred. Until labor begins, there is no rationale for withholding all intake. The client should void before insertion of the prostaglandin gel. It is recommended the client stay in bed for only one hour. The client should void on her own and not need a catheter.
Planning
Physiological Integrity
Application

22.5 Under which of the following circumstances would the nurse remove prostaglandins from the client's cervix? (Select all that apply.)
a. contractions every five minutes.
b. nausea and vomiting.
c. late decelerations.
d. contractions every 90 seconds.

Answers: b, c, d
Rationale: The main reasons to remove prostaglandins from a client's cervix are nausea and vomiting, decelerations, and hyperstimulation of the cervix. Contractions every 5 minutes are consistent with the plan of induction.
Evaluation
Physiological Integrity
Application

22.6 Bishop's scoring system for cervical readiness includes cervical dilatation, consistency, position, and which of the following? (Select all that apply.)
a. station.
b. lie.
c. fetal presenting part.
d. cervical effacement.

Answers: a, d
Rationale: Fetal lie and presenting part are not part of the scoring system for the Bishop scale.
Assessment
Health Promotion and Maintenance
Application

22.7 The client is recovering from delivery that included a midline episiotomy. Her perineum is swollen and sore. The client is asking for her ice pack to be refreshed. The best response from the nurse is:
a. "I'll get you one right away."
b. "You only need to use one ice pack."
c. "You need to leave it off for at least 20 minutes and then reapply."
d. "I'll bring you an extra so that you can change it when you are ready."

Answer: c
Rationale: Optimal effects from the use of an ice pack occur when it is applied for 20 to 30 minutes and then removed for at least 20 minutes before being reapplied.
Implementation
Physiological Integrity
Application

22.8 The caregiver responsible for the care of the client has determined the need for the use of forceps. The client's cervix is dilated to 10 cm, and the fetus is at a +2 station. What category of forceps application would the nurse anticipate being used? a. input. b. low. c. mid. d. outlet.	Answer: b Rationale: Low forceps are applied when the leading edge of the fetal head is at a +2 station. Input is not a term associated with the use of forceps. Midforceps are applied when the fetal head is engaged. Outlet forceps are applied when the fetal skull has reached the perineum. Planning Physiological Integrity Analysis
22.9 Which of the following would be a contraindication to the induction of labor? a. placenta previa. b. isoimmunization. c. diabetes mellitus. d. premature rupture of membranes.	Answer: a Rationale: Placenta previa is a contraindication to the induction of labor. Cesarean section usually is the preferred method of delivery for placenta previa. Isoimmunization, diabetes, and premature rupture of membranes are all indications for induction. Planning Physiological Integrity Analysis
22.10 Which of the following is an appropriate nursing diagnosis for a postpartal mother with lacerations from a forceps delivery? a. alteration in body image related to scar formation. b. high risk for infection related to lochia and decreased perineal and birth canal integrity. c. alteration in nutrition—more than body requirements related to increased appetite. d. self-care deficit related to poor opportunity for independence.	Answer: b Rationale: Alteration in nutrition and self-care deficit are not related to the problem of lacerations in the postpartal period. While the mom may have concerns about eventual scar formation, the priority is to prevent infection during the postpartal period. Diagnosis Health Promotion and Maintenance Analysis
22.11 After being in labor for several hours with no progress, your client is diagnosed with CPD (cephalopelvic disproportion), and must have a cesarean section. Your client is worried that she will not be able to attempt to have any future children vaginally. After sharing this information with her care provider, you would anticipate that your client would receive what type of incision? a. transverse. b. suprapubic. c. classic. d. vertical.	Answer: a Rationale: The lower uterine segment incision most commonly used for cesarean section is the transverse incision. The suprapubic and classic incision are types of vertical incisions. The vertical incision is associated with increased risk of uterine rupture in subsequent pregnancies so is not commonly used. Planning Physiological Integrity Application
22.12 The client demonstrates understanding of the implications for future pregnancies secondary to her classical uterine incision when she states: a. "The next time I have a baby, I can try to deliver vaginally." b. "The risk of rupturing my uterus is too high for me to have any more babies." c. "Every time I have a baby, I will have to have a cesarean delivery." d. "I can only have one more baby."	Answer: c Rationale: A classical uterine incision is made in the upper uterine segment, and has an increased risk of rupture in subsequent pregnancy, labor, and birth. Therefore, subsequent deliveries will be done by cesarean. The number of subsequent pregnancies is not limited to one. Evaluation Physiological Integrity Analysis

22.13 The client is being prepped for a cesarean delivery in the operating room. The doctor is present. What is the last assessment the nurse should make just prior to the client being draped for surgery?
a. maternal temperature.
b. maternal urine output.
c. vaginal exam.
d. fetal heart tones.

Answer: d
Rationale: Fetal heart tones are assessed just prior to the start of surgery because the supine position can lead to fetal hypoxia. The supine position would not cause an abnormality in maternal temperature or maternal urine output. There would be no indication that a vaginal exam should be performed.
Assessment
Safe, Effective Care Environment
Application

22.14 Amnioinfusion has been ordered for your client in an attempt to alleviate which type of fetal heart rate decelerations?
a. early.
b. moderate.
c. late.
d. variable.

Answer: d
Rationale: Amnioinfusion can be used when cord compression is suspected. Cord compression usually is associated with variable decelerations. Early decelerations require no intervention, and late decelerations are consistent with head compression. Amnioinfusion does not relieve head compression. *Moderate* is not a descriptor used to identify decelerations.
Implementation
Safe, Effective Care Environment
Application

22.15 The client is scheduled for an elective cesarean section due to fetal malposition. An important aspect of postoperative teaching would be:
a. the importance of early ambulation.
b. the need for bed rest the first 48 hours.
c. to limit pain medication in breastfeeding mothers.
d. to only take shallow breaths to decrease abdominal pain.

Answer: a
Rationale: Deep breathing promotes respiratory health after surgery. Pain medication should be taken to the degree that the mother is comfortable enough to care for the baby and herself. Bed rest places the mother at risk for deep vein thrombosis, and gastrointestinal and respiratory problems.
Implementation
Safe, Effective Care Environment
Application

CHAPTER 23

23.1 A nurse is delegating care of postpartum clients to a licensed vocational nurse (LVN). Which postpartum client is at the highest risk for postpartum bleeding from uterine atony and should not be delegated to an LVN's care?
a. a breastfeeding postpartum client.
b. a postpartum client who began early ambulation.
c. the client who delivered vaginally after a prolonged labor.
d. a primiparous client.

Answer: c
Rationale: The client at highest risk for postpartum hemorrhage because of uterine atony is the client who had a prolonged labor. Other factors that slow uterine involution and may interfere with contraction of the uterus during the postpartum period include: anesthesia or excessive analgesia, difficult birth, grand multiparity, a full bladder, and incomplete expulsion of all of the placenta or fragments of the membranes. Therefore, a primiparous client, one who is breastfeeding, and one who ambulates early would be at lower risk for postpartum hemorrhage and would be appropriate to delegate to an LVN's care.
Planning
Safe Effective Care Environment
Analysis

23.2 Because of the great concern to many postpartum clients, the nurse includes which of the following subjects in the teaching plan?
a. puerperal tachycardia.
b. striae and cholasma.
c. diastasis of the recti muscles.
d. HELLP syndrome.

Answer: c
Rationale: Diastasis of the recti muscles can be improved with abdominal tightening exercises and is best taught when the mother is receptive to instruction during the postpartum assessment. Puerperal tachycardia might indicate a complication because pulse rates normally slow after birth. Striae and cholasma are normal skin changes in the pregnant woman. HELLP syndrome is a medical condition based on abnormal lab values.
Implementation
Health Promotion and Maintenance
Application

23.3 On the first postpartum day, the nurse teaches the client about breastfeeding. Two hours later, the client seems to remember very little of the teaching. The nurse understands this memory lapse to be due to: a. the taking-hold phase. b. postpartum hemorrhage. c. the taking-in phase. d. epidural anesthesia.	Answer: c Rationale: The taking-in phase, which occurs during the first day or two following birth, is characterized by a passive and dependent affect, and the mother also might be in need of food and rest. The taking-hold phase occurs by the second or third day, when the mother is ready to resume control of life and is open to teaching. Postpartum hemorrhage is a serious complication and will need medical intervention. Epidural anesthesia is a pharmacologic approach to pain control. Diagnosis Psychosocial Integrity Analysis
23.4 The nurse determines the fundus of a postpartum client to be boggy. Initially, the nurse should: a. document the findings. b. catheterize the client. c. massage gently and reassess. d. call the physician immediately.	Answer: c Rationale: Massage gently and reassess would be the initial intervention to prevent postpartum hemorrhage. Document findings would come after the reassessment and evaluation. Catheterizing the client may be indicated if assessment reveals a full bladder and inability to void, but not as an initial intervention. Calling the physician immediately is not necessary until more data are obtained. Implementation Physiological Integrity Application
23.5 The nurse assesses for Homans' sign by: a. extending the foot and inquiring about calf pain. b. extending the leg and inquiring about foot pain. c. flexing the knee and inquiring about thigh pain. d. dorsiflexing the foot and inquiring about calf pain.	Answer: d Rationale: Dorsiflexing the foot and inquiring about calf pain is the correct way to assess for Homans' sign. The pain is caused by stretching of inflamed vessels in the calf. Extending the foot and inquiring about the calf would exert a stretch on the vessels. Extending the leg and inquiring about foot pain and flexing the knee and inquiring about thigh pain are incorrect assessment procedures for Homans' sign. Assessment Health Promotion and Maintenance Application
23.6 The nurse would expect a physician to prescribe the following medication if a postpartum client was having heavy bleeding and a boggy uterus: a. methylergonovine maleate (Methergine). b. Rh immune globulin (RhoGAM). c. terbutaline (Brethine). d. docusate (Colace).	Answer: a Rationale: Methergine is the drug used for the prevention and control of postpartum hemorrhage. RhoGAM suppresses Rh isoimmunization and is used when the client is Rh negative. Terbutaline is used as a tocolytic. Docusate is a stool softener. Diagnosis Physiological Integrity Analysis
23.7 A postpartum client has inflamed hemorrhoids. Which of the following nursing interventions would be appropriate? a. encourage sitz baths. b. position the client in the supine position. c. avoid stool softeners. d. decrease fluid intake.	Answer: a Rationale: Encourage sitz baths is the correct approach because moist heat decreases inflammation and provides for comfort. Positioning the client in a supine position would just increase the pressure on the hemorrhoids. Avoiding stool softeners would put the client at risk for constipation and increase the likelihood of increased inflammation. Decreasing fluid intake also would put the client at risk for constipation. Positioning the client in the supine position would not help the condition. Decreasing fluid intake would be contraindicated in reducing inflammation. Implementation Physiological Integrity Application
23.8 The nurse assesses the postpartum client who has not had a bowel movement by the third postpartum day. Which of the following nursing interventions would be appropriate? a. encourage patience; it will happen soon. b. eat a low-fiber diet.	Answer: d Rationale: Obtain an order for a stool softener is the correct intervention by the third day. The client may fear having a bowel movement due to perineal soreness, and stool softeners would increase bulk and moisture in the fecal material, allowing for more comfortable evacuation. Encourage patience; it will happen soon is not addressing the client's needs, and could increase the chance for constipation. Eating a low-fiber diet would not increase bulk or moisture in the stool. Decreasing fluid intake would decrease moisture in the fecal material.

c. decrease fluid intake.	Implementation
d. obtain an order for a stool softener.	Physiological Integrity
	Application

23.9 Every time the nurse enters the room of a postpartum client who gave birth three hours ago, the client asks something else about her birth experience. The nurse would: a. answer questions quickly and try to divert her attention to other subjects. b. review documentation of the birth experience and discuss it with her. c. contact the physician to warn him the client might want to file a lawsuit due to her preoccupation with her birth experience. d. submit a referral to social services because you are concerned about obsessive behavior.	Answer: b Rationale: Review documentation of the birth experience and discuss it with her so the client can integrate the experience. Three hours after birth, the mother needs to talk about her perceptions of her labor and delivery. Answering questions quickly and trying to divert her attention to other subjects trivializes her questions and does not allow her to sort out the reality from her fantasized experience. Contacting the physician to warn him that the client might want to file a lawsuit due to her preoccupation with her birth experiences is an incorrect action. This is normal behavior. Submitting a referral to social services because you are concerned about obsessive behavior is an incorrect action because this behavior is normal. Implementation Psychosocial Integrity Application

23.10 The postpartum nurse is caring for a client who gave birth to full-term twins earlier today. The nurse will know to assess for symptoms of: a. increased blood pressure. b. hypoglycemia. c. postpartum hemorrhage. d. postpartum infection.	Answer: c Rationale: Postpartum hemorrhage is correct. This client is at risk for hemorrhage due to overdistention of the uterus with twins and possible slower uterine involution. Increased blood pressure would cause vasoconstriction and is not identified in this client. Hypoglycemia would not be a usual assessment to make following delivery for the mother—possibly for the infants. Postpartum infection would be assessed through odor of lochia and uterine pain and would not be expected this soon after delivery. Assessment Physiological Integrity Application

23.11 A postpartum client asks the nurse to weigh her. The nurse expects an initial weight loss of: a. 10 to 12 pounds. b. 5 to 8 pounds. c. 15 to 20 pounds. d. 12 to 15 pounds.	Answer: a Rationale: Ten to 12 pounds is the usual initial weight loss. This weight is lost with the birth of the infant and the expulsion of the placenta and the amniotic fluid. Five to 8 pounds might be the loss after a preterm birth. Fifteen to 20 pounds might be the loss from a multiple birth. Twelve to 15 pounds is close but does not match the usual weight of placenta, amniotic fluid, and full-term infant weight. Assessment Health Promotion and Maintenance Application

23.12 A nurse is caring for several postpartum clients. Which client is demonstrating a problem attaching to her newborn? a. the client who is discussing how her boy looks like her father. b. the client who is singing softly to her baby. c. the client who continues to touch her baby with only her fingertips. d. the client who picks her baby up when he cries.	Answer: c Rationale: During the attachment process the client should proceed from fingertip touch, to palmar contact, to enfolding the infant close to her own body. If the client continues to touch only with her fingertips she may not be developing adequate early attachment. Other signs of developing early attachment include: pointing out family traits or characteristics seen in the newborn, speaking to the baby frequently and affectionately (singing), and being sensitive to the newborn's needs (picking the baby up when the baby cries). Assessment Psychosocial Integrity Analysis

23.13 Put the following components specific to postpartum examination of a client in the proper sequential order: a. L-lochia. b. E-emotional.	Answer: d, f, h, g, a, e, c, b Rationale: The components for remembering the sequential order are based on the term BUBBLEHE. Start at the head and consistently assess each part using the same technique and order.

c. H-Homans'/hemorrhoids. d. B-breast. e. E-episiotomy/lacerations. f. U-uterus. g. B-bowel. h. B-bladder. Write your answer in the box below. ☐	Implementation Health Promotion and Maintenance Application
23.14 The nurse is caring for a postpartal client who is experiencing afterpains following the birth of her third child. Which of the following comfort measures should the nurse implement to decrease her pain? (Select all that apply.) a. offer warm blankets for her abdomen. b. call the physician to report this finding. c. inform her that this is not normal, and she will need an oxytocic agent. d. massage the fundus of the uterus gently and observe lochia for clots. e. administer a mild analgesic at bedtime to assure rest.	Answers: a, d, e Rationale:The nurse should offer comfort measures that address the discomfort of afterpains—warm blankets, massage, and a mild analgesic will decrease pain. It is not necessary to call the physician, or to inform the client that this is not normal and she will need an oxytocic agent. Implementation Physiological Integrity Analysis
23.15 A nurse is preparing to discharge a postpartum client. The nurse notes on her chart that she is nonimmune to rubella. The nurse: a. administers a rubella vaccine prior to discharge. b. instructs the client to obtain a rubella vaccine after 1 month has elapsed. c. charts this information in the discharge summary notes. d. takes no action because none is needed.	Answer: a Rationale: If the postpartum client is nonimmune to rubella, a rubella vaccine is administered prior to discharge.The client should not be instructed to wait for 1 month. Simply charting the information or taking no action is not appropriate. Implementation Health Promotion and Maintenance Application

CHAPTER 24

24.1 The postpartum nurse applies which of the following adult learning principles to the discharge teaching of postpartum clients? a. demonstration of skills. b. classroom lectures and one-on-one teaching. c. use of television and videos. d. sensory involvement and active participation.	Answer: d Rationale: Sensory involvement and active participation are two of the keys in adult learning because they actively involve the clients in the learning. Demonstration of skills is done by the nurse, and classroom lectures, one-one teaching, and use of television and videos—while helpful when used as part of the teaching plan—do not actively involve the client in learning. Implementation Health Promotion and Maintenance Application
24.2 The postpartum client has chosen to bottlefeed her infant. Nursing actions that aid in lactation suppression include: a. warm showers BID. b. pumping milk TID. c. ice packs to the axillary area of each breast QID. d. avoidance of wearing a bra for 5 to 7 days.	Answer: c Rationale: Ice packs to the axillary area of each breast for 20 minutes, four times daily, should begin soon after birth.This provides mechanical inhibition of lactation.Warm showers BID, pumping milk TID, and avoiding a bra for 5 to 7 days actually increase the flow of breast milk. Implementation Health Promotion and Maintenance Application

24.3 On the second day postpartum, the client experiences engorgement. To relieve her discomfort, the nurse should encourage the client to:
a. remove her bra.
b. apply heat to the breasts.
c. apply ice packs to the breasts.
d. limit breastfeeding to BID.

Answer: c
Rationale: Applying ice packs to the breasts relieves discomfort through the numbing effect of ice. Removing her bra and applying heat only serve to increase breast milk, and limiting breastfeeding to BID actually would decrease the flow of breast milk eventually and would not serve to decrease the discomfort of mother or infant.
Implementation
Physiological Integrity
Application

24.4 The breastfeeding client asks the nurse about appropriate contraception. The nurse would state:
a. "Breastfeeding has many effects on sexual intercourse."
b. "IUDs are easy to use and easy to insert prior to sexual intercourse."
c. "Breastfeeding hampers ovulation, but to be safe use condoms."
d. "Breastfeeding hampers ovulation, so no contraception is needed."

Answer: c
Rationale: Breastfeeding hampers ovulation, but to be safe, use condoms is the correct response. Breastfeeding increases the hormone prolactin, which hampers the release of the hormonal feedback system that induces ovulation. However, it is not a guarantee, and many things can interfere. Stating that IUDs are easy to use and easy to insert prior to sexual intercourse is incorrect because IUDs can only be placed by a healthcare provider in a clinic situation. Breastfeeding has many effects on sexual intercourse is not a clear explanation. The woman may spurt milk at the time of orgasm, but otherwise there is no effect. Breastfeeding hampers ovulation so no contraception is needed is incorrect.
Implementation
Health Promotion and Maintenance
Application

24.5 A client is preparing to take a sitz bath for the first time. The nurse will:
a. allow the client privacy during the sitz bath time.
b. place a call bell well within reach and check on the client frequently.
c. discourage the client from taking a sitz bath.
d. check on the client after the sitz bath.

Answer: b
Rationale: The warm, moist heat and warm environment of the sitz bath may cause the client to faint. A call bell should be placed within reach and the client should be checked on frequently to maintain safety. Allowing the client privacy and not checking until after the sitz bath does not assure safety. Warm or cool sitz bathes are recommended to assist in perineal healing and reduction of discomfort.
Implementation
Physiological Integrity
Application

24.6 A postpartum client has just received a rubella vaccination. The client understands the teaching associated with administration of this vaccine when she states:
a. "I will need another vaccination in 3 months."
b. "I must avoid getting pregnant for 3 months."
c. "This will prevent me from getting chickenpox."
d. "This will protect my newborn from getting the measles."

Answer: b
Rationale: The client is to avoid pregnancy for 3 months after receiving the rubella vaccine. The client will not need another vaccination in 3 months. The vaccination prevents measles not chickenpox. The vaccination will only protect the client receiving it, therefore, the newborn will not be protected until the child receives his or her own vaccination.
Evaluation
Health Promotion and Maintenance
Analysis

24.7 The nurse assesses the postpartum client to have moderate lochia rubra with clots. Which of the following nursing interventions would be appropriate?
a. assess fundus and bladder status.
b. catheterize the client.
c. administer Methergine IM per order.
d. contact the physician immediately.

Answer: a
Rationale: Assess the fundus and bladder status first. Moderate lochia, even with clots, might be due to the client's supine position for several hours, or to other factors. Catheterizing the client may be an intervention if the bladder is full and the client is unable to void, but it is not the initial intervention. It is not necessary to administer Methergine IM per order or contact the physician immediately because the situation does not warrant this intervention.
Implementation
Physiological Integrity
Application

24.8 Which nursing action is appropriate for the postpartum client who has received Percocet 1 tablet PO? a. increase the IV fluid rate. b. encourage diversion activities. c. ambulate the client. d. reassess pain level in 30 minutes.	Answer: d Rationale: Reassess pain level in 30 minutes indicates that the nurse knows Percocet has its peak effect between 30 to 60 minutes from administration. Increasing the IV fluid rate might hydrate the client but does not affect the absorption of Percocet. Ambulating the client and encouraging diversion activities might be helpful but would not affect the assessment of Percocet's pain-relieving capabilities. Implementation Physiological Integrity Application
24.9 Which of the following statements by the nursing student would require further teaching concerning rubella vaccine? a. "Clients should be assessed for allergies to eggs." b. "Breastfeeding mothers should not receive the vaccine." c. "Clients should avoid pregnancy for 3 months following vaccination." d. "Some clients develop a slight rash after vaccination."	Answer: b Rationale: Breastfeeding mothers should not receive the vaccine is an incorrect response. The nursing student needs to review the purpose of rubella vaccine, which is to increase the immunity in the mother. It does not affect her breastfeeding or her infant. Exposure to rubella in a nonimmune mother who is in her first trimester can result in congenital defects and fetal death. Clients should be assessed for allergies to eggs, clients should avoid pregnancy for 3 months following vaccination, and some clients develop a slight rash after vaccination all are teaching points when administering rubella vaccine. Evaluation Physiological Integrity Analysis
24.10 RhoGAM is given to the postpartum client for the purpose of: a. preventing congenital birth defects through vaccination. b. preventing or avoiding the chronic state of infection of hepatitis B. c. preventing sensitization from the fetomaternal transfusion of Rh-positive fetal red blood cells. d. preventing the spread of group B streptococcal infection in the client's neonate.	Answer: c Rationale: Preventing sensitization from the fetomaternal transfusion of Rh-positive fetal red blood cells is the correct purpose for administering a RhoGAM injection to an Rh− mother who delivered an Rh+ infant. Preventing congenital birth defects through vaccination is related to rubella vaccination. Preventing or avoiding the chronic state of infection of hepatitis B refers to the hepatitis vaccine (Heptivax), and preventing the spread of group B streptococcal infection in the client's neonate refers to the use of antibiotics in the mother during and after birth. Planning Physiological Integrity Application
24.11 The nurse instructs the postpartum client she can resume light housekeeping after the: a. second week at home. b. first week at home. c. six-week postpartum checkup. d. second day at home.	Answer: a Rationale: The postpartum client can resume light housekeeping after the second week at home. The second day or even within the first week is too early to resume this type of activity. However, it's not necessary to wait until after the six-week postpartum checkup to resume light housekeeping. Planning Health Promotion and Maintenance Application
24.12 The nurse is caring for a client who had a cesarean birth four hours ago. Which of the following interventions would the nurse implement at this time? (Select all that apply.) a. administer analgesics as needed. b. encourage her to ambulate to the bathroom to void. c. encourage leg exercises every 2 hours. d. encourage client to cough and deep-breathe every 2 to 4 hours. e. encourage the use of breathing, relaxation, and distraction.	Answers: a, c, d, e Rationale: Administering analgesics as needed, encouraging leg exercises every 2 hours, encouraging the client to cough and deep-breathe every 2 to 4 hours, and encouraging the use of breathing, relaxation, and distraction all address the client's nursing care needs and are similar to needs of other surgical clients. Encouraging her to ambulate to the bathroom to void might be an intervention done on the first or second day postpartum. Implementation Physiological Integrity Application

24.13 The nurse is caring for a client who delivered by cesarean birth. The client received a general anesthetic. The nurse would encourage which of the following in order to prevent or minimize abdominal distention? (Select all that apply.)
a. increased intake of cold beverages.
b. leg exercises every 2 hours.
c. abdominal tightening.
d. ambulation.
e. eating a high-protein general diet.

Answers: b, c, d
Rationale: Leg exercises every 2 hours, abdominal tightening, and ambulation all serve to prevent or minimize abdominal distention in a surgical client who received a general anesthetic. Increased intake of cold beverages and eating a high-protein general diet would increase the distention through increase of gas and constipation.
Implementation
Physiological Integrity
Application

24.14 Which of the following best describes the advantage of patient-controlled analgesia (PCA) for the client following a cesarean birth?
a. The client receives a bolus of the analgesia when pressing the button.
b. The client experiences pain relief within 30 minutes.
c. The client feels a greater sense of control and less dependence on the nursing staff.
d. The client can deliver as many doses of the medication as needed.

Answer: c
Rationale: The client feels a greater sense of control and less dependence on the nursing staff is correct. The preset pump has a time lockout so the client cannot deliver another dose until a specified period of time has elapsed, but it allows the client to do the administering. The client receives a bolus of analgesia when pressing the button is incorrect. The bolus is given by the healthcare provider at the beginning of therapy and is not repeated. The client experiences pain relief within 30 minutes applies to oral pain medications. IV pain medications have rapid pain relief. The client is locked out of delivering as many doses as desired by the preset time lockout in the pump.
Diagnosis
Physiological Integrity
Application

24.15 The nurse is caring for a client who plans to relinquish her baby for adoption. The nurse would implement which of the following approaches to care? (Select all that apply.)
a. encourage the client to see and hold her infant.
b. encourage the client to express her emotions.
c. respect any special requests for the birth.
d. acknowledge the grieving process in the client.
e. allow for access to the infant if the client requests it.

Answers: b, c, d, e
Rationale: Encouraging the client to express emotions, respecting any special request for the birth, acknowledging the grieving process, and allowing for access to the infant at the client's request are all aspects of providing care for the client who decides to relinquish her infant. Encouraging the client to see and hold her infant does not respect the client's right to refuse interaction and might make her feel guilty for not wanting to see the infant.
Implementation
Psychosocial Integrity
Application

CHAPTER 25

25.1 The charge nurse is analyzing a postpartum client's risk for hemorrhage. Which client has the highest risk for postpartum hemorrhage?
a. client who went overdue and delivered vaginally.
b. client who delivered by a scheduled cesarean delivery.
c. client who had oxytocin augmentation of labor.
d. client who delivered vaginally at 36 weeks.

Answer: c
Rationale: Uterine atony is a cause of postpartal hemorrhage. A contributing factor that can cause uterine atony is oxytocin augmentation of labor. The client who was overdue, the client who delivered by cesarean, and the client who delivered vaginally at 36 weeks are not as high risk for postpartum hemorrhage.
Assessment
Physiological Integrity
Analysis

25.2 A client had a cesarean birth 3 days ago. She has tenderness, localized heat, and redness of the left leg. She is afebrile. As a result of these symptoms, the nurse recognizes that the client will most likely be: a. encouraged to ambulate freely. b. given aspirin 650 mg by mouth. c. given Methergine IM. d. placed on bed rest.	Answer: d Rationale: Placed on bed rest would be correct because these symptoms indicate the presence of superficial thrombophlebitis. The treatment involves bed rest and elevation of the affected limb, analgesics, and use of elastic support hose. Encouraged to ambulate freely is incorrect because that would increase the inflammation. Aspirin 650 mg by mouth has anticoagulant properties but usually is not necessary unless complications occur. Methergine is given only for postpartum hemorrhage and would only cause vasoconstriction of an already inflamed vessel. Assessment Health Promotion and Maintenance Analysis
25.3 The postpartum client is concerned about mastitis because she experienced it with her last baby. Preventive measures the nurse could teach include: a. wearing a tight-fitting bra. b. limiting feedings to QID. c. frequent breastfeeding. d. forcing fluids.	Answer: c Rationale: Frequent breastfeeding is important because complete emptying of the breasts prevents engorgement and stasis. Wearing a tight-fitting bra would mechanically suppress lactation, as would limiting feedings to QID. Forcing fluids is not necessary. Implementation Health Promotion and Maintenance Application
25.4 A postpartum client reports sharp, shooting pains in her nipple during breastfeeding and flaky, itchy skin on her breasts. The nurse suspects: a. nipple soreness. b. engorgement. c. mastitis. d. letdown reflex.	Answer: c Rationale: Mastitis is characterized by late-onset nipple pain, followed by shooting pains during and between feedings. The skin of the affected breast becomes pink, flaking, and pruritic. Nipple soreness, engorgement, and the letdown reflex do not share these symptoms. Assessment Health Promotion and Maintenance Analysis
25.5 Which relief measure would be most appropriate for a postpartum client with thrombophlebitis? a. urge ambulation. b. apply ice to the leg. c. remove blankets from the bed. d. massage her calf.	Answer: c Rationale: Removing blankets from the bed would decrease pressure and thus increase comfort on the affected leg. Urging ambulation would increase discomfort. Applying ice to the leg is contraindicated in thrombophlebitis treatment because it can cause vasoconstriction, increasing pain. Massaging the calf is contraindicated because it can cause a breakup of a clot and put the client at risk for a pulmonary embolus. Planning Physiological Integrity Application
25.6 The most appropriate nursing diagnosis for a client with postpartum deep vein thrombosis is: a. fluid volume excess related to tissue edema. b. sleep pattern disturbance related to tissue hypoxia. c. risk for infection related to obstructed venous return. d. altered tissue perfusion related to obstructed venous return.	Answer: d Rationale: Altered tissue perfusion related to obstructed venous return is the correct diagnosis because it identifies the underlying cause. Fluid volume excess related to tissue edema and sleep pattern disturbance related to tissue hypoxia are incorrect because they do not identify the underlying cause. Risk for infection related to obstructed venous return might be a possible diagnosis if complications of infection are present. Diagnosis Physiological Integrity Application
25.7 To prevent the spread of infection, the nurse teaches the postpartum client to: a. address pain early. b. change peri-pads frequently. c. avoid overhydration. d. report symptoms of uterine cramping.	Answer: b Rationale: Changing peri-pads frequently prevents contamination of the perineum and risk of infection. Wiping from front to back and good hygiene practices also are important. Addressing pain early and reporting symptoms of uterine cramping would not be a preventive action for infection. Avoiding overhydration actually would increase the risk for infection by not providing adequate fluids to flush the kidneys and bladder. Implementation Physiological Integrity Application

25.8 The nurse understands that the optimal position for a postpartum client with endometritis is:
a. semi-Fowler's.
b. Trendelenburg.
c. side-lying.
d. supine.

Answer: a
Rationale: Semi-Fowler's position would be the better position for a client with endometritis because the sitting position would decrease the discomfort. Trendelenburg position would be used only in case of shock. Side-lying and supine would only increase the pressure on the abdomen and increase pain.
Implementation
Physiological Integrity: Reduction of Risk Potential
Application

25.9 Which method of assessment would best indicate that a client has a urinary complication?
a. urine pH.
b. calculation of output.
c. urine-specific gravity.
d. calculation of intake.

Answer: b
Rationale: Calculation of output would provide a better assessment of complete emptying of the bladder because overdistention can cause trauma to the bladder, displace the uterus, and cause infection. Urine pH and urine-specific gravity can be used to identify certain conditions but would not be part of the initial assessment. Calculation of intake is incorrect.
Assessment
Physiological Integrity
Application

25.10 The postpartum client states that she doesn't understand why she can't enjoy being with her baby. The nurse is concerned about postpartum:
a. psychosis.
b. infection.
c. depression.
d. blues.

Answer: c
Rationale: Postpartum depression is characterized by feelings of failure and self-accusation among others. Postpartum psychosis is more severe and includes hallucinations and irrationality not represented in this situation. Postpartum infection has nothing to do with this situation. Postpartum blues is characterized by mild depression interspersed with happier feelings and is self-limiting.
Assessment
Psychosocial Integrity
Analysis

25.11 The childbirth educator revises the curriculum to include postpartum depression preventative measures. Topics will include:
a. encouraging planning in the prenatal period for the postnatal period.
b. review of historical cases of postpartum psychosis.
c. importance of counseling for all postpartum mothers.
d. prophylactic administration of Paxil.

Answer: a
Rationale: Encouraging planning in the prenatal period for the postpartal period is the correct response. Offering realistic information and anticipatory guidance and debunking myths about the perfect mother or perfect newborn might help prevent postpartum depression. Reviewing historical cases of postpartum psychosis will serve only to scare parents. Importance of counseling for all postpartum mothers is not necessary, because postpartum depression only affects 7% to 30% of all postpartum women in North America. Prophylactic administration of Paxil is not recommended. Treatment needs to be individualized.
Planning
Psychosocial Integrity
Application

25.12 The nurse is caring for a postpartum client who had an estimated blood loss of 500 mL following a vaginal birth. What is the best clinical measure of the client's actual blood loss?
a. the clinical estimation of blood loss at time of birth.
b. a decrease in the hematocrit of 10 points between the time of admission and the time of postbirth.
c. the amount of saturation of the linens during and after the birth.
d. a decrease in blood pressure and increase in pulse after birth.

Answer: b
Rationale: A decrease in the hematocrit of 10 points between the time of admission and the time of postbirth is seen by many clinicians as more reliable in estimating the actual blood loss. The clinical estimation of blood loss at the time of birth often is obscured by blood mixing with amniotic fluid and oozing onto the sterile drapes or getting sponged away. The amount of saturation of the linens during and after the birth is incorrect for this reason. A decrease in blood pressure and an increasing pulse rate after birth do not appear until as much as 1800 to 2100 mL have been lost and shortly before the woman becomes hemodynamically unstable.
Assessment
Physiological Integrity
Analysis

25.13 Which of the following would indicate the presence of a perineal hematoma? (Select all that apply.) a. ecchymosis. b. edema. c. vaginal bleeding. d. tenseness of tissues. e. elevated temperature.	Answers: a, b, d Rationale: Ecchymosis, edema, and tenseness of tissues overlying the hematoma are characteristic signs of perineal hematomas. Vaginal bleeding is nonspecific to identifying a hematoma, and elevated temperature can be due to a variety of reasons, such as dehydration or mastitis. Assessment Physiological Integrity Application
25.14 The nurse inspects the perineum of a postpartal client using the REEDA scale. Put the following signs in the appropriate order according to this scale. a. discharge. b. ecchymosis. c. approximation. d. redness. e. edema.	Answer: d, e, b, a, c Rationale: The REEDA scale helps the nurse remember to consider all of these signs of perineum healing while performing a perineal check. Assessment Physiological Integrity Application
25.15 A postpartal client recovering from a deep vein thrombosis is being discharged. What areas of teaching on self-care and anticipatory guidance should the nurse discuss with the client? (Select all that apply.) a. avoid crossing of her legs. b. avoid prolonged standing or sitting. c. take frequent walks. d. take a daily aspirin dose of 650 mg. e. avoid long car trips.	Answers: a, b, c Rationale: Avoid crossing of legs because of the pressure it causes. Avoid prolonged standing or sitting, which contributes to venous stasis. Take frequent walks to promote venous return. Taking a daily aspirin increases anticoagulant activity and should be avoided if the client is being treated with other anticoagulants. Avoiding long car trips is not necessary. The client should be told to take frequent breaks during car trips but not to avoid them entirely. Planning Physiological Integrity Application

CHAPTER 26

26.1 A postpartum client calls the clinic to report that her 3-day-old baby girl has a spot of blood on her diaper. The nurse explains to the client that this is due to: a. withdrawal of maternal hormones. b. a urinary infection. c. an immature immune system. d. physiologic jaundice.	Answer: a Rationale: As maternal hormones clear the newborn, it is not unusual to find blood on the diapers of a female newborn. This is referred to as pseudomenstruation. An immature immune system or a urinary infection does not cause pseudomenstruation. Physiologic jaundice is due to an accelerated destruction of fetal RBCs, impaired conjugation of bilirubin, and an increase in bilirubin reabsorption from the intestinal tract. Implementation Physiological Integrity Application
26.2 Which of the following nursing interventions would protect the newborn from the most susceptible form of heat loss? a. placing the newborn away from air currents. b. pre-warming the examination table. c. drying the newborn thoroughly. d. removing wet linens from the isolette.	Answer: c Rationale: The most susceptible form of heat loss is evaporation. Evaporation occurs when water is converted to a vapor. Drying the newborn thoroughly immediately after birth or after a bath will prevent heat loss by evaporation. Placing the newborn away from air currents reduces heat loss by convection. Pre-warming the examination table reduces heat loss by conduction. Removing wet linens from the isolette that are not in direct contact with the newborn reduces heat loss by radiation. Implementation Health Promotion and Maintenance Application
26.3 A 2-day-old newborn is asleep, and the nurse assesses the apical pulse to be 88 bpm. What would be the most appropriate nursing action based on this assessment finding?	Answer: c Rationale: An apical pulse rate of 88 bpm is within the normal range of a sleeping full-term newborn. The average resting heart rate in the first week of life is 110 to 150 bpm. The heart rate may drop to 85 bpm during sleep in a full-term newborn.

a. call the physician. b. administer oxygen. c. document the finding. d. place newborn under the radiant warmer.	Assessment Physiological Integrity Application
26.4 A telephone triage nurse gets a call from a postpartum client concerned about jaundice. The client's newborn is 37 hours old. What data would the nurse need to gather first? a. stool characteristics. b. fluid intake. c. skin color. d. bilirubin level.	Answer: c Rationale: Yellow coloration of the skin and sclera are signs of physiologic jaundice that appear after the first 24 hours postnatally. Inspection of the skin would be the first step in assessing for jaundice. Skin color begins to appear yellow once the serum levels of bilirubin are about 4 to 6 mg/dL. Assessment Physiological Integrity Analysis
26.5 Which of the following nursing interventions would protect the newborn from heat loss by convection? a. placing the newborn away from air currents. b. pre-warming the examination table. c. drying the newborn thoroughly. d. removing wet linens from the isolette.	Answer: a Rationale: Placing the newborn away from air currents reduces heat loss by convection. Drying the newborn thoroughly immediately after birth or after a bath will prevent heat loss by evaporation. Pre-warming the examination table reduces heat loss by conduction. Removing wet linens from the isolette that are not in direct contact with the newborn reduces heat loss by radiation. Implementation Physiological Integrity Application
26.6 The nurse has assessed four newborn's respiratory rates immediately following birth. Which of the following respiratory rates would require further assessment by the nurse? a. 60 breaths per minute. b. 70 breaths per minute. c. 64 breaths per minute. d. 28 breaths per minute.	Answer: d Rationale: The normal range for respirations of a newborn within 2 hours after birth is 60 to 70 breaths per minute. If respirations drop below 30 breaths per minute when the infant is at rest, the nurse should notify the physician. Assessment Physiological Integrity Application
26.7 The student nurse notices that a newborn weighs less today compared with the newborn's birth weight 3 days ago. The nursing instructor explains that newborns lose weight following birth due to: a. a shift of intracellular water to extracellular spaces. b. loss of meconium stool. c. a shift of extracellular water to intracellular spaces. d. the sleep-wake cycle.	Answer: a Rationale: A shift of intracellular water to extracellular space account for the 5% to 10% of weight loss during the first few days of life. Loss of meconium stool and the sleep-wake cycle do not affect this amount of weight loss. Implementation Physiological Integrity Application
26.8 A postpartum client calls the nursery to report that her 3-day-old newborn has passed a bright green stool. The nurse's best response is: a. "Take your newborn to the pediatrician." b. "There may be a possible food allergy." c. "Your newborn has diarrhea." d. "This is to be expected."	Answer: d Rationale: By the third day of life, the newborn's stools appear thin brown to green in color. The green color of stool is not due to food allergies or characterized as diarrhea but is a transitional stool consisting of part meconium and part fecal material. Implementation Health Promotion and Maintenance Application
26.9 At birth, an infant weighed 8 pounds 4 ounces. Three days later he weighs 7 pounds 15 ounces. What conclusion should the nurse draw regarding this newborn's weight?	Answer: b Rationale: This newborn's weight loss is within normal limits. During the first 5 to 10 days of life, caloric intake often is insufficient for weight gain. Therefore, there may be a weight loss of 5% to 10% in term newborns.

a. weight loss is excessive. b. weight loss is within normal limits. c. weight gain is excessive. d. weight gain is within normal limits.	Evaluation Health Promotion and Maintenance Analysis
26.10 At birth, an infant weighed 6 pounds 12 ounces. Three days later, he weighs 5 pounds 2 ounces. What conclusion should the nurse draw regarding this newborn's weight? a. weight loss is excessive. b. weight loss is within normal limits. c. weight gain is excessive. d. weight gain is within normal limits.	Answer: a Rationale: This newborn has lost more than 10% of the birth weight. This newborn's weight loss is excessive. During the first 5 to 10 days of life, caloric intake often is insufficient for weight gain. Therefore, there may be a weight loss of 5% to 10% in term newborns. Evaluation Health Promotion and Maintenance Analysis
26.11 The student nurse notices that the newborns sleep peacefully in the nursery, although the environment is noisy and well lit. The nursing instructor explains that this newborn behavior is: a. habituation. b. orientation. c. self-quieting. d. due to sleep-alert states.	Answer: a Rationale: Habituation is the newborn's ability to process and respond to visual and auditory stimulation. The capacity to ignore repetitious disturbing stimuli is a newborn defense mechanism readily apparent in the noisy, well-lit nursery. Orientation is the newborn's ability to be alert to, follow, and fixate on complex visual stimuli that are appealing and attractive. Self-quieting ability is the newborn's ability to quiet and comfort herself by sucking on her fist. Assessment Psychosocial Integrity Analysis
26.12 The student nurse notices that the newborn seems to focus on his mother's eyes. The nursing instructor explains that this newborn behavior is: a. habituation. b. orientation. c. self-quieting. d. due to sleep-alert states.	Answer: b Rationale: Orientation is the newborn's ability to be alert to, follow, and fixate on complex visual stimuli that are appealing and attractive, such as a mother's eyes. Habituation is the newborn's ability to process and respond to visual and auditory stimulation. Self-quieting ability is the newborn's ability to quiet and comfort himself by sucking on his fist. Assessment Psychosocial Integrity Analysis
26.13 A postpartum mother questions if the environmental temperature should be warmer in the baby's room at home. The nurse responds that the environmental temperature should be warmer for the newborn. This response by the nurse is based on which of the following newborn characteristics that affect the establishment of a neutral thermal environmental? (Select all that apply.) a. newborns have a decrease in subcutaneous fat. b. newborns have a thick epidermis layer. c. flexed posture of the term newborn. d. blood vessels are closer to the skin. e. newborns have an increase in subcutaneous fat.	Answers: a, c, d Rationale: The normal newborn will require a higher environmental temperature in order to maintain a thermoneutral environment. Decreased subcutaneous fat, blood vessels closer to the skin, and a thin epidermis layer all are characteristics that affect the newborn's neutral thermal environment. The flexed posture of the newborn reduces heat loss by decreasing the surface area that is exposed to the environment. Implementation Physiological Integrity Application
26.14 The nurse is caring for a client who was given meperidine (Demerol) during labor. In planning care for the client's newborn, the nurse would closely assess the newborn's: a. body temperature. b. stool pattern. c. bilirubin level. d. urine output.	Answer: a Rationale: Certain drugs such as meperidine (Demerol) may prevent the metabolism of brown fat. Therefore, when meperidine (Demerol) is given to a laboring woman, the newborn may be at risk for hypothermia. Planning Physiological Integrity Application

26.15 The nurse is caring for a newborn 30 minutes after birth. During an assessment of respiratory function, the following data is collected. Which of the following assessment findings would the nurse report as abnormal? (Select all that apply.)
a. respiratory rate of 66 breaths per minute.
b. periodic breathing with pauses of 25 seconds.
c. chest and abdomen movements are synchronous.
d. grunting on expiration.
e. nasal flaring.
f. acrocyanosis.

Answers: b, d, e
Rationale: Immediately after birth and for the next two hours, normal respiratory rate is 60 to 70 breaths per minute. Abdominal movements that are synchronous with the chest movements are normal. Acrocyanosis is normal for several hours after birth. Abnormal findings that should be reported to the physician include periodic breathing with pauses more than 20 seconds (apnea), grunting on expiration, and nasal flaring.
Assessment
Physiological Integrity
Analysis

CHAPTER 27

27.1 A nursing instructor is demonstrating an assessment on a newborn for the nursing students using the Ballard gestational assessment tool. The nurse explains that which of the following tests should be performed after the first hour of birth?
a. arm recoil.
b. square window sign.
c. scarf sign.
d. popliteal angle.

Answer: a
Rationale: Recoil time is slower in fatigued newborns. Therefore, arm recoil is best elicited after the first hour of birth so the newborn can recover from the stress of birth. Square window, scarf sign, and popliteal angle are assessments performed by the examiner, where arm recoil is a response by the newborn.
Assessment
Health Promotion and Maintenance
Analysis

27.2 Before the nurse begins to dry the newborn off after birth, which of the following assessment findings should the nurse document to ensure an accurate gestational rating on the Ballard gestational assessment tool?
a. amount and area of vernix coverage.
b. creases on the sole.
c. size of the areola.
d. body surface temperature.

Answer: a
Rationale: Drying the baby after birth will disturb the vernix and potentially alter the score when using the Ballard gestational assessment tool. The nurse first should document the amount and coverage of the vernix before drying the newborn. Creases on the sole and size of the areola are not affected by drying of the newborn. Body surface temperature is not part of the Ballard gestational assessment tool.
Implementation
Health Promotion and Maintenance
Application

27.3 A new mother is concerned about a mass on the newborn's head. The nurse assesses this to be a cephalhematoma. Which of the following characteristics would indicate a cephalhematoma? (Select all that apply.)
a. The mass appeared on the second day after birth.
b. The mass appears larger when the newborn cries.
c. The head appears asymmetrical.
d. The mass appears only on one side of the head.
e. The mass overrides the suture line.

Answers: a, d
Rationale: A cephalhematoma is a collection of blood resulting from ruptured blood vessels between the surface of a cranial bone and the periosteal membrane. It can appear between the first and second day after birth and does not increase in size when the newborn cries. Cephalhematomas can be unilateral or bilateral but do not cross the suture lines. Molding causes the head to appear asymmetrical; this is due to the overriding of cranial bones during labor and birth.
Assessment
Physiological Integrity: Physiological Adaptation
Application

27.4 During an assessment of a 12-hour-old newborn, the nurse notices pale pink spots on the nape of the neck. The nurse documents this finding as: a. nevus vasculosus. b. nevus flammeus. c. telangiectatic nevi. d. a Mongolian spot.	Answer: c Rationale: Telangiectatic nevi (stork bites) are pale pink or red spots that appear on the eyelids, nose, lower occipital bone, or the nape of the neck. Nevus vasculosus (strawberry mark) is a capillary hemangioma. Nevus flammeus (port-wine stain), a capillary angioma, is located directly below the epidermis. Mongolian spots are macular areas of bluish-black pigmentation on the dorsal area of the buttocks. Assessment Health Promotion and Maintenance Application
27.5 The nurse desires to demonstrate to a new family their infant's individuality. Which assessment tool would be most appropriate for the nurse to use? a. Brazelton Neonatal Behavioral Assessment Scale. b. Ballard Maturity Scale. c. Dubowitz Gestational Age Scale. d. Ortolani maneuver.	Answer: a Rationale: The Brazelton Neonatal Behavioral Assessment Scale assesses the newborn's state changes, temperament, and individual behavior patterns. The Ballard Maturity Scale and the Dubowitz are tools that assess external physical characteristics and neurological or neuromuscular development. The Ortolani maneuver is an assessment technique that rules out the possibility of congenital hip dysplasia. Implementation Health Promotion and Maintenance Application
27.6 The nurse attempts to elicit the Moro reflex on a newborn and assesses movement of the right arm only. Based on this finding, the nurse immediately assesses the: a. Ortolani maneuver. b. Babinski reflex. c. clavicle. d. Gallant reflex.	Answer: c Rationale: When the Moro reflex is elicited, the newborn will straighten both arms and hands outward while the knees are flexed, then slowly return the arms to the chest, as in an embrace. If this response is not elicited, the nurse will assess the clavicle. If the clavicle is fractured, the response will be demonstrated on the unaffected side only. Ortolani maneuver is an assessment technique that rules out the possibility of congenital hip dysplasia. Babinski reflex tests for upper neuron abnormalities. Trunk incurvation (Gallant reflex) is seen when the newborn is prone and the pelvis is turned to the stimulated side when the spine is stroked. Assessment Physiological Integrity Application
27.7 The nurse is making an initial assessment of the newborn. Which of the following data would be considered normal? a. chest circumference 32.5 cm, head circumference 31.5 cm. b. chest circumference 30 cm, head circumference 29 cm. c. chest circumference 38 cm, head circumference 31.5 cm. d. chest circumference 32.5 cm, head circumference 36 cm.	Answer: a Rationale: The average circumference of the head at birth is 32 to 37 cm. Average chest circumference ranges from 30 to 35 cm at birth. The circumference of the head is approximately 2 cm greater than the circumference of the chest at birth. Assessment Health Promotion and Maintenance Analysis
27.8 A new parent reports to the nurse that the baby looks cross-eyed several times a day. The nurse teaches the parents that this finding should resolve in: a. 2 months. b. 2 weeks. c. 1 year. d. 4 months.	Answer: d Rationale: The newborn might demonstrate transient strabismus caused by poor neuromuscular control of the eye muscles. This will gradually regress in 3 to 4 months. Implementation Health Promotion and Maintenance Application
27.9 A nurse is instructing a new mother on how to take an axillary temperature. The nurse knows the mother understands when she states that the thermometer should be held in place for: a. 1 minute. b. 3 minutes. c. 5 minutes. d. 10 minutes.	Answer: b Rationale: Axillary temperatures are the preferred method for assessing newborn temperature. The thermometer should remain in place for 3 minutes, unless an electronic thermometer is used. Evaluation Health Promotion and Maintenance Application

27.10 The nurse assesses the newborn's ears to be parallel to the outer and inner canthus of the eye. The nurse documents this finding to be:
a. a normal position.
b. a possible chromosomal abnormality.
c. facial paralysis.
d. prematurity.

Answer: a
Rationale: The top of the ear (pinna) should be parallel to the outer and inner canthus of the eye in the normal newborn. Low-set ears may indicate a chromosomal abnormality.
Assessment
Health Promotion and Maintenance
Application

27.11 The student nurse attempts to take the vital sign of the newborn, but the newborn is crying. What nursing intervention would be appropriate?
a. placing a gloved finger in the newborn's mouth.
b. taking the vital signs.
c. waiting until the newborn stops crying.
d. placing a hot water bottle in the isolette.

Answer: a
Rationale: To soothe a newborn during assessment or other procedures, place a gloved finger into the newborn's mouth. Crying will increase heart rate and respiratory rate so vitals should not be taken when the newborn is crying. Assessment of vitals needs to be done at regularly timed intervals so waiting until the newborn stops crying may be too long of a delay. A hot water bottle should not be placed next to the newborn because of a potential risk for burns.
Implementation
Health Promotion and Maintenance
Application

27.12 The nurse suspects clubfoot in the newborn. It is appropriate to:
a. adduct the foot and listen for a click.
b. move the foot to midline and determine resistance.
c. extend the foot and observe for pain.
d. dorsiflex the foot and release to observe for tremors.

Answer: b
Rationale: Clubfoot is suspected when the foot will not turn to a midline position or align readily. Adducting the foot and listening for a click is not an assessment that is done. Extending the foot and observing for pain will not determine or rule out clubfoot. Dorsiflexing the foot and releasing is an assessment that would show reflex status.
Assessment
Health Promotion and Maintenance
Application

27.13 A mother is concerned because the anterior fontanelle swells when the newborn cries. What would the nurse include in her teaching to a new mother about the normal findings concerning the fontanelles? (Select all that apply.)
a. The fontanelles may swell with crying.
b. The fontanelles may be depressed.
c. The fontanelles may pulsate with the heartbeat.
d. The fontanelles may bulge.
e. The fontanelles may swell when stool is passed.

Answers: a, c, e
Rationale: Newborn fontanelles can swell when the newborn cries or passes a stool, or can pulsate with the heartbeat; all of these findings are normal. Bulging fontanelles signify increased intracranial pressure, and depressed fontanelles indicate dehydration.
Implementation
Health Promotion and Maintenance
Application

27.14 The nurse assesses four newborns. Which assessment finding would place a newborn at risk for developing physiologic jaundice?
a. cephalhematoma.
b. Mongolian spots.
c. telangiectatic nevi.
d. molding.

Answer: a
Rationale: A cephalhematoma is a collection of blood resulting from ruptured blood vessels between the surface of a cranial bone and the periosteal membrane. The red blood cells present in the cephalhematoma begin to break down, which can lead to an increase in bilirubin levels in the blood. Mongolian spots are macular areas of bluish-black pigmentation on the dorsal area of the buttocks. Telangiectatic nevi are pale pink or red spots found on the eyelids, nose, lower occipital bone, or nape of the neck. Molding is caused by overriding of the cranial bones.
Assessment
Physiologic Integrity
Analysis

27.15 A mother of a 16-week-old infant calls the clinic and is concerned because she cannot feel the posterior fontanelle on her infant. Which of the responses by the nurse would be most appropriate?
a. "It is normal for the posterior fontanelle to close by 8 to12 weeks after birth."
b. "Bring your infant to the clinic immediately."
c. "This is due to overriding of the cranial bones during labor."
d. "Your baby must be dehydrated."

Answer: a
Rationale: This is a normal finding at 16 weeks. The posterior fontanelle closes within 8 to 12 weeks. Overriding of the cranial bones is referred to as molding and will diminish within a few days following birth. Fontanelles may be depressed when the infant is dehydrated.
Implementation
Health Promotion and Maintenance
Application

CHAPTER 28

28.1 The nurse is caring for a newborn who recently was circumcised. Which nursing intervention is appropriate following the procedure?
a. NPO for four hours following procedure.
b. observe for urine output.
c. wrap dry gauze tightly around the penis.
d. keep the newborn in the nursery for the next four hours.

Answer: b
Rationale: After a circumcision, it is important for the nurse to observe for the first voiding to evaluate for urinary obstruction related to penile injury and/or edema. The newborn does not need to be NPO, gauze should not be wrapped tightly around the penis, and the newborn can return to the mother's room.
Implementation
Health Promotion and Maintenance
Application

28.2 In planning care for a new family immediately after birth, which procedure would the nurse most likely withhold for one hour to allow time for the family to bond with the newborn?
a. eye prophylaxis medication.
b. drying the newborn.
c. vital signs.
d. vitamin K injection.

Answer: a
Rationale: Eye prophylaxis medication may be withheld for one hour following birth. This allows for eye contact between the newborn and the family, which enhances parent–newborn bonding. Vital signs and drying the newborn after birth are essential nursing interventions and should not be withheld. Vitamin K usually is given within one hour following birth, but will not interfere with eye contact between parent and newborn.
Planning
Health Promotion and Maintenance
Analysis

28.3 The nurse teaches the parents of an infant who recently was circumcised to observe for bleeding. What should the parents be taught to do if bleeding does occur?
a. wrap the diaper tightly.
b. remove the Vaseline dressing and observe in one hour.
c. apply gentle pressure to the site with gauze.
d. apply a new Vaseline gauze dressing.

Answer: c
Rationale: Bleeding is not normal after a circumcision. If bleeding occurs, the caregiver should use sterile gauze to apply gentle pressure at the bleeding site. It can't be observed for an hour because the bleeding may not stop spontaneously. Petroleum ointment (Vaseline gauze) helps protect the granulation tissue but won't stop any bleeding. When diapering, ensure that the diaper is not so tight as to cause pain.
Implementation
Health Promotion and Maintenance
Application

28.4 A nurse is instructing the nursing students about the procedure for vitamin K administration. What information should be included? (Select all that apply.)
a. gently massage the site after injection.
b. use a 22 gauge 1-inch needle.
c. inject in the vastus lateralis muscle.

Answers: a, c, d
Rationale: Vitamin K is given IM in the vastus lateralis muscle using a 25 gauge, 5/8-inch needle at a 90-degree angle. Aspirate, then slowly inject the solution, remove needle, and gently massage the site with an alcohol swab.
Implementation
Health Promotion and Maintenance
Application

d. cleanse site with alcohol prior to injection.
e. inject at a 45-degree angle.
f. do not aspirate.

28.5 A postpartum mother is concerned that her newborn has not had a stool since birth. The newborn is 18 hours old. The nurse's best response is: a. "I will call your pediatrician immediately." b. "Passage of the first stool within 48 hours is normal." c. "Your newborn may not have a stool until the third day." d. "Your newborn must be dehydrated."	Answer: b Rationale: The passage of the first stool within 48 hours is normal. Decreased urinary output and depressed fontanelles indicate dehydration. Implementation Health Promotion and Maintenance Application
28.6 The nurse is preparing a newborn for a circumcision. Which of the following data would be important for the nurse to report to the physician prior to the procedure? a. The mother took anticoagulants prenatally. b. The mother is breastfeeding the newborn. c. The newborn's Apgar scores were 8 and 9. d. The newborn has had six wet diapers within the last 12 hours.	Answer: a Rationale: Bleeding is a potential problem with circumcisions. A newborn may be susceptible to bleeding problems if the mother took anticoagulants during pregnancy. Apgar scores, breastfeeding, and six wet diapers are normal findings and would not affect circumcision. Planning Health Promotion and Maintenance Analysis
28.7 Appropriate nursing interventions for the application of erythromycin ophthalmic ointment (Ilotycin Ophthalmic) include: a. massaging eyelids gently following application. b. irrigating eyes after instillation. c. using a syringe to apply ointment. d. preceding instillation with irrigation.	Answer: a Rationale: The nurse squeezes the tube to instill the ointment into the lower conjunctival sac of each eye. Following application of Ilotycin Ophthalmic ointment, the eyelids should be massaged gently to distribute the ointment evenly. The eyes should not be irrigated before or after instillation. The ointment is not applied with a syringe. Implementation Health Promotion and Maintenance Application
28.8 The nurse assesses the newborn and the following behaviors are noted: nasal flaring, facial grimacing, and excessive mucus. The nurse is most concerned about: a. neonatal jaundice. b. polycythemia. c. neonatal hyperthermia. d. respiratory distress.	Answer: d Rationale: Nasal flaring, facial grimacing, and excessive mucus are signs of respiratory distress. A high bilirubin would be an indication of jaundice. An excess of red blood cells would be noted with polycythemia and a high temperature would indicate hyperthermia. Assessment Physiological Integrity Application
28.9 To promote infant security in the hospital, the nurse instructs the parents of a newborn to: a. keep the baby in the room at all times. b. check identification of all personnel who transport the newborn. c. place a "No Visitors" sign on the door. d. keep the baby in the nursery at all times.	Answer: b Rationale: Practicing safety measures and providing information to parents are important steps to prevent infant abduction. Parents should be instructed to check identification of all personnel who transport the newborn. Newborns will need to return to the nursery at times; therefore, following all safety procedures will increase the safety of all newborns during their hospital stay. A "No Visitors" sign would not assure safety. Implementation Safe, Effective Care Environment Application

28.10 A nurse is instructing a new mother on circumcision care with a Plastibell. The nurse knows the mother understands when she states that the Plastibell should fall off within: a. 2 days. b. 10 days. c. 8 days. d. 14 days.	Answer: a Rationale: The Plastibell should fall off within 8 days. The mother should be instructed to consult the physician if the Plastibell remains on longer than 8 days. Implementation Health Promotion and Maintenance Application
28.11 A new family decides not to have their newborn circumcised. What should the nurse teach regarding uncircumcised care? a. The foreskin will be retractable at 2 months. b. Retract the foreskin and clean thoroughly. c. Avoid retracting the foreskin. d. Use soap and Betadine to cleanse the penis daily.	Answer: c Rationale: The foreskin is not fully retractable until around the age of 3 to 5 years. When retraction has occurred, daily gentle washing of the glans with soap and water is sufficient. Implementation Health Promotion and Maintenance Application
28.12 A postpartum client calls the nursery to report that her newborn's umbilical cord stump is draining and has a foul order. The nurse's best response is: a. "Take your newborn to the pediatrician." b. "Cover the cord stump with gauze." c. "Apply Betadine around the cord stump." d. "This is normal during healing."	Answer: a Rationale: The nurse is responsible for instructing the parents on cord care and when to report problems. Signs and symptoms of infection around the umbilical stump include: foul smell, redness, drainage, localized heat and tenderness, or bleeding. These signs and symptoms should be reported to the physician. It is not recommended to cover the cord stump with gauze or the diaper. Betadine is not used on the cord stump. Implementation Health Promotion and Maintenance Application
28.13 The nurse is analyzing various teaching strategies that can be used to teach new mothers about newborn care. To enhance learning, which teaching method should the nurse implement? a. select videos on various topics of newborn care. b. organize a class that includes first-time mothers only. c. have mothers return in one week when they feel more rested. d. schedule time for one-to-one teaching in the mother's room.	Answer: d Rationale: The most effective educational method is one-to-one teaching while the nurse is in the mother's room. Individual teaching allows the nurse to answer specific questions. The other methods would not assure one-to-one teaching. Planning Health Promotion and Maintenance Analysis
28.14 The nurse has just assisted the father in bathing the newborn 2 hours after birth. The nurse explains to the father that the newborn must remain in the radiant warmer. This is based on which of the following assessment data? a. heart rate 120. b. temperature 96.8°F. ⌐36 c. respiratory rate 50. d. temperature 99.6°F. 37.5	Answer: b Rationale: After the first bath, the temperature is rechecked. If the temperature falls below 97.5°F, the nurse returns the newborn to the radiant warmer. The re-warming process is gradual, to prevent hypothermia. Heart rate and respiratory rate are within normal limits for a newborn 2 hours old. Evaluation Health Promotion and Maintenance Application

28.15 The nurse has instructed a new mother on quieting activities for her newborn. The nurse knows the mother understands when she overhears the mother tell the father to:
a. hold the newborn in an upright position.
b. massage the hands and feet.
c. swaddle the newborn in a blanket.
d. make eye contact while talking to the newborn.

Answer: c
Rationale: Swaddling (wrapping) the newborn in a blanket provides a sense of security, and is effective in quieting a crying baby. Massaging the hands and feet, holding the newborn upright, and talking to the newborn are waking activities.
Evaluation
Health Promotion and Maintenance
Application

CHAPTER 29

29.1 A new mother is concerned her newborn is not gaining enough weight. To encourage proper weight gain, the mother should be instructed to:
a. dilute formula with water.
b. offer 12 to 32 oz of formula every 24 hours.
c. offer formula every 6 to 8 hours.
d. provide skim milk exclusively.

Answer: b
Rationale: From birth to 2 months of age, the newborn should take between 6 to 8 feedings consisting of approximately 2 to 4 ounces of formula per 24 hours. When formula is overdiluted, the infant will not receive adequate nutrients to ensure proper weight gain. Formula-fed newborns should be fed every 3 to 4 hours but should not go longer than 4 hours between feedings. Skim milk should not be offered to newborns before 1 year of age.
Implementation
Health Promotion and Maintenance
Application

29.2 A nurse is demonstrating the proper steps for breastfeeding a newborn to a client. Put these steps in a logical order that would assist the client in placing the newborn to her breast.
a. tickle newborn's lips with the nipple.
b. bring newborn to breast.
c. newborn opens mouth wide.
d. have newborn face mother tummy to tummy.
e. position newborn so the newborn's nose is at level of the nipple.

Answer: e, d, a, c, b
Rationale: To facilitate successful breastfeeding, the nurse may encourage the mother to follow these steps: Position newborn so the newborn's nose is at level of the nipple; have newborn face mother tummy to tummy; tickle newborn's lips with the nipple; wait until newborn opens mouth wide; and then bring newborn to breast.
Implementation
Health Promotion and Maintenance
Application

29.3 A premature newborn is unable to suck at the breast. The nurse plans care for the mother and has arranged for the mother to use an electric pump at least:
a. two times in a 24-hour period.
b. four times in a 24-hour period.
c. six times in a 24-hour period.
d. eight times in a 24-hour period.

Answer: d
Rationale: An electric pump may be used at least eight times a day. This will help a new mother establish and increase her milk supply until the newborn can breastfeed.
Planning
Physiological Integrity
Application

29.4 A nurse is teaching a new mother how to encourage a sleepy baby to breastfeed. All of the following activities are taught except:
a. providing skin-to-skin contact.
b. swaddling the newborn in a blanket.
c. unwrapping the newborn.
d. allowing the newborn to feel and smell the mother's breast.

Answer: b
Rationale: Activities that encourage a sleepy newborn to breastfeed include: unwrapping the newborn; providing skin-to-skin contact between mother and newborn; and allowing the mother to rest with the newborn near her breast so the newborn can feel and smell the mother's breast.
Implementation
Health Promotion and Maintenance
Application

29.5 Which of the following mothers definitely should be counseled against breastfeeding?
a. a mother with a poorly balanced diet.
b. a mother who is overweight.
c. a mother who is HIV-positive.
d. a mother who has twins.

Answer: c
Rationale: Women with HIV or AIDS are counseled against breastfeeding. A newborn whose mother has a poor diet may need to receive supplements. Mothers who are overweight or have twins can be encouraged to breastfeed.
Planning
Physiological Integrity
Analysis

29.6 A mother states that her breasts leak between feedings. Which of the following may contribute to the letdown reflex in breastfeeding mothers?
a. pain with breastfeeding.
b. number of hours passed since last feeding.
c. the newborn's cry.
d. maternal fluid intake.

Answer: c
Rationale: A newborn's cry can stimulate the letdown reflex in breastfeeding mothers. Maternal fluid intake and too many hours between feeding can affect milk supply. Pain with breastfeeding is associated with improper positioning.
Diagnosis
Physiological Integrity
Application

29.7 When a breastfeeding mother complains that her breasts are leaking milk, the nurse could offer which effective intervention?
a. decrease the number of minutes the newborn is at the breast per feeding.
b. decrease the mother's fluid intake.
c. place absorbent pads in the bra.
d. administer oxytocin.

Answer: c
Rationale: Absorbent breast pads can be worn in the bra to help absorb secretions from leaking breasts during letdown. Decreasing the number of minutes the newborn is at the breast, decreasing fluid intake, and administering oxytocin would be contraindicated for a breastfeeding client.
Implementation
Physiological Integrity
Application

29.8 To thaw breast milk that has been frozen, parents should be taught to:
a. run cool water over the bottle.
b. use the microwave briefly.
c. place the bottle in boiling water.
d. place the bottle in the refrigerator for 24 hours.

Answer: a
Rationale: Initially run cool water over the container, then gradually add warm until the milk is thawed. Breast milk should not be thawed in hot or boiling water, in the refrigerator for an extended time (24 hours), or placed in the microwave.
Implementation
Physiological Integrity
Application

29.9 A nurse is evaluating the diet plan of a breastfeeding mother and determines her intake of fruits and vegetables is inadequate. Which of the following strategies would be recommended to the mother that would be beneficial for the newborn?
a. stop breastfeeding.
b. provide vitamin supplements to the newborn.
c. offer whole milk.
d. supplement with skim milk.

Answer: b
Rationale: The mother may continue to breastfeed, but the caregiver may choose to prescribe additional vitamins for the newborn. Whole milk and skim milk are not recommended during the first year of life.
Implementation
Physiological Integrity
Analysis

29.10 A triage nurse receives a call from a mother of an obese infant who appears pale, sweaty, and irritable. What data would the nurse need to gather next?
a. newborn's daily iron intake.
b. number of wet diapers a day.
c. skin color.
d. bilirubin level.

Answer: a
Rationale: An obese newborn who appears pale in color, diaphoretic, and irritable should be assessed for iron deficiency. The number of wet diapers a day would provide information concerning hydration. Skin color and bilirubin level would provide information about jaundice.
Assessment
Physiological Integrity
Analysis

29.11 The nurse encourages a new mother to feed the newborn as soon as the newborn shows interest. The nurse bases this recommendation on which of the following benefits of early feedings? (Select all that apply.)
a. Stimulates peristalsis.
b. Colostrum is thinner than mature milk.
c. Enhances maternal-infant attachment.
d. Decreases the risk of jaundice.
e. Colostrum contains a high amount of calories.

Answers: a, c, d
Rationale: Early breastfeeding stimulates peristalsis, decreases the risk of jaundice, and enhances maternal-infant attachment. Colostrum contains fewer calories than mature milk and is a yellowish or creamy-appearing fluid that is thicker than mature milk.
Implementation
Health Promotion and Maintenance
Analysis

29.12 A mother is concerned that her newborn doesn't appear to be alert enough to feed and is very irritable. Which of the following data documented in the mother's birth record might contribute to this newborn's behavior?
a. length of labor was eight hours.
b. epidural during labor.
c. blood pressure of 114/82
d. short second stage of labor.

Answer: b
Rationale: Some newborns whose mothers received epidurals in labor may experience a delay in normal feeding patterns. These newborns have been noted to be irritable and have decreased visual skills and alertness. A normal length of labor and normal vital signs during labor are not factors related to early feeding patterns.
Assessment
Health Promotion and Maintenance
Analysis

29.13 A nurse is performing an assessment on an infant whose mother states she props the bottle during feeding. Based on this information, what would the nurse include in her assessment?
a. otoscopic exam of the ear drum.
b. bowel sounds.
c. vital signs.
d. skin assessment.

Answer: a
Rationale: If the infant is fed horizontally, positional otitis media may develop. This is due to milk and nasal mucus blocking the eustachian tube. Assessment of the abdomen, skin, and vital signs is not affected by the position of the feeding.
Assessment
Physiological Integrity
Analysis

29.14 The nurse is assisting a mother to feed her newborn. The newborn has been crying. The nurse suggests that prior to feeding, the mother should:
a. offer a pacifier.
b. burp the newborn.
c. unwrap the newborn.
d. stroke the newborn's spine and feet.

Answer: b
Rationale: If a newborn has been crying prior to feeding, air might have been swallowed; therefore, the newborn should be burped before feeding. Time should be taken to calm the newborn prior to feeding. Unwrapping the newborn and stroking the spine and feet stimulate the newborn.
Implementation
Physiological Integrity
Application

29.15 The nurse is caring for a new breastfeeding mother who is from Pakistan. The nurse plans her care so that the newborn is offered the breast on the:
a. day of birth.
b. first day after birth.
c. second day after birth.
d. third to fourth day after birth.

Answer: d
Rationale: It is important for the nurse to understand the impact of culture on specific feeding practices. Women from Pakistan do not offer colostrum to their newborns. They begin breastfeeding only after the milk flow has been established, which typically occurs on the third to fourth day after birth.
Planning
Psychosocial Integrity
Application

30.1 A nurse is caring for a newborn of a diabetic mother. Which of the following should be included in the nurse's plan of care for this newborn?
a. offer more frequent feedings.
b. provide glucose water exclusively.
c. evaluate blood glucose levels at 12 hours after birth.
d. assess for hypothermia.

Answer: a
Rationale: Newborns of diabetic mothers can require more frequent feedings. If normal levels of glucose cannot be maintained, the newborn might require intravenous infusions of D10W, along with oral feedings, to maintain normoglycemia. Onset of hypoglycemia occurs 1 to 3 hours after birth. Blood glucose levels should be checked hourly during the first 4 hours and then at 4-hour intervals until the risk peak has passed. Hypothermia is more common in SGA newborns, due to diminished subcutaneous fat.
Planning
Physiological Integrity
Analysis

30.2 A 38-week newborn is found to be small for gestational age. Which of the following nursing interventions should be included in the care of this newborn?
a. monitor for feeding difficulties.
b. assess for facial paralysis.
c. monitor for signs of hyperglycemia.
d. maintain a warm environment.

Answer: d
Rationale: Hypothermia is a common complication of the SGA newborn, therefore, the newborn's environment must remain warm to decrease heat loss. SGA newborns are more prone to hypoglycemia. LGA newborns are more difficult to arouse to a quiet alert state and can have feeding difficulties. They often are prone to birth trauma, such as facial paralysis, due to cephalopelvic disproportion.
Implementation
Physiological Integrity: Reduction of Risk Potential
Analysis

30.3 A mother of a premature newborn questions why a gavage feeding catheter is placed in the mouth of the newborn and not in the nose. The nurse's best response is:
a. "Most newborns are nose breathers."
b. "The tube will elicit the sucking reflex."
c. "A smaller catheter is preferred for feedings."
d. "Most newborns are mouth breathers."

Answer: a
Rationale: Most newborns are nose breathers, therefore, an orogastric catheter is preferable. A small catheter is used for a nasogastric tube to minimize airway obstruction. Gavage feedings are used when newborns have a poorly coordinated suck, swallow reflex, or are ill.
Implementation
Physiological Integrity
Application

30.4 A nurse is analyzing assessment findings on four different newborns. Which assessment finding on a newborn might suggest a congenital heart defect?
a. apical heart rate of 140 beats per minute.
b. respiratory rate of 40.
c. acrocyanosis.
d. cyanosis of the buccal membranes.

Answer: d
Rationale: Cyanosis of the buccal membranes is not a normal finding in a newborn and could indicate a congenital heart defect. Apical heart rate of 140, respiratory rate of 40, and acrocyanosis (cyanosis of the extremities) are normal assessment findings for newborns.
Assessment
Physiological Integrity
Analysis

30.5 The nurse is caring for a newborn born to a drug-addicted mother. Which of the following assessment findings would be common for this newborn? (Select all that apply.)
a. hyperirritability.
b. decreased muscle tone.
c. exaggerated reflexes.
d. depressed respiratory effort.
e. transient tachypnea.

Answers: a, c, e
Rationale: Newborns born to drug-addicted mothers exhibit hyperirritability, exaggerated reflexes, and transient tachypnea.
Assessment
Physiological Integrity
Application

30.6 A 3-month-old, former 25-week premature baby has been exposed to prolonged oxygen therapy. Due to oxygen therapy, the nurse explains to the parents, their infant is at a higher risk for: a. visual impairment. b. hypercalcemia. c. cerebral palsy. d. sensitive gag reflex.	Answer: a Rationale: Premature infants are at greater risk for developing complications related to prolonged oxygen therapy, such as retinopathy, which can lead to visual impairment. Hypocalcemia is more common in premature infants, as is an absent or decreased gag reflex. Cerebral palsy may be due to decreased oxygen. Implementation Physiological Integrity Analysis
30.7 During discharge planning of a drug-dependent newborn, the nurse explains to the mother how to: a. place the newborn in a prone position. b. limit feedings to three a day to decrease diarrhea. c. place supine and operate a home apnea monitoring system. d. wean the newborn off the pacifier.	Answer: c Rationale: Drug-dependent newborns are at a higher risk for SIDS. Therefore, the newborn should sleep in a supine position, and a home apnea monitoring system should be implemented. A pacifier may be offered to provide non-nutritive sucking. Small, frequent feedings are recommended. Planning Physiological Integrity Application
30.8 A nurse is teaching the parents of a newborn who has been exposed to HIV how to care for the newborn at home. Which of the following instructions should the nurse emphasize? (Select all that apply.) a. proper handwashing techniques. b. provide three feedings per day. c. place soiled diapers in a sealed plastic bag. d. wear gloves when diapering. e. rectal temperatures are preferred.	Answers: a, c, d Rationale: The nurse should instruct the parents on proper handwashing techniques, on proper disposal of soiled diapers, and to wear gloves when diapering. Small, frequent meals are recommended. Taking rectal temperatures is to be avoided because it may stimulate diarrhea. Implementation Safe, Effective Care Environment Application
30.9 The nurse is teaching the parents of a PKU infant how to care for the infant at home. Teaching includes information about: a. special formulas for the infant. b. cataract problems. c. respiratory problems. d. administration of thyroid medication.	Answer: a Rationale: Teaching should include information about special diets that limit intake of phenylalanine. Special formulas low in phenylalanine include Lofenalac, Minafen, and Albumaid XP. The PKU infant exhibits signs of CNS damage if treatment is not begun by 1 month of age. Cataracts are associated with infants who have galactosemia. Thyroid medication is given to infants with congenital hypothyroidism. Implementation Physiological Integrity Application
30.10 The nurse is assessing a drug-dependent newborn. Which symptom would require further assessment by the nurse? a. occasional watery stools. b. spitting up after feeding. c. unrelieved irritability. d. positive Babinski's reflex.	Answer: c Rationale: Unrelieved irritability may be an indicator for drug withdrawal. An occasional watery stool, spitting up after some feeding, and a positive Babinski's reflex can be associated with the normal newborn. Assessment Physiological Integrity Analysis
30.11 In planning care for the fetal alcohol syndrome (FAS) newborn, which of the following interventions would the nurse include? a. allow extra time with feedings. b. assign different personnel to the newborn each day. c. place the newborn in a well-lit room. d. monitor for hyperthermia.	Answer: a Rationale: Newborns with fetal alcohol syndrome have feeding problems and are prone to heat loss; therefore, extra time and patience are needed for feeding. Provide consistency of staff when working with the newborn and keep environmental stimuli to a minimum. Planning Physiological Integrity Application

30.12 A NICU nurse plans care for a preterm newborn that will provide opportunities for development. Which of the following interventions support development of a preterm newborn in a NICU? (Select all that apply.)
a. schedule care throughout the day.
b. silence alarms quickly.
c. place a blanket over the top portion of the incubator.
d. do not offer a pacifier.
e. dim lights.

Answers: b, c, e
Rationale: Silencing alarms quickly, placing a blanket over the top portion of the incubator, and dimming the lights are supportive interventions that can support development of a preterm newborn. Care should be clustered to minimize the number of times the newborn is disturbed. Pacifiers can be offered because they provide opportunities for non-nutritive sucking.
Implementation
Physiological Integrity
Application

30.13 The nurse is caring for a 2-hour-old newborn whose mother is diabetic. The nurse assesses that the newborn is experiencing tremors. What nursing action has the highest priority?
a. obtain a blood calcium level.
b. take the newborn's temperature.
c. obtain a bilirubin level.
d. place a pulse oximeter on the newborn.

Answer: a
Rationale: Tremors are the classical sign for hypocalcemia. Diabetic mothers tend to have decreased serum magnesium levels at term. This could cause secondary hypoparathyroidism in the infant. Bilirubin level, body temperature, and oxygen saturation also might be necessary to monitor but do not present with tremors in the newborn.
Implementation
Physiological Integrity
Analysis

30.14 A nurse assesses the gestational age of a newborn. She explains to the parents that the newborn is premature. All of the following assessment findings are congruent with prematurity except:
a. cry is weak and feeble.
b. clitoris and labia minora are prominent.
c. strong sucking reflex.
d. lanugo is plentiful.

Answer: c
Rationale: Assessment findings that indicate prematurity include weak cry, lanugo that is plentiful and widely distributed, and a prominent clitoris and labia minora. A strong sucking reflex is found in normal term newborns.
Assessment
Physiological Integrity
Analysis

30.15 Interventions provided by the nurse caring for a post-term newborn can include all of the following except:
a. provision of warmth.
b. frequent monitoring of blood glucose.
c. observation of respiratory status.
d. restriction of breastfeeding.

Answer: d
Rationale: Provision of warmth, frequent monitoring of blood glucose, and observation of respiratory status are important interventions for post-term newborns. These interventions can help prevent common complications such as hypoglycemia, cold stress, and hypoxia. Breastfeeding is encouraged.
Implementation
Physiological Integrity
Application

CHAPTER 31

31.1 The visiting nurse evaluates a 2-day-old breastfed newborn at home and notes the baby appears jaundiced. When explaining jaundice to the parents, the nurse would tell them:
a. "Jaundice is nothing to worry about."
b. "Some newborns require phototherapy."
c. "Jaundice is a medical emergency."
d. "Jaundice is always a sign of liver disease."

Answer: b
Rationale: Physiologic jaundice is a normal process that may occur after 24 hours of life in about half of healthy newborns. It is not a sign of liver disease. Physiological jaundice may require phototherapy.
Implementation
Physiological Integrity
Application

31.2 A nurse explains to new parents that their newborn has developed respiratory distress syndrome (RDS). The nurse bases this assessment on all of the following data except: a. grunting respirations. b. nasal flaring. c. respiratory rate of 40 during sleep. d. chest retractions.	Answer: c Rationale: Respiratory rate of 40 during sleep is normal. Grunting with respirations, nasal flaring, and chest retractions are characteristics of RDS. Assessment Physiological Integrity Application
31.3 A client in labor is found to have meconium-stained amniotic fluid upon rupture of membranes. At delivery, the nurse anticipates that the priority nursing intervention is to: a. deliver the neonate on its side with head up, to facilitate drainage of secretions. b. suction the oropharynx when the newborn's head is delivered. c. prepare for the immediate use of positive pressure to expand the lungs. d. monitor the client's temperature.	Answer: b Rationale: After the birth of the head, while the shoulders and chest are still in the birth canal, the newborn's oropharynx is suctioned by the birth attendant. The newborn is not delivered on its side, positive pressure is not used to expand lungs, and the client's temperature has nothing to do with meconium-stained amniotic fluid. Planning Safe, Effective Care Environment Application
31.4 The nurse is evaluating the effectiveness of phototherapy on a newborn. Which of the following evaluations indicate a therapeutic response to phototherapy? a. normal temperature is maintained by the newborn. b. bilirubin level of 14 mg/dL. c. decreased reflexes. d. skin blanches yellow.	Answer: a Rationale: Expected outcomes of phototherapy include normal temperature readings, bilirubin levels less than 6 mg/dL, normal reflexes, and skin that does not appear yellow. Evaluation Physiological Integrity Analysis
31.5 The parents of a preterm newborn desire to visit their baby in the NICU. All of the following statements by the nurse will support the parents as they visit their newborn except: a. "Your newborn likes to be touched." b. "Stroking the newborn will help with stimulation." c. "Visits must be scheduled between feedings." d. "Your baby loves her pink blanket."	Answer: c Rationale: Statements that encourage the parents to touch and stroke the newborn will help parents become more familiar and bond with their preterm newborn. Comments that personalize the baby will tell the parents their baby is unique and special. The nurse always should encourage parents to visit and get to know their newborn, even in the NICU. Implementation Psychosocial Integrity Application
31.6 The nurse prepares to admit to the nursery a newborn whose mother had meconium-stained amniotic fluid. The nurse knows this newborn may require: a. initial resuscitation. b. vigorous stimulation at birth. c. phototherapy immediately. d. an initial feeding of iron-enriched formula.	Answer: a Rationale: Newborns who have aspirated meconium may require resuscitation to establish adequate respiratory effort. Stimulation at birth should be avoided to minimize respiratory movements. Phototherapy is not required immediately. Typically, bilirubin levels rise after the first 24 hours of life. Oral feedings may be withheld until respirations are normal. The newborn might require intravenous fluids. Planning Physiological Integrity Application

31.7 The nurse notes that a 36-hour-old newborn's serum bilirubin level is 14 mg/dL. What nursing intervention would be included in the plan of care for this newborn?
a. continue to observe.
b. begin phototherapy.
c. begin blood exchange transfusion.
d. stop breastfeeding.

Answer: b
Rationale: Physiological jaundice is normal but will need to be treated and might require phototherapy. Newborns may continue to breastfeed. Newborns with a bilirubin of 20 mg/dL or above might need an exchange transfusion.
Implementation
Physiological Integrity
Analysis

31.8 Which of the following assessment findings by the nurse would require obtaining a blood glucose level on the newborn?
a. jitteriness of the newborn.
b. newborn sucking on fingers.
c. lusty cry.
d. axillary temperature of 98.

Answer: a
Rationale: Jitteriness of the newborn is associated with hypoglycemia and would require close monitoring of blood glucose levels. Sucking on fingers, lusty cry, and axillary temperature of 98 are all normal findings.
Evaluation
Physiological Integrity
Application

31.9 A newborn is receiving phototherapy. Which intervention would be most important?
a. measurement of head circumference.
b. encouraging the mother to stop breastfeeding.
c. stool guaiac testing.
d. assessment of hydration status.

Answer: d
Rationale: Newborns being treated for jaundice experience a fluid volume deficit due to an increase in insensible water loss and frequent loose stools. Phototherapy does not alter head circumference. Breastfeeding most likely can be continued, and the stools do not need to be tested for blood (guaiac testing).
Implementation
Physiological Integrity
Application

31.10 The nurse is caring for a newborn with jaundice. The parents question why the newborn is not under the phototherapy lights. The nurse explains that the fiber optic blanket is beneficial because: (Select all that apply.)
a. lights can stay on all of the time.
b. the eyes do not need to be covered.
c. the lights will need to be removed for feedings.
d. newborns do not get overheated.
e. weight loss is not a complication of this system.

Answers: a, b, d, e
Rationale: Benefits of the fiber optic blanket are that newborns do not get overheated, weight loss is not a complication of this system, the eyes do not have to be covered, and the lights can stay on all of the time.
Implementation
Physiological Integrity
Application

31.11 During newborn resuscitation, effectiveness of bag and mask ventilations can be determined by:
a. the rise and fall of the chest.
b. sudden wakefulness.
c. urinary output.
d. adequate thermoregulation.

Answer: a
Rationale: With proper resuscitation, effectiveness is observed by visualizing the rise and fall of the chest. Sudden wakefulness, urinary output, and adequate thermoregulation are not associated with effectiveness of bag and mask ventilations.
Assessment
Physiological Integrity
Analysis

31.12 A nurse is caring for a newborn on a ventilator who has respiratory distress syndrome (RDS). The nurse informs the parents that the newborn is improving. Which of the following data supports the nurse's assessment?
a. decreased urination.
b. pulmonary vascular resistance increases.
c. increased P_{CO_2}.
d. increased urination.

Answer: d
Rationale: Increased urination may be an indication that the newborn's condition is improving. As fluid moves out of the lungs and into the bloodstream, alveoli open and kidney perfusion increases, thereby increasing urine output. Pulmonary vascular resistance increases with hypoxia. Increased P_{CO_2} results from alveolar hypoventilation.
Assessment
Physiological Integrity
Analysis

31.13 A nursing instructor is demonstrating how to perform a heel stick on a newborn. To obtain an accurate capillary hematocrit reading, the nursing instructor tells the students to:
a. warm the heel prior to obtaining blood.
b. use a previous puncture site.
c. cool the heel prior to obtaining blood.
d. use a sterile needle and aspirate.

Answer: a
Rationale: The heel is warmed prior to obtaining the blood. This will help to decrease falsely high values. A microlance is used for puncture in an unpunctured site.
Implementation
Physiological Integrity
Application

31.14 Antibiotics have been ordered for a newborn with an infection. Which of the following interventions would the nurse prepare to implement? (Select all that apply.)
a. obtain skin cultures.
b. restrict parental visits.
c. evaluate bilirubin levels.
d. administer oxygen as ordered.
e. observe for signs of hypoglycemia.

Answers: a, c, d, e
Rationale: The nurse will encourage parents to visit and implement the following: Assist in obtaining skin cultures, evaluate bilirubin levels, administer oxygen as ordered, and observe for signs of hypoglycemia.
Implementation
Physiological Integrity
Application

31.15 The nurse assesses that a newborn's skin has a ruddy appearance and the peripheral pulses are decreased. The nurse suspects polycythemia. Which of the following lab reports might indicate that the newborn has polycythemia?
a. venous hemoglobin level greater than 26 g/dL.
b. bilirubin level of 6 mg/dL.
c. venous hemoglobin level less than 12 g/dL.
d. blood glucose level of 44 mg/dL.

Answer: a
Rationale: A venous hemoglobin level greater than 26 g/dL indicates polycythemia. A venous hemoglobin level less than 12 g/dL indicates anemia. Bilirubin level and blood glucose levels are within normal range.
Analysis
Physiological Integrity: Reduction of Risk Potential
Analysis

CHAPTER 32

32.1 A postpartum family desires to return home 24 hours after birth. Which of the following newborn criteria would require a longer hospital stay?
a. gestational age of 38 weeks AGA.
b. one stool passed, urination documented.
c. one feeding with documented proper sucking, swallowing, and breathing.
d. choice of pediatrician and follow-up plan of care documented.

Answer: c
Rationale: One feeding with documented proper sucking, swallowing, and breathing is not enough time to determine if the infant and/or mother will have any problems. It may take longer than 2 days to develop and identify any problems. Breastfeeding may not be well established prior to 48 hours, and problems can lead to dehydration and poor breastfeeding. Gestational age of 38 weeks AGA, one stool passed and urination documented, and the choice of pediatrician and follow-up plan of care being documented are not reasons to require a longer hospital stay.
Assessment
Health Promotion and Maintenance
Application

32.2 Which of the following safety devices is most appropriate for the nurse making home visits?
a. personal handgun.
b. cellular phone.
c. can of mace.
d. map of the area.

Answer: b
Rationale: Cellular phones provide a means of contact and are advisable for the nurse to carry. A map of the area should be checked before leaving for a visit, and the route traced. Personal handguns and a mace are not permissible or legal for nurses to carry on home visits.
Planning
Safe, Effective Care Environment
Application

32.3 To prevent sudden infant death syndrome (SIDS), the nurse encourages the parents of a term infant to place the infant in what position when the infant is sleeping? a. on the parents' waterbed. b. swaddled in the infant swing. c. on his back. d. on his stomach.	Answer: c Rationale: On his back is correct. Research has shown that sleeping on the back decreases the risk of SIDS. On the parents' waterbed, on the stomach, or swaddled in the infant swing can increase the risks of SIDS. Implementation Health Promotion and Maintenance Application
32.4 The nurse understands that the infant's position should be changed periodically during the early months of life to prevent: a. muscle contractures. b. respiratory distress. c. permanently flattened areas of the skull. d. esophageal reflux.	Answer: c Rationale: Permanently flattened areas of the skull can occur if the infant is consistently in one position because the skull bones are soft in the early months of life. Muscle contractures would not occur with periodic changing of the infant's position. Respiratory distress and esophageal reflux would indicate complications and may not be affected by periodic position changes. Implementation Health Promotion and Maintenance Application
32.5 A new mother asks the nurse how to trim her newborn's fingernails. The nurse instructs the mother to: a. use blunt-ended cuticle scissors to shorten the nails. b. use fingernail clippers to shorten the nails. c. let the nails grow until the newborn is 4 weeks old. d. bring the newborn to the pediatrician to have the nails trimmed.	Answer: a Rationale: Using blunt-ended cuticle scissors to shorten the nails is important because the infant fingernails are very soft and can adhere to the skin of the fingers. A blunt-ended scissors would prevent cutting the skin. Use of fingernail clippers to shorten the nails is not recommended, as they might cut the skin. Letting the nails grow and bringing the newborn to the pediatrician are not appropriate responses. Implementation Physiological Integrity Application
32.6 A nurse is making a postpartum visit to a family. The new father asks the nurse if it is all right to take the baby to the river this weekend. The nurse encourages the father to: a. cover the infant with dark blankets to block the sun. b. protect the infant with light clothing. c. uncover the infant's head to prevent hyperthermia. d. avoid taking the infant outdoors for six months.	Answer: b Rationale: Protecting the infant with light clothing is enough to prevent overheating and sun-damaging effects. Covering the infant with dark blankets to block the sun would cause overheating and is not necessary. Uncovering the infant's head to prevent hyperthermia could actually cause hypothermia because infants lose much of their body heat through the head. Avoiding taking the infant outdoors for six months is not necessary or practical. Implementation Safe, Effective Care Environment Application
32.7 A postpartum client calls the telephone triage nurse and reports that her 2-month-old infant has a fever. She asks the nurse what to give the baby. The nurse suggests: a. Tylenol. b. aspirin. c. Advil. d. Motrin.	Answer: a Rationale: Tylenol is the medication recommended by pediatricians for its antipyretic action, and also because it has a minimum of side effects in the proper form and dose. Aspirin, while also an antipyretic, has many other actions and side effects and would not be recommended. Advil and Motrin are similar nonsteroidal anti-inflammatory drugs (NSAIDS) and are not recommended for infants. Implementation Physiological Integrity Application

32.8 The nurse teaches the breastfeeding mother that the newborn may have one stool every few days due to: a. fluid loss through diaphoresis. b. high fiber content of breast milk. c. decreased fluid intake in breastfeeding infants. d. increased digestibility of breast milk.	Answer: d Rationale: Increased digestibility of breast milk causes infants to have one stool every few days. Fluid loss through diaphoresis and decreased fluid intake in breastfeeding infants are usually caused by illness. Breast milk does not have a high fiber component. Implementation Health Promotion and Maintenance Application
32.9 A parent is concerned about spoiling her newborn. The telephone triage nurse teaches the mother that: a. newborns can be manipulative, so caution is advised. b. meeting the infant's needs develops a trusting relationship. c. spoiling occurs when an infant is rocked to sleep every night. d. crying is good for a baby, and letting them cry it out is advised.	Answer: b Rationale: Meeting the infant's needs develops a trusting relationship. Picking babies up when they cry teaches them that adults try to meet their needs and are responsive to them. This helps build a sense of trust in humankind. Newborns can be manipulative so caution is advised, spoiling occurs when an infant is rocked to sleep every night and crying is good for a baby and letting the infant cry it out is advised are incorrect. Implementation Psychosocial Integrity Application
32.10 The breastfeeding postpartum client reports sore nipples to the nurse making a home visit. The assessment with the highest priority is: a. infant positioning. b. use of the breast shield. c. use of breast pads. d. type of soap used.	Answer: a Rationale: Infant positioning is a critical factor in nipple soreness. Changing positions alters the focus of greatest stress and promotes more complete breast emptying. Use of the breast shield, use of breast pads, and type of soap used are not critical factors in nipple soreness. Assessment Physiological Integrity Application
32.11 The new mother hesitantly asks the nurse at the six-week postpartum visit about resumption of sexual activity. To promote comfort, the nurse suggests: a. the female superior position. b. using Vaseline for lubrication. c. the male superior position. d. douching before and after, to avoid infection.	Answer: a Rationale: The female superior position puts the least amount of pressure against the healing perineum, and creates more control of movement for the woman. Using Vaseline for lubrication is not recommended. KY jelly is the recommended lubricant. The male superior position creates more pressure on the perineum, and douching before and after to avoid infection is never recommended. Implementation Health Promotion and Maintenance Application
32.12 A nurse is teaching a class on newborn safety. The nurse knows a parent needs further teaching when she states: a. "I will place my baby to sleep on his back." b. "I have removed all the pillows from the crib." c. "I plan to air the baby's room daily." d. "I have a down comforter for the baby."	Answer: d Rationale: The baby should not be covered with blankets, sheets, or down comforters. It is appropriate to place the baby to sleep on his or her back, to remove pillows from the crib, and to assure plenty of ventilation (air the room on a daily basis) to the infant. Evaluation Health Promotion and Maintenance Analysis
32.13 The nurse is teaching new parents about sponge baths for their infants. Put the following actions in the order in which they would be done in a sponge bath. a. wet the chest, back, and arms with a washcloth.	Answer: c, b, a, d, e Rationale: The correct way of proceeding with a sponge bath is to start with the cleanest area first, which is the eyes, and then proceed in a cephalocaudal manner. Implementation Health Promotion and Maintenance Application

b. wash the ears and the remainder of the baby's face. c. gently wipe each eye from inner to outer corner. d. cleanse the genital area with soap and water. e. wash the hair using a small amount of mild shampoo.	
32.14 The newborn demonstrates several different sleep-wake states after the initial periods of reactivity. The nurse assessing a newborn notes that the infant has regular breathing and no movement except for sudden body jerks. The nurse documents this state as: a. light sleep. b. quiet alert. c. active alert. d. deep sleep.	Answer: d Rationale: Deep sleep is characterized by regular breathing and no movement. Normal household noise will not awaken the infant. Quiet alert and active alert are both characterized by involvement with the environment, moving, and smiling. Light sleep is characterized by irregular breathing and fine muscular twitching. Diagnosis Psychosocial Integrity Application
32.15 Before a newborn and mother are discharged from the hospital, the nurse informs the parents about the normal screening tests for newborns. Which of the following reasons are good ones for having the screening test done? a. The tests will prevent infants from developing phenylketonuria. b. The tests will detect such disorders as hypertension and diabetes. c. The tests will detect disorders that cause mental retardation, physical handicaps, or death if left undiscovered. d. The tests will prevent sickle cell anemia and galactosemia.	Answer: c Rationale. The normal screening tests for newborns are done to detect disorders that cause mental retardation, physical handicaps, or death if left undiscovered. The testing will not prevent any disorders, and will not detect hypertension or diabetes. Planning Physiological Integrity Application

CHAPTER 33

33.1 While in the pediatrician's office for their child's 12-month well child exam, the parents ask the nurse for advice on age-appropriate toys for their child. Based on the child's developmental level, the nurse should suggest which types of toys? (Select all that apply.) a. soft toys that can be manipulated and mouthed. b. toys that can pop apart and go back together. c. jack-in-the-box toys. d. toys with black-and-white patterns. e. push-and-pull toys.	Answers: b, c, e Rationale: Both gross and fine motor skills are becoming more developed, and children at this age enjoy toys that can help them refine these skills. They tend to enjoy more colorful toys at this age and are more mobile, thus they have less interest in placing toys in their mouth and more interest in toys that can be manipulated. Implementation Health Promotion and Maintenance Application
33.2 A mother of a 6-year-old boy who recently had surgery for the removal of his tonsils and adenoids complains that he has begun sucking his thumb again. The nurse caring for the child should assure the mother that this is a normal	Answer: c Rationale: The correct answer is *regression*, which is a return to an earlier behavior. Repression is the involuntary forgetting of uncomfortable situations, rationalization is an attempt to make unacceptable feelings acceptable, and fantasy is a creation of the mind to help deal with an unacceptable fear.

response for a child who has undergone surgery, and that it is a coping mechanism that children use called: a. repression. b. rationalization. c. regression. d. fantasy.	Diagnosis Psychosocial Integrity Application
33.3 While being comforted in the emergency room, the 7-year-old sibling of a pediatric trauma victim blurts out to the nurse, "It's all my fault! When we were fighting yesterday, I told him I wished he was dead!" The nurse, realizing that the child is experiencing magical thinking, should respond by: a. asking the child if he would like to sit down and drink some water. b. sitting the child down in an empty room with markers and paper so that he can draw a picture. c. calmly discussing the catheters, tubes, and equipment that the client requires, and explaining to the sibling why the client needs them. d. reassuring the child that it is normal to get angry and say things that we do not mean, but that we have no control over whether an accident happens.	Answer: d Rationale: Magical thinking is the belief that events occur because of one's thoughts or actions, and the most therapeutic way to respond to this is to correct any misconceptions that the child may have and reassure him that he is not to blame for any accident or illness. The other options would not be therapeutic at this time. Implementation Psychosocial Integrity Application
33.4 While analyzing the development of a 9-month-old infant, the nurse asks the mother if the child actively looks for toys when they are placed out of sight. The nurse is determining if the infant has developed: a. object permanence. b. centration. c. transductive reasoning. d. conservation.	Answer: a Rationale: A child who has developed object permanence has the ability to understand that even though something is out of sight, it still exits. Centration is when a child focuses only on one particular aspect of a situation. Transductive reasoning is when a child connects two events in a cause–effect relationship because they have occurred at the same time. Conservation is when a child knows that matter is not changed when its form is altered. Diagnosis Health Promotion and Maintenance Analysis
33.5 Utilizing Urie Bronfenbrenner's ecologic theory of development, the nurse caring for a child would discuss the parents' work environment as part of an assessment of that child's: a. macrosystem. b. exosystem. c. mesosystem. d. chronosystem.	Answer: b Rationale: A child's exosystem is composed of the settings that influence a child even though she is not in daily contact with that system. Political and cultural beliefs comprise a child's macrosystem, the relationships of one microsystem to another involve a child's mesosystem, and the chronosystem involves the perspective of time in the child's life. Assessment Health Promotion and Maintenance Application
33.6 The parents of a 1-month-old infant are concerned that this baby seems different from their other child and ask the nurse if this is normal. The nurse informs them that it is normal for babies to have different temperaments, and that according to the temperament theory of Stella Chess and Alexander	Answer: c Rationale: "Slow-to-warm-up" children adapt slowly to new situations and initially will withdraw. Showing regularity in patterns of eating is a characteristic of an "easy" child, and displaying a predominantly negative mood and commonly having intense reactions to the environment are characteristics of "difficult" children. Implementation Health Promotion and Maintenance Application

Thomas, one of the characteristics of the "slow-to-warm-up" child is that he: a. shows a regularity in patterns of eating. b. displays a predominately negative mood. c. initially reacts to new situations by withdrawing. d. commonly has intense reactions to the environment.	
33.7 While counseling the parents of a 6½-month-old infant, the most appropriate toy for the nurse to suggest would be a: a. soft, fluid-filled ring that can be chilled in the refrigerator. b. colorful rattle. c. "jack-in-the-box" toy. d. push-and-pull toy.	Answer: a Rationale: Teething toys would be appropriate for this age. The rattle might be better enjoyed by a 3- to 6-month-old infant, and the "jack-in-the-box" and push-and-pull toys are better suited for a 9- to 12-month-old child. Implementation Health Promotion and Maintenance Application
33.8 A nurse is assessing language development in all the infants presenting at the doctor's office for well child visits. The child that would be expected to be verbalizing the words "dada" and "mama" is the child between the ages of: a. 3 to 5 months. b. 6 to 8 months. c. 9 to 12 months. d. 13 to 18 months.	Answer: c Rationale: A child should be able to verbalize "mama" or "dada" to identify her parents by 1 year of age. Evaluation Health Promotion and Maintenance Analysis
33.9 Prior to giving an intramuscular injection to a 2½-year-old child, the most appropriate statement by the nurse would be: a. "We will give you your shot when your mommy comes back." b. "This is medicine that will make you better. First we will hold your leg, then I will wipe it off with this magic cloth that kills the germs on your leg right here, then I will hold the needle like this and say 'one, two, three … go' and give you your shot. Are you ready?" c. "It is all right to cry, I know that this hurts. After we are done you can go to the box and pick out your favorite sticker." d. "This is a magic sword that will give you your medicine and make you all better."	Answer: c Rationale: The most appropriate response would be to acknowledge the child's feelings and give her something to look forward to (picking out a sticker). Waiting for the mother to come back would be inappropriate because toddlers do not have an understanding of time. Giving elaborate descriptions and using colorful language are inappropriate. The instructions should not end with a "are you ready" statement because the toddler will say no. You also don't want to frighten and/or confuse the child by using statements such as use of a magic sword. Planning Health Promotion and Maintenance Application
33.10 While planning a lecture on healthy lifestyle choices for a high school class, the school nurse should be aware that the following statement is most supported by current research: a. children with lower self-efficacy scores tend to have a lower consumption of high-fat foods.	Answer: c Rationale: Current research supports the validity of the statement, "children with lower self-efficacy scores have been associated with more frequent violent behaviors than have children with higher self-efficacy scores." Research findings contradict the other statements. Planning Health Promotion and Maintenance Analysis

b. the most effective way to prevent or lower obesity rates in adolescents is to present them with facts about dietary intake.
c. children with lower self-efficacy scores have been associated with more frequent violent behaviors than children with higher self-efficacy scores.
d. approaches that address choices, consciousness, efficacy, and behavioral factors are unlikely to encourage adaptation of healthy lifestyles in adolescents.

33.11 Two 3-year-olds are playing in a hospital playroom together. One is working on a puzzle while the other is stacking blocks. The mother of one of the children scolds them for not sharing their toys. The nurse counsels this mother that this is normal developmental behavior for this age, and that the term for it is:
a. cooperative play.
b. associative play.
c. parallel play.
d. solitary play.

Answer: c
Rationale: Parallel play is when two or more children play together, each engaging in his own activities. Cooperative play is when children demonstrate the ability to cooperate with others and to play a part in order to contribute to a unified whole. Associative play is characterized by children interacting in groups and participating in similar activities. Solitary play is when a child plays alone.
Implementation
Health Promotion and Maintenance
Application

33.12 A neonatal nurse who encourages parents to hold their baby and provides opportunities for Kangaroo Care most likely is demonstrating concern for which aspect of the infant's psychosocial development?
a. attachment.
b. assimilation.
c. centration.
d. resilience.

Answer: a
Rationale: Attachment is a strong emotional bond between a parent and child that forms the foundation for the fulfillment of the basic need of trust in the infant. Assimilation describes the child's incorporation of new experiences, centration is the ability to consider only one aspect of a situation at a time, and resilience is the ability to maintain healthy function even under significant stress and adversity.
Implementation
Psychosocial Integrity
Application

33.13 The nurse, talking with the parents of a toddler who is struggling with toilet training, reassures them that their child is demonstrating a typical developmental stage that Erikson described as:
a. "trust versus mistrust."
b. "autonomy versus shame and doubt."
c. "initiative versus guilt."
d. "industry versus inferiority."

Answer: b
Rationale: Erikson's stage of "autonomy versus shame and doubt" marks a period of time when the toddler is trying to gain some independence while still wanting to please adults.
Implementation
Health Promotion and Maintenance
Application

33.14 A 14-year-old with cystic fibrosis suddenly becomes noncompliant with the medication regime. The intervention by the nurse that would most likely improve compliance would be to:
a. give the child a computer-animated game that presents information on the management of cystic fibrosis.
b. arrange for the physician to sit down and talk to the child about the risks related to noncompliance with medications.

Answer: c
Rationale: Providing an adolescent with positive role models who are in her peer group is the intervention most likely to improve compliance. Interest in games may begin to wane, adults' opinions may be viewed negatively and challenged, and threatening punishment may further incite rebellion.
Planning
Health Promotion and Maintenance
Application

---

c. set up a meeting with some older teens with cystic fibrosis who have been managing their disease effectively.

d. discuss with the child's parents the privileges that can be taken away, such as cell phone, if compliance fails to improve.

33.15 While trying to inform a 5-year-old girl about what will occur during an upcoming CAT scan, the nurse notices that the child is engaged in a collective monologue, talking about a new puppy. The nurse's best response would be:

a. "Please stop talking about your puppy. I need to tell you about your CT scan."

b. Ignore the child's responses and continue discussing the procedure.

c. "I'll come back when you are ready to talk with me more about your CT scan."

d. "You must be so excited to have a new puppy! They are so much fun. Now let me tell you again about going downstairs in a wheelchair to a special room."

Answer: d
Rationale: When a child becomes engaged in a collective monologue, it is best to respond to the content of her conversation and then attempt to reinsert facts about the content that needs to be covered.
Implementation
Health Promotion and Maintenance
Application

CHAPTER 34

34.1 A 6-year-old, recently diagnosed with asthma, also has a peanut allergy. The nurse instructs the family to not only avoid peanuts, but also to check food label ingredients carefully for peanut products and to make sure dishes and utensils are adequately washed prior to food preparation. The mother asks why this is specific for her child. The nurse should reply that in comparison with other children, this child has a higher risk for:

a. urticaria.

b. diarrhea.

c. anaphylaxis.

d. headache.

Answer: c
Rationale: Children with food allergies can experience all of the listed reactions to a particular food, but the child who also has asthma is most at risk for death secondary to anaphylaxis caused by a food allergy.
Implementation
Physiological Integrity
Application

34.2 The mother of a premature infant born at 32 weeks' gestation expresses the desire to breastfeed her child. An appropriate suggestion by the nurse would be:

a. "Mothers who cannot directly breastfeed should talk with and stroke their infants during gavage feedings, as this can help facilitate milk letdown."

b. "The letdown reflex is best initiated by having the baby suck at the breast."

c. "Pumping should be done no more than three times daily, making sure to empty each breast completely."

Answer: d
Rationale: It is best for the mother to initiate the letdown reflex by stimulating the breast prior to feeding so that the infant will not have to suck as hard, which can burn unnecessary calories. Breast pumping should be done at least five or more times per day to ensure an adequate supply of milk. The sooner the mother can begin breast pumping postpartum, the more likely she is to produce an adequate milk supply.
Implementation
Health Promotion and Maintenance
Application

---

d. "The mother should begin pumping by six hours postpartum to ensure adequate milk production."	
34.3 While teaching the parents of a newborn about infant care and feeding, the nurse instructs the parents to: a. delay supplemental foods until the infant is 4 to 6 months old. b. delay supplemental foods until the infant reaches 15 pounds or greater. c. begin diluted fruit juice at 2 months of age but wait 3 to 5 days before trying a new food. d. add rice cereal to the nighttime feeding if the infant is having difficulty sleeping after 2 months of age.	Answer: a Rationale: Four to 6 months is the optimal age to begin supplemental feedings because earlier feeding of non-formula foods is not needed by the infant and does not promote sleep. Earlier feeding of non-formula foods, regardless of the infant's weight, is more likely to cause the development of food allergies and is not well tolerated by infants because the necessary tongue control is not well developed and they lack the digestive enzymes to take in and metabolize many food products. Implementation Health Promotion and Maintenance Application
34.4 During a 4-month-old's well child checkup, the nurse discusses introduction of solid foods into the infant's diet and concerns for foods commonly associated with food allergies. Therefore, the parents are instructed to delay until after 1 year of age introduction of: a. strawberries, eggs, and wheat. b. honey, tomatoes, and spinach. c. carrots, beets, and spinach. d. squash, pork, and tomatoes.	Answer: a Rationale: Strawberries, eggs, and wheat, along with corn, fish, and nut products, are all foods that have commonly been associated with food allergies. Honey can contain botulism spores, which cannot be detoxified by the infant less than 1 year old but it is not an allergic reaction. Carrots, beets, and spinach contain nitrates and should not be given before 4 months old. Squash and tomatoes are okay to try after an infant is 4 to 6 months old, but should be given one at a time and 3 to 5 days after starting a new food. Pork can be tried after the infant is 8 to 10 months old, as meats are harder to digest and have a high protein load. Implementation Health Promotion and Maintenance Application
34.5 While teaching a health promotion class to a group of parents of children in a Head Start class, the nurse informs the parents that the most common preventable chronic infectious disease in U.S. children is: a. hepatitis A. b. dental decay. c. human immunodeficiency virus. d. herpes.	Answer: b Rationale: By 2 to 4 years of age, 17% of U.S. children have already had dental decay, and by the age of 8, 52% of children have experienced dental decay, making this the most common preventable chronic infectious disease in U.S. children. Implementation Health Promotion and Maintenance Application
34.6 The mother of a 2-year-old is concerned because her child does not seem interested in eating. The child is drinking about 5 to 6 cups of whole milk per day and 1 cup of fruit juice. When the weight-to-height percentile is calculated, the child is in the 90th to 95th percentile. What would be the best advice for the nurse to give this mom? a. eliminate the fruit juice from the child's diet. b. offer healthy snacks, presented in a creative manner, and let the child choose what she wants to eat without pressure from the parents. c. change from whole milk to 2% milk and decrease milk consumption to 3 to 4 cups per day and the fruit juice to $\frac{1}{2}$ cup per day, offering water if the child is still thirsty in between.	Answer: c Rationale: Toddlers require a maximum of about 1 L of milk per day. This toddler is consuming most of her calories from the milk, and thus is not hungry. The high fat content of the milk and the high sugar content of the fruit juice also are contributing to the child's higher weight-to-height percentile. Decreasing the amount and fat content of the milk and decreasing the intake of fruit juice will decrease calories and make the child hungry for other foods. The other advice is also appropriate but did not address the problem of excessive milk consumption. Implementation Health Promotion and Maintenance Analysis

d. make sure that the child is getting adequate opportunities for exercise, as this will increase her appetite and help lower her weight-to-height percentile.	
34.7 A nurse is talking to the mother of an exclusively breastfed African-American 3-month-old infant who was born in late fall. The nurse would want to make sure that this child is receiving: a. iron. b. vitamin D. c. fluoride. d. calcium.	Answer: b Rationale: An infant's iron stores are usually adequate until about 4 to 6 months of age. The infant should be receiving sufficient amounts of calcium from breast milk, and fluoride supplementation, if needed, does not begin until the child is approximately 6 months old. This infant will have limited exposure to sunlight, and thus vitamin D, because of the infant's dark skin and decreased sun exposure in the fall and winter months. Planning Health Promotion and Maintenance Analysis
34.8 A vegetarian adolescent has been placed on iron supplementation secondary to a diagnosis of iron deficiency anemia. To increase the absorption of iron, the nurse would instruct the teen to take the supplement with: a. black or green tea. b. orange juice. c. milk. d. tomato juice.	Answer: b Rationale: Acidity increases absorption of iron. Foods containing phosphorus, such as in milk; oxalates, such as in tomatoes; and tannins, such as in teas, all decrease absorption of iron. Implementation Physiological Integrity Application
34.9 A 6-year-old child has been newly diagnosed with cystic fibrosis. During discharge teaching, the nurse is instructing the parents on nutritional requirements specifically related to the child's decreased ability to absorb fats. The nurse teaches the family that the child will need supplementation with vitamins that are fat-soluble, such as: a. riboflavin. b. vitamin K. c. thiamin. d. vitamin B_{12}.	Answer: b Rationale: Vitamin K is fat soluble. Riboflavin, vitamin B_{12}, and thiamin are all water-soluble vitamins, and their absorption is not related to availability of dietary fat. Implementation Health Promotion and Maintenance Application
34.10 The nurse is caring for an infant receiving tube feedings exclusively. An important nursing intervention for this infant is: a. keeping the mouth suctioned and free of secretions. b. providing a pacifier for non-nutritive sucking. c. putting small amounts of formula on the infant's lips. d. giving glycerin suppositories as needed to maintain bowel function.	Answer: b Rationale: It is important to maintain the infant's sucking reflex when he is not orally fed, and the non-nutritive sucking from the pacifier helps facilitate this. The other interventions are not necessary and would be irritating to the infant. Planning Physiological Integrity Application
34.11 While teaching parents of a newborn about normal growth and development, the nurse informs them that their child's weight should: a. triple by 6 months of age. b. double by 1 year of age. c. double by 5 months of age. d. triple by 9 months of age.	Answer: c Rationale: Normal weight gain for an infant would be to have doubled in weight by 5 months of age. It would be abnormal for the infant's weight only to have doubled by 1 year of age or to have tripled by either 6 months or 9 months of age. Implementation Health Promotion and Maintenance Application

34.12 The nurse is teaching the parents of a 4-month-old infant about good feeding habits. The nurse emphasizes the importance of holding the baby during feeding and not letting the infant go to sleep with the bottle, as this is most likely to increase the incidence of both dental caries and:

a. otitis media.
b. aspiration.
c. malocclusion problems.
d. sleeping disorders.

Answer: a
Rationale: It has been shown in numerous studies that allowing an infant to fall asleep with a bottle in his mouth causes pooling of the formula in the mouth, which increases the risk of both dental caries and otitis media. There have been limited data to date showing a positive correlation to bottle propping and increased risk of aspiration, malocclusions, and sleeping disorders.
Implementation
Health Promotion and Maintenance
Application

34.13 The parents of a 2½-year-old are concerned about their child's finicky eating habits. While counseling the parents, the nurse would accurately make which statements? (Select all that apply.)

a. "The child is experiencing physiologic anorexia, which is normal for this age group."
b. "A general guideline for food quantity at a meal is ¼ cup of each food per year of age."
c. "It is more appropriate to assess a toddler's nutritional demands over a one-week period rather than a 24-hour one."
d. "Nutritious foods should be made available at all times of the day, so that the child is able to 'graze' whenever he is hungry."
e. "The toddler should drink 16 to 24 ounces of milk daily."

Answers: a, c, e
Rationale: Physiologic anorexia is caused when the extremely high metabolic demands of infancy slow to keep pace with the slower growth of toddlerhood, and it is a very normal finding at this age. It is not unusual for toddlers to have food jags where they only want one or two food items for that day. It is more helpful to look at what their intake has been over a week instead of a day. Two to three cups of milk per day are sufficient for a toddler, and more than that can decrease their desire for other foods and lead to dietary deficiencies. The correct general guideline for food quantity is one tablespoon of each food per year of age, and food should be offered only at meal and snack times. Children should sit at the table while eating to encourage socialization skills.
Implementation
Health Promotion and Maintenance
Application

34.14 The nurse has been providing nutritional guidance to the parents of an 18-month-old. The comment by a parent that would prompt the nurse to provide the parent with further education is:

a. "We allow our child to drink only pasteurized apple cider."
b. "We take the meat out of the freezer, and then allow it to thaw on the counter for 2 to 3 hours before cooking it thoroughly."
c. "We always wash our hands well before any food preparation."
d. "We use separate utensils for preparing raw meat and preparing fruits, vegetables, and other foods."

Answer: b
Rationale: All of the other practices—washing hands, using separate utensils, and not serving unpasteurized apple cider—help to prevent infection with foodborne pathogens. Allowing meat to sit out on a counter may cause the bacteria counts to increase quickly and cooking the meat may not effectively destroy all of the bacteria. Frozen meat should be thawed in the refrigerator prior to cooking.
Evaluation
Health Promotion and Maintenance
Analysis

34.15 During a well-child physical, a 16-year-old girl has a normal history and physical except for an excessive amount of tooth enamel erosion, a greater-than-normal number of filled cavities, and calluses on the back of her hand. Her body mass index is in the 50th to 75th percentile for her age. The nurse would be most concerned about:

Answer: c
Rationale: The erosion of tooth enamel, dental caries, and calluses on the back of her hand all most likely are due to frequent vomiting of gastric acids, which is common with this disorder as part of a "binge–purge" cycle. Anorexia nervosa is an eating disorder where adolescents literally starve themselves to prevent weight gain, also exercising excessively and using laxatives and diuretics to lose weight. Anorexia usually manifests as extreme weight loss and an obsession with food. Kwashiorkor is a protein deficiency, usually from malnutrition, that

a. anorexia nervosa.
b. kwashiorkor.
c. bulimia nervosa.
d. marasmus.

manifests as generalized edema. Marasmus is a lack of energy-producing calories that can be seen in anorexia, and this causes emaciation, decreased energy levels, and retarded development.
Diagnosis
Physiological Integrity
Application

CHAPTER 35

35.1 The nurse is taking a health history from the family of a 3-year-old child. The statement or question by the nurse that would be most likely to establish rapport and elicit an accurate response from the family is:
a. "Does any member of your family have a history of asthma, heart disease, or diabetes?"
b. "Hello, I would like to talk with you and get some information on you and your child."
c. "Tell me about the concerns that brought you to the clinic today."
d. "You will need to fill out these forms; make sure that the information is as complete as possible."

Answer: c
Rationale: Asking the parents to talk about their concerns is an open-ended question, and one that will establish rapport and give the nurse an understanding of the parent's perceptions. Beginning with a question about family history of diseases does not establish rapport. Introducing oneself before asking the parents for information is likely to establish rapport, but it doesn't give the nurse an understanding of the parent's perceptions. Simply asking the parents to fill out forms is very impersonal, and more information is likely to be obtained and clarified by the nurse directing the interview.
Assessment
Health Promotion and Maintenance
Application

35.2 The nurse is questioning a 10-year-old child to assess the level of cognitive development. The question by the nurse that would best determine cognitive development would be:
a. "What books have you read lately?"
b. "What classes are you taking, and what are your grades in them?"
c. "What is your least favorite class?"
d. "What grade are you in?"

Answer: b
Rationale: Asking about what kind of classes and the grades that the child is receiving in those classes would give the nurse an indication of how the child is developing cognitively. Many children have not been encouraged to read books, and while the types of books read would be a good indication of cognitive development, lack of interest in reading would not necessarily indicate poor cognitive development. Determining classes the child does not enjoy would be helpful, but not the best determinant of poor cognitive development. Grade level is also a good indication of cognitive development, but there could be many different reasons that a child has been held back in school that are not related to cognitive development.
Assessment
Health Promotion and Maintenance
Analysis

35.3 Place the following in the appropriate sequence when assessing a toddler:
a. examination of eyes, ears, and throat.
b. auscultation of chest.
c. palpation of abdomen.
d. developmental assessment.

Answer: d, b, c, a
Rationale: In examining toddlers, in order to build their trust and cooperation, it usually is best to go from least invasive to most invasive. Developmental assessment involves visual inspection and activities that toddlers view as games. Auscultation is less threatening to toddlers than palpation, especially if the nurse uses the stethoscope on a parent or a toy first. The most uncomfortable, most invasive exam for toddlers is the examination of the eyes, ears, and throat, and so this should be performed last.
Assessment
Health Promotion and Maintenance
Analysis

35.4 A 15-year-old girl is seen for a school physical. Her weight is 121 pounds, and her height is 64 inches. The

Answer: 20.7
Rationale: To calculate the body mass index, take the weight in kilograms and divide by the height in meters, squared. To convert weight from pounds to

nurse would calculate her body mass index (BMI) to be: _____.	kilograms, divide by 2.2; 121 pounds divided by 2.2 = 55 kilograms. To convert the height in inches to meters, multiply by 0.0254; 64 inches multiplied by 0.0254 = 1.63 meters. 1.63 meters squared = 2.66 meters squared. 55 kilograms divided by 2.66 meters squared = 20.7 (BMI). Assessment Health Promotion and Maintenance Application
35.5 While assessing a 10-month-old African-American infant, the nurse notices that the sclerae have a yellowish tint. Which organ system would the nurse suspect as having an ongoing disease process? a. cardiac. b. respiratory. c. hepatic. d. genitourinary.	Answer: c Rationale: This infant's sclerae are showing signs of jaundice, which most likely is secondary to a failure or malfunction of the liver or hepatic system. Cyanosis of the skin and mucous membranes are generally signs of problems with the cardiac and/or respiratory system. Tenting of the skin and dry mucous membranes could be signs of dehydration, and edema could be a sign of fluid overload. Both of these conditions could be secondary to problems with functioning of the genitourinary system. Diagnosis Physiological Integrity Analysis
35.6 A nurse, caring for a 9-year-old, notices some swelling in the child's ankles. The nurse presses against the ankle bone for five seconds, then releases the pressure, noticing a markedly slow disappearance of the indentation. Due to these physical findings the nurse would suspect a problem with the: a. respiratory system. b. renal system. c. musculoskeletal system. d. integumentary system.	Answer: b Rationale: Dependent, pitting edema, especially in the lower extremities, can be a symptom of kidney disorder so the renal system is affected. The renal system would be suspected before the respiratory, musculoskeletal, or integumentary system. Diagnosis Physiological Integrity Analysis
35.7 A mother of a 2-month-old is worried about a "soft spot" on the top of her infant's head. The nurse informs her that this is a normal physical finding called the anterior fontanelle, and that it will remain open until: a. 2 to 3 months of age. b. 6 to 9 months of age. c. 12 to 18 months of age. d. approximately 2 years of age.	Answer: c Rationale: The anterior fontanelle is located at the top of the head, and is the opening at the intersection of the suture lines. As the infant grows, the suture lines begin to fuse and the anterior fontanelle closes at about 12 to 18 months of age. Implementation Health Promotion and Maintenance Application
35.8 While inspecting a 5-year-old child's ears, the nurse notes that the right pinna protrudes outward, and that there is a mass behind the right ear. In light of these findings, the vital sign parameter that the nurse would be most concerned with would be: a. temperature. b. heart rate. c. respirations. d. blood pressure.	Answer: a Rationale: Swelling behind an ear could indicate mastoiditis, and the presence of a fever would indicate a higher index of suspicion for this. There also could be changes in other vital sign parameters, but they would not be specific for the presence of infection. Assessment Physiological Integrity Analysis

35.9 A nurse is assessing a 5-year-old child. Which assessment finding is abnormal? a. simultaneous rise of the chest and abdomen on inspiration. b. anteroposterior diameter smaller than the lateral diameter. c. bronchovesicular breath sounds. d. a protruding sternum.	Answer: d Rationale: A protruding sternum is an abnormal chest shape and is called pigeon chest (pectus carinatum). In children less than 6 years old, the chest and abdomen rise simultaneously because the diaphragm is the primary breathing muscle. The anteroposterior diameter becomes smaller than the lateral diameter after around 1 year of age. Bronchovesicular breath sounds are normal. Assessment Health Promotion and Maintenance Application
35.10 A very concerned 14-year-old boy presents to the clinic because of an enlargement of his left breast. Except for the breast enlargement, the rest of the history and physical is reported as normal. The most appropriate intervention for the nurse to implement next would be to inform the child that: a. a pediatric endocrine consult is being arranged. b. the health practitioner is arranging a surgical consult for him. c. this is a normal finding in adolescent males, and that the breast tissue generally regresses by the time of full sexual maturity. d. his condition is related to a high-fat diet, and that limiting fat intake usually will resolve the enlargement over a period of a couple of months.	Answer: c Rationale: Gynecomastia, or breast enlargement, is a normal finding in adolescent males, is not related to diet or endocrine abnormalities, and does not require surgery. Implementation Health Promotion and Maintenance Application
35.11 A nurse is reviewing normal and abnormal heart sounds. The nurse recognizes a child has an abnormal heart sound if: a. there is a sinus arrhythmia (heart rate is faster on inspiration and slower on expiration). b. a third heart sound is heard. c. the S1 is heard best in the mitral area of the heart d. the S1 and S2 heart sounds are muffled.	Answer: d Rationale: S1 and S2 heart sounds should be crisp. Muffling may indicate a heart defect of congestive heart failure. Sinus arrhythmia and a third heart sound is normal in children. The S1 is heard best in the mitral area of the heart. Implementation Physiological Integrity Analysis
35.12 The nurse is completing a physical examination of a 4-year-old child. The best position to place the child in for assessment of the genitalia would be: a. frog-leg position. b. right side-lying. c. supine, legs at a 50-degree angle. d. prone position, knees drawn up under body.	Answer: a Rationale: Having the child lie supine, flexing her knees and pulling them up to a frog-legged position, allows for accurate assessment of the genitalia, and is the better-tolerated position in the majority of children. Implementation Health Promotion and Maintenance Application
35.13 An assessment finding that would indicate developmental dysplasia of the hip would be a: a. 1-month-old with flat soles and prominent fat pads.	Answer: d Rationale: Asymmetric thigh and gluteal folds are positive findings for developmental dysplasia of the hip requiring follow-up with x-rays. A positive Babinski's reflex and flat soles are normal findings for 2-week-to 1-month-old infants. Metatarsus varus is an in-toeing of the feet that usually occurs secondary to intrauterine positioning and

b. 2-week-old with a positive Babinski's reflex.
c. 1-week-old with metatarsus varus.
d. 1½-month-old with asymmetric thigh and gluteal folds.

frequently resolves on its own. It can be an indication of a talipes (clubfoot) condition and does not necessarily mean the infant has developmental dysplasia of the hip.
Assessment
Physiological Integrity
Application

35.14 During an examination, a nurse asks a 5-year-old child to repeat his address. The nurse most likely is evaluating:
a. recent memory.
b. language development.
c. remote memory.
d. social skill development.

Answer: c
Rationale: Asking children to remember addresses, phone numbers, and dates assesses remote memory development. To evaluate recent memory, the nurse would have the child name something and then ask him to name it again in 10 to 15 minutes. Listening to how the child talks and his sentence structure evaluates his language development, and assessing how he interacts with others evaluates social skill development.
Assessment
Health Promotion and Maintenance
Application

35.15 A school nurse is conducting a health education class for middle school girls. The nurse knows further teaching is needed if a student states:
a. "I should begin to see hair in the pubic area before my breasts start to develop."
b. "I understand girls develop earlier than boys."
c. "I understand that sexual maturity can vary as to when it occurs."
d. "The beginning of breast development is around 10 years of age for Caucasian girls."

Answer: a
Rationale: Breast development precedes other pubertal changes. Girls begin to experience sexual maturity earlier than boys. Sexual maturity can vary with race and ethnicity, environmental conditions, geographic location, and nutrition. The beginning of breast development is around 10 years of age for Caucasian girls and 9 years of age for African-American girls.
Evaluation
Health Promotion and Maintenance
Analysis

CHAPTER 36

36.1 A concerned parent calls the school nurse because of changes in his 15-year-old adolescent's behavior. In counseling the parents, the nurse would inform them that the behavior that is most likely to be abnormal and indicate possible substance abuse is the adolescent's:
a. buying baggy, over-sized clothing at thrift shops and dying her hair a dark black shade.
b. becoming very involved with participating with friends on a basketball team, never seeming to be home, and when she is home, preferring to be in her room with the door shut.
c. receiving numerous detentions lately from teachers for sleeping in class.
d. becoming very moody, dramatically crying, and weeping one minute and then cheerful and excited the next.

Answer: c
Rationale: Mood swings, experimenting with clothes and hair, and periodically distancing themselves from their parents, preferring involvement with their peers, all are normal adolescent behaviors. While most teens do prefer staying up late, they usually are not so tired that they would fall asleep during the day, especially while engaged in classroom activities. This behavior is abnormal and might indicate involvement with substance abuse or an underlying pathology.
Assessment
Psychosocial Integrity
Analysis

36.2 During a well child exam, the parents of a 4-year-old child inform the nurse that they are thinking of buying a television for their child's bedroom and ask for advice as to whether this is appropriate. The best response from the nurse would be:

a. "Research has shown that children with a television in their bedroom spend significantly less time playing outside than other children do, and physical inactivity in children has been linked to many chronic diseases, such as obesity and type 2 diabetes."

b. "Research has shown that watching educational television shows improves a child's performance in school."

c. "Don't buy a television for your child's room; he is much too young for that."

d. "It is okay for your child to have a television in his room as long as you limit the amount of time he watches it to less than 2 hours per day."

Answer: a

Rationale: Young children need to be physically active at this age. "Research has shown that children with a television in their bedroom spend significantly less time playing outside than other children do, and physical inactivity in children has been linked to many chronic diseases, such as obesity and type 2 diabetes" is the best response, because it gives the parents an evidence-based rationale for not placing a television in the child's room. "Don't buy a television for your child's room, he is much too young for that" does not give parents a rationale, and might seem opinionated to them. While there may be some truth in the comment "Research has shown that watching educational television shows improves a child's performance in school," this statement might encourage increased television watching by the child, and the child's developmental need for physical activity is greater than the benefit that he might obtain by watching educational programs. "It is okay for your child to have a television in his room as long as you limit the amount of time he watches it to less than 2 hours per day" is correct in that limiting television viewing to less than 2 hours per day is appropriate, but the probability of this occurring with a television in the child's room is low, and the child most likely will be watching much more than 2 hours per day.
Implementation
Health Promotion and Maintenance
Application

36.3 A high school student calls to ask the nurse for advice on how to care for a new naval piercing. The nurse should reply:

a. "Apply warm soaks to the area for the first 2 days to minimize swelling."

b. "Do not move or turn the jewelry for the first 3 days."

c. "Avoid contact with another person's bodily fluids until the area is well healed."

d. "Apply lotion to the area, rubbing gently, to prevent skin from becoming dry and irritated."

Answer: c

Rationale: Until the piercing has healed, it is a non-intact area of skin that has the potential for infection, especially from contact with bodily fluids from someone else. Ice, not warm soaks, should be applied to the area for the first 2 days to minimize the swelling. The jewelry needs to be gently rotated several times per day to aid healing. Lotion can provide a medium for bacteria, and rubbing at the site can cause irritation to the area.
Implementation
Health Promotion and Maintenance
Application

36.4 While working at a weekend "free clinic," the nurse is assessing a 3-year-old when the mother of the child confides that it has been very difficult providing for her family of four children on her limited budget, and that she is not sure that she has enough money to buy food for the rest of the month, let alone the antibiotic that is needed for the child's ear infection. The intervention by the nurse that would be most beneficial for the child and this family is:

a. giving the mother enough free samples of the antibiotic for the recommended course of treatment.

b. putting the mother in contact with a local agency that provides food on a regular basis to needy families and helps them access other resources in the community.

c. talking with the mother about the factors that increase a child's risk of acquiring an ear infection.

Answer: b

Rationale: While all of these are good interventions, putting the mother in contact with a local agency will meet the family's basic need for food and connect the parent to a resource that could supply her with the antibiotic for her child. Giving the mother enough free samples of the antibiotic would treat the immediate problem of the ear infection, but not the more far-reaching effects of malnutrition. A family's basic needs must be met before health promotion can be effective, and so talking with the mother about the factors that increase a child's risk of acquiring an ear infection and about the importance of a balanced diet would not be the most beneficial intervention for this family at this time.
Planning
Health Promotion and Maintenance
Analysis

d. talking with the mother about the importance of a balanced diet in the growth and development of children, and providing her with a list of inexpensive, nutritious foods.	
36.5 A 7-year-old child has been seen in the pediatric clinic three times in the last 2 months for complaints of abdominal pain. Physical exam and all ordered lab work have been normal. The statement or question by the nurse working with this child that would help determine the etiology of this child's abdominal pain is: a. "Have there been any changes in your child's school or home life recently?" b. "Tell me what your child usually eats on a normal day." c. "Are your child's immunizations up to date?" d. "Has your child had any fevers or viral illnesses in the last 3 months?"	Answer: a Rationale: With a normal exam and lab work, there is a high probability that this child's abdominal pain is stress-related, and it is important to identify the possible stressors in this child's life to aid in diagnosis and treatment, the other questions are also important to ask, but are not as relevant to this child's symptoms as "Have there been any changes in your child's school or home life recently?" Implementation Psychosocial Integrity Application
36.6 A recently divorced mother, who must return to work, is concerned about the effects of placing her child in daycare full-time. In counseling the mother, the nurse knows that the factor that is most influential in determining whether daycare has a positive or negative effect on the child is: a. the ratio of daycare workers to children. b. the closeness of the parent–child relationship. c. the amount of time that the children spend playing outside. d. the cleanliness of the facility.	Answer: b Rationale: While the ratio of childcare workers to the children, the cleanliness of the facility, and how much time the children are able to spend playing outdoors all can contribute to whether childcare is a positive or negative experience, the closeness of the parent–child relationship is more likely to impact how resilient the child is, and this has a greater impact on the effects of the childcare experience. Implementation Psychosocial Integrity Analysis
36.7 A 7-year-old child is being seen in the clinic for a well-child visit. The parent of the child reports that the child is timid, seems anxious, and actually fears going to school. The nurse should counsel the parent that the child may be: a. a victim of a bully. b. bullying other children at school. c. doing poorly in math class. d. doing poorly in physical education class.	Answer: a Rationale: Children who are bullied are commonly timid, anxious, and fear going to school. Bullies are aggressive, impulsive, and need to dominate others. A child who was doing poorly in math or physical education class would not fear going to school. Implementation Health Promotion and Maintenance Application
36.8 The nurse is giving a health promotion class to adolescents. In counseling an adolescent about lifestyle choices, the nurse discusses the fact that the most preventable cause of adult death in the United States is: a. alcohol use. b. obesity. c. tobacco use. d. cocaine use.	Answer: c Rationale: Although all of these factors are preventable causes of mortality in the United States, tobacco use accounts for 430,000 deaths annually and is the most preventable cause of adult death. Implementation Health Promotion and Maintenance Application

36.9 The school nurse is planning a smoking prevention program for middle school students. The strategy that is most likely to be effective in preventing middle school children from smoking is:
a. having a local high school basketball star come talk to the students about the importance of not smoking.
b. having the school's biology teacher demonstrate the pathophysiology of the effects of smoking tobacco on the body.
c. developing colorful posters with catchy slogans and placing them all over the school.
d. having a pledge campaign with prizes awarded where students sign contracts saying that they will not use tobacco products.

Answer: a
Rationale: While all of the above strategies are good, the most effective strategy would be to have a local high school basketball star talk to the students about the importance of not smoking, because students at this age are more likely to listen to and attempt to emulate someone of their own peer group whom they respect and look up to. Information from adults, posters, and signed contracts are not as likely to influence children of this age as is the pressure of their peers.
Implementation
Health Promotion and Maintenance
Analysis

36.10 A 14-year-old presents in the clinic with a naval piercing that is warm, red, and painful to the touch. In planning care for this adolescent, the nurse would be aware that the skin pathogens most likely to have caused this infection would be:
a. *E. coli* and *Neisseria*.
b. *Staphylococcus* and *E. coli*.
c. *Streptococcus* and *Staphylococcus*.
d. *Neisseria* and *Staphylococcus*.

Answer: d
Rationale: *Neisseria* and *Staphylococcus* are the skin pathogens that are most often cultured from infected body piercing sites. *E-coli* is associated with urinary tract infections. *Streptococcus* is associated with throat infections.
Diagnosis
Health Promotion and Maintenance
Application

36.11 A community nurse makes visits to several families. Which risk factor, if present, in a family would be of a concern to the nurse because of a potential for abusive behavior to a child?
a. a single parent who works full-time.
b. a father of a child who tells the nurse he believes in harsh discipline, just like his own father used with him.
c. a family who has several relatives living within the neighborhood.
d. A family who reports they know it's too early to start to potty train the 2-year-old.

Answer: b
Rationale: The highest risk factor in this case is a father who believes in a tradition of harsh discipline. A single parent working full-time would be providing financial stability, a family with relatives living close by would not be socially isolated, and a family who understands it's too early to potty train a 2-year-old has realistic expectations of the developmental level of a child.
Assessment
Health Promotion and Maintenance
Analysis

36.12 While taking the history of a 10-year-old child, the parents admit to owning firearms. Appropriate safety measures for the nurse to suggest would be: (Select all that apply.)
a. using gun locks on all firearms in the house.
b. taking the child to a shooting range for lessons on how to use a gun properly.
c. storing the guns and ammunition in separate places.
d. keeping all the guns in a locked cabinet.

Answers: a, c, d
Rationale: Statistics show that about 75% of unintentional deaths and suicides are committed with firearms found in the home. The safety measures of using gun locks, keeping the gun and ammunition separate, and putting the guns in a locked cabinet at least will make the guns less accessible. Telling a child that a gun is "dangerous" and not to be touched probably will make it more fascinating. Even with knowledge of the proper use of a firearm, a 10-year-old child's judgment might not be mature enough to prevent misuse of it.
Implementation
Health Promotion and Maintenance
Application

e. explaining the dangers of a gun to the child and telling her or him explicitly to never touch it.	
36.13 A mother of two children, an 8-year-old and a 10-year-old, tells you that her husband recently has been deployed to the Middle East. The mother is concerned about the children's interest in constantly watching TV news coverage of activities in the Middle East. The most appropriate suggestion for the nurse to make to this mother would be: a. "Allow the children to watch as much television as they want. This is how they are coping with their father's absence." b. "It will just take some time to adjust to their father's absence, then everything will return to normal." c. "The less that you discuss this, the quicker the children will adjust to their father's absence. Try to keep them busy, and use distractions to keep their mind off of it." d. "Spend time with your children and take cues from them about how much they want to discuss."	Answer: d Rationale: Constant viewing of the TV coverage of the war may increase the children's anxiety and fear for their father's safety. The mother should be aware that even though the children might appear to have adjusted, there may be delayed reactions or regressions in behavior. Children need to be able to discuss their feelings and concerns with an adult; otherwise, their emotional distress may increase. Implementation Psychosocial Integrity Analysis
36.14 The nurse works in a pediatric unit. In working with a parent who is suspected of Munchausen syndrome by proxy, it is very important for the nurse to: a. confront the parent with concerns of possible abuse. b. carefully document parent–child interactions. c. try to keep the parent separated from the child as much as possible. d. explain to the child that her parent is causing their illness, and that the health team will prevent them from being harmed.	Answer: b Rationale: Munchausen syndrome by proxy is very difficult to prove, and evidence provided by the careful documentation of the nursing staff can be very influential. Care must be taken not to make the parent suspicious and to keep him in the hospital until enough evidence is collected. Confronting the parent or separating him from his child may alienate him and cause him to leave with his child. Talking to the child about the healthcare team's suspicions might be confusing and frightening for the child. Implementation Safe, Effective Care Environment Application
36.15 A child is admitted to the hospital unit with physical injuries. The nurse is taking the child's history. The statement by the parent that would be most suspicious for abuse is: a. "I did not realize that my baby was able to roll over yet, and I was just gone a minute to check on dinner when the baby rolled off of the couch and onto our tile floor." b. "The baby's 18-month-old brother was trying to pull the baby out of the crib and dropped the baby on the floor." c. "I placed the baby in the infant swing. His 6-year-old brother was running through the house and	Answer: b Rationale: All of the statements made by the parent are plausible from a developmental perspective except the statement "The baby's 18-month-old brother was trying to pull the baby out of the crib and dropped the baby on the floor." Developmentally, it would be very difficult for an 18-month-old child to pull an infant out of a crib. Assessment Psychosocial Integrity Analysis

604 NCLEX-RN® Test Questions   © 2007 Pearson Education, Inc.

tripped over the swing, causing it to fall."

d. "I feel so bad. I was holding the baby in one arm and some towels in the other and did not see my toddler's toys on the floor. I tripped, and when I fell, the baby slipped out of my arms."

CHAPTER 37

37.1 A nurse is helping the parents of 2-year-old twins cope with the daily demands of life in an active household. Which of these strategies should the nurse use?
a. health maintenance.
b. health promotion.
c. partner development.
d. health supervision.

Answer: b
Rationale: In health promotion, nurses partner with families to promote family strategies in the areas of lifestyle and coping. The definitions of health maintenance and health supervision make the other answers incorrect. Partner development is simply a distractor, and should be ignored.
Implementation
Health Promotion and Maintenance
Application

37.2 A nurse says to the mother of a 6-month-old infant, "Does the baby sit without assistance and is the baby crawling?" Which process is the nurse using in this interaction?
a. health promotion.
b. health maintenance.
c. disease surveillance.
d. developmental surveillance.

Answer: d
Rationale: The question asked by the nurse is seeking information about developmental milestones; therefore, the nurse is involved in developmental surveillance. While health promotion and health maintenance activities are related to developmental surveillance, this question is looking specifically at the milestones; therefore, the answers health promotion and health maintenance are incorrect. The questions asked in the stem are not classified as disease surveillance questions.
Assessment
Health Promotion and Maintenance
Analysis

37.3 A parent says to a nurse, "How do you know when my child needs these screening tests the doctor just mentioned?" Which response should the nurse make to the parent?
a. "Screening tests are administered at the ages when a child is most likely to develop a condition."
b. "Screening tests are done in the new-born nursery, and from these results, additional screening tests are ordered throughout the first two years of life."
c. "Screening tests are most often done when the doctor suspects something is wrong with the child."
d. "Screening tests are done at each office visit."

Answer: a
Rationale: "Screening tests are administered at ages when a child is most likely to develop a condition" provides a definition for screening tests. The remaining answers all provide incorrect information to the parent. Abnormal newborn screening tests require immediate follow-up. Screening tests are done to detect the possibility of problems, and are not done when a problem is suspected. Screening tests are not done at each office visit.
Implementation
Health Promotion and Maintenance
Application

37.4 A pediatric nurse who is employed in a busy ambulatory clinic setting is informed by the nurse manager that average nursing time allocated for each child and family is being reduced to 10 minutes to manage the clinic more efficiently. The nursing activities must include a nursing assessment and discussion on anticipatory guidance. Which of these

Answer: d
Rationale: With limited time for each visit, the nurse should focus on anticipatory guidance strategies that will benefit the parent and child most during that office visit. Limiting assessment and education to 10 minutes, performing anticipatory guidance prior to history taking, and suggesting that parents complain to a nurse manager might be destructive to the needs of the children and parents and might adversely affect the operation of the nursing unit.
Implementation
Safe, Effective Care Environment
Application

strategies should the nurse utilize in the plan of care delivery?
a. attempt to complete the assessment and education in 10 minutes but extend the time whenever the nurse deems necessary.
b. plan to do the anticipatory guidance first since either the nurse practitioner or the physician can perform the assessment of the child.
c. ask each parent to complain to the nurse manager that there is not adequate time to talk with the nurse at each visit.
d. focus anticipatory guidance strategies on topics that the parent or child has expressed as an area of interest.

37.5 A new mother has been taught that her infant needs to be seen in the pediatrician's office for the initial healthcare visit. The mother asks the nurse what the purpose of this visit will be. The nurse explains that during this initial visit, the nurse will: (Select all that apply.)
a. discuss policies related to provision of care.
b. evaluate the parents' understanding of the services offered.
c. determine if the parents' and healthcare provider's personalities are compatible.
d. determine if the parents are child abusers.
e. determine whether the parents will make their infant obese.

Answers: a, b, c
Rationale: The initial visit should help to acquaint the parents to office policies and services offered by the office, and to determine if the parents and provider will get along well. Only under very unusual circumstances would the healthcare providers be able to determine whether the parents are potential child abusers and whether the parents will tend to overfeed the infant and place the infant at risk for obesity.
Implementation
Health Promotion and Maintenance
Analysis

37.6 A nurse assesses the height and weight measurements on an infant and documents these measurements at the 75th percentile. The nurse notes that the measurements 2 months ago were at the 25th percentile. How should the nurse interpret these data?
a. the infant is not gaining enough weight.
b. the infant has gained a significant amount of weight.
c. the previous measurements were most likely inaccurate.
d. these measurements most likely are inaccurate.

Answer: b
Rationale: A comparison of these two sets of measurements shows that the infant has crossed two percentiles, going from the 25th to the 75th percentile, and has gained a significant amount of weight. This rationale makes all remaining answers incorrect.
Evaluation
Health Promotion and Maintenance
Application

37.7 An infant is growing slowly and the weight on the growth chart has remained at the −2 standard deviation (−2 SD). Which of these interventions takes priority?
a. ask for a recall of the infant's intake in the previous day.
b. question the mother about development milestones.

Answer: a
Rationale: The nurse needs to obtain a nutritional history on this infant. Obtaining a 24-hour dietary recall on the infant is most appropriate. Questioning developmental milestones would not lead to any conclusions about the problem presented. There is no indication for reporting this parent to Child Protective Services. Providing instruction on dietary intake without a nutritional history would not be appropriate.
Assessment
Health Promotion and Maintenance
Analysis

c. report the case to Child Protective Services. d. firmly instruct the family about appropriate dietary intake for the infant.	
37.8 The nurse is working with first-time parents. Which of these activities will the nurse suggest to encourage the development of good muscle tone? a. surrounding the infant with toys and other stimulating items to encourage motor movement. b. putting the infant to bed each night at 8 P.M., even if the infant protests with crying. c. swaddling the infant. d. placing the infant in an infant seat rather than lying down in a crib.	Answer: a Rationale: Encouraging movement best assists the infant to obtain good muscle tone. Swaddling the infant, while calming for a young infant, restricts movement. The bedtime has nothing to do with development of infant muscle tone. Implementation Health Promotion and Maintenance Application
37.9 A nurse is assessing an 11-month-old infant, and notes that the infant's height and weight are at the 5th percentile on the growth chart. Family history reveals that the two siblings are at the 50th percentile for height and at the 75th percentile for weight. Psychosocial history reveals that the parents are separated and are planning to divorce. Which of these nursing diagnoses takes priority? a. alteration in growth pattern related to parental anxiety. b. alteration in growth pattern secondary to familial short stature. c. nutritional intake: excessive secondary to maternal feeding patterns. d. at risk for constitutional growth delay as related to decreased appetite.	Answer: a Rationale: The scenario reveals parental anxiety due to marital problems. The most appropriate nursing diagnosis is alteration in growth patterns related to parental anxiety. There is no data that indicate familial short stature. Since height and weight are at the 5th percentile, there is no indication of increased nutritional intake. This infant is not at risk for constitutional growth delay. Diagnosis Health Promotion and Maintenance Analysis
37.10 A 27-month-old toddler who is in the pediatric office for a well-child visit begins to cry the moment he is placed on the examination table. The parent attempts to comfort the toddler, but nothing is effective. Which of these actions by the nurse takes priority? a. instruct the father to hold the toddler down tightly to complete the examination. b. allow the toddler to sit on the parent's lap and begin the assessment. c. allow the toddler to stand on the floor until the crying stops. d. ask another nurse in the office to hold the toddler since the parent is not able to control the toddler's behavior.	Answer: b Rationale: Toddlers are most comfortable when sitting with the parents. Much of the examination can be completed in this way. Allowing the toddler to stand on the floor is inappropriate. A nurse can assist if the parent is unable to hold the child during the examination of the throat and ears to prevent injury from movement. Implementation Health Promotion and Maintenance Application
37.11 Which of these developmental milestones should the nurse expect to find in children who are between 2 and 3 years old? (Select all that apply.)	Answers: b, c, e Rationale: Children between the ages of 2 and 3 years old can do the selected activities. Children between the ages of 3 and 4 years old feed themselves. Children between the ages of 4 and 5 years old can throw a ball overhead.

a. always feeds self. b. scribbles and draws on paper. c. kicks a ball. d. throws ball overhand. e. goes up and down stairs.	Assessment Health Promotion and Maintenance Analysis
37.12 A nurse instructs a parent of a preschooler to use the "five-a-day" rule for feeding the preschooler, a rule that relates to: a. chicken and at least two servings of red meat per week. b. milk and milk products. c. fruits and vegetables. d. breads and cereals.	Answer: c Rationale: Five servings of fruits and vegetables each day are needed for toddlers and preschoolers to help boost the immune system, provide regular bowel patterns, and promote healthy hair and nails. Implementation Health Promotion and Maintenance Application
37.13 A parent says to a nurse, "My 4-year-old has five cavities." The nurse informs the parent that early-childhood cavities is related to which of these? a. strong familial history of dental caries. b. inadequate preventive care, including brushing the teeth and eating habits. c. increased intake of iron supplements. d. fluoride intake in water and in toothpaste.	Answer: b Rationale: Early childhood caries are related to inadequate preventive care, which can include diet, brushing, and feeding habits. Dental caries is not hereditary. Iron intake is not related to dental caries. While fluoride intake is needed for strong, healthy teeth, poor dental hygiene is responsible for dental caries. Implementation Health Promotion and Maintenance Analysis
37.14 Parents of a preschool-age child report that they find it necessary to spank the child at least once a day. Which response should the nurse make to the parents? a. "Spanking is one form of discipline, however, you want to be certain that you do not leave any marks on the child." b. "Let's talk about other forms of discipline that have a more positive effect on the child." c. "Can you try only spanking the child every other day for one week and see how that affects the child's behavior?" d. "I think you are not parenting your child properly, so let's talk about ways to improve your parenting skills."	Answer: b Rationale: The behavior reported by the parent was excessive. The only response that is appropriate is to seek a more positive way of influencing behavior in this age child. To suggest spanking is an appropriate form of discipline is inappropriate, especially when the parent is describing daily spanking of the child. Implementation Health Promotion and Maintenance Application
37.15 A parent questions how her toddler plays with other toddlers. The nurse's best description of the differences in play between the toddler and the preschooler is: a. toddlers play "side by side," while preschoolers play cooperatively. b. toddlers play house and imitate adult roles, while preschoolers become the "Mom or Dad" while playing house. c. toddlers play cooperatively, while preschoolers play interactive games. d. there are no differences between toddlers and preschoolers since both play cooperatively.	Answer: a Rationale: Toddlers, although they will play "side by side" with another child, do not interact with the child during play. Preschoolers play cooperatively with other children. Implementation Health Promotion and Maintenance Analysis

38.1 A nurse observes the parent–child interaction during a 6-year-old's well child checkup and notes that the parent speaks harshly to the child and uses negative remarks when speaking with the nurse. Which statement by the nurse would be most beneficial?

a. "Perhaps you should leave the room so that I can speak with your child privately."
b. "I am going to refer you for counseling since your interactions with your child seem so negative."
c. "Let's talk privately. Let's discuss the way you speak with your child and possible ways to be more positive."
d. Addressing the child, the nurse says, "Are you unhappy when Mommy talks to you like this?"

Answer: c
Rationale: The best approach to this encounter would be for the nurse to discuss concerns with the parent privately, since the nurse wants to help the parent develop a good relationship with the child. The child should not be a part of this conversation. Since the child is only 6 years old, it would be difficult to ask the parent to leave the room. If the nurse also wants to speak alone with the child, the nurse perhaps would escort the child to another area and speak briefly with the child. Referring to counseling without a discussion with the parent is not appropriate. The nurse should not ask the child if she is "unhappy" with the parent.
Implementation
Health Promotion and Maintenance
Application

38.2 The nurse in a hospital unit must develop a comprehensive plan of care for a school-age child. The question the nurse will ask the child that will be most helpful in data collection related to nutrition is:

a. "What did you have to eat so far today?"
b. "What is your favorite grocery store?"
c. "Do you eat school lunches or pack a lunch from home each day?"
d. "How do you feel about your weight and the way you look?"

Answer: d
Rationale: The best way to obtain information to include in the plan of care is to use a broad opening question. It also is important to ask information about the way the child feels about his body image. Asking about eating habits and food selection at a grocery store or school contribute to the nutritional history but are not the most helpful individual aspects in establishing a comprehensive plan of care.
Assessment
Health Promotion and Maintenance
Analysis

38.3 A nurse obtains a nutritional health history from a 10-year-old child. Which of these food selections, if consumed on a regular basis, should lead the nurse to become concerned about the need for improving oral hygiene?

a. peanuts and crackers.
b. sorbet and yogurt.
c. gummy bears and licorice.
d. fluoridated water.

Answer: c
Rationale: Food items that stick to the teeth lead to dental caries. Items such as gummy bears and licorice stick to the teeth and lead to dental caries. Foods such as peanut butter, crackers, sorbet, and yogurt do not stick to the teeth and are not considered foods that increase dental caries. Fluoridated water has been shown to decrease the incidence of dental caries.
Evaluation
Health Promotion and Maintenance
Analysis

38.4 A report from the school psychologist indicates that a 10-year-old child often is teased by his classmates, and said to the psychologist, "I know I am not as good as them, so I just play by myself at recess every day." The nurse knows that the child most likely has a:

a. poor body image.
b. self-determined concept.
c. good sense of self-worth.
d. decreased self-esteem.

Answer: d
Rationale: The child's statement reveals no interaction with other children during play periods, therefore, the child's self-esteem is low. There are no data in this scenario to indicate that the child has a problem with body image since there is no information related to why other children are teasing the child. This child would not have a good sense of self-worth, and a self-determined concept is merely a distractor.
Evaluation
Health Promotion and Maintenance
Analysis

38.5 The school health nurse is working with a parent–child group discussing sex education. Which statement by a parent or child requires further teaching by the nurse?
a. "I know girls can develop early. I was only 8 years old when I developed breasts."
b. "I plan to speak with my daughter about her sexuality only after she reads the books I purchased for her."
c. "My school nurse talked with us about getting a period," the child giggles.
d. "My friends like to talk about sex. Lots of us have older sisters who dress sexy."

Answer: d
Rationale: The school-age child who is being influenced by an older sibling is at risk for inappropriate behaviors and needs further teaching. Girls can begin secondary sex characteristic development at 8 years old, and it is appropriate for a parent to discuss concepts of sexuality after the child completes some appropriate reading. School-age children often laugh or giggle after discussions at school about secondary sex characteristics.
Evaluation
Health Promotion and Maintenance
Analysis

38.6 A nurse is planning to present a lecture/discussion on health maintenance to adolescents in their High School Health Class. Which of these should the nurse include in the presentation? Select all that apply.
a. Limiting refined sugar and high fat intake.
b. Include 2-3 servings of dairy products daily to enhance bone formation.
c. Resources for treatment of eating disorders for all adolescents.
d. Type II diabetes mellitus and insulin resistence.
e. The importance of decreasing calcium intake once full adult height is achieved.

Answer: a, b
Rationale: A general presentation should focus on normal expected behaviors for health promotion such as limiting refined sugar intake and including dairy in the diet. Discussing eating disorders and diabetes mellitus is not appropriate for health promotion activities. Decreasing calcium would not be a recommendation for teenagers.
Planning
Health Promotion and Maintenance
Application

38.7 The school health nurse is evaluating the home environment of several children as it relates to child safety. The nurse visits the home of each child and gathers the following data. Which of these activities places a child at the greatest risk for bodily harm?
a. The parents are in a methadone program.
b. The parents consume alcohol on a daily basis.
c. The child is permitted to take target practice with a revolver unsupervised.
d. The child is a latchkey child.

Answer: c
Rationale: Of all the activities mentioned, the child who is playing with guns is most at risk for injury. The other inappropriate behaviors, such as drug and alcohol use or past use, also place the child at risk, but the use of firearms is more risky. A latchkey child needs special attention, but in the situations given is not at the highest risk.
Assessment
Health Promotion and Maintenance
Analysis

38.8 The mother of a 12-year-old child informs the nurse that the child's father died from sudden cardiac death at 44 years old. Which of these laboratory tests should the nurse anticipate the physician to order?
a. CBC with differential.
b. lipid profile.
c. chest x-ray.
d. EEG.

Answer: b
Rationale: This child should have a lipid profile completed at 12 years old, and based on the results, further testing might be needed. The CBC is routine but will not give information related to cardiac disease. A routine chest x-ray might be ordered by the physician but will not provide relevant information at this time. An EEG (electroencephalogram) reveals information about brain activity, not cardiac status.
Evaluation
Health Promotion and Maintenance
Application

38.9 The school nurse is teaching a class about safety. The nurse will teach the children that they should wear protective athletic gear when participating in selected activities. Which of these activities require protective athletic gear? (Select all that apply.) a. skateboarding. b. football. c. swimming. d. lacrosse. e. acrobatic tricks	Answers: a, b, d Rationale: Any sport that includes body contact requires a child to wear protective equipment. These include skateboarding, football, and lacrosse. Swimming and acrobatics do not have any requirements for protective equipment. Evaluation Health Promotion and Maintenance Application
38.10 A 15-year-old female adolescent's body mass index (BMI) is 27.5. The adolescent's height is 5 feet, 2 inches, and she weighs 160 pounds. The girl's menses began when she was 12 years old. School performance has been spotty. The priority client teaching would be related to: a. nutritional intake. b. school performance. c. adolescent mini mental health status examination. d. menstrual cycle.	Answer: a Rationale: The BMI for this client is too high, placing the adolescent at risk for cardiovascular disease, hypertension, and diabetes mellitus later in life. Therefore, a question about nutritional intake is the most important question to ask this client at this time. The only choice related to BMI is nutritional intake. Assessment Health Promotion and Maintenance Analysis
38.11 The school nurse performs screenings on all students in the high school. In addition, the nurse will perform selected screenings on individual teenagers. When planning the screenings for the year, the nurse will include screening all teenagers for: (Select all that apply.) a. scoliosis. b. tanner staging. c. blood pressure measurement. d. hepatitis B profile serology. e. chest x-ray.	Answers: a, b, c Rationale: Routine screening for adolescents includes checking for scoliosis, tanner staging to determine if the progression of secondary sex characteristics is normal, and blood pressure measurements. The hepatitis B profile is needed only once prior to administration of hepatitis B vaccine; however, this is not a required screening for all adolescents. A chest x-ray is not a routine screening test for adolescents. Planning Health Promotion and Maintenance Application
38.12 A nursing history on a 16-year-old female reveals that the adolescent takes a multivitamin with 0.5 mg of fluoride and 0.4 mg of folic acid each day. The concern the nurse should bring to the attention of the physician is the: a. presence of fluoride in the multivitamin. b. amount of fluoride in the multivitamin is too low. It should be 1.0 mg each day. c. intake of folic acid. d. need for a daily iron tablet.	Answer: a Rationale: Fluoride supplementation is not recommended for teenagers. Fluoride supplementation should be stopped at 12 years old. There are no data to support iron recommendations for the client in this scenario. Folic acid is recommended for all women of childbearing age to prevent neural tube defects. Evaluation Health Promotion and Maintenance Analysis
38.13 An adolescent who recently moved to a new school in a different town presents to an ambulatory care center and describes the following: "I have no friends in my new school, and I no longer want to go to college. I know	Answer: b Rationale: The adolescent obviously is lonely with the move to the new school. The nurse should focus on appropriate coping methods that will enhance good mental health outcomes for the child. It would not be appropriate to discuss the importance of a college education at this time since the adolescent must deal with the loss of friends and developing new friends first. The parent–child

I will be lonely there too." Which of these takes priority when speaking with the adolescent?
a. helping the adolescent realize the value of post-secondary education.
b. promotion of healthy mental health outcomes.
c. acknowledgement of the fact that it takes several months to make new friends at a new school, due to adolescent exclusion behaviors.
d. the adolescent should consider the importance of remaining in a close parent–child relationship during these stressful times.

relationship should not be used as a substitute for the development of new peer relationships.
Evaluation
Health Promotion and Maintenance
Application

38.14 An obese adolescent who adamantly denies sexual activity has a positive pregnancy test that was performed in the adolescent clinic. The appropriate nursing statement to the adolescent is:
a. "Tell me how you feel about your body image."
b. "When was your last menstrual cycle (LMP)?"
c. "Let's discuss some activities that you have done within the past few months that could possibly lead to pregnancy."
d. "Were you involved in a date rape and are you hesitant to speak about it?"

Answer: c
Rationale: The nurse must help the adolescent realize that previous behaviors have led to a positive pregnancy test. The only response by the nurse that will accomplish this goal is for the nurse to ask a direct question in which the nurse and client search for an answer.
Implementation
Health Promotion and Maintenance
Application

38.15 A nurse should review the immunization record for hepatitis B status as a priority for which of these adolescents? An adolescent who:
a. has chronic acne.
b. has overuse injuries from playing varsity sports.
c. has chronic asthma.
d. is planning on getting a tattoo.

Answer: d
Rationale: The adolescent who is most at risk in the scenario presented is the teen who is planning on getting a tattoo. Adolescents with chronic acne or asthma do not have an increased risk for hepatitis B since transmission has nothing to do with a diagnosis of acne. Overuse of muscles while playing sports is not related to development of hepatitis B.
Evaluation
Health Promotion and Maintenance
Application

CHAPTER 39

39.1 A community nurse is conducting an assessment on a family. Which assessment tool will the nurse use that requires family members to complete a questionnaire?
a. the HOME Inventory.
b. the Friedman Family Assessment Tool (FFAM).
c. the Family APGAR
d. the Calgary Family Assessment Model.

Answer: c
Rationale: The Family APGAR is a quick five-item questionnaire that may be used as an initial screening tool for family assessment. The five-item questionnaire can be administered quickly to family members over 10 years of age. All family members are asked to complete a separate copy of the questionnaire.
The HOME Inventory is an assessment tool developed to measure the quality and quantity of stimulation and support available to the child in the home environment. Data are collected using interview and observation. The Friedman Family Assessment Tool and the Calgary Family Assessment Model are tools used by the nurse to collect data. They do not require family members to fill out questionnaires.
Planning
Health Promotion and Maintenance
Application

39.2 Several children have arrived at the walk-in clinic of a primary care facility. The child the nurse should assess first is: a. a 2-month-old with a two-day history of diarrhea. b. a 2-year-old who has been pulling at his ear. c. a 6-year-old who is wheezing and short of breath. d. a 10-year-old with a sore throat.	Answer: c Rationale: While all of the children need to be seen, the child who has symptoms of respiratory distress should be seen right away. Waiting a while to be seen should not affect the other children adversely, but a child who is experiencing respiratory difficulty could become worse quickly. Assessment Safe, Effective Care Environment Analysis
39.3 A 16-year-old client has a long leg cast secondary to a fractured femur. To effectively facilitate the adolescent's return to school, the school nurse should: a. meet with teachers and administrators at the school to make sure entrances and classrooms are wheelchair-accessible. b. develop an individualized health plan (IHP) that focuses on long-term needs of the adolescent. c. meet with all of the other students prior to the student's return to school to emphasize the special needs of the injured teen. d. meet with parents of the injured student to encourage homebound schooling until a short leg cast is applied.	Answer: a Rationale: An adolescent with a long leg cast secondary to a fractured femur will be dependent on a wheelchair for mobility. It is essential that the environment be wheelchair-accessible prior to the adolescent's return to school. While an IHP might be developed, short-term needs would be the focus. It is not necessary to meet with all of the students to discuss the adolescent's needs. There is no reason to encourage the child to stay at home for schooling if he is ready to return. Planning Physiological Integrity Application
39.4 The community health nurse is planning an education session for recently hired teachers at a childcare center. It is most important that the nurse teach the staff: a. the schedule for immunizations. b. principles of infection control. c. how to interpret healthcare records. d. how to take a temperature.	Answer: b Rationale: While all of the information is nice to know, it is most essential that teachers know principles of infection control to decrease the spread of germs that can cause disease in young children. Planning Health Promotion and Maintenance Application
39.5 Prior to returning to school, an individualized health plan (IHP) will be developed for the child: a. who has recently developed a penicillin allergy. b. newly diagnosed with insulin-dependent diabetes mellitus. c. who has been treated for head lice. d. who has missed 2 weeks of school due to mononucleosis.	Answer: b Rationale: An IHP that ensures appropriate management of the child's healthcare needs must be developed for a child newly diagnosed with a chronic illness such as diabetes. A child who is allergic to penicillin will not receive this medication anymore, and therefore should not encounter any problems related to it at school. A child who has been treated for head lice can return to school and does not need an IHP. While a child who has missed 2 weeks of school will need to make arrangements for makeup work, an IHP is not needed. Planning Safe, Effective Care Environment Analysis
39.6 The school nurse assesses a child with a history of asthma who has an acute onset of wheezing. The initial action by the nurse is to: a. call 911 to request emergency medical assistance. b. call the child's parents to come and pick up the child.	Answer: c Rationale: A child with a history of asthma might have episodes of wheezing that can be controlled by prompt use of the child's rescue inhaler. An inhaler should be readily available in the school setting for a child previously diagnosed with asthma. This should be tried first. Emergency personnel should be notified if the inhaler does not provide relief, and the child is in respiratory distress. Parents can be notified if the child does not feel well, but this is not the initial action. Having the child lie down likely will worsen his condition.

c. have the child use his metered dose inhaler. d. have the child lie down to see if the symptoms subside.	Implementation Physiological Integrity Analysis
39.7 The telephone triage nurse receives a call from a parent who states that her 18-month-old is making a crowing sound when he breathes and is hard to wake up. The nurse should: a. obtain the history of the illness from the parent. b. advise the parent to hang up and call 911. c. make an appointment for the child to see the healthcare provider. d. reassure the parent and provide instructions on home care for the child.	Answer: b Rationale: The nurse should immediately recognize the symptoms of severe upper respiratory distress and advise the parent to call 911. The other actions would be appropriate in nonemergency situations. Assessment Physiological Integrity Analysis
39.8 The home health nurse is providing care to a 2-week-old infant, and notes that the infant has a necklace with a charm around his neck. The parents state that they believe the charm will keep the infant healthy. The nurse should: a. respect the parents' wishes and leave the necklace in place. b. remove the necklace and inform the parents that it is dangerous. c. report the parent to social services for endangering the child. d. ask the parents to remove the necklace.	Answer: a Rationale: Families of different cultural backgrounds may have specific beliefs about health care. These beliefs may differ from those of the nurse. The nurse should honor the practices of the family. To do otherwise would lead to loss of trust from the family. The nurse can provide anticipatory guidance to the family that includes safety principles as the infant grows. Assessment Safe, Effective Care Environment Application
39.9 A 5-year-old child who has had a tracheostomy for several years is scheduled to begin kindergarten in the fall. The teacher is concerned about this child being in her class and consults the school nurse. The nurse should: a. make arrangements for the child to go to a special school. b. ask the parents of the child to provide a caregiver during school hours. c. recommend that the child be home-schooled. d. teach the teacher how to care for the child in the classroom.	Answer: d Rationale: Public Law 94-142 and Public Law 99-457 ensure that all children with disabilities ages 3 to 21 will receive a free education. The child may need little extra attention while in the school setting since she has had the tracheostomy for several years. The teacher should be taught how to care for the child, if needed, and taught the signs of distress. If needed, a health aide may be assigned to the child, but this is not the responsibility of the parents. Planning Safe, Effective Care Environment Analysis
39.10 A 2-month-old infant with bronchopulmonary dysplasia is being prepared for discharge from the neonatal intensive care unit. He will continue to receive oxygen via nasal cannula at home. Prior to discharge, the home health nurse assesses the home. Which of the following findings poses the greatest risk to this infant? a. small toys strewn on the floor. b. a wood stove used for heating.	Answer: b Rationale: Assessment of the home environment is essential prior to discharge of a medically fragile infant. The use of a wood stove poses great risk to the infant who already has fragile lungs. Small toy pieces and paint peeling from the wall will pose a choking risk to the older infant who is crawling. Ear infections are not contagious. Assessment Safe, Effective Care Environment Analysis

c. a sibling who has an ear infection.
d. paint peeling on the walls.

39.11 A child who is dependent on a ventilator is being discharged from the hospital. Prior to discharge, the home health nurse discusses development of an emergency plan of care with the family. Which of the following is the most essential part of the plan? a. acquisition of a backup generator. b. designation of an emergency shelter site. c. provision for an alternate heating source if power is lost. d. notifying the power company that the child is on life support.	Answer: a Rationale: Prior to discharge to home, it is essential that the family acquire a generator so that the child's life support will continue to function effectively should power be lost. While all other actions are very important, it is most essential that the ventilator has power to continue to function at all times. Planning Safe, Effective Care Environment Analysis
39.12 Prior to accepting an assignment as a home health nurse, the nurse must realize that: a. all decisions will be made by the healthcare provider. b. the family will adapt their lifestyle to the needs of the nurse. c. independent decisions regarding emergency care of the child will be made by the nurse. d. the family is in charge.	Answer: d Rationale: The home health nurse must realize that the family is in charge. The nurse must be flexible and adaptable to the lifestyle of the family. The family must provide informed consent for emergency care. Planning Safe, Effective Care Environment Application
39.13 An assessment of a community has been conducted. The assessment revealed that the number of serious injuries in children has doubled in the past year. Based on this information, the most appropriate community nursing diagnosis is: a. noncompliance related to inappropriate use of child safety seats. b. risk for injury related to inadequate use of bicycle helmets. c. altered family processes related to hospitalization of an injured child. d. knowledge deficit related to injury prevention in children.	Answer: d Rationale: All of these diagnoses might be appropriate in specific situations, but knowledge deficit related to injury prevention in children is the only one that is general to the problem as a whole and is, therefore, the most appropriate community nursing diagnosis. Diagnosis Safe, Effective Care Environment Analysis
39.14 Which of the following aspects of an emergency medical services system is most indicative that EMS providers are prepared to provide emergency care to children? a. placement of small stretchers in emergency vehicles. b. lists of hospitals in the area that treat children. c. staff education related to assessment and treatment of children of all ages. d. pediatric-sized equipment and supplies.	Answer: c Rationale: While size-appropriate equipment and a list of hospitals that treat children are essential parts of an EMS system, the aspect that is most indicative that EMS providers actually are prepared to take care of children is evidence of education related to assessment and emergency treatment. Evaluation Safe, Effective Care Environment Analysis

39.15 A group of nursing students are discussing job options. One of the students states that a position as a school nurse sounds interesting. In discussing the roles of the school nurse, the students will include: (Select all that apply.)
a. screening for head lice.
b. prescribing antibiotics for streptococcal pharyngitis.
c. developing a plan for emergency care of injured children.
d. diagnosing an ear infection.
e. teaching a class on wellness to teachers and staff.

Answers: a, c, e
Rationale: Screening of students for certain conditions; educating students, teachers, and staff; and developing emergency plans are all roles of the school nurse. Diagnosing acute illness and prescribing medication for a new illness are beyond the scope of practice for the school nurse unless the nurse is licensed as an advanced practice nurse.
Implementation
Safe, Effective Care Environment
Analysis

CHAPTER 40

40.1 The parents of a critically injured child wish to stay in the room while the child is receiving emergency care. The nurse should:
a. escort the parents to the waiting room and assure them that they can see their child soon.
b. allow the parents to stay with the child.
c. ask the physician if the parents can stay with the child.
d. tell the parents that they do not need to stay with the child.

Answer: b
Rationale: Parents should be allowed to stay with their child if they wish to do so. This position is supported by the Emergency Nurses Association and is a key aspect of family-centered care.
Implementation
Psychosocial Integrity
Application

40.2 The charge nurse on a hospital unit is developing plans of care related to separation anxiety. The charge nurse recognizes the hospitalized child at highest risk to experience separation anxiety when parents cannot stay is the:
a. 6-month-old.
b. 18-month-old.
c. 3-year-old.
d. 4-year-old.

Answer: b
Rationale: While all of these children can experience separation anxiety, the young toddler is at highest risk. Toddlers are the group most at risk for a stressful experience when hospitalized. Separation from parents increases this risk greatly.
Diagnosis
Psychosocial Integrity
Application

40.3 It happens that a group of children on one hospital unit are suffering separation anxiety. When determining the stages of separation anxiety, the nurse recognizes the child in the despair phase is the child who:
a. plays with toys when parents are not around.
b. screams and cries when parents leave.
c. appears to be happy and content with staff.
d. lies quietly in bed.

Answer: d
Rationale: Children in the stage of despair appear sad, depressed, or withdrawn. A child who is lying in bed might be exhibiting any of these. Screaming and crying are components of the stage of protest. The young child who appears to be happy and content with everyone and the child who plays with toys when parents are not around are in the stage of denial.
Assessment
Psychosocial Integrity
Application

40.4 A 4-year-old is seen in the clinic for a sore throat. The most likely causative agent in the child's mind is that he:
a. was exposed to someone else with a sore throat.

Answer: c
Rationale: Preschoolers understand some concepts of being sick, but not the cause of illness. They are likely to think that they are sick as a result of something that they have done. They frequently will view illness as punishment. This child

b. did not eat the right foods. c. yelled at his brother. d. did not take his vitamins.	does not yet understand that he can become sick from exposure to someone else who is sick. The other two answers can be factors in some illnesses, but are beyond the thinking of a 4-year-old. Assessment Psychosocial Integrity Analysis
40.5 The charge nurse is concerned with reducing the stressors of hospitalization. The nursing intervention that is most helpful in decreasing the stressors for the toddler is to: a. assign the same nurse to the toddler as much as possible. b. let the child listen to an audiotape of the mother's voice. c. place a picture of the family at the bedside. d. encourage a parent to stay with the child.	Answer: d Rationale: While all of the interventions are appropriate for the hospitalized toddler, presence of a parent is most important. Separation from parents is the major stressor for the hospitalized toddler. Implementation Psychosocial Integrity Analysis
40.6 The nurse is working with a school-age child who is hospitalized. In planning care that will promote a sense of industry in this child, the nurse will: a. allow the child to assist with her care. b. encourage parents to participate in the child's care. c. give the child a detailed scientific explanation of the illness. d. speak to the child in a high-pitched voice.	Answer: a Rationale: Allowing the child to participate in care will decrease the sense of loss of control and increase a sense of industry. While parents certainly can participate in their child's care, it does not increase the child's sense of control. School-age children in general will not understand detailed scientific explanations. Change in voice tone is appropriate when talking to very young children. Implementation Psychosocial Integrity Application
40.7 The nurse is caring for a client in the pediatric intensive care. The parents have expressed anger over the nursing care their child is receiving. The nursing intervention most appropriate for these parents would be to: a. ask the physician to talk with the family. b. explain to the parents that their anger is affecting their child, so they will not be allowed to visit the child until they calm down. c. acknowledge the parents' concerns and collaborate with them regarding the care of their child. d. call the chaplain to sit with the family.	Answer: c Rationale: Hospitalization of the child in a pediatric intensive care unit is a great stressor for parents. If the parents feel that they are not informed or involved in the care of their child, they may become angry and upset. Calling the physician or chaplain may be appropriate at some point, but the nurse must assume the role of supporter in this situation to promote a sense of trust. Telling the parents that they cannot visit their child will only increase their anger. Implementation Psychosocial Integrity Application
40.8 The nurse needs to administer a medication to a 4-year-old. The medication is available only in tablet form. The nurse should: a. place the tablet on the child's tongue and give the child a drink of water. b. break the tablet in small pieces and ask the child to swallow the pieces one by one.	Answer: c Rationale: A 4-year-old is not mature enough to swallow a pill or pieces of a pill. The medication should be crushed and mixed with a very small amount of food, not juice. Implementation Physiological Integrity Application

c. crush the tablet and mix it in a teaspoon of applesauce. d. crush the tablet and mix it in a cup of juice.	
40.9 A 2-year-old child recently diagnosed with a seizure disorder will be discharged home on an anticonvulsant. Which of the following actions by the mother best demonstrates understanding of how to give the medication? The mother: a. verbalizes how to give the medication. b. acknowledges understanding of written instruction. c. draws up the medication correctly in an oral syringe and administers it to the child. d. observes the nurse draw up the medication and administer it to the child.	Answer: c Rationale: Verbalization of how to give the medication and acknowledging understanding of written instructions are methods that might be used, but they do not actually demonstrate understanding. Observing the nurse draw up and administer the medication may be used in the teaching process. The best way for the mother to demonstrate understanding is to actually draw up and give the medication. Evaluation Safe, Effective Care Environment Application
40.10 The nurse must perform a procedure on a toddler. The technique most appropriate when performing the procedure is to: a. ask the mother to restrain the child during the procedure. b. ask the child if it is okay to start the procedure. c. perform the procedure in the child's hospital bed. d. allow the child to cry or scream.	Answer: d Rationale: While the toddler will need to be restrained, the parent should not be the one to do this. The nurse should avoid giving the child a choice if there is no choice. The treatment room should be utilized for the procedure, so that the hospital bed remains a safe place. The child should be allowed to cry or scream during the procedure. Planning Psychosocial Integrity Application
40.11 A 5-year-old is in the playroom when the respiratory therapist arrives on the pediatric unit to give the child a scheduled breathing treatment. The nurse should: a. reschedule the treatment for a later time. b. show the respiratory therapist to the playroom so the treatment may be performed. c. postpone the treatment until the next scheduled time. d. assist the child back to his room for the treatment, but reassure him that he may return when the procedure is completed.	Answer: d Rationale: Procedures should not be performed in the playroom. Scheduled respiratory treatments should be performed on time, but the child should be allowed to return to the playroom as soon as the procedure is completed. Implementation Psychosocial Integrity Application
40.12 The nurse is working with a hospitalized preschool-age child. The nurse is planning activities to reduce anxiety in this child. The most appropriate action by the nurse is to: a. provide the child with a doll and safe medical equipment. b. read a story to the child. c. use an anatomically correct doll to teach the child about the illness. d. talk to the child about the hospitalization.	Answer: a Rationale: Therapeutic play is a means of anxiety reduction in the hospitalized child. Allowing the child to play with safe medical equipment is an age-appropriate method through which the child can express feelings, thereby reducing anxiety. Anatomically correct dolls are not age-appropriate. Reading a story to the child does not allow for expression of feelings. Talking to the child might be beneficial, but it does not allow for active release of frustration and anxiety. Implementation Psychosocial Integrity Application

40.13 A child is being discharged from the hospital after a three-week stay following a motor vehicle accident. The mother expresses concern about caring for the child's wounds at home. She has demonstrated appropriate technique with medication administration and wound care. The priority nursing diagnosis is:

a. knowledge deficit of home care.

b. altered family processes related to hospitalization.

c. parental anxiety related to care of the child at home.

d. risk for infection related to presence of healing wounds.

Answer: c

Rationale: While all of the diagnoses might have been appropriate at some point, the current focus is the mother's anxiety about caring for the child at home. The priority is to develop a plan to assist in relieving the anxiety.

Diagnosis

Psychosocial Integrity

Analysis

40.14 An infant has been NPO for surgery for 4 hours and does not have an intravenous line. The nurse receives a call from the operating room with the information that the surgery has been postponed due to an emergency. The nurse should:

a. feed the infant 4 oz of formula.

b. reassure the parents that it will not be much longer before surgery.

c. allow the parents to feed the infant an ounce of oral rehydration solution.

d. call the physician to see if the infant needs to have an intravenous line started.

Answer: d

Rationale: The infant who is NPO is at high risk for dehydration. The nurse does not know how much longer it will be before surgery. The nurse cannot make the decision to feed the infant independently. Feeding the infant could postpone the surgery further should an operating room become available sooner than expected. It is best to keep the infant NPO and consult the physician to see if an intravenous line is needed.

Planning

Physiological Integrity

Analysis

40.15 The nurse is working with an adolescent who will be admitted to the hospital in 2 days. The appropriate nursing intervention to prepare the adolescent for hospitalization is to: (Select all that apply.)

a. provide the adolescent with written material about the hospitalization.

b. provide an opportunity for the adolescent to talk with a peer who has had a similar experience.

c. teach the parents what to expect, so the information can be shared with the adolescent.

d. provide an opportunity for the teen to try on surgical attire.

e. explain the adolescent's upcoming surgery using an anatomically correct doll.

Answers: a, b, e

Rationale: Adolescents benefit from a different approach than do younger children when being prepared for hospitalization. Written materials, anatomically correct dolls, and talking to peers who have had similar experiences are all appropriate for the adolescent. The adolescent should be taught firsthand what to expect during the hospitalization. Dressing up in surgical attire is appropriate for the younger child.

Planning

Psychosocial Integrity

Application

CHAPTER 41

41.1 The nurse caring for a child who is sedated, unconscious, and on a mechanical ventilator can expect to include which of the following nursing interventions in the nursing care plan?

a. active range of motion (ROM) exercises.

Answer: b

Rationale: The child who is unconscious is unable to take anything by mouth and will need IV therapy for hydration. The nurse may perform passive ROM exercises on the child, but the child is incapable of doing active ROM exercises. The child would not be permitted to be transferred to a wheelchair or to take whirlpool baths.

---

b. maintenance of intravenous (IV) hydration. c. out-of-bed transfer to wheelchair. d. whirlpool baths.	Implementation Physiological Integrity Application
41.2 The parents of a 2-year-old child who sustained severe head trauma from falling out of a second-story window are arguing in the pediatric intensive care unit (PICU) and are blaming each other for the child's accident. The best nursing diagnosis for this family is: a. parental role conflict related to protecting the child. b. hopelessness related to the child's deteriorating condition. c. anxiety related to the critical care unit environment. d. family coping: compromised, related to the child's critical injury.	Answer: d Rationale: The parents are displaying ineffective coping behaviors as a family. Parental role conflict does not refer to the parents' argument in the PICU, but means a parent is conflicted or confused about some aspect of the parental role. Each parent might be experiencing hopelessness, frustration, and anxiety, but they are not coping well as a family unit. Diagnosis Psychosocial Integrity Analysis
41.3 A 6-year-old child is in the pediatric intensive care unit (PICU) with a fractured femur and head trauma. The child was not wearing a helmet while riding his new bicycle on the highway and collided with a car. The nurse can expect which of the following nursing diagnoses with parents of this child? (Select all that apply.) a. guilt related to lack of child supervision and safety precautions. b. family coping: compromised, related to the critical injury of the child. c. parental role conflict related to child's injuries and PICU policies. d. knowledge deficit, home care of fractured femur. e. anger related to feelings of helplessness.	Answers: a, b, c, e Rationale: All of these nursing diagnoses except knowledge deficit are possible in this situation. Although planning for discharge begins with admission, it is too early to begin teaching the parents about home care. The astute and experienced PICU nurse is prepared to recognize current problems and intervene appropriately. Diagnosis Psychosocial Integrity Analysis
41.4 The nurse must prepare parents to see their adolescent daughter in the pediatric intensive care unit (PICU). The child arrived by life flight after experiencing multiple traumas in a car accident involving a suspected drunk driver. At this time, the priority nursing statement would be: a. "Don't worry, everything will be okay. We will take excellent care of your child." b. "You should press charges against the drunk driver." c. "Your child's leg was crushed and might have to be amputated." d. "Your child's condition is very critical; her face is swollen, and she might not look like herself."	Answer: d Rationale: The priority is to prepare the parents for the child's changed appearance. The nurse must not offer false reassurance nor project future stressful events. Truthful statements about the child's condition can be introduced after the parents have seen the child and grasped the situation. The nurse supports the family, but remains nonjudgmental about accident details. Implementation Psychosocial Integrity Application

41.5 An adolescent with cystic fibrosis is intubated with an endotracheal tube. The most appropriate nursing diagnosis is:
a. potential for imbalanced nutrition, more than body requirements related to inactivity.
b. anxiety related to leaving chores undone at home.
c. potential for fear of future pain related to medical procedures.
d. powerlessness (moderate) related to inability to speak or communicate with friends.

Answer: d
Rationale: The adolescent values communication with peers and might feel frustrated that she cannot speak to them while intubated. The adolescent is present-, not future-, oriented and is unlikely to worry about household chores or future unknown procedures. The adolescent with cystic fibrosis is likely to be underweight and is unlikely to take in more calories than needed while intubated.
Diagnosis
Psychosocial Integrity
Analysis

41.6 The nurse is working with a 3-year-old child in Bryant's traction for a fractured femur. A pain assessment scale, such as the oucher scale, can be useful to the nurse caring for this child because use of a pain assessment scale:
a. provides continuity and consistency in assessing and monitoring the child's pain.
b. decreases anxiety in the child.
c. increases the child's comfort level.
d. reduces the child's fear of painful procedures.

Answer: a
Rationale: The purpose of a pain assessment scale is to assess and monitor pain. Using an assessment scale cannot reduce the child's anxiety or fear, nor increase the child's comfort level. The nurse can reduce anxiety or fear and increase the child's comfort level by implementing appropriate nursing interventions based on assessment scale data.
Implementation
Psychosocial Integrity
Analysis

41.7 A 16-year-old boy has a stiff neck, headache, fever of 103°F, and purpuric lesions on his legs. He is admitted to the hospital for treatment of suspected meningococcemia. Although the adolescent's physical needs take priority at the present time, the nurse can expect which of the following to be the most significant psychological stressor for this adolescent?
a. separation from parents and home.
b. separation from friends and permanent changes in appearance.
c. fear of painful procedures and bodily mutilation.
d. fear of getting behind in schoolwork.

Answer: b
Rationale: Adolescents are developing their identity and rely most on their friends. They are concerned about their appearance and how they look compared with their peers. Separation from parents and home is the main psychological stressor for infants and toddlers. Preschoolers fear pain and bodily mutilation. School-age children are developing a sense of industry and fear getting behind in schoolwork.
Assessment
Psychosocial Integrity
Application

41.8 A school bus carrying children in grades K–12 crashed into a ravine. The critically injured children were transported by ambulance and admitted to the pediatric intensive care unit (PICU). The nurse is concerned about calming the frightened children. The most effective nursing intervention to achieve this goal is which of the following?
a. tell the children that the physicians are competent.
b. assure the children that the nurses are caring.
c. explain that the PICU equipment is state of the art.
d. call the children's parents to come into the PICU.

Answer: d
Rationale: A sense of physical and psychological security is best achieved by the presence of parents. Children at all developmental levels look first to their parents or whoever acts as their parents for safety and security. Healthcare providers, no matter how competent or caring, cannot substitute for parents. Children often cannot recognize nor care about state-of-the-art equipment.
Implementation
Psychosocial Integrity
Application

41.9 A 12-year-old child with congenital heart block codes in the emergency room. The parents witness this and stare at the resuscitation scene unfolding before them. The best nursing intervention in this situation is which of the following?
a. ask the parents to leave.
b. ask the parents to help bag the child.
c. ask the parents to sit near the child's face and hold his hand.
d. ask the parents to stand at the foot of the cart to watch.

Answer: c
Rationale: Parents should be helped to support their child through emergency procedures, if they are able. Parents never should be asked to take part in emergency efforts unless absolutely necessary. Merely watching the resuscitation serves no purpose for the child. If the parents interfere with resuscitation efforts, or are unable to tolerate the situation, they can be asked to leave later.
Implementation
Psychosocial Integrity
Application

41.10 The nurse is working with children in hospice care. The mother of a young child with cancer talks with the nurse about the future holiday celebrations she will miss with her child. The nurse assesses that the mother is experiencing:
a. actual loss.
b. anticipatory loss.
c. perceived loss.
d. loss.

Answer: b
Rationale: Anticipatory loss is experienced before the loss actually transpires. Actual loss is a real loss objectively confirmed by others. A perceived loss is subjectively experienced by a person but cannot be confirmed by others. Loss is a general term for something of value being changed, no longer available, or no longer able to be experienced by an individual.
Assessment
Psychosocial Integrity
Application

41.11 A 3-year-old child with severe head trauma is intubated and on a respirator. The child has three flat electroencephalograms (EEG) done 24 hours apart. The electrocardiogram (EKG) shows a rate of 90 beats per minute in a normal sinus rhythm. The nurse assesses these findings as:
a. heart–lung death.
b. cerebral death.
c. imminent death.
d. natural death.

Answer: b
Rationale: Cerebral death, or brain death, is the irreversible cessation of all brain functions, including those of the cerebral cortex and brain stem, manifested by the absence of brain waves on EEG. Heart–lung death, the irreversible cessation of cardiorespiratory functions, has not occurred because the child is being mechanically ventilated. Imminent death means physical death is inevitable within a period of time. Natural death is allowing cessation of all body functions without extraordinary medical interventions.
Assessment
Physiological Integrity
Analysis

41.12 A 10-year-old boy was killed in a car accident. His 16-year-old brother was the driver of the car. At the brother's checkup a year later, he confides to the nurse that he has thoughts of killing himself to be with his brother. The nurse assesses that this adolescent may be experiencing:
a. anticipatory grief.
b. disenfranchised grief.
c. dysfunctional grief.
d. resolved grief.

Answer: c
Rationale: Plans of suicide to reunite with a deceased loved one are a sign of dysfunctional grief, grief that is unhealthy, unresolved, or inhibited. Anticipatory grief is grieving for a future loss. Disenfranchised grief involves grief that cannot be shared with or acknowledged by others. Resolved grief occurs when the bereaved person has gone through the mourning process, adapted to the loss of a loved one, and begins to enjoy life again.
Assessment
Psychosocial Integrity
Analysis

41.13 The emergency room nurse is talking with a preschooler about the death of the child's parents in an airplane crash. The preschooler asks, "Can I talk to my mommy and daddy?" The nurse responds, "They were killed, and cannot talk to you anymore." However, the nurse realizes that preschoolers may:
a. believe death is permanent.
b. believe the parents will not come back home.

Answer: d
Rationale: Preschoolers engage in magical thinking and may believe they wished or caused the death of their parents. Preschoolers do not have a concept of death as permanent, therefore, they might expect their parents to return home.
Implementation
Psychosocial Integrity
Application

---

c. engage in reality-based thinking.
d. believe deaths are their fault.

41.14 A terminally ill 10-year-old child asks the nurse, "What is it like to die? Will I be an angel? I think my parents know I am dying, but they don't talk to me about it." The nurse knows the child is dying, but the parents have not discussed this with the nurse. The nurse assesses the child and family to be at what level of understanding of the impending death of the child?
a. closed awareness.
b. open awareness.
c. mutual pretense.
d. denial.

Answer: c
Rationale: The parents and child are carrying on a mutual pretense. They know the child is dying but cannot discuss it with each other. In closed awareness, the child and family are unaware of impending death or believe the child will recover. Open awareness is characterized by open and comfortable communication among the child, family, and the healthcare team. Denial is the refusal of parents and child to believe the child will die.
Assessment
Psychosocial Integrity
Analysis

41.15 The hospital nurses, after attending a conference on nursing burnout, discuss among themselves strategies to use when working with families of dying children. Which of the following would be helpful? (Select all that apply.)
a. planning the child and family's care alone as the primary nurse.
b. participating in team decisions to decide the dying child's plan of care.
c. declining the family's invitation to attend the child's funeral.
d. participating in a mentoring relationship with experienced hospice nurses.
e. participating in support groups with mental health professionals.

Answers: b, d, e
Rationale: Team decisions, mentorship, and support groups all alleviate the responsibility of providing nursing care and coping with the death of a child alone. Planning the child's care alone might result in an excessive burden of guilt. Distancing oneself from the family may result in unresolved grief.
Implementation
Psychosocial Integrity
Application

CHAPTER 42

42.1 The nurse is admitting an 8-year-old Vietnamese child who hit a parked car while riding a bike. The child has a fracture of the left radius and femur in addition to a fractured orbit. The child is stoic and denies pain. The most appropriate initial action by the nurse is to:
a. use the FLACC scale to determine the child's pain level.
b. tell the child to ring the call bell if the leg starts hurting.
c. administer pain medication now and continue on a regular basis.
d. ask the child's parents to notify the nurse if the child complains of pain.

Answer: c
Rationale: Based on the type of injuries the child has, pain will be present. Analgesics should be given on a scheduled basis so that the pain does not get out of control. The FLACC scale is not the most appropriate tool to use with an 8-year-old. The child's stoic expression is likely to be culturally related, and the child might not admit to hurting. While asking the parents to call the nurse is not inappropriate, it is not the most appropriate initial action.
Implementation
Physiological Integrity
Analysis

42.2 During the nurse's initial assessment of a school-aged child, the child reports a pain level of 6 out of 10. The child is lying quietly in bed watching television. The nurse should:
a. administer prescribed analgesic.
b. ask the child's parents if they think the child is hurting.
c. reassess the child in 15 minutes to see if the pain rating has changed.

Answer: a
Rationale: School-age children are old enough to report their pain level accurately. A pain score of 6 is an indication for prompt administration of pain medication. The child might be trying to be brave, or might be lying still because movement is painful.
Assessment
Physiological Integrity
Application

d. do nothing, since the child appears to be resting.	
42.3 A 10-year-old has been receiving morphine every 2 hours for postoperative pain as ordered. The medication relieves the pain for approximately 90 minutes and then the pain returns. The nurse should: a. tell the child that pain medication cannot be administered more frequently than every 2 hours. b. reposition the child and quietly leave the room. c. inform the parents that the child is dependent on the medication. d. call the physician to see if the child's orders for pain medication can be changed.	Answer: d Rationale: The nurse has the responsibility to relieve the child's pain. The child has been receiving the prescribed medication on a regular basis. The physician should be called to see if the child's orders can be changed. This child might do well with PCA. Oral medications such as acetaminophen and NSAIDS can be given with morphine to provide optimum pain relief. Implementation Physiological Integrity Application
42.4 The nurse is working in a pediatric surgical unit. In discussing patient-controlled analgesia in a pre-op parental meeting, the nurse would explain that PCA is most appropriate for the: a. developmentally delayed 16-year-old post-op bone surgery. b. 5-year-old post-op tonsillectomy. c. 10-year-old who has a fractured femur and concussion from a bike accident. d. 12-year-old post-op spinal fusion for scoliosis.	Answer: d Rationale: Patient controlled analgesia (PCA) is most appropriate in children 5 years old and older. Children must be able to press the button, and to understand that they will receive pain medicine by pushing the button. PCA generally is prescribed for clients who will be hospitalized for at least 48 hours. Children who are developmentally delayed or have suffered head trauma would not be candidates for PCA. Implementation Physiological Integrity Analysis
42.5 A 2-year-old is hospitalized with a fractured femur. In addition to pain medication, which of the following will best provide pain relief for this child? a. parents' presence at the bedside. b. age-appropriate toys. c. deep breathing exercises. d. providing videos for the child to watch.	Answer: a Rationale: Parents' presence at the bedside reduces anxiety and subsequently reduces pain. Although play and other methods of distraction might be somewhat effective, they do not equal the comfort that parents' presence provides, especially in a 2-year-old who is also at high risk for separation anxiety. Planning Physiological Integrity Application
42.6 The nurse is caring for a 2-year-old child in the postoperative period. The pain assessment tool most appropriate for assessment of pain intensity in a 2-year-old is the: a. FLACC behavioral pain assessment scale. b. faces pain scale. c. oucher scale. d. poker chip tool.	Answer: a Rationale: The FLACC scale is an appropriate tool for infants and young children who cannot self-report pain. The faces scale, oucher scale, and the poker tool are all self-report scales. Assessment Physiological Integrity Application
42.7 The nurse is caring for a child who has a long leg cast. The child complains of increasing pain in the toes of the foot in the cast. The nurse's initial action is to: a. call the physician to report increasing pain. b. administer pain medication. c. reposition the child in bed. d. check to see if the cast is too tight.	Answer: d Rationale: While all of the actions are appropriate, the nurse's initial action is to assess for external factors that might be causing pain. Assessment Physiological Integrity Application

42.8 A hospitalized 3-year-old needs to have an IV restarted. The child begins to cry when carried into the treatment room by the mother. The most appropriate nursing diagnosis is:
a. ineffective individual coping related to an invasive procedure.
b. anxiety related to anticipated painful procedure.
c. fear related to the unfamiliar environment.
d. knowledge deficit of the procedure.

Answer: b
Rationale: This aged child is not old enough to understand the need for an IV infusion. The stem indicates that the child has been through this painful procedure before, and his reaction to entering the treatment room is based on anticipation of repeat discomfort. The child's behavior is appropriate for this aged child.
Diagnosis
Psychosocial Integrity
Analysis

42.9 A parent asks the nurse if there is anything that can be done to reduce the pain that his 3-year-old experiences each morning when blood is drawn for lab studies. The most appropriate method the nurse can suggest to relieve pain associated with the venipuncture is:
a. intravenous sedation 15 minutes prior to the procedure.
b. EMLA cream applied to skin at least 1 hour prior to the procedure.
c. use of guided imagery during the procedure.
d. use of muscle relaxation techniques.

Answer: b
Rationale: Sedation generally is not used with quick minor procedures such as venipuncture. A 3-year-old is too young to participate in techniques such as muscle relaxation and guided imagery. EMLA cream is shown to be effective in providing topical anesthesia if applied at least 1 hour prior to the procedure.
Implementation
Physiological Integrity
Application

42.10 As an advocate for the child undergoing bone marrow aspiration, the nurse would most appropriately suggest:
a. general anesthesia.
b. sedation prior to and during the procedure.
c. intravenous narcotics 10 minutes before the procedure.
d. oral pain medication for discomfort after the procedure.

Answer: b
Rationale: It is important for the child undergoing repeated procedures to be sedated prior to and during the initial procedure. General anesthesia is not necessary for bone marrow aspiration alone. Narcotics alone will not provide appropriate sedation to keep the child from remembering the procedure. While oral pain medication post-procedure is not inappropriate if discomfort exists, it is not the best answer. The child will have great anxiety and discomfort during the procedures and prior to future procedures.
Implementation
Psychosocial Integrity
Application

42.11 A 5-year-old is being discharged from the outpatient surgical center. Which statement by the parent would indicate the need for further teaching?
a. "I can expect my child to have some pain for the next few days."
b. "I will plan to give my child pain medicine around the clock for the next day or so."
c. "Since my child just had surgery today, I can expect the pain level to be higher tomorrow."
d. "I will call the office tomorrow if the pain medicine is not relieving the pain."

Answer: c
Rationale: Increasing pain can be a sign of complication, and should be reported to the physician. If the parent makes the statement in answer c, the nurse should clarify expectations for pain control. The child is expected to have some pain for a few days after surgery and should receive pain medication on a scheduled basis. If prescribed medication is not relieving the pain to a satisfactory level, the physician should be notified.
Evaluation
Physiological Integrity
Analysis

42.12 The nurse is caring for a child who has been sedated for a painful procedure. The priority nursing activity for this child is:
a. allowing parents to stay with the child.
b. monitoring pulse oximetry.

Answer: c
Rationale: When the child is sedated for a procedure, it is very important for the nurse actually to visualize the child and her effort of breathing. Although equipment is important and is used routinely during sedation, it does not replace the need for visual assessment. Parents may be allowed to stay with the child, but assessment of breathing effort must take priority.

---

c. assessing the child's respiratory effort. d. placing the child on a cardiac monitor.	Implementation Physiological Integrity Application
42.13 The nurse is preparing to perform a heel stick on a newborn. The most appropriate complementary therapy for the nurse to plan to use for the newborn to decrease pain during this quick but painful procedure is: a. swaddling. b. sucrose pacifier. c. massage. d. holding the infant.	Answer: b Rationale: Sucrose provides short-term natural pain relief and is most appropriate for use in newborns to decrease pain associated with a quick procedure. The other measures are more appropriate following the procedure or as an adjunct to pain medication for ongoing pain or distress. Planning Physiological Integrity Application
42.14 A 3-year-old is hospitalized following surgery for a ruptured appendix. During assessment of the child, the nurse notes that the child is sleeping. Vital signs are as follows: temperature 97.8 axillary, pulse 90, respirations 12, and blood pressure 100/60. Based on this assessment, the nurse concludes that the child is: a. comfortable, and the pain is controlled. b. in shock secondary to blood loss during surgery. c. experiencing respiratory depression secondary to opioid administration for postoperative pain. d. sleeping to avoid pain associated with surgery.	Answer: c Rationale: Respiratory depression secondary to opioid use is most likely to occur when the child is sleeping. A respiratory rate of 12 is well below normal for a 3-year-old. The other vital signs are within normal limits for a sleeping 3-year-old. Evaluation Physiological Integrity Analysis
41.25 A 5-year-old is hospitalized with a fractured femur. Which of the following assessment tools are appropriate for this age child? (Select all that apply.) a. faces pain scale. b. oucher scale. c. visual analog scale. d. CRIES scale. e. poker chip tool.	Answers: a, b, e Rationale: A 5-year-old should be able to use the faces and oucher scale to choose which face best matches his pain level. The child also should be able to count and understand the concepts of the poker chip tool. The CRIES Scale was developed for preterm and full-term neonates. A 5-year-old is not old enough to use the visual analog scale. Assessment Physiological Integrity Application

CHAPTER 43

43.1 A nurse is taking care of four different pediatric clients. The client with the greatest risk for dehydration is the child: a. over 2 years of age with migraine headaches. b. under 2 years of age with tachypnea. c. over 2 years of age with a broken arm. d. under 2 years of age with cellulitis of the left leg.	Answer: b Rationale: The pediatric client with the greatest risk is under 2 years of age and has a condition that increases insensible fluid loss. The pediatric client with a chronic or acute condition that does not directly affect the GI or electrolyte system is at a lower risk than a client with a condition that increases insensible water loss—in this case, tachypnea. Planning Safe, Effective Care Environment Analysis

43.2 The nurse is assessing an infant brought to the clinic because of diarrhea. The infant is alert, but has dry mucous membranes. Which other sign indicates the infant still is in the early or mild stage of dehydration?

a. tachycardia.
b. bradycardia.
c. increased blood pressure.
d. decreased blood pressure.

Answer: a
Rationale: Tachycardia is a sign that indicates mild dehydration. Bradycardia and increased blood pressure are not signs of dehydration. Decreased blood pressure is not a sign of mild dehydration. Decreased blood pressure indicates moderate-to-severe dehydration.
Assessment
Physiological Integrity
Analysis

43.3 A 1-month-old infant is admitted to the emergency room with severe diarrhea. Which of the following assessments suggests the infant is severely dehydrated?

a. skin moist and flushed; mucous membranes dry.
b. low specific gravity of urine; skin color pale.
c. fontanelles depressed; capillary refill greater than 3 seconds.
d. high specific gravity of urine; moist mucous membranes.

Answer: c
Rationale: Two signs of severe dehydration are depressed fontanelles and capillary refill time greater than 3 seconds. Moist, flushed skin; moist mucous membranes; and low specific gravity of urine are not signs of dehydration. Dry mucous membranes and pale skin color are signs of mild, not severe, dehydration.
Assessment
Physiological Integrity
Analysis

43.4 The nurse is expecting the admission of a child with severe isotonic dehydration. Which intravenous fluid should the nurse anticipate the doctor to order initially to replace fluids?

a. D5W.
b. 0.9% normal saline (NS).
c. albumin.
d. D5 0.2% (1/4) normal saline.

Answer: b
Rationale: 0.9% normal saline (NS) maintains Na and chloride at present levels. D5W can lower sodium levels, and so would not be used initially to replace fluids in severe isotonic dehydration. Albumin is used to restore plasma proteins. D5 0.2% (1/4) normal saline would be used later, as maintenance fluids.
Implementation
Physiological Integrity
Application

43.5 Parents of an infant with slow weight gain ask the nurse if they can feed their baby a high-concentrated formula. An appropriate response given by the nurse would be:

a. "A higher-concentrated formula could lead to dehydration because of high sodium content. Let's discuss other strategies."
b. "An undiluted formula concentrate could be given to help the child gain weight. Let's look at brands."
c. "Evaporated milk could be given to the infant instead of the current formula you're using."
d. "A higher-concentrated formula could be given for daytime feedings. Let's work on a schedule."

Answer: a
Rationale: Parents and caregivers of bottle-fed babies should be taught never to give undiluted formula concentrate or evaporated milk due to the high-sodium content.
Implementation
Physiological Integrity
Application

43.6 The nurse has just finished a parent teaching session on preventing heat-related illnesses for children who exercise. Which statement by a parent indicates understanding of preventive techniques taught?

a. "Hydration should occur at the end of an exercise session."

Answer: d
Rationale: During activity, stopping for fluids every 15 to 20 minutes is recommended. Hydration should occur before and during the activity, not just at the end. A combination of water and sports drinks is best to replace fluids during exercise. Light-colored, light clothing is best to wear during exercise activities. Wearing of dark colors can increase sweating.
Evaluation
Health Promotion and Maintenance
Analysis

---

b. "Water is the drink of choice to replenish fluids."
c. "Wearing dark clothing during exercise is recommended."
d. "During activity, stop for fluids every 15 to 20 minutes."

43.7 A child is being treated for dehydration with intravenous fluids. The child currently weighs 13 kg and is estimated to have lost 7% of her normal body weight. The nurse is double-checking the IV rate the physician has ordered. The formula the physician used was maintenance fluids: 1000 mL for 10 kg of body weight plus 50 cc for every kg over 10 for 24 hours. Replacement fluid is the percentage of lost body weight x 10 per kg of body weight. According to the calculation for maintenance and replacement fluid, this child's hourly IV rate for 24 hours should be: _____.

Answer: 86
Rationale: Maintenance needs for 13 kg is 1,000 + (50 × 3), or 1,150 mL/24 hr. Add to this the replacement fluid loss = 7 (percent of total body weight lost) × 10 = 70 mL/kg/24hr (70 × 13 = 910). 1,150 + 910 = 2,060 for 24 hours. 2060/24 = 86 mL per hour.
Implementation
Physiological Integrity
Application

43.8 In the morning, a nurse receives a report on four pediatric clients, each of whom has some form of fluid volume excess. The nurse should check which child first? The child with:
a. periorbital edema, normal respiratory rate.
b. tachypnea and pulmonary congestion.
c. dependent and sacral edema, regular pulse.
d. hepatomegaly, normal respiratory rate.

Answer: b
Rationale: A child with respiratory distress should be the first client the nurse checks after receiving the report. The child with periorbital edema and normal respiratory rate, the child with dependent and sacral edema and regular pulse, and the child with hepatomegaly and normal respiratory rate are more stable than the child with tachypnea and pulmonary congestion.
Implementation
Safe, Effective Care Environment
Application

43.9 The nurse is caring for a child on bed rest who has severe edema in the left lower leg due to blocked lymphatic drainage. A priority nursing diagnosis would be:
a. risk for imbalanced nutrition: less than body requirements.
b. risk for impaired skin integrity.
c. risk for altered body image.
d. risk for activity intolerance.

Answer: b
Rationale: The highest-priority problem is skin integrity. Nutrition, body image, and activity intolerance would not take priority over the integrity of the skin for this scenario.
Diagnosis
Safe, Effective Care Environment
Application

43.10 An infant is in the hospital for hypernatremia. The most appropriate means of collecting urine for a specific gravity test is by:
a. placing cotton balls in the diaper and then (wearing gloves) squeezing a drop of urine from the cotton balls onto the specific gravity test strip.
b. performing a sterile in-and-out catheterization to collect urine for the specific gravity test strip.
c. placing a urine collection bag on the infant.
d. inserting a Foley catheter to obtain a sterile urine specimen for the specific gravity test strip.

Answer: a
Rationale: Urine for a specific gravity test should be collected by placing cotton balls in the diaper. Only a small amount of clean (uncontaminated from stool) urine is needed to do a specific gravity test. An in-and-out catheter or a Foley catheter would be invasive for this clean collection of a small amount of urine. A urine bag can be irritating to the skin and would not be appropriate for collecting a small amount of urine for a specific gravity test.
Implementation
Physiological Integrity
Application

43.11 A nurse is planning care for a child with hyponatremia. The nurse, delegating care of this child to an LVN, cautions the LVN that the child should be watched for: a. seizures. b. bradycardia. c. respiratory distress. d. hyperthermia.	Answer: a Rationale: A child with hyponatremia is at risk for seizures. Bradycardia, respiratory distress, and hyperthermia are not risks of hyponatremia. Planning Safe, Effective Care Environment Analysis
43.12 A 6-year-old child is hypokalemic. The nurse is helping the child choose menu items. The nurse would encourage this child to select: a. hamburger with french fries. b. pizza with a fruit plate. c. chicken strips with chips. d. fajita with rice.	Answer: b Rationale: Pizza with a fruit plate should be encouraged because fruit (bananas, apricots, cantaloupe, cherries, peaches, and strawberries) have high amounts of potassium, and a child is likely to eat this combination. The other choices would not be as high in potassium. Intervention Physiological Integrity Application
43.13 A child is admitted to the hospital for hypercalcemia and is placed on diuretic therapy. Which diuretic would the nurse expect to give? a. hydrochlorothiazide (Aquazide). b. spironolactone (Aldactone). c. furosemide (Lasix). d. mannitol (Osmitrol).	Answer: c Rationale: Furosemide (Lasix) is the diuretic used to aid in excretion of calcium. Thiazide diuretics (hydrochlorothiazide) decrease calcium excretion, and should not be given to the hypercalcemic client. Mannitol (Osmitrol) is a diuretic used to decrease cerebral edema, and is not routinely used to aid in excretion of calcium. Spironolactone (Aldactone) is a potassium-sparing diuretic, and would not be effective for excretion of calcium. Planning Physiological Integrity Application
43.14 A child with croup has an increased PCO_2, a decreased pH, and a normal HCO_3 blood gas value. The nurse interprets this as uncompensated: a. respiratory acidosis. b. respiratory alkalosis. c. metabolic acidosis. d. metabolic alkalosis.	Answer: a Rationale: If the pH is decreased and the PCO_2 is increased with a normal HCO_3, it is uncompensated respiratory acidosis. Also, croup can be a disease process that causes respiratory acidosis. Respiratory alkalosis, uncompensated, has an increased pH, decreased PCO_2 and normal HCO_3; metabolic acidosis, uncompensated, has a decreased pH, normal PCO_2, and normal HCO_3; and metabolic alkalosis, uncompensated, has an increased pH, normal PCO_2, and increased HCO_3. Planning Physiological Integrity Analysis

43.15 The nurse is completing the intake and output record for a child admitted for fluid volume deficits. The child has had the following intake and output during the shift:
Intake:
    4 oz of Pedialyte
    1/2 of an 8 oz cup of clear orange Jell-O
    2 graham crackers
    200 mL of D5 1/2 sodium chloride IV
    Output:
    345 mL of urine
    50 mL of loose stool
How many milliliters should the nurse document as the client's intake? _____.
	Answer: 440
	Rationale: Pedialyte, Jell-O, and IV fluid would be calculated for intake. The child has had 240 mL orally and 200 mL intravenously for a total of 440.
	Implementation
	Physiological Integrity
	Application

44.1 A nurse has begun an infusion of intravenous immunoglobulin (IVIG) to a child who has combined immunodeficiency disease. The infusion should be stopped if the child:

a. experiences a mild headache.
b. voids clear yellow urine.
c. develops severe shaking, chills, and fever.
d. complains of being "thirsty."

Answer: c
Rationale: Hypersensitivity reaction can be seen with IVIG. The infusion should be started slowly and increased if there is no reaction. Shaking, chills, and fever can indicate a reaction. A mild headache is an adverse side effect of IVIG but not a severe reaction. Thirst is not an indication of a reaction. Voiding clear yellow urine is a normal finding.
Implementation
Physiological Integrity
Application

44.2 A nurse is administering an intramuscular vaccination to an infant who has Wiskott-Aldrich syndrome (WAS). Because of this syndrome, this infant is at higher risk for:

a. pain at the injection site.
b. bleeding at the injection site.
c. redness and swelling at the injection site.
d. mild rash at the injection site.

Answer: b
Rationale: Wiskott-Aldrich syndrome is characterized by thrombocytopenia, with bleeding tendencies appearing during the neonatal period. The syndrome would not put the child at higher risk for pain, redness, swelling, or rash at the injection site.
Diagnosis
Physiological Integrity
Analysis

44.3 A nurse is planning care for a child with human immunodeficiency virus (HIV). The highest-priority nursing problem for this child is:

a. risk for infection.
b. risk for fluid volume deficit.
c. ineffective thermoregulation.
d. ineffective tissue perfusion, peripheral.

Answer: a
Rationale: A child with HIV is at risk for a myriad of bacterial, viral, fungal, and opportunistic infections because of the effect of the virus on the immune system. Risk for fluid volume deficit, ineffective thermoregulation, and ineffective tissue perfusion, peripheral, would not be priority problems with this disease process.
Diagnosis
Safe, Effective Care Environment
Application

44.4 A child is receiving didanosine, a nucleoside reverse transcriptase inhibitor, for human immunodeficiency virus (HIV). The lab value the nurse should monitor is:

a. potassium.
b. sodium.
c. red blood cell count.
d. glucose.

Answer: c
Rationale: Didanosine causes bone marrow suppression with resulting anemia. Red blood cell counts are monitored at least monthly for changes. Potassium and sodium are electrolytes, and glucose is a laboratory test for checking diabetes. Didanosine does not affect these values.
Assessment
Physiological Integrity
Application

44.5 A child with the human immunodeficiency virus is started on sulfamethoxazole and trimethoprim (Bactrim) for *pneumocystis carinii pneumonia* (PCP) prophylaxis. The recommended dose is based on the trimethoprim (TMP) component and is 15 to 20 mg TMP/kg/day in divided doses every 6 to 8 hours. The child weighs 6.8 kg. What is the highest dose of TMP he can receive a day? _____.

Answer: 136
Rationale: 6.8×20 mg $= 136$ mg/day.
Implementation
Physiological Integrity
Application

44.6 The immunization a child with acquired immunodeficiency syndrome (AIDS) should not receive is the:

a. diphtheria and tetanus toxoids and acellular pertussis vaccine (DTaP).
b. *Haemophilus influenzae* type B (HIB conjugate vaccine).

Answer: c
Rationale: A child with an immune disorder should not be immunized with a live varicella vaccine because of the risk of contracting the disease. DTaP, HIB, and hepatitis B vaccinations are not live vaccines and should be given on schedule.
Implementation
Health Promotion and Maintenance
Application

c. varicella vaccine. d. hepatitis B vaccine (Hep B).	
44.7 A child with human immunodeficiency virus (HIV) also has oral candidiasis. Mouth care for this child should be with: a. normal saline. b. Listerine. c. Scope. d. viscous lidocaine.	Answer: a Rationale: The mouth care should be with a nonalcohol base. Normal saline can keep the child's lips and mouth moist. Listerine and Scope are commercial mouth rinses that can have an alcohol base and cause drying of the membranes. Viscous lidocaine causes numbing, and could depress the gag reflex in a younger child. Implementation Physiological Integrity Application
44.8 A problem the nurse anticipates for a family who has a child with acquired immunodeficiency syndrome (AIDS) is: a. anticipatory grieving. b. family coping, compromised. c. risk for impaired parenting. d. parental role conflict.	Answer: a Rationale: AIDS is not curable so the problem nurses can anticipate, for all families, is anticipatory grieving. Compromised family coping, risk for impaired parenting, and parental role conflict may be present, but further information is needed to anticipate these problems. Diagnosis Psychosocial Integrity Application
44.9 An adolescent has systemic lupus erythematosus (SLE). An action by the adolescent that indicates acceptance of body changes with SLE would be that the teen: a. refuses to attend school. b. doesn't want to attend any social functions. c. discusses the body changes with a peer. d. discusses the body changes with healthcare personnel only.	Answer: c Rationale: Peer interaction is important to the teen. Being able to discuss the changes to his body with a peer indicates acceptance of the change in body image. Discussing changes only with healthcare personnel does not indicate the teen has adjusted to body image changes. Refusing to go to school and not going to social functions indicate nonacceptance of the changes to body image. Evaluation Psychosocial Integrity Analysis
44.10 A school-age child with rheumatoid arthritis asks the nurse to recommend an exercise activity. The nurse should recommend: a. softball. b. football. c. swimming. d. basketball.	Answer: c Rationale: Swimming helps to exercise all of the extremities without putting undue stress on joints. Softball, football, and basketball could exacerbate joint discomfort. Implementation Health Promotion and Maintenance Application
44.11 The nurse is caring for a child with rheumatoid arthritis. A nonpharmacological measure to reduce the joint pain is: a. moist heat. b. elevation of the extremity. c. massage. d. immobilization.	Answer: a Rationale: Moist heat can promote relief of pain and decrease joint stiffness. Elevation of the extremity would not have an effect on reducing pain in rheumatoid arthritis. Massage of extremities should be avoided because of the potential risk for emboli. Immobilization can lead to contractures, and range of motion to the involved joint should be maintained. Implementation Physiological Integrity Analysis
44.12 The nurse is caring for a child who experiences an anaphylactic shock reaction. The nurse should place the child: a. in the Trendelenburg position. b. in the high Fowler's position.	Answer: d Rationale: Flat, with legs slightly elevated is the position that is used for a client experiencing shock. This allows for the blood pressure to be maintained during this critical time. The Trendelenburg position no longer is recommended for the treatment of shock. The position causes abdominal organs to press against the

c. in the reverse Trendelenburg position. d. flat, with legs slightly elevated.	diaphragm, which impedes respirations and decreases coronary artery filling. High Fowler's and reverse Trendelenburg are positions that have the head elevated. This position is not effective to maintain a blood pressure when shock is occurring. Implementation Physiological Integrity Application
44.13 You are the nurse in charge on a hospital unit over the weekend. A nurse technician is showing symptoms of latex sensitivity. You should: a. send the nurse technician to a department that does not use latex products. b. contact the employee health department in the facility and obtain latex-free products for the nurse technician. c. wait until Monday to report the problem to the supervisor of the unit. d. assign the nurse technician nonpatient care duties.	Answer: b Rationale: When symptoms of sensitivity to latex occur on exposure, the employee health department of the facility should be contacted, and latex-free products should be supplied. The other options are not realistic because the nurse technician may experience exposure on another unit (no hospital unit can be latex-free), waiting until Monday does not solve the problem, and assigning the nurse technician nonpatient duties might not be possible. Implementation Safe, Effective Care Environment Application
44.14 A child with a myelomeningocele has a latex allergy. Which product should not be used for a dressing change for this child? a. 4 × 4 gauze. b. transpore tape. c. elastroplast. d. duoderm.	Answer: c Rationale: Elastroplast is a product that frequently contains latex. 4 x 4 gauze, transpore tape, and duoderm are latex-safe. Implementation Physiological Integrity Application
44.15 A child has been placed on a corticosteroid for a rash caused by graft-versus-host disease. A side effect of the steroid the nurse should monitor is: a. hyperglycemia. b. renal toxicity. c. hepatic toxicity. d. seizures.	Answer: a Rationale: Hyperglycemia is a side effect of steroid therapy. Renal and hepatic toxicity and seizures are not side effects associated with steroid therapy. Assessment Physiological Integrity Analysis

CHAPTER 45

45.1 A nurse is providing information to a group of new mothers. The nurse would explain that newborns and young infants are more susceptible to infection because they have: a. high levels of maternal antibodies to diseases to which the mother has been exposed. b. passive transplacental immunity from maternal immunoglobulin G. c. immune systems that are not fully mature at birth. d. been exposed to microorganisms during the birth process.	Answer: c Rationale: Newborns have a limited storage pool of neutrophils and plasma proteins to defend against infection. Newborns' and young infants' high levels of maternal antibodies, passive transplacental immunity, and exposure to microorganisms during the birth process all are true statements but are incorrect answers because they do not explain the susceptibility of newborns and young infants to infection. Implementation Physiological Integrity Analysis

45.2 A 3-year-old child is lying in a fetal position. The child has pale skin, glassy eyes, and a flat affect. The child is irritable and refuses food and fluids. The child's vital signs are a temperature of 40.1°C (104.2°F), pulse of 120/min, and respirations of 28/min. The best, most comprehensive description of this child's condition is:

a. toxic.
b. feverish.
c. flushed.
d. tired.

Answer: a
Rationale: The child described as having a toxic appearance is one with a high temperature, lethargy, irritability, poor skin perfusion, hypoventilation or hyperventilation, and cyanosis. The child has a high fever, and the child may be tired, but these words are not the best, most comprehensive description of the child's condition. The term "flushed" is incorrect because it indicates a reddish appearance to the skin. The child has pale skin, which would be a white appearance to the skin.
Assessment
Physiological Integrity
Analysis

45.3 The nurse prepares the second diphtheria, tetanus toxoid, and acellular pertussis (DTAP) and second inactivated polio vaccine (IPV) immunization injections for an infant who is 4 months old. Provided a separate injection site is used for all injections, the nurse also may give which of the following immunizations during the same well child care appointment?

a. varicella (Var).
b. influenza (TIV).
c. measles, mumps, rubella (MMR).
d. *haemophilus influenzae* type B (HIB).

Answer: d
Rationale: *Haemophilus influenzae* type B (HIB) vaccine is given at 2, 4, 6, and 12 to 15 months of age (four doses). None of the other vaccines can be given to a 4-month-old infant. Influenza (TIV) vaccine may be given yearly to infants between 6 months and 3 years of age. Measles, mumps, and rubella (MMR) vaccine is given at 12 to 15 months and 4 to 6 years of age (two doses). Varicella (Var) is given at 12 to 18 months or anytime up to 12 years (one dose) and for 13 years and older (two doses, 4 to 8 weeks apart).
Implementation
Health Promotion and Maintenance
Application

45.4 A mother refuses to have her child immunized with measles, mumps, and rubella (MMR) vaccine because she believes that letting her infant get these diseases will help him fight off other diseases later in life. The nurse's most appropriate response to this mother is to:

a. honor her request because she is the parent.
b. explain that antibodies can fight many diseases.
c. tell her that not immunizing her infant might protect pregnant women.
d. explain that if her child contracts measles, mumps, or rubella, he could have very serious and permanent complications from these diseases.

Answer: d
Rationale: Explaining that if her child contracts measles, mumps, or rubella, he could have very serious and permanent complications from these diseases is correct because measles, mumps, and rubella all have potentially serious sequelae, such as encephalitis, brain damage, and deafness. Honoring her request is not correct, because the nurse has a professional duty to explain that the mother's belief about immunizations is erroneous and may result in harm to her infant. Explaining that antibodies can fight many diseases is not correct because the body makes antibodies that are specific to antigens of each disease. Antibodies for one disease cannot fight another disease. Telling her that not immunizing her infant might protect pregnant women is not correct, because immunizing the infant with MMR vaccine will help protect pregnant women from contracting rubella by decreasing the transmission. If a pregnant woman should contract rubella, her fetus can be severely damaged with congenital rubella syndrome.
Implementation
Health Promotion and Maintenance
Application

45.5 A parent reports that her 5-year-old child, who has had all recommended immunizations, had a mild fever one week ago and now has bright red cheeks and a lacy red rash on the trunk and arms. The nurse recognizes that this child may have:

a. chickenpox (varicella).
b. German measles (rubella).
c. roseola (exanthem subitum).
d. fifth disease (erythema infectiosum).

Answer: d
Rationale: Fifth disease manifests first with a flu-like illness, followed by a red "slapped cheek" sign. Then a lacy maculopapular erythematous rash spreads symmetrically from the trunk to the extremities, sparing the soles and palms. Chickenpox (Varicella) and German measles (rubella) are unlikely if the child had all recommended immunizations. The rash of varicella progresses from papules to vesicles to pustules. The rash of rubella is a pink maculopapular rash that begins on the face and progresses downward to the trunk and extremities. Roseola typically occurs in infants, and begins abruptly with a high fever, followed by a pale pink rash starting on the trunk and spreading to the face, neck, and extremities.
Diagnosis
Physiologic Integrity
Analysis

45.6 The nurse prepares a DTaP (diphtheria, tetanus toxoid, and acellular pertussis) immunization for a 6-month-old infant. To administer this injection safely, the nurse chooses which of the following needles (size and length), injection type, and injection site?
a. 25 gauge 5/8-inch needle, IM (intramuscular), anterolateral thigh.
b. 22 gauge 1–2 inch needle, IM (intramuscular), ventrogluteal.
c. 25 gauge 5/8-inch needle, ID (intradermal), deltoid.
d. 25 gauge 3/4-inch needle, SQ (subcutaneous), anterolateral thigh.

Answer: a
Rationale: The dose of DTaP is 0.5 cc or 0.5 mL, to be given with a 22 to 25 gauge, 5/8- to 3/4-inch needle, IM (intramuscularly). The only safe intramuscular injection site for a 6-month-old infant is the anterolateral thigh.
Planning
Physiologic Integrity
Analysis

45.7 A goal of *Healthy People 2010* is full immunization of 95% of children in kindergarten and first grade in the United States. To help reach this goal, the school nurse can teach families about which of the following?
a. a minor illness with a low-grade fever is a contraindication to receiving an immunization.
b. vaccines should be given one at a time for optimum active immunity.
c. premature infants and low-birth-weight infants should receive half doses of vaccines for protection from communicable diseases.
d. the risks of communicable diseases and the risks and benefits of vaccines from vaccine information statements as required by the National Vaccine Injury Act of 1986 and 1993.

Answer: d
Rationale: The risks and benefits of vaccines far outweigh the risks from communicable diseases and the resulting complications. A minor illness is not a contraindication to immunization. Giving vaccines one at a time will result in many missed opportunities. Half doses of vaccines should not be given routinely to premature and low-birth-weight infants.
Implementation
Health Promotion and Maintenance
Application

45.8 A 2-year-child with a fever is prescribed amoxicillin clavulanate 250 mg/5 cc TID PO × 10 days for otitis media. To guard against antibiotic resistance, the nurse instructs the parent to:
a. administer a loading dose for the first dose.
b. measure the prescribed dose in a household teaspoon.
c. give the antibiotic for the full 10 days.
d. stop the antibiotic if the child is afebrile.

Answer: c
Rationale: Antibiotics must be administered for the full number of days ordered to prevent mutation of resistant strains of bacteria. A loading dose was not ordered. A household teaspoon may contain less than 5 cc, and the full dose must be given. Stopping the antibiotic before the prescribed time will permit remaining bacteria to reproduce, and the otitis media will return, possibly with antibiotic-resistant organisms. The absence of a fever is not an indication that all bacteria are killed or are not reproducing.
Implementation
Physiologic Integrity
Application

45.9 The hospital has just provided its nurses with information about biologic threats and terrorism. After completing the course, a group of nurses are discussing their responsibility in relation to terrorism. The nurses who correctly understood the presentation are the ones who identify their action to be:
a. separating clients according to cultural, religious, or ethnic group.
b. disposing of blood-contaminated needles in the sharps container.

Answer: c
Rationale: The CDC must be contacted to investigate the source of serious infections and determine if a terrorist threat exists. Discrimination based on cultural, religious, or ethnic group is immoral, illegal, and will do nothing to stop terrorism. Proper disposal of blood-contaminated needles in the sharps container and initiating isolation precautions for a hospitalized client with methicillin-resistant *Staphylococcus aureus* (MRSA) are appropriate nursing actions but do not relate to terrorism.
Implementation
Health Promotion and Maintenance
Application

c. notifying the Centers for Disease Control (CDC) if a large number of persons with the same life-threatening infection present to the emergency room.
d. initiating isolation precautions for a hospitalized client with methicillin-resistant *Staphylococcus aureus* (MRSA).

45.10 The hospital has instructed its nurses that they must participate in disease surveillance associated with infectious agents. The nurses are warned that which disease(s) is/are likely to be the weapons of terrorists?
a. severe acute respiratory syndrome (SARS).
b. plague, anthrax, smallpox.
c. rubella, mumps, chickenpox.
d. Rocky Mountain spotted fever, Lyme disease.

Answer: b
Rationale: Plague, anthrax, and smallpox are choices of terrorists because they are highly contagious and lethal diseases that can kill large numbers of people in a relatively short time. SARS is a rare infectious disease. Rubella, mumps, and chickenpox are childhood communicable diseases that are not usually fatal. Rocky Mountain spotted fever and Lyme disease are caused by ticks endemic to wooded areas.
Assessment
Health Promotion and Maintenance
Analysis

45.11 The school nurse is trying to prevent the spread of a flu virus through the school. Infection control strategies that may be employed include: (Select all that apply.)
a. teaching parents safe food preparation and storage techniques.
b. withholding immunizations for children with compromised immune systems.
c. sanitizing toys, telephones, and doorknobs to kill pathogens.
d. separating children with infections from well children.
e. teaching children to wash their hands after using the bathroom.

Answers: c, d, e
Rationale: To prevent the spread of communicable diseases, microorganisms must be killed, or their growth controlled. Sanitizing toys and all contact surfaces, separating children with infections, and teaching children to wash their hands all control the growth and spread of microorganisms. Teaching parents safe food preparation and storage techniques is another tool to prevent the spread of microorganisms, but is not related to the flu virus. Immunizations should not be withheld from immunocompromised children, and this is not an infection control strategy.
Implementation
Safe, Effective Care Environment
Application

45.12 The nurse is teaching a prenatal class about infant care. The nurse emphasizes that parents should call their healthcare provider immediately if their infant: (Select all that apply.)
a. is 4 months old, received a DTaP immunization yesterday, and has a temperature of 38.0°C (100.4°F).
b. is under 3 months old and has a temperature over 40.1°C (104.2°F).
c. is difficult to awaken.
d. has purple spots on the skin.
e. has a stiff neck.

Answers: b, c, d, e
Rationale: Infants under 3 months of age have limited ability to develop antibodies to fight infection, and a fever as high as 40.1°C indicates a serious infection. All of these signs in infants and children of any age may indicate meningitis. A mild fever in the 4-month-old who received a DTaP immunization yesterday and has a temperature of 38.0°C (100.4°F) is incorrect because the fever is expected as the body develops antibodies in response to antigens in the immunization.
Implementation
Health Promotion and Maintenance
Application

45.13 A parent is given a prescription of amoxicillin for his 1-year-old son. The prescription reads amoxicillin 125mg/5mL PO TID × 10 days. What is the total volume in mL of amoxicillin that must be dispensed? _____.

Answer: 150 mL
Rationale: 125 mg/5 mL × TID (three times per day) = 15mL
15 mL × 10 days = 150 mL
Implementation
Physiologic Integrity
Analysis

45.14 The hospital admitting nurse is taking a history on a child's illness from the parents. The nurse concludes that the parents treated their 6-year-old child appropriately for a fever when they reported that they:
a. used aspirin.
b. alternated acetaminophen with ibuprofen.
c. put the child in a tub of cold water.
d. offered generous amounts of fluids frequently.

Answer: d
Rationale: The body's need for fluids increases during a febrile illness. Aspirin has been associated with Reye's syndrome, and should not be given to children with a febrile illness. Alternating acetaminophen with ibuprofen has no benefit and might result in an overdose. Putting the child in a tub of cold water will chill the child and cause shivering, a response that will increase body temperature.
Evaluation
Physiologic Integrity
Application

45.15 A mother brings her 4-month-old infant in for a routine checkup and vaccinations. The mother reports that the 4-month-old was exposed to a brother who has the flu. In this case the nurse will:
a. withhold the vaccinations.
b. give the vaccinations as scheduled.
c. withhold the DTaP vaccination but give the others as scheduled.
d. give the infant the flu vaccination but withhold the others.

Answer: b
Rationale: Recent exposure to an infectious disease is not a reason to defer a vaccine. There is no reason to withhold any of the vaccinations due at this time. The flu vaccination would not routinely be given to a 4-month-old.
Implementation
Health Promotion and Maintenance
Application

CHAPTER 46

46.1 A nurse is assessing infants for visually related developmental milestones. The infant who is showing a delay in meeting an expected milestone is the:
a. 4-month-old who has a social smile.
b. 8-month-old who has just begun to inspect her own hand.
c. 12-month-old who stacks blocks.
d. 7-month-old who picks up a raisin by raking.

Answer: b
Rationale: An 8-month-old who has just begun to inspect her own hand is delayed. The infant usually inspects her own hand beginning at 3 months. A 4-month-old with a social smile, a 12-month-old who stacks blocks, and a 7-month-old who picks up raisins by raking all are showing appropriate visually related milestones.
Assessment
Health Promotion and Maintenance
Analysis

46.2 A neonate has been diagnosed with a herpes simplex viral infection of the eye. The nurse will prepare to administer:
a. fluoroquinolone eyedrops or ointment.
b. intravenous penicillin.
c. oral erythromycin.
d. parenteral acyclovir and vidarabine ophthalmic ointment.

Answer: d
Rationale: Neonatal herpes simplex virus is treated vigorously with parenteral acyclovir for 14 days or longer and topical ophthalmic medication (trifluridine, iododeoxyuridine, or vidarabine). Fluoroquinolone eyedrops are used to treat bacterial eye infections. Intravenous penicillin treats selected bacterial infections. Oral erythromycin is used to treat chlamydial eye infections.
Planning
Physiological Integrity
Application

46.3 The nurse suspects that a toddler has a visual disorder caused by abnormal musculature. To detect this disorder, the nurse would perform a(n):
a. cover/uncover test.
b. ophthalmologic exam.
c. vision acuity exam.
d. pupil reaction to light test.

Answer: a
Rationale: The cover/uncover test can detect abnormal musculature of the eye that can lead to asymmetric eye movement. An ophthalmologic eye exam allows the practitioner to view the internal structures of the eye, not abnormal musculature. Vision acuity is used to test for myopia. Pupil reaction to light tests neurological status.
Assessment
Health Promotion and Maintenance
Application

46.4 The nurse is caring for four clients. The client with the highest risk of developing retinopathy of prematurity is the: a. 30-week-gestation infant who was in an oxyhood for 12 hours and weighed 1,800 g. b. 32-week-gestation infant who needed no oxygen and weighed 1,850 g. c. 28-week-gestation infant who has been on long-term oxygen and weighed 1,400 g. d. 28-week-gestation infant who was on short-term oxygen and weighed 1,420 g.	Answer: c Rationale: The 28-week infant on oxygen weighing 1,400 g has the highest risk of retinopathy of prematurity because of gestational age (28 weeks or less), weight (less than 1,500 g), and oxygen therapy. The other neonates have fewer risk factors. Diagnosis Physiological Integrity Analysis
46.5 A nurse is caring for a visually impaired 20-month-old who has not begun to walk. An appropriate nursing diagnosis for this child would be: a. delayed growth and development. b. impaired physical mobility. c. self-care deficit. d. impaired home maintenance.	Answer: a Rationale: A 20-month-old child who is not walking is delayed in growth and development. The child's mobility is not due to a physiological problem so impaired mobility is not appropriate. Self-care deficit does not apply to this age of child. There are not enough data to determine if home maintenance is impaired. Diagnosis Physiological Integrity Application
46.6 A nurse is caring for a visually impaired 10-year-old child. The nursing intervention with the highest priority for this child during the admission process would be: a. explaining playroom policies. b. orienting the child to where furniture is placed in the room. c. letting the child touch equipment that will be used during the hospitalization. d. taking the child on a tour of the unit.	Answer: b Rationale: The priority intervention is to orient the child to furniture placement in the room. This is priority because it addresses basic safety for a visually impaired client. Policies, handling equipment, and tours can be done at a later time. Implementation Safe, Effective Care Environment Application
46.7 An infant has acute otitis media. The nurse will teach the parents to: a. keep the baby in a flat-lying position during sleep. b. administer acetaminophen (Tylenol) to relieve discomfort. c. administer a decongestant. d. place baby to sleep with a pacifier.	Answer: b Rationale: An infant with a bulging tympanic membrane because of acute otitis media will have pain. Parents are taught to administer acetaminophen (Tylenol) to relieve the discomfort associated with acute otitis media. A flat-lying position may exacerbate the discomfort. Elevating the head slightly is recommended. Decongestants are not recommended for treatment of acute otitis media. Placing infants to sleep with a pacifier can increase the incidence of otitis media. Implementation Physiological Integrity Application
46.8 The nurse has taught a group of parents how to care for their children who have had tympanostomy tubes inserted. The nurse will know the parents understand how to care for their child's tympanostomy tubes if they: (Select all that apply.) a. encourage the child to drink generous amounts of fluids. b. administer a decongestant for 1 to 2 weeks following surgery. c. restrict the child to quiet activities after surgery.	Answers: a, c, e Rationale: The correct responses include: encouraging the child to drink generous amounts of water, restricting the child to quiet activities after surgery, and avoiding water in ears at bath time. Incorrect responses include administering a decongestant for 1 to 2 weeks following surgery and limiting the diet to soft bland foods. Decongestants are not needed after surgery, and a regular diet should be resumed. Evaluation Health Promotion and Maintenance Analysis

d. limit diet to soft, bland foods. e. avoid getting excessive water in the ears during bath time.	
46.9 The nurse can assist a child who has a mild hearing loss and reads lips to adapt to hospitalization by: a. dimming the lights in the hospital room. b. speaking in a loud voice. c. using long sentences. d. touching the child lightly before speaking.	Answer: d Rationale:The nurse can facilitate hospital adaptation of a child who has a hearing loss and can lip-read by obtaining the child's visual attention by lightly touching the child before communicating. Speaking in a loud voice, using long sentences, and dimming lights would be inappropriate. Implementation Psychosocial Integrity Application
46.10 A school child has an epistaxis. The school nurse appropriately intervenes by: a. tilting the child's head forward, squeezing the nares below the nasal bone, and applying ice to the nose. b. tilting the child's head back, squeezing the bridge of the nose, and applying a warm moist pack to the nose. c. lying the child down and applying no pressure or ice or warm pack. d. immediately packing the nares with a cotton ball soaked with Neo-Synephrine.	Answer: a Rationale:The correct initial treatment for a nosebleed is to tilt the head forward, squeeze the nares below the nasal bone for 10 to 15 minutes, and apply ice to the nose or the back of the head.Tilting the child's head back may cause the blood to trickle down the throat.Warmth can cause an increase in bleeding because of vasodilation. Lying the child down without application of pressure to the nares may not stop the bleeding.A cotton ball soaked with Neo-Synephrine would be used only if the bleeding will not stop with pressure and ice. Implementation Physiological Integrity Application
46.11 A nurse who is planning to teach school-age children about the "common cold" should include the information that: a. vaccinations can prevent contraction of a nasopharyngitis virus. b. antibiotics will eliminate the nasopharyngitis virus. c. proper handwashing can prevent the spread of the infection. d. aspirin should be taken for alleviation of fever if the "common cold" is contracted.	Answer: c Rationale: Proper handwashing should be taught to school-age children to reduce the spread of the "common cold" virus. No vaccine can prevent the common cold.Antibiotics are not used to treat viral infections.Aspirin should not be taken for fever because of its association with Reye's syndrome. Planning Health Promotion and Maintenance Analysis
46.12 A child has been diagnosed with group A beta-hemolytic streptococcus (GABHS) infection of the throat.The nurse should teach the parents to: a. complete the entire course of antibiotics. b. keep the child NPO. c. continue normal activities. d. not allow the child to gargle with salt water.	Answer: a Rationale: It is important for parents to complete the entire course of antibiotics for GABHS infections. Nothing by mouth, or NPO, status is not recommended, because the child needs to stay hydrated. The child should rest, and use of warm saltwater gargles is recommended. Implementation Physiological Integrity Application
46.13 The nurse has completed post-op discharge teaching to the parents of a child who has had a tonsillectomy.The nurse will know the parents understand the teaching if they state, "We'll: a. call the physician for any indication of ear pain." b. plan on administering acetaminophen (Tylenol) for pain."	Answer: b Rationale:Acetaminophen (Tylenol) is recommended for pain after a tonsillectomy. Citrus juices should be avoided for the first week. Ear pain might be experienced 4 to 8 days after a tonsillectomy and does not indicate an ear infection. Children do not need to be confined to bed.They can return to school in 10 days. Evaluation Physiological Integrity Analysis

c. be sure to give our child adequate amounts of citrus juices." d. keep our child on bed rest for 10 days after the surgery."	
46.14 The child has had a tonsillectomy earlier today and now is awake and tolerating fluids. The child asks for something to "eat." The most appropriate food would be: a. orange slices. b. lemonade. c. grapefruit juice. d. applesauce.	Answer: d Rationale: Soft foods such as applesauce can be added as tolerated to a diet following a tonsillectomy. Citric juices and citric fruits should be avoided because they can cause a burning sensation in the throat. Implementation Physiological Integrity Application
46.15 During an admission assessment, the nurse notes that the child has impaired oral mucous membranes. A nursing intervention aimed at resolving the problem would be: a. administering topical analgesics. b. promoting an adequate intake of nutrients. c. administering antibiotics as ordered. d. using lemon and glycerin for oral hygiene.	Answer: b Rationale: Adequate intake of fluids and nutrients promotes the intactness of the oral mucous membrane tissue, which is the desired outcome for an impaired oral mucous membrane problem. Lemon and glycerin can dry the oral mucous membrane, which is not desirable. Administration of antibiotics or topical analgesics is a medical intervention that might be performed but does not assure that impaired tissue will be resolved. Implementation Physiological Integrity Application

CHAPTER 47

47.1 The nurse is performing a respiratory assessment on a pediatric client. Identify the area where the nurse would assess for substernal retractions.

Answer: The correct spot is directly under the sternum (a). The alternate spots are: suprasternal (b—above the sternum), intercostal (c— between the ribs), or subcostal (d—under the ribs).
Rationale: The substernal area is under the sternum. Retractions in this area can occur when the child is experiencing mild respiratory distress. As the child becomes more distressed, the retractions can appear in the intercostal areas, suprasternal, and supraclavicular areas.
Assessment
Physiological Integrity
Application

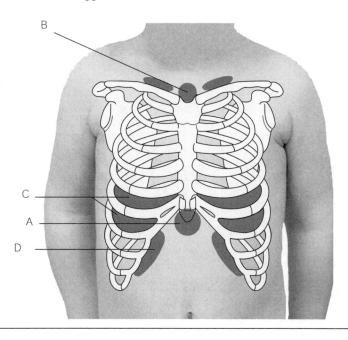

47.2 A child is showing signs of acute respiratory distress. The child should be positioned: a. upright. b. side-lying. c. flat. d. low Fowler's.	Answer: a Rationale: Upright is correct because it allows for optimal chest expansion. Side-lying, flat, and low Fowler's (head up slightly) do not allow for as optimal chest expansion as does the upright position. Implementation Physiological Integrity Application
47.3 A nurse delegates the task of infant vital sign assessment to a nurse technician. The nurse should instruct the technician to: a. report any infant using abdominal muscles to breathe. b. report any infant with a breathing pause that lasts 10 seconds or less. c. count respirations for 15 seconds and multiply by 4 to get the rate for 1 minute. d. report any infant with a breathing pause that lasts 20 seconds or longer.	Answer: d Rationale: The abnormal assessment finding for vital signs the nurse should instruct a nurse technician to report is any breathing pause by an infant lasting longer than 20 seconds. This can indicate apnea, and could lead to an apparent life-threatening event (ALTE). A breathing pause of 10 seconds or less is called periodic breathing, and is a normal pattern for an infant. Respirations should be counted for 1 minute, not 15 seconds. It's normal for infants to use abdominal muscles for breathing. Assessment Safe, Effective Care Environment Analysis
47.4 Supportive care for the family of an infant with sudden infant syndrome (SIDS) includes: a. interviewing parents to determine the cause of the SIDS incident. b. allowing parents to hold, touch, and rock the infant. c. sheltering the parents from grief by not giving them any personal items of the infant's, such as footprints. d. advising parents that an autopsy is not necessary.	Answer: b Rationale: The parents should be allowed to hold, touch, and rock the infant, giving them a chance to say good-bye to their baby. The other options are nontherapeutic. Implementation Psychosocial Integrity Application
47.5 A child is admitted to the hospital with the diagnosis of laryngotracheo-bronchitis (LTB). The nurse should be prepared to: a. administer nebulized epinephrine and oral or IM dexamethasone. b. administer antibiotics and assist with possible intubation. c. swab the throat for a throat culture. d. obtain a sputum specimen.	Answer: a Rationale: Nebulized epinephrine and dexamethasone are given for LTB. Antibiotic administration and possible intubation are associated with epiglottitis. Throat cultures are not obtained for LTB because it is viral, and swabbing the throat could cause complete obstruction to occur. Sputum specimens will not assist in the diagnosis of LTB. Planning Physiological Integrity Analysis
47.6 A child is admitted with epiglottitis, and needs an x-ray. The nurse orders the x-ray to be done: a. by transporting the child to the x-ray department on a cart. b. portable in the unit's waiting room. c. portable in the child's hospital room. d. by transporting the child to the x-ray department in a parent's arms.	Answer: c Rationale: The x-ray should be portable so that the child remains on the pediatric unit, near equipment and personnel who can perform emergency airway interventions. Traveling to the x-ray department takes the child away from emergency equipment and trained personnel who can perform emergency airway interventions. Implementation Safe, Effective Care Environment Application
47.7 The nurse is teaching a group of infants' mothers about the benefits of immunizations. The nurse will explain that the life-threatening disease	Answer: b Rationale: The *Haemophilus influenzae* type B (Hib) immunization can assist in prevention of epiglottitis. Hepatitis B; measles, mumps, and rubella; and the polio virus are not causative agents for epiglottitis.

epiglottitis can be prevented by immunizing against: a. measles, mumps, and rubella (MMR). b. *Haemophilus influenzae* type B (Hib). c. hepatitis B. d. polio.	Planning Health Promotion and Maintenance Analysis
47.8 A nurse is assessing an infant. The assessment that might indicate the infant's respiratory status is worsening is: a. acrocyanosis. b. an arterial CO_2 of 40. c. periorbital edema. d. grunting respirations with nasal flaring.	Answer: d Rationale: Grunting respirations with nasal flaring indicate respiratory status is becoming worse. Acrocyanosis (cyanosis of the extremities) is a normal finding in an infant. A CO_2 of 40 is within a normal range. Periorbital edema does not necessarily mean deterioration in respiratory status. Assessment Physiological Integrity Analysis
47.9 An appropriate nursing diagnosis for an infant with acute bronchiolitis due to respiratory syncytial virus would be: a. activity intolerance. b. decreased cardiac output. c. pain, acute. d. tissue perfusion, ineffective (peripheral).	Answer: a Rationale: Activity intolerance is a problem because of the imbalance between oxygen supply and demand. Cardiac output is not compromised during an acute phase of bronchiolitis. Pain usually is not associated with acute bronchiolitis. Tissue perfusion (peripheral) is not affected by this respiratory disease process. Diagnosis Physiological Integrity Application
47.10 A child is admitted to the hospital with pneumonia. The child's oximetry reading upon admission to the pediatric floor is 88. The priority nursing activity for this child would be to: a. obtain a blood sample to send to the lab for electrolyte analysis. b. begin oxygen per nasal cannula at 1 liter. c. medicate for pain. d. begin administration of intravenous fluids.	Answer: b Rationale: Pulse oximetry reading should be 92 or greater. Oxygen by nasal cannula at 1 liter should be started initially. Medicating for pain, administering IV fluids, and sending lab specimens can be done once the child's oxygenation status has been addressed. Implementation Safe, Effective Care Environment Application
47.11 A child is on rifampin (Rimactane) for treatment of tuberculosis. The parents call the clinic and report that the child's urine is orange. The nurse should advise the parents to: a. bring the child to the clinic for a urinalysis. b. bring the child to the clinic for an x-ray of the kidneys. c. expect orange-colored urine while the child is on rifampin. d. encourage the child to drink cranberry juice.	Answer: c Rationale: Rifampin can color the urine orange so the parents and child should be taught that this is an expected side effect. It does not mean the child has a urinary tract infection, and a urinalysis, x-ray, or encouragement of cranberry juice would not be options. Implementation Physiological Integrity Application
47.12 A physician has changed a child's asthma medication to salmeterol (Serevent). The mother asks the nurse what this drug will do. The nurse should explain that salmeterol (Serevent) is used to treat asthma because the drug: a. is an anti-inflammatory. b. decreases mucous production.	Answer: d Rationale: Salmeterol (Serevent) is a long-acting beta 2-agonist that acts by bronchodilating. Steroids are anti-inflammatory, anticholinergics decrease mucous production, and antihistamines control allergic rhinitis. Implementation Physiological Integrity Analysis

c. controls allergic rhinitis. d. is a bronchodilator.	
47.13 Following parental teaching, the nurse is evaluating the parents' understanding of environmental control for their child's asthma management. Teaching has been understood by the parents if they state: a. "We will replace the carpet in our child's bedroom with tile." b. "We're glad the dog can continue to sleep in our child's room." c. "We'll be sure to use the fireplace often to keep the house warm in the winter." d. "We'll keep the plants in our child's room dusted."	Answer: a Rationale: Control of dust in the child's bedroom is an important aspect of environmental control for asthma management. When possible, pets and plants should not be kept in the home. Smoke from fireplaces should be eliminated. Evaluation Health Promotion and Maintenance Analysis
47.14 A newborn is suspected of having cystic fibrosis. As the child is being prepared for transfer to a pediatric hospital, the mother asks the nurse what symptoms made the physician suspect cystic fibrosis. The nurse would reply that the clinical manifestation of cystic fibrosis that is seen first is: a. steatorrheac stools. b. constipation. c. meconium ileus. d. rectal prolapse.	Answer: c Rationale: Newborns with cystic fibrosis may present in the first 48 hours with meconium ileus. Steatorrhea, constipation, and rectal prolapse can be signs of cystic fibrosis seen in an older infant or child. Assessment Physiological Integrity Analysis
47.15 The nurse is teaching the parents of a newly diagnosed cystic fibrosis client how to administer the pancreatic enzymes. The nurse will advise the parents to administer the enzymes: a. B.I.D. b. with meals and large snacks. c. every 6 hours around the clock. d. Q.I.D.	Answer: b Rationale: Pancreatic enzymes are administered with meals and large snacks. A scheduled time would not be appropriate because the enzymes are used to assist in digestion of nutrients. Implementation Physiological Integrity Application

CHAPTER 48

48.1 The nurse has admitted a child with a cyanotic heart defect. The nurse would expect to find the initial lab result to show a: a. high hemoglobin. b. low hematocrit. c. high white blood cell count. d. low platelet count.	Answer: a Rationale: The child's bone marrow responds to chronic hypoxemia by producing more red blood cells to increase the amount of hemoglobin available to carry oxygen to the tissues. This occurs in cases of cyanotic heart defects. Therefore, the hematocrit would not be low, the white blood cell count would not be high (unless an infection is present), and the platelets would be normal. Assessment Physiological Integrity Analysis

48.2 A child has been admitted to the hospital unit in congestive heart failure (CHF). Symptoms related to this admission diagnosis would include: a. weight loss. b. bradycardia. c. tachycardia. d. increased blood pressure.	Answer: c Rationale:Tachycardia is a sign of congestive heart failure (CHF), because the heart attempts to improve cardiac output by beating faster. Bradycardia is a serious sign and can indicate impending cardiac arrest. Blood pressure does not increase in CHF, and the weight, instead of decreasing, increases because of retention of fluids. Assessment Physiological Integrity Analysis
48.3 An infant is in for ligation of a patent ductus arteriosus. On the accompanying picture identify the area that will be ligated. 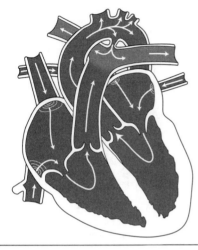	Answer:The correct label is on the area where the patent ductus arteriosus is present. Incorrect: atrial areas, ventricular areas, or pulmonic artery area as it exits the right ventricle. Rationale:When the ductus arteriosus is ligated, the area is where the ductus is patent (area off the aorta).The other areas would not be effective (atrials, ventricles, or pulmonic artery as it exits the right ventricle). Assessment Physiological Integrity Application
48.4 A toddler has been started on Lanoxin for cardiac failure. If the child develops digoxin toxicity, the first sign the nurse might note would be: a. lowered blood pressure. b. tinnitus. c. ataxia. d. nausea and vomiting.	Answer: d Rationale: Early signs of digoxin toxicity are nausea and vomiting. Digoxin toxicity does not cause lowered blood pressure, tinnitus (ringing in the ears), or ataxia (unsteady gait). Assessment Physiological Integrity Analysis
48.5 The nurse is checking peripheral perfusion to a child's extremity following a cardiac catheterization. If there is adequate peripheral circulation, the nurse would find that the extremity: a. is cool, with a capillary refill of greater than 3 seconds. b. has a palpable dorsalis pedis pulse but an absent posterior tibial pulse. c. has decreased sensation, with an absent dorsalis pedis pulse. d. is warm, with a capillary refill less than 3 seconds.	Answer: d Rationale:The nurse checks the extremity to determine adequacy of circulation following a cardiac catheterization.An extremity that is warm, with capillary refill less than 3 seconds, has adequate circulation. Other indicators of adequate circulation include: palpable pedal (dorsalis and posterior tibial) pulses, adequate sensation, and pink in color. If the capillary refill takes more than 3 seconds, any of the pedal pulses are absent, or the extremity is cool, cyanotic, or lacking sensation, circulation might not be adequate. Assessment Physiological Integrity Analysis

48.6 The nurse has admitted a child with a ventricular septal defect to the unit. An appropriate nursing diagnosis for this child is: a. impaired gas exchange related to pulmonary congestion secondary to the increased pulmonary blood flow. b. fluid volume, deficient related to hyperthermia secondary to the congenital heart defect. c. acute pain related to the effects of a congenital heart defect. d. hypothermia related to decreased metabolic state.	Answer: a Rationale: Because of the increased pulmonary congestion, impaired gas exchange would be an appropriate nursing diagnosis. Ventricular septal defects do not cause pain, fever, or deficient fluid volume. Diagnosis Physiological Integrity Analysis
48.7 The nurse is teaching parents about care for their child after cardiac surgery. The nurse includes in the information that any child who has undergone cardiac surgery should: a. be restricted from most play activities. b. receive prophylactic antibiotics for any dental, oral, or upper respiratory tract procedures. c. not receive routine immunizations. d. have a fever for several weeks following the surgery.	Answer: b Rationale: Parents should be taught that the child should receive prophylactic antibiotics to prevent endocarditis, according to the American Heart Association. The child should live a normal and active life following repair of a cardiac defect. Immunizations should be provided according to the schedule. Any unexplained fever should be reported. Implementation Health Promotion and Maintenance Application
48.8 An infant with tetralogy of Fallot is having a hypercyanotic episode (TET spell). Which of the following nursing interventions should the nurse implement? (Select all that apply.) a. place the child in knee-chest position. b. draw blood for a serum hemoglobin. c. administer oxygen. d. administer morphine and propranolol intravenously as ordered. e. administer Benadryl as ordered.	Answers: a, c, d Rationale: When an infant with tetralogy of Fallot has a hypercyanotic episode, interventions should be geared toward decreasing the pulmonary vascular resistance. Therefore, the nurse would place in knee-chest position (to decrease venous blood return from the lower extremities) and administer oxygen, morphine, and propranolol (to decrease the pulmonary vascular resistance). The nurse would not draw blood until the episode had subsided because unpleasant procedures are postponed. Benadryl is not appropriate for this child. Implementation Safe, Effective Care Environment Application
48.9 An infant has been diagnosed with a mild cyanotic heart defect. Surgery to correct the defect will not be performed for at least 2 years. The nurse teaches the parents that a child with a mild cyanotic heart defect should: a. maintain normal activity. b. be placed on bed rest. c. not be given antipyretics. d. have a low-grade fever until the defect is repaired.	Answer: a Rationale: A child with a mild cyanotic heart defect should be treated as normally as possible, without activity adjustment. Bed rest would not be recommended. Fevers are treated with antipyretics, so that dehydration is avoided. Low-grade fever is not a normal finding in a child with a mild cyanotic heart defect and could be a sign of infective endocarditis. Implementation Health Promotion and Maintenance Application

48.10 The nurse finds that an infant has stronger pulses in the upper extremities than in the lower extremities and higher blood pressure readings in the arms than in the legs. This could be indicative of what heart defect? a. patent ductus arteriosus. b. atrial septal defect. c. transposition of the great vessels. d. coarctation of the aorta.	Answer: d Rationale: Coarctation of the aorta may present with stronger pulses in the upper extremities than in the lower extremities and higher blood pressure readings in the arms than in the legs because of obstruction to circulation to the lower extremities. Assessment Physiological Integrity Analysis
48.11 A child has had a heart transplant. The nurse recognizes that postoperative teaching has been successful when the parents state that the child is on cyclosporine A to: a. reduce serum cholesterol level. b. prevent rejection c. treat hypertension. d. treat infections.	Answer: b Rationale: Cyclosporine A is given to prevent rejection. Lovastatin is given to reduce serum cholesterol level, calcium channel blockers can be used to treat hypertension, and an antibiotic can be given to treat an infection. Evaluation Physiological Care Analysis
48.12 An athletic activity the nurse could recommend for a school-age child with pulmonary artery hypertension is: a. cross-country running. b. soccer. c. golf. d. basketball.	Answer: c Rationale: A child with pulmonary artery hypertension should have exercise tailored to avoid dyspnea. Golf would be less exertional than soccer, basketball, or cross-country running. Implementation Health Promotion and Maintenance Application
48.13 A child is admitted with infective endocarditis. The nurse is prepared to: a. start an intravenous. b. place the child in contact isolation. c. place the child on seizure precautions. d. assist with a lumbar puncture.	Answer: a Rationale: Infective endocarditis is treated with intravenous antibiotics for 2 to 8 weeks. It is not contagious so the child is not placed in contact isolation. Seizures are not a risk of infective endocarditis. A lumbar puncture is not a diagnostic test done for infective endocarditis. Planning Physiological Integrity Application
48.14 A diagnosis of rheumatic fever is being ruled out for a child. The nurse teaches the parents that the lab test to check for a recent streptococcal infection is: a. a throat culture. b. antistreptolysin-O (ASLO). c. erythrocyte sedimentation rate. d. C-reactive protein.	Answer: b Rationale: The lab test for antistreptococcal antibodies is an antistreptolysin-O (ASLO). An erythrocyte sedimentation rate and a C-reactive protein can indicate inflammation. A culture can indicate a current streptococcal infection. Assessment Physiological Integrity Analysis
48.15 A nursing intervention for a stable infant who has supraventricular tachycardia is: a. application of ice to the face. b. administration of intravenous adenosine (Adenocard). c. administration of intravenous amiodarone (Cardarone). d. preparation for cardioversion.	Answer: a Rationale: Supraventricular tachycardia episodes initially are treated with vagal maneuvers to slow the heart rate when the infant is stable. In infants, the application of ice or iced saline solution to the face can reduce the heart rate. Adenosine or amiodarone may be given when the vagal maneuvers are unsuccessful. Cardioversion is used in an urgent situation. Implementation Physiological Integrity Application

49.1 The nurse is evaluating the activity tolerance of a 9-month-old with iron-deficiency anemia. The finding that indicates the child is tolerating activity is:
a. tachycardia.
b. decreased alertness.
c. respiratory rate less than 50 with activity.
d. muscle weakness.

Answer: c
Rationale: Iron-deficiency anemia can result in less oxygen reaching the cells and tissues, causing activity intolerance. An indication that a 9-month-old child is tolerating activity and iron-deficiency anemia is resolving would be maintaining a respiratory rate of less than 50 (within a normal range for this age) during activity. Tachycardia, decreased alertness, and muscle weakness all are signs that iron-deficiency anemia is not resolving and activity tolerance is not improving.
Evaluation
Physiological Integrity
Analysis

49.2 Parents understand the nurse's teaching with regard to prevention of iron-deficiency anemia if they:
a. feed their infant with a formula that is not iron-fortified.
b. start iron-fortified infant cereal at 4 to 6 months of age.
c. introduce cow's milk at 6 months of age.
d. limit vitamin C consumption after 1 year of age.

Answer: b
Rationale: Starting iron-fortified infant cereal at 4 to 6 months of age is recommended for prevention of iron deficiency in children. Infants who are not breastfed should get iron-fortified formula. Cow's milk should not be introduced until 12 months of age. Vitamin C should be started at 6 to 9 months of age and continued because foods rich in vitamin C improve iron absorption.
Evaluation
Health Promotion and Maintenance
Analysis

49.3 A child has been diagnosed with sickle cell disease. The parents are unsure how their child contracted the disease. The nurse should explain that the:
a. mother and the father of the child have the sickle cell trait.
b. mother of the child has the trait but the father doesn't.
c. father of the child has the trait but the mother doesn't.
d. mother of the child has sickle cell disease, but the father doesn't have the disease or the trait.

Answer: a
Rationale: Sickle cell disease is an autosomal recessive disorder—both parents must have the trait in order for a child to have the disease.
Assessment
Health Promotion and Maintenance
Analysis

49.4 You are the nurse in charge on a pediatric unit. A child with sickle cell disease, in splenic sequestration crisis, is being admitted. You would assign this patient to a:
a. semi-private room.
b. reverse isolation room.
c. contact isolation room.
d. private room.

Answer: d
Rationale: Splenic sequestration can be life-threatening, and there is profound anemia. The child does not need an isolation room but should not be placed in a room with any child who may have an infectious illness. The private room is appropriate for this child.
Implementation
Safe, Effective Care Environment
Application

49.5 The nurse would expect to administer this drug for a sickle cell pain crisis:
a. morphine sulfate (Duramorph).
b. meperidine (Demerol).
c. acetaminophen (Tylenol).
d. ibuprofen (Advil).

Answer: a
Rationale: The pain during a sickle cell pain crisis is severe, and morphine is needed for pain control around the clock or by patient-controlled analgesia (PCA). Meperidine is not used for pain control for clients with sickle cell pain crisis because it could cause seizures. Acetaminophen and ibuprofen are used for mild pain and would not be effective for the severe pain experienced by a child in sickle cell pain crisis.
Implementation
Physiological Integrity
Application

49.6 The nurse is teaching parents how to prevent a sickle cell crisis in the child with sickle cell disease. The nurse will explain that precipitating factors contributing to a sickle cell crisis include: (Select all that apply.) a. fever. b. dehydration. c. regular exercise. d. altitude. e. increased fluid intake.	Answers: a, b, d Rationale: Fever, dehydration, and altitude are precipitating factors contributing to a sickle cell crisis. Regular exercise and increased fluid intake are recommended activities for a child with sickle cell disease and will not contribute to a sickle-cell crisis. Assessment Health Promotion and Maintenance Analysis
49.7 The nurse is administering packed red blood cells to a child with sickle cell disease. The nurse knows that a transfusion reaction most likely will occur: a. 6 hours after the transfusion is given. b. within the first 20 minutes of administration of the transfusion. c. at the end of the administration of the transfusion. d. never—blood reactions to transfusions do not occur.	Answer: b Rationale: Blood reactions can occur as soon as the blood transfusion begins, or within the first 20 minutes. The nurse should remain with the child for the first 20 minutes of the transfusion. Assessment Physiological Integrity Analysis
49.8 A child who has ß-thalassemia is receiving numerous blood transfusions. The child also is receiving deferoxamine (Desferal) therapy. The parents ask how the deferoxamine will help their child. The nurse explains that the deferoxamine (Desferal) is given to: a. prevent blood transfusion reactions. b. stimulate red blood cell production. c. provide vitamin supplement. d. prevent iron overload.	Answer: d Rationale: Iron overload can be a side effect of a hypertransfusion therapy. Deferoxamine (Desferal) is an iron-chelating drug that binds excess iron so it can be excreted by the kidneys. It does not prevent blood transfusion reactions, stimulate red blood cell production, or provide vitamin supplement. Planning Physiological Integrity Analysis
49.9 A child recently has been diagnosed with aplastic anemia. Support for the family should include: a. referrals to support groups and social services. b. short-term support. c. genetic counseling. d. nutrition counseling.	Answer: a Rationale: Families require support in dealing with a child who has a life-threatening disease. They should be referred to support groups for counseling, if indicated, and to social services. The support will be long-term in nature. Aplastic anemia is not a genetically transmitted disease. Nutrition counseling is not a priority and might or might not be needed with aplastic anemia. Planning Psychosocial Integrity Application
49.10 A school-age child with hemophilia falls on the playground and goes to the nurse's office with superficial bleeding above the knee. The nurse should: a. apply a warm, moist pack to the area. b. perform some passive range-of-motion to the affected leg. c. apply pressure to the area for at least 15 minutes. d. keep the affected extremity in a dependent position.	Answer: c Rationale: If a hemophiliac child experiences a bleeding episode, superficial bleeding should be controlled by applying pressure to the area for at least 15 minutes. Ice, not heat, should be applied. The extremity should be immobilized and elevated, so passive range of motion and keeping the extremity in a dependent position would not be appropriate interventions at this time. Implementation Physiological Integrity Application

49.11 A child with hemophilia plans on participating in a bicycling club. The nurse should recommend that the child:
a. consider a swim club instead of the bicycling club.
b. wear kneepads, elbow pads, and a helmet while bicycling.
c. participate only in the social activities of the club.
d. not join the club.

Answer: b
Rationale: Children with hemophilia should be encouraged to participate in non-contact sports activities. Bicycling is an excellent option and is recommended, along with swimming. The child should always use kneepads, elbow pads, and a helmet when participating in a physical sport. Participating only in the social aspects of the club would not encourage physical activity. Discouraging a child from joining a club would not foster growth and development.
Implementation
Health Promotion and Maintenance
Application

49.12 The nurse is caring for a child with disseminated intravascular coagulation (DIC). A priority nursing intervention for this child is:
a. frequent ambulation.
b. maintenance of skin integrity.
c. monitoring of fluid restriction.
d. preparation for x-ray procedures.

Answer: b
Rationale: Impairment of skin integrity can lead to bleeding in DIC. The child with DIC should be placed on bed rest. Fluids need to be monitored but will not be restricted, and DIC is not diagnosed with x-ray examination but by serum lab studies.
Implementation
Physiological Integrity
Application

49.13 A priority nursing diagnosis for the child with idiopathic thrombocytopenic purpura (ITP) is:
a. risk for injury (bleeding).
b. ineffective breathing pattern.
c. nausea.
d. fluid volume deficit.

Answer: a
Rationale: ITP is the most common bleeding disorder in children, so risk for injury (bleeding) is the priority nursing diagnosis. The disease process usually does not cause ineffective breathing patterns, nausea, or fluid volume deficits.
Diagnosis
Physiological Integrity
Analysis

49.14 A child with meningococcemia is being admitted to the pediatric intensive care unit. This child should be placed in a:
a. semi-private room.
b. private room, but not isolation.
c. private room, in protective isolation.
d. private room, in respiratory isolation.

Answer: d
Rationale: Meningococcemia follows an infection with *Neisseria meningitidis*. *N. meningitidis* is transmitted through airborne droplets so the child should be placed in a private room in respiratory isolation. A private room with protective isolation (child is essentially kept in a "bubble") would not be appropriate.
Planning
Safe, Effective Care Environment
Application

49.15 A child who has undergone hematopoietic stem cell transplantation (HSCT) is ready for discharge. It is important that the nurse teach the family to:
a. keep the child on a low-calcium diet.
b. return the child to school within 6 weeks.
c. practice good handwashing.
d. avoid obtaining influenza vaccinations.

Answer: c
Rationale: Handwashing is essential to prevent the spread of infection. The child should be placed on calcium supplements to reduce the risk of osteopenia. The child can't return to school for 6 to 12 months after an HSCT. In-hospital or in-home schooling is required. The child and the family should be encouraged to get yearly influenza vaccinations.
Implementation
Health Promotion and Maintenance
Application

50.1 A child has been diagnosed with a Wilms' tumor, and is being treated with chemotherapy. Since many chemotherapeutic agents cause bone marrow depression, prior to administering the chemotherapy, the nurse will determine if this child has any infection-fighting capability by monitoring the:
a. hemoglobin.
b. red blood cell count.
c. absolute neutrophil count (ANC).
d. platelets.

Answer: c
Rationale: The absolute neutrophil count (ANC) uses both the segmented (mature) and band (immature) neutrophils as a measure of the body's infection-fighting capability. Red blood cell count, hemoglobin, and platelets cannot determine infection-fighting capabilities.
Assessment
Physiological Integrity
Analysis

50.2 A child has cancer and has been treated with chemotherapy. The latest lab value indicates the white blood cell count is very low. The nurse would expect to administer:
a. filgrastim (Neupogen).
b. ondansetron (Zofran).
c. oprelvekin (Neumega).
d. epoietin (human recombinant erythropoietin).

Answer: a
Rationale: Filgrastim (Neupogen) increases production of neutrophils by the bone marrow. Ondansetron (Zofran) is an antiemetic, oprelvekin (Neumega) increase platelets, and epoietin (human recombinant erythropoietin) stimulates red blood cell (RBC) production.
Implementation
Physiological integrity
Analysis

50.3 The child is receiving chemotherapy for acute lymphocytic leukemia. The nurse recognizes that a potential oncological emergency for this child would be tumor lysis syndrome. The nurse will monitor this child for:
a. thrombocytopenia and leukocytosis.
b. oliguria and altered levels of consciousness.
c. respiratory distress and cyanosis.
d. upper-extremity edema and neck vein distension.

Answer: b
Rationale: Tumor lysis causes a metabolic emergency. Because of electrolyte imbalance, the signs can be oliguria and altered levels of consciousness. Thrombocytopenia and leukocytosis occur with a hematological emergency. Space-occupying lesions can cause respiratory distress and cyanosis, upper-extremity edema, and neck vein distension.
Assessment
Physiological Integrity
Analysis

50.4 The nurse works in an oncology clinic. A preschool-age child is being seen in the clinic, and the nurse anticipates a diagnosis of cancer. The nurse prepares for the common reaction preschool-age children often have to a diagnosis of cancer, which is:
a. acceptance, especially if able to discuss the disease with children their own age.
b. thoughts that they caused their illness and are being punished.
c. understanding of what cancer is and how it is treated.
d. unawareness of what the illness is.

Answer: b
Rationale: Preschool-aged children might think they caused their illness. Adolescents find contact with others who have gone through their experience helpful. School-age children can understand a diagnosis of cancer. Infants and toddlers are unaware of the severity of the disease.
Assessment
Psychosocial Integrity
Analysis

50.5 The nurse is monitoring the urine-specific gravity and pH on a child receiving chemotherapy. The nurse will try to maintain the urine values at:
a. spec gravity 1.030; pH 6.
b. spec gravity 1.030; pH 7.5.

Answer: d
Rationale: Because the breakdown of malignant cells releases intracellular components into the blood, and electrolyte imbalance causes metabolic acidosis, the urine-specific gravity should remain at less than 1.010 and the pH at 7 to 7.5. A specific gravity higher than 1.010 can mean fluid intake is not high enough, and a pH of less than 7 means acidosis.

c. spec gravity 1.005; pH 6. d. spec gravity 1.005; pH 7.5.	Assessment Physiological Integrity Analysis
50.6 The antiemetic drug ondansetron (Zofran) is being administered to a child receiving chemotherapy. It should be administered: a. only if the child experiences nausea. b. after the chemotherapy has been administered. c. before chemotherapy administration, as a prophylactic measure. d. never—this antiemetic is not effective for controlling nausea and vomiting associated with chemotherapy.	Answer: c Rationale: The antiemetic ondansetron (Zofran) should be administered before chemotherapy, as a prophylactic measure. Giving it after the child has nausea or at the end of chemotherapy treatment does not help with preventing nausea. It is the drug of choice for controlling nausea caused by chemotherapy agents. Implementation Physiological Integrity Application
50.7 A child has thrombocytopenia secondary to chemotherapy treatments. The nurse should not: a. administer intramuscular (IM) injections. b. perform oral hygiene. c. monitor intake and output. d. use palpation as a component of assessment.	Answer: a Rationale: When the child is thrombocytopenic (decreased platelets) from chemotherapy, the nurse should not administer IM injections because of the risk of bleeding. Oral hygiene care should be done with a soft toothbrush, and intake and output monitored for any abnormalities. Gentle palpation still should be included in physical assessments. Assessment Physiological Integrity Application
50.8 A child undergoing chemotherapeutic treatment for cancer is being admitted to the hospital for fever and possible sepsis. Cultures, antibiotics, and acetaminophen (Tylenol) have been ordered for this child. Which order should the nurse do first? a. administer the antibiotics. b. administer the Tylenol. c. obtain the cultures. d. any of the three.	Answer: c Rationale: Obtain the cultures first because management of infections is critical, and since a child on chemotherapy has lowered immune status, unusual agents can be identified. Cultures can help identify the causative agents before treatment is started. Administering antibiotics and Tylenol can affect identification of the causative agent. Implementation Safe, Effective Care Environment Application Difficulty: 3
50.9 The nurse is admitting a client with an infratentorial brain tumor. The nurse is teaching the parents about the tumor. Identify the area of the brain the nurse should show the parents where this type of tumor occurs:	Answer: Correct mark is below the tentorium area (brainstem gliomas, medulloblastoma, cerebellar astrocytoma, ependymoma). Incorrect mark would be above the tentorium area (cerebral astrocytoma, ependymoma, optic nerve glioma). Rationale: Infratentorial tumors are below the tentorium line (cerebellum area). Tumors occurring here are: brainstem gliomas, medulloblastoma, cerebellar

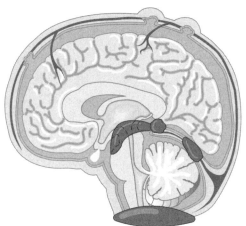

astrocytoma, and ependymoma. These tumors make up around one-half of all brain tumors, yet occur in about one-third (lower area) of the brain. The supratentorial tumors occur above the tentorium line (cerebrum area). These include: cerebral astrocytoma, ependyoma, optic nerve glioma. The supratentorial tumors make up one-half of all brain tumors and occur in the two-thirds (upper area) of the brain.

Assessment

Physiological Integrity

Application

50.10 A 24-hour urine for vanillylmandelic acid (VMA) has been ordered on a child suspected of having neuroblastoma. The nurse begins the collection:

a. at 0700.

b. after the next time the child voids.

c. at bedtime.

d. when the order is noted.

Answer: b

Rationale: A 24-hour urine collection is started after the child voids. That specimen is not saved, but all subsequent specimens in that 24-hour period should be collected. It would not be an accurate collection of 24 hours of urine if the collection began at 0700, at bedtime, or when the order is noted.

Intervention

Physiological Integrity

Application

50.11 A child has been diagnosed with a Wilms' tumor. Preoperative nursing care would involve:

a. careful bathing and handling.

b. monitoring of behavioral status.

c. maintenance of strict isolation.

d. administration of packed red blood cells.

Answer: a

Rationale: The tumor should never be palpated. Careful bathing and handling are important nursing considerations. Palpating the tumor can cause a piece of the tumor to dislodge. The child's behavior will not be affected by a Wilms' tumor. The tumor does not cause excessive lowering of WBCs or RBCs, so strict isolation or administration of packed red blood cells is not usually a nursing intervention.

Implementation

Safe, Effective Care Environment

Application

50.12 An adolescent is receiving methotrexate chemotherapy after undergoing limb salvage surgery for osteogenic sarcoma. The nurse knows the teen understands the purpose of leucovorin therapy after the methotrexate if the teen says:

a. "I'm glad I only need one dose of the leucovorin."

b. "I don't have any pain, so I won't need to take the leucovorin this time."

c. "I know I will be taking the leucovorin every 6 hours for about the next 3 days."

d. "I don't have any nausea, so I won't need the leucovorin."

Answer: c

Rationale: Leucovorin (citrovorum factor) is a form of folic acid that helps to protect normal cells from the destructive action of methotrexate. It is started within 24 hours of methotrexate administration and is given along with hydration therapy. Usual administration is every 6 hours up to 72 hours, or until serum methotrexate is at the desired level.

Evaluation

Physiological Integrity

Analysis

50.13 A child recently has been diagnosed with leukemia. The child's sibling is expressing feelings of anger and guilt. This reaction by the sibling is:

a. abnormal, and she should be referred to a psychologist.

b. unusual, as the illness doesn't affect the sibling.

c. unexpected, as the cancer is easily treated.

d. normal, as the sibling is affected too, and anger and guilt are expected feelings.

Answer: d

Rationale: A diagnosis of cancer affects the whole family, and initial feelings experienced by the sibling might be anger and guilt. Seldom will the sibling be unaffected; however, the response is not abnormal.

Assessment

Psychosocial Integrity

Analysis

50.14 A child with rhabdomyosarcoma is to undergo radiation therapy after surgical removal of the tumor. The parents should be taught to:
a. apply sunscreen to the area when the child is exposed to sunlight.
b. vigorously scrub the area when bathing.
c. remove any markings left after each radiation treatment.
d. apply lotion to the area before radiation therapy.

Answer: a
Rationale: Radiation therapy causes the skin in that area to be sensitive. Sunscreen should be applied so that sunburns are avoided. Vigorous scrubbing and removing the radiation markings are not recommended. Lotion can increase the chance of a radiation burn when applied before the treatment.
Implementation
Physiological Integrity
Application

50.15 The child has been admitted to the hospital unit newly diagnosed with retinoblastoma. The nurse would expect to see:
a. a red reflex.
b. yellow sclera.
c. a white pupil.
d. blue-tinged sclera.

Answer: c
Rationale: The first sign of retinoblastoma is a white pupil. The red reflex is absent. Yellow sclera is a sign of jaundice, not retinoblastoma. Blue-tinged sclera is a sign of osteogenesis imperfecta, not retinoblastoma.
Assessment
Health Promotion and Maintenance
Analysis

CHAPTER 51

51.1 The nurse is measuring the abdominal girth of a child with abdominal distention. Identify the area on the child's abdomen where the tape measure should be placed for an accurate abdominal girth.

Answer: a
Rationale: An abdominal girth should be taken around the largest circumference of the abdomen—in this case, just above the umbilicus. The circumferences below the umbilicus, below the sternum, or across the symphysis pubis would not be accurate abdominal girths.

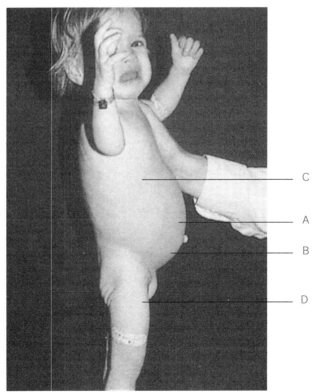

a. just above the umbilicus, around the largest circumference of the abdomen. b. below the umbilicus. c. just below the sternum. d. across the symphysis pubis.	Assessment Health Promotion and Maintenance Application
51.2 The nurse is planning post-op care for an infant after a cleft lip repair. The plan should include: a. prone positioning. b. suctioning with a Yankauer device. c. supine or side-lying positioning. d. avoidance of soft elbow restraints.	Answer: c Rationale: Integrity of the suture line is essential for post-op care of cleft lip repair. The infant should be placed in a supine or side-lying position to avoid rubbing the suture line on the bedding. The prone position should be avoided. A Yankauer suction device is made of hard plastic and could cause trauma to the suture line. Suctioning should be done with a small soft suction catheter. Soft elbow restraints may be used to prevent the infant from touching the incisional area. Planning Safe, Effective Care Environment Application
51.3 An infant has been born with an esophageal atresia and tracheoesophageal fistula. What is a priority pre-op nursing diagnosis? a. risk for aspiration related to regurgitation. b. acute pain related to esophageal defect. c. ineffective infant feeding pattern related to uncoordinated suck and swallow. d. ineffective tissue perfusion: Gastrointestinal related to decreased circulation.	Answer: a Rationale: Depicted is the most common type of esophageal atresia and tracheoesophageal fistula, where the upper segment of the esophagus ends in a blind pouch and a fistula connects the lower segment to the trachea. Preoperatively, there is a risk of aspiration of gastric secretions from the stomach into the trachea because of the fistula that connects the lower segment of the esophagus to the trachea. Pain usually is not experienced preoperatively with this condition. The infant is always kept NPO preoperatively, so ineffective feeding pattern would not apply. Tissue perfusion is not a problem with this condition. Diagnosis Physiological Integrity Analysis
51.4 The nurse is evaluating an infant's tolerance of a feeding post-pyloromyotomy. Which finding indicates the infant is not tolerating the feeding? a. need for burping after 30 cc. b. presence of bowel sounds. c. passing gas. d. emesis.	Answer: d Rationale: An infant is not tolerating feedings after a pyloromyotomy if emesis is present. Burping after 30 cc, presence of bowel sounds, and the passing of gas would be expected findings following a pyloromyotomy, and would indicate tolerance of the feeding. Evaluation Physiological Integrity Analysis
51.5 An infant, born with an omphalocele defect, is being admitted to the intensive care nursery. The nurse in charge should instruct the nursing technician to prepare a: a. warmer. b. crib. c. feeding of formula. d. bilirubin light.	Answer: a Rationale: Omphalocele is a congenital malformation in which intra-abdominal contents herniate through the umbilical cord. The infant may lose heat through the viscera—a warmer is indicated to prevent hypothermia. The crib would not provide adequate maintenance of temperature control. The infant is NPO preoperatively, and might or might not need a bilirubin light before surgery. Planning Safe, Effective Care Environment Application

51.6 The parents have understood the nurse's teaching with regard to colostomy stoma care for their infant if they state:
a. "We will change the colostomy bag with each wet diaper."
b. "We will use adhesive enhancers when we change the bag."
c. "We will watch for skin irritation around the stoma."
d. "We will expect a small amount of bleeding after cleansing the area around the stoma."

Answer: c
Rationale: Skin irritation around the stoma should be assessed—it might indicate leakage. Physical or chemical skin irritation can occur if the appliance is changed too frequently, or with each wet diaper. Adhesive enhancers should be avoided on the skin of newborns. Their skin layers are thin, and removal of the appliance can strip off the skin. Also, adhesive contains latex, and its constant use is not advised due to risk of latex allergy development. Bleeding usually is attributable to excessive cleaning.
Evaluation
Health Promotion and Maintenance
Analysis

51.7 A nurse is preparing for the delivery of a newborn with a known diaphragmatic hernia defect. The equipment the nurse prepares is:
a. intubation setup.
b. appropriate bag and mask.
c. sterile gauze and saline.
d. soft arm restraints.

Answer: a
Rationale: A diaphragmatic hernia (protrusion of abdominal contents into the chest cavity through a defect in the diaphragm) is a life-threatening condition. Intubation is required immediately so the newborn's respiratory status can be stabilized. A bag and mask will not be adequate to ventilate a newborn with this condition. The defect is not external so sterile gauze and saline are not needed. Soft arm restraints are not immediately necessary.
Implementation
Physiological Integrity
Application

51.8 The nurse is administering several medications to an infant with neurologic impairment and delay. The medication that utilizes a proton pump inhibitor administered for gastroesophageal reflux is:
a. omeprazole (Prilosec).
b. ranitidine (Zantac).
c. phenytoin (Dilantin).
d. glycopyrrolate (Robinul).

Answer: a
Rationale: Omeprazole (Prilosec) utilizes a proton pump inhibitor that blocks the action of acid-producing cells and is used to treat gastroesophageal reflux. Ranitidine (Zantac) causes the stomach to produce less acid and may be used to treat gastroesophageal reflux, but it is a histamine-2 receptor blocker. Phenytoin (Dilantin) is an anticonvulsant used to treat seizures, and glycopyrrolate (Robinul) is an anticholinergic agent used to inhibit excessive salivation.
Implementation
Physiological Integrity
Analysis

51.9 A newborn has been diagnosed with Hirschsprung's disease. The parents ask the nurse about the symptoms that lead to this diagnosis. The nurse should explain that common symptoms are:
a. acute diarrhea—dehydration.
b. failure to pass meconium—abdominal distention.
c. currant jelly, gelatinous stools—pain.
d. projectile vomiting—altered electrolytes.

Answer: b
Rationale: Hirschsprung's disease is the absence of autonomic parasympathetic ganglion cells in the colon, which prevents peristalsis at that portion of the intestine. In newborns, the symptoms include abdominal distention and failure to pass meconium. Acute diarrhea and dehydration are symptons characteristic of gastroenteritis. Currant jelly, gelatinous stools, and pain are symptoms of intussusception, and projectile vomiting and altered electrolytes are symptoms of pyloric stenosis.
Assessment
Physiological Integrity
Analysis

51.10 A child with severe gastroenteritis is being admitted to a semiprivate room on the pediatric unit. The nurse in charge should place this client with which roommate?
a. an infant with meningitis.
b. a child with fever and neutropenia.
c. another child with gastroenteritis.
d. a child recovering from an appendectomy.

Answer: c
Rationale: Gastroenteritis can be viral or bacterial and can be infectious. It is best to cohort children with this infectious process. Good handwashing is essential to prevent the spread. An infant with meningitis, a child with fever and neutropenia and a child recovering from an appendectomy should not be placed with another child with an infectious process.
Implementation
Safe, Effective Care Environment
Application

51.11 The nurse is preparing to ambulate an 11-year-old child who has had an appendectomy. In addition to pharmacological pain management, the nurse can use which nonpharmacological pain management strategy for this client?

a. a heating pad.
b. a warm, moist pack.
c. a pillow to splint the incisional area.
d. an ice pack.

Answer: c
Rationale: Splinting the incisional area while moving can be a nonpharmacological strategy to decrease discomfort after an appendectomy. Heat and ice are not used on the incisional area, as they can impair the healing process of the wound.
Implementation
Physiological Integrity
Application

51.12 A neonate is being fed 20 mL every 3 hours by orogastric gavage. At the beginning of this feeding, the nurse aspirates 15 mL of gastric residual. The nurse should:

a. withhold the feeding and notify the physician.
b. replace the residual and continue with the full feeding.
c. replace the residual, but only give 5 mL of the feeding.
d. withhold the feeding and check the residual in 3 hours.

Answer: a
Rationale: Residual of more than half the amount of feeding indicates a feeding intolerance and could be a sign of necrotizing enterocolitis. Early detection of enterocolitis is essential, and aggressive management is required. Therefore, the physician should be notified of this finding. The amount of residual is too much to replace and continue with the feeding, and waiting for 3 hours to recheck the residual could delay treatment of a serious condition.
Implementation
Physiological Integrity
Application

51.13 A child with inflammatory bowel disease is taking prednisone daily. The family should be taught to administer the prednisone:

a. between meals.
b. 1 hour before meals.
c. at bedtime.
d. with meals.

Answer: d
Rationale: Prednisone, a corticosteroid, can cause gastric irritation. It should be administered with meals to reduce the gastric irritation.
Implementation
Physiological Integrity
Application

51.14 The nurse has taught the parents of a child with celiac disease about allowed foods. The nurse should explain that which of the following would be an allowed meal?

a. pizza with milk.
b. spaghetti and meat sauce with juice.
c. hot dog on a bun with a shake.
d. fruit plate with Gatorade.

Answer: d
Rationale: A child with celiac disease needs a gluten-free diet. Included on the list are: fruits, meats, rice, and vegetables, including corn. Excluded are: bread, cake, doughnuts, cookies, crackers, and many processed foods that might contain hidden gluten. Therefore, the child would be allowed to have the fruit plate with Gatorade.
Implementation
Health Promotion and Maintenance
Application

51.15 Parents have understood strategies to reduce risk of lead exposure for their child if they state:

a. "We will provide our child with frequent snacks high in iron and calcium."
b. "We will avoid washing any surfaces that have peeling paint."
c. "We will store leftovers in a ceramic pot."
d. "We can continue to use our traditional medicine treatment, Azarcon, for any GI upset."

Correct: a
Rationale: Snacks and meals high in iron and calcium should be encouraged. Lead is absorbed more readily on an empty stomach. Any surface with peeling paint should be washed with a damp sponge. Ceramic pots, if fired improperly, could contain lead. Food should not be prepared or stored in them. Azarcon, a traditional medicine used to treat a colic-like illness, can contain large amounts of lead.
Evaluation
Health Promotion and Maintenance
Analysis

52.1 The nurse is performing a newborn assessment on a male infant with hypospadias. Identify which picture depicts the expected assessment finding.

Answer: a
Rationale: In hypospadias, the urethral canal is open on the ventral surface of the penis. In epispadias, the canal is open on the dorsal surface.
Assessment
Physiological Integrity
Application

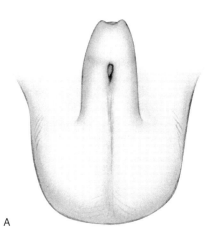

A

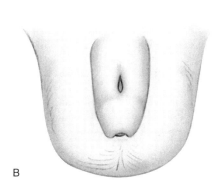

B

52.2 A nurse is preparing to admit a child with possible obstructive uropathy. The nurse should expect to draw what labs on this child?
a. platelet count.
b. BUN and creatinine.
c. partial thromboplastin time (PTT).
d. blood culture.

Answer: b
Rationale: The BUN and creatinine are serum lab tests for kidney function. Obstructive uropathy is a structural or functional abnormality of the urinary system that interferes with urine flow and results in urine backflow into the kidneys; therefore, the BUN and creatinine will be elevated. Platelet count and partial thromboplastin time (PTT) are drawn when a bleeding disorder is suspected. A blood culture is done when an infectious process is suspected.
Planning
Physiological Integrity
Application

52.3 Discharge instructions for care of a child just having had an orchiopexy should include:
a. information to the parents about the child resuming normal vigorous activities.
b. discussion with the parents about the low incidence of testicular malignancy and no further need for any follow-up.
c. explanation to the parents about the need for loose and nonrestrictive clothing.
d. reassurance to the parents that infertility is not a future risk.

Answer: c
Rationale: Orchiopexy is the surgical correction for cryptorchidism (failure of the testes to descend into the scrotal sac). Discharge instructions should include the information about the need for loose and nonrestrictive clothing in order to avoid pressure to the post-op site. The risk of testicular cancer is 35 to 50 times greater in men with a history of cryptorchidism. Long-term planning includes teaching the child to perform monthly testicular examinations once puberty has been reached. Vigorous activities such as straddling toys, riding bicycles, or rough play should be avoided for up to 2 weeks following surgery, to promote healing and prevent injury. A discussion of fertility and the possible need for fertility testing is important since cryptorchidism increases the risk of infertility.
Intervention
Health Promotion and Maintenance
Application

52.4 Which of the following symptoms is characteristic of a preschool-age child with a urinary tract infection?
a. foul-smelling urine, elevated BP, hematuria.
b. severe flank pain, nausea, headache.

Answer: d
Rationale: Clinical manifestations of a urinary tract infection in a preschool-age child include fever, urgency, and dysuria. While hematuria may be present, there is no elevated BP, headache, or vertigo.
Assessment
Physiological Integrity
Analysis

c. headache, hematuria, vertigo.
d. urgency, dysuria, fever.

52.5 The nurse teaches parents that the anticholinergic drug used to treat enuresis is: a. desmopressin acetate (DDAVP). b. oxybutynin (Ditropan). c. imipramine (Tofranil). d. spironolactone (Aldactone).	Answer: b Rationale: Oxybutynin (Ditropan) is an anticholinergic that relaxes the smooth muscle of the bladder, allowing for an increase in bladder capacity and a delay in the initial desire to void. Desmopressin acetate (DDAVP) is a vasopressin, imipramine (Tofranil) is a tricyclic antidepressant, and spironolactone (Aldactone) is a potassium-sparing diuretic. Intervention Physiological Integrity Application
52.6 A child has been admitted to the hospital unit with a diagnosis of minimal change nephritic syndrome. The clinical manifestations will include which of the following? a. hematuria, bacteriuria, weight gain. b. gross hematuria, albuminuria, fever. c. massive proteinuria, hypoalbuminemia, edema. d. hypertension, weight loss, proteinuria.	Answer: c Rationale: Nephrotic syndrome is an alteration in kidney function secondary to increased glomerular basement membrane permeability to plasma protein. It is characterized by massive proteinuria, hypoalbuminemia, and edema. While hematuria and hypertension may be present, they are not pronounced. Gross hematuria and hypertension are associated with glomerulonephritis. Bacteriuria and fever are associated with a urinary tract infection. Because of the edema, a weight gain, not a weight loss, would be seen. Assessment Physiological Integrity Analysis
52.7 A child with nephrotic syndrome is severely edematous. The doctor has placed him on bed rest. An important nursing intervention for this child would be to: a. reposition the child every 2 hours. b. monitor BP every 2 hours. c. encourage fluids. d. limit visitors.	Answer: a Rationale: A child with severe edema, on bed rest, is at risk for altered skin integrity. To prevent skin breakdown, the child should be repositioned every 2 hours. Vital signs are taken every 4 hours, fluids need to be monitored and should not be encouraged, and the child needs social interaction so visitors should not be limited. Intervention Physiological Integrity Application
52.8 A child with nephritic syndrome has been placed on prednisone. The nurse knows that for this syndrome, the administration will be: a. daily for 6 weeks, then 6 weeks of alternate-day doses. b. daily for 1 week. c. on a short-burst schedule. d. infrequently.	Answer: a Rationale: Prednisone, a corticosteroid with anti-inflammatory action, is administered daily for 6 weeks and then 6 weeks of alternate-day doses. Daily for 1 week and short-burst therapy would not be effective for treating nephrotic syndrome. Prednisone is frequently used to treat nephrotic syndrome. Implementation Physiological Integrity Application
52.9 A child is admitted with acute glomerulonephritis. The nurse would expect the urinalysis during this acute phase to show which of the following? a. bacteriuria, hematuria. b. hematuria, proteinuria. c. bacteriuria, increased specific gravity. d. proteinuria, decreased specific gravity.	Answer: b Rationale: Glomerulonephritis is an inflammation of the glomeruli of the kidneys. The clinical manifestation of glomerulonephritis is grossly bloody hematuria with mild to moderate proteinuria. Bacteriuria is not present, and because the urine is concentrated, the specific gravity is increased. Assessment Physiological Integrity Analysis

52.10 A 4-year-old has acute glomerulonephritis and is admitted to the hospital. An appropriate nursing diagnosis for this child would be: a. risk for injury related to loss of blood in urine. b. fluid volume excess related to decreased plasma filtration. c. risk for infection related to hypertension. d. altered growth and development related to a chronic disease.	Answer: b Rationale: The fluid is excessive, and fluid and electrolyte balance should be monitored. There is no risk for injury because the blood loss in the urine is not such that it causes anemia. While a risk for infection may be present, it is not related to the hypertension. Growth and development are not normally affected because this is an acute process, not a chronic one. Diagnosis Physiological Integrity Analysis
52.11 A child with acute glomerulonephritis is in the playroom and experiences blurred vision and headache. Which of the following actions should be taken by the nurse? a. check the urine to see if hematuria has increased. b. obtain a BP on the child—notify the physician. c. reassure the child and encourage bed rest until the headache improves. d. obtain serum electrolytes and send urinalysis to the lab.	Answer: b Rationale: Blurred vision and headache may be signs of encephalopathy, a complication of acute glomerulonephritis. A BP should be obtained and the physician notified. The physician may decide to order an antihypertensive to bring down the BP. This is a serious complication, and delay in treatment could mean lethargy and seizures. Therefore, the other options (checking urine for hematuria, encouraging bed rest, and obtaining serum electrolytes) do not directly address the potential problem of encephalopathy. Implementation Safe, Effective Care Environment Application
52.12 A child in renal failure has hyperkalemia. The nurse plans to instruct the child and her parents to avoid the following foods: a. bananas, carrots, and green leafy vegetables. b. chips, cold cuts, and canned foods. c. spaghetti and meat sauce, breadsticks. d. hamburger on a bun, cherry Jell-O.	Answer: a Rationale: Bananas, carrots, and green leafy vegetables are high in potassium. Chips, cold cuts, and canned foods are high in sodium but not necessarily potassium. Spaghetti and meat sauce with breadsticks, hamburger on a bun, and cherry Jell-O would be acceptable choices for a low-potassium diet. Planning Health Promotion and Maintenance Application
52.13 A child has undergone a kidney transplant and is receiving cyclosporine. The parents ask the nurse about the reason for the cyclosporine. The nurse should explain that the drug is given to: a. boost immunity. b. suppress rejection. c. decrease pain. d. improve circulation.	Answer: b Rationale: Cyclosporine is given to suppress rejection. It doesn't boost immunity, decrease pain, or improve circulation. Intervention Physiological Integrity Application
52.14 A child is undergoing hemodialysis. The child should be monitored closely for: a. shock. b. hypertension. c. neutropenia. d. headaches.	Answer: a Rationale: Rapid changes in fluid and electrolyte balance during hemodialysis can lead to shock. Other complications to watch for are thromboses and infection. Hypertension, neutropenia, and headaches are not clinical manifestations associated with hemodialysis. Assessment Physiological Integrity Application

52.15 A child is scheduled for a kidney transplant. The nurse has completed the pre-op teaching to prepare the child and parents for the surgery and post-op considerations. The nurse will know the parents realistically understand the transplantation process that is involved with a kidney transplant if they state:

a. "We know it's important to see that our child takes prescribed medications after the transplant."

b. "We'll be glad we won't have to bring our child in to see the doctor again."

c. "We're happy our child won't have to take any more medicine after the transplant."

d. "We understand our child won't be at risk anymore for catching colds from other children at school."

Answer: a
Rationale: It is important the nurse emphasize compliance with treatments that will need to be followed after the transplant. Follow-up appointments will be necessary, as will medications and general health promotion.
Evaluation
Health Promotion and Maintenance
Analysis

CHAPTER 53

53.1 A child has been diagnosed with epilepsy and is on daily phenytoin (Dilantin). Client education should include:

a. fluid intake.

b. good dental hygiene.

c. a decrease in vitamin D intake.

d. taking the medication with milk.

Answer: b
Rationale: Because phenytoin (Dilantin) can cause gingival hyperplasia, good dental hygiene should be encouraged. Fluid intake does not affect the drug's effectiveness, an adequate intake of vitamin D should be encouraged, and phenytoin (Dilantin) should not be taken with dairy products.
Planning
Physiological Integrity
Application

53.2 A 2-year-old starts to have a tonic-clonic seizure while in a crib in the hospital. The child's jaws are clamped. The most important nursing action at this time is to:

a. place a padded tongue blade between the child's jaws.

b. stay with the child and observe his respiratory status.

c. prepare the suction equipment.

d. restrain the child to prevent injury.

Answer: b
Rationale: During a seizure, the nurse remains with the child, watching for complications. The child's respiratory rate should be monitored. Be sure nothing is placed in the child's mouth during a seizure. Suction equipment already should be set up at the bedside before a seizure begins. The child should not be restrained during a seizure.
Implementation
Physiological Integrity
Application

53.3 A lumbar puncture is being done on an infant suspected to have meningitis. If the infant has bacterial meningitis, the nurse would expect the cerebral spinal fluid to show:

a. an elevated white blood cell count.

b. an elevated red blood cell count.

c. normal glucose.

d. a decreased white blood cell count.

Answer: a
Rationale: The lumbar puncture is done to obtain cerebral spinal fluid. An elevated white blood cell count is seen with bacterial meningitis. The red blood cell count is not elevated, and the glucose is decreased in meningitis.
Assessment
Physiological Integrity
Analysis

53.4 The nurse is planning care for a school-age child with bacterial meningitis. Which of the following should be included? a. keep environmental stimuli at a minimum. b. avoid giving pain medications that could dull sensorium. c. measure head circumference to assess developing complications. d. have the child move her head from side to side at least once every 2 hours.	Answer: a Rationale: A quiet environment should be maintained because noise can disturb a child with meningitis. Pain medications are appropriate to give and should be used when needed. Measuring head circumference would only be appropriate for a child less than 2 years. Excessive head movement should be avoided because it can increase irritation of the meninges. Planning Physiological Integrity Application
53.5 If an intramuscular injection is administered to a child who has Reye's syndrome, the nurse should watch for: a. bleeding at the injection site. b. infection at the injection site. c. poor absorption. d. itching at the injection site.	Answer: a Rationale: Prothrombin time is prolonged in Reye's syndrome, putting the child at risk for bleeding from an injection site. Infection, poor absorption, and itching at the site would not be risks associated with Reye's syndrome. Evaluation Physiological Integrity Application
53.6 A nurse is doing a post-op assessment on an infant who has just had a ventroperitoneal shunt placed for hydrocephalus. Which assessment would indicate a malfunction in the shunt? a. incisional pain. b. movement of all extremities. c. negative Brudzinski sign. d. bulging fontanelle.	Answer: d Rationale: A bulging fontanelle would be an abnormal finding and could indicate that the shunt is malfunctioning. Incisional pain, movement of all extremities, and negative Brudzinski sign all are normal findings after a ventroperitoneal shunt has been placed. Assessment Physiological Integrity Analysis
53.7 An infant has just been born with a myelomeningocele. The infant has been admitted to the neonatal intensive care unit. The nursing tech is preparing an open crib for this infant. The nurse should: a. not say anything—the tech is doing an appropriate action. b. stop the tech and ask her to prepare a warmer for this infant. c. remind the tech to include adequate warm blankets in the crib. d. ask the tech to place a hat and warm gown for the infant in the crib.	Answer: b Rationale: An infant with a myelomeningocele has a vertebral defect that can cause loss of body temperature and also difficulty in thermoregulation. It would not be appropriate to place the infant in a crib. Implementation Safe, Effective Care Environment Application
53.8 An important nursing intervention when caring for an infant with a myelomeningocele in the pre-op stage would be: a. place infant supine to decrease pressure on the sac. b. apply a heat lamp to facilitate drying and toughening of the sac. c. measure head circumference daily to identify developing hydrocephalus. d. apply a diaper to prevent contamination of the sac.	Answer: c Rationale: The infant should be monitored for developing hydrocephalus, so the head circumference should be monitored daily. The infant will be placed prone, not supine, and the defect will be protected from trauma or infection. Therefore, applying heat and a diaper around the defect would not be recommended. A sterile saline dressing may be used to cover the sac to maintain integrity. Intervention Physiological Integrity Application

53.9 A child with a myelomeningocele corrected at birth is now 5 years old. What is a priority nursing diagnosis for a child with corrected spina bifida at this age?
a. risk for infection.
b. risk for impaired tissue perfusion—cranial.
c. risk for altered urinary elimination.
d. risk for altered comfort.

Answer: c
Rationale: A child with spina bifida will continue to have a risk for altered urinary elimination because the bowel and bladder sphincter controls are affected. Urinary retention is a problem so bladder interventions are initiated early to prevent kidney damage. Risk for infection, impaired tissue perfusion, and altered comfort are not problems once surgery, to close the defect, has been performed.
Diagnosis
Physiological Integrity
Analysis

53.10 The nurse should suspect a child has cerebral palsy if the parent says:
a. "My 6-month-old baby is rolling from back to prone now."
b. "My 3-month-old fails to smile at me."
c. "My 8-month-old can sit without support."
d. "My 10-month-old is not walking."

Answer: b
Rationale: Children with cerebral palsy are delayed in meeting developmental milestones. The infant who fails to smile at 3 months of age is showing a delay. The social smile usually appears at around 6 weeks of age. A baby rolls over from back to prone at 6 months, sits without support at 8 months, and walks at 12 months.
Evaluation
Physiological Integrity
Analysis

53.11 A nurse is caring for a child who has recently been diagnosed with cerebral palsy. The major goals of therapy for this child will include:
a. reversal of degenerative processes that have occurred.
b. curing the underlying defect causing the disorder.
c. preventing the spread to individuals in close contact with the child.
d. promoting optimum development.

Answer: d
Rationale: Recognition of the disorder is important so that optimal development can be maintained. Cerebral palsy cannot be reversed or cured. It is not caused by a contagious process so there is no risk of spread.
Planning
Safe, Effective Care Environment
Analysis

53.12 A child has sustained a traumatic brain injury and is being monitored in the pediatric intensive care unit. The nurse is using the Glasgow Coma Scale to assess the child. What will the nurse be assessing for? (Select all that apply.)
a. eye opening.
b. verbal response.
c. motor response.
d. head circumference.
e. pulse oximetry.

Answers: a, b, c
Rationale: The Glasgow Coma Scale for infants and children score parameters related to eye opening, verbal response, and motor response. The maximum score is 15, indicating the highest level of neurological functioning. Head circumference and pulse oximetry are not included on the scale.
Assessment
Physiological Integrity
Analysis

53.13 A child with a mild traumatic brain injury is being sedated with a mild sedative so that pain and anxiety are minimized. The nurse should:
a. place a continuous pulse oximetry monitor on the child.
b. place the child in a room away from the nurse's station.
c. allow for several visitors to remain at the child's bedside.
d. use soft restraints if the child becomes confused.

Answer: a
Rationale: When a child is sedated, respiratory status should be monitored with a pulse oximetry machine. The child should be close to the nurse's station so that frequent monitoring can be done. Several visitors at the bedside would increase the child's anxiety. Soft restraints may increase agitation.
Intervention
Safe, Effective Care Environment
Application

53.14 A child has sustained a basilar skull fracture. The nurse should watch for: a. cerebral spinal fluid leakage from the nose or ears. b. headache. c. transient confusion. d. periorbital ecchymosis.	Answer: a Rationale: Cerebral spinal fluid leakage could be present from the nose or ears and, if it persists, might indicate that surgical repair will be needed. Headache, transient confusion, and periorbital ecchymosis are findings that commonly are present with a basilar skull fracture but do not indicate that surgical repair will be needed. Assessment Physiological Integrity Analysis
53.15 A child has experienced a near-drowning episode and is admitted to the pediatric intensive care unit. The parents express guilt over the near-drowning of their child. The nurse's best response is: a. "You will need to watch the child more closely." b. "Tell me more about your feelings." c. "The child will be fine, so don't worry." d. "Why did you let the child almost drown?"	Answer: b Rationale: In near-drowning cases, the nurse should be nonjudgmental and should provide a forum for parents to express feelings of guilt. Telling the parents to watch the child more closely or asking them why they let the child almost drown is judgmental. Saying the child will be fine might not be true. The nurse should reassure the parents that the child is receiving all possible medical treatment. Intervention Psychosocial Integrity Application

CHAPTER 54

54.1 A nurse is caring for four clients in the hospital. Which client should the nurse refer for play therapy? a. adolescent with asthma. b. preschool child hospitalized with injuries sustained in a traumatic motor vehicle accident. c. school-age child having an appendectomy. d. infant with sepsis.	Answer: b Rationale: Play therapy often is used with preschool- and school-age children who are experiencing anxiety, stress, and other specific nonpsychotic mental disorders. In this case, the child who experienced a traumatic motor vehicle accident should be referred for play therapy. The adolescent with asthma, the school-age child having an appendectomy, and the infant with sepsis do not have as high a need for play therapy as the preschool-age child surviving a car accident. Intervention Psychosocial Integrity Application
54.2 A child with autism is being admitted to the hospital because of recent vomiting and diarrhea. Upon admission, the nurse should: a. take the child on a tour of the whole unit. b. take the child to the playroom immediately. c. orient the child to the hospital room, keeping noise and distractions to a minimum. d. admit the child to a four-bed unit.	Answer: c Rationale: Autistic children interpret and respond to the environment differently than other individuals do. The child needs to be oriented to new settings and adjusts best to a quiet, controlled environment. A hospital room with only one other child is best. Intervention Psychosocial Integrity Application
54.3 A nurse is planning preoperative teaching for a child scheduled to have a tonsillectomy. The child has a history of attention deficit hyperactivity disorder (ADHD). The nurse plans to: a. give instructions verbally and use a picture pamphlet, repeating points more than once. b. conduct the teaching in a playroom setting with several other children present.	Answer: a Rationale: A teaching session for a child with ADHD should foster attention. Giving instructions verbally and in written form, repeating points, will improve learning for a child with ADHD. The environment needs to be quiet, with minimal distractions. A child will have difficulty concentrating if allowed to interrupt frequently. Distractions such as noise from a television should be minimized. Planning Health Promotion and Maintenance Analysis

c. allow the child to interrupt the teaching session frequently. d. play a television show in the background.	
54.4 A child is taking Adderall (amphetamine mixed salts) for attention deficit hyperactivity disorder (ADHD). The parents should be instructed to administer the medication: a. at bedtime. b. before lunch. c. with the evening meal. d. early in the morning.	Answer: d Rationale: A side effect of Adderall can be insomnia. Administering the medication early in the day can help alleviate the effect of insomnia. Intervention Physiological Integrity Application
54.5 A child with attention deficit hyperactivity disorder is interested in playing the drums in the school band. The school nurse should: a. recommend the child take private lessons and not join the band. b. encourage the child to join the band. c. consult with the physician about allowing the child to participate in band activities. d. discourage the child from playing in the band.	Answer: b Rationale: A child with ADHD can lack connectedness with other children. Participation in a school activity where the rules of working with others can be learned should be encouraged. Implementation Health Promotion and Maintenance Application
54.6 A child is being evaluated for depression. An assessment tool the nurse expects the psychologist to use is the: a. Denver Developmental Screening Test. b. Revised Children's Manifest Anxiety Scale. c. Parent Developmental Questionnaire. d. Disruptive Behavior Disorders Rating Scale.	Answer: b Rationale: The Revised Children's Manifest Anxiety Scale is a tool used to assess for depression. The Denver Developmental Screening Test and the Parent Developmental Questionnaire are tools used to assess development. The Disruptive Behavior Disorders Rating Scale is used to assess for autism. Assessment Health Promotion and Maintenance Analysis
54.7 A nurse is calculating the maximum recommended dose a 9-year-old child with depression can receive for sertraline (Zoloft). The recommended pediatric dose for sertraline (Zoloft) is 1.5 to 3 mg/kg/day. If the child weighs 31 kg, the maximum recommended dose for this child would be how many mg? _____.	Answer: 93 Rationale: The maximum recommended dose for sertraline (Zoloft) is 3 mg/kg/day. If the child weighs 31 kg it would be $3 \times 31 = 93$ mg/day. Implementation Safe, Effective Care Environment Application
54.8 The priority nursing diagnosis for a child with bipolar disorder who has suicidal ideas would be: a. powerlessness related to mood instability. b. social isolation related to disorder. c. risk for injury related to suicidal ideas. d. impaired social interaction.	Answer: c Rationale: The priority for a child with bipolar disorder and suicidal ideas is safety. Risk for injury would be the nursing diagnosis that would address safety for the child. The other diagnoses have a lower priority. Diagnosis Safe, Effective Care Environment Analysis

54.9 An adolescent child with panic disorder is taking paroxetine (Paxil), a serotonin reuptake inhibitor (SSRI). The child tells the nurse she often takes diet pills because she is trying to lose weight. The nurse should advise the child to:

a. continue with the paroxetine (Paxil) and the diet pills.
b. stop both the paroxetine (Paxil) and the diet pills.
c. discontinue use of the diet pills while taking the paroxetine (Paxil).
d. discuss use of the diet pills with a pharmacist.

Answer: c
Rationale: Serotonin syndrome, the serious and life-threatening side effect of SSRIs, can develop when the drug is taken with diet pills, Saint John's wort, other antidepressants, alcohol, or LSD. In this case, the diet pills should be discontinued in order to avoid serotonin syndrome. The Paxil should not be discontinued and waiting to discuss the use of diet pills with a pharmacist would not be an appropriate option.
Intervention
Physiological Integrity
Application

54.10 Parents tell the nurse their child has the following behaviors: excessive handwashing, counting objects, and hoarding substances. The nurse knows this behavior is characteristic of:

a. depression.
b. separation anxiety disorder.
c. obsessive-compulsive disorder.
d. bipolar disorder.

Answer: c
Rationale: Common behaviors of obsessive-compulsive disorder are excessive handwashing, counting objects, and hoarding substances. These practices may take 1 or more hours each day.
Assessment
Physiological Integrity
Analysis

54.11 A nurse is concerned about the safety of a suicidal child and wants to be prepared for the use of physical restraints if necessary. The nurse should:

a. obtain a physician's order and follow the institution's policy for use of restraints.
b. apply the restraints and then obtain a physician's order later.
c. apply the restraints if parental permission is obtained.
d. ask for the child's permission before applying the restraints.

Answer: a
Rationale: Restraints are used only when ordered by the physician and interdisciplinary team caring for the child. Physical restraint is only a short-term approach to providing immediate safety, if necessary. It would not be appropriate to apply the restraints and then obtain a physician's order. Even if permission is given by the parent and/or child, a physician's order still needs to be obtained.
Planning
Safe, Effective Care Environment
Analysis

54.12 A nurse is doing developmental assessments on several children in the daycare setting. Which child indicates a delay in meeting developmental milestones?

a. an 18-month-old toddler unable to phrase sentences.
b. a kindergartener unable to button his shirt.
c. a 1-year-old unable to sit still for a short story.
d. a 2-year-old unable to cut with scissors.

Answer: b
Rationale: A developmental milestone that can indicate learning disability if not met is a kindergartener unable to button. The inability to phrase sentences is considered a delay if not done at $2\frac{1}{2}$ years; inability to sit still for a short story is considered a delay if the child is 3 to 5 years old; and being unable to cut with scissors is considered a delay if not achieved by kindergarten age.
Assessment
Health Promotion and Maintenance
Analysis

54.13 Parents of a child recently diagnosed with Down syndrome relate to the nurse that they "feel guilty about causing the condition." The best response by the nurse is:

a. "Down syndrome is a condition caused by an extra chromosome, and it really is not known why it occurs."

Answer: a
Rationale: The therapeutic and accurate response is that Down syndrome is a condition caused by an extra chromosome, but it's not known why it occurs. The other responses are nontherapeutic and/or inaccurate.
Intervention
Psychological Integrity
Application

b. "Down syndrome is a condition that is genetically transmitted from both the father and the mother."

c. "Down syndrome is a condition that is carried on the X chromosome, so it came from the mother."

d. "Down syndrome is caused by birth trauma, not by genetics."

54.14 A child with profound mental retardation has been admitted to the hospital for an appendectomy. The nurse recognizes that the IQ of this child is:

a. between 50 and 70.
b. below 20.
c. between 35 and 50.
d. between 20 and 35.

Answer: b
Rationale: Profound retardation is described as an intelligence quotient (IQ) below 20. Mild mental retardation is described as an IQ between 50 and 70; moderate retardation as an IQ between 35 and 50; and severe retardation as an IQ between 20 and 35.
Assessment
Health Promotion and Maintenance
Analysis

54.15 The family of a child with mental retardation is expressing difficulty with managing the care needs of the child. The nursing diagnosis appropriate for this situation is:

a. hopelessness related to the terminal condition of the child.

b. compromised family coping related to the child's developmental variations.

c. family processes dysfunctional related to the child with mental retardation.

d. parenting, impaired related to poor parenting skills.

Answer: b
Rationale: The family is compromised, but not dysfunctional. Hopelessness and impaired parenting are not appropriate in the given situation.
Diagnosis
Psychosocial Integrity
Analysis

CHAPTER 55

55.1 The nurse has completed parent education related to treatment for a child with congenital clubfoot. The nurse knows that parents need further teaching when they state:

a. "We're happy this is the only cast our baby will need."

b. "We'll watch for any swelling of the feet while the casts are on."

c. "We'll keep the casts dry."

d. "We're getting a special car seat to accommodate the casts."

Answer: a
Rationale: Serial casting is the treatment of choice for congenital clubfoot. The cast is changed every 1 to 2 weeks. Parents should be watching for swelling while the casts are on, keeping the casts dry, and using a car seat to accommodate the casts.
Evaluation
Physiological Integrity
Analysis

55.2 An infant has just returned from surgery for correction of bilateral congenital clubfeet. The infant has bilateral long leg casts. The toes on both feet appear edematous, but there is color, sensitivity, and movement to them. The nurse should:

a. call the physician to report the edema.

b. elevate the legs on pillows.

c. apply a warm, moist pack to the feet.

d. encourage movement of toes.

Answer: b
Rationale: The legs should be elevated on a pillow for 24 hours to promote healing and help with venous return. Some amount of swelling can be expected so it would not be appropriate to notify the physician, especially if the color, sensitivity, and movement remained normal. Ice, not heat, should be applied. An infant would not be able to follow directions to move her toes, and in this case, it would not be as effective as elevating the legs on pillows.
Intervention
Physiological Integrity
Application

55.3 The nurse in the newborn nursery is doing the admission assessment on a neonate. Which area in the accompanying picture is an abnormal finding indicating the neonate may have congenital hip dysplasia?

Answer: a
Rationale: A sign of congenital hip dysplasia in the infant would be asymmetry of the gluteal and thigh fat folds. The right side in this picture is not affected. The top of the left buttock shows no sign of abnormality.
Assessment
Physiological Integrity
Application

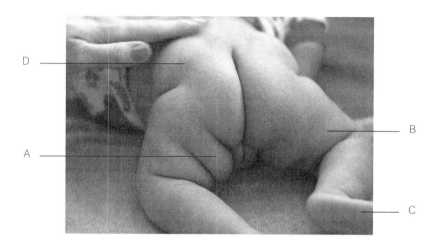

55.4 The nurse is teaching a family how to care for an infant in a Pavlik harness to treat congenital developmental dysplasia of the hip. The nurse will include in the parental education instructions to:
a. apply lotion or powder to minimize skin irritation.
b. put clothing over the harness for maximum effectiveness of the device.
c. check at least two or three times a day for red areas under the straps.
d. place the diaper over the harness, preferably using a thin, superabsorbent disposable diaper.

Answer: c
Rationale: The brace should be checked two or three times a day for red areas under the straps. Lotion or powder can contribute to skin breakdown. A light layer of clothing should be under the brace, not over it. The diaper also should be under the brace.
Intervention
Physiological Integrity
Application

55.5 The nurse is caring for a child in Bryant's skin traction. An appropriate nursing intervention for this child would be to:
a. remove the adhesive traction straps daily to prevent skin breakdown.
b. check the traction frequently to assure that proper alignment is maintained.

Answer: b
Rationale: The traction apparatus should be checked frequently to assure that proper alignment is maintained. The adhesive straps should not be removed. The child should be positioned supine, and frequent repositioning is necessary to prevent complications of immobility.
Intervention
Physiological Integrity
Application

c. position the child prone to maintain good alignment. d. move the child as infrequently as possible to maintain traction.	
55.6 The nurse has completed discharge teaching for the family of a child diagnosed with Legg-Calvé-Perthes disease. The nurse knows further teaching is needed about the condition if the family states: a. "We're glad this will only take about 6 weeks to correct." b. "We understand swimming is a good sport for Legg-Calvé-Perthes." c. "We know to watch for areas on the skin that the brace might rub." d. "We understand abduction of the affected leg is important."	Answer: a Rationale: The treatment generally takes approximately 2 years. Swimming is a good activity to increase mobility. A brace might be worn so skin irritation should be monitored. The leg should be kept in the abducted position. Evaluation Physiological Integrity Analysis
55.7 A school health nurse is screening for scoliosis. What assessment findings would the nurse look for? (Select all that apply.) a. uneven shoulders and hips. b. a one-sided rib hump. c. prominent scapula. d. lordosis. e. pain	Answers: a, b, c Rationale: The classic signs of scoliosis include uneven shoulders and hips, a one-sided rib hump, and prominent scapula. Lordosis and pain are not present with scoliosis. Assessment Health Promotion and Maintenance Application
55.8 A child must wear a brace for correction of scoliosis. The nursing diagnosis that should be included in this child's plan of care is: a. risk for impaired skin integrity. b. risk for altered growth and development. c. risk for impaired mobility. d. risk for impaired gas exchange.	Answer: a Rationale: The skin should be monitored for breakdown in any area the brace may rub. The other diagnoses would not be priority and should be corrected by the wearing of the brace. Diagnosis Physiological Integrity Analysis
55.9 A child has just returned from surgery after a spinal fusion surgery. The nurse should check for signs of: a. increased intracranial pressure. b. seizure activity. c. impaired pupillary response during neurological checks. d. impaired color, sensitivity, and movement to lower extremities.	Answer: d Rationale: When the spinal column is manipulated, there is a risk for impaired color, sensitivity, and movement to lower extremities. The other signs are of neurological impairment and are not high-risk with spinal surgery. Intervention Physiological Integrity Application
55.10 A child has been admitted to the hospital with osteomyelitis. The nurse would expect to administer which intravenous antibiotic for this child? a. ampicillin or penicillin. b. vancomycin or clindamycin. c. gentamicin or tobramycin. d. rifampin.	Answer: b Rationale: Medical management of osteomyelitis begins with intravenous administration of a broad-spectrum antibiotic. Treatment is influenced by the possibility of methicillin-resistant *S. aureus* (MRSA), so beginning antibiotics are usually vancomycin or clindamycin. Gentamicin and tobramycin are aminoglycosides, and rifampin is used to treat tuberculosis. Evaluation Physiological Integrity Analysis

55.11 A nurse notes a blue sclera during a newborn assessment. The infant should be checked for: a. Marfan's syndrome. b. achondroplasia. c. *osteogenesis imperfecta.* d. muscular dystrophy.	Answer: c Rationale: Clinical manifestations of *osteogenesis imperfecta* include a blue sclera. This is not present in Marfan's syndrome, achondroplasia, or muscular dystrophy. Assessment Physiological Integrity Analysis
55.12 Care for an infant with *osteogenesis imperfecta* should include: a. support of the trunk and extremities when moving. b. traction care. c. cast care. d. post-op spinal surgery care.	Answer: a Rationale: With *osteogenesis imperfecta*, nursing care focuses on preventing fractures. Because the bones are fragile, the entire body must be supported when the child is moved. Traction, casts, and spinal surgery are not routinely done for *osteogenesis.* Intervention Physiological Integrity Application
55.13 A 12-year-old boy with Duchenne's muscular dystrophy is being seen in the clinic for a routine health visit. An appropriate nursing diagnosis for this client would be: a. risk for impaired mobility related to hypertrophy of muscles and possible loss of ability to ambulate. b. risk for infection related to altered immune system. c. risk for impaired skin integrity related to paresthesia to lower extremities. d. risk for altered comfort related to effects of muscular dystrophy disease.	Answer: a Rationale: Nursing care for muscular dystrophy focuses on promoting independence and mobility for this progressive, incapacitating disease. Risk for infection, risk for impaired skin integrity, and risk for altered comfort are not as high a priority as risk for impaired mobility. Diagnosis Physiological Integrity Analysis
55.14 A child has experienced a sprain of the right ankle. The school nurse should: a. apply ice to the extremity. b. apply a warm, moist pack to the extremity. c. perform passive range-of-motion to the extremity. d. lower the extremity to below the level of the heart.	Answer: a Rationale: For the first 24 hours after a sprain, rest, ice, compression, and elevation should be followed. Therefore, the nurse should apply ice to the extremity. Intervention Physiological Integrity Application
55.15 A nurse is assessing a child after an open reduction of a fractured femur. A sign that compartment syndrome could be occurring would be: a. a pink, warm extremity. b. pain relieved by pain medication. c. dorsalis pedis pulse present. d. prolonged capillary refill time with loss of paresthesia.	Answer: d Rationale: The major serious complication post fracture reduction is compartment syndrome. A prolonged capillary refill time with loss of paresthesia is a sign of compartment syndrome. Pink, warm extremity; pain relieved by medication; and a present dorsalis pedis pulse would all be normal findings post fracture reduction. Assessment Physiological Integrity Analysis

56.1 A child with growth hormone deficiency will be receiving a daily subcutaneous injection of biosynthetic growth hormone. The parents are being trained to administer the injection. It is important for the nurse to instruct the parents to:

a. avoid cleaning the area with alcohol before giving the injection.
b. use only the legs for injection sites.
c. delay giving the injection by 1 day if the child becomes upset.
d. rotate the injection sites.

Answer: d
Rationale: Lipoatrophy can occur at growth hormone injection sites; therefore, the sites should be rotated. The area should be cleansed with alcohol. The arms, thighs, abdomen, and fatty part of the buttocks can be used for injection sites, and the injection should be given at the same time every day so a routine is established. This minimizes the trauma of receiving daily injections. Delaying giving the injection will only heighten the child's anxiety.
Intervention
Physiological Integrity
Application

56.2 A child with diabetes insipidus has been admitted to the pediatric unit. The nurse would expect the child's lab value to demonstrate:

a. hyperglycemia.
b. hypernatremia.
c. hypercalcemia.
d. hypoglycemia.

Answer: b
Rationale: In all forms of diabetes insipidus, serum sodium can increase to pathologic levels, so hypernatremia can occur and should be treated. The glucose level is not affected so hypoglycemia and hyperglycemia are not caused by diabetes insipidus. Hypercalcemia (high calcium) does not occur with this endocrine disorder.
Assessment
Physiological Integrity
Analysis

56.3 A nurse taking a daily weight on a child with diabetes insipidus notes the child has lost 2 pounds in 24 hours. The nurse should:

a. continue to monitor the child.
b. notify the physician regarding the weight loss.
c. chart the weight and report the loss to the next shift.
d. do nothing more than chart the weight, as this would be a normal finding.

Answer: b
Rationale: With diabetes insipidus, the child might have severe fluid volume deficit. A weight loss of 2 pounds indicates a loss of 1 L of fluid so the physician should be notified and the fluids replaced either orally or intravenously. This is a significant loss in a 24-hour period so continuing to monitor, charting the weight and reporting to the next shift, and doing nothing would prolong treatment.
Intervention
Safe, Effective Care Environment
Application

56.4 The nurse is caring for a child with syndrome of inappropriate antidiuretic hormone (SIADH) disorder. Which of the following interventions should the nurse implement for this child? (Select all that apply.)

a. encouragement of fluids.
b. strict intake and output.
c. administration of ordered diuretics.
d. specific gravity of urine.
e. weight on admission, but not daily.

Answers: b, c, d
Rationale: SIADH results from an excessive amount of serum antidiuretic hormone, causing water intoxication and hyponatremia. Intake and output should be monitored strictly; diuretics such as furosemide (Lasix) are administered to eliminate excess body fluid; and urine-specific gravity is monitored. Fluids are restricted to prevent further hemodilution. Daily weights should be obtained to monitor fluid balance.
Implementation
Physiological Integrity
Application

56.5 An adolescent girl with Graves' disease is admitted to the hospital. The nurse expects to find which of the following clinical manifestations characteristic of Graves' disease (hyperthyroidism) present?

a. weight gain, hirsutism, and muscle weakness.
b. dehydration, metabolic acidosis, and hypotension.

Answer: c
Rationale: Graves' disease (hyperthyroidism) occurs when thyroid hormone levels are increased, resulting in excessive levels of circulating thyroid hormones. Clinical manifestations include tachycardia, fatigue, and heat intolerance. Weight gain, hirsutism, and muscle weakness are signs of Cushing's syndrome. Dehydration, metabolic acidosis, and hypertension are signs of congenital adrenal hyperplasia. Hyperglycemia, ketonuria, and glucosuria are signs of diabetes.
Assessment
Physiological Integrity
Analysis

c. tachycardia, fatigue, and heat intolerance. d. hyperglycemia, ketonuria, and glucosuria	
56.6 A child will require lifelong cortisol replacement therapy following the removal of adrenal glands. The family should be taught: a. to discontinue the injections after 1 week. b. that hydrocortisone is available only in oral form so the medication will need to be held if the child has nausea or vomiting. c. to take the hydrocortisone on an empty stomach. d. to administer the medication early in the morning or every other day in the morning.	Answer: d Rationale: Administering the medication early in the morning or every other day causes fewer symptoms and mimics the normal diurnal pattern of cortisol secretion. The injections should not be discontinued abruptly. Injectable hydrocortisone is available, and should be kept on hand if the child is unable to take the medication by mouth. Cortisone should be taken with food. Intervention Physiological Integrity Application
56.7 A nurse is planning care for a child with adrenal insufficiency (Addison's disease). The priority nursing diagnosis is: a. risk for deficient fluid volume. b. risk for injury secondary to hypertension. c. acute pain. d. imbalance nutrition: more than body requirements.	Answer: a Rationale: Adrenal insufficiency can cause fluid deficit. The goal of care is to maintain fluid and electrolyte balance while normal levels of corticosteroids and mineral corticoids are established. Therefore, acute pain and imbalanced nutrition: more than body requirements are not priority nursing diagnoses. A symptom of adrenal insufficiency is hypotension, not hypertension. Planning Physiological Integrity Analysis
56.8 A child has been admitted to the hospital unconscious. The child has a history of insulin-dependent diabetes mellitus (IDDM), and according to the child's mother, he took a normal dose of insulin this morning with breakfast. At school, the child had two pieces of birthday cake and some ice cream at a class birthday party. What is the likely reason for this child's unconscious state? a. metabolic alkalosis. b. metabolic ketoacidosis. c. insulin shock. d. insulin reaction.	Answer: b Rationale: Metabolic acidosis or ketoacidosis could have occurred because of the excessive intake of sugar with no additional insulin. The body burns fat and protein stores for energy when no insulin is available to metabolize glucose. Altered consciousness occurs as symptoms progress. Metabolic alkalosis, insulin shock, and insulin reaction would not be happening in this case. Assessment Physiological Integrity Analysis
56.9 The child has been diagnosed with insulin-dependent diabetes mellitus. The nurse has taught the child the difference between insulin shock and diabetic hyperglycemia. The nurse knows that the child understood the teaching when the child states that the characteristics of diabetic hyperglycemia would be: a. tremors and lethargy. b. hunger and hypertension. c. thirst and flushed skin. d. shakiness and pallor.	Answer: c Rationale: Thirst and flushed skin are characteristic of diabetic hyperglycemia. Tremors, lethargy, hunger, shakiness, and pallor are characteristic of hypoglycemia. Hypertension is not a sign associated with hyperglycemia or hypoglycemia. Assessment Physiological Integrity Analysis

56.10 The nurse is administering an 0800 dose of NPH insulin to an insulin-dependent diabetic child. Based on when the insulin peaks, the child would be at greatest risk for a hypoglycemic episode between:
a. breakfast and lunch.
b. bedtime and breakfast the next morning.
c. 0830 to a midmorning snack.
d. lunch and dinner.

Answer: d
Rationale: NPH is intermediate-acting insulin that peaks in 6 to 12 hours. If administered at 0800, the risk of a hypoglycemic reaction would be between lunch and dinner. A hypoglycemic reaction between breakfast and lunch would be associated with short-acting insulin; between bedtime to breakfast the next morning with long-acting insulin; and 0830 to a midmorning snack with rapid-acting insulin.
Planning
Physiological Integrity
Application

56.11 During the summer many children are more physically active. What changes in the management of the child with diabetes should be taught as a result of more exercise?
a. increased food intake.
b. decreased food intake.
c. increased need for insulin.
d. decreased risk of insulin reaction.

Answer: a
Rationale: Increased physical activity requires adequate caloric intake to prevent hypoglycemia so food intake should be increased. Increased activity would not require decreased food intake, and it would not result in a decreased risk of insulin reaction. Exercise causes the insulin to be used more efficiently so increased insulin would not be needed.
Implementation
Physiological Integrity
Application

56.12 You are teaching the parent of a diabetic preschool-age child about management of the disease. The parent should be told to allow the preschool child to:
a. administer all the insulin injections.
b. pick which finger to stick for glucose testing.
c. draw up the insulin dose.
d. test blood glucose.

Answer: b
Rationale: The preschool-age child's need for autonomy and control can be met by allowing the child to pick which finger to stick for glucose testing. Administering the insulin, drawing up the dose, and testing blood glucose should not be done until the child is middle or later school-age.
Intervention
Health Promotion and Maintenance
Application

56.13 A child is being seen in the clinic with a possible diagnosis of type 2 diabetes. The mother asks what the physician uses to make the diagnosis. The nurse would explain that type 2 diabetes is suspected if the child has obesity, acanthosis nigricans, and a blood glucose level without fasting, on two separate occasions, above:
a. 120.
b. 80.
c. 200.
d. 50.

Answer: c
Rationale: Blood glucose levels at or above 200 mg/dL without fasting are diagnostic of diabetes.
Assessment
Physiological Integrity
Analysis

56.14 A child with Turner's syndrome tells the nurse she feels different from her peers. The nurse should respond with:
a. "Tell me more about the feelings you are experiencing."
b. "These feelings are not unusual and should pass soon."
c. "You'll start to grow soon so don't worry."
d. "You seem to be upset about your disease."

Answer: a
Rationale: The lack of growth and sexual development associated with Turner's syndrome present problems with psychosocial development. Self-image, self-consciousness, and self-esteem are affected by the girl's perception of her body and how she differs from peers. The nurse should encourage more expression of the girl's feelings. Responding that the feelings will pass, that she'll start to grow, or that she is upset about the disease would not be therapeutic.
Intervention
Psychosocial Integrity
Application

56.15 A parent of a newborn asks the nurse why a heel stick is being done on the baby to test for phenylketonuria (PKU). The nurse responds that: a. screening for PKU is required, and detection can be done before symptoms develop. b. the infant has high-risk characteristics. c. because the infant was born by cesarean, a PKU test is necessary. d. because the infant was born by vaginal delivery, a PKU is recommended.	Answer: a Rationale: Screening for phenylketonuria is required by law in every state. It is not done according to high-risk characteristics or type of delivery. Intervention Health Promotion and Maintenance Application

CHAPTER 57

57.1 The nurse caring for a 3-month-old infant with eczema is planning nursing care for this infant. The nurse should focus on: a. maintaining adequate nutrition. b. keeping the baby content. c. preventing infection of lesions. d. applying antibiotics to lesions.	Answer: c Rationale: Nursing care should focus on preventing infection of lesions. Due to impaired skin barrier function and cutaneous immunity, an infant with eczema is at greater risk for the development of skin infections by organisms. Maintaining adequate nutrition and keeping the infant content are not as high priority. Antibiotics are not routinely applied to the lesions. Implementation Physiological Integrity Application
57.2 A child has eczema. Nursing interventions would include use of what? a. hydrocortisone ointment 1%. b. nystatin topical ointment. c. Lotrimin ointment. d. Silvadene cream.	Answer: a Rationale: Topical corticosteroids are used to reduce inflammation when the child has eczema. Hydrocortisone 1% is usually the drug of choice. Nystatin and Lotrimin ointments are used to treat fungal infections. Silvadene cream is used for burns. Implementation Physiological Integrity Analysis
57.3 The nurse is examining a 12-month-old who was brought to the clinic for persistent diaper rash. The nurse finds perianal inflammation, with bright red, scaly plaques and small papules. Satellite lesions are also present. This is most likely caused by which of the following? a. impetigo (staph). b. *Candida albicans* (yeast). c. urine and feces. d. infrequent diapering.	Answer: b Rationale: *Candida albicans* frequently is the underlying cause of severe diaper rash. When a primary or secondary infection with *Candida albicans* occurs, the rash has bright red, scaly plaques with sharp margins. Small papules and pustules might be seen, along with satellite lesions. Even though diaper dermatitis can be caused by impetigo, urine, feces, and infrequent diapering, the lesions and persistent characteristics are common for *Candida*. Assessment Health Promotion and Maintenance Analysis
57.4 An infant, age 2 months, has a candidial diaper rash. The medication the nurse will give this infant will most likely be: a. bacitracin ointment. b. hydrocortisone ointment. c. Desitin. d. nystatin given topically and orally.	Answer: d Rationale: Diaper candidiasis is treated with an antifungal cream (nystatin). An oral antifungal agent may be given to clear the candidiasis from the intestines. Bacitracin is for an infection caused by staphylococcus. Mild diaper rash is treated with a barrier such as Desitin. Moderate diaper rash is treated with hydrocortisone ointment. Implementation Physiological Integrity Application

57.5 The nurse is teaching a group of adolescents about care for acne. The nurse should include: (Select all that apply.)
a. wash skin with mild soap and water twice a day.
b. use astringents and vigorous scrubbing.
c. avoid picking or squeezing the lesions.
d. apply tretinoin (Retin-A) liberally.
e. avoid sun exposure if on tetracycline.

Answers: a, c, e
Rationale: The adolescent should be taught to wash skin with mild soap and water twice a day, to avoid picking or squeezing acne lesions, and to avoid sun exposure if on tetracycline. Using astringents and vigorous scrubbing can exacerbate acne. Tretinoin (Retin-A) should be applied sparingly (pea-sized dose).
Implementation
Health Promotion and Maintenance
Application

57.6 A child has been hospitalized with a severe case of impetigo contagiosa. What antibiotic(s) will the nurse expect to be prescribed?
a. dicloxacillin (Pathocil).
b. rifampin (Rifadin).
c. sulfamethoxazole and trimethoprim (Bactrim).
d. metronidazole (Flagyl).

Answer: a
Rationale: A systemic antibiotic will be given for severe impetigo because it is a bacterial infection. Dicloxacillin is used in treatment of skin and soft tissue infections. It is specific for treating staphylococcal infections. Rifampin is an antitubercular agent, sulfamethoxazole and trimethoprim are used as a prophylaxis against *Pneumocystis carinii* pneumonia (PCP), and metronidazole is used to treat anaerobic and protozoic infections.
Planning
Physiological Integrity
Application

57.7 An infant has a severe case of oral thrush (*Candida albicans*). A priority nursing diagnosis for this client is:
a. activity intolerance related to oral thrush.
b. airway clearance ineffective related to mucus.
c. ineffective infant feeding pattern related to discomfort.
d. ineffective breathing pattern related to oral thrush.

Answer: c
Rationale: An infant with oral thrush might refuse to nurse or feed because of discomfort and pain. Prompt treatment is necessary so that the infant can resume a normal feeding pattern. Activity intolerance, ineffective airway clearance, and ineffective breathing patterns are not usual associated problems.
Diagnosis
Health Promotion and Maintenance
Analysis

57.8 Parents understand the teaching a nurse has done with regard to care of their child with tinea capitis (ringworm of the scalp) if they state:
a. "We will give the griseofulvin on an empty stomach."
b. "We're glad ringworm isn't transmitted from person to person."
c. "Once the lesion is gone, we can stop the griseofulvin."
d. "We will give the griseofulvin with milk or peanut butter."

Answer: d
Rationale: Parents are advised to give oral griseofulvin with fatty foods, such as milk or peanut butter, to enhance absorption. The medication must be used for the entire prescribed period, even if the lesions are gone. All members of the family and household pets should be assessed for fungal lesions because person-to-person transmission is common.
Evaluation
Health Promotion and Maintenance
Analysis

57.9 The school nurse is conducting pediculosis capitis (head lice) checks. A child with a "positive" head check would have:
a. white, flaky particles throughout the entire scalp region.
b. maculopapular lesions behind the ears.
c. lesions in the scalp that extend to the hairline or neck.
d. white sacs attached to the hair shafts in the occipital area.

Answer: d
Rationale: Evidence of pediculosis capitis includes white sacs (nits) that are attached to the hair shafts, frequently in the occiput area. Lesions may be present from itching, but the positive sign is evidence of nits. Lice and nits must be distinguished from dandruff, which appears as white flaky particles.
Assessment
Health Maintenance and Maintenance
Analysis

57.10 A nurse is applying a 5% permethrin lotion to a toddler with scabies. The nurse applies the lotion: a. to the scalp only. b. over the entire body, from the chin down, as well as the scalp and forehead. c. only on the areas with evidence of scabies activity. d. only on the hands.	Answer: b Rationale: Treatment of scabies involves application of a scabicide, such as 5% permethrin lotion, over the entire body, from the chin down. The scabicide also is applied to the scalp and forehead of younger children, avoiding the face. Implementation Health Promotion and Maintenance Application
57.11 A child has sustained a severe burn. When the medical team arrives on the scene, the highest priority for this child at this time would be: a. start intravenous fluids. b. provide for relief of pain. c. establish an airway. d. place a Foley catheter.	Answer: c Rationale: The first step in burn care is to ensure that the child has an airway, is breathing, and has a pulse. Implementation Safe, Effective Care Management Application
57.12 The priority nursing diagnosis during the acute phase of burn injury for a child who has a third-degree circumferential burn of the right arm would be: a. risk for infection. b. risk for altered tissue perfusion. c. risk for altered nutrition: less than body requirements. d. impaired physical mobility.	Answer: b Rationale: When the burn is circumferential, blood flow can become restricted due to edema and result in tissue hypoxia; therefore, the priority diagnosis is a risk for altered tissue perfusion to the extremity. Infection, nutrition, and mobility would have second priority in this case. Diagnosis Safe, Effective Care Environment Analysis
57.13 During the recovery/management phase of burn treatment, which of the following is the most common complication seen in children? a. shock. b. metabolic acidosis. c. burn wound infection. d. asphyxia.	Answer: c Rationale: Infection of the burned area is a frequent complication in the recovery management phase. A goal of burn wound care is protection from infection. Assessment Physiological Integrity Application
57.14 The nurse explains to the parents of a child with a severe burn that wearing of an elastic pressure garment (Jobst stocking) during the rehabilitative stage can help with the prevention of: a. poor circulation. b. hypertrophic scarring. c. pain control. d. formation of thrombus in the burn area.	Answer: b Rationale: During the rehabilitation stage, Jobst or pressure garments are used to reduce development of hypertrophic scarring and contractures. Planning Physiological Integrity Application
57.15 A child has sustained a minor burn. The nurse should teach the family that the child's diet should be high in: a. fats. b. protein. c. minerals. d. carbohydrates.	Answer: b Rationale: Parents should be taught that management of a minor burn requires a high-calorie, high-protein diet. This is necessary to meet the increased nutritional requirements of healing. Implementation Health Promotion and Maintenance Application

ANIMATION AND VIDEO ASSETS ON STUDENT CD-ROM

<table>
<tr><td>

Chapter 3—Reproductive Anatomy and Physiology
Animation: 3-D Female Pelvis
Animation: 3-D Male Pelvis

Chapter 4—Health Promotion for Women
Animation: Oral Contraceptive
Video: Spousal Abuse

Chapter 7—Conception and Fetal Development
Animation: Conception
Animation: Cell Division
Animation: Oogenesis
Animation: Spermatogenesis
Animation: Oogenesis and Spermatogenesis Compared
Animation: Matching Oogenesis and Spermatogenesis
Animation: Placenta Formation
Animation: Embryonic Heart Formation and Circulation
Animation: Embryonic Heart Formation and Circulation

Chapter 17—Processes and Stages of Labor and Birth
Video: Fetal Lie
Animation: Rupturing Membranes
Video: First Stage of Labor
Video: First Stage of Labor: Transition
Video: Second Stage of Labor: Part 1
Video: Second Stage of Labor: Part 2
Video: Delivery of Placenta

Chapter 20—Pharmacologic Pain Relief
Video: Epidural Placement

Chapter 22—Birth-Related Procedures
Video: Vacuum Extractor
Video: Cesarean Birth—Postpartum Epidural Placement
Video: Cesarean Birth—Types of Incisions
Video: Cesarean Birth—Delivery of Infant
Video: Cesarean Birth Videos—Postpartum Assessment: Cesarean Section

Chapter 23—Postpartal Adaptation and Nursing Assessment
Video: Postpartum Assessment
Nursing in Action: Postpartum Assessment

Chapter 28—Normal Newborn: Needs and Care
Video: Newborn Care

Chapter 29—Newborn Nutrition
Nursing In Action: Breastfeeding

Chapter 31—The Newborn at Risk: Birth-Related Stressors
Nursing in Action: Care of the Infant Receiving Phototherapy

Chapter 33—Growth and Development
Video: Growth and Development

Chapter 34—Infant, Child, and Adolescent Nutrition
Video: Breastfeeding and First Foods
Video: Nutritional Status
Video: Children and Overweight

</td><td>

Video: Anorexia Nervosa
Nursing in Action: Administering a Gavage/Tube Feeding

Chapter 35—Pediatric Assessment
Animation: Otoscope Examination
Animation: Mouth and Throat Examination
3D Animation: Eye
Animation: Movement of Joints
Nursing in Action: Pediatric Assessment

Chapter 36—Social and Environmental Influences on the Child
Video: Violence in the Media
Video: Extreme Sports
Video: Identifying Child
Video: Smoking & Smoking Cessation
Video: Identifying Youth Who Abuse Drugs & Alcohol Use

Chapter 37—Health Promotion and Health Maintenance for the Infant and Young Child
Video: Making the Pacifier Decision
Video: Temper Tantrums

Chapter 38—Health Promotion and Health Maintenance for the Older Child and Adolescent
Video: Teen Mental and Spiritual Health

Chapter 39—Nursing Considerations for the Child and Family in the Community
Video: Disaster Preparedness
Video: EMS for Children

Chapter 40—Nursing Considerations for the Hospitalized Child
Video: Treatment Room

Chapter 41—The Child with a Life-Threatening Condition and End-of-Life Care
Video: Presenting Bad News to Families
Video: Involving Family in NICU Setting
Video: Parental Reactions to Death of a Child

Chapter 42—Pain Assessment and Management in Children
Animation: Morphine
Video: Pain Management Kit
Video: Pain Perception
Nursing in Action: Conscious Sedation Monitoring
Nursing in Action: Administering Client-Controlled Analgesia (PCA) Pumps

Chapter 43—The Child with Alterations in Fluid, Electrolyte, and Acid-Base Balance
Animation: Acid-Base Balance

Chapter 44—The Child with Alterations in Immune Function
Video: AIDS/HIV
Animation: HIV Infection/Transmission
Animation: Methotrexate

</td></tr>
</table>

Chapter 46—The Child with Alterations in Eye, Ear, Nose, and Throat Function
Video: 3D Eye/Eye Anatomy
Video: 3D Ear/Ear Anatomy
Animation: Middle Ear Dynamics
Video: Otitis Media
Animation: Ear Abnormalities
Nursing in Action: Child with a Sore Throat
Nursing in Action: Ophthalmic, Otic, and Nasal Medication Administration

Chapter 47—The Child with Alterations in Respiratory Function
Video: SIDS

Chapter 48—The Child with Alterations in Cardiovascular Function
Animation: Congenital Heart Defects
Animation: Digoxin
Animation: Heart Sounds
Normal Heart Sounds: Infant—4 months
Normal Heart Sound: Child—12 years old
Normal Heart Sound: Child—100 Beats per Minute
Physiological S2 split: Child—12 years old
Fixed S2 split
Continuous Murmur Caused by Patent Ductus Arteriosus
Non-continuous Systolic Murmur Caused by Hypertrophic Cardiomyopathy
Normal Physiological Arrhythmia
Animation: Blood Pressure

Chapter 49—The Child with Alterations in Hematologic Function
Drag & Drop Animation: Circulatory System
Drag & Drop Animation: Types of Blood Cells
Video: Administering Blood or Blood Products
Animation: Sickle Cell Anemia

Chapter 50—The Child with Alterations in Cellular Growth
Video: Cancer Overview
Video: Leukemia

Chapter 51—The Child with Alterations in Gastrointestinal Function
Animation: Digestive System
Video: Stool Toileting: Refusals and Rewards
Animation: Activated Charcoal
Animation: Lead Poisoning
Nursing in Action: Ostomy Care Questions

Chapter 52—The Child with Alterations in Genitourinary Function
Animation: Renal Function
Video: Circumcision
Animation: Furosemide
Video: Sexually Transmitted Infections

Chapter 53—The Child with Alterations in Neurologic Function
3-D Animation: Brain and Brainstem
Video: Seizure Disorders
Video: Living with Spina Bifida
Animation: Coup-Contrecoup Injury
Animation: Diazepam

Chapter 54—The Child with Alterations in Cognitive and Mental Health Function
Video: ADD/ADHD
Video: Down Syndrome

Chapter 55—The Child with Alterations in Musculoskeletal Function
Animation: Muscle Physiology

Chapter 56—The Child with Alterations in Endocrine Function
Animation: Physiology of Diabetes
Video: Adolescent Diabetes and Quality of Life
Animation: Responding to Hypoglycemia

Chapter 57—The Child with Alterations in Skin Integrity
Drag & Drop Animation: Layers of the Skin
Animation: Integumentary Repair
Nursing in Action: Burn Wound Care

IMAGE LIBRARY POWERPOINT FILES

Selected illustrations, photographs, and tables from the student text have been provided in Microsoft PowerPoint format for your use in class lectures and discussions. They can be accessed by clicking on the "Image Library" or lecture notes PowerPoints links on the Instructor's Resource CD-ROM. The items listed here may be found in the PowerPoint files.

Chapter 1: Maternal, Newborn, and Child Health Nursing
Figure 1.1: A certified nurse-midwife confers with her client.
Figure 1.2: Children need to be involved actively in decisions regarding their care when appropriate.
Figure 1.3: Uninsured children by race, Hispanic origin, and age: 2003.
Figure 1.4: Infant mortality rates by race: United States, 1940–2002.

Chapter 2: Culture and the Family
Figure 2.1: Single-parent families account for nearly one-third of all U.S. families.
Figure 2.2: Preschoolers from various cultural backgrounds play together.
Figure 2.3: Many cultures value the input of grandparents and other elders in the family or group.
Figure 2.4: Today very few communities are limited to one culture.
Figure 2.5: Infant massage.
Figure 2.6: During pregnancy, therapeutic touch is often helpful in easing pain and reducing anxiety.

Chapter 3: Reproductive Anatomy and Physiology
Figure 3.1: Sexual differentiation.
Figure 3.2: Physiologic changes leading to onset of puberty.
Figure 3.3: Female external genitals, longitudinal view.
Figure 3.4: Female internal reproductive organs.
Figure 3.5: Structures of the uterus.
Figure 3.6: Pelvic blood supply.
Figure 3.7: Uterine muscle layers.
Figure 3.8: Uterine ligaments.
Figure 3.9: Fallopian tubes and ovaries.
Figure 3.10: Pelvic bones with supporting ligaments.
Figure 3.11: Muscles of the pelvic floor.
Figure 3.12: Female pelvis.
Figure 3.13: Pelvic planes: Coronal section and diameters of the bony pelvis.
Figure 3.14: Anatomy of the breast: Sagittal view of left breast.
Figure 3.15: Female reproductive cycle: Interrelationships of hormones with the four phases of the uterine cycle and the two phases of the ovarian cycle in an ideal 28-day cycle.
Figure 3.16: Various stages of development of the ovarian follicles.
Figure 3.17: Blood supply to the endometrium (cross-sectional view of the uterus).
Figure 3.18: Male reproductive system, sagittal view.
Figure 3.19: Schematic representation of a mature spermatozoon.

Chapter 4: Health Promotion for Women
Figure 4.1: Sample basal body temperature chart.
Figure 4.2: A, Unrolled condom with reservoir tip. B, Correct use of a condom.
Figure 4.3: A, The female condom. B, Remove condom and applicator from wrapper by pulling up on the ring. C, Insert condom slowly by gently pushing the applicator toward the small of the back. D, When properly inserted, the outer ring should rest on the folds of skin around the vaginal opening, and the inner ring (closed end) should fit loosely against the cervix.
Figure 4.4: Inserting the diaphragm.
Figure 4.5: A cervical cap.
Figure 4.6: The contraceptive sponge is moistened well with water and inserted into the vagina with the concave portion positioned over the cervix.
Figure 4.7: The Mirena Intrauterine System, which releases levonorgestrel gradually, may be left in place for up to 5 years.
Figure 4.8: The NuvaRing vaginal contraceptive ring. Courtesy of Organon, Inc.
Figure 4.9: Positions for inspection of the breasts.
Figure 4.10: Procedure for breast self-examination.
Figure 4.11: Screening for domestic violence should be done privately.

Chapter 5: Common Gynecologic Problems
Figure 5.1: Depiction of the clue cells characteristically seen in bacterial vaginosis.
Figure 5.2: The hyphae and spores of *Candida albicans*, the fungus responsible for vulvovaginal candidiasis.
Figure 5.3: Microscopic appearance of *Trichomonas vaginalis*.
Figure 5.4: Condylomata acuminata on the vulva.
Figure 5.5: The nurse provides information for the woman during preoperative teaching.
Table 5.1: The Bethesda System for Classifying Pap Smears
Nursing Practice 5.2

Chapter 6: Special Reproductive Issues for Families
Figure 6.1: Flow chart for management of the infertile couple.
Figure 6.2: A, A monophasic, anovulatory basal body temperature (BBT) chart. B, A biphasic BBT chart illustrating probable time of ovulation, the different types of testing, and the time in the cycle that each would be performed.
Figure 6.3: A, Spinnbarkeit (elasticity). B, Ferning pattern. C, Lack of ferning.
Figure 6.4: Sperm passage through cervical mucus.
Figure 6.5: Assisted reproductive techniques.
Figure 6.6: Normal female karyotype.
Figure 6.7: Normal male karyotype.
Figure 6.8: Karyotype of a male who has trisomy 21, Down syndrome.
Figure 6.9: A boy with Down syndrome.
Figure 6.10: Infant with Turner syndrome at 1 month of age.
Figure 6.11: Autosomal dominant pedigree.
Figure 6.12: Autosomal recessive pedigree.
Figure 6.13: X-linked recessive pedigree.
Figure 6.14: A, Genetic amniocentesis for prenatal diagnosis is done at 14 to 16 weeks' gestation. B, Chorionic villus sampling is done at 8 to 10 weeks, and the cells are karyotyped within 48 to 72 hours.
Figure 6.15: Dermatoglyphic patterns of the hands in A, a normal individual, and B, a child with Down syndrome.

Figure 31.10: Infant receiving phototherapy via overhead bilirubin lights.

Figure 31.11: Newborn on fiberoptic "bili" mattress and under phototherapy lights.

Figure 31.12: Maladaptive and adaptive parental responses during crisis period, showing unhealthy and healthy outcomes.

Figure 31.13: This 25 weeks' gestational age infant with respiratory distress syndrome may be frightening for her parents to see for the first time due to the technology that is attached to her.

Figure 31.14: Mother of this 26 weeks' gestational age, 600-g baby begins attachment through fingertip touch.

Figure 31.15: This mother of a 35 weeks' gestational age infant with respiratory distress syndrome is spending time with her newborn and meeting the baby's need for cuddling.

Figure 31.16: Cobedding of twins facilitates delivery of care and parent interaction with healthcare members.

Table 31.1: Clinical Assessments Associated with Respiratory Distress

Table 31.3: Instructional Checklist for In-Room Phototherapy

Chapter 32: Home Care of the Postpartum Family

Figure 32.1: Nurse arriving for a home visit.

Figure 32.2: Various positions for holding an infant. A, Cradle hold. B, Upright position. C, Football hold.

Figure 32.3: Babies should be placed on their backs to sleep.

Figure 32.4: When bathing the newborn, it is important to support the head. Wet babies are very slippery.

Figure 32.5: Two basic cloth diaper shapes. Dotted lines indicate folds.

Figure 32.6: Mothers with sore nipples can leave bra flaps down after feedings to promote air drying and prevent chapping.

Chapter 33: Growth and Development

Figure 33.1: In normal cephalocaudal growth, the child gains control of the head and neck before the trunk and limbs.

Figure 33.2: Children exposed to pleasant stimulation and who are supported by an adult will develop and refine their skills faster.

Figure 33.3: Bronfenbrenner's ecologic theory of development views the individual as interacting within five levels or systems.

Figure 33.4: Fetal alcohol syndrome.

Figure 33.5: Body proportions at various ages.

Figure 33.6: This toddler has learned to ride a Big Wheel, which he is doing right into the street.

Figure 33.7: Preschoolers continue to develop more advanced skills such as kicking a ball without falling down.

Figure 33.8: These preschoolers are participating in associative play, which means they can interact.

Figure 33.9: Jasmine is participating in dramatic play with a nurse while her mother looks on.

Figure 33.10: A, School-age children may take part in activities that require practice.

Figure 33.11: School-age girls and boys enjoy participating in sports.

Figure 33.12: The nurse can help the child and family accept and adjust to new circumstances.

Figure 33.13: Social interaction between children of same and opposite sex is as important inside the acute care setting as it is outside.

Table 33.5: Nine Parameters of Personality

Table 33.6: Patterns of Temperament

Chapter 34: Infant, Child, and Adolescent Nutrition

Figure 34.1: The Food Guide Pyramid is used to provide teaching about amounts of foods recommended for daily intake.

Figure 34.2: Early childhood caries.

Figure 34.3: The baby who has developed the ability to grasp with thumb and forefinger should receive some foods that can be held in the hand.

Figure 34.4: Toddlers should sit at a table or in a high chair to eat, to minimize the chance of choking and to foster positive eating patterns.

Figure 34.5: Preschoolers learn food habits by eating with others.

Figure 34.6: The nurse accurately measures the child and then places height and weight on appropriate growth grids for the child's age and gender.

Figure 34.7: The nurse is interviewing a child about foods eaten in the last day.

Figure 34.8: Most Head Start centers participate in screening programs to identify children at risk for anemia.

Figure 34.9: Infants with failure to thrive may not look severely malnourished, but they fall well below the expected weight and height norms for their age.

Figure 34.10: This young lady began to have symptoms of anorexia at age 12 years.

Figure 34.11: This child has returned to school following surgery.

Teaching Highlights 34.3: Foodborne Safety Guidelines

Chapter 35: Pediatric Assessment

Figure 35.1: Examination of the child begins from the first contact.

Figure 35.2: Tenting of the skin associated with poor skin turgor.

Figure 35.3: Capillary refill technique.

Figure 35.4: A, Inspecting for head lice with a fine-tooth comb. B, Nits on hair.

Figure 35.5: Draw an imaginary line down the middle of the face over the nose and compare the features on each side.

Figure 35.6: External structures of the eye.

Figure 35.7: Draw an imaginary line across the medial canthi and extend it to each side of the face to identify the slant of the palpebral fissures.

Figure 35.8: The eyes of this boy with Down syndrome show a Mongolian slant.

Figure 35.9: Begin the eye muscle examination with inspection of the extraocular movements.

Figure 35.10: The cover-uncover test.

Figure 35.11: Normal fundus.

Figure 35.12: To detect the correct placement of the external ears, draw an imaginary line through the medial and lateral canthi of the eye toward the ear.

Figure 35.13: To restrain an uncooperative child, place the child prone on the examining table.

Figure 35.14: To straighten the auditory canal, pull the pinna back and up for children over 3 years of age.

Figure 35.15: Cross-section of the ear.

Figure 35.16: A, Weber test.

Figure 35.17: Technique for examining nose.

Figure 35.18: The structures of the mouth.

Figure 35.19: Typical sequence of tooth eruption for both deciduous and permanent teeth.

Figure 35.20: The neck is palpated for enlarged lymph nodes around the ears, under the jaw, in the occipital area, and in the cervical chain of the neck.

Figure 35.21: Intercostal spaces and ribs are numbered to describe the location of findings.

Figure 35.22: The sternum and spine are the vertical landmarks used to describe the anatomic location of findings.

Figure 35.23: Two types of abnormal chest shape.

Figure 35.24: One example of a sequence for auscultation of the chest.

Figure 35.25: A, Indirect percussion.

Figure 35.26: Normal resonance patterns expected over the chest.

Figure 35.27: Sound travels in the direction of blood flow.

Figure 35.28: Topographic landmarks of the abdomen.

Figure 35.29: Sequence for indirect percussion of the abdomen.

Figure 35.30: Anatomic structures of the female genital and perineal area.

Figure 35.31: Palpating the scrotum for descended testicles and spermatic cords.

Chapter 36: Social and Environmental Influences on the Child

Figure 36.1: The special relationship between a father about to be deployed in the military and his young daughter is clear.

Figure 36.2: Most children will spend time in childcare settings.

Figure 36.3: Approximately 70% of children have tried smoking by their high school years.

Figure 36.4: Methamphetamine is a popular drug because it can be manufactured with items that are available to the lay public.

Figure 36.5: Physical inactivity is a growing problem among children and can contribute to poor health.

Figure 36.6: What protective gear should children use for skateboarding?

Figure 36.7: Talk openly with adolescents about their health and teach them to avoid health risks connected with tattoos and piercing.

Figure 36.8: Therapeutic strategies with young children involve various methods of communication, such as dramatic play and art.

Chapter 37: Health Promotion and Health Maintenance for the Infant and Young Child

Figure 37.1: A, The nurse is providing a health supervision visit in the child's home after discharge from the hospital for an acute illness. B, A nurse is providing information to a child visiting a mobile healthcare van.

Figure 37.2: The nurse plays many roles in providing health promotion and health maintenance for children.

Figure 37.3: Follow all directions for performing the Denver II assessment and for interpreting responses.

Figure 37.5: This 18-month-old toddler is having a blood screening test to detect iron deficiency anemia.

Figure 37.6: The nurse begins assessment of the infant's family when they are seen in the waiting room and called in for care.

Figure 37.7: Weighing and measuring length during health supervision visits provides important information about the child's nutrition and general development.

Figure 37.8: Interactions between the parent and infant provide clues to mental health.

Figure 37.9: The approach to examination of the toddler or preschooler is important in order to elicit cooperation.

Figure 37.10: This toddler enjoys motor activity that uses large muscle groups.

Table 37.2: Nutrition Teaching for Health Promotion and Health Maintenance Visits

Chapter 38: Health Promotion and Health Maintenance for the Older Child and Adolescent

Figure 38.1: This school-age child is receiving teaching from the nurse about food choices.

Figure 38.2: Everyone needs to be physically active.

Figure 38.3: School-age children often enjoy hikes with family, clubs, or other groups.

Figure 38.4: A student with diabetes is showing the school nurse how to programs her insulin pump.

Figure 38.5: This boy is learning about the effects of smoking on the body through the concrete experience of examining a model of the lungs.

Figure 38.6: Parents often accompany teens with a healthcare problem in for the examination.

Figure 38.7: This teen girl is an avid "boarder."

Figure 38.8: Teens often become associated with causes.

Figure 38.9: Adolescents often drive motorized vehicles and may be at risk for injury if not properly prepared or protected.

Chapter 39: Nursing Considerations for the Child and Family in the Community

Figure 39.1: A visit to the home when all family members are present provides the best information for completion of an assessment tool such as the Home Observation for Measurement of the Environment (HOME).

Figure 39.2: Nurses carefully assess children in the office setting who present with an acute care illness.

Figure 39.3: The school is often the setting for screening tests of large groups of students to identify those that may have a problem that interferes with Learning.

Figure 39.4: Assess the childcare center's environment for safety hazards.

Figure 39.5: Nurses provide both short-term and long-term services to families in the home setting.

Figure 39.6: Children with chronic conditions may have a visible or nonvisible health condition, or nonvisible until an acute episode of their condition makes the condition visible.

Figure 39.7: Nurses often assume a larger role in working with children and families with a chronic health condition, and educating the family to manage diabetes type 1 is an important role of this pediatric nurse, who is also a certified diabetes educator.

Figure 39.8: Because some children need medications or other therapies during school hours, the parents and child, school nurse, teacher, and school administrators develop a plan to manage the child's condition during school hours.

Figure 39.9: Daily caregiving demands of the child who is medically fragile continue 24 hours a day, 7 days a week.

Chapter 40: Nursing Considerations for the Hospitalized Child

Figure 40.1: Allowing the child to dress up as a doctor or a nurse helps prepare the child for hospitalization.

Figure 40.2: The child's anxiety and fear often will be reduced if the nurse explains what is going to happen and demonstrates how the procedure will be done by using a doll.

Figure 40.3: Jasmine's parents are taking the time to prepare her for hospitalization by reading a book recommended by the nurse.

Figure 40.4: The nurse is monitoring a young child who is in a short-stay unit for treatment of dehydration and fever.

Figure 40.5: Rehabilitation units provide an opportunity for the child to relearn tasks like walking and climbing stairs.

Figure 40.6: A, Volunteers such as this foster grandmother can provide stimulation and nurturing to help young children adapt to lengthy hospitalizations. B, Child life specialists plan activities for young children in the hospital to facilitate play and stress reduction.

Figure 40.7: The nurse can use a simple gender-specific outline drawing of a child's body to encourage children to draw what they think about their medical problem.

Figure 40.8: A child life specialist works with children being treated for cancer.

Figure 40.9: Hospitals may have pet therapy from specially trained animals to provide comfort and distraction during health care.

Figure 40.10: A, Age-appropriate play will help the child adjust to hospitalization and care. B, Having the child play with dolls that have "disabilities" similar to his or her own will help the child adjust.

Figure 40.11: Having interaction with other hospitalized adolescents and maintaining contact with friends outside the hospital are very important so that the teenager does not feel isolated and alone.

Figure 40.12: Shriners Hospital in Spokane, Washington, has a special classroom and teacher for children undergoing a lengthy hospital stay, enabling them to remain current with their schoolwork.

Figure 40.13: This child has just undergone surgery and is in the PICU.

Figure 40.14: This child with chronic medical problems is being cared for at home.

Chapter 41: The Child with a Life-Threatening Condition and End-of-Life Care

Figure 41.1: Jooti feels pain, hears noises, has her sleep disrupted, and has limited mobility because of all the equipment attached to her.

Figure 41.2: By their very nature, PICUs are ominous and sterile.

Figure 41.3: In times of crisis, everyone likes to know that someone is in charge and who that person is.

Figure 41.4: During the sibling's visit to the ill child, it is important to talk with the sibling and answer any questions in an honest manner at a level the child can understand.

Figure 41.5: It is important that parents and siblings feel comfortable communicating with the seriously ill child.

Figure 41.6: The toddler with a life-limiting condition recognizes that he feels bad and that routines are different.

Figure 41.7: Nurses need to express grief in a supportive environment after a child's death.

Chapter 42: Pain Assessment and Management in Children

Figure 42.1: Neonatal characteristic facial responses to pain include bulged brow, eyes squeezed shut, furrowed nasolabial creases, open lips, pursed lips, stretched mouth, taut tongue, and a quivering chin.

Figure 42.3: The Faces Pain Rating Scale is valid and reliable in helping children to report their level of pain.

Figure 42.6: When painful procedures are planned, use EMLA cream to anesthetize the skin where the painful stick will be made.

Table 42.2: Physiologic Consequences of Unrelieved Pain in Children

Table 42.9: NSAIDs and Recommended Doses for Children and Adolescents

Table 42.10: Characteristics of Light and Deep Sedation

Chapter 43: The Child with Alterations in Fluid, Electrolyte, and Acid-Base Balance

Figure 43.1: The major body fluid compartments.

Figure 43.2: Normal routes of fluid excretion from infants and children.

Figure 43.3: Use of an overhead warmer or phototherapy increases insensible fluid excretion through the skin, thus increasing the fluid intake needed.

Figure 43.4: The use of a volume control device with an intravenous saline solution is important to prevent a sudden extracellular fluid volume overload.

Figure 43.5: If isotonic fluid containing sodium is given too rapidly or in too great an amount, an extracellular fluid volume excess will develop.

Figure 43.6: This infant with congenital heart disease has signs of generalized edema.

Figure 43.7: Edematous tissue is easily damaged.

Figure 43.8: A, Water balance is maintained by the simple passage of molecules from greater to lesser concentration across cell membranes. B, Sodium levels are maintained by an active transport system, the sodium-potassium pump, which moves these electrolytes across cell membranes in spite of their concentration.

Figure 43.9: Because this child has a nasogastric tube in place, it is important to monitor his potassium levels.

Figure 43.10: This child may develop respiratory acidosis or respiratory alkalosis.

Figure 43.11: This child, who has muscular dystrophy, uses a "turtle" respirator at home to assist with breathing.

Figure 43.12: With any postoperative or immobilized child, it is important to monitor urine output to detect oliguria.

Figure 43.13: Teaching parents to use safety latches on cabinets to keep aspirin away from small children can help prevent one cause of metabolic acidosis.

Table 43.1: Electrolyte Concentrations in Body Fluid Compartments

Table 43.12: Risk Factor Assessment for Fluid Imbalances

Table 43.13: Risk Factor Assessment for Electrolyte Imbalances

Pathophysiology Illustrated 43.3: Pottassium Ions

Pathophysiology Illustrated 43.5: Buffer Responses to Acid and Base

Pathophysiology Illustrated 43.6: The Bicarbonate Buffer System

Pathophysiology Illustrated 43.7: The Kidneys and Metabolic Acids

Figure 49.3: Many of these red blood cells show an elongated crescent shape characteristic of sickle cell anemia.
Figure 49.4: Red blood cell appearance in β-thalassemia.
Figure 49.5: The child undergoing bone marrow transplantation is hospitalized in a special unit while receiving chemotherapy before the transfusion.
Table 49.2: White Blood Cells and Their Functions
Pathophysiology Illustrated 49.1: Sickle Cell Anemia

Chapter 50: The Child with Alterations in Cellular Growth

Figure 50.1: Percentage of primary tumors by site of origin for different age groups.
Figure 50.2: Computed tomography (CT) can be a frightening procedure for children.
Figure 50.3: Chemotherapy protocol.
Figure 50.4: One of the most common threats to a child's body image at any age is hair loss induced by chemotherapy. Use of hats can improve self-concept.
Figure 50.5: The child with cushingoid changes frequently has a rounded face and prominent cheeks.
Figure 50.6: The child with cancer depends on parents and family members to provide support. Nurses can assist families and draw upon their strengths to help the child.
Figure 50.7: Survivors of childhood cancer.
Figure 50.8: A child in a pediatric oncology clinic giving injections to a doll.
Figure 50.9: A vascular access device allows chemotherapeutic agents to be administered without the need for repeated "sticks" to the child.
Nursing Practice 50.10: Laboratory Values in Leukemia
Pathophysiology Illustrated 50.3: Brian Tumors
Pathophysiology Illustrated 50.4: Hodgkin's Disease

Chapter 51: The Child with Alterations in Gastrointestinal Function

Figure 51.1: A, Unilateral cleft lip. B, Bilateral cleft lip.
Figure 51.2: A, Repaired unilateral cleft lip (see Fig. 51.1A). B, Repaired bilateral cleft lip (see Fig. 51.1B).
Figure 51.3: A gastrostomy tube is used to feed the child with a gastrointestinal disorder such as esophageal atresia.
Figure 51.5: The newborn with gastroschisis has abdominal contents located outside the abdominal wall.
Figure 51.6: The umbilical hernia of the newborn usually closes as the muscles strengthen in later infancy and childhood.
Figure 51.7: Nursing strategies to address altered perceptions of body image and increased feelings of dependence are important when working with adolescents who have ostomies.
Figure 51.8: The child with celiac disease commonly shows failure to grow and wasting of extremities.
Pathophysiology Illustrated 51.1: Esophageal Artesia and Tracheoesophageal Fistula
Pathophysiology Illustrated 51.2: Pyloric
Stenosis Pathophysiology Illustrated 51.4: Viral Hepatitis

Chapter 52: The Child with Alterations in Genitourinary Function

Figure 52.1: The kidneys are located between the twelfth thoracic (T12) and third lumbar (L3) vertebrae.
Figure 52.2: This child has bladder exstrophy, noted by extrusion of the posterior bladder wall through the lower abdominal wall.

Figure 52.3: Hypospadias and epispadias.
Figure 52.4: This boy has generalized edema, a characteristic finding in nephrotic syndrome.
Figure 52.5: A color wheel, such as the one shown here, can be used as a guide in standardizing descriptions of urine color.
Figure 52.6: This child is undergoing hemodialysis.
Clinical Manifestations 52.3: Acute Versus Chronic Renal Failure
Pathophysiology Illustrated 52.1: Obstruction Sites in the Urinary System
Pathophysiology Illustrated 52.2: Acute Renal Failure

Chapter 53: The Child with Alterations in Neurologic Function

Figure 53.1: Transverse section of the brain and spinal cord.
Figure 53.2: A, Decorticate posturing, characterized by rigid flexion, is associated with lesions above the brainstem in the corticospinal tracts. B, Decerebrate posturing, distinguished by rigid extension, is associated with lesions of the brainstem.
Figure 53.3: Pupil findings in various neurologic conditions with altered consciousness.
Figure 53.4: A child who has a seizure when standing should be gently assisted to the floor and placed in a side-lying position.
Figure 53.5: The child with bacterial meningitis assumes an opisthotonic position, with the neck and the head hyperextended, to relieve discomfort.
Figure 53.6: To test for Kernig sign, raise the child's leg with the knee flexed.
Figure 53.7: To test Brudzinski sign, flex the child's head while in a supine position.
Figure 53.8: In communicating hydrocephalus, an excessive amount of cerebrospinal fluid accumulates in the subarachnoid space, producing the characteristic head enlargement seen here.
Figure 53.9: A ventriculoperitoneal shunt, commonly used to treat children with hydrocephalus, is usually placed at 3 to 4 months of age.
Figure 53.10: Lumbosacral myelomeningocele is caused by a neural tube defect that results in incomplete closure of the vertebral column.
Figure 53.11: Help determine the best assistive device for the child to gain the most independence for mobilizing and to promote development.
Figure 53.12: In craniosynostosis, the head shape is dependent upon which sutures are involved.
Figure 53.13: A child having a baclofen pump filled.
Figure 53.14: A child with cerebral palsy has abnormal muscle tone and lack of physical coordination.
Figure 53.15: Mechanics of injury to the spinal cord
Figure 53.16: Splints are often used to prevent contractures, thus maintaining optimal functioning of the child's hands or feet.
Table 53.1: Summary of Anatomic and Physiologic Differences Between Children and Adults
Table 53.3: Glasgow Coma Scale for Assessment of Coma in Infants and Children
Table 53.6: Anticonvulsants Used to Treat Seizure Disorders
Table 53.7: Stages of Reye Syndrome
Growth and Development 53.1: Cues in the Glasgow Coma Scale Assessment

ANSWERS TO CRITICAL THINKING IN ACTION ACTIVITY QUESTIONS

The following are suggested answers to the Critical Thinking in Action Activity Questions that appear at the end of each chapter of the textbook and on the Student CD-ROM.

CHAPTER 1

CRITICAL THINKING IN ACTION

You are working as a prenatal nurse in a local clinic. Before entering a client's room, you review the chart for pertinent information such as cultural background, significant family members, weeks of gestation, test results, birth plan, and education for health promotion. You greet each client and family members by name and ask how they are coping with the pregnancy. Depending on the trimester of the pregnancy, you review the discomforts or concerns of the mother/family and what they may expect. You examine the mother, including fundal height, fetal heart rate and fetal position if appropriate, maternal blood pressure, weight gain, and urine analysis. With each client, you discuss the community resources available such as prenatal classes, lactation consultants, and prenatal exercise/yoga classes. Based upon the information you obtain, you might refer the mother to social services or the WIC program as appropriate. At the end of the clinic session, you review the clients with the collaborating physician.

1. How would you define the terms *family* and *family-centered care?*	Answer: Family is those persons defined by the mother. For example, the family of a single mother may include her mother, her sister, another relative, a close friend, a lesbian partner, or the father of the child. Many cultures also recognize the importance of extended families, and several family members may provide care and support.
	Family-centered care is characterized by an emphasis on the family and the family's choices about their birth experience. Fathers and partners are active participants; siblings are encouraged to visit and meet the newest family member, and they may even attend the birth. Care is designed to meet the emotional, social, and developmental needs of children and families seeking health care.
2. Describe how the nursing process provides the framework for the delivery of direct nursing care.	Answer: The nurse assesses the mother and identifies the nursing diagnoses that describe the responses of the individual and family to the pregnancy or illness. The nurse then implements and evaluates nursing care. The care is designed to meet specific physical and psychosocial needs.
3. How would you describe the concept of community-based care?	Answer: A "seamless" system of family-centered, comprehensive, coordinated health care, health education, and social services. The system requires coordination as clients move from primary-care services to acute-care facilities and then back into the community.
4. How would you describe culturally competent care?	Answer: Culture develops from socially learned beliefs, lifestyles, values, and integrated patterns of behavior that are characteristic of the family, cultural group, and community. Conflicts can occur within a family when traditional rituals and practices of the family do not conform to current healthcare practices. Nurses need to be sensitive to the potential implications for the client's health care. When cultural values are not part of the nursing care plan, the client may be forced to decide whether the family's beliefs should take priority over the healthcare professional's guidance.

CHAPTER 2

CRITICAL THINKING IN ACTION

While working in an inner-city clinic for adolescents, you meet a new client, a 14-year-old Latina girl named Juanita. She is accompanied by her parents. None of them speak English. Through a translator, Juanita tells you that she recently moved here with her grandparents. They have brought her here today because she has a sore throat. The curandero they took her to see prescribed the herbal remedy echinacea, but her throat is still sore. The rapid test you perform for strep throat is positive, and the nurse practitioner prescribes an antibiotic.

1. According to the national standards for culturally and linguistically appropriate services in health care set by the government, what are examples of important standards of care you as the nurse can provide in the care of this adolescent?	Answer: You should provide respectful care in their preferred language (getting an interpreter if needed), attend ongoing cultural sensitivity training, provide language brochures in their preferred language, and evaluate if the client is satisfied with the services you provided.

2. How can you, as the nurse, take steps to achieve cultural competence?	Answer: The first step is to evaluate your own feelings about people from other cultures. You can also examine your own personal background to determine what values and beliefs you have. This will help identify what values and beliefs you have that are similar to and different from other cultures.
3. How would you, as the nurse, be able to address some of the disparities that can exist when this client comes to the clinic?	Answer: You can prevent any barriers to the access of health care in your clinic. The barriers this family may encounter are lack of health insurance, hours available, transportation problems, and providing a trusting relationship.
4. What are some examples of common food preferences in the Latino-American culture?	Answer: The use of corn, cheese, and beans is common in this population.

CHAPTER 3

CRITICAL THINKING IN ACTION

You are working in the OB/GYN clinic when Sally Smith, a 17-year-old teenager, comes in complaining of irregular menses. She believes her periods are really "messed up" and interfering with her active schedule. She wants them to be more regular and asks you for birth control. She tells you that she is a member of the swimming team and is a senior in high school. She says she is planning to start community college next year to obtain an associate degree in computer technology. You assess Sally's history as follows: menarche began at age 12; periods occur every 28 to 32 days. She usually experiences cramping in the first 2 days and the flow lasts 4 to 5 days. She uses an average of 4 to 5 tampons a day during her period. She has never been hospitalized, has no prior medical problems, and is up to date on her immunizations except for meningitis.

1. Based on your knowledge of menstruation, how would you describe Sally's menstrual cycle?	Answer: Sally has described a normal menstrual cycle. While there is some variability in frequency, it is not outside the normal range for a teenager.
2. What is your primary goal in discussing Sally's menstrual cycle with her?	Answer: It is important to reassure Sally that her menstrual cycle is normal. Your role is to provide accurate information and assist in clarifying misconceptions so that Sally will develop a positive self-image.
3. What information would you give Sally relating to her menstrual cycle?	Answer: The menstrual cycle length is determined from the first day of one menses to the first day of the next. Normal length is 25 to 35 days. The amount of flow is approximately 30 mL per period. Flow is heavier at first and lightens toward the end of the period. The length of menses may last 2 to 8 days.
4. What important request does Sally have?	Answer: Of utmost importance is the request for birth control. Sally may be considering becoming sexually active and needs contraception. Teenagers often have difficulty asking for what they really want. This is an ideal situation to bring up issues of sexuality.
5. Sally expresses problems dealing with the cramping she experiences with the first 2 days of her menses. What would you suggest to Sally to cope with the discomfort?	Answer: Relief may be obtained with oral contraception, prostaglandin inhibitors such as ibuprofen, aspirin, naproxen, and measures such as regular exercise, rest, heat, and good nutrition with an emphasis on vitamins B and E.

CHAPTER 4

CRITICAL THINKING IN ACTION

You are working at a local clinic when Joy Lang, age 20, presents for her first pelvic exam. You obtain the following GYN history: LMP 6/12, menarche age 12, menstrual cycle 28 to 30 days lasting 4 to 5 days, heavy one day, then lighter. She tells you that she needs to use superabsorbent tampons on the first day of her period and then she switches to a regular absorbency tampon for the remaining days. She confirms that she changes the tampon every 6 to 8 hours, never leaving it in overnight. She denies premenstrual syndrome, dysmenorrhea, or medical problems and says that she is not taking any medication on a regular schedule. She tells you that she recently got married, but would like to wait before getting pregnant. She'd like to discuss birth control methods. Joy tells you that doctors make her nervous and she admits to being anxious about her first pelvic exam.

1. What steps would you take to reduce Joy's anxiety relating to the pelvic exam?	Answer: Perform the head-to-toe exam leaving the pelvic exam for last to establish trust. Involve Joy as an active participant in the examination. Explain the sensations she may feel. Use the opportunity to teach about the body and its function. Invite Joy to visualize her external and internal genitalia by using a mirror.

2. What position is best to relax Joy's abdominal muscles for the pelvic exam?	Answer: Assist Joy in the semisitting position with her hands either at her sides or over her chest. The stirrups should be at a comfortable length for her height.
3. What precaution should be taken when obtaining a Pap smear?	Answer: No lubricant is used with the speculum as it can interfere with the laboratory results.
4. Explain the purpose of the Pap smear.	Answer: The purpose of the test is to screen for the presence of cellular abnormalities by obtaining a sample containing cells from the cervix and the endocervical canal.
5. What factors do you include in a discussion of the type of birth control that Joy could practice?	Answer: The discussion should explore available choices, advantages, disadvantages, effectiveness, side effects, contraindications, and long-term effects. Outside factors influence the choice of contraception such as cultural practices, religious beliefs, attitudes and personal preferences, cost effectiveness, misinformation, practicality of method, and self-esteem.

CHAPTER 5

CRITICAL THINKING IN ACTION

Linda Knoll, 35 years old, presents to you at the GYN clinic for her annual physical and pelvic exam. You obtain the following menstrual history: LMP 8 days ago. Periods occur every 29 days and last 5 days. She tells you that she uses superabsorbent tampons during the first 2 days of her period and then changes to regular absorbency tampons for the duration, and that she currently has an IUD in place for contraception. She tells you that her husband has been complaining for the last few months that she seems irritable, tense, and moody near "that time of the month." Linda admits that she doesn't feel well before her period and describes having low pelvic discomfort, breast tenderness, "bloating," and some constipation. She seems to cry easily 2 to 3 days before her period. She has noticed this pattern over the last 4 or 5 months. You recognize these symptoms as related to premenstrual syndrome (PMS). Linda asks you if these changes are due to female hormones.

1. How would you answer Linda's question concerning female hormones?	Answer: Although there is no known cause for PMS, one study suggests there is a complex interrelationship among ovarian hormones and stress-related hormones. Many women believe PMS to be psychologic, but the result of the study provided information that actual physiologic changes occur.
2. After reviewing Linda's diet with her, what would you recommend to help?	Answer: Counsel Linda to restrict her intake of foods containing methylxanthines, such as chocolate, cola, and coffee; restrict her intake of alcohol, nicotine, red meat, and foods containing salt and sugar; increase her intake of complex carbohydrates and protein; and increase the frequency of meals.
3. Linda has an IUD in place. What other type of contraceptive might help reduce the symptoms of PMS?	Answer: Low-dose oral contraceptives.
4. What other activities can you suggest to help Linda reduce PMS symptoms?	Answer: A program of aerobic exercises such as fast walking, jogging, or aerobic dancing is generally beneficial.
5. What should you tell Linda about using tampons during heavy menstrual flow?	Answer: Tampons should be used during the day; change to pads at night when flow is lighter to decrease the risk of toxic shock syndrome.

CHAPTER 6

CRITICAL THINKING IN ACTION

Marie Neives, age 19, presents while you are working at a Planned Parenthood Clinic. She is there for a GYN exam and tells you that she is sexually active with her boyfriend but doesn't want to become pregnant. Since she lives at home with her parents, she does not want to use "the pill" because her mother might find out. Marie asks you for information concerning fertility awareness. You obtain a menstrual history as follows: menarche age 12, cycle every 28 days lasting 5 days, dysmenorrhea the first 2 days with moderate flow. She has had one sexual partner. She states her boyfriend doesn't like to use condoms and that she has been lucky so far in not getting pregnant. You assist the nurse practitioner with a physical and pelvic exam. The results show that Marie is essentially healthy. The nurse practitioner asks you to review with Marie the basal body temperature (BBT) method of fertility awareness.

1. Explore with Marie "natural family planning." How would you explain this to her?	Answer: Natural family planning is based on an understanding of the changes that occur throughout a woman's ovulatory cycle. This method requires periods of abstinence and recording of certain events throughout the cycle; cooperation of the partners is important.
2. Briefly explain why the basal body temperature (BBT) method can predict ovulation.	Answer: Basal temperature for the woman in the preovulatory phase is usually below 36°C. As ovulation approaches, production of estrogen peaks and may cause a slight drop, then a rise in the basal temperature. After ovulation, progesterone production rises. It causes a 0.3°C to 0.6°C sustained rise in basal temperature. Just before or coincident with the onset of menses, the temperature falls below 36°C.
3. Describe to Marie the procedure for obtaining BBT.	Answer: Using a BBT thermometer, the woman chooses one site (oral, vaginal, or rectal), which she uses consistently. She takes her temperature for 5 minutes every day before arising and before starting any activity, including smoking. The result is recorded on a BBT chart, and the temperature dots are connected to form a graph. She shakes the thermometer down and cleans it in preparation for use the next day.
4. To avoid conception, when do you tell Marie to abstain from unprotected intercourse?	Answer: If her periods are regular, she should abstain or use protection (condoms) 3 days before and 3 days after the anticipated day of ovulation.

CHAPTER 7

CRITICAL THINKING IN ACTION

You are working at the local clinic when Frances, a 28-year-old G2 P1001 at 11 weeks' gestation, comes into the office. Frances tells you that early in the first trimester, her husband experienced a flu-like syndrome and that he was later diagnosed with cytomegalovirus (CMV) pneumonia . She tells you that his physician found an enlarged supraclavicular lymph node and an ulcer on one tonsil. Laboratory testing revealed elevated liver enzymes. Further testing led to the discovery of positive cytomegalovirus (CMV) IgM levels. She has come today with symptoms including night sweats, persistent sore throat, joint pain, headache, vomiting, and fatigue. You obtain vital signs of temperature 99°F, pulse 90, respirations 14, BP 110/70. Her physical exam is normal; no lymphadenopathy is present. Her weight gain is 2 lb even with nausea and some vomiting. She is worried that her husband's illness could be related to her current symptoms.

1. How would you respond to Frances's concern?	Answer: Frances's symptoms may be attributable to normal pregnancy or possibly to a flu virus. The physician will probably order serologic tests for CMV IgM and IgG. The test will determine if Frances has been exposed to CMV, has an acute or recent infection, or is immune.
2. Frances asks you if her baby is formed. How would you discuss the three stages of development?	Answer: The preembryonic stage consists of the first 14 days after the ovum is fertilized, the embryonic stage covers the period from day 15 until the end of the eighth week, and the fetal stage extends from the end of the eighth week until birth.
3. Frances asks when her baby is most vulnerable for abnormal growth or structure. How would you answer?	Answer: During the embryonic stage when tissues differentiate into essential organs and the main external features develop, the embryo is most vulnerable.
4. Frances asks what stage her baby is in. What would you tell her?	Answer: At 11 weeks your baby is considered a fetus and all the organs are present.

CHAPTER 8

CRITICAL THINKING IN ACTION

Terry Dole, a 38-year-old G1, P0000, at 6 weeks' gestation, presents to you at the OB clinic for her first prenatal visit with the certified nurse-midwife (CNM). One of the first decisions facing Terry is the selection of a healthcare provider. The midwife explains the various options available to Terry at the clinic related to the differences in educational preparation, skill level, practice characteristics, and general philosophy of CNMs and obstetricians. Terry tells you that she has been married for 6 years and works as a massage therapist. You obtain the following data: BP 110/70, temperature 97°F, pulse 76, respirations 12, weight 140 lb, height 5'7". The physical and pelvic exams are essentially normal. The CNM asks you to teach Terry about birth plans.

1. Discuss the advantages of a birth plan.	Answer: A birth plan helps couples set priorities. It identifies areas that they want to incorporate into their own birth experience. By writing down preferences, prospective parents identify aspects of the childbearing experience that are most important to them.

2. Discuss the disadvantages of a birth plan.	Answer: At times expectations cannot be met because of the unavailability of some choices in the community, limitations set by insurance providers, or unexpected problems during pregnancy or birth.
3. Explain the role of a doula.	Answer: Doula roles and responsibilities include providing specific labor support skills; offering guidance and encouragement; assisting mothers to cover gaps in their care; building a team relationship; and encouraging communication between patient, nursing staff, and medical caregivers.
4. What gender differences are there in moving toward parenthood?	Answer: Women, especially working women, experience appreciably more change than do men in the transition to parenthood. Women tend to feel responsible for their children's success and happiness. They also internalize the distress experienced by those to whom they are closest, particularly family members.

CHAPTER 9

CRITICAL THINKING IN ACTION

Twenty-two-year old Jean Simmons is an aerobic instructor, G0, P0000 in her first trimester of pregnancy. She presents to you at the local clinic complaining of frequent nausea, urinary frequency, and fatigue. You obtain her vital signs as 108/60, 97°F, pulse 68, respirations 12, weight 125 lb, height 64 inches. Her urine tests negative for ketones, albumin, leukocytes, and sugar. You note that Jean has lost 3 lb since her last visit. You assist the certified nurse-midwife with a physical exam, the findings of which are essentially normal. Jean says that while she knows it could become an issue, she would like to continue working as an aerobic instructor for as long as she possibly can during the pregnancy. You identify Jean's complaints as normal discomforts of pregnancy and proceed with prenatal education.

1. What advice would you suggest to cope with the nausea of pregnancy?	Answer: Eat crackers or dry toast before arising; avoid causative foods and odors; eat small, frequent meals and dry foods with fluids between meals; avoid greasy or highly seasoned foods.
2. What advice might you suggest to cope with urinary frequency?	Answer: Do not cut back on fluids; void when urge is experienced; increase fluid intake during the day.
3. What teaching would be important relating to exercise in pregnancy?	Answer: Decrease intensity of exercise as pregnancy progresses and stop when fatigued. Avoid high-risk activities or activities that require good balance and coordination. Avoid prolonged overheating. Keep heart rate at or below 140 beats per minute. Wear supportive shoes and supportive bra.
4. What symptoms related to exercise should Jean report to her physician?	Answer: Extreme fatigue, dizziness or faintness, sudden sharp pain, difficulty in breathing, nausea and vomiting, pain, vaginal bleeding, and excessive muscle soreness.

CHAPTER 10

CRITICAL THINKING IN ACTION

Wendy Stodard, age 40, G3, P0020 comes to the obstetrician's office where you are working for a prenatal visit. Wendy had experienced two spontaneous abortions followed by a D&C at 14 and 15 weeks' gestation during the previous year. She has a history of *Chlamydia* infection 3 years ago, which was treated with azithromycin. She is at 10 weeks' gestation. Wendy tells you that she is afraid of losing this pregnancy as she did previously. She says she has been experiencing some mild nausea, breast tenderness, and fatigue, which did not occur with her other pregnancies. You assist the obstetrician with an ultrasound. The gestational sac is clearly seen, fetal heartbeat is observed, and crown-to-rump measurements are consistent with gestational age of 10 weeks. The pelvic exam demonstrates a closed cervix and positive Goodell's, Hegar's, and Chadwick's signs. You discuss with Wendy the signs of a healthy pregnancy.

1. What signs are reassuring with this pregnancy?	Answer: The ultrasound showed a gestational sac with a fetus consistent with gestational age, and the fetus has a heartbeat. Breast tenderness, nausea, and fatigue confirm a pregnancy hormone level consistent with a normal pregnancy.
2. What symptoms should be reported to the obstetrician immediately?	Answer: Vaginal bleeding or cramping, painful urination, severe vomiting or diarrhea, fever higher than 101°F, low abdominal pain located on either side or in the middle of the abdomen, lightheadedness, and dizziness, particularly if accompanied by shoulder pain.
3. What is the frequency of antepartal visits?	Answer: Every 4 weeks for the first 28 weeks' gestation; every 2 weeks until 36 weeks' gestation; after week 36, every week until childbirth.

CHAPTER 11

CRITICAL THINKING IN ACTION

Thirty-seven-year-old Cathy Sommers, G1, P0000, presents to you, with her husband, at the OB physician's office at 32 weeks' gestation. Cathy tells you that she and her husband are practicing lawyers with their own firm. The couple delayed starting a family because it has been important to them to advance their careers and establish their firm. Cathy had an amniocentesis at 18 weeks' gestation because of her advanced maternal age, and the results ruled out chromosomal abnormalities. The couple knows that the baby is a boy and are anticipating a vaginal birth. Cathy tells you that she is experiencing more fatigue, leg cramps, and shortness of breath when climbing stairs. The physical exam including a negative Homans' sign is within normal limits with the exception of slight ankle edema. Her weight is 150 lb, temperature 98.6°F, pulse 88, respirations 16, BP 126/70. You discuss pregnancy discomforts in the third trimester with Cathy and her husband.

1. What measures can you suggest to cope with fatigue?	Answer: Encourage adequate sleep and rest periods. Explore ways to arrange work to allow frequent rest periods. Encourage good posture, wearing of low-heeled shoes, and pelvic rock exercises to ease backaches. Suggest ways to reduce insomnia with the use of pillows and raising the head of the bed.
2. Discuss measures to decrease leg cramps.	Answer: Avoid stretching her legs, pointing her toes, walking excessively, and lying on her back. Demonstrate how to massage legs and buttocks to her husband.
3. Discuss the physiologic changes underlying dyspnea.	Answer: The uterus presses up against the abdominal organs and diaphragm, preventing full expansion of the lungs. Relief will occur in the ninth month when the baby drops into the pelvis.
4. Review Braxton Hicks contractions.	Answer: Around the sixth month, the uterus begins painless irregular contractions. No cervical dilatation occurs. The contractions may increase the tone of the uterine muscle in preparation for labor.

CHAPTER 12

CRITICAL THINKING IN ACTION

Sandra Hill is a 17-year-old at 12 weeks' gestation with her first pregnancy. She presents to you accompanied by her mother. Her mother tells you that Sandra is an active teenager who plays sports and has been taking dance lessons for 5 years. She maintains a "B+" in school. Sandra voices concern about potential weight gain during pregnancy. She tells you that this was not a planned pregnancy and she has ambivalent feelings about it. You become concerned as she tells you that she has reduced her caloric intake over the last few months to try to keep her weight down and camouflage her pregnancy. You do a nutritional assessment and find that she is deficient in calcium, iron, and protein. Sandra seems to have irregular eating patterns and she admits to often skipping breakfast. She asks why she has to gain so much weight when you explain the nutritional needs of her baby during the pregnancy.

1. Discuss weight distribution in pregnancy.	Answer: The average distribution is as follows: 11 lb fetus, placenta, and amniotic fluid; 2 lb uterus; 4 lb increased blood volume; 3 lb breast tissue; and 5 to 10 lbs maternal stores.
2. Discuss foods that will increase calcium, protein, and iron in her diet.	Answer: A diet that includes 4 cups of milk or servings of fortified orange juice, legumes, nuts, dried fruit, and dark green leafy vegetables will increase calcium. Red meat or dairy products will increase protein. She should take prenatal vitamins to ensure adequate iron and folate intake.
3. Explain why folate supplementation is important.	Answer: Prenatal folate supplementation significantly reduces the risk of neonatal neural tube defects.
4. What criteria will measure adequate caloric intact during pregnancy?	Answer: A satisfactory weight gain.

CHAPTER 13

CRITICAL THINKING IN ACTION

Sixteen-year-old Linda Perez and her mother present to you at the OB clinic for Linda's first prenatal visit. You determine that Linda is 20 weeks pregnant. Her weight is 135 lb, height 5'4", temperature 98°F, pulse 80, respirations 14, BP 100/64. You assess that Linda's mother has type 2 diabetes, and that her siblings are healthy. Linda admits to having one sexual partner and says she has never been hospitalized. Her immunizations are up to date and she's never used tobacco or recreational drugs. To date, the father of the baby is not involved. Mrs. Perez is clearly upset over the fact that Linda's pregnancy is so far advanced without her knowledge. Linda is very quiet and speaks only when questioned directly. You do your best to try to establish a trusting relationship with Linda and her mother by providing an atmosphere where issues can be discussed.

1. What psychologic factors contribute to teenage pregnancy?	Answer: "Magical thinking," feelings of invincibility, and limited abstract thought processes contribute to the incidence of unplanned pregnancy.
2. Explore reasons why teenagers delay prenatal care.	Answer: Teenagers deny signs and symptoms of pregnancy, feel embarrassed to admit their inability to use birth control, or misuse birth control.
3. Linda's mother asks you what factors facilitate adolescent pregnancies.	Answer: Adolescent pregnancies can be related to cultural norms, peer interaction, immature cognitive abilities, psychologic needs, increasing societal acceptance, and unprotected coitus.
4. You assess that Linda has some anxiety concerning the birth process. She states she is not interested in prenatal classes because she is single and does not want to have natural childbirth. Your best response would be:	Answer: Prenatal classes can teach you relaxation methods and benefits and risks of pain relief methods. This will help you to make the best decision for you. You can bring whoever is going to be with you in labor—a friend, the father of the baby, or your mother.

CHAPTER 14

CRITICAL THINKING IN ACTION

Jane Adams, a 23-year-old, G3, P2, at 37 weeks' gestation, presents to you in the birthing unit complaining of "vaginal pressure" but no contractions. You assess her and find that her history includes being HIV positive for 2 years, second-trimester cocaine and marijuana use, missed appointments, anemia (HCT 28%), and a positive syphilis serology. Jane tells you that she has other children and that they are being cared for by her mother, who has legal custody of them. You admit Jane and place her on the fetal monitor for evaluation of fetal well-being and contraction patterns. The monitor shows you that the fetal heart rate baseline is 120 to 130 with no decelerations; contractions are mild and irregular lasting 20 to 30 seconds. You obtain vital signs of BP 130/88, temperature 97.0°F, pulse 88, respirations 14. A vaginal exam determines that Jane is 7 cm dilated at +1 station with intact membranes. She asks you if being HIV positive will affect her labor.

1. Discuss the prophylactic regimen for the prevention of HIV transmission to the fetus during labor.	Answer: To prevent transmission of the HIV virus to the neonate, a loading dose of zidovudine is given; followed by a continuous infusion of the medication until delivery.
2. Discuss the transmission of HIV to the fetus during pregnancy and birth.	Answer: Transmission of HIV to the fetus can occur antenatally through the placenta, or intrapartum through contact with infected maternal blood or secretions.
3. Identify the emotional impact of HIV infection or other STIs on the woman.	Answer: Their story is often one of fear, anxiety, frustration, anger, shame, and guilt.
4. On postpartum day 2, you inform Jane that her infant is HIV antibody positive. How would you clarify the results?	Answer: Because of placental passage of antibodies, infants born to HIV-seropositive mothers will test positive for HIV antibodies whether or not the neonate is actually infected. Positive viral blood cultures are necessary to confirm the diagnosis of HIV infection in the newborn.

CHAPTER 15

CRITICAL THINKING IN ACTION

Carol Smith, a 40-year-old, single, G2, P0010, presents to you while you are working in the birthing unit, at 32 weeks' gestation. Her chief complaint is severe headache, nausea, and trouble seeing. She describes "blackened areas" in her visual fields bilaterally. Her prenatal record reveals long-term substance abuse, depression, and hypertension currently treated with nifedipine 60 mg by mouth once in the morning. You note that she has had two prenatal visits with this pregnancy. You determine her blood pressure to be 170/110; deep tendon reflexes are 3+, clonus negative. She has general edema and 3+ proteinuria. You place Carol on the external fetal monitor to observe for fetal well-being and any contractions. You position her on her left side with her head elevated and use pillows for comfort. You observe that the fetal heart rate is 143 to 148 with decreased long-term variability. No fetal heart rate decelerations or accelerations are noted. The uterus is soft, and no contractions are palpated or noted on the fetal monitor. Carol asks you why she should stay on her left side.

1. How would you explain the importance of the left-side lying position when on bed rest?	Answer: This position decreases pressure on the vena cava, increasing venous return, circulatory volume, and placenta and renal perfusion. Improved renal flow helps to decrease angiotension II levels, promotes diuresis, and lowers blood pressure.
2. You administer nifedipine 10 mg sublingual and a loading dose of magnesium sulfate 4 gm IV piggyback to the main IV line of Ringer's lactate. What findings would indicate that Carol has therapeutic levels of magnesium?	Answer: You observe for diminished reflexes, decreased respiratory rate, slurring of speech, awkwardness of movement, and decreased appetite.
3. What signs of magnesium toxicity should you monitor Carol for?	Answer: Absent deep tendon reflexes, difficulty swallowing, drooling, respirations below 10 and decreased urine output less than 30 cc/hour. Calcium gluconate should be at the bedside to reverse magnesium toxicity.
4. Carol asks if magnesium sulfate will affect her infant. How would you answer her?	Answer: The newborn may exhibit poor muscle tone, suppressed respiratory effort at birth, and poor sucking. These effects subside as the newborn excretes the drug over 3 to 4 days.
5. Which signs of premature labor would you ask Carol to notify you of if she experiences?	Answer: Uterine contractions that occur every 10 minutes or less with or without pain; mild menstrual-like cramps low in the abdomen; constant or intermittent feeling of pelvic pressure that feels like the baby is pressing down; rupture of membranes; or constant or intermittent low back pain.

CHAPTER 16

CRITICAL THINKING IN ACTION

Patricia Adams is a 20-year-old, married, G2, P0010 at 36 weeks' gestation with gestational diabetes. She presents to you during her prenatal visit with a complaint of decreased fetal movement for the "last day or so." Her OB history includes a 13 lb weight gain, hematocrit of 29%, diastolic BP ranging 80 to 96 mm Hg, and 1+ proteinuria. A 19-week ultrasound demonstrated no fetal anatomic defects. A hemoglobin A1c at 23 weeks was 5.8%. Patricia has had weekly NST since 28 weeks' gestation. You place Patricia on the fetal monitor for an NST. You obtain vital signs of temperature 97°F, pulse 88, respirations 14, BP 130/88. After 30 minutes you observe that the fetal heart rate baseline is 160 to 165, long-term variability is decreased, and repetitive variable decelerations are occurring. No contractions are noted. The fetus is very active. You notify the physician of the fetal heart rate baseline and unsatisfactory NST. The physician orders a biophysical profile (BPP) for fetal well-being. You describe and explain the biophysical profile test to Patricia.

1. How would you describe and explain the biophysical profile test?	Answer: The BPP provides additional information about fetal health. Real-time ultrasound allows visualization of the fetus in its environment and fetal activities. The BPP measures acute and chronic markers of fetal well-being. The five biophysical characteristics are fetal breathing movements, gross body movements, fetal tone reactive, fetal heart rate, and amniotic fluid volume. These five characteristics are evaluated and scored as present (2) or absent (0). Patricia's baby's highest score could only be 8 because of the unsatisfactory NST.
2. To heighten Patricia's awareness of fetal movement, how would you instruct her to do a daily fetal movement record (FMR)?	Answer: For consistency, the FMR should be done the same time each day. Most fetal movement tends to be in the evening. Start by recording the day and time; then lie in the left lateral position, preferably after a meal or when the baby is most active. Place your hand over the abdomen to feel the baby's movement. Mark every movement the baby makes. Remain in this position until you have counted 10 movements. Record the end time. Bring the card with you to your next visit.
3. Explain when Patricia should contact her care provider.	Answer: If 10 movements are not obtained within 3 hours; if overall, the fetus's movements are slowing, and it takes much longer each day to note 10 movements; if there are no movements in the morning; or if there are fewer than 3 movements in 8 hours.
4. Discuss the significance of fetal movement.	Answer: Maternal perception of fetal movement correlates with fetal well-being. From 24 weeks until term, frequency of fetal movement is consistent if the fetus is not compromised. Decreased fetal movement is associated with more complications during the intrapartum period or in the newborn after birth.

5. Explore factors that decrease fetal movements.	Answer: Fetal and placental factors that influence fetal movement include congenital abnormalities, decreased placenta perfusion due to maternal disease, and fetal demise. Maternal use of barbiturates, alcohol, methadone, narcotics, or cigarettes will decrease fetal movements. Decreased movement may also be due to fetal sleep cycles or to inactivity during a particular time of day.

CHAPTER 17

CRITICAL THINKING IN ACTION

Ann Nelson, a 28-year-old, G2, P0010 at 41 weeks' gestation, is admitted to the birthing unit where you are working. She is here for cervical ripening and induction of labor due to postdate pregnancy and decreased amniotic fluid volume. A review of her prenatal chart reveals a pertinent history of infertility (Clomid-induced pregnancy) and asthma (treated with inhalers on a PRN basis). The Doppler picks up a fetal heart rate of 120 bpm. You place Ann on the electronic fetal monitor and obtain the following data: BP 126/76, temperature 98°F, pulse 82, respirations 16; vaginal exam reveals a 20% effaced cervix, 1 cm dilatation in the posterior position, and vertex at −2 station. The fetal monitor shows a fetal heart rate baseline of 120 to 128 with occasional variable decelerations, accelerations to 140 with fetal activity. No contractions are noted on the monitor or palpated. Ann asks you what to expect with "cervical ripening" using prostaglandin gel.

1. Discuss the action of prostaglandin gel.	Answer: The prostaglandin gel is expected to soften and efface the cervix, change the cervix from posterior to midposition, and provide cervical dilatation. If uterine activity is initiated, it is expected to improve the fetal station as well.
2. Ann asks you why cervical ripening and induction of labor are recommended for her and her baby. How would you best respond to her?	Answer: Postdate pregnancy is associated with perinatal morbidity and mortality such as neonatal jaundice, neonatal low blood sugar, temperature instability, respiratory distress, meconium aspiration syndrome, birth trauma secondary to macrosomia, and neonatal asphyxia.
3. Ann asks how she will know if she is getting contractions. How would you answer her?	Answer: Uterine contractions are felt in the lower abdominal wall and in the area over the lower lumbar and upper sacrum region. It may start in the front and radiate to the back, or start in the back and radiate to the front. In the latent stage, it may feel like cramping.
4. Discuss the difference between mild, moderate, and strong contractions.	Answer: During the peak of the contraction, the uterine fundus is palpated to estimate the intensity of the contraction. During mild contraction, the uterine wall can be indented easily; during a strong contraction, the uterine wall cannot be indented. A contraction of moderate intensity falls between mild and strong.
5. Describe the latent phase of labor.	Answer: The latent phase of labor starts with the beginning of regular uterine contractions, which are usually mild, lasting 30 seconds with a frequency of 10 to 20 minutes. The contractions progress to moderate ones, lasting 30 to 40 seconds with a frequency of 5 to 7 minutes. The cervix begins to efface and dilate.

CHAPTER 18

CRITICAL THINKING IN ACTION

Cindy Bell, a 20-year-old gravida 2 para 1, 40 weeks' gestation, presents to you in the birthing unit with contractions every 5 to 7 minutes. She is accompanied by her husband. Spontaneous rupture of membranes occurred 2 hours prior to admission. Cindy tells you that the fluid was colorless and clear. You orient Cindy and her family to the birthing room and perform a physical assessment, documenting the following data: Vital signs are normal. A vaginal exam reveals that the cervix is 75% effaced, 4 cm dilated with a vertex at −1 station in the LOP position. You place Cindy on an external fetal monitor. The fetal heart rate baseline is 140–147 with accelerations to 156, no decelerations are noted. Contractions are 5 to 6 minutes apart, of moderate intensity, and lasting 40 to 50 seconds. Cindy states she would like to stay out of bed as long as possible because lying down seems to make the contractions more painful, especially in her back.

1. Discuss the benefits of ambulation in labor.	Answer: Ambulation may assist in labor progression by stimulating contractions and allowing gravity to help with the descent of the fetus. Ambulating may be more comfortable for the woman and may give her a sense of independence and control.
2. Cindy would like her daughter to be present for the baby's birth. What would you discuss with her about the impact of having a young sibling present during labor and birth?	Answer: It is important that a young child have her own support person whose sole responsibility is tending to the child's needs. This person must be prepared to interpret what is happening for the child and to intervene when necessary. Being present at the birth seems to increase siblings' acceptance of the new baby.

3. What fetal heart rate assessment will best ensure fetal well-being during the period Cindy is ambulating?	Answer: Perform intermittent auscultation every 15 minutes with an ultrasound or a fetoscope. Listen to the fetal heart during a contraction and 30 seconds after the contraction to identify nonreassuring heart pattern.
4. When a nonreassuring fetal heart pattern is detected, what remedial nursing intervention is carried out?	Answer: Change position, preferably on the left side, give IV fluids, administer oxygen by tight-fitting mask, discontinue oxytocics, and notify the physician.
5. What are indications for continuous fetal monitoring in labor?	Answer: Indications include previous history of a stillbirth at 38 or more weeks' gestation, presence of a complication of pregnancy, induction of labor, preterm birth, decreased fetal movement, nonreassuring fetal status, meconium-stained amniotic fluid, and trial of labor following a previous cesarean birth.

CHAPTER 19

CRITICAL THINKING IN ACTION

Anita Grey, a 22-year-old primigravida at 40 weeks' gestation, is admitted to you in the birthing center in labor. Anita was sent from her physician's office after being evaluated at her prenatal visit. While in the office, she was assessed to be 4 cm dilated, 100% effaced, vertex at 0 station with bulging membranes. She tells you that her husband is on his way to the birthing center, and she is anxious for him to arrive. A review of her prenatal record shows no complications affecting this pregnancy. Anita's vital signs are within normal limits. You assess the fetal heart rate and contraction pattern with the fetal monitor and observe a fetal heart rate of 140 to 150 bpm with accelerations to 160s. Contractions are every 3 to 4 minutes lasting 30 seconds of moderate intensity by palpation. Anita seems to be tolerating the contractions well, but still seems anxious about her husband's arrival.

1. What steps can you take to reduce the stress and anxiety of the laboring woman and her family?	Answer: You introduce yourself and escort the woman and her family to the birthing room and provide an orientation that includes location of restrooms, public phones, and nurse call or emergency call system. You explain the monitor equipment and other unfamiliar technology. You provide an environment that is quiet and feels safe.
2. When you notify the physician/midwife, what pertinent information should the report contain?	Answer: Pertinent information includes parity, cervical dilatation and effacement, station, presenting part, status of membranes, contraction pattern, fetal heart rate, abnormal vital signs, any significant prenatal history, and her preference for pain relief.
3. What support measures can you give in the active phase of labor?	Answer: Support and encourage breathing patterns, provide a quiet environment, provide reassurance, keep couple informed of progress. Promote comfort with back rubs, sacral pressure, and cool cloths. Assist with position changes, support with pillows, and effleurage. Provide ice chips for dry mouth. Encourage to void every 1 to 2 hours. Offer shower/whirlpool/warm bath if available.
4. What measures can be used to decrease discomfort/pain as labor progresses?	Answer: Ensure general comfort, provide information to decrease anxiety, use specific supportive relaxation techniques, encourage controlled breathing, and administer pharmacologic agents as ordered by physician/CNM.
5. What observations reflect the physiologic manifestations of pain?	Answer: Assess for increased pulse and respiratory rates, dilated pupils, increased blood pressure, and muscle tension.

CHAPTER 20

CRITICAL THINKING IN ACTION

Sandra, a 26-year-old G1, P0000, is in active labor when she presents to you at the birthing center. She has been in labor for 5 hours and is clearly tired and seems to be having difficulty coping with the pain. Her contractions are occurring every 2 to 4 minutes lasting 50 to 60 seconds, and are moderate to strong in intensity. You assess the fetal heart rate of 120 to 130 with early decelerations; moderate long-term variability is present. Sandra's vital signs are stable and her laboratory results are within normal limits. She is requesting an epidural analgesia for pain control. A vaginal exam demonstrates the cervix is 100% effaced, 6 cm dilated with the vertex at 0 station in the LOT position. You notify the physician of Sandra's wish for pain relief and labor progress. You review the client's record for written consent for regional analgesia and assist the anesthesiologist with the procedure.

1. Discuss the advantages of regional analgesia.	Answer: Regional analgesia relieves discomfort during labor and birth. The woman is fully awake and can participate in the birth process.

2. Describe the nursing responsibility during the administration of regional analgesia.	Answer: Provide hydration with 500 to 1000 mL of intravenous solution and encourage the woman to void prior to starting the procedure; assist her with positioning during and after the procedure; monitor and assess maternal vital signs and respiratory status; monitor analgesic effect and determine fetal well-being. Provide reassurance and thorough explanations to help decrease anxiety and fear.
3. Discuss the side effects of regional analgesia.	Answer: The anesthetic agents may interfere with blood pressure stability, leg movements, and the ability to void. Some women experience pruritus, nausea, and vomiting.
4. What are the absolute contraindications for an epidural block?	Answer: Contraindications are client refusal, infection at the site of needle puncture, coagulopathies, specific drug allergies to the agents being used, and hypovolemic shock.
5. How do you assist Sandra with the second stage of labor when she cannot feel her contractions?	Answer: Help her to get into a pushing position and place her hand on her abdomen to feel when a contraction begins. Instruct her to bear down with the contraction. Give her extra assistance by holding her legs up and apart. Inform her when the contraction is over and encourage her to lay back and rest until the next contraction begins.

CHAPTER 21

CRITICAL THINKING IN ACTION

June Dice, a 25-year-old G3, P1011, is admitted to you in labor and delivery at 38 weeks' gestation with a moderate amount of dark red vaginal bleeding. June's prenatal history is significant for late prenatal care (20 weeks' gestation by ultrasound) and cocaine abuse. An ultrasound is done upon admission that demonstrates a marginal placenta abruption. You place June on the fetal monitor and observe a fetal heart rate baseline of 146 to 155 with accelerations to 166 with fetal movement. There are occasional mild variable decelerations with a quick return to baseline. Contraction pattern is interpreted as an irritable uterus. An intravenous infusion with Ringer's lactate is started with a #18 intracath. June's vital signs are within normal limits. Her hematocrit is 29%. You assist the physician with a vaginal exam to rupture membranes and insert a fetal scalp electrode and intrauterine pressure catheter. A small amount of light yellow-green amniotic fluid is observed. The exam shows June is 4 cm dilated, 50% effaced, vertex at -1 station. You follow protocol and start an oxytocin induction/augmentation. June is asking why oxytocin is needed.

1. Explain the goal of labor induction/augmentation in response to June's question.	Answer: The goal of oxytocin augmentation/induction is to establish an adequate contraction pattern that would promote cervical dilatation. A contraction pattern of three contractions in 10 minutes lasting 40 to 60 seconds with an intensity of 25 to 75 mm Hg intrauterine pressure is adequate for labor progression.
2. Explain potential risk factors associated with oxytocin induction of labor.	Answer: Observe for uterine hyperstimulation (contractions occurring more frequently than every 2 minutes or lasting longer than 90 seconds), uterine hyperactivity (tachysystole, skewed contractions, polysystole, coupled contractions, tetanic contractions), uterine hypertonus (elevated resting tone, greater than or equal to 20 mm Hg), uterine rupture, and nonreassuring fetal heart rate patterns.
3. You observe a nonreassuring fetal heart rate of 144 to 150 with decreased variability and persistent late decelerations with each contraction. What interventions would you immediately take?	Answer: Assist the woman to turn to a left lateral position, increase the rate of the IV infusion, discontinue oxytocin, and administer oxygen by tight face mask. Perform a vaginal examination for fetal scalp stimulation to obtain further information about the condition of the fetus. Notify the physician of your observations.
4. What supportive actions are taken to decrease the risk of hypofibrinogenemia?	Answer: You would obtain blood work for type and cross match for blood transfusions, evaluating the blood clotting mechanism (pt, ptt, and fibrin index), platelet and hemoglobin counts, and provide intravenous fluids.
5. What complications might be present in the newborn at birth?	Answer: Anemia and hypoxia.

CHAPTER 22

CRITICAL THINKING IN ACTION

Betsy Jones, a 28-year-old G1, P0, at 39 weeks' gestation, and her husband present to you in the labor suite for an external cephalic version procedure by her obstetrician. You introduce yourself and review her record for any significant risk factors or contraindications to the version procedure. Her prenatal chart is significant in that the fetus has been in a persistent frank breech position. You encourage Betsy and her husband to express their understanding and expectations of the procedure. You discuss certain criteria to be met prior to the procedure and obtain vital signs as follows: temperature 98.8°F, pulse 88, respirations 14, BP 110/80, urine screening negative for sugar, albumin, and ketones. You place Betsy on the external electronic fetal monitor, which demonstrates a fetal heart rate baseline of 140 to 152 with moderate long-term variability. There are no contractions observed by the monitor or Betsy. After explaining how to record fetal movement on the monitor, you proceed with an NST.

1. Explain the contraindications to the version procedure.	Answer: The woman has no pregnancy problems such as uterine anomalies, uncontrolled preeclampsia, or third-trimester bleeding. There are no complications of pregnancy such as ruptured membranes, oligohydramnios, hydramnios, or placenta previa present. There is no previous cesarean birth or other significant uterine surgery. The pregnancy is a singleton gestation with no fetal abnormalities, such as intrauterine growth restriction, nuchal cord, or nonreassuring fetal heart rate.
2. Discuss the criteria that should be met prior to performing external version.	Answer: The pregnancy is 36 weeks' gestation or more. The fetal breech is not engaged. An ultrasound is done to locate the placenta and confirm fetal presentation. A nonstress test is reactive.
3. How would you explain to Betsy and her husband what to expect during the version procedure?	Answer: Explain that before the version begins, you will help her into a comfortable semisitting position on the labor bed. You will start an intravenous line to give her medications if necessary. She will receive an injection of terbutaline to relax the uterus. If she has severe pain or there is a significant slowing or deceleration of the fetal heart rate, the procedure will be discontinued. There is the possibility of failure of the version and slight risk of cesarean birth if the fetal heart rate becomes nonreassuring.
4. What support would you give Betsy during the procedure?	Answer: You continue to monitor maternal blood pressure, pulse, and comfort level frequently. Fetal well-being is ascertained before, intermittently during, and for 30 minutes following the procedure, using electronic fetal monitoring, ultrasound, or both. Because the procedure can be uncomfortable, encourage the mother to take slow deep breaths and relax her abdominal muscles. Use distractions and speak in a calm reassuring voice to help decrease fear and anxiety.
5. Explain postversion discharge teaching.	Answer: Explain to the mother how to monitor for contractions. Describe mild, moderate, and strong contractions. Teach the mother to observe and record fetal kick counts. Advise the mother to notify her physician if her water breaks or if she experiences any vaginal bleeding or signs of labor.

CHAPTER 23

CRITICAL THINKING IN ACTION

Janet Burns, a 25-year-old G3, P3, is 2 hours past a low forceps vaginal birth with a right medial lateral episiotomy of a live 8 lb baby boy. You obtain vital signs of BP 118/70, temperature 98.8°F, pulse 76, respirations 14. You observe the fundus is +1 finger above the umbilicus and slightly to the right. Her episiotomy is slightly ecchymotic and well approximated without edema or discharge. Ice has been applied to the episiotomy for the last 20 minutes. Lochia rubra is present and a pad was saturated in 90 minutes. Janet has an intravenous of Ringer's lactate with 10 units of Pitocin infusing at 100 mL/hr in her lower left arm and is complaining of moderate abdominal cramping. She tells you that she is very tired and requests some pain medication so she can sleep for a while.

1. What nursing assessment is of immediate concern?	Answer: A uterus that is above the umbilicus and deviated to the side may indicate that the bladder is full and Janet needs to urinate. Women often lose their sense of bladder fullness and urge to void after a long second stage with the fetus pressing down on the bladder and meatus. Using nursing interventions, you assist Janet to void. You determine if she has any difficulty urinating or emptying her bladder. After Janet voids, you reassess the uterus for firmness and location. You should not feel the bladder in the lower abdomen.
2. Discuss care of her episiotomy and perineum.	Answer: Demonstrate and describe how to use the perineal rinse bottle to spray warm water from the front (at the symphysis pubis) to the back (around the anus) and pat dry with toilet paper. Encourage the use of witch hazel pads or analgesia ointment over the episiotomy. Apply the pad from front to back. Ice wrapped in gauze can be applied to the episiotomy to decrease edema and discomfort.
3. What other self-care measures could you advise?	Answer: Advise she should call for assistance the first time she gets out of bed as she might experience some dizziness. Encourage the woman to request analgesic medications for discomfort for afterbirth or episiotomy pain. Encourage fluids and snacks. Demonstrate gentle uterine massage and explain changes in lochia. Encourage frequent perineal pad change and use of the perineal rinse bottle, especially after voiding. Keep the perineum clean and dry. Encourage frequent rest periods.

4. Discuss postpartal occurrences that may cause special concern for the mother.	Answer: Explain that a gush of blood that sometimes occurs when she first gets up is due to pooling of blood in the vagina when a woman lies down for a period of time. As the body attempts to eliminate excess fluids that were present during pregnancy, night sweats might occur. Afterbirth pains are more common in multiparas due to uterine contractions.
5. Janet expressed concern about her episiotomy healing. What information can you offer?	Answer: Provide information about the location of the episiotomy. Explain that the sutures will not have to be removed. The sutures will dissolve slowly over the next few weeks as the tissue heals. By the time the sutures are dissolved, the tissues are strong and the incision edges will not separate.

CHAPTER 24

CRITICAL THINKING IN ACTION

Wendy Calahan, a 31-year-old G3, P2, gave birth to an 8.5 lb baby boy by primary cesarean birth for failure to progress. The baby's Apgar scores were 9 and 9 at 1 and 5 minutes. The baby was admitted to the newborn nursery for transitional observation. Wendy was transferred to the postpartum unit where you assume her care. You introduce yourself and orient her to the room, call bell, and safety measures. You perform an initial assessment, with all findings within normal limits. Wendy tells you she is very tired and would like to rest while her baby is in the nursery. Her husband and family have left the hospital after spending time with her in the recovery room but will return later. She admits she is disappointed that she could not give birth vaginally even though she pushed for 2 hours. She says, "This baby was just too big."

1. How would you discuss with Wendy the need for frequent assessments after birth?	Answer: Explain that you will assess the mother's fundus, lochia, dressing, vital signs, and comfort level every 30 minutes for the next hour, then every hour for 2 hours, and every 4 hours during the rest of her stay to monitor her transition from pregnant to nonpregnant condition.
2. Explain "maternity or baby blues."	Answer: Maternity or baby blues are transient, emotional disturbances commonly occurring around the second or fourth postpartum day, lasting a few hours to 2 weeks. Physiologic factors are rapid hormonal changes, lack of sleep and less effective sleep, and increased energy expenditure.
3. Explore activities to minimize maternity blues.	Answer: Suggest that the mother allow family and friends to help with household tasks and care for older children. She should get plenty of rest, eat a well-balanced diet, drink plenty of fluids but limit caffeine intake, continue taking her prenatal vitamins, perform light exercise daily, ensure some personal time and adult relationships, and avail herself of support groups and other community resources.
4. Discuss concerns of a woman experiencing her second pregnancy.	Answer: Concern for the first child may cause grieving over the dyadic relationship with the first child and her anticipation of the first child's pain. Managing the care of two children may cause a mother to feel overwhelmed. She may have increased expectations of the first child and may doubt her own ability to love two children equally. The second pregnancy may not be as exciting or as desired as the first.
5. Discuss behaviors that inhibit paternal attachment.	Answer: Observe for difficulty adjusting to a new dependent, for failure to relate to the infant, for escape mechanisms such as alcohol and drugs, and for separation from mother and infant because of business or military responsibilities.

CHAPTER 25

CRITICAL THINKING IN ACTION

Betty Jones, a 32-year-old, G4, P2012, is admitted to the postpartum unit after a precipitous birth of a preterm (35 weeks' gestation) 4 lb baby girl followed by a postpartum tubal ligation. Betty's vital signs and postpartum assessment are within normal limits. She has an abdominal dressing that is dry and intact, and she is able to void. Her IV with 10 units of Pitocin is infusing well in her lower left arm. She admits to 3 on a pain scale of 10. Betty admits to active use of crack cocaine throughout her pregnancy and smoked it most recently 5 hours before she gave birth. She is HIV positive with a CD^4 count of 726 cells/mm^3 and was treated with zidovudine during the pregnancy, labor, and birth. She also has a history of genital herpes and had been treated for chlamydia during the pregnancy. Her infant has been admitted to the special care nursery because of her preterm status. Betty anticipates her baby will be taken into foster care when discharged from the nursery. Wishing to establish as much of a relationship with her infant as possible before that happens, she asks if she can breastfeed the baby while she is in the hospital.

1. What is your response to Betty's request to breastfeed her infant?	Answer: HIV is present in breast milk. Vertical transmission is doubled by breastfeeding. This concern overrides Betty's concern about attachment. You can increase her sense of involvement with her baby with encouraging her to visit her baby and assist with bottle feedings, changing diapers, and touching and holding her baby. Betty's desire to parent her baby would be best supported by seeking drug treatment and carefully following an HIV medical regimen.

2. Over the course of the first postpartum day, Betty appears lethargic and spends most of her time sleeping. After her evening visitors leave, you observe that she is highly energetic and excitable. Would urine testing be useful to help determine if Betty has used cocaine this evening?	Answer: Urine toxicology would not be useful. By her own report, Betty has used cocaine prior to her admission. Other observations may be more useful such as increase in blood pressure and pulse. Your suspicions necessitate further follow-up including social, community, and drug rehabilitation services.
3. Discuss supportive nursing care for infants born of HIV-positive mothers.	Answer: Care involves providing comfort, keeping the newborn well nourished and protected from opportunistic infections, providing good skin care to prevent skin rashes, and facilitating growth, development, and attachment. Caregivers should wear gloves during all diaper changes and examinations. Handwashing is crucial for all newborns at risk for AIDS.
4. Betty wishes for an early discharge from the hospital. What physical criteria must be met before leaving the hospital?	Answer: Betty has to have normal vital signs, appropriate involution of the uterus, and appropriate amount of lochia without evidence of infection. Episiotomy is approximated with a decrease in edema or bruising. She is able to void, pass flatus, and take fluids and food without difficulty. She has received rubella vaccine or RhoGAM if indicated.
5. Discuss when she should contact her physician/CNM after her discharge.	Answer: Betty should notify her caregiver if she experiences a sudden, persistent, or spiking fever; a change in the character of the lochia, such as a foul odor, bright-red bleeding, passage of large clots, or excessive amounts; evidence of increased breast tenderness with reddened areas accompanied by malaise; pain in the calf of her leg with tenderness and redness; urinary frequency or burning with urination; or incapacitating postpartal depression.

CHAPTER 26

CRITICAL THINKING IN ACTION

Sandra Dee, a 21-year-old, G1, P0000, at 36 weeks' gestation, has been in labor for the last 12 hours and is fully dilated with caput visible on the perineum. The fetal heart rate is 148 to 152 with early deceleration down to 142 with contraction and pushing. Her contractions are 4 to 5 minutes apart of good quality. Sandra's mother and sister are present for the birth. Her prenatal record shows no significant pregnancy problems or complications, and her vital signs have been stable within normal limits. Sandra has received two doses of Stadol for a total of 2 mg IV for pain relief during her labor. The last dose was given 2 hours ago. You assist with the vaginal birth of a live baby without an episiotomy. You observe the sex and time as the midwife places the infant girl on the mother's abdomen, suctions out the baby's mouth and nose, and proceeds to clamp the cord. You dry and stimulate the infant to breathe, remove the wet blanket and replace it with a dry one, and place the infant skin to skin on the mother's chest. You assess the need for infant resuscitation. The baby has a lusty cry spontaneously less than 30 seconds after birth. You palpate the cord obtaining a heart rate of 120, and observe that the baby's chest and face are pink, and the legs and arms are flexed with open fist.

1. Explain the changes that must occur in the infant's cardiopulmonary system at birth.	Answer: Pulmonary ventilation is established through lung expansion with the first inspiration in response to mechanical, chemical, thermal, and sensory changes associated with birth. A marked increase in pulmonary circulation occurs as PO_2 rises in the alveoli, relaxing pulmonary arteries and triggering a decrease in pulmonary vascular resistance.
2. What criteria do you look for when you assess the newborn for adequate cardiopulmonary adaptation at birth?	Answer: You determine that the infant's airway is clear. The infant has a good quality cry (has respirations). The infant's color is pink and the muscle tone is good (arms and legs are flexed with fists open or clenched). You use the Apgar score at 1 and 5 minutes to monitor that the infant's condition is stable or improving.
3. What steps do you take to maintain a neutral thermal environment at birth?	Answer: The delivery room should be warm. You would ensure any equipment/ linens to be used on the infant are warmed. Place the infant under a radiant heater or skin to skin on the mother's abdomen or chest. Dry the infant with a warm blanket immediately after birth, remove the wet blanket, and cover the infant with a dry blanket. Place a warm cap on the infant's head.
4. Sandra plans to breastfeed. When would you initiate the first feeding?	Answer: The newborn has the first period of reactivity approximately 30 minutes after birth. During this period the infant is awake and alert. This is a natural time to have the mother and infant together. You assist the mother to bring the infant to the breast. The infant may root and latch on or just root and lick the nipple.
5. Discuss nursing actions that can decrease the probability of high bilirubin levels in the newborn.	Answer: Maintain the infant's skin temperature at 97.8°F or above; monitor for stooling in character and amount; encourage early feeding to promote intestinal elimination and ensure adequate caloric intake.

CHAPTER 27

CRITICAL THINKING IN ACTION

Susan Pine, a 21-year-old G2, now P1011, delivers a 39-week-old female newborn. The vaginal birth is assisted with a vacuum extractor. The prenatal record is significant for an increase of maternal blood pressure to 140/ 90 on the day of birth. Susan is treated with magnesium sulfate during her labor and has an epidural analgesia for the pain of labor. The baby's Apgar is 8 and 9 at 1 and 5 minutes, and she has been admitted to the newborn nursery. The newborn's admission exam is normal except for a 2 cm round caput. Now, 8 hours later, the baby's condition is stable and she needs to be bottle-fed. You take her to her mother's room where you observe that Susan does not reach out to take her from you. She seems unsure when handling her baby. Susan asks you about the swelling on her baby's head and wonders if it will ever go away.

1. How would you explain the cause of Susan's baby's caput succedaneum?	The swelled area is from the vacuum extraction of the baby's head at birth. The pressure of the vacuum caused compression of blood vessels in the baby's scalp, which caused an increase in tissue fluids and a small amount of bleeding under the skin. The swelled area feels soft and mushy, but this will be absorbed after a few days.
2. Compare the difference between a cephalhematoma and caput succedaneum.	Answer: Cephalhematoma does not cross a suture line, whereas a caput succedaneum does. Caput succedaneum is present at birth; cephalhematomas emerge as defined hematomas between the first and second day.
3. Explore with Susan her baby's reflexes and state of alertness.	Answer: Show the mother the grasping, Moro, rooting, sucking, and stepping reflexes to demonstrate what her baby can do. Point out that in the quiet awake state, her baby is alert and fixates on her face and attends to her voice. Advise that this is the best time to interact with the baby.
4. Susan asks you how she will know what her baby needs. How would you respond?	Answer: Crying is the infant's main method of communicating. Heat, cold, or hunger stimulates the baby to wakefulness. Crying lets you know that she is awake and wants attention. By responding to the baby's cry, the mother will learn what different cries mean such as if the baby is cold, is hungry, or just wants to be held.

CHAPTER 28

CRITICAL THINKING IN ACTION

Alice Fine, age 32, G1, now P1001, spontaneously delivers a 7.25 lb baby girl over a median episiotomy. The baby's Apgar scores are 7 and 9 at 1 and 5 minutes. The baby is suctioned, stimulated, and given free flow oxygen at birth. As the nurse on duty, you admit baby Fine to the newborn nursery, place her under a radiant heater, and perform a newborn assessment. You obtain the vital signs of temperature 97°F, heart rate 128, respirations 55. A physical exam demonstrates no abnormalities, and you note that there were no significant problems with the pregnancy, the mother's blood type is A+, and she plans to bottle-feed. You monitor the baby until her vital signs are stable and then take him to the mother's room for his first bottle-feeding at 60 minutes old.

1. How would you review measures to promote the safety of the newborn from abduction?	Answer: Inform the mother that the identification bands will be checked each time the baby is brought to her room. She should allow only the people with the proper birthing unit identification to remove the baby from the room. Only the parents or a person with identification bands should bring the baby to the nursery. Advise her not to leave the baby alone in the room.
2. How would you explain the technique to suction the newborn with a bulb syringe?	Answer: Explain to the mother that most newborns are obligatory nose breathers for the first months of life. Newborns can cough or sneeze to clear their airway. However, during the first few days of life, the newborn has increased mucus. Gentle suction with a bulb syringe may be needed. You turn the baby on its side, squeeze the syringe, place the tip in the side (by the cheek) of the mouth, release the bulb, and then squeeze the mucus out onto a tissue. Gently do the same to each nostril. The bulb should be rinsed out after each use.
3. Describe the care of the newborn's cord.	Answer: Instruct the mother to keep the cord clean and dry; fold down the diaper to avoid covering the cord stump, which will prevent soiling of the area and promote drying. Contact your physician if you observe signs of infection such as a foul smell, redness and drainage, localized warmth and tenderness, or bleeding.
4. How would you review bottle-feeding with the mother?	Answer: The infant is held for all feedings to provide social and physical contact. Point the nipple directly into the infant's mouth directly on top of the tongue. The nipple should be full of formula at all times to prevent ingestion of extra air. The infant is burped at intervals, preferably at the middle and end of the feeding. Gently pat or stroke the infant's back while holding him upright on the shoulder or in a sitting position on the mother's lap. Advise the mother that newborns frequently regurgitate small amounts of feeding that initially may be due to excessive mucus; keep a "burp cloth" available.

CHAPTER 29

CRITICAL THINKING IN ACTION

Patty Kline, age 28, G1, now P1, delivers a 7.3 lb baby girl by spontaneous vaginal birth over a median episiotomy. The newborn's Apgar scores are 8 and 9 at 1 and 5 minutes. The infant is suctioned in the nose and mouth and given free flow oxygen on the mother's abdomen. Patty received an epidural during labor and birth. Patty initiated breastfeeding within the first hour after the birth, but at that time the newborn did not latch on. The infant was held to the mother's breast, rooted, and licked the nipple. You are the nurse caring for the infant at 2 hours of age. The admission assessment is significant for asymmetric head with a 3 cm caput succedaneum. The infant's temperature is stable. You bring the infant to the mother's room to assist her with breastfeeding.

1. Describe clues that indicate the infant is ready to breastfeed with the mother.	Answer: Early clues that indicate an infant is interested in feeding include hand-to-mouth or hand-passing-mouth motion, whimpering, sucking, and rooting. Advise the mother that crying is a late sign of hunger and may make it more difficult to get the infant latched on if she waits for the infant to cry.
2. How would you explain how to position the infant at the breast?	Answer: The mother should be in a comfortable position with her arms supported. Unwrap the blanket so that the infant is close to the mother's breast. Turn the infant's entire body toward the mother with the infant's mouth adjacent to the mother's nipple. The infant's ear, shoulder, and hip should be in direct alignment. Bring the infant to the mother's breast; tickle the infant's lower lip with her nipple until the infant opens her mouth wide. Direct the nipple straight into the infant's mouth so that during sucking the infant's jaw compresses the ducts directly beneath the areola.
3. Explain what to observe for the infant's proper latch on.	Answer: The infant's nose and chin should touch the breast. If the breast occludes the infant's airway, lifting up the breast will clear the nares. The infant's lips should be relaxed and flanged outward with the tongue over the lower gum.
4. Explain the basics of milk production.	Answer: Breast milk is produced according to demand. The milk is stored in the sinus under the areola. The mother requires adequate fluids to replenish her supply. The milk supply is best established by frequent feedings every $1\frac{1}{2}$ to 2 hours. The letdown reflex for the release of milk is initiated by the infant's sucking.
5. Explore helpful measures the mother can attempt in support of breastfeeding.	Answer: Suggest that the infant is awake before attempting to feed; alternate the breast at which the feeding begins; rotate the infant's position at the breast to avoid trauma to the nipples and improve emptying of the ducts. During early feedings, the infant should be offered both breasts at each feeding to stimulate the supply-demand response. Avoid supplementary formula-feeding and pacifiers until lactation is established to prevent nipple confusion in the infant.

CHAPTER 30

CRITICAL THINKING IN ACTION

As the nurse on duty, you are caring for baby Erin, a 38-week IDM female born by repeat cesarean birth to a 32-year-old G3, now P3, mother. Erin's Apgar scores are 7 and 9 at 1 and 5 minutes. At 2 hours of age, the baby has an elevated respiratory rate of 100 to 110, heart rate of 165 with Grade II/VI intermittent machinery murmur and mild cyanosis. She is now receiving 30% oxygen and has a respiratory rate of 70 to 80. The baby's clinical course, chest x-ray, and lab results are all consistent with transient tachypnea of the newborn and patent ductus arteriosus. The mother calls you to ask about how her baby is doing. She tells you that her last child was born at 30 weeks and had to be hospitalized for 6 weeks. She says, "I really tried to do it right this time," and asks you if this baby will have the same respiratory problem.

1. What should you tell the mother?	Answer: It is important to give the mother clear, factual information regarding the type, cause, and usual course of the infant's respiratory problems. You explain that the infant's laboratory test, chest x-ray, and clinical course are indicative of transient tachypnea of the newborn. Respiratory distress syndrome is probably not the problem since the infant is not premature.
2. What can you do to facilitate mother–infant attachment?	Answer: When transporting the mother from the recovery room, have the mother stop at the nursery so she can see and if possible touch her infant. Give the mother pictures so she can show her baby to visitors and family members. Ask her if she has a name for the infant and call the infant by name.

3. Discuss the emotional response of parents to the birth of an ill or at-risk infant.	Answer: The birth of an ill or at-risk infant is a serious crisis for parents. Each parent experiences an acute grief reaction, which follows the loss of the fantasized perfect baby. Parents express grief as shock, disbelief, denial of reality, anger toward self and others, guilt, blame, and concern for the future.
4. Discuss the four psychologic tasks essential for coping with the stress of an at-risk newborn and providing a basis for the maternal-infant relationship (also see the discussion in Chapter 31).	Answer: (1) The mother experiences anticipatory grief in preparation for the possible loss of her infant while hoping for her survival. (2) Acknowledgment of the mother's failure to produce a term or perfect newborn expressed as anticipatory grief and depression lasting until the chance of survival is secure. (3) Resumption of the process of relating to the infant. (4) Understanding of the potential special needs and growth pattern of the at-risk infant.
5. Baby Flynn is being discharged tomorrow. Review the elements of discharge and home care instructions.	Answer: Teach the parents routine well-baby care such as bathing, taking a temperature, cord care, preparing formula, and safety for the infant. Arrange for medical follow-up care; make the appointment if possible.

CHAPTER 31

CRITICAL THINKING IN ACTION

Rebecca Prince, age 21, G2, now P2, gives birth to a 5 lb baby at 38 weeks' gestation by primary cesarean birth for fetal distress. The infant's Apgar scores are 7 and 9 at 1 and 5 minutes. The infant is suctioned and given free flow oxygen at birth, then is admitted to the newborn nursery for transitional care and does well. You are the nurse caring for baby Prince at 36 hours old. You review the newborn's record and note that the baby's blood type is A+ and his mother is O+. Rebecca wants to breastfeed. You are performing a shift assessment on Baby Prince when you observe the infant has a unilateral cephalhematoma and is lethargic. You blanch the skin over the sternum and observe a yellow discoloration of the skin. Lab tests reveal a serum bilirubin level of 12 mg/dL, hematocrit 55%, a mildly positive direct Coombs' test, and a positive indirect Coombs' test. Baby Prince is diagnosed with hyperbilirubinemia secondary to ABO incompatibility and cephalhematoma. You provide phototherapy by fiber-optic blanket around the trunk of the infant and take the baby to his mother's room.

1. How would you explain the purpose of phototherapy with the mother?	Answer: Exposure of the newborn to high-intensity light decreases serum bilirubin levels in the skin by facilitating biliary excretion of unconjugated bilirubin. The infant's bilirubin will be lowered by excretion in the stool and urine.
2. Describe the care the mother can give to the newborn.	Answer: Encourage the mother to breastfeed the newborn every 2 to 3 hours to increase the intestinal motility, promote the excretion of unconjugated bilirubin through the clearance of stools, and prevent dehydration. Advise the mother that the infant's stool will change to loose and green color due to the bilirubin. Request that the mother track the number of stools and voids.
3. Discuss the advantage of the fiber-optic blanket phototherapy for the newborn.	Answer: Phototherapy can be provided to the newborn while allowing the newborn to be more accessible to the mother for feedings, holding, and diapering. The blanket eliminates the need for eye patches and allows the newborn to be fully clothed and wrapped, which decreases heat loss. Use of the blanket is less alarming to the parents.
4. Newborns up to 1 month of age are susceptible to organisms that do not cause significant disease in older children. Explore the circumstances that cause susceptibility to infection.	Answer: The newborn's immunologic systems are immature. They lack the complex factors involved in effective phagocytosis and the ability to localize infection or to respond with a well-defined recognizable inflammatory response. All newborns lack IgM immunoglobulin to protect against bacteria because it does not cross the placenta.
5. Describe how to distinguish between oral thrush and milk curds.	Answer: Differentiate white plaque of candidal infection from milk curds by rubbing a cotton tip applicator to the suspect plaque. If it is thrush, removal of the white areas causes raw bleeding areas.

CHAPTER 32

CRITICAL THINKING IN ACTION

Jane Benne, age 23, gravida 1 para 1, gave birth by cesarean for cephalopelvic disproportion to a healthy 7 lb 1 oz baby boy 5 days ago. You are making a home visit 2 days after Jane was discharged from the hospital to her two-story home. When you arrive, the baby is sleeping in a bassinet in Jane's bedroom on the second level. Jane has been trying to breastfeed and complains to you of sore nipples and swollen breasts. She is also having problems getting the baby to latch on and says that she has been supplementing her baby's feedings with a bottle because she is afraid her baby is not getting enough milk from her breasts alone. She also mentions that the baby seems more satisfied after she gives the bottle and seems to sleep longer. You ask her how she has been feeling, and she tells you that she is very tired and upset about her body not making enough milk to feed her child. You assess Jane's breasts and find them to be full and firm, but the nipples are cracked and blistered.

1. What is your focus in the home postpartum visit?	Answer: Home care is focused on assessment, teaching, and counseling the mother and her family rather than on physical care. You assess the mother and infant for signs of complications; the parents' adaptation to the new baby and their skill in bathing, dressing, handling, and comforting the newborn; and the safety of the home environment. You provide answers to questions about infant feedings, provide support and encouragement, and address the need for referrals.
2. What counseling can you give Jane regarding her sore nipples?	Answer: Suggest Jane express some of her milk to soften the breast so the baby can latch on. Observe that the baby is positioned correctly on the breast and alternate positions are used with each feeding. Observe that the nipple and some of the areola is in the baby's mouth. Encourage the mother to hold the baby closely during feedings so the nipple is not constantly being pulled. Assess for breast engorgement and for an inverted nipple. Advise the mother to end the feeding when the baby's sucking slows, before he has a chance to chew on the nipple. Remove the baby from the breast by placing a finger between the baby's gums to ensure the suction is broken. Suggest Jane can apply ice to the nipples and areola for a few minutes before feeding to promote nipple erectness and numb the tissue initially. Air-dry the breasts after feeding to toughen the nipples and promote healing.
3. What suggestion do you give Jane regarding supplemental bottle-feedings?	Answer: Supplemental bottle-feeding for the breastfeeding infant may weaken or confuse the infant's sucking reflex or decrease the infant's interest in breastfeeding. Infants suck differently on a rubber nipple and tend to push the mother's nipple out of their mouth in subsequent breastfeeding attempts. This is frustrating for the mother and baby, so the mother should avoid introducing the bottle until breastfeeding is well established.
4. Explain your assessment of Jane's abdominal incision and provide suggestions for healing.	Answer: Assess the incision for signs of infection such as redness, severe pain, edema, poor tissue approximation, and drainage. Expect some bruising and tenderness. Advise Jane to keep the incision clean and dry. She should allow warm water to flow over the incision in the shower and pat dry the incision. Suggest bringing the baby downstairs during the day to decrease the need to climb stairs frequently. Ask if her husband could carry the bassinet down for the day and up at night. Encourage Jane to rest when the baby sleeps.
5. How would you discuss the baby's voiding patterns to ensure adequate hydration?	Answer: Infants normally void five to eight times a day. Fewer than six to eight wet diapers may indicate the newborn needs more breastfeeding sessions.

CHAPTER 33

CRITICAL THINKING IN ACTION

You encounter a 12-month-old child, Julia, while working in the developmental clinic. Her mother tells you that their family practice physician had concerns that Julia might have a developmental delay. She was a full-term baby, and there were no complications throughout the mother's pregnancy or delivery. Julia's mother tells you that she has a generally shy and slow-to-warm-up temperament. She makes little eye contact with you and prefers to sit on her mother's lap and cling to her arms if a stranger gets close. The baby in the video is demonstrating some of the skills Julia is able to accomplish. She is able to pick up small objects, babble, crawl, and use her pincer grasp. She is not able to walk, hold a crayon, or speak any words. Julia clearly has a developmental delay.

1. What are some examples of toys you can suggest to Julia's parents based on her developmental level (not based on her age)?	Answer: Large blocks, jack-in-the-box, push and pull toys, and toys that pop apart and back together.
2. What are some examples of hazards you can advise Julia's mother to avoid based on her developmental level?	Answer: Provide gates so Julia does not crawl to places where a fall could occur. Keep the poison control number by the phone and keep poisons and medicines locked. Always use a properly fitted car seat and make sure Julia is not able to remove her own seatbelt.
3. What is a suggestion you can give the parents about dealing with a child like Julia who has a shy or slow-to-warm-up temperament?	Answer: Suggest that they let Julia adapt to new environments slowly. Introduce her to new people by having the parents remain present at first. After several sessions, the parents can leave for a short time and then return.

CHAPTER 34

CRITICAL THINKING IN ACTION

A mother is seeing the pediatric nurse practitioner you are working with for her son Jonathan's 3-month, well-baby checkup at the local community health clinic. The baby is in the 90th percentile for weight and in the 50th percentile for height and is fed Similac formula with iron. According to the medical history, Jonathan had RSV when he was 1 month old and there are smokers in the house. The nurse practitioner has asked you to educate the mother about feeding her 3-month-old baby. The mother has raised concerns that the baby is not sleeping through the night, and the baby's grandmother has suggested adding cereal to his bottle at night to help him sleep. Jonathan has met all developmental milestones and has not yet developed teeth.

1. What type of advice can you give the mother about adding cereal to the bottle?	Answer: Infants should not be given any solid foods until they are between 4 to 6 months old. Developmentally, they are not able to manage spoon feeding well, they have all nutrients met by the formula being fed, and early introduction of solid food may increase the chance that the baby could develop an allergy. There is no evidence that early cereal feeding helps a baby sleep through the night. Cereal is the first food that is usually given, and Jonathan should be fed it with a spoon, not added to the bottle, after 4 months old.
2. Why is rice cereal recommended as the first food to introduce when Jonathan is able to start solid foods?	Answer: Because it has a low allergenic potential, it is easy to digest, and it contains iron.
3. What is the reason only iron-fortified formula or breast milk is recommended for the entire first year of life for Jonathan, rather than cow milk?	Answer: Jonathan should not be given cow milk under 1 year of age due to the fact it can cause gastric irritation, leading to bleeding and anemia. This can also interfere with the absorption of some nutrients. Both breast milk and infant formulas meet all nutrient requirements and are digested well by nearly all infants.
4. Based on Jonathan's height and weight percentiles on the growth chart, his mother wonders if he should be put on a "diet." What would be the appropriate response to her concern?	Answer: Based on Jonathan's age he should have between 3 to 4 ounces every 3 to 4 hours. Some infants will drink more and sometimes less based on their own needs. Ask how much Jonathan is drinking and how often he feeds. Provide suggestions for normal patterns if it appears the family is offering excess milk. Encourage her return for the next visit so that height and weight monitoring can continue.

CHAPTER 35

CRITICAL THINKING IN ACTION

It is a relatively calm night in the children's hospital emergency room when a 6-month-old infant named Colby is brought in by emergency personnel from an automobile accident. Colby was in his infant, rear-facing car seat, riding with his parents when another car rear-ended them. The parents were not hurt and did not need to go to the hospital. The father immediately called 911 on his cell phone after the accident. When the ambulance arrived at the emergency room, you were given the report from the EMT. He stated that Colby was alert and quiet in his father's arms when they arrived on the scene, and he did not have any obvious signs of trauma. He is being brought to the hospital to make sure he did not sustain any injuries from the accident. His vital signs are as follows: temperature 98.9°F, respirations 40, pulse 110, and his blood pressure is 95/55. Colby is alert with no apparent distress. His pupils are equal, round, and reactive to light. His anterior fontanelle is flat, and he has equal movements of extremities. His breath sounds are clear and equal bilaterally. His heart sounds have a regular rate and rhythm without murmur. He voided around 2 hours ago, before the accident.

1. The fontanelles are an extremely important body part to examine in children. In the scenario with Colby, it can give an indication if there is increased intracranial pressure related to the accident. How can you describe the placement of the fontanelles, and when should they close and become impalpable? Also, describe why the head would be more likely to sustain injury in an infant like Colby versus an adult.	Answer: Infants have a posterior fontanelle located between the sagittal suture and lambdoid suture, and it should close by 3 months old. The anterior fontanelle is located between the coronal suture and sagittal suture and will close usually by 18 months old. The head is proportionately larger than an adult, and the neck muscles are less able to support the head.

2. After reviewing the scenario, what can you tell the parents about Colby's vital signs and stability at this time? What is the difference between adult vital signs and Colby's vital signs?	Answer: They can be told that based on Colby's vital signs, everything appears normal and stable at this time. The heart rate is faster in infants due to their higher metabolic rate and cardiac output being rate-dependent, not stroke dependent. The normal heart rate in Colby's age group is 80 to 130 beats per minute and the normal heart rate for adults is 60 to 100 beats per minute. The respiratory rate is faster in infants due to their higher metabolic rate and proportionately greater need for oxygen. The normal respiratory rate for an infant is 30 to 60 breaths per minute and gradually decreases into adulthood to 12 to 20 breaths per minute. The normal blood pressure for children varies based on their age and height.
3. Describe what structures in the chest and abdominal area of Colby's body would be of concern with the type of accident he sustained.	Answer: The spleen, liver, and lungs would be the main structures of concern with Colby. The spleen and liver can be easily traumatized due to a lack of much protection from an infant's ribs and abdomen. The ribs are mostly cartilage at this age and do not easily fracture. However, forces from a severe crash can be transmitted to the lung tissue under the ribs and cause bruising or a pneumothorax. The infant car seat has a 5-point harness to help spread forces from a crash over the chest and abdomen and help protect the chest and abdomen.
4. If a heart murmur were to be found on examination of Colby, what would be the five ways to describe it?	Answer: The heart murmur should be described by intensity, location, if it radiates, when it occurs (timing), and quality of the sound.

CHAPTER 36

CRITICAL THINKING IN ACTION

You are working at the inpatient adolescent psychiatric unit where there are approximately 20 teens between the ages of 12 and 17 years old. The teens are admitted for several different diagnoses, including: depression, suicide attempts, bipolar disorders, and eating disorders. The nurses are in charge of medication administration, vital signs, unit safety issues, physical assessments, and basic therapeutic interventions. You are working with a client named Cindy, 15 years old, who was admitted due to a suicide attempt and has been given a dual diagnosis of bulimia nervosa and depression. She has had extreme weight loss and gain over the past year and is currently 67 inches tall and weighs 140 pounds. She has stated she tried to commit suicide with a knife due to being upset with the loss of a boyfriend. She thought she was fat and was trying to lose weight by laxative use and vomiting after meals. There is a family history of depression and substance abuse, but Cindy denies any substance use. She lives with her mother and has no contact with her father. She does not feel she has anyone to discuss her feelings with and states her mother is gone from the house frequently. Cindy admits to often eating fast food and snacking on other junk food and soda. She has been in the hospital for 2 weeks and was resistant to treatment at first, but seems to be improving with therapy and medication. She has lost 3 pounds while she has been hospitalized, and her vital signs are usually: temperature 98.7°F, pulse 70, respirations 12, and blood pressure 110/70. Review the content on bulimia in Chapter 34 to help you answer these questions.

1. What are some of the signs of bulimia Cindy may exhibit?	Answer: Cindy may frequently visit the restroom immediately after eating. She may be preoccupied with her body size. She may have erosion of tooth enamel, calluses on the back of her hand from inducing vomiting, abdominal distention, and she may have an electrolyte imbalance.
2. What can you tell the mother about Cindy's vital signs and stability at this time? How can you explain the weight loss?	Answer: She can be told that based on Cindy's vital signs, everything appears normal and stable at this time. She appears to be responding to therapy, and her weight loss could be due to the balanced food intake she is receiving while in the hospital.
3. What behavioral signs of bulimia should be part of your nursing assessment of Cindy while she is hospitalized?	Answer: The nurse should watch for visiting the bathroom within 30 minutes after eating, hiding or giving away food, and calluses on the hands.
4. What are the treatment recommendations for Cindy?	Answer: Cindy's physiological state should be stabilized with expected outcomes to include: healthy mucous membranes, healed skin lesions, and electrolyte balance. Cindy should receive behavior modification focusing on a normal eating pattern. She should also receive psychotherapy, including treatment of depression if needed. Family therapy and group therapy with other teens may be beneficial for Cindy.

CHAPTER 37

CRITICAL THINKING IN ACTION

Quinton and his mother have come into the office for his 2-year-old well-child checkup. During the visit you learn that his mother stays home with him during the day, and his father often works overtime. His only significant medical history incident was when he had stitches placed in his forehead for falling on the edge of a table when he was 15 months old. There is a family history of attention deficit disorder and Crohn's disease. His height is in the 75th percentile, weight is in the 50th percentile, and body mass index is between the 25th and 50th percentiles. His temperature is 98.9°F and his pulse is 80. He is described by his parents as a picky eater and tends to eat the same foods frequently. They also say he tends to eat well on some days and other days will hardly eat anything. On the days he is not eating well, his mother will often resort to giving him soda or a sugary snack just so he is "getting something." Quinton sleeps about 7 hours per night and his mother usually ends up sleeping with him because he continues to fight going to sleep after being put to bed. He does not have a regular bedtime or rest routine, and he will usually nap in the car during the day. His mother tells you that her only break during the day when she is at home with Quinton is when he is watching television in his bedroom so he often watches 2 to 4 hours per day. Quinton has a soft stool every day and has not showed any interest in potty training at this time. He is developmentally able to go up and down stairs, kick a ball, scribble on paper, and is able to speak in 3 to 4 word sentences. During the visit at the office, it is obvious his parents have difficulty controlling him and frequently make threats and offer bribes to get him to behave properly. He starts screaming and kicking when his parents set limits on his behavior in the office, and his parents say they are frequently exhausted and do not know what to do about his high energy level. They also are concerned because they feel like the discipline methods they have been using are not working, and he is getting into so many things in the home that they are concerned he may hurt himself. They have used spanking and time-outs, but they do not seem to improve his behavior. They think he may have some type of medical condition like attention deficit disorder considering it does run in their family.

1. At 2 years of age, a consistent routine will help a toddler behave more appropriately. What are some of the things you can tell Quinton's mother regarding his sleep and nutrition habits to help establish a better routine?	Answer: It is recommended that Quinton gets an adequate amount of 10 hours of sleep per night with one nap at this age, and it would be helpful to establish a routine to do this. The sleep patterns should be at the same time everyday and should follow a similar routine. The routine may include a story, brushing teeth, bath, and the parent should leave the room after the routine is done. A transitional object, such as a blanket, may be helpful to provide comfort. Quinton should be offered healthy, low-sugar choices for food at each meal, including snacks. He should be offered a food from each of the four food groups at most meals. Advise the parents that his appetite may vary daily, which is normal at this age. If he is offered nutritious foods on a regular basis, he will eat when he is hungry.
2. How can you advise Quinton's mother about positive approaches to disciplining him?	Answer: Limit the rules to those that are essential and provide an environment that is a place where the child will be less prone to redirection. Use distraction as a first approach and praise the child for choosing a new activity. Spend time interacting with the child several times a day and praise positive behavior. Question the parents about Quinton's physical activity. Several daily play periods and outside activity are needed to channel his energy. Television should be limited to no more than 2 hours daily, and the television should not be in his room.
3. How can you advise Quinton's mother about disciplining him when it is needed?	Answer: Give Quinton one warning to change his behavior, and if he does not change, place him in time out. Give him 1 minute per year of age in time out and then direct Quinton to a positive activity. If the behavior is aggressive towards others, immediately remove him from the situation and put him in time out. Encourage him to use words instead of hitting, biting, or throwing toys.
4. What are some suggestions you can give Quinton's mother about handling his temper tantrums?	Answer: The parents should learn when a temper tantrum is about to occur and distract or hold him at that time. Separate the child from others and put him in time out. Do not "give in" to what the child wants. Let him have his tantrum and then reward him for being able to regain control. Encourage the use of words to express his feelings.

CHAPTER 38

CRITICAL THINKING IN ACTION

Tammy is a 13 year old coming into the office for her yearly checkup and she has never been in the hospital or had surgery. She is a good student and is excited to start seventh grade next year. She has not had any immunizations since going into kindergarten. Tammy arrives with her mother, with whom she lives; she has no contact with her biological father. Her mother decides to stay in the waiting room, but did note on the written history form that there is a family history of high cholesterol and heart disease in family members under 50 years old. Tammy's mother is a single parent working full time with two other children at home. Tammy's body mass index is in the 85th percentile and she passed her hearing and vision tests. Her blood pressure is 115/70 and her urinalysis shows blood, but Tammy has her menses today. Tammy has a period every month and menarche started at 10 years old. Her menses lasts 5 to

7 days and she denies experiencing cramping or excessively heavy menses. Tammy enjoys being a member of the volleyball team and is involved in a church youth group. She does not get to spend much time with her friends because she watches her two younger siblings in the afternoons while her mother is at work. When her mother is away, she admits to sitting and playing video games or watching TV most of the day. Tammy says she has had a boyfriend but denies sexual activity. She also denies any experimentation with substance use.

1. What vaccines is Tammy due for at this age if she has not already received them?	Answer: Varicella (if Tammy never had chickenpox), Td, MMR II, meningococcal, hepatitis A (if required in their state), and hepatitis B series are all recommended.
2. Based on the information you collected about Tammy, what are some areas of recommended health teaching?	Answer: She will need teaching on nutrition, exercise, immunizations, support systems, limiting TV time to less than 2 hours per day, injury prevention, sexual activity, and substance use.
3. A dietary assessment demonstrates that Tammy frequently skips meals and eats fast food almost daily. What are some of the suggestions you can give Tammy to improve her nutritional status?	Answer: She should incorporate the following into her daily lifestyle: • Five fruits and vegetables and three servings of dairy per day. • Use whole grain products and limit sugar and high-fat foods. • Eat three balanced meals per day and eat with her family when possible. • Also assess for eating disorders and address if necessary.
4. What are some of the injury prevention topics you can discuss with Tammy?	Answer: Topics to be discussed would include: safe practices when riding in cars with friends, limiting sun exposure, water safety, fire and firearm safety, avoiding loud music, and abuse issues.

CHAPTER 39

CRITICAL THINKING IN ACTION

Gavin is a 9 month old coming into the clinic for his well-child checkup. The clinic is set up to see teen mothers and their babies for well-child visits and immunizations. Diane, his mother, has been bringing him there since he was born. Gavin qualifies for healthcare coverage through the Medicaid system in their state. He was born full term and has never been in the hospital or had surgery. Diane is still attending high school and plans to graduate this year. She and Gavin are living with her boyfriend's (Gavin's father) parents until they can raise enough money to live on their own. Gavin's father does not come to the well-baby visits. Gavin attends child care while his mother is at school. He is up-to-date on immunizations so far, and there is no significant family medical history, but there is smoking in the home. Gavin is walking since he is able to point, wave, clap. He is able to drink from a cup and put objects into a cup. He has been growing and thriving at an appropriate pace. Diane describes him as a good eater and tells you that he is currently on whole milk. He has soft stools daily and 5 to 6 wet diapers per day. He sleeps through the night and takes two naps per day. Diane describes him as an extremely active child and has worked on childproofing everything in the house.

1. What is the role of the nurse in caring for Gavin and his parents in the clinic?	Answer: Performing a nursing assessment and screening tests, assisting the physician with the examination and diagnostic tests, developing a nursing diagnosis and developing a care plan that includes immunizations and patient education for health promotion, and linking the family to community resources.
2. What data does the nurse collect to perform a family assessment?	Answer: The nurse collects data on all people residing in the household and their family relationship; family structure, roles and values; cultural customs related to childrearing; faith-based affiliations; support system network; communication patterns; and home and environment.
3. What strengths and stressors are likely to be present in this family?	Answer: • **Strengths:** Father is involved, father's family is supportive since that is the mother's and child's home, mother still attending high school, she has healthcare coverage, child appears healthy, and the mother has worked to make the environment safe for an active child. • **Stressors:** Teen mother, parents are not married, and limited finances.
4. What are the elements of a healthcare or medical home?	Answer: Family-centered care with a trusting relationship with the child and family, continuity of care from birth through adolescence, family-centered health promotion and health maintenance, and interaction with community agencies and coordination of care with all of the child's healthcare providers.

CHAPTER 40

CRITICAL THINKING IN ACTION

Today, the hospital is sponsoring an orientation day for a group of children preparing to have surgery. One 8-year-old girl, Lauren, is extremely nervous about getting a tonsillectomy. Both her parents are with her today, and she clings to them. You decide to ask Lauren to draw a picture of a person. Lauren seems excited to do this and draws a person with a lot of detail, which, you analyze afterwards, demonstrates that she has a cognitive level of a 9-year-old. You next ask Lauren to describe what all the parts are in the human body. You ask her to describe what is inside them to see what she understands about the body. When she is asked about the head, she says, "There are gooey brains in there." When asked about the heart and what would happen if she didn't have a heart, she says, "A person would die in the hospital like grandpa." After hearing this comment you see it as a good opportunity to discuss her fears of the hospital. She states that she is afraid that she is going to die like her grandpa did when his heart stopped beating. You explain that her procedure is different than that of her grandpa. You read a book to Lauren entitled, *Why Am I Going to the Hospital?* by Lyle Stuart. Lauren appears to relax and asks to see the place for surgery. You let Lauren dress up like a surgeon, touch the instruments, and give the family the tour. You offer more suggestions on books they could read before coming back for surgery and suggest getting a doll to practice playing doctor on at home. You provide phone numbers for the parents if they have additional questions.

1. Describe the role of a child life specialist.	Answer: The role of a child life specialist includes the following: • Plans age-appropriate activities. • Plans activities based on feelings. • May stay with the child during a painful procedure. • Focuses on the emotional needs of the hospitalized child.
2. Besides the types of techniques used with Lauren to help her deal with her feelings based on her age, what are examples of other techniques that can be used?	Answer: The following techniques may be incorporated: • Make up stories about her problem. • Encourage listening to her favorite music in the hospital. • Use puppets to describe feelings. • Provide pet therapy.
3. Describe the concept of rooming in.	Answer: The parent stays in the child's room and performs tasks needed in the care of the child. Some hospitals have cots or built-in beds to provide a place for the parent to sleep. Communication with the parent by the nurse is extremely important so the parent is supported and is involved at the desired level.
4. After surgery what assessments are needed to monitor Lauren for signs of infection?	Answer: Vital signs, respiratory status, and effectiveness of pain control measures provide clues about possible infection.

CHAPTER 41

CRITICAL THINKING IN ACTION

Kelly is a 24-week-old premature baby born to her parents, Shawn and Lori, who are of Navajo Indian descent. The mother had a premature rupture of membranes and Kelly was kept alive by life support. Kelly's condition is extremely critical with her weight at 500 grams. You know that when infants are this small and their condition critical, any amount of touch can be extremely stressful to their bodies. The mother has been pumping and freezing breast milk for future use. The parents are encouraged to assist the nurse in any way they can, but they are not able to touch Kelly. The parents have been educated about how critical Kelly's condition is and the machines and medications being used. They still have confusion and uncertainty about the situation. The grandparents have been helping care for Roseanne, Kelly's 7-year-old sister, and she has visited her sister once. The parents have not left the hospital at all. On the third day of life, Kelly gained weight and started to show an increase in activity. The parents thought this could be a positive sign, but the nurse explained that the weight gain was from swelling, and the increased activity was from agitation as Kelly struggled to breathe. When the parents were at the bedside, Kelly started to become cyanotic, and her oxygen saturation level dropped to the 60s. Several nurses, doctors, and respiratory therapists tried to save her, but were unsuccessful. This was an extremely devastating loss to all the medical personnel and family involved.

1. What are some of the stressors Kelly experienced while in the hospital?	Answer: The stressors would include the following: • Painful, invasive procedures. • Immobilization because of all the equipment attached to her. • Sensory overload. • Sleep deprivation.

2. What are the stages of grief a family is likely to experience with Kelly's situation?	Answer: They will progress through stages of shock and disbelief; anger and guilt; deprivation and loss; anticipatory waiting; and readjustment or mourning.
3. What are some of the strategies that can be used when helping Kelly's sibling deal with the loss of her sister?	Answer: Insert Table 41.3.
4. What are some of the strategies for helping Kelly's parents deal with losing her?	Answer: Insert Table 41.7.

CHAPTER 42

CRITICAL THINKING IN ACTION

A 12-year-old boy, Kevin, is recovering from a four-wheeler accident on the medical surgical unit at a local children's hospital. He was riding the four-wheeler unsupervised and without permission while his parents were at work. He suffered an abdominal injury requiring surgery, three broken bones, and several lacerations that needed stitches. His parents are very worried about his injuries and at the same time angry with him for not following the rules. Kevin appears expressionless in his hospital bed, but cries and grimaces at any slight movement. When asked on a scale of 1 to 10 (10 being the most pain) how much pain he is feeling, he says a 10. His parents are reluctant to let him have any pain medications because they fear he may become dependent on the medication. His father states that Kevin be a man and tolerate the pain, and thinks that enduring the pain will teach him a lesson about responsibility. The nurse explains that pain management is necessary to improve Kevin's healing, help him mobilize sooner, and potentially shorten his hospital stay. She explains the physiological consequences of ineffective pain management and discusses how the medication will help him sleep and rest. She explains that some pain medications can be addicting, but the chances of Kevin becoming addicted to pain medications for this injury are extremely rare. She also reviews the nonpharmacological methods of relieving pain. The parents are still reluctant about giving Kevin the medications but agree to conform to the doctor's orders.

1. What are some of the potential physiological consequences to letting Kevin be in pain?	Answer: Insert Table 42.2.
2. What are some examples of opioid analgesics available to Kevin?	Answer: Insert Table 42.7.
3. What are some examples of NSAIDs available to Kevin?	Answer: Insert Table 42.8.
4. What are the signs and symptoms of opioid withdrawal, and how long should it take for Kevin to be weaned off an opioid?	Answer: It may take 2 to 4 weeks to wean him off an opioid. Insert Table 42.9.

CHAPTER 43

CRITICAL THINKING IN ACTION

Ten-month-old Devin is brought to the emergency room at 3:00 AM for respiratory distress by ambulance. He is usually healthy and has no history of respiratory distress or asthma. His parents state that he was experiencing a cough and stuffy nose for the past week and developed a fever over 103°F during the night. He woke up crying with a frightening cough and could barely catch his breath so the parents called 911. Devin's assessment in the emergency room included: respiratory rate 55 per minute with moderate retractions, temperature 103.2°F, and heart rate of 120 beats per minute with regular rhythm. Auscultation revealed wheezing and rhonchi throughout all lung fields. He was administered a nebulizer treatment with albuterol 0.5 mL and 2 mL of normal saline. His respiratory rate decreased to 40 breaths per minute after the treatment and retractions improved. The arterial blood gas measurements showed an increased PCO_2, a decreased pH, and a normal HCO_3. A diagnosis of upper respiratory infection and croup syndrome and resultant respiratory acidosis is made. Devin was admitted for monitoring and has improved vital signs and respiratory effort the next morning.

1. What are some of the other possible causes of respiratory acidosis in children such as Devin?	Answer: Common causes could be pneumonia, asthma, aspiration, and epiglottitis.

2. What are some of the signs and symptoms of respiratory distress and the central nervous system problems associated with Devin's particular acid-base imbalance?	Answer: The signs and symptoms of respiratory distress are increased respiratory rate, skin retractions in the truncal area, nasal flaring, and grunting. The central nervous conditions that could be complications of his acid-base imbalance are: confusion, lethargy, and headache.
3. Devin's heart rate and rhythm are monitored closely in the hospital. What is the reason for these assessments?	Answer: With respiratory acidosis, tachycardia and cardiac arrhythmias may develop.
4. What is the treatment for Devin's acid-base imbalance?	Answer: The treatment for respiratory acidosis involves treating the underlying cause. Breathing treatments are effective to decrease bronchospasm.
5. What are some of the measures taken in the hospital to ensure Devin's safety?	Answer: Keep side rails raised, turn and position Devin regularly, and evaluate his mental status. Report changes in condition promptly.

CHAPTER 44

CRITICAL THINKING IN ACTION

You are working at a pediatrician's office when 11-year-old Nirah and his parents come in. The husband, wife, and Nirah are all human immunodeficiency virus (HIV) positive. Nirah does not know he is HIV positive, but he has been very compliant with taking his antiretroviral medications. However, he recently developed a cough and the parents decided to visit the pediatrician's office.

The pediatrician finds that Nirah has a fever of 102°F, respiratory rate of 60 breaths per minute, no visible retractions during respiration, and a pulse of 120 beats per minute. The physician decides to admit him to the hospital to perform a comprehensive assessment and monitor medication effects. After the laboratory tests and radiographs are completed in the hospital, the physician tells the family that Nirah has pneumonia and a streptococcal infection of the throat. Nirah is started on intravenous antibiotics, and improvement is apparent after three days of treatment. You monitor Nirah frequently and have him deep breathe. You also teach the parents how to encourage deep-breathing exercises.

1. How does HIV interfere with normal functioning of the child's immune system?	Answer: The HIV virus destroys the body's T cells. Once the T cells are destroyed, the body cannot fight infection.
2. What are some of the measures of infection control for Nirah while he is hospitalized with HIV?	Answer: The methods of infection control include the following: • Assess every 2 to 4 hours for fever, breath sounds, and skin/mucous membrane lesions. • Perform deep breathing exercises every 2 to 4 hours; perform respiratory assessment before and after these sessions. • Employ strict hand hygiene measures. • Do not place fresh flowers in the room. • Avoid visitors with illness. • Allow Nirah to have regular rest periods. • Administer intravenous antibiotics as ordered.
3. How can you promote Nirah's respiratory function?	Answer: Encourage coughing and deep breathing every 2 to 4 hours. Teach Nirah to blow cotton balls with a straw, blow bubbles, or blow a pinwheel.
4. When children, especially those with an immune system problem, are on antibiotics, they can develop thrush (*Candida* in the mouth). What is the treatment to prevent this side effect?	Answer: The treatment is mouth care every 2 to 4 hours with a non-alcohol-based solution, such as normal saline or lemon-glycerin swabs. Nirah can be taught to do this, and the nurse should continue to check for lesions.

CHAPTER 45

CRITICAL THINKING IN ACTION

Keisha, 7 years old, and Brandon, 1 year old, are brought to the pediatric clinic both needing immunizations. Even though Brandon is sick today, their mother would still like Keisha to have her immunizations, and she would also like both kids to have a complete checkup before their vaccines to make sure they are healthy. You examine Keisha's vital signs as 80th percentile in height, 40th percentile in weight, temperature 98.9°F, blood pressure 105/62, urinalysis with a trace of leukocytes, and she passes her hearing and vision screening. She seems extremely anxious about having to get a needle. There is evidence of eczema and allergic rhinitis.

You examine Brandon while he clings to his mother. His vital signs are: temperature 102°F, respiratory rate of 30 breaths per minute, and heart rate of 90 beats per minute. Brandon's exam exhibits evidence of a coxsackievirus, evidenced by grayish, papulovesicular, ulcerative lesions in his mouth. This type of illness does not respond to antibiotics. You advise the mother to avoid others because it is contagious and to offer cool drinks and bland foods. She is also told warm saline mouth rinses would be helpful, to observe for dehydration, and to give ibuprofen or acetaminophen as needed.

1. Since Brandon has been into the office several times for various infections, what education can be given to his mother to reduce the chance of future infections?	Answer: All of the following are important to tell Brandon's mother: • Use disposable tissues and discard. • Wash her hands frequently when caring for both children, and teach Brandon to wash hands. • Do not share eating utensils or eat food off of each other's plates. • Wipe the food preparation areas with a disinfectant. • Wash dishes in hot water and soap.
2. Keisha has eczema and allergic rhinitis. Would this be a contraindication to giving vaccines?	Answer: Only when an allergy to a vaccine component exists would allergy be a contraindication to the vaccines.
3. What are questions the nurse should ask the mother before administering vaccines to Keisha to make sure there are no contraindications to giving them?	Answer: Keisha's mother should be asked about the following: • Does Keisha have allergies to anything? • Has Keisha ever had a reaction to a vaccine in the past? • Does Keisha have any neurological or immune system problems? • Has Keisha taken a steroid in the past 3 months? • Has Keisha received a blood transfusion or immune globulin in the past year?
4. What should the mother be told about caring for Keisha after her vaccines?	Answer: The mother should be provided with the following information: • Vaccine information sheets (VIS) for each administered vaccine should be given. • The injection sites may be red and painful to touch. Use ice and acetaminophen to help reduce this problem. It should improve in 1 to 2 days. • A mild fever may develop within a few days after the vaccine. • Watch for severe reactions to the vaccine, such as: hives or swelling, trouble breathing, neurological problems, or other reactions mentioned on the VIS. • Call 911 for severe reactions and your healthcare provider for any other reactions Keisha has that concern you.
5. How should the mother be told to manage Brandon's fever?	Answer: Insert "Teaching Highlights: Guidelines for Evaluating and Treating Fever in Children."

CHAPTER 46

CRITICAL THINKING IN ACTION

You are working at a children's urgent care facility when a couple enters carrying their screaming 9-month-old child, Becky. The parents are worried as Becky has been crying steadily for the past 2 hours. You ask about recent illnesses or injuries and learn that she has had only two colds in her life, and the most recent was about a week ago.

You assess Becky's vital signs as follows: weight 19 pounds (8.6 kilograms), temperature 101°F, respirations 60 breaths per minute without retractions, and heart rate 120 beats per minute. She does not have any rashes or evidence of injuries, and upon examination, she appears well nourished but clearly in distress. Her heart rate is regular and breath sounds are equal bilaterally and clear to auscultation. Both tympanic membranes are red and bulging. Her abdomen is soft and without organomegaly. The nurse practitioner diagnoses bilateral acute otitis media and administers analgesic ear drops and ibuprofen in the office. Within 15 minutes, Becky has settled down, stopped crying, and is resting in her father's arms. The family is sent home with instructions to administer analgesics and return within 48 hours for further assessment.

1. What are the three main organisms that may have caused Becky's otitis media?	Answer: Becky's otitis media was likely caused by *Streptococcus pneumoniae*, *Haemophilus influenzae*, or *Moraxella catarrhalis*.
2. What are some of the guidelines you can give Becky's parents about otitis media treatment?	Answer: The child should be treated for pain and reevaluated within 48 to 72 hours. If there is no improvement, an antibiotic may then be administered.

3.	The mother says she has family members who have had tubes placed in their ears because of ear infections and wants to know if this something that Becky will need to have done.	Answer: Ear tubes or tympanotomy tubes are not needed unless the middle ear effusion has persisted longer than 3 months or the infection keeps recurring. At this time surgical treatment is not recommended.
4.	What are some methods parents can use to prevent future otitis media?	Answer: The nurse should educate the parents about the following: • Position infant upright when feeding. • Eliminate smoke and dust around Becky. • Limit exposure to children who have colds and other infections. • Provide Becky with adequate rest, exercise, and proper nutrition.

CHAPTER 47

CRITICAL THINKING IN ACTION

Adam and his mother have come to speak with you to discuss the plan of care for his asthma. Adam, 7 years old, has a history of episodic wheezing and nebulizer treatments, but he was never hospitalized for asthma until last week. He was treated in the emergency department and kept 2 days. His parents were educated about how to manage his mild persistent asthma.

His mother has brought a doctor's order along with Adam's albuterol MDI, his peak flow meter, spacer, and his asthma action plan. She tells you that he is also completing a dose of oral steroids and was placed on Singulair to help prevent the asthma. You discuss the peak flow meter, the guidelines, and what type of action to take as needed. Based on his height of 48 inches, his peak flow meter green zone is 160–128, his yellow zone is 128–80, and his red zone is 80 or below. If he is having problems, he is to take his albuterol MDI with spacer, two puffs every 4 to 6 hours as needed.

1.	What are some of the side effects associated with Adam's albuterol MDI?	Answer: The common side effects of using albuterol are: tachycardia, nervousness, nausea, vomiting, and headaches.
2.	What is the benefit to using a spacer on Adam's albuterol MDI?	Answer: The spacer will help Adam coordinate inspiration with the release of the medication to get the albuterol into his lungs. The spacer captures the medication and offers a longer time frame to get the medication into his body while he inhales. It is less time consuming than the nebulizer treatment for the appropriate aged child.
3.	What are the signs of respiratory distress to observe for with Adam?	Answer: Adam should be watched for an increased respiratory rate and effort, retractions, cyanosis, and nasal flaring.
4.	Describe the pathophysiology with asthma and why Adam had an asthma attack.	Answer: When Adam has an asthma attack, breathing becomes difficult as the airway narrows due to constriction of the smooth muscles or becomes obstructed by swelling and mucous production in the bronchioles. Gas exchange in the alveoli becomes impaired. Refer to the illustration for more clarification on the pathophysiology. Refer to "Pathophysiology Illustrated: Asthma" on page 1415 in Chapter 47.

CHAPTER 48

CRITICAL THINKING IN ACTION

You are working in the hospital when Samantha, a 2-day-old infant is diagnosed with a continuous, systolic, grade 3, heart murmur in the pulmonic area of the chest. This is the parents' first child and they are extremely worried about their 6-week premature baby. Samantha has full, bounding pulses and weighed 5 lb 6 oz at birth, but has lost 3 ounces in the past 2 days. The day after Samantha was born, the parents are told about her heart murmur and that an echocardiogram, ECG, and chest x-ray are needed to determine the cause. The tests show that she has a patent ductus arteriosus (PDA). The physician has prescribed three doses of a medication to aid in the closure of the duct. You explain that her vital signs and urine output will need to be monitored closely for decreases while she is on this medicine.

Several days later the heart murmur is still heard; the medicine did not work. The parents want to avoid surgery if possible, and the doctor explains if the ductus closes by the time she is 9 to 12 months old, and she is without symptoms, surgery could be avoided. If the PDA is not corrected, her life span will be shortened. She is discharged from the hospital, thriving and breastfeeding well, and the doctor advises about watching for poor weight gain, swelling, intercostal retractions, and breathing more than 60 times per minute. A follow-up appointment is made for 1 week later.

1. How would you explain a PDA to the parents?	Answer: You could explain this is something that happens more frequently in premature infants than in full-term infants. The PDA is a blood vessel that is open the entire time of gestation, but closes usually within a few days after the infant is born to allow the blood to flow through the heart like it normally would.
2. What was the most likely cause of Samantha's weight loss? Is it the PDA that caused the weight loss?	Answer: All infants have the potential to lose up to 10% of their body weight after they are born. They should gain it back by the time they are 2 weeks old. The chances of the weight loss being related to the PDA are unlikely.
3. What is the physiological reason Samantha's life span would be shortened if she does not get surgical correction of her PDA?	Answer: She would eventually develop pulmonary hypertension and vascular obstructive disease.
4. How would you describe congestive heart failure?	Answer: The cardiac output is inadequate to support the body's needs. See also "Clinical Manifestations: Congestive Heart Failure" on page 1441 in Chapter 48.

CHAPTER 49

CRITICAL THINKING IN ACTION

Frederick is admitted to the hospital with severe abdominal pain. He has been hospitalized for treatment of sickle cell anemia several times in the past and now, as an 8 year old, he and his mother are very familiar with the routine. The disease is stable most of the time, but about twice annually he is admitted to the hospital for complications of the disorder. His mother expresses how upsetting it is to watch her son suffering pain from the disease. In the hospital a priority of nursing intervention is to control Frederick's pain. The doctor diagnoses that the abdominal pain is caused by sickled cells in the spleen. Frederick's hemoglobin is 6 g/dL, so a blood transfusion is ordered. Fluids and oxygen are also administered. Frequent vital signs and other monitoring are performed to identify any infections.

1. Besides correcting the anemia, what is another reason Frederick would be given a transfusion?	Answer: To make the sickled blood less viscous.
2. How would you explain what is happening to Frederick's spleen that is causing the abdominal pain?	Answer: The red blood cells are forming in the shape of a sickle, collecting in the spleen, and causing a blockage.
3. In what way does sickle cell anemia affect the various systems of the body?	Answer: Due to the sickling of the cells, all body systems can become affected. Refer to "Pathophysiology Illustrated: Sickle Cell Anemia" on page 1496 in Chapter 49 to see how this can be demonstrated.
4. When giving a blood transfusion to Frederick, should warm or cold blood be given? What is the reason for your answer?	Answer: The blood should be warmed to room temperature because cold blood can increase sickling of RBCs.

CHAPTER 50

CRITICAL THINKING IN ACTION

Seven-year-old Christina is brought to the hospital with a strange rash, lethargy, and fever. Blood is drawn, and the results are abnormal. The hematologist confirms that Christina has acute lymphoblastic leukemia (ALL), the most common childhood cancer. Her parents are in shock and disbelief about the news; she seems too young. Christina is immediately admitted to the hospital and put on an IV with orders for more blood work.

Christina's blood work demonstrates the following: hemoglobin 9g/dL, leukocytes 20,000/mm^3, and platelets 90,000/mm^3. Chemotherapy was initiated and precautions were taken to avoid infections. Recommendations for Christina include daily rest times, generous amounts of water, intake of healthy foods, and avoidance of sun exposure.

The parents are happy when Christina comes home even though she is still on chemotherapy. The hematologist advises them to keep a suitcase packed because it is not uncommon to return to the hospital due to a chemotherapy complication. The parents are also reminded to take care of themselves and to get away and relax on occasion. This will help them deal with Christina's therapy more efficiently.

1. What are some of the common side effects to chemotherapy?	Answer: Bone marrow suppression, nausea and vomiting, anorexia and weight loss, mouth ulcers, constipation, pain.
2. What is the reason it is important to check daily weights on Christina?	Answer: Daily weights help check hydration and nutrition status.
3. What signs of infection should the parents be told to report to the doctor while Christina is on chemotherapy?	Answer: Temperature above 101°F, cough, runny nose, tugging at ears, redness or drainage around central lines, pain.
4. What are some developmentally appropriate techniques you can encourage that will assist Christina to deal with her illness?	Answer: You can encourage her to practice giving medicine to a doll, provide therapeutic play when she comes for chemotherapy, and read stories about children with cancer.

CHAPTER 51

CRITICAL THINKING IN ACTION

Ryan, a 3 year old, was last seen at 2 years of age, and appears today for a well-child checkup. He is in the 10th percentile for height (last visit height was in the 25th percentile), and he is in the 5th percentile for weight (while he was in the 10th percentile on the last visit). A developmental assessment shows that Ryan has only a limited vocabulary. When asked to draw a circle, he only scribbles. Although he can run, his mother says he cannot kick a ball. The physical exam is unremarkable, except that he is found to be thin, but active. The mother says he is usually healthy. When asked about Ryan's environment, his mother tells you they moved into an old house and have been doing some restoration.

The nurse practitioner performs some blood work and orders a CBC with differential, lead screening test, and sedimentary rate. The blood test results show Ryan has a hemoglobin of 9g/dL and a lead level of 30 mcg/dL. The nurse practitioner recommends that Ryan be taken to a specialist at the local university due to the high lead level, and he is treated with chelation therapy. The public health department visits the home and finds high lead levels in the paint. The family is assisted to find alternative housing. After the lead level is lowered, Ryan is referred to an early intervention program for treatment of developmental delays. Iron supplementation is started and the family is instructed in high-iron foods.

1. What is the primary risk factor that Ryan has for lead poisoning?	Answer: The primary risk factor is living in an older home that is having remodeling work.
2. What are some of the signs of lead poisoning Ryan is exhibiting?	Answer: He is having a growth delay, anemia, constipation, vomiting, decreased concentration, and a delay in his developmental milestones.
3. What should Ryan's family be told regarding the role of the health department in treating the lead toxicity?	Answer: The health department assesses the living situation and provides family education about how to control the sources of lead affecting Ryan in the home.
4. How does chelation therapy alter lead levels?	Answer: Chelation is the administration of chemicals that bind with lead in the body so that it can be excreted.

CHAPTER 52

CRITICAL THINKING IN ACTION

Kendra, a 2-year-old who appears ill, is brought into the urgent care center for a skin rash, fever, irritability, and edema. Her father is concerned she might also be dehydrated because she has had a decreased urine output. The doctor determines her skin rash does not blanche when pressure is applied and notes a purplish color. Last week, Kendra was treated for an episode of abdominal pain, diarrhea, and vomiting. The doctor immediately admits her to the hospital and orders a urine culture, blood work, and stool tests. The stool comes back positive for the strain of *E. coli* usually found in contaminated hamburger meat. Kendra has hemolytic uremic syndrome (HUS) and is in acute renal failure (ARF). She also has a low hemoglobin, elevated BUN and creatinine, hematuria, and electrolyte imbalances.

Kendra is given medication for her electrolyte imbalances, antihypertensive medications, and is placed on a high-calorie, high-carbohydrate diet with restrictions on protein, sodium, potassium, and phosphorus. You explain to her parents the extreme importance of adhering to her dietary and fluid restrictions to help keep her electrolytes and fluid level balanced. You educate them that in some cases children with HUS need dialysis and some children have long-term kidney damage. You teach them how to take her blood pressure and how to observe for edema so that Kendra can be monitored after she goes home.

1. How is drug administration adjusted for Kendra since she has ARF? What is an important nursing role when administering various medications to her?	Answer: The dosages in children with ARF are adjusted because the kidneys cannot excrete drugs as efficiently as normal. It is extremely important to know the signs of toxicity when administering these medications to Kendra.
2. What is the reason ARF develops in HUS?	Answer: ARF develops because of blood clotting in the arterioles. The hemolyzed red blood cells have a toxic effect on renal tubular cells, which leads to acute tubular necrosis.
3. What is one way Kendra's condition could have been prevented?	Answer: By completely cooking beef to 155°F throughout.
4. Renal failure is characterized by azotemia and oliguria. Describe what this is.	Answer: Azotemia occurs when the nitrogenous wastes accumulate in the blood. Oliguria occurs when urine output decreases to less than 1 mL/kg/hr.

CHAPTER 53

CRITICAL THINKING IN ACTION

Abigail, a 3-year-old with myelodysplasia, is seen every few months with her parents in the multidisciplinary spina bifida clinic where you work. Her lesion is at the L3 level, so she can flex her hips and extend her knees, but her ankles and toes are paralyzed. She uses full leg braces and a walker to mobilize, and she has minimal sensation in her lower legs and feet. Her bladder and bowel sphincters are also affected so Abigail and her parents have worked hard to establish bowel control through a high-fiber diet and by establishing specific times for bowel evacuation. Abigail's parents have learned to perform intermittent self-catheterization for bladder control to reduce the risk for kidney damage.

Her health history reveals she has experienced a case of acute otitis media since her last visit and responded well to antibiotics. Her legs are well protected by stockings to reduce rubbing by her braces. Her gait is becoming steadier with the walker, and her parents are encouraging exercise of her arms and upper trunk with swimming.

You encourage Abigail's parents to promote her cognitive development with age-appropriate games and interactions with her siblings.

1. What are the safety issues to discuss with Abigail's parents about spina bifida?	Answer: Insert "Teaching Highlights: Safety for the Children with Spina Bifida" on page 1700.
2. Describe spina bifida.	Answer: A congenital neural tube defect that can occur anywhere along the spine.
3. Identify important health promotion issues to discuss with Abigail's parents.	Answer: Insert "Health Promotion 53.1: The Children with Myelodysplasia."
4. Describe the difference between meningocele and myelomeningocele.	Answer: A myelomeningocele contains spinal cord or nerve roots in the sac, and the meningocele does not.

CHAPTER 54

CRITICAL THINKING IN ACTION

Douglas, a 5-year-old autistic child, comes into the office for his annual checkup and school immunizations of diphtheria-tetanus-acellular-pertussis, inactivated polio vaccine, and measles-mumps-rubella. He is very combative and it takes four people to help hold him and administer the vaccines. He will be attending a special school for children with autism and similar disorders. Diagnosed at 3 years old, he has never been in the hospital or had surgery. It is extremely difficult to examine him as he does not like to be touched. During prior visits in the office Douglas has stood facing the wall and twisting his hands. He continues to be combative for most of the exam, even with the use of decreased stimuli, communication, and slow movements, but you are able to assess that his blood pressure is 95/53. He is in the 50th percentile for both height and weight and his temperature is 99°F.

His mother says he is usually cooperative at home, but when they go out, he becomes aggressive when people get near him. She says that she feels isolated being at home with him all the time since she knows of no one who can watch him. His father was killed in a car accident a year ago, and she has found it difficult dealing with this by herself. You give her information about local support groups for children with autism and about local psychiatrists who can treat autism with types of medication to help control aggressive behavior. You also supply her with contact information for counselors in the area to help her deal with her own stress. She is appreciative of your help and support and looks forward to being able to send Douglas to school.

1. The mother has questions about the MMR vaccine and whether it causes autism. What can you tell her about that? Would you administer the vaccine today?	Answer: The research shows there is no association linking the MMR with incidence of autism. Autism is not a contraindication to receiving the MMR and Douglas should receive the vaccine today.
2. What can you tell the mother about safety issues with Douglas?	Answer: Autistic children need to be supervised at all times, especially at bath time, to ensure they are not harmed. Helmets and mittens can offer some protection with certain activities.
3. How can you enhance communication with Douglas when he comes into the office?	Answer: Use speech if possible and look for other ways to communicate such as pictures, computers, or sign language. Encourage his mother to bring comfort objects from home when he comes to the office.

CHAPTER 55

CRITICAL THINKING IN ACTION

Peter, now 7 years old, was diagnosed at 5 years with Duchenne muscular dystrophy. His parents are well informed about the disease since they had an older son who died of the disorder at 19 years. They first suspected the diagnosis when Peter did not walk until 19 months and had frequent falls. At the present time, he walks on his toes but is able to ambulate well with leg braces. Today, Peter is visiting the specialty clinic for children with muscular dystrophies. His braces will be checked for fit and performance, physical therapy will be performed, and he will attend a group session with other school-age children. During these visits, the parents also meet in a support group with other families and receive instruction and resources to help them with Peter's health management. As a nurse in the clinic, you perform a physical and mental assessment on Peter. All findings are within normal limit although he has had some constipation and several upper respiratory infections. You learn that he has an individualized education plan (IEP) in place at school that allows for periods of rest and physical therapy; the parents report that he is at grade level and excels at computer modeling.

1. What are the main roles of the nurse working with Peter in the specialty clinic?	Answer: The nurse should perform an assessment, promote independence for Peter and his parents, and provide resources and psychosocial support. A report should be sent to the school nurse.
2. Children with muscular dystrophy often get to a standing position by mainly using arm muscles. What is the name of this maneuver?	Answer: Gower's maneuver.
3. What are some of the tests performed to see if a child has muscular dystrophy and what are the expected results?	Answer: The tests used are serum enzyme assay, muscle biopsy, and electromyography. It would be expected to see an elevated serum creatine kinase, and the muscle biopsy would show a lack of the muscle protein, dystrophin.
4. Who can Peter expect to meet with on the days he goes to the specialty clinic for muscular dystrophy?	Answer: The team members should include: doctors, nurses, physical and occupational therapists, a nutritionist, genetic counselor, and social worker.

CHAPTER 56

CRITICAL THINKING IN ACTION

Fourteen-year-old Amanda is admitted to the hospital with newly diagnosed type 1 diabetes mellitus. She had initially been taken to her doctor's office for enuresis, polyphagia, polydipsia, and lethargy, but when assessed, her urinalysis had glucose and ketones and she had a weight loss of 15 pounds.

Upon admission to the hospital where you work, a full assessment is performed and the following vital signs are documented: weight of 115 pounds, temperature of 98.8°F, respiratory rate of 40 breaths per minute, heart rate of 90 beats per minute, and BP 106/63. She has dry mucous membranes, but skin turgor is brisk. Blood is drawn immediately and will continue to be drawn every hour until she is stable. After determining Amanda's developmental level, you decide she is able to understand the nutritional guidelines associated with type 1 diabetes and how to, under adult supervision, perform blood glucose monitoring as well as how to draw up and administer insulin. Amanda and her parents spend most of the time in the hospital learning survival skills for managing her diabetes.

Daily education and monitoring will occur in the diabetes clinic until the family is confident about taking care of Amanda. Regular follow-up visits will be scheduled with the diabetes nurse educator and endocrinologist.

1. What is the most likely blood work done on Amanda when admitted to the hospital for type 1 diabetes?	Answer: The most likely lab work performed is blood gases, glucose, and electrolytes.
2. How should the family be told to manage hypoglycemic episodes?	Answer: See "Teaching Highlights: Treating Hypoglycemic Episodes."
3. What should the parents be told about preventing diabetic ketoacidosis in Amanda?	Answer: See "Teaching Highlights: Preventing DKA."
4. How often should blood glucose monitoring be performed once the condition is stabilized?	Answer: The blood glucose should be checked four times a day and once a week at 3 AM.

CHAPTER 57

CRITICAL THINKING IN ACTION

Twelve-year old Rebecca is admitted to the burn unit after being scalded by spilling boiling spaghetti water on her legs and feet when attempting to carry the pot to the sink. The burn is classified as moderate with a mixture of partial thickness and full thickness covering a BSA of 12%. IV fluids are started in the emergency department and a continuous infusion of morphine is given for pain. Her temperature is 101°F. The initial debridement of the burns is performed in the operating room so that Rebecca is anesthetized and does not feel pain from the procedure. Following debridement, Rebecca is put on a high-calorie, high-protein diet to help meet her increased nutritional requirements. Wound care is performed twice a day so the burn site can be inspected for signs of infection and for development of eschar. Pain medication for wound care is provided through the IV. After the burn site is cleaned, antibiotic cream and a dressing are applied. Rebecca's nutritional intake and urine output are carefully monitored while she is hospitalized. Physical therapy is initiated to maintain range of motion and to prevent contractures. The nurse talks with Rebecca and her family about what to expect as the burns heal. Education of the family includes signs and symptoms of infection and the expected need for skin grafts over the full-thickness burn sites. After a few days in the hospital, Rebecca is discharged with daily follow-up in the burn clinic for wound care.

1. What is the most likely type of IV fluids started on Rebecca in the hospital and why?	Answer: Lactated Ringer's or normal saline solutions are the preferred fluids. Other solutions, such as D5W, can increase the risk for hyponatremia, cerebral edema, and seizures.
2. What is the reason it is important to monitor Rebecca's urine output?	Answer: Urine output should be monitored to make sure the cardiovascular and renal systems have adequate hydration. There is an initial loss of fluids through the wounds and fluid shifting to the interstitial spaces, which can cause an imbalance of fluids.
3. What is the reason Rebecca needed her extremities elevated and distal pulses checked frequently?	Answer: Elevation reduces distal edema and promotes circulation. Edema can constrict blood flow and prevent the burn from healing properly.
4. What are the goals of burn wound care for Rebecca?	Answer: Burn wound care will speed debridement, protect viable tissue, prevent infection, conserve heat and fluids, and control scarring.
5. Why is it important to monitor burns that have eschar?	Answer: Eschar that completely circles an extremity can constrict circulation and cause tissue hypoxia.

TRANSITION GUIDE

London, Ladewig, Ball, Binder: *Maternal-Newborn & Child Nursing,* 1e

to

London, Ladewig, Ball, Binder: *Maternal & Child Nursing Care,* 2e

London, et al. 1e	Pg	London, et al. 2e	Pg
Unit I		Unit 1	
Introductory Concepts		Family-Centered Care: Introductory Concepts	
Chapter 01 Maternal, Newborn, and Child Health Nursing	3	Chapter 01 Maternal, Newborn, and Child Health Nursing	2
Nursing Roles in Maternal-Child Nursing	4	Nursing Roles in Maternal-Child Nursing	3
Family-Centered Maternal-Child Care	5	Family-Centered Maternal-Child Care	4
Access to Health Care	8	Access to Health Care	8
Culturally Competent Care	9	Culturally Competent Care	8
Statistical Data and Maternal-Child Care	9	Statistical Data and Maternal-Child Care	9
Legal Considerations in Maternal-Child Nursing	11	Legal Considerations in Maternal-Child Nursing	11
Ethical Issues in Maternal-Child Nursing	14	Ethical Issues in Maternal-Child Nursing	14
Evidence-Based Practice in Maternal-Child Nursing	16	Evidence-Based Practice in Maternal-Child Nursing	17
		Chapter 02 Culture and the Family	21
		The Family	22
		Cultural Influences Affecting the Family	24
		Culture and Nursing Care	30
		Complementary and Alternative Therapies and the Family	34
Unit II		Unit 2	
The Reproductive Years and Beyond		The Reproductive Years and Beyond	
Chapter 02 Reproductive Anatomy and Physiology	21	Chapter 03 Reproductive Anatomy and Physiology	44
Puberty	23	Puberty	45
Female Reproductive System	23	Female Reproductive System	46
Female Reproductive Cycle	34	Female Reproductive Cycle	59
Male Reproductive System	38	Male Reproductive System	63
Chapter 03 Women's Health Care	43	Chapter 04 Health Promotion for Women	70
Nursing Care in the Community	44	Nursing Care in the Community	71
The Nurse's Role in Addressing Issues of Sexuality	44		
Menstruation	45	Menstruation	72
Contraception	47	Contraception	75
Clinical Interruption of Pregnancy	56		
Recommended Gynecologic Screening Procedures	56	Health Promotion for Women	85
Menopause	59	Menopause	88
Violence against Women	61	Violence against Women	92
		Chapter 05 Common Gynecologic Problems	100
Care of the Woman with a Benign Disorder of the Breast	65	Care of the Woman with a Benign Disorder of the Breast	101

© 2007 Pearson Education, Inc.

London, et al. 1e	Pg	London, et al. 2e	Pg
Iron Deficiency Anemia	1103	Iron Deficiency Anemia	1492
Normocytic Anemia	1104	Normocytic Anemia	1493
Sickle Cell Anemia	1105	Sickle Cell Anemia	1494
β-Thalassemia	1112		
Hemophilia	1114	Hemophilia	1505
Von Willebrand Disease	1116	Von Willebrand Disease	1507
Disseminated Intravascular Coagulation	1117	Disseminated Intravascular Coagulation	1508
Idiopathic Thrombocytopenic Purpura	1117	Idiopathic Thrombocytopenic Purpura	1508
Meningococcemia	1117	Meningococcemia	1509
Chapter 45 The Child with Alterations in Cellular Growth	1121	Chapter 50 The Child with Alterations in Cellular Growth	1516
Anatomy and Physiology of Pediatric Differences	1122	Anatomy and Physiology of Pediatric Differences	1517
Childhood Cancer	1122	Childhood Cancer	1517
Brain Tumors	1140	Brain Tumors	1546
Neuroblastoma	1143	Neuroblastoma	1549
Wilms' Tumor (Nephroblastoma)	1145	Wilms' Tumor (Nephroblastoma)	1552
Bone Tumors	1146	Bone Tumors	1553
Leukemia	1148	Leukemia	1556
Soft Tissue Tumors	1151	Soft Tissue Tumors	1559
Impact of Cancer Survival	1155		
Chapter 46 The Child with Alterations in Gastrointestinal Function	1159	Chapter 51 The Child with Alterations in Gastrointestinal Function	1569
Anatomy and Physiology of Pediatric Differences	1160	Anatomy and Physiology of Pediatric Differences	1570
Cleft Lip and Cleft Palate	1160	Cleft Lip and Cleft Palate	1571
Esophageal Atresia and Tracheoesophageal Fistula	1167	Esophageal Atresia and Tracheoesophageal Fistula	1579
Pyloric Stenosis	1169	Pyloric Stenosis	1582
Gastroesophageal Reflux	1172	Gastroesophageal Reflux	1584
Omphalocele	1173	Omphalocele and Gastroschisis	1587
Intussusception	1174	Intussusception	1588
Hirschsprung's Disease	1174	Hirschsprung's Disease	1589
Anorectal Malformations	1175	Anorectal Malformations	1590
Diaphragmatic Hernia	1176	Diaphragmatic Hernia	1591
		Umbilical Hernia	1591
Preoperative Care	1177	Preoperative Care	1593
Postoperative Care	1178	Postoperative Care	1593
Appendicitis	1178	Appendicitis	1593
Necrotizing Enterocolitis	1180	Necrotizing Enterocolitis	1595
Meckel's Diverticulum	1181	Meckel's Diverticulum	1597
Inflammatory Bowel Disease	1182	Inflammatory Bowel Disease	1597
Peptic Ulcer	1184	Peptic Ulcer	1599
Gastroenteritis (Acute Diarrhea)	1185	Gastroenteritis (Acute Diarrhea)	1601
Constipation	1189	Constipation	1603
Colic	1193	Colic	1609
Rumination	1193	Rumination	1609
Celiac Disease	1194	Celiac Disease	1610
Lactose Intolerance	1195	Lactose Intolerance	1611
Short Bowel Syndrome	1195	Short Bowel Syndrome	1611

London, et al. 1e	Pg	London, et al. 2e	Pg
Biliary Atresia	1196	Biliary Atresia	1612
Viral Hepatitis	1197	Viral Hepatitis	1613
Cirrhosis	1201	Cirrhosis	1617
Abdominal Trauma	1201	Abdominal Trauma	1618
Poisoning	1202	Poisoning	1619
		Ingestion of Foreign Objects	1621
Lead Poisoning	1204	Lead Poisoning	1622
Chapter 47 The Child with Alterations in Genitourinary Function	1209	Chapter 52 The Child with Alterations in Genitourinary Function	1628
Anatomy and Physiology of Pediatric Differences	1210	Anatomy and Physiology of Pediatric Differences	1629
		Urinary System	1629
		Reproductive System	1630
Bladder Exstrophy	1211	Bladder Exstrophy	1630
Hypospadias and Epispadias	1211	Hypospadias and Epispadias	1631
Obstructive Uropathy	1212	Obstructive Uropathy	1632
		Urinary Tract Infection	1635
		Enuresis	1637
Nephrotic Syndrome	1218	Nephrotic Syndrome	1639
Renal Failure	1222	Acute Renal Failure	1643
		Chronic Renal Failure	1649
		Peritoneal Dialysis	1655
		Hemodialysis	1655
		Kidney Transplantation	1658
Polycystic Kidney Disease	1233		
Hemolytic-Uremic Syndrome	1233		
Acute Postinfectious Glomerulonephritis	1234		
Phimosis	1238	Phimosis	1662
Cryptorchidism	1238	Cryptorchidism	1662
Inguinal Hernia and Hydrocele	1239	Inguinal Hernia and Hydrocele	1663
Testicular Torsion	1239	Testicular Torsion	1664
Chapter 48 The Child with Alterations in Eye, Ear, Nose, and Throat Function	1242	Chapter 46 The Child with Alterations in Eye, Ear, Nose, and Throat Function	1348
Anatomy and Physiology of Pediatric Differences	1243	Anatomy and Physiology of Pediatric Differences	1349
Infectious Conjunctivitis	1244	Infectious Conjunctivitis	1351
Periorbital Cellulitis	1245	Periorbital Cellulitis	1352
Visual Disorders	1245	Visual Disorders	1352
		Color Blindness	1354
Retinopathy of Prematurity	1248	Retinopathy of Prematurity	1354
Visual Impairment	1251	Visual Impairment	1359
Injuries of the Eye	1253	Injuries of the Eye	1362
Otitis Media	1254	Otitis Media	1363
		Otitis Externa	1367
Hearing Impairment	1259	Hearing Impairment	1370
Injuries of the Ear	1263	Injuries of the Ear	1376
Epistaxis	1263	Epistaxis	1377
Nasopharyngitis	1264	Nasopharyngitis	1378
Sinusitis	1265	Sinusitis	1379
Pharyngitis	1265	Pharyngitis	1379

London, et al. 1e	Pg	London, et al. 2e	Pg
Growth Hormone Deficiency (Hypopituitarism)	1352	Growth Hormone Deficiency (Hypopituitarism)	1808
Hyperpituitarism	1353	Hyperpituitarism	1811
Diabetes Insipidus	1353	Diabetes Insipidus	1811
		Syndrome of Inappropriate Antidiuretic Hormone (SIADH)	1813
Precocious Puberty	1355	Precocious Puberty	1813
Hypothyroidism	1355	Hypothyroidism	1814
Hyperthyroidism	1357	Hyperthyroidism	1815
		Hyperparathyroidism	1817
		Hypoparathyoidism	1818
Cushing Syndrome	1358	Cushing Syndrome	1818
Congenital Adrenal Hyperplasia	1359	Congenital Adrenal Hyperplasia	1819
Adrenal Insufficiency (Addison's Disease)	1361	Adrenal Insufficiency (Addison Disease)	1821
Pheochromocytoma	1362	Pheochromocytoma	1822
Diabetes Mellitus	1362	Diabetes Mellitus	1822
		Diabetic Ketoacidosis	1837
		Hypoglycemia	1839
		Type 2 Diabetes	1840
Gynecomastia	1376	Gynecomastia	1842
Amenorrhea	1377	Amenorrhea	1842
Turner's Syndrome	1377	Turner Syndrome	1843
Klinefelter's Syndrome	1378	Klinefelter Syndrome	1844
		Inborn Errors of Metabolism	1844
Phenylketonuria	1379	Phenylketonuria	1845
Galactosemia	1380	Galactosemia	1846
Maple Syrup Urine Disease	1380	Maple Syrup Urine Disease	1847
Chapter 52 The Child with Alterations in Skin Integrity	1383	Chapter 57 The Child with Alterations in Skin Integrity	1853
Anatomy and Physiology of Pediatric Differences	1384	Anatomy and Physiology of Pediatric Differences	1854
Skin Lesions	1385	Skin Lesions	1855
Wound Healing	1385	Wound Healing	1856
Contact Dermatitis	1386	Contact Dermatitis	1858
Diaper Dermatitis	1387	Diaper Dermatitis	1859
Seborrheic Dermatitis	1388	Seborrheic Dermatitis	1860
Drug Reactions	1388	Drug Reactions	1864
		Acne	1864
Eczema (Atopic Dermatitis)	1390	Eczema (Atopic Dermatitis)	1860
Impetigo	1395	Bacterial Infections	1869
Folliculitis	1396		
Cellulitis	1396		
		Viral Infectious Disorders	1872
Pediculosis Capitis (Lice)	1397	Pediculosis Capitis (Lice)	1874
Scabies	1398	Scabies	1877
Fungal Infections	1398	Fungal Infections	1873
		Vascular Tumors (Hemangiomas)	1878
Pressure Ulcers	1399	Pressure Ulcers	1878
Burns	1402	Burns	1879
Sunburn	1412	Sunburn	1892

London, et al. 1e	Pg	London, et al. 2e	Pg
Hypothermia	1412	Hypothermia	1892
Frostbite	1413	Frostbite	1894
Bites	1413	Bites	1894
Contusions	1416	Contusions	1897
Foreign Bodies	1416	Foreign Bodies	1898
		Lacerations	1898
Chapter 53 The Child with Alterations in Mental Health	1418	Chapter 54 The Child with Alterations in Cognitive and Mental Health Function	1725
Psychotherapeutic Management of Children and Adolescents	1419		
Autistic Spectrum Disorder	1423	Pervasive Developmental Disorders	1731
Attention Deficit Disorder and Attention Deficit Hyperactivity Disorder	1425	Attention Deficit Disorder and Attention Deficit Hyperactivity Disorder	1735
Mental Retardation	1429	Mental Retardation	1752
Schizophrenia	1433	Schizophrenia	1750
Depression	1434	Depression	1740
Bipolar Disorder (Manic-Depression)	1437	Bipolar Disorder (Manic-Depression)	1742
Generalized Anxiety	1437	Generalized Anxiety	1744
		Separation Anxiety Disorder	1745
Panic Disorder	1438	Panic Disorder	1745
Obsessive-Compulsive Disorder	1438	Obsessive-Compulsive Disorder	1745
School Phobia	1438	School Phobia	1746
Posttraumatic Stress Disorder	1439	Post-traumatic Stress Disorder	1746
		Suicide	1748
Conversion Reaction	1440	Conversion Reaction	1746
		Tic Disorders and Tourette Syndrome	1750
		Learning Disabilities	1751